【英汉对照全译本】

DEMOCRACY IN AMERICA

论 美 国 民 主

[法]托克维尔 著

朱尾声 译

马高霞 译校

（一）

中国社会科学出版社

图书在版编目(CIP)数据

论美国民主/〔法〕托克维尔著;朱尾声译.—北京:
中国社会科学出版社,2007.8
(西方学术经典译丛)
ISBN 978-7-5004-6291-0

Ⅰ.论… Ⅱ.①托…②朱… Ⅲ.民主—研究—美国
Ⅳ.D771.209

中国版本图书馆 CIP 数据核字(2007)第 097674 号

出版策划　曹宏举
责任编辑　钟　芳
责任校对　修广平
技术编辑　李　建

出版发行　中国社会科学出版社
社　　址　北京鼓楼西大街甲 158 号　　　邮　编　100720
电　　话　010—84029450(邮购)
网　　址　http://www.csspw.cn
经　　销　新华书店
印　　刷　北京京晟纪元印刷有限公司
版　　次　2007 年 8 月第 1 版
印　　次　2007 年 8 月第 1 次印刷
开　　本　630×970　1/16
印　　张　112.25
字　　数　1204 千字
定　　价　212.00 元

出版说明

为了进一步促进中西文化交流,构建全新的西学思想平台,我们出版了这套《西方学术经典译丛》(英汉对照全译本)。本译丛精选西方学术思想流变中最有代表性的部分传世名作,由多位专家学者选目,内容涵盖了哲学、宗教学、政治学、经济学、心理学、法学、历史学等人文社会科学领域,收录了不同国家、不同时代、不同体裁的诸多名著。

本译丛系根据英文原著或其他文种的较佳英文译本译出,在国内第一次以英汉对照的形式出版。与以往译本不同的是,本译丛全部用现代汉语译出,尽量避免以往译本时而出现的文白相间、拗口难懂的现象;另外出于尊重原作和正本清源的目的,本译本对原作品内容一律不做删节处理,全部照译。以往译本由于时代和社会局限,往往对原作品有所删节,因此,本译本也是对过去译本的补充和完善。

为加以区别,原文中的英文注释,注释号用①、②……形式表示;中文译者注释则以〔1〕、〔2〕……形式表示。至于英译本中出现的原文页码和特殊索引等问题,中文译者在"译者后记"中将予以解释、说明。另外,在英文原著或原英译本中,有一些表示着重意义的斜体或大写等字体,考虑到读者可以在英汉对照阅读中注意到,在本译文中没有照样标出,还望读者理解。

中国社会科学出版社

Democracy in America

By *Alexis de Tocqueville*

本书根据 Alfred A. Knopf, Inc. 1976 年版本译出

CONTENTS

目　录

（一）

(二)

(三)

FIRST BOOK　Influence Of Democracy On The Action Of Intellect In The United States

第一部　民主对美国民智行为的影响

（四）

SECOND BOOK　Influence Of Democracy On

The Feelings Of The Americans

第二部　民主对美国民情的影响

THIRD BOOK   Influence Of Democracy On Manners Properly So Called

第三部   民主对民情的影响

（五）

FOURTH BOOK Influence Of Democratic Ideas

And Feelings On Political Society

第四部 民主思想的影响和政治社会的观念

To The Twelfth Edition

However sudden and momentous the events which we have just beheld so swiftly accomplished, the author of this book has a right to say that they have not taken him by surprise. His work was written fifteen years ago, with a mind constantly occupied by a single thought — that the advent of democracy as a governing power in the world's affairs, universal and irresistible, was at hand. Let it be read over again and there will be found on every page a solemn warning that society changes its forms, humanity its condition, and that new destinies are impending. It was stated in the very Introduction to the work that "the gradual development of the principle of equality is a providential fact. It has all the chief characteristics of such a fact: it is universal, it is durable, it constantly eludes all human interference, and all events as well as all men contribute to its progress. Would it be wise to imagine that a social movement the causes of which lie so far back can be checked by the efforts of one generation? Can it be believed that the democracy which has overthrown the feudal system and vanquished kings will retreat before tradesmen and capitalists? Will it stop now that it is grown so strong and its adversaries so weak?"

He who wrote these lines in the presence of a monarchy which had been rather confirmed than shaken by the Revolution of 1830 may now fearlessly ask again the attention of the public to his work. And he may be permitted to add that the present state of affairs gives to his book an immediate interest and a practical utility that it had not when it was first published. Royalty was then in power; it has now been overthrown. The institutions of America, which were a subject only of curiosity to monarchical France, ought to be a subject of study for republican France. It is not force alone, but good laws, that give stability to a new government. After the combatant comes the legislator; the one has pulled down, the other builds up; each has his office.

第十二版序

尽管那些我们仿佛刚刚经历过的出乎意料的重大的事件匆匆结束了,这部书的作者还是会说这些事情并没有使他感到惊讶。他的著作是在15年前写的,当时他头脑就一直被一个单一的思想占据着——那就是民主以统治力量的身份出现在世界事务中,那么广泛而且势不可挡。再读这部作品,文中每一页都透漏着社会变革和新的社会命运即将到来的郑重警示。本书的绪论中说道:平等原则的逐步发展是一件幸事。他有其所应有的一切重要特质:广泛、持久、避开了一切民族冲突,所有的人与事都为其进步服务。如果我们设想深藏其后的社会前进的起因是可以通过一代人的努力研究得到的,这样的设想是明智的吗? 我们可以相信推翻了封建制度和没落君王的民主在面对商人和资本家时会退缩吗? 民主势力的壮大和其对立方削弱的局势目前会改变吗?

1830年大革命的爆发证实了那些描写君主政体统治的作者现在可以毫无顾忌地再次号召大家关注他的作品了。也许他应该被允许给自己的著作补充一点:现状赋予其作品的意义和对现实的作用,这些都是他在第一次出版的时候没有具备的作用。曾经是王室掌握的权力现如今被推翻了。曾经使法国王室感到好奇的美国的社会制度,成为共和制下的法国研究的对象。这不仅是在武力方面,也是在法律完备方面,使得新政府得以维护社会的稳定。战士下场,立法者登场,他们一个专于推倒,另一

Though it is no longer a question whether we shall have a monarchy or a republic in France, we are yet to learn whether we shall have a convulsed or a tranquil republic, whether it shall be regular or irregular, pacific or warlike, liberal or oppressive, a republic that menaces the sacred rights of property and family, or one that honors and protects them both. It is a fearful problem, the solution of which concerns not France alone, but the whole civilized world. If we save ourselves, we save at the same time all the nations which surround us. If we perish, we shall cause all of them to perish with us. According as democratic liberty or democratic tyranny is established here, the destiny of the world will be different; and it may be said that this day it depends upon us whether the republic shall be everywhere finally established or everywhere finally overthrown.

Now, this problem, which among us has but just been proposed for solution, was solved by America more than sixty years ago. The principle of the sovereignty of the people, which we enthroned in France but yesterday, has there held undivided sway for over sixty years. It is there reduced to practice in the most direct, the most unlimited, and the most absolute manner. For sixty years the people who have made it the common source of all their laws have increased continually in population, in territory, and in opulence; and — consider it well—it is found to have been, during that period, not only the most prosperous, but the most stable, of all the nations of the earth. While all the nations of Europe have been devastated by war or torn by civil discord, the American people alone in the civilized world have remained at peace. Almost all Europe was convulsed by revolutions; America has not had even a revolt. The republic there has not been the assailant, but the guardian, of all vested rights; the property of individuals has had better guarantees there than in any other country of the world; anarchy has there been as unknown as despotism.

Where else could we find greater causes of hope, or more instructive lessons? Let us look to America, not in order to make a servile copy of the institutions that she has established, but to gain a clearer view of the polity that will be the best for us; let us

个专于建立,都有自己的职责。尽管在法国,我们应该拥护君主政体还是共和政体已不需要再讨论,但我们还不知道我们应该拥有动荡或者平稳的共和政体,它的发展是规范的还是杂乱无章的,是和平的还是纷乱的,是自由的还是强权的,是威胁到财产和家族神圣权利的,还是对两者保护和尊敬的。这是一个严肃的问题,它的解决不仅仅牵扯到法国,而是涉及整个文明社会。如果我们拯救了自己,我们也就拯救了邻族。一旦我们毁灭,就会给其他民族带来灭顶之灾。民主的自由和民主的暴政的建立会给世界带来完全不同的局面;或者可以说,这也关系到我们今天,关系到我们是否能够建立起完全的共和政体或者将其彻底推翻。

如今,在我们中间刚刚提出的这一问题,早在60多年前美国人就已经解决了。人民主权的原则,在法国刚刚被创建,而在美国已坚定地统治了60多年。人民主权以最直接、最自由和最彻底的方式在美国得以实行。60年来,美国人民将其作为立法的根本,在其影响下,美国在人口、领土、财富方面都取得了极大的提高;在那个时期,人民主权统治下的美国不仅比世界所有的其他国家更繁荣,而且更稳定。在欧洲国家都被战争所毁坏、被内讧所分裂的时候,唯独美国人民保持了和平状态。几乎整个欧洲都被革命撼动的时候,美国甚至没有发生一场暴动。共和政体在美国不仅没有侵犯其他权利,反而成了既得权利的捍卫者;个人的财产在美国得到了比世界上其他任何国家更好的保护;无政府主义和专制在美国都不存在。

还有其他地方可以使我们得到更大的希望,获得更多的启发吗?我们学习美国,并不是为了照搬它所建立的一切,而是要对国家组织结构有更清楚地认识,以建立适合我们的政体;我们学

look there less to find examples than instruction; let us borrow from her the principles, rather than the details, of her laws. The laws of the French republic may be, and ought to be in many cases, different from those which govern the United States; but the principles on which the American constitutions rest, those principles of order, of the balance of powers, of true liberty, of deep and sincere respect for right, are indispensable to all republics; they ought to be common to all; and it may be said beforehand that wherever they are not found, the republic will soon have ceased to exist.

1848

习美国,更多的是要得到启发而不是学习他们的实例;我们应该从美国汲取法律的原理而不是细节。法国的共和体制下的法律,可以或者说应该在许多方面有别于美国的法律,但是美国政体所依附的那些原则,如遵守秩序的原则、权力均等的原则、真正自由的原则以及对权力的深厚诚挚尊敬的原则,是任何共和政体都不可缺少的;这些原则是所有共和政体都应当具备的,而且可以这么说,如果不建立这些原则,共和政体最终还是会走向灭亡。

1848 年

FIRST PART

Author's Introduction

Among the novel objects that attracted my attention during my stay in the United States, nothing struck me more forcibly than the general equality of condition among the people. I readily discovered the prodigious influence that this primary fact exercises on the whole course of society; it gives a peculiar direction to public opinion and a peculiar tenor to the laws; it imparts new maxims to the governing authorities and peculiar habits to the governed.

I soon perceived that the influence of this fact extends far beyond the political character and the laws of the country, and that it has no less effect on civil society than on the government; it creates opinions, gives birth to new sentiments, founds novel customs, and modifies whatever it does not produce. The more I advanced in the study of American society, the more I perceived that this equality of condition is the fundamental fact from which all others seem to be derived and the central point at which all my observations constantly terminated.

I then turned my thoughts to our own hemisphere, and thought that I discerned there something analogous to the spectacle which the New World presented to me. I observed that equality of condition, though it has not there reached the extreme limit which it seems to have attained in the United States, is constantly approaching it; and that the democracy which governs the American communities appears to be rapidly rising into power in Europe. Hence I conceived the idea of the book that is now before the reader.

It is evident to all alike that a great democratic revolution is going

上　卷

绪　论

我在美国停留期间,在那些众多的新奇的事物当中,最吸引我注意力的,莫过于人们之间地位的平等。我欣然发现这一重要事实的巨大影响力贯穿整个社会进程;它为大众指明了珍贵的舆论方向,为法律提供了宝贵的主旨;它给统治阶层以新的箴言,使被统治阶层享有独特的习惯。

我很快就认识到,这种巨大的影响不仅覆盖了这个国家的政治特性和法律,它对国民社会和政治统治都具有深刻的影响。它使人们有了自己的意见,得以产生新的观点,树立新的习惯并且修正一切不是它所产生的东西。我对美国的社会研究得越深,就越体会到这种平等的社会地位是其他一切衍生的基础,是我所做观察的终结点。

然后我把思绪转向了我们的半球。我看到了一些和这个新大陆所展示给我的情形类似的东西存在着。我认为,人们之间平等的地位,尽管没能像在美国所得到的那样的彻底,但也在不断地向这个方向前进着;统治着美国社会的民主政治在欧洲的实力也得到了飞速的成长。因此,那时我就开始构思读者现在看到的这本书。

很明显,一场伟大的民主革命正在我们中间进行着,但是人

— 3 —

on among us, but all do not look at it in the same light. To some it appears to be novel but accidental, and, as such, they hope it may still be checked; to others it seems irresistible, because it is the most uniform, the most ancient, and the most permanent tendency that is to be found in history.

I look back for a moment on the situation of France seven hundred years ago, when the territory was divided among a small number of families, who were the owners of the soil and the rulers of the inhabitants; the right of governing descended with the family inheritance from generation to generation; force was the only means by which man could act on man; and landed property was the sole source of power.

Soon, however, the political power of the clergy was founded and began to increase: the clergy opened their ranks to all classes, to the poor and the rich, the commoner and the noble; through the church, equality penetrated into the government, and he who as a serf must have vegetated in perpetual bondage took his place as a priest in the midst of nobles, and not infrequently above the heads of kings.

The different relations of men with one another became more complicated and numerous as society gradually became more stable and civilized. Hence the want of civil laws was felt; and the ministers of law soon rose from the obscurity of the tribunals and their dusty chambers to appear at the court of the monarch, by the side of the feudal barons clothed in their ermine and their mail.

While the kings were ruining themselves by their great enterprises, and the nobles exhausting their resources by private wars, the lower orders were enriching themselves by commerce. The influence of money began to be perceptible in state affairs. The transactions of business opened a new road to power, and the financier rose to a station of political influence in which he was at once flattered and despised.

Gradually enlightenment spread, a reawakening of taste for literature and the arts became evident; intellect and will contributed to success; knowledge became an attribute of government, intelligence a social force; the educated man took part in affairs of state.

The value attached to high birth declined just as fast as new

们对它的看法却相去甚远。一些人认为它的出现异乎寻常,是很偶然的,因而仍希望它能够被遏制;一些人则认为它是必然的,因为它有最统一、最古老以及在历史长河中最持久的发展趋势。

我回过头看700年前法国的社会面貌,那个被一小撮拥有土地、统治居民的家族瓜分版图的时期;统治的权力连同遗产的继承被家族子孙世代相传;权力是人们得以制服他人的唯一途径;而只有拥有的地产才是权力的唯一来源。

不久以后,神职人员政治权利建立了并逐渐增强:他们对所有人都敞开门户,无论穷人还是富户,不分平民和贵族;平等通过教会渗入统治阶层。奴隶本须生活在永久的奴役的状态中,现在可以凭借牧师的身份在贵族中争得一席之地,并且还常常会成为国王的座上客。

社会越来越稳定越来越开明,人们之间的关系却变得越来越多样,越来越复杂。因此人们就产生了对民法的需要;法律大臣迅速从法官席中阴暗的角落崛起,走出落满灰尘的房间,并开始出现在了君主的庭院,坐在身着貂皮盔甲的封建男爵的旁边。

当国王的势力逐渐被自己的野心掏空,而贵族也把自己的精力耗费在无止境的内讧上时,下层的人们正通过商业不断地充实着自己的实力。金钱开始在政治事务中显示力量。商业开启了一条新的通往权力的道路,地位上升,左右政治社会金融家上升到了影响政治社会的地位,并同时受到人们的追捧和鄙视。

随着开明教化的广泛传播,人们再度激发了对文学艺术的兴趣。人们靠智力和意志取得成功,知识成了为政的手段,智慧则变成一种社会力量,文人参与到国家事务中来。

随着新的通往权力道路的发现,人们出身的贵贱的重要性也

avenues to power were discovered. In the eleventh century, nobility was beyond all price; in the thirteenth, it might be purchased. Nobility was first conferred by gift in 1270, and equality was thus introduced into the government by the aristocracy itself.

In the course of these seven hundred years it sometimes happened that the nobles, in order to resist the authority of the crown or to diminish the power of their rivals, granted some political power to the common people. Or, more frequently, the king permitted the lower orders to have a share in the government, with the intention of limiting the power of the aristocracy.

In France the kings have always been the most active and the most constant of levelers. When they were strong and ambitious, they spared no pains to raise the people to the level of the nobles; when they were temperate and feeble, they allowed the people to rise above themselves. Some assisted democracy by their talents, others by their vices. Louis XI and Louis XIV reduced all ranks beneath the throne to the same degree of subjection; and finally Louis XV descended, himself and all his court, into the dust. As soon as land began to be held on any other than a feudal tenure, and personal property could in its turn confer influence and power, every discovery in the arts, every improvement in commerce of manufactures, created so many new elements of equality among men. Henceforward every new invention, every new want which it occasioned, and every new desire which craved satisfaction were steps towards a general leveling. The taste for luxury, the love of war, the rule of fashion, and the most superficial as well as the deepest passions of the human heart seemed to co-operate to enrich the poor and to impoverish the rich. From the time when the exercise of the intellect became a source of strength and of wealth, we see that every addition to science, every fresh truth, and every new idea became a germ of power placed within the reach of the people. Poetry, eloquence, and memory, the graces of the mind, the fire of imagination, depth of thought, and all the gifts which Heaven scatters at a venture turned to the advantage of democracy; and even when they were in the possession of its adversaries,

迅速减弱。11 世纪贵族的身份至高无上,而到了 13 世纪,如果想要,人们就可以买得到这样的身份。1270 年贵族的头衔开始被作为礼物授予,因此平等的观念也被贵族自己引入到政府的统治当中。

在这 700 年期间,一些贵族为了反抗国王的统治或削弱敌对方的势力,常常会准许平民拥有一些政治权利。或者,更经常发生的是,国王为了限制贵族势力的无限扩大,允许下层阶级参与政府统治。

在法国,国王总是最活跃、最坚决的平均主义者。当他们实力强大野心勃勃的时候,就很慷慨地授予一些人贵族身份;当他们势力衰落无能为力的时候,竟允许有人拥有比他们更高的衔位。这样,一些国王因为自己的才干,而一些则是因为自己的昏庸,帮助了民主的发展,像路易十一和路易十四两位国王就将国王下面所有的等级都划为同一等;而路易十五却将自己和自己的王朝一道付与尘土。一旦土地摆脱了封建制度下的占有,个人财产可以带来影响力和权力,人们在艺术领域的每一个发现,在工商业中获得每一次进步,都为人们的平等创造出新的元素。自此之后,每一次新的发明,每一次对机遇的渴盼,每一次满足欲望的新的期望都向着普遍平等的目标前进。对奢华的体验,战争的热爱,流行的规则,人类最肤浅的情感和最深厚的激情的追求,都仿佛联合起来,既使穷人变得富足,也使富人变得贫穷。对知识加以运用便能得到力量和财富的时期开始后,只要是有人存在的地方,科学的每一点进步,每一件新的知识甚至每一个新的想法都跟权力的增长息息相关。诗情、口才、记忆力、美好的心灵、创造的激情、思想的深度,以及所有那些上天随机给予人们的天赋,都成为民主的优势所在;即使这些天赋为其敌对方所有,也能

they still served its cause by throwing into bold relief the natural greatness of man. Its con-quests spread, therefore, with those of civilization and knowledge; and literature became an arsenal open to all, where the poor and the weak daily resorted for arms.

In running over the pages of our history, we shall scarcely find a single great event of the last seven hundred years that has not promoted equality of condition.

The Crusades and the English wars decimated the nobles and divided their possessions: the municipal corporations introduced democratic liberty into the bosom of feudal monarchy; the invention of firearms equalized the vassal and the noble on the field of battle; the art of printing opened the same resources to the minds of all classes; the post brought knowledge alike to the door of the cottage and to the gate of the palace; and Protestantism proclaimed that all men are equally able to find the road to heaven. The discovery of America opened a thousand new paths to fortune and led obscure adventurers to wealth and power.

If, beginning with the eleventh century, we examine what has happened in France from one half-century to another, we shall not fail to perceive that at the end of each of these periods a twofold revolution has taken place in the state of society. The noble has gone down the social ladder, and the commoner has gone up; the one descends as the other rises. Every half-century brings them nearer to each other, and they will soon meet.

Nor is this peculiar to France. Wherever we look, we perceive the same revolution going on throughout the Christian world. The various occurrences of national existence have everywhere turned to the advantage of democracy: all men have aided it by their exertions, both those who have intentionally labored in its cause and those who have served it unwittingly; those who have fought for it and even those who have declared themselves its opponents have all been driven along in the same direction, have all labored to one end; some unknowingly and some despite themselves, all have been blind instruments in the hands of God.

The gradual development of the principle of equality is, therefore, a providential fact. It has all the chief characteristics of such a fact: it is universal, it is lasting, it constantly eludes all human interference, and all events as well as all men contribute to its progress.

够通过他们显示人性的伟大并且仍然为民主服务。所以,民主征服的领域随着文明开化的进程和知识的传播而扩展;而文学也成了大众的军械厂,以供那些贫穷弱小的势力汲取力量。

历史的书页不停地翻过,我们发现在过去的 700 年中每一件重大事件的发生无不推进着平等的进程。

十字军东征和几次与英国的战争杀害了大批贵族,分散了他们的财产;地方自治把民主自由带进了封建君主政体的辖区;火力武器的发明使各封臣与贵族在战场上处于势均力敌的平等地位;印刷术开启了所有阶层人们的智慧源泉;邮政使知识传遍平民的小屋和宫殿的大门;新教宣扬所有的人们在前往天堂的路上都处于平等的地位。美洲的发现,开通了无数条通往财富的道路,并引领众多的探险家走向财富和力量。

如果我们从 11 世纪后半期开始考察法国的面貌,我们会发现每过 50 年,社会体制都会发生一次双重的革命。贵族的地位不断地下滑而平民的身份则处于上升态势;一个下降必然另一个上升。每过 50 年,它们之间的距离就缩短一些,直到完全平等。

这也不是只在法国出现过。在所有基督教国家里,同样的革命都在上演。国内发生的各类事件都转向对民主有利的一面:所有的人们,无论是主动的帮助,还是无心的行为,都为促进民主的发展贡献了自己的力量;那些为民主而战的人们,甚至宣称自己是民主之敌的人们都被同一个目标所牵引,共同致力于这一目标;人们要么不由自主,要么不知不觉地成为上帝手中驯服的工具。

因此,平等原则得以缓慢的发展正是顺应天意。这一事实的主要特性在于:它是普遍的、持续的、总能避开人类的干涉并且得到了所有人和物的支持。

Would it, then, be wise to imagine that a social movement the causes of which lie so far back can be checked by the efforts of one generation? Can it be believed that the democracy which has overthrown the feudal system and vanquished kings will retreat before tradesmen and capitalists? Will it stop now that it has grown so strong and its adversaries so weak?

Whither, then, are we tending? No one can say, for terms of comparison already fail us. There is greater equality of condition in Christian countries at the present day than there has been at any previous time, in any part of the world, so that the magnitude of what already has been done prevents us from foreseeing what is yet to be accomplished.

The whole book that is here offered to the public has been written under the influence of a kind of religious awe produced in the author's mind by the view of that irresistible revolution which has advanced for centuries in spite of every obstacle and which is still advancing in the midst of the ruins it has caused. It is not necessary that God himself should speak in order that we may discover the unquestionable signs of his will. It is enough to ascertain what is the habitual course of nature and the constant tendency of events. I know, without special revelation, that the planets move in the orbits traced by the Creator's hand. If the men of our time should be convinced, by attentive observation and sincere reflection, that the gradual and progressive development of social equality is at once the past and the future of their history, this discovery alone would confer upon the change the sacred character of a divine decree. To attempt to check democracy would be in that case to resist the will of God; and the nations would then be constrained to make the best of the social lot awarded to them by Providence.

The Christian nations of our day seem to me to present a most alarming spectacle; the movement which impels them is already so strong that it cannot be stopped, but it is not yet so rapid that it cannot be guided. Their fate is still in their own hands; but very soon they may lose control.

那么,我们就可以简单地认为久有渊源的社会发展的起因,可以通过一代人的努力被遏制吗?我们就可以相信民主在推翻封建体制、打败国王之后,会在商人和资本家面前退缩吗?就像我们相信他会在自己发展壮大到如此强壮的时候,在自己的对手衰落的时候,反而戛然而止吗?

那么,我们将何去何从?在我们依然对对比的结果失去信心的时候,没人能说得清楚。在基督教国家中,目前身份平等的程度比以往任何时候,世界上任何地区都高,以至于已完成的部分让我们无法估算到还有什么有待我们去完成。

呈现在读者面前的这部作品,全文都受到作者所感受的因不可抵抗的革命所产生的类似宗教敬畏心理的影响。这场革命排除了一切障碍,经历了上百年的发展并仍旧踩踏着它战胜的废墟前进。上帝希望人们能够发现他为表达自己的意愿而显示的一些征兆,但这并不需要他亲自开口说话。只需要人们能够确知自然发展的客观规律和事物发展的趋势即可。因为我知道,行星不需要任何启示,也会按照上帝为它规划的轨迹运行。经过仔细地观察和认真地反思,当代的人们如果相信社会地位平等的缓慢发展进程既是过去的历史,也是历史的未来,那么单是这一发现就赋予这场革命以至高无上的神启性质。企图遏止民主的行为就是违抗神的旨意;国家也将会按照神所授予的社会状态来发展。

我们这个时代信奉基督教的国家,在我看来显示了最令人担忧的景象;席卷这些国家的革命运动的力量是如此巨大,根本就不可能停止下来,但是其发展速度也还没有快到无法控制的局面。他们的命运现在仍然控制在自己的手中;但是很快就会挣脱束缚。

The first of the duties that are at this time imposed upon those who direct our affairs is to educate democracy, to reawaken, if possible, its religious beliefs; to purify its morals; to mold its actions; to substitute a knowledge of statecraft for its inexperience, and an awareness of its true interest for its blind instincts, to adapt its government to time and place, and to modify it according to men and to conditions. A new science of politics is needed for a new world.

This, however, is what we think of least; placed in the middle of a rapid stream, we obstinately fix our eyes on the ruins that may still be descried upon the shore we have left, while the current hurries us away and drags us backward towards the abyss.

In no country in Europe has the great social revolution that I have just described made such rapid progress as in France; but it has always advanced without guidance. The heads of the state have made no preparation for it, and it has advanced without their consent or without their knowledge. The most powerful, the most intelligent, and the most moral classes of the nation have never attempted to control it in order to guide it. Democracy has consequently been abandoned to its wild instincts, and it has grown up like those children who have no parental guidance, who receive their education in the public streets, and who are acquainted only with the vices and wretchedness of society. Its existence was seemingly unknown when suddenly it acquired supreme power. All then servilely submitted to its caprices; it was worshipped as the idol of strength; and when afterwards it was enfeebled by its own excesses, the legislator conceived the rash project of destroying it, instead of instructing it and correcting its vices. No attempt was made to fit it to govern, but all were bent on excluding it from the government.

The result has been that the democratic revolution has taken place in the body of society without that concomitant change in the laws, ideas, customs, and morals which was necessary to render such a revolution beneficial. Thus we have a democracy without anything to lessen its vices and bring out its natural advantages;

目前,压在领导者身上最迫切的任务,就是对民主加以引导,如果可能的话,再度唤醒对民主的信仰;净化民主精神;塑造民主行为;为没有经验的民主灌输国家管理的知识,使其摆脱盲目的本能,了解真正的民主利益,使民主政体因地因时制宜,并根据对象和环境的真实情况加以修正。一个全新的世界需要新的政治科学。

但是,这些问题我们很少想过;置身于迅猛发展的历史激流中,迫不得已被激流推离岸边,卷入深渊,但我们仍然顽强地紧盯着岸边那依稀可见的残垣断壁。

欧洲唯有法国,像我所描述的,发生了取得巨大进步的社会变革,但也是一个没有引导的进程。国家领导人对它的发生没有丝毫准备,革命的发生既没有得到他们的认可,也没有为他们所了解。这个国家最具权力、最有智慧、最高尚的阶层从未试图去控制它、指引它。民主的天然本性没有得到任何约束,它自己成长起来了,就像那些没有父母指教的孩子,他们混迹于市井并在那里学到了社会丑陋悲惨的一面。民主不知不觉就忽然获得了极大的力量。所有的人就屈从它任性的行为;人们把它当作力量的象征加以膜拜;后来它由于自己无节制的行为而走向了衰弱,立法者没有对它加以引导,纠正它的恶习,就草率决定将它扼杀。没有人企图去挽救它,使它适用于政府的统治,而所有的立法者都想将它排挤出局。

结果就是,社会实体内虽然发生了民主革命,但是法律、观念、习俗和道德并没有发生任何有利于民主革命的改变,而这些正是对革命有益所必需的变化。因此,我们并没能对民主做出任何举动从而减轻其恶习,并引出其天然的优势;我们虽然认识了

and although we already perceive the evils it brings, we are ignorant of the benefits it may confer.

While the power of the crown, supported by the aristocracy, peaceably governed the nations of Europe, society, in the midst of its wretchedness, had several sources of happiness which can now scarcely be conceived or appreciated. The power of a few of his subjects was an insurmountable barrier to the tyranny of the prince; and the monarch, who felt the almost divine character which he enjoyed in the eyes of the multitude, derived a motive for the just use of his power from the respect which he inspired. The nobles, placed high as they were above the people, could take that calm and benevolent interest in their fate which the shepherd feels towards his flock; and without acknowledging the poor as their equals, they watched over the destiny of those whose welfare Providence had entrusted to their care. The people, never having conceived the idea of a social condition different from their own, and never expecting to become equal to their leaders, received benefits from them without discussing their rights; They became attached to them when they were clement and just and submitted to their exactions without resistance or servility, as to the inevitable visitations of the Deity. Custom and usage, moreover, had established certain limits to oppression and founded a sort of law in the very midst of violence.

As the noble never suspected that anyone would attempt to deprive him of the privileges which he believed to be legitimate, and as the serf looked upon his own inferiority as a consequence of the immutable order of nature, it is easy to imagine that some mutual exchange of goodwill took place between two classes so differently endowed by fate. Inequality and wretchedness were then to be found in society, but the souls of neither rank of men were degraded.

Men are not corrupted by the exercise of power or debased by the habit of obedience, but by the exercise of a power which they believe to be illegitimate, and by obedience to a rule which they consider to be usurped and oppressive.

On the one side were wealth, strength, and leisure, accompanied

民主所带来的弊端，但是却没能意识到它的好处。

当王权在贵族阶级的支持下平安无事地统治着欧洲国家时，陷于悲惨境地的社会还存在着一些在我们今天看来无法想象和认同的幸福的来源。一些臣民的力量，对皇族的专政来说，是不可跨越的障碍。对君主来说，他从民众眼中所感受到的近乎神圣的崇拜，使他觉得很享受，从而也激励他公正地运用自己的权力。贵族呢，高高在上的地位，使得他们像牧羊人对待自己的羊群那样，用平静和慈善的心境对待人民的命运。他们并不认为穷人与自己的地位是平等的，他们关心这些穷人的命运，只是因为上帝把这些人的幸福托付给了自己。他们从未想过会有与自己现有的社会状况不同的社会环境的存在，他们也从未想过会与自己的首领们享有平等的地位，在接受他们的好处的时候根本不考虑他们拥有的权利；他们爱戴仁慈公正的首领，对那些严苛的首领也逆来顺受，毫不反抗，将之视为是上帝赐予的惩罚。此外，习惯和其运用，也为暴政规定了一定的限制，并在暴政中建立了一系列的法规。

因为贵族从未怀疑过有人企图夺取他所认为自己拥有的合法特权，而奴隶也将自己低下的地位视为上帝的安排，是不可改变的自然规律使然，因此也就不难想象两个被赋予不同命运的阶级之间出于善意而发生的相互的关系。不平等和悲惨的状况在社会中虽存在，但是两个阶层人民的灵魂还没有堕落。

人们之所以堕落变坏，并不是因为统治者行使的权力，或者他们习惯于服从，而是因为统治者行使了他们认为违法的权力或者因为被迫服从他们认为是侵夺和压迫的行为。

一边是集财富、权势和休闲于一身，伴之以对奢华的追求，

by the pursuit of luxury, the refinements of taste, the pleasures of wit, and the cultivation of the arts; on the other were labor, clownishness, and ignorance. But in the midst of this coarse and ignorant multitude it was not uncommon to meet with energetic passions, generous sentiments, profound religious convictions, and wild virtues.

The social state thus organized might boast of its stability, its power, and, above all, its glory.

But the scene is now changed. Gradually the distinctions of rank are done away with; the barriers that once severed mankind are falling; property is divided, power is shared by many, the light of intelligence spreads, and the capacities of all classes tend towards equality. Society becomes democratic, and the empire of democracy is slowly and peaceably introduced into institutions and customs.

I can conceive of a society in which all men would feel an equal love and respect for the laws of which they consider themselves the authors; in which the authority of the government would be respected as necessary, and not divine; and in which the loyalty of the subject to the chief magistrate would not be a passion, but a quiet and rational persuasion. With every individual in the possession of rights which he is sure to retain, a kind of manly confidence and reciprocal courtesy would arise between all classes, removed alike from pride and servility. The people, well acquainted with their own true interests, would understand that, in order to profit from the advantages of the state, it is necessary to satisfy its requirements. The voluntary association of the citizens might then take the place of the individual authority of the nobles, and the community would be protected from tyranny and license.

I admit that, in a democratic state thus constituted, society would not be stationary. But the impulses of the social body might there be regulated and made progressive. If there were less splendor than in an aristocracy, misery would also be less prevalent; the pleasures of enjoyment might be less excessive, but those of comfort would be more general; the sciences might be less perfectly cultivated, but ignorance would be less common; the ardor of the feelings would be constrained, and the habits of the nation softened; there would be more vices and fewer crimes.

高雅的品位,智慧的快乐和艺术的教化;另一边则只有劳动、粗野和无知。但是,在这无知粗鄙的人群中,也不乏精力充沛的激情,高尚的情操,深厚的宗教信仰以及质朴的德行。

这样的社会状态因此被一些夸张的稳定的状态、强大的实力和最重要的荣誉所包围着。

但是这一景象已经改变了。阶级之间的差异已逐渐消失;曾经存在的严峻障碍已经消除;财产和权力被瓜分,智慧的光明四处传播,所有阶级的地位也趋于平等。社会变得民主化,民主的统治已缓慢平稳地被引入制度和习惯当中。

我可以想象这样一个社会,人们可以以平等的地位爱护和尊敬法律,人人都是制定法律的主人。在这样的社会中,政府的权威应被视为是必需的,而不是神圣不可侵犯的;在这样的社会中,人们对地方长官的忠心不很强烈,但是出于理性的感情。每人都有权保留自己的权利,所有的阶级之间都应充满自信、互相礼让,而不再有傲慢和卑屈;每一个知道自己真正利益的人都会了解,为了从社会获得好处,就必须满足它的要求。公民之间自愿的联合可能取代各个贵族的权威,社会也会受到保护从而不受暴政和特权的侵害。

我承认,这样构成的民主社会也许不稳定,但是将会对社会实体的推动力加以规范并促进其发展。即使这样做不比贵族体制有更多的好处,但其带来的不幸的影响也会小得多;在民主社会,人们享受的幸福不会过多,但是其得到的福利却更普及;科学也许不会特别突出,但是人们无知的程度将会大大减少;人们激烈的感情将会受到约束,但是社会的行为会更加平稳;也许还会有更多的恶习出现,但是人们的犯罪能得以减少。

In the absence of enthusiasm and ardent faith, great sacrifices may be obtained from the members of a commonwealth by an appeal to their understanding and their experience; each individual will feel the same necessity of union with his fellows to protect his own weakness; and as he knows that he can obtain their help only on condition of helping them, he will readily perceive that his personal interest is identified with the interests of the whole community. The nation, taken as a whole, will be less brilliant, less glorious, and perhaps less strong; but the majority of the citizens will enjoy a greater degree of prosperity, and the people will remain peaceable, not because they despair of a change for the better, but because they are conscious that they are well off already.

If all the consequences of this state of things were not good or useful, society would at least have appropriated all such as were useful and good; and having once and forever renounced the social advantages of aristocracy, mankind would enter into possession of all the benefits that democracy can offer.

But here it may be asked what we have adopted in the place of those institutions, those ideas, and those customs of our forefathers which we have abandoned.

The spell of royalty is broken, but it has not been succeeded by the majesty of the laws. The people have learned to despise all authority, but they still fear it; and fear now extorts more than was formerly paid from reverence and love.

I perceive that we have destroyed those individual powers which were able, single-handed, to cope with tyranny; but it is the government alone that has inherited all the privileges of which families, guilds, and individuals have been deprived; to the power of a small number of persons, which if it was sometimes oppressive was often conservative, has succeeded the weakness of the whole community.

The division of property has lessened the distance which separated the rich from the poor; but it would seem that, the nearer they draw to each other, the greater is their mutual hatred and the more vehement the envy and the dread with which they resist each other's claims to power; the idea of right does not exist for either party, and force affords to both the only argument for the present and the only guarantee for the future.

没有狂热激烈的信仰,国民所受到的教育和他们的经验也会让他们做出伟大的奉献;每个个体都能体会到大家联合起来保护单个弱小个体的必要性;大家都明白只有帮助别人才能获得别人的帮助,他就能体会到自己的利益与群体的利益是一致的。整个国家也许会少了一些光芒和荣耀,也许实力也会有所削弱;但是大多数公民就会享受到更多的繁荣,人民就会保持和平的状态,这并不是因为他们不希望变得更好,而是因为他们觉得自己已经很富足。

假使这种状态下事物的发展并不都很好或很有用,但至少对社会来说是具备使其得到很好的发展的条件。社会一旦永远拒绝了贵族提供的在社会中的有利条件,人们就可以完全享受民主所带来的好处了。

这里也许有人发问,我们用什么来取代我们所遗弃的前辈们的制度、思想和习惯。

王权的魅力遭到破坏,但是还没能被法律至高无上的权威取代。人们蔑视所有的权威,但却仍然对它怀着恐惧的心理;而且人们担心所付出的代价,远远多于之前敬畏和尊崇权威时所付出的代价。

我认识到我们破坏了一些原来可以单独与暴政相抗衡的力量;但是政府却独自继承了所有从家庭、行会和个体所得来的特权;对一小部分人的权力来说,虽说偶尔具压迫性但通常还是很保守,但战胜了民众的软弱。

富人与穷人的财富差距减小了;但事实是,随着两者之间差距的减小,他们之间滋生了更多仇恨和更强烈的嫉妒,以及对对方对权力的追求的恐惧心理;权力的观念在两者中都不存在,权势是他们目前争夺的重心,也是未来的唯一保障。

The poor man retains the prejudices of his forefathers without their faith, and their ignorance without their virtues; he has adopted the doctrine of self-interest as the rule of his actions without understanding the science that puts it to use; and his selfishness is no less blind than was formerly his devotion to others. If society is tranquil, it is not because it is conscious of its strength and its well-being, but because it fears its weakness and its infirmities; a single effort may cost it its life. Everybody feels the evil, but no one has courage or energy enough to seek the cure. The desires, the repinings, the sorrows, and the joys of the present time lead to nothing visible or permanent, like the passions of old men, which terminate in impotence.

We have, then, abandoned whatever advantages the old state of things afforded, without receiving any compensation from our present condition; we have destroyed an aristocracy, and we seem inclined to survey its ruins with complacency and to accept them. The phenomena which the intellectual world presents are not less deplorable. The democracy of France, hampered in its course or abandoned to its lawless passions, has overthrown whatever crossed its path and has shaken all that it has not destroyed. Its empire has not been gradually introduced or peaceably established, but it has constantly advanced in the midst of the disorders and the agitations of a conflict. In the heat of the struggle each partisan is hurried beyond the natural limits of his opinions by the doctrines and the excesses of his opponents, until he loses sight of the end of his exertions, and holds forth in a way which does not correspond to his real sentiments or secret instincts. Hence arises the strange confusion that we are compelled to witness.

I can recall nothing in history more worthy of sorrow and pity than the scenes which are passing before our eyes. It is as if the natural bond that unites the opinions of man to his tastes, and his actions to his principles, was now broken; the harmony that has always been observed between the feelings and the ideas of mankind appears to be dissolved and all the laws of moral analogy to be abolished.

Zealous Christians are still found among us, whose minds are nurtured on the thoughts that pertain to a future life, and who

穷人保留着先辈们的偏见和无知,却没能继承他们的信仰和德行;他继承了利己的原则作为他行为的准则,但却没有理解其实践的含义;他的自私的盲目程度并不比之前在其他方面的盲目程度更少。社会之所以保持稳定,不是因为它对自己的实力和良好的秩序有自知之明,而是因为它对自己的虚弱的状况感到心虚;任何一个动作都会使它丧命。每个人都感到了这一不幸,但是却没人有勇气或足够的精力去寻求医治。人们对现状的渴望、抱怨、悲痛和快乐,并没能带来任何实质性的和持续的效果,像老年人产生的激情一样,在达到预想的效果之前便终结了。

我们在抛弃了昔日体制的各项优势后,并没能从现在条件中给予弥补;我们破坏了贵族的统治,然后却表现得对这些被破坏的东西恋恋不舍而希望停留在其中。文明社会所展示的这一现象真是令人叹息。法国的民主在其进程中受到阻碍,之后又毫无约束地任凭激情使然,推翻了任何阻碍其发展的事物,不能推翻的则使其动摇。民主的统治不是被逐渐引入或者和平的建立起来的,而是一直在混乱中前进,在冲突中煽动起来的。在斗争的高潮时,大家都急于战胜压制对方的言论和敌对者的行为,从而超出了自己判断的自然极限,以至于看不到其追求的终点,表达了一些与自己的真实情感或笃厚天性不符的行为或言论。以至于引起了我们之后被迫见到的异常混乱。

历史留给我回忆的悲痛和遗憾莫过于从我们眼前溜走的景象。仿佛那种使人们的观点和他的品味、行为与原则相联系在一起的天然纽带被破坏;人们情感和思想之间的和谐被解散,所有法律在道德上的相似之处被废止。

我们中间仍然存在着热心的基督教徒,他们以相信来世生

readily espouse the cause of human liberty as the source of all moral greatness. Christianity, which has declared that all men are equal in the sight of God, will not refuse to acknowledge that all citizens are equal in the eye of the law. But, by a strange coincidence of events, religion has been for a time entangled with those institutions which democracy destroys; and it is not infrequently brought to reject the equality which it loves, and to curse as a foe that cause of liberty whose efforts it might hallow by its alliance.

By the side of these religious men I discern others whose thoughts are turned to earth rather than to heaven. These are the partisans of liberty, not only as the source of the noblest virtues, but more especially as the root of all solid advantages; and they sincerely desire to secure its authority, and to impart its blessings to mankind. It is natural that they should hasten to invoke the assistance of religion, for they must know that liberty cannot be established without morality, nor morality without faith. But they have seen religion in the ranks of their adversaries, and they inquire no further; some of them attack it openly, and the rest are afraid to defend it.

In former ages slavery was advocated by the venal and slavish-minded, while the independent and the warm-hearted were struggling without hope to save the liberties of mankind. But men of high and generous character are now to be met with, whose opinions are directly at variance with their inclinations, and who praise that servility and meanness which they have themselves never known. Others, on the contrary, speak of liberty as if they were able to feel its sanctity and its majesty, and loudly claim for humanity those rights which they have always refused to acknowledge.

There are virtuous and peaceful individuals whose pure morality, quiet habits, opulence, and talents fit them to be the leaders of their fellow men. Their love of country is sincere, and they are ready to make the greatest sacrifices for its welfare. But civilization often finds them among its opponents; they confound its abuses with its benefits, and the idea of evil is inseparable in their minds from that of novelty.

活的宗教精神指导生活,他们乐于支持人类的自由,因为这是所有伟大道德的源泉。基督教宣称,上帝面前人人平等,也不会反对公民在法律面前的平等。但是,由于一些事件发生异常地巧合,宗教一度被扯到了民主所破坏的制度一边,因此它开始反对其所热爱的平等,并以敌对者的身份诅咒自由;而它如果与自由联合,则会使自由变得神圣不可侵犯。

在这些基督徒的周围,我见识了另一些想法实际的人们。这些自由的支持者,不仅仅是因为自由是高尚品质的源泉,更多的则是因为自由是所有利益的基础;他们真心希望保护自由的权力,并将其祝福给予全人类。很自然地他们急切想要得到宗教的帮助,因为他们相信自由的建立少不了道德的建设,而道德不能没有信仰。但是宗教已经与他们背道而驰,于是他们也就不再抱什么希望;于是一些人开始正面的攻击,而另一些人则不敢拥护它了。

过去的几个世纪中,奴隶制度都为那些具有奴性思想的人们所推崇,而一些能够独立思考和热心的人们则毫无希望地一直为捍卫人类的自由而努力斗争。但如今那些出身高贵道貌岸然的人,持有与他们的高贵身份完全不符的观点,赞扬那些他们完全不熟悉的奴性和卑鄙的习性。另一些人则与他们完全相反,整天把自由挂在嘴边,仿佛他们已经感受到自由的圣洁和不可侵犯的权威,并大声地向人们呼吁着一些他们自己都不了解的权力。

一些道德高尚爱好和平的人们,他们的完美的品行、稳健的习性、富裕的地位以及自身的才干使他们成为同胞们的领袖,他们对国家的爱是真诚的,他们时刻准备着为国家的富强奉献自己的一切。但是他们常常把文明社会视为自己的敌人;他们使其弊端和利益混淆,在他们的头脑中,邪恶的思想总是伴随着一些新鲜的事物出现。

Near these I find others whose object is to materialize mankind, to hit upon what is expedient without heeding what is just, to acquire knowledge without faith, and prosperity apart from virtue; claiming to be the champions of modern civilization, they place themselves arrogantly at its head, usurping a place which is abandoned to them, and of which they are wholly unworthy.

Where are we, then?

The religionists are the enemies of liberty, and the friends of liberty attack religion; the high-minded and the noble advocate bondage, and the meanest and most servile preach independence; honest and enlightened citizens are opposed to all progress, while men without patriotism and without principle put themselves forward as the apostles of civilization and intelligence.

Has such been the fate of the centuries which have preceded our own? and has man always inhabited a world like the present, where all things are not in their proper relationships, where virtue is without genius, and genius without honor; where the love of order is confused with a taste for oppression, and the holy cult of freedom with a contempt of law; where the light thrown by conscience on human actions is dim, and where nothing seems to be any longer forbidden or allowed, honorable or shameful, false or true?

I cannot believe that the Creator made man to leave him in an endless struggle with the intellectual wretchedness that surrounds us. God destines a calmer and a more certain future to the communities of Europe. I am ignorant of his designs, but I shall not cease to believe in them because I cannot fathom them, and I had rather mistrust my own capacity than his justice.

There is one country in the world where the great social revolution that I am speaking of seems to have nearly reached its natural limits. It has been effected with ease and simplicity; say rather that this country is reaping the fruits of the democratic revolution which we are undergoing, without having had the revolution itself. The emigrants who colonized the shores of America in the beginning of the seventeenth century somehow separated the democratic principle from all the principles that it had to contend with in the old communities of Europe, and transplanted it alone to the New World.

除了这些，我还发现了另外一些人，他们的目的是将人类唯物化，他们只关注有利的一面，而不关心其是否公正，他们不带任何信仰观念去获取知识，他们所谓的幸福也和道德无关；打着拥护现代文明社会的旗帜，他们毫不客气地把自己置于领导者的地位，侵占了这个他们本不配占有的位置。

那么，我们又处于什么样的境地呢？

宗教狂热者是自由的敌人，而自由的朋友又反过来攻击宗教；贵族和品德高尚的人提倡奴役，而卑鄙且出身卑贱的人则崇尚独立；诚实开明的公民反对所有的进步，而没有爱国精神和原则的人则将自己视为文明和智慧的传道者。

难道这就是几百年来引领着我们的命运的天数吗？人们一直都生活在像现在这样的环境里吗？所有的事物都不在自己本来的关系网中，人们的美德与天赋无关，而天赋的一切与荣耀无关；在这个混乱的关系网中，对社会秩序的热爱与镇压混为一谈，对自由的圣洁的崇拜与法律相违背；人们行为的道德光芒昏暗，没有任何东西能够再被禁止或允许，感到荣耀或羞耻、虚假或真实？

我不认为造物主造人是为了让人陷入永无止境的，与像现在缠绕在我们身边的这样的知识贫乏的斗争中。上帝给欧洲社会安排了一个更加平静和稳定的未来。我不知道他的安排，但我不会因为自己无法探知就停止对这些安排的信任，因为我宁肯怀疑自己的智慧也不会怀疑上帝的公正。

我所说的这场伟大社会革命，世界上有一个国家似乎已经接近了它的自然极限。这场革命的实现显得很简易；甚至可以说，这个国家没有发生我们进行的民主革命，就直接收到了这场革命的成果。17世纪初在美洲定居的移民，从他们在欧洲旧社会所反对的一切原则中析出民主原则，并把它单独移植到新大陆。在这

It has there been able to spread in perfect freedom and peaceably to determine the character of the laws by influencing the manners of the country.

It appears to me beyond a doubt that, sooner or later, we shall arrive, like the Americans, at an almost complete equality of condition. But I do not conclude from this that we shall ever be necessarily led to draw the same political consequences which the Americans have derived from a similar social organization. I am far from supposing that they have chosen the only form of government which a democracy may adopt; but as the generating cause of laws and manners in the two countries is the same, it is of immense interest for us to know what it has produced in each of them.

It is not, then, merely to satisfy a curiosity, however legitimate, that I have examined America; my wish has been to find there instruction by which we may ourselves profit. Whoever should imagine that I have intended to write a panegyric would be strangely mistaken, and on reading this book he will perceive that such was not my design; nor has it been my object to advocate any form of government in particular, for I am of the opinion that absolute perfection is rarely to be found in any system of laws. I have not even pretended to judge whether the social revolution, which I believe to be irresistible, is advantageous or prejudicial to mankind. I have acknowledged this revolution as a fact already accomplished, or on the eve of its accomplishment; and I have selected the nation, from among those which have undergone it, in which its development has been the most peaceful and the most complete, in order to discern its natural consequences and to find out, if possible, the means of rendering it profitable to mankind. I confess that in America I saw more than America; I sought there the image of democracy itself, with its inclinations, its character, its prejudices, and its passions, in order to learn what we have to fear or to hope from its progress.

In the first part of this work I have attempted to show the distinction that democracy, dedicated to its inclinations and tendencies and abandoned almost without restraint to its instincts, gave to the laws the course it impressed on the government, and in general the control which it exercised over affairs of state. I have sought to discover the evils and the advantages which it brings. I have examined

里,民主原则得到自由成长,并在影响民情的过程中和平地确立了法律的性质。

我毫不怀疑,不久的将来,我们也会像美国一样实现近乎完全的平等。但我并不能从中断言,我们从与美国相似的社会结构中,必然得出与美国相同的政治结果。我并不认为他们所采用的政府形式是民主政体的唯一选择;但是,由于两个国家中立法和民情的起因是相同的,那么最引起我们注意的就是它在两个国家中造成的不同后果。

这不仅仅是为了满足我研究美国的好奇心理,尽管也是合理的;我的目的在于找到能够给我们带来有益的启示。如果有人认为我在写一篇颂词,那就完全误会了,而且如果他读了我的书,就会了解那不是我的目的;而且我也没有想去吹捧任何一种政治形式,因为我一直认为,没有哪一种法律体系是完美的。我甚至没想去判断我认为不可抵挡的这场社会变革是有利的还是有害的。我认为这场变革事实上已经结束了,或者说即将结束。而且我从众多经历这一变革的国家中选择这个将革命进行得最和平最彻底的国家,是为了看清它所导致的自然结果,或者有可能的话,找到使革命有利于人类的方法。我承认,我虽然观察的是美国,可是又不局限于美国;我在美国找到了民主本身的形象,了解了民主的倾向、它的特性、它的偏颇之处和它的激情,这一切都是为了了解我们应该对它持有什么样的希望和担心。

在本书的第一部分,我试图说明一点区别,那就是民主按照自己的意向发展,在几乎没有受到任何对它的本能的限制下,法律进程对政府造成的影响,对政治事务的普遍控制力,对法律指出的方向。我希望找出它所带来的危害和利益。我研究了美国用以指导民

the safeguards used by the Americans to direct it, as well as those that they have not adopted, and I have undertaken to point out the factors which enable it to govern society.

My object was to portray, in a second part, the influence which the equality of conditions and democratic government in America exercised on civil society, on habits, ideas, and customs; but I grew less enthusiastic about carrying out this plan. Before I could have completed the task which I set for myself, my work would have become purposeless. Someone else would before long set forth to the public the principal traits of the American character and, delicately cloaking a serious picture, lend to the truth a charm which I should not have been able to equal. [1]

I do not know whether I have succeeded in making known what I saw in America, but I am certain that such has been my sincere desire, and that I have never, knowingly, molded facts to ideas, instead of ideas to facts.

Whenever a point could be established by the aid of written documents, I have had recourse to the original text, and to the most authentic and reputable works. [2] I have cited my authorities in the notes, and anyone may verify them. Whenever opinions, political customs, or remarks on the manners of the country were concerned, I have endeavored to consult the most informed men I met

---

[1] At the time I published the first edition of this work, M. Gustave de Beaumont, my traveling-companion in America, was still working on his book entitled *Marie, ou l' Esclavage aux Etats-Unis*, which has since appeared. M. de Beaumont's primary purpose was to portray clearly and accurately the position of Negroes in Anglo-American society. His work will throw a new and vivid light on the question of slavery, a vital one for all united republics. I am not certain whether I am mistaken, but it seems to me that M. de Beaumont's book, after having vitally interested those who will put aside their emotions and regard his descriptions dispassionately, should have a surer and more lasting success among those readers who, above all else, desire a true picture of actual conditions.

[2] Legislative and executive documents have been furnished to me with a kindness which I shall always remember with gratitude. Among the American statesmen who have thus helped my researches, I will mention particularly Mr. Edward Livingston, then Secretary of State, afterwards Minister Plenipotentiary at Paris. During my stay in Washington, he was kind enough to give me most of the documents which I possess relating to the Federal government. Mr. Livingston is one of the few men whose writings cause us to conceive an affection for them, whom we admire and respect even before we come to know them personally, and to whom it is a pleasure to give recognition.

主以及一些他们没有采用的预防措施,并且发现了它之所以能够统治社会的原因。

在第二部分中,我的目的是指出美国作家所描述的平等地位和民主统治对市民社会在民情、思想和习俗方面的影响;但是我已没有那么多热心去完成这个计划。在我完成自己设定的这个任务之前,我的工作就变得没有目的性。不久就还会有人给读者描述美国人性格的主要的特质,并且勾勒了一幅严肃的画面,给事实赋予迷人的色彩,这些我没办法达到。①

我不知道我是否成功地将我眼中的美国展现在大家的面前,但我确信这是我最诚挚的愿望,我绝没有让事实成就观点,而是让观点以事实为依据。

只要有需要借助文字材料的观点,我都会找到原文,并且尽量找那些最有权威最有名的作品。②注释中有我引用的典据,大家可以核实。在涉及一些看法、政治习惯和国家民情的时候,我都会尽力去咨询那些我见到的最博学的人。碰到一些问题的难点

---

① 当这部作品第一版出版的时候,与我一起去美国的同伴 M. 古斯塔夫·德·博蒙特还在创作他随后面世的《玛丽》。他创作的主要目的是要清楚准确地描述黑人在英裔美国人中的社会处境。他在书中会对关乎整个联邦共和国的奴隶制所存在的问题加以全新地、生动地阐述。我不知道是不是我自己搞错了,但是在我看来,博蒙特的著作,在引起了那些没有感情的和对他的描述感到失望的人们的兴趣之余,在那些强烈地希望获取真实的情况的读者中间将会引起更确信更持久的胜利。

② 我会永远感激那些好心提供给我立法和行政资料的人们。在这些帮助我做调查的美国政治家们中,我要特别提一下,美国国务卿、M. 爱德华·利文斯通先生,后来成为驻巴黎全权大臣。在我停留在华盛顿期间,我所拥有的大多数关于联邦政府的资料都是他在这一期间慷慨提供给我的。利文斯通是少数几个我通过阅读他们的作品而对他们产生好感的人之一。他在我们还未谋面之前就得到了我的钦佩和尊敬,是一位使人们很高兴结交的人。

with. If the point in question was important or doubtful, I was not satisfied with one witness, but I formed my opinion on the evidence of several witnesses. Here the reader must necessarily rely upon my word. I could frequently have cited names which either are known to him or deserve to be so in support of my assertions; but I have carefully abstained from this practice. A stranger frequently hears important truths at the fireside of his host, which the latter would perhaps conceal from the ear of friendship; he consoles himself with his guest for the silence to which he is restricted, and the shortness of the traveler's stay takes away all fear of an indiscretion. I carefully noted every conversation of this nature as soon as it occurred, but these notes will never leave my writing-case. I had rather injure the success of my statements than add my name to the list of those strangers who repay generous hospitality they have received by subsequent chagrin and annoyance.

I am aware that, notwithstanding my care, nothing will be easier than to criticize this book should anyone care to do so.

Those readers who may examine it closely will discover, I think, in the whole work a dominant thought that binds, so to speak, its several parts together. But the diversity of the subjects I have had to treat is exceedingly great, and it will not be difficult to oppose an isolated fact to the body of facts which I cite, or an isolated idea to the body of ideas I put forth. I hope to be read in the spirit which has guided my labors, and that my book may be judged by the general impression it leaves, as I have formed my own judgment not on any single consideration, but upon the mass of evidence.

It must not be forgotten that the author who wishes to be understood is obliged to carry all his ideas to their utmost theoretical conclusions, and often to the verge of what is false or impracticable; for if it be necessary sometimes to depart in action from the rules of logic, such is not the case in discourse, and a man finds it almost as difficult to be inconsistent in his language as to be consistent in his conduct.

I conclude by pointing out myself what many readers will consider the principal defect of the work. This book is written to favor

和有疑问的地方,我不会仅仅满足于自己的见识,而是根据大量的证据形成我的见解。我的读者可以相信我所说的一切。我本可以在文中经常提到一些知名人士或者必要的人的名字来支持我的主张,但我没有这样做。陌生人往往是在主人的炉火旁听到最真实的事实,这些事实也许他对自己的朋友也不曾提过,而为了打破主人与客人之间沉默的拘谨,并且因为客人短暂的停留消除了他的顾忌,所以客人才能听到。我总是在这样自然的谈话从开始的时候就变得很警觉并开始认真地加以注意,但是这些从没用笔记过。我宁愿使我的著作失去一些光彩,也不愿成为使热情接待自己的主人在事后觉得懊悔烦恼的人之一。

我明白,尽管我很小心,可是如果有人想批评这本书,那他完全可以做得到。再没有比这更容易的事情了。

仔细研究过我的书的人就会发现,我认为,整本书由一个中心思想将几个小章节贯穿在一起。可是,我不得不讨论的课题之间的差异是很大的,所以要想用一个独立的事实来引证我所引用的一组事实,或者说一个独立的观点证明我提出的一系列的观点是很容易的。我希望读者也能有与我写作这部书同样的精神来读它,并根据读后的整体印象来评价它,就像我一样,凭着大量的事实作依据,而不是单纯根据思考作评判。

我们必须铭记,作者想要得到大家的理解,就必须将它的思想做出最理性的总结,却常常濒临错误或不实际的边缘;因为有时虽可以在行动上偏离逻辑的规则,但是在论述中却万万不能。而一个人要想在言语上前后不符,与想在行动上前后一致一样,都是很难的。

最后,我自行指出一个许多读者将会认为是我的书中的一个

no particular views, and in composing it I have entertained no design of serving or attacking any party. I have not undertaken to see differently from others, but to look further, and while they are busied for the morrow only, I have turned my thoughts to the whole future.

主要的错误:写这本书没有任何想要支持某一派言论的目的。在构思这本书的时候,我也从没想过要服务于某一派,或者攻击某一派。我并不是跟大家看到的不一致,而是我看得更远,当他们都在忙于明天的事务时,我的思维已经在考虑将来。

CHAPTER I

Exterior Form Of North America

North America *divided into two vast regions, one inclining to wards the Pole, the other towards the Equator—Valley of the Mississippi— Traces found there of the revolutions of the globe—Shore of the Atlantic Ocean, on which the English colonies were founded—Different aspects of North and of South America at the time of their discovery—Forests of North America - Prairies - Wandering tribes of natives—Their outward appearance, customs, and languages—Traces of an unknown people.*

North America presents in its external form certain general features which it is easy to distinguish at the first glance.

A sort of methodical order seems to have regulated the separation of land and water, mountains and valleys. A simple but grand arrangement is discoverable amid the confusion of objects and the prodigious variety of scenes.

This continent is almost equally divided into two vast regions. One is bounded on the north by the Arctic Pole, and on the east and west by the two great oceans. It stretches towards the south, forming a triangle, whose irregular sides meet at length above the great lakes of Canada. The second region begins where the other terminates, and includes all the remainder of the continent. The one slopes gently towards the Pole, the other towards the Equator.

The territory included in the first region descends towards the north with a slope so imperceptible that it may almost be said to form a plain. Within the bounds of this immense level tract there are neither high mountains nor deep valleys. Streams meander through it irregularly; great rivers intertwine, separate, and meet again, spread into vast marshes, losing all trace of their channels in the labyrinth of waters they have themselves created, and thus at length, after innumerable windings, fall into the Polar seas. The great lakes which bound this first region are not walled in, like most of those in the Old World, between

第一章　北美的外貌

北美分为两大地区,一个伸向北极,一个延向赤道。密西西比河大峡谷见证了这个区域历史变迁的痕迹——在建有英国殖民地的大西洋沿岸——北美和南美在被发现时有着不同的外观——北美的森林——牧场——和四处漂泊的土著部落——而这些部落的外表、习俗和语言早已随着历史消失得无影无踪。

北美在外貌上有一个易于分辨的特点。

陆地和水域、山脉和河谷,都被布置得井然有序。在这种简单而壮观的安排中,既有景物的杂乱,又有景色的多变。

北美被划分为几乎同样的两大地区。一个伸向北极,东西各临大洋。它向南伸展,形成一个三角形。三角形的两个不等边,交汇在加拿大五大湖下方。第二个地区始于第一个地区的终点,包括大陆的所有剩余部分。一个地区微微斜向北极,另一个地区微微斜向赤道。第一个地区的大地在缓缓地向北下降,它的斜度不易被察觉,几乎可以说这是一片平原。

在这片广阔的平地上既没有高山,也没有深谷。河流蜿蜒它从这里流过,一些河流有时聚合,又有时分开,它们流向沼泽地带,消失在它们自身造成的水乡迷宫之中;经过这样地千回百转,最后流入北极的海中。与旧大陆不同,这第一个地区的各个大湖

hills and rocks. Their banks are fiat and rise but a few feet above the level of their waters, each thus forming a vast bowl filled to the brim. The slightest Change in the structure of the globe would cause their Waters to rush either towards the Pole or to the tropical seas.

The space that lies between these two chains of mountains contains 228,843 square leagues. [1]Its surface is therefore about six times as great as that of France. [2]

This vast territory, however, forms a single valley, one side of which descends from the rounded summits of the Alleghenies, while the other rises in an uninterrupted course to the tops of the Rocky Mountains. At the bottom of the valley flows an immense river, into which you can see, flowing from all directions, the waters that come down from the mountains. In memory of their native land, the French formerly called this river the St. Louis. The Indians, in their pompous language, have named it the Father of Waters, or the Mississippi.

The Mississippi takes its source at the boundary of the two great regions of which I have spoken, not far from the highest point of the plateau that separates them. Near the same spot rises another river, [3] which empties into the Polar seas. The course of the Mississippi is at first uncertain: it winds several times towards the north, whence it rose, and only at length, after having been delayed in lakes and marshes, does it assume its definite direction and flow slowly onward to the south.

Sometimes quietly gliding along the chalky bed that nature has assigned to it, sometimes swollen by freshets, the Mississippi waters over 1,032 leagues in its course. [4] At the distance of 600 leagues[5]from its mouth this river attains an average depth of 15 feet; and it is navigated by vessels of 300 tons for a course of nearly 200

---

[1]　1,341,649 miles. See Darby's *View of the United States*, p. 499. I have reduced these miles to leagues of 2,000 toises.

[2]　France is 35,181 square leagues.

[3]　Red River [of the North].

[4]　2,500 miles, 1,032 leagues. *See Description of the United States*, by Warden, Vol. I, p. 169.

[5]　1,364 miles, 563 leagues. See ibid. , Vol. I, p. 169.

的周围没有群山峭壁,湖岸平坦,只比水面高出几英尺。因此,每个湖就像盛满水的大碗:地球构造的微微变动,会致使湖水不是流入北极,就是流入热带海洋。

两条山脉之间的空隙约为 228843 平方里格,[①]因此它的面积约为法国的六倍。[②]

然而,在这个广大的地域内却形成一个大河谷,河谷的一侧从阿勒格尼山脉的圆形峰顶向下,同时,它的另一侧沿着落基山脉的各大顶峰上升。一条巨大的河流流淌在大河谷的底部,这里的水来自高山上的流水,从四面八方汇入其中。法国人为了纪念他们的国土,曾把这条河流称为圣路易河;而印第安人,则夸张的称之为"水之父"或密西西比河。

密西西比河发源于我在前面所说的两大地区的交界处,距分隔这两大地区的高原的最高点不远。在这附近还有另一条河,[③]它流入北极的海洋。密西西比河本身的河道在起初似乎并不确定。它曾经多次流向北方,在流经湖区和沼泽后才稳定流向,最后缓缓向南流去。

有时,密西西比河在大自然的黏土质河床中静静地流过,有时因暴雨而变成洪流,流程约 1032 里格。[④] 在离河口近 600 里格处,[⑤]水深平均已达 15 英尺。可承载 300 吨的船舶航行 200 里格左右。

---

① 1341649 里格。见《达比看美国》,第 499 页。约等于 2000 突阿斯。

② 法国 35181 平方里格。

③ 红河。

④ 2500 英里,1032 里格。见瓦登著:《美利坚合众国描述》一书,第一卷,第 169 页。

⑤ 1364 英里,563 里格。参考书目如上,第一卷,第 169 页。

leagues. One counts, among the tributaries of the Mississippi, one river of 1,300 leagues,① one of 900,② one of 600,③ one of 500,④ four of 200,⑤ not to speak of a countless multitude of small streams that rush from all directions to mingle in its flow.

The valley which is watered by the Mississippi seems to have been created for it alone, and there, like a god of antiquity, the river dispenses both good and evil. Near the stream nature displays an inexhaustible fertility; the farther you get from its banks, the more sparse the vegetation, the poorer the soil, and everything weakens or dies. Nowhere have the great convulsions of the globe left more evident traces than in the valley of the Mississippi. The whole aspect of the country shows the powerful effects of water, both by its fertility and by its barrenness. The waters of the primeval ocean accumulated enormous beds of vegetable mold in the valley, which they leveled as they retired. Upon the right bank of the river are found immense plains, as smooth as if the tiller had pased over them with his roller. As you approach the mountains, the soil becomes more and more unequal and sterile; the ground is, as it were, pierced in a thousand places by primitive rocks, which appear like the bones of a skeleton whose flesh has been consumed by time. The surface of the earth is covered with a granitic sand and irregular masses of stone, among which a few plants force their growth and give the appearance of a green field covered with the ruins of a vast edifice. These stones and this sand disclose, on examination, a perfect analogy with those that compose the arid and broken summits of the Rocky Mountains. The flood of waters which washed the soil to the bottom of the valley afterwards carried away portions of the rocks themselves; and these, dashed and bruised against the neighboring cliffs, were left scattered like wrecks at their feet.⑥

---

① The Missouri. See *Description of the United states*, by Warden., Vol. I, p. 132 (1,278 leagues).

② The Arkansas. See ibid., Vol. I, p. 188 (877 leagues).

③ The Red River. See ibid., Vol. I, p. 190 (598 leagues).

④ The Ohio. See ibid., Vol. I, p. 192 (490 leagues).

⑤ The Illinois, St. Pierre, St. Francis, Des Moines. The above measurements are based on the legal mile (statute mile) and on the postal league of 2,000 toises.

⑥ See Appendix A.

据计算,在密西西比河的支流中,有一条长约 1300 里格,[①]一条长 900 里格,[②]一条长 600 里格,[③]一条长 500 里格,[④]四条长 200 里格。[⑤] 至于从四面八方流入其中的无数小河,就不必细说了。

这条让密西西比河流经的河谷,好像专门为它而创造的。这条河就像神一样既象征善良,也象征邪恶。在大河附近,有着用之不竭的肥沃的土地;离河越远,草木也就越稀疏,土地也就越贫瘠,万物也就越来越弱,直到死去。地球上的任何巨大变动所留下的痕迹,都不如密西西比河谷的明显。这个地区的一切,包括肥沃与贫瘠都是在水的作用下产生的。古时的大洋,为河谷沉积下厚厚一层适于植物生长的沃土,而且非常平坦。河的右岸被发现是巨大的平原,平坦得就像有人用碌子滚过一样。当你离山越近,土地也就变得越不平坦和越贫瘠。在这里,到处可见锋利的岩石,它们就像一架架骨架立在那里,而肉体早已被时间吞噬。地球的表面被一层沙子和一些形状不规则的岩石所覆盖。一些植物艰难地生长,好不容易才可以冒出绿色的幼芽。就像被一片巨大的并且破烂的废墟覆盖着。据考察,这些岩石和沙子,在成分上与落基山顶的沙石一样。在谷底沉积出土地以后,洪水冲洗着河谷底部的沙土,并把一部分岩石从山上冲下来。这些岩石你推我打,互相冲击与碰撞,最后都支离破碎地停在山脚下。[⑥]

---

① 密苏里州。见瓦登著:《美利坚合众国描述》,第一卷,第 132 页。(1278 里格)。

② 阿肯色州。参考书目同上书,第一卷,第 188 页(877 里格)。

③ 红河。参考书目同上书,第一卷,第 190 页(598 里格)。

④ 俄亥俄州。参考书目同上书,第一卷,第 192 页(490 里格)。

⑤ 伊利诺伊州,圣皮埃尔,圣佛朗西斯。以上测量结果依据法律规定的单位,依据旧的测量单位为 2000 突阿斯。

⑥ 见附件 A。

The valley of the Mississippi is, on the whole, the most magnificent dwelling-place prepared by God for man's abode; and yet it may be said that at present it is but a mighty desert.

On the eastern side of the Alleghenies, between the base of these mountains and the Atlantic Ocean, lies a long ridge of rocks and sand, which the sea appears to have left behind as it retired. The average breadth of this territory does not exceed 48 leagues; [1] but it is about 300 leagues in length. [2] This part of the American continent has a soil that offers every obstacle to the husbandman, and its vegetation is scanty and unvaried.

Upon this inhospitable coast the first united efforts of human industry were made. This tongue of arid land was the cradle of those English colonies which were destined one day to become the United States of America. The center of power still remains here; while to the west of it the true elements of the great people to whom the future control of the continent belongs are gathering together almost in secrecy.

When Europeans first landed on the shores of the West Indies, and afterwards on the coast of South America, they thought themselves transported into those fabulous regions of which poets had sung. The sea sparkled with phosphoric light, and the extraordinary transparency of its waters disclosed to the view of the navigator all the depths of the ocean, [3] Here and there appeared little islands perfumed with odoriferous plants, and resembling baskets of flowers floating on the tranquil surface of the ocean. Every object that met the sight in this enchanting region seemed prepared to satisfy the wants or contribute to the pleasures of man. Almost all the trees were loaded with nourishing fruits, and those which were useless as food delighted the eye by the brilliance and variety of their colors.

---

[1]　100 miles.

[2]　About 900 miles

[3]　Malte-Brun tells us (Vol. III, p. 726) that the water of the Caribbean Sea is so transparent that corals and fish are discernible at a depth of sixty fathoms. The ship seemed to float in air, the navigator became giddy as his eye penetrated through the crystal flood and beheld submarine gardens, or beds of shells, or gilded fishes gliding among tufts and thickets of seaweed.

总之,密西西比河大河谷是上帝赐予人们的最好住所。但在目前,它还是一大片荒漠。

在阿勒格尼山的东侧,位于这条山脉和大西洋之间的,是一条由岩石和沙子构成的岩石脊,好像是海水退泻时留下来的,这个地带的平均宽度只有 48 里格,①但它的长度却达 300 里格。②美洲大陆这一部分土地,为开垦者制造了种种困难。植物贫瘠,种类单调。

正是在这一片荒芜贫瘠的海岸,出现了第一批工业制造者。也正是这片土地,成为那些英国殖民地的摇篮,它们命中注定有朝一日会成为今天的美国。现在权力中心仍然在这里。而在它的西面,将来就要掌握的这个伟大民族的真正元素正在秘密地聚集起来。

当欧洲人最初登上西印度群岛的海岸,以及不久以后又登上南美大陆的时候,他们以为来到了诗人们歌颂的童话般的地方。海面上波光粼粼,海水清澈得使航海者可以看到海底。隐约中一个又一个的小岛密布在海面,③传来阵阵芳香。在这个地方,所有的一切,都像是为了满足人们的需求与快乐而准备的。大部分树木都负载着丰硕的果实,而一些不能食用的果实则会因缤纷的色彩取悦于人。丛林里生长着芬芳的柠檬树、野生的无花果树、

---

① 100 英里。

② 大约 900 英里。

③ 马特·希恩说(第三卷第 726 页;指英文原版页码——译者),加勒比海的水域非常清澈,人们甚至可以透过 60 英尺的深水分辨出珊瑚和鱼。行驶在上面的船,就像漂浮在天空中一样,航海家们都会觉得晕眩,他们的眼睛甚至可以透过透明的海水看到水下花园、大片的贝壳和在海草丛中穿梭的鱼。

In groves of fragrant lemon trees, wild figs, flowering myrtles, acacias, and oleanders; which were bung with festoons of various climbing plants, covered with flowers, a multitude of birds unknown in Europe displayed their bright plumage, glittering with purple and azure, and mingled their warbling with the harmony of a world teeming with life and motion. ①

Underneath this brilliant exterior death was concealed. But this fact was not then known, and the air of these climates had an indefinably enervating influence, which made man cling to the present, heedless of the future.

North America apeared under a very different aspect: there everything was grave, serious, and solemn; it seemed created to be the domain of intelligence, as the South was that of sensual delight. A turbulent and foggy ocean washed its shores. It was girt round by a belt of granitic rocks or by wide tracts of sand. The foliage of its woods was dark and gloomy, for they were composed of firs, larches, evergreen oaks, wild olive trees, and laurels.

Beyond this outer belt lay the thick shades of the central forests, where the largest trees which are produced in the two hemispheres grow side by side. The plane, the catalpa, the sugar maple, and the Virginian poplar mingled their branches with those of the oak, the beech, and the lime.

In these, as in the forests of the Old World, destruction was perpetually going on. The ruins of vegetation were heaped upon one another; but there was no laboring hand to remove them, and their decay was not rapid enough to make room for the continual work of reproduction. Climbing plants, grasses, and other herbs forced their way through the mass of dying trees; they crept along their bending trunks, found nourishment in their dusty cavities, and a passage beneath the lifeless bark. Thus decay gave its assistance to life, and their respective productions were mingled together. The depths of these forests were gloomy and obscure, and a thousand rivulets, undirected in their course by human industry, preserved in them a constant moisture. It was rare to meet with flowers, wild fruits, or birds beneath their shades. The fall of a tree overthrown by age, the rushing torrent of a cataract, the lowing of the buffalo, and the howling of the wind were the only sounds that broke the silence of nature.

---

① See Appendix B.

圆叶的桃金娘树、带刺的金合欢树和夹竹桃树,它们被很多藤条连接起来,上面盖满了鲜花。一群群在欧洲没有见过的鸟展翅飞翔,它们的羽毛呈现出美丽的深红色和天蓝色,在蓝天中用充满活力的声音鸣叫着。①

在这种辉煌的外表之下隐藏着死亡,但人们当时并未察觉,反而沉湎于这种环境的气氛之中。这种环境使人只顾眼前而不管将来,人们并不知道未来会有什么消极影响。

北美有着不同的情形。在这里,一切都是严肃、郑重和庄严的。仿佛这里是为使智力成为统治者而被创造的,而南美则是为使肉体有享受之处而被创造的。汹涌多雾的海洋冲洗着岸边,海岸仿佛被花岗岩的石块和沙粒给系上一条腰带。这里的树木繁密,有红松、落叶松、常绿栎、野橄榄和桂树。

穿越这第一条腰带之后,便进入中央森林。在这里,东西两半球所出产的巨大乔木并肩生长,法国梧桐、梓树、糖枫、弗吉尼亚白杨与栎树、山毛榉、椴树枝叶交相呼应。

在这些旧世界森林里,毁灭在不断地进行。弃枝和残木日积月累,堆积的到处都是,但没有人去收拾它们,以致它们的腐烂速度赶不上新树的生长。蔓生植物和杂草克服了重重困难爬上倒木,从这些朽木身上附着的尘土中吸取养分,为自己的生长打开一条道路。因此,死亡帮助了生命。生与死好像有意混合和交换它们的成果。森林的深处幽暗朦胧,人们尚未发现的千百条小溪使森林里永远潮湿。在这里,很少能看到鲜花、野果或鸟。一棵老朽树木的倒地声,一条河流的跌水声,野牛的叫声,风声,是打破这里的沉寂的唯一声音。

---

① 见附件 B。

To the east of the great river the woods almost disappeared; in their stead were seen prairies of immense extent. Whether Nature in her infinite variety had denied the germs of trees to these fertile plains, or whether they had once been covered with forests, subsequently destroyed by the hand of man, is a question which neither tradition nor scientific research has been able to answer.

These immense deserts were not, however, wholly untenanted by men. Some wandering tribes had been for ages scattered among the forest shades or on the green pastures of the prairie.

From the mouth of the St. Lawrence to the Delta of the Mississippi, and from the Atlantic to the Pacific Ocean, these savages possessed certain points of resemblance that bore witness to their common origin; but at the same time they differed from all other known races of men;[1] they were neither white like the Europeans, nor yellow like most of the Asiatics, nor black like the Negroes. Their skin was reddish brown, their hair long and shining, their lips thin, and their cheekbones very prominent. The languages spoken by the North American tribes had different vocabularies, but all obeyed the same rules of grammar. These rules differed in several points from such as had been observed to govern the origin of language. The idiom of the Americans seemed to be the product of new combinations, and bespoke an effort of the understanding of which the Indians of our days would be incapable.[2]

The social state of these tribes differed also in many respects from all that was seen in the Old World. They seem to have multiplied freely in the midst of their deserts, without coming in contact with

---

[1] With the progress of discovery, some resemblance has been found to exist between the physical conformation, the language, and the habits of the Indians of North America, and those of the Tungus, Manchus, Mongols, Tatars, and other wandering tribes of Asia. The land occupied by these tribes is not very distant from Behring's Strait, which allows of the supposition that at a remote period they gave inhabitants to the desert continent of America. But this is a point which has not yet been clearly elucidated by science. See Malte-Brun, Vol. V. ; the works of Humboldt; Fischer; *Conjecture sur l'origine des Américains*; Adair: *History of the American Indians.*

[2] See Appendix C.

在大河以东,森林逐渐消失;取而代之的是广袤无垠的大草地。到底是大自然在这千变万化中不肯给这些沃野撒下树种,还是覆盖这片沃野的森林曾经被人破坏? 这是一个无论是传说还是科学研究都未能解答的问题。

但是,这一望无际的荒凉土地,并不是从来没有人烟。一些云游四方的部落,曾有好几个世纪分布在森林的树荫下或大草地的绿野上。

从圣劳伦斯河河口到密西西比州,从大西洋到太平洋,居住在这里的原始人类有着一些相似的特质。虽然这些特质足以使我们相信他们有相同的起源,但是他们似乎又与我们所知的其他各类人种都有区别。[①] 他们既不像欧洲人那样有白色的皮肤,也没有多数亚洲人所拥有的那种黄色的皮肤,更不是黑人。他们生有古铜色的皮肤,浅黄色的头发,薄薄的嘴唇和凸出的颧骨。这里各个部落的所说的口语词汇虽有区别,但是又都遵从着统一的语法规则。这些语法规则与最初用以规范语言的规则又不尽相同。美洲土著的方语渗入了一些新的成分,而他们对这些新成分的创造远远超出了如今的印第安人所能达到的智力水平。[②]

这些部族的社会状况,在许多方面也与旧大陆不同。他们仿佛一直在自己的荒凉天地里自由繁殖,从来未与比他们更开化的

---

① 人们又进一步发现,北美印第安人和通古斯人、满人、蒙古人、鞑靼等其他一些游牧种族在肢体语言和生活习性上也存在一些相似之处。而这些部落所占领的土地距白令海峡不远,这就又产生了一种假想,在远古时代,此地的居民有可能向美国的中部迁徙。但是这一点猜想还未经科学证实。在德国著名科学家洪堡的著作中,就提到过美国印第安人的历史这一课题。

② 见附件 C。

other races more civilized than their own. Accordingly, they exhibited none of those indistinct, incoherent notions of right and wrong, none of that deep corruption of manners, which is usually joined with ignorance and rudeness among nations who, after advancing to civilization, have relapsed into a state of barbarism. The Indian was indebted to no one but himself; his virtues, his vices, and his prejudices were his own work; he had grown up in the wild independence of his nature.

If in polished countries the lowest of the people are rude and uncivil, it is not merely because they are poor and ignorant, but because, being so, they are in daily contact with rich and enlightened men. The sight of their own hard lot and their weakness, which is daily contrasted with the happiness and power of some of their fellow creatures, excites in their hearts at the same time the sentiments of anger and of fear: the consciousness of their inferiority and their dependence irritates while it humiliates them. This state of mind displays itself in their manners and language; they are at once insolent and servile. The truth of this is easily proved by observation: the people are more rude in aristocratic countries than elsewhere; in opulent cities than in rural districts. In those places where the rich and powerful are assembled together, the weak and the indigent feel themselves oppressed by their inferior condition. Unable to perceive a single chance of regaining their equality, they give up to despair and allow themselves to fall below the dignity of human nature.

This unfortunate effect of the disparity of conditions is not observable in savage life: the Indians, although they are ignorant and poor, are equal and free.

When Europeans first came among them, the natives of North America were ignorant of the value of fiches, and indifferent to the enjoyments that civilized man procures for himself by their means. Nevertheless there was nothing coarse in their demeanor; they practiced habitual reserve and a kind of aristocratic politeness.

Mild and hospitable when at peace, though merciless in war beyond any known degree of human ferocity, the Indian would expose himself to die of hunger in order to succor the stranger who

种族接触过。因此,他们那里一点也不像曾经一度文明而后又堕入野蛮状态的民族那样是非不明和善恶不分,更不像后者那样因无知和败俗而腐化堕落。印第安人的一切都是自生自长的:他们的德行,他们的恶习,他们的偏见,都是他们本身的产物。他们是在天然的野生独立状态下成长起来的。

在文明开化的国家,社会底层的人们之所以变得粗野不文明,不仅仅是由于他们本身的无知和贫困,而且还由于在这种生活状况下,他们每天与文明人和富人接触。他们苦难和菲薄的生活,每天都在同某些同胞的幸福和权势作出鲜明的对照。内心的愤怒和恐惧,自卑感和依附感,即使他们恼火,又使他们觉得屈辱。这种内心状态体现在他们的言行举止上,就变成了既傲慢又卑屈的神态。这个事实通过观察很容易得到证实。生活在贵族制度国家的人们比在其他任何地方都更粗野;而繁华城市里的人,又比乡间人粗野。在有钱有势的人聚集的地方,软弱和贫穷的人由于地位卑下而受压迫。这些人找不到机会使自己重新获得平等,他们便完全处于绝望之中,而自甘践踏作为人的尊严。

这种由于身份悬殊而造成不平等待遇的情况对野蛮人的社会不适用。印第安人尽管贫穷无知,但彼此间都是平等和自由的。

欧洲人最初来到北美的时候,那里的土著居民对财富的价值一无所知,对文明人利用财富获得的享受也毫不在意。但是,他们的举止毫不粗野,反而习惯于谦让持重,表现出一种贵族式的彬彬有礼的风度。

平日里印第安人温和好客,作战时却又表现出令人难以想象的残忍无情。他们可以为了搭救一个夜里敲门求宿的路人,甘冒

asked admittance by night at the door of his hut; yet he could tear in pieces with his hands the still quivering limbs of his prisoner. The famous republics of antiquity never gave examples of more unshaken courage, more haughty spirit, or more intractable love of independence than were hidden in former times among the wild forests of the New World. ① The Europeans produced no great impression when they landed upon the shores of North America; their presence engendered neither envy nor fear. What influence could they possess over such men as I have described? The Indian could live without wants, suffer without complaint, and pour out his death-song at the stake. ② Like all the other members of the great human family, these savages believed in the existence of a better world, and adored, under different names, God, the Creator of the universe. Their notions on the great intellectual truths were in general simple and philosophical. ③

Although we have here traced the character of a primitive people, yet it cannot be doubted that another people, more civilized and more advanced in all respects, had preceded it in the same regions.

An obscure tradition which prevailed among the Indians on the borders of the Atlantic informs us that these very tribes formerly dwelt on the west side of the Mississippi. Along the banks of the

---

① We learn from President Jefferson (*Notes on Virginia*, p. 148), that among the Iroquois, when attacked by a superior force, aged men refused to fly. or to survive the destruction of their country; and they braved death like the ancient Romans when their capital was sacked by the Gauls. Further on (p. 150), he tells us that "there is no example of an Indian, who, having fallen into the hands of his enemies, begged for his life; on the contrary, the captive sought to obtain death at the hands of his conquerors by the use of insult and provocation. "

② See *Histoire de la Louisiane*, by Lepage Dupratz; Charlevoix: *Histoire de la Nouvelle France*; Lettres du Rev. G. Heckewelder, *Transactions of the* American Philosophical Society, Vol. I; Jefferson: *Notes on Virginia*, pp. 135-90. What is said by Jefferson is of special weight on account of the personal merit of the writer, of his peculiar position, and of the matter-of-fact age in which he lived.

③ See Appendix D.

饿死自己的危险。他们也可以亲手撕裂战俘还在颤抖的四肢。古代的那些非常出名的共和国就从未表现得像当时隐居在新大陆荒野森林里的人们那样,具有无可比拟的毫不气馁的勇气、高傲的精神和坚定的独立信念。① 欧洲人最初在北美登陆时,当地人的生活并没有受到太大的影响。陌生人的出现既没有引起他们的嫉妒,也没有引起他们的恐惧。那么,究竟欧洲人的登陆给土著人带来了什么样的影响呢?印第安人在生活中很容易得到满足,即使忍受再多的苦难也不会埋怨。② 对于生死的态度也很坦然。和所有伟大的民族一样,这些原始的人们坚信美好世界的存在,并且以各自的形式信仰创造万物的上帝。③

尽管我们在这里追述了这些原始人类的特征,但是毋庸置疑,还存在着另一个在许多方面都比他们更开化、更进步的民族。这个民族在这片土地上曾远远领先着他们。

有一个传说悄悄地在大西洋沿岸的印第安部落蔓延着。传说这些部族原先住在密西西比河以西的地方。现在在俄亥俄河

---

① 我们可以从杰斐逊总统的陈述中得见一斑,他说,对易洛魁族人来说,如果他们遇到了强大武力的袭击,连老人们也不会弃城逃命,更不会在被别人践踏损毁的城中苟延残喘,他们会英勇地战死,就像当初古罗马人面对自己被高卢人洗劫一空的城池时一样(摘自《弗吉尼亚笔记》中第148页)。"印第安人如果不幸落入敌人的手中,他们决不会向敌人摇尾乞怜保全性命;相反,他们会不断挑拨侮辱对方以求一死。"(摘自《弗吉尼亚笔记》第150页)

② 见理培杜让所著的《路易斯安那州的历史》;查理王的著作《法国历史》;《美洲社会哲学录》第一卷;杰斐逊《弗吉尼亚笔记》,第135~190页。杰斐逊是一位道德品质高尚的作家,他独特的视角和写实的风格使其具有极其重要的分量。

③ 见附件D。

Ohio, and throughout the central valley, there are frequently found, at this day, tumuli raised by the hands of men. On exploring these heaps of earth to their center, it is usual to meet with human bones, strange instruments, arms and utensils of all kinds, made of metal, and destined for purposes unknown to the present race.

The Indians of our time are unable to give any information relative to the history of this unknown people. Neither did those who lived three hundred years ago, when America was first discovered, leave any accounts from which even a hypothesis could be formed. Traditions, those perishable yet ever recurrent monuments of the primitive world, do not provide any light. There, however, thousands of our fellow men have lived; one cannot doubt that. When did they go there, what was their origin, their destiny, their history? When and how did they disappear? No one can possibly tell.

How strange it appears that nations have existed and afterwards so completely disappeared from the earth that the memory even of their names is effaced! Their languages are lost; their glory is vanished like a sound without an echo; though perhaps there is not one which has not left behind it some tomb in memory of its passage. Thus the most durable monument of human labor is that which recalls the wretchedness and nothingness of man.

Although the vast country that I have been describing was inhabited by many indigenous tribes, it may justly be said, at the time of its discovery by Europeans, to have formed one great desert. The Indians occupied without possessing it. It is by agricultural labor that man appropriates the soil, and the early inhabitants of North America lived by the produce of the chase. Their implacable prejudices, their uncontrolled passions, their vices, and still more, perhaps, their savage virtues, consigned them to inevitable destruction. The ruin of these tribes began from the day when Europeans landed on their

两岸和整个中央盆地，人们还常常可以发现堆起的坟墓。挖开这些古冢，通常可以见到有人骨、奇形怪状的器皿、武器、金属制造的各种器具和一些不知道用途的工具。

现在的印第安人已经不能提供任何关于这个早已消失的民族的历史资料。300 年前第一次发现美洲时生活在那里的人，也没能留下任何线索据以做出猜测。远古时代继承下来的传统，因为不断地经历被破坏和再恢复的循环，也没能给我们任何启示。但是，有一点是确信的。那就是我们千千万万的同类的确在那里生活过。可是，他们是什么时候到那里的呢？他们的起源、他们的命运、他们的历史究竟是怎样的呢？他们是在何时，怎样被消灭的呢？没有一个人能够说得清楚。

真是奇怪！一些曾经存在的民族，竟从地球上消失得如此彻底，以至于他们的族名都在人们的记忆中被抹去！他们的语言早已失传，他们的辉煌也像没有回应的声音那样消逝得干干净净。也许还有一样东西可以使我们想起他们，那就是他们留下的坟墓。那才是为人类虚无、苦难的生活和劳作留下的最经久的纪念。

尽管我描述的这个广袤土地上当时住有一些土著部落，但仍然可以公正地说，在它被欧洲人发现的时候还是一片荒芜。印第安人虽然在那里居住，但并没有真正地拥有它。因为只有通过农业劳作人们才能真正的与土地融为一体。而北美的先民却以狩猎为生。他们根深蒂固的偏见，他们不可遏止的激情，他们的种种恶习，也许还要再加上野蛮品行，使得他们踏上了一条不可避免的毁灭之路。这些部族的灭亡始于欧洲人登上他们海岸的那一天，后来又一直继续进行着，直至今天正接近于尾声。上帝在

shores; it has proceeded ever since, and we are now witnessing its completion. They seem to have been placed by Providence amid the riches of the New World only to enjoy them for a season; they were there merely to wait till others came. Those coasts, so admirably adapted for commerce and industry; those wide and deep rivers; that inexhaustible valley of the Mississippi; the whole continent, in short, seemed prepared to be the abode of a great nation yet unborn.

In that land the great experiment of the attempt to construct society upon a new basis was to be made by civilized man; and it was there, for the first time, that theories hitherto unknown, or deemed impracticable, were to exhibit a spectacle for which the world had not been prepared by the history of the past.

把他们安置在新大陆这片富饶土地上时,似乎只给了他们暂时使用获益的权利。他们住在那里,仿佛是在等待接替者的到来。那些十分适于经商和工业的海岸,那些深水河流,那条用之不竭的密西西比河大河谷,总之,整个这片大陆,好像都是为一个伟大民族的来临而准备的。

就是在这里,文明人开始尝试着在一个全新的基础上建造社会。也是在这里,首次应用了当时人们尚不理解或认为行不通的理论,使世界呈现出过去没有出现过的壮观。

CHAPTER II

Origin Of The Anglo-americans,
And Importance Of This Origin In
Relation To Their Future Condition

Utility of knowing the origin of nations, in order to understand their social condition and their laws — America the only country in which the starting-point of a great people has been clearly observable— In what respects all who emigrated to British America were similar—In what they differed—Remark applicable to all the Europeans who established themselves on the shores of the New World—Colonization of Virginia—Colonization of New England—Original character of the first inhabitants of New England—Their arrival—Their first laws Their social contract—Penal code borrowed from the Hebrew legislation—Religious Fervor—Republican spirit—Intimate union of the spirit of religion with the spirit of liberty.

A Man has come into the world; his early years are spent without notice in the pleasures and activities of childhood. As he grows up, the world receives him when his manhood begins, and he enters into contact with his fellows. He is then studied for the first time, and it is imagined that the germ of the vices and the virtues of his maturer years is then formed.

This, if I am not mistaken, is a great error. We must begin higher up; we must watch the infant in his mother's arms; we must see the first images which the external world casts upon the dark mirror of his mind, the first occurrences that he witnesses; we must hear the first words which awaken the sleeping powers of thought,

第二章　英裔美国人的根源及其
对他们未来的重要影响

　　了解一个民族的来源,有利于理解其社会的状况和其法律的形成——美洲是唯一可以查清一个伟大民族的源流的地区——当初移居英属美洲的人们在一些方面彼此相似——又在一些方面彼此不同——对于当初定居在新大陆海岸的一切欧洲人的评论——弗吉尼亚殖民地——新英格兰殖民地——新英格兰首批居民初始的特性——他们的到来——他们的首批法律——社会契约——借用摩西立法的刑法典——宗教热情——共和精神——宗教精神和自由精神的紧密结合。

　　一个人生到世上来,他的童年是在欢乐和玩耍中度过的,人们不会过多地注意他的言行是否得当。随着他逐渐长大进入成年,开始同其他成年人交往,这个世界才开始接受他。这时候,人们开始注意他,而他在成年后所沾染的恶习和德行也逐渐成形。

　　如果我没弄错的话,上面的这个看法其实是个极大的错误。如果我们要理解支配一个人一生的偏见、习惯和激情的来源,我们就应当追溯他的过去,应当考虑到他在母亲怀抱中的婴儿时期,应当观察外界曾投在他懵懂的心灵上的影像,应当考虑到他最初所接触的事物,应当倾听唤醒他沉睡的思维能力的最初的话

and stand by his earliest efforts if we would understand the prejudices, the habits, and the passions which will rule his life. The entire
man is, so to speak, to be seen in the cradle of the child.

The growth of nations presents something analogous to this; they
all bear some marks of their origin. The circumstances that accompanied their birth and contributed to their development affected the
whole term of their being.

If we were able to go back to the elements of states and to examine the oldest monuments of their history, I doubt not that we should
discover in them the primal cause of the prejudices, the habits, the
ruling passions, and, in short, all that constitutes what is called the
national character. We should there find the explanation of certain
customs which now seem at variance with the prevailing manners; of
such laws as conflict with established principles; and of such incoherent opinions as are here and there to be met with in society, like those
fragments of broken chains which we sometimes see hanging from the
vaults of an old edifice, supporting nothing. This might explain the
destinies of certain nations which seem borne on by an unknown force
to ends of which they themselves are ignorant. But hitherto facts have
been lacking for such a study: the spirit of analysis has come upon
nations only as they matured; and when they at last conceived of contemplating their origin, time had already obscured it, or ignorance
and pride had surrounded it with fables behind which the truth was
hidden.

America is the only country in which it has been possible to witness the natural and tranquil growth of society, and where the influence exercised on the future condition of states by their origin is clearly distinguishable.

At the period when the peoples of Europe landed in the New
World, their national characteristics were already completely
formed; each of them had a physiognomy of its own; and as they
had already attained that stage of civilization at which men are led
to study themselves, they have transmitted to us a faithful picture
of their opinions, their manners, and their laws. The men of the
sixteenth century are almost as well known to us as our contemporaries. America, consequently, exhibits in the broad light of day the
phenomena which the ignorance or rudeness of earlier ages con-

语和他最初的奋斗。人的一生,可以说是三岁看老。

民族的发展与此类似;他们或多或少都带着其起源所留有的痕迹。伴随他们出生,帮助他们成长的环境会影响他们的一生。

如果我们能够退回到构成一个国家的基础,考察他们最古老的历史遗存,我肯定我们会从这些历史中发现造成偏见、习惯和生活中的主要喜好,简单地说,就是所有构成所谓民族性的最初的原因。据此,我们知道了造成与今天主流的行为不同的习惯的原因;找到造成现有的法律与建立的原则抵触的原因;找到社会上到处充斥的一些不连贯的看法的原因。这些不连贯的观点,就像我们平常看到在旧的建筑物的拱顶上垂落下来的断掉的链条,禁不住任何支撑。由此我们也许可以用来解释一些国家,他们承受着莫名的力量将他们推向自己也不知道的结局。但是,到目前为止,这些事实还缺少这样的研究:只有成熟的民族,才会产生这样的分析的精神;而当他们最终开始深思自己的起源时,时间早已使这些事实变得模糊,又或者被无知和骄傲用一些传奇的故事将真实的情况隐藏。

只有在美国,人们才可能见证其自然稳健的社会发展历程,才可能清楚地划分出他们的起源对其未来发展的影响。

早在欧洲人登上新大陆之前,他们的民族特性已经形成;每个民族都有其自己的特性;进入文明社会后人们开始学习研究自己,并留给我们一幅有关他们的观点、行为和法律的真实画面。我们像了解自己同时代的人们一样,也同样了解生活在 15 世纪的人们的生活状况。因此,美国使之前由于无知和野蛮造成的景象大白于天下。今天的人们似乎注定比我们的祖先能了解更多人类的事实;美国建成的时间距现在不久,因此我们得以详细地

ceals from our researches. The men of our day seem destined to see further than their predecessors into human events; they are close e-nough to the founding of the American settlements to know in detail their elements, and far enough away from that time already to be able to judge what these beginnings have produced. Providence has given us a torch which our forefathers did not possess, and has allowed us to discern fundamental causes in the history of the world which the ob-scurity of the past concealed from them. If we carefully examine the social and political state of America, after having studied its history, we shall remain perfectly convinced that not an opinion, not a cus-tom, not a law, I may even say not an event is upon record which the origin of that people will not explain. The readers of this book will find in the present chapter the germ of all that is to follow and the key to almost the whole work.

The emigrants who came at different periods to occupy the terri-tory now covered by the American Union differed from each other in many respects; their aim was not the same, and they governed them-selves on different principles.

These men had, however, certain features in common, and they were all placed in an analogous situation. The tie of language is, per-haps, the strongest and the most durable that can unite mankind. All the emigrants spoke the same language; they were all children of the same people. Born in a country which had been agitated for centuries by the struggles of faction, and in which all parties had been obliged in their turn to place themselves under the protection of the laws, their political education had been perfected in this rude school; and they were more conversant with the notions of right and the principles of true freedom than the greater part of their European contemporaries. At the period of the first emigrations the township system, that fruitful germ of free institutions, was deeply rooted in the habits of the English; and with it the doctrine of the sovereignty of the people had been intro-duced into the very bosom of the monarchy of the house of Tudor.

The religious quarrels which have agitated the Christian world were then rife. England had plunged into the new order of things with headlong vehemence. The character of its inhabitants, which had al-ways been sedate and reflective, became argumentative and austere. General information had been increased by intellectual contests, and the mind had received in them a deeper cultivation. While religion was the topic of discussion, the morals of the people became more pure.

了解其基础,但我们距离其建成的时间又不足以使我们得以正确判定这样的起源创造了怎样的结果。上帝给予我们先辈们所没能拥有的启示,使我们学会分辨世界历史的基本起因,从而使之前模糊的历史大白于天下。在研究了美国历史之后,再仔细地研究美国社会和政治状况,我们就会完全相信,在美国,没有哪个见解、习惯、法律,我甚至可以说没有哪个事件,是人们无法从这个社会的起源中找到解释的。读者可从本书这个章节中找到随后提到的所有事物的萌芽以及开启整部作品的钥匙。

来自不同时期占据不同领域的移民,尽管都在美国联邦统治下,却在很多方面有着各自不同的特点;他们各有各的目的,各自统治所依据的原则也不尽相同。

但是,他们也存在一些共性,而且他们生活的环境也有许多类似之处。语言应该说是最强有力和最持久地将人类联系在一起的纽带。所有的移民都操着相同的语言;他们拥有相同的祖先。出生在一个因为派系之间的斗争而经历了百年来动荡的国家,而最终大家都不得不屈从于法律对自己权益的捍卫,他们的政治教育也在这个粗野的环境中得到良好的培养;他们比欧洲同时代更多的人们都更了解权利的含义和真正的自由法则。在第一次移民时期,乡镇组织,这一自由体制的原体,就深深地扎根在英国人的习性之中;在此基础上,人民主权原则的学说也传入了都铎王朝的核心。

搅乱了基督教世界的宗教纷争开始越传越广。英国头脑一热,也掺和了进来。它的一度稳重善于思考的居民变得很严肃并善于争辩。人们在这一智力竞赛中大大增长了知识,头脑也得到了更进一步的训练。人们的道德随着以宗教作为主题的讨论而

All these national features are more or less discoverable in the physiognomy of those Englishmen who came to seek a new home on the opposite shores of the Atlantic.

Another observation, moreover, to which we shall have occasion to return later, is applicable not only to the English, but to the French, the Spaniards, and all the Europeans who successively established themselves in the New World. All these European colonies contained the elements, if not the development, of a complete democracy. Two causes led to this result. It may be said that on leaving the mother country the emigrants had, in general, no notion of superiority one over another. The happy and the powerful do not go into exile, and there are no surer guarantees of equality among men than poverty and misfortune. It happened, however, on several occasions, that persons of rank were driven to America by political and religious quarrels. Laws were made to establish a gradation of ranks; but it was soon found that the soil of America was opposed to a territorial aristocracy. It was realized that in order to clear this land, nothing less than the constant and self-interested efforts of the owner himself was essential; the ground prepared, it became evident that its produce was not sufficient to enrich at the same time both an owner and a farmer. The land was then naturally broken up into small portions, which the proprietor cultivated for himself. Land is the basis of an aristocracy, which clings to the soil that supports it; for it is not by privileges alone, nor by birth, but by landed property handed down from generation to generation that an aristocracy is constituted. A nation may present immense fortunes and extreme wretchedness; but unless those fortunes are territorial, there is no true aristocracy, but simply the class of the rich and that of the poor.

All the British colonies had striking similarities at the time of their origin. All of them, from their beginning, seemed destined to witness the growth, not of the aristocratic liberty of their mother country, but of that freedom of the middle and lower orders of which the history of the world had as yet furnished no complete example.

In this general uniformity, however, several marked divergences could be observed, which it is necessary to point out.

变得更加纯净。那些到大西洋彼岸寻找新的安身之处的人们的脸上都或多或少地带着这一民族特征的印记。

除此之外,我们在后面还会提到的另一个观察结果,不仅适用于英国人,也同样适用于法国人、西班牙人以及其他一些成功地在新大陆站稳脚跟的欧洲国家的人民。所有这些欧洲殖民地,即使没有发展完全民主的萌芽,也保留着民主的萌芽。这一结果的出现有两个原因。移民者在异国他乡很少会产生高人一等的感觉。大家都认为幸福的和有权势的人们是不会背井离乡的。贫穷和悲苦是地位平等最好的保障。然而有些时候,也有一些富人因为政治和宗教的分歧而被流放到美国。他们制定法律以维护等级秩序,但是不久就发现在美国,贵族统治受到了人们的抵触。于是人们开始意识到,为了开发这片土地,只有拥有者自己不断地坚持和努力才是一切的根本;土地是有限的,很明显它的产出并不足以同时满足地主和农民。然后土地就被划分成更小的小块,由所有者自己耕种。土地是贵族统治的基础。贵族与支撑他的土地密不可分,而这里既没有贵族赖以存在的特权,也没有其赖以存在的身份制度。但是如果土地可以被世代相传,那就会形成贵族制度。一个民族可能会出现大批的富人和许多穷人;但除非这些财富是归属于土地的,否则就不会存在真正的贵族,而仅仅是富人阶层和穷人阶层之分而已。

所有的英国殖民地在最初的时候都是极其相似的。他们从最初开始,就似乎注定要去见证自由的发展,而这一自由却不是如他们祖国贵族的自由,而是中下层阶级人民的自由,而这种自由在之前的世界历史中从未有过完整的模型。

尽管状况相似,但是还是有一些必须指出的显著差异。庞大

Two branches may be distinguished in the great Anglo-American family, which have hitherto grown up without entirely commingling: the one in the South, the other in the North.

Virginia received the first English colony; the immigrants took possession of it in 1607. The idea that mines of gold and silver are the sources of national wealth was at that time singularly prevalent in Europe; a fatal delusion, which has done more to impoverish the European nations who adopted it, and has cost more lives in America, than the united influence of war and bad laws. The men sent to Virginia ① were seekers of gold, adventurers without resources and without character, whose turbulent and restless spirit endangered the infant colony ② and rendered its progress uncertain. Artisans and agriculturists arrived afterwards; and, although they were a more moral and orderly race of men, they were hardly in any respect above the level of the inferior classes in England. ③ No lofty views, no spiritual conception, presided over the foundation of these new settlements. The colony was scarcely established when slavery was introduced; 4 this was the capital fact which was to exercise an immense influence on the character, the laws, and the whole future of the South. Slavery, as I shall afterwards show, dishonors labor; it introduces idleness into society, and with idleness, ignorance and pride, luxury and distress. It enervates the powers of the mind and benumbs the activity of

---

① The charter granted by the crown of England in 1609 stipulated, among other conditions that the adventurers should pay to the crown a fifth of the produce of all gold and silver mines. *See Life of* Washington, by Marshall, Vol. I, pp. 18-66.

② A large portion of the adventurers, says Stith (*History of Virginia*), were unprincipled young men of family, whom their parents were glad to ship off in order to save them from an ignominious fate, discharged servants, fraudulent bankrupts, debauchees, and others of the same class, people more apt to pillage and destroy than to promote the welfare of the settlement. Seditious leaders easily enticed this band into every kind of extravagance and excess. See for the history of Virginia the following works: *History of Virginia, from the First Settlements in the Year* 1624, *by Smith*; *History of Virginia*, by William Stith; *History of Virginia, from the Earliest Period*, by Beverley, translated into French in 1807.

③ It was not till some time later that a certain number of rich English landholders came to establish themselves in the colony.

的英裔美国人家族至今仍没能完全融合而有着不同成长经历的两大分支:一支生长在南部,另一支在北部。

　　第一个英国殖民地在弗吉尼亚州,1607 年移民占领了这片土地。这个时期,欧洲还一心迷恋于开采金矿可使国家致富的思想;这一致命的错误思想,使得那些轻信的欧洲国家的人民比战争和残酷的法律所造成的贫困更甚,而美国则因此比战争和残酷的法律下丧失的生命还要多得多。前往弗吉尼亚的都是些淘金人,①这些人无财无德。他们浮躁狂乱的性格时刻威胁着这片稚嫩的土地并使得它的发展极不稳定②。随后,一些工匠和农民来到了这里,尽管他们显得比较有涵养守秩序,可在各个方面还是摆脱不了英格兰下等人的习性③。他们缺乏对新的殖民制度建设以高尚的观点和深刻思想的指导。殖民地刚建起来,就引进了奴隶制度;这给日后南方的发展造成了极大的影响,是他们性格、法律等其他一切行为形成的最主要的事件。奴隶制度,正如我随后描述的那样,是耻辱的劳动,这给社会带来了懒散、无知、骄狂、奢侈和苦难;它使人们在精神上萎靡不振,行动上软弱无力。奴隶

---

　　①　1609 年英格兰皇室通过的宪章中的规定,值得一提的是,规定淘金人要向皇室缴纳其所得到的所有金银矿产的 15%。见《华盛顿的生命》,马歇尔著,第一卷第 18~66 页。

　　②　斯蒂斯说,大部分淘金者都是家族中不守德行的年轻人,他们的家人很愿意将他们送走,以免他们走入歧途,还有一些被撵走的仆人、假破产者、浪荡子和其他一些同一阶层的人们,他们更适合进行掠夺和破坏,而不是促进殖民地的社会安全。具有煽动性的领导者很容易就教唆这些人进行各种过度的言行。以下著作描述了弗吉尼亚的历史:史密斯著《弗吉尼亚的历史:自 1624 年第一批定居者至今》;威廉·斯蒂斯著《弗吉尼亚的历史》;贝弗利著《最早以来的弗吉尼亚史》,1807 年译为法文。

　　③　直到后来一些富裕的英国地主来到殖民地发展。

man. The influence of slavery, united to the English character, explains the manners and the social condition of the Southern states.

On this same English foundation there developed in the North very different characteristics. Here I may be allowed to enter into some details.

In the English colonies of the North, more generally known as the New England states, ① the two or three main ideas that now constitute the basis of the social theory of the United States were first combined. The principles of New England spread at first to the neighboring states; they then passed successively to the more distant ones; and at last, if I may so speak, they *interpenetrated* the whole confederation. They now extend their influence beyond its limits, over the whole American world. The civilization of New England has been like a beacon lit upon a hill, which, after it has diffused its warmth immediately around it, also tinges the distant horizon with its glow.

The foundation of New England was a novel spectacle, and all the circumstances attending it were singular and original. Nearly all colonies have been first inhabited either by men without education and without resources, driven by their poverty and their misconduct from the land which gave them birth, or by speculators and adventurers greedy of gain. Some settlements cannot even boast so honorable an origin; Santo Domingo was founded by buccaneers; and at the present day the criminal courts of England supply the population of Australia.

The settlers who established themselves on the shores of New England all belonged to the more independent classes of their native country. Their union on the soil of America at once presented the singular phenomenon of a society containing neither lords nor common people, and we may almost say neither rich nor poor. These men possessed, in proportion to their number, a greater mass of intelligence than is to be found in any European nation of our own time. All, perhaps without a single exception, had received a good education, and

① The New England states are those situated to the east of the Hudson. They are now six in number: (1) Connecticut, (2) Rhode Island, (3) Massachusetts, (4) New Hampshire, (5) Vermont, (6) Maine.

制度的影响与英国人的性格结合起来,就能解剖出美国南方的社会状况与方式。

同样是英国人建立的殖民地,南北却有着截然不同的特征。在此我可以细细道来。

人们普遍称北部英格兰殖民地为新英格兰,[①]由两三个主要观点构成了美利坚合众国社会原理的基础。新英格兰的这些思想首先传到了其邻近的州;接着又传到了距离更远的那些州;直到最后,如果我说得没错的话,传遍了整个联邦。如今,他们的影响力更是远远超出其国土范围,席卷整个美洲世界。新英格兰的文明像一座高山上的大火,为周围释放温暖的同时,也把光芒带给了远处的人们。

新英格兰的建立对人们来说是一幅全新的景象,它所有的状况都是独一无二。几乎所有殖民地的居民都没有受过教育,没有家业,他们从自己的国家来到这里,多半都是因为贫穷和流放的,要么就是一些投机者和冒险家,希望在这里获得财富。一些殖民地的居民甚至不敢说出其出身;海盗们建起了圣多明各。就是现在,英格兰法庭还是把罪犯遣往澳大利亚。

那些定居在新英格兰沿岸的居民都是在自己的国家中属于比较独立阶层的人们。他们在美国土地上形成的联合,立刻呈现了一个奇特的景象。在这样的社会中,没有大领主和平民之分,几乎可以说是没有穷人和富人之分。按照比例来说,那些人中文明程度高的人,比我们现今欧洲国家的更多些。他们无一例外的都接受了良好的教育,其中一些有才华有作为的人甚至闻名

---

① 新英格兰各州位于哈德森以东。现有六个州,分别是:(1)康涅狄格,(2)罗德岛州,(3)马萨诸塞州,(4)新汉普郡,(5)佛蒙特州,(6)缅因州。

many of them were known in Europe for their talents and their acquirements. The other colonies had been founded by adventurers without families; the immigrants of New England brought with them the best elements of order and morality; they landed on the desert coast accompanied by their wives and children. But what especially distinguished them from all others was the aim of their undertaking. They had not been obliged by necessity to leave their country; the social position they abandoned was one to be regretted, and their means of subsistence were certain. Nor did they cross the Atlantic to improve their situation or to increase their wealth; it was a purely intellectual craving that called them from the comforts of their former homes; and in facing the inevitable sufferings of exile their object was the triumph of an idea. The immigrants, or, as they deservedly styled themselves, the Pilgrims, belonged to that English sect the austerity of whose principles had acquired for them the name of Puritans. Puritanism was not merely a religious doctrine, but corresponded in many points with the most absolute democratic and republican theories. It was this tendency that had aroused its most dangerous adversaries. Persecuted by the government of the mother country, and disgusted by the habits of a society which the rigor of their own principles condemned, the Puritans went forth to seek some rude and unfrequented part of the world where they could live according to their own opinions and worship God in freedom.

A few quotations will throw more light upon the spirit of these pious adventurers than all that we can say of them. Nathaniel Morton,[①] the historian of the first years of the settlement, thus opens his subject:

"Gentle Reader, I have for some lengths of time looked upon it as a duty incumbent especially on the immediate successors of those that have had so large experience of those many memorable and signal demonstrations of God's goodness, viz. the first beginners of this Plantation in New England, to commit to writing his gracious dispensations on that behalf; having so many inducements thereunto, not only otherwise, but so plentifully in the Sacred Scriptures: that so, what we have seen, and what our fathers have told us (Psalm lxxviii. 3, 4), we may not hide from our children,

---

① *New England's Memorial* (Boston, 1826), p. 14. See also *Hutchinson's History*, Vol. II, p. 440.

欧洲各国。其他还有一些殖民地由一些单身的冒险者们建成;新英格兰的移民有良好的社会秩序和道德理念;他们刚登上这片荒芜的海岸时,只有自己的妻儿相伴。但是真正将他们与其他的居民划分开来的,还是他们的目的。他们不是因为生活所迫而来到这里;他们所丢弃的社会地位是优越的;他们也有自己稳定的生活来源。他们来新英格兰的目的,并不是为了提升自己的社会地位,也不是为了谋取财富;只是一种单纯的对文明的渴望,促使他们离开自己舒适的国度,面对流放生活带来的苦难,他们唯一的目标就是获得理想的胜利。这些移民,或者是他们自己喜欢的称谓朝圣者,他们的教派因教义严格而得名清教。清教不仅仅是一个宗教的教义,它在很多方面都与大多数完全民主的和共和的理论是一致的。因此,它给自己树立了很多敌人。清教徒遭到自己国家政府的迫害,感到社会习俗有损于自己教义的严格,于是一道远走他乡以期寻找一处蛮夷荒芜之地,以得以按照自己的方式生活并自由要崇拜上帝。

摘几段引文将比我们的赘述更能说明这些虔诚的冒险家的精神。纳萨尼尔莫顿,①这个历史学家在描述早期定居的生活时,是这样开始的:

"尊敬的读者,长久以来,把上帝所给予的大量难以忘怀的恩赐记录下来,以使经历和见证过这一切的人们的后代永远记得上帝的仁慈,是我一直以来义不容辞的职责。凡是我们见到的,凡是我们从父辈那里听到的,都应当让我们的子女知道,以使我们

---

① 《新英格兰录》(波士顿,1826 年),第 14 页。见哈金森著《历史》第二卷,第 440 页。

showing to the generations to come the praises of the Lord; that especially the seed of Abraham his servant, and the children of Jacob his chosen (Psalm cv. 5, 6), may remember his marvellous works in the beginning and progress of the planting of New England, his wonders and the judgments of his mouth; how that God brought a vine into this wilderness; that he cast out the heathen, and planted it; that he made room for it and caused it to take deep root; and it filled the land (Psalm lxxx. 8, 9). And not only so, but also that he hath guided his people by his strength to his holy habitation, and planted them in the mountain of his inheritance in respect of precious Gospel enjoyments: and that as especially God may have the glory of all unto whom it is most due; so also some rays of glory may reach the names of those blessed Saints, that were the main instruments and the beginning of this happy enterprise."

It is impossible to read this opening paragraph without an involuntary feeling of religious awe; it breathes the very savor of Gospel antiquity. The sincerity of the author heightens his power of language. In our eyes, a well as in his own, it was not a mere party of adventurers gone forth to seek their fortune beyond seas, but the germ of a great nation wafted by Providence to a predestined shore.

The author continues, and thus describes the departure of the first Pilgrims: [1]

"So they left that goodly and pleasant city of Leyden, which had been their resting-place for above eleven years; but they knew that they were pilgrims and strangers here below, and looked not much on these things, but lifted up their eyes to heaven, their dearest country, where God hath prepared for them a city (Heb. xi. 16), and therein quieted their spirits. When they came to Delfs-Haven they found the ship and all things ready; and such of their friends as could not come with them followed after them, and sundry came from Amsterdam to see them shipt, and to take their leaves of them. One night was spent with little sleep with the most, but with friendly entertainment and Christian discourse, and other real expressions of true Christian love.

---

① *New England's Memorial*, p. 22.

的后代懂得赞颂上帝;使上帝的仆人亚伯拉罕的后裔和上帝的选民雅各的子孙(《诗篇》第 105 篇第 5、6 节)永远记住上帝在新英格兰种植地最初和发展过程中的奇妙作为、他所说的奇迹和做出的断言。要使他们知道上帝如何把葡萄带到荒野,如何把异教徒撵走并栽上葡萄,如何整备出种葡萄的用地,把秧苗的根深深植入土内,以及后来又如何让葡萄爬蔓而布满大地。不仅如此,还要让他们知道上帝如何引导他的子民走向他的圣所,而定居在他遗赐的山间、这些事实一定要使他们知道,以使上帝得到他应得的荣誉,让上帝的荣光也能被及作为工具为他服务的圣徒们的可敬名字。"

读罢这段开头,油然而生一种对宗教的敬畏之情;呼吸吐纳之间伴着古老的《圣经·新约》的气息。作者真挚的感情增强了其文字的力量。在我们看来,和作者所看到的一样,他们不仅仅是一群冒险者漂洋过海寻找财富,而且是上帝赐予其这片命定的海岸,并且成长为伟大民族的创造者。

作者接着这般描述前几批朝圣者们出发时的情景,说:[1]

"于是,他们离开了自己优美舒适的城市,在那里他们已经生活了 11 年多;但他们是心安理得的,因为他们知道自己此生是朝圣者和异乡人。他们不留恋世间的东西,而是眼望上苍,上帝已在那里为他们准备了城市,那里才是他们亲爱的故乡,他们的灵魂将在那里得到安宁。他们终于到达停着船只的代夫特港口。岸上站满了不能随他们同行的亲友。还有各式各样从阿姆斯特丹赶来看他们远航并为他们送行的人。大家一夜没睡,在倾吐友

---

[1] 《新英格兰录》,第 22 页。

The next day they went on board, and their friends with them, where truly doleful was the sight of that sad and mournful parting, to hear what sighs and sobs and prayers did sound amongst them; what tears did gush from every eye, and pithy speeches pierced each other's heart, that sundry of the Dutch strangers that stood on the Key as spectators could not refrain from tears. But the tide (which stays for no man) calling them away, that were thus loth to depart, their Reverend Pastor, falling down on his knees, and they all with him, with watery cheeks commended them with most fervent prayers unto the Lord and his blessing; and then with mutual embraces and many tears they took their leaves one of another, which proved to be the last leave to many of them."

The emigrants were about 150 in number, including the women and the children. Their object was to plant a colony on the shores of the Hudson; but after having been driven about for some time in the Atlantic Ocean, they were forced to land on the arid coast of New England, at the spot which is now the town of Plymouth. The rock is still shown on which the Pilgrims disembarked. ①

"But before we pass on," continues our historian,' ② "let the reader with me make a pause, and seriously consider this poor people's present condition, the more to be raised up to admiration of God's goodness towards them in their preservation: for being now passed the vast ocean, and a sea of troubles before them in expectation, they had now no friends to welcome them, no inns to entertain or refresh them, no houses, or much less towns, to repair unto to seek for succour: and for the season it was winter, and they that know the winters of the country know them to be sharp and violent, subject to cruel and fierce storms, dangerous to travel to known places, much

---

① This rock has become an object of veneration in the United States. I have seen bits of it carefully preserved in several towns of the Union. Does not this sufficiently show how all human power and greatness are entirely in the soul? Here is a stone which the feet of a few poor fugitives pressed for an instant, and this stone becomes famous; it is treasured by a great nation, a fragment is prized as a relic. But what has become of the doorsteps of a thousand palaces? Who troubles himself about them?

② *New England's Memorial*, p. 35.

情、诚恳交心和表达基督徒的真正慈爱的谈话中度过一夜。第二天,他们上船了,可是亲友们还想在船上陪伴他们一会儿,甲板上到处是悲伤的离别场面,叹息声、呜咽的呼声夹杂着人们的祷告声;人们泪如泉涌,彼此说着感人的话语。这悲伤的画面,使得站在一旁的陌生人都禁不住热泪盈眶。开船的信号发出来了(潮汐不等人啊),分别的时候到了,尊贵的牧师先跪了下来,大家跟着跪下来,眼泪汪汪,仰望天空,祈求上帝赐福;最后,他们互相拥抱,哭泣着互道珍重,对他们大多数人来说这也将是永别。"

这批移民有 150 多人,加上妇女和儿童。他们的目的是在今美国纽约州东部海岸开垦一片殖民地;但是在大西洋中漂泊了一段时间后,不得不在新英格兰贫瘠的海岸登陆,登陆点正是现在的普利茅斯。那里仍然有一块岩石,标记着移民者登陆的地点。[①]

"但是在我们长篇大叙之前,"我们这位历史学家接着写道,[②]"请读者跟我一起暂停一下,让我们来仔细考虑一下这些穷苦的人们当时的状况,赞美上帝对他们的仁慈:他们现在已经跨越了大西洋,呈现在眼前的是他们预料中的一系列的问题。这里没有亲人朋友的欢呼声,没有旅馆入住得以休养,没有房子,甚至没有小镇可以求援。当时正是严冬,了解这个地方冬天的气候的人们都知道,这里的冬天是冷冽的,伴有暴风雪。在这样的天气中去熟悉

---

① 这块岩石受到美国人民的崇拜。我在联盟中许多城镇都见到仔细保存着的这块大石的碎片。这难道还不足以说明人类的力量和伟大是如何在人们的精神中发挥作用的吗? 这是一块记载着一些穷困的逃亡者的足迹的石头,并且它很有名气;它被一个伟大民族视若珍宝,每一块碎片都被当作是一块遗物。但是,什么样的石头最终变为了宫殿的台阶? 又是谁使得自己为他们烦恼呢?

② 《新英格兰录》,第 35 页。

more to search unknown coasts. Besides, what could they see but a hideous and desolate wilderness, full of wilde beasts, and wilde men? and what multitudes of them there were, they then knew not: for which way soever they turned their eyes (save upward to Heaven) they could have but little solace or content in respect of any outward object; for summer being ended, all things stand in appearance with a weather-beaten face, and the whole country, full of woods and thickets, represented a wild and savage hew; if they looked behind them, there was the mighty ocean which they had passed, and was now as a main bar or gulph to separate them from all the civil parts of the world. "

It must not be imagined that the piety of the Puritans was merely speculative, or that it took no cognizance of the course of worldly affairs. Puritanism, as I have already remarked, was almost as much a political theory as a religious doctrine. No sooner had the immigrants landed on the barren coast described by Nathaniel Morton than it was their first care to constitute a society, by subscribing the following Act:[1]

"IN THE NAME OF GOD. AMEN. We, whose names are underwritten, the loyal subjects of our dread Sovereign Lord King James, &c. &c. , Having undertaken for the glory of God, and advancement of the Christian Faith, and the honour of our King and country, a voyage to plant the first colony in the northern parts of Virginia; Do by these presents solemnly and mutually, in the presence of God and one another, covenant and combine ourselves together into a civil body politick, for our better ordering and preservation, and furtherance of the ends aforesaid: and by virtue hereof do enact, constitute, and frame such just and equal laws, ordinances, acts, constitutions, and offices, from time to time, as shall be thought most meet and convenient for the general good of the Colony: unto which we promise all due submission and obedience," etc.

This happened in 1620, and from that time forwards the emigration went on. The religious and political passion which ravaged the British Empire during the whole reign of Charles I drove fresh crowds of sectarians every year to the shores of America.

---

① The emigrants who founded the state of Rhode Island in 1638, those who landed at New Haven in 1637, the first settlers in Connecticut in 1639, and the founders of Providence in 1640 began in like manner by drawing up a social contract, which was acceded to by all the interested parties. See Pitkin's *History*, pp. 42 and 47.

的地方都很危险,更别说去寻找陌生的海岸了。除此之外,周围入眼皆是荒无人烟,到处都是野兽和野人。他们不知道这些野兽和人到底有多少:眼望苍天才能够得到一点慰藉和想到外面的世界时的满足;在自己的家乡,夏天结束的时候,所有的东西都好像被太阳晒得红彤彤的,到处是森林和灌木丛,人们大力地开采;可是如果向后看,只有他们穿越的浩瀚的海洋,阻断了他们与文明世界的一切联系。"

不要认为清教徒的虔诚仅仅是说在嘴上,也不要以为他们不谙世事。正如我所说过的,清教的教义既是宗教学说,又是政治理论。因此,移民们在刚刚登上纳撒尼尔·莫尔顿描述的贫瘠的海岸,第一件关心的事情就是建立自己的社会。他们立即通过一项公约,①内称:

"以上帝的名义,阿门。我们,在下面签名的人,上帝忠诚的子民,为了上帝的荣耀,为了发扬基督教的信仰和祖国的荣誉,漂洋过海来到弗吉尼亚北部开拓第一个殖民地;我们谨在上帝的面前,对着在场的这些妇女,通过彼此庄严表示的同意,现约定将我们全体组成政治社会,以管理我们自己和致力于实现我们的目的。我们将根据这项契约颁布法律、法令和命令,并视需要而任命我们应当服从的行政官员。"

这个事件发生在1620年,从那时起,移民的工作就一直没停过。查尔斯一世统治期间,宗教和政治的热情使英国王权的统治动荡不安,每年都要往美国送一批新的宗教主义者。英国清教徒

---

① 1638年发现了罗德岛的移民,那些1637年登陆纽黑文的移民,1639年康涅狄格的第一批定居者,以及1640年普罗维登斯的创造者开始起草一份由所有有志于此的州参加的社会契约。见培特金:《历史》,第42页、47页。

In England the stronghold of Puritanism continued to be in the middle classes; and it was from the middle classes that most of the emigrants came. The population of New England increased rapidly; and while the hierarchy of rank despotically classed the inhabitants of the mother country, the colony approximated more and more the novel spectacle of a community homogeneous in all its parts. A democracy more perfect than antiquity had dared to dream of started in full size and panoply from the midst of an ancient feudal society.

The English government was not dissatisfied with a large emigration which removed the elements of fresh discord and further revolutions. On the contrary, it did everything to encourage it and seemed to have no anxiety about the destiny of those who sought a shelter from the rigor of their laws on the soil of America. It appeared as if New England was a region given up to the dreams of fancy and the unrestrained experiments of innovators.

The English colonies (and this is one of the main causes of their prosperity) have always enjoyed more internal freedom and more political independence than the colonies of other nations; and this principle of liberty was nowhere more extensively applied than in the New England states.

It was generally allowed at that period that the territories of the New World belonged to that European nation which had been the first to discover them. Nearly the whole coast of North America thus became a British possession towards the end of the sixteenth century. The means used by the English government to people these new domains were of several kinds: the king sometimes appointed a governor of his own choice, who ruled a portion of the New World in the name and under the immediate orders of the crown;[1] this is the colonial system adopted by the other countries of Europe. Sometimes grants of certain tracts were made by the crown to an individual or to a company,[2] in which case all the civil and political power fell into the hands of one or more persons, who, under the inspection and control of the

---

[1] This was the case in the state of New York.

[2] Maryland, the Carolinas, Pennsylvania, and New Jersey were in this situation. See Pitkin's *History*, Vol. I, pp. 11-31.

的来源主要还是中层阶级的人们；并且大多数移民也都属于中层阶级。大量的移民使新英格兰的人口数量剧增；当祖国的居民仍被按照等级制度专政地划分开来的时候，殖民地在各个方面已经越来越多地呈现出同一化的新局面。与旧制度相比更显完美的民主，在旧制度下几乎不敢想象，而今却也从全副武装的古老的封建社会整装出发了。

英国政府并没有不满意，因为大量的移民带走了社会动荡和进一步发生革命的基本因素。反过来说，它很支持移民这件事并毫不担心那些为逃避本国法律而到美国寻找保护的人们的命运。仿佛新英格兰是一块充满神奇的梦想可以让改革者毫无限制地作为的地方。

英国的殖民地一直都比其他国家的殖民地享有更多的内部自由和政治独立（这也是它们繁荣的一个主要原因）；而且，再没有其他地方的自由原则可以像在新英格兰州实施得这样广阔。

那时候大家已经达成共识，新大陆的疆域属于首先发现它的欧洲国家。因此到了 16 世纪末，北美洲几乎所有的海岸都成了英国的领土。当时英国政府对这些新领地的统治分几种方式：有时是国王亲自任命一名官员，这名官员以国王的名义统治新大陆的一部分领域并直接受国王的控制，①这一殖民体系为欧洲其他国家所采用；还有就是国王将大片领土分给个人或公司②，以这种方式的话，相应的民事和政治权利也就落到了一个或者许多人

---

① 这是纽约州的一个案例。

② 马里兰、卡罗来纳、宾夕法尼亚和新泽西当时都处于这样的环境。见培特金：《历史》第一卷，第 11 ~ 31 页。

crown, sold the lands and governed the inhabitants. Lastly, a third system consisted in allowing a certain number of emigrants to form themselves into a political society under the protection of the mother country and to govern themselves in whatever was not contrary to her laws. This mode of colonization, so favorable to liberty, was adopted only in New England. ①

In 1628 ② a charter of this kind was granted by Charles I to the emigrants who went to form the colony of Massachusetts. But, in general, charters were not given to the colonies of New England till their existence had become an established fact. Plymouth, Providence, New Haven, Connecticut, and Rhode Island ③ were founded without the help and almost without the knowledge of the mother country. The new settlers did not derive their powers from the head of the empire, although they did not deny its supremacy; they constituted themselves into a society, and it was not till thirty or forty years afterwards, under Charles II, that their existence was legally recognized by a royal charter.

This frequently renders it difficult, in studying the earliest historical and legislative records of New England, to detect the link that connected the emigrants with the land of their forefathers. They continually exercised the rights of sovereignty; they named their magistrates, concluded peace or declared war, made police regulations, and enacted laws, as if their allegiance was due only to God. ④

---

① See the work entitled *Historical Collection of State Papers and Other Authentic Documents Intended as Materials for a History of the United States of America*, by Ebenezer Hazard, printed at Philadelphia, 1792, for a great number of documents relating to the commencement of the colonies, which are valuable for their contents and their authenticity; among them are the various charters granted by the English crown, and the first acts of the local governments.

See also the analysis of all these charters given by Mr. Story, Judge of the Supreme Court of the United States, in the Introduction to his *Commentaries on the Constitution of the United States*. It is proved by these documents that the principles of representative government and the external forms of political liberty were introduced into all the colonies almost from their origin. These principles were more fully acted upon in the North than in the South, but they existed everywhere.

② See Pitkin's *History*, p. 35. Also, the *History of the Colony of Massachusetts Bay*, by Hutchinson, Vol. I, p. 9.

③ See ibid. , pp. 42, 47.

④ The inhabitants of Massachusetts had deviated from the forms that are preserved in the criminal and civil procedure of England; in 1650 the name of the king was not yet put at the head of the decrees of justice. See Hutchinson, Vol. I, p. 452.

手中,这些人在国王的监督和控制下变卖土地,统治居民;最后,第三种方法,由一批得到许可的移民自己组成一个政治社会并受到其祖国的保护,他们在不违背祖国法律的前提下自己管理自己的事务。这种殖民地统治方式,有利于自由的发展,也只为新大陆采用。①

1628 年②查理一世就为准备建立马萨诸塞州的移民们颁布了一则具有这种性质的特许状。但是,新英格兰的其他殖民地都是在其统治已既成事实之后,才颁布了相应的特许状。像普利茅斯、普罗维登斯、新港、康涅狄格和罗德埃兰州③的建立没有得到其祖国的帮助,甚至根本就是在他们毫不知情的情况下建立起来的。新的居民尽管没有否认国王的权力至上,但也没从他那里得到权力;他们自己组建了社会,并且直到三四十年后查理二世统治时期,他们的存在才通过王室的特许状得到了法律的认可。

因此,在研究早期新英格兰的历史法律著作时,就常常会发现很难找到移民和其原来祖国之间的联系。他们依然行使自己的主权;他们可以任命官员,宣布和谈或开战,制定公安规定,制定法律。他们似乎只对上帝忠诚。④

---

①　见著作《州论文和其他权威资料以作美国历史材料的历史收集》,埃比尼泽·哈泽德著,费城 1792 年出版,一大批关于殖民地的初始的文献,具有有价值的内容和其真实性;在这些著作中,有英国皇室颁布的不同的宪章,以及地方政府实行的第一部法令。

以及斯托里先生,美国联邦最高法院法官,对所有的宪章的分析,在他对联邦宪法的解说的引言中。这些文件证实了代议制的原理和政治自由的外在形式被所有的殖民地从最初开始就被引入。这些原则尽管到处存在,但在北部比在南部等到了更充分地实施。

②　见培特金:《历史》第 35 页。以及哈金森著《马萨诸塞州殖民地史》第一卷,第 9 页。

③　如上,第 42、47 页。

④　马萨诸塞州的居民偏离了英国保留的刑事和民事程序的形式。1650 年国王的名字不再置于司法判决的开头。见哈金森著《马萨诸塞州殖民地史》,第一卷,第 452 页。

Nothing can be more curious and at the same time more instructive than the legislation of that period; it is there that the solution of the great social problem which the United States now presents to the world is to be found.

Among these documents we shall notice as especially characteristic the code of laws promulgated by the little state of Connecticut in 1650. [1]

The legislators of Connecticut [2] begin with the penal laws, and, strange to say, they borrow their provisions from the text of Holy Writ.

"Whosoever shall worship any other God than the Lord," says the preamble of the Code, "shall surely be put to death. " This is followed by ten or twelve enactments of the same kind, copied verbatim from the books of Exodus, Leviticus, and Deuteronomy. Blasphemy, sorcery, adultery, [3] and rape were punished with death; an outrage offered by a son to his parents was to be expiated by the same penalty. The legislation of a rude and half-civilized people was thus applied to an enlightened and moral community. The consequence was, that the punishment of death was never more frequently prescribed by statute, and never more rarely enforced.

The chief care of the legislators in this body of penal laws was the maintenance of orderly conduct and good morals in the community;

---

[1] *Code* of 1650, p. 28 (Hartford, 1830).

[2] See also in Hutchinson's *History*, Vol. I, pp. 435-6, the analysis of the penal code adopted in 1648 by the colony of Massachusetts. This code is drawn up on the same principles as that of Connecticut.

[3] Adultery was also punished with death by the law of Massachusetts: and Hutchinson (Vol. I, p. 441) says that several persons actually suffered for this crime. On this subject he quotes a curious anecdote of what took place in the year 1663. A married woman had had criminal intercourse with a young man; her husband died, and she married the lover. Several years had elapsed when the public began to suspect the previous intercourse of this couple; they were thrown into prison, put to trial, and very narrowly escaped capital punishment.

这时期制定的法律最让人好奇也最具有指导意义;现在美国呈现在世界公众面前的重大社会问题,在这些法律中都能找到解决的途径。

在这些法规中,我们尤其应该引起注意的,是 1650 年一个小州康涅狄格颁布的一部法典。[1]

康涅狄格的立法者们[2]最初制定的是刑法,奇怪的是,他们竟然引用《圣经》的原文作为法律条文。

"凡信仰除上帝以外的其他诸神,"法典的导言中如是说,"处以死刑。"有十或十二条同类的条文,都是逐字摘自《出埃及记》、《利未记》和《申命记》的原文。亵渎神灵、施巫术、通奸[3]和强奸都处死刑;子女虐待父母的,被处以相等的刑罚。就这样,一部野蛮未完全开化的民族制定的法律,被文明开化道德秩序井然的社会所采用。这样造成的结果就是,死刑被最大限度的使用并强制执行。

对于这一刑法体系,立法者主要关注的就是其对有序社会秩序的引导和良好道德风尚的维护;因此,他们一直很注重人们

---

① 1650 年法典,第 28 页(哈特福德,1830)。

② 见哈金森:《历史》第一卷,第 435～436 页,1648 年马萨诸塞州刑法典分析。这部刑法典编撰的原则与康涅狄格的一致。

③ 马萨诸塞州法律规定通奸亦判死刑;哈金森(第一卷第 441 页)说,确实有一些犯此罪的遭受此刑罚。就此论题,他还引用了一个 1663 年发生的奇怪的案件。一位已婚女性与一名男子有着非法的交往;她的丈夫死后,她与自己的情人结婚。许多年后,公众开始调查这对夫妇从前的违法行为;他们被关进监狱接受审讯,最后勉强逃脱了惩罚。

thus they constantly invaded the domain of conscience, and there was scarcely a sin which was not subject to magisterial censure. The reader is aware of the rigor with which these laws punished rape and adultery; intercourse between unmarried persons was likewise severely repressed. The judge was empowered to inflict either a pecuniary penalty, a whipping, or marriage [1] on the misdemeanants, and if the records of the old courts of New Haven may be believed, prosecutions of this kind were not infrequent. We find a sentence, bearing the date of May 1, 1660, inflicting a fine and reprimand on a young woman who was accused of using improper language and of allowing herself to be kissed. [2] The Code of 1650 abounds in preventive measures. It punishes idleness and drunkenness with severity. [3] Innkeepers were forbidden to furnish more than a certain quantity of liquor to each consumer; and simple lying, whenever it may be injurious, [4] is checked by a fine or a flogging. In other places the legislator, entirely forgetting the great principles of religious toleration that he had himself demanded in Europe, makes attendance on divine service compulsory, [5] and goes so far as to visit with severe punishment, [6] and even with death, Christians who chose to worship God according to a ritual differing from his own. [7]

---

[1]　Code of 1650, p. 48. It appears sometimes to have happened that the judges inflicted these punishments cumulatively, as is seen in a sentence pronounced in 1643 (*New Haven Antiquities.* p. 114), by which Margaret Bedford, convicted of loose conduct, was condemned to be whipped and afterwards to marry Nicolas Jemmings, her accomplice.

[2]　*New Haven Antiquities*, p. 104. See also Hutchinson's *History*, Vol. I, p. 435, for several causes equally extraordinary.

[3]　*Code of* 1650, pp. 50, 57.

[4]　Ibid. , p. 64.

[5]　Ibid. , p. 44.

[6]　This was not peculiar to Connecticut. See, for instance, the law which, on September 13, 1644, banished the Anabaptists from Massachusetts (*Historical Collection of* State Papers, Vol. I, p. 538). See also the law against the Quakers, passed on October 14, 1656. "Whereas. " says the preamble, "an accursed race of heretics called Quakers has sprung up," etc. The clauses of the statute inflict a heavy fine on all captains of ships who should import Quakers into the country. The Quakers who may be found there shall be whipped and imprisoned with hard labor. Those members of the sect who should defend their opinions shall be first fined, then imprisoned, and finally driven out of the province. *Historical Collection of State Papers*, Vol. I, p. 630.

[7]　By the penal law of Massachusetts, any Catholic priest who should set foot in the colony after having been once driven out of it was liable to capital punishment.

的道德领域,几乎没有一件罪过不受到惩罚的。读者已经知道了法律惩治强奸犯和通奸犯的严厉性;未婚男女之间的交往也受到同样严厉的禁止。法官有权对这些罪犯处以罚款、刑罚或迫使他们结婚。[①] 如果纽黑文那时的法庭记录准确的话,这种判决并不少见。我们找到了一条 1660 年 5 月 1 日的判决,一位少妇因为言语轻佻并被人吻了一下而被处以罚款和申诉。[②] 1650 年的法典中包含了许多预防性的惩罚措施。该法典对懒怠的人和酗酒的人课以严厉的惩罚。[③] 酒店严禁向每位顾客提供超过一定数量的酒水;仅是一个谎言,无论何时只要它产生了危害的结果[④],都处以罚款或鞭笞。在其他方面,立法者完全忘记了其在欧洲所要求的宗教自由,而强迫人们信教,[⑤]直至处以严厉的惩罚。[⑥] 甚至基督教徒根据与其礼仪完全不同的形式信仰上帝就会被处死。[⑦]

---

① 1650 年法典,第 48 页。有时还会发生这样的情况,法官的判决会因年长日久而加重处罚,像 1643 年宣布的一些判决(纽黑文遗迹,114 页),玛格丽特·贝格福德犯行为放纵罪,被判处鞭笞并嫁给同案犯尼古拉斯·吉明。

② 纽黑文遗迹,第 104 页。见哈金森:《历史》第一卷,第 435 页,一些原因同样奇特。

③ 1650 年法典,第 50、57 页。

④ 如上,第 64 页。

⑤ 如上,第 44 页

⑥ 这在康涅狄格并不罕见。比如说,1644 年 9 月 13 日的法律将再洗礼派教徒从马萨诸塞州放逐(州论文的历史收集,第一卷,第 538 页)。还有1656 年 10 月 14 日通过的反对教友派信徒的法律。"然而"导言中说,"被称为教友派信徒一个受诅咒的种族出现了"等。法律条款还规定了对所有的搭载教友派信徒入国的船长处以重金罚款。对发现的教友派信徒处以鞭笞和苦力监禁。这些教派的成员,如果维护其教义,则会被处以罚款,然后监禁,最终驱除出境。《州论文和其他权威资料以作美国历史材料的历史收集》第一卷,第 630 页。

⑦ 马萨诸塞州刑法规定,所有天主教徒,一旦被逐出本教后踏入殖民地,就必须缴纳罚款。

Sometimes, indeed, the zeal for regulation induces him to descend to the most frivolous particulars: thus a law is to be found in the same code which prohibits the use of tobacco. [1] It must not be forgotten that these fantastic and oppressive laws were not imposed by authority, but that they were freely voted by all the persons interested in them, and that the customs of the community were even more austere and puritanical than the laws. In 1649 a solemn association was formed in Boston to check the worldly luxury of long hair. [2]

These errors are no doubt discrecditable to human reason; they attest the inferiority of our nature, which is incapable of laying firm hold upon what is true and just and is often reduced to the alternative of two excesses. In strict connection with this penal legislation, which bears such striking marks of a narrow, sectarian spirit and of those religious passions which had been warmed by persecution and were still fermenting among the people, a body of political laws is to be found which, though written two hundred years ago, is still in advance of the liberties of our age.

The general principles which are the groundwork of modern constitutions, principles which, in the seventeenth century, were imperfectly known in Europe, and not completely triumphant even in Great Britain, were all recognized and established by the laws of New England: the intervention of the people in public affairs, the free voting of taxes, the responsibility of the agents of power, personal liberty, and trial by jury were all positively established without discussion.

These fruitful principles were there applied and developed to an extent such as no nation in Europe has yet ventured to attempt.

In Connecticut the electoral body consisted, from its origin, of the whole number of citizens; and this is readily to be understood. [3]

---

[1] *Code* of 1650, p. 96.

[2] *New England's Memorial*, p. 316. See Appendix E.

[3] Constitution of 1638, p. 17.

实际上,有些时候,对一些制度的狂热使得他作出一些不该做的事情:于是在法典中就有了禁烟的法条。① 有一点要记得,这些荒诞严厉的法律并不是由当权者强制执行的,而是由全体当事人投票表决的,社会的习俗远比法律的规定严厉和富有清教性质得多。1649 年波士顿庄严地成立了劝阻人们留长发的奢华行为的协会。②

这样的偏颇,无疑有辱于人类的理性。这也证实了人类的劣根性,不能一直坚守真理和正义而常常陷入其相反的一面。虽然与具有明显的狭隘的宗派精神的特点,以及具有酝酿在人们当中为迫害行为所激发的宗教热情烙印的刑法有一定的联系,这部制定于 200 多年前的政治方面的法律,仍然领先于我们现代的自由主义精神。

作为现代宪法和原则基础的一般原则,在欧洲并不为人所知,甚至在大不列颠也没有取得广泛的认可,而在新英格兰得到大家的公认和确立:人们可以参与公共事务、自由投票决定赋税、行政官员职责的确定、人身的自由和陪审团制度都毫无异议地一致通过并得以确立。

这些富有成效的原则在新英格兰得以实施并进一步发展,而在欧洲却没有任何一个国家敢冒险尝试。

康涅狄格州一开始就是全体公民都有选举权,而且这一做法得到了大家的理解。③ 在这个年轻的国度,人们财富均等,并

---

① 1650 年法典,第 96 页。
② 《新英格兰录》,第 316 页。见附件 E。
③ 1638 年宪法,第 17 页。

In this young community there was an almost perfect equality of fortune, and a still greater uniformity of opinions. ① In Connecticut at this period all the executive officials were elected, including the governor of the state. ② The citizens above the age of sixteen were obliged to bear arms; they formed a national militia, which appointed its own officers, and was to hold itself at all times in readiness to march for the defense of the country. ③

In the laws of Connecticut, as well as in all those of New England, we find the germ and gradual development of that township independence which is the life and mainspring of American liberty at the present day. The political existence of the majority of the nations of Europe commenced in the superior ranks of society and was gradually and imperfectly communicated to the different members of the social body. In America, on the contrary, it may be said that the township was organized before the county, the county before the state, the state before the union.

In New England, townships were completely and definitely constituted as early as 1650. The independence of the township was the nucleus round which the local interests, passions, rights, and duties collected and clung. It gave scope to the activity of a real political life, thoroughly democratic and republican. The colonies still recognized the supremacy of the mother country; monarchy was still the law of the state; but the republic was already established in every township.

The towns named their own magistrates of every kind, assessed themselves, and levied their own taxes. ④ In the New England town the law of representation was not adopted; but the affairs of the community were discussed, as at Athens, in the marketplace, by a general assembly of the citizens.

In studying the laws that were promulgated at this early era of the American republics, it is impossible not to be struck by the legislator's knowledge of government and advanced theories.

---

① In 1641 the General Assembly of Rhode Island unanimously declared that the government of the state was a democracy, and that the power was vested in the body of free citizens, who alone had the right to make the laws and to watch their execution. *Code* of 1650, p. 70.

② Pitkin's *History*, p. 47.

③ Constitution of 1638, p. 12.

④ *Code* of 1650, p. 80.

且具有高度统一的意见。① 这个时期的康涅狄格,所有的行政官员都由选举产生,包括那些州的官员。② 年满 16 岁的公民人人都有义务参军;他们组成了州的民兵队伍,拥有自己的指挥官,时时备战以保卫国家。③

在康涅狄格甚至全新英格兰的法律中,我们发现了在今天看来是美国自由主义的生命和起因的乡镇独立的萌芽及其缓慢发展。政治生活在大多数欧洲国家都产生在社会上层阶级,然后逐渐且不完全地扩展到社会其他不同阶层的人们中间。在美国刚好相反,美国的乡镇体系的建立早于县的建立,县又比州的建立早,最后才由州组成了联邦。

在新英格兰,1650 年就建立了完整的乡镇体系。当地的利益、情感、权力和职责都是围绕着地方自治而存在的。它促成了真正、彻底的民主和共和的政治生活。殖民地仍然承认其宗主国至高无上的权力;君主政体仍然被写在各州的法律内;但共和政体在各州都已完全建立起来。

城镇自行任命其各类官员,规定自己的税则并且自行征收赋税。④ 在新英格兰的城镇没有采用代议制的法律;但是像雅典一样,社会事务在公共场合召开公民大会讨论解决。

研究美国共和政体早期的法律,一定会被美国立法者对于政府管理的才能和先进的理论所撼动。他们对于社会对公民承担

---

① 1641 年,罗德岛州公民大会一致通过并宣布,州政府是民主政体,所有权利掌握在自由公民手中,公民有权制定法律并监督执行。1650 年法典,第 70 页。

② 《培特金史》,第 47 页。

③ 1638 年宪法,第 12 页。

④ 1650 年法典,第 80 页。

The ideas there formed of the duties of society towards its members are evidently much loftier and more comprehensive than those of European legislators at that time; obligations were there imposed upon it which it elsewhere slighted. In the states of New England, from the first, the condition of the poor was provided for; ① strict measures were taken for the maintenance of roads, and surveyors were appointed to attend to them; ② records were established in every town, in which the results of public deliberations and the births, deaths, and marriages of the citizens were entered; ③ clerks were directed to keep these records; ④ officers were appointed to administer the properties having no claimants, and others to determine the boundaries of inherited lands, and still others whose principal functions were to maintain public order in the community. ⑤ The law enters into a thousand various details to anticipate and satisfy a crowd of social wants that are even now very inadequately felt in France.

But it is by the mandates relating to public education that the original character of American civilization is at once placed in the clearest light. ⑥ "Whereas," says the law, "Satan, the enemy of mankind, finds his strongest weapons in the ignorance of men, and whereas it is important that the wisdom of our fathers shall not remain buried in their tombs, and whereas the education of children is one of the prime concerns of the state, with the aid of the Lord. . ." Here follow clauses establishing schools in every township and obliging the inhabitants, under pain of heavy fines, to support them. Schools of a superior kind were founded in the same manner in the more populous districts. The municipal authorities were bound to enforce the sending of children to school by their parents; they were empowered to inflict fines upon all who refused compliance; and in cases of continued resistance, society assumed the place of the parent, took possession of the child, and deprived the father of those natural rights which he used to so bad a purpose. ⑦ The reader will undoubtedly have remarked the preamble of these enactments:

---

① Code of 1650. , p. 78.
② Ibid. , p. 49.
③ See Hutchinson's History, Vol. I, p. 455.
④ *Code* of 1650, p. 86.
⑤ Ibid. , p. 40.
⑥ Ibid. , p. 90.
⑦ Ibid. , p. 83.

的职责构成的想法明显比那时欧洲的立法者的立意更加崇高,更加全面;他们为社会规定的义务,至今仍然被一些地方所忽视。在新英格兰州,从最初开始,就对穷人实施救济;①并采取严格的措施养护道路,并指派检查员参与措施实施;②每个乡镇都建立起了各种公文记事簿,记录公民大会商议的结果,以及公民的出生、死亡时间和婚姻状态;③设置文书保管这些记录;④一些官员被任命管理无人认领的财产,还有的处断地产继承的划分,还有一部分官员的主要任务就是维护社会秩序稳定。⑤法律规定了上千条条文预料社会事务,满足社会需要,这甚至在现在的法国都没有全部实现。

但是,美国民主本质最突出的特点,在于其有关公共教育的指令。⑥"然而,"法律规定,"鉴于人类的敌人撒旦,借助人类的无知为其最强有力的武器,鉴于祖辈的智慧再不会被埋没,鉴于儿童的教育是本州的核心问题之一,在上帝的帮助下……"接着是一些条款,规定在每个州都兴建学校,要求公民有义务出资办学。高一级中学以同样的方式建在人口密集州。市政当局应当强制父母要孩子接受教育;对不服从的父母处以罚款;如果父母继续违抗,社会便承担其家长的责任,并剥夺其用于不良目的对孩子的天赋权利。⑦ 读者从这一法令的导言中可知:在美国,宗教是通

---

① 1650 年《法典》,第 78 页。

② 如上,第 49 页。

③ 见《哈金森史》第一卷,第 455 页。

④ 1650 年《法典》,第 86 页。

⑤ 如上,第 40 页。

⑥ 如上,第 90 页。

⑦ 如上,第 83 页。

in America religion is the road to knowledge, and the observance of the divine laws leads man to civil freedom.

If, after having cast a rapid glance over the state of American society in 1650, we turn to the condition of Europe, and more especially to that of the Continent, at the same period, we cannot fail to be struck with astonishment. On the continent of Europe at the beginning of the seventeenth century absolute monarchy had everywhere triumphed over the ruins of the oligarchical and feudal liberties of the Middle Ages. Never perhaps were the ideas of right more completely overlooked than in the midst of the splendor and literature of Europe; never was there less political activity among the people; never were the principles of true freedom less widely circulated; and at that very time those principles which were scorned or unknown by the nations of Europe were proclaimed in the deserts of the New World and were accepted as the future creed of a great people. The boldest theories of the human mind were reduced to practice by a community so humble that not a statesman condescended to attend to it; and a system of legislation without a precedent was produced offhand by the natural originality of men's imaginations. In the bosom of this obscure democracy, which had as yet brought forth neither generals nor philosophers nor authors, a man might stand up in the face of a free people, and pronounce with general applause the following fine definition of liberty:

"Concerning liberty, I observe a great mistake in the country about that. There is a twofold liberty, natural (I mean as our nature is now corrupt) and civil or federal. The first is common to man with beasts and other creatures. By this, man, as he stands in relation to man simply, hath liberty to do what he lists; it is a liberty to evil as well as to good. This liberty is incompatible and inconsistent with authority, and cannot endure the least restraint of the most just authority. The exercise and maintaining of this liberty makes men grow more evil, and in time to be worse than brute beasts: *omnes sumus licentiâdeteriores.* This is that great enemy of truth and peace, that wild beast, which all the ordinances of God are bent against, to restrain and subdue it. The other kind of liberty I call civil or federal; it may

往知识的道路,遵循神的戒律使人们获得自由。

"在对 1650 年美国的社会状况作了简单的回顾之后,再将视线转向在同一时期的欧洲,尤其是新大陆,我们很难不感到惊讶。17 世纪初期的欧洲大陆君主专制政体在中世纪寡头政治和封建统治的废墟上一统天下。大概,权利的观念从来没有像在欧洲大放异彩和文艺繁荣的时期这样被人完全忽视,人民从来没有像这一时期更少参加政治生活,真正自由的思想从来没有像这一时期更少占据人的头脑。而这一时期那些为欧洲民族鄙视甚至根本不知道的思想在新大陆受到欢迎并且日后为一个伟大民族奉为信条。人类思想创造的最大胆的理论竟在没有任何政治家谦逊地关注它的国家中受到如此的轻视而最终取得成功;而一个全新的立法体系也完全依靠人们独创精神的想象力而建立了起来。在这个没有过将军、哲学家和作家,被民主的阴影笼罩着的时期,一个人,敢于面对着一群自由的人们站起来,在大家的喝彩声中,发表以下关于自由的定义的精彩言论:

我在一个自称自由的国家发现了一个重要的错误。民主具有双重性:天性使然的民主(就像我们被遭到破坏的天性一样)和民情或联邦下的民主。第一种对于人类、野兽或者其他生物来说很普通。这个,只要是人,就可以自由地行使自己的意愿。这种自由既可以是邪恶的也可以是崇高的。这种自由与权威相悖,即使是最公正的权威的限制也与它不相容。要行使并保证这种自由,就会使人变得日益邪恶,甚至会变得比野兽还残忍。这种民主的自由是真理和和平最强大的敌人,为上帝的法令所反对、抵御和征服。另一种形式的自由我称为民情或联邦下的民主,也可以称为道德规范下的自由。在道德法意义上的上帝与人之间的

also be termed moral, in reference to the covenant between God and man, in the moral law, and the politic covenants and constitutions, among men themselves. This liberty is the proper end and object of authority, and cannot subsist without it; and it is a liberty to that only which is good, just, and honest. This liberty you are to stand for, with the hazard not only of your goods, but of your lives, if need be. What soever crosseth this, is not authority, but a distemper thereof. This liberty is maintained and exercised in a way of subjection to authority; it is of the same kind of liberty wherewith Christ hath made us free. " ①

I have said enough to put the character of Anglo-American civilization in its true light. It is the result (and this should be constantly kept in mind) of two distinct elements, which in other places have been in frequent disagreement, but which the Americans have succeeded in incorporating to some extent one with the other and combining admirably. I allude to the *spirit* of *religion* and the *spirit of liberty*.

The settlers of New England were at the same time ardent sectarians and daring innovators. Narrow as the limits of some of their religious opinions were, they were free from all political prejudices.

Hence arose two tendencies, distinct but not opposite, which are everywhere discernible in the manners as well as the laws of the country.

Men sacrifice for a religious opinion their friends, their family, and their country; one can consider them devoted to the pursuit of intellectual goals which they came to purchase at so high a price. One sees them, however, seeking with almost equal eagerness material wealth and moral satisfaction; heaven in the world beyond, and well-being and liberty in this one.

Under their hand, political principles, laws, and human institutions

---

① Mather's *Magnalia Christi Americana*, Vol. II, p. 13. This speech was made by Winthrop; he was accused of having committed arbitrary actions during his magistracy, but after having made the speech, of which the above is a fragment, he was acquitted by acclamation, and from that time forwards he was always re-elected Governor of the state. See *Marshall*, Vol. I, p. 166.

契约,以及人类之间的政治盟约和惯例。这一自由正是权威所希望达到的圆满结局和最终目的,也是必不可少的;这是只有向善、公正和诚实才享有的自由。这是你不仅用失去财物的危险,如果有必要,甚至冒着生命的危险所捍卫的自由。任何阻挡它的都是遭到抵制的。这一自由的行使和维护是在权威的保障下实现的;是与上帝赐予我们的权利一致的。"①

我所讲的已足以准确地展现英裔美国社会文明的真实状况。这种文明是两种完全相反的元素同时作用的结果(这一来源我们必须牢记在心),而这两种来源在其他的地方必然会产生无休止的矛盾,而在美国却成功地使其在一定意义上予以融合并取得令人称赞的效果。我所说的这两种元素就是宗教精神和自由精神。

新英格兰的居民既是狂热的宗派主义者同时又是改革创新者。尽管他们在宗教意见上有局限性,但是却坦诚接受一切政治意见。

因此就产生了两种倾向,有差异但不对立,这一不同在民情和州的法律中都显而易见。

人们出于宗教的信仰而抛弃了他们的朋友、家庭和国家;有些人认为他们对于追求这种精神上的享受付出的代价太高。但是人们又可以看到他们对于物质的追求和精神的追求同样充满热情:天堂远在我们之上,而幸福和自由却在身边。

在他们认为,政治原则、法律和人为的机构都是可以按照人

---

① 马瑟的《美国风物志》第二卷,第13页。演讲者是温斯罗普;他被指控在位期间滥用职权,但是在作了以上摘录了一部分的演讲之后,由于得到了大家的拥护而被无罪释放。并在此之后一直被选为州长。见《马歇尔》第一篇第一卷第166页。

seem malleable, capable of being shaped and combined at will. As they go forward, the barriers which imprisoned society and behind which they were born are lowered; old opinions, which for centuries had been controlling the world, vanish; a course almost without limits, a field without horizon, is revealed: the human spirit rushes forward and traverses them in every direction. But having reached the limits of the political world, the human spirit stops of itself; in fear it relinquishes the need of exploration; it even abstains from lifting the veil of the sanctuary; it bows with respect before truths which it accepts without discussion.

Thus in the moral world everything is classified, systematized, foreseen, and decided beforehand; in the political world everything is agitated, disputed, and uncertain. In the one is a passive though a voluntary obedience; in the other, an independence scornful of experience, and jealous of all authority. These two tendencies, apparently so discrepant, are far from conflicting; they advance together and support each other.

Religion perceives that civil liberty affords a noble exercise to the faculties of man and that the political world is a field prepared by the Creator for the efforts of mind. Free and powerful in its own sphere, satisfied with the place reserved for it, religion never more surely establishes its empire than when it reigns in the hearts of men unsupported by aught beside its native strength.

Liberty regards religion as its companion in all its battles and its triumphs, as the cradle of its infancy and the divine source of its claims. It considers religion as the safeguard of morality, and morality as the best security of law and the surest pledge of the duration of freedom. ①

---

① See Appendix F.

们的意愿变形并重新组合的。他们认为社会所产生的阻碍其发展的障碍低头了;统治了世界几百年的旧观念不复存在了;展现出一条几乎没有限制的大道,一片没有尽头的空间:人类的思想直向前冲,从各个方向向他们涌来。但是一旦进入了政治社会的范围,人类的思想就主动停止了;怀着担心的心理,放弃了改革的需求,甚至拒绝撩起圣殿的面纱,毕恭毕敬地跪倒在真理的面前。

因此,在精神世界中,一切都按部就班,有条不紊,预先得知并有计划地实施;而在政治世界中,一切都充满了不安,正义和不确定性。在前一个世界中,是消极然而自愿的服从,而在后者则是轻视经验和蔑视一切权威的独立。这两者之间,表面看充满差异和矛盾,但实际上却是互相促进共同发展。

宗教认为,公民自由需要人的权利的高尚行使,而政治世界是上帝为人们的头脑提供的竞技场所。自由和权利停留在自己的圈子里,并满足于自己的状况,宗教的最完全的确立的标志,就是当它在统治人们的心灵的时候,除了其自然的力量之外不需要借助其他外力。

自由将宗教视为其所有战争和胜利中的伙伴,视为它童年时的摇篮和满足要求的神圣的来源。他认为宗教是道德的守卫者,而道德是法律最好的维护者和保卫自由的最可靠的保证。①

———————

① 见附件F。

Reasons For Certain
Anomalies Which The Laws
And Customs Of The Anglo-Americans Present

Remains of aristocratic institutions amid the most complete democracy Why? — Careful distinction to be drawn between what is of Puritanical and what of English origin.

The reader is cautioned not to draw too general or too absolute an inference from what has been said. The social condition, the religion, and the customs of the first immigrants undoubtedly exercised an immense influence on the destiny of their new country. Nevertheless, they could not found a state of things originating solely in themselves: no man can entirely shake off the influence of the past; and the settlers, intentionally or not, mingled habits and notions derived from their education and the traditions of their country with those habits and notions that were exclusively their own. To know and to judge the Anglo-Americans of the present day, it is therefore necessary to distinguish what is of Puritanical and what of English origin.

Laws and customs are frequently to be met with in the United States which contrast strongly with all that surrounds them. These laws seem to be drawn up in a spirit contrary to the prevailing tenor of American legislation; and these customs are no less opposed to the general tone of society. If the English colonies had been founded in an age of darkness, or if their origin was already lost in the lapse of years, the problem would be insoluble.

I shall quote a single example to illustrate my meaning. The civil and criminal procedure of the Americans has only two means of action, committal or bail. The first act of the magistrate is to exact security from the defendant or, in case of refusal, to incarcerate him; the ground of the accusation and the importance of the charges against him are then discussed.

It is evident that such a legislation is hostile to the poor and favorable only to the rich. The poor man has not always security to produce,

英裔美国人的法律和习俗中
表现出的一些异常现象的原因

贵族制度在最完全的民主中的残留——为什么——对于何谓清教徒的东西何谓英国的东西,仔细地加以区分。

读者要避免从以上的叙述中得出过于一般化或绝对的结论。社会状况、宗教和第一批移民者的习俗都毫无疑问对他们新建立的州产生了巨大的影响。然而,新社会的建立并非完全起因于这些东西:没有人能够完全摆脱过去的影响;这些定居者有意或者无意地,就把自己在祖国受到的教育和习俗的影响所产生的习惯和观念和自己固有的习惯和观念混在一起。要了解和评判今天的英裔美国人,就必须区分清楚什么是清教的东西,什么是英国的东西。

在美国,法律和习惯常常会与周围的事物格格不入。这些法律秉着与普遍流行的美国立法的旨意相悖的精神而制定,那些习惯也与社会的基调完全不合。如果说英国的殖民地建立在遥远的古代,又或者他们的起源业已在过去的年月中迷失,那么这个矛盾就不可调和了。

我可以引用一个例子来阐述我的想法。美国的民事和刑事诉讼程序,对被告人的处置只规定两种办法:收监和保释。诉讼开始时法官首先要求被告人交付保释金,如被告人拒不交纳,则将他收监关押。然后,再审理被控告的事实或罪状的轻重。

显而易见,这样的立法敌视穷人,而只对富人有利。穷人并非总是有钱可交保释金,即使在民事案件中也是如此;假如他被

even in a civil case; and if he is obliged to wait for justice in prison, he is speedily reduced to distress. A wealthy person, on the contrary, always escapes imprisonment in civil cases; nay, more, if he has committed a crime, he may readily elude punishment by breaking his bail. Thus all the penalties of the law are, for him, reduced to fines. [1] Nothing can be more aristocratic than this system of legislation. Yet in America it is the poor who make the law, and they usually reserve the greatest advantages of society to themselves. The explanation of the phenomenon is to be found in England; the laws of which I speak are English, [2] and the Americans have retained them, although repugnant to the general tenor of their legislation and the mass of their ideas.

Next to its habits the thing which a nation is least apt to change is its civil legislation. Civil laws are familiarly known only to lawyers, whose direct interest it is to maintain them as they are, whether good or bad, simply because they themselves are conversant with them. The bulk of the nation is scarcely acquainted with them; it sees their action only in particular cases, can with difficulty detect their tendency, and obeys them without thought.

I have quoted one instance where it would have been easy to adduce many others. The picture of American society has, if I may so speak, a surface covering of democracy, beneath which the old aristocratic colors sometimes peep out.

---

[1] Crimes no doubt exist for which bail is inadmissible, but they are few in number.

[2] See Blackstone and Delolme, Bk. I, ch. 10.

迫在狱中等候公正的裁决,那他就会很快沦落到悲惨的境地。相反,富人在民事案件中总是可以逃避关押。更有甚者,他们虽然犯了罪,却可轻易逃避应受的惩罚,因为交了保释金以后,他们可以躲藏起来。因此可以说,法律上规定的惩罚,对于富人来说只不过是罚款而已。① 没有什么比这样的立法体系更具有贵族化的特性。但是,在美国,是穷人制定法律,因此他们总是将社会的最大利益留给自己。在英国可以发现对这一现象的解释,因为我所讲的法律本是来自英国的。② 尽管在彼此立法的宗旨上和许多思想方面存在差异,美国人还是保留了它们。

一个国家最难修改的事物,除了人们的习惯,就是民法了。只有搞法律的人才能懂民法,他们的兴趣就在于保持民法的原样,不论是好的还是坏的法律,只因为他们对法律太熟悉了。国家中的大部分人很难了解法律;他们只能在一些特别的案例中觉察到法律的存在,但很难识别其倾向,并且毫不犹豫地服从法律。

这只是我引用的一个例证,我还能举出很多其他的例子。如果我可以这样说,美国社会的画面,遮盖了民主的光芒,而在民主之下,时时会窥见久远的贵族制度的身影。

---

① 也有一些犯罪不能交保证金,但是数量很少。
② 见布莱斯通和迪洛英,第一卷,第10章。

CHAPTER Ⅲ
Social Condition Of
The Anglo-Americans

Social condition is commonly the result of circumstances, sometimes of laws, oftener still of these two causes united; but when once established, it may justly be considered as itself the source of almost all the laws, the usages, and the ideas which regulate the conduct of nations: whatever it does not produce, it modifies.

If we would become acquainted with the legislation and the manners of a nation, therefore, we must begin by the study of its social condition.

The Striking Characteristic Of
The Social Condition Of The
Anglo-Americans Is Its
Essential Democracy

The first immigrants of New England Their equality Aristocratic laws introduced in the South Period of the Revolution — Change in the laws of inheritance — effects produced by this change Democracy carried to its utmost limits in the new states of the West — Equality of mental endowments.

Many important observations suggest themselves upon the social condition of the Anglo-Americans; but there is one that takes precedence of all the rest. The social condition of the Americans is eminently democratic; this was its character at the foundation of the colonies, and it is still more strongly marked at the present day.

第三章 英裔美国人的社会状况

社会状况一般是由社会环境或法律造成的结果,而更多的是这两者同时作用的结果;但是社会环境一旦形成,就被理所应当地认为是规范各州行为大部分法律、习惯,或者观念产生的根源:即使不是它所产生的,也经过其修改。

因此,要了解一个国家法律制定的过程和民情,我们就必须从研究这个国家的社会状况开始。

英裔美国人社会状况的显著特点,
在于其民主的本质

新英格兰最早的移民——他们之间的平等——南部推行的贵族的法律——革命时期——继承法的改革——该改革所产生的作用——民主在新英格兰西部各州得到其最大的发展——学识上的平等。

在许多基于英裔美国人社会状况的重要的观察中,有一种居于前列:美国社会的状况是非常的民主的;这是由其殖民地建立初始的性质决定的,而在今天表现得尤为强烈。

I have stated in the preceding chapter that great equality existed among the immigrants who settled on the shores of New England. Even the germs of aristocracy were never planted in that part of the Union. The only influence which obtained there was that of intellect; the people became accustomed to revere certain names as representatives of knowledge and virtue. Some of their fellow citizens acquired a power over the others that might truly have been called aristocratic if it had been capable of transmission from father to son.

This was the state of things to the east of the Hudson: to the southwest of that river, and as far as the Floridas, the case was different. In most of the states situated to the southwest of the Hudson some great English proprietors had settled who had imported with them aristocratic principles and the English law of inheritance. I have explained the reasons why it was impossible ever to establish a powerful aristocracy in America; these reasons existed with less force to the southwest of the Hudson. In the South one man, aided by slaves, could cultivate a great extent of country; it was therefore common to see rich landed proprietors. But their influence was not altogether aristocratic, as that term is understood in Europe, since they possessed no privileges; and the cultivation of their estates being carried on by slaves, they had no tenants depending on them, and consequently no patronage. Still, the great proprietors south of the Hudson constituted a superior class, having ideas and tastes of its own and forming the center of political action. This kind of aristocracy sympathized with the body of the people, whose passions and interests it easily embraced; but it was too weak and too shortlived to excite either love or hatred. This was the class which headed the insurrection in the South and furnished the best leaders of the American Revolution.

At this period society was shaken to its center. The people, in whose name the struggle had taken place, conceived the desire of exercising the authority that it had acquired; its democratic tendencies were awakened; and having thrown off the yoke of the mother country, it aspired to independence of every kind. The influence of individuals gradually ceased to be felt, and custom and law united to produce the same result.

　　我在上一章中已经说过定居在新英格兰海岸的移民之间存在着平等,甚至是贵族制的萌芽也从未在合众国这一部分出现过。唯一影响到那里的就只有知识;人们开始崇拜一些人的名字,认为他们是具有知识和品德的人物的代表。他们中间的一些公民取得了高于其他公民的权力,并且这种权力能够有世袭的性质,也许真的可以被称为贵族的权力。

　　美国赫德森河流以东的情形当时是这样的;而在这条河流的西南部,一直到佛罗里达,情形跟这里完全不同。在赫德森河西南部的大多数州,有很多英国大地主都定居在那里,他们随之也带来了自己的贵族制度原则和英国的继承法。我在前面已经解释过美国不可能建立贵族制度的原因,这些原因在赫德森河西南部的威力就弱了很多。在南部,个人可以有很多奴隶帮助他种植大面积的土地,在这里富有的土地主很平常。但是他们的影响力与贵族地主的完全不同,因为他们还没有特权,并且,他们的土地都是由奴隶耕种的,他们与奴隶之间不存在租赁关系,所以也就没有了对奴隶的保护责任。这些赫德森河南部的大地主形成了一个上层阶级,拥有他们自己的观念和品味,并形成了一个政治活动中心。这些贵族与人民大众很容易产生共鸣,很容易接受人们的热情和利益的观念;但是他们实力太弱并且生命力短暂,不能激起人们爱憎的感情。就是这样的阶层,领导了南部的起义并且产生了美国革命最杰出的领袖。

　　在这一时期,社会处于大动荡之中。人民,开始了以自己的名义发动的起义,并希望运用自己在斗争中获得的权利;他们的民主的倾向被唤醒;他们立志在各个方面获得独立,并抛弃了祖国对他们的各种束缚。个人的影响逐渐失去作用,社会习惯和法律也开始向同一目标发展。

But the law of inheritance was the last step to equality. I am surprised that ancient and modern jurists have not attributed to this law a greater influence on human affairs. ① It is true that these laws belong to civil affairs; but they ought, nevertheless, to be placed at the head of all political institutions; for they exercise an incredible influence upon the social state of a people, while political laws show only what this state already is. They have, moreover, a sure and uniform manner of operating upon society, affecting, as it were, generations yet unborn. Through their means man acquires a kind of preternatural power over the future lot of his fellow creatures. When the legislator has once regulated the law of inheritance, he may rest from his labor. The machine once put in motion will go on for ages, and advance, as if self-guided, towards a point indicated beforehand. When framed in a particular manner, this law unites, draws together, and vests property and power in a few hands; it causes an aristocracy, so to speak, to spring out of the ground. If formed on opposite principles, its action is still more rapid; it divides, distributes, and disperses both property and power. Alarmed by the rapidity of its progress, those who despair of arresting its motion endeavor at least to obstruct it by difficulties and impediments. They vainly seek to counteract its effect by contrary efforts; but it shatters and reduces to powder every obstacle, until we can no longer see anything but a moving and impalpable cloud of dust, which signals the coming of the Democracy. When the law of inheritance permits, still more when it decrees, the equal division of a father's property among all his children, its effects are of two kinds: it is important to distinguish them from each other, although they tend to the same end.

---

① I understand by the law of inheritance all those laws whose principal object it is to regulate the distribution of property after the death of its owner. The law of entail is of this number: it certainly prevents the owner from disposing of his possessions before his death; but this is solely with the view of preserving them entire for the heir. The principal object, therefore, of the law of entail is to regulate the descent of property after the death of its owner; its other provisions are merely means to this end.

继承法却使平等迈出了重要的一步。我很惊讶,古代和现代的法理学家们没有使继承法在民事方面产生更大的影响。① 而这些法律的确属于民事的范畴;但是也应该被置于政治制度的首列;因为他们的运用对社会状况会发生巨大的影响,而政治方面的法律只是社会情况的表现形式。此外,继承法是以稳妥和始终如一的方式作用于社会,并对还未出生的世世代代产生影响。通过继承法,人们就获得了一种超自然的力量,得以控制未来的人类。立法者一旦将继承法制定出来,他就可以休息了。因为继承法的施行就像一部机器的运行,一旦开动,就会成年累月连续不断地运行下去,而且如果是自动导向的话,还会向着已经设定的目标自动提升。如果限定一定的方式制定该法律,那么法律就会把财产和权力联合起来,集中到一起并最终归于个别人手中;可以说,它使贵族浮出水面;按另一种原则制定,它的发展速度会更快;但是这时它是分裂、分化和分割财产和权势。有时它的发展惊人,在人们觉得无法制止它的时候,甚至要想办法设置一些困难和障碍减缓其发展。但随即发现想通过抵制的方法阻碍其发展是徒劳无功的;它伴随着民主前进的号角将所有的阻碍一一击碎并化为灰烬,直到最后只剩一团烟尘。当继承法承认并判决儿女如何公平地继承父亲的遗产的时候,会产生两种结果:尽管这两种结果的目的都是相同的,但是将两者之间清楚地划分还是很重要的。

———————

①　通过继承法,我了解到所有那些法律树立的原则的目的都是为了规范被继承人死后的遗产划分。限定继承法确保财产拥有者在其死之前处理其财产;但是这项法律只考虑到为继承者保留全部的遗产。该原则的目的就是为了规范财产拥有者死后其财产的继承;它所包含的其他的规定也只是为了这一目的。

As a result of the law of inheritance, the death of each owner brings about a revolution in property; not only do his possessions change hands, but their very nature is altered, since they are parceled into shares, which become smaller and smaller at each division. This is the direct and as it were the physical effect of the law. In the countries where legislation establishes the equality of division, property, and particularly landed fortunes, have a permanent tendency to diminish. The effects of such legislation, however, would be perceptible only after a lapse of time if the law were abandoned to its own working; for, supposing the family to consist of only two children (and in a country peopled as France is, the average number is not above three), these children, sharing between them the fortune of both parents, would not be poorer than their father or mother.

But the law of equal division exercises its influence not merely upon the property itself, but it affects the minds of the heirs and brings their passions into play. These indirect consequences tend powerfully to the destruction of large fortunes, and especially of large domains.

Among nations whose law of descent is founded upon the right of primogeniture, landed estates often pass from generation to generation without undergoing division; the consequence of this is that family feeling is to a certain degree incorporated with the estate. The family represents the estate, the estate the family, whose name, together with its origin, its glory, its power, and its virtues, is thus perpetuated in an imperishable memorial of the past and as a sure pledge of the future.

When the equal partition of property is established by law, the intimate connection is destroyed between family feeling and the preservation of the paternal estate; the property ceases to represent the family; for, as it must inevitably be divided after one or two generations, it has evidently a constant tendency to diminish and must in the end be completely dispersed. The sons of the great landed proprietor, if they are few in number, or if fortune befriends them, may indeed entertain the hope of being as wealthy as their father, but not of possessing the same property that he did; their riches must be composed of other elements than his. Now, as soon as you divest the landowner of that interest in the preservation of his estate which he derives from association, from tradition, and from family pride, you may be certain that, sooner or later, he will dispose of it;

继承法使得每一位所有者的死亡都引发一场关于财产的革命;并不仅仅是财产的拥有者改变了,它们的性质也跟着变化了,因为他们被平均地分配,并随着每一次的分配越来越少。这就是法律带来的直接的也是物质方面的结果。在立法规定平均分配的国家,财产,尤其是地产必然会一直向着减小的趋势发展。如果让立法自由发展,其立法效果只有经过时间的洗礼才能为人们觉察得到;因为,设想一个家庭如果只有两个孩子(例如在法国这样的国家,每个家庭的孩子的数量平均不超过三个),这些孩子平分父母的财产,就会变得比他们的父母富裕。

但是平均分配的法律并不只是对财产起作用,而且对继承者的思想也产生了作用,激起他们的创业激情。这样带来的间接后果,就使得大量的财富遭到破坏,尤其是对大地主来说。

对继承法建立在长子继承权基础上的国家,土地不动产不会随着世袭的传递被分化,这样就导致家庭因素与地产合为一体。家族就代表该地产,地产就是家庭,家庭的姓氏、起源、荣耀、权力和德行与土地融为一体。土地使家庭成为不可磨灭的印记并成为家庭未来可靠的保证。

当法律建立起财产均等分配的规定之后,家族声誉与保存父辈地产之间的密切关系遭到了破坏;财产不再代表家族,因为经过一两代它必然划分,并且一直沿着逐渐变小直至最终消失的趋势发展。如果大地产主的儿子数量少或者依靠财富的帮助,也许有希望和他们的父辈一样富裕,但始终不会拥有和父辈一样多的财产;他们的财富组成的成分跟父辈的不一样。如今,一旦剥夺了大地主因占有地产而获得感情、传统和家庭荣耀方面的利益,人们就可以确信,迟早他会卖掉地产;因为卖掉的话,就可以获得

for there is a strong pecuniary interest in favor of selling, as floating capital produces higher interest than real property and is more readily available to gratify the passions of the moment.

Great landed estates which have once been divided never come together again; for the small proprietor draws from his land a better revenue, in proportion, than the large owner does from his; and of course he sells it at a higher rate. [1] The reasons of economy, therefore, which have led the rich man to sell vast estates will prevent him all the more from buying little ones in order to form a large one.

What is called family pride is often founded upon an illusion of self-love. A man wishes to perpetuate and immortalize himself, as it were, in his great-grandchildren. Where family pride ceases to act, individual selfishness comes into play. When the idea of family becomes vague, indeterminate, and uncertain, a man thinks of his present convenience; he provides for the establishment of his next succeeding generation and no more. Either a man gives up the idea of perpetuating his family, or at any rate he seeks to accomplish it by other means than by a landed estate.

Thus, not only does the law of partible inheritance render it difficult for families to preserve their ancestral domains entire, but it deprives them of the inclination to attempt it and compels them in some measure to co-operate with the law in their own extinction. The law of equal distribution proceeds by two methods: by acting upon things, it acts upon persons; by influencing persons, it affects things. By both these means the law succeeds in striking at the root of landed property, and dispersing rapidly both families and fortunes. [2]

---

[1] I do not mean to say that the small proprietor cultivates his land better, but he cultivates it with more ardor and care; so that he makes up by his labor for his want of skill.

[2] Land being the most stable kind of property, we find from to time rich individuals who are disposed to make great sacrifices in order to obtain it and who willingly forfeit a considerable part of their income to make sure of the rest. But these are accidental cases. The preference for landed property is no longer found habitually in any class except among the poor. The small landowner, who has less information, less imagination, and less prejudice than the great one, is generally occupied with the desire of increasing his estate: and it often happens that by inheritance, by marriage, or by the chances of trade he is gradually furnished with the means. Thus, to balance the tendency that leads men to divide their estates, there exists another, which incites them to add to them. This tendency, which is sufficient to prevent estates from being divided ad *infinitum*, is not strong enough to create great territorial possessions, certainly not to keep them up in the same family.

大量的金钱,而流动资金可以产生比地产更高的利润,并且更能满足他们现实的欲望。

大地产一旦被分割就不会再合并;而与大地主相比,小地主从其土地中获得的收益会更多;因此小地主的土地售价也就高一些。① 所以,导致大地主变卖大量土地的这一经济原因,也将会阻止其为了集聚土地而从小地主手中购买土地。

所谓的家族声誉,常常是建立在满足人们自私心理的基础上的。人们总是希望自己能够在自己的子孙心里永存不朽。家族荣誉如果消失了,那么个人的自私心理就会活跃起来。当家族的概念变得模糊不明确时,甚至不确定时,人们就开始只考虑自己的利益了。他只为自己的下一代考虑,而不会考虑更多。人们放弃兴旺家族的想法或者考虑用其他途径兴旺自己的家族,而不是从地产方面考虑了。

这样一来,遗产划分的法律不仅仅使得家族很难保留住祖先遗留下来的完整的财产,而且使得他们丧失了获得完整继承的企图,并从某种程度上被迫与法律联合加速其自身的灭亡。平等分配的法律有两种途径:通过作用于物而对人产生作用;通过对人的影响来改变物。这两种方法都使得法律在撼动地产的根基方面取得了胜利,加速了家族和其财富的毁灭。②

---

① 我并不是说小地主对他的土地耕种得更好,而是说他更用心更有激情,所以他凭借自己的劳动弥补了技术的不足。

② 土地是最稳定的财产,我们发现有为了得到土地宁愿付出巨大牺牲的富人,他们用收入的大半换取另一半的稳定。但这种现象很少见。除了穷人,在其他阶层中人们已不再承认土地至上的权利。由于获得的信息少,缺乏想象力,而且相对大地主来说少有偏见,一些小地主通常还都希望扩大自己的地产:他们常常通过继承、婚姻或者交易的手段逐渐富裕起来。如此一来,为了平衡人们分割地产的趋势,还有另一种煽动他们扩大地产的趋势的存在。这种趋势,虽能够阻止土地无止境地分割,但并不足以形成大的领土占有,更不能使大面积的土地归属同一家族。

Most certainly it is not for us, Frenchmen of the nineteenth century, who daily witness the political and social changes that the law of partition is bringing to pass, to question its influence. It is perpetually conspicuous in our country, overthrowing the walls of our dwellings, and removing the landmarks of our fields. But although it has produced great effects in France, much still remains for it to do. Our recollections, opinions, and habits present powerful obstacles to its progress.

In the United States it has nearly completed its work of destruction, and there we can best study its results. The English laws concerning the transmission of property were abolished in almost all the states at the time of the Revolution. The law of entail was so modified as not materially to interrupt the free circulation of property. [1] The first generation having passed away, estates began to be parceled out; and the change became more and more rapid with the progress of time. And now, after a lapse of a little more than sixty years, the aspect of society is totally altered; the families of the great landed proprietors are almost all commingled with the general mass. In the state of New York, which formerly contained many of these, there are but two who still keep their heads above the stream; and they must shortly disappear. The sons of these opulent citizens have become merchants, lawyers, or physicians. Most of them have lapsed into obscurity. The last trace of hereditary ranks and distinctions is destroyed; the law of partition has reduced all to one level.

I do not mean that there is any lack of wealthy individuals in the United States; I know of no country, indeed, where the love of money has taken stronger hold on the affections of men and where a profounder contempt is expressed for the theory of the permanent equality of property. But wealth circulates with inconceivable rapidity, and experience shows that it is rare to find two succeeding generations in the full enjoyment of it.

This picture, which may, perhaps, be thought to be overcharged, still gives a very imperfect idea of what is taking place in the new states of the West and Southwest. At the end of the last century a few bold adventurers began to penetrate into the valley of the Mississippi, and the mass of the population very soon began to

---

① See Appendix G.

最确定的就是这并不符合我们法国的国情。19 世纪的法国人虽天天目睹了继承法给政治和社会带来的变革,但他们仍然怀疑它的影响力。在我们国家它的影响显著存在,使人们拆掉自己的院墙,抹去土地之间的界限。但是尽管它给法国带来了巨大的影响,但是还有很多需要去做。我们的记忆、观念和习惯给它的发展设置了重重障碍。

而在美国,它几乎完成了所有的毁坏工作,而我们也可以学到其后果。在独立战争时期,美国的所有州几乎都废止了英国的继承法。限定继承法已被修改为不得影响财产的自由流通。① 第一代人逝去后,地产就被分割;而且这种变化随着时间的推移速度变得越来越快。60 多年后的今天,社会的各个层面都发生了巨大的变化,那些大地产家庭都混迹于人海中已不可查。纽约州以前有许多这样的大地主,如今尚存的仅有两家,然而不久也必然会消失。这些富裕的家庭的孩子如今都成了商人、律师和医生,但大多数都默默无闻。世袭等级的最后的印记和区别也被毁灭了,继承法将所有的等级都化为平等。

我并不是说美国不再有拥有大量资产的富人,我知道事实上没有一个国家比美国人对于金钱的热爱更强烈,或者更轻视财产永远平等的理论。但是,财富以难以置信的速度运转着,而且实践证明,没有哪个相继的两代人都是富人的。

我所描述的这幅画面,读者也许会觉得过于夸大,但实际上还不足以展现当时西部和西南部各州发生的景象。上世纪末,一些大胆的探险家进入了密西西比大峡谷,接着很快便迁徙来了大

---

① 见附件 G。

move in that direction; communities unheard of till then suddenly appeared in the desert. States whose names were not in existence a few years before, claimed their place in the American Union; and in the Western settlements we may behold democracy arrived at its utmost limits. In these states, founded offhand and as it were by chance, the inhabitants are but of yesterday. Scarcely known to one another, the nearest neighbors are ignorant of each other's history. In this part of the American continent, therefore, the population has escaped the influence not only of great names and great wealth, but even of the natural aristocracy of knowledge and virtue. None is there able to wield that respectable power which men willingly grant to the remembrance of a life spent in doing good before their eyes. The new states of the West are already inhabited, but society has no existence among them.

It is not only the fortunes of men that are equal in America; even their acquirements partake in some degree of the same uniformity. I do not believe that there is a country in the world where, in proportion to the population, there are so few ignorant and at the same time so few learned individuals. Primary instruction is within the reach of everybody; superior instruction is scarcely to be obtained by any. This is not surprising; it is, in fact, the necessary consequence of what I have advanced above. Almost all the Americans are in easy circumstances and can therefore obtain the first elements of human knowledge.

In America there are but few wealthy persons; nearly all Americans have to take a profession. Now, every profession requires an apprenticeship. The Americans can devote to general education only the early years of life. At fifteen they enter upon their calling, and thus their education generally ends at the age when ours begins. If it is continued beyond that point, it aims only towards a particular specialized and profitable purpose; one studies science as one takes up a business; and one takes up only those applications whose immediate practicality is recognized.

In America most of the rich men were formerly poor; most of those who now enjoy leisure were absorbed in business during their youth; the consequence of this is that when they might have had a taste for study, they had no time for it, and when the time is at their disposal, they have no longer the inclination.

量的人口：一些从未听说过的乡镇忽然出现在这片荒凉之地。一些前几年连名字都没有的州，也要求加入美国联邦；而西部的一些定居群落则将民主发挥得淋漓尽致；在一些偶然被发现的州上，其居民都是新近迁来的人们。大家彼此之间都不认识，即使是最近的邻居，也互不知对方的底细。因此，在美洲大陆的这块土地上，居民不会受到一些有名的姓氏或者以财富和贵族的学识及德行带来的影响。那里也没有因在人们面前终其一生行善而获得被人们尊敬的权力。西部的各州虽已有人居住，但是他们还没有形成社会。

在美国，不仅财富均等，他们的学识程度也相当。我不相信世界上有这样的国家，与其居民相比，有这么少无知的人同时又有这么少有学识的人。在美国，人人都接受初等教育，但是受高等教育的人却很少。这并不奇怪，事实上，这正是我上面所提到的一切的必然结果。几乎所有的美国人生活环境都很好，所以就很轻易受到初等教育。

在美国，几乎没有很富裕的人；几乎所有的美国人都必须工作。现在，几乎所有的工作都要求有学徒经历。所以美国人只能在很年轻的时候接受普及教育。15岁就开始工作，所以他们受教育的机会在法国人刚刚开始的时候就结束了。即使有人能够继续接受教育，也都是学某些特殊技能或者为了一定的目的；人们学习科学就像是学习一门手艺，只接受一些立刻就可以见效的实用型的技能。

在美国，所有的富人都是从穷人开始的；大多数现在得以享受生活的人，在其年轻的时候都需要拼命地工作；这就使得当他们想学习的时候没时间，而有时间的时候又没有了学习的欲望。

There is no class, then, in America, in which the taste for intellectual pleasures is transmitted with hereditary fortune and leisure and by which the labors of the intellect are held in honor. Accordingly, there is an equal want of the desire and the power of application to these objects.

A middling standard is fixed in America for human knowledge. All approach as near to it as they can; some as they rise, others as they descend. Of course, a multitude of persons are to be found who entertain the same number of ideas on religion, history, science, political economy, legislation, and government. The gifts of intellect proceed directly from Cod, and man cannot prevent their unequal distribution. But it is at least a consequence of what I have just said that although the capacities of men are different, as the Creator intended they should be, the means that Americans find for putting them to use are equal.

In America the aristocratic element has always been feeble from its birth; and if at the present day it is not actually destroyed, it is at any rate so completely disabled that we can scarcely assign to it any degree of influence on the course of affairs. The democratic principle, on the contrary, has gained so much strength by time, by events, and by legislation, as to have become not only predominant, but all-powerful. No family or corporate authority can be perceived; very often one cannot even discover in it any very lasting individual influence.

America, then, exhibits in her social state an extraordinary phenomenon. Men are there seen on a greater equality in point of fortune and intellect, or, in other words, more equal in their strength, than in any other country of the world, or in any age of which history has preserved the remembrance.

Political Consequences Of
The Social Condition Of The Anglo-Americans

The political consequences of such a social condition as this are easily deducible.

It is impossible to believe that equality will not eventually find its way into the political world, as it does everywhere else. To conceive of men remaining forever unequal upon a single point, yet equal on all others, is impossible; they must come in the end to be equal upon all.

美国没有将对知识的喜爱连同其世袭的财富和享乐一起继承的阶层,从而形成以脑力劳动为荣的阶层。可见,美国人既没有专心从事脑力劳动的意志,也没有专心从事这一劳动的毅力。

美国人的知识处于中等水平。所有人都接近这个水平,要么略高要么略低。大多数人都拥有相同的宗教信仰、历史、知识、政治经济、立法和政府。智力是上帝直接赐予的,人们无力抗拒其不公平性。但是至少我前面描述的情形可以得出,尽管人们的智力水平不同,就像上帝安排的那样,但其发展的条件是相等的。

美国自始就一直存在着微弱的贵族成分,如果时至今日仍未能真正消除,从某种意义上说也几乎无力再对社会事务产生任何影响。相反,民主的原则在经历了时间、事件和法律的考验后,获得了巨大的力量,不仅仅能产生影响,而且集聚了所有的力量于一身。在美国没有哪个家族或者团体可以产生影响力,甚至持久的个人的影响力也不多见。

美国展示出其独特的社会面貌。与世界上任何其他国家,或者历史上的任何时代相比,美国人民在财富和知识方面都享受到了更大的平等,换句话说,享受到更大的力量的平等。

英裔美国人社会状况的政治结果

如此社会状况会产生的政治后果是很容易推断的。

人们不会相信,政界将不会像社会其他方面那样可以最终实现平等。就如同相信人们可以满足于在社会的其他方面享受平等,而仅保持某一方面不平等一样,很难以让人信服。人们最终会要求实现完全的平等。

Now, I know of only two methods of establishing equality in the political world; rights must be given to every citizen, or none at all to anyone. For nations which are arrived at the same stage of social existence as the Anglo-Americans, it is, therefore, very difficult to discover a medium between the sovereignty of all and the absolute power of one man: and it would be vain to deny that the social condition which I have been describing is just as liable to one of these consequences as to the other.

There is, in fact, a manly and lawful passion for equality that incites men to wish all to be powerful and honored. This passion tends to elevate the humble to the rank of the great; but there exists also in the human heart a depraved taste for equality, which impels the weak to attempt to lower the powerful to their own level and reduces men to prefer equality in slavery to inequality with freedom. Not that those nations whose social condition is democratic naturally despise liberty; on the contrary, they have an instinctive love of it. But liberty is not the chief and constant object of their desires; equality is their idol: they make rapid and sudden efforts to obtain liberty and, if they miss their aim, resign themselves to their disappointment; but nothing can satisfy them without equality, and they would rather perish than lose it.

On the other hand, in a state where the citizens are all practically equal, it becomes difficult for them to preserve their independence against the aggressions of power. No one among them being strong enough to engage in the struggle alone with advantage, nothing but a general combination can protect their liberty. Now, such a union is not always possible.

From the same social position, then, nations may derive one or the other of two great political results; these results are extremely different from each other, but they both proceed from the same cause.

The Anglo-Americans are the first nation who, having been exposed to this formidable alternative, have been happy enough to escape the dominion of absolute power. They have been allowed by their circumstances, their origin, their intelligence, and especially by their morals to establish and maintain the sovereignty of the people.

到如今,我只知道有两种方法可以使政界实现平等:要么是全体公民享有权利;要么剥夺他们所有的权利。因为,一个社会如果像美国这样发展到如今的社会状况,就很难找到折中的方法解决人民主权和个人专政的矛盾。同时,也很难否认,我所描述的社会状况会倾向于两种情况的哪一种。

事实上,有一种雄壮且合法的获得平等的激情鼓舞着人们,希望大家都变得强大并受到尊重。这种激情致力于使卑贱的人们获得尊贵阶级同等的权利;但是也同时存在人类对平等的阴暗的追求,这种阴暗的心理促使弱者企图削弱别人的权利,使他们沦落到与自己同等的水平,宁愿让大家拥有受束缚的平等,而不愿拥有自由的阶级差别。这并不是说那些社会状况民主的民族就轻视自由;相反,他们对自由有一种本能的热爱。但是自由并不是他们主要不变的追求;平等才是他们所向往的:他们迅速突击以期获得自由,如果失败了,就会心灰意冷;但是没有了平等,任何东西都不能使他们感到满意,他们珍惜平等,不会将它丢失。

但从另一方面说,在人人真实地获得平等的地方,他们就很难再反抗当局对他们的独立的侵犯。他们中没有人足以强壮到单枪匹马在斗争中占据优势,只有联合起来才能保护他们的自由。但是,这样的联合并不总是存在。

因此,在同样的社会背景下,同一个国家可能得出两种政治结果:这两种结果完全不同于彼此,但是他们都出自同一本源。

英裔美国人是第一个面临这样艰难的抉择而有幸逃脱专制统治的民族。他们的环境、他们的本源、他们的知识、他们的智慧,特别是他们的民情,使他们得以建立和维护人民主权。

CHAPTER IV

The Principle Of The Sovereignty
Of The People Of America

It Dominates *the whole society in America — Application made of
this principle by the Americans even before their Revolution — Development given to it by that Revolution — Gradual and irresistible extension
of the elective qualification.*

Whenever the political laws of the United States are to be discussed, it is with the doctrine of the sovereignty of the people that we
must begin.

The principle of the sovereignty of the people, which is always to
be found, more or less, at the bottom of almost all human institutions, generally remains there concealed from view. It is obeyed without being recognized, or if for a moment it is brought to light, it is
hastily cast back into the gloom of the sanctuary.

"The will of the nation" is one of those phrases, that have been
most largely abused by the wily and the despotic of every age. Some
have seen the expression of it in the purchased suffrages of a few of
the satellites of power; others, in the votes of a timid or an interested
minority; and some have even discovered it in the silence of a people,
on the supposition that the fact of submission established the right to
command.

In America the principle of the sovereignty of the people is neither
barren nor concealed, as it is with some other nations; it is recognized
by the customs and proclaimed by the laws; it spreads freely, and arrives without impediment at its most remote consequences. If there is a
country in the world where the doctrine of the sovereignty of the people

第四章　美国的人民主权原则

人民主权原则支配了整个美国社会——早在大革命之前这一原则就在美国得以实施——革命促进其发展——缓慢但是必然扩大范围的选举资格。

只要讨论到美国的政治方面的法律，我们就必须先从人民主权原则谈起。

人民主权原则一直以来都或多或少地存在于几乎所有人类社会制度的底层，通常隐而不现。人们不认可它，但是都遵守其原则，即使偶尔出现，也会立即被人们推于圣殿的深处。

"民族意志"是每个时代的那些阴谋家和实施暴政的人们所滥用的口号中的一句。在一些当权人物为竞选买选票的过程中常常会听到这句话；另一些在少数人出于私利和畏惧为别人拉票时会被用到。还有一些人对于人民对此表示的沉默也认为是其表现形式之一，认为人们的屈服使得这种发号施令的权利得以确立。

在美国，人民主权原则跟在其他国家不一样，既没有表现得没有成效也没有表现得很隐蔽；它为民情所承认并且为法律所宣布，它得到了自由的传播和毫无阻碍地发展的极限。如果说世界上有一个国家，其人民民主的原则得到了公正的评判，其在社会

can be fairly appreciated, where it can be studied in its application to the affairs of society, and where its dangers and its advantages may be judged, that country is assuredly America.

I have already observed that, from their origin, the sovereignty of the people was the fundamental principle of most of the British colonies in America. It was far, however, from then exercising as much influence on the government of society as it now does. Two obstacles, the one external, the other internal, checked its invasive progress.

It could not ostensibly disclose itself in the laws of colonies which were still forced to obey the mother country; it was therefore obliged to rule secretly in the provincial assemblies, and especially in the townships.

American society at that time was not yet prepared to adopt it with all its consequences. Intelligence in New England and wealth in the country to the south of the Hudson (as I have shown in the preceding chapter) long exercised a sort of aristocratic influence, which tended to keep the exercise of social power in the hands of a few. Not all the public functionaries were chosen by popular vote, nor were all the citizens voters. The electoral franchise was everywhere somewhat restricted and made dependent on a certain qualification, which was very low in the North and more considerable in the South.

The American Revolution broke out, and the doctrine of the sovereignty of the people came out of the townships and took possession of the state. Every class was enlisted in its cause; battles were fought and victories obtained for it; it became the law of laws.

A change almost as rapid was effected in the interior of society, where the law of inheritance completed the abolition of local influences.

As soon as this effect of the laws and of the Revolution became apparent to every eye, victory was irrevocably pronounced in favor of the democratic cause. All power was, in fact, in its hands, and resistance

事务中的运用得以被研究,能够对其存在的危险性和优势做出判断,那么这个国家一定是美国。

我前面已经说过,从最初开始,人民主权就是美国大部分英国殖民地的基础原则。但是当时人民主权原则实施的影响还远不如现在这么大。有两个原因阻碍了它的进一步发展,有外部的原因,也有内部的原因。

它之所以没能见诸于殖民地的法律之中,是因为当时殖民地还必须服从于其宗主国;因此它不得不偷偷地仅在各地的人民大会中存在,特别是在乡镇政府中存在。

美国社会当时还没有准备好接受一切有关人民主权的原则以及它所带来的所有后果。新英格兰的文化水平和赫德森河南部的富裕条件(如我在前一章节中描述的那样),长久以来一直受到贵族制度的影响,社会权利一直都掌握在少数人的手中。并不是所有的政府官员都由普选产生,也不是所有的公民都有投票权。各地的选举机构受到不同的限制并具备一定的资格,而这一资格在北部要求很低而在南部相对来说要求更多。

美国大革命爆发之后,人民主权原则从乡镇政府中跳出来,上升到各州的统治。每一个阶级都从本身考虑参与其中;人们举着维护人民主权的旗帜互相发动战争并获得胜利;人民主权原则成了法律的法律。

社会内部立刻发生了巨大的变化,继承法完全废除了地方政府的影响。

法律和革命所产生的作用为人们所发现时,民主已宣布了其取得的彻底胜利。事实上,所有的权力都已掌握在人民民主的手中,所有的反抗已无济于事。上层阶级服从之后所遭受的不可避

was no longer possible. The higher orders submitted without a murmur and without a struggle to an evil that was thenceforth inevitable. The ordinary fate of falling powers awaited them: each of their members followed his own interest; and as it was impossible to wring the power from the hands of a people whom they did not detest sufficiently to brave, their only aim was to secure its goodwill at any price. The most democratic laws were consequently voted by the very men whose interests they impaired: and thus, although the higher classes did not excite the passions of the people against their order, they themselves accelerated the triumph of the new state of things; so that, by a singular change, the democratic impulse was found to be most irresistible in the very states where the aristocracy had the firmest hold. The state of Maryland, which had been founded by men of rank, was the first to proclaim universal suffrage[①] and to introduce the most democratic forms into the whole of its government.

When a nation begins to modify the elective qualification, it may easily be foreseen that, sooner or later, that qualification will be entirely abolished. There is no more invariable rule in the history of society: the further electoral rights are extended, the greater is the need of extending them; for after each concession the strength of the democracy increases, and its demands increase with its strength. The ambition of those who are below the appointed rate is irritated in exact proportion to the great number of those who are above it. The exception at last becomes the rule, concession follows concession, and no stop can be made short of universal suffrage.

At the present day the principle of the sovereignty of the people has acquired in the United States all the practical development that the imagination can conceive. It is unencumbered by those fictions that are thrown over it in other countries, and it appears in every possible form, according to the exigency of the occasion. Sometimes the laws are made by the people in a body, as at Athens; and sometimes its representatives, chosen by universal suffrage, transact business in its name and under its immediate supervision.

---

① Amendment made to the Constitution of Maryland in 1801 and 1809.

免的苦难,不敢有任何抱怨和反抗。权力的丧失是他们普遍的命运:他们的每个成员都有其自己追逐的利益;因为他们没有憎恨到有勇气从人民手中夺得权力,他们的唯一的目的就是维持与人们的友好。结果最民主的法律也得到了被其所削弱利益的阶级的投票:这样,上层阶级虽没有刺激人们反抗他们所建立的秩序的激情,他们自己却加速了新的社会状态的胜利建立;然而,仅仅通过一场改革,民主的推动力就在曾被贵族制度牢固统治的国家表现出势不可挡的发展趋势。马里兰州本是由贵族阶层建立的,而它也是最早宣布普选①和将最民主的体系引进其整个政府统治的州。

当一个国家开始修改其选举资格的时候,那就意味着,这一资格限制迟早会被完全推翻。这是支配社会发展的不变规律之一;随着选举权利的进一步扩大,人们对于其扩展的要求就更强烈;因为在每一次让步之后,民主的权利都会增强,它的要求也会随着其势力的增长而增多。没有选举权的人们希望获得选举权的野心与有选举权的人的多少成正比。最后,例外逐渐变成规则,随着连连让步,直到达到全普选的结果。

到了今天,人民主权的原则已在美国获得人们所想到的一切的实际的发展。它并没有受到在其他国家被架空的状况所带来的影响的阻碍,它根据具体的情况以各种可能的形式存在着。有时,法律由某一人民团体来制定,像在雅典;有时由普选的议员代表人民,以人民的名义办理政务并接受人民的直接监督。

----

①　1801 年至 1809 年对马里兰宪法的修正。

In some countries a power exists which, though it is in a degree foreign to the social body, directs it, and forces it to pursue a certain track. In others the ruling force is divided, being partly within and partly without the ranks of the people. But nothing of the kind is to be seen in the United States; there society governs itself for itself. All power centers in its bosom, and scarcely an individual is to be met with who would venture to conceive or, still less, to express the idea of seeking it elsewhere. The nation participates in the making of its laws by the choice of its legislators, and in the execution of them by the choice of the agents of the executive government; it may almost be said to govern itself, so feeble and so restricted is the share left to the administration, so little do the authorities forget their popular origin and the power from which they emanate. The people reign in the A-merican political world as the Deity does in the universe. They are the cause and the aim of all things; everything comes from them, and everything is absorbed in them. [①]

---

① See Appendix H.

　　有一些国家,其政权可以说是由外部加于社会的,社会不仅要按它的指示行动,而且要被迫按照一定的道路前进。还有一些国家,其统治力量是分开的,有些阶层可以参与权力,有些阶层则不可以。美国绝没有这种情形,在那里,社会是由自己管理,并为自己而管理。所有的权力都归社会所有,几乎没有一个人敢于产生到处去寻找权力的想法,更不用说敢于提出这种想法了。人民以推选立法人员的办法参与立法工作,以挑选行政人员的办法参与执法工作。可以说是人民自己治理自己,而留给政府的那部分权力也微乎其微,并且薄弱得很,何况政府还要受人民的监督,服从建立政府的人民的权威。人民之对美国政界的统治,犹如上帝之统治宇宙。人民是一切事物的原因和结果,凡事皆出自人民,并用于人民。①

---

①　见附件 H。

CHAPTER V

Necessity Of Examining The Condition Of The States Before That Of The Union At Large

In the following chapter the form of government established in America on the principle of the sovereignty of the people will be examined; what are its means of action, its hindrances, its advantages, and its dangers. The first difficulty that presents itself arises from the complex nature of the Constitution of the United States, which consists of two distinct social structures, connected, and, as it were, encased one within the other; two governments, completely separate and almost independent, the one fulfilling the ordinary duties and responding to the daily and indefinite calls of a community, the other circumscribed within certain limits and only exercising an exceptional authority over the general interests of the country. In short, there are twenty-four small sovereign nations, whose agglomeration constitutes the body of the Union. To examine the Union before we have studied the states, would be to adopt a method filled with obstacles. The form of the Federal government of the United States was the last to be adopted; and it is in fact nothing more than a summary of those republican principles which were current in the whole community before it existed, and independently of its existence. Moreover, the Federal government, as I have just observed, is the exception; the government of the states is the rule. The author who should attempt to exhibit the picture as a whole before he had explained its details would necessarily fall into obscurity and repetition.

The great political principles which now govern American society undoubtedly took their origin and their growth in the state. We must know the state, then, in order to gain a clue to the rest.

第五章 在详尽地叙述联邦政府之前,有必要先来研究各州过去的状况

在接下来的这一章中,我们将考察美国根据人民主权原则建立的政府形式、行动方式、障碍、进步和危险。美国宪法的复杂性是其遇到的第一个困难。美国有两个不同的社会结构,这两个社会结构互相结合,而且可以说是互相嵌入对方。美国有两个截然不同和几乎完全独立的政府:一个是负责执行普通职责和处理日常事务一般性政府;另一个是拥有特殊权限,只管辖全国性的一些重大问题的政府。简单地讲,美国内部还存在着 24 个拥有各自主权的小国,是它们构成了联邦这个大整体。在研究各州之前要先考察联邦,这对于我们来讲,是一个充满困难的做法。美国联邦政府的形式是最后出现的,实际上,它什么都不是,只不过是共和制度的变革,只是对那些不依赖于它的存在,并在它之前就通行于社会的那些政治原则的总结。而且正如我刚才讲过的,联邦政府是一个特例,而各州的政府才具有一般性。如果在解释这幅图画的细节之前,作者就将其全景展示给大家,他必然在有些地方含糊不清和出现重复。

目前统治美国社会的那些伟大政治原则无疑是在各州产生和发展的。因此,我们必须了解州,以便更好地掌握解决其余一切问题的线索。就制度的外观来看各州,都具有同样的特征。

The states that now compose the American Union all present the same features, as far as regards the external aspect of their institutions. Their political or administrative life is centered in three focuses of action, which may be compared to the different nervous centers that give motion to the human body. The township is the first in order, then the county, and lastly the state.

The American System Of Townships

Why the author begins the examination of the political institutions with the township —Its existence in all nations — Difficulty of establishing and preserving municipal independence — Its importance — Why the author has selected the township system of New England as the main topic of his discussion.

It is not without intention that I begin this subject with the township. The village or township is the only association which is so perfectly natural that, wherever a number of men are collected, it seems to constitute itself.

The town or tithing, then, exists in all nations, whatever their laws and customs may be: it is man who makes monarchies and establishes republics, but the township seems to come directly from the hand of God. But although the existence of the township is coeval with that of man, its freedom is an infrequent and fragile thing. A nation can always establish great political assemblies, because it habitually contains a certain number of individuals fitted by their talents, if not by their habits, for the direction of affairs. The township, on the contrary, is composed of coarser materials, which are less easily fashioned by the legislator. The difficulty of establishing its independence rather augments than diminishes with the increasing intelligence of the people. A highly civilized community can hardly tolerate a local independdnce, is disgusted at its numerous blunders, and is apt to despair of success before the experiment is completed. Again, the immunities of townships, which have been obtained with so much difficulty, are least of all protected against the encroachments of the supreme power.

各州的政治或行政管理都集中在三个不同的行政中心上,这三个中心可以被比做是指挥人体活动的不同的神经中枢。它们依次是乡镇、县和州。

美国的乡镇组织

为什么作者要从乡镇开始考察政治制度——乡镇在所有国家的存在——实现和保持乡镇独立的困难——以及其重要性——为什么作者要选择新英格兰的乡镇组织作为其讨论的主题。

我把乡镇作为考察的起点,并不是一种漫无目的的决定。乡村或乡镇是自然界中唯一联合体,这种联合体不论有多少人集聚,都能自发地组织起来。

因此,乡镇组织存在于所有的国家,不管这个国家的法律和风俗习惯如何。建立君主政体和创造共和政体的是人,而乡镇却似乎由上帝所创造。尽管乡镇自有人类以来就已经存在,但它的自由却不常见并且非常脆弱。一个国家总是能够举行大的政治集会,因为它通常拥有一定数量的人民,他们的文化水平已经发展到一定程度并被赋予处理公务的能力。而乡镇则相反,它是由一些粗俗的人组成的,他们通常都不能理解立法者的用心。实现乡镇独立的困难不但没有减少,反而随着人类的进步、人民文化水平的提高而增加了。一个高度文明的社会,几乎不能忍受地方的独立,在对乡镇的众多错误做法的试验中,在还没有等到结果时,它就对前途充满了绝望。乡镇自由在各种自由中是最难实现的,它也最容易受到国家政权的威胁。全靠自身维持的乡镇组织,绝对斗不过庞大的中央政府。

They are unable to struggle, single-handed, against a strong and enterprising government, and they cannot defend themselves with success unless they are identified with the customs of the nation and supported by public opinion. Thus until the independence of townships is amalgamated with the manners of a people, it is easily destroyed; and it is only after a long existence in the laws that it can be thus amalgamated. Municipal freedom is not the fruit of human efforts; it is rarely created by others, but is, as it were, secretly self-produced in the midst of a semi-barbarous state of society. The constant action of the laws and the national habits, peculiar circumstances, and, above all, time, may consolidate it; but there is certainly no nation on the continent of Europe that has experienced its advantages. Yet municipal institutions constitute the strength of free nations. Town meetings are to liberty what primary schools are to science; they bring it within the people's reach, they teach men how to use and how to enjoy it. A nation may establish a free government, but without municipal institutions it cannot have the spirit of liberty. Transient passions, the interests of an hour, or the chance of circumstances may create the external forms of independence, but the despotic tendency which has been driven into the interior of the social system will sooner or later reappear on the surface.

To make the reader understand the general principles on which the political organization of the counties and townships in the United States rests, I have thought it expedient to choose one of the states of New England as an example, to examine in detail the mechanism of its constitution, and then to cast a general glance over the rest of the country.

The township and the county are not organized in the same manner in every part of the Union; it is easy to perceive, however, that nearly the same principles have guided the formation of both of them throughout the Union. I am inclined to believe that these principles have been carried further and have produced greater results in New England than elsewhere. Consequently they stand out there in higher relief and offer greater facilities to the observations of a stranger.

The township institutions of New England form a complete and regular whole; they are old; they have the support of the laws and the still stronger support of the manners of the community, over which they exercise a prodigious influence. For all these reasons they deserve our special attention.

除非认同于全民族的习惯并获得公共舆论的支持,乡镇组织才能有效地保护自己。乡镇自由在还没有融入民俗的情况下是很易于被摧毁的;但只要它能在法律下长期存在,它就能成为民俗的一部分。因此,乡镇自由并不是人力的结果。也就是说,人力几乎不可能创造它。它是在半野蛮的社会中悄悄地自己发展起来的。法律、民俗、社会环境和时间的持续作用,使它更加巩固。在欧洲大陆的所有国家中,几乎可以说没有一个国家知道乡镇自由。然而,乡镇却是体现自由人民的力量的地方。乡镇组织的自由,如同小学生的学习。乡镇组织带给人民很多自由,并教导人民怎样享受自由和很好的让自由为他们服务。国家可以建立一个自由的政府,在没有乡镇组织的条件下,它就不会有自由的精神。片刻的激情、暂时的兴趣或环境的机遇可以创造出独立的外在形式,但潜伏在社会机体内部的专制迟早都会重新浮出水面。

为了使读者清楚地了解美国的乡镇和县的政治机构建立的一般原则,我认为最好是拿新英格兰的一个州为例,先详细考察这个州的机构与体制,然后再去了解其余的州。

联邦各州的乡镇和县并不是按照同一方式建立起来的。但也不难看出,在整个联邦,乡镇和县的创建,却差不多完全基于同样的原则。但我认为,这些原则在新英格兰要比在其他地方推行得更广和更有成果。因此,可以说它们在新英格兰表现得最为突出,而且对于陌生人也最易于观察。

新英格兰的乡镇组织形成了一个完整而有秩序的群体,它们建立的时间最长。它们受到法律和社会的民俗的强烈支持,这些使它变得更强有力。它对全社会起着异常巨大的影响。由于这些原因,它值得了我们的特别关注。

Limits Of The Township

The township of New England holds a middle place between the *commune* and the *canton* of France. Its average population is from two to three thousand, [①] so that it is not so large, on the one hand, that the interests of its inhabitants would be likely to conflict, and not so small, on the other, but that men capable of conducting its affairs may always be found among its citizens.

Powers Of The Township In New England

The people the source of all power in the township as elsewhere — Manages its own affairs — No municipal council — The greater part of the authority vested in the selectmen — How the selectmen act Town meeting — Enumeration of the officers of the township — Obligatory and remunerated functions.

In the township, as well as everywhere else, the people are the source of power; but nowhere do they exercise their power more immediately. In America the people form a master who must be obeyed to the utmost limits of possibility.

In New England the majority act by representatives in conducting the general business of the state. It is necessary that it should be so. But in the townships, where the legislative and administrative action of the government is nearer to the governed, the system of representation is not adopted. There is no municipal council; but the body of voters, after having chosen its magistrates, directs them in everything

---

① In 1830 there were 305 townships in the state of Massachusetts, and 610,014 inhabitants; which gives an average of about 2,000 inhabitants to each township.

乡镇的规模

新英格兰的乡镇处在法国的区和乡之间,其平均人口数为两三千人。① 因此,一方面乡镇的面积并未大得或小得使全体居民的利益发生冲突;另一方面,它的居民人数也总能从其伙伴中间选出优秀的行政管理人员。

新英格兰的乡镇的权利

新英格兰的乡镇政权同其他地方一样,人民是乡镇一切权力的源泉,乡镇自己处理主要事务——没有乡镇议会——乡镇的大权主要掌握在行政委员的手里——行政委员是怎样工作的——乡镇居民大会——乡镇官员的种类列举——义务官职和有酬官职。

乡镇组织,像其他任何地方,其权力的源泉是人民,但其他任何地方的权力的行使都不像这里这样迅速。在美国,人民是主人,而各方面都必须尽最大的可能去讨好他们。

在新英格兰,公民是通过代表参与州的公共事务的。这样做有其一定的必要性,因为公民没有办法直接参与公共事务,但在乡镇,政府的立法和行政工作都是就近在被治者的面前完成的,所以没有采用代议制。这里没有乡镇议会。但选举团在任命其行政官员之后,便在所有事情上都领导他们,其工作程序之简便,

_____

① 1830 年,马萨诸塞共有 305 个乡镇,610014 名居民;平均每个乡镇有 2000 名居民。

that exceeds the simple and ordinary execution of the laws of the state. ①

This state of things is so contrary to our ideas, and so different from our customs that I must furnish some examples to make it intelligible.

The public duties in the township are extremely numerous and minutely divided, as we shall see farther on; but most of the administrative pnwer is vested in a few persons, chosen annually, called "the selectmen." ②

The general laws of the state impose certain duties on the selectmen, which they may fulfill without the authority of their townsmen, but which they can neglect only on their own responsibility. The state law requires them, for instance, to draw up a list of voters in their townships; and if they omit this duty, they are guilty of a misdemeanor. In all the affairs that are voted in town meeting, however, the selectmen carry into effect the popular mandate, as in France the *maire* executes the decree of the municipal council. They usually act upon their own responsibility and merely put in practice principles that have been previously recognized by the majority. But if they wish to make any change in the existing state of things or to undertake any new enterprise, they must refer to the source of their power. If, for instance, a school is to be established, the selectmen call a meeting of the voters on a certain day at an appointed place.

---

① The same rules are not applicable to the cities, which generally have a mayor, and a corporation divided into two bodies; this, however, is an exception that requires the sanction of a law. — See the Act of February 22, 1822, regulating the powers of the city of Boston. *Laws of Massachusetts*, Vol. II, p. 588. It frequently happens that small towns, as well as cities, are subject to a peculiar administration. In 1832, 104 townships in the state of New York were governed in this manner. Williams's Register.

② Three selectmen are appointed in the small townships, and nine in the large ones. See *The Town Officer*, p. 186. See also the principal laws of Massachusetts relating to selectmen: law of February 20, 1786, Vol. I, p. 219; February 24, 1796, Vol. I, p. 488; March 7, 1801, Vol. II, p. 45; June 16, 1795, Vol. I, p. 475; March 12, 1808, Vol. II, p. 186; February 28, 1787, Vol. I, p. 302; June 22, 1797, Vol. I, p. 539.

远远胜过州的执行法律。①

这种制度是如此违背我们的想法,又如此的不同于我们的习惯,所以我必须提出一些例证,以使它变得更加清楚。

乡镇的公共事务是极其繁多而又分工细致的,这个在稍后会详细讨论。但是,大部分的行政权都掌握在少数人手里,这些人就是每年一选的"行政委员"。②

州的常规法律对行政委员规定了一定的职责。他们可以不必经过本乡镇人民的认可来执行这些职务。但如果玩忽职守,则由他们自己负责。例如,州的法律要求他们上报本乡镇的选民名单。如果他们疏忽了这个责任,就犯有渎职罪。但是,对于需要由乡镇政权处理的一切事务,行政委员是代表人民意志的执行者,比如在法国,市镇长就像是市镇议会决议的执行者一样。他们通常对自己的公务负责,只是在工作中要按本乡镇居民早先通过的原则办事。但是,如果他们想对已经存在的事务做任何更改,或计划一项新的事业,那就必须请示赋予给他们的权力的上级。比如说,打算创办一所学校。这时,几位行政委员就要找一个特定的日子,在事先规定的场所召集全体选民开

---

① 同样的规定在一些城市并不适合,这些城市一般有一名市长和一个由两个科组成的公所,但是,这些规定是需要法律认可的。——见 1822 年 2 月 22 日的法令,调整了波士顿市的权力。《马萨诸塞法律》第二卷,第 588 页。小城镇和城市一般会有较独特的行政部门。在 1832 年,纽约的很多州都已这种方式被统治。威廉纪录。

② 小乡镇任命三个行政委员,而大乡镇则任命九个。——《见乡镇官员》,第 186 页,同样见马萨诸塞关于行政委员的主要法律:1786 年 2 月 20 日的法令,第一卷,第 219 页;1796 年 2 月 24 日的法令,第一卷,第 448 页;1801 年 3 月 7 日的法令,第二卷,第 45 页;1795 年 6 月 16 日的法令,第一卷,第 475 页;1808 年 3 月 12 日的法令,第二卷,第 186 页;1787 年 2 月 28 日的法令,第一卷,第 302 页;1797 年 6 月 22 日的法令,第一卷,第 539 页。

They explain the urgency of the case; they make known the means of satisfying it, the probable expense, and the site that seems to be most favorable. The meeting is consulted on these several points; it adopts the principle, marks out the site, votes the tax, and confides the execution of its resolution to the selectmen.

The selectmen alone have the right of calling a town meeting; but they may be required to do so. If ten citizens wish to submit a new project to the assent of the town, they may demand a town meeting; the selectmen are obliged to comply and have only the right of presiding at the meeting. [1] These political forms, these social customs, doubtless seem strange to us in France. I do not here undertake to judge them or to make known the secret causes by which they are produced and maintained. I only describe them.

The selectmen are elected every year, in the month of March or April. The town meeting chooses at the same time a multitude of other town officers, [2] who are entrusted with important administrative functions. The assessors rate the township; the collectors receive the tax. A constable is appointed to keep the peace, to watch the streets, and to execute the laws; the town clerk records the town votes, orders, and grants. The treasurer keeps the funds. The overseers of the poor perform the difficult task of carrying out the poor-laws. Committeemen are appointed to attend to the schools and public instruction; and the surveyors of highways, who take care of the greater and lesser roads of the township, complete the list of the principal functionaries. But there are other petty officers still; such as the parish committee, who audit the expenses of public worship; fire wardens, who direct the efforts of the citizens in case of fire; tithing-men,

---

[1] See *Laws of Massachusetts*, Vol. I, p. 150. Law of March 25, 1786.
[2] Ibid.

会。他们在会上会解释事件的紧急性,并向大家说明满足此项要求的办法,需要多少款项,适合建立的场所。大会就这一切问题进行讨论之后,便制定出原则,选定地点,筹集费用,然后由行政委员执行以上决定。

只有行政委员具有号召举行乡镇居民大会的权力,但其他人也可以要求他们召开。如果有十名选民希望提出一项新的计划并要求乡镇会议的支持,他们就可以请求行政委员召开乡镇居民大会。而行政委员必须答应他们的要求,并且有权主持会议。[①]在法国,这些政治形势和社会习惯对我们而言无疑是很陌生的。在此,我既不想对它们进行评论,也不想说明它们之所以产生和发展的内在原因。我只是把它们叙述一下而已。

行政委员在每年4月或5月选举一次。同时,乡镇居民大会还选出其他一些官员来担任乡镇的某些重要行政职务。[②] 其中有:数名负责评估居民财产的财产评估员;数名负责按评估的财产收税的税收员;一名负责维持治安、巡逻街道和执行法律的警察;一名负责会议记录的审议事项和管理户籍乡镇文书的文员;一名负责管理乡镇的财务的司库。除了以上这些官员之外,还有一名负责执行济贫法的济贫工作检查员,他的任务是非常艰巨的;还有几名负责管理学校和国民教育的委员;和几名负责大小道路的一切管理工作的道路管理员。以上就是乡镇管理方面的主要官员的列表。但是在乡镇组织中,还有其他一些官员,有几名负责管理宗教事务费用的教区管理员,以及各种各样的视察员,例如有的负责组织公民救火,有的组织人力看护林木,有的协

---

① 见《马萨诸塞法律》,1786年3月25日的法令,第一卷,第150页。

② 出处同上。

hog-reeves, fence-viewers, timber-measurers, and sealers of weights and measures. ①

There are, in all, nineteen principal offices in a township. Every inhabitant is required, on pain of being fined, to undertake these different functions, which, however, are almost all paid, in order that the poorer citizens may give time to them without loss. In general, each official act has its price, and the officers are remunerated in proportion to what they have done.

Life In The Township

Everyone the best judge of his own interest — Corollary of the principle of the sovereignty of the people — Application of these doctrines in the townships of America — The township of New England is sovereign in all that concerns itself alone, and subject to the state in all other matters — Duties of the township to the state — In France the government lends its agents to the commune — In America it is the reverse.

I have already observed that the principle of the sovereignty of the people governs the whole political system of the AngloAmericans. Every page of this book will afford new applications of the same doctrine. In the nations by which the sovereignty of the people is recognized, every individual has an equal share of power and participates equally in the government of the state. Why, then, does he obey society, and what are the natural limits of this obedience? Every individual is always supposed to be as well informed, as virtuous, and as strong as any of his fellow citizens. He obeys society, not because he is inferior to those who conduct it or because he is less capable than

---

① All these magistrates actually exist; their different functions are all detailed in a book called *The Town Officer*, by Isaac Goodwin (Worcester, 1827), and the *General Laws of Massachusetts* in 3 vols. (Boston, 1823).

助公民解决修建庭院时可能遇到的困难,有的负责测量森林,有的负责检查度量衡器具。①

一个乡镇共有 19 名主要官员。每个居民都被要求担当各种不同的职务,违者罚款。但是,这些职务大部分都是有报酬的,为的是能使贫穷的公民在付出时间的情况下不受损失。总的来讲,每项公务都有其固定的报酬,按官员完成的工作量的多少来计酬。

乡镇的生活

每个人都是自己利益的最好裁决者——人民主权原则的必然结果——这些学说在美国乡镇的应用——新英格兰的乡镇只在与本身利益有关的一切事务上享有主权,在其他事务上则服从于州——乡镇对州的责任——在法国,政府把官员借给村镇,在美国是乡镇把官员借给政府。

我在前面已经讲过,人民主权原则统治着英籍美国人的整个政治制度。这本书的每一页,都会为读者提供这个理论的某些新的应用。在推行人民主权原则的国家,每一个人都享有同等的权利,平等地参与国家政府的管理。因此每一个人在其学识涵养和才能方面也与大家相等。那么,他们为什么要屈从于社会呢? 而这种服从的自然界限又是什么呢? 每一个人的文化程度、道德修养和能力也被认为是与其他同胞相等的。个人服从社会,并不是因为他比管理社会的那些人低劣,也不是因为他管理自己

---

① 实际上,所有这些官员都存在着;他们不同的职务都在一本名为《乡镇官员》的书中(艾萨克·顾得 1827 年写于伍斯特),和马萨诸塞的编为三卷的一般法律中(波士顿,1823)被详细列出。

any other of governing himself, but because he acknowledges the utility of an association with his fellow men and he knows that no such association can exist without a regulating force. He is a subject in all that concerns the duties of citizens to each other; he is free, and responsible to God alone, for all that concerns himself. Hence arises the maxim, that everyone is the best and sole judge of his own private interest, and that society has no right to control a man's actions unless they are prejudicial to the common weal or unless the common weal demands his help. This doctrine is universally admitted in the United States. I shall hereafter examine the general influence that it exercises on the ordinary actions of life; I am now speaking of the municipal bodies.

The township, taken as a whole, and in relation to the central government, is only an individual, like any other to whom the theory I have just described is applicable. Municipal independence in the United States is therefore a natural consequence of this very principle of the sovereignty of the people. All the American republics recognize it more or less, but circumstances have peculiarly favored its growth in New England.

In this part of the Union political life had its origin in the townships; and it may almost be said that each of them originally formed an independent nation. When the kings of England afterwards asserted their supremacy, they were content to assume the central power of the state. They left the townships where they were before; and although they are now subject to the state, they were not at first, or were hardly so. They did not receive their powers from the central authority, but, on the contrary, they gave up a portion of their independence to the state. This is an important distinction and one that the reader must constantly recollect. The townships are generally subordinate to the state only in those interests which I shall term *social*, as they are common to all the others. They are independent in all that concerns themselves alone; and among the inhabitants of New England I believe that not a man is to be found who would acknowledge that the state has any right to interfere in their town affairs.

的能力不如别人。而是因为他明白与同胞联合起来才是非常有利的,知道如果没有管理权力的作用,社会就不可能存在。因此,在同每个公民应该负责的一切事务上,他也必须服从;而在与他本身有关的一切事务上,他却是拥有主动权。也就是说,他的自由,只对上帝负责。因此产生了如此格言:每个人都是其自己利益的最好的和唯一的裁判。社会无权控制个人的行动,除非社会感到自己被个人的行为侵害或必须要求个人协助时。这个学说,在美国是被普遍承认的。我准备以后再考察它对日常生活行为产生的影响,而现在只谈谈它对乡镇产生的影响。

在整体观察乡镇和中央政府的关系时,就会发现乡镇也如同其他行政区,像是由个人来行使自己权利。我刚才叙述的原理,也适用于乡镇和其他行政区。因此,美国乡镇的独立是人民主权原则的自然结果。所有美国的共和制政府都或多或少承认乡镇的独立。但是在新英格兰,环境则特别有利于这一学说的发展。

在联邦的这一部分,政治生活开始于乡镇。甚至可以说,每个乡镇最初都是一个独立国。后来,当英国的几位国王相继维护他们的主权的时候,他们也只限于州一级的权力。他们让乡镇恢复了先前的样子。尽管新英格兰的乡镇是从属于州的,但起初它们决非这样或几乎不是这样的。它们并没有从中央集权那里得到权力;相反,它们却把自己的一部分独立让给了州。这是一个重大的差别,请读者千万要记住。乡镇一般只在我称之为社会的利益上,即在各乡镇共享的利益上服从于州,而在与其本身有关的一切事务上是独立的。我认为在新英格兰的居民中,没有一个

The towns of New England buy and sell, sue and are sued, augment or diminish their budgets, and no administrative authority ever thinks of offering any opposition. ①

There are certain social duties, however, that they are bound to fulfill. If the state is in need of money, a town cannot withhold the supplies; ② if the state projects a road, the township cannot refuse to let it cross its territory; if a police regulation is made by the state, it must be enforced by the town; if a uniform system of public instruction is enacted, every town is bound to establish the schools which the law ordains. ③ When I come to speak of the administration of the laws in the United States, I shall point out how and by what means the townships are compelled to obey in these different cases; I here merely show the existence of the obligation. Strict as this obligation is, the government of the state imposes it in principle only, and in its performance the township resumes all its independent rights. Thus, taxes are voted by the state, but they are levied and collected by the township; the establishment of a school is obligatory, but the township builds, pays for, and superintends it. In France the state collector receives the local imposts; in America the town collector receives the taxes of the state. Thus the French government lends its agents to the commune; in America the township lends its agents to the government. This fact alone shows how widely the two nations differ.

Spirit Of The Townships Of New England

How the township of New England wins the affections of its inhabitants — Difficulty of creating local public spirit in Europe — The rights and duties of the American township favorable to it — Sources of

---

① See *Laws of Massachusetts*, law of March 23, 1786, Vol. I, p. 250.

② Ibid. , law of February 20, 1786, Vol. I, p. 217.

③ Ibid. , law of June 25, 1789, Vol. I, p. 367, and of March 8, 1827, Vol. III, p. 179.

人会承认州有权干涉乡镇的事务。因此,在新英格兰的乡镇,买卖东西,打官司,或增减预算,州当局从来不曾想过要加以干涉。①

但是,对于一些特定的社会性的义务,它们必须履行职责。如果州需要钱,乡镇就不能拒绝提供帮助;②如果州想修建一条道路,乡镇就不能不让道路从其境内通过;如果州制定了一项公安条例,乡镇就必须予以执行;如果州想在全州范围内实行统一的教育制度,乡镇就得按照法律规定设立相应的学校。③ 当我叙述到美国的行政组织时,我将会谈到乡镇是怎样和通过什么途径服从上述规定的。在这里,我只想指出有这种义务存在性。这种义务是必须尽的,但州政府只是在原则上规定它,而在执行的时候,乡镇一般又恢复了它的一切个体独立权。比如,征税是由议会表决的,但是负责征收税款的却是乡镇;设立学校是州的义务,但却是乡镇花钱建立和管理学校。在法国,由国家的税务人员去征收地方的税;而在美国,则由乡镇的税务人员去征收州的税。也就是说,法国的中央政府把它的官员借给了村镇;而在美国,则是乡镇把它的官员借给了州政府。仅仅是这个事实,就足以表明两个社会的差别是如何之大了。

新英格兰的乡镇精神

新英格兰的乡镇为什么会赢得居民的爱戴——在欧洲形成地方乡镇精神的困难——美国乡镇的权利和义务有利于乡镇精

---

① 见《马萨诸塞法律》,1786 年 3 月 23 日的法令,第一卷,第 250 页。

② 出处同上,1786 年 2 月 20 日的法令,第一卷,第 217 页。

③ 出处同上,1789 年 6 月 25 日的法令,第一卷,第 367 页,和 1827 年 3 月 8 日的法令,第三卷,第 179 页。

local attachment in the United States — How town spirit shows itself in New England — Its happy effects.

In America not only do municipal bodies exist, but they are kept alive and supported by town spirit. The township of New England possesses two advantages which strongly excite the interest of mankind: namely, independence and authority. Its sphere is limited, indeed; but within that sphere its action is unrestrained. This independence alone gives it a real importance, which its extent and population would not ensure.

It is to be remembered, too, that the affections of men generally turn towards power. Patriotism is not durable in a conquered nation. The New Englander is attached to his township not so much because he was born in it, but because it is a free and strong community, of which he is a member, and which deserves the care spent in managing it. In Europe the absence of local public spirit is a frequent subject of regret to those who are in power; everyone agrees that there is no surer guarantee of order and tranquillity, and yet nothing is more difficult to create. If the municipal bodies were made powerful and independent, it is feared that they would become too strong and expose the state to anarchy. Yet without power and independence a town may contain good subjects, but it can have no active citizens. Another important fact is that the township of New England is so constituted as to excite the warmest of human affections without arousing the ambitious passions of the heart of man. The officers of the county are not elected, and their authority is very limited. Even the state is only a second-rate community whose tranquil and obscure administration offers no inducement sufficient to draw men away from the home of their interests into the turmoil of public affairs. The Federal government confers power and honor on the men who conduct it, but these individuals can never be very numerous. The high station of the Presidency can only be reached at an advanced period of life; and the other Federal functionaries of a high class are generally men who have been favored by good luck or have been distinguished in some other career. Such cannot be the permanent aim of the ambitious. But the township, at

神的形成——乡镇在美国比在其他国家有更大的特点——乡镇
精神在新英格兰是怎样表现的——乡镇精神产生的有利的效果。

在美国,乡镇制度不仅存在,而且有乡镇精神的支持和鼓励。
新英格兰的乡镇有两个可以强烈刺激人们进取的优点,那就是独
立和权力。不错,它的范围是有限的,但在这个范围内,乡镇的活
动是不受限制的。当人口和面积还不足以使乡镇独立时,这种活
动自由的独立性,就已使乡镇占有实际上非常重要的地位。

必须承认,人们通常爱慕权势。而且可以看到,爱国主义在
一个被征服的国家里是不会长久的。新英格兰居民之所以爱慕
乡镇,并不是因为他们生于那里,而是因为他们认为乡镇是一个
自由而强大的集体。他们是乡镇的成员,而乡镇也值得他们细心
管理。在欧洲,很遗憾的是统治者本人就常常缺乏乡镇精神,几
乎每个人都认为乡镇精神是维持安定和公共秩序的一个重要保
障,但不知道怎么去培养它。他们害怕乡镇强大和独立以后会篡
夺中央的权力,使国家处于无政府状态。但是,如果不让乡镇强
大和独立,就不会有积极而活跃的公民。另一个重要事实是:新
英格兰的乡镇组织得很好,既能吸引居民的爱戴,又不会刺激他
们贪婪的欲望。县的官员不是选举产生的,他们的权力也非常有
限。甚至州也只有次要的权限,它的平静的和无关紧要的行政权
力不能带来足够的诱惑,驱使人们离开自己感兴趣的事业而投奔
到混乱的公共事务中。联邦政府为管理人员授予权力和荣誉,但
此类人并不是很多。总统是在达到一定的年龄之后才能取得的
最高职位。至于联邦政府的其他高级官员,可能是由于好运的降
临,也可能是由于他们在某些领域获得过杰出的成绩。这些并不
能成为他们雄心壮志的最终目标。但是乡镇,这个日常生活关系

the center of the ordinary relations of life, serves as a field for the desire of public esteem, the want of exciting interest, and the taste for authority and popularity; and the passions that commonly embroil society change their character when they find a vent so near the domestic hearth and the family circle.

In the American townships power has been distributed with admirable skill, for the purpose of interesting the greatest possible number of persons in the common weal. Independently of the voters, who are from time to time called into action, the power is divided among innumerable functionaries and officers, who all, in their several spheres, represent the powerful community in whose name they act. The local administration thus affords an unfailing source of profit and interest to a vast number of individuals. The American system, which divides the local authority among so many citizens, does not scruple to multiply the functions of the town officers. For in the United States it is believed, and with truth, that patriotism is a kind of devotion which is strengthened by ritual observance. In this manner the activity of the township is continually perceptible; it is daily manifested in the fulfillment of a duty or the exercise of a right; and a constant though gentle motion is thus kept up in society, which animates without disturbing it. The American attaches himself to his little community for the same reason that the mountaineer clings to his hills, because the characteristic features of his country are there more distinctly marked; it has a more striking physiognomy.

The existence of the townships of New England is, in general, a happy one. Their government is suited to their tastes, and chosen by themselves. In the midst of the profound peace and general comfort that reign in America, the commotions of municipal life are infrequent. The conduct of local business is easy. The political education of the people has long been complete; say rather that it was complete when the people first set foot upon the soil. In New England no tradition exists of a distinction of rank; no portion of the community is tempted to oppress the remainder; and the wrongs that may injure isolated individuals are forgotten in the general contentment that prevails. If the government has faults (and it would no doubt be easy to point out some), they do not attract notice, for the government really

的中心,才是人们的求名思想、获致实利的需要、掌权和求荣的爱好之所向。经常困扰社会的这种激情要是发生在壁炉旁边时,即所谓家庭内部时,性质就不一样了。

于是,在美国的乡镇,人们试图用巧妙的技巧来分离权力,目的是为了最大限度上使多数人参与公共事务。结果,选民的任务是经常开会审议乡镇的管理措施,而各式各样的官职,则独立于选民之外,在一定的职权范围内代表权力很大的乡镇自治体,并以这个自治体的名义行动。因此,地方行政组织为广大人民群众提供了可以享受到的利益。美国的制度把乡镇政权同时分给这么多公民,它并不害怕扩大乡镇官员的职权。我们有理由认为,在美国,爱国主义是通过实践而养成的一种眷恋故乡的感情。这样,乡镇生活可以说每时每刻都在使人感到与自己有着密切的关系,每天每日都有着一项义务的履行或一次权利的行使。这样的乡镇生活,使社会一直会勇往直前而又不致打乱其稳定的秩序。美国人依恋其乡镇同山区居民热爱其山水是一样的,因为故乡的那种与众不同的特殊气质使他们感到依依不舍。

一般说来,新英格兰的乡镇生活是幸福的。乡镇政府根据居民的喜好由他们自己选择。在生活安定和物资充裕的美国,乡镇的暴动是不常见的,因此地方的事务容易管理。此外,长期以来人民受到了政治教育,或者说在人们刚刚落脚于这个地方的时候就开始受到了这种教育。在新英格兰,从来没有明显的等级区分。因此,乡镇中没有一部分人压迫另一部分人的现象,即使是对孤立的个人进行的罚治,也会在征得全体居民同意后撤销。如果政府有了缺点(要指出这种缺点无疑是很容易的),人们也不耿耿于怀,因为管理实际上是根据被治理的人的喜好而进行的,所

emanates from those it governs, and whether it acts ill or well, this fact casts the protecting spell of a parental pride over its demerits. Besides, they have nothing wherewith to compare it England formerly governed the mass of the colonies; but the people was always sovereign in the township, where its rule is not only an ancient, but a primitive state.

The native of New England is attached to his township because it is independent and free: his co-operation in its affairs ensures his attachment to its interests; the well-being it affords him secures his affection; and its welfare is the aim of his ambition and of his future exertions. He takes a part in every occurence in the place; he practices the art of government in the small sphere within his reach; he accustoms himself to those forms without which liberty can only advance by revolutions; he imbibes their spirit; he acquires a taste for order, comprehends the balance of powers, and collects clear practical notions on the nature of his duties and the extent of his rights.

The Counties Of New England

The division of the counties in America has considerable analogy with that of the *arrondissements* of France. The limits of both are arbitrarily laid down, and the various districts which they contain have no necessary connection, no common tradition or natural sympathy, no community of existence; their object is simply to facilitate the administration.

The extent of the township was too small to contain a system of judicial institutions; the county, therefore, is the first center of judicial action. Each county has a court of justice, [1] a sheriff

---

① See *Laws of Massachusetts*, law of February 14, 1821, Vol. I, p. 551.

以不管好坏,他们都得认可,以此来表示他们做主人的自豪感。没有什么东西可以与这种自豪感相比。英国从前虽是统治全体殖民地的,但殖民地的人民却一直自己管理乡镇的事务。因此,乡镇人民的主权不仅古老,而且自始就已存在。

新英格兰的居民眷恋他们的乡镇,因为乡镇是独立并自由的;他们关心乡镇的利益,因为他们参加乡镇的管理;他们热爱自己的乡镇,因为他们不能不珍惜自己的命运。乡镇的幸福安定是他们的雄心壮志和远大抱负的最终目标,乡镇发生的每一件事情都与他们息息相关。他们在力所能及的有限范围内,尝试着去管理社会,使自己习惯于自由的组织形式,而没有这种组织形式,自由只有靠革命来实现。他们体会到这种组织形式的精神,产生了遵守秩序的需求,理解了权力和谐的优点,并对他们的义务的性质和权利范围形成明确而切合实际的概念。

新英格兰的县

美国在县的划分上与法国的很相似——县的建制纯系出于行政考虑——没有代议制的任何因素——由非选举的官员治理美国的县,这同法国的县有许多类似之处。无论是美国的县还是法国的县,都是随意划定的。县虽然是个整体,但在其所包括的各个部分之间既没有必然的联系,没有共同的传统道德和自然习性,也没有联邦的存在。建立县的主要目的是为了方便行政权的实施。

乡镇的面积太小,以至于无法建立成套的司法体系。因此,县就成了司法体系的第一中心。每县都有一个法院、①一名执行

---

① 见《马萨诸塞法律》,1821 年 2 月 14 日的法令,第一卷,第 551 页。

to execute its decrees, and a prison for criminals. There are certain wants which are felt alike by all the townships of a county; it is therefore natural that they shnuld be satisfied by a central authority. In Massachusetts this authority is vested in the hands of several magistrates, who are appointed by the governor of the state, with the advice①of his council. ② The county commissioners have only a limited and exceptional authority, which can be used only in certain predetermined cases. The state and the townships possess all the power requisite for ordinary and public business. The county commissioners can only prepare the budget; it is voted by the legislature;③ there is no assembly that directly or indirectly represents the county. It has, therefore, properly speaking, no political existence.

A twofold tendency may be discerned in most of the American constitutions, which impels the legislator to concentrate the legislative and to divide the executive power. The township of New England has in itself an indestructible principle of life; but this distinct existence could only be fictitiously introduced into the county, where the want of it has not been felt. All the townships united have but one representation, which is the state, the center of all national authority; beyond the action of the township and that of the state, it may be said that there is nothing but individual action.

The Administration Of Government In New England

Administration not perceived in America — Why? — The Europeans believe that liberty is promoted by depriving the social authority of some of its rights; the Americans, by dividing its exercise — Almost all the administration confined to the township, and

---

① *See Laws of Massachusetts.*, law of February 20, 1819, Vol. II, p. 494.

② The council of the governor is an elective body.

③ See Laws of Massachusetts, law of November 2, 1791, Vol. I, p. 61.

法律的司法官员和一座关押犯人的监狱。有些设施是一个县的所有乡镇差不多都感到需要的,所以很自然的它们会满足于建立中央政权。在马萨诸塞州,这个机关的大权掌握在为数不多的几个官员之手,他们是州长根据州长议会的提议①而任命的。② 县的行政官员仅仅只有有限和特殊的权力,而且只能在为数极少的预先规定的事件中行使。州与乡镇拥有一切负责日常和公共事务的权力。县的行政官员只编制本县的预算,然后由立法机关通过;③县里没有直接或间接的代表本县的议会。因此,确切地说,这里没有政治生活。

美国大部分州的宪法,都有一种双重倾向:一方面驱使立法者分散行政权,另一方面又让立法者集中立法权。新英格兰的乡镇,自身有其不可破坏的生活原则,但又需要把乡镇的生活虚构于县的活动之中。结果,谁也没有感到乡镇在县里发生作用。在州内,能够代表全体乡镇的只有一个机构,那就是作为全州权力中心的州政府。除了乡镇活动和全州活动以外,可以说只有个人活动。

新英格兰的政府行政组织

在美国感觉不到有行政——为什么?——欧洲人认为自由是要靠剥夺某些人的公共权利来促进的,而美国人认为要靠分散某些人的权利来建立——几乎所有的行政工作都可以说归乡镇

---

① 见《马萨诸塞法律》,1819 年 2 月 20 日的法令,第二卷,第 494 页。

② 统治者委员会是由选举产生的。

③ 见《马萨诸塞法律》,1791 年 11 月 2 日的法令,第一卷,第 61 页。

*divided among the town officers — No trace of an administrative hier-
archy perceived, either in the township or above it Why this is the case
— How it happens that the administration of the state is uniform —
Who is empowered to enforce the obedience of the township and the
county to the law — The introduction of judicial power into the administration — Consequence of the extension of the elective principle to all
functionaries — The justice of the peace in New England — By whom
appointed — County officer: ensures the administration of the townships
— Court of sessions — Its mode of action Who brings matters before
this court for action — Right of inspection and indictment parceled out
like the other administrative functions — Informers encouraged by the
division of fines.*

Nothing is more striking to a European traveler in the United
States than the absence of what we term the government, or the administration. Written laws exist in America, and one sees the daily
execution of them; but although everything moves regularly, the mov-
er can nowhere be discovered. The hand that directs the social machine is invisible. Nevertheless, as all persons must have recourse to
certain grammatical forms, which are the foundation of human language, in order to express their thoughts; so all communities are o-
bliged to secure their existence by submitting to a certain amount of
authority, without which they fall into anarchy. This authority may be
distributed in several ways, but it must always exist somewhere.

There are two methods of diminishing the force of authority in a
nation. The first is to weaken the supreme power in its very principle,
by forbidding or preventing society from acting in its own defense under certain circumstances. To weaken authority in this manner is the
European way of establishing freedom.

The second manner of diminishing the influence of authority does
not consist in stripping society of some of its rights, nor in paralyzing
its efforts, but in distributing the exercise of its powers among various
hands and in multiplying functionaries, to each of whom is given the
degree of power necessary for him to perform his duty. There may be
nations whom this distribution of social powers might lead to anarchy,
but in itself it is not anarchical. The authority thus divided is, indeed, rendered less irresistible and less perilous, but it is not destroyed.

所有,由乡镇官员掌管——无论是在乡镇或是在更上层的等级,均见不到行政等级森严的痕迹——为什么会这样——而州行政权又是怎样统一的——谁授权使乡镇和县的行政服从法律——司法权被引进到行政部门——选举原则扩展到一切官职的后果——新英格兰的治安法官——由谁任命——县的官员:确保乡镇的行政权——地方法院——其行使的方式——谁把案件提交法院审理——监督权和起诉权像其他一切行政职务一样被多人掌管——以分得罚款的办法鼓励检举。

让欧洲旅行者最为吃惊的,是美国并没有我们通常所说的政府或行政组织。美国有成文的法律,而且人们每天都在执行它。虽然一切事件都在有规律地进行着,但你到处都看不到指挥者。直接操纵社会机器的那只手是看不见的。但是,正如人们为了表达自己思想而需要依靠人类语言基础的语法结构一样,一切社会为了求得生存也不得不服从于某种权威,而没有这种权威,社会就会陷于无政府状态。这种权威可能有不同的表现形式,但它必定始终在某处存在着。

一般有两种方法可以削弱国家权威的力量。第一种是禁止和阻止当局在特定情况下的自我维护,以便从根本上减弱当局的权力。欧洲人用这种方法削弱权威,通常是为了建立自由。

第二种是缩小权威的影响:不去剥夺当局的某些权力或不去使当局的权力瘫痪,而是把社会权力分给许多人掌握,并增设官职,使每一官职只有履行职务时所必要的权限。有些国家在用这种方法分散当局的权力时可能导致无政府状态,但这种做法本身却不是无政府主义的。不错,用这种方法分散权威之后,权威的作用便减少了其不可抗拒性和危险性,但权威本身并没有被摧毁。美国的革命,反映了人们对自由的热爱,而不是对独立盲目和没有限制的渴求。

The Revolution of the United States was the result of a mature and reflecting preference for freedom, and not of a vague or illde-fined craving for independence. It contracted no alliance with the turbulent passions of anarchy, but its course was marked, on the contrary, by a love of order and law.

It was never assumed in the United States that the citizen of a free country has a right to do whatever he pleases; on the contrary, more social obligations were there imposed upon him than anywhere else. No idea was ever entertained of attacking the principle or con-testing the rights of society; but the exercise of its authority was di-vided, in order that the office might be powerful and the officer in-significant, and that the community should be at once regulated and free. In no country in the world does the law hold so absolute a lan-guage as in America; and in no country is the right of applying it vested in so many hands. The administrative power in the United States presents nothing either centralized or hierarchical in its consti-tution; this accounts for its passing unperceived. The power exists, but its representative is nowhere to be seen.

I have already mentioned that the independent townships of New England were not under guardianship, but took care of their own pri-vate interests; and the municipal magistrates are the persons who ei-ther execute the laws of the state or see that they are executed. ① Be-sides the general laws the state sometimes passes general police regulations; but more commonly the townships and town officers, conjointly with the justices of the peace, regulate the minor de-tails of social life, according to the necessities of the different lo-calities, and promulgate such orders as concern the health of the community and the peace as well as morality of the citizens. ②

---

① See *The Town-Officer*, especially at the words SELECTMEN, ASSES-SORS, COLLECTORS, SCHOOLS, SURVEYORS OF HIGHWAYS. I take one example in a thousand: the state prohibits traveling on Sunday without good rea-son; the tithing-men, who are town officers, are required to keep watch and to execute the law. See *Laws of Massachusetts*, law of March 8, 1792, Vol. I, p. 410.

The selectmen draw up the lists of voters for the election of the governor, and transmit the result of the ballot to the state secretary of state. Ibid. , law of February 24, 1796, Vol. I, p. 488.

② Thus, for instance, the selectmen authorize the construction of drains, and point out the proper sites for slaughterhouses and other trades which are a nui-sance to the neighborhood. See ibid. , law of June 7, 1785, Vol. I, p. 193.

这个革命没有受到无政府的暴动激情的支持,相反,它是在爱好秩序和法律的口号下进行的。

我们不能认为在美国这个自由的国家,人们可以有权为所欲为。相反,这里施加于人们的社会义务要比其他地方多得多,人们从来没有想过从根本上打击当局的权力和否定它的权限,而只是把权限的行使分给许多人,以确保当局的权力会更强,而官员的权力会减弱,以使社会永远秩序井然而又保持自由。世界上没有一个国家的法律像美国那样绝对专制,也没有一个地方像美国那样把权力分掌在如此众多的人们手中。美国的行政权结构既不是中央集权的,也不是逐级分权的。它在行使的过程中是不为人察觉的,原因是行政权虽然存在,但不知道它的代表在何处。

我在前面已经讲过,新英格兰乡镇的独立是不受任何上级机关监护的。但是,因为它们是自行处理本乡镇的事务的,乡镇的行政委员们也往往监督执行或亲自执行全州性的法律。① 除了全州性的普通法律以外,州有时也颁布一些全州性的治安条例。但在一般情况下,是由乡镇当局或乡镇官员共同负责治安,根据不同地方的不同需要,规定本地的社会生活细则,宣布有关公共健康、社会安定和公民道德的守则。② 最后,乡镇的行政委员们也可

① 见城镇官员,特别是行政委员,财产评估员,收税人,学校和调查者这些词条。我举个例子:国家禁止人们在没有合适原因的情况下在周日旅游;作为乡镇官员的收税人必须严格服从法律。见《马萨诸塞法》,1792 年 3月 8 日的法令,第一卷,第 410 页。

行政委员将草拟选举统治者的选举名单,并把选举结果递交给国家秘书处。出处同上,1796 年 2 月 24 日的法令,第一卷,第 488 页。

② 例如,行政委员有权批准排水道的建造,并确定合适的地点和处理与周围的关系。出处同上,1785 年 6 月 7 日的法令,第一卷,第 193 页。

Lastly, these town magistrates provide, of their own accord and without any impulse from without, for those unforeseen emergencies which frequently occur in society. ①

It results from what I have said that in the state of Massachusetts the administrative authority is almost entirely restricted to the township, ② and that it is there distributed among a great number of individuals. In the French commune there is properly but one official functionary — namely, the *maire*; and in New England we have seen that there are nineteen. These nineteen functionaries do not, in general, depend one upon another. The law carefully prescribes a circle of action to each of these magistrates; within that circle they are all-powerful to perform their functions independently of any other authority. If one looks higher than the township, one can find scarcely a trace of an administrative hierarchy. It sometimes happens that the county officers alter a decision of the townships or town magistrates, ③ but in general the authorities of the county have no right to interfere with the authorities of the township ④ except in such matters as concern the county.

The magistrates of the township, as well as those of the county, are bound in a small number of predetermined cases to communicate their acts to the central government. ⑤ But the central govern-

---

① For example, the selectmen, conjointly with the justices of the peace, take measures for the security of the public in case of contagious diseases. Ibid. , law of June 22, 1797, Vol. I, p. 539.

② I say *almost*, for there are many incidents in town life which are regulated by the justices of peace in their individual capacity, or by an assembly of them in the chief town of the county; thus, licenses are granted by the justices. See ibid. , law of February 28, 1797, Vol. I, p. 297.

③ Thus, licenses are granted only to such persons as can produce a certificate of good conduct from the selectmen. If the selectmen refuse to give the certificate, the party may appeal to the justices assembled in the court of sessions, and they may grant the license. See ibid. , law of March 12, 1808, Vol. II, p. 186. The townships have the right to make by-laws, and to enforce them by fines, which are fixed by law; but. these by-laws must be approved by the court of sessions. Ibid. , law of March 25, 1786, Vol. I, p. 254.

④ In Massachusetts the county magistrates are frequently called upon to investigate the acts of the town magistrates; but it will be shown farther on that this investigation is a consequence, not of their administrative, but of their judicial power.

⑤ Thus, the town school committees are obliged to make an annual report to the secretary of the state on the condition of the schools. See ibid. , law of March 10, 1827, Vol. III, p. 183.

以不受任何外来的指示,而自行处理乡镇经常发生的但又无法预见的一些紧急事项。①

　　根据我前面讲的可以知道,在马萨诸塞州,行政权几乎全被乡镇所控制,②并被分散在许多人的手里。在法国的乡镇,严格来讲应该只有一个行政官员,即所谓的乡长或镇长。而在新英格兰,至少要有19种官员。一般说来,这19种官员彼此之间并不互相依靠。法律为这些官员中的每个人规定了职权范围。在这个范围内,他们是拥有全部权力去履行自己职责的。如果把视线移到乡镇的上级,也很难看到行政等级的痕迹。有时,县的官员也修改乡镇或其行政委员做出的决定,③但总的说来,县的行政官员无权干预乡镇官员的行动,④除非这些事务关系到全县的利益。

　　乡镇的行政官员和县的行政官员,在极少数的预先规定事务上要同时向州政府的官员报告他们的处理结果。⑤ 但是,州政府并不派专门的代理去制定全州性的治安条例,去颁布

---

　　① 例如,行政委员要对公共安全与和平负责,并采取措施防止社会隐患的发生。出处同上,1797 年 6 月 22 日的法令,第一卷,第 539 页。

　　② 可以说,乡镇生活中有很多小事件发生,而这些小事件都被人们自己的和平正义感或他们在主要城镇的集会所克服。由治安法官颁布许可证。出处同上,1797 年 2 月 28 日的法令,第一卷,第 297 页。

　　③ 然而,这些许可证仅仅是由行政委员以证书的形式颁发给那些具有良好行为的人。如果行政委员拒绝颁发此证书,政党可呼请司法官员们开会,并颁发这些许可证。出处同上,1808 年 3 月 12 日的法令,第 2 卷,第 186 页。乡镇有权制定议事程序,并且通过法律范围内的罚金来强化这些程序;但是,这些程序必须经过法庭的审议,才能被通过。出处同上,1786 年 3 月 25 日的法律,第一卷,第 254 页。

　　④ 在马萨诸塞,县的官员会经常调查乡镇官员的行为;但是这种调查带来的结果往往是他们司法权的体现,而不是他们行政权的体现。

　　⑤ 乡镇负责学校的委员会有义务根据学校情况向国家秘书处上交年分析报告。出处同上,1827 年 3 月 10 日的法令,第三卷,第 183 页。

ment is not represented by an agent whose business it is to publish police regulations and ordinances for the execution of the laws, or to keep up a regular communication with the officers of the township and the county, or to inspect their conduct, direct their actions, or reprimand their faults. There is no point that serves as a center to the radii of the administration.

How, then, can the government be conducted on a uniform plan? And how is the compliance of the counties and their magistrates or the townships and their officers enforced? In the New England states the legislative authority embraces more subjects than it does in France; the legislator penetrates to the very core of the administration; the law descends to minute details; the same enactment prescribes the principle and the method of its application, and thus imposes a multitude of strict and rigorously defined obligations on the secondary bodies and functionaries of the state. The consequence of this is that if all the secondary functionaries of the administration conform to the law, society in all its branches proceeds with the greatest uniformity. The difficulty remains, how to compel the secondary bodies and administrative officials to conform to the law. It may be affirmed in general that society has only two methods of enforcing the execution of the laws: a discretionary power may be entrusted to one of them of directing all the others and of removing them in case of disobedience; or the courts of justice may be required to inflict judicial penalties on the offender. But these two methods are not always available.

The right of directing a civil officer presupposes that of cashiering him if he does not obey orders, and of rewarding him by promotion if he fulfills his duties with propriety. But an elected magistrate cannot be cashiered or promoted. All elective functions are inalienable until their term expires. In fact, the elected magistrate has nothing to expect or to fear except from his constituents; and when all public offices are filled by ballot, there can be no series of official dignities, because the double right of commanding and of enforcing obedience can never be vested in the same person, and because the power of issuing an order can never be joined to that of inflicting a punishment or bestowing a reward.

The communities, therefore, in which the secondary officials of the government are elected are inevitably obliged to make great use of judicial penalties as a means of administration. This is not evident at

执行法律的命令,或者和县和乡镇的行政官员经常保持联系,或者去检查他们的活动,去指导他们的行为和谴责他们的错误。因此,并不存在以行政权的半径所辐射的圆心。

那么,政府怎样按照一个统一的计划去指导社会呢? 又怎么能使县或乡镇的行政官员服从他们的决定呢? 在新英格兰各州,立法机构的权力所涉及的范围比法国要广泛。立法者的权力几乎到达了行政当局的内部。法律也规定到事情的细节;同一法律既规定原则,又规定原则的应用方法;上级单位的法律,还给下属单位及其官员施加了一系列严格而细密的义务。这样做的结果是,只要一切行政下属单位和全体官员依法行事,社会的各个部分的行动就会在最大程度上一致。但还有一个问题,那就是如何能够迫使下属单位及其官员遵守法律。事实证明,社会只拥有两种迫使官员遵守法律办法:可以赋予这些官员中的一个官员指导其他官员,并在他们不服从时罢免其独断的权力;或者,可以要求法院惩治违法的官员。但是,这两种办法不总是有用。

指导一个官员的权力,应该在他不遵守规则时罢免他,在他全心全意全部履行完职责时奖赏他。但是,对于一个民选的行政委员,行政当局既不能罢免,又不能提升,因为所有经选举产生的官员,在他们的任期未满以前,他的权力是不可剥夺的。实际上,所有经选举产生的行政委员不会畏惧任何事情,除了他自己的选民。在这种条件下,官员之间就不会存在真正的等级差别,因为发号施令权和镇压反抗的双重权力不会集中于一人之手,指挥权也不会与奖惩权合并于一人之身。

因此,那些通过选举制度任用政府的下层官员的国家,必然要广泛使用司法权力作为行政措施。这种情形不是非常明显的。统治者们把实行选举制度视为第一次让步,把允许法官惩治

first sight; for those in power are apt to look upon the institution of e-
lective officials as one concession, and the subjection of the elected
magistrate to the judges of the land as another. They are equally a-
verse to both these innovations; and as they are more pressingly solic-
ited to grant the former than the latter, they accede to the election of
the magistrate and leave him independent of the judicial power. Nevertheless, the second of these measures is the only thing that can possibly counterbalance the first; and it will be found that an elective authority that is not subject to judicial power will sooner or later either e-
lude all control or be destroyed. The courts of justice are the only
possible medium between the central power and the administrative
bodies; they alone can compel the elected functionary to obey, without violating the rights of the elector. The extension of judicial power
in the political world ought therefore to be in the exact ratio of the extension of elective power; if these two institutions do not go hand in
hand, the state must fall into anarchy or into servitude.

It has always been remarked that judicial habits do not render
men especially fitted for the exercise of administrative authority. The
Americans have borrowed from their fathers, the English, the idea of
an institution that is unknown on the continent of Europe: I allude to
that af justices of the peace.

The justice of the peace is a sort of middle term between the
magistrate and the man of the world, between the civil officer and the
judge. A justice of the peace is a well-informed citizen, though he is
not necessarily learned in the law. His office simply obliges him to
execute the police regulations of society, a task in which good sense
and integrity are of more avail than legal science. The justice introduces into the administration, when he takes part in it, a certain taste
for established forms and publicity, which renders him a most unserv-
iceable instrument for despotism; and, on the other hand, he is not a
slave of those legal superstitions which render judges unfit members of
a government. The Americans have adopted the English system of justices of the peace, depriving it of the aristocratic character that distinguishes it in the mother country. The governor of Massachusetts[1]

---

[1] Later on we shall see the nature of the governor's functions; here it is
enough to note that the governor represents the entire executive power of the state.

选举产生的行政官员视为第二次让步。他们对这两种新办法都是很不情愿的,但在众多的压力下,他们宁愿选用前者,也不愿选择后者。所以他们同意选举官员,而让选举出来的官员独立于法官之外。但是,只有同时采用两种办法,才能使它们彼此抵消,保持平衡,因为情况十分清楚,不受司法权监管的被选举权迟早会失去控制或被取消。在中央政权和经选举产生的行政单位之间,只有法院可以充当调停人。并且他们能够强迫民选的官员顺从和使他们不违背选民的权利。因此,司法权向政界的扩张,应当与被选举权的扩张协调起来,如果这两者不携手前进,国家必将陷于无政府状态或一部分人压迫另一部分人的状态。

一直以来,人们总是认为司法体制不适合锻炼公民行使行政权的能力。美国人从他们的祖辈英国人那里学来了一种与欧洲大陆实行的制度完全不同的制度。我指的是设置治安法官。

治安法官在处理民众与行政官员之间和行政机关与法院之间的纠纷时始终站在中间的立场。治安法官应是一位知识渊博的公民,但不必精通法律。他只负责维持社会治安,他在工作方面对社会良知的需求远远大于对法律知识的需求。在治安法官参加国家行政管理工作的时候,可为管理工作带来照章办事和凡事向群众公布的作风,而这种作风是防止专横的最强大武器。但是,他们不应成为迷信法律的奴隶,因为这样会使行政官员对政府的行政管理产生惰性。美国人采用了英国的治安法官制度,但却剥夺了它在母国的那种显赫的贵族气质。马萨诸塞的州长,①

---

① 稍后,我们会看到统治者职能的本性;这里我们可以清楚地知道,统治者代表州的全部执行权力。

appoints a certain number of justices of the peace in every county, whose functions last seven years. ① He further designates three individuals from the whole body of justices, who form in each county what is called the court of sessions. The justices take a personal share in the public administration; they are sometimes entrusted with administrative functions in conjunction with elected officers; ② they sometimes constitute a tribunal before which the magistrates summarily prosecute a refractory citizen, or the citizens inform against the abuses of the magistrate. But it is in the court of sessions that they exercise their most important functions. This court meets twice a year, in the county town; in Massachusetts it is empowered to enforce the obedience of most ③ of the public officers. ④ It must be observed that in Massachusetts the court of sessions is at the same time an administrative body, properly 30 called, and a political tribunal. It has been mentioned that the county is a purely administrative division. The court of sessions presides over that small number of affairs which, as they concern several townships, or all the townships of the county in common, cannot be entrusted to any one of them in particular. In all that concerns county business the duties of the court of sessions are purely administrative; and if in its procedure it occasionally introduces judicial

---

① See Constitution of Massachusetts, Chap. II, section 1, paragraph 9; Chap. II, paragraph 3.

② Thus, as one example among many others, a stranger arrives in a township from a country where a contagious disease prevails, and he falls ill. Two justices of the peace can, with the assent of the selectmen, order the sheriff of the county to remove and take care of him. *Laws of Massachusetts*, law of June 22, 1797, Vol. I, p. 540. In general the justices interfere in all the important acts of the administration and give them a semi-judicial character.

③ I say *most* of them because certain administrative misdemeanors are brought before the ordinary tribunals. If, for instance, a township refuses to tee, it is liable to a heavy fine. But this penalty is pronounced by the supreme judicial court or the court of common pleas. See ibid. , law of March 10, 1827, Vol. III, p. 190. For the failure of the town to make provision for military supplies, see ibid. , law of February 21, 1822, Vol. II, p. 570.

④ In their individual capacity the justices of the peace take a part in the business of the counties and townships. In general the most important acts of the town can be performed only with the concurrence of some one of them.

为本州的各县任命一定数量的任期为七年的治安法官。① 另外，他又从每县的治安法官中指定三个人，由他们组成地方法院。个别的治安法官也参与一般行政工作。有时，他们也连同民选的官员一起被委以一定的行政职务；②有时，他们会组成临时法庭，接受行政官员对拒不履行义务的公民的控诉或公民对行政官员的违法行为的检举。但是，地方法院才是治安法官执行其主要职务的场所。地方法院每年在县城开庭两次。在马萨诸塞州，这个法院有权迫使大多数③民选的官员④服从。应当指出，在马萨诸塞州，地方法院既是行政组织，同时也是政治法庭。我们已经说过，县仅仅是一个行政区域。地方法院只主持很少量的事务，这些事务只与大部分乡镇或全体乡镇有关，因而不能由任何一个乡镇单独处理。在涉及全县性的工作时，地方法院的工作纯属行政性的。地方法院在处理工作的过程所以要经常采取司法程序，那只

---

① 见《马萨诸塞宪法》，第二章，第一部分，第九段；第二章，第三段。

② 举一个例子，一个陌生人，从传染疾病流行的县来到乡镇后也患上了疾病。两个治安法官可在行政委员的允许下，命令县的治安官将他带走并照顾他。马萨诸塞法律，1797 年 6 月 22 日的法令，第一卷，第 540 页。总之，治安法官可参与所有关于行政的重要行为，并进行中间调停。

③ 我讲了这么多关于他们，是因为一些行政轻罪是由普通法院审理的。例如，如果一个乡镇拒绝在学校方面的应有开支，它将会受到很重的惩罚。但这种惩罚是由最高司法法庭或普通民事法庭宣判。出处同上，1827 年 3 月 10 日的法令，第三卷，第 190 页。而乡镇缺乏对军队需求的供给，出处同上，1822 年 2 月 21 日的法令，第二卷，第 570 页。

④ 治安法官依靠其个人能力参与县与乡镇的事务。一般情况下，县的一些重要举措在经过治安法官同意后就可执行。

forms, it is only with a view to its own information, ① or as a guarantee to those for whom it acts. But when the administration of the township is brought before it, it acts as a judicial body and only in some few cases as an administrative body. ②

The first difficulty is to make the township itself, an almost independent power, obey the general laws of the state. I have stated that assessors are annually named by the town meetings to levy the taxes. If a township attempts to evade the payment of the taxes by neglecting to name its assessors, the court of sessions condemns it to a heavy fine. ③ The fine is levied on each of the inhabitants; and the sheriff of the county, who is the officer of justice, executes the mandate. Thus in the United States, government authority, anxious to keep out of sight, hides itself under the forms of a judicial sentence; and its influence is at the same time fortified by that irresistible power which men attribute to the formalities of law.

These proceedings are easy to follow and to understand. The demands made upon a township are, in general, plain and accurately defined; they consist in a simple fact, or in a principle without its application in detail. ④But the difficulty begins when it is not the obedience of the township, but that of the town officers, that is to be

---

① These affairs may be brought under the following heads: (1) the erection of prisons and courts of justice; (2) the county budget, which is afterwards voted by the state legislature; (3) the distribution of the taxes so voted; (4) grants of certain patents; (5) the building and repair of the county roads.

② Thus, when a road is under consideration, the court of sessions decides almost all questions regarding the execution of the project with the aid of a jury.

③ See *Laws of Massachusetts*, law of February 20, 1786, Vol. I, p. 217.

④ There is an indirect method of enforcing the obedience of a township. Suppose that the funds which the law demands for the maintenance of the roads have not been voted; the town surveyor is then authorized, *ex officio*, to levy the supplies. As he is personally responsible to private individuals for the state of the roads, and indictable before the court of sessions, he is sure to employ the extraordinary right which the law gives him against the township. Thus, by threatening the officer, the court of sessions exacts compliance from the town. See ibid. , law of March 5, 1787, Vol. I, p. 305.

是为了便于自己处理工作,①和让被审理的官员明白处理的法律根据。但在需要审理乡镇的行政官员时,它几乎总是作为司法机关而工作,并且只是在极少数情况下才以行政机关的身份出现。②

在这方面遇到的第一个困难,是如何使乡镇这个几乎是独立的政权实体服从州的一般法律。我们已经说过,乡镇每年要任命一定人数的财产估价员来征收税款。如果乡镇试图以不任命财产估价员的办法来逃避纳税的义务,地方法院这时可对这样的乡镇实施巨额罚款。③ 罚款按法院的判决分派给全体居民。县的司法官是执法人员,由他执行判决。因此,在美国,行政当局好像喜欢躲在幕后进行仔细观察,使自己隐藏在司法判决的形式下。这样,行政当局由于拥有被人们视为合法的这种几乎不可抗拒的权力的权限就更大了。

这样的做法是不难推行而且容易被人接受的。一般说来,要求乡镇的事情,都是清清楚楚和以明文规定的。这种规定很简单,并不复杂,或只写出原则,而不列出细节。④ 但是,当要使乡镇服从时,或者要使乡镇官员服从时,都会遇到困难。一个公共官

---

① 这些事件如下:(1)监狱和司法法庭的建造;(2)由国家立法机构通过的国家预算;(3)关于税的分配的通过;(4)一定专利的许可;(5)建筑与道路的修复。

② 当需要修路或建路时,法院通过陪审团可作出关于这个项目的一切决定。

③ 见《马萨诸塞法》,1786 年 2 月 20 日的法令,第一卷,第 217 页。

④ 有一个间接的方法可以使乡镇更加服从。假设,法律需要用来维持公路的基金没有被通过;乡镇检查员有权进行征收。因为对于国家公路方面的问题,他可凭借大众的力量向地方法院起诉,法律赋予他可反对乡镇的特殊权利。通过对官员的恐吓,地方法院迫使乡镇顺从。出处同上,1787 年 3 月 5 日的法令,第一卷,第 305 页。

enforced. All the reprehensible actions which a public functionary can commit are reducible to the following heads:

He may execute the law without energy or zeal;

He may neglect what the law requires;

He may do what the law forbids.

Only the last two violations of duty can come before a legal tribunal; a positive and appreciable fact is the indispensable foundation of an action at law. Thus, if the selectmen omit the legal formalities usual at town elections, they may be fined. [1] But when the officer performs his duty unskillfully, or obeys the letter of the law without zeal or energy, he is out of the reach of judicial interference. The court of sessions, even when clothed with administrative powers, is in this case unable to enforce a more satisfactory obedience. The fear of removal is the only check to these quasi-offenses, and the court of sessions does not originate the town authorities; it cannot remove functionaries whom it does not appoint. Moreover, a perpetual supervision would be necessary to convict the officer of negligence or lukewarmness. Now, the court of sessions sits but twice a year, and then only judges such offenses as are brought to its notice. The only security for that active and enlightened obedience which a court of justice cannot enforce upon public functionaries lies in their arbitrary removal from office. In France this final security is exercised by the *heads of the administration*; in America it is obtained through the principle of *election*.

Thus, to recapitulate in a few words what I have described.

If a public officer in New England commits a *crime* in the exercise of his functions, the ordinary courts of justice are *always* called upon to punish him.

If he commits a *fault in his administrative capacity*, a purely administrative tribunal is empowered to punish him; and if the affair is important or urgent, the judge does what the functionary should have done. [2]

---

[1] *Laws of Massachusetts*, Vol. II, p. 45.

[2] If, for instance, a township persists in refusing to name its assessors, the court of sessions nominates them; and the magistrates thus appointed are invested with the same authority as elected officers. See ibid. , the law of February 20, 1787, previously cited.

员可能做出的应受责备的行为,可以归纳为以下几种:

他在履行法定的义务时不热心或不卖力气;

他可能忽略了法律规定的义务;

最后,他可能做出法律禁止的事情。

只有后两种失职行为会被法院追究,但要以确凿可查的事实作为审理的依据。然而,乡镇的行政委员在乡镇进行选举的时候,也会忽略法律规定的手续。这时,他可能被罚款。[①] 但是,在官员履行职责不熟练时,或在执行法律的规定时不热心和不卖力时,他完全不会受到法律的处分。虽然地方法院被授予行政权,但在这种情况下它也无力迫使这些官员完全服从。只有害怕被撤免的心理可能阻止这样的轻微犯罪,但地方法院没有使乡镇政权害怕的行为,它不能罢免非它任命的官员。并且,对一些玩忽职守和消极懈怠的官员,进行经常的监督是非常必要的。但是,地方法院每年只开庭两次,不负监督的责任,只审理被检举的应予斥责的违法事件。只有坚决罢免公共官员的举措,才是迫使他们切实而积极地服从的唯一保证,而用一般的司法措施是无法办到的。在法国,我们从行政等级制度中看到了这种保证;而在美国,则可从选举制度中找到。

现在,我想用简短的几句话对前面所描述的进行简单地总结:

新英格兰的公共官员在执行职务中犯罪时,普通法院可以随时惩罚他们;

如果他犯有行政过错,只有纯粹的行政性的法庭有权处分他们,要是情节严重或事关紧要,则法官应做出其作为一个法官应做的处理。[②]

---

① 《马萨诸塞法》第二卷,第45页。

② 例如,假如一个乡镇坚持拒绝任命其评估员,那么地方法院将进行任命;行政官员与行政委员具有同等的权力。出处同上,1787年2月20日的法令,前面曾引用过。

Lastly, if the same individual is guilty of one of those intangible offenses which human justice can neither define nor appreciate, he annually appears before a tribunal from which there is no appeal, which can at once reduce him to insignificance and deprive him of his charge. This system undoubtedly possesses great advantages, but its execution is attended with a practical difficulty, which it is important to point out.

I have already observed that the administrative tribunal which is called the court of sessions has no right of inspection over the town officers. It can interfere only when the conduct of a magistrate is specially brought under its notice; and this is the delicate part of the system. The Americans of New England have no public prosecutor for the court of sessions, [1] and it may readily be perceived that it would be difficult to create one. If an accusing magistrate had merely been appointed in the chief town of each county and had been unassisted by agents in the townships, he would not have been better acquainted with what was going on in the county than the members of the court of sessions. But to appoint his agents in each township would have been to center in his person the most formidable of powers, that of a judicial administration. Moreover, laws are the children of habit, and nothing of the kind exists in the legislation of England. The Americans have therefore divided the offices of inspection and complaint, as well as all the other functions of the administration. Grand jurors are bound by the law to apprise the court to which they belong of all the misdemeanors which may have been committed in their county. [2] There are certain great offenses that are officially prosecuted by the state; [3] but more frequently the task of punishing delinquents devolves upon the fiscal officer, whose province it is to receive the fine; thus the treasurer of the township is charged with the prosecution of such administrative offenses as fall under his notice. But a more especial appeal is made by American legislation to the private interest of each citizen; [4]

---

[1] I say the court of sessions because in common courts there is an officer who exercises some of the functions of a public prosecutor.

[2] The grand jurors are, for instance, bound to inform the court of the bad state of the roads. *Laws of Massachusetts*, Vol. I, p. 308.

[3] If, for instance, the treasurer of the county holds back his accounts. Ibid. , Vol. I, p. 400.

[4] Thus, to take one example out of a thousand, if a private individual breaks his carriage or is injured in consequence of the badness of a road, he can sue the township or the county for damages at the sessions. Ibid. , Vol. I, p. 309.

最后,如果同样的公共官员犯了难以断定的罪行之一,而上述法庭又无法确定其是否有罪时,可在当年交由一个不准上诉的法庭去审理。这个法庭可以立即剥夺他的权力,收回他的任命书而罢他的官。这个制度本身无疑是有很大好处的,但必须指出的是,它在执行时也会遇到很大的困难。

我已经说过,被称作是地方法院的行政性法院无权监察乡镇的行政官员。只在受理案件之后,才能有这种权限。这也正是这个制度的弱点。新英格兰的美国人没有专门为地方法院工作的检察官,[①]而且我们也应当看到,只设置一名检察官对他们也有难处。如果只在县城设置一名检察官,而在乡镇却没有他的助理,他不可能比地方法院的成员更熟悉全县的情况。但是如果在每个乡镇都为他设置助理,那又会把行政和司法大权都集中于他一人之手。而且,法律是习惯的产物,而英国的立法也从来没有类似的规定。因此,像其他一切行政职务一样,美国人也把监察权与起诉权分开。大陪审团的成员必须依法将本县可能发生的各类犯罪行为通知给他们所服务的法院。[②] 一些特定的重大罪行,由相应的高级检察机关起诉。[③] 对违法者的处分,经常是由财务官员执行,即负责收纳被处的罚款。因此,乡镇的财务主管查出违法事件时,大部分可由他自己直接起诉。但是,美国的立法特别重视每个公民的个人权益。[④]

---

① 我之所以讲地方法院是因为在普通法庭中,有一名行使检察官职能的官员。

② 例如,陪审员有义务报告法庭一些不良州的罪行。《马萨诸塞法》第一卷,第308页。

③ 假设一个国家的财务主管拒绝报账。出处同上,第一卷,第400页。

④ 举一个例子,如果一个人因不良的公路状况而损坏了自己的车,并使自己受伤,他可以就此控诉其乡镇或县。出处同上,第一卷,第309页。

and this great principle is constantly to be met with in studying the laws of the United States. American legislators are more apt to give men credit for intelligence than for honesty; and they rely not a little on personal interest for the execution of the laws. When an individual is really and sensibly injured by an administrative abuse, his personal interest is a guarantee that he will prosecute. But if a legal formality be required which, however advantageous to the community, is of small importance to individuals plaintiffs may be less easily found; and thus, by a tacit agreement, the laws may fall into disuse. Reduced by their system to this extremity, the Americans are obliged to encourage informers by bestowing on them a portion of the penalty in certain cases; ① and they thus ensure the execution of the laws by the dangerous expedient of degrading the morals of the people.

Above the county magistrates there is, properly speaking, no administrative power, but only a power of government.

General Remarks On Administration in The United States

Differences of the states of the Union in their systems of administration — Activity and perfection of the town authorities decreases towards the South — Power of the magistrates increases; that of the voter diminishes — Administration passes from the township to the county — States of New York; Ohio; Pennsylvania — Principles of administration applicable to the whole Union — Election of public officers,

---

① In cases of invasion or insurrection, if the town officers neglect to furnish the necessary stores and ammunition for the militia, the township may be condemned to a fine of from 1,000 to 2,700 francs. It may readily be imagined that, in such a case, it might happen that no one would care to prosecute. Hence the law adds that "any citizen may enter a complaint for offences of this kind, and that half the fine shall belong to the prosecutor." See ibid. , law of March 6, 1810, Vol. II, p. 236. The same clause is frequently found in the *Laws of Massachusetts*. Not only are private individuals thus incited to prosecute the public officers, but the public officers are encouraged in the same manner to bring the disobedience of private individuals to justice. If a citizen refuses to perform the work which has been assigned to him upon a road, the road-surveyor may prosecute him, and, if he is convicted, the surveyor receives half the penalty for himself. See the law previously cited, Vol. I, p. 308.

这也是我们在研究美国的法律时经常见到的主要原则。美国的立法者们更愿意相信人们的理智,而不愿意相信人们的忠诚。因此,为了法律的顺利执行,他们总是重视私人权益。但也不难想见,如果所规定的法律条款只对社会有利,而对个人却没有任何好处,那谁也不愿意去作原告。因此,通过大家心照不宣的想法,这个法律应该被废止。美国人的制度使他们走上了这样的极端。在这种情况下,美国人便不得不鼓励检举,①使检举人根据某些条件分得一部分罚款。这是一种以败坏风尚为代价来保证法律执行的有害办法。

当然,县的行政官员的上级就没有行政权,而只有统治权了。

美国行政概况

联邦各州之间在行政制度上的差别——越往南方,乡镇当局活动的积极性和精确性就会减少——官员的权力越大,选民的权力就越小——行政权由乡镇过渡到县——纽约州、俄亥俄州、宾夕法尼亚州——行政原则被应用到全联邦——公共官员的选举

---

① 当有外国侵入或发生国内叛乱的时候,如果乡镇官员拒绝对军队提供必要的储备与弹药,乡镇有权对其进行 1000～2700 法郎的罚金。在类似的事件中,没有人会去控诉。因此,法律补充道:"任何公民可对犯罪行为进行控诉,并且罚金的一半归检察官所有。"出处同上,1810 年 3 月 6 日的法令,第二卷,第 236 页。同样的条款在《马萨诸塞法》中屡次出现。在这里,不只是公民有权起诉公共官员,并且公共官员也有权起诉不守法的公民。如果一个公民拒绝执行分配给它的在道路中的工作,道路检察官有权起诉他,并且在起诉成功的情况下,检察官可以将罚金的一半归为己有。见前面引用的法律,第一卷,第 308 页。

*and inalienability of their functions — Absence of gradation of ranks —
Introduction of judicial procedures into the administration.*

I have already said that, after examining the constitution of the
township and the county of New England in detail, I should take a
general view of the remainder of the Union. Townships and town arrangements exist in every state, but in no other part of the Union is a
township to be met with precisely similar to those of New England.
The farther we go towards the South, the less active does the business
of the township or parish become; it has fewer magistrates, duties,
and rights; the population exercises a less immediate influence on affairs; town meetings are less frequent, and the subjects of debate less
numerous. The power of the elected magistrate is augmented and that
of the voter diminished, while the public spirit of the local communities is less excited and less influential. ① These differences may be
perceived to a certain extent in the state of New York; they are very
evident in Pennsylvania; but they become less striking as we advance
to the Northwest. The majority of the immigrants who settle in the
Northwestern states are natives of New England, and they carry the
administrative habits of their mother country with them into the country which they adopt. A township in Ohio is not unlike a township in
Massachusetts.

We have seen that in Massachusetts the mainspring of public administration lies in the township. It forms the common center of the
interests and affections of the citizens. But this ceases to be the case
as we descend to the states in which knowledge is less generally diffused, and where the township consequently offers fewer guarantees
of a wise and active administrative. As we leave New England,
therefore, we find that the importance of the town is gradually transferred to the county, which becomes the center of administration

---

① For details, see the Revised Statutes of the State of New York, Part I,
chap. xi, "Of the powers, duties and privileges of towns," Vol. I, pp. 336-64.

See, in the *Digest of the Laws of Pennsylvania*, the words Assessors, Collector, Constables, Overseer Of The Poor, Supervisors Of Highways. And in the *Acts
of a General Nature of the State of Ohio*, the Act of February 25, 1834, relating
to townships, p. 412. And note the special provisions relating to various town officials such as Township's Clerks, Trustees, Overseers Of The Poor, Fence-viewers, Appraisers Of Property, Township's Treasurer, Supervisors Of Highways.

及他们职位的终身性——没有等级制度——司法手段被用于行政机构。

我在前面已经讲过,在详细考察过新英格兰的乡镇和县的组织以后,我可以概述联邦的其余部分。每个州都有乡镇并实行乡镇自治,但每个州的乡镇并不与新英格兰的乡镇完全一样。越往南方,乡镇的自治程度越低,乡镇的官员以及他们的权限和职责也会越少,居民对乡镇事务的影响也不像其他地方那样直接,乡镇居民大会的召开也会变少,而大会讨论的问题的范围也越小。因此,民选官员的权力较大,而选民的权力较小,地方乡镇的自治精神也较差和影响不大。① 这种差别在纽约州开始出现,而到宾夕法尼亚州便已十分明显,但是在未涉及过西北地区以前,还不会对这种差别感到吃惊。定居在西北各州的移民,大部分来自新英格兰,他们把母国的行政习惯带到了这里。俄亥俄州的乡镇同马萨诸塞州的极其相似。

我们已经知道,在马萨诸塞,公共行政的大权掌握在乡镇手里。乡镇是人们的利益和感情眷恋的中心。但向南方各州看去,乡镇便不再是这样的中心了。在这些州里,教育还不太普及,所以培养出来的人才不多,能胜任行政工作的人较少。因此,当我们离开新英格兰时,我们就会发现行政工作几乎全部转移到县里。县变成了主

---

① 关于细节,见纽约州已修正过的法规,第一部分,第十一章,"乡镇的权力,职责和特权,"第一卷,第 336～364 页。

见宾夕法尼亚法律对财产评估员,征税者,警察,监督人员和高速路检察员等词条的解释。在俄亥俄州的法律中,1834 年 2 月 25 日的法令,有关乡镇的,第 412 页。有一些关于各种乡镇官员职位的特殊描述,例如乡镇秘书,理事会成员,监督人员,围栏观众,财产评估员,乡镇财务主管,高速路检察员。

and the intermediate power between the government and the citizen. In Massachusetts the business of the county is conducted by the court of sessions, which is composed of a quorum appointed by the governor and his council; but the county has no representative assembly, and its expenditure is voted by the state legislature. In the great state of New York, on the contrary, and in those of Ohio and Pennsylvania, the inhabitants of each county choose a certain number of representatives, who constitute the assembly of the county. ① The county assembly has the right of taxing the inhabitants to a certain extent; and it is in this respect a real legislative body. At the same time it exercises an executive power in the county, frequently directs the administration of the townships, and restricts their authority within much narrower bounds than in Massachusetts. Such are the principal differences which the systems of county and town administration present in the Federal states. Were it my intention to examine the subject in detail, I should have to point out still further differences in the executive details of the several communities. But I have said enough to show the general principles on which the administration in the United States rests. These principles are differently applied; their consequences are more or less numerous in various localities, but they are always substantially the same. The laws differ and their outward features change, but the same spirit animates them. If the township and the county are not everywhere organized in the same manner, it is at least true that in the United States the county and the township are always based upon the same principle: namely, that everyone is the best judge of what concerns himself alone, and the most proper person to supply his own wants. The township and the county are therefore bound to take care of their special interests; the state governs, but does not execute the laws. Exceptions to this principle may be met with, but not a contrary principle.

---

① See the *Revised Statutes of the State of New York*, *Part I*, *chap.* xi, Vol. I, p. 340; ibid. , chap. xii, p. 366; also in the *Acts of the State of Ohio*, an act relating to county commissioners, February 25, 1824, p. 263. See the *Digest of the Laws of Pennsylvania*, at the words COUNTY-RATES and LEVIES, p. 170.

In the state of New York each township elects a representative, who has a share in the administration of the county as well as in that of the township.

要行政中心,形成介于州政府和普通公民之间的权力机关。在马萨诸塞,县的事务由地方法院主持。地方法院须由经州长及其委员会商议并任命的数名官员组成。县不设议会,它的预算由州立法机关投票表决。而在像纽约这样的大州,以及在俄亥俄州和宾夕法尼亚州,每县的居民选出一定数量的代表,这些代表的会议便是县的具有代议制性质的议会。① 县的议会在一定范围内有权向居民征税,而在这一方面它代表着真正的立法机关。同时,它又行使县的行政权,领导乡镇的大部分行政工作,把乡镇的权力限制在比马萨诸塞乡镇的权力更小的范围之内。这就是联邦各州在县和乡镇的组织方面呈现的主要差别。如果我有意考察这些执行方法的细节,还会发现更多的不同点。但是,我的目的不是讲述美国的行政权。我以为我所讲述的,已经足以说明美国的行政工作是以哪些原则为根据的。这些原则被应用到不同的地方,其结果也会或多或少地有些不同,但其本质都是一样的。法律的内容在变化,法律的对外特性也在变化,但给予法律以活力的仍是同一精神。如果乡镇和县不是处处都以同样的方式建立起来的,但至少在美国,乡镇和县是建立在同一原则上的:也就是说,每个人都是仅与自身利益有关的事情的最好裁决者,并且是满足自身需求的最合适人选。因此,乡镇和县只负责照顾人们的公共利益,而州政府只负责统治,而不管法律的执行。在应用这一原则时也有例外,但不能反对这一原则。

---

① 见纽约州已修正过的法规,第一部分,第十一章,第一卷,第 340 页;出处同上,第十二章,第 366 页;同样见俄亥俄州关于国家官员的 1824 年 2 月 25 日的法规,第 263 页。见《宾夕法尼亚法律》中的"县费率"和"征税"词条,第 170 页。

在纽约州,每个乡镇都会选出一名享有县和乡镇的行政管理的代表。

The first result of this doctrine has been to cause all the magistrates to be chosen either by the inhabitants or at least from among them. As the officers are everywhere elected or appointed for a certain period, it has been impossible to establish the rules of a hierarchy of authorities; there are almost as many independent functionaries as there are functions, and the executive power is disseminated in a multitude of hands. Hence arose the necessity of introducing the control of the courts of justice over the administration, and the system of pecuniary penalties, by which the secondary bodies and their representatives are constrained to obey the laws. One finds this system from one end of the Union to the other. The power of punishing administrative misconduct, or of performing, in urgent cases, administrative acts, has not, however, been bestowed on the same judges in all the states. The AngloAmericans derived the institution of justices of the peace from a common source; but although it exists in all the states, it is not always turned to the same use. The justices of the peace everywhere participate in the administration of the townships and the counties, [①] either as public officers or as the judges of public misdemeanors; but in most of the states the more important public offenses come under the cognizance of the ordinary tribunals.

Thus the election of public officers, or the inalienability of their functions, the absence of a gradation of powers, and the introduction of judicial action over the secondary branches of the administration are the principal and universal characteristics of the American system from Maine to the Floridas. In some states (and that of New York has advanced most in this direction) traces of a centralized administration begin to be discernible. In the state of New York the officers of the

---

① In some of the Southern states the county courts are charged with all the detail of the administration. See the *Statutes of the State of Tennessee*, at Arts. JUDICIARY, TAXES, etc.

　　这个原则产生的第一结果,全体行政官员是由居民自己选择,或至少从自己人当中选择。各处的行政官员都是经选举或任命产生的,因此在各处都不会产生等级制度。因此,几乎是有多少官职就有多少独立的官员。行政权被分散到许多人之手。既然各处都不能建立行政等级制度,并且行政官员都是选举产生的,并在任期结束以前不得罢免其职位,所以就必须建立某种制裁行政官员的制度。于是便产生了罚款制度,将下属机构及其代表限制在法律的约束内。在美国,上上下下,各个地方都在采用这种制度。不过,在所有的州,惩治行政犯罪或采取紧急行政措施的权力,并不集中于同一个法官之手。英籍美国人吸收的治安法官制度,都是出于同一来源。尽管各州都存在这样的制度,但并非出于同一使用目的。各地的治安法官参与乡镇和县的行政工作:①有时作为公共官员亲自处理行政工作,有时又作为法官审理行政犯罪行为。但在大多数州,重大的行政犯罪案件由普通法院审理。

　　由此可见,实行行政官员的选举和在任期未满之前不能罢免的制度,不存在行政等级制度,将司法手段用于下属的行政部门——这就是美国从缅因到佛罗里达实行的行政制度的主要特点。在某些州里,开始看到行政权集中的迹象。纽约州是在这条道路上走在最前面的。在纽约州,州政府的官员对下属县和乡镇

---

　　①　在一些南方的州,县级法院掌管一切行政细节。见田纳西法规有关人文,司法和税则等。

central government exercise, in certain cases, a sort of inspection or control over the secondary bodies. ① At other times they constitute a sort of court of appeal for the decision of affairs. ② In the state of New York judicial penalties are less used than in other places as a means of administration; and the right of prosecuting the offenses of public officers is vested in fewer hands. ③ The same tendency is faintly observable in some other states; ④ but in general the prominent feature of the administration in the United States is its excessive decentralization.

---

① For instance, the direction of public instruction is centralized in the hands of the government. The legislature names the members of the university, who are denominated regents; the governor and lieutenant governor of the state are necessarily of the number. (*Revised Statutes [of the state of New York]*, Vol. I, p. 456.) The regents of the university annually visit the colleges and academies and make their report to the legislature. Their superintendence is not inefficient, for several reasons: the colleges, in order to become corporations, stand in need of a charter, which is only granted on the recommendation of the regents; every year funds are distributed by the state, for the encouragement of learning, and the regents are the distributors of this money. See *Revised Statutes*, chap. xv, "Public Instruction," Vol. I, p. 455. The school commissioners are obliged to send an annual report to the general superintendent of the schools. Ibid. , p. 488. A similar report is annually made to the same person on the number and condition of the poor. Ibid. , p. 631.

② If anyone conceives himself to be wronged by the school commissioners (who are town officers), he can appeal to the superintendent of the primary schools, whose decision is final. *Revised Statutes*, Vol. I, p. 487.

Provisions similar to those above cited are to be met with from time to time in the laws of the state of New York; but in general these attempts at centralization are feeble and unproductive. The great authorities of the state have the right of watching and controlling the subordinate agents, without that of rewarding or punishing them. The same individual is never empowered to give an order and to punish disobedience; he has, therefore, the right of commanding without the means of exacting compliance. In 1830 the Superintendent of Schools, in his annual report to the legislature, complained that several school commissioners, notwithstanding his application, had neglected to furnish him with the accounts which were due. He added that "if this omission continues, I shall be obliged to prosecute them, as the law directs, before the proper tribunals. "

③ Thus, the district attorney is directed to. recover all fines below the sum of fifty dollars, unless such a right has been specially awarded to another magistrate. *Revised Statutes*, Part I, chap. x, Vol. I, p. 383.

④ Several traces of centralization may be discovered in Massachusetts; for instance, the committees of the town schools are directed to make an annual report to the secretary of state. *Laws of Massachusetts*, Vol. I, p. 367.

的管理,有时可以说就是监督和控制。[1] 有时,州政府的官员也可以成立一种审理上诉案件的上诉法院。[2] 在纽约州,用司法处分作为行政手段的情况少于其他州,而对行政犯罪行为的起诉权则掌握在少数人手里。[3] 在其他某些州,也刚刚出现这种倾向。[4] 但从全面来看,仍可以说过度的地方分权,是美国公共行政的突出特点。

---

[1]　例如,政府集中掌握着对公众的指导权。立法机构任命学院成员,并命名他们为摄政者;州的统治者与副统治者在数量上是一定的。(修正过的纽约州法律,第一卷,第456页。)学院的摄政者每年会访问大学和一些专科院校,并向立法机构递交其报告。有几个原因可以说明他们的负责人不是无能力的:大学要想变成社团,必须要有一个章程,而这个章程只能是由摄政者推荐的;州每年会分配一定的基金以鼓励学习,而摄政者就是基金的分配者。见《修正法规》,第十五章,"公共指导,"第一卷,第455页。学校的委员必须向学校的一般主管上交年分析报告。出处同上,第488页。同样的报告也适用于贫困者的数量和状况。出处同上,第631页。

[2]　如果有人认为学校委员是错误的(乡镇官员),他可以向有最终判决权的初级学校提出上诉。已《修正法规》,第一卷,第487页。条款与前面引用过的类似,并不时地与纽约州的法律碰面;但是一般来说,这些关于集权的尝试是微弱的和无效果的。州的最高权威有权监视和控制其下级人员,不会奖赏或惩罚他们。同样的,个人从来不会被赋予发布命令和惩治不守法居民权力;因此,他有命令权,但不会强迫别人服从。在1830年学校官员对立法机构的年报告中,他抱怨有一些学校的委员在财政方面玩忽职守,忘记了他们本应上缴的款项。他还补充道"如果这种错误继续发生,我将在法律的程序下对他们进行起诉。"

[3]　检察官可以恢复金额在50美元以下的罚款,除非这个权力被赋予其他的行政官员。以《修正法规》,第一部分,第十章,第一卷,第383页。

[4]　马萨诸塞还留有中央集权的踪迹,乡镇学校的委员要向州秘书处递交年报告。《马萨诸塞法》,第一卷,第367页。

Of The State

I Have described the townships and the administration; it now remains for me to speak of the state and the government. This is ground I may pass over rapidly without fear of being misunderstood, for all I have to say is to be found in the various written constitutions, copies of which are easily to be procured. These constitutions rest upon a simple and rational theory; most of their forms have been adopted by all constitutional nations, and have become familiar to us.

Here, then, I have only to give a brief account; I shall endeavor afterwards to pass judgment upon what I now describe.

Legislative Power Of The State

Division of the legislative body into two houses — Senate — House of representatives — Different functions of these two bodies.

The legislative power of the state is vested in two assemblies, the first of which generally bears the name of the Senate.

The Senate is commonly a legislative body, but it sometimes becomes an executive and judicial one. It takes part in the government in several ways, according to the constitution of the different states; [1] but it is in the nomination of public functionaries that it most commonly assumes an executive power. It partakes of judicial power in the trial of certain political offenses, and sometimes also in the decision of certain civil cases. [2] The number of its members is always small.

The other branch of the legislature, which is usually called the House of Representatives, has no share whatever in the administration and takes a part in the judicial power only as it impeaches public functionaries before the Senate. The members of the two houses are nearly everywhere subject to the same conditions of eligibility. They are chosen in the same manner, and by the same citizens. The only difference which exists between them is that the term for which the Senate is chosen

---

[1] In Massachusetts the senate is not invested with any administrative functions.

[2] As in the state of New York.

关于州

我已讲述了乡镇及其行政,现在再来讲州及其政府。关于州的问题,我可以一笔带过,而不怕人们费解。我所讲的一切,都是写在每个人均可读懂的各州的成文宪法里的。而且,这些宪法本身都是以一个简明而合理的学说为基础的。其中的大部分条款,已为一切立宪国家所采用,并为我们所熟知。

因此,我在这里只做简单的陈述。以后,我再对我所叙述的一切进行评述。

州的立法权

立法机构分为两院——参议院——众议院——这两个院的不同职能。

州的立法权属于两院,一般将第一个称为参议院。参议院通常是立法机关,但有时也变为行政和司法机关。

根据各州宪法的规定,参议院以各种不同的方式参与行政工作,[①]但它一般是在官员竞选的时候进入行政权的领域。在审理某些政治案件时,有时在审理某些民事案件时,它也分享司法权。[②] 参议员的人数总是不多的。

另一个立法机关,通称为众议院,它不享有任何行政权,只在向参议院控告公职人员时享有司法权。两院议员的当选条件,在各州几乎都是一样的。他们都是按照同样的方式,由同样的公民选举出来的。两者之间的唯一差别,是参议员的任

---

① 在马萨诸塞,参议院不具备任何行政职能。
② 如同纽约州。

is, in general, longer than that of the House of Representatives. The latter seldom remain in office longer than a year; the former usually sit two or three years. By granting to the senators the privilege of being chosen for several years, and being renewed seriatim, the law takes care to preserve in the legislative body a nucleus of men already accustomed to public business, and capable of exercising a salutary influence upon the new-comers. By this separation of the legislative body into two branches, the Americans plainly did not desire to make one house hereditary and the other elective, one aristocratic and the other democratic. It was not their object to create in the one a bulwark to power, while the other represented the interests and passions of the people. The only advantages that result from the present constitution of the two houses in the United States are the division of the legislative power, and the consequent check upon political movements; together with the creation of a tribunal of appeal for the revision of the laws. Time and experience, however, have convinced the Americans that, even if these are its only advantages, the division of the legislative power is still a principle of the greatest necessity. Pennsylvania was the only one of the United States which at first attempted to establish a single House of Assembly, and Franklin himself was so far carried away by the logical consequences of the principle of the sovereignty of the people as to have concurred in the measure; but the Pennsylvanians were soon obliged to change the law and to create two houses. Thus the principle of the division of the legislative power was finally established, and its necessity may henceforward be regarded as a demonstrated truth. This theory, nearly unknown to the republics of antiquity, first introduced into the world almost by accident, like so many other great truths, and misunderstood by several modem nations, has at length become an axiom in the political science of the present age.

The Executive Power Of The State

Office of governor in an American state — His relation to the legislature — His rights and his duties — His dependence on the people.

The executive power of the state is *represented* by the governor. It is not by accident that I have used this word; the governor *represents*

期一般长于众议员。后者的任期很少超过一年,前者通常任期二年或三年。法律所以授予参议员以任期长和连选连任的特权,是因为要在立法机关内保存一些已经熟悉公务和能够对新当选参议员发生有利影响的核心人物。美国人在把立法机关分为两院时,根本就未想把其中的一个建成为世袭的,另一个建成为选举的。他们也未曾想使其中的一个变成贵族的机构,另一个变成民主的代表。他们的目的也不是让第一个支持政权,而让第二个支持民意和人民的利益。把立法权力分开,因而抑制了国会的活动,并建立了审查法律的上诉法院——这就是美国现行的两院制带来的唯一好处。时间和经验使美国人发现,带来这种好处的司法权分割还是一种急需。在整个合众国中,唯有宾夕法尼亚州曾首先试图建立单一的议会。富兰克林本人在人民主权原则的逻辑推理的驱使下,同意了这项方案。但是不久,宾夕法尼亚又不得不修改法律,而成立了两个议院。于是,司法权分散的原则又得到承认,所以人们今后可以认为,必须使立法权分属数个立法机构,乃是一个已被证明的真理。这个几乎为古代的共和国一无所知的理论,如同许许多多的伟大真理一样,在刚一出世的时候曾被许多现代国家所误解,但终于作为今日政治科学的一项公理而被传播开来。

州 的 行 政 权

一个美国的州长——他与立法机构的关系——他的权利和职责——他对人民的依靠。

州的行政权以州长为代表。我使用"代表"这个词,并非出于偶然。州长确实代表着行政权,但他只享有他所拥有的权力中的

this power; although he enjoys but a portion of its rights. The supreme magistrate, under the title of governor, is the official moderator and counselor of the legislature. He is armed with a veto or suspensive power, which allows him to stop, or at least to retard, its movements at pleasure. He lays the wants of the country before the legislative body, and points out the means that he thinks may be usefully employed in providing for them; he is the natural executor of its decrees in all the undertakings that interest the nation at large. ① In the absence of the legislature, the governor is bound to take all necessary steps to guard the state against violent shocks and unforeseen dangers. The whole military power of the state is at the disposal of the governor. He is the commander of the militia and head of the armed force. When the authority which is by general consent awarded to the laws is disregarded, the governor puts himself at the head of the armed force of the state, to quell resistance and restore order. Lastly, the governor takes no share in the administration of the townships and counties, except through the appointment of justices of the peace, whom he cannot afterwards dismiss. ② The governor is an elected magistrate, and is generally chosen for one or two years only, so that he always continues to be strictly dependent upon the majority who returned him.

Political Effects Of
Decentralized Administration
In The United States

Necessary distinction between a centralized government and a centralized administration — Administration not centralized in the United States: great centralization of the government — Some bad consequences resulting to the United States from the extremely decentralized administration — Administrative advantages of this order of things — The power that administers is less regular, less enlightened, less learned, but much greater than in Europe — Political advantages of this order of things — In the United States the country makes itself

---

① Practically speaking, it is not always the governor who executes the plans of the legislature; it often happens that the latter, in voting a measure, names special agents to superintend its execution.

② In some of the states justices of the peace are not appointed by the governor.

某些部分。被称为州长的这位最高官员,既是立法机构的仲裁者,又是它的咨询师。他以否决权为武器,可以随意停止或至少推迟司法机构的活动。他向立法机构提出国家的需要,并指出他认为可以满足这些需要的有效方法。他是立法机构对于与全州有关的一切活动所做的决定的自然执行者。[①]在立法机构休会的时候,州长必须采取有效的措施来保护州,以防止它被动乱和意外危险所袭击。全州的军事大权都由州长控制。他既是军队的司令员,又是武装力量的首长。当人们依法同意的州的权威被人否认时,州长可以统帅全州的武装力量来镇压反抗并恢复正常的秩序。最后,州长不参与乡镇和县的行政工作,除非在参与治安法官的任命时,而治安法官经他任命以后,他却无权罢免。[②]州长是经过选举产生的,一般的任期为一年或二年,因此他总是处在选举他的大多数选民的严密监视之下。

美国的行政分权的政治效果

政府集权和行政集权之间的必要的差别——美国不实行行政集权,大权都掌握在政府手里——严重的行政分权给美国带来的不良影响——这种做法对行政工作的好处——管理社会的行政人员不如欧洲的正规、文明和有学识,但他们的权力却大于欧洲——这种做法在政治上的好处——在美国,国家意识表现于各

---

① 确切地说,并不总是统治者在执行立法机构的方案;而常常是由立法机构推选出一个措施,任命特殊的代理来监督其执行过程。

② 一些州的治安法官不是由统治者任命的。

felt everywhere Support given to the government by the community —
Provincial institutions more necessary in proportion as the social condi-
tion becomes more democratic — Reason for this.

"Centralization" is a word in general and daily use, without any
precise meaning being attached to it. Nevertheless, there exist two
distinct kinds of centralization, which it is necessary to discriminate
with accuracy. Certain interests are common to all parts of a nation,
such as the enactment of its general laws and the maintenance of its
foreign relations. Other interests are peculiar to certain parts of the
nation, such, for instance, as the business of the several townships.
When the power that directs the former or general interests is concentrated in one place or in the same persons, it constitutes a centralized
government. To concentrate in like manner in one place the direction
of the latter or local interests, constitutes what may be terled a centralized administration.

Upon some points these two kinds of centralization coincide, but
by classifying the objects which fall more particularly within the province of each, they may easily be distinguished. It is evident that a
centralized government acquires immense power when united to centralized administration. Thus combined, it accustoms men to set their
own will habitually and completely aside; to submit, not only for
once, or upon one point, but in every respect, and at all times. Not
only, therefore, does this union of power subdue them compulsorily,
but it affects their ordinary habits; it isolates them and then influences
each separately.

These two kinds of centralization assist and attract each other,
but they must not be supposed to be inseparable. It is impossible to i-
magine a more completely centralized government than that which existed in France under Louis XIV; when the same individual was the
author and the interpreter of the laws, and the representative of
France at home and abroad, he was justified in asserting that he constituted the state. Nevertheless, the administration was much less
centralized under Louis XIV than it is at the present day.

In England the centralization of the government is carried to great
perfection; the state has the compact vigor of one man, and its will puts
immense masses in motion and turns its whole power where it pleases.

个方面——社会对政府的支持——社会变得越民主,就越需要完善地方组织——原因是什么。

"集权"是人们很常用的一个词,但它并没有任何精确的定义。实际上有两种性质非常不同的集权,对此我们有必要分辨清楚。有一些特定的利益是与全国各地都有关的,比如像颁布一项全国性法律和与别国的外交关系。另一些利益,则与全国的某一特定区域有关,比如对一些乡镇的建设事业。如果把第一类事情的领导权集中于同一个地方或同一个人的手中,这就是政府集权。而把以同样方式集中第二类事情的领导权的做法叫做行政集权。

这两种集权在某些情况下纯属巧合,但如果从总体上来观察它们各自管辖的对象时,便不难把两者区别开来。很明显,如果政府集权与行政集权结合起来,那它就获得了无限的权力。这样,它便会使人们长期地并完全地习惯于把自己的意愿搁置到一边,这种习惯不仅仅是暂时的或只在一个问题上的,而且是无时无刻地对所有问题的服从。因此,这种联合不仅能使人民屈从于它们,而且能影响到人民的日常习惯。它先把人民彼此孤立起来,然后再逐个击破,使他们服从。

这两种集权相互支持并相互吸引,但是它们是绝对不能被分开的。我们不能想象会出现比法国路易十四时期所拥有的强大的政府集权还要大的政权;当制定国家的法律和解释国家法律的是同一个人,他在对内和对外方面都能代表法国。他总是有理的,并且他就是国家。然而,在路易十四统治时代,行政集权却大大不如今天。

在英格兰,政府集权已经发展到了最完美的状态:国家就像一个单独的行动的人,它可以随意把广大的群众鼓动起来,将自己的全部权力集中并投放在它想指向的任何地方。但在用了五

But England, which has done such great things for the last fifty years, has never centralized its administration. Indeed, I cannot conceive that a nation can live and prosper without a powerful centralization of government. But I am of the opinion that a centralized administration is fit only to enervate the nations in which it exists, by incessantly diminishing their local spirit. Although such an administration can bring together at a given moment, on a given point, all the disposable resources of a people, it injures the renewal of those resources. It may ensure a victory in the hour of strife, but it gradually relaxes the sinews of strength. It may help admirably the transient greatness of a man, but not the durable prosperity of a nation.

Observe that whenever it is said that a state cannot act because it is not centralized, it is the centralization of the government that is spoken of. It is frequently asserted, and I assent to the proposition, that the German Empire has never been able to bring all its powers into action. But the reason is that the state has never been able to enforce obedience to its general laws; the several members of that great body always claimed the right, or found the means, of refusing their co-operation to the representatives of the common authority, even in the affairs that concerned the mass of the people; in other words, there was no centralization of government. The same remark is applicable to the Middle Ages; the cause of all the miseries of feudal society was that the control, not only of administration, but of government, was divided among a thousand hands and broken up in a thousand different ways. The want of a centralized government prevented the nations of Europe from advancing with energy in any straightforward course.

I have shown that in the United States there is no centralized administration and no hierarchy of public functionaries. Local authority has been carried farther than any European nation could endure without great inconvenience, and it has even produced some disadvantageous consequences in America. But in the United States the centralization of the government is perfect; and it would be easy to prove that the national power is more concentrated there than it has ever been in the old nations of Europe. Not only is there but one legislative body in

十年的时间来完成了如此伟大事业的英国,并没有实行行政集权。实际上,我不能设想一个国家在没有强大的政府集权下会很好的生存下去,甚至会繁荣富强。但我认为,行政集权只能使国家逐步走向衰弱,因为它在不断消磨人们的精神与意志。不错,在一定的时代和一定的地区,行政集权可能把国家一切可以使用的力量集结起来,但会损害这些力量的再生。它可能迎来战争的胜利,但会缩短政权的寿命。因此,它可能对一个人的转瞬即逝的伟大很有帮助,但对一个国家的持久繁荣却无能为力。

值得注意的是,每当谈及一个国家因为没有实行集权而无所作为的时候,这个被谈论的对象几乎总是指政府集权。有人一再指出,德意志帝国从来没有使它的力量带来可能取得的一切好处。我同意这个说法。但是,原因是什么呢? 因为国家从来没能使全国人民服从全国的一般法律;因为这个大机构中的一些成员总是有权利或机会去拒绝同全国最高当局的代表合作,甚至在关系到全体人民的利益时也是如此;换句话说,是因为它没有政府集权。这种说法也同样适用于中世纪。因为封建社会所出现的种种苦难,就是由于行政权和统治权,都被分掌在许多人之手和被分割成许多部分。欧洲各国都没有采用政府集权,这就妨碍了他们生气勃勃地奔向任何一个目标的激情。

我们已经讲过,在美国并没有行政集权,而且也很难看见等级制度的痕迹。美国的地方分权已经达到任何一个欧洲国家所不能容忍的地步;而且这种分权在美国国内也产生了一些不良后果。但在美国,政府集权也发展到了很高的水平;而且很容易证明,美国的国家权力比欧洲以往任何一个君主国家都要集中。每个州不仅只有一个立法机构,而且只有一个可以创造本州政治生

each state, not only does there exist but one source of political authority, but numerous assemblies in districts or counties have not, in general, been multiplied lest they should be tempted to leave their administrative duties and interfere with the government. In America the legislature of each state is supreme; nothing can impede its authority, neither privileges, nor local immunities, nor personal influence, nor even the empire of reason, since it represents that majority which claims to be the sole organ of reason. Its own determination is therefore the only limit to its action. In juxtaposition with it, and under its immediate control, is the representative of the executive power, whose duty it is to constrain the refractory to submit by superior force. The only symptom of weakness lies in certain details of the action of the government. The American republics have no standing armies to intimidate a discontented minority; but as no minority has as yet been reduced to declare open war, the necessity of an army has not been felt. The state usually employs the officers of the township or the county to deal with the citizens. Thus, for instance, in New England the town assessor fixes the rate of taxes; the town collector receives them; the town treasurer transmits the amount to the public treasury; and the disputes that may arise are brought before the ordinary courts of justice. This method of collecting taxes is slow as well as inconvenient, and it would prove a perpetual hindrance to a government whose pecuniary demands were large. It is desirable that, in whatever materially affects its existence, the government should be served by officers of its own, appointed by itself, removable at its pleasure, and accustomed to rapid methods of proceeding. But it will always be easy for the central government, organized as it is in America, to introduce more energetic and efficacious modes of action according to its wants. The want of a centralized government will not, then, as has often been asserted, prove the destruction of the republics of the New World; far from the American governments being not sufficiently centralized, I shall prove hereafter that they are too much so. The legislative bodies daily encroach upon the authority of the government, and their tendency, like that of the French Convention, is to appropriate it entirely to themselves. The social power thus centralized is constantly changing hands, because it is subordinate to the power of the people. It often forgets the maxims of wisdom and foresight in the consciousness of its strength. Hence arises its danger. Its vigor, and not its impotence, will probably be the cause of its ultimate destruction.

活的政权机关;同时,也不允许数个县的议会联合行动,以防止它们企图超越自己的行政职权而干涉政府工作。在美国,每个州的立法机构都是至高无上的,没有任何力量可以妨碍它们的工作。无论是特权,还是地方豁免权,无论是个人影响,还是理性的权威,都阻止不了它的前进,因为它代表着自认为是唯一的理性机构的大多数。因此,它可以根据自己的意志而为所欲为。和它并排前进并受它控制的,是行政权的代表,它负责以强力迫使不满分子屈服。只在政府工作的某些细节方面,还存在一些弱点。美国的各共和州,没有用以镇压少数派的常备军,但这些少数派至今还没有发展到可以发动战争或使州感到要必须建立一支强大军队的地步。州会经常雇佣乡或县的官员同公民打交道。比如,在新英格兰,由乡财产估价员计算税额,由乡税收员征收应交付的税金,由乡司库将收到的税款转交到州库,由普通法院审理税务纠纷。这样的征税办法不仅很慢而且不方便,会经常妨碍政府在大量需款时的工作。一般认为,凡与政府的生存有重大关系的事务,都应由政府自己任命和可以随时撤换的善于迅速处理工作的官员担任。但是,像美国建立起来的那种中央政府,很容易根据需要而采取比较有力和有效的行动手段。因此,并不像人们所宣称的那样,因为美国没有实行中央集权,新大陆的各共和州将会自行灭亡。美国各州的政府并不是集权不够,在后面,我可以证明是因为它们过于集权了。立法机构每天都在吞噬着政府的各种权力,而这种趋势,就像法国的国民公会试图把一切权力都集中到自己手里一样。而社会权力的集中却经常容易改变,因为它是从属于人民的权力。它们会经常忘记理智的格言,其行为也缺乏一定的远见性。它的危险之处也在于此。导致它有朝一日灭亡的,不是它的软弱无能,而正是它的力量本身。

The system of decentralized administration produces several different effects in America. The Americans seem to me to have overstepped the limits of sound policy in isolating the administration of the government; for order, even in secondary affairs, is a matter of national importance. [1] As the state has no administrative functionaries of its own, stationed on different points of its territory, to whom it can give a common impulse, the consequence is that it rarely attempts to issue any general police regulations. The want of these regulations is severely felt and is frequently observed by Europeans. The appearance of disorder which prevails on the surface leads one at first to imagine that society is in a state of anarchy; nor does one perceive one's mistake till one has gone deeper into the subject. Certain undertakings are of importance to the whole state; but they cannot be put in execution, because there is no state administration to direct them. Abandoned to the exertions of the towns or counties, under the care of elected and temporary agents, they lead to no result, or at least to no durable benefit. The partisans of centralization in Europe are wont to maintain that the government can administer the affairs of each locality better than the citizens can do it for themselves. This may be true when the central power is enlightened and the local authorities are ignorant; when it is alert and they are slow; when it is accustomed to act and they to obey. Indeed, it is evident that this double tendency must augment with the increase of centralization, and that the readiness of the one and the incapacity of the others must become more and more

---

[1] The authority that represents the state ought not, I think, to waive the right of inspecting the local administration, even when it does not itself administer. Suppose, for instance, that an agent of the government was stationed at some appointed spot in each county to prosecute the misdemeanors of the town and county officers, would not a more uniform order be the result, without in any way compromising the independence of the township? Nothing of the kind, however, exists in America: there is nothing above the county courts, which have, as it were, only an incidental knowledge of the administrative offenses they ought to repress.

　　行政分权制度在美国产生了几种不同的影响。在我看来,美国人几乎把行政从政府完全独立出来;在这个问题上,他们好像越出了常轨,违反了常识,因为即使在一些次要的事情上,全国也该有一个统一的制度。① 由于州并没有将其自己的行政官员指派到其境内各行政区划担任固定职务,从而不能建立共同的惩罚制度,结果也就很少想到颁布全州统一的治安条例。但是,颁布这种条例是非常需要的。欧洲人却不能在美国见到这种条例。这种表面上的无秩序状态,起初会使欧洲人认为美国社会处于完全无政府状态;而在他们深入观察事物的本质以后,就会发现原来的认识是不正确的。一些特定的事情相对于全州来说是很重要的,但却不能落实于行动,因为没有管理它们的全州性行政组织。把这些事情交给乡镇或县的由选举产生的暂时代理人去办理,结果不是一事无成,就是持续不了多久。欧洲的集权主义的拥护者们坚持认为,由中央政府管理地方的行政事务,会比由地方行政的当局官员自己管理要好。当中央集权是有知的,而地方当局是无知的时候;当前者是积极活跃的,而后者是消极迟缓的时候;当前者是惯于发布命令的,而后者是惯于服从的时候,这种说法也许是正确的。甚至很明显的,随着中央集权的加强,这种向两极发展的趋势也会随之增加,即一方的权能日益加大,而另一方则日趋无能。但是,当人民像美国人那样是有知的,是关

---

　　① 我认为,代表州的权威不应该放弃检查地方行政的权力,甚至是在它自己不管理的时候。例如,假设一个政府的代理驻守在每个县的指定地点,以处罚乡镇和县的官员的罪行,其结果是不会成为更统一的规则的,这在任何方面有可能缓解乡镇的独立吗? 当然这种事在美国不会发生:因为那里的任何事务都不会高于国家法院。国家法院只需对很小的甚至很偶然的行政上的攻击进行镇压。

prominent. But I deny that it is so when the people are as enlightened, as awake to their interests, and as accustomed to reflect on them as the Americans are. I am persuaded, on the contrary, that in this case the collective strength of the citizens will always conduce more efficaciously to the public welfare than the authority of the government. I know it is difficult to point out with certainty the means of arousing a sleeping population and of giving it passions and knowledge which it does not possess; it is, I am well aware, an arduous task to persuade men to busy themselves about their own affairs. It would frequently be easier to interest them in the punctilios of court etiquette than in the repairs of their common dwelling. But whenever a central administration affects completely to supersede the persons most interested, I believe that it is either misled or desirous to mislead. However enlightened and skillfull a central power may be, it cannot of itself embrace all the details of the life of a great nation. Such vigilance exceeds the powers of man. And when it attempts unaided to create and set in motion so many complicated springs, it must submit to a very imperfect result or exhaust itself in bootless efforts.

Centralization easily succeeds, indeed, in subjecting the external actions of men to a certain uniformity, which we come at last to love for its own sake, independently of the objects to which it is applied, like those devotees who worship the statue and forget the deity it represents. Centralization imparts without difficulty an admirable regularity to the routine of business; provides skillfully for the details of the social police; represses small disorders and petty misdemeanors; maintains society in a *status quo* alike secure from improvement and decline; and perpetuates a drowsy regularity in the conduct of affairs which the heads of the administration are wont to call good order and public tranquillity; [1]

---

[1] China appears to me to present the most perfect instance of that species of well-being which a highly centralized administration may furnish to its subjects. Travelers assure us that the Chinese have tranquillity without happiness, industry without improvement, stability without strength, and public order without public morality. The condition of society there is always tolerable, never excellent. I imagine that when China is opened to European observation, it will be found to contain the most perfect model of a centralized administration that exists in the universe.

心自己利益的,是惯于思考自身利益的时候,我就会否认这种情况的出现。相反,在这种条件下,我确信公民的集体力量永远会比政府的权力创造出更大的社会福利。我知道,在某种条件下是很难找到一个能唤醒沉睡的民族的办法,并使他们拥有前所未有的激情和知识;我也相信,说服人们应为自己的工作去努力也并不是件容易的事;让人们学习宫廷礼法的细节,往往比让他们去修理公众住宅更易于引起他们的兴趣。但是,我也认为,当中央政府的行政部门一定要替代下级机构的工作时,它不是在自误,也是在误人。不管一个中央政府是如何精明能干,它也不能依靠自己去了解一个大国生活的一切细节。因为这样的工作超过了人们的能力。当它试图要独力创造那么多发条并使它们发动的时候,其结果要不是很不完美,就是徒劳无益地消耗自己的精力。

实际上,中央集权很容易使人们在表面上的行动保持一致。这种一致虽然出于爱戴中央集权,但人们却不知这种集权的目的何在,好比信神的人们在拜祭神像时而忘记了神像所代表的是哪位神仙一样。结果,中央集权可以轻而易举地维护国家日常事务的秩序时,详尽地制定出全国公安条例的细则,及时镇压小规模的叛乱和惩治轻微的犯罪行为,使社会维持在一个既没有本质上的进步又不会真正落后的状态中,让整个社会永远处于被官员们惯于称之为良好秩序和社会安宁的那种昏昏欲睡的循规蹈矩的状态中;①

---

① 在我看来,中国是代表高度行政集权的最好例子。旅行者们自信的告诉我们,中国人的生活很平静,但缺少快乐,他们有自己的工业,但缺少改进,发展很稳定,但没有士气,他们有自己的公共规则,但缺乏公共道德。那里的社会状况是过得去的,但绝不是完美的。我认为,当中国对欧洲人实行开放政策时,它就被认为是天底下将行政集中行使得最完美的国家。

in short, it excels in prevention, but not in action. Its force deserts it when society is to be profoundly moved, or accelerated in its course; and if once the co-operation of private citizens is necessary to the furtherance of its measures, the secret of its impotence is disclosed. Even while the centralized power, in its despair, invokes the assistance of the citizens, it says to them: "You shall act just as I please, as much as I please, and in the direction which I please. You are to take charge of the details without aspiring to guide the system; you are to work in darkness; and afterwards you may judge my work by its results. " These are not the conditions on which the alliance of the human will is to be obtained; it must be free in its gait and responsible for its acts, or (such is the constitution of man) the citizen had rather remain a passive spectator than a depdndent actor in schemes with which he is unacquainted.

It is undeniable that the want of those uniform regulations which control the conduct of every inhabitant of France is not infrequently felt in the United States. Gross instances of social indifference and neglect are to be met with; and from time to time disgraceful blemishes are seen, in complete contrast with the surrounding civilization. Useful undertakings which cannot succeed without perpetual attention and rigorous exactitude are frequently abandoned; for in America, as well as in other countries, the people proceed by sudden impulses and momentary exertions. The European, accustomed to find a functionary always at hand to interfere with all he undertakes, reconciles himself with difficulty to the complex mechanism of the administration of the townships. In general it may be affirmed that the lesser details of the police, which render life easy and comfortable, are neglected in America, but that the essential guarantees of man in society are as strong there as elsewhere. In America the power that conducts the administration is far less regular, less enlightened, and less skillful, but a hundredfold greater than in Europe. In no country in the world do the citizens make such exertions for the common weal. I know of no people who have established schools so numerous and efficacious, places of public worship better suited to the wants of the inhabitants,

总之,中央集权善于预防,而短于主动创新。当它激起社会发生巨大动荡,或加速社会的前进步伐时,它便会失去控制的力量。如果它的各项措施都需要公民的帮助,那么它的弱点就会马上暴露出来,中央集权立即处于无能为力的状态。有时,中央集权的政府在万不得已的时候,也会恳求公民的帮助,但它却向公民们说:"你们必须按照我的意愿行动,我想叫你们做多少你们就要做多少,并且你们的行为要让我满足。你们只负责那些细节的管理,而不要妄想去指导整体。你们要不闻不问地工作;等以后再根据结果来评定我的所作所为。"这样的条件怎么能使人们愿意帮助它呢!人们需要行动自由,愿意对自己的行为负责。因此,人们宁肯停在那里不动,也不愿意盲目地走向他们一无所知的去处。

不可否认的,这种指导每个法国人生活习惯的那种统一制度在美国并不常见。有时遇到一些证明社会对人冷漠和不够关心的实例,时不时地也会看到一些抵触周围的文明环境的污点。一些有益的事业却得不到永久的关注和严格的实施,以至都被半途而废;因为在美国也同在其他国家一样,人民的行动有时也是出于一时的冲动和片刻的激情。欧洲人习惯于找一位几乎可以承办一切事务的官员,所以他们很难采用美国的那种复杂的乡镇行政制度。一般可以被证实的是能够使人民的生活安逸和舒畅的公安细则,在美国是被忽略了的;但在社会对人的主要保障上,美国也同其他国家是一样强的。在美国,各州行使的权力不如欧洲条理分明和富于教育指导作用,但却大于欧洲的百倍。世界上没有一个国家能为社会福利事业做出如此大的贡献。我还不知道有哪个国家设立了如此之多和如此有效的学校,其建筑的教堂如此适合于居民的需要,其修筑的乡间公路保养得如此完好。因

or roads kept in better repair. Uniformity or permanence of design, the minute arrangement of details, ① and the perfection of administrative system must not be sought for in the United States; what we find there is the presence of a power which, if it is somewhat wild, is at least robust, and an existence checkered with accidents, indeed, but full of animation and effort.

Granting, for an instant, that the villages and counties of the United States would be more usefully governed by a central authority which they had never seen than by functionaries taken from among them; admitting, for the sake of argument, that there would be more security in America, and the resources of society would be better employed there, if the whole administration centered in a single arm — still the political advantages which the Americans derive from their decentralized system would induce me to prefer it to the contrary plan. It profits me but little, after all, that a vigilant authority always protects the tranquillity of my pleasures and constantly averts all dangers from my path, without my care or concern, if this same authority is the absolute master of my liberty and my life, and if it so monopolizes movement and life that when it languishes everything languishes around it, that when it sleeps everything must sleep, and that when it dies the state itself must perish.

---

① A writer of talent who, in a comparison of the finances of France with those of the United States, has proved that ingenuity cannot always supply the place of the knowledge of facts, justly reproaches the Americans for the sort of confusion that exists in the accounts of the expenditure in the townships; and after giving the model of a departmental budget in France, he adds: "We are indebted to centralization, that admirable invention of a great man, for the order and method which prevail alike in all the municipal budgets, from the largest city to the humblest commune." Whatever may be my admiration of this result, when I see the communes of France, with their excellent system of accounts, plunged into the grossest ignorance of their true interests, and abandoned to so incorrigible an apathy that they seem to vegetate rather than to live; when, on the other hand, I observe the activity, the information, and the spirit of enterprise in those American townships whose budgets are neither methodical nor uniform, I see that society there is always at work. I am struck by the spectacle; for, to my mind, the end of a good government is to ensure the welfare of a people, and not merely to establish order in the midst of its misery. I am therefore led to suppose that the prosperity of the American townships and the apparent confusion of their finances, the distress of the French communes and the perfection of their budget, may be attributable to the same cause. At any rate, I am suspicious of a good that is united with so many evils, and I am not averse to an evil that is compensated by so many benefits.

此,不必到美国去找外观上的一致性和持久性,去找对细节的详尽安排以及行政手续的完善规定;①我们在那里看到的是一种力量,这种力量虽然有些粗犷,但却是无比强大的,它的存在伴随着意外的发生,但却充满了生机和进取精神。

　　比如说如果美国的乡村和县城被它们永远没有使用过的中央政权管理,也许会比由它们从当地选出的官员管理更为有效。如果要我判断的话,我相信美国全国的行政被集中于一个人之手时,会把美国治理得更加安全,会使美国的社会资源利用得更为合适和合理。尽管美国人从地方分权制度中获得了政治好处,但我仍然主张采用相反的制度。即使存在一个常在的权威当局,它经常保护我的快乐不被干扰,排除我前进道路上的一切危险,从来不让我担心,如果这个当局是我的自由和生命的绝对主人,如果它垄断了整个社会的活动和生活,以至于当它无精打采时周围的一切也跟着无精打采,当它睡觉时周围的一切也得睡觉,当它死去时周围的一切也得灭亡,那它对我又有什么好处呢?

────────────

① 一位有才能的作家,在对比了法国的财政系统和美国的财政系统后,证明了智谋不可能总是掩盖住实事,并责备美国乡镇的账目在消费支出上的混乱。在给出法国一个部门预算的范例后,他补充道:"我们感谢这种由伟人发明出来的中央集权制度,因为它的规则与方法盛行于所有的市政规则中,上至大城市,小到最底层的群体。"不管我为什么会敬佩这样的结果,当我看见法国人带着他们完美的账目系统,而完全忽视他们真正利益的存在,并中止了其一贯的冷漠,与其说他们在生活,不如说他们是在无所事事地过活;而另一方面,在我考察美国乡镇事业的活动、信息和精神时,发现它们的预算既不是有序的,也不是统一的,而它们的社会却总是在前进。我深深地被眼前的这种景象所震惊;在我看来,一个优秀的政府应该为人民的幸福事业奋斗,而不是在大众的痛苦上建立规则。因此,我认为,美国乡镇的繁荣和其财政的表面混乱,法国人民的不幸和其完美的预算系统都来自同一原因。不管怎样,我不相信建立在罪恶之上的完美,但我不反对在众多利益补偿下的罪恶。

There are countries in Europe where the native considers himself as a kind of settler, indifferent to the fate of the spot which he inhabits. The greatest changes are effected there without his concurrence, and (unless chance may have apprised him of the event) without his knowledge; nay, more, the condition of his village, the police of his street, the repairs of the church or the parsonage, do not concern him; for he looks upon all these things as unconnected with himself and as the property of a powerful stranger whom he calls the government. He has only a life interest in these possessions, without the spirit of ownership or any ideas of improvement. This want of interest in his own affairs goes so far that if his own safety or that of his children is at last endangered, instead of trying to avert the peril, he will fold his arms and wait till the whole nation comes to his aid. This man who has so completely sacrificed his own free will does not, more than any other person, love obedience; he cowers, it is true, before the pettiest officer, but he braves the law with the spirit of a conquered foe as soon as its superior force is withdrawn; he perpetually oscillates between servitude and license.

When a nation has arrived at this state, it must either change its customs and its laws, or perish; for the source of public virtues is dried up; and though it may contain subjects, it has no citizens. Such communities are a natural prey to foreign conquests; and if they do not wholly disappear from the scene, it is only because they are surrounded by other nations similar or inferior to themselves; it is because they still have an indefinable instinct of patriotism; and an involuntary pride in the name of their country, or a vague reminiscence of its bygone fame, suffices to give them an impulse of self-preservation.

Nor can the prodigious exertions made by certain nations to defend a country in which they had lived, so to speak, as strangers be adduced in favor of such a system; for it will be found that in these cases their main incitement was religion. The permanence, the glory, or the prosperity of the nation had become parts of their faith,

在欧洲的一些国家,本土居民认为自己是外来的移民,所以毫不关心他们居住的地方的命运。国内发生的一些重大变化都与他们无关,甚至他们并不了解这种变化是怎样发生的(除非他们被告知这些变化)。更有甚者,他们对自己村庄的状况、街道的治安、教堂的翻修和教士的处境都无动于衷。他们认为,这一切事情与他们毫无关系,应由被他们称作政府的强大的第三者管理。他们仅仅是这些财产的终身受益者,对这些财产既无占有的思想,又无任何改善的念头。这种对自己不关心的态度,竟然发展到当他们本身或其子女的安全受到危险时,他们非但不去试图排除危险,反而束手等待全国来帮助的地步。这些人虽然愿意完全牺牲自己的自由意志,但决不会比其他人更愿意服从。不错,他们在一个小军官面前都会畏缩屈服,但当部队撤退以后,他们就像战胜了敌人似敢于冒犯法纪。因此,他们将永远踌躇在奴役和任性之间。

当一个国家达到这样的地步,它必须既改变民情又改变法律,否则就将灭亡;因为它的公共道德的源泉已经枯竭;它虽然尚存臣民,但已无公民。这样的国家自然会成为外国征服的猎物;如果它还没有从世界的舞台上消失,那仅仅是因为周围的国家与它类似或者还不如它;它仍然有一种无法定义的爱国本能;或一种不经意间产生的自豪感,或一种对过去荣誉的模糊回忆,但这些东西实际上于事无补,只能使它在受压迫的时候产生自我保护的冲动。

如果想以某些民族曾为保卫他们称作是外来人居住的国家而做过巨大的贡献来证明他们是爱祖国的,那也是错误的,因为你将发现宗教几乎总是他们当时的主要动力。国家的永存、荣誉和繁荣昌盛都属于他们信仰的一部分,而在保卫祖国的时候就等

and in defending their country, they defended also that Holy City of which they were all citizens. The Turkish tribes have never taken an active share in the conduct of their affairs, but they accomplished stupendous enterprises as long as the victories of the Sultan were triumphs of the Mohammedan faith. In the present age they are in rapid decay because their religion is departing and despotism only remains. Montesquieu, who attributed to absolute power an authority peculiar to itself, did it, as I conceive, an undeserved honor; for despotism, taken by itself, can maintain nothing durable. On close inspection we shall find that religion, and not fear, has ever been the cause of the longlived prosperity of an absolute government. Do what you may, there is no true power among men except in the free union of their will; and patriotism and religion are the only two motives in the world that can long urge all the people towards the same end.

Laws cannot rekindle an extinguished faith, but men may be interested by the laws in the fate of their country. It depends upon the laws to awaken and direct the vague impulse of patriotism, which never abandons the human heart; and if it be connected with the thoughts, the passions, and the daily habits of life, it may be consolidated into a durable and rational sentiment. Let it not be said that it is too late to make the experiment; for nations do not grow old as men do, and every fresh generation is a new people ready for the care of the legislator.

It is not the *administrative*, but the *political* effects of decentralization that I most admire in America. In the United States the interests of the country are everywhere kept in view; they are an object of solicitude to the people of the whole Union, and every citizen is as warmly attached to them as if they were his own. He takes pride in the glory of his nation; he boasts of its success, to which he conceives himself to have contributed; and he rejoices in the general prosperity by which he profits. The feeling he entertains towards the state is analogous to that which unites him to his family, and it is by a kind of selfishness that he interests himself in the welfare of his country.

于保卫他们作为其公民的神圣城市。土耳其人从来不参加社会事务的管理，但只要他们认为苏丹们的征服就是穆罕默德教的胜利，他们就会完成一些艰巨的任务。目前，这个宗教在快速地衰落，因为只有专制制度还活在他们那里。孟德斯鸠认为是他自己使专制制度具有了独特的威力，我认为他不配享有这个荣誉。专制制度本身只能依靠自己，不能维持很久。当我们认真地考察一下，就会发现使专制政府长期兴盛的是宗教，而不是它的威吓力量。不管你会怎么想，除了人们的意志可以自由联合以外，你再也不会在人类中间找到其他的真正的强大力量。而且在世界上，只有爱国主义或宗教能够使全体公民持久地奔向同一目标前进。

法律已不能重新点燃已经熄灭的信仰，但能使人们关心自己国家的命运。法律能够唤醒和指导人们心中模糊存在的爱国本能，而这种爱国本能从来都没有被人们遗弃；如果把这种本能与思想、激情和日常习惯结合起来，它就会被巩固成一种持久的和理性的感情。而且决不能说试图唤醒这种本能的实验已经来不及了；因为国家不会像人类那样迅速衰落。每一代新人在一个国家出生时，是作为准备掌握立法工作的新人而出现的。

美国最使我钦佩的，不是它的地方分权的行政效果，而是这种分权的政治效果。在美国，到处都可以感到国家利益的存在；这是全联邦每个公民共同关心的目标。居民关心国家的每一项利益就像关心自己的利益一样。他们以国家的光荣而自豪，并夸耀国家获得的成就，相信自己对国家的成就也有所贡献；他为国家的繁荣昌盛而高兴，并为自己从这种富强中获得的好处而深感欣慰。他们对国家的感情好比是对自己家庭的感情，而且是一种自私的心理促使他们去关心国家的幸福。

To the European, a public officer represents a superior force; to an American, he represents a right. In America, then, it may be said that no one renders obedience to man, but to justice and to law. If the opinion that the citizen entertains of himself is exaggerated, it is at least salutary; he unhesitatingly confides in his own powers, which appear to him to be all-sufficient. When a private individual meditates an undertaking, however directly connected it may be with the welfare of society, he never thinks of soliciting the co-operation of the government; but he publishes his plan, offers to execute it, courts the assistance of other individuals, and struggles manfully against all obstacles. Undoubtedly he is often less successful than the state might have been in his position; but in the end the sum of these private undertakings far exceeds all that the government could have done. As the administrative authority is within the reach of the citizens, whom in some degree it represents, it excites neither their jealousy nor hatred; as its resources are limited, everyone feels that he must not rely solely on its aid. Thus when the administration thinks fit to act within its own limits, it is not abandoned to itself, as in Europe; the duties of private citizens are not supposed to have lapsed because the state has come into action, but everyone is ready, on the contrary, to guide and support it This action of individuals, joined to that of the public authorities, frequently accomplishes what the most energetic centralized administration would be unable to do. [1]

It would be easy to adduce several facts in proof of what I advance, but I had rather give only one, with which I am best acquainted. In America the means that the authorities have at their disposal for the discovery of crimes and the arrest of criminals are few. A state police does not exist, and passports are unknown. The criminal police of the United States cannot be compared with that of France; the magistrates and public agents are not numerous; they do not always initiate the measures for arresting the guilty; and the examinations of prisoners are rapid and oral. Yet I believe that in no country does crime

---

[1] See Appendix I.

　　欧洲人认为公共官员是至高权力的代表,而美国人则认为公共官员就是行使公民的权利。因此可以说,在美国绝不是人服从人,而是人服从正义或法律。如果他们对自己也往往有一种夸大,那也几乎总是有益的看法。他们会毫不犹豫地相信自己的力量,并认为这种力量是不可抵抗的。假如一个人想做一番事业,而且这项事业与社会公益有着直接的关系,他也从不会考虑去联合政府的力量;他把计划公布出来后,便自己去执行,或请其他个人的力量来协助,并尽力排除一切障碍。毫无疑问,他的成功率会远远低于有州政府协助时的结果。但是从长远观点来看,一切私人事业的总结果却大大超过政府可能做出的成果。由于行政当局只管民事,所以既不会引起人们的羡慕,又不会引起人们的厌恶;但因为它的权力范围有限,所以大家认为不能只依靠它去办各项事业。因此,当行政机关行使它的职权时,它不会像在欧洲那样全靠自己;也不必担心公民会不行使义务,因为州会对此采取行动。相反,每个人都将扶持、指导和支援行政机关。个人的努力与社会力量结合,常会完成最集权和最强大的行政当局所完不成的工作。①

　　我可以举出许多事实来证明上述的一切,但在此我只想列举一个我最熟悉的事例来证明。在美国,权力机构拥有的发现罪行和追捕罪犯的手段极少。美国没有行政勤务警察,也不知护照为何物。美国的司法警察比不上法国的;地方官员和公共官员的人数很少;他们不总是经常提出追捕罪犯的措施;对罪犯的审讯很迅速,而且只是口头问讯。我认为,没有一个国家的罪犯会像在美国那样少于漏网。因为每个人都认为提供犯罪

---

　　①　见附录 I。

more rarely elude punishment. The reason is that everyone conceives himself to be interested in furnishing evidence of the crime and in seizing the delinquent. During my stay in the United States I witnessed the spontaneous formation of committees in a county for the pursuit and prosecution of a man who had committed a great crime. In Europe a criminal is an unhappy man who is struggling for his life against the agents of power, while the people are merely a spectator of the conflict; in America he is looked upon as an enemy of the human race, and the whole of mankind is against him.

I believe that provincial institutions are useful to all nations, but nowhere do they appear to me to be more necessary than among a democratic people. In an aristocracy order can always be maintained in the midst of liberty; and as the rulers have a great deal to lose, order is to them a matter of great interest. In like manner an aristocracy protects the people from the excesses of despotism, because it always possesses an organized power ready to resist a despot. But a democracy without provincial institutions has no security against these evils. How can a populace unaccustomed to freedom in small concerns learn to use it temperately in great affairs? What resistance can be offered to tyranny in a country where each individual is weak and where the citizens are not united by any common interest? Those who dread the license of the mob and those who fear absolute power ought alike to desire the gradual development of provincial liberties.

I am also convinced that democratic nations are most likely to fall beneath the yoke of a centralized administration, for several reasons, among which is the following:

The constant tendency of these nations is to concentrate all the strength of the government in the hands of the only power that directly represents the people; because beyond the people nothing is to be perceived but a mass of equal individuals. But when the same power already has all the attributes of government, it can scarcely refrain from penetrating into the details of the administration, and an opportunity of doing so is sure to present itself in the long run, as was the case in France. In the French Revolution there were two impulses in opposite directions, which must never be confounded; the one was favorable to liberty, the other to despotism. Under the ancient monarchy the king

的证据和擒拿罪犯,与自己的利害有着密切的关系。我在旅美期间,曾亲眼见证在一个发生重大案件的县的居民,为追捕犯人和把他送交法院惩治而自动组织了一个委员会。在欧洲,罪犯在逃时被官员擒获,算他自己倒霉,居民在这场斗争中只是旁观者;但在美国,罪犯都被视为人类的敌人,全人类都会攻击他。

我认为地方分权制度对于所有国家都是有益的,但没有一个国家会比民主制国家的人民更需要他。在贵族阶层中,只有维持一定的秩序,才能永远确保自由。由于统治阶级因混乱造成的损失较多,所以他们特别关心秩序。也可以说,贵族体制可以保护人民逃避专制的过分压迫,而总是拥有有组织的可以随时反抗暴君的强大力量。但是没有地方分权制度的民主政体,不会有抵抗这种灾难的任何保障。老百姓在小事情上都没有学会使用民主,又怎么可能在大事情上很好地运用它呢?在每个人都软弱无权且未被任何共同的利益联合起来的国家里怎么能抵抗暴政呢?因此,害怕人民造反和恐惧政府专制的人,都应该同样渴望能逐步发展地方的自由。

我也同样确信,民主制国家更易于陷入行政集权的束缚。而导致这种结果的原因很多,但最主要的是:

这些国家的恒久趋势是集中政府的一切直接代表人民的唯一权力,因为除了人民之外,再也没有什么了,但这个人民不过是一大群完全平等的个人。但是,当这个权力机关一旦具有政府的一切属性的时候,它几乎不可能阻止设法干预行政工作的细节,而且久而久之,它决不会找不到这样干的机会。这种情况在法国就发生过。在法国大革命期间,有两股完全相反并始终不能混淆的力量:一个倾向于自由,一个倾向于专制。在古代的君主专制下,国王是唯一可以制定法律的人。但在君主专权的时候,残缺不全的

was the sole author of the laws; and below the power of the sovereign certain vestiges of provincial institutions, half destroyed, were still distinguishable. These provincial institutions were incoherent, ill arranged, and frequently absurd; in the hands of the aristocracy they had sometimes been converted into instruments of oppression. The Revolution declared itself the enemy at once of royalty and of provincial institutions; it confounded in indiscriminate hatred all that had preceded it, despotic power and the checks to its abuses; and its tendency was at once to republicanize and to centralize. This double character of the French Revolution is a fact which has been adroitly handled by the friends of absolute power. Can they be accused of laboring in the cause of despotism when they are defending that centralized administration which was one of the great innovations of the Revolution? [1] In this manner popularity may be united with hostility to the rights of the people, and the secret slave of tyranny may be the professed lover of freedom.

I have visited the two nations in which the system of provincial liberty has been most perfectly established, and I have listened to the opinions of different parties in those countries. In America I met with men who secretly aspired to destroy the democratic institutions of the Union; in England I found others who openly attacked the aristocracy; but I found no one who did not regard provincial independence as a great good. In both countries I heard a thousand different causes assigned for the evils of the state, but the local system was never mentioned among them. I heard citizens attribute the power and prosperity of their country to a multitude of reasons, but they *all* placed the advantages of local institutions in the foremost rank. Am I to suppose that when men who are naturally so divided on religious opinions and on political theories agree on one point (and that one which they can best judge, as it is one of which they have daily experience) they are all in error? The only nations which deny the utility of provincial liberties are those which have fewest of them; in other words, only those censure the institution who do not know it.

---

[1] See Appendix K.

地方分权制度仍然依稀可见。这种地方分权制度是很不一致的，并且常常显得荒谬可笑。但在贵族体制下，这种制度有时竟变成压迫的工具。法国大革命同时宣布，它本身既反对君主政体，又反对地方分权制度。它不加选择地仇恨先前发生的一切，既仇恨专制权力，又仇恨可以遏止这种暴政的措施。革命的趋势既是共和主义的，又是中央集权化的。法国大革命的这种双重性，是专制权力的友人最好精心引用的事实。当他们在保卫行政集权的时候，你根本不能说他们是在为专制制度效劳，因为他们说自己是在保卫大革命的主要革新之一。① 这样，民众和敌人，即自由的公开爱好者和暴政的隐蔽仆人，便都可以享有人民的权利了。

我曾经访问过两个地方自由制度高度发达的国家，并细心地聆听过这些国家的两个不同政党的意见。在美国，我发现有人想暗中破坏联邦的民主制度；在英国，我发现有人明目张胆地反对贵族体制。但我发现没有一个国家的人民会不认为地方自由是一件大好事。在这两个国家，我听到人们把国家的弊端归咎于许多因素，但他们从来不把地方自由归为其内。我还听到公民们说他们国家的强大和繁荣有一大堆原因，但他们在列举优点时都把地方自由放在首位。我发现，尽管他们在宗教教义和政治学说方面显然不同，但在他们每天目睹的、因而可以做出正确判断的唯一事实上却意见一致。我的这个发现会是错的吗？只有地方自治制度不发达或根本不实行这种制度的国家，才否认这种制度的好处。换句话说，只有不懂得这个制度的人，才会谴责这个制度。

---

① 见附录 K。

CHAPTER VI

Judical Power In The United States, And Its Influence On Political Society

The Angl O-americans have retained the characteristics of judicial power which are common to other nations — They have, however, made it a powerful political organ — How — In what the judicial system of the Anglo-Americans differs from that of all other nations — Why the American judges have the right of declaring laws to be unconstitutional — How they use this right Precattions taken by the legislator to prevent its abuse.

I Have thought it right to devote a separate chapter to the judicial authorities of the United States, lest their great political importance should be lessened in the reader's eyes by merely incidental mention of them. Confederations have existed in other countries besides America; I have seen republics elsewhere than upon the shores of the New World alone: the representative system of government has been adopted in several states of Europe; but I am not aware that any nation of the globe has hitherto organized a judicial power in the same manner as the Americans. The judicial organization of the United States is the institution which a stranger has the greatest difficulty in understanding. He hears the authority of a judge invoked in the political occurrences of every day, and he naturally concludes that in the United States the judges are important political functionaries; nevertheless, when he examines the nature of the tribunals, they offer at the first glance nothing that is contrary to the usual habits and privileges of those bodies; and the magistrates seem to him to interfere in public affairs only by chance, but by a chance that recurs every day.

When the Parliament of Paris remonstrated, or refused to register

第六章 美国的司法权以及它 对政治社会的影响

英籍美国人维持了司法的特有通性,这点在其他国家也是一样的——但他们使司法权变成了强大的政治权力——怎样变的呢——英籍美国人的司法制度在哪些方面与其他所有国家不同为什么美国法官有权宣布法律违宪——他们又是怎样利用这项权力——立法者为了防止滥用这项权力而采取的措施。

我准备计划用一个独立章节来讨论美国的司法权。以免读者会因我简单的一笔带过而忽略美国司法权的政治作用,除了美国之外,联邦的组织已相继在其他国家出现。共和政体不单存在于新大陆的海岸,而且也出现在世界上其他地方。欧洲好几个国家已采用代议制形式。但我认为,迄今为止,世界上任何一个国家,还没有像美国这样建立过司法权。使一个外人最难理解的是美国的司法组织。因为几乎每天发生的所有政治事件都是要求助于法官的权威的。所以,他自然会得出结论说,法官在美国是很强大的政治势力之一。当他继续考察法院的特性时,他一眼就可以看清这些特性与一般的程序没什么区别。法官好像只是偶尔干预公共事务,但这种偶然性却是天天出现。

当巴黎的最高法院驳回或拒绝政府的法案或法令的备案时,

an edict, or when it summoned a functionary accused of malversation to its bar, its political influence as a judicial body was clearly visible; but nothing of the kind is to be seen in the United States. The Americans have retained all the ordinary characteristics of judicial authority and have carefully restricted its action to the ordinary circle of its functions.

The first characteristic of judicial power in all nations is the duty of arbitration. But rights must be contested in order to warrant the interference of a tribunal; and an action must be brought before the decision of a judge can be had. As long, therefore, as a law is uncontested, the judicial authority is not called upon to discuss it, and it may exist without being perceived. When a judge in a given case attacks a law relating to that case, he extends the circle of his customary duties, without, however, stepping beyond it, since he is in some measure obliged to decide upon the law in order to decide the case. But if he pronounces upon a law without proceeding from a case, he clearly steps beyond his sphere and invades that of the legislative authority.

The second characteristic of judicial power is that it pronounces on special cases, and not upon general principles. If a judge, in deciding a particular point, destroys a general principle by passing a judgment which tends to reject all the inferences from that principle, and consequently to annul it, he remains within the ordinary limits of his functions. But if he directly attacks a general principle without having a particular case in view, he leaves the circle in which all nations have agreed to confine his authority; he assumes a more important and perhaps a more useful influence than that of the magistrate, but he ceases to represent the judicial power.

The third characteristic of the judicial power is that it can act only when it is called upon, or when, in legal phrase, it has taken cognizance of an affair. This characteristic is less general than the other two; but, not with standing the exceptions, I think it may be regarded as essential. The judicial power is, by its nature, devoid of action; it must be put in motion in order to produce a result. When it is called upon to repress a crime, it punishes the criminal; when a wrong is to

或当它本身传讯一个被控渎职的官员时,司法权的政治作用会很明显的表现出来。但在美国,却看不到这类事情。美国人仍然保留了司法权的一切众所周知的特征。他们严格地把司法权局限于有章可循的范围之内。

司法权的第一特征在所有国家都表现为对案件进行调停。要使法院发挥作用,就得有争讼的案件。要使法官进行裁判,就得有提交审理的诉讼案件。因此,要是没有依法提出诉讼的案件,司法权便发挥不到其作用。它的存在就更失去了意义。当法官审理一个案件而斥责与此案件有关的法律时,他只是扩大了自己的职权范围,而并非越出了这个范围,因为在审理案件之前,他一定要对该项法律进行一定的判断。但如果在法官开始审理案件之前就对此法律有一定看法,那他就是完全的越权,侵犯了立法权。

司法权的第二个特征,是审理特殊案件,而不能对全国的一般原则进行宣判。当法官判决某一特殊案件,由于他认为某些一般原则的一切推论都不适合而认为其无效并加以破坏时,他并没有越出应有的职权范围。但是,当法官直接指责一般原则或在没有审核特殊案件时而破坏一般原则,他就越出了所有国家都同意应予限制的法官的职权范围,因为他擅自取得了比一般官员更重要而且或许是更有用的权限,但他却因此也不再代表司法权。

司法权的第三个特征,是只有它在被请求的时候,或用法律的术语来讲,只有在它审案件的时候,它才采取行动。这个特征不如其他两个普遍。尽管会存在一些例外,但我认为,这个特征仍然可以被看作是最重要的。司法权的特性是其自身不是主动的。要想有结果,就一定得推动它,使它行动。当它审理犯罪案件时,它就惩罚犯罪的人;当它需要纠正一个非法行为,它就加以纠正;当它审

be redressed, it is ready to redress it; when an act requires interpretation, it is prepared to interpret it; but it does not pursue criminals, hunt out wrongs, or examine evidence of its own accord. A judicial functionary who should take the initiative and usurp the censureship of the laws would in some measure do violence to the passive nature of his authority.

The Americans have retained these three distinguishing characteristics of the judicial power: an American judge can pronounce a decision only when lhtigation has arisen, he is conversant only with special cases, and he cannot act until the cause has been duly brought before the court. His position is therefore exactly the same as that of the magistrates of other nations; and yet he is invested with immense political power. How does this come about? If the sphere of his authority and his means of action are the same as those of other judges, whence does he drive a power which they do not possess? The cause of this difference lies in the simple fact that the Americans have acknowledged the right of judges to found their decisions on the *Constitution* rather than on the laws. In other words, they have permitted them not to apply such laws as may appear to them to be unconstitutional.

I am aware that a similar right has been sometimes claimed, but claimed in vain, by courts of justice in other countries; but in America it is recognized by all the authorities; and not a party, not so much as an individual, is found to contest it. This fact can be explained only by the principles of the American constitutions. In France the constitution is, or at least is supposed to be, immutable; and the received theory is that no power has the right of changing any part of it. [1] In England the constitution may change continually, [2] or rather it does not in reality exist; the Parliament is at once a legislative and a constituent assembly. The political theories of America are more simple and more rational. An American constitution is not supposed to be immutable, as in France; nor is it susceptible of modification by the

---

[1] See Appendix L.
[2] See Appendix M.

查一项需要解释的法案时,它就予以解释。但是,它不能自己去追捕罪犯、调查非法行为和纠察事实。如果它主动出面并以法律的检查者的身份行动,那它就有超越权力的嫌疑。

美国人保存了司法权的这三个显著特征。只有当有人起诉的时候,美国的法官才能审理案件。这点没有例外,只受理特殊案件,而且总是要在接到起诉书后才采取行动。因此,美国的法官跟其他国家的司法官员没什么不同,但他们被授予巨大的政治权力。这是怎样产生的呢? 如果他们的权力范围和他们行使权力的手段与其他国家的法官没有不同,那他们为什么又拥有其他国家法官所没有的权力呢? 其原因就在于:美国人认为法官对公民进行判决的权力是根据宪法,而不是根据法律。换句话说,美国人允许法官可以不使用那些在他们认为是违宪的法律。

事实上,其他国家的法院有时也要求过类似的权力,但它们从来没有成功过。而在美国,各方面都承认法官的这项权力,没有一个政党,甚至是一个个人对此提出过异议。这个现象可从美国宪法规定的这项原则中得到解释。在法国,宪法是不可修改的,至少被认为是不可修改的;没有任何权威能对宪法做任何修改。① 在英国,国会有权修改宪法。因此,在英国,宪法是可以不断被修改的,②或者说它根本没有真正地存在过。国会既是立法机关,又是制宪机构。而在美国,政治理论是比较简单和比较合理的。美国的宪法并不像在法国那样被认为是不可修改的,但也不像在英国那样可被社会的公认权威所修改。它是在完全公平

①　见附录 L。
②　见附录 M。

ordinary powers of society, as in England. It constitutes a detached whole, which, as it represents the will of the whole people, is no less binding on the legislator than on the private citizen, but which may be altered by the will of the people in predetermined cases, according to established rules. In America the Constitution may therefore vary; but as long as it exists, it is the origin of all authority, and the sole vehicle of the predominating force.

It is easy to perceive how these differences must act upon the position and the rights of the judicial bodies in the three countries I have cited. If in France the tribunals were authorized to disobey the laws on the ground of their being opposed to the constitution, the constituent power would in fact be placed in their hands, since they alone would have the right of interpreting a constitution of which no authority could change the terms. They would therefore take the place of the nation and exercise as absolute a sway over society as the inherent weakness of judicial power would allow them to do. Undoubtedly, as the French judges are incompetent to declare a law to be unconstitutional, the power of changing the constitution is indirectly given to the legislative body, since no legal barrier would oppose the alterations that it might prescribe. But it is still better to grant the power of changing the constitution of the people to men who represent (however imperfectly) the will of the people than to men who represent no one but themselves.

It would be still more unreasonable to invest the English judges with the right of resisting the decisions of the legislative body, since the Parliament which makes the laws also makes the constitution; and consequently a law emanating from the three estates of the realm can in no case be unconstitutional. But neither of these remarks is applicable to America. In the United States the Constitution governs the legislator as much as the private citizen: as it is the first of laws, it cannot be modified by a law; and it is therefore just that the tribunals should obey the Constitution in preference to any law. This condition belongs to the very essence of the judicature; for to select that legal obligation by which he is most strictly bound is in some sort the natural right of every magistrate.

In France the constitution is also the first of laws, and the judges have the same right to take it as the ground of their decisions; but were they to exercise this right, they must perforce encroach on rights more sacred than their own: namely, on those of society, in whose

的基础上建立的,代表全体人民的意志,立法者和普通公民均须遵守;但可以根据规定的程序,在预先规定的条件下,按照人民的意志加以修改。因此,美国的宪法是可以变动的,但只要它存在一天,一切机构和个人都得服从它。只有它拥有统治的权威。

因此可以很容易地发现,这些差异一定会影响我所说的这三个国家的司法机关的地位和权力。如果在法国,法院可以以法律违宪为理由而不服从法律,那么,法国的制宪权实际上就将被法院控制,因为只有它们将会有权解释谁也无权更改其条例的宪法。因此,它们将会代替国家和统治社会,并且司法权所固有的弱点也会允许它们这样做。毋庸置疑,法国的法官无法宣布法律违宪,所以法国的宪法修改权便间接地落在了立法机关,因为没有合法的障碍来阻止它修改宪法。但是还是应该把宪法的修改权赋予能代表人民意志的人,这样总比赋予除了代表自己谁也不能代表的人为好。

如果赋予英国法官以抵制立法机构的意志的权利,那将更加不合理,因为制定法律的议会同时也制定宪法,因此,凡由这三个地方公布的法律,都不能认为是违宪的。但是这两个推论都不适用于美国。在美国,宪法不仅制约着普通公民,同样也制约着立法者。因此,美国的宪法是一切法律之首,是其他任何法律所不能修改的。由此可见,法院在执行法律的时候必须要先服从宪法。这正是司法权的本质,即法官在选择合法的处置办法时,要从其中选择最合乎根本大法的办法,乃是他的天然权利。

在法国,宪法同样是一切法律之首,法官也有权以它作为判决的基础;但在行使这项权力时,他们又有可能侵犯比这项权力更为神圣的其他权力,即侵犯他们所代表的国家的权力。在这种

name they are acting. In this case reasons of state clearly prevail over ordinary motives. In America, where the nation can always reduce its magistrates to obedience by changing its Constitution, no danger of this kind is to be feared. Upon this point, therefore, the political and the logical reason agree, and the people as well as the judges preserve their privileges.

Whenever a law that the judge holds to be unconstitutional is invoked in a tribunal of the United States, he may refuse to admit it as ` rule; this power is the only one peculiar to the American magistrate, but it gives rise to immense political influence. In truth, few laws can escape the searching analysis of the judicial power for any length of time, for there are few that are not prejudicial to some private interest or other, and none that may not be brought before a court of justice by the choice of parties or by the necessity of the case. But as soon as a judge has refused to apply any given law in a case, that law immediately loses a portion of its moral force. Those to whom it is prejudicial learn that means exist of overcoming its authority, and similar suits are multiplied until it becomes powerless. The alternative, then, is, that the people must alter the Constitution or the legislature must repeal the law. The political power which the Americans have entrusted to their courts of justice is therefore immense, but the evils of this power are considerably diminished by the impossibility of attacking the laws except through the courts of justice. If the judge had been empowered to contest the law on the ground of theoretical generalities, if he were able to take the initiative and to censure the legislator, he would play a prominent political part; and as the champion or the antagonist of a party, he would have brought the hostile passions of the nation into the conflict. But when a judge contests a law in an obscure debate on some particular case, the importance of his attack is concealed from public notice; his decision bears upon the interest of an individual, and the law is slighted only incidentally. Moreover, although it is censured, it is not abolished; its moral force may be diminished, but its authority is not taken away; and its final destruction can be accomplished only by the reiterated attacks of judicial functionaries.

情况下,普通原因必须让步于国家原因。在美国,国家永远可以通过修改宪法的办法使法官服从,所以不必害怕这种危险。因此,在这一点上,政治和逻辑是一致的,而人民和法官也都保存了他们各自的特权。

因此,在要求美国的法院承认一项在法官看来是违宪的法律时,法官有权拒绝。这项权利虽然是美国法官所特有的,但却有着巨大的政治影响。实际上,很少有法律能够长期逃脱法官的验证分析,因为法律很少不涉及私人利益,而且诉讼当事人在涉及他的利益时也可以和必然向法院提出异议。但是,当法官在办案中拒绝应用某项法律之日起,这项法律便将立即失去其一部分道德力。这时,那些利益受损的人就会想尽方法不去履行该项法律所规定的义务,以导致此类诉讼案件开始增加,而该项法律也将变得无力。结果就出现了这样的选择,不是人民修改宪法,就是立法机构宣布废除该项法律,两者必选其一。虽然美国人赋予法院强大的政治权力,但如果法院强迫他们服从的时候,他们也可以通过司法手段来抵制,这样就可以大大减少这种权力的弊端。如果法官可以根据理论基础抵制法律,如果他可以自主行动和责难立法者,那他就在政治方面扮演了重要的角色,变成某一政党的支持者或反对者,激起全国人民参加斗争的激情。但是,当法官在一件不甚重要的政治纠纷和特殊案件中抵制法律的时候,其抵制的重要性可能吸引不了公众的注意力。这时,他的决定只能影响到个别人的利益,而法律也只是附带性地受到了损害。还有,它仅仅是受到损害,并不至于被废除,因为只是它的道德力被减弱了,而它的权威性还没有被剥夺。它最终的废除只有经过一步一步地抵制和在无数判例的反复验证

It will be seen, also, that by leaving it to private interest to censure the law, and by intimately uniting the trial of the law with the trial of an individual, legislation is protected from wanton assaults and from the daily aggressions of party spirit. The errors of the legislator are exposed only to meet a real want; and it is always a positive and appreciable fact that must serve as the basis of a prosecution.

I am inclined to believe this practice of the American courts to be at once most favorable to liberty and to public order. If the judge could attack the legislator only openly and directly, he would sometimes be afraid to oppose him; and at other times party spirit might encourage him to brave it at every turn. The laws would consequently be attacked when the power from which they emanated was weak, and obeyed when it was strong; that is to say, when it would be useful to respect them, they would often be contested; and when it would be easy to convert them into an instrument of oppression, they would be respected. But the American judge is brought into the political arena independently of his own will. He judges the law only because he is obliged to judge a case. The political question that he is called upon to resolve is connected with the interests of the parties, and he cannot refuse to decide it without a denial of justice. He performs his functions as a citizen by fulfilling the precise duties which belong to his profession as a magistrate. It is true that, upon this system, the judicial censorship of the courts of justice over the legislature cannot extend to all laws indiscriminately, in as much as some of them can never give rise to that precise species of contest which is termed a lawsuit; and even when such a contest is possible, it may happen that no one cares to bring it before a court of justice. The Americans have often felt this inconvenience; but they have left the remedy incomplete, lest they should give it an efficacy that might in some cases prove dangerous. Within these limits the power vested in the American courts of justice of pronouncing a statute to be unconstitutional forms one of the most powerful barriers that have ever been devised against the tyranny of political assemblies.

下才有效。并且不难看出,允许私人弹劾法律,把对法律的审判与对人的审判紧密结合起来,还会保证法制不致轻易地受到攻击。也同样确保法制不再天天遭到政党的侵略。立法者的错误只有在遇到实际的需要时才会暴露出来,即必须实事求是和有据可查,因为这要作为审理案件的依据。

我非常相信,美国法院的这种做法对自由和公共秩序都十分有利。如果法官只能正面地或公开地攻击立法者,他有时就不敢这样做;而在另一些时候,党派精神又会给他勇气,让他敢于去做。结果,制定法律的权力机关软弱时,法律就会受到攻击;当这个机关强大时,人们便会老老实实地服从法律。也就是说,当人们感到尊重法律对自己最有好处时,他们常常会攻击法律;而当法律容易转变成压迫工具体时,他们反而会尊重法律。但是,美国的法官是不由自主地被拉上政治舞台的。他们审视法律,是因为有要审理的案件,一些需要他们解决的政治问题都与政党的利益息息相关,而他们又不能拒不审理。只要他们不否认正义,他们就不能拒不审理。作为法官,他们在执行职业的职责时,就相当于在尽公民的义务。不错,在这种制度下,法院对立法机构进行的司法弹劾,是不能毫无顾忌地涉及所有法律的,因为有些法律决不会引起那种称之为诉讼的针锋相对的斗争。尽管有可能出现这种争端,也没有人愿意把它递交到法院解决。美国人也常常会感到这种办法的不便,但他们宁愿修修补补,不作彻底修正,唯恐完全修正之后会在一些案件上产生危险的后果。美国法院所特有的这种在有限范围内可以宣布某项法律违宪的权力,也是迄今为止人们为反对议会政治的专横而筑起的强大壁垒之一。

Other Powers Granted To Amrican Judges.

In the United States all the citizens have the right of indicting the public functionaries before the ordinary tribunals — How they use this right ART. 75 of the French Constitution of the year VIII The Americans and the English cannot understand the purport of this article.

It is hardly necessary to say that in a free country like America all the citizens have the right of indicting public functionaries before the ordinary tribunals, and that all the judges have the power of convicting public officers. The right granted to the courts of justice of punishing the agents of the executive government when they violate the laws is so natural a one that it cannot be looked upon as an extraordinary privilege. Nor do the springs of government appear to me to be weakened in the United States by rendering all public officers responsible to the tribunals. The Americans seem, on the contrary, to have increased by this means that respect which is due to the authorities, and at the same time to have made these authorities more careful not to offend. I was struck by the small number of political trials that occur in the United States, but I had no difficulty in accounting for this circumstance. A prosecution, of whatever nature it may be, is always a difficult and expensive undertaking. It is easy to attack a public man in the journals, but the motives for bringing him before the tribunals must be serious. A solid ground of complaint must exist before anyone thinks of prosecuting a public officer, and these officers are careful not to furnish such grounds of complaint when they are afraid of being prosecuted.

This does not depend upon the republican form of American institutions, for the same thing happens in England. These two nations do not regard the impeachment of the principal officers of state as the guarantee of their independence. But they hold that it is rather by minor prosecutions, which the humblest citizen can institute at any time, that liberty is protected, and not by those great judicial procedures which are rarely employed until it is too late.

In the Middle Ages, when it was very difficult to reach offenders, the judges inflicted frightful punishments on the few who were arrested; but this did not diminish the number of crimes.

授予美国法官的其他权力

在美国,所有公民都有权向普通法院控告公共官员——他们怎样使用这项权利——法国第八年宪法的第七十五条——美国人和英国人都无法理解这一条的意义。

不知是否有必要谈一谈在像美国这样自由的国家,所有公民都有权向普通法院的法官控告公共官员,所有的法官也都有权处罚公共官员。而法院处罚违反法律的行政官员是他们的自然权力,并非是授予法院的特权。我认为,美国让全体公共官员对法院负责,并没有削弱政府的权力。相反,美国人在这样做的时候,却使政府应当享有的尊重得到加强,而政府也更加注意工作,以免遭到控诉。我从来没有见到哪个国家的政治诉讼案件像美国那样少,而且我也不难说明其原因。任何形式的诉讼案件都是一件困难和费钱的事。在报纸杂志上攻击一个普通人很容易,但要把他告到法庭去受审,就不得不小心谨慎。因此,要依法对一个官员起诉,就得有控诉他的充分的正当理由。但如果官员害怕被控诉,他就绝对不会向人们提供这样的理由。

这种现象并不是由美国的共和制度所决定的,因为同样的情况也可以在英国发生。这两个国家的人民都不曾认为把国家的主要官员置于法院的监督之下,他们的独立就有了保证。他们认为要想确保自由,与其依靠他们从未求助过的或很晚才能提出的繁琐的诉讼程序,不如依靠普通老百姓在任何时候都可以提出的简单的诉讼程序。

在中世纪时是很难抓住在逃罪犯的,法官在逮捕了几个罪犯之后,往往要对这些落网的人实施严酷的刑罚,但这并没有减少

It has since been discovered that when justice is more certain and more mild, it is more efficacious. The English and the Americans hold that tyranny and oppression are to be treated like any other crime, by lessening the penalty and facilitating conviction.

In the year VIII of the French Republic a constitution was drawn up in which the following clause was introduced: "Art. 75. All the agents of the government below the rank of ministers can be prosecuted for offenses relating to their several functions only by virtue of a decree of the council of state; in which case the prosecution takes place before the ordinary tribunals." This clause survived the Constitution of the year VIII and is still maintained, in spite of the just complaints of the nation. I have always found a difficulty in explaining its meaning to Englishmen or Americans, and have hardly understood it myself. They at once perceived that, the council of state in France being a great tribunal established in the center of the kingdom, it was a sort of tyranny to send all complainants before it as a preliminary step. But when I told them that the council of state was not a judicial body in the common sense of the term, but an administrative council composed of men dependent on the crown, so that the king, after having ordered one of his servants, called a prefect, to commit an Judicial Power in the United States injustice, has the power of commanding another of his servants, called a councillor of state, to prevent the former from being punished. When I showed them that the citizen who has been injured by an order of the sovereign is obliged to ask the sovereign's permission to obtain redress, they refused to credit so flagrant an abuse and were tempted to accuse me of falsehood or ignorance. It frequently happened before the Revolution that a parliament issued a warrant against a public officer who had committed an offense. Sometimes the royal authority intervened and quashed the proceedings. Despotism then showed itself openly, and men obeyed it only by submitting to superior force. It is painful to perceive how much lower we are sunk than our forefathers, since we allow things to pass, under the color of justice and the sanction of law, which violence alone imposed upon them.

犯罪数。后来被证明,审判越是正确和温和,就越是有效。英国人和美国人认为,应把暴政和压迫都视为犯罪,所以他们简化了审讯程序,并减轻了刑罚。

法国第八年公布了一部宪法,其中第七十五条写道:"部长级以下的政府官员因职务关系而犯罪时,只有根据行政法院的决定才可以被捕。这时,可向普通法院起诉。"第八年宪法已经被废除了,但这一条并没有废除,至今仍被保留,而且每天都会遭到公民的抱怨。我发现很难向英国人和美国人解释,并试图叫他们理解这第七十五条的意义,因为连我自己都很难懂。他们曾经以为,法国的行政法院是王国中央设立的一个大法院,而首先要把所有的原告都推到那里去,在他们看来是一种暴政。但是,当我告诉他们行政法院不是一般意义上的司法机构,而是一个成员直接隶属于国王的行政机构,所以当国王命令他的一个叫做省长的臣仆违法之后,可以命令另一个叫做行政法院法官的臣仆去使前者免受惩处的时候;当我向他们解释公民是因为君主的命令而受到损害,而只能向君主本人要求损失赔偿的时候,他们根本无法相信天下会有如此荒谬的事情。在大革命以前的法国君主政体时代,经常是由最高法院下令逮捕犯罪的公共官员。有时王权会进行干涉,拒绝诉讼。于是,这种暴政便暴露出它的真面目,但人们只是在压力之下才服从于它。我们会不情愿地发现,我们又后退回到我们祖先所处的状态,因为在今天,依靠暴力而强加于人的事情,在正义与法律的掩盖下得到了合法的名义。

CHAPTER VII
Political Jurisdiction
In The United States

Definition of political jurisdiction — What is understood by political jurisdiction in France, in England, and in the United States — In America the political judge has to do only with public officers — He more frequently decrees removal from office than an ordinary penalty — Political jurisdiction as it exists in the United States is, not withstanding its mildness, and perhaps in consequence of that mildness, a most powerful instrument in the hands of the majority.

I Understand by political jurisdiction that temporary right of pronouncing a legal decision with which a political body may be invested.

In absolute governments it is useless to introduce any extraordinary forms of procedure; the prince, in whose name an offender is prosecuted, is as much the sovereign of the courts of justice as of everything else, and the idea that is entertained of his power is of itself a sufficient security. The only thing he has to fear is that the external formalities of justice should be neglected and that his authority should be dishonored, from a wish to strengthen it. But in most free countries, in which the majority can never have the same influence over the tribunals as an absolute monarch, the judicial power has occasionally been vested for a time in the representatives of the people. It has been thought better temporarily to merge the functions of the different authorities than to violate the necessary principle of the unity of government.

England, France, and the United States have established this political jurisdiction by law; and it is curious to see the different use that these three great nations have made of it. In England and in France the House of Lords and the Chamber of Peers constitute the highest criminal court [1] of their respective nations; and although

---

[1] The House of Lords in England is also the court of last resort in certain civil cases. See *Blackstone*, Bk. III, ch. 4.

第七章 美国的政治审判

对政治审判的定义——在法国、英国和美国,人们是怎样理解政治审判的——在美国,政治法官只审理公共官员——在他的判决中,撤职多于普通的刑罚——美国的政治审判是温和的,但也许正是由于这种温和,才使它成为控制多数的最强大武器。

另外我认为,政治审判是一种暂时的权力,是被授予审判权的政治团体所进行的判决。

在专制政府统治下,给审判规定专门的程序是没有用的,因为起诉人是以君主的名义控诉被告的,而君主是法院和全国的主人,他认为除了自己所拥有的权力以外,已没有必要再去寻找其他保障。他唯一害怕的,是人民一贯坚持司法制度的表面手续和由于主张按手续办事而有损于他的权威。但在大部分自由国家,多数表决对法院的影响从来没有像君主专断对法院的影响那样大,司法权往往由人民的代表在任期内行使。有人认为,把这些不同权力暂时融合在一起,总比破坏国家统一的必要原则为好。

英国、法国和美国,都在各自法律的基础上建立了政治审判。并且这三个大国对于政治审判有着各自不同的运用。在英国和法国,由贵族院组成国家的最高刑事法庭。① 尽管这个法庭通常并不

---

① 英国的贵族院在一些特定的案件中是最后一个可以起诉的法庭。见《黑石》,第三卷,第四章。

they do not habitually try all political offenses, they are competent to try them all. Another political body has the right of bringing the accusation before the Peers; the only difference which exists between the two countries in this respect is that in England the Commons may impeach whom so ever they please before the Lords, while in France the Deputies can employ this mode of prosecution only against the ministers of the crown. In both countries the upper house may make use of all the existing penal laws of the nation to punish the delinquents.

In the United States as well as in Europe one branch of the legislature is authorized to impeach and the other to judge: the House of Representatives arraigns the offender, and the Senate punishes him. But the Senate can try only such persons as are brought before it by the House of Representatives, and those persons must belong to the class of public functionaries. Thus the jurisdiction of the Senate is less extensive than that of the Peers of France, while the right of impeachment by the Representatives is more general than that of the Deputies. But the great difference which exists between Europe and America is that in Europe the political tribunals can apply all the enactments of the penal code, while in America, when they have deprived the offender of his official rank and have declared him incapable of filling any political office for the future, their jurisdiction terminates and that of the ordinary tribunals begins. Suppose, for instance, that the President of the United States has committed the crime of high treason; the House of Representatives impeaches him, and the Senate degrades him from office; he must then be tried by a jury, which alone can deprive him of liberty or life. This accurately illustrates the subject we are treating. The political jurisdiction that is established by the laws of Europe is intended to reach great offenders, whatever may be their birth, their rank, or their power in the state; and to this end all the privileges of a court of justice are temporarily given to a great political assembly. The legislator is then transformed into a magistrate; he is called upon to prove, to classify, and to punish the offense; and as he exercises all the authority of a judge, the law imposes upon him all the duties of that high office and requires all the formalities of justice. When a public functionary is impeached before an English or a French political tribunal and is found guilty, the sentence deprives him *ipso facto* of his functions and may pronounce him incapable of resuming them or any others for the future.

But in this case the political interdict is a consequence of the sentence, and not the sentence itself. In Europe, then, the sentence of a political tribunal is a judicial verdict rather than an administrative measure. In the United States the contrary takes place;

审理一切政治罪行,但它也有权这样做。另一个政治团体是享有起诉权的众议院。两国在这方面存在的唯一差别是:在英国,众议院可向贵族院控诉任何它想要控诉的人;而在法国,众议院只能向贵族院控诉国王和大臣。此外,两国的贵族院都可按本国的规定依照刑法打击犯罪分子。

美国的情况和欧洲一样,这两个司法机构一个享有上诉权,而另一个则享有判决权。也就是众议院指控罪犯,参议院处罚罪犯。但是,参议院只能对众议院追诉的财物进行查封,而众议院只能向参议院控告公职人员。因此,美国参议院的权限远远比不上法国贵族院的权限那么大,而美国众议院的起诉权则要比众议院的权限大。但是,美国与欧洲之间的最大差别在于:在欧洲,政治法院可以使用刑法的一切条款;而在美国,政治法院剥夺犯人原来担任的职位,并宣布他将来不得担当任何公职以后,就算完成其任务,而下一步则递交到普通法院处理。假如美国总统犯了叛国大罪,众议院先对他进行弹劾,接着由参议院宣布罢免他的职务。然后,他必须到陪审团出庭受审,因为只有这里可以剥夺他的自由或生命。这实际就恰恰证明了我们所讨论的问题。欧洲人在依法进行政治审判时,都是审理大型的罪犯,不管罪犯是什么出身、什么等级或在国内拥有什么至高无上的权力。这就需要临时组织一个大的政治审判团,并授予它法院的一切特权。当一个公共官员在英国或法国的政治法庭面前被起诉有罪,这时会根据事实给他判罪。甚至可以宣布他将来不得担当任何公职。

但是,政治上的罢免是判决的结果,而不是对职务本身的判决。因此,在欧洲,与其说政治审判是一种行政措施,不如说它是一种司法判决。美国的情况却与此不同。尽管参议院的决定在

and although the decision of the Senate is judicial in its form, since the Senators are obliged to comply with the rules and formalities of a court of justice; although it is judicial also, in respect to the motives on which it is founded, since the Senate is generally obliged to take an offense at common law as the basis of its sentence; yet the political judgment is rather an administrative than a judicial act. If it had been the intention of the American legislator really to invest a political body with great judicial authority, its action would not have been limited to public functionaries, since the most dangerous enemies of the state may not have any public functions; and this is especially true in republics, where party influence has the most force and where the strength of many a leader is increased by his exercising no legitimate power.

If the American legislator had wished to give society itself the means of preventing great offenses by the fear of punishment, according to the practice of ordinary justice, all the resources of the penal code would have been given to the political tribunals. But he gave them only an imperfect weapon, which can never reach the most dangerous offenders, since men who aim at the entire subversion of the laws are not likely to murmur at a political interdict.

The main object of the political jurisdiction that obtains in the United States is therefore to take away the power from him who would make a bad use of it and to prevent him from ever acquiring it again. This is evidently an administrative measure, sanctioned by the formalities of a judicial decision. In this matter the Americans have created a mixed system; they have surrounded the act that removes a public functionary with all the securities of a political trial, and they have deprived political condemnations of their severest penalties. Every link of the system may easily be traced from this point; we at once perceive why the American constitutions subject all the civil functionaries to the jurisdiction of the Senate, while the military, whose crimes are nevertheless more formidable, are exempted from that tribunal. In the civil service none of the American functionaries can be said to be removable; the places that some of them occupy are inalienable, and the others are chosen for a term which cannot be shortened. It is therefore necessary to try them all in order to deprive them of their authority. But military officers are dependent on the chief magistrate of the state, who is himself a civil functionary;

形式上是司法性的,因为参议院必须根据司法机构的规定与程序进行判断。从判决的理由来看,参议院的判决也是司法性的,因为一般说来,参议院必须以普通法上规定的罪行作为它判决的根据;所以美国的政治审判与其说是司法行为,不如说是行政措施。如果说美国立法者的主要目的实际上是将司法大权作为一个政治机构武装起来使用,那么这个政治机构就不会把自己的行动只限于对付公共官员,因为对于国家来说,其最危险的敌人并不可能担任任何职位。在实行共和政体的国家,情况更是如此,因为这些国家的政党的最大利益是控制权力,而且往往是势力越大越非法夺权。

如果美国立法当局为了防止犯罪而赋予社会本身以法官的身份去惩治重大罪行的权力,那么政治法院的措施也要根据刑法典的一切规定来进行。但是,这仅仅是给了政治法院一个不完善的武器,而且这个武器根本不能打击最危险的犯罪行为,因为对于那些企图推翻法律本身的人来说,行政撤职处分的作用并不大。

因此,美国政治审判的主要目的,是剥夺那些滥用权限的官员的权力,并且防止这个公民以后再有机会获得这种权力。很显然,这是一种具有司法判决形式的行政措施。因此,美国人在这方面创造了一种混合制度。他们的政治审判只可以做行政撤职处分,而无权进行严厉的惩罚。这项规定贯穿于整个政治审判制度。因此我们可以发觉,为什么美国及其各州的宪法中规定,只有文职官员受参议院的司法管辖,而把可能犯大罪的军人排除在外。在文职方面,美国可以说没有能被撤职的官员,因为对于一些官员实行的是终身制,而另一些官员在他们当选后的任期内不能罢免。要想剥夺他们的权力,只有交给法院处理。但是,军人直接属于国家元首的级别,而国家元首本身就是文职官员。如果给国家元

and the decision that condemns him is a blow to them all. ①

If we now compare the American and the European systems, we shall meet with differences no less striking in the effects which each of them produces or may produce. In France and England the jurisdiction of political bodies is looked upon as an extraordinary resource, which is only to be employed in order to rescue society from unwonted dangers. It is not to be denied that these tribunals, as they are constituted in Europe, violate the conservative principle of the division of powers in the state and threaten incessantly the lives and liberties of the subject. The same political jurisdiction in the United States is only indirectly hostile to the division of powers; it cannot menace the lives of the citizens, and it does not hover, as in Europe, over the heads of the whole community, since it reaches those only who have voluntarily submitted to its authority by accepting office. It is at the same time less formidable and less efficacious; indeed, it has not been considered by the legislators of the United States as an extreme remedy for the more violent evils of society, but as an ordinary means of government. In this respect it probably exercises more real influence on the social body in America than in Europe. We must not be misled by the apparent mildness of American legislation in all that relates to political jurisdiction. It is to be observed, in the first place, that in the United States the tribunal that passes judgment is composed of the same elements, and subject to the same influences, as the body which impeaches the offender, and that this gives an almost irresistible impulse to the vindictive passions of parties. If political judges in the United States cannot inflict such heavy penalties as those in Europe, there is the less chance of their acquitting an offender; the conviction, if it is less formidable, is more certain. The principal object of the political tribunals of Europe is to punish the offender; of those in America, to deprive him of his power. A political sentence in the United States may therefore be looked upon as a preventive measure; and there is no reason for tying down the judges to the exact definitions of criminal law. Nothing can be more alarming than the vagueness with which political offenses, properly so called, are described

---

① An officer cannot be removed from his grade, but he can be relieved of his command.

首判罪,那么就等于是在打击全体文武官员吗?①

　　如果我们比较一下美国和欧洲的制度,将会明显地发现在它们各自产生的效果方面的不同。在法国和英国,政治审判被看作是一种超常的资源,它仅仅用来拯救在遭重大灾难时的社会。毋庸置疑,欧洲实行的这种政治审判违背了权力的分配原则,并且经常威胁着人民的自由和生命。同样的,这种政治审判在美国只是间接地侵犯了分权的原则,它绝不会威胁到公民的生存。它也不像在欧洲那样盘旋在社会的上空,因为它只打击因渎职犯罪而被它惩治的人。同时,它既不是让人害怕的,也不是效果很明显的。实际上,它并没有被美国的立法机构看作是防治社会重大弊端的良方,而只把它作为政府的一般管理手段。从这个观点来看,它在美国对社会产生的影响比它在欧洲对社会产生的影响更加真实。当然,我们也不能为美国立法在政治审判方面所做的温和表现所迷惑。首先应当指出,美国所用来进行政治审判的法庭,在其成员和其所受的影响上与负责刑事审判的法庭处于同等水平,这就为政党之间的互相报复提供了一种几乎无法抵抗的动力。美国的政治法官不能像欧洲的政治法官那样判决重大刑罚,他们做无罪宣判的情况也很少。使人确信的是他们所做的判决并不可怕,但很切合实际。欧洲的政治审判的主要目的是惩罚罪犯。而在美国则主要是为了剥夺罪犯的权力。美国的政治审判可以被看作是一种预防措施。因此,政治法官不必被限制在刑法的条条框框里。任何一种法律都不会比美国法律在给按照意思的政治罪下定义时表现的似是而非更使人惊讶的

---

① 　一个官员不可能被革职,但可以被免除其命令的权力。

in the laws of America. Article II, Section 4 of the Constitution of the United States runs thus: "The President, Vice President, and all civil officers of the United States shall be removed from office on impeachment for, and conviction of, treason, bribery, *or other high crimes and misdemeanors.*" Many of the constitutions of the states are even less explicit. "Public officers," says the Constitution of Massachusetts, "shall be impeached for misconduct or maladministration." ①The Constitution of Virginia declares that "all the civil officers who shall have offended against the State by maladministration, corruption, or other high crimes, may be impeached by the House of Delegates." In some of the states the constitutions do not specify any offenses, in order to subject the public functionaries to an unlimited responsibility. ② I venture to affirm that it is precisely their mildness that renders the American laws so formidable in this respect. I have shown that in Europe the removal of a functionary and his political disqualification are the consequences of the penalty he is to undergo, and that in America they constitute the penalty itself. The consequence is that in Europe political tribunals are invested with terrible powers which they are afraid to use, and the fear of punishing too much hinders them from punishing at all. But in America no one hesitates to inflict a penalty from which humanity does not recoil. To condemn a political opponent to death in order to deprive him of his power is to commit what all the world would execrate as a horrible assassination, but to declare that opponent unworthy to exercise that authority and to deprive him of it, leaving him uninjured in life and limb, may seem to be the fair issue of the struggle. But this sentence, which it is so easy to pronounce, is not the less fatally severe to most of those upon whom it is inflicted. Great criminals may undoubtedly brave its vain rigor, but ordinary offenders will dread it as a condemnation that destroys their position in the world, casts a blight upon their honor, and condemns them to a shameful inactivity worse than death. In the United States the influence exercised upon the progress of society by the jurisdiction of political bodies is the more powerful in proportion as it seems less frightful.

---

① Chap. I, section 2, § 8.
② See the Constitutions of Illinois, Maine, Connecticut, and Georgia.

了。《美利坚合众国宪法》第二条第四项写道:"总统、副总统和合众国的一切文职官员,凡因叛国罪、贿赂罪或其他重罪轻罪的弹劾并被判定有罪时,应被罢免其职位。"而大部分州的宪法,对政治罪描述得更不明确。《马萨诸塞州宪法》写道:"一些渎职和施政不善的官员应被责罚。"①《弗吉尼亚州宪法》写道:"因施政不善、贪污或其他重罪轻罪而使本州受损失的一切官员,将受州众议院的弹劾。"有些州的宪法根本没有对任何一种罪行进行罗列,这就将巨大的责任压在公共官员身上。这就使公共官员承担了无限的责任。② 但是,我敢断言,正是美国法律的这种温和性,使它在这方面显得如此可怕。我已经表示过:在欧洲,对一个官员的撤职和剥夺政治权力,是他受到刑罚的结果,而在美国,这种处分本身就是刑罚。结果,就出现了,在欧洲,虽然赋予了政治法院以令人可怕的权力,但它却害怕不知如何使用,并且因害怕惩罚过重,而根本就不去惩罚。但是在美国,没有人会犹豫去实施一种根本不会对人身造成痛苦的惩罚;对于判处政治敌人死刑而为了剥夺其权力的做法,则被视为是一种可怕的暗杀;美国人认为,宣布政敌不配行使其权力而剥夺他的权力,同时让他自由和不伤害他的生命,才是斗争的最公正的结果。但是,这种十分容易作出的判决,对于被处罚的大多数人来说,也是极其痛苦的。一些重大罪犯可能根本不把判决放在眼里;而普通犯人则会非常害怕,他把这种宣判看成是使他失去地位和名誉扫地的判决,认为这种判决让其过着生不如死的生活。因此,美国的政治审判对社会生活的影响虽然不太可

---

① 第一章,第二部分,第八节。
② 见伊利诺伊、缅因、康涅狄格和佐治亚州的宪法。

It does not directly coerce the subject, but it renders the majority more absolute over those in power; it does not give to the legislature an unbounded authority that can be exerted only at some great crisis, but it establishes a temperate and regular influence, which is at all times available. If the power is decreased, it can, on the other hand, be more conveniently employed, and more easily abused. By preventing political tribunals from inflicting judicial punishments, the Americans seem to have eluded the worst consequences of legislative tyranny rather than tyranny itself; and I am not sure that political jurisdiction, as it is constituted in the United States, is not, all things considered, the most formidable weapon that has ever been placed in the grasp of a majority. When the American republics begin to degenerate, it will be easy to verify the truth of this observation by remarking whether the number of political impeachments is increased. ①

---

① See Appendix N.

怕,但实际上是很厉害的。政治审判不直接强加于被治者,但它是使为政者获得多数选票的非常重要的手段。它不授予立法机构以只有在危急时期才能行使的无限大权,而是让它随时具有可行使的适度的常规权力。如果授予的权力不够大,虽然便于行使,同时也容易被滥用。因此,美国人为了阻止让政治法院作刑事判决,与其说是他们为了躲避立法暴政本身,不如说是为了躲避立法暴政所产生的可怕后果。总而言之,我不确定美国实行的政治审判,是不是多数迄今掌握过的武器中的最强大武器。当美国的共和政体开始衰败的时候,人们可以很容易的检验我的说法,因为只要看一看是否政治审判的数量有所增加就可以了。①

①　见附录 N。

CHAPTER VIII
The Federal Constitution

I have hitherto considered each state as a separate whole and have explained the different springs which the people there put in motion, and the different means of action which it employs. But all the states which I have considered as independent are yet forced to submit, in certain cases, to the supreme authority of the Union. The time has now come to examine the portion of sovereignty that has been granted to the Union, and to cast a rapid glance over the Federal Constitution.

History Of The Federal Constitution

Origin of the first Union — Its weakness — Congress appeals to the constituent authority — Interval of two years between this appeal and the promulgation of the new Constitution.

The thirteen colonies, which simultaneously threw off the yoke of England towards the end of the last century, had, as I have already said, the same religion, the same language, the same customs, and almost the same laws; they were struggling against a common enemy; and these reasons were sufficiently strong to unite them to one another and to consolidate them into one nation. But as each of them had always had a separate existence and a government within its reach, separate interests and peculiar customs had sprung up which were opposed to such a compact and intimate union as would have absorbed the individual importance of each in the general importance of all.

第八章　联邦宪法

以上,我介绍了作为一个单独整体的各州,也解释了各州人民采用的不同制度和他们所应用的行动手段。但是,被我作为独立体考察的各州,在某些情况下必须服从一个最高的当局。现在,我们就来考察联邦政府所特有的主权,并简单地看看联邦的宪法。

联邦宪法的历史

第一个联邦的起源——它的弱点——国会对制宪权力的求助——从向制宪权的求助到公布新宪法的出现和颁布的时间间隔在两年内。

在上一个世纪末,13个殖民地同时摆脱了英国的束缚,正如我讲过的,有着相同的宗教、相同的语言、相同的生活习性和几乎相同的法律,他们与共同的敌人进行斗争,而这些理由足够强壮到把他们彼此联合起来,结成为一个单一的独立国家。但是,由于它们一开始就以单独的个体存在,各自拥有其独立的政府,所以就形成了自己特有的利益和生活习惯,他们会厌烦于使自己的重要性消失于全体的重要性中的这种坚定而完全的联合。

Hence arose two opposite tendencies, the one prompting the Anglo-A-mericans to unite, the other to divide, their strength.

As long as the war with the mother country lasted, the principle of union was kept alive by necessity; and although the laws that constituted it were defective, the common tie subsisted in spite of their imperfections. ① But no sooner was peace concluded than the faults of this legislation became manifest, and the state seemed to be suddenly dissolved. Each colony became an independent republic, and assumed an absolute sovereignty. The Federal government, condemned to impotence by its Constitution and no longer sustained by the presence of a common danger, witnessed the outrages offered to its flag by the great nations of Europe, while it was scarcely able to maintain its ground against the Indian tribes, and to pay the interest of the debt which had been contracted during the War of Independence. It was already on the verge of destruction when it officially proclaimed its inability to conduct the government and appealed to the constituent authority. ②

If America ever approached (for however brief a time) that lofty pinnacle of glory to which the proud imagination of its inhabitants is wont to point, it was at this solemn moment, when the national power abdicated, as it were, its authority. All ages have furnished the spectacle of a people struggling with energy to win its independence; and the efforts of the Americans in throwing off the English yoke have been considerably exaggerated. Separated from their enemies by three thousand miles of ocean, and backed by a powerful ally, the United States owed their victory much more to their geographical position than to the valor of their armies or the patriotism of their citizens. It would be ridiculous to compare the American war to the wars of the French Revolution, or the efforts of the Americans to those of the French when France, attacked by the whole of Europe, without money, without credit, without allies, threw forward a twentieth part of her population

---

① See the Articles of the first Confederation, formed in 1778. This Constitution was not adopted by all the states until 1781. See also the analysis given of this Constitution in *The Federalist*, from No. 15 to No. 22 inclusive, and Story's *Commentaries on the Constitution of the United States*, pp. 85-115.

② Congress made this declaration on February 21, 1787.

因此,产生了两个互相对立的趋势:一个趋势迫使英籍美国人走向联合,而另一个趋势则让他们走向分裂。

只要同母国战争下去,联合的原则就变得非常重要。虽然最初建立这种联合的法律还存在着缺点。但共同的利益却不顾这些缺点而继续存在着。① 但自和平结盟以后,最初立法的缺点便暴露无遗:国家好像一下子就解体了。每个殖民地都成了一个独立共和国,都要求享有绝对完全的主权。邦联政府被它的宪法弄得像被判了死刑一样,不再以共同的危险感作为它的支柱,眼睁睁地看着悬挂在自己船舶上的国旗被欧洲大国侮辱,却一点办法都没有,而且当时几乎不可能去对付印第安人和支付在独立战争时期所欠的债款的利息。当邦联政府徘徊在毁灭的边缘时,它正式宣布自己的无能,并向宪制权求助。②

如果说美国有一时期曾达到了这一荣誉的顶点,那就是使它的居民一直向我们显示其自豪的想象力的,就正是在国家权力自动放弃统治权的最高潮时期。在任何时代,都会出现一个民族为争取独立而进行的坚强斗争,何况美国人为摆脱英国人的束缚所做的努力又被过分夸大。美国和它的敌人被距离3000英里的大洋隔开,又有一个强大的同盟者支持。美国人的胜利主要是依赖它的地理位置,其次才是由于它的军队士气或公民爱国心。将美国的独立战争与法国大革命相比是荒谬可笑的,或美国人的努力怎么比得上法国人所做的努力呢,当法国在抵抗全欧的侵略时,它一没有财力,二又无处借债,再加上根本没有同盟者,投入二十分之一的人力去迎敌,用一只

---

① 见第一次联盟时的宪法。这部宪法形成于1778年。在1781年以前这部宪法并没有被所有的州所采用。同样见联邦人士对这部宪法的分析,(包括从第15~20页)和斯得瑞对美国宪法的评论,第85~115页。

② 1787年2月21日对这次大会的宣言。

to meet her enemies and with one hand carried the torch of revolution beyond the frontiers, while she stifled with the other a flame that was devouring the country within. But it is new in the history of society to see a great people turn a calm and scrutinizing eye upon itself when apprised by the legislature that the wheels of its government are stopped, to see it carefully examine the extent of the evil, and patiently wait two whole years until a remedy is discovered, to which it voluntarily submitted without its costing a tear or a drop of blood from mankind.

When the inadequacy of the first Constitution was discovered, America had the double advantage of that calm which had succeeded the effervescence of the Revolution, and of the aid of those great men whom the Revolution had created. The assembly which accepted the task of composing the second Constitution was small;[1] but George Washington was its President, and it contained the finest minds and the noblest characters that had ever appeared in the New World. This national Convention, after long and mature deliberation, offered for the acceptance of the people the body of general laws which still rules the Union. All the states adopted it successively.[2] The new Federal government commenced its functions in 1789, after an interregnum of two years. The Revolution of America terminated precisely when that of France began.

Summary Of The Federal Constitution.

Division of authority between the Federal government and the states – The government of the states is the rule, the Federal government the exception.

The first question which awaited the Americans was so to divide the sovereignty that each of the different states which composed the Union should continue to govern itself in all that concerned its internal prosperity, while the entire nation, represented by the Union,

---

[1] It consisted of fifty-five members; Washington, Madison, Hamilton, and the two Morrises were among the number.

[2] It was not adopted by the legislatures, but representatives were elected by the people for this sole purpose; and the new Constitution was discussed at length in each of these assemblies.

手去猛烈的扑灭燃烧在国内的大火,而用另外一只手在国外挥舞火焰。但是,当立法者告知一个伟大的民族,说他们政府的车轮已经不能在运转后,仍能平静地、不慌不忙地进行自省,深入检查罪恶的原因,足足用了两年时间去寻找问题的根源和补救措施,而在找到补救办法时又能不流一滴泪、不流一滴血地自愿服从它,倒使人觉得这是社会历史上的一件新鲜事。

当第一部联邦宪法的缺点被发现时,美国人昔日的那股政治激情只是部分地消沉下去,宣告制定宪法是在 1787 年 2 月 21 日,而且参与制定宪法的所有伟大人物仍然健在。负责起草第二部宪法的制宪会议虽然人数很少,[①]但却聚集了新大陆当时最精明、最高尚的人物,而乔治·华盛顿就是它的主席。经过全国委员会的长期的深思熟虑,终于建立起人民接受的并至今仍然治理着美国的那部基本大法。所有的州都相继接受了它。[②] 经过两年的无人统治时期,新的联邦政府于 1789 年开始工作。因此,美国革命结束之际,正是法国大革命开始之时。

联邦宪法概要

联邦当局与州当局间的权力划分,州政府负责制定普通法,而联邦政府以制定普通法为例外。

美国人面临的第一个难题,就是对主权的划分既能使组成联邦的各州继续在一切关于本州的繁荣有关的事务上管理自己,又

---

① 它包括 55 个成员;华盛顿、麦迪逊、汉密尔顿和两个莫利斯城市也被包括在内。

② 它并没有被立法机构所采用,但是人民为了一个目的而选举的典型代表;新宪法也最终在每个集会中被讨论。

should continue to form a compact body and to provide for all general exigencies. The problem was a complex and difficult one. It was as impossible to determine beforehand, with any degree of accuracy, the share of authority that each of the two governments was to enjoy as to foresee all the incidents in the life of a nation.

The obligations and the claims of the Federal government were simple and easily definable because the Union had been formed with the express purpose of meeting certain great general wants; but the claims and obligations of the individual states, on the other hand, were complicated and various because their government had penetrated into all the details of social life. The attributes of the Federal government were therefore carefully defined, and all that was not included among them was declared to remain to the governments of the several states. Thus the government of the states remained the rule, and that of the confederation was the exception. [1]

But as it was foreseen that, in practice, questions might arise as to the exact limits of this exceptional authority, and it would be dangerous to submit these questions to the decision of the ordinary courts of justice, established in the different states by the states themselves, a high Federal court was created,[2] one of whose duties was to maintain the balance of power between the two rival governments

---

[1] See amendment to the Federal Constitution; *The Federalist*, No. 31; Story, p. 711; Kent's *Commentaries*, Vol. I, p. 364. It is to be observed that whenever the *exclusive* right of regulating certain matters is not reserved to Congress by the Constitution, the states may legislate concerning them till Congress sees fit to act. For instance, Congress has the right of making a general law on bankruptcy, which, however, it has not done. Each state is then at liberty to make such a law for itself. This point, however, has been established only after discussion in the law courts, and may be said to belong more properly to jurisprudence.

[2] The action of this court is indirect, as I shall hereafter show.

能使联邦所代表的全国政府仍然作为一个整体和满足全国性的需要。这是一个复杂并且不容易解决的问题。要想事先用一个准确而又全面的方法对分享主权的两个政府的权限进行划分，是根本不可能的。

谁能预见一个国家的一切事件呢？联邦政府的义务和权利是简单而又容易界定的，因为联邦的形成就是为了解决某些重大的特定需要；但各个州的义务和权利就变得复杂而多样了，因为州政府已经深入到了社会生活的细枝末节。因此，当时对联邦政府的职权做出了明确而谨慎的规定，并宣布凡规定中没有包括的事项均属州政府的职权。结果，州政府以制定普通法为常规，而联邦政府以制定普通法为例外。①

但是，当时就曾预见到，实际上有些问题可能不在为这个例外的政府明确规定的职权范围内，而递交给各州自己的普通法院去解决又会有危险，所以就设立一个联邦最高法院。② 它的职权之一就是在两种互相竞争的政府之间维护宪法规定的分权。在人民之间，每个人民都只是作为单个的人而存在的；而一个国家为了使对外联合变得更加方便，

---

① 见对联邦宪法的修改《联邦党人文集》，第31篇；《斯得瑞的评论》，第711页；肯特：美国法释义，第一卷，第364页。当宪法没有为国会保留可以控制某些事务的专权时，州可以自己制定相关的法律直到国会认为已适合去实施行动。例如，国会有权制定关于破产的一般法律，但它一直没有完成。于是，每个州都可自由地自主制定这类法律。当然，这点是经法院讨论后才制定的，并且据说是更适合法律效应的举措。

② 这个法院的行动是间接的，关于这点我将在后面阐述。

as it had been established by the Constitution. ①

Powers Of The Federal Government.

Power of declaring war, making peace, and levying general taxes vested in the Federal government — What part of the internal policy of the country it may direct — The government of the Union in some respects more centralized than the king's government in the old French monarchy.

The people in themselves are only individuals; and the special reason why they need to be united under one government is that they may appear to advantage before foreigners. The exclusive right of making peace and war, of concluding treaties of commerce, raising armies, and equipping fleets, was therefore granted to the Union. ② The necessity of a national government was less imperiously felt in the conduct of the internal affairs of society; but there are certain general interests that can only be attended to with advantage by a general authority. The Union was invested with the power of controlling the monetary system, carrying the mails, and opening the great roads that were to unite the different parts of the country. ③ The independence of the government of each state in its sphere was recognized;

---

① It is thus that *The Federalist*, No. 45, explains this division of sovereignty between the Union and the states: "The powers delegated by the Constitution to the Federal government are few and defined. Those which are to remain in the State governments are numerous and indefinite. The former will be exercised principally on external objects, as war, peace, negotiation, and foreign commerce. The powers reserved to the several States will extend to all the objects which, in the ordinary – course of affairs, concern the internal order and prosperity of the State." I shall often have occasion to quote *The Federalist* in this work. When the bill which has since become the Constitution of the United States was before the people and the discussions were still pending, three men who had already acquired a portion of that celebrity which they have since enjoyed —John Jay, Hamilton, Madison — undertook together to explain to the nation the advantages of the measure that was proposed. With this view, they published in a journal a series of articles, which now form a complete treatise. They entitled their journal *The Federalist*, a name which has been retained in the work. *The Federalist* is an excellent book, which ought to be familiar to the statesmen of all countries, though it specially concerns America.

② See Constitution, Article I, Sections 8, 10, § 1; *The Federalist*, Nos. 41 and 42; Kent's *Commentaries*, Vol. I, pp. 207 ff. ; Story, p. 338-82, 409-26.

③ Several other powers of the same kind exist, such as that of legislating on bankruptcy and granting patents. The necessity of confiding such matters to the Federal government is obvious enough.

则特别需要一个统一的政府。①

联邦政府的权力

联邦政府被授予宣战,媾和征税的权力——它指导着国家内部政策的哪些部分——联合政府在某些方面比法国的君主专政更加集中。

人民本身只是单个的群体;他们之所以迫切需要统一在一个政府下,是因为这样会使他们在外人面前显得强大。联邦政府被授予宣战、媾和、缔结商约、征集军队和筹建舰队的专权。②在指导社会的内部事务方面,并不如此迫切需要一个全国政府。尽管如此,还是有一些与全国利益有关的问题,只有交给一个总的当局才能得到有效的处理。因此,联邦政府被授予控制与金钱有关的系统,管理全国的邮政,有权建设将全国各部分连接起来的交通干线。③ 一般说来,各州政府在本州境内是自主的。但是,它可能滥用这种独立,并因其莽撞的措施而危害全联邦的安全。

---

① 在《联邦党人文集》第45条中,已确切解释了联邦与州之间的主权划分;"宪法授予联邦政府的权力是小量并有限的。而保留给州政府的权力是巨大和无限的。联邦政府主要处理对外事务,如战争、和平、交涉和对外贸易。而一些州的权力则会扩大到所有的方面,如内部秩序和州的繁荣。"我常常会在这部著作里引用《联邦党人文集》。当这个已经作为美国联邦宪法的议案在当时还受到人们的质疑,并迫切需要讨论时,三位知名人士——约翰、汉密尔顿、麦迪逊共同向国家解释了这项议案的进步性。鉴于此,他们在报纸上发表了一系列的文章,这些文章目前已形成了一个完整的理论。他们把这些理论命名为《联邦党人文集》。《联邦党人文集》是一本完美的著作,它关系着整个美国,所有国家的政治家都应熟知它。

② 见宪法,第一篇,第八部分;《联邦党人文集》,第41页和第42页;肯特:《美国法释义》第一卷,第207页;《斯得瑞的评论》,第338～382页,第409～426页。

③ 还存在着同一类的另外几种权力,如对破产的立法权和专利权。

yet the Federal government was authorized to interfere in the internal affairs of the states ① in a few predetermined cases in which an indiscreet use of their independence might compromise the safety of the whole Union. Thus, while the power of modifying and changing their legislation at pleasure was preserved to each of the confederate republics, they are forbidden to enact ex post facto laws or to grant any titles of nobility. Lastly, as it was necessary that the Federal government should be able to fulfill its engagements, it has an unlimited power of levying taxes. ②

In examining the division of powers as established by the Federal Constitution, remarking on the one hand the portion of sovereignty which has been reserved to the several states, and on the other the share of power which has been given to the Union, it is evident that the Federal legislators entertained very clear and accurate notions respecting the centralization of government. The United States form not only a republic but a confederation; yet the national authority is more centralized there than it was in several of the absolute monarchies of Europe. I will cite only two examples.

Thirteen supreme courts of justice existed in France, which, generally speaking, had the right of interpreting the law without appeal; and those provinces that were styled *pays d' État* were authorized to refuse their assent to an impost which had been levied by the sovereign, who represented the nation. In the Union there is but one tribunal to interpret, as there is one legislature to make, the laws; and a tax voted by the representatives of the nation is binding upon all the citizens. In these two essential points, therefore, the Union is more centralized than the French monarchy, although the Union is only an assemblage of confederate republics.

In Spain certain provinces had the right of establishing a system of custom-house duties peculiar to themselves, although that privilege

---

① Even in these cases its interference is indirect. The Union interferes by means of the tribunals, as will hereafter be shown.

② Constitution, Article I, Sections 8, 9, and 10; *The Federalist*, Nos. 30 - 36 inclusive; ibid., Nos. 41, 42, 43, 44; Kent's *Commentaries*, Vol. I, pp. 207, 381; *Story*, pp. 329, 514.

在发生这种罕见的现象时,事先就有明文规定,准许联邦政府干预其州的内部事务。①因此,加入联邦的各州虽然有权修改或改订自己的立法,但不准追究既往的法律,不得在本州内组织贵族集团。最后,为使联邦政府能够实现其契约,而赋予它无限制的征税权。②

当认真考察联邦宪法规定的分权制度时,一方面要考察分给各个州的那部分主权,另一方面要考察联邦留有的那部分大权,这时我们不难发现联邦的立法者都对我在前面提出的有关政府集权方面的问题,具有十分清晰和理性的认识。美国不仅是一个共和国,而且是一个联邦。在这里,国家权威在某些方面甚至比当时欧洲一些君主专制大国还要集权。我这里只举两个例子。

法国共有十三个最高法院,它们大部分都对法律拥有解释权,而且不允许上诉。另外,一些被称为"国中国"(pays d'Etat)的省份,在负责代表国家的最高当局制定税法时,有权拒绝同最高当局合作。而在美国,正如只有一个机构可以拥有制定法律大权一样,这里也只有一个法院对法律拥有解释权。众议院的表决和每个公民都有关系。因此,在这两个主要点上,美国比旧法兰西王国还要集权,虽然美国只是一个联合了数个共和国的集合体。

在西班牙,某些省份有权建立自己的税法制度,而这项权力在本质上是属于国家的。在美国,只有国会有权对各州之间的

---

① 其干预即使在这种事件中也是间接的。联邦通过法庭的形式干预,我在后面将解释这点。

② 宪法,第一篇,第8、9、10部分;《联邦党人文集》,第30～36条款;出处同上,第41、42、43、44条;肯特:《美国法释义》第一卷,第207～381页;《概论》,第329、514页。

belongs, by its very nature, to the national sovereignty. In America Congress alone has the right of regulating the commercial relations of the states with each other. The government of the confederation is therefore more centralized in this respect than the Kingdom of Spain. It is true that the power of the crown in France or Spain was always able to obtain by force whatever the constitution of the country denied, and that the ultimate result was consequently the same; but I am here discussing the theory of the constitution.

After having settled the limits within which the Federal government was to act, the next point was to determine how it should be put in action.

Legislative Powers Of The Federal Government.

Division of the legislative body into two branches — Difference in the manner of forming the two houses — The principle of the independence of the states predominates in the formation of the Senate — That of the sovereignty of the nation in the composition of the House of Representatives — Singular effect of the fact that a constitution can be logical only when the nation is young.

The plan which had been laid down beforehand in the constitutions of the several states was followed, in many respects, in the organization of the powers of the Union. The Federal legislature of the Union was composed of a Senate and a House of Representatives. A spirit of compromise caused these two assemblies to be constituted on different principles. I have already shown that two interests were opposed to each other in the establishment of the Federal Constitution. These two interests had given rise to two opinions. It was the wish of one party to convert the Union into a league of independent states, or a sort of congress, at which the representatives of the several nations would meet to discuss certain points of common interest. The other party desired to unite the inhabitants of the American colonies into one and the same people and to establish a government that should act as the sole representative of the nation, although in a limited sphere. The practical consequences of these two theories were very different.

If the object was that a league should be established instead of a national government, then the majority of the states, instead of the majority of the inhabitants of the Union, would make the laws; for every state, great or small, would then remain in full independence and enter the Union upon a footing of perfect equality. If, however, the inhabitants of the United States were to be considered as belonging to one and the same nation, it would be natural that the majority of the citizens of the Union should make the law.

商业关系进行调整。因此,在这一点上,联邦政府的政权比西班牙王国还要集中。实际上,在法国和西班牙,王权总是能在必要的时候凭借武力做到王国宪法无权做到的事情。虽然其结果都是一样的,但我在这里讨论的是宪法的理论。

在了解了联邦政府的明确活动范围之后,下一步就是要考察它是如何活动的。

联邦政府的立法权

立法机构分为两部分——两院的建立方式不同——州独立的原则在建立参议院方面取得胜利——国家主权在组建众议院方面占主导地位——宪法只在国家初建时合乎逻辑,在组建联邦的权力机关时,许多方面都遵循了各州宪法早已定下的制度。

联邦政府的立法机构由参议院和众议院构成。一种和解的精神,使这两个议院按照不同的原则组成。我已经讲过,在起草联邦宪法时,曾有两种互相对立的利益。这两种利益产生了两种意见。一些人想把联邦建成一个各自独立的联盟,或一种召集各州代表在一起讨论共同利益的议会。而另一些人想把美洲各殖民地的全体居民联合成为一个单一的国家,并建立一个政府,这个政府即使权力范围有限,但也能在这个范围内作为国家的唯一单独代表而活动。这两种理论的实践结果将是不大相同的。

如果其目的是建立一个联盟,而不是一个全国政府,则法律的制定将取决于州的多数票,而不取决于联邦人民的多数票,每个州不论其大小,都将保留自己的独立政权的特点,并以完全平等的资格加入联邦。如果把美国的所有居民看作是属于同一国家,法律的制定当然由决定于公民的多数票决定。当然,一些较

Of course, the lesser states could not subscribe to the application of this doctrine without in fact abdicating their existence in respect to the sovereignty of the confederation, since they would cease to be a coequal and coauthoritative power and become an insignificant fraction of a great people. The former system would have invested them with excessive authority, the latter would have destroyed their influence altogether. Under these circumstances the result was that the rules of logic were broken, as is usually the case when interests are opposed to arguments. The legislators hit upon a middle course which brought together by force two systems theoretically irreconcilable.

The principle of the independence of the states triumphed in the formation of the Senate, and that of the sovereignty of the nation in the composition of the House of Representatives. Each state was to send two senators to Congress, and a number of representatives proportioned to its population. [1]It results from this arrangement that the state of New York has at the present day thirty-three representatives, and only two senators; the state of Delaware has two senators, and only one representative; the state of Delaware is therefore equal to the state of New York in the Senate, while the latter has thirty-three times the influence of the former in the House of Representatives. Thus the minority of the nation in the Senate may paralyze the decisions of the majority represented in the other house, which is contrary to the spirit of constitutional government.

These facts show how rare and difficult it is rationally and logically to combine all the several parts of legislation. The course of time always gives birth to different interests, and sanctions different principles, among the same people; and when a general constitution is to be established, these interests and principles are so many natural obstacles to the rigorous application of any political system with all its

---

[1] Every ten years Congress fixes anew the number of representatives which each state is to furnish. The total number was 69 in 1789, and 240 in 1833. A-merican Almanac (1834), p. 194.

The Constitution decided that there should not be more than one representative for every 30,000 persons; but no minimum was fixed on. Congress has not thought fit to augment the number of representatives in proportion to the increase of population. The first Act which was passed (April 14, 1792) on the subject (see Story: Laws of the United States, Vol. I, p. 235) decided that there should be one representative for every 33,000 inhabitants.

小的州如同意实行这种主张,就必须在涉及联邦主权时完全放弃自己的独立存在,而由同联邦完全平等的政权变为其微不足道的一部分。前一种制度会把它们交给一个不合理的政权,而后一种办法又会将它们毁坏。在这样的局面下,即当利害与理论发生对立时,理论总是无法立足,而不得不服从现实。所以,立法者采取了一种中立的态度,将理论上无法共存的两种制度强行协调在一起。

州独立的原则在组建参议院方面获得胜利,而国家主权在组建众议院方面占居优势。每个州都要向国会选派两名参议员,而众议院的议员人数则根据人口的比例来定。[①]根据这样的规定,现在纽约州有 33 名众议员,但只有两名参议员;而特拉华州有两名参议员,但只有一名众议员。因此,特拉华州与纽约州在参议院数目平等;但就众议院而言,纽约州的影响是特拉华州的 33 倍。因此,参议院的少数票会使众议院的多数票失效,而这是与立宪政府的精神背道而驰的。

这些事实表明,要在参议院和众议院之间按逻辑地并合理地将立法工作的各个部分连接起来是多么的复杂和困难。随着时间的流逝,在同一个国家里,总会产生不同的利益和各种各样的权利。当制定宪法时,这些利益和原则就会互相对立,成为任何一项政治原则达到某些效果时的自然障碍。因此,只有在社会初

---

① 每隔 10 年,国会将重新确定各州的代表。在 1789 年,代表总数为 69 人,而在 1833 年发展到 240 人。出自 1834 年的《美国年鉴》,第 194 页。

宪法规定,代表的人数不能多于每 3 万人中选一个,但没有规定最小数量。国会并不曾想要根据人口的增长来增加代表数量。第一次关于这项提案的通过是在 1792 年 4 月 14 日。提案规定在每 3.3 万名居民中推选一名代表(见斯得瑞:《美国法律》第一卷,第 235 页)。

consequences. The early stages of national existence are the only periods at which it is possible to make legislation strictly logical; and when we perceive a nation in the enjoyment of this advantage, we should not hastily conclude that it is wise, but only remember that it is young. When the Federal Constitution was formed, the interest of independence for the separate states and the interest of union for the whole people were the only two conflicting interests that existed among the AngloAmericans, and a compromise was necessarily made between them.

It is just to acknowledge, however, that this part of the Constitution has not hitherto produced those evils which might have been feared. All the states are young and contiguous; their customs, their ideas, and their wants are not dissimilar; and the differences which result from their size are not enough to set their interests much at variance. The small states have consequently never leagued themselves together in the Senate to oppose the designs of the larger ones. Besides, there is so irresistible an authority in the legal expression of the will of a people that the Senate could offer but a feeble opposition to the vote of the majority expressed by the House of Representatives.

It must not be forgotten, moreover, that it was not in the power of the American legislators to reduce to a single nation the people for whom they were making laws. The object of the Federal Constitution was not to destroy the independence of the states, but to restrain it. By acknowledging the real power of these secondary communities (and it was impossible to deprive them of it) they disavowed beforehand the habitual use of compulsion in enforcing the decisions of the majority. This being laid down, the introduction of the influence of the states into the mechanism of the Federal government was by no means to be wondered at, since it only attested the existence of an acknowledged power, which was to be humored and not forcibly checked.

A Further Difference
Between The Senate And
The House Of Representatives

The Senate named by the state legislatures; the Representatives by the people — Double election of the former; single election of the latter — Term of the different offices — Peculiar functions of each house.

The Senate differs from the other house not only in the very

期,才能使法律严格地遵循逻辑。当我们看到一个国家在享受自己的进步时,千万不要忙于下结论,说它是明智的,而应当切记它还处于年轻阶段。在联邦宪法形成后,英籍美国人之间仍存在着相互对立的两种利益:各州的独自利益和联邦的全国利益。必须使这两种利益调和。

但是应当承认,迄今为止,联邦宪法的这一部分并未产生人们曾经担心的可怕后果。所有的州都很年轻,并且彼此关系密切,他们有着一样的风俗习惯、思想和需求。因大小或强弱造成的差距,还不足以使它们的利益过于悬殊。因此,这些小州从未在参议院联合起来反对大州的提案。而且,表达全国意志的法律条文具有不可抗拒的力量,以致面对众议院的多数表决,参议院亦无力反对。

另外,不能忘记,美国的立法机构只被赋予代表人民立法权,而没有权力将人民组成一个单一国家。联邦宪法的目的,不是取消各州的独立存在,而只是对此稍加限制。因此,立法机构在向第二级政权下放一项实权(而且不能再收回来)时,就已经放弃了强制它们服从多数表决意志的做法。有了这项规定,各州的影响力要进入联邦政府就没有什么反常的了,只是确认已成为事实,即对已被承认的权力只能支持,而不能压制。

参议院与众议院的其他差别

参议员由州立法机关提名选举——由人民提名选出众议员——对参议院实行第二次级复选——对众议员则实行一次选举——两种议员的不同任期——职权。

参议院与众议院的不同,不仅表现在代表制度的原则方面,

principle of representation, but also in the mode of its election, in the term for which it is chosen, and in the nature of its functions. The House of Representatives is chosen by the people, the Senate by the legislatures of the states; the former is directly elected, the latter is e-lected by an elected body; the term for which the representatives are chosen is only two years, that of the senators is six. The functions of the House of Representatives are purely legislative, and the only share it takes in the judicial power is in the impeachment of public officers. The Senate co-operates in the work of legislation and tries those political offenses which the House of Representatives submits to its decision. It also acts as the great executive council of the nation; the treaties that are concluded by the President must be ratified by the Senate; and the appointments he may make, in order to be legally effective, must be approved by the same body. [1]

The Executive Power[2]

Dependence of the President — He is elective and responsible — Free in his own sphere, under the inspection, but not under the direction, of the Senate — His salary fixed at his entry into office — Suspensive veto.

The American legislators undertook a difficult task in attempting to create an executive power dependent on the majority of the people and nevertheless sufficiently strong to act without restraint in its own sphere. It was indispensable to the maintenance of the republican form of government that the representative of the executive power should be subject to the will of the nation.

The President is an elective magistrate. His honor, his property, his liberty, and his life are the securities which the people have for the temperate use of his power. But in the exercise of his authority he is not perfectly independent; the Senate takes cognizance of his relations with foreign powers, and of his distribution of public appointments, so that he can neither corrupt nor be corrupted.

---

[1] See *The Federalist*, Nos. 52-66 inclusive; Story, pp. 199-314; Constitution, Article I, Sections 2 and 3.

[2] *The Federalist*, Nos. 66-77 inclusive; Constitution, Article II; Story, pp. 315, 518-780; Kent's *Commentaries*, p. 255.

而且表现在选举的方式、参议员的任期和职权的特性方面。众议院由人民选举,而参议院由各州的立法机构选举。前者是直接选举,而后者是经两个阶段选举产生。众议员的任期只有两年,而参议员的任期为六年。众议院只具有立法权,它所享有的司法权仅仅是对公共官员的弹劾。参议院与立法机构合作,审理众议院向它起诉的政治罪案件。它同时也是全国的最高行政机构,总统签署的条约必须经它批准才能生效。总统所作的任命,也必须经这个机构的同意才能最后生效。①

行政权②

总统的依靠——总统的选举和责任——总统在其职权范围内的自由——参议院只监察总统,而不指导总统——总统的薪金在他任职时确定——暂停否决权。

美国的立法者所面临的一项艰难的难以胜任的任务,就是要设立一种既依靠多数,又有足够的力量在自己的职权范围内自由行事的行政权。这对维护国家的共和制度是必不可少的,要求行政权必须代表全国人民的意志。

总统是经选举产生的最高行政官。他的荣誉、财产、自由以及他的生命,要求他要不断地正确行使自己的权力来报答人民。而且在他行使权力时,他并不是完全独立的:参议院既监督他与外国的关系,又监督他的公共的任命,所以他既不能自行贿赂,也不能被人贿赂。联邦的立法者们看到,如果赋予行政权的稳定性和权力比不上各州所赋予它的稳定性和力量,行政

---

① 见《联邦党人文集》,第 52～66 条;《斯得瑞的评论》,第 199～314 页;宪法,第一篇,第 2、3 部分。

② 见《联邦党人文集》,第 66～77 条;宪法,第二篇;《斯得瑞的评论》,第 315 页和第 518～780 页;肯特:《美国法释义》,第 255 页。

The legislators of the Union acknowledge that the executive power could not fulfill its task with dignity and advantage unless it enjoyed more stability and strength than had been granted it in the separate states.

The President is chosen for four years, and he may be re-elected, so that the chances of a future administration may inspire him with hopeful undertakings for the public good and give him the means of carrying them into execution. The President was made the sole representative of the executive power of the Union; and care was taken not to render his decisions subordinate to the vote of a council, a dangerous measure which tends at the same time to clog the action of the government and to diminish its responsibility. The Senate has the right of annulling certain acts of the President; but it cannot compel him to take any steps, nor does it participate in the exercise of the executive power.

The action of the legislature on the executive power may be direct, and I have just shown that the Americans carefully obviated this influence; but it may, on the other hand, be indirect. Legislative assemblies which have the power of depriving an officer of state of his salary encroach upon his independence; and as they are free to make the laws, it is to be feared lest they should gradually appropriate to themselves a portion of that authority which the Constitution had vested in his hands. This dependence of the executive power is one of the defects inherent in republican constitutions. The Americans have not been able to counteract the tendency which legislative assemblies have to get possession of the government, but they have rendered this propensity less irresistible. The salary of the President is fixed, at the time of his entering upon office, for the whole period of his magistracy. The President, moreover, is armed with a suspensive veto, which allows him to oppose the passing of such laws as might destroy the portion of independence that the Constitution awards him. Yet the struggle between the President and the legislature must always be an unequal one, since the latter is certain of bearing down all resistance by persevering in its plans; but the suspensive veto forces it at least to reconsider the matter, and if the motion be persisted in, it must then be backed by a majority of two thirds of the whole house. The veto, moreover, is a sort of appeal to the people. The executive power, which without this security might have been secretly oppressed, adopts this means of pleading its cause and stating its motives. But if the legislature perseveres in its design, can it not always overpower all

权便不能严肃而有效地完成自己的任务。

总统任期四年,连选时可以连任。为了能让自己连任,他会积极投身于公共福利事业并使其变为现实。总统是联邦行政权的独一无二的代表,并阻止他的思想意志服从于一个委员会的意志,因为这是一种既会削弱政府行动,又会降低执政者责任的危险做法。参议院有权废除总统的某些法令,但不能强迫总统采取行动和分享总统的行政权。

立法机构对行政权采取的行动可能是直接的,我们刚才已经讲过,美国人总是设法阻止这种做法。而这种行动也可能是间接的。立法机构有权撤销州公共官员的薪金,以此剥夺他们的一部分独立;而立法机构作为法律的主要制定者,使公职人员经常担心它们会逐渐将总统依照宪法授予他们的那部分权力拿走。行政权的这种受制性,是共和制度固有的缺欠之一。美国人一直未能取消立法机构想要控制政府的趋势,但他们却使这种趋势变得不那么难以抗拒。总统的薪金在他任职之时就被确定下来,而且在他的整个任职期间都有效。此外,总统还有暂停否决权作为他的武器,这种否决权可以使那些可能损害宪法赋予他的独立性的法律获得通过。但总统与立法机构之间的斗争是永远不会平等的,因为后者如要坚持它的方案,可以战胜总统的抵抗,但暂停否决权至少可以迫使立法机构重新考虑它的提案,而且在重新审议议案时必须有三分之二的多数支持才可通过。此外,暂停否决权也是对人民的一种呼吁。这样,行政权对可能在失去这项保障后并同时暗中受到压迫后提出申辩,让人民知道它的理由。但是,如果立法机构仍然坚持它的提案,它总能战胜所有的抵制吗?对于这个问题,我认为:任何国家的宪法,不管它的性质

resistance? I reply that in the constitutions of all nations, of whatever kind they may be, a certain point exists at which the legislator must have recourse to the good sense and the virtue of his fellow citizens. This point is nearer and more prominent in republics, while it is more remote and more carefully concealed in monarchies; but it always exists somewhere. There is no country in which everything can be provided for by the laws, or in which political institutions can prove a substitute for common sense and public morality.

In What The Position Of A President Of The United States Differs From That Of A Constitutional King Of France

Executive power in the United States as limited and exceptional as the sovereignty that it represents — Executive power in France, like the state's sovereignty, extends to everything — The King a branch of the legislature — The President the mere executor of the law — Other differences resulting from the duration of the two powers — The President checked in the exercise of executive authority — The King independent in its exercise – In spite of these differences, France is more a-kin to a republic than the Union to a monarchy — Comparison of the number of public officers depending upon the executive power in the two countries.

The executive power has so important an influence on the destinies of nations that I wish to dwell for an instant on this portion of my subject in order more clearly to explain the part it sustains in America. In order to form a clear and precise idea of the position of the President of the United States it may be well to compare it with that of one of the constitutional kings of France. In this comparison I shall pay but little attention to the external signs of power, which are more apt to deceive the eye of the observer than to guide his researches. When a monarchy is being gradually transformed into a republic, the executive power retains the titles, the honors, the etiquette, and even the funds of royalty long after its real authority has disappeared. The English, after having cut off the head of one king, and expelled another from his throne, were still wont to address the successors of those princes only upon their knees. On the other hand, when a republic

如何,都要求立法者必须依靠公民的意志和德行。这一点在共和制国家是比较容易实行和突出的,但在君主国则比较难于实行,并且总是被掩藏起来。但是,这一点一定只是存在于某一方面。没有一个国家的法律能够为一切做准备,没有一个国家的制度能够代替大众的意志和公共道德。

美国总统的地位在哪些地方
与法国的立宪国王不同

美国的行政权像其有代表性的国家主权一样,总是有限和例外的——法国的行政权像国家主权一样,可以扩及到一切事务——国王是立法者之一——总统仅仅是法律的执行者——两种权力的任期产生的其他差别——总统被束缚在行政权的范围内——国王在行使权力时是自主的——尽管有此种种不同,但法国更接近共和制,而美国更近似君主国——比较两国依赖于行政权的官员人数。

行政权对国家命运的影响很大,所以在这里我必须先详细讨论一下它在美国占有什么地位。为了对美国总统的地位有个清晰明确的概念,最好拿美国总统的地位同欧洲的一个立宪君主国国王的地位作一比较。在比较中,我不太注重权力的外在标志,因为这种标志容易转移研究者的视线,对研究者的引导作用非常小。当一个君主国逐渐变为共和国的时候,虽然行政权仍使国王保留着头衔、荣誉,甚至财富,但实际上王权已经消失了很久。英国人斩了一位国王的首级,把另一位国王从宝座上撵走以后,他们依然习惯于跪着对这些君主的继承人谈话。另一方面,当共和国落到了个人的控制之下,这个独裁者却依然能够

falls under the sway of a single man, the demeanor of the sovereign remains as simple and unpretending as if his authority was not yet paramount. When the emperors exercised an unlimited control over the fortunes and the lives of their fellow citizens, it was customary to call them Cæsar in conversation; and they were in the habit of supping without formality at their friends' houses. It is therefore necessary to look below the surface.

The sovereignty of the United States is shared between the Union and the states, while in France it is undivided and compact; hence arises the first and most notable difference that exists between the President of the United States and the King of France. In the United States the executive power is as limited and exceptional as the sovereignty in whose name it acts; in France it is as universal as the authority of the state. The Americans have a Federal and the French a national government.

This cause of inferiority results from the nature of things, but it is not the only one; the second in importance is as follows. Sovereignty may be defined to be the right of making laws. In France, the King really exercises a portion of the sovereign power, since the laws have no weight if he refuses to sanction them; he is, moreover, the executor of all they ordain. The President is also the executor of the laws; but he does not really co-operate in making them, since the refusal of his assent does not prevent their passage. He is not, therefore, a part of the sovereign power, but only its agent. But not only does the King of France constitute a portion of the sovereign power; he also contributes to the nomination of the legislature, which is the other portion. He participates in it through appointing the members of one chamber and dissolving the other at his pleasure; whereas the President of the United States has no share in the formation of the legislative body and cannot dissolve it. The King has the same right of bringing forward measures as the chambers, a right which the President does not possess. The King is represented in each assembly by his ministers, who explain his intentions, support his opinions, and maintain the principles of the government. The President and his ministers are alike excluded from Congress, so that his influence and his opinions can only penetrate indirectly into that great body. The King of France is therefore on an equal footing with the legislature,

生活俭朴,不尚虚荣,作风谦逊,好像自己并未处于万人之上。当皇帝们控制大权,并对自己国民的财产和生存进行专横统治时,人民在谈话中通常称他们为恺撒,而他们本人却又能屈尊到朋友家里做客。因此,很有必要看清面纱底下的真相。

在美国,主权由联邦和各州共同分享;而在法国,主权是不可分割的。美国总统与法国国王最大的最主要的不同就由此产生。在美国,行政权像其所代表的国家主权一样,是有限的和例外的;而在法国,行政权像国家主权一样,可以扩及一切事务。美国人有一个联邦政府,而法国人则有一个全国政府。

这就是这种由此自然产生的美国总统地位不如法国国王地位的第一个原因,但不是唯一原因。第二个重要原因,是关于将主权定义为制定法律的权限。在法国,国王实际上是执行权力的象征,因为法律在未经过国王批准前就不能生效。同时,他也是法律的执行者。美国总统虽然也是法律的执行者,但他实际不参加法律的制定工作,因为他的否决并不妨碍法律的存在。因此,他绝不是权力的化身,而只是权力的代理人。在法国,国王不仅是权力的化身,而且也参加立法机构的任命,这也是他的权力的一部分。他参加国会的一个议院的议员提名,并能以自己的意志终止另一个议院议员的任期。而美国总统不参加立法机构的组建工作,也不能撤销立法机构。国王与国会共同分享法律的提案权。总统却没有这样的权力。国王在国会的两院中各有其一定人数的代表,这些代表会解释他的观点,支持他的意见,并维持他在政府的制度。而总统和他的同党则不能成为国会的议员,他们都被排除在国会之外。他只能通过间接的办法使自己的影响和意见进入国会。因此,法国的国王与立法机构的地位是一样的,

which can no more act without him than he can without it. The President is placed beside the legislature like an inferior and dependent power.

Even in the exercise of the executive power, properly so called, the point upon which his position seems to be most analogous to that of the King of France, the President labors under several causes of inferiority. The authority of the King in France has, in the first place, the advantage of duration over that of the President; and durability is one of the chief elements of strength; nothing is either loved or feared but what is likely to endure. The President of the United States is a magistrate elected for four years. The King in France is a hereditary sovereign.

In the exercise of the executive power the President of the United States is constantly subject to a jealous supervision. He may prepare, but he cannot conclude, a treaty; he may nominate, but he cannot appoint, a public officer. ① The King of France is absolute within the sphere of executive power.

The President of the United States is responsible for his actions; but the person of the King is declared inviolable by French law.

Nevertheless, public opinion as a directing power is no less above the head of the one than of the other. This power is less definite, less evident, and less sanctioned by the laws in France than in America; but it really exists there. In America it acts by elections and decrees; in France it proceeds by revolutions. Thus, notwithstanding the different constitutions of these two countries, public opinion is the predominant authority in both of them. The fundamental principle of legislation, a principle essentially republican, is the same in both countries, although its developments may be more or less free and its consequences different. Thus I am led to conclude that France with its King is nearer akin to a republic than the Union with its President is to a monarchy.

---

① The Constitution has left it doubtful whether the President is obliged to consult the Senate in the removal as well as in the appointment of Federal officers. *The Federalist* (No. 77) seems to establish the affirmative; but in 1789 Congress formally decided that as the President was responsible for his actions, he ought not to be forced to employ agents who had forfeited his esteem. See Kent's *Commentaries*, Vol. I, p. 289.

立法机构没有国王不能活动,而国王离开立法机构也不能活动。而总统就像一个低级的和从属的权力,被置于立法机构之外。

在行政权的执行上,总统的地位似乎与法国国王的地位很接近。但即使在行使这项权力的时候,总统也由于种种原因而地位低下。首先,法国国王的权力在任期上就优于美国总统的权力。而任期又是权力的一项重要因素。似乎是越长久的东西就越会得到爱戴和敬畏。美国总统的任期是四年,而法国国王则是一个世袭的君主。

美国总统在行使行政权时,会始终受到一种嫉妒性的监督。他可以缔结但不能批准条约,他可以提名但不能任命官员。① 而法国国王在行政权的行使方面是绝对有效的。

美国总统对自己的行为负责;但是法国的法律规定国王的人身是不可侵犯的。

当然,不管是法国国王还是美国总统,都要受到作为一种指导力量的舆论的影响。这个力量在法国不如在美国那样明显,被完全认可,没有正式在法律里注明,但它确实存在着。在美国,这种力量通过选举和法令发生作用,而在法国则通过革命发生作用。尽管两国的宪法不同,但它们在一点上是相同的,即公共舆论实际上都是具有统治作用的力量。因此,立法的原则和法律的原动力在两国都是一样的,尽管这个原动力在两国的发展上有过于自由和不够自由之别,而发展的结果又总是有所不同。从本性来说,这个原动力实质上是共和主义的。所以我认为,法国的国王制度近似于共和国,而美国的总统制接近于君主国。

---

① 宪法让人们产生疑惑,总统在对联邦官员的撤除与任命上是否非要请示参议院的。《联邦党人文集》(第77条)似乎对此持肯定的态度;但是1789年的国会已正式决定,总统有权对自己的行为负责,它不应被迫雇佣已经失去其地位的代理。见肯特:《美国法释义》第一卷,第289页。

In all that precedes I have touched only upon the main points of distinction; if I could have entered into details, the contrast would have been still more striking.

I have remarked that the authority of the President in the United States is only exercised within the limits of a partial sovereignty, while that of the King in France is undivided. I might have gone on to show that the power of the King's government in France exceeds its natural limits, however extensive these may be, and penetrates in a thousand different ways into the administration of private interests. Among the examples of this influence may be quoted that which results from the great number of public functionaries, who all derive their appointments from the executive government. This number now exceeds all previous limits; it amounts to 138,000 ① nominations, each of which may be considered as an element of power. The President of the United States has not the exclusive right of making any public appointments, and their whole number scarcely exceeds 12,000. ②

Accidental Causes Which May Increase The Influence Of Executive Government

External security of the Union — Army of six thousand men — Few ships — The President has great prerogatives, but no opportunity of exercising them — In the prerogatives which he does exercise he is weak.

IF the executive government is feebler in America than in France, the cause is perhaps more attributable to the circumstances than to the laws of the country.

It is chiefly in its foreign relations that the executive power of a nation finds occasion to exert its skill and its strength. If the existence

---

① The sums annually paid by the state to these officers amount to 200,000,000 francs.

② Each year an almanac called the *National Calendar* is published in the United States. It gives the names of all Federal office-holders. This number is extracted from the *National Calendar* for 1833.

It results from this comparison that the King of France has eleven times as many places at his disposal as the President, although the population of France is not much more than one and one-half times that of the Union.

在前面的叙述中,我只是着重指出了主要的不同点。如果要深入细节,则对比的结果还会更让人吃惊。

我已经指出,美国总统的权力只限于在其拥有的那部分主权内行使,而法国国王的权力则是不可分割的。我可以证明,尽管法国国王的统治权已经大得惊人,超越其自然范围,并通过无数方式深入到私人利益的管理。除了国王统治权的这个影响之外,我还能指出任用大批公共官员所带来的后果。这些公共官员,几乎都是代替国王行使行政权的。现在,法国公共官员的总数已超过以往任何时期,高达 13800 人,①而其中的每个人都被视为权力的分子。美国总统没有任用公共官员的专权,而且任用的人数也没有超过 1200 人。②

可使政府行政权影响增强的偶然原因

美国的对外安全政策——6000 人的军队——少数的军舰——总统虽拥有特权,却没有机会行使它们——有行使特权的机会时,总统也会显得很软弱。

如果说美国的行政权不如法国的强大,其原因与其说在于国家的法律,不如说在于环境。

一个国家行使行政权的技巧和力量的机会,主要表现在它同外国打交道的时候。如果美国的生存不断受到威胁,如果它的主

① 州每年付给官员酬金的总数大概是 2 亿法郎。

② 美国每年会出版一本名为《国家年鉴》的书。它记载了所有联邦官员的姓名。这个数字来自 1833 年的国家年鉴。

这种对比的结果是,法国国王对很多职位的控制是美国总统的 11 倍,尽管法国的人口仅仅是联邦的 1.5 倍。

of the Union were perpetually threatened, if its chief interests were in daily connection with those of other powerful nations, the executive government would assume an increased importance in proportion to the measures expected of it and to those which it would execute. The President of the United States, it is. true, is the commander-in-chief of the army, but the army is composed of only six thousand men; he commands the fleet, but the fleet reckons but few sail; he conducts the foreign relations of the Union, but the United States is a nation without neighbors. Separated from the rest of the world by the ocean, and too weak as yet to aim at the dominion of the seas, it has no enemies, and its interests rarely come into contact with those of any other nation of the globe. This proves that the practical operation of the government must not be judged by the theory of its constitution. The President of the United States possesses almost royal prerogatives, which he has no opportunity of exercising; and the privileges which he can at present use are very circumscribed. The laws allow him to be strong, but circumstances keep him weak.

On the other hand, the great strength of the loyal prerogative in France arises from circumstances far more than from the laws. There the executive government is constantly struggling against immense obstacles, and has immense resources in order to overcome them; so that it is enlarged by the extent of its achievements, and by the importance of the events it controls, without modifying its constitution. If the laws had made it as feeble and as circumscribed as that of the American Union, its influence would soon become still more preponderant.

Why The President Of The United States Does Not Need A Majority In The Two Houses In Order To Carry On The Govepnment

It is an established axiom in Europe that a constitutional king cannot govern when opposed by the two branches of the legislature. But several Presidents of the United States have been known to lose the majority in the legislative body without being obliged to abandon the supreme power and without inflicting any serious evil upon society. I have heard this fact quoted to prove the independence and the power of the executive government in America;

要利益每天都同其他大国的利益息息相关。则行政权的权威性将随着人们对它的期待和它自己的作为而增高。不错,美国总统是军队的统帅,但这只军队只有 6000 名士兵。他也指挥舰队,但这支舰队只有几艘军舰。他处理一切与外国的关系,但美国并没有邻居。它与世界的其余大洲被汪洋大海隔开,而它统治海洋的能力还很差。它没有敌人,它的利益只是偶尔同地球上其他国家的利益冲突。这就证明了实际操作并不能以宪法理论来判断。美国总统拥有至高无上的特权,但他却没有机会使用。目前他所拥有的权限是非常有限的,至今也只能在极其有限的范围内行使。法律容许他强大,但环境使他软弱无力。

另一方面,法国国王所拥有的皇家特权多数来自环境,而不是来自法律。在法国,行政权不断与巨大的障碍进行斗争,并用严厉的手段去克服这些障碍。它不用去修改宪法,就能凭着它所处理的事务的广泛性和它所主管的事件的重要性来增加自己的力量。假如法律使它也像在美国那样软弱无力和限制重重,它的影响不用多久也会因环境而大大加强。

美国总统为了执行政府工作
为什么不需要在两院取得多数

在欧洲,一个立宪君主的意见如果遭到立法机构两院的反对,他就不能进行统治,这已经成为公理。但是美国有好几位总统曾在立法机构失去多数,但并未被迫放弃权力,也未给社会造成严重的灾难。我听说这个事实被用来证明美国行政权的不依赖性和有力性。但是,只要稍加思考,我们就会发现情况恰恰相

a moment's reflection will convince us, on the contrary, that it is a proof of its weakness.

A king in Europe requires the support of the legislature to enable him to perform the duties imposed upon him by the constitution, because those duties are enormous. A constitutional king in Europe is not merely the executor of the law, but the execution of its provisions devolves so completely upon him that he has the power of paralyzing its force if it opposes his designs. He requires the assistance of the legislative assemblies to make the law, but those assemblies need his aid to execute it. These two authorities cannot function without each other, and the mechanism of government is stopped as soon as they are at variance.

In America the President cannot prevent any law from being passed, nor can he evade the obligation of enforcing it. His sincere and zealous co-operation is no doubt useful in carrying on public affairs, but is not indispensable. In all his important acts he is directly or indirectly subject to the legislature, and of his own free authority he can do but little. It is therefore his weakness, and not his power, that enables him to remain in opposition to Congress. In Europe harmony must reign between the crown and the legislature, because a collision between them may prove serious; in America this harmony is not indispensable, because such a collision is impossible.

Election Of The President

The dangers of the elective system increase in proportion to the extent of the prerogative — This system possible in America because no powerful executive authority is required — How circumstances favor the establishment of the elective system — Why the election of the President does not change the principles of the government — Influence of the election of the President on secondary functionaries.

The dangers of the system of election, applied to the chief of the executive government of a great people, have been sufficiently exemplified by experience and by history. I wish to speak of them in reference to America alone.

反,这个事实只能证明美国的行政权是软弱无力的。

欧洲的君主,要求得到立法机构的支持并实现宪法赋予他的巨大的任务。欧洲的立宪君主不仅仅是法律的执行者,他们还要设法使法律的执行完全符合自己的意愿,如果法律有反对他们的地方,他们可以使法律失效。他需要立法机构制定法律,但这些机构则需要君主的辅助来执行法律。这两个权力机关彼此缺了对方都不能生存,一旦双方对立,政府的车轮就要停止转动。

在美国,总统无权阻止法律的制定,他也无权回避执行法律的义务。他真挚热心地合作,对于政府在公共事务的工作的执行上无疑是有用的,但也并非必不可少。他的一切重要举措,都直接或间接受到立法机构的控制,而当他能够完全自由的行使权力时,他又几乎什么都不能做。因此,使他能够同立法机构作对的,只是他的软弱,而非他的力量。在欧洲,国王与国会必须和睦相处,因为两者之间发生冲突可能是严重的;而在美国,这种和睦非常不重要,因为他们不可能发生斗争。

总统的选举

选举制度的危险性的增加与特权的扩张是成正比的——在美国,这种制度可能是因为缺少对行政权威性的需求——谈一谈这种危险——环境对选举制度会产生怎样的影响——为什么对总统的选举制度不能改变政府的原则——对次要官员选举的影响。

选举制度的危险已经体现在大多数人在对执行政府的首脑的选举上,这一点已经充分地被历史和经验所证明。我想在此谈谈美国的选举制度。

These dangers may be more or less formidable in proportion to the place that the executive power occupies and to the importance it possesses in the state; and they may vary according to the mode of election and the circumstances in which the electors are placed. The most weighty argument against the election of a chief magistrate is that it offers so splendid a lure to private ambition and is so apt to inflame men in the pursuit of power that when legitimate means are wanting, force may not infrequently seize what right denies. It is clear that the greater the prerogatives of executive authority are, the greater is the temptation; the more the ambition of the candidates is excited, the more warmly are their interests espoused by a throng of partisans who hope to share the power when their patron has won the prize. The dangers of the elective system increase, therefore, in the exact ratio of the influence exercised by the executive power in the affairs of the state. The revolutions of Poland are attributable not solely to the elective system in general, but to the fact that the elected monarch was the sovereign of a powerful kingdom.

Before we can discuss the absolute advantages of the elective system, we must make preliminary inquiries as to whether the geographical position, the laws, the habits, the customs, and the opinions of the people among whom it is to be introduced will permit the establishment of a weak and dependent executive government; for to attempt to render the representative of the state a powerful sovereign, and at the same time elective, is, in my opinion, to entertain two incompatible designs. To reduce hereditary royalty to the condition of an elective authority, the only means that I am acquainted with are to circumscribe its sphere of action beforehand, gradually to diminish its prerogatives, and to accustom the people by degrees to live without its protection. But this is what the republicans of Europe never think of doing; as many of them hate tyranny only because they are exposed to its severity, it is oppression and not the extent of the executive power that excites their hostility; and they attack the former without perceiving how nearly it is connected with the latter.

Hitherto no citizen has cared to expose his honor and his life in order to become the President of the United States, because the power of that office is temporary, limited, and subordinate. The prize of fortune must be great to encourage adventurers in so desperate a game.

选举制度的危险或多或少地与行政权所处的环境,以及它在州政府的重要性有关;它会因为选举方式和选举者当时所处的环境的不同而改变。人们无理由地谴责国家首脑选举制度的论据,是说这种制度对于野心家具有非常吸引人的诱惑力,十分强烈地激发野心家去争权夺利,以致合法的手段往往不能满足他们的需要,而当权力行将离开他们时,他们就要使用武力。显而易见,行政权越大,诱惑力也就越大;候选人的野心越强,就越有二流的野心家来支持他,因为这群二流野心家也希望在他们的候选人获胜后分享权力。因此,选举制度的危险与行政权对国家事务影响的加强成正比。波兰的历次革命不仅仅是因为一般选举制度,而且还因为当选的官员成了一个大君主国的首脑。

在讨论选举制度的绝对好处之前,我们总要先去了解一下,打算采用选举制度的国家的地理位置、法律、习惯、国情和民意是否允许在这个国家建立一个软弱而又依赖的行政政府,因为在我看来,既想让国家的代表人拥有强大的权力,又想由选举产生这个代表人,这是两种互相对立的意愿。据我所知,要使世袭的王权过渡到一般选举政体,只有一个可行的办法,那就是先限制王权的活动范围,再一步步地取消它的特权,然后使人民逐渐习惯于在没有王权的保护下也能生活。但是,欧洲的共和主义者们从来没有这样想过。他们当中的许多人之所以憎恨暴政,是因为他们遭受过暴政的欺压。刺激到他们仇恨的是暴政,而并非是行政权的广泛,当他们在攻击前者时,并没有察觉其实这两者的关系是非常密切的。

至今还没有见到过任何一个人甘愿冒着荣誉和生命的风险去争当美国总统,因为总统的职位是暂时的,受到限制和制约的。赌场上必须有大注,绝望的赌徒才能孤注一掷。至今还没有一个

No candidate has as yet been able to arouse the dangerous enthusiasm or the passionate sympathies of the people in his favor, for the simple reason that when he is at the head of the government, he has but little power, little wealth, and little glory to share among his friends; and his influence in the state is too small for the success or the ruin of a faction to depend upon his elevation to power.

The great advantage of hereditary monarchies is that, as the private interest of a family is always intimately connected with the interests of the state, these state interests are never neglected for a moment; and if the affairs of a monarchy are not better conducted than those of a republic, at least there is always someone to conduct them, well or ill, according to his capacity. In elective states, on the contrary, the wheels of government cease to act, as it were, of their own accord at the approach of an election, and even for some time previous to that event. The laws may, indeed, accelerate the operation of the election, which may be conducted with such simplicity and rapidity that the seat of power will never be left vacant; but notwithstanding these precautions, a break necessarily occurs in the minds of the people.

At the approach of an election the head of the executive government thinks only of the struggle that is coming on; he no longer has anything to look forward to; he can undertake nothing new, and he will only prosecute with indifference those designs which another will perhaps terminate. "I am so near the time of my retirement from office," said President Jefferson, on January 21, 1809, six weeks before the election [sic; actually, six weeks before he left office], "that I feel no passion, I take no part, I express no sentiment. It appears to me just to leave to my successor the commencement of those measures which he will have to prosecute, and for which he will be responsible. " On the other hand, the eyes of the nation are centered on a single point; all are watching the gradual birth of so important an event.

The wider the influence of the executive power extends, the greater and the more necessary is its constant action, the more fatal is the term of suspense; and a nation that is accustomed to the government or, still more, one used to the administration of a powerful executive authority would be infallibly convulsed by an election. In the United States the action of the government may be slackened with impunity, because it is always weak and circumscribed.

候选人能够激起人民的热烈同情和激烈情感去支持他。原因很简单：因为他当上政府首脑后，只能使他的朋友们分享到很少一点权力、财富和荣誉，而且他在国内的影响很小，不足以决定他的本派人在他当权时的事业成败。

世袭君主政体有一个巨大好处：就是个人的家族利益总与国家利益息息相关，所以一时一刻也不会置国家利益于不顾。如果这种君主国的事务主持的没有共和国的好，但是不管好坏，总会有一个人在尽力主持。可是相反地，选举首脑的国家，一临近选举，甚至在选举前的一段时间，政府的车轮就仿佛自行停止转动了。不错，可以制定适当的法律，促进选举或使选举立即进行完毕，即不让行政权出现空位；但是，即使如此预防，人们也不会理解立法者的苦心，仍然会认为行政权处于空位。

一临近选举，行政权的首脑只考虑即将来临的斗争。他不再向前看，他不会开始任何新的活动，而只会漠不关心地处理那些也许将由另一个人来结束的工作。杰斐逊总统于 1809 年 1 月 21 日（选举前六个星期）写道："现在，我已如此接近我的退职期限，我已经失去了激情，以致我可以不再参加实际工作，而只提出我的建议。我觉得，让我的后任主动采取他将实行和要负责的措施，是正当的。"另一方面，全国上上下下人们的目光都集中于一点：瞪眼看着生命在逐步孕育中的痛楚。

如果行政权实施的范围越大，它的活动的经常性就越多和越有必要，则由此产生的危险也越严重。在一个已经习惯于受政府统治或者说是受行政权威管理的国家，必然会在选举中受到剧烈的震动。在美国，行政权的行使可能会因为其松弛而不受谴责，因为这种行为本来就是软弱无力和受到重重限制的。

One of the principal vices of the elective system is that it always introduces a certain degree of instability into the internal and external policy of the state. But this disadvantage is less acutely felt if the share of power vested in the elected magistrate is small. In Rome the principles of the government underwent no variation although the consuls were changed every year, because the Senate, which was a hereditary assembly, possessed the directing authority. In most of the European monarchies, if the king were elective, the kingdom would be revolutionized at every new election. In America the President exercises a certain influence on state affairs, but he does not conduct them; the preponderating power is vested in the representatives of the whole nation. The political maxims of the country depend, therefore, on the mass of the people, not on the President alone; and consequently in America the elective system has no very prejudicial influence on the fixity of the government. But the want of fixed principles is an evil so inherent in the elective system that it is still very perceptible in the narrow sphere to which the authority of the President extends.

The Americans have admitted that the head of the executive power, in order to discharge his duty and bear the whole weight of responsibility, ought to be free to choose his own agents and to remove them at pleasure; the legislative bodies watch the conduct of the President more than they direct it. The consequence is that at every new election the fate of all the Federal public officers is in suspense. It is sometimes made a subject of complaint that in the constitutional monarchies of Europe the fate of the humbler servants of an administration often depends upon that of the ministers. But in elective governments this evil is far greater; and the reason therefor is very obvious. In a constitutional monarchy successive ministries are rapidly formed; but as the principal representative of the executive power is never changed, the spirit of innocation is kept within bounds; the changes that take place are in the details of the administrative system rather than in its principles; but to substitute one system for another, as is done in America every four years by law, is to cause a sort of revolution. As to the misfortunes which may fall upon individuals in consequence of this state of things, it must be allowed that the uncertain tenure of the public offices does not produce the evil consequences in America which might be expected from it elsewhere.

选举制度的一个主要弊端,就是当政府首脑是由选举产生时,几乎总要在国家的内外政策方面出现一段不稳定时期。而且,这一弊端的严重程度,跟当选首脑被赋予的权力的大小成正比。在古罗马,尽管执政官每年一换,但政府的工作原则始终不变,因为议院是世袭机构,并控制着直接权力。而且,在欧洲的大多数君主国,如果国王是选举的,王国则在每次进行新选举时都会改变面貌。在美国,总统虽对国务有一定的影响,但他并不主持国务,主要的权力掌握在代表全国人民的议员之手。因此,能够改变政治准则的是全国人民,而不是总统个人。结果,美国的选举制度就没有对政府的稳定性产生极为不利的影响。但是,缺乏稳定性毕竟是选举制度的一个固有缺欠,以致这个缺欠在总统的本来就很小的活动范围内表现得更加明显。

美国人已经认可了行政权的首脑为了履行职务和承担全国责任的重担,应有充分的自由去亲自挑选其自己的党派并能随意撤免他们;立法机构主要应当监督而不是指导总统,但结果却变成:只要进行新的选举,全体联邦官员的命运就好像处于悬而不定的状态中。在欧洲的君主立宪国,人们常常会抱怨一个行政机关的小职员的命运决定于大臣们的命运。而在选举制度的国家,这种情况更为严重。其实原因很简单:在君主立宪国,接任的大臣很快就能上任,而行政权的主要代表并没有改变,改革精神也有一定范围。因此,这种国家的行政权的变化主要表现在细节方面,而不表现在原则方面。不是用一种制度去代替另一种制度,因而不致引起一场革命。而在美国,却是每隔四年依法进行这样的革命。至于说这种立法自然会给个人造成的不幸,我们必须承认公共官员命运的不固定性在美国还未产生在别处出现的灾难。

It is so easy to acquire an independent position in the United States that the public officer who loses his place may be deprived of the comforts of life, but not of the means of subsistence.

I remarked at the beginning of this chapter that the dangers of the elective system, applied to the head of the state, are augmented or decreased by the peculiar circumstances of the people which adopts it. However the functions of the executive power may be restricted, it must always exercise a great influence upon the foreign policy of the country; for a negotiation cannot be opened or successfully carried on otherwise than by a single agent. The more precarious and the more perilous the position of a people becomes, the more absolute is the want of a fixed and consistent external policy, and the more dangerous does the system of electing the chief magistrate become. The policy of the Americans in relation to the whole world is exceedingly simple; and it may almost be said that nobody stands in need of them, nor do they stand in need of anybody. Their independence is never threatened. In their present condition, therefore, the functions of the executive power are no less limited by circumstances than by the laws; and the President may frequently change his policy without involving the state in difficulty or destruction. Whatever the prerogatives of the executive power may be, the period which immediately precedes an election, and that during which the election is taking place, must always be considered as a national crisis, which is perilous in proportion to the internal embarrassments and the external dangers of the country. Few of the nations of Europe could escape the calamities of anarchy or of conquest every time they might have to elect a new sovereign. In America society is so constituted that it can stand without assistance upon its own basis; nothing is to be feared from the pressure of external dangers; and the election of the President is a cause of agitation, but not of ruin.

Mode Of Election

Skill of the American legislators shown in the mode of election adopted by them — Creation of a special electoral body — Separate votes of these electors — Case in which the House of Representatives is called upon to choose the President — Results of the twelve elections that have taken place since the Constitution was established.

在美国,寻找自食其力的生活出路容易得像丢掉官职一样。虽然丢官后有时会过不上舒适生活,但绝不会由此失去谋生之道。

我在本章的开头讲过,选举制度的危险性在于对政府首脑的选举上,而这又因采用这一制度的国家所处环境的不同而有所区别。尽管行政权的范围受到限制,但它对国家的外交政策却有极大的影响,因为除非由一个代理经手,否则谈判就无法开始和顺利进行。人民的处境变得越是不稳定和危险,就越是需要一项稳定持续的对外政策。这样,对国家首脑采用选举制度,也会更加危险。美国人对全世界的政策是非常简单的,几乎可以认为没有人需要他们,他们也不需要任何人。他们的独立从未受到过威胁。因此,从他们目前的情况来看,行政权的职能既受环境的限制,又受法律的限制。总统可以经常改变他的政策,但国家不会因此而遭殃或毁灭。不管如何选举行政权的首脑,选举之前和选举时期,都会被认为是全国的危险时期。一个国家的内忧越大,它的外患也就越大,而这时的国家会更有危机感并更有危险。欧洲的少数国家每逢选举新首脑时,很少有不被人征服和陷入无政府状态的。在美国,社会被组织得不需要帮助即能自立。美国从来没有遇到过外患。它的总统选举总是激励人心的大事,而非导致毁灭的举动。

选举方式

美国的立法者在选择选举方式时表现的才能——创立一种特殊的选举团体——这些独特的选举独立投票——众议院在什么情况下应召去选举总统——自现行宪法建立以来十二次选举的概要。

Besides the dangers that are inherent in the system, many others may arise from the mode of election; but these may be obviated by the precautions of the legislator. When a people met in arms on some public spot to choose its head, it was exposed to all the chances of civil war resulting from such a mode of proceeding, besides the dangers of the elective system in itself. The Polish laws, which subjected the election of the sovereign to the veto of a single individual, suggested the murder of that individual or prepared the way for anarchy.

In the examination of the institutions and the political as well as social condition of the United States. we are struck by the admirable harmony of the gifts of fortune and the efforts of man. That nation possessed two of the main causes of internal peace; it was a new country, but it was inhabited by a people grown old in the exercise of freedom. Besides, America had no hostile neighbors to dread; and the American legislators, profiting by these favorable circumstances, created a weak and subordinate executive power, which could without danger be made elective. It then remained for them only to choose the least dangerous of the various modes of election; and the rules that they laid down upon this point admirably correspond to the securities which the physical and political constitution of the country already afforded. Their object was to find the mode of election that would best express the choice of the people with the least possible excitement and suspense. It was admitted, in the first place, that the simple majority should decide the point; but the difficulty was to obtain this majority without an interval of delay, which it was most important to avoid. It rarely happens that an individual can receive at the first trial a majority of the suffrages of a great people; and this difficulty is enhanced in a republic of confederate states, where local influences are far more developed and more powerful. The means by which it was proposed to obviate this second obstacle was to delegate the electoral powers of the nation to a body that should represent it.

除了选举制度固有的危险之外,还有许多其他的是来自选举方式,但这些可以通过立法者的预防而消除。当全国人民带着武装到公共场所去选他们的首脑时,除了有选举制度本身存在的危险之外,还特别有由于选举方式而产生的内战的危险。当波兰的法律允许国王的选举可被一个个体否决时,这项法律就等于是对这个个体的谋杀,或预先规定了无政府状态。

在深入研究美国的机构和认真观察这个国家的政治与社会状况以后,我们发现人们在那里的发迹与他们的能力是极其一致的。美国是一个新兴的国家,但它的人民却在很久以前就已习惯于这种内部的和平与自由:这是其内部秩序得以维持的两个主要原因。而且,美国没有前来恐吓它的敌人。美国的立法者,受益于这些有利的环境,因而不难创立一个软弱而有依附性的行政权,使他们的行政权在不会带来危险的情况下,也能采用选举制度,而又不致带来危险。留给他们需要做的,只是从不同的选举制度中选择危险性最小的制度,使在这方面规定的准则恰恰符合本国的自然条件和政治制度所提供的保障。他们首要的目的是找到一种合适的选举方式,这种方式既能够充分表达人民的真正意愿,又不至于过分激发人民的情感。首先,他们采用了以简单多数通过法律的办法。但这还是比较难做到,因为人们为了获得这个多数并不害怕拖延时间,但立法者却尽量避免拖延时间。事实上,在一个大国进行选举时,很少有人能在第一轮投票即获得多数。在地方势力的影响非常发达和有力的数州联合而成的共和国中,这种困难变得更大。为了消除这第二个障碍而提出的方法,是将全国人民的选举权委任给一个可以代表全国人民的机构。这种选举方式,使大多数的机会增加,因为选举的人数越少,

This mode of election rendered a majority more probable; for the fewer the electors are, the greater is the chance of their coming to an agreement. It also offered an additional probability of a judicious choice. It then remained to be decided whether this right of election was to be entrusted to the legislature itself, the ordinary representative of the nation, or whether a special electoral college should be formed for the sole purpose of choosing a President . The Americans chose the latter alternative, from a belief that those who were chosen only to make the laws would represent but imperfectly the wishes of the nation in the election of its chief magistrate; and that, as they are chosen for more than a year, the constituency they represented might have changed its opinion in that time. It was thought that if the legislature was empowered to elect the head of the executive power, its members would, for some time before the election, be exposed to the maneuvers of corruption and the tricks of intrigue; whereas the special electors would, like a jury, remain mixed up with the crowd till the day of action, when they would appear for a moment only to give their votes.

It was therefore determined that every state should name a certain number of electors,[1] who in their turn should elect the President; and as it had been observed that the assemblies to which the choice of a chief magistrate had been entrusted in elective countries inevitably became the centers of passion and cabal; that they sometimes usurped powers which did not belong to them; and that their proceedings, or the uncertainty which resulted from them, were sometimes prolonged so much as to endanger the welfare of the state, it was determined that the electors should all vote on the same day, without being convoked to the same place. [2] This double election rendered a majority probable, though not certain; for it was possible that the electors might not, any more than their constituents, come to an agreement. In that case it would be necessary to have recourse to one of three measures: either to appoint new electors, or to consult a second time those already appointed, or to give the election to another authority. The first two of these alternatives, independently of cision and to perpetuate an agitation which must always be accompanied with danger.

---

[1] As many as it sends members to Congress. The number of electors at the election of 1833 was 288 (the *National Calendar*).

[2] The electors of the same state assemble, but they transmit to the central government the list of their individual votes, and not the mere result of the vote of the majority.

就越容易在意见上达成一致。这种办法也便于人们作出良好的选择。然而,是应该把选举权委任给本身代表全国人民意愿的立法机构呢?还是需要成立一个以选举总统为唯一目的的选举团呢?美国人选择了后者。他们认为,让那些已经被赋予制定法律的人再负责选举全国的首席行政官,只能不全面地代表民意;另外,他们当选为议员已经超过一年,而他们所代表的选民这时可能改变了主意。美国人认为,如果立法机构被赋予选举行政首脑的权力,议员们会在选举前的一段长时间内受贿和参与阴谋活动,而这些特别选举人也会像陪审团的成员一样,和群众混合在一起,不为人所知,只有在他们应当行动时才只用上几分钟时间投投票而已。

因此,决定每州必须提出一定名额的选举人,[①]并委任他们去选举总统。但是,可以想象得到,实行选举制的国家的这种负责选举政府首脑的团体,不可避免地要成为争吵和策划阴谋的中心。它们有时会篡夺不属于它的权力;而它的不确定性和随之而来的争吵不休,又有时会危及到国家的幸福。于是美国人决定,选举者必须在同一天投票,而不把他们召集在一个地方。[②]这种双重选举方式有助于多数,但并不保证一定能行,因为选举者事后采取下列方法之一作为援助:重新任命新的选举人,由原来的选举人再次协商,或交给另一个权力当局去选举。前两种办法除不够可靠外,还会最终决定延迟,必然带来无尽无休的可怕争吵和危

---

① 它向国会输送尽可能多的成员。在 1833 年的选举中,选举者的数量为 288 位(出自《国家年鉴》)。

② 选举者虽然来自同一集会,但他们向中央政府递交各自的选举名单,并且不仅仅是大多数选举的结果。

The third expedient was therefore adopted, and it was agreed that the votes should be transmitted. sealed, to the president of the Senate, and that they should be opened and counted on an appointed day, in the presence of the Senate and the House of Representatives. If none of the candidates has received a majority, the House of Representatives then proceeds immediately to elect the President; but with the condition that it must fix upon one of the three candidates who have the highest number of votes in the electoral college. ①

Thus it is only in case of an event which cannot often happen, and which can never be foreseen, that the election is entrusted to the ordinary representatives of the nation; and even then, they are obliged to choose a citizen who has already been designated by a powerful minority of the special electors. It is by this happy expedient that the respect due to the popular voice is combined with the utmost celerity of execution, and with those precautions which the interests of the country demand. But the decision of the question by the House of Representatives does not necessarily offer an immediate solution of the difficulty; for the majority of that assembly may still be doubtful, and in that case the Constitution prescribes no remedy. Nevertheless, by restricting the number of candidates to three, and by referring the matter to the judgment of an enlightened public body, it has smoothed all the obstacles ② that are not inherent in the elective system itself.

In the forty-four years that have elapsed since the promulgation of the Federal Constitution, the United States have twelve times chosen a President. Ten of these elections took place at once by the simultaneous votes of the special electors in the different states. The House of Representatives has only twice exercised its conditional privilege of deciding in cases of uncertainty: the first time was at the election of Mr. Jefferson in 1801; the second was in 1825, when Mr. J. Quincy Adams was named.

---

① In this case it is the majority of the states, and not the majority of the members, that decides the question; so that New York has no more influence in the debate than Rhode Island. Thus the citizens of the Union are first consulted as members of one and the same community; and if they cannot agree, recourse is had to the division of the states, each of which has a separate and independent vote. This is one of the singularities of the Federal Constitution, which can be explained only by the jar of conflicting interests.

② Jefferson, in 1801, was not elected until the thirty-sixth ballot.

险。因此,他们采用了第三种办法,并规定将选票密封后送交参议院议长,在一个指定的日子,当着参议员和众议员的面开封计票。如果没有一个候选人获得多数,则立即由众议院直接选举总统,但为众议院规定了权力范围。众议员只能从原来得票最多的三个候选人当中选定一个人为总统。①

所以,像前面所讲的那样,只是在极少数和很难预见的情况下,选举总统的权力才会交给众议员去执行,而且他们不得不从特殊选举者的强有力多数指定的人当中选定一人为总统。这是一种很好的权宜办法,它把对人民的意愿的尊敬,迅速地同进行选举和国家利益完美地协调起来了。但是,让众议员分享解决问题的权力,也不一定能够解决一切困难,因为在众议院能否获得多数仍有疑问,而且宪法对此没有提供补救办法。不过,由于规定了必备的候选人资格,把议员的人数限定为三人,让一个摆脱了偏见束缚的机构去任命,所以这种办法尽可能地排除了一切障碍。至于其他一些障碍,则是选举制度本身所固有的了。②

自联邦宪法建立后44年以来,美国已选过12次总统。有10次是由各州的特别选举人在本州投票后便选出的。众议院只行使过两次它可以分享的这种特殊权力:第一次是在1801年杰斐逊总统的选举上,第二次是在1825年昆西·亚当斯总统的选举上。

---

① 既然这样,决定问题本质的是州的大多数,而不是成员的大多数;所以,纽约对争辩的影响不会多于罗德岛。因此,联邦的公民的选举首先是被看作一个成员和同一组织被查阅的;如果他们不能协调,就必须对州进行划分,每一个被分割的组织有其独立的选票。这是联邦宪法的一个卓越之处,并且只能被相互发生冲突的利益所解释。

② 在1801年,杰斐逊总统直到第36票才当选成功。

Crisis Of The Election

The election may be considered as a moment of national crisis—Why? —Passions of the people—Anxiety of the President—Calm which succeeds the agitation of the election.

I Have shown what the circumstances are that favored the adoption of the elective system in the United States and what precautions were taken by the legislators to obviate its dangers. The Americans are accustomed to all kinds of elections; and they knew by experience the utmost degree of excitement which is compatible with security. The vast extent of the country and the dissemination of the inhabitants render a collision between parties less probable and less dangerous there than elsewhere. The political circumstances under which the elections have been carried on have not as yet caused any real danger. Still, the epoch of the election of the President of the United States may be considered as a crisis in the affairs of the nation.

The influence which the President exercises on public business is no doubt feeble and indirect; but the choice of the President, though of small importance to each individual citizen, concerns the citizens collectively; and however trifling an interest may be, it assumes a great degree of importance as soon as it becomes general. In comparison with the kings of Europe, the President possesses but few means of creating partisans; but the places that are at his disposal are sufficiently numerous to interest, directly or indirectly, several thousand electors in his success. Moreover, political parties in the United States are led to rally round an individual in order to acquire a more tangible shape in the eyes of the crowd, and the name of the candidate for the Presidency is put forward as the symbol and personification of their theories. For these reasons parties are strongly interested in winning the election, not so much with a view to the triumph of their principles under the auspices of the President elect as to show by his election that the supporters of those principles now form the majority.

For a long while before the appointed time has come, the election becomes the important and, so to speak, the all-engrossing topic

选举的紧急时期

选举总统的时期可被看作是全国的紧急时期——为什么？——人民的激情——总统的忧虑——选举热潮之后的平静。

我已讲过环境对美国的选举制度起到一定有利作用,并指出立法机构为消除这种制度的危险而采取的预防措施。美国人已经习惯于各种各样的选举。他们从经验中了解了满足安全要求的最大限度的激情。美国的幅员辽阔和居民分散,使政党间之冲突不像在其他国家那样明显和具有破坏性。在选举时形成的政治环境,至今还未引发过任何真正的危险。但是,仍可把美国选举总统的时期看作全国的紧急时期。总统对公共事务的影响,无疑是微弱的和有依赖性的。总统的选举对每个公民来讲可能并不非常重要,但对全体公民却十分重要。要知道,不管一项利益是怎样微不足道,当它一旦成为普遍利益,就会获得巨大的重要性。同欧洲的国王相比,美国的总统几乎没有权力创建自己的政党。但是,由他任免的职位,却多得足以使成千上万的选民直接或间接地关心总统的成败。此外,美国的政党也和其他国家一样,感到需要团结在一个人的周围,以便更容易为群众所理解。因此,它们一般都以总统候选人的名字作为旗号来为自己服务,让这个人去具体实现本党的理论。因为这些原因,能在选举中获益则成为他们最关心的利益,但不是依靠当选总统来使自己的原则获胜,而是通过总统的当选证明自己的学说获得了多数。

在指定的选举日到来之前的很长一段时期内,选举变得越来越重要,而且可以说是举国上下唯一关心的大事。因此,各党派又有

of discussion. Factional ardor is redoubled, and all the artificial passions which the imagination can create in a happy and peaceful land are agitated and brought to light. The President, moreover, is absorbed by the cares of self-defense. He no longer governs for the interest of the state, but for that of his re-election; he does homage to the majority, and instead of checking its passions, as his duty commands, he frequently courts its worst caprices. As the election draws near, the activity of intrigue and the agitation of the populace increase; the citizens are divided into hostile camps, each of which assumes the name of its favorite candidate; the whole nation glows with feverish excitement; the election is the daily theme of the press, the subject of private conversation, the end of every thought and every action, the sole interest of the present. It is true that as soon as the choice is determined, this ardor is dispelled, calm returns, and the river, which had nearly broken its banks, sinks to its usual level; but who can refrain from astonishment that such a storm should have arisen?

Re-election Of The President

When the head of the executive power is re-eligible, it is the state that is the source of intrigue and corruption — The desire to be re-elected is the chief aim of a President of the United States — Disadvantage of the reelection peculiar to America — The natural evil of democracy is that it gradually subordinates all authority to the slightest desires of the majority — The re-election of the President encourages this evil.

Were the legislators of the United States right or wrong in allowing the re-election of the President? At first sight is seems contrary to all reason to prevent the head of the executive power from being elected a second time. The influence that the talents and the character of a single individual may exercise upon the fate of a whole people, especially in critical circumstances or arduous times, is well known. A law preventing the re-election of the chief magistrate would deprive the citizens of their best means of ensuring the prosperity and the security of the

了加倍的热情,所有能够想象出来的激情,又在这时于一个幸福和平的国家里躁动起来。而这时的总统,则专心于自我保护。他不再为国家的利益去处理政务,只为再次当选而忙碌。他为了获得选民而百般讨好,但不像他的职责所要求的那样,他并没有控制自己的激情,反而经常任意发作。随着选举的临近,各种阴谋活动又积极活动起来,而选举的热潮也在不断地扩大。公民们被分成很多对立的阵营,每个阵营都高举自己候选人的旗帜。这时,全国到处都处在兴奋发热中,选举成了报纸的头条新闻,私人交谈的内容,一切行动的目的,一切思想的中心和当前的唯一兴趣。不错,选举的结果一经公布,这种热情随即消失,一切又恢复平静,而看来似乎即将决堤的河水,又静静地淌流在原来的河道里,但是,这场风暴如果已经刮大了,又有谁能不感到惊奇呢?

总统的连选连任

容许行政权首脑连选连任,说明政府本身在变质和有人搞阴谋和腐化——连选连任的愿望统治着美国总统的整个思想——连选连任在美国有其特别害处——民主的自然弊端在于使一切权力逐渐屈服于多数的微小愿望——总统的连选连任助长了这种弊端。

美国的立法者当初容许总统连选连任,是正确还是错误?乍一看来,不准行政权首脑连选连任,似乎是不合理的。谁都知道一个人的才能和品格会对整个国家的命运产生什么影响,特别是当国家处在危机环境和紧要关头的时候!一个禁止公民连选连任首席行政官的法律,会剥夺公民帮助国家繁荣和拯救国家的

commonwealth; and, by a singular inconsistency, a man would be excluded from the government at the very time when he had proved his ability to govern well.

But if these arguments are strong, perhaps still more powerful reasons may be advanced against them. Intrigue and corruption are the natural vices of elective government; but when the head of the state can be re-lected, these evils rise to a great height and compromise the very existence of the country. When a simple candidate seeks to rise by intrigue, his maneuvers must be limited to a very narrow sphere; but when the chief magistrate enters the lists, he borrows the strength of the government for his own purposes. In the former case the feeble resources of an individual are in action; in the latter the state itself, with its immense influence, is busied in the work of corruption and cabal. The private citizen who employs culpable practices to acquire power can act in a manner only indirectly prejudicial to the public prosperity. But if the representative of the executive descends into the combat, the cares of government dwindle for him into second-rate importance, and the success of his election is his first concern. All public negotiations, as well as all laws, are to him nothing more than electioneering schemes; places become the reward of services rendered, not to the nation, but to its chief; and the influence of the government, if not injurious to the country, is at least no longer beneficial to the community for which it was created. It is impossible to consider the ordinary course of affairs in the United States without perceiving that the desire to be re-elected is the chief aim of the President; that the whole policy of his administration, and even his most indifferent measures, tend to this object; and that, especially as the crisis approaches, his personal interest takes the place of his interest in the public good. The principle of re-eligibility renders the corrupting influence of elective government still more extensive and pernicious. It tends to degrade the political morality of the people and to substitute management and intrigue for patriotism.

In America it injures still more directly the very sources of national existence. Every government seems to be afflicted by some evil inherent in its nature, and the genius of the legislator consists in having a clear view of this evil. A state may survive the influence of a

最好方法。而且可能产生一种异常的矛盾，即当一个人证明其有很好的管理才能时，却被排除于政府之外。

但是，如果这些论点非常有力，也许还会有更有力的论点去反驳它们。阴谋和腐败是民选政府的自然弊端。当国家首脑可以连选连任时，这种弊端将会无限扩大，并危及到国家本身的生存。当一个普通候选人想依靠阴谋来达到目的时，他的动机只能被限制到极其有限的范围内；但当国家主要官员出现于候选人名单中，他会借助政府的力量去达到个人的目的。在前一种情况下，候选人只拥有极其微弱的手段；而在后一种情况下，则是国家本身用其强大的影响去搞阴谋和腐败。利用应受谴责的阴谋诡计去获得权力的普通公民，只能间接地损害国家的繁荣；而行政权的代表也参与到竞争中，就会使政府将其主要注意力移到次要工作上去，而把自己的选举看成是当前最重要的事情。所有的外交谈判和法律在他们面前已变得不重要，他们只一心关心选举。政府官员照样得报酬，但他们已经不是为国家服务，而是为其首领服务了。同时，政府的活动如果不违反国家的利益，至少也不再使社会受益。但是，政府的活动只应当为国家效劳。连选连任的渴望支配着总统的思想，他的一切行政方针，以至于他的一举一动都指向这个目标，特别是当选举即将来临的时候，他自己的私人利益就代替了全国的普遍利益。看不到这一切，就不能认识美国总统处理国务的常规。连选连任的原则，使民选政府的腐败影响变得越来越广泛和危险。它在败坏人民的政治道德，以阴谋诡计冒充爱国行为。

在美国，这项原则仍旧直接打击着国家生存的基础。每个政府本身都有一种似乎与其生存原则相联系的自然弊端，而天才的

host of bad laws, and the mischief they cause is frequently exaggerated; but a law that encourages the growth of the canker within must prove fatal in the end, although its bad consequences may not be immediately perceived.

The principle of destruction in absolute monarchies lies in the unlimited and unreasonable extension of the royal power, and a measure tending to remove the constitutional provisions that counterbalance this influence would be radically bad even if its immediate consequences were unattended with evil. By parity of reasoning, in countries governed by a democracy, where the people is perpetually drawing all authority to itself, the laws that increase or accelerate this action directly attack the very principle of the government.

The greatest merit of the American legislators is that they clearly discerned this truth and had the courage to act up to it. They conceived that a certain authority above the body of the people was necessary, which should enjoy a degree of independence in its sphere without being entirely beyond the popular control; an authority which would be forced to comply with the *permanent* determinations of the majority, but which would be able to resist its caprices and refuse its most dangerous demands. To this end they centered the whole executive power of the nation in a single arm; they granted extensive prerogatives to the President and armed him with the veto to resist the encroachments of the legislature.

But by introducing the principle of re-election they partly destroyed their work; they conferred on the President a great power, but made him little inclined to use it. If ineligible a second time, the President would not be independent of the people, for his responsibility would not cease; but the favor of the people would not be so necessary to him as to induce him to submit in every respect to its desires. If re-eligible (and this is especially true at the present day, when political morality is relaxed and when great men are rare), the President of the United States becomes an easy tool in the hands of the majority. He adopts its likings and its animosities, he anticipates its wishes, he forestalls its complaints, he yields to its idlest cravings, and instead

立法者应该能清楚地认识这一弊端。一个国家可能因废除许多不良法律而存在下去，但不良法律的恶劣影响也常常会被夸大。一些会助长危险的法律，尽管其危害作用不能马上被人发现，但它们不能长期使危险不发作。

专制君主国破灭的原因，在于王权的无限的和不合理的扩张。因此，即使采取措施，拿走宪法中使王权加重的砝码，当这些措施长期不发生作用时，它们也将极其有害。同样，在民主开始居于统治地位和人民逐渐将一切事情主管起来的国家里，那些使人民的活动日益活跃和日益不可抗拒的法律，也会直接打击政府的生存。

美国立法者们的最大的价值，在于他们清楚地认识到这个事实，并有勇气付诸行动。他们认为，除了人民的权力之外，还要有一定数量的执行权力的机构。这些机构虽不是完全独立于人民的，但在自己的职权范围内享有一定程度的自由，他们既要被迫服从人民中的多数的一致决定，又可以制止这个多数的无理取闹和拒绝其危险的要求。为了达到这个目的，美国的立法者把全国的行政权集中于一个人手里，并赋予总统广泛的特权，用否决权把总统武装起来，以便抵抗立法机构的侵犯。

但是，由于可以采用总统连选连任的原则，立法者又部分地破坏了自己的工作。他们授予总统巨大的权力，但使总统很少能使用到这些大权。如果总统的第二次竞选失败，他也不会脱离人民，因为对人民的责任并没有终止。但对他来说，为向人民讨好，也不必非得完全遵从人民的意愿。如果可以连选连任（这在现今社会是很真实的，当政治道德放松警惕和伟人不多的时候）美国总统就会变成多数手中的工具。他要爱多数之所爱，恨多数之所恨；他要以多数的愿望为己任，为多数的抱怨打抱不平，多数的一小点企求，他也得服从；立法者本希望

of guiding it, as the legislature intended that he should do, he merely follows its bidding. Thus, in order not to deprive the state of the talents of an individual, those talents have been rendered almost useless; and to retain an expedient for extraordinary perils, the country has been exposed to continual dangers.

Federal Courts Of Justice[①]

Political importance of the judiciary in the United States — Difficulty of treating this subject — Utility of judicial power in confederations — What tribunals could be introduced into the Union — Necessity of establishing Federal courts of justice — Organization of the national judiciary — The Supreme Court — In what it differs from all other known tribunals.

I have examined the legislative and executive power of the Union, and the judicial power now remains to be considered; but here I cannot conceal my fears from the reader. Their judicial institutions exercise a great influence on the condition of the AngloAmericans, and they occupy a very important place among political institutions, properly so called: in this respect they are peculiarly deserving of our attention. But I am at a loss how to explain the political action of the American tribunals without entering into some technical details respecting their constitution and their forms of proceeding; and I cannot descend to these minutiæ without wearying the reader by the natural dryness of the subject. Yet how can I be clear and at the same time brief? I can scarcely hope to escape these different evils. Ordinary

---

① See Chapter VI, entitled "Judicial Power in the United States." This chapter explains the general principles of the American judiciary. See also the Federal Constitution, Article III; *The Federalist*, *Nos.* 78-83 *inclusive*; *Constitutional Law*, *Being a View of the Practise and Jurisdiction of the Courts of the United States*, by Thomas Sergeant; Story, pp. 134-62; 489511, 581, 668. See the organic law of September 24, 1789, in the collection entitled *Laws of the United States*, by Story, Vol. I, p. 53.

他领导多数,而他却唯唯诺诺,屈从于多数。因此,立法者本不想埋没人们的才能,但结果却使这些人几乎成了废物;立法者本想为这种特殊环境采取一种对策,而结果却使全国经常处于频频的危险之中。

联邦系统法院①

美国司法权的政治重要性——在对待这个问题时的困难——司法权在全联邦的实用性——哪些法院通行于全联邦——设立全联邦性法院的必要性——联邦司法工作的组织——最高法庭——最高法院与我们所知道的其他法院有什么不同。

我已经分析了美国的立法权和行政权,还留有司法权等着我们考虑。在这里,我不能对读者隐藏我的担心:因为我的讲解可能很无趣。司法制度对英籍美国人的命运产生了重大影响,它在政治机构中占有非常重要的地位。因此可以说,它特别值得我们重视。但是,我不知道怎么解释美国法院的政治作用,因为我们并不了解美国法院的组织体系和审判程序的某些技术细节,并且在讲解这些细节时怎能不使读者对这种本来就枯燥无味的题目而更加扫兴呢?所以,怎样才能进行清楚并简单扼要的讲解呢?我几乎没有回避过这些繁杂的难题。一般的读者会抱怨我

① 见第六章的《美国司法权》。这一章讲述了美国司法部门的一般原则。同样见联邦宪法,第三篇;《联邦党人文集》,第 78~83 条;宪法是美国法院行使司法权的依据;《斯得瑞的评论》,第 134~162、489~511、581、668 页。见 1789 年 9 月 24 日的组织法,斯得瑞的美国法律集合,第一卷,第 53 页。

readers will complain that I am tedious, lawyers that I am too concise. But these are the natural disadvantages of my subject, and especially of the point that I am now to discuss.

The great difficulty was, not to know how to constitute the Federal government, but to find out a method of enforcing its laws. Governments have generally but two means of overcoming the opposition of the governed: namely, the physical force that is at their own disposal, and the moral force that they derive from the decisions of the courts of justice.

A government which should have no other means of exacting obedience than open war must be very near its ruin, for one of two things would then probably happen to it. If it was weak and temperate, it would resort to violence only at the last extremity and would connive at many partial acts of insubordination; then the state would gradually fall into anarchy. If it was enterprising and powerful, it would every day have recourse to physical strength, and thus would soon fall into a military despotism. Thus its activity and its inertness would be equally prejudicial to the community.

The great end of justice is to substitute the notion of right for that of violence and to place a legal barrier between the government and the use of physical force. It is a strange thing, the authority that is accorded to the intervention of a court of justice by the general opinion of mankind! It clings even to the mere formalities of justice, and gives a bodily influence to the mere shadow of the law. The moral force which courts of justice possess renders the use of physical force very rare and is frequently substituted for it; but if force proves to be indispensable, its power is doubled by the association of the idea of law.

A federal government stands in greater need than any other of the support of judicial institutions, because it is naturally weak and exposed to formidable opposition. ① If it were always obliged

---

① Federal laws are those which most require courts of justice, and at the same time those which have most rarely established them. The reason is that confederations have usually been formed by independent states, which had no real intention of obeying the central government; and though they readily ceded the right of command to the central government, they carefully reserved the right of noncompliance to themselves.

的单调和乏味,而法学家们则会认为我讲得过于简要。但是,这些是我在书中的自然的缺陷,特别是现在叙述的这部分。

最大的困难不在于了解怎样组织联邦政府,而在于知道美国是怎样使人们服从联邦的法律的。一般说来,各国政府只有两种制止造反的手段:政府本身拥有的物质力量;法院的判决给予政府的道德力量。

如果一个政府到了只有依靠武力才能使人们服从其法律的地步,这个政府也快接近灭亡了。这时可能出现两种情况,一是如果政府是软弱而有节制的,只在迫不得已时才动用武力,并对局部的接二连三的反抗行为置之不理时,这个国家将逐渐陷入无政府状态;二是如果政府是有魄力的并强大的,每天都使用武力手段,这个国家很快就会变成一个纯粹的军事专制国家。政府的消极被动和积极主动,对社会都同样具有致命的害处。

司法工作的最大目的,是用权力观念代替暴力观念,在政府管理与物质力量使用之间设立合法的屏障。人们一致认为给与法院的干涉力量,是一件奇怪的事情。当法院不复存在的时候,这个力量还十分强大地存在于司法程序上,使人们隐约觉得法院好像依然存在于无形之中。法院具有的道义力量会时常代替物质力量,并使物质力量极少为国家所使用。但当最后不得不使用武力时,武力还会因与道义力量结合而使自己的力量倍增。

联邦政府比其他任何形式的政府更想得到司法部门的支持,因为它天生软弱无力,并遭到强大的反对。① 如果它在一开始就

---

① 联邦法律比其他任何法律都更需要司法法庭的支持。而同时又很少去确立司法法庭。因为联邦是由各个独立的州组成的,这些州并没有真正想完全服从中央政府的指令;虽然各个州愿意将指挥权割让给中央政府,但他们仍谨慎地为自己保留了不服从的权力。

to resort to violence in the first instance, it could not fulfill its task. The Union, therefore, stood in special need of a judiciary to make its citizens obey the laws and to repel the attacks that might be directed against them. But what tribunals were to exercise these privileges? Were they to be entrusted to the courts of justice which were already organized in every state? Or was it necessary to create Federal courts? It may easily be proved that the Union could not adapt to its wants the judicial power of the states. The separation of the judiciary from the other powers of the state is necessary for the security of each and the liberty of all. But it is no less important to the existence of the nation that the several powers of the state should have the same origin, follow the same principles, and act in the same sphere; in a word, that they should be correlative and homogeneous. No one, I presume, ever thought of causing offenses committed in France to be tried by a foreign court of justice in order to ensure the impartiality of the judges. The Americans form but one people in relation to their Federal government; but in the bosom of this people divers political bodies have been allowed to exist, which are dependent on the national government in a few points and independent in all the rest, which have all a distinct origin, maxims peculiar to themselves, and special means of carrying on their affairs. To entrust the execution of the laws of the Union to tribunals instituted by these political bodies would be to allow foreign judges to preside over the nation. Nay, more; not only is each state foreign to the Union at large, but it is a perpetual adversary, since whatever authority the Union loses turns to the advantage of the states. Thus, to enforce the laws of the Union by means of the state tribunals would be to allow not only foreign, but partial judges to preside over the nation. But the number, still more than the mere character, of the state tribunals made them unfit for the service of the nation. When the Federal Constitution was formed, there were already thirteen courts of justice in the United States which decided causes without appeal. That number has now increased to twenty-four. To suppose that a state can exist when its fundamental laws are subjected to four-and-twenty different interpretations at the same time is to advance a proposition contrary alike to reason and to experience.

经常使用武力反对暴力,那它将不能完成自己的任务。因此,联邦特别需要设立法院,以使公民服从它的法律或保护公民不受侵犯。但是,什么样的法院才能行使这些权力呢?每个州都早已有了自己的司法当局,它还需要这些法院的帮助吗?它需要建立直属于联邦的司法当局吗?不难证明,联邦无法使各州早已建立的司法当局适应于它的需要。在每个州内,司法权与其他权力的分离,对州的安全和自由都是必要的。但是,各州的几种权力应当有同样的来源,遵循同样的原则,并在同样的范围内行使权力。总之,就是应当互相关联和性质相同的。我猜测没有一个人曾经想过,为了得到法官的公正判决,而要求把在法国犯下的罪行送交外国法院审判。从美国人和联邦政府的关系来说,美国是一个统一民族,但这个民族却允许只有某些方面服从于全国政府,而在其余一切方面都独立于全国政府的政治组织。这些政治组织都有自己不同的来源、独自的宗旨和特殊的执行方式。将联邦法律的执行工作交给这些政治组织所设立的法院,无疑是让外国法官审理本国事务。更加严重的是,每个州和整个联邦的关系好像是两个外国,而且永远是对立的,因为联邦所丧失的权力都被各州夺去了。因此,在允许各州的法院执行联邦的法律时,这不仅等于把国家交给外国法官审理,而且还是交给了带有偏见的法官。另外,州法院的性质也使州法院不能为国家目的服务,而州法院的数目之多,则会使它们如此。在制定联邦宪法的时候,美国已设有 13 个法院,这些法院在宣判之后不得向联邦上诉。现在,这个数目已增至 24 个。既要对国家的主要法律做 24 种解释和应用,又要让国家继续存在,这怎么能办到! 这样的制度既没有道理,又没有经验。

The American legislators therefore agreed to create a Federal judicial power to apply the laws of the Union and to determine certain questions affecting general interests, which were carefully defined beforehand. The entire judicial power of the Union was centered in one tribunal, called the Supreme Court of the United States. But to facilitate the expedition of business, inferior courts were added to it, which were empowered to decide causes of small importance without appeal, and, with appeal, causes of more magnitude. The members of the Supreme Court are appointed neither by the people nor by the legislature, but by the President of the United States, acting with the advice of the Senate. In order to render them independent of the other authorities, their office was made inalienable; and it was determined that their salary, when once fixed, should not be diminished by the legislature. ① It was easy to proclaim the principle of a Federal judiciary, but difficulties multiplied when the extent of its jurisdiction was to be determined.

---

① The Union was divided into districts, in each of which a resident Federal judge was appointed, and the court in which he presided was termed a "District Court." Each of the judges of the Supreme Court annually visits a certain portion of the country, in order to try the most important causes on the spot; the court presided over by this magistrate is styled a "Circuit Court." Lastly, all the most serious cases of litigation are brought, either directly or by appeal before the Supreme Court, which holds a solemn session once a year, at which all the judges of the circuit courts must attend. The jury was introduced into the Federal courts in the same manner and for the same cases as into the courts of the states.

It will be observed that no analogy exists between the Supreme Court of the United States and our Cour de Cassation. The Supreme Court has original, the *Cour de Cassation* only appellate jurisdiction. The Supreme Court is in fact, as is the *Cour de Cassation*, a unique tribunal responsible for establishing a uniform jurisprudence; but the Supreme Court judges of the fact as well as the law and makes a final judgment without recourse to another tribunal, two things which the *Cour de Cassation* cannot do.

See the organic law of September 24, 1789, *Laws of the United States*, by Story, Vol. I, p. 53.

因此,美国的立法者决定创立一个联邦司法当局,以实施联邦的法律,并仔细审查曾经涉及全国利益的案件。于是,联邦的全部司法权都掌握在一个叫做"美国最高法院"的法院手里。为了便于审理政务,这个法院又设立一些下属法院,把一些不太重要的案件交给它们判决,或对一些重大的申诉做初审判决。最高法院的成员既不由人民决定,也不由立法机构决定,而由美国总统征求参议院同意后任命。为了赋予最高法院独立权,不受其他权力当局的影响,而决定最高法院法官为终身制,并规定他们的工资一经确定,就不受司法机构的核查。① 简要讲述联邦司法制度的原则是很容易的,但要深入讲解它的职权时,便会遇到一大堆的困难。

---

①　联邦被分割成很多区域,每个区域都会任命自己的联邦法官,由联邦法官主持的法庭被称作是"地方法院"。每年,最高法院的法官都会对这些地区的部分地方法院进行访问;为了对这些地方最重要的一些案件进行审察。由一个行政官员主持法庭的这种形式被认为是"巡回法庭"。最终,这个法庭将审理所有的不管是直接的还是已经上诉到最高法院的诉讼案件,这种巡回法庭的所有法官都必须参加的审判每年举行一次。巡回法官被以同样的方式和同样的原因像被引入州法庭那样,被介绍到联邦法庭。我们仔细观察将会发现,美国的最高法院与我们法国的最高法院间并没有任何相似之处。

美国的最高法院具有一切特权,而法国的只具有上诉管辖权。实际上,美国的最高法院和法国的最高法院都是唯一负责建立统一的法律的法庭;但是美国最高法院在对实事与法律作出最终判决时不需求助于其他法庭,而法国的最高法院却不能做到。

见 1789 年 9 月 24 日,美国的组织法,斯得瑞的《美国法律》第一卷,第 53 页。

Means Of Determining The
Jurisdiction Of The Federal Courts

Difficulty of determining the jurisdiction of the different courts of justice in confederations — The courts of the Union obtained the right of fixing their own jurisdiction — In what respects this rule attacks the portion of sovereignty reserved to the several states — The sovereignty of these states restricted by the laws and by the interpretation of the laws — Danger thus incurred by the several states more apparent than real.

As the Constitution of the United States recognized two distinct sovereignties, in presence of each other, represented in a judicial point of view by two distinct classes of courts of justice, the utmost care taken in defining their separate jurisdictions would have been insufficient to prevent frequent collisions between those tribunals. The question then arose to whom the right of deciding the competency of each court was to be referred.

In nations that constitute a single body politic, when a question of jurisdiction is debated between two courts, a third tribunal is generally within reach to decide the difference; and this is effected without difficulty because in these nations questions of judicial competence have no connection with questions of national sovereignty. But it was impossible to create an arbiter between a superior court of the Union and the superior court of a separate state, which would not belong to one of these two classes. It was therefore necessary to allow one of these courts to judge its own cause and to take or to retain cognizance of the point that was contested. To grant this privilege to the different courts of the states would have been to destroy the sovereignty of the Union, *de facto* after having established it; *de jure* for the interpretation of the Constitution would soon have restored to the states that portion of independence of which the terms of the Constitution deprived them. The object of creating a Federal tribunal was to prevent the state courts from deciding, each after its own fashion, questions affecting the national interests, and so to form a uniform body of jurisprudence for the interpretation of the laws of

规定联邦法院司法权的方法

规定联邦各法院的司法权的困难——联邦法院有权规定自己的司法权——这项规定在哪些方面侵犯了让给各州的那部分主权——这些州的主权受到法律和被法律解释的限制——各州由此遇到的危险实际上并不如表面看来那样严重。

首先,美国的宪法承认两种不同的主权同时存在,而在司法制度方面,这两种主权又以两种不同性质的法院为代表,所以即使十分细心地规定两种性质的法院各自的审理权,也不能够防止两者之间经常发生冲突。所以,在这种情况下,应当把决定法院司法权的权力交给谁。

在政治组织单一的国家,当两个法院之间为司法权争议时,一般都会由第三个法庭出面仲裁。这样,问题就很容易解决,因为在这样的国家里,司法权限问题与国家主权问题没有什么牵连。但是在美国,要想在州的最高法院和联邦的最高法院之间设立一个既不属于前者又不属于后者的仲裁系统是不可能的。因此,必须使这两个法院中的一个法院有自己判决的权力,并有权受理或拒绝受理案件。但是如果将这项特权授予各州的法院,那就等于破坏联邦的主权,所以这样做是不可能的;因为州的法院获得宪法解释权后,很快就会恢复以前被宪法的有关条款夺去的那部分独立性。创建联邦最高法院的目的,是为了防止各州的法院用其自己的方式解决涉及全国利益的问题,并建立一个统一的可以解释联邦法律的司法仲裁机构。如果各州的法院拒绝审理本

the Union. This end would not have been attained if the courts of the several states, even while they abstained from deciding cases avowedly Federal in their nature, had been able to decide them by pretending that they were not Federal. The Supreme Court of the United States was therefore invested with the right of determining all questions of jurisdiction. ①

This was a severe blow to the sovereignty of the states, which was thus restricted not only by the laws, but by the interpretation of them, by one limit which was known and by another which was unknown, by a rule which was certain and one which was arbitrary. It is true, the Constitution had laid down the precise limits of the Federal supremacy; but whenever this supremacy is contested by one of the states, a Federal tribunal decides the question. Nevertheless, the dangers with which the independence of the states is threatened by this mode of proceeding are less serious than they appear to be. We shall see hereafter that in America the real power is vested in the states far more than in the Federal government. The Federal judges are conscious of the relative weakness of the power in whose name they act; and they are more inclined to abandon the right of jurisdiction in cases where the law gives it to them than to assert a privilege to which they have no legal claim.

Different Cases Of Jurisdiction

The matter and the party are the first conditions of the Federal jurisdiction — Suits in which ambassadors are engaged — Or the Union — Or a separate state — By whom tried — Causes resulting from

---

① In order to diminish the number of these suits, however, it was decided that in a great many Federal causes the courts of the states should be empowered to decide conjointly with those of the Union, the losing party having then a right of appeal to the Supreme Court of the United States. The Supreme Court of Virginia contested the right of the Supreme Court of the United States to judge an appeal from its decisions, but unsuccessfully. See Kent's *Commentaries*, Vol. I, pp. 300, 370, et seq. ; Story's Commentaries, p. 646; and the organic law of 1789, *Laws of the United States*, Vol. I, p. 53.

应属于自己负责的案件,说它是属于联邦管辖的,或把本应属于联邦管辖的案件硬说成是属于自己管辖的,那么这个目的是根本无法达到的。因此,美国的最高法院被赋予解决一切司法权问题的权力。①

这对州的主权是一次严厉的打击。这样一来,州的主权不仅受到法律的限制,而且受到法律解释的限制,既受一个已知范围的限制,又受一个未知范围的限制,既受明文规定的限制,又受专横权力的限制。确实如此,宪法已被联邦主权限定了明确的范围;但同时又规定:一旦联邦的主权与州的主权发生冲突,应由联邦法院来判决。尽管如此,这样的规定可能对州的主权有一定的威胁性,但可能并不像表面看到的那样严重。以后我们还将看到,美国各州实际拥有的权力远远大于联邦政府的权力。联邦的法官们已经感觉到以他们自己的名义行使的权力比较软弱。他们受理依法有权审理的案件时,如果附带为他们规定了一些不合理要求,他们宁愿放弃审判权而不予受理。

联邦法院审理的各种案件

案件与诉讼当事人是联邦法院审判的首要条件——有关外国大使的诉讼案件——或联邦的诉讼案件——或各个州的诉讼案件——由谁审判——因联邦法律引发的诉讼——为什么要由,

---

① 为了减少此类诉讼事件的发生,州的法庭被赋予和联邦法庭共同解决诸多联邦问题的权力,败诉的一方可以向美国最高法院上诉。弗吉尼亚的最高法庭会与美国最高法庭争辩对此种上诉的决定,但最终会以失败而告终。见肯特:《美国法释义》第一卷,第 300 页,第 370 页;见斯得瑞的《评论》,第 646 页;见 1789 年《美国组织法》第一卷,第 53 页。

the laws of the Union — Why judged by the Federal tribunals — Causes relating to the non-performance of contracts tried by the Federal courts — Consequences of this arrangement.

After establishing the competence of the Federal courts the legislators of the Union defined the cases that should come within their jurisdiction. It was determined, on the one hand, that certain parties must always be brought before the Federal courts, without regard to the special nature of the suit; and, on the other, that certain causes must always be brought before the same courts, no matter who were the parties to them. The party and the cause were therefore admitted to be the two bases of Federal jurisdiction.

Ambassadors represent nations in amity with the Union, and whatever concerns these personages concerns in some degree the whole Union. When an ambassador, therefore, is a party in a suit, its issue affects the welfare of the nation, and a Federal tribunal is naturally called upon to decide it. The Union itself may be involved in legal proceedings, and in this case it would be contrary to reason and to the customs of all nations to appeal to a tribunal representing any other sovereignty than its own; the Federal courts alone, therefore, take cognizance of these affairs. When two parties belonging to two different states are engaged in a suit, the case cannot with propriety be brought before a court of either state. The surest expedient is to select a tribunal which can excite the suspicions of neither party, and this is naturally a Federal court. When the two parties are not private individuals, but states, an important political motive is added to the same consideration of equity. The quality of the parties, in this case, gives a national importance to all their disputes; and the most trifling litigation between two states may be said to involve the peace of the whole Union. [1]

---

[1] The Constitution also says that the Federal courts shall decide "controversies between a State and the citizens of another State." And here a most important question arose, whether the jurisdiction given by the Constitution in cases in which a state is a party extended to suits brought against a state as well as by it, or was exclusively confined to the latter. The Supreme Court decided in the affirmative. The decision created general alarm among the states which feared that they would be subjected to Federal justice in spite of themselves. An amendment was proposed and ratified by which the power was entirely taken away so far as it regards suits brought against a state by the citizens of another. See Story's *Commentaries*, p. 624.

联邦法院审理——由于不履行合同而引起的诉讼由联邦法院审理——这种安排的结果。

在确定联邦法院的能力和权限后,美国的立法者又规定了联邦法院审理案件的范围。一方面,他们规定了只能由联邦法院审理的诉讼人的范围,而不管诉讼的内容是什么。另一方面,他们又规定了只能由联邦法院审判的案件的范围,而不管诉讼人是谁。因此,诉讼当事人和案件是联邦法院审判的两个基本条件。

外国大使代表联邦的友好国家;凡是和他们有关的案件,在某种程度上也可以说是涉及全联邦的案件。因此,当外国大使为诉讼的一方时,这种诉讼一定关系到国家的利益,而自然应由联邦法院审理判决。联邦本身也可能卷入诉讼案件。这时,它如果在向代表联邦本身主权的法院控诉之后,又到其他法院去起诉,则是不合乎道理,并违反国家惯例的。因此,这种案件只能由联邦法院自行审理判决。当两个不同州的不同诉讼人纷纷诉讼时,将案件交给任何一州的法院审理都是不合适的。最可行的办法,是挑选一个不会引起两方中的任何一方怀疑的法院,而这个法院自然就是联邦法院。当诉讼的双方不是个人而是州时,除了上述的公平理由之外,还应当加上一项政治理由。这时,两方的性质便使整个诉讼具有了全国影响。两州之间微不足道的争端,都将影响全国的和平。①

---

①　宪法同时还规定,联邦法院应对:"一个州与另一个州之间的争论"进行协调。但是,这就产生了一个很重要的问题,宪法赋予联邦法院的这种权力是否是为了防止一个州对另一个州的侵犯或排斥。最高法院将进行正面判决。这种判决给那些担心会不由自主地屈从于联邦司法决定的州敲响了警钟。于是,关于这个权力的修正案被批准,只要这种权力被看作是一个州对另一个州的侵犯,它将被完全剥夺。见斯得瑞的《评论》,第624页。

The nature of the cause frequently prescribes the rule of competency. Thus, all questions which concern maritime affairs evidently fall under the cognizance of the Federal tribunals. [1] Almost all these questions depend on the interpretation of the law of nations, and in this respect they essentially interest the Union in relation to foreign powers. Moreover, as the sea is not included within the limits of any one state jurisdiction rather than another, only the national courts can hear causes which originate in maritime affairs. The Constitution comprises under one head almost all the cases which by their very nature come before the Federal courts. The rule that it lays down is simple, but pregnant with an entire system of ideas and with a multitude of facts. It declares that the judicial power of the Supreme Court shall extend to all cases in law and equity *arising under the laws of the United States*. Two examples will put the intention of the legislator in the clearest light. The Constitution prohibits the states from making laws on the value and circulation of money. If, notwithstanding this prohibition, a state passes a law of this kind, with which the interested parties refuse to comply because it is contrary to the Constitution, the case must come before a Federal court, because it arises under the laws of the United States. Again, if difficulties arise in the levying of import duties that have been voted by Congress, the Federal court must decide the case, because it arises under the interpretation of a law of the United States.

This rule is in perfect accordance with the fundamental principles of the Federal Constitution. The Union, as it was established in 1789, possesses, it is true, a limited sovereignty; but it was intended that within its limits it should form one and the same people. [2] Within those limits the Union is sovereign. When this point is established and admitted, the inference is easy; for if it is acknowledged that the United States, within the bounds prescribed by their Constitution, constitute

---

① As, for instance, all cases of piracy.

② This principle was, in some measure, restricted by the introduction of the several states as independent powers into the Senate, and by allowing them to vote separately in the House of Representatives when the President is elected by that body. But these are exceptions, and the contrary principle is the rule.

诉讼的性质常常可以决定竞争的原则。比如,凡与海商有关的问题,都应由联邦系统法院解决。① 几乎所有的问题都依赖于国家法律的解释,从这个方面来看,这类问题都要涉及整个联邦与外国的关系。而且,海上也不像在陆地那样能够划定司法管辖区,所以要有一个能够审理海上诉讼案件的国家法院。联邦宪法几乎把所有在性质上属于联邦法院判决的诉讼,都定在一个项目之内。对这方面做出的规定虽很简单,但人们可以从中看到有关整个系统的想法和大量的事实。美国的宪法规定,最高法庭的司法权力可以审理以合众国法律为基础的一切诉讼。举两个例子,就可以清楚地明白立法者的意图。例如,宪法禁止各州制定有关货币流通和货币价值的法律,但如果有一个州不顾这项禁令,通过了一项类似的法律,而有关机构可能因其违宪而拒绝执行,这就需要由联邦法院来处理,因为处理这种行为的方法存在于联邦的法律之内。再例如,国会规定了一项进口税,但在征税时遇到了困难,这时联邦法院也要判决此案,因为诉讼的原因在于对联邦法律的解释上。

这项规定完全符合联邦宪法的基本原则。不错,联邦自1789年建立以后,只拥有有限的主权,但宪法又规定联邦必须在这个范围形成一个单一制的统一国家。② 也就是在这个范围内,它是一个主权国家。在这个观点被建立和同意后,其余的问题就容易解决了;因为如果承认美国是由宪法规定的拥有主权的国家,就

① 例如,所有盗版事件。

② 在某种程度上,这个原则受到一些进入到参议院的具有独立主权的州的限制,同时当竞选总统时,也会受到这些州在众议院所具有的独立选举权的限制。但是,这些只是特殊情况,而与其相反的原则才是主要规则。

but one people, it is impossible to refuse them the rights which belong to other nations. But it has been allowed, from the origin of society, that every nation has the right of deciding by its own courts those questions which concern the execution of its own laws. To this it is answered that the Union is in such a singular position that in relation to some matters it constitutes but one people, and in relation to all the rest it is a nonentity. But the inference to be drawn is that in the laws relating to these matters the Union possesses all the rights of absolute sovereignty. The difficulty is to know what these matters are; and when once it is settled (and in speaking of the means of determining the jurisdiction of the Federal courts I have shown how it was settled), no further doubt can arise; for as soon as it is established that a suit is Federal — that is to say, that it belongs to the share of sovereignty reserved by the Constitution to the Union — the natural consequence is that it should come within the jurisdiction of a Federal court.

Whenever the laws of the United States are attacked, or whenever they are resorted to in self-defense, the Federal courts must be appealed to. Thus the jurisdiction of the tribunals of the Union extends and narrows its limits exactly in the same ratio as the sovereignty of the Union augments or decreases. I have shown that the principal aim of the legislators of 1789 was to divide the sovereign authority into two parts. In the one they placed the control of all the general interests of the Union, in the other the control of the special interests of its component states. Their chief concern was to arm the Federal government with sufficient power to enable it to resist, within its sphere, the encroachments of the several states. As for these communities, the general principle of independence within certain limits of their own was adopted on their behalf; there the central government cannot control, nor even inspect, their conduct. In speaking of the division of authority, I observed that this latter principle had not always been respected, since the states are prevented from passing certain laws which apparently belong to their own particular sphere of interest. When a state of the Union passes a law of this kind, the citizens who are injured by its execution can appeal to the Federal courts.

Thus the jurisdiction of the Federal courts extends, not only to all the cases which arise under the laws of the Union, but also to those which arise under laws made by the several states in opposition to the Constitution. The states are prohibited from making *ex posto*

得赋予它一切其他国家所拥有的权力。但是,自有国家以来,人们就一致认为每个民族都有权在本国的法院审理有关本国法律执行的问题。但有人却反驳说,联邦在这一点上处于独特的地位,它在一些方面可以说是一个国家,而在其余一切方面它又算不上一个国家。结果是只在一些和法律有关的方面上,它有权成为拥有完整主权的国家。但困难在于如何知道这些方面是什么。这个问题一旦解决(在前面叙述联邦法庭的司法审判方式时,已经解释过这一点是如何解决的),就不会再有什么疑问了;因为只要确定一件诉讼属于联邦法院管辖范围之内,也就是说按宪法规定这是属于联邦的主权时,诉讼自然应由联邦法院审理判决。

　　每当联邦的法律受到侵犯时,或要采取手段保卫这些法律时,联邦法院应出面协调。因此,联邦法院的司法权是随着联邦主权的增加或减少而相应地扩大或缩小的。我们已经讲过,立法者在1789年的主要目的,是把主权分成两个不同的部分,让其中一方掌管联邦的一切共同利益,而另一方掌管各州的一切独自利益。立法者目前最关心的,是用足够的权力将联邦政府武装起来,使它能在自己的职权范围内抵抗来自各州的侵犯。至于对各州,立法者们则采取了各州在各自范围内享有自由的普遍原则。中央政府不能指导,甚至不能检查它们的行为。在讲述权力划分的那部分时,我已经指出后项原则并不总是受到尊重的。因为一些州无权制定法律,尽管这些法律在表面看来只与一个州的利益有关。如果联邦的某个州颁布了类似的法律,则因执行此项法律而受害的公民可向联邦法院控诉。

　　因此,联邦法院的司法权不仅扩及到由于联邦法律而提出的一切诉讼,而且也扩及到每个州因为制定违宪的法律所造成的诉讼。禁止各州颁布在刑法方面的法律。被这种法律判刑的人,

facto laws in criminal cases; and any person condemned by virtue of a law of this kind can appeal to the judicial power of the Union. The states are likewise prohibited from making laws that may impair the obligation of contracts. ① If a citizen thinks that an obligation of this kind is impaired by a law passed in his state, he may refuse to obey it and may appeal to the Federal courts. ②

This provision appears to me to be the most serious attack upon the independence of the states. The rights accorded to the Federal government for purposes obviously national are definite and easily understood; but those with which this clause invests it are neither clearly appreciable nor accurately defined. For there are many political laws that affect the existence of contracts, which might thus furnish a pretext for the encroachments of the central authority.

Procedure Of The Federal Courts

Natural weakness of the judicial power in confederations —

---

① It is perfectly clear, says Mr. Story (*Commentaries*, p. 503), that any law which enlarges. abridges, or in any manner changes the intention of the parties, resulting from the stipulations in the contract, necessarily impairs it. He gives in the same place a very careful definition of what is understood by a contract in Federal jurisprudence. The definition is very broad. A grant made by the state to a private individual and accepted by him is a contract, and cannot be revoked by any future law. A charter granted by the state to a company is a contract, and equally binding on the state as on the grantee. The clause of the Constitution here referred to ensures, therefore, the existence of a great part of *acquired rights*, but not of all. Property may legally be held, though it may not have passed into the possessor's hands by means of a contract; and its possession is an acquired right, not guaranteed by the Federal Constitution.

② A remarkable instance of this is given by Mr. Story (p. 508). Dartmouth College in New Hampshire had been founded by a charter granted to certain individuals before the American Revolution, and its trustees formed a *corporation* under this charter. The legislature of New Hampshire had, without the consent of this corporation, passed an act changing the terms of the original charter of the college, and transferring all the rights, privileges, and franchises derived from the old charter to new trustees appointed under the act. The constitutionality of the act was contested, and the cause was carried up to the Supreme (Federal) Court, where it was held, that since the original charter was an inviolable contract between the state and the incorporators, the new law could not change the terms of this charter without violating acquired rights as in a contract, and that therefore it violated Article I, Section 10 of the Constitution of the United States.

可以向联邦法院上诉。各州也不得颁布破坏合同义务的法律。①
一个公民确信自己的合同权益被本州的法律损害时,他可以拒绝
服从该法,并向联邦法院控诉。②

　　我认为这项规定对各州主权的打击最为严重。为了明显的
国家利益而授予联邦政府的权力,是明确的和易于理解的。但我
刚才讲的这条宪法规定间接给予联邦政府的权力是难于理解的,
而且它的范围也不明确。实际上,有许多政治性法律影响了合同
的成立,并且由此侵犯了中央主权。

联邦法院的诉讼程序

联邦法院的固有的弱点——立法者应该更多地让个人而

---

　　① 　斯德瑞先生在其《评论》中(第503页)已经明确地讲过,任何由于
合同规定而扩大、缩减或改变政党意图的法律都必定会损害它。他同时也
为联邦法律合同所能理解的范围下了定义。这个定义涉及很广。州对个人
的认可和个人的接受是一种合同,并且不可以被以后的任何法律撤销。州
对某个公司的租赁许可也是一种合同,这种合同不仅受出租者的约束,同时
也受州的约束。因此,宪法的条款在这里代表确保大部分被要求的权力,但
不是全部。虽然财产可能通过合同的方式过户到持有者的名下,但也可能
被合法阻止;对财产的拥有是一种权力,但不受联邦宪法保护。

　　② 　斯得瑞(第508页)曾经在这个问题上举过一个很显著的例子。在
美国革命之前,新罕布什尔的达特茅斯学院是建立在与某些人的特定的租
赁协议上的,并且这些人在这份契约下形成了社团理事会。新罕布什尔的
立法机构未经社团理事会的批准,通过了一项改变学院最初协议的法令,这
项法令将先前协议中的所有权力、特权和参政权转交到其任命的新理事会
的名义下。这项法令引起颇多争议,并被告到最高联邦法庭受理,因为最初
的那份建立在州与合作者之间的租赁协议是不可更改的,新法律不能对协
议的任何条款进行更改,因此,这种做法违背了美国宪法第一篇,第10部
分。

Legislators ought, as much as possible, to bring private individuals, and not states, before the Federal courts — How the Americans have succeeded in this — Direct prosecution of private individuals in the Federal courts — Indirect prosecution of the states which violate the laws of the Union — The decrees of the Supreme Court enervate, but do not destroy, state laws.

I have shown what the rights of the Federal courts are, and it is no less important to show how they are exercised. The irresistible authority of justice in countries in which the sovereignty is undivided is derived from the fact that the tribunals of those countries represent the entire nation at issue with the individual against whom their decree is directed; and the idea of power is thus introduced to corroborate the idea of right. But it is not always so in countries in which the sovereignty is divided; in them the judicial power is more frequently opposed to a fraction of the nation than to an isolated individual, and its moral authority and physical strength are consequently diminished. In Federal states the power of the judge is naturally decreased and that of the justiciable parties is augmented. The aim of the legislator in confederate states ought therefore to be to render the position of the courts of justice analogous to that which they occupy in countries where the sovereignty is undivided; in other words, his efforts ought constantly to tend to maintain the judicial power of the confederation as the representative of the nation, and the justiciable party as the representative of an individual interest.

Every government, whatever may be its constitution, requires the means of constraining its subjects to discharge their obligations and of protecting its privileges from their assaults. As far as the direct action of the government on the community is concerned, the Constitution of the United States contrived, by a master stroke of policy, that the Federal courts, acting in the name of the laws, should take cognizance only of parties in an individual capacity. For, as it had been declared that the Union consisted of one and the same people within the limits laid down by the Constitution, the inference was that the government created by this Constitution, and acting within these limits, was invested with all the privileges of a national government, of which one of the principal is the right of transmitting its injunctions directly to the private citizen. When, for instance, the Union votes an impost, it does not apply to the states for the levying of it, but to every American citizen, in proportion to his assessment. The Supreme Court, which is empowered to enforce the execution of this law of the Union, exerts its influence not upon a refractory state, but upon the private taxpayer; and, like the judicial power of other nations, it acts only upon the person of an individual.

不是让州参与联邦法院——美国是怎样成功做到这一点的——联邦法院对私人的诉讼的直接审理——对违反联邦法律的州进行间接判决——最高法院只能削弱各州的法律判决,而不做废除它们的判决。

我已经讲过联邦法院都拥有什么权力,现在来谈一谈它们是如何行使这些权力的。在主权未被分割的国家,来自国家的法院的不可抗拒的司法权在处分违反法律的个人时代表整个国家。在这里,权力的概念与确定权力的概念结合在一起。但是,在主权被分割的国家里,情况并非总是这样。在这种国家里,与司法机构最常打交道的不是孤立的个人,而是国家中的各个党派。结果,道德权力和物质力量被大大减弱。因此,在联邦国家里,司法机构的权力自然会减弱,而受审人的力量却逐渐强大。在联邦制国家里,立法者的目标应该是使法院获得类似在主权未被分为两部分的国家里的那样的地位,换句话说,通过立法者的努力,应当使司法机构代表国家,使受审者代表个人利益。

每个政府,不管其组成机构如何,都要统治其被统治者,以强迫他们履行义务;它也要保护自己,以防止被统治者的侵犯。关于政府强迫社会人民服从法律的直接行动,按美国宪法的规定,联邦法院执行法律时只以个人为受审主体。既然已经宣布联邦是享有宪法规定的那部分主权的单一制统一国家,所以政府是根据这部宪法创立的,并在其范围内行使权力,它还享有全国政府拥有的一切权力,而其中最主要的权力是向公民直接发号施令。比如当政府公布征税的法令时,这就不是向各州征收,而是按规定的税率向每个应纳税的美国公民征收。最高法院被赋予确保联邦的这项法令顺利实施的任务,它不能判决抗税的州,而只能判决违法的纳税人。同其他国家的司法机构一样,联邦的司法机构

It is to be observed that the Union chose its own antagonist; and as that antagonist is feeble, he is naturally worsted.

But the difficulty increases when the proceedings are not brought forward *by*, but *against* the Union. The Constitution recognizes the legislative power of the states; and a law enacted by that power may violate the rights of the Union. In this case a collision is unavoidable between that body and the state which has passed the law, and it only remains to select the least dangerous remedy, The general principles that I have before established show what this remedy is. [1]

It may be conceived that in the case under consideration the U-nion might have sued the state before a Federal court, which would have annulled the act; this would have been the most natural proceeding. But the judicial power would thus have been placed in direct opposition to the state, and it was desirable to avoid this predicament as much as possible. The Americans hold that it is nearly impossible that a new law should not injure some private interests by its provisions. These private interests are assumed by the American legislators as the means of assailing such measures as may be prejudicial to the Union, and it is to these interests that the protection of the Supreme Court is extended.

Suppose a state sells a portion of its public lands to a company, and that a year afterwards it passes a law by which the lands are otherwise disposed of and that clause of the Constitution which prohibits laws impairing the obligation of contracts is thereby violated. When the purchaser under the second act appears to take possession, the possessor under the first act brings his action before the tribunals of the Union and causes the title of the claimant to be pronounced null and void. [2] Thus, in point of fact, the judicial power of the Union is contesting the claims of the sovereignty of a state; but it acts only indirectly and upon an application of detail. It attacks the law in its consequences, not in its principle, and rather weakens than destroys it.

---

[1] See Chapter VI, on "The Judicial Power in America."
[2] See Kent's Commentaries, Vol. I, p. 387.

也只能处分个人。很明显,联邦在这方面可以自己选择对手。它的对手通常是软弱的,所以自然就会屈服。

但是,当联邦不是进攻而是自卫的时候,困难就增加了。宪法承认各州的立法权,而这些州制定的法律又可能侵犯联邦的权力。这时,联邦与制定法律的各个州之间难免会发生主权冲突。为了解决冲突,只能选择危险最小的办法。在我前面讲过的总原则中,已经表明了这种处理办法。①

根据通常的想法,在上面提到的这种案件中,联邦一定要向联邦法院控诉侵略它的州,而联邦法院也会废除该州制定的法律。这是最合乎情理的处理方式。但是,这样一来,联邦法院就会与该州处于直接对立的状态,所以联邦法院会尽可能避免这种情况的发生。美国人认为,一项新法律的执行是不可能不损害一些私人利益的。美国的立法者们认为,这种私人利益可以抵制各个州用立法方式损害联邦,所以最高法院在立法时保护了这种利益。

假如,一个州向一个公司出卖了一块公共土地,而一年后它又以一项新的法令把这块土地归为它的范围内。这样,它就破坏了宪法中有关禁止更改依合同而获得的权利的条款。当依据新的法令的土地购买者要求占有土地时,那么在旧的法令中的先前的土地占有者可以向联邦法院起诉,并要求联邦法院判决新的土地占有者是无效的。② 因此,事实上联邦司法权与州的主权发生了争执。但是,联邦司法机构只是间接地向州进攻。它的进攻是法律的结果,而不是它的原则。它只是削弱它的效力,而不是废除那项法令。

---

① 见第六章的《美国的司法权》。
② 见肯特:《美国法释义》第一卷,第387页。

The last case to be provided for was that each state formed a corporation enjoying a separate existence and distinct civil rights, and that it could therefore sue or be sued before a tribunal. Thus a state could bring an action against another state. In this instance the Union was not called upon to contest a state law, but to try a suit in which a state was a party. This suit was perfectly similar to any other cause except that the quality of the parties was different; and here the danger pointed out at the beginning of this chapter still exists, with less chance of being avoided. It is inherent in the very essence of Federal constitutions that they should create parties in the bosom of the nation which present powerful obstacles to the free course of justice.

High Rank Of The Supreme Court Among The Great Powers Of State

No nation ever constituted so great a judicial power as the Americans — Extent of its prerogatives — Its political influence — The tranquillity and the very existence of the Union depend on the discretion of the seven Federal judges.

When we have examined in detail the organization of the Supreme Court and the entire prerogatives which it exercises, we shall readily admit that a more imposing judicial power was never constituted by any people. The Supreme Court is placed higher than any other known tribunal, both by the nature of its rights and the class of justiciable parties which it controls.

In all the civilized countries of Europe the government has always shown the greatest reluctance to allow the cases in which it was itself interested to be decided by the ordinary course of justice. This repugnance is naturally greater as the government is more absolute; and, on the other hand, the privileges of the courts of justice are extended with the increasing liberties of the people; but no European nation has yet held that all judicial controversies, without regard to their origin, can be left to the judges of common law.

In America this theory has been actually put in practice; and the Supreme Court of the United States is the sole tribunal of the nation. Its power extends to all cases arising under laws and treaties

最后一个需要假设的案例是,美国的各州都是联合享有公民权的独立存在的自治体,它们既可以向法院起诉,又可以被控诉于法院。比如,一个州可以向法院控告另一个州。在这种情况下,联邦并不会攻击州所公布的法令,只是诉讼当事人均为州而已。这种案件与其他案件没有两样,除了诉讼当事人的性质不同而已。这里,在本章开始时指出的危险依然存在,而且很难有机会避免。这是联邦体制固有的危险,已成为使一些司法机构难于对抗的强大阻力。

最高法院在各州的大权中居于高位

没有一个国家曾像美国那样的拥有如此强大的司法权——特权范围的扩大——它的政治影响——联邦的安定与生存取决于七位联邦法官的明辨能力。

当我们细细考察过最高法院的组织和他们所执行的全部特权之后,就不难发现其他任何国家都从来没有创制过如此强大的司法权。美国的最高法院,无论从其职权的性质来说,还是从其控制的受审人的范围来说,均远远高于其他已知的法院。

在欧洲的所有文明国家,政府向来极其反对将与其本身利益相关的案件交由司法机构审理。政府越是专制,这种反抗情绪自然就越大。但在另一方面,随着人民自由的与日俱增,法院的职权范围也日益扩大。但是,至今还没有一个欧洲国家想过,一切有争辩的问题,不管其起因如何,都可以提交执行普通法的法官审理。

在美国,这个理论已经被付诸实施。美国的最高法院在全国是唯一的。它的权力范围扩及到一切与国家权力机关制定的

made by the national authorities, to all cases of admiralty and maritime jurisdiction, and, in general, to all points that affect the law of nations. It may even be affirmed that, although its constitution is essentially judicial, its prerogatives are almost entirely political. Its sole object is to enforce the execution of the laws of the Union; and the Union regulates only the relations of the government with the citizens, and of the nation with foreign powers; the relations of citizens among themselves are almost all regulated by the sovereignty of the states.

A second and still greater cause of the preponderance of this court may be adduced. In the nations of Europe the courts of justice are called upon to try only the controversies of private individuals; but the Supreme Court of the United States summons sovereign powers to its bar. When the clerk of the court advances on the steps of the tribunal and simply says: "The State of New York *versus* The State of Ohio," it is impossible not to feel that the court which he addresses is no ordinary body; and when it is recollected that one of these parties represents one million, and the other two millions of men, one is struck by the responsibility of the seven judges, whose decision is about to satisfy or to disappoint so large a number of their fellow citizens.

The peace, the prosperity, and the very existence of the Union are vested in the hands of the seven Federal judges. Without them the Constitution would be a dead letter: the executive appeals to them for assistance against the encroachments of the legislative power; the legislature demands their protection against the assaults of the executive; they defend the Union from the disobedience of the states, the states from the exaggerated claims of the Union, the public interest against private interests, and the conservative spirit of stability against the fickleness of the democracy. Their power is enormous, but it is the power of public opinion. They are all-powerful as long as the people respect the law; but they would be impotent against popular neglect or contempt of the law. The force of public opinion is the most intractable of agents, because its exact limits cannot be defined; and it is not less dangerous to exceed than to remain below the boundary prescribed.

法律和条约有关的问题。有关海商方面的问题,凡涉及国际法的问题,均属于它管理。甚至必须承认,尽管它的组织完全是司法性的,但它的特权却几乎是政治性的。它唯一的目标就是执行联邦的法律,而联邦政府的任务则是调整政府和人民之间的关系,以及与外国间的关系。至于公民之间的关系,则几乎全由各州的主管机关负责。

使美国最高法院拥有这种至高权力的第二个原因是:欧洲各国的法院只审理私人间的案件,而美国最高法院,可以说能够审理州的主权。当法院的官员登上法庭的大堂,简单地宣告"纽约州控告俄亥俄州"时,使人不得不感到这个大堂不是一般的法庭。而当你再仔细想想这两方中的一方代表着一百万人,另一方也许代表着二百万人时,便不由自主地感到这七位法官的责任十分重大,因为他们的判决要使如此众多的子民有悲有喜。

联邦的和平、繁荣与安定,全都系于这七位联邦法官之手。没有他们,宪法只是一纸空文。行政权也依靠他们去抵制立法机构的侵犯,而立法机构也需要他们的保护,以使自己不受行政权的进攻。他们保护着联邦,并使各州服从于联邦,而各州则依靠他们抵制联邦的过分要求。公共利益依靠他们去抵制私人利益,而私人利益则依靠他们去抵制公共利益。保守派依靠他们去抵制民主派的大胆与放纵,而民主派则依靠他们去抵制保守派的顽固。他们的权力是巨大的,但这是来自于公共舆论的权力。只要人民尊重法律,他们的力量就会无限大;而如果人民无视或轻蔑法律,他们就无能为力。公共舆论的力量是最难于驾驭的力量,因为它的权限是说不清楚的,而且界限以内的危险,也不是总低于界限以外的危险。

Not only must the Federal judges be good citizens, and men of that information and integrity which are indispensable to all magistrates, but they must be statesmen, wise to discern the signs of the times, not afraid to brave the obstacles that can be subdued, nor slow to turn away from the current when it threatens to sweep them off, and the supremacy of the Union and the obedience due to the laws along with them.

The President, who exercises a limited power, may err without causing great mischief in the state. Congress may decide amiss without destroying the Union, because the electoral body in which the Congress originates may cause it to retract its decision by changing its members. But if the Supreme Court is ever composed of imprudent or bad men, the Union may be plunged into anarchy or civil war.

The original cause of this danger, however, does not lie in the constitution of the tribunal, but in the very nature of federal governments. We have seen that in confederate states it is especially necessary to strengthen the judicial power, because in no other nations do those independent persons who are able to contend with the social body exist in greater power, or in a better condition to resist the physical strength of the government. But the more a power requires to be strengthened, the more extensive and independent it must be made; and the dangers which its abuse may create are heightened by its independence and its strength. The source of the evil is not, therefore, in the constitution of the power, but in the constitution of the state which renders the existence of such a power necessary.

In What Respects The Federal Constitution Is Superior To That Of The States

How the Constitution of the Union can be compared with that of the states — Superiority of the Constitution of the Union attributable to the wisdom of the Federal legislators — Legislature of the Union less dependent on the people than that of the states — Executive power more independent in its sphere — Judicial power less subjected to the will of the majority — Practical consequence of these facts — The dangers inherent in a democratic government diminished by the Federal legislators, and increased by the legislators of the states.

The Federal Constitution differs essentially from that of the states

因此,联邦法官不仅应当是品行端正、德高望重、博闻强识的公民,具有一切行政官所必备的品质,而且必须是国务活动家。他们要善于分辨时代的特性,勇于克服一切困难,力挽有可能把他们本人与联邦的主权和法律的尊严一起卷走的狂澜。

总统只行使有限的权力,所以他犯的错误可能不会损害到州。国会的失误可能不会破坏到联邦,因为权力大于国会的选举团可以通过改选议员的办法改变国会的状况。但是,如果最高法院是由轻率冒失或腐化堕落的分子组成,联邦就有陷入无政府状态或引起内战的危险。

但是,这种危险的起因并不在于法庭的组织,而在于联邦政府本身的特质。我们知道,联邦国家特别需要建立强有力的司法权,而其他体制的国家并不需要像联邦制国家那样建立强有力的司法权,因为那里的个人在同国家权力斗争时不能处在较强或较好的地位去抵抗政府动用武力。不过,一个政权越是需要加强,它就越是需要扩大和独立,这时因滥用职权所造成的危险也就越大。因此,这种危险的根源并不在于这个政权的组织,而在于建立这个政权的国家的体制本身。

联邦宪法在哪些方面比各州宪法优越

联邦宪法怎样与各州宪法做比较——联邦宪法之所以优越,是因为联邦立法者的聪明才智——联邦立法机构不像各州立法机构那样过于依赖人民——行政权在其行使范围内比较独立——司法权很少服从多数的意志——实际的后果——联邦立法者使民主制政府固有的危险减少了,而州的立法者却使它增加。

联邦宪法在其所要达到的目的上,与各州宪法有本质上的区

in the ends which it is intended to accomplish; but in the means by which these ends are attained a greater analogy exists between them. The objects of the governments are different, but their forms are the same; and in this special point of view there is some advantage in comparing them with each other.

I am of opinion, for several reasons, that the Federal Constitution is superior to any of the state constitutions.

The present Constitution of the Union was formed at a later period than those of the majority of the states, and it may have profited by this additional experience. But we shall be convinced that this is only a secondary cause of its superiority, when we recollect that eleven new states have since been added to the Union, and that these new republics have almost always rather exaggerated than remedied the defects that existed in the former constitutions. The chief cause of the superiority of the Federal Constitution lay in the character of the legislators who composed it. At the time when it was formed, the ruin of the Confederation seemed imminent, and its danger was universally known. In this extremity the people chose the men who most deserved the esteem rather than those who had gained the affections of the country. I have already observed that, distinguished as almost all the legislators of the Union were for their intelligence, they were still more so for their patriotism. They had all been nurtured at a time when the spirit of liberty was braced by a continual struggle against a powerful and dominant authority. When the contest was terminated, while the excited passions of the populace persisted, as usual, in warring against dangers which had ceased to exist, these men stopped short; they cast a calmer and more penetrating look upon their country; they perceived that a definitive revolution had been accomplished, and that the only dangers which America had now to fear were those which might result from the abuse of freedom. They had the courage to say what they believed to be true, because they were animated by a warm and sincere love of liberty; and they ventured to

别,而在实现这个目的的手段上,又与各州宪法极为相似。联邦政府和州政府的任务不同,但它们在组织形式上却是一样的。因此,从这个特有的现象来看,把联邦宪法和各州宪法进行比较是有好处的。

我认为,联邦宪法在整体上高于任何一个州的宪法,其原因是多方面的。

联邦的现行宪法,比大多数州的制定时期要晚,所以它能从这些额外的经验中获得好处。但是,这仅仅是其主权优越性的一个次要原因,因为当我们想到自联邦宪法制定以来又有十一个州新加入美利坚合众国,而这些新参加进来的州又总是夸大它们对先前各州宪法的缺点所做的补救。联邦宪法所以优越的主要原因,在于立法者们的品格。在联邦宪法形成的时候,各州的联盟好像接近于毁灭。并且这种危险是众所周知的。在这个危急时刻,人民选择了最值得他们尊敬的人,而没有去选择他们最喜爱的人。我在前面已经讲过,联邦的立法者们几乎都以他们的智慧著称,而且更以他们的爱国精神著称。他们是在提倡社会自由的氛围中成长起来的。这时的自由精神正在同强大的专横的权力机构进行持续不断的斗争。当这场斗争结束时,人们在斗争中奋起的激情并没有被击灭,它仍在同已经不复存在的危险作战,于是立法者们呼吁人们要冷静下来,让他们以锐利的眼光观察国家的形势,他们发觉一场决定性的革命已经完成,而目前美国人最担心的可能是由于对自由的滥用而引发的灾难。他们敢于说出自己的真实想法,因为在他们的内心深处,对自由怀有真挚的和炽烈的爱。他们敢于提倡节制自由,因为他们真诚地不想使自由

propose restrictions, because they were resolutely opposed to destruction. ①

Most of the state constitutions assign one year for the duration of the House of Representatives and two years for that of the Senate, so that members of the legislative body are constantly and narrowly tied down by the slightest desires of their constituents. The legislators of the Union were of opinion that this excessive dependence of the legislature altered the nature of the main consequences of the representative system, since it vested not only the source of authority, but the government, in the people. They increased the length of the term in order to give the representatives freer scope for the exercise of their own judgment.

The Federal Constitution, as well as the state constitutions, divided the legislative body into two branches. But in the states these two branches were composed of the same elements and elected in the same manner. The consequence was that the passions and inclinations of the populace were as rapidly and easily represented in one chamber as in the other, and that laws were made

---

① At this time the celebrated Alexander Hamilton, who was one of the principal founders of the Constitution, ventured to express the following sentiments in *The Federalist*, No. 71:

"There are some who would be inclined to regard the servile pliancy of the Executive to a prevailing current, either in the community or in the legislature, as its best recommendation. But such men entertain very crude notions, as well of the purposes for which government was instituted, as of the true means by which the public happiness may be promoted. The republican principle demands, that the deliberative sense of the community should govern the conduct of those to whom they entrust the management of their affairs; but it does not require an unqualified complaisance to every sudden breeze of passion, or to every transient impulse which the people may receive from the arts of men who flatter their prejudices to betray their interests. It is a just observation, that the people commonly *intend the public good*. This often applies to their very errors. But their good sense would despise the adulator who should pretend that they always *reason right* about the *means* of promoting it. They know from experience that they sometimes err; and the wonder is, that they so seldom err as they do, beset, as they continually are, by the wiles of parasites and sycophants; by the snares of the ambitious, the avaricious, the desperate; by the artifices of men who possess their confidence more than they deserve it, and of those who seek to possess rather than to deserve it. When occasions present themselves in which the interests of the people are at variance with thier inclinations, it is the duty of the persons whom they have appointed to be the guardians of those interests to withstand the temporary delusion, in order to give them time and opportunity for more cool and sedate reflection. Instances might be cited, in which a conduct of this kind has saved the people from very fatal consequences of their own mistakes, and has procured lasting monuments of their gratitude to the men who had courage and magnanimity enough to serve them at the peril of their displeasure."

破灭。①

大部分州的宪法规定众议员的任期为一年,而参议员的任期为两年。因此,立法机构的成员可以经常并最严格地受制于选民的最微小愿望。但是,联邦的立法者们认为,立法机构的这种过度依赖性,使代议制的主要成果改变了性质,因为这种依赖性不仅把权力的基础交给了人民,而且也把政府交给了人民。他们把联邦议员的任期加长,以使议员能有更广泛的自由行使其职权。

联邦宪法和各州的宪法一样,把立法机构分成两院。但在各州,这两个部分的构成方式和选举方式都相同。结果,多数的激情和意志能够很容易地在这一院或那一院反映出来,并能迅速地在这两个院找到代言人和工具,这就给法律的制定工作带来了粗

---

① 这时,参与宪法的创立者之一,著名的亚历山大·汉密尔顿先生在《联邦党人文集》第71条中,大胆地发表了如下评论:

"有些人会以为行政部门对于社会上或立法机构中潮流能够屈从顺应,乃是其最大的美德。但是,此种人对于所以要设置政府的宗旨,以及对于促进人民幸福的真正手段,都是理解得十分粗浅的。共和制度的原则,要求接受社会委托管理其事务的人,能够体察社会意志,并据以规范本人行为,但并不要求无条件顺应人民群众的一切突发激情或一时冲动,因为这些很可能是由那些善于迎合人民偏见而实则出卖其利益的人所阴谋煽动的。人民普遍的是从公益出发的。但这一点亦常用来说明人民群众的错误。但是,人民群众从常识出发会蔑视阿谀奉承的人,这些人胡说人民群众无时不能正确找出促进公益的手段。人民群众从自己的经验知道他们自己有时候会犯错误;人民群众终日受那些寄生虫和马屁精的欺骗,受野心家、贪污犯、亡命徒的坑害,受那些不值得信任却为人所信任的人,以及不应得而巧取豪夺的人的耍弄,他们经常受到这样一些干扰,却并不常犯错误,毋宁说是个奇迹。在人民群众的意向同他们本身利益出现差异的情况下,受命维护人民利益者的职责应该是抵制这种一时误会,以便给予人民群众时间和机会去进行冷静认真的反省。这种做法曾经使人民群众免遭其本身错误所造成的严重后果,并使有勇气和雅量为人民利益服务而不惜引致人民不快的人长期受到人民群众感激和纪念,这样的先例是不难枚举的。"

with violence and precipitation. By the Federal Constitution the two houses originate in like manner in the choice of the people; but the conditions of eligibility and the mode of election were changed in order that if, as is the case in certain nations, one branch of the legislature should not represent the same interests as the other, it might at least represent more wisdom. A mature age was necessary to become a Senator, and the Senate was chosen by an elected assembly of a limited number of members.

To concentrate the whole social force in the hands of the legislative body is the natural tendency of democracies; for as this is the power that emanates the most directly from the people, it has the greater share of the people's overwhelming power, and it is naturally led to monopolize every species of influence. This concentration of power is at once very prejudicial to a well-conducted administration and favorable to the despotism of the majority. The legislators of the states frequently yielded to these democratic propensities, which were invariably and courageously resisted by the founders of the Union.

In the states the executive power is vested in the hands of a magistrate who is apparently placed upon a level with the legislature, but who is in reality only the blind agent and the passive instrument of its will. He can derive no power from the duration of his office, which terminates in one year, or from the exercise of prerogatives, for he can scarcely be said to have any. The legislature can condemn him to inaction by entrusting the execution of its laws to special committees of its own members, and can annul his temporary dignity by cutting down his salary. The Federal Constitution vests all the privileges and all the responsibility of the executive power in a single individual. The duration of the Presidency is fixed at four years; the salary cannot be altered during this term; the President is protected by a body of official dependents and armed with a suspensive veto: in short, every effort was made to confer a strong and independent position upon the executive authority, within the limits that were prescribed to it.

In the state constitutions, the judicial power is that which is the most independent of the legislative authority; nevertheless, in all the states the legislature has reserved to itself the right of regulating the emoluments of the judges, a practice that necessarily subjects them to its immediate influence. In some states the judges are appointed only temporarily, which deprives them of a great

暴性和轻率性。联邦宪法也规定联邦的两院由人民选举,但候选资格和选举方式已被改变。目的是要能像在其他国家一样,使立法机构中的一支,即使不代表不同于另一支的利益,至少也能代表更丰富的才智。必须达到规定的成熟年龄,才能当选为参议员。而议员是由一个首先被选举出来的人数不多的会议负责选举的。

将整个社会的力量集中到立法机构之手,是民主制度的自然趋势。既然立法机构的权力直接来自人民,它也同样分享人民所拥有的一切大权。因此,立法机构自然会有一种惯于垄断一切权力的倾向。这种权力的集中,既有害于有利政策的实施,又为多数的专制奠定了基础。州的立法者们经常屈从于民主的这种习性,而联邦的立法者们则一直是抵制这种行为的。

各州的行政权掌握在地方行政长官即州长的手里,他们表面上似乎与立法机构平起平坐,但实际只是立法机构的盲目代理人和被动工具。他从其任职期限内是吸取不到力量的,因为他的任期只有一年。或者从他的特权中吸取?但他又毫无特权可言。立法机构可以把自己所订法律的执行工作交给自己内部成立的专门委员会去办理,它还可以用停薪的办法,暂时废除行政长官。联邦宪法把其行政权的所有特权和责任集中到一个人的手上,即总统。总统的任期为四年,在任职期间不得扣发他的薪金,他有专门的保卫侍从,并享有暂时否决权。简单地讲,就是宪法在详细地规定执行权的范围以后,又尽量设法使他在这个范围内享有强大的独立地位。

在各州的宪法中,司法权是一切权力中最不受立法权限制的权力。但是,所有州的立法机构都保留了调整法官薪水的权力,这就必然将法官置于立法机构的直接影响之下。在某些州里,法官只是被临时任命的,这就剥夺了法官的大部分权力和自由。

portion of their power and their freedom. In others the legislative and judicial powers are entirely confounded. The Senate of New York, for instance, constitutes in certain cases the superior court of the state. The Federal Constitution, on the other hand, carefully separates the judicial power from all the others; and it provides for the independence of the judges, by declaring that their salary shall not be diminished, and that their functions shall be inalienable.

The practical consequences of these different systems may easily be perceived. An attentive observer will soon notice that the business of the Union is incomparably better conducted than that of any individual state. The conduct of the Federal government is more fair and temperate than that of the states; it has more prudence and discretion, its projects are more durable and more skillfully combined, its measures are executed with more vigor and consistency.

I recapitulate the substance of this chapter in a few words.

The existence of democracies is threatened by two principal dangers: namely, the complete subjection of the legislature to the will of the electoral body, and the concentration of all the other powers of the government in the legislative branch.

The development of these evils has been favored by the legislators of the states; but the legislators of the Union have done all they could to render them less formidable.

Characteristics Of The Federal Constitution Of The United States Of America As Compared With All Other Federal Constitutions

The American Union appears to resemble all other confederations — Yet its effects are different — Reason for this — In what this Union differs from all other confederations — The American government not a Federal but an imperfect national government.

The United States of America does not afford the first or the only instance of a confederation, several of which have existed in modern Europe, without referring to those of antiquity. Switzerland, the Germanic Empire, and the Republic of the Low Countries either have been or still are confederations. In studying the constitutions of these different countries one is surprised to see that the powers with which they invested the federal government are nearly the same as those awarded by the American Constitution to the government of the United States.

在另一些州里,立法权和司法权是完全混在一起的。例如,纽约州的参议院就是该州的审理某些案件的最高法庭。联邦宪法则与此不同,它把司法权同其他一切权力完全分开。另外,它宣布法官的薪金是固定的,法官的职权是不得改变的,从而给予法官以独立的地位。

这些不同系统的实际效果是很容易被察觉的。细心的观察家可以立即看到,联邦的政务比任何一个州都处理得好。联邦政府在实施政务方面比各州要公正和稳妥。它的看法比较明智,它的计划比较持久和合理,它的措施执行得比较灵活和一致。

我用简单的几句话就可以对这一章做出总结。

民主制度的存在受到两大危险的威胁:第一,立法权完全屈服于选举团的意志;第二,政府的所有其他权力都向立法权靠拢。

州的立法者使这两大危险进一步发展,而联邦的立法者则尽力减弱了它们。

美利坚合众国宪法与其他
一切联邦制国家宪法有什么不同

美国的联邦表面上似乎与其他一切联邦一样——但是他们的作用不同——为什么会这样——这个联邦在哪些方面与其他一切联邦不同——美国政府并不是一个联邦政府,而是一个不完善的国家政府。

美利坚合众国并不是联邦制度的第一个或唯一的例子。即使不涉及古代,就是在现代的欧洲,也存在过数个联邦。瑞士、德意志帝国、尼德兰共和国,都曾经是或今天仍为联邦。在研究这些不同联邦的宪法时,会惊异地发现,它们授予各自联邦政府的权力,

They confer upon the central power the same rights of making peace and war, of raising money and troops, and of providing for the general exigencies and the common interests of the nation. Nevertheless, the federal government of these different states has always been as remarkable for its weakness and inefficiency as that of the American Union is for its vigor and capacity. Again, the first American Confederation perished through the excessive weakness of its government; and yet this weak government had as large rights and privileges as those of the Federal government of the present day, and in some respects. even larger. But the present Constitution of the United States contains certain novel principles which exercise a most important influence, although they do not at once strike the observer.

This Constitution, which may at first sight be confused with the federal constitutions that have preceded it, rests in truth upon a wholly novel theory, which may be considered as a great discovery in modern political science. In all the confederations that preceded the American Constitution of 1789, the states allied for a common object agreed to obey the injunctions of a federal government; but they reserved to themselves the right of ordaining and enforcing the execution of the laws of the union. The American states which combined in 1789 agreed that the Federal government should not only dictate the laws, but execute its own enactments. In both cases the right is the same, but the exercise of the right is different; and this difference produced the most momentous consequences. In all the confederations that preceded the American Union the federal government, in order to provide for its wants, had to apply to the separate governments; and if what it prescribed was disagreeable to any one of them, means were found to evade its claims. If it was powerful, it then had recourse to arms; if it was weak, it connived at the resistance which the law of the union, its sovereign, met with, and did nothing, under the plea of inability. Under these circumstances one of two results invariably followed: either the strongest of the allied states assumed the privileges of the federal authority and ruled all the others in its name; ①

---

① This was the case in Greece when Philip undertook to execute the decrees of the Amphictyons; in the Low Countries, where the province of Holland always gave the law; and, in our own time in the Germanic Confederation, in which Austria and Prussia make themselves the agents of the Diet and rule the whole confederation in its name.

同美国宪法赋予合众国政府的权力是完全相同的。他们也赋予中央政府以媾和权、宣战权、税收权和征兵权，应付全国危机和为全国谋求共同利益的权力。但是，这些不同国家的联邦政府几乎都是软弱和无效率的，而只有美国的联邦政府能够果断而有力地处理政务。并且，美国的第一个联邦之所以未能存在下去，也是因为它的政府过于软弱。然而，这样一个如此软弱的政府，却拥有同今天的美国政府一样大的特权，甚至在某些方面它享有更大的特权。因此，美国现行的宪法包括了几项新的原则。这些原则起初没有引起人们的注意，但后来却产生了十分深远的影响。

这部宪法，初看上去好像与以前的几部宪法没有什么不同，但实际上是出自一个全新的理论。我们应当把这个理论看作是现今政治科学中的一大发现。在美国1789年宪法之前建立的所有联邦，为了共同的目标联合起来共同遵守一个联邦政府的法令，但他们却保留了自己调整和实施联邦法律的权力。1789年联合起来的美国各州，不仅同意联邦政府有权颁布法律，而且同意由它自己执行。这两种情况下的权力都是一样的，只是行使权力的方式不同了。但是，这种不同却产生了极其悬殊的结果。在今天的美国联邦政府之前建立的所有联邦中，他们为了满足自己的需要，必须求助于各加盟政府。如果它规定的政策遭到某一加盟政府反对，这个加盟政府总能找到回避的办法。如果联邦政府的力量强大，它会求助于武力；假如它的力量软弱，它只有任由法律的摆布而自认无能。在这种情况下，不是联邦中最强大的加盟政府攫取联邦的政权，以联邦的名义向其他加盟政府发号施令；①

---

① 这种情况也发生在希腊，当菲利浦同意执行与邻近各邦联盟的法令时；像荷兰这样的底层国家常常会向法律让步；并且，在当时的德意志联盟中，奥地利与普鲁士使它们自己成为会议的代表，并统治着整个联邦。

or the federal governmentwas abandoned by its natural supporters, anarchy arose between the confederates, and the union lost all power of action. ①

In America the subjects of the Union are not states, but private citizens: the national government levies a tax, not upon the state of Massachusetts, but upon each inhabitant of Massachusetts. The old confederate governments presided over communities, but that of the Union presides over individuals. Its force is not borrowed, but self-derived; and it is served by its own civil and military officers, its own army, and its own courts of justice. It cannot be doubted that the national spirit, the passions of the multitude, and the provincial prejudices of each state still tend singularly to diminish the extent of the Federal authority thus constituted and to facilitate resistance to its mandates; but the comparative weakness of a restricted sovereignty is an evil inherent in the federal system. In America each state has fewer opportunities and temptations to resist; nor can such a design be put in execution (if indeed it be entertained) without an open violation of the laws of the Union, a direct interruption of the ordinary course of justice, and a bold declaration of revolt; in a word, without taking the decisive step that men always hesitate to adopt.

In all former confederations the privileges of the union furnished more elements of discord than of power, since they multiplied the claims of the nation without augmenting the means of enforcing them; and hence the real weakness of federal governments has almost always been in the exact ratio of their nominal power. Such is not the case in the American Union, in which, as in ordinary governments, the Federal power has the means of enforcing all it is empowered to demand.

The human understanding more easily invents new things than new words, and we are hence constrained to employ many improper and inadequate expressions. When several nations form a permanent league and establish a supreme authority, which, although

---

① Such has always been the situation of the Swiss Confederation, which would have perished ages ago but for the mutual jealousies of its neighbors.

就是联邦政府放弃自己的权力,使联邦陷入无政府状态,继而便失去活动的能力。①

在美国,联邦所统治的不是各州,而是各州的公民。比如说,在联邦要征税时,它不是向州政府征收,例如马萨诸塞,而是向州的居民征收。以前的联邦政府负责主持加盟政府的事务,而现在的美国联邦政府则负责公民个人的事务。它的力量不是借来的,而是靠自己取得的。它有自己的行政人员、军队、法院和司法人员。毋庸置疑,民族的精神、群众的激情和各州的地方偏见,仍在有力地抑制着联邦的权限,制造一些反对联邦意志的中心。主权有限的联邦,并没有强大到可以自由行使其拥有的全部权力的地步。但是,这正是联邦制度固有的缺陷之一。

美国的各州很少有造反的机会和图谋。如果某个州要造反,也只能以公开抵抗联邦的法律、破坏正常的司法程序和举行暴动的形式进行。一句话,在人们采取这个步骤之前总是犹豫不决的。在以前的联邦制国家里之所以要赋予联邦政府各种各样的权力,是出于进行战争,而不是出于治国,因为这些权力会增加联邦政府的要求,而联邦政府却没有实现这些要求的举措。因此,联邦政府的真正弱点,与它们名义上权力的增加成正比。美国的联邦却不是这样的。像大部分一般政府一样,美国的联邦政府能够去做它有权做到的一切。

人们在对新事物的理解上往往比发明新词还要容易,所以我们只好使用一些不够确切的词汇和不够全面的说法。有些国家

---

①　在很早以前就已经灭亡的瑞士联邦的情形就总是如此,它们与其邻国之间相互妒忌。

it cannot act upon private individuals like a national government, still acts upon each of the confederate states in a body, this government, which is so essentially different from all others, is called Federal. Another form of society is afterwards discovered in which several states are fused into one with regard to certain common interests, although they remain distinct, or only confederate, with regard to all other concerns. In this case the central power acts directly upon the governed, whom it rules and judges in the same manner as a national government, but in a more limited circle. Evidently this is no longer a federal government, but an incomplete national government, which is neither exactly national nor exactly federal; but the new word which ought to express this novel thing does not yet exist.

Ignorance of this new species of confederation has been the cause that has brought all unions to civil war, to servitude, or to inertness; and the states which formed these leagues have been either too dull to discern, or too pusillanimous to apply, this great remedy. The first American Confederation perished by the same defects.

But in America the confederate states had been long accustomed to form a portion of one empire before they had won their independence; they had not contracted the habit of governing themselves completely; and their national prejudices had not taken deep root in their minds. Superior to the rest of the world in political knowledge, and sharing that knowledge equally among themselves, they were little agitated by the passions that generally oppose the extension of federal authority in a nation, and those passions were checked by the wisdom of their greatest men. The Americans applied the remedy with firmness as soon as they were conscious of the evil; they amended their laws and saved the country.

成立了永久性联盟,并建立了最高权力机构。尽管这个机构不能像一个全国政府那样直接管理公民个人,但却能对每个加盟政府直接采取行动。这个与其他一切政府性质根本不同的机构,便是联邦政府。在之后出现的另外一种社会组织形式里,几个政府只是在一些共同的利益方面才真正结合为一体,尽管在其他方面仍保持独立或一些仅存联盟关系。在这种情况下,中央政府像一切全国政府一样,直接管理被统治者、行政官员和司法人员,但却是在有限的范围内。显然,这个政府不再是联邦政府,而是一个不完全的国家政府。因此,确切地说,它既不是全国政府,也不是联邦政府。但是,我们现在只能说到此,因为可以表达这个新事物的新词目前还不存在。

由于还不了解这种新式的联邦,所以过去的所有联邦不是导致内战和征服,就是陷入毫无生气的状态。加盟的国家不是没有知识去制定解除其弊端的方策,就是缺乏勇气去采取这种方策。美国的第一个邦联,也是由于有这种缺陷而解体的。

但在美国,联邦的各州在获得独立以前,曾长期属于同一帝国。因此,它们还没有形成完全独立自主的习惯,民族的偏见也没有根深蒂固,但却优越于世界的其余部分。彼此的文明程度不相上下,它们的人民一般很少有扩大联邦权力的强烈激情,即使有这样的激情,也被它们的几位伟大人物所克制。同时,美国人发现弊端后,便坚决采取补救的办法。他们修改了法律,拯救了自己的国家。

Advantages Of The Federal System In General, And Its Special Utility In America

Happiness and freedom of small nations—Power of great nations—Great empires favorable to the growth of civilization—Strength often the first element of national prosperity—Aim of the federal system to unite the twofold advantages resulting from a small and from a large territory—Advantages derived by the United States from this system— The law adapts itself to the exigencies of the population; population does not conform to the exigencies of the law—Activity, progress, the love and enjoyment of freedom, in American communities—Public spirit of the Union is only the aggregate of provincial patriotism—Principles and things circulate freely over the territory of the United States—The Union is happy and free as a little nation, and respected as a great one.

In small states, the watchfulness of society penetrates everywhere, and a desire for improvement pervades the smallest details; the ambition of the people being necessarily checked by its weakness, all the efforts and resources of the citizens are turned to the internal well-being of the community and are not likely to be wasted upon an empty pursuit of glory. The powers of every individual being generally limited, his desires are proportionally small. Mediocrity of fortune makes the various conditions of life nearly equal, and the manners of the inhabitants are orderly and simple. Thus, all things considered, and allowance being made for the various degrees of morality and enlightenment, we shall generally find more persons in easy circumstances, more contentment and tranquillity, in small nations than in large ones.

When tyranny is established in the bosom of a small state, it is more galling than elsewhere, because, acting in a narrower circle, everything in that circle is affected by it. It supplies the place of those great designs which it cannot entertain, by a violent or exasperating interference in a multitude of minute details; and it leaves the political world, to which it properly belongs, to meddle with the arrangements of private life. Tastes as well as actions are to be regulated; and the families of the citizens, as well as the state, are to be governed. This invasion of rights occurs but seldom, however, freedom being in

邦制的一般优点和它在美国的特殊效用

小国享有的幸福与自由——大国的力量——大帝国有利于文明的发展——实力是国家繁荣的首要因素——联邦制度的目的在于把大领域的长处与小领域的长处结合起来——美国从联邦制度中获得的好处——法律的制定必须符合人民的需求,人民不遵守法律的苛求——美国人民的积极性与进取性以及他们对自由的热爱和享受——联邦的公共精神仅仅是地方爱国主义的集合——社会准则等在美国境内的自由的传播。

联邦既像小国一样自由和幸福,又像大国一样受人尊敬。在小国,社会的警惕性遍及全国各地,渴求进步的欲望已深入到最微小的事物;在人民的野心因其弱点而被必要地阻止时,人民的所有努力和智慧几乎全部用于国内的福利事业,而不会浪费于对虚荣的追求。通常,每个人的能力都是有限的,所以他们的欲望也就相对很小;财富的平庸,使他们的生活状况几乎平等,并且,人民的生活习惯也有序而朴素。因此,总的说来,尽管道德和文化水平会以各种不同的程度出现,小国的人民一般都比大国的人民容易谋生和安居乐业。

当暴政在小国发生时,它将比任何地方都要施虐,因为它的实施是在相对较小的范围内,而小范围内的所有一切事物都会被影响。它无法很好地施展雄才大略,而只能凭借暴力和骚动去干预一大堆小事。它把它的统治从所谓的政治界渗入到私人生活。它不但控制着人们的喜好,还控制着人们的行动。在统治了国家以后,它又想统治家庭。但是,这种情况并不多见,因为自由毕竟

truth the natural state of small communities. The temptations that the government offers to ambition are too weak and the resources of private individuals are too slender for the sovereign power easily to fall into the grasp of a single man; and should such an event occur, the subjects of the state can easily unite and overthrow the tyrant and the tyranny at once by a common effort.

Small nations have therefore always been the cradle of political liberty; and the fact that many of them have lost their liberty by becoming larger shows that their freedom was more a consequence of their small size than of the character of the people. The history of the world affords no instance of a great nation retaining the form of republican government for a long series of years;[①]and this has led to the conclusion that such a thing is impracticable. For my own part, I think it imprudent for men who are every day deceived in relation to the actual and the present, and often taken by surprise in the circumstances with which they are most familiar, to attempt to limit what is possible and to judge the future. But it may be said with confidence, that a great republic will always be exposed to more perils than a small one.

All the passions that are most fatal to republican institutions increase with an increasing territory, while the virtues that favor them do not augment in the same proportion. The ambition of private citizens increases with the power of the state; the strength of parties with the importance of the ends they have in view; but the love of country, which ought to check these destructive agencies, is not stronger in a large than in a small republic. It might, indeed, be easily proved that it is less powerful and less developed. Great wealth and extreme poverty, capital cities of large size, a lax morality, selfishness, and antagonism of interests are the dangers which almost invariably arise from the magnitude of states. Several of these evils scarcely injure a monarchy, and some of them even contribute to its strength and duration. In monarchical states the government has its peculiar strength; it may use, but it does not depend on, the community; and the more numerous the people, the stronger is the prince. But the only security that a republican government possesses against these evils lies in the support of the majority. This support is not, however, proportionably

---

① I do not speak of a confederation of small republics, but of a great consolidated republic.

是小国所固有的长处。小国政府提供给野心家的诱惑太少,而公民个人的智慧又极其有限,所以国家大权容易被一个人独揽。不过,当这种情况发生时,老百姓也会很自然地联合起来,通力合作,推翻暴君和暴政。

因此,小国自古以来就是政治自由的摇篮。而事实证明,很多小国有时随着自身的强大而丢失了这种自由。所以,政治自由来源于国家规模的小,而并非是因为其人民的性格。世界历史没有提供过任何关于一个大国长期实行共和制度的例证。① 这个结论说明这样的事情是不可能的。就我个人的观点,我认为如果一个人终日回避现实,对自己熟悉的事情又常常表示惊讶,试图限制可能发生的事物并判断未来,那未免过于荒唐。但可以肯定地说,大共和国总是比小共和国容易暴露危机。

热爱共和制度的一切激情,随着领土的扩大而增强;而支持这种激情的德行,则不会同步增长。个人的野心随着国家力量的增强而增长,政党的力量随着其所定目的的重要性的增大而增强,但是可以抵制这种破坏性力量的爱国心,在大共和国就不如小共和国那么强烈。而且也不难证明,大共和国的爱国心缺乏力量并发展缓慢。贫富的悬殊,城市的巨大化,道德败坏,自私自利和利益的冲突,几乎都是因国家的巨大化而引发的后果。这些危险中的大多数不会伤害到君主国的生存,而少数的几个甚至能延长其寿命。在君主国家,政府有一种特殊的力量;政府可以利用人民,但不依赖人民。人口越多,君王的力量也就越强。但是,共和制政府拥有的唯一安全举措就是依靠多数的支持去克服这些

---

① 我不是要讲小共和制国家的联邦,而是要讲一个强大的共和制国家。

greater in a large republic than in a small one; and thus, while the means of attack perpetually increase, in both number and influence, the power of resistance remains the same; or it may rather be said to diminish, since the inclinations and interests of the people are more diversified by the increase of the population, and the difficulty of forming a compact majority is constantly augmented. It has been observed, moreover, that the intensity of human passions is heightened not only by the importance of the end which they propose to attain, but by the multitude of individuals who are animated by them at the same time. Everyone has had occasion to remark that his emotions in the midst of a sympathizing crowd are far greater than those which he would have felt in solitude. In great republics, political passions become irresistible, not only because they aim at gigantic objects, but because they are felt and shared by millions of men at the same time.

It may therefore be asserted as a general proposition that nothing is more opposed to the well-being and the freedom of men than vast empires. Nevertheless, it is important to acknowledge the peculiar advantages of great states. For the very reason that the desire for power is more intense in these communities than among ordinary men, the love of glory is also more developed in the hearts of certain citizens, who regard the applause of a great people as a reward worthy of their exertions and an elevating encouragement to man. If we would learn why great nations contribute more powerfully to the increase of knowledge and the advance of civilization than small states, we shall discover an adequate cause in the more rapid and energetic circulation of ideas and in those great cities which are the intellectual centers where all the rays of human genius are reflected and combined. To this it may be added that most important discoveries demand a use of national power which the government of a small state is unable to make: in great nations the government has more enlarged ideas, and is more completely disengaged from the routine of precedent and the selfishness of local feeling; its designs are conceived with more talent and executed with more boldness.

In time of peace the well-being of small nations is undoubtedly more general and complete; but they are apt to suffer more acutely from the calamities of war than those great empires whose distant frontiers may long avert the presence of the danger from the mass of the people, who are therefore more frequently afflicted than ruined by the contest.

危险。然而,这种支持并不与共和国的大小成正比;因此,当攻击手段的数量和影响不断增加时,抵抗的力量依旧保持不变,甚至可以说在减弱,因为随着人口的增加,人民的志趣和兴趣也随之变化,也就越难形成一个巩固的群体。也可以证明,人们激情的高涨,不仅取决于其目标的重要性,而且有赖于受激情鼓舞的人数的多少。每个人都会感觉到,他的情绪在与志同道合的人相聚时会比在他自己独处时高涨很多。在大共和国里,政治激情之所以变得不可抗拒,不仅是因为其目标的宏伟,而且还因为在同一时间里这种激情以同样的方法鼓舞着千百万人。

因此,可以一般地说,再也没有比大帝国更反对人民的幸福和自由的了。但是,我们不得不承认大国也有其独特的好处。如同大国对权力的欲望比别处强烈一样,个人的荣誉感在大国也比在别处强烈,因为他们在广大人民的喝彩声中会找到他们将要为之奋斗的目标,而且这个目标还在一定程度上能鼓舞他们自我前进。因此我们可以知道,为什么大国比小国能更快地开化,更快地推广文明的进步。我们还可以发现,在大国思想能在一切方面迅速而强烈地得到响应,观点可以比较自由地传播,其大城市是人类理性之光大放异彩和聚焦的巨大知识中心。还需要补充的是重大的发明都需要强大的国力,而小国的政府是无力实施的。在大国,政府一般都有丰富的理想,可以广泛地打破陈规旧套和地方本位主义。其思想也大多富有创意,并敢于实施。

在和平时期的小国,国内的福利事业无疑是普遍和完整的,但小国在战争中,将比大国承受更多的灾难。在大国,由于领土辽阔,所以即使战争不断,也能使人民群众少受灾难。而对于人民来说,与其说战争是灾难的原因,不如说它是亡国的原因。

But in this matter, as in many others, the decisive argument is the necessity of the case. If none but small nations existed, I do not doubt that mankind would be more happy and more free; but the existence of great nations is unavoidable.

Political strength thus becomes a condition of national prosperity. It profits a state but little to be affluent and free if it is perpetually exposed to be pillaged or subjugated; its manufactures and commerce are of small advantage if another nation has the empire of the seas and gives the law in all the markets of the globe. Small nations are often miserable, not because they are small, but because they are weak; and great empires prosper less because they are great than because they are strong. Physical strength is therefore one of the first conditions of the happiness and even of the existence of nations. Hence it occurs that, unless very peculiar circumstances intervene, small nations are always united to large empires in the end, either by force or by their own consent. I do not know a more deplorable condition than that of a people unable to defend itself or to provide for its own wants. The federal system was created with the intention of combining the different advantages which result from the magnitude and the littleness of nations; and a glance at the United States of America discovers the advantages which they have derived from its adoption.

In great centralized nations the legislator is obliged to give a character of uniformity to the laws, which does not always suit the diversity of customs and of districts; as he takes no cognizance of special cases, he can only proceed upon general principles; and the population are obliged to conform to the requirements of the laws, since legislation cannot adapt itself to the exigencies and the customs of the population, which is a great cause of trouble and misery. This disadvantage does not exist in confederations; Congress regulates the principal measures of the national government, and all the details of the administration are reserved to the provincial legislatures. One can hardly imagine how much this division of sovereignty contributes to the well-being of each of the states that compose the Union. In these small communities, which are never agitated by the desire of aggrandizement or the care of self-defense, all public authority and private energy are turned towards internal improvements. The central government of each state, which is in immediate relationship with the citizens, is daily apprised of the wants that arise in society; and new projects are proposed every year, which are discussed at town meetings or by the legislature, and which are transmitted by the press to stimulate

还有一个问题,即在这里也和其他许多地方一样,最主要的是应当研究事物的必然性。如果只有小国的存在,人类无疑会更加自由和幸福。但是,大国的存在是不可避免的。

政治力量变成国家繁荣富强的条件。如果一个国家天天被人掠夺或侵略,那么空有富裕和自由的形象又有什么用处。如果别国统治了大海并规定各项世界贸易条例,那么本国的制造业和工商业又有什么用处。小国之所以往往贫穷,不是因为它很小,而是因为它很弱。大国之所以繁荣,也不是因为它很大,而是因为它很强。因此,力量一直是国家幸福,甚至是生存的主要条件之一。于是,除非有特殊环境干涉,小国总是要自愿或被迫联合起来,成为大国的一员。我不知道还有什么境况比一个国家既不能自卫又不能自给更可怜的了。因此,联邦制度的建立就是为了把因国家之大而产生的好处和因国家之小而产生的好处结合起来。考察一下美利坚合众国,就会发现采用这种制度所获得的一切好处。

在中央集权的大国,立法者有义务使各项法律具有一致性,而不能总带有地域和习俗的差异。立法者绝不处理特殊事件,只能按一般原则立法,这样,人民就不得不遵守法律,因为法律不可能服从人民的要求和习俗,而这正是国家动乱和苦难的一大原因。这种弊端不会发生在联邦制国家里,因为国会只制定全国性的主要法令,而法令的细节则留给地方立法机构去规定. 我们很难想象主权的这种划分对联邦的每个成员带来的好处有多大。在这些小社会中,人们从不会为扩张和自卫而担忧,所有的公共权威和个人精力都用于内部的改进。由于每个成员的中央政府都站在本国居民的一边,所以能够经常了解到社会的需要。它还每年提出新的计划,提交本国的议会或立法机构讨论,然后由媒

the zeal and to excite the interest of the citizens. This spirit of improvement is constantly alive in the American republics, without compromising their tranquillity; the ambition of power yields to the less
refined and less dangerous desire for wellbeing. It is generally believed in America that the existence and the permanence of the republican form of government in the New World depend upon the existence
and the duration of the federal system; and it is not unusual to attribute a large share of the misfortunes that have befallen the new states of
South America to the injudicious erection of great republics instead of
a divided and confederate sovereignty.

It is incontestably true that the tastes and the habits of republican
government in the United States were first created in the townships
and the provincial assemblies. In a small state, like that of Connecticut, for instance, where cutting a canal or laying down a road is a
great political question, where the state has no army to pay and no
wars to carry on, and where much wealth or much honor cannot be
given to the rulers, no form of government can be more natural or
more appropriate than a republic. But it is this same republican spirit, it is these manners and customs of a free people, which have been
created and nurtured in the different states, that must be afterwards
applied to the country at large. The public spirit of the Union is, so to
speak, nothing more than an aggregate or summary of the patriotic
zeal of the separate provinces. Every citizen of the United States
transfers, so to speak, his attachment to his little republic into the
common store of American patriotism. In defending the Union he defends the increasing prosperity of his own state or county, the right of
conducting its affairs, and the hope of causing measures of improvement to be adopted in it which may be favorable to his own interests;
and these are motives that are wont to stir men more than the general
interests of the country and the glory of the nation.

On the other hand, if the temper and the manners of the inhabitants especially fitted them to promote the welfare of a great republic,
the federal system renders their task less difficult. The confederation
of all the American states presents none of the ordinary inconveniences
resulting from large associations of men. The Union is a great republic
in extent, but the paucity of objects for which its government acts as-
similates it to a small state. Its acts are important, but they are rare.

体将讨论的结果发布出来,以刺激公民的热情和兴趣。这种要求改进的精神一直存在于美国的共和制度中,而且从来没有引起过动乱。追求权力的野心被热爱公益的精神所取代,激情更为洋溢,但很少带来危险。美国人普遍认为,新大陆的共和制度之所以能够存在和长久延续,有赖于联邦制度的存在和长久延续。而南美的一些新兴国家之所以长期沉沦,主要是因为它们总想建立强大的共和国而不实行主权分享。

大家都知道,在美国对共和制度的尝试和应用首先开始于乡镇和地方议会内部。例如,在康涅狄格这样的小州,挖掘运河和铺筑道路已经是关系政治的大问题了,它不需要供养军队,也不进行战争。它的统治者们既没有太多的报酬,也没有很高的荣誉。在这里,再没有任何一种政府形式比共和制度更自然和更合情合理的了。于是,正是这种共和精神,即一个自由民族的风气和习惯,在各个州产生和发展起来,而后又顺利地通行于全国了。从某种意义上来说,联邦的公共精神无疑是地方爱国主义的集合或总结。也可以说,每个美国公民都把自己对小共和国的爱慕之情转移到对共同祖国的热爱上了。在保卫联邦时,他们也就等于在保卫自己州县的繁荣昌盛,保卫了参与治理国家大事的权利,保卫了他们希望联邦拟出一定会使他们富裕的改进措施的心愿;这一切,通常比全国的共同利益和国家的荣誉更能激发人心。

另一方面,如果居民的习性和风气能够促进一个大国的繁荣富强,那么联邦制度会把这项任务的困难减少到最低程度。美国各州的共和制度,没有出现大多数人群常见的弊端。从领土的面积来说,联邦是一个大共和国;但从它管理事务之少来说,它又无异于一个小共和国。它的作为是很重要的,但为数不多。

As the sovereignty of the Union is limited and incomplete, its exercise is not dangerous to liberty; for it does not excite those insatiable desires for fame and power which have proved so fatal to great republics. As there is no common center to the country, great capital cities, colossal wealth, abject poverty, and sudden revolutions are alike unknown; and political passion, instead of spreading over the land like a fire on the prairies, spends its strength against the interests and the individual passions of every state. Nevertheless, tangible objects and ideas circulate throughout the Union as freely as in a country inhabited by one people. Nothing checks the spirit of enterprise. The government invites the aid of all who have talents or knowledge to serve it. Inside of the frontiers of the Union profound peace prevails, as within the heart of some great empire; abroad it ranks with the most powerful nations of the earth: two thousand miles of coast are open to the commerce of the world; and as it holds the keys of a new world, its flag is respected in the most remote seas. The Union is happy and free as a small people, and glorious and strong as a great nation.

Why The Federal Systhemis Is Not Practicable For All Natlons, And How The Anglo-amerlcans Were Enabled To Adopt lt.

Every federal system has inherent faults that baffle the efforts of the legislator—The federal system is complex —It demands a daily exercise of the intelligence of the citizens—Practical knowledge of government common among the Americans —Relative weakness of the government of the Union another defect inherent in the federal system—The Americans have diminished without remedying it—The sovereignty of the separate states apparently weaker, but really stronger, than that of the Union—Why—Natural causes of Union, then, must exist between confederate nations besides the laws—What these causes are among the Anglo-Americans—Maine and Georgia, separated by a distance of a thousand miles, more naturally united than Normandy and Brittany—War the main peril of confederations— This proved

由于联邦的主权是有限的和不完整的,所以对主权的行使不会危及到自由;它也不会激起对大共和国有致命危险的那种对名利和权力的永不知足的欲望。因为这里没有一个共同的中心,没有巨大的城市,没有巨额的财富,没有贫困的底层,也没有突然爆发的革命。政治激情不是像野火燎原那样顿时遍及全国,而是逐渐蔓延开来去反对每个州的自私和偏见。然而,在美国,工作和思想的自由传播就如同单一制国家一样,没有任何东西能抑制事业的进取精神。政府邀请所有有才能和有知识的人为他服务。在整个联邦境内,就像在由同一个帝国统治的国家内部一样,到处是和平的气息。在国外,它与地球上的各大强国并驾齐驱:它有 2000 英里的对全世界外商公开的海岸;由于它掌握了通向新世界的钥匙,所以它的国旗在遥远的海边也受到尊敬。联邦既像一个小国那样自由和幸福,又像一个大国那样光荣和强大。

为什么联邦制不能适用于所有国家,而英籍美国人又是怎样采用它的。

每个联邦制度都有立法者克服不了的固有缺点——联邦制度的复杂性——它要经常利用公民的才智——美国人在治国方面的实际知识——联邦政府的相对软弱性,联邦制度的另一个固有缺陷——美国人减弱了这一缺陷,但并没有从根本上补救它——各州的主权表面上比联邦的主权小,而实际上比它强大——为什么——除了法律因素以外,还有联邦的一些自然因素——英裔美国人有哪些这种原因——缅因州与佐治亚州相距1000 英里,但大联合比诺曼底与布列塔尼联合更为自然——战争是对联邦制的主要危险——美国本身的例子可以证明这一点——

even by the example of the United States—The Union has no great wars to fear—Why—Dangers which Europeans would incur if they adopted the federal system of the Americans.

When, after many efforts, a legislator succeeds in exercising an indirect influence upon the destiny of nations, his genius is lauded by mankind, while, in point of fact, the geographical position of the country, which he is unable to change, a social condition which arose without his co-operation, customs and opinions which he cannot trace to their source, and an origin with which he is unacquainted exercise so irresistible an influence over the courses of society that he is himself borne away by the current after an ineffectual resistance. Like the navigator, he may direct the vessel which bears him, but he can neither change its structure, nor raise the winds, nor lull the waters that swell beneath him.

I have shown the advantages that the Americans derive from their federal system; it remains for me to point out the circumstances that enabled them to adopt it, as its benefits cannot be enjoyed by all nations. The accidental defects of the federal system which originate in the laws may be corrected by the skill of the legislator, but there are evils inherent in the system which cannot be remedied by any effort. The people must therefore find in themselves the strength necessary to bear the natural imperfections of their government.

The most prominent evil of all federal systems is the complicated nature of the means they employ. Two sovereignties are necessarily in presence of each other. The legislator may simplify and equalize as far as possible the action of these two sovereignties, by limiting each of them to a sphere of authority accurately defined; but he cannot combine them into one or prevent them from coming into collision at certain points. The federal system, therefore, rests upon a theory which is complicated at the best, and which demands the daily exercise of a considerable share of discretion on the part of those it governs. A proposition must be plain, to be adopted by the understanding of a people. A false notion which is clear and precise will always have more power in the world than a true principle which is obscure or involved. Thus it happens that parties, which are like small communities in the heart of the nation, invariably adopt some principle or name

没有什么大战会使联邦害怕——为什么——欧洲国家采取美国的联邦制时可能发生的危险。

当经过了很多努力后，一个立法者能成功地对本国的命运产生一点间接的影响，他的才华会立刻得到颂扬。其实，能对社会的发展经常发生不可抗拒影响的，倒是他无力改变的该国的地理位置，在他以前就已存在的该国的社会情况，他已无法考察其来源的该国的民情和思想，他已无法知道的该国的起源。对这种不可抗拒的影响，他的反抗也是没有用的，最后连自己都会被卷走。立法者像航海家一样，他可以指挥他所乘的船只，但他却改变不了船的结构，他既不能呼风唤雨，也不能平息在他脚下咆哮的大洋。

我已经讲过美国人从他们的联邦制中获得的好处。接下来我要指出的是哪些东西使他们得以采用这种制度，因为这个制度并未使所有国家受益。联邦制度中的一些偶然缺陷是来自法律的，它可由立法者人为地更正；但还有一些缺陷则是制度本身所固有的，并非人力所能克服。因此，采用这种制度的人民，应当具备必要的力量来容忍在这种制度的统治下所固有的缺陷。

所有联邦制度的固有缺陷中，最突出的是其所采用的手段的复杂性。两种主权在这种制度下必然会共存。立法者尽可能地使这两种主权的活动简单和平等，把两者限制在各自明确规定的活动范围之内；但他们无法阻止两者互为影响，更无法防止它们在某个方面发生冲突。因此，联邦制度拥有一套复杂的理论。这套理论的应用，要求被统治者每天都得运用他们对这套理论具有的知识。一般说来，人民必须掌握几个简单的概念。一个清晰明确的错误的观念往往比一个含糊复杂的正确观念更有力。因此，一些类似于大国中的小国的政党，总是不择手段地利用并不完全代

as a symbol, which very inadequately represents the end they have in view and the means that they employ, but without which they could neither act nor exist. The governments that are founded upon a single principle or a single feeling which is easily defined are perhaps not the best, but they are unquestionably the strongest and the most durable in the world.

In examining the Constitution of the United States, which is the most perfect federal constitution that ever existed, one is startled at the variety of information and the amount of discernment that it presupposes in the people whom it is meant to govern. The government of the Union depends almost entirely upon legal fictions; the Union is an ideal nation, which exists, so to speak, only in the mind, and whose limits and extent can only be discerned by the understanding. After the general theory is comprehended, many difficulties remain to be solved in its application; for the sovereignty of the Union is so involved in that of the states that it is impossible to distinguish its boundaries at the first glance. The whole structure of the government is artificial and conventional, and it would be ill adapted to a people which has not been long accustomed to conduct its own affairs, or to one in which the science of politics has not descended to the humblest classes of society. I have never been more struck by the good sense and the practical judgment of the Americans than in the manner in which they elude the numberless difficulties resulting from their Federal Constitution. I scarcely ever met with a plain American citizen who could not distinguish with surprising facility the obligations created by the laws of Congress from those created by the laws of his own state, and who, after having discriminated between the matters which come under the cognizance of the Union and those which the local legislature is competent to regulate, could not point out the exact limit of the separate jurisdictions of the Federal courts and the tribunals of the state.

The Constitution of the United States resembles those fine creations of human industry which ensure wealth and renown to their inventors, but which are profitless in other hands. This truth is exemplified by the condition of Mexico at the present time. The Mexicans were desirous of establishing a federal system, and they took the Federal Constitution of their neighbors, the AngloAmericans, as their model and copied it almost entirely. [1] But ion represented by although they had borrowed the letter of the law, they could not

---

[1] See the Mexican Constitution of 1824.

表它们所追求的目的和所使用的手段的名义或主义当旗号;而没有这个旗号,它们既不能存在,也无法开展活动。一个建立在容易界定的简单原则或学说之上的政府或许不是最好的政府,但无疑是最强大和最长命的政府。

但是,当我们研究迄今为止世界上存在的最完美的联邦制宪法——美国宪法时,却对于这个宪法种类繁多的条款和要求被统治者必须具有识别能力感到吃惊。联邦政府几乎完全依赖于法律的虚构。联邦是一个理想国,可以说它只存在于人的头脑里,它的版图和范围也完全凭感觉去辨别。当总的理论被理解之后,很多实际应用方面的难题还有待解决,因为联邦主权与各州主权互相交错,不可能一眼就分清其界限。政府的构造是复杂的,只有长期以来惯于自治和政治知识普及到社会下层的民族,才适于采用这套办法。我对美国人在解决来自联邦宪法的无数难题方面表现的高超知识和能力,真是佩服得五体投地。我见过的美国人中,没有一个不能轻而易举地把国会的法律为他规定的义务与自己州的法律分给他的义务区分开来,也没有一个不能在区分属于联邦的普通法院审理的案件和应由地方的司法机构处理的事件之后指出联邦法院管辖权的起点和州法院管辖权的终点。

美国的联邦宪法好像那些精美的艺术品,它们能赋予创造者财富和荣誉,但落到他人之手后就会变得毫无用处。墨西哥的现况就能很好的证明这个问题。墨西哥人渴望建立联邦制度,于是把他们的邻居英籍美国人的联邦宪法作为范本,并几乎全部照抄过来。① 但是,他们只抄来了宪法的条文,却不能把给予宪法以生

---

① 见 1824 年的墨西哥宪法。

carry over the spirit that gives it life. They were involved in ceaseless embarrassments by the mechanism of their dual government; the sovereignty of the states and that of the Union perpetually exceeded their respective privileges and came into collision; and to the present day Mexico is alternately the victim of anarchy and the slave of military despotism.

The second and most fatal of all defects, and that which I believe to be inherent in the federal system, is the relative weakness of the government of the Union. The principle upon which all confederations rest is that of a divided sovereignty. Legislators may render this partition less perceptible, they may even conceal it for a time from the public eye, but they cannot prevent it from existing; and a divided sovereignty must always be weaker than an entire one. The remarks made on the Constitution of the United States have shown with what skill the Americans, while restraining the power of the Union within the narrow limits of a federal government, have given it the semblance, and to a certain extent the force, of a national government. By this means the legislators of the Union have diminished the natural danger of confederations, but have not entirely obviated it.

The American government, it is said, does not address itself to the states, but transmits its injunctions directly to the citizens and compels them individually to comply with its demands. But if the Federal law were to clash with the interests and the prejudices of a state, it might be feared that all the citizens of that state would conceive themselves to be interested in the cause of a single individual who refused to obey. If all the citizens of the state were aggrieved at the same time and in the same manner by the authority of the Union, the Federal government would vainly attempt to subdue them individually; they would instinctively unite in a common defense and would find an organization already prepared for them in the sovereignty that their state is allowed to enjoy. Fiction would give way to reality, and an organized portion of the nation might then contest the central authority.

The same observation holds good with regard to the Federal jurisdiction. If the courts of the Union violated an important law of a state in a private case, the real though not the apparent contest would be between the aggrieved state represented by a citizen and the Union

命的精神也照搬过来。因此,他们的双重政府的车轮便陷入了时停时转的窘境。各州的主权和联邦的主权时常超越宪法为它们规定的范围,所以双方总是发生冲突,直到今天,墨西哥还陷于从无政府状态到军人专制,再从军人专制回到无政府状态的循环之中。

在所有的缺陷中,第二个致命的而且我认为也是来自联邦制度所固有的重大缺陷,是联邦政府的相对软弱性。所有联邦制国家所依据的原则是对主权进行划分。立法者们把这种划分规定得不够明确,他们有时甚至对公众隐瞒这种划分,但他们不能阻止它的存在;并且,被划分的主权永远比完整的主权软弱。我们在讲述美国宪法时已经知道,美国人是如何巧妙地在把联邦的权力限制在联邦政府的狭小职权范围内的同时,又能使联邦政府具有全国中央政府的外貌,而且在某些方面使它具有全国中央政府的权力的。联邦的立法者们也同样巧妙地减轻了联邦制的固有危险,但未能完全消除。

据说,美国政府并不直接与各州打交道,而是直接把它的法令传达给公民,并强迫公民服从国家的要求。但是,如果联邦的法律触犯了一个州的利益和惯例,它也许会害怕在处罚拒绝服从该项法律的人时,整个州的公民会认为是等于侵害他们自己的利益。如果这个州的全体公民也认为联邦的处罚同时和同样地侵害了他们;如果联邦政府企图分化他们并加以制服;他们会本能地自己联合起来抵抗,并会认为他们州分享的那部分主权将为他们做主。

这时,虚构的东西就要向现实让步,而一个有组织的权力当局可以向中央政权挑战,联邦的司法权也是如此。假如联邦的法院在审理一个私人案件时侵犯了一个州的一项重要法律,尽管表面上双方会很平静,但实际上却是由一个公民做代表的受害

represented by its courts of justice. ①

He would have but a partial knowledge of the world who should imagine that it is possible by the aid of legal fictions to prevent men from finding out and employing those means of gratifying their passions which have been left open to them. The American legislators, though they have rendered a collision between the two sovereignties less probable, have not destroyed the causes of such a misfortune. It may even be affirmed that, in case of such a collision, they have not been able to ensure the victory of the Federal element. The Union is possessed of money and troops, but the states have kept the affections and the prejudices of the people. The sovereignty of the Union is an abstract being, which is connected with but few external objects; the sovereignty of the states is perceptible by the senses, easily understood, and constantly active. The former is of recent creation, the latter is coeval with the people itself. The sovereignty of the Union is factitious, that of the states is natural and self-existent, without effort, like the authority of a parent. The sovereignty of the nation affects a few of the chief interests of society; it represents an immense but remote country, a vague and ill-defined sentiment. The authority of the states controls every individual citizen at every hour and in all circumstances; it protects his property, his freedom, and his life; it affects at every moment his well-being or his misery. When we recollect the traditions, the customs, the prejudices of local and familiar attachment with which it is connected, we cannot doubt the superiority of a power that rests on the instinct of patriotism, so natural to the human heart.

----

① For instance, the Union possesses by the Constitution the right of selling unoccupied lands for its own profit. Suppose that the state of Ohio should claim the same right in behalf of certain tracts lying within its own boundaries, upon the plea that the Constitution refers only to those lands which do not belong to the jurisdiction of any particular state, and consequently should choose to dispose of them itself. The litigation would be carried on, it is true, in the names of the purchasers from the state of Ohio and the purchasers from the Union, and not in the names of Ohio and the Union. But what would become of this legal fiction if the Federal purchaser was confirmed in his right by the courts of the Union while the other competitor was ordered to retain possession by the tribunals of the state of Ohio?

州和由法院做代表的联邦之间的争讼。①

如果有人认为,给予人们以满足其激情的手段,他们就可以在法律的假设的帮助下,通过认识法和运用法而控制住激情,那么这说明他在这个世界上还经验不足。美国的立法者虽然已经尽可能地使两种主权之间的冲突减到最小,但并不能完全消除冲突的原因。甚至可以断言,在两种主权发生冲突时,他们也许还保证不了联邦主权获胜。联邦拥有财力和部队,但各州可保持人民的爱好和习惯。主权是一个抽象的存在,只与少数的对外事务有关。各州的主权是可以被人们完全感觉到的,并易于理解,人们每时每刻都能感觉到它在行动。前者是新的事物,后者是与人民本身同时产生的。联邦主权是人工创造的,各州主权是自然存在的,就像家长的权力一样,不必费力就能建立起来。联邦主权只影响到社会的一些重大问题上的利益;它代表一个幅员辽阔的国家,它代表一种模糊不清的感情。各州的主权似乎每时每刻在任何环境下都控制着每个公民,它保护着公民的财产、自由以及他们的生命,它无时无刻不在影响每个公民的安危。各州主权所依靠的是人民的传统和习惯,是地方的偏见,是地方和家庭的私心。我们怎能怀疑这种爱国主义的优越性呢,它已深深扎根于人们的心里。

---

① 例如,宪法赋予联邦可以为了自己的利益任意出售未被占领的土地的权力。让我们试想如果俄亥俄州也要求同样的权利,出售自己的范围内的土地,那么对于这种请求宪法只能涉及一些在司法上不属于任何州的土地,而最终还会选择由他们自己处置。由此便会引发争论,到底是以俄亥俄州的买主的名义,而不以俄亥俄州的名义? 还是以联邦的买主的名义,而不以联邦的名义? 那么最终是由联邦法庭所承认的联邦的收购具有合法性是有效的? 还是由俄亥俄州法庭承认的俄亥俄州的收购具有合法性是有效的呢?

Since legislators cannot prevent such dangerous collisions as occur between the two sovereignties which coexist in the Federal system, their first object must be, not only to dissuade the confederate states from warfare, but to encourage such dispositions as lead to peace. Hence it is that the Federal compact cannot be lasting unless there exists in the communities which are leagued together a certain number of inducements to union which render their common dependence agreeable and the task of the government light. The Federal system cannot succeed without the presence of favorable circumstances added to the influence of good laws. All the nations that have ever formed a confederation have been held together by some common interests, which served as the intellectual ties of association.

But men have sentiments and principles as well as material interests. A certain uniformity of civilization is not less necessary to the durability of a confederation than a uniformity of interests in the states that compose it. In Switzerland the difference between the civilization of the Canton of Uri and that of the Canton of Vaud is like the difference between the fifteenth and the nineteenth centuries; therefore, properly speaking, Switzerland has never had a federal government. The union between these two cantons exists only on the map; and this would soon be perceived if an attempt were made by a central authority to prescribe the same laws to the whole territory.

The circumstance which makes it easy to maintain a Federal government in America is not only that the states have similar interests, a common origin, and a common language, but that they have also arrived at the same stage of civilization, which almost always renders a union feasible. I do not know of any European nation, however small, that does not present less uniformity in its different provinces than the American people, which occupy a territory as extensive as one half of Europe. The distance from Maine to Georgia is about one thousand miles; but the difference between the civilization of Maine and that of Georgia is slighter than the difference between the habits of Normandy and those of Brittany. Maine and Georgia, which are placed at the opposite extremities of a great empire, have therefore more real inducements to form a confederation than Normandy and Brittany, which are separated only by a brook The geographical position of the country increased the facilities that the American legislators derived from the usages and customs of the inhabitants; and it is to this circumstance that the adoption and the maintenance of the Federal system are mainly attributable.

The most important occurrence in the life of a nation is the breaking out of a war. In war a people act as one man against foreign

　　既然立法者不能阻止在联邦制度中并存的两种主权发生危险的冲突，那他们就必须尽一切努力使联合起来的各州远离战争，并鼓励那种能导致和平的态度。因此，除非联邦的参加者之间存在着许多能使联邦联合并团结的因素，否则联邦的公约就不会持续很久。同样，联邦制要想获得成功，不仅要有良好的法律，而且要有有利的环境。所有组成联邦的成员国家都必须拥有一些共同的利益，而这些共同的利益就形成了它们联合的精神纽带。

　　但是，除了物质利益以外，人还有思想和感情。对于一个联邦的持久存在，一定的文明的结合不亚于各成员间利益的结合。在瑞士的沃州和乌里州之间，文明的差别就像19世纪与15世纪之不同；因此，严格地说来，瑞士从来没有过联邦政府。这两个州之间的瑞士联邦，只存在于地图上。如果中央政府试图对全瑞士实行同样的法律，这种情况就会立刻被证明。

　　有一个事实非常有利地维护了美国建立的联邦政府。各州不仅有相似的利益、相同的起源和语言，而且还处于同样的文明水平，这便使它们的联合几乎永远成为容易的事情。我不知道是否有一个欧洲小国，其不同地区间的同质性高于面积相当于大半个欧洲的美国。缅因州到佐治亚州的距离大约为1000英里，但它们之间的文明差异却小于诺曼底和布列塔尼间的这种差异。因此，位于一个大帝国的两端的缅因和佐治亚，却比仅有一溪之隔的诺曼底和布列塔尼更自然地容易结成联邦。国家的地理位置增加了立法者从居民的风气与习惯中获得的这种便利性，也正是国家的地理位置，有利于联邦制度的建立和保持。

　　在能够影响一个国家的生活的所有事件中，最重要的是战争。在战争当中，一个国家的人民要团结得像一个人似的，为保

nations in defense of their very existence. The skill of the government, the good sense of the community, and the natural fondness that men almost always entertain for their country may be enough as long as the only object is to maintain peace in the interior of the state and to favor its internal prosperity; but that the nation may carry on a great war the people must make more numerous and painful sacrifices; and to suppose that a great number of men will of their own accord submit to these exigencies is to betray an ignorance of human nature. All the nations that have been obliged to sustain a long and serious warfare have conse quently been led to augment the power of their government Those who have not succeeded in this attempt have been subjugated. A long war almost always reduces nations to the wretched alternative of being abandoned to ruin by defeat or to despotism by suecess. War therefore renders the weakness of a government most apparent and most alarming; and I have shown that the inherent defect of federal governments is that of being weak.

The federal system not only has no centralized administration, and nothing that resembles one, but the central government itself is imperfectly organized, which is always a great cause of weakness when the nation is opposed to other countries which are themselves governed by a single authority. In the Federal Constitution of the United States, where the central government has more real force than in any other confederation, this evil is still extremely evident. A single example will illustrate the case.

The Constitution confers upon Congress the right of "calling forth the militia to execute the laws of the Union, suppress insurrections, and repel invasions"; and another article declares that the President of the United States is the commander-in-chief of the militia. In the war of 1812 the President ordered the militia of the Northern states to march to the frontiers; but Connecticut and Massachusetts, whose interests were impaired by the war, refused to obey the command. They argued that the Constitution authorizes the Federal government to call forth the militia in case of *insurrection or invasion*; but in the present instance there was neither invasion nor insurrection. They added that the same Constitution which conferred upon the Union the right of calling the militia into active service reserved to the states that of naming the officers; and consequently (as they understood the clause) no officer of the Union had any right to command the militia, even during war, except the President in person:and in this case they were ordered to join an army commanded

卫自己国家的生存而共同打击敌人。如果问题仅仅是要维持国内和平和促进国家繁荣,那么只要政府治理有方,被统治者通情达理,人民经常怀有爱国的自然情感,也就够了。但是,当一个国家打一场大战时,人民就得付出大量的牺牲和遭受数不尽的苦难。认为大多数人会自愿服从这种社会要求,那么这是对人性的一种无知的表现。因此,凡是参加过持久并激烈的大战的国家,几乎全都身不由己地去加强政府的力量。而在大战中失败的国家便被征服。一场长期的战争必然会导致两种结果,一种是国家因失败而灭亡,另一种就是国家因胜利而导致专政,二者必居其一。因此,战争使政府的弱点暴露得更加明显和危险,而且我已经说过,联邦制国家政府的固有缺陷就是它的过于软弱。

联邦制度不仅没有中央行政集权和类似的东西,而且中央政府本身也只是不完整的组织结构,这就是为什么当这样的国家与实行统一的中央集权的国家交战时会如此软弱的一大原因。在美国的联邦宪法中,中央政府虽然比其他任何联邦制政府都有实权,但它的缺陷依然显而易见。一个简单的例子就可以证明这种情况。

美国宪法授权国会以下权力:"可以向各州召集士兵,以平息内乱或抵抗外来侵略";另外一条法令宣称美国总统为合众国陆海军总司令。在1812年战争中,总统曾命令北方的士兵进军前线,但康涅狄格和马萨诸塞却拒不执行,因为它们的利益曾受到过战争的损害。这两个州指出,宪法规定只有在发生内乱和外来侵略时联邦政府才有权召集士兵,而现在既无内乱又无外来侵略。它们还补充说,授权联邦可以召集民兵的同一宪法,也为各州保留了任命军官的权利,因此,按照它们对宪法的理解,除了总统本人以外,没有一个联邦军官有权指挥士兵,即使是在战争中。

by another individual. These absurd and pernicious doctrines received the sanction not only of the governors and the legislative bodies, but also of the courts of justice in both states; and the Federal government was forced to raise elsewhere the troops that it required. ①How does it happen, then, that the American Union, with all the relative perfection of its laws, is not dissolved by the occurrence of a great war? It is because it has no great wars to fear. Placed in the center of an immense continent, which offers a boundless field for human industry, the Union is almost as much insulated from the world as if all its frontiers were girt by the ocean. Canada contains only a million inhabitants, and its population is divided into two inimical nations. The rigor of the climate limits the extension of its territory, and shuts up its ports during the six months of winter. From Canada to the Gulf of Mexico a few savage tribes are to be met with, which retire, perishing in their retreat, before six thousand soldiers. To the south the Union has a point of contact with the empire of Mexico; and it is hence that serious hostilities may one day be expected to arise. But for a long while to come the uncivilized state of the Mexican people, the depravity of their morals, and their extreme poverty will prevent that country from ranking high among nations. As for the powers of Europe, they are too distant to be formidable. ②

The great advantage of the United States does not, then, consist in a Federal Constitution which allows it to carry on great wars, but in a geographical position which renders such wars extremely improbable. No one can be more inclined than I am to appreciate the advantages of the federal system, which I hold to be one of the combinations

---

① Kent's *Commentaries*, Vol. I, p. 244. I have selected an example that relates to a time long after the promulgation of the present Constitution. If I had gone back to the days of the Confederation, I might have given still more striking instances. The whole nation was at that time in a state of high enthusiasm; the Revolution was represented by a man who was the idol of the people; but at that very period, Congress, to say the truth, had no resources at all at its disposal. Troops and supplies were perpetually wanting. The best-devised projects failed in their execution, and the Union, constantly on the verge of destruction, was saved by the weakness of its enemies far more than by its own strength.

② See Appendix O.

在这种情况下,士兵被命令加入只有一个人指挥的军队中。赞同这种荒谬且有害说法的,不仅有两州的政府和立法机构,而且有两州的法院;于是,联邦政府只好到别处去招募所需的军队。[①] 但是,为什么只靠相对完整的法制保护的美国联邦,却没有毁于一场大战呢? 那是因为还没有发生真正危害到他们生存的战争。美国位于一个广袤无垠的大陆的中部,他为人类事业的发展提供了无限的空间,两侧的大洋几乎使它与世隔绝。加拿大仅有一百万居民,而且是由两个互相敌对的民族构成。气候的寒冷限制了它的领土扩张,并且在冬季的六个月中,它的港口是不对外开放的。从加拿大到墨西哥湾,其间还有数个野蛮部族,在6000名士兵面前处于半灭亡的状态。在南部,美国与墨西哥帝国接壤;有朝一日,这里也许会发生大战。但是,由于墨西哥人的文明还不够开化、加上道德的腐败和国家的极度贫穷,这些都会阻止他们早日跻身于大国之林。至于欧洲各国,由于它们离美国太远,也不足为惧。[②]

因此,美国的一大优势并不在于它有一部可以使它顶得住大战的联邦宪法,而在于它处在一个不会发生威胁到它利益的战争的地理位置。没有人比我更赏识联邦制度的优点。我认为,联邦

---

① 见肯特的《评论》第一卷,第244页。这里我选了一个发生在宣布现今宪法后很长一段时间里的例子。如果我能回到联邦时代,我会给出更好的例子。在那时,整个民族都处于极高的热情中,领导革命的人被人民拜为偶像。但实际上,国会在那段时间根本没有可供其部署的人员。军队和物品永远是急需的。他们的完美计划最终也以失败而告终,联邦已经处于崩溃的边缘,与其让联邦依靠自己的力量解救自己,不如让他们依靠敌人的软弱来解救自己。

② 见附录O。

most favorable to the prosperity and freedom of man. I envy the lot of those nations which have been able to adopt it; but I cannot believe that any confederate people could maintain a long or an equal contest with a nation of similar strength in which the government is centralized. A people which, in the presence of the great military monarchies of Europe, should divide its sovereignty into fractional parts would, in my opinion, by that very act abdicate its power, and perhaps its existence and its name. But such is the admirable position of the New World that man has no other enemy than himself, and that, in order to be happy and to be free, he has only to determine that he will be so.

制度是最有利于人类繁荣和自由的强大组织形式之一。我羡慕那些已经采用这个制度的国家。但我又总是不能相信，实行联邦的国家能够在力量相等的条件下与一个实行中央集权制度的强国进行长期的斗争。在我看来，一个国家在面对欧洲的几个强大军事君主国时，将主权分成两个部分，简直就等于放弃自己的政权，或许可以说是放弃了自己的生存和名望。但是新大陆的令人向往之处，就在于人们在那里没有别的敌人，而恰恰可以自我奋斗。只要你去追求，就能获得想要的幸福和自由。

DEMOCRACY IN AMERICA

论 美 国 民 主

[法]托克维尔　著

朱尾声　译

马高霞　译校

（二）

中国社会科学出版社

CHAPTER IX
How It Can Be Strictly Said That The People Govern In The United States

Thus far I have examined the institutions of the United States; I have passed their legislation in review and have described the present forms of political society in that country. But above these institutions and beyond all these characteristic forms, there is a sovereign power, that of the people, which may destroy or modify them at its pleasure. It remains to be shown in what manner this power, superior to the laws, acts; what are its instincts and its passions, what the secret springs that retard, accelerate, or direct its irresistible course, what the effects of its unbounded authority, and what the destiny that is reserved for it.

How It Can Be Strictly Said That The People Govern In The United States

In America the people appoint the legislative and the executive power and furnish the jurors who punish all infractions of the laws. The institutions are democratic, not only in their principle, but in all their consequences; and the people elect their representatives *directly*, and for the most part *annually*, in order to ensure their dependence. The people are therefore the real directing power; and although the form of goverenment is representative, it is evident that the opinions, the prejudices, the interests, and even the passions of the people are hindered by no permanent obstacles from exercising a perpetual influence on the daily conduct of affairs. In the United States the majority governs in the name of the people, as is the case in all

第九章　为什么可以严格地说
美国是由人民统治的

前面我曾考察过美国的规章制度；也回顾了他们的立法机构，并描述了国家现行的政治形势。但是，在这所有的制度和体系之外，还存在着一个强大的力量，那就是人民，它们能随兴修改甚至瓦解已存在的制度。人民的权力在某些行为的执行上比法律还有力；什么是它的本能与激情，又是什么神秘的源泉在延缓着、促进着甚至是控制着它不可抗拒的力量，它无限权力的影响，等待它的命运又是怎样的。

从严格意义上讲，为什么是人民统治着美国

在美国，由人民任命立法者和执法者，并充当着惩罚一切非法行为的审判员的角色。社会的各项制度，不论是在其原则上，还是在其影响上，都是民主的；并且，当人民对他们的代表进行直接的和普遍一年一次的选举时，就是为了确保代表们能完全受制于人民。因此，人民才是真正的直接领导力量；尽管政府的形式是代议制的，但是很明显的，人民的观念、偏见、利益，甚至是激情对日常生活所产生的普遍的影响，都不会遇到任何永久的阻碍。在美国，大多数统治者都代表着人民的利益，这就如同其他所有

countries in which the people are supreme. This majority is principally composed of peaceable citizens, who, either by inclination or by
interest, sin cerely wish the welfare of their country. But they are surrounded by the incessant agitation of parties, who attempt to gain their
co operation and support.

国家一样,人民是至高无上的。这个多数主要由平静温和的公民组成,他们不是由于自己的爱好,就是出于自己的利益,并且真诚的希望自己的国家能幸福。但是他们不断地被一些善于煽动他们的政党包围着,以企图与他们合作,并得到他们的支持。

CHAPTER X

Parties In The United States

Great distinction to be made between parties—Parties that are to each other as rival nations—Parties properly so called—Difference between great and small parties—Epochs that produce them—Their characteristics—America has had great parties—They are extinct—Federalists—Republicans—Defeat of the Federalists—Difficulty of creating parties in the United States—What is done with this intention—Aristocratic or democratic character to be met with in all parties—Struggle of General Jackson against the Bank of the United States.

A great distinction must be made between parties. Some countries are so large that the different populations which inhabit them, although united under the same government, have contradictory interests, and they may consequently be in a perpetual state of opposition. In this case the different fractions of the people may more properly be considered as distinct nations than as mere parties; and if a civil war breaks out, the struggle is carried on by rival states rather than by factions in the same state.

But when the citizens entertain different opinions upon subjects which affect the whole country alike, such, for instance, as the principles upon which the government is to be conducted, then distinctions arise that may correctly be styled parties. Parties are a necessary evil in free governments; but they have not at all times the same character and the same propensities.

At certain periods a nation may be oppressed by such insupportable evils as to conceive the design of effecting a total change in its political constitution; at other times, the mischief lies still deeper and

第十章　美国的政党

政党之间的大分类——政党之间就如同是相互敌对的国家——真正意义上的政党——大政党与小政党之间的差别——政党产生于哪个时代——他们的特点——美国曾有过的大政党——他们已不复存在——联邦党——共和党——联邦党的失败——在美国建立政党的困难——为建立政党所做过的一切——在一切政党中都可见到的贵族性或民主性——杰克逊将军反对美国银行的斗争。

首先,我必须对政党进行一次大分类。有些国家地处广大,其中也聚集着不同的居民,尽管把人民都联合在同一政权下,但他们仍有相互对立的利益,因此,人民便会处于一种永久的对立状态中。在这种情况下,人民中的不同派别,便很可能被看作是不同的国家,而不仅仅是政党;假如爆发一场内战,与其说这是不同派别之间的斗争,不如说这是敌对国家之间的较量。

但当公民们在遇到一些会影响整个国家的问题时,比如说政府将采用那些总的施政原则时,他们就会产生不同的意见,于是具有自己风格的政党便产生了。政党是自由政府必有的灾难;而它们在任何时候都不具有相同的特性和相同的倾向。

在一定的时候,国家可能深受这种灾难的压迫,于是就会设想能完全改变其政治结构的有效局面;还有些时候,灾难来的更

the existence of society itself is endangered. Such are the times of great revolutions and of great parties. But between these epochs of misery and confusion there are periods during which human society seems to rest and mankind to take breath. This pause is, indeed, only apparent, for time does not stop its course for nations any more than for men; they are all advancing every day towards a goal with which they are unacquainted. We imagine them to be stationary only when their progress escapes our observation, as men who are walking seem to be standing still to those who run.

But however this may be, there are certain epochs in which the changes that take place in the social and political constitution of nations are so slow and imperceptible that men imagine they have reached a final state; and the human mind, believing itself to be firmly based upon sure foundations, does not extend its researches beyond a certain horizon. These are the times of small parties and of intrigue.

The political parties that I style great are those which cling to principles rather than to their consequences; to general and not to special cases; to ideas and not to men. These parties are usually distinguished by nobler features, more generous passions, more genuine convictions, and a more bold and open conduct than the others. In them private interest, which always plays the chief part in political passions, is more studiously veiled under the pretext of the public good; and it may even be sometimes concealed from the eyes of the very persons whom it excites and impels.

Minor parties, on the other hand, are generally deficient in political good faith. As they are not sustained or dignified by lofty purposes, they ostensibly display the selfishness of their character in their actions. They glow with a factitious zeal; their language is vehement, but their conduct is timid and irresolute. The means which they employ are as wretched as the end at which they aim. Hence it happens that when a calm state succeeds a violent revolution, great men seem

加深重,以至于社会本身的存在都要受到威胁。而这些时候正是发生大革命和出现大政党的时代。但是在这些灾难和混乱的时代交替之间,社会似乎可以暂时休息,而人类也可以稍稍喘口气了。其实,这种平静只是表面上的,不论是对于国家还是对于人类,时间都是不会停止脚步的;国家和人类每天都在向一个他们自己并不熟悉的目标前进。所以当我们觉得国家和人类是停止前进的时候,那是因为我们没有察觉到他们的运动,就如同跑着的人看走着的人时,感觉走着的人是原地不动的。

但是无论怎样,国家的政治结构和社会情况都在发生着变化,这些变化有时太慢而使人觉得难以察觉,甚至使人们认为自己已经处于最佳状态;这时,人类的思想也以为自己是建立在坚实可靠的基础之上,不再把眼光扩展到已定的视野之外。这正是一些小政党开始活动和秘密沟通的时候。

我意义上的大政党,是重视原则强于重视结果的;重视一般强于重视特别;相信思想高于相信人民。这些政党与其他政党相比,一般都具有显著的特征,高尚的激情,真实的信念以及大胆和公开的举止。在政治激情中经常产生巨大作用的私人利益,在这里被十分巧妙地掩盖于公共利益之下;有时甚至能瞒过被它们刺激并驱使行动的人们的眼睛。

小党则于此不同,它们一般缺乏良好的政治信念。也没有支持它们的或是被他们尊敬的崇高的目标,所以在他们的行为中,它们的性格就明显地表现出自私自利的一面。它们洋溢着虚伪的热情;它们的言词过于激烈,但行动却胆小并优柔寡断。它们采用的手段,同它们所抱的目的一样,都是令人不快的。因此,在一场暴力革命发生后而出现平静时期时,伟大的人物便好像突然消失了,人类思想的力量也被隐藏起来了。大政党使社会震

suddenly to disappear and the powers of the human mind to lie concealed. Society is convulsed by great parties, it is only agitated by minor ones; it is torn by the former, by the latter it is degraded; and if the first sometimes save it by a salutary perturbation, the last invariably disturb it to no good end.

America has had great parties, but has them no longer; and if her happiness is thereby considerably increased, her morality has suffered. When the War of Independence was terminated and the foundations of the new government were to be laid down, the nation was divided between two opinions—two opinions which are as old as the world and which are perpetually to be met with, under different forms and various names, in all free communities, the one tending to limit, the other to extend indefinitely, the power of the people. The conflict between these two opinions never assumed that degree of violence in America which it has frequently displayed elsewhere. Both parties of the Americans were agreed upon the most essential points; and neither of them had to destroy an old constitution or to overthrow the structure of society in order to triumph. In neither of them, consequently, were a great number of private interests affected by success or defeat: but moral principles of a high order, such as the love of equality and of independence, were concerned in the struggle, and these sufficed to kindle violent passions. The party that desired to limit the power of the people, endeavored to apply its doctrines more especially to the Constitution of the Union, whence it derived its name of *Federal*. The other party, which affected to be exclusively attached to the cause of liberty, took that of *Republican*. America is the land of democracy, and the Federalists, therefore, were always in a minority; but they reckoned on their side almost all the great men whom the War of Independence had produced, and their moral power was very considerable. Their cause, moreover, was favored by circumstances. The ruin of the first Confederation had impressed the people with a dread of anarchy, and the Federalists profited by this transient disposition of the multitude. For ten or twelve years, they were at the head of affairs, and they were able to apply some, though not all, of their principles; for the hostile current was be

荡,而小政党仅仅使社会骚动;前者使社会分裂,后者使社会堕落;如果前者有时因善意的打乱社会秩序而拯救了社会,后者会因为经常扰乱社会而对社会毫无益处。

美国曾经有过几个大党,但都已不复存在;如果它的快乐会因此而增加,那么它的道德将会承受很大的痛苦。当独立战争结束和新政府即将成立的时候,全国被持有两种意见的两个阵营划分开来——这两种意见同世界一样古老,但在所有自由的社会中却以不同的形式和各种各样的名称出现。一种意见倾向于限制人民的权力,而另一种则希望无限扩大人民的权力。两种意见之间的斗争,在美国从来不具有暴力性,而这种暴力性却经常出没于其他地方。美国的两个党派在一些本质问题上的意见都是一致的;他们双方谁也不会为了胜利而去破坏旧的社会体制和推翻整个社会结构。因此,任何一方都不会把大多数人民的个人利益与本派的胜利或失败联系在一起。但类似于热爱平等和独立这样的道德原则会吸引两派在斗争中的极大注意。而这就足以促使他们产生狂热的激情。那些想要限制人民权力的政党,努力使自己的学说更加适用于联邦宪法,由此得名为联邦党。而另一个政党,则非常的向往于自由,便挂上了共和党的名号。美国是民主的国家,因此联邦党总是占据少数;但是他们几乎把独立战争造就出来的伟大人物都拉到他们这一边,并且他们的道德力量也相当具有影响。更何况环境也对他们有利。第一次联合的瓦解,还深深地影响着人们,使他们害怕陷入无政府状态,联邦党也从大多数人的这种短暂的性情中获得了好处。在 10 年到 12 年的时间里,他们领导着国家的事务,并使他们的原则得以应用,尽管不是全部;随着敌人的日益强大,他们也终于无力反对,并以失败而

coming from day to day too violent to be checked. In 1801 the Republicans got possession of the government: Thomas Jefferson was elected President; and he increased the influence of their party by the weight of his great name, the brilliance of his talents, and his immense popularity.

The means by which the Federalists had maintained their position were artificial, and their resources were temporary; it was by the virtues or the talents of their leaders, as well as by fortu nate circumstances, that they had risen to power. When the Republicans attained that station in their turn, their opponents were overwhelmed by utter defeat. An immense majority declared itself against the retiring party, and the Federalists found themselves in so small a minority that they at once despaired of future success. From that moment the Republican or Democratic Party has pro ceeded from conquest to conquest, until it has acquired absolute supremacy in the country. The Federalists, perceiving that they were vanquished, without resource, and isolated in the midst of the nation, fell into two divisions, of which one joined the victorious Republicans, and the other laid down their banners and changed their name. Many years have elapsed since they wholly ceased to exist as a party.

The accession of the Federalists to power was, in my opinion, one of the most fortunate incidents that accompanied the formation of the great American Union: they resisted the inevitable propensities of their country and their age. But whether their theories were good or bad, they had the fault of being inapplicable, as a whole, to the society which they wished to govern, and that which occurred under the auspices of Jefferson must therefore have taken place sooner or later. But their government at least gave the new republic time to acquire a certain stability, and afterwards to support without inconvenience the rapid growth of the very doctrines which they had combated. A considerable number of their principles, moreover, were embodied at last in the political creed of their opponents; and the Federal Constitution, which subsists at the present day, is a lasting monument of their patriotism and their wisdom. Great political parties, then, are not to be met with in the United States at the present time. Parties, indeed, may be found which threaten the future of the Union; but there is none which seems to contest the present form of

告终。1801 年,共和党掌握了国家政权:托马斯·杰斐逊当选为总统;并且依靠自己伟大的名誉、卓越的才能和受欢迎的广度为自己的政党获得了更多的支持。

联邦党用以维持他们地位的方法是虚假的,不可靠的,对他们的支持也是暂时的;他们之所以能够执政,是依靠他们统治者的品德和才能,以及对他们有利的环境。在轮到共和党执政以后,他们便作为对手被彻底的打败。有极大多数人宣称他们反对这个已经败退的政党,这时的联邦党立即发现自己已经成为极其微小的一部分,并对未来的胜利充满了绝望。从此以后,共和党或民主党派便开始了一个又一个的征服,直到最后控制了国家的最高权力。联邦党感到自己已被征服,失去了支持,在国内陷于孤立状态,于是分裂为两部分:一部分参加了胜利的共和党中,另一部分放下了他们的旗帜,并改变了名称。在过去的许多年中,他们已完全不再以政党的形式存在。

我认为,联邦党之所以能掌握政权,实际上是伴随伟大的美国联邦的成立而出现的最幸运的偶然事件之一:他们抵制了他们国家和他们那个时代的一些无法抵抗的习性。但是无论他们的理论是好还是坏,总的说来是有一个缺点的,那就是它不适用于他们想要去统治的社会。所以在这种预兆下,杰斐逊迟早要去治理这个社会。但是,联邦党政府至少给了新共和国一定的时间来达到自我稳定,之后毫无困难地支持了它所反对的学说的迅速发展。而且它的相当多的信条也最终被体现在对手的政治信条中;现今仍在被美国人使用的联邦宪法,是他们的爱国主义和智慧的不朽的里程碑。因此,在现今的美国已经看不到大政党了。但仍旧存在着许多威胁着联邦未来的政党;然而没有一个政党对政府

government or the present course of society. The parties by which the Union is menaced do not rest upon principles, but upon material interests. These inter ests constitute, in the different provinces of so vast an empire, rival nations rather than parties. Thus, upon a recent occasion the North contended for the system of commercial prohibition, and the South took up arms in favor of free trade, simply because the North is a manufacturing and the South an agricultural community; and the restrictive system that was profitable to the one was prejudicial to the other.

In the absence of great parties the United States swarms with lesser controversies, and public opinion is divided into a thousand minute shades of difference upon questions of detail. The pains that are taken to create parties are inconceivable, and at the present day it is no easy task. In the United States there is no religious animosity, because all religion is respected and no sect is predominant; there is no jealousy of rank, because the people are everything and none can contest their authority; lastly, there is no public misery to serve as a means of agitation, because the physical position of the country opens so wide a field to industry that man only needs to be let alone to be able to accomplish prodigies. Nevertheless, ambitious men will succeed in creating parties, since it is difficult to eject a person from authority upon the mere ground that this place is coveted by others. All the skill of the actors in the political world lies in the art of creating parties. A political aspirant in the United States begins by discerning his own interest, and discovering those other interests which may be collected around and amalgamated with it. He then contrives to find out some doctrine or principle that may suit the purposes of this new association, which he adopts in order to bring forward his party and secure its popularity: just as the imprimatur of the king was in former days printed upon the title page of a volume and was thus incorporated with a book to which it in no wise belonged. This being done, the new party is ushered into the political world.

To a stranger all the domestic controversies of the Americans at first appear to be incomprehensible or puerile, and he is at a loss

目前的组织形式和社会发展的总方向表示反对。那些对美国的未来有所威胁的党派所依靠的不是它们的原则，而是它们的物质利益。在如此幅员辽阔的帝国的不同地区，与其说这种利益形成了政党，不如说这种利益形成了敌对的国家。拿最近的一个例子来说，最近北方主张采取贸易禁运政策，而南方则拿起武器去保护贸易自由，而这仅仅是因为北方是工业区，而南方是农业区；而禁运政策对一方有利，对另一方有害。

　　在缺乏大党存在的时候，美国上上下下都被许多小党所包围，且公共舆论在对一些细小问题的看法上，也形成了许多不同的见解。建立政党时遇到的困难几乎都不存在；但在今天，建党就不是一件容易的事了。在美国，没有宗教仇恨，因为所有的宗教都会被人尊重，没有一个教派占居统治地位；也没有阶级间的妒忌，因为人民就是一切，没有任何人敢反对人民的权力；最后，美国的公众不受剥削之苦，因为国家的物质状况为工业发展开辟了无限广阔的道路，人们只要自己动手，就能创造出奇迹。但是，也有些人存在企图建立政党的野心，因为他们知道，只凭自己的愿望想上台，很难把台上的人拉下来。因此，在政界中，行动者的全部技巧都用于创建政党。在美国，一个政治家首先要学会辨别自己的利益，并发现可以把哪些类似的利益聚集到自己的周围合并起来。于是，他会去努力寻找适于这种新设想的学说或原则，目的是促进其政党的前进和威望：这就像以前在出版书籍时要在书名页印上国王的出版许可一样，虽然这个许可与该书的内容毫不相干，但却硬被和书连在一起。这一切做完以后，新的政党便进入政界。

　　对于一个陌生者，美国国内的所有纠纷，乍一看来是不可理

whether to pity a people who take such arrant trifles in good earnest or to envy that happiness which enables a community to discuss them. But when he comes to study the secret propensities that govern the factions of America, he easily perceives that the greater part of them are more or less connected with one or the other of those two great divisons which have always existed in free communities. The deeper we penetrate into the inmost thought of these parties, the more we perceive that the object of the one is to limit and that of the other to extend the authority of the people. I do not assert that the ostensible purpose or even that the secret aim of American parties is to promote the rule of aristocracy or democracy in the country; but I affirm that aristocratic or democratic passions may easily be detected at the bottom of all parties, and that, although they escape a superficial observation, they are the main point and soul of every faction in the United States.

To quote a recent example, when President Jackson attacked the Bank of the United States, the country was excited, and parties were formed; the well-informed classes rallied round the bank, the common people round the President. But it must not be imagined that the people had formed a rational opinion upon a question which offers so many difficulties to the most experienced statesmen. By no means. The bank is a great establishment, which has an independent existence; and the people, accustomed to make and unmake whatsoever they please, are startled to meet with this obstacle to their authority. In the midst of the perpetual fluctuation of society, the community is irritated by so permanent an institution and is led to attack it, in order to see whether it can be shaken, like everything else.

Remalns Of The Aristocratic Party In The United States.

Secret opposition of wealthy individuals to democracy—Their retirement—Their taste for exclusive pleasures and for luxury at home

解的和不成熟的。他不知道自己是应当可怜这个民族把这类烦琐小事当成正经大事,还是应当羡慕他们在为国家命运操劳时的幸福。但是,当他细心研究支配着美国各党派的隐秘的原因时,就不难发现这些大党派都或多或少地与两大党有联系,而这两大党自自由社会成立以来就把人们分成了两派,它们不是靠近这一党,就是亲近那一党。越是深入了解这些党派的内心的想法,就会越多的发现他们中的一方是为了限制人民的权力,而另一方则是致力于扩大人民的权力。我并不是在宣称美国政党的公开目的,甚至是美国政党为了促进贵族政治或民主政治在国内占居优势的隐蔽的目的;而是说贵族政治或民主政治的激情易于在一切政党的内心深处被发现。尽管这种激情能够逃脱人们的视野,但它们仍然是美国政党的重点和灵魂。

我举一个最近的例子:当总统杰克逊攻击美国银行时,国家在骚动,这时便形成了政党;上层阶级一般都站在银行一边,而普通人民则站在总统一边。你以为人民能从如此简单的、而有经验的在难以解决的问题的纷扰中找到可以证明自己的意见是正确的理由吗? 不,他们不能。但是,银行是一个独立存在的巨大机构;而习惯于推翻或建立一切权力的人民却会如此吃惊于对它毫无办法。在社会的永无止境的波荡起伏中,这个牢固的据点向人民发起挑战,它想看一看自己是否也能像其他东西一样继续活动下去。

贵族党在美国的残余

一些贵族对民主的秘密反对——他们的退隐——他们在家享受着独有的快乐与奢华——他们在外微行简出——他们对人

—Their simplicity abroad—Their affected condescension towards the people.

It sometimes happens in a people among whom various opinions prevail that the balance of parties is lost and one of them obtains an irresistible preponderance, overpowers all obstacles, annihilates its opponents, and appropriates all the resources of society to its own use. The vanquished despair of success, hide their heads, and are silent. The nation seems to be governed by a single principle, universal stillness prevails, and the prevailing party assumes the credit of having restored peace and unanimity to the country. But under this apparent unanimity still exist profound differences of opinion, and real opposition.

This is what occurred in America; when the democratic party got the upper hand, it took exclusive possession of the conduct of affairs, and from that time the laws and the customs of society have been adapted to its caprices. At the present day the more affluent classes of society have no influence in political affairs; and wealth, far from conferring a right, is rather a cause of unpopularity than a means of attaining power. The rich abandon the lists, through unwillingness to contend, and frequently to contend in vain, against the poorer classes of their fellow citizens. As they cannot occupy in public a position equivalent to what they hold in private life, they abandon the former and give themselves up to the latter; and they constitute a private society in the state which has its own tastes and pleasures. They submit to this state of things as an irremediable evil, but they are careful not to show that they are galled by its continuance; one often hears them laud the advantages of a republican government and democratic institutions when they are in public. Next to hating their enemies, men are most inclined to flatter them.

Mark, for instance, that opulent citizen, who is as anxious as a Jew of the Middle Ages to conceal his wealth. His dress is plain, his demeanor unassuming; but the interior of his dwelling glitters with luxury, and none but a few chosen guests, whom he haughtily styles his equals, are allowed to penetrate into this sanctuary. No European noble is more exclusive in his pleasures or more jealous of the smallest advantages that a privileged station confers. But the same individual

民的虚伪的殷勤。

在各种舆论盛行的国家,有时党派之间的平衡被打破,并使其中的一个政党占居不可抗拒优势,它将摧毁一切障碍,消灭它的政敌,迫使所有的社会资源都为它所用。被征服的政党对成功感到绝望之后,便暂时退隐,默不作声。全国似乎被统制在一个单一的思想下,沉寂在一片宁静中,胜利的党高呼着,是它们给国家赢得了荣誉,给国家带来了和平与和谐。但是,在这种表面和谐的下面,依然存在着深刻的分歧和实质的对抗。

这就是美国所发生的现实情况;当民主党占居优势时,它就独揽处理国务的大权,随后,它又不断地按照自己的想法去改变社会的民情和法律。在今天的美国,越是富有的社会阶级就越不参加政治活动;而财富,已更多的成为人们在政界中失去势力的原因,而不是使人从政治活动中获得足够的权力。因此,富人宁愿离开官场,以免同最贫困公民进行斗争,而这些斗争是他们所不情愿的并往往是徒劳的。由于他们在公共生活中不能占有他们在私人生活中同样的地位,所以便放弃前者,而埋头于后者;他们在美国社会中形成了一个具有自己的爱好和乐趣的特殊群体。他们承认这种社会情况是一种不可补救的罪恶,但是他们很小心地不表现出这种罪恶给他们带来的不满;因此,人们常常听见他们在公众面前赞扬共和党政府的温和和民主制度良好。这几乎就等于在憎恨敌人之后又向敌人诌媚。

举个例子,有这样一个富人,他就像中世纪的一个犹太人一样喜欢隐藏自己的财富。他的服装朴素,他的行为谦逊;但他的住宅内部却十分豪华,除了几个他自鸣得意地称为好友的宾客,谁也不能进入这座圣殿。没有一个欧洲贵族比他享有更独享的快乐,他对特权地位带来的任何一点好处都表示嫉妒。但是,当他

crosses the city to reach a dark countinghouse in the center of traffic, where everyone may accost him who pleases. If he meets his cobbler on the way, they stop and con verse; the two citizens discuss the affairs of the state and shake hands before they part.

But beneath this artificial enthusiasm and these obsequious attentions to the preponderating power, it is easy to perceive that the rich have a hearty dislike of the democratic institutions of their country. The people form a power which they at once fear and despise. If the maladministration of the democracy ever brings about a revolutionary crisis and monarchical institutions ever become practicable in the United States, the truth of what I advance will become obvious.

The two chief weapons that parties use in order to obtain success are the newspapers and public associations.

穿过城市的街道,到位于市中心的黑暗的小破房来做生意时,人人都可自由地同他交谈。假如他在途中遇到他的修鞋匠,他们还会停下来寒暄几句;这两位公民在谈论国家大事,并在分别时互相握手道别。

在这种虚情假意的后面,在这种对当权人士的阿谀奉承的背后,我们很容易看到富人对他们国家的民主制度怀有极大的厌恶之情。人民形成了一股既让他们害怕又让他们藐视的力量。假如民主的弊政会一旦引发政治危机,假如君主制度有一天在美国可行,人们马上就会发现我在上面所说的是正确的。

政党为了取胜而使用的两大武器,是报纸和公众组织。

CHAPTER XI

Liberty Of The Press In The United States

Difficulty of restraining the liberty of the press—Particular reasons that some nations have for cherishing this liberty—The liberty of the press a necessary consequence of the sovereignty of the people as it is understood in America—Violent language of the periodical press in the United States—The periodical press has some peculiar instincts, proved by the example of the United States—Opinion of the Americans upon the judicial repression of the abuses of the press—Why the press is less powerful in America than in France.

The influence of the liberty of the press does not affect political opinions alone, but extends to all the opinions of men and modifies customs as well as laws. In another part of this work I shall attempt to determine the degree of influence that the liberty of the press has exercised upon civil society in the United States and to point out the direction which it has given to the ideas as well as the tone which it has imparted to the character and the feelings of the Anglo-Americans. At present I propose only to examine the effects produced by the liberty of the press in the political world.

I confess that I do not entertain that firm and complete attach ment to the liberty of the press which is wont to be excited by things that are supremely good in their very nature. I approve of it from a consideration more of the evils it prevents than of the advantages it en sures.

If anyone could point out an intermediate and yet a tenable position between the complete independence and the entire servitude of o pinion, I should perhaps be inclined to adopt it, but the difficulty is to discover this intermediate position. Intending to correct the licentiousness of the press and to restore the use of orderly language, you first try the offender by a jury; but if the jury acquits him, the opinion which was that of a single individual becomes the opinion of the

第十一章　美国的出版自由

限制出版自由的困难——某些国家珍爱这种自由的特殊原因——出版自由是美国所理解的人民主权的必然结果——美国期刊使用的激烈的言词——用美国的例子可以证明，期刊有其特殊的本性——美国人对司法当局处分出版违章的看法——出版界在美国为什么不如在法国强大有力。

出版自由的影响不仅涉及政治观点，还扩及到有关人民的一切见解，它还能改变国家的民情和法律。在这本书的另一部分，我将试图定义出版自由对美国社会产生影响的程度，并指出它对美国人的思想的指导性以及它传递给英籍美国人性格和思想上的习性。

在这里，我只想考察出版自由对政界产生的影响。凭良心讲，我对出版自由的爱好并不容易那种因事物本身十分良好而产生的完全坚定的爱好。我之所以爱好出版自由，主要是因为它能阻止弊端，其次才是因为它本身的好处。

假如有谁能在思想的完全独立和全部被奴役之间指出一个可使我相信的中间立场，我或许会倾向于这个立场，但是，困难就在于找出这个中间立场。现在，假定让你试图纠正出版社的肆无忌惮，并恢复语言的有序的使用，你会首先把犯罪人送交陪审团；但如果陪审团宣判他无罪，会使本来只是一个人的意见变成整个

whole country. Too much and too little has therefore been done; go
farther, then. You bring the delinquent before permanent magistrates; but even here the cause must be heard before it can be decided; and the very principles which no book would have ventured to a-
vow are blazoned forth in the pleadings, and what was obscurely hinted at in a single composition is thus repeated in a multitude of other
publications. The language is only the expression and, if I may so
speak, the body of the thought, but it is not the thought itself. Tribunals may condemn the body, but the sense, the spirit of the work is
too subtle for their authority. Too much has still been done to recede,
too little to attain your end; you must go still farther. Establish a censorship of the press. But the tongue of the public speaker will still
make itself heard, and your purpose is not yet accomplished; you
have only increased the mischief. Thought is not, like physical
strength, dependent upon the number of its agents; nor can authors
be counted like the troops that compose an army. On the contrary,
the authority of a principle is often increased by the small number of
men by whom it is expressed. The words of one strong-minded man
addressed to the passions of a listening assembly have more power
than the vociferations of a thousand orators; and if it be allowed to
speak freely in any one public place, the consequence is the same as
if free speaking was allowed in every village. The liberty of speech
must therefore be destroyed as well as the liberty of the press. And
now you have succeeded, everybody is reduced to silence. But your
object was to repress the abuses of liberty, and you are brought to the
feet of a despot. You have been led from the extreme of independence
to the extreme of servitude without finding a single tenable position on
the way at which you could stop.

There are certain nations which have peculiar reasons for cherishing the liberty of the press, independently of the general motives that
I have just pointed out. For in certain countries which profess to be
free, every individual agent of the government may violate the laws
with impunity, since the constitution does not give to those who are

国家的意见。因此,你要办的事情是太多,可是办成的又太少,所以你还得继续办下去。你又把违法者送交地方行政长官面前;但在这里法官在判决前必须听取被告的陈述;原来没有敢于公开写进书里的东西在这时作为辩护词被宣布,原来隐晦地写在单个文章里的话也要重复出现于其他许多出版物中。要是让我说,语言仅仅是思想的一种表达方式,它并不能代表思想本身。法庭只是惩罚了思想的外壳,而被告的思想和精神却逃脱了惩罚,仍在被告的身上发生着微妙的作用。因此,依然还有很多事情等着你去办,而能达到目的的也依然太少;你仍旧需要继续办下去。最后,你给出版社设立了审查制度。但是,公共议长岂不是要因此而忙得不可开交?因此,你的目的还是不能达到;你仅仅是增加了自己的苦恼。思想不像物质力量要依赖于其作用者;而作家也不像组成军队的士兵。而与一切强大物质力量相反,思想的威力却往往因其表述思想的人数的较少而增强。一个有思想的人在鸦雀无声的听众会上所做的激情的讲话,比一千个演说家的大喊大叫还有力量。如果人们被允许能在公共场所自由演说,其结果会和被允许在每个村镇自由演说是一样的。因此,讲演自由会像写作自由那样被破坏掉。这次,你的目的达到了,人人都保持着沉默。但是,你原本的目的是什么呢?是要压制自由的泛滥,而你却被带到一个暴君的脚下。你从极端的自主走到极端的屈从,而在如此漫长的途中,连一个可供歇一歇的站脚处都没有遇到。

有一些国家,除我方才指出的一般原因之外,还有一些特殊原因使它们不得不实行出版自由。在一些声称自由的国家,每个政府工作人员都可能触犯法律而又不受惩罚,因为它们的宪法并没有给予被压迫者以向法院控告官员的权利。在这种情况下,出

injured a right of complaint before the courts of justice. In this case the liberty of the press is not merely one of the guarantees, but it is the only guarantee of their liberty and security that the citizens possess. If the rulers of these nations proposed to abolish the independence of the press, the whole people might answer: Give us the right of prosecuting your offenses before the ordinary tribunals, and perhaps we may then waive our right of appeal to the tribunal of public opinion.

In countries where the doctrine of the sovereignty of the people ostensibly prevails, the censorship of the press is not only dangerous, but absurd. When the right of every citizen to a share in the government of society is acknowledged, everyone must be presumed to be able to choose between the various opinions of his contemporaries and to appreciate the different facts from which inferences may be drawn. The sovereignty of the people and the liberty of the press may therefore be regarded as correlative, just as the censorship of the press and universal suffrage are two things which are irreconcilably opposed and which cannot long be retained among the institutions of the same people. Not a single individual of the millions who inhabit the United States has as yet dared to propose any restrictions on the liberty of the press. The first newspaper over which I cast my eyes, upon my arrival in America, contained the following article:

In all this affair, the language of Jackson [the President] has been that of a heartless despot, solely occupied with the preservation of his own authority. Ambition is his crime, and it will be his punishment, too. intrigue is his native element, and intrigue will confound his tricks, and deprive him of his power. He governs by means of corruption, and his immoral practices will redound to his shame and confusion. His conduct in the political arena has been that of a shameless and lawless gamester. He succeeded at the time; but the hour of retribution approaches, and he will be obliged to disgorge his winnings, to throw aside his false dice, and to end his days in some retirement, where he may curse his madness at his leisure; for repentance is a virtue with which his heart is likely to remain forever unacquainted. (VINCENNES *Gazette.*)

Many persons in France think that the violence of the press originates in the instability of the social state, in our political passions and the general feeling of uneasiness that consequently prevails; and it is therefore

版自由就不仅是公民的自由和安全的保障之一,而且是这方面的唯一保障。如果这些国家的统治者提议宣布废除出版自由,全体人民可以这样回答:给我们在普通法庭面前处罚犯罪官员的权力,或许我们会同意不到舆论的法院去揭露你们的罪行。

在完全按人民主权理论施政的国家,设立出版审查制度不仅危险,而且极其荒谬。当每个公民都享有参与管理国家事务的权力时,那么每个公民就要认为自己有能力对同时代人的各种意见进行选择,对认识之后能够指导他们的行为的各种事实进行鉴别。因此,人民主权和出版自由被看作是关系密切的两件事,而出版检查和普选则是互相对立的两件事,无法在同一个国家的政治制度中长期共存下去。生活在美国境内的上百万人中,至今还没有一个人敢于提议限制出版自由。我抵达美国后看到的第一份报纸,其中包括以下一篇文章:

在整个事件中,杰克逊(总统)使用的语言,是冷酷无情,一心一意为了保全自己权力的一个暴君的语言。野心是他的罪行,他也将因此受到惩罚。搞阴谋是他的本性,但阴谋也将打乱他的计划和夺去他的权力。他以腐败的方式统治,他的不道德的行为将增加他的羞耻之心和混淆是非。他登上政治舞台,就像一个毫无廉耻而又目无天法的赌徒来到赌场。他成功了,但他受报应的时间也越来越近,他必须被迫把他赢到手的东西退回来,扔掉他虚伪的面具,尽早退休,在退休后,他可能在空闲时咒骂自己过去为什么发疯;但忏悔并不是能使他的良心有所发现的一种德行。(文森斯报。)

在法国,许多人认为,出版的暴力来自社会情况的不稳定性,来自我们的政治激情,来自随之而来的普遍不安;因此,人们一直希望社会能尽快恢复到一定程度的宁静,报刊也将抛弃它目前的

supposed that as soon as society has re sumed a certain degree of composure, the press will abandon its present vehemence. For my own part, I would willingly attribute to these causes the extraordinary ascendancy which the press has acquired over the nation; but I do not think that they exercise much influence on its language. The periodical press appears to me to have passions and instincts of its own, independent of the circumstances in which it is placed; and the present condition of America corroborates this opinion.

America is perhaps, at this moment, the country of the whole world that contains the fewest germs of revolution; but the press is not less destructive in its principles there than in France, and it displays the same violence without the same reasons for indignation. In America as in France it constitutes a singular power, so strangely composed of mingled good and evil that liberty could not live without it, and public order can hardly be maintained against it. Its power is certainly much greater in France than in the United States, though nothing is more rare in the latter country than to hear of a prosecution being instituted against it. The reason for this is perfectly simple: the Americans, having once admitted the doctrine of the sovereignty of the people, apply it with perfect sincerity. It was never their intention out of elements which are changing every day to create institutions that should last forever; and there is consequently nothing criminal in an attack upon the existing laws, provided a violent infraction of them is not intended. They are also of the opinion that courts of justice are powerless to check the abuses of the press, and that, as the subtlety of human language perpetually eludes judicial analysis, offenses of this nature somehow escape the hand which attempts to seize them. They hold that to act with efficacy upon the press it would be necessary to find a tribunal not only devoted to the existing order of things, but capable of surmounting the influence of public opinion; a tribunal which should conduct its proceedings without publicity, which should pronounce its decrees without assigning its motives, and punish the intentions even more than the language of a writer. Whoever should be able to create and maintain a tribunal of this kind would waste his time in prosecuting the liberty of the press; for he would be the absolute master of the whole community and would be as free to rid himself of the authors as of their writings. In this question, therefore, there is no medium between servitude and license; in order to enjoy the inestimable benefits that the liberty of the press ensures, it is necessary to submit to the inevitable evils that it creates, To expect

热烈之情。至于我，虽然愿意把报刊对我国发生的巨大影响归因于上述各项；但并不认为这些因素曾对报刊的语言起过很大影响。报刊对于我来说是不管在什么环境下，都能保持其特有的激情和本性；而美国目前的情况，就恰恰证明了我的观点。

现在，美国可能是世界上最难发起革命的国家；但在这里，报刊在原则上的破坏性也不比法国的少，美国报刊的暴力虽与法国相同，但其激起人民愤怒的原因则与法国不同。在美国，如同在法国，报刊构成了一种把善与恶混在一起的非凡的力量，没有它自由就不能存在，而有了它公共秩序才得以维持。应当指出的是，美国报刊的力量不如法国的强大，但在美国，却很少见到司法当局惩治报刊的事件。这个原因很简单：美国人承认了人民的主权学说，并真诚地加以应用。他们从来没有想过，用每天都在变化的因素能创造出永久存在的制度；因此，对现行法律的攻击是不属于犯罪的，只要它不是以暴力违法。另外，他们还认为，法院无力查核报刊的滥用，而人类语言的微妙差别，又总能逃脱司法当局的检查，所以这种性质的罪行几乎都能从企图抓住它们的手下溜走。于是他们认为，为了能够有效地对付报刊，就必须有一个专门的法庭，这个法庭不仅要专心致力于维护现有的秩序，而且能够克服公共舆论的影响；这个法庭要在审案时不公开，在宣判时不陈述处罚理由，惩处的主要对象是意图而不是作家的语言。不管谁有权建立和维持这样的法庭来追诉出版的自由，我认为都是在浪费时间；因为这个法庭将是整个社会的绝对统治者，它可以随意把作家连同他的著作一起除掉。因此，在这个问题上，并没有什么中介能存在于屈从和许可之间；为了能够享用出版自由提供的大量益处，必须忍受它所造成的不可避免的痛苦，

to acquire the former and to escape the latter is to cherish one of those illusions which commonly mislead nations in their times of sickness when, tired with faction and exhausted by effort, they attempt to make hostile opinions and contrary principles coexist upon the same soil.

The small influence of the American journals is attributable to several reasons, among which are the following:

The liberty of writing, like all other liberty, is most formidable when it is a novelty, for a people who have never been accustomed to hear state affairs discussed before them place implicit confidence in the first tribune who presents himself. The AngloAmericans have enjoyed this liberty ever since the foundation of the colonies; moreover, the press cannot create human passions, however skillfully it may kindle them where they exist. In America political life is active, varied, even agitated, but is rarely affected by those deep passions which are excited only when material interests are impaired; and in the United States these interests are prosperous. A glance at a French and an American newspaper is sufficient to show the difference that exists in this respect between the two nations. In France the space allotted to commercial advertisements is very limited, and the news intelligence is not considerable, but the essential part of the journal is the discussion of the politics of the day. In America three quarters of the enormous sheet are filled with advertisements, and the remainder is frequently occupied by political intelligence or trivial anecdotes; it is only from time to time that one finds a corner devoted to passionate discussions like those which the journalists of France ev eryday give to their readers.

It has been demonstrated by observation, and discovered by the sure instinct even of the pettiest despots, that the influence of a power is increased in proportion as its direction is centralized. In France the press combines a twofold centralization; almost all its power is centered in the same spot and, so to speak, in the same hands, for its organs are far from numerous. The influence upon a skeptical nation of a public press thus constituted must be almost unbounded. It is an enemy with whom a government may sign an occasional truce, but which it is difficult to resist for any length of time.

想得到好处而又要逃避痛苦,这是导致国家患病时常有的幻想之一,这时,国家已疲于斗争,力量衰竭,它企图找到一个使敌对意见与相反原则在同一块土地上共存的方法。

美国报刊的影响力所以很小,有许多原因。下面会列举一些:

写作自由与其他自由一样,在它还是新事物时最令国家害怕,从来不习惯听到别人在自己面前讨论国家大事的人民,完全相信第一个出现的法院。英籍美国人自从建立殖民地之初就享有写作自由了;但是,报刊不能创造人类的激情,尽管它能巧妙的点燃人的激情。大家知道,美国的政治生活是积极的、多样的,甚至是动荡的,但很少会受到狂暴激情的影响。当物质利益发生冲突而不能妥协时,也很少掀起狂暴的激情;何况在美国这种利益是容易得到满足的。只要看一下法国和美国的报刊,就可以足够地辨别这两国在这个问题上存在的差别。在法国,报刊上登载商业广告的版面非常有限,甚至商业新闻也不怎么多,报纸最重要的版面,都是在讨论当日的政治问题。在美国,一份大报的四分之三版面全是广告,其余的部分经常是政治新闻或短小的趣闻轶事;翻来翻去之后,才能在人们不注意的角落,看到我们法国报刊每天为读者刊登的引起热烈讨论的题材,字数也不多。

任何力量,越集中使用于一个方向,其效果就越大。这是已经被观察者所证明的一般自然规律,而一些微不足道的暴君也凭借他们可靠的本能,发现了这个规律的存在。在法国,报刊兼有双重的集中;报刊几乎将其所有的力量都集中于一点,也可以说是,集中于几个人之手,因为它的机构为数很少。对一个疑心重重的国家的公共报刊的影响必然是接近无限的。它是政府的敌人,政府可以与它建立或长或短的休战协定,但与它长期共处是

Neither of these kinds of centralization exists in America. The U-nited States has no metropolis; the intelligence and the power of the people are disseminated through all the parts of this vast country, and instead of radiating from a common point they cross each other in every direction; the Americans have nowhere established any central direction of opinion, any more than of the conduct of affairs. This difference arises from local circumstances and not from human power; but it is owing to the laws of the Union that there are no licenses to be granted to printers, no securities demanded from editors, as in France, and no stamp duty, as in France and England. The consequence is that nothing is easier than to set up a newspaper, as a small number of subscribers suffices to defray the expenses.

Hence the number of periodical and semi-periodical publications in the United States is almost incredibly large. The most enlightened Americans attribute the little influence of the press to this excessive dissemination of its power; and it is an axiom of political science in that country that the only way to neutralize the effect of the public journals is to multiply their number. I cannot see how a truth which is so self-evident should not already have been more generally admitted in Europe. I can see why the persons who hope to bring about revolutions by means of the press should be desirous of confining it to a few powerful organs, but it is inconceivable that the official partisans of the existing state of things and the natural supporters of the laws should attempt to diminish the influence of the press by concentrating its power. The governments of Europe seem to treat the press with the courtesy which the knights of old showed to their opponents; having found from their own experience that centralization is a powerful weapon, they have furnished their enemies with it in order doubtless to have more glory for overcoming them.

In America there is scarcely a hamlet that has not its newspaper.

不容易的。

我方才讲的这两种集中，没有一个存在于美国。美国没有大城市；人民的才智和力量散布于这片广大国土的每一处，人类智慧之光不是从一个共同的中心向四外散射，而是在各处交互辉映；美国人在任何方面都不设置思想的总方针和工作的总方针。这些不同都并非来自人力，而是取决于当地的环境；但美国法律在这方面也起了作用。在美国就如同在法国一样，既不向印刷业发放执照，也不向作家提供任何保障措施，而没有付邮资的义务又和法国和英国相似。因此，没有什么比创办报刊更容易的了，只要有少量的订户，就足以应付报刊的开销。

所以美国定期期刊和半定期期刊的种类多得让人感到吃惊。很见多识广的美国人，认为美国报刊的影响力之所以很小，是因为出版力量的过度分散；因此，在美国政治科学中有一个定理：唯一可以抵消公共报刊影响的方法，是增加报刊的数量。我真不明白，这样一个显而易见的真理，为什么还未在法国被普遍承认。因此，我不难理解，那些想依靠报刊的力量进行革命的人，为什么要把报刊限制在几个强大的机构中，但是，那些对现存事务的状态的官方维护者和现行法律的天然支持者，为什么会想试图集中报刊的权力而减弱其影响力，这就变得有些不可思议了。欧洲各国政府对付报刊的方法，就如同是中世纪的骑士对付敌人的办法；丰富的经验告诉他们，集中才是最强大和最有力的武器，而它们为自己的敌人提供这些武器，无疑是为了在对付敌人时获得更大的荣誉。

在美国，几乎没有一个小村镇没有自己的报纸。我们可以想

It may readily be imagined that neither discipline nor unity of action can be established among so many combatants, and each one consequently fights under his own standard. All the political journals of the United States are, indeed, arrayed on the side of the administration or against it; but they attack and defend it in a thousand different ways. They cannot form those great currents of opinion which sweep away the strongest dikes. This division of the influence of the press produces other consequences scarcely less remarkable. The facility with which newspapers can be established produces a multitude of them; but as the competition prevents any considerable profit, persons of much capacity are rarely led to engage in these undertakings. Such is the number of the public prints that even if they were a source of wealth, writers of ability could not be found to direct them all. The journalists of the United States are generally in a very humble position, with a scanty education and a vulgar turn of mind. The will of the majority is the most general of laws, and it establishes certain habits to which everyone must then conform; the aggregate of these common habits is what is called the class spirit (*esprit de corps*) of each profession; thus there is the class spirit of the bar, of the court, etc. The class spirit of the French journalists consists in a violent but frequently an eloquent and lofty manner of discussing the great interests of the state, and the exceptions to this mode of writing are only occasional. The characteristics of the American journalist consist in an open and coarse appeal to the passions of his readers; he abandons principles to assail the characters of individuals, to track them into private life and disclose all their weaknesses and vices.

Nothing can be more deplorable than this abuse of the powers of thought. I shall have occasion to point out hereafter the influence of the newspapers upon the taste and the morality of the American people, but my present subject exclusively concerns the political world. It cannot be denied that the political effects of this extreme license of the press tend indirectly to the maintenance of public order. Individuals who already stand high in the esteem of their fellow citizens are afraid to write in the newspapers, and they are thus deprived of the

象要在这么多的战士中间建立有序并统一的行动,是不可能的。因此,每个人都在自己标榜的旗帜下战斗,各自发挥其能力。的确,美国的所有政治报刊不会联合起来支持或反对政府的情形;但它们却以各种各样不同的方法攻击政府或保护政府。因此,美国的报纸无法形成强大的可以冲垮牢固的大坝的洪流。报刊影响的这种分散,还暴露出另外一些显而易见的后果。办报很容易,所以人人都可以去办报;但是由于竞争妨碍了报纸可能获得的利益,因而使精明强干的实业家很少参与这类事业。再者,由于报刊的样数太多,即使办报是一条可以谋财的路子,有能力的作家也难于靠它发财。因此,美国的报人一般都处在比较低的地位,他们没有受过很高的教育,思维也不是很灵活。由大多数的意志决定一切,并建立每个人应当遵行的行动守则;把这些共同习惯汇总起来,就是我们通常所指的行业精神;于是,有律师业的行业精神、法院的行业精神等。法国报业的行业精神是用猛烈的,但常常又是雄辩的和高尚的方式讨论国家大事,有时,没能这样经常坚持下去,那是说明任何一种规律都存在着其例外性。美国报人的特征,是以公开的、粗暴的方法刺激读者的激情;他们不会侮辱个人的性格,甚至攻击人家的私人生活,揭露他们的所有弱点和缺陷。

　　没有什么事情会比对思想自由的滥用更令人表示惋惜。以后,我还要找机会来谈报纸在美国人民的爱好和道德方面产生的影响,而目前我的话题只能涉及政治世界。所以只能对这种影响进行简单地描述。不可否认,对出版界采取这种放任做法的政治效果,曾间接地对公共安宁的维持有所加强。因此,那些得到自己同胞们的较高尊敬的人都害怕在报纸发表文章,他们怕因此

most powerful instrument that they can use to excite the passions of the multitude to their own advantage. ①

The personal opinions of the editors have no weight in the eyes of the public. What they seek in a newspaper is a knowledge of facts, and it is only by altering or distorting those facts that a journalist can contribute to the support of his own views.

But although the press is limited to these resources, its influence in America is immense. It causes political life to circulate through all the parts of that vast territory. Its eye is constantly open to detect the secret springs of political designs and to summon the leaders of all parties in turn to the bar of public opinion. It rallies the interests of the community round certain principles and draws up the creed of every party; for it affords a means of intercourse between those who hear and address each other without ever coming into immediate contact. When many organs of the press adopt the same line of conduct, their influence in the long run becomes irresistible, and public opinion, perpetually assailed from the same side, eventually yields to the attack. In the United States each separate journal exercises but little authority; but the power of the periodical press is second only to that of the people. ②

The opinions *established in the United States under the influence of the liberty of the press are frequently more firmly rooted than those which are formed elsewhere under the sanction of a censor.*

In the United States democracy perpetually brings new men to the conduct of public affairs, and the administration consequently seldom preserves consistency or order in its measures. But the general

---

① They write in the papers only when they choose to address the people in their own name; as, for instance, when they are called upon to repel calumnious imputations or to correct a misstatement of facts.

② See Appendix P.

而失去最强有力武器,这些武器正是他们为了自己利益而去刺激大众激情的。[①]

由此可见,作家的个人观点,在大众的眼中是无足轻重的。读者想从报纸上了解到的,是对事实的报道,而只有通过改变或扭曲那些事实,一个新闻工作者才能在支持自己的观点方面有所贡献。

但是,虽然报刊被限制在有限的资源里,但它在美国的影响是巨大的。它使政治生活传播于这个辽阔领土的各个地方。它经常睁大眼睛努力侦察政治意图的秘密动力,把所有政党的领导们依次推上公共舆论的裁判所。它把社会的利益集结到某种特定的原则周围,并为每个政党勾画出自己的信仰;它为那些彼此听到对方声音并交谈过,但未曾谋面的政党提供了一个可以互相交流的方式。当报刊的许多机构在同一指导理论上前进时,它们的影响在时间的洪流中就变得是不可抗拒的,而始终被另一个方面控制的舆论,也最终屈服在它们的攻击下。在美国,每一家独立的报纸都拥有少部分自己的权力;但期刊的权力要大于报纸的权力,它是仅次于最有权威的人民的权力的。[②]

受美国出版自由的环境的影响而形成的见解常常比在其他地方受检查制度影响而形成的见解更根深蒂固。

美国的民主制度永远不断地在推出新人去参与国务的管理,所以政府的管理就很难一致和有序的进行。但是,该国政府的总原则却比其他多数国家稳定,而控制社会的主要观念也比其他多。

---

① 作家只有在代表人民利益时,才在报纸上发表文章;例如,当人民需要他们对一些罪责进行责难或抨击一些伪证时。

② 见附录 P。

principles of the government are more stable and the chief opinions which regulate society are more durable there than in many other countries. When once the Americans have taken up an idea, whether it be well or ill founded, nothing is more difficult than to eradicate it from their minds. The same tenacity of oqinion has been observed in England, where for the last century greater freedom of thought and more invincible prejudices have existed than in any other country of Europe. I attribute this to a cause that may at first sight appear to have an opposite tendency: namely, to the liberty of the press. The nations among whom this liberty exists cling to their opinions as much from pride as from conviction. They cherish them because they hold them to be just and because they chose them of their own free will; and they adhere to them, not only because they are true, but because they are their own. Several other reasons conduce to the same end.

It was remarked by a man of genius that "ignorance lies at the two ends of knowledge." Perhaps it would have been more correct to say that strong convictions are found only at the two ends, and that doubt lies in the middle. The human intellect, in truth, may be considered in three distinct states, which frequently succeed one another.

A man believes firmly because he adopts a proposition without inquiry. He doubts as soon as objections present themselves. But he frequently succeeds in satisfying these doubts, and then he begins again to believe. This time he has not a dim and casual glimpse of the truth, but sees it clearly before him and advances by the light it gives. ①

When the liberty of the press acts upon men who are in the first of these three states, it does not immediately disturb their habit of believing implicitly without investigation, but it changes every day the objects of their unreflecting convictions. The human mind continues to discern but one point at a time upon the whole intellectual horizon, and that point is constantly changing. This is the period of sudden revolutions. Woe to the generations which first abruptly adopt the

---

① It may be doubted, however, whether this rational and self-guiding conviction arouses as much fervor or enthusiastic devotion in men as does their first dogmatical belief.

当美国人采纳了这种思想，不管它是对还是错，就再也没有比彻底地从人们头脑里根除它更难的了。同样的事实也见于英国，这个国家在过去一百多年中，曾有过比欧洲其他任何国家更自由的思想和更坚固的偏见。我认为，这个现象是来自于猛的看来好像是本应阻止这个现象产生的事实，也就是出版自由。实行这种自由的国家，高傲对其见解的影响与自信相同。他们珍爱这种见解，是因为他们认为这一见解是公正的并且是体现他们自由意愿的；他们坚持这种见解，不仅是因为它是真实的，而且是因为它是属于自己的。还有几个其他的原因。

一位伟人曾经说过："无知处于知识的两端。"或者这样说更为正确，强烈自信处于两端，而怀疑处在中间。实际上，人类的智慧可以被看作是三个不同的阶段，这三个阶段又总是成功地衔接在一起。

一个人之所以会对某件事深信不疑，是因为他没有进行调查就接受了它。当异议出现在他面前时，他就会立刻产生怀疑。但他常常能够克服这些怀疑，于是又开始相信。这一次，他不是含糊不清和随随便便地去认识真理，而是切切实实地去考察真理，并紧随着真理光芒前进。①

当出版自由遵照智力水平尚处在第一阶段的人们的思想行事时，它没有立即打乱人们的不经过调查研究就坚信不疑的习惯，而只能逐渐地改变他们不加思考就轻信的事物。因此，在智力的整个发展过程中，人类思想的辨别能力在逐步地向前发展，但被认识的那一点也在不断改变。这就是革命爆发时期的到来。于是，这就会给最先突然接受出版自由的那一

---

① 值得我们怀疑的是，人们的这种理性的和自我引导的信任是否会比主导人们内心的第一信仰更能激起人们的热情与激情。

freedom of the press.

The circle of novel ideas, however, is soon traveled over. Experience comes to undeceive men and plunges them into doubt and general mistrust. We may rest assured that the majority of mankind will always remain in one of these two states, will either believe they know not wherefore, or will not know what to believe. Few are those who can ever attain to that other state of rational and independent conviction which true knowledge can produce out of the midst of doubt.

It has been remarked that in times of great religious fervor men sometimes change their religious opinions; whereas in times of general skepticism everyone clings to his old persuasion. The same thing takes place in politics under the liberty of the press. In countries where all the theories of social science have been contested in their turn, men who have adopted one of them stick to it, not so much because they are sure of its truth as because they are not sure that there is any better to be had. In the present age men are not very ready to die for their opinions, but they are rarely inclined to change them; there are few martyrs as well as few apostates.

Another still more valid reason may be adduced: when no opinions are looked upon as certain, men cling to the mere instincts and material interests of their position, which are naturally more tangible, definite, and permanent than any opinions in the world.

It is a very difficult question to decide whether an aristocracy or a democracy governs the best. But it is certain that democracy annoys one part of the community and that aristocracy oppresses another. It is a truth which is self-established, and one which it is needless to discuss, that "you are rich and I am poor."

代人带来痛苦。

用不了多久,一系列新的思想又陆续而来。经验让人们醒悟,使他们陷入怀疑和普遍不信任之中。我们可以确认,大多数人的思想都总是停留在下述两个阶段之一:不是相信根本不知其所以然的东西,就是不知到底该信什么。而只有很少数人能达到另一个阶段,在这个阶段中有真知冲破怀疑的干扰所产生的理性的和独立的自信。

但也有人曾经指出,在宗教受到极大的拥护并盛行的时代,人们有时会改变他们的宗教信仰;而在普遍怀疑的时代,大家却都深深地坚持着自己原先的信条。同样的情形也见于出版自由盛行时的政治。当社会科学理论在轮番角逐时,如果有人采纳其中之一并死死坚持着,那也不是因为人们确信它就是真理,而是因为人们不知道还会有什么能比它更好。在现今这个时代,人们不会轻易地为自己的见解献身,但也不会轻易地改变自己的见解;牺牲者和背叛者都是同样的少之又少的。

还有一个更为强而有力的理由需要引证:当人们不确定某种见解时,最终总是要联系自己现有状态下的本能和物质利益,因为本能和物质利益比见解更实实在在,更明确肯定,更永久。

我们很难讲清楚,究竟是民主制度统治的好,还是贵族制度统治的好。但有一点是明确的,那就是民主制度使社会上的一部分人苦恼,而贵族制度则压迫了另一部分人。"你富了,我就穷了",这是一个自行成立和无需讨论的真理。

CHAPTER XII

Political Associations In The United States

Daily use which the Anglo-Americans make of the right of association—Three kinds of political associations—How the Americans apply the representative system to associations—Dangers resulting to the state—Great Convention of 1831 relative to the tariff—Legislative character of this Convention—Why the unlimited exercise of the right of association is less dangerous in the United States than elsewhere—Why it may be looked upon as necessary—Utility of associations among a democratic people.

In no country in the world has the principle of association been more successfully used or applied to a greater multitude of objects than in America. Besides the permanent associations which are established by law under the names of townships, cities, and counties, a vast number of others are formed and maintained by the agency of private individuals.

The citizen of the United States is taught from infancy to rely upon his own exertions in order to resist the evils and the difficulties of life; he looks upon the social authority with an eye of mistrust and anxiety, and he claims its assistance only when he is unable to do without it. This habit may be traced even in the schools, where the children in their games are wont to submit to rules which they have themselves established, and to punish misdemeanors which they have themselves defined. The same spirit pervades every act of social life. If a stoppage occurs in a thoroughfare and the circulation of vehicles is hindered, the neighbors immediately form themselves into a deliberative body; and this extemporaneous assembly gives rise to an executive power which remedies the inconvenience before anybody has thought of re curring to a pre-existing authority superior to that of the

第十二章 美国的政治社团

英籍美国人对社团权力的日常应用——三种类型的政治社团——美国人如何将代议制应用到社团中——这对国家的危险——1831年关于关税问题的大会——这次大会的立法特性——为什么对社团权力的无限应用在美国不如在其他地方危险——为什么可以认为这样做是必要的——社团在民主国家的效用。

世界上没有一个国家像美国那样有组织社团的原则，并能成功地把这一强大行动手段用于多种多样的目的。除了依法以乡、镇、市、县的名义建立的永久性社团以外，还有许多以个人名义建立和发展起来的社团。

美国的居民从小就被教育要依靠自己的努力去克服生活的苦难和解决生活中的困难；他们用一种不信任和焦虑的眼光来看待社会的权威机构，只在走投无路的时候才求助于它。这种习惯是他们在上小学的时候就被培养起来的，孩子们在学校里做游戏时要服从自己制定的规则，处罚由他们自己限定的违规行为。同样的精神也体现在社会生活的每个细节上。假如公路上发生阻塞，车辆拥挤并因此不能通行，附近的人就会自动组织起来研究解决办法；这种临时的集会，可以选出一个执行机构，在没有人去向有关主

persons immediately concerned. If some public pleasure is concerned, an association is formed to give more splendor and regularity to the entertainment. Societies are formed to resist evils that are exclusively of a moral nature, as to diminish the vice of intemperance. In the United States associations are established to promote the public safety, commerce, industry, morality, and religion. There is no end which the human will despairs of attaining through the combined power of individuals united into a society.

I shall have occasion hereafter to show the effects of association in civil life; I confine myself for the present to the political world. When once the right of association is recognized, the citizens may use it in different ways.

An association consists simply in the public assent which a number of individuals give to certain doctrines and in the engagement which they contract to promote in a certain manner the spread of those doctrines. The right of associating in this fashion almost merges with freedom of the press, but societies thus formed possess more authority than the press. When an opinion is represented by a society, it necessarily assumes a more exact and explicit form. It numbers its partisans and engages them in its cause; they, on the other hand, become acquainted with one another, and their zeal is increased by their number. An association unites into one channel the efforts of divergent minds and urges them vigorously towards the one end which it clearly points out.

The second degree in the exercise of the right of association is the power of meeting. When an association is allowed to establish centers of action at certain important points in the country, its activity is increased and its influence extended. Men have the opportunity of seeing one another; means of execution are combined; and opinions are maintained with a warmth and energy that writ ten language can never attain. Lastly, in the exercise of the right of political association there is a third degree: the partisans of an opinion may unite in electoral bodies and choose delegates to represent them in a central assembly. This is, properly speaking, the application of the representative

管当局报告事故之前,这个机构就开始解决问题了。假如是有关公共庆祝活动,这种自动组织的活动小组,不仅会给活动增辉,还会使活动有规律的进行。而且,还有一些组织是为了反对各类败坏道德的行为的组织。比如,把大家组织起来反对酗酒。在美国,也有为促进公共安全、商业、工业、道德和宗教的社团。人们的意愿一定会通过个人力量与社会力量的结合得到满足。以后,我会再找机会讲述社团对公民生活产生的作用。

但目前,我的任务是只谈政界。一旦当社团的权力被承认,公民们就可以用各种不同方式去行使它。

一个社团可以简单的由若干人组成,这些人都一致赞成某一学说或主张,并用他们签署的某项约定使该学说或主张以某种方式得到促进。因此,社团权力在这种方式上与写作自由几乎没有什么不同,但是,早期形成的社团要比出版界拥有更大的权力。当一种见解由一个社团来代表时,它必须具备更明确和更清晰的形式。这个社团要拥有它自己的成员,并让他们为本社团的事业贡献力量。而成员们也会因此彼此相互了解,他们的热情也会随着人数的增加而增强。社团努力把不同人们的不同思想连结在一起,促使他们精力旺盛地朝着由它清楚的指明的方向前进。

行使社团权力的第二阶段,是行使集会权。当一个政治社团被允许在国家的某个重要地点建立其活动中心,它的活动会增加,它的影响也会扩大。在那里,人们有机会互相见面;并将各种执行手段结合起来;各种见解可以用文字永远无法达到的力量和热情向外传播。最后,行使政治社团权力的第三阶段是:同一见解的支持者们可以联合起来,组成选举团,选出在中央集会中可以代表他们的社团。这就可以说将代议制的体系应用到政党

system to a party.

Thus, in the first instance, a society is formed between individuals professing the same opinion, and the tie that keeps it together is of a purely intellectual nature. In the second case, small assemblies are formed, which represent only a fraction of the party. Lastly, in the third case, they constitute, as it were, a separate nation in the midst of the nation, a government within the government. Their delegates, like the real delegates of the majority, represent the whole collective force of their party, and like them, also, have an appearance of nationality and all the moral power that results from it. It is true that they have not the right, like the others, of making the laws; but they have the power of attacking those which are in force and of drawing up beforehand those which ought to be enacted.

If, among a people who are imperfectly accustomed to the exercise of freedom, or are exposed to violent political passions, by the side of the majority which makes the laws is placed a minority which only deliberates and gets laws ready for adoption, I cannot but believe that public tranquillity would there incur very great risks. There is doubtless a wide difference between proving that one law is in itself better than another and proving that the former ought to be substituted for the latter. But the imagination of the multitude is very apt to overlook this difference, which is so apparent to the minds of thinking men. It sometimes happens that a nation is divided into two nearly equal parties, each of which affects to represent the majority. If, near the directing power, another power is established which exercises almost as much moral authority as the former, we are not to believe that it will long be content to speak without acting; or that it will always be restrained by the abstract consideration that associations are meant to direct opinions, but not to enforce them, to suggest but not to make the laws. The more I consider the independence of the press in its principal consequences, the more am I convinced that in the modern world it is the chief and, so to speak, the constitutive element of liberty. A nation that is determined to remain free is therefore right in demanding, at any price, the exercise of this independence. But the unlimited liberty of political association cannot be entirely assimilated to the liberty of the press. The one is at the same time less necessary and more dangerous than the other. A nation may confine it within

中了。

因此,第一,社会应建立在拥护同一见解的人之间,并且这些人要在彼此之间建立纯思想的联系;第二,他们要组成一些只代表本党的小团体;第三,他们要建立一个国家中的国家,政府中的政府。他们的代表在表面上好像是代表着真实的大多数,而实际上他们只代表自己的支持者,他们的支持者也好像拥有以代表国家和由此而来的所有道德权力的外表。事实上,这些支持者不能像其他人那样具有制定法律的权力;但他们拥有攻击现行的法律并协助他们草拟法律的权利。

如果一个民族完全没有行使自由的习惯,或暴露于猛烈的政治激情下,而在它的多数立法者的旁边,只有少数的负责审议和监督采纳,那我不能不认为它的公共秩序会处于严重的危险之中。要证明一项法律本身比另一项法律好,与证明前一项法律应代替后一项法律,无疑是有很大不同的。但是,大多数人的智慧又会聪明的发现这一差别,他就不会再去考虑大众的想法了。有时,一个国家被分成两个势力相当的两派,每派都争着抢着要去代表多数。如果在直接领导权之旁再建立一个无论是道义还是权威都几乎与它相同的权力,我们当然不会认为众人还会为直接领导权这种长期只说不干地做法所蒙骗;认为社团是为了指导舆论而不是要强制舆论,是要审议法律而不是立法,就成为形而上学的想法。我越深入考察出版自由的主要影响,便越是深深的相信它在现代世界里是自由的最主要的,也可以说是最基本的组成部分。因此,一个国家要是决定保卫自由,那么它绝对要要求人们全力行使独立权力。但是,政治社团的无限自由又不完全类似于出版自由。前者不像后者那么必需,但却比后者危险。一个国家可能会把社团自由限制在一定范

certain limits without forfeiting any part of its self-directing power; and it may sometimes be obliged to do so in order to maintain its own authority.

In America the liberty of association for political purposes is unlimited. An example will show in the clearest light to what an extent this privilege is tolerated.

The question of a tariff or free trade has much agitated the minds of Americans. The tariff was not only a subject of debate as a matter of opinion, but it affected some great material interests of the states. The North attributed a portion of its prosperity, and the South nearly all its sufferings, to this system. For a long time the tariff was the sole source of the political animosities that agitated the Union.

In 1831, when the dispute was raging with the greatest violence, a private citizen of Massachusetts proposed, by means of the newspapers, to all the enemies of the tariff to send delegates to Philadelphia in order to consult together upon the best means of re storing freedom of trade. This proposal circulated in a few days, by the power of the press, from Maine to New Orleans. The opponents of the tariff adopted it with enthusiasm; meetings were held in all quarters, and delegates were appointed. The majority of these delegates were well known, and some of them had earned a considerable degree of celebrity. South Carolina alone, which afterwards took up arms in the same cause, sent sixty-three delegates. On the 1st of October 1831 this assembly, which, according to the American custom, had taken the name of a Convention, met at Philadelphia; it consisted of more than two hundred members. Its debates were public, and they at once assumed a legislative character; the extent of the powers of Congress, the theories of free trade, and the different provisions of the tariff were dis cussed. At the end of ten days the Convention broke up, having drawn up an address to the American people in which it declared: (1) that Congress had not the right of making a tariff, and that the existing tariff was unconstitutional; (2) that the prohibition of free trade was prejudicial to the interests of any nation, and to those of the American people especially.

It must be acknowledged that the unrestrained liberty of political association has not hitherto produced in the United States the fatal results that might perhaps be expected from it elsewhere. The right of

围内,并且不会失去对其中任何一部分的控制权;而有时,国家为了维护自己的权威也可能被迫这样做。

在美国,以政治为目的的结社自由是不受限制的。有一个例子可以非常清楚地显示出这项权力被容许的扩大的程度是多么惊人。

关税问题和贸易自由问题曾使美国人感到极大的不安,关税制度不仅对舆论产生了影响,而且对物质利益也产生了不小的影响。北方把它的一部分繁荣归功于关税制度,而南方则把它的一切灾难栽到关税制度的头上。曾经有很长一段时间,关税制度一直是使当时美国不安的唯一政治激情的来源。

1831 年,当发生最激烈的争论的时候,一名马萨诸塞州的公民提出了一个建议,即通过报纸的形式告知现行税制的所有反对者们,请他们派代表到费城,共同解决恢复贸易自由的办法。这项提议,通过报刊的力量,没过多久就从缅因州传到新奥尔良。现行税制的反对者们热忱地采纳了这项建议;他们到处开会,并选举自己的代表。这些代表都是知名人士,有的人还具有极高的名望。单单是南卡罗来纳州就派去 63 名代表,它们还为此问题拿起了武器。1831 年 10 月 1 日,一个按照美国人的习惯取名为全国代表大会的大会,于费城召开;参加大会的共有 200 多人。会上在公开的进行辩论,大会立刻呈现出立法的特性;会上讨论了国会的职权范围、自由贸易理论和不同条款的税则。第十天,在草拟一封致美国人民的信后,大会闭幕了。信中这样说道:(1)国会无权制定关税税则,现行税则是违反宪法的;(2)自由贸易的禁令对任何国家均无利益,特别是对美国。

但必须承认,迄今为止,政治社团的无限自由并没有在美国产生严重的后果,而这种后果也许在别处会发生。社团的权力是

association was imported from England, and it has always existed in America; the exercise of this privilege is now incorporated with the manners and customs of the people. At the present time the liberty of association has become a necessary guarantee against the tyranny of the majority. In the United States, as soon as a party has become dominant, all public authority passes into its hands; its private supporters occupy all the offices and have all the force of the administration at their disposal. As the most distinguished members of the opposite party cannot surmount the barrier that excludes them from power, they must establish themselves outside of it and oppose the whole moral au thority of the minority to the physical power that domineers over it. Thus a dangerous expedient is used to obviate a still more formidable danger.

The omnipotence of the majority appears to me to be so full of peril to the American republics that the dangerous means used to bridle it seem to be more advantageous than prejudicial. And here I will express an opinion that may remind the reader of what I said when speaking of the freedom of townships. There are no countries in which associations are more needed to prevent the despotism of faction or the arbitrary power of a prince than those which are democratically constituted. In aristocratic nations the body of the nobles and the wealthy are in themselves natural associations which check the abuses of power. In countries where such associations do not exist, if private individuals cannot create an artificial and temporary substitute for them I can see no permanent protection against the most galling tyranny; and a great people may be oppressed with impunity by a small faction or by a single individual.

The meeting of a great political convention (for there are conventions of all kinds), which may frequently become a necessary measure, is always a serious occurrence, even in America, and one that judicious patriots cannot regard without alarm. This was very perceptible in the Convention of 1831, at which all the most distinguished members strove to moderate its language and to restrain its objects within certain limits. It is probable that this Convention exercised a great influence on the minds of the malcontents and prepared them for the open revolt against the commercial laws of the Union that took place in 1832.

It cannot be denied that the unrestrained liberty of association for political purposes is the privilege which a people is longest in learning

从英国输入到美国的,自输入之后就一直存在着;现在,对这项权力的行使,已被固定在美国人的习惯和风气里。在现今这个时代,反对多数专制的一项必要措施就是社团自由。在美国,一旦一个政党开始统治后,所有的国家大权就都落于它的手中;它的同党也将谋得一官半职,控制一切有组织的力量。反对党的最杰出的人物也不能克服把他们排除在政权以外的种种障碍,反对党只能在野,发动少数的全部道德权威去反对统治他们的强大物质力量。可见,这是用一种危险的办法去避免另一种更为可怕的危险。

在我看来,多数的无限权威充满了对美国共和制度的危害,以致使我认为用来束缚它的那个危险手段还好一些。在这里,我想表达一些观点,它使读者可以想起我在本书第一部分讲述乡镇自由时所说的话。那就是:再没有比社会民主国家更需要用社团自由去防止政党专制或国王的专权的了。在贵族制国家,贵族和富人是在制止滥用职权方面形成了一个天然的社团。在这种社团不存在的国家,如果人们之间不能创造出仿造的和暂时的类似的社团,我没有发现有任何可以防止暴政的举措;另外,一个伟大的民族可能不是要受一个小派别的压迫,就是要受到独夫政权的压迫。

一个大型的政治集会很有可能成为一种必要的手段(有各种人参加),即使在美国也总是件严肃的事,使一些明智的爱国者感到惊讶。这种情况可清楚地体现在1831年的大会中,参加大会的所有杰出人物,都尽量使自己的语言温和,并将自己的目标有所限制。这次大会对不满政府措施的人产生了很大影响,促使他们在1832年对联邦商业法进行了公开造反。

不能否认,以政治为目的的社团的无限自由,是人们在长期中学会行使的特权。如果这种自由没有让国家陷入无政府状态,也

how to exercise. If it does not throw the nation into anarchy, it perpetually augments the chances of that calamity. On one point, however, this perilous liberty offers a security against dangers of another kind; in countries where associations are free, secret societies are unknown. In America there are factions, but no conspiracies.

Different ways *in which the right of association is understood in Europe and in the United States—Different use which is made of it.*

The most natural privilege of man, next to the right of acting for himself, is that of combining his exertions with those of his fellow creatures and of acting in common with them. The right of association therefore appears to me almost as inalienable in its nature as the right of personal liberty. No legislator can attack it without impairing the foundations of society. Nevertheless, if the liberty of association is only a source of advantage and prosperity to some nations, it may be perverted or carried to excess by others, and from an element of life may be changed into a cause of destruction. A comparison of the different methods that associations pursue in those countries in which liberty is well understood and in those where liberty degenerates into license may be useful both to governments and to parties.

Most Europeans look upon association as a weapon which is to be hastily fashioned and immediately tried in the conflict. A society is formed for discussion, but the idea of impending action prevails in the minds of all those who constitute it. It is, in fact, an army; and the time given to speech serves to reckon up the strength and to animate the courage of the host, after which they march against the enemy. To the persons who compose it, resources which lie within the bounds of law may suggest themselves as means of success, but never as the only means.

Such, however, is not the manner in which the right of association is understood in the United States. In America the citizens who form the minority associate in order, first, to show their numerical strength and so to diminish the moral power of the majority; and, secondly, to stimulate competition and thus to discover those arguments that are most fitted to act upon the majority; for they always

可以说它在每一分每一秒都会增加这种灾难的发生。但是,这个如此危险的自由,却在一点上提供了反对危险的保障;那就是在社团自由的国家,结社行为都是公开的。在美国,只有派系斗争,而没有搞阴谋者。

欧洲和美国对社团权力在理解上的差异——它们对社团权力的不同使用。

人们最自然的特权是把自己的力量同自己的同志的力量联合起来的共同活动的自由,是仅次于自己活动的权力。因此,在我看来,社团的权力在性质上几乎与个人自由的权力是一样不可剥夺的。没有一个立法者能在不损坏社会基础的情况下攻击社团的权力。但是,如果说社团自由在一些国家仅仅是进步和繁荣的源泉,那么在另一些国家又可能因为对社团自由的滥用和歪曲而使它由一种积极行为变成具有破坏性的行为。在我看来,对能很好理解自由的国家的社团和滥用自由的国家的社团所经常采用的不同方法进行比较,对于政府和政党是有很大好处的。

大多数欧洲人把社团看作是在战斗中匆匆忙忙组织起来而马上投入战场的武器。在结社时应当明确目的,但急于行动的思想却限制了创办人的头脑。实际上,一个社团就如同是一支军队;向士兵讲话,是为了激发军人的力量和鼓舞他们的士气,让他们勇敢地冲向敌人。社团的组织者们认为,合法的手段可能会让他们走向成功,但这决不是迈向成功的唯一途径。

但是,美国人却不是这样理解这种社团权力。在美国,占居少数地位的美国公民之所以结社,首先是为了显示自己巨大的力量,同时也为了削弱多数的道德权力;其次是为了刺激竞争,从而

entertain hopes of drawing over the majority to their own side, and then controlling the supreme power in its name. Political associations in the United States are therefore peaceable in their intentions and strictly legal in the means which they employ; and they assert with perfect truth that they aim at success only by lawful expedients.

The difference that exists in this respect between Americans and Europeans depends on several causes. In Europe there are parties which differ so much from the majority that they can never hope to acquire its support, and yet they think they are strong enough in themselves to contend against it. When a party of this kind forms an association, its object is not to convince, but to fight. In America the individuals who hold opinions much opposed to those of the majority can do nothing against it, and all other parties hope to win it over to their own principles. The exercise of the right of association becomes dangerous, then, in proportion as great parties find themselves wholly unable to acquire the majority. In a country like the United States, in which the differences of opinion are mere differences of hue, the right of association may remain unrestrained without evil consequences. Our inexperience of liberty leads us to regard the liberty of association only as a right of attacking the government. The first notion that presents itself to a party, as well as to an individual, when it has acquired a consciousness of its own strength is that of violence; the notion of persuasion arises at a later period, and is derived from experi ence. The English, who are divided into parties which differ essentially from each other, rarely abuse the right of association because they have long been accustomed to exercise it. In France the passion for war is so intense that there is no undertaking so mad, or so injurious to the welfare of the state that a man does not consider himself honored in defending it at the risk of his life.

But perhaps the most powerful of the causes that tend to mitigate the violence of political associations in the United States is universal suffrage. In countries in which universal suffrage exists, the majority is never doubtful, because neither party can reasonably pretend to represent that portion of the community which has not voted. The associations know as well as the nation at large that they do not represent

找出最适合作用于多数的论据;因为他们总希望劝说多数站在自己这一边,然后再以多数的名义控制最高权力。因此,美国政治社团的宗旨是温和的,而其手段则是严格合乎法律的;由于它们只想通过合法的计策取胜,所以一般都讲真话。

美国人和欧洲人在这方面的差异,来自多种原因。在欧洲,有些政党完全与多数背道而行,这就使它们永远都别想得到多数的支持,但这些政党又认为自己已经足够强壮来与多数抗衡。当这种类型的政党形成社团时,它们的目的并不是要说服,而只是要进行战斗。在美国,与多数的观点相背离的人,绝对不是多数的对手,因为其余所有的人都想赢得多数的支持。因此,当社团的行使权越是安全,大党就越是不可能成为多数。像在美国这样的国家,各种不同的意见只有细微的差别,社团权力可以不带任何罪恶结果的无限地存在下去。我们对自由的无知,使我们仅仅把社团自由看作是一种能攻击政府的权利。一个党派就如同一个个体,当它在感觉到自己的强大后而产生的第一个想法,就是用权力来让大家信服;而劝说的观念,是在很久以后需要有一定的经验的积累才能实现的。英国人在因意见不同而形成的各种各样的派别中,很少滥用社团权力,因为他们已经习惯于长期行使这项权力。而在有着如此强烈的好战激情的法国,人们都发疯似地参与关于国家安危的大事,他们认为因为国家战死是光荣的。

但在美国,最有力的可能缓和政治社团暴力的因素,也许是普选权。在实行普选的国家,多数从来都是不被怀疑的,因为任何一个政党都不可能伪装成没有选举它的选民的代表。因此,各个社团和人民大众都知道,那样的政党并不是多数的代表。这也是由它们存在的实事所决定的;因为如果它们真的是多数的代

the majority. This results, indeed, from the very fact of their existence; for if they did represent the preponderating power, they would change the law instead of soliciting its reform. The consequence of this is that the moral influence of the government which they attack is much increased, and their own power is much enfeebled.

In Europe there are few associations which do not affect to represent the majority, or which do not believe that they represent it. This conviction or this pretension tends to augment their force amazingly and contributes no less to legalize their measures. Violence may seem to be excusable in defense of the cause of oppressed right. Thus it is, in the vast complication of human laws, that extreme liberty sometimes corrects the abuses of liberty, and that extreme democracy obviates the dangers of democracy. In Europe associations consider themselves, in some degree, as the legislative and executive council of the people, who are unable to speak for themselves; moved by this belief, they act and they command. In America, where they represent in the eyes of all only a minority of the nation, they argue and petition.

The means that associations in Europe employ are in accordance with the end which they propose to obtain. As the principal aim of these bodies is to act and not to debate, to fight rather than to convince, they are naturally led to adopt an organization which is not civic and peaceable, but partakes of the habits and maxims of military life. They also centralize the direction of their forces as much as possible and entrust the power of the whole party to a small number of leaders.

The members of these associations respond to a watchword, like soldiers on duty; they profess the doctrine of passive obedience; say, rather, that in uniting together they at once abjure the exercise of their own judgment and free will; and the tyrannical control that these societies exercise is often far more insupportable than the authority possessed over society by the government which they attack. Their moral force is much diminished by these proceedings, and they lose the sacred character which always attaches to a struggle of the oppressed against their oppressors. He who in given cases consents to

表,它们本身就可以随意修改法律,又何苦整日企求改革法律呢?结果是受到它们攻击的政府的道德权力被大大加强了,而它们自己的这种力量却被大大地削弱了。

在欧洲,几乎没有一个社团不认为或相信自己是多数意志的代表。这种自信和自命不凡,在以惊人的速度扩大着它们的力量,并使它们的手段在不知不觉中合法化。这种暴力在抵制压制它的权利的时候似乎是值得原谅的。正因为如此,在巨大的复杂的人类法律中,极端自由有时反而能控制对自由的滥用,而极端民主有时反而能使民主摆脱危险。欧洲的社团在一定程度上总把自己看成是无法为自己发表意见的人民的立法机构和执行机构;并在这种想法的指导下去行动和发号施令。在美国,人人都认为社团是代表少数人民利益的,所以在那里,社团只能通过辩论和请愿。

在欧洲,各国社团所使用的手段,与它们想要达到的目的是一致的。这些社团的主要目的是行动而不是无端的辩论,是战斗而不是说服,所以它们自然要建立一种一点都不具有城市化与和平化的组织,但一定要带有军事生活的习惯和准则。它们还尽可能的集中领导自己的下属,并把组织的一切权力交给几个少数的领袖。

这些社团的成员对命令的服从,要如同战场上的士兵一样严格;他们信奉消极服从的理论;或者再准确点,他们一旦联合在一起,就立刻放弃了对自己的判断力和自由意志的行驶;因此,在这些社团内部所实行的专制统治,常常比它们所攻击的政府对社会实行的专制统治还要让人无法忍受。它们的道义力量被大大的减弱,它们也失去了被压迫者在反对压迫者的斗争中所具有的神圣的特性。心甘情愿地服从于同伙中的某几个人并奴隶般地

obey his fellows with servility and who submits his will and even his thoughts to their control, how can he pretend that he wishes to be free?

The Americans have also established a government in their associations, but it is invariably borrowed from the forms of the civil administration. The independence of each individual is recognized; as in society, all the members advance at the same time towards the same end, but they are not all obliged to follow the same track. No one abjures the exercise of his reason and free will, but everyone exerts that reason and will to promote a common undertaking.

受他们控制,情愿双手奉送出自己的意志、甚至是思想由他人控制的人,还怎么敢伪称他希望自由呢?

美国人也同样在自己的社团中建立统治组织,但是,它会不变的套用和平的统治组织。在社团中,对个人独立的认可,就像在社会里一样,所有成员在同一时刻朝着同一个目标迈进,但并非都要按照同一种模式前进。没有人放弃自己的判断力和自由意志,但每个人都要用自己的判断力和意志去促进公共事业的发展。

CHAPTER XIII

Government Of The Democracy In America

I am well aware of the difficulties that attend this part of my subject; but although every expression which I am about to use may clash, upon some points, with the feelings of the different parties which divide my country, I shall still speak my whole thought. In Europe we are at a loss how to judge the true character and the permanent instincts of democracy, because in Europe two conflicting principles exist and we do not know what to attribute to the principles themselves and what to the passions that the contest produces. Such is not the case in America, however; there the people reign without impediment, and they have no perils to dread and no injuries to avenge. In America democracy is given up to its own propensities; its course is natural and its activity is unrestrained; there, consequently, its real character must be judged. And to no people can this inquiry be more vitally interesting than to the French nation, who are blindly driven onwards, by a daily and irresistible impulse, towards a state of things which may prove either despotic or republican, but which will assuredly be democratic.

Universal Suffrage

I have already observed that universal suffrage has been adopted in all the states of the Union; it consequently exists in communities

第十三章　美国的民主政府

　　我清楚地知道在讨论我的主题的这部分时,会遇到很多困难;尽管在这一章中,我所使用的每一句表达,都有可能在某些方面刺痛使我国分裂的各个政党。但我还要说出我的全部想法。在欧洲,我们不知该如何判断民主的真理性和不变性,因为在欧洲,存在着两个互相对立的原则,我们无法知道哪些争论是来自主义本身,而哪些争论又是由争论所产生的激情而引发的。而在美国就不会发生这种情形,在那里,人民不受任何阻碍地对国家进行统治,他们既不需要担心会发生什么危险,也不需要在乎是否有什么损害需要报复。因此,美国的民主是按照其习性所行事的;它的过程是自然的,它的一切活动是不受限制的;因此,美国的民主才具有最真实的特性。这项研究对法国比对任何国家都更有用有益,因为每天,我们每天都在一种无法抵抗的运动的驱动下毫无目的地向前走。是走向专制还是走向共和呢? 我们无法知道,但社会情况必定会向着民主的方向前进。

普选权

　　我在前面说过,普选权已被全联邦的所有国家所采用;任何

that occupy very different positions in the social scale. I have had opportunities of observing its effects in different localities and among races of men who are nearly strangers to each other in their language, their religion, and their modes of life; in Louisiana as well as in New England, in Georgia as in Canada. I have remarked that universal suffrage is far from producing in America either all the good or all the evil consequences which may be expected from it in Europe, and that its effects generally differ very much from those which are attributed to it.

The Choice Of The People, And The Instinctive Preferences Of The American Democracy

In the United States the ablest men are rarely placed at the head of affairs—Reason for this peculiarity—The envy which prevails in the lower orders of France against the higher classes is not a French but a purely democratic feeling—Why the most distinguished men in America frequently seclude themselves from public affairs.

Many people in Europe are apt to believe without saying it, or to say without believing it, that one of the great advantages of universal suffrage is that it entrusts the direction of affairs to men who are worthy of the public confidence. They admit that the people are unable to govern of themselves, but they aver that the people always wish the welfare of the state and instinctively designate those who are animated by the same good will and who are the most fit to wield the supreme authority. I confess that the observations I made in America by no means coincide with these opinions. On my arrival in the United States I was surprised to find so much distinguished talent among the citizens and so little among the heads of the government. It is a constant fact that at the present day the ablest men in the United States are rarely placed at the head of affairs; and it must be acknowledged that such has been the result in proportion as democracy has exceeded all its former limits. The race of American statesmen has evidently dwin dled most remarkably in the course of the last fifty years.

Several causes may be assigned for this phenomenon. It is impossible, after the most strenuous exertions, to raise the intelligence

一个人,不管其社会地位的高低,都享有这项权利。在一些不同的地区,在因语言、宗教和生活习性差异很多而彼此几乎形同外国人的一些种族之间;在路易斯安那和新英格兰,在佐治亚和加拿大,我都曾有机会看到实施普选权的一些影响。我曾说过,普选权在美国还远远没有产生人们所期望它在欧洲产生的一切幸福与罪恶,它在美国的实施效果一般也因原因的不同而不同。

人民的选择和美国民主的本能的选择

在美国,很少有能干的人出任公职——产生这种独特性的原因——法国下层阶级对上层阶级所怀的嫉妒心不是法国人特有的感情,而是一种单纯的民主的感情——在美国,为什么一些最杰出的人往往使自己远离公共事务。

在欧洲,许多人不是嘴上不说而心里默默的相信,就是心里根本就不相信而嘴上却要说:普选权的最大好处之一,是赋予最受公众信任的人指导公共事务的权力。他们认为人民是不能统治自己,但人民衷心希望国家富强;人民的爱好决不妨害他们推选同他们怀有同样愿望和最适合行使至高权力的人去主持政务。我承认我在美国看到的一切绝不是与这些观点相符合。在我刚到美国时,就非常吃惊地发现真正杰出的人才大多存在于被治者中间,而很少存在于统治者当中。在今天的美国,最能干的人士很少去参与国家事务,已是一个普遍的实事;而且必须承认,这也是随着民主超过其先前所有的界限而引发的后果。很明显,在过去的 50 年里,美国的政治家们已经很明显的减少了。

有一些原因可以用来解释这个现象。尽管做了许多努力,但还

of the people above a certain level. Whatever may be the facilities of acquiring information, whatever may be the profusion of easy methods and cheap science, the human mind can never be instructed and developed without devoting considerable time to these objects.

The greater or lesser ease with which people can live without working is a sure index of intellectual progress. This boundary is more remote in some countries and more restricted in others, but it must exist somewhere as long as the people are forced to work in order to procure the means of subsistence; that is to say, as long as they continue to be the people. It is therefore quite as difficult to imagine a state in which all the citizens are very well informed as a state in which they are all wealthy; these two difficulties are correlative. I readily admit that the mass of the citizens sincerely wish to promote the welfare of the country; nay, more, I even grant that the lower classes mix fewer considerations of personal interest with their patriotism than the higher orders; But it is always more or less difficult for them to discern the best means of attaining the end which they sincerely desire. Long and patient observation and much acquired knowledge are requisite to form a just estimate of the character of a single individual. Men of the greatest genius often fail to do it, and can it be supposed that the common people will always succeed? The people have neither the time nor the means for an investigation of this kind. Their conclusions are hastily formed from a superficial inspection of the more prominent features of a question. Hence it often happens that mountebanks of all sorts are able to please the people, while their truest friends frequently fail to gain their confidence.

Moreover, democracy not only lacks that soundness of judgment which is necessary to select men really deserving of their confidence, but often have not the desire or the inclination to find them out. It cannot be denied that democratic institutions strongly tend to promote the feeling of envy in the human heart; not so much because they afford to everyone the means of rising to the same level with others as because those means perpetually disappoint the persons who employ them. Democratic institutions awaken and foster a passion for equality which they can never entirely satisfy. This complete equality eludes

是不可能使人民的文化达到一定的水平。尽可能简化人们的学习内容,丰富教育方法,使学习走上正轨,这些都很容易做到;但如果人们不能增加其学习时间,就仍旧不能学到知识和发挥学到的知识。

因此,人们不需劳动而能生活的安逸程度的多少,就决定着他们获取知识的一定量的时间。这个时间在某些国家是比较充足的;而在另一些国家,就显得有些紧张。但只要人们为了生存而迫于工作,这个时间就一定会存在;也就是说,人类一直作为真正的人而生活。因此,我们既无法想象一个社会里的所有人都知识渊博,又无法想象同一个国家里的所有公民都腰缠万贯;这两种不可能是互相联系的。我承认,广大的人民大众都真心地希望国家能富强;我还愿意更进一步承认,社会的底层阶级在这个愿望中掺杂的自己的私念,一般说来少于上层阶级。但是,他们却总是很难辨别出什么是达到他们衷心希望的目的所用的最佳方法。为了能完全认清一个人的个性,必须要长期和耐心的观察,并进行各种分析。一些伟大的天才常常失败于这样去做,而普通人就能成功地做到吗? 人民既没有时间也没有合适的办法去做这项工作。他们的结论总是对问题突出特性的肤浅研究而匆匆忙忙做出的。因此,各种骗子能够用尽花样取悦于人民并得到人民的信任,而人民的最忠实的朋友却往往不能让人民信服。

另外,民主不但缺乏人们在选择他们可以信任的人时的那种稳固的判断性,而且有时人们也不愿和不想通过民主的方式选举。不可否认,民主制度强烈地促发着人们心中的嫉妒之情;与其说这是因为民主制度为每个人提供了可以拉近自己与他人距离的方法,不如说是因为人们总是觉得不能找到合适的方法去运用它。民主制度唤醒和助长了永远无法完全满足的一种渴望平

the grasp of the people at the very moment when they think they have grasped it, and "flies," as Pascal says, "with an eternal flight"; the people are excited in the pursuit of an advantage, which is more precious because it is not sufficiently remote to be unknown or sufficiently near to be enjoyed. The lower orders are agitated by the chance of success, they are irritated by its uncertainty; and they pass from the enthusiasm of pursuit to the exhaustion of ill success, and lastly to the acrimony of disappointment. Whatever transcends their own limitations appears to be an obstacle to their desires, and there is no superiority, however legitimate it may be, which is not irksome in their sight.

It has been supposed that the secret instinct which leads the lower orders to remove their superiors as much as possible from the direction of public affairs is peculiar to France. This is an error, however; the instinct to which I allude is not French, it is democratic; it may have been heightened by peculiar political circumstances, but it owes its origin to a higher cause.

In the United States the people do not hate the higher classes of society, but are not favorably inclined towards them and carefully exclude them from the exercise of authority. They do not fear distinguished talents, but are rarely fond of them. In general, everyone who rises without their aid seldom obtains their favor.

While the natural instincts of democracy induce the people toreject distinguished citizens as their rulers, an instinct not less strong induces able men to retire from the political arena, in which it is so difficult to retain their independence, or to advance without becoming servile. This opinion has been candidly expressed by Chancellor Kent, who says, in speaking with high praise of that part of the Constitution which empowers the executive to nominate the judges: "It is indeed probable that the men who are best fitted to discharge the duties of this high office would have too much reserve in their manners, and too much austerity in their principles, for them to be returned by the majority at an election where universal suffrage is adopted."[1]Such were the opinions which were printed without contradiction in America in the year 1830!

---

[1] Kent's *Commentaries*, Vol. I, p. 272.

等的热情。这种完全的平等,总是在人们以为得到它的一刹那,便从人们的手中溜走了,用帕斯卡尔的话来说,就是"消失了","永远的消逝了";人们经常兴奋于对一些重大利益的追求,而这些利益远得使人够不到,却又近得足以使人摸到。人们会在成功的可能性大时而自我陶醉;同时也会在成功的不确定性大时而懊恼与沮丧;他们付诸所有的热忱精疲力竭地追逐着成功,而最终带给他们的是无情的绝望。凡是某些事物在某一点上超出他们的能力范围,都被他们看作是阻碍他们实现愿望的绊脚石,不管这些东西是多么有权威并合法化,他们都一概不予理睬。

许多人认为,这种引导下层阶级把他们的上层从指导公务的职位上拉下来的秘密本能,只见于法国。但这是一个误解;我所说的这个本能,不是法国人所固有的,而是民主体制下的本能;特殊的政治环境或许可以促进这种本能,但它不能创造这种本能。

在美国,人民并不会仇视社会的高层阶级,只是不太喜欢他们,设法阻止他们行使权力。人民不怕杰出的天才,但对这种人不会加以重用。一般说来,凡是没有天才头脑而上升的人,都不会赢得人民的赞扬。

一方面是民主的天然本能诱导人们拒绝让杰出人物当权,另一方面又有一种不亚于这种本能的力量在使这些人远离政界,因为他们想在政界中保持独立和免于堕落是很难的。法官肯特就十分坦率地表达过这种思想。我提到的这位著名作家在盛赞联邦宪法授权总统提名法官的条款之后说:"最能履行职责的人,也许为了不在普选中当选而行动上有所保留,并在原则上非常严谨。"[①]这是在 1830 年发表于美国而且没有人反对的观点。我

① 肯特:《美国法释义》第 1 卷,第 272 页。

I hold it to be sufficiently demonstrated that universal suffrage is by no means a guarantee of the wisdom of the popular choice. Whatever its advantages may be, this is not one of them.

Causes Which May Partly Correct These Tendencies Of The Democracy

Contrary effects produced on nations as on individuals by great dangers—Why so many distinguished men stood at the head of affairs in America fifty years ago—Influence which intelligence and morality exercise upon the popular choice—Example of New England—States of the Southwest—How certain laws influence the choice of the people—Election by an elected body—Its effects upon the composition of the Senate.

When serious dangers threaten the state, the people frequently succeed in selecting the citizens who are the most able to save it It has been observed that man rarely retains his customary level in very critical circumstances; he rises above or sinks below his usual condition, and the same thing is true of nations. Extreme perils sometimes quench the energy of a people instead of stimulating it; they excite without directing its passions; and instead of clearing they confuse its powers of perception. The Jews fought and killed one another amid the smoking ruins of their temple. But it is more common, with both nations and individuals, to find extraordinary virtues developed from the very imminence of the danger. Great characters are then brought into relief as the edifices which are usually concealed by the gloom of night are illuminated by the glare of a conflagration. At those dangerous times genius no longer hesitates to come forward; and the people, alarmed by the perils of their situation, for a time forget their envious passions. Great names may then be drawn from the ballot box.

I have already observed that the American statesmen of the present day are very inferior to those who stood at the head of affairs fifty years ago. This is as much a consequence of the circumstances as of the laws of the country. When America was struggling in the high

只想用这些话证明,普选权绝不会成为人们做出最明智的选择的保证。尽管普选权有许多优点,但并不在这里。

能够部分纠正民主的这种秉性的因素

巨大的危险对国家和人民产生的反面影响——为什么50年前美国有那么多杰出人物在参与政务——教育和道德对大众的选择产生的影响——新英格兰的例子——西南部各州——某些法律是怎样影响人民的选择的——两级选举制度——这种选举制度对参议院的结构所产生的影响。

当国家面临巨大危险的时候,人民总是能成功地选出最能拯救国家的公民。我们可以看到,一个人很少能在紧要关头的面前还保持常态;他不是高于其常态,就是低于其常态。国家的情形也是如此。极端的危险有时不但不会去激发人民的力量,反而会压制它;这种危险虽能促发人民的激情,却没有对这种激情加以正确地引导;它虽能触及人民的思想,但没有完全地唤醒它,犹太人就曾经互相厮杀在他们的一片战火的神殿废墟之中。但最常见的,是一些国家和个人在危难临近的时候,会做出惊人的抵制危险的行动。这时,一些伟大的人物出现了,就像一座座耸立在黑夜中的大楼,顿时被一场大火照亮。在这种危机时刻,天才们不再犹豫不决,奋勇地向前进;而处于苦难中的人民,也会被这危险的情形所惊动而暂时忘却他们的嫉妒之情。这时,从选票箱里捡出伟人的名字已不是件稀奇的事。

我已经讲过,美国今天的政治家,远远不如50年前政治家优秀。我们不能把这种现象仅仅归因于法律,环境也对它造成了一

cause of independence to throw off the yoke of another country, and
when it was about to usher a new nation into the world, the spirits of
its inhabitants were roused to the height which their great objects required. In this general excitement distinguished men were ready to
anticipate the call of the community, and the people clung to them for
support and placed them at their head. But such events are rare, and
it is from the ordinary course of affairs that our judgment must be
formed.

　　If passing occurrences sometimes check the passions of democracy, the intelligence and the morals of the community exercise an influence on them which is not less powerful and far more permanent.
This is very perceptible in the United States. In New England, where
education and liberty are the daughters of morality and religion, where
society has acquired age and stability enough to enable it to form principles and hold fixed habits, the common people are accustomed to
respect intellectual and moral superiority and to submit to it without
complaint, although they set at naught all those privileges which
wealth and birth have introduced among mankind. In New England,
consequently, the democracy makes a more judicious choice than it
does elsewhere. But as we descend towards the South, to those states
in which the constitution of society is more recent and less strong,
where instruction is less general and the principles of morality, religion, and liberty are less happily combined, we perceive that talents
and virtues become more rare among those who are in authority.

　　Lastly, when we arrive at the new Southwestern states, in which
the constitution of society dates but from yesterday and presents only
an agglomeration of adventurers and speculators, we are amazed at the
persons who are invested with public authority, and we are led to ask
by what force, independent of legislation and of the men who direct
it, the state can be protected and society be made to flourish. There
are certain laws of a democratic nature which contribute, nevertheless, to correct in some measure these dangerous tendencies of democracy. On entering the House of Representatives at Washington, one is struck by the vulgar demeanor of that great assembly.
Often there is not a distinguished man in the whole number. Its

定的影响。当美国在为独立这项伟大的事业而奋斗时,它要设法摆脱另一个国家的束缚,而当它以一个新国家的面孔出现在新世界时,它的全体人民的精神已经达到他们的伟大目标所要求的高度。在全国还出于兴奋状态的时候,杰出的人物已准备迎合人民的呼声,而人民也举手支持他们,并把他们置于自己的监督之下。但是,这样的事情毕竟很少,我们还必须思考到事物的另一方面,然后再做判断。

如果这种已逝的事件有时会抑制民主的激情,而人们的知识和道德水平将对激情的发展趋势发生不仅强大而且持久的影响。这种情况在美国是常见的。在新英格兰,教育和自由产生于道德和宗教,而需要足够长时期的稳定性才能建立起来的社会,已形成自己的一套道德标准和生活习惯,所以人民大众已习惯于尊重知识和道德的权威性,并无怨无悔地加以服从,尽管他们从来都是不在乎财富和显赫的家族在人们中间造成的优势的。因此,民主在新英格兰比在其他地方可做出更好的选择。但是,当我们一直往南走,就看到不同的情况。南方各州的社会结构形成得较晚且不够牢固,教育不够普及,道德、宗教和自由的原则还不能很好地结合在一起。因此,我们会发现,一些能干和品德兼优的人在那些州的政府里是很少见的。

最后,当我们到达建立不久的西南部各州时,这里的社会结构中存在的全是冒险家和投机家的庄园,我们深深地吃惊于管理社会的大权被控制在几个人的手中,并在心中暗自思量:除了立法机构和人的独立以外,有什么力量能使国家发达和社会繁荣呢?有些具有民主性质的法律,在某些方面也曾纠正了民主的危险本能。当你进入华盛顿的众议院大厅时,你会非常惊讶地发现这个大会议厅里的人们的言谈举止怎么会如此的粗俗。那里的

members are almost all obscure individuals, whose names bring no associations to mind. They are mostly villagelaw yers, men in trade, or even persons belonging to the lower classes of society. In a country in which education is very general, it is said that the representatives of the people do not always know how to write correctly. At a few yards distance is the door of the Senate, which contains within a small space a large proportion of the celebrated men of America. Scarcely an individual is to be seen in it who has not had an active and illustrious career: the Senate is composed of eloquent advocates, distinguished generals, wise magistrates, and statesmen of note, whose arguments would do honor to the most remarkable parliamentary debates of Europe.

How comes this strange contrast, and why are the ablest citizens found in one assembly rather than in the other? Why is the former body remarkable for its vulgar elements, while the latter seems to enjoy a monopoly of intelligence and talent? Both of these assemblies emanate from the people; both are chosen by universal suffrage; and no voice has hitherto been heard to assert in America that the Senate is hostile to the interests of the people. From what cause, then, does so startling a difference arise? The only reason which appears to me adequately to account for it is that the House of Representatives is elected by the people directly, while the Senate is elected by elected bodies. The whole body of the citizens name the legislature of each state, and the Federal Constitution converts these legislatures into so many electoral bodies, which return the members of the Senate. The Senators are elected by an indirect application of the popular vote; for the legislatures which appoint them are not aristocratic or privileged bodies, that elect in their own right, but they are chosen by the totality of the citizens; they are generally elected every year, and enough new members may be chosen every year to determine the senatorial appointments. But this transmission of the popular authority through an assembly of chosen men operates an important change in it by

成员中几乎没有杰出的人才,大家都是无名之辈,他们的姓名只会在我们的脑海里稍纵即逝,永远不会给我们留下任何印象。他们大部分是乡村律师和商人,甚至是社会最下层阶级的人们。在这个教育几乎达到普及的国家,据说人民的代表并非都是能够正确的书写的。仅隔几步的距离,就是参议院大厅的大门。但在这个不大的会议厅里,却聚集了大部分著名的美国人。在这里,你见到的每个人都具有活跃的和显赫的职业:他们当中有善于雄辩的大律师、著名的将军、英明的行政官和著名的国务活动家。这个会议厅里的一切争论,都可与欧洲各国国会的最出色的辩论相媲美。

怎么会出现这么强烈的两种对比呢? 为什么有才干的人只见于参议院而不见于众议院? 又为什么后者只有一些粗俗的人,而前者却充满了天才和名人呢? 这两个议院都来自人民;并且都是由普选产生;而且迄今为止,在美国,还没有发现有人痛斥参议院与人民的利益是敌对的。那么,是什么因素导致如此惊人的差异的产生呢? 在我看来,只有一个原因可以解释这个问题,那就是:众议院是经人民直接选举而产生的,而参议院则是经两级选举而产生的。每个州的全体公民共同对本州的立法机构进行选举,而联邦宪法又将各州的立法机构转变为很多选举团,由这些选举团选举参议员。当然,参议员也是间接地代表普选的结果,这是因为:各州的选举参议员的立法机构,并不是贵族团体或有选举特权的团体,它实际上是为各州的全体公民服务的;各州的立法机构一般每年选举一次,全体公民通过改选立法机构使其成员得到更新,以达到控制选举参议员的作用。但是,当这个选举团在表达人民的意志时,可能会使人民的意志在精确其判断力和

refining its discretion and improving its choice. Men who are chosen in this manner accurately represent the majority of the nation which governs them; but they represent only the elevated thoughts that are current in the community and the generous propensities that prompt its nobler actions rather than the petty passions that disturb or the vices that disgrace it.

The time must come when the American republics will be obliged more frequently to introduce the plan of election by an elected body into their system of representation or run the risk of perishing miserably among the shoals of democracy.

I do not hesitate to avow that I look upon this peculiar system of election as the only means of bringing the exercise of political power to the level of all classes of the people. Those who hope to convert this institution into the exclusive weapon of a party, and those who fear to use it, seem to me to be equally in error.

Influence Which The American Democracy Has Exercised On The Laws Relating To Elections

When elections are rare, they expose the state to a violent crisis— When they are frequent, they keep up a feverish excitement—The Americans have preferred the second of these two evils—Mutability of the laws—Opinions of Hamilton, Madison, and Jefferson on this subject.

When elections recur only at long intervals, the state is exposed to violent agitation every time they take place. Parties then exert themselves to the utmost in order to gain a prize which is so rarely within their reach; and as the evil is almost irremediable for the candidates who fail, everything is to be feared from their disappointed ambition. If, on the other hand, the legal struggle is soon to be repeated, the defeated parties take patience.

When elections occur frequently, their recurrence keeps society in a feverish excitement and gives a continual instability to public affairs. Thus, on the one hand, the state is exposed to the perils of a revolution, on the other to perpetual mutability; the former system

改善自己的决定方面发生重要的改变。因此,在这种方式下被选举出来的参议员真实地代表了统治国家的多数;但是,他们只代表流行于国内的严肃的思想和促进其贵族行为的大量的倾向,而不是代表常常扰乱国家的小规模的激情和侮辱国家名誉的邪念。

不难看到,将来总有一天,美国的各共和州会被迫把采用两级选举的选举制度引入它们的代表制度中。否则,它们就有可能掉进民主的陷阱而遭受苦难的危险。

对于这一点,我始终坚信不疑。我认为两级选举是使各阶层人民都可以同等的享用政治自由权力的唯一方法。不管是希望把这个手段变成政党所特有的武器的人,还是对这一手段有所畏惧的人,在我看来都是错误的。

美国民主在选举法方面产生的影响

当选举变得稀少而罕见时,它会对国家造成重大危险——当选举变得频繁时,它会使全国处于激动不已的状态——美国人偏向于这两种弊端中的后者——法律的易变性——汉密尔顿、麦迪逊和杰斐逊对这个问题的看法。

在选举的间隔期长时,每次选举都有使国家发生动乱的危险。这时,所有的政党都将尽自己最大努力,像是要抓住一个他们很难得到的奖励;而选举的失败对于候选人来说是一种无法救治的创伤,所以当他们的野心没能达到目的时,他们就无所畏惧了。但是,如果这种合法的斗争很快就能重新再来一次,那么失败的政党便有了耐心。

当选举频繁地出现时,它的再次发生会使社会动荡不安,使公共政务处于持续的常变状态。因此,一方面,国家有面临爆发革命

threatens the very existence of the government, the latter prevents any steady and consistent policy. The Americans have preferred the second of these evils to the first; but they were led to this conclusion by instinct more than by reason, for a taste for variety is one of the characteristic passions of democracy. Hence their legislation is strangely mutable.

Many Americans consider the instability of their laws as a necessary consequence of a system whose general results are beneficial. But no one in the United States affects to deny the fact of this instability or contends that it is not a great evil.

Hamilton, after having demonstrated the utility of a power that might prevent or at least impede the promulgation of bad laws, adds: "It may perhaps be said, that the power of preventing bad laws includes that of preventing good ones, and may be used to the one purpose as well as to the other. But this objection will have little weight with those who can properly estimate the mischiefs of that inconstancy and mutability in the laws which form the greatest blemish in the character and genius of our governments. " (*Federalist*, No. 73.)

And again, in No. 62 of the same work, he observes: "The facility and excess of law-making seem to be the diseases to which our governments are most liable. "

Jefferson himself, the greatest democrat whom the democracy of America has as yet produced, pointed out the same dangers. "The instability of our laws," said he, "is really a very serious inconvenience. I think that we ought to have obviated it by deciding that a whole year should always be allowed to elapse between the bringing in of a bill and the final passing of it. It should afterwards be discussed and put to the vote without the possibility of making any alteration in it; and if the circumstances of the case required a more speedy decision, the question should not be decided by a simple majority, but by a majority of at least two thirds of each house. "[1]

---

[1] Letter to Madison, December 20, 1787, translation of M. Conseil.

的危险,而另一方面,国家可能处于永久的不稳定中;第一种制度威胁到政府的存在,第二种制度则影响到政府稳固和一贯的政策。相对于这两种弊端,美国人更愿意忍受第二种;但是产生这种结论的主要是依靠他们的本能,而并非是出于理性的思考,对变化的喜好是民主的特有激情之一。结果,导致美国的立法具有很特殊的易变性。

大多数美国人认为,他们法律的不稳定性是一种结果普遍有益处的制度的必然结果。但是在美国人,没有一个人会否认这种易变性的事实或争论说它不是一个大弊端。

汉密尔顿在论证一项可能阻止或至少是推迟不良法律的颁布的权力后,补充说:"也许有人会说,阻止颁布不良法律的权力同时也会阻止颁布良好法律的权力,它或许可以被用于这个目的,也有可能被用于另一目的。但这个反对意见,对于能够正确评价法律的不稳定性和多变性的坏处的人来说,并不是十分重要的。法律的不稳定性已经成为我国政府的特性和宗旨方面的最大弊端。"(《联邦党人文集》第 73 篇。)

同样的,在《联邦党人文集》第 62 篇中,他指出:"立法的便利性和过渡性,似乎是我国政府的最倾向于的病症。"

杰斐逊本人是迄今为止出现在美国的民主制度下的最伟大的民主主义者,他也指出过同样的危险。他说:"我国法律的不稳定性确实是一个非常严重的弊病。我觉得我们应当废除它,也就是要这样规定,在提出一项法案之后,允许它在一年内被批准实施。法案应交付讨论,在没有反对意见的情况下进行表决。如果情况紧急要求对该法案进行快速的决定,这也不能单凭简单多数的决定,而至少应以两院各自的三分之二多数通过。"①

---

① 1787 年 12 月 20 日给麦迪逊的信中,由康斯尔先生翻译。

Public Officers Under The Control
Of The American Democracy

Simple exterior of American public officers—No official costume—
All public officers are remunerated—Political consequences of this sys-
tem—No public career exists in America—Results of this fact.

Public officers in the United States are not separate from the
mass of citizens; they have neither palaces nor guards nor ceremonial
costumes. This simple exterior of persons in authority is connected not
only with the peculiarities of the American character, but with the
fundamental principles of society. In the estimation of the democracy
a government is not a benefit, but a necessary evil. A certain degree
of power must be granted to public officers, for they would be of no
use without it. But the ostensible semblance of authority is by no
means indispensable to the conduct of affairs, and it is needlessly offensive to the susceptibility of the public. The public officers themselves are well aware that the superiority over their fellow citizens
which they derive from their authority they enjoy only on condition of
putting themselves on a level with the whole community by their manners. A public officer in the United States is uniformly simple in his
manners, accessible to all the world, attentive to all requests, and o-
bliging in his replies. I was pleased by these characteristics of a democratic government; I admired the manly independence that respects
the office more than the officer and thinks less of the emblems of authority than of the man who bears them.

I believe that the influence which costumes really exercise in an
age like that in which we live has been a good deal exaggerated. I
never perceived that a public officer in America, while in the discharge of his duties, was the less respected because his own merit was
set off by no adventitious signs. On the other hand, it is very doubtful
whether a peculiar dress induces public men to respect themselves
when they are not otherwise inclined to do so. When a magistrate
snubs the parties before him, or indulges his wit at their expense, or
shrugs his shoulders at their pleas of defense, or smiles complacently
as the charges are enumerated (and in France such instances are not
rare), I should like to deprive him of his robes of office, to see

美国民主统治下的公共官员

美国公共官员的简朴——没有官方的制服——所有公共官员均有报酬——这样做的政治后果——美国没有终身公职——这个实事的后果。

美国的公共官员,同公民大众没有什么区别;他们既没有宫殿和卫士,也没有统一的制服。权威人士的这种对外的简朴作风,这不仅关系到美国人的品质,而且还关系到美国社会的基本原则。从民主的角度去评估,政府不会带来任何好处,而是一个必然的灾难。官员们必须被授予一定的权力,因为如果没有这种权力他们将一无是处。但是,权力的外表现象,决非工作所必不可少的,而且会让公众很厌恶。公共官员自己心里很明白,赋予他们向其他人发号施令的权利,是以不能使他们自己的言谈举止高于整体社会为前提的。美国的公共官员作风朴实,和蔼可亲,问话时态度温和,答话时也从不严肃。我对民主政府的这些特性感到很满意;我崇拜在这里所见到的所有男子汉气概,那就是重视职责多于重视职位、重视人品甚于重视权力外表。

我认为制服在一百多年来所产生的影响已经被极大地夸张了。我在美国从来没有见到一个公共官员在执行公务时因穿着不合身份而被蔑视或受到他人耻笑的情形。另外,我也十分怀疑是否公务人员在虚伪地穿上制服时就能受到人们特别的尊重,因为我不相信人们是靠衣着而不是靠人品来判断一个人。当一些行政官员待人冷淡或放纵自己的花销,或耸一耸肩膀表示反对,或在沾沾自喜地下达指令时(在法国,这样的例子并不稀少),我

whether, when he is reduced to the garb of a private citizen, he would not recall some portion of the natural dignity of mankind. No public officer in the United States has an official costume, but every one of them receives a salary. And this, also, still more naturally than what precedes, results from democratic principles. A democracy may allow some magisterial pomp and clothe its officers in silks and gold without seriously compromising its principles. Privileges of this kind are transitory; they belong to the place and not to the man. But if public officers are unpaid, a class of rich and independent public functionaries will be created who will constitute the basis of an aristocracy; and if the people still retain their right of election, the choice can be made only from a certain class of citizens.

When a democratic republic requires salaried officials to serve without pay, it may safely be inferred that the state is advancing towards monarchy. And when a monarchy begins to remunerate such officers as had hitherto been unpaid, it is a sure sign that it is approaching a despotic or a republican form of government. The substitution of paid for unpaid functionaries is of itself, in my opinion, sufficient to constitute a real revolution.

I look upon the entire absence of unpaid offices in America as one of the most prominent signs of the absolute dominion which democracy exercises in that country. All public services, of whatever nature they may be, are paid; so that everyone has not merely a right, but also the means of performing them. Although in democratic states all the citizens are qualified to hold offices, all are not tempted to try for them. The number and the capacities of the candidates more than the conditions of the candidateship restrict the choice of the electors.

In nations where the principle of election extends to everything, no political career can, properly speaking, be said to exist. Men arrive as if by chance at the post which they hold, and they are by no means sure of retaining it. This is especially true when the elections are held annually. The consequence is that in tranquil times public

真想上前去剥下他们的制服，一直剥到让他们赤裸裸的露出作为一个公民的真正模样，看这是否能使他们想起人类应当受到尊敬。美国的公共官员都没有统一的制服，但却领取薪水。这一点比起上述各点更明显的是自然来自民主原则。民主制度准许一些官员炫耀自己，用丝绸和黄金装扮自己，但不得严重违背民主的原则。这样的特权只是暂时的；而且是属于特定的职位，并不真正属于个人。但是，如果不对公务人员付薪水，一个富有和独立的公务人员阶级就会产生，这样就形成了一个贵族基础；这时，即使人民还对选举权有所保留，其选择也必定会被限制在一些特定的公民中。

如果一个民主共和国把公务人员的薪俸制改为无偿制，我可以肯定地说，这个国家正在向君主政体迈进。而当一个君主国开始补偿实行无偿制的官员时，这无疑标志着这个国家不是在向着专制政体前进就是向着共和政体前进。因此，在我看来，用薪俸制公务人员来取代无偿制公务人员，这本身就足够形成一场真正的革命。

我把美国整个缺乏对官员不付薪水这个举动，看成是民主在该国产生绝对统治效用的最明显标志之一。不管是什么性质的公共服务，都要有报酬；因此，每个人不仅有权为公共服务，而且也是履行自己权利的一种方法。在民主国家，虽然每个公民都有资格出任公职，但也不是全体公民都想要去出任的。这不是因为候选人的条件不够，而是因为候选人的人数和能力限制着选举者的选择。

在选举原则扩展到一切事物的国家，严格说来没有永存的政治生涯。人们出任公职，多半来自偶然的原因，任何人都别想能永久地保住其职位。这种情况在每年进行一次的选举中尤其真实。因此，在相对安宁的时期，野心家对公职并不重视。在美国，

functions offer but few lures to ambition. In the United States those who engage in the perplexities of political life are persons of very moderate pretensions. The pursuit of wealth generally diverts men of great talents and strong passions from the pursuit of power; and it frequently happens that a man does not undertake to direct the fortunes of the state until he has shown himself incompetent to conduct his own. The vast number of very ordinary men who occupy public stations is quite as attributable to these causes as to the bad choice of democracy. In the United States I am not sure that the people would choose men of superior abilities even if they wished to be elected; but it is certain that candidates of this description do not come forward.

Arbitrary Power Of Magistrates [①] Under The Rule Of American Democracy

For what reason the arbitrary power of magistrates is greater in absolute monarchies and in democratic republics than it is in limited monarchies—Arbitrary power of the magistrates in New England.

In two kinds of government the magistrates exercise considerable arbitrary power: namely, under the absolute government of an individual, and under that of a democracy. This identical result proceeds from very similar causes. In despotic states the fortune of no one is secure; public officers are not more safe than private persons. The sovereign, who has under his control the lives, the property, and sometimes the honor of the men whom he employs, thinks he has nothing to fear from them and allows them great latitude of action because he is convinced that they will not use it against him.

In despotic states the sovereign is so much attached to his power that he dislikes the constraint even of his own regulations, and likes to see his agents acting irregularly and, as it were, by chance in order to be sure that their actions will never counteract his desires.

---

① I here use the word *magistrates* on its widest sense; I apply it to all officers to whom the execution of the laws is entrusted.

参与到混沌的政治生活里的人,都是没什么抱负的人。而有着优秀才能和巨大野心的人,都远离对政权的追求,而执著于对财富的追求;由于觉得自己没能力经营好自己的事业而去负责领导国家事务的,倒是大有人在。而之所以有大量平庸之辈担任了公职,正是由于这些原因以及对民主的不良选择。在美国,我不确定人民是否会选举那些有卓越才能的人,即使这些人很希望被选中;但可以肯定的是这种候选人是不会出来竞选的。

美国民主统治下的行政官的专断权[①]

是什么原因使行政官的专权在专制君主国和民主共和国要比在立宪君主国强大——新英格兰行政官的专权。

存在着两种政府有权对行政官授予很多专权,这两种政府分别是:只由一个人统治的绝对政府,和在民主制度下的政府。这个同样的结果,来自一些几乎相同的原因。在专制国家,人们的命运无法得到保障;而官员的命运并不会比私人的命运有更多的保障。君主不仅对他所雇佣的人们的生命财产加以控制,有时还控制着他们的荣誉。他认为这些人没什么可恐惧的,还赋予这些人很大的可以自由行动的权利,因为他确信他们不会滥用这种自由来反对他。

在专制国家,君主非常依恋自己的权力,他厌恶强制的制度,以至于把这种厌恶发展到自己制定的规则上,在他看来,他的臣民的一些很小的越轨行为是出于偶然,并相信这不是臣民们存心想要反抗他的。

———————

① 这里,我使用了行政官员的最广泛的含义;我将这个词用于可行使法律权的所有官员。

In democracies, as the majority has every year the right of taking away the power of the officers whom it had appointed, it has no reason to fear any abuse of their authority. As the people are always able to signify their will to those who conduct the government, they prefer leaving them to their own free action instead of prescribing an invariable rule of conduct, which would at once fetter their activity and the popular authority. It may even be observed, on attentive consideration, that, under the rule of a democracy the arbitrary action of the magistrate must be still greater than in despotic states. In the latter the sovereign can immediately punish all the faults with which he becomes acquainted, but he cannot hope to become acquainted with all those which are committed. In democracies, on the contrary, the sovereign power is not only supreme, but universally present. The American functionaries are, in fact, much more free in the sphere of action which the law traces out for them than any public officer in Europe. Very frequently the object which they are to accomplish is simply pointed out to them, and the choice of the means is left to their own discretion.

In New England, for instance, the selectmen of each township are bound to draw up the list of persons who are to serve on the jury; the only rule which is laid down to guide them in their choice is that they are to select citizens possessing the elective franchise and enjoying a fair reputation. [①] In France the lives and liberties of the subjects would be thought to be in danger if a public officer of any kind was entrusted with so formidable a right. In New England the same magistrates are empowered to post the names of habitual drunkards in public houses and to prohibit the inhabitants of a town from supplying them with liquor. [②] Such a censorial power would be revolting to the

---

① See the law of February 27, 1813, *General Collection of the Laws of Massachusetts*, Vol. II, p. 331. It should be added, that the jurors are afterwards drawn from these lists by lot.

② Law of February 28, 1787. See *General Collection of the Laws of Massachusetts*, Vol. I, p. 302. The text is as follows: "The select-men of each township shall post in the shops of tavern-keepers, inn-keepers, and tradesmen a list of persons known to be drunkards, gamblers, and who are accustomed to spend their time and their money in such places; and the proprietor of the aforesaid establishments who, after posting such notice, shall allow the aforesaid persons to drink or gamble on his premises, or sell them spiritous liquors, shall be subject to a fine."

在民主国家,多数每年都有权从他们以前任命的官员手里收回权力,所以他们没什么理由要去担心那些人会滥用职权。人们总是能够让执政者知道他们对政府的意见,所以他们更愿意让执政者充分发挥自己的能力,而不愿意用一套死规矩去束缚执政者,因为这样的死规矩不但限制着执政者,同时也限制着他们自己。但是,只要对此稍加研究,就会发现民主制度下的行政官的专权比专制国家还要大。在专制的国家,君主可以对他所发现的一切犯法行为即刻采取措施,但不能保证的是,他能够随时发现应被惩治的一切犯法行为。而在民主国家,君主的权力不仅极高,而且普遍存在。实际上,在法律所限定的范围内,美国公务人员所享有的行动的自由比欧洲的任何官员都更加广泛。一般都会明确地告诉他们哪些任务是必须完成的,而方法由他们自己定。

比如,在新英格兰,由各乡镇的行政委员负责起草陪审员的名单;唯一指导他们选择的原则就是,陪审员的选择必须在享有选举权和拥有良好名望的公民中进行。①在法国,如果一个公务人员被授予如此可怕的权力,那么人们必定会认为老百姓的生命和自由将变得危险了。在新英格兰,乡镇的行政委员还有权把酗酒者的名字张贴在显眼的地方,禁止居民向他们提供酒类。②这种苛

---

①　见1813年2月27日的法律,《马萨诸塞法律集刊》第2卷,第331页。应当补充一点,陪审员多数从这张表中拟定。

②　1787年2月28日的法律,见《马萨诸塞法律集刊》第1卷,第302页。原文如下:"每个乡镇的行政委员应当在酒吧、客栈和小商店门前各贴一张名单,上面记有酗酒者、赌博者和经常喜欢出没于此类场所的人的姓名;如果这些经营者看到通知后,仍然纵容让这些人在他们的地盘上酗酒、赌博或出售酒给这些人,那么经营者将被罚款。"

population of the most absolute monar nies; here, however, it is submitted to without difficulty.

Nowhere has so much been left by the law to the arbitrary determination of the magistrate as in democratic republics, because they have nothing to fear from arbitrary power. It may even be asserted that the freedom of the magistrate increases as the elective franchise is extended and as the duration of the term of office is shortened. Hence arises the great difficulty of converting a democratic republic into a monarchy. The magistrate ceases to be elective, but he retains the rights and the habits of an elected officer, which lead directly to despotism.

It is only in limited monarchies that the law which prescribes the sphere in which public officers are to act regulates all their measures. The cause of this may be easily detected. In limited monarchies the power is divided between the king and the people, both of whom are interested in the stability of the magistrate. The king does not venture to place the public officers under the control of the people, lest they should be tempted to betray his interests; on the other hand, the people fear lest the magistrates should serve to oppress the liberties of the country if they were entirely dependent upon the crown; they cannot, therefore, be said to depend on either the one or the other. The same cause that induces the king and the people to render public officers independent suggests the necessity of such securities as may prevent their independence from encroaching upon the authority of the former or upon the liberties of the latter. They consequently agree as to the necessity of restricting the functionary to a line of conduct laid down beforehand and find it to their interest to impose upon him certain regulations that he cannot evade.

Instability Of The Administration In The United States

In America the public acts of a community frequently leave fewer traces than the actions within a family—Newspapers the only historical remains—Instability of the administration prejudicial to the art of government.

刻的权限,在最专制的君主国,也会遭到人民的厌恶;但在新英格兰,却不费吹灰之力地就被人服从了。

任何一个地方的法律,都不可能像民主共和国那样使行政官具有如此惊人的权力,因为它们认为这种专权没有可怕之处。甚至可以说,随着选举权的日益扩大和官员的任期日益缩短,行政官比以前更加自由了。因此,要想把一个民主共和国改变为君主国,将是非常困难的。如果人民不再对行政官进行选举,但却依旧保留着民选的行政官的权限和习惯,那就会引发专制。

只有在立宪君主国,法律在限定官员的行动范围的同时,还要指导官员的每一行动。这种做法的原因很简单。在立宪君主国,由国王和人民共同分享权力,他们都希望行政官的职位保持稳定。国王不敢让人民来控制行政官的命运,以免行政官员会违背王权的利益;而另一方面,人民则害怕行政官员会完全依赖国王,从而压制国家的自由;因此,既不能让行政官员完全站到国王那一边,也不能让行政官员完全支持人民。使国王和人民都允许官员保持独立的这一原因,也在使国王和人民不断寻找可以制止官员滥用这种独立的方法,以阻止官员侵犯王权的利益和人民的自由。因此,双方达成协定,认为首先必须限制官员的行动范围,并且要为官员制定一套他们无法逃避的规则。

美国行政的不稳定性

在美国,人们在社会公共事务方面留下的痕迹往往比不上他们在家庭事务方面留下的痕迹——报纸是唯一的历史资料——行政的不稳定性为什么对政府的施政艺术毫无益处。

The authority which public men possess in America is so brief and they are so soon commingled with the ever changing population of the country that the acts of a community frequently leave fewer traces than events in a private family. The public administration is, so to speak, oral and traditional. But little is committed to writing, and that little is soon wafted away forever, like the leaves of the Sibyl, by the smallest breeze.

The only historical remains in the United States are the news-papers; if a number be wanting, the chain of time is broken and the present is severed from the past. I am convinced that in fifty years it will be more difficult to collect authentic documents concerning the social condition of the Americans at the present day than it is to find remains of the administration of France during the Middle Ages; and if the United States were ever invaded by barbarians, it would be nec-essary to have recourse to the history of other nations in order to learn anything of the people who now inhabit them.

The instability of administration haspenetrated into the habits of the people; it even appears to suit the general taste, and no one cares for what occurred before his time: no methodical system is pursued, no archives are formed, and no documents are brought together when it would be very easy to do so. Where they exist, little store is set up-on them. I have among my papers several original public documents which were given to me in the public offices in answer to some of my inquiries. In America society seems to live from hand to mouth, like an army in the field. Nevertheless, the art of administration is un-doubtedly a science, and no sciences can be improved if the discover-ies and observations of successive generations are not connected to-gether in the order in which they occur. One man in the short space of his life remarks a fact, another conceives an idea; the former in-vents a means of execution, the latter reduces a truth to a formula; and mankind gathers the fruits of individual experience on its way and gradually forms the sciences. But the persons who conduct the admin-istration in America can seldom afford any instruction to one another; and when they assume the direction of society, they simply possess those attainments which are widely disseminated in the community,

　　在美国,公众人物所拥有的权力是如此短暂,以至于他们很快便会回到每天都在改变面貌的人民大众中去,所以他们在社会公共事务方面留下的痕迹往往比不上他们在家庭事务方面留下的痕迹。美国的公共行政管理,几乎全是依靠口述和传统的形式进行。没有书面上的规定,即使曾经有过一些,也像古代女巫写在棕榈树叶上的预言,在一阵微风轻拂后,就消失得无影无踪了。

　　报纸美国的唯一历史资料;如果报纸缺少了一期,时间的锁链就会断裂,现在和过去就无法连接上了。我确信,当50年后我们再想去收集有关今天美国社会详情的文件,将难于寻找法国中世纪行政管理的文件;如果有一天,美国遭到野蛮人的侵略,要想知道今天居住在这里的人民的一些事情,那就只能依靠其他国家的历史资料了。

　　行政管理的不稳定性已渗入到人民的日常生活习惯中;甚至可以说,它已经迎合了大众的口味,没有人会去关心在他以前发生的事情:没有人再对管理的方法进行深入研究,也没有人对经验进行细心的总结,收集文献本来是件很容易的事,但也根本没有人会去做它。偶然落到人们手里的文件很少能被保留住。我手里的仅有的几份原始材料,还是一些行政部门为了对我关于某些官员的提问而给我的答复。美国的社会似乎每天都在勉强度日,就像一支战斗中的军队。然而,毫无疑问,行政管理技术是一门科学,并且如果每代人民没有把他们发现和观察到的经验流传下来,所有的科学都不会进步发展。人们在短暂的一生中,有的人注重实践,有的人相信理论;前者在发明执行方法,后者在创造理论;人类就是这样,在前进过程中不断收集自己的不同经验果实,并逐渐建立起各门科学。美国行政管理人员根本不互相学

and no knowledge peculiar to themselves. Democracy, pushed to its furthest limits, is therefore prejudicial to the art of government; and for this reason it is better adapted to a people already versed in the conduct of administration than to a nation that is uninitiated in public affairs. This remark, indeed, is not exclusively applicable to the science of administration. Although a democratic government is founded upon a very simple and natural principle, it always presupposes the existence of a high degree of culture and enlightenment in society. ①
At first it might be supposed to belong to the earliest ages of the world, but maturer observation will convince us that it could come only last in the succession of human history.

Charges Levied By The State Uuder The Rule Of The American Democracy

In all communities citizens are divisible into certain classes—Habits of each of these classes in the direction of public finances—Why public expenditure must tend to increase when the people govern—What renders the extravagance of a democracy less to be feared in America—Public expenditure under a democracy.

Before we can tell whether a democratic government is economical or not we must establish a standard of comparison. The question would be of easy solution if we were to draw a parallel between a democratic republic and an absolute monarchy. The public expenditure in the former would be found to be more considerable than in the latter; such is the case with all free states compared with those which are not so. It is certain that despotism ruins individuals by preventing them from producing wealth much more than by depriving them of what they have already produced; it dries up the source of riches, while it usually respects acquired property. Freedom, on the contrary, produces

---

① It is unnecessary to observe that I speak here of the democratic form of government as applied to a people and not merely to a tribe.

习,并提出建议;而且,他们在指导社会工作时,只凭借在社会上广泛流传的经验知识,而很少有指导该项工作所必备的专业知识。因此,被推广到行政管理工作的民主,反而对政府管理有害;就这一点来说,民主更适用于那些精通行政管理的国家,而不适用于缺乏行政管理的国家。而且,这个论断并不只适用于行政科学。尽管民主政府可以建立在简单和自然的原则上,但它总是需要社会有很高程度的文明和开化。[①] 最初,人们还以为这种政府只是存在于遥远的古代;但是,随着后来的深入考察,才确信这种政府只能出现于社会发展的最终阶段。

美国民主统治下的公共开支

在任何社会,公民都被分为几个阶级——每个阶级都有控制国家财政的欲望——为什么人民主政时公共开支会必然增加——是什么使美国人对民主制度造成的浪费并不害怕——民主制度下的公共开支。

在我们想要分辨一个民主政府是否节约之前,我们必须界定一个可以进行比较的标准。对比一个民主共和国与一个专制君主国后,就会使这个问题变得容易解决了。这时,我们将会发现,前者的公共开支远远大于后者的;而且,这种情况在比较一切自由国家与不自由国家时也是一样的。我们可以确定,专制制度使人民贫穷的主要原因,不是它夺去人民的创造成果而是它妨碍人民制造财富;而是它明明已经知道财源已经被耗尽,却还是只看重

---

① 我们不必再考察,我这里所讲的政府民主形式是适用于人类的,而不仅仅是相对于原始部落的。

far more goods than it destroys; and the nations which are favored by free institutions invariably find that their resources increase even more rapidly than their taxes.

My present object is to compare free nations with one another and to point out the influence of democracy upon the finances of a state. Communities as well as organic bodies are subject in their formation to certain fixed rules from which they cannot depart. They are composed of certain elements that are common to them at all times and under all circumstances. The people may always be mentally divided into three classes. The first of these classes consists of the wealthy; the second, of those who are in easy circumstances; and the third is composed of those who have little or no property and who subsist by the work that they perform for the two superior orders. The proportion of the individuals in these several divisions may vary according to the condition of society, but the divisions themselves can never be obliterated.

It is evident that each of these classes will exercise an influence peculiar to its own instincts upon the administration of the finances of the state. If the first of the three exclusively possesses the legislative power, it is probable that it will not be sparing of the public funds, because the taxes which are levied on a large fortune only diminish the sum of superfluities and are, in fact, but little felt. If the second class has the power of making the laws, it will certainly not be lavish of taxes, because nothing is so onerous as a large impost levied upon a small income. The government of the middle classes appears to me the most economical, I will not say the most enlightened, and certainly not the most generous, of free governments.

Let us now suppose that the legislative authority is vested in the lowest order: there are two striking reasons which show that the tendency of the expenditures will be to increase, not to diminish. As the great majority of those who create the laws have no taxable property, all the money that is spent for the community appears to be spent to their advantage, at no cost of their own; and those who have some little property readily find means of so regulating the taxes that they weigh upon the wealthy and profit the poor, although the rich cannot take the same advantage when they are in possession of

既得的财产。与此相反的是,自由所创造出来的财富比它所毁掉的要多很多;享受过自由好处的国家,会发现其财源总比税收增长迅速。

我目前的任务,是要对比各种自由的国家,并指出民主对各国财政所产生的影响。社会就好比是一个有机体,在组织上必须服从他们无法违背的固定原则。社会是由无论何时何地都存在的一定成分组成的。人类常常被分为三个阶级。第一个阶级由富人组成;第二个阶级,是由那些虽然不是富人但又无需为生活担忧的人组成;而第三个阶级的人,只拥有很少财产或根本没有财产,他们完全要依靠为前两个阶级劳动才得以维持生活。这三类人的人数,可能因社会情况的不同而变化,但不能否认每个社会里都有这三类人。

显而易见,每个阶级在管理国家财政方面都有其特定的标准。假如第一个阶级拥有国家的立法权,那么要想节省公共开支就有些不大可能了,因为对大额财产的征税仅仅是其财富很小一部分,事实上,他们根本不会在乎的。再假如是由第二个阶级制定国家的法律,这时,他们肯定不会挥霍国家的税收,因为对小额财产征收高额税金可以说是他们最大的灾难了。在我看来,中间阶级的政府是自由政府中最节约的,但我不能肯定它是自由政府中最有知识和最慷慨的政府。

现在,让我们猜想是第三个阶级总揽了制定法律的大权:这里有两个明显的原因表示公共开支只会增加,不会减少。首先,制定法律的人大部分没有可以征税的财产,国家的公共开支在表面上似乎只是为他们服务的,而决不会伤害他们;其次,有些小钱的人不难找到办法,把赋税的负担完全转移到富人身上,而仅仅让穷人获利。这种情况在富人当政时是不可

the government.

In countries in which the poor① have the exclusive power of making the laws, no great economy of public expenditure ought to be expected; that expenditure will always be considerable, either because the taxes cannot weigh upon those who levy them, or because they are levied in such a manner as not to reach these poorer classes. In other words, the government of the democracy is the only one under which the power that votes the taxes escapes the payment of them.

In vain will it be objected that the true interest of the people is to spare the fortunes of the rich, since they must suffer in the long run from the general impoverishment which will ensue. Is it not the true interest of kings also, to render their subjects happy, and of nobles to admit recruits into their order on suitable grounds? If remote advantages had power to prevail over the passions and the exigencies of the moment, no such thing as a tyrannical sovereign or an exclusive aristocracy could ever exist.

Again, it may be objected that the poor never have the sole power of making the laws; but I reply that wherever universal suffrage has been established, the majority unquestionably exercises the legislative authority; and if it be proved that the poor always constitute the majority, may it not be added with perfect truth that in the countries in which they possess the elective franchise they possess the sole power of making the laws? It is certain that in all the nations of the world the greater number has always consisted of those persons who hold no property, or of those whose property is insufficient to exempt them from the necessity of working in order to procure a comfortable subsistence. Universal suffrage, therefore, in point of fact does invest the poor with the government of society.

The disastrous influence that popular authority may sometimes exercise upon the finances of a state was clearly seen in some of the democratic republics of antiquity, in which the public treasure was exhausted in order to relieve indigent citizens or to supply games and theatrical amusements for the populace. It is true that the representative system was then almost unknown, and that at the present time

---

① The word *poor* is used here and throughout the remainder of this chapter in a relative, not in an absolute sense. Poor men in America would often appear rich in comparison with the poor of Europe; but they may with propriety be styled poor in comparison with their more affluent countrymen.

能发生的。

因此,在穷人垄断制定法律大权的国家,①不能期望会减少公共开支;这项开支是相当巨大的,这是因为立法征税的人可能不履行纳税义务,或者说他们不让赋税的负担转嫁到穷人身上。换句话讲,民主政府是唯一能使立法征税的人摆脱纳税义务的政府。

你的反对是无用的,因为使人民保护富人的财产才是人民的真正利益所在,否则人民必须长期忍受接踵而来的痛苦。而且,国王幸福了,人民不也就幸福了吗?贵族的利益不也是随时随地为人民开放吗?如果此刻的激情和要求可以被长远的利益所掩盖,那么暴君统治或专横的贵族制度就永远不会出现了。

也许会有人提出,穷人从来没有制定法律的权力;我的回答会是,无论他们建立了多么普遍的制度,法律的制定权仍然掌握在多数手里;如果能够证明多数是由穷人构成的,那也可以补充道:穷人能在实行选举制度的国家垄断制定法律的大权吗?不错,迄今为止,世界上的所有国家的绝大多数人是没有财产的,或者只拥有少数的可以让他们在不劳动时也可以维持生活的财产。因此,普选制度实际上是把管理社会的大权交到穷人手中。

民权有时可能对国家财政发生灾难性影响,在古代的一些民主共和国,这一点就已经很清楚了。在这些共和国,国库的公共开支几乎完全被花在救济贫困的公民或为人民提供休闲时的娱乐设施上。事实上,代议制在古代几乎是不被人知的,而在今天,

---

① 贯穿于整章并用在这里的单词"穷人",只是相对意义上的穷人,并不是绝对意义上的穷人。美国的穷人在和法国的穷人相比时,常常会显示出富裕;但把他们和其同乡人比较时,就会代表真正意义上的穷人。

the influence of popular passions is less felt in the conduct of public affairs; but it may well be believed that in the end the delegate will conform to the principles of his constituents and favor their propensities as much as their interests.

The extravagance of democracy is less to be dreaded, however, in proportion as the people acquire a share of property, because, on the one hand, the contributions of the rich are then less needed, and, on the other, it is more difficult to impose taxes that will not reach the imposers. On this account universal suffrage would be less dangerous in France than in England, where nearly all the taxable property is vested in the hands of a few. America, where the great majority of the citizens possess some fortune, is in a still more favorable position than France.

There are further causes that may increase the amount of public expenditure in democratic countries. When an aristocracy governs, those who conduct the affairs of state are exempted, by their very station in society, from any want: content with their lot, power and renown are the only objects for which they strive; placed far above the obscure crowd, they do not always clearly perceive how the well-being of the mass of the people will redound to their own grandeur. They are not, indeed, callous to the sufferings of the poor; but they cannot feel those miseries as acutely as if they were themselves partakers of them. Provided that the people appear to submit to their lot, the rulers are satisfied and demand nothing further from the government. An aristocracy is more intent upon the means of maintaining than of improving its condition.

When, on the contrary, the people are invested with the supreme authority, they are perpetually seeking for something better, because they feel the hardship of their lot. The thirst for improvement extends to a thousand different objects; it descends to the most trivial details, and especially to those changes which are accompanied with considerable expense, since the object is to improve the condition of the poor, who cannot pay for the improvement. Moreover, all democratic communities are agitated by an ill-defined excitement and a kind of feverish impatience that creates a multitude of innovations, almost all of which are expensive.

人民的激情已很难表现在公共事务方面;但可以断定,随着时间的流逝,代表们总会按照选民的要求行事,以他们的爱好和利益为出发点。

另外,随着人民的财富积累越来越多,民主的铺张浪费也将按比例地减少,因为当人民富裕以后,首先是不再需要富人的施舍,其次是如果要增加赋税,自己也必定会受损失。从这一点来说,法国的普选制度将比英国普选制度产生较少危险,因为在英国,有少数人控制了几乎所有的应当缴税的财产。在美国,绝大多数人都有财产,其社会地位也比法国人更加有利。

还有一些可能增加民主国家公共开支的因素。当贵族政府管理国家事务时,他们因为自己特殊的社会地位而免于匮乏。他们满足于自己的权势,并把向社会要求更多的权力和名誉作为自己的奋斗目标;他们高踞于人民大众之上,从来没有清楚地了解到人民大众的安宁幸福是怎样促进他们的荣华富贵的。不错,他们也确实感觉到了穷人的苦难;但他们对于这种苦难的感受并不如穷人那样切实。只要人民能够安于现状,统治者们便心满意足并不再向政府索求什么了。贵族阶级更希望维持现状而不是改进现状。

反之,当国家大权被控制在人民手中时,统治者们会寻求更好的统治方式,因为他们知道生活的艰难。这时,改革的精神将影响到各行各业;深入到最琐碎的细节,特别会体现在需要耗以资金的事业上,因为改善穷人的生活状况正是这种事业的目的所在,而这又是穷人自己所无法办到的。而且,所有的民主社会都被鼓舞着,这种鼓舞来自一种目标并不明确的奋进精神,和一阵不断追求各种革新的热情,这种热情几乎总是要以金钱为代价。

In monarchies and aristocracies those who are ambitious flatter the natural taste which the rulers have for power and renown and thus often incite them to very costly undertakings. In democracies, where the rulers are poor and in want, they can be courted only by such means as will improve their well-being, and these improvements cannot take place without money. When a people begin to reflect on their situation, they discover a multitude of wants that they had not before been conscious of, and to satisfy these exigencies recourse must be had to the coffers of the state. Hence it happens that the public charges increase in proportion to the civilization of the country, and taxes are augmented as knowledge becomes more diffused. The last cause which renders a democratic government dearer than any other is that a democracy does not always lessen its expenditures even when it wishes to do so, because it does not understand the art of being economical. As it frequently changes its purposes, and still more frequently its agents, its undertakings are often ill-conducted or left unfinished; in the former case the state spends sums out of all proportion to the end that it proposes to accomplish; in the latter the expense brings no return.

Tendencles Of The American Democracy As Regards The Salaries Of Public Officers

In democracies those who establish high salaries have no chance of profiting by them—Tendency of the American democracy to increase the salaries of subordinate officers and to lower those of the more important functionaries-Reason for this—Comparative statement of the salaries of public officers in the United States and in France.

There is a powerful reason that usually induces democracies to economize upon the salaries of public officers. Those who fix the amount of the salaries, being very numerous, have but little chance of obtaining office so as to be in receipt of those salaries. In aristocratic countries, on the contrary, the individuals who appoint high salaries have almost always a vague hope of profiting by them. These appointments may be looked upon as a capital which they create for their own use, or at least as a resource for their children.

It must be allowed, moreover, that a democratic state is most

在君主政体和贵族政体下,野心家们为了迎合主政者对权势和名誉的自然喜好,经常促使主政者去从事一些成本巨大的事业。在穷人主政的民主国家,主政者只会设法增进社会的福利事业,而这种事业的实施不能没有资金。另外,当人民对自身的处境开始思索时,总会产生很多当初并不曾想到的需要,而使这些需要得到满足,就必须依靠国家的帮助。因此,一般说来,随着社会文明程度的提升,国家的公共开支也会增加,而随着教育程度地普及,税额也会跟着上升。最后,还有一个常使民主政府比其他政府更加可贵的因素,那就是民主政府虽然有时打算节省开支,但它却总是无法实现,因为它没有节约的技巧。由于民主政府经常改变自己的目标和频繁更换它的人员,所以它的事业经常不能前后很好地联系在一起或经常半途而废;在第一种情况下,国家虽花了钱,但并没有达到预期的效果;在第二种情况下,国家花了钱,但一无所获。

美国民主在规定公务人员薪俸方面表现的趋势

在民主制度下,建立高薪制度的人并无机会从中受益——美国民主的趋势是增加下级公务人员的薪俸和降低高级公务人员的薪俸——这样做的原因——对比美国公务人员和法国公务人员的薪俸。

通常有一个重大原因能使民主制度节省公共官员的薪水。在民主制度下,有很多人能规定薪水制度,但其中却很少有人有机会从中获利。相反的,在贵族国家,规定高薪制度的人几乎总怀有一丝希望能从中获利。这是他们为自己创造的财富,或至少是为其子女创造的财源的源泉。

但是不得不承认,民主国家对其主要公共官员也是极其吝

parsimonious towards its principal agents. In America the secondary officers are much better paid and the higher functionaries much worse than elsewhere.

These opposite effects result from the same cause: the people fix the salaries of the public officers in both cases, and the scale of remuneration is determined by a comparison with their own wants. It is held to be fair that the servants of the public should be placed in the same easy circumstances as the public themselves;① but when the question turns upon the salaries of the great officers of state, this rule fails, and chance alone guides the popular decision. The poor have no adequate conception of the wants which the higher classes of society feel. The sum which is scanty to the rich appears enormous to him whose wants do not extend beyond the necessities of life; and in his estimation, the governor of a state, with his twelve hundred or two thousand dollars a year, is a fortunate and enviable being. ② If you try to convince him that the representative of a great people ought to appear with some splendor in the eyes of foreign nations, he will at first assent to your assertion; but when he reflects on his own humble dwelling and the small earnings of his hard toil, he remembers all that he could do with a salary which you judge to be insufficient, and he is startled and almost frightened at the view of so much wealth. Besides,

---

① The easy circumstances in which lower officials are placed in the United States result also from another cause, which is independent of the general tendencies of democracy: every kind of private business is very lucrative, and the state would not be served at all if it did not pay its servants well. The country is in the position of a commercial house, which is obliged to meet heavy competition, notwithstanding its inclination to be economical.

② Ohio, which has a million inhabitants, gives its governor a salary of $1,200 or 6,504 francs.

啬的。在美国,下级公务人员的薪俸要比其他国家的高很多,但高级公务人员的薪俸却远远不如其他国家的。

这两个相反的现象,来自同一个原因。在这两种情形下,是人民根据自己的需要,在下级公务人员和高级公务人员的贡献做出对比后而规定公共官员的薪俸的。并且人民也切实地感觉到,在社会生活富裕的情况下,应当让公共官员也一起分享这种宽裕的生活;①但是,在规定国家的高级公共官员薪俸时,这个想法便失去了其效用,而完全是由随意决定的。穷人对社会的高层阶级的生活需要并没有完全足够的概念。一笔在富人眼中很微不足道的款项,而对穷人来讲就是一笔非常巨大的财富,因为后者只要能够满足日常生活需要就很知足了;在他们看来,一个每年收入在6000法郎的州长,就已经是很幸福和很值得羡慕的人了。② 假如你想要劝说他们,让他们知道一个代表在替自己国家与外国人会面时,应该显示出应有的气派,他们在最初可能对你的看法完全肯定;但当他们想到自己简陋的住所和靠辛苦的劳动才能得到的很少的收入时,看到用你以为是微不足道的财富也可以让他做出一番事业时,他就会对这样一笔财富感到非常惊讶,甚至被吓得说不出话来。另外,下级公共官员与人民几乎

---

① 美国低级官员的宽裕环境出自另一原因,它是不依赖于民主制度的一般趋势的:各种与私人利益有关的事业都是有报酬的,如果国家没有给为它服务的官员很好的薪俸,那么将没人为它效劳。我们处在一个竞争激烈的商品社会时期,尽管大环境是提倡经济节约的。

② 俄亥俄州有近百万居民,它们统治者的薪俸是1200美金或6540法郎。

the secondary public officer is almost on a level with the people, while the others are raised above them. The former may therefore excite his sympathy, but the latter begin to arouse his envy.

This is clearly seen in the United States, where the salaries seem, if I may so speak, to decrease as the authority of those who receive them is augmented. ①

Under the rule of an aristocracy, on the contrary, the high officers receive munificent salaries, while the inferior ones often have not more than enough to procure the necessaries of life. The reason for this fact is easily discoverable from causes very analogous to those that I have just pointed out. As a democracy is unable to conceive the pleasures of the rich or to witness them without envy, so an aristocracy is slow to understand the privations of the poor, or rather is unacquainted with them. The poor man is not, properly speaking, of the same kind as the rich one, but a being of another species. An aristocracy therefore cares but little for the condition of its subordinate agents; and their salaries are raised only when they refuse to serve for too scanty a remuneration.

It is the parsimonious conduct of democracy towards its principal officers that has caused more economical propensities to be attributed

---

① To render this assertion perfectly evident, it will suffice to examine the scale of salaries of the agents of the Federal government. I have added the salaries of the corresponding officers in France to complete the comparison.

UNITED STATES		FRANCE	
Treasury Department		Ministé re de Finances	
Messenger	$ 700	Messenger	1,500 fr.
Clerk with lowest salary	$ 1,000	Clerk with lowest salary	1,000 to 1,800 fr.
Clerk with highest salary	$ 1,600	Clerk with lowest salary	3,200 to 3,600 fr.
Chief Clerk	$ 2,000	Secretary-General	20,000 fr.
Secretary of State	$ 6,000	The Minister	80,000 fr.
The President	$ 25,000	The King	12,000,000 fr.

I have perhaps done wrong in selecting France as my standard of comparison. In France, as the democratic tendencies of the nation exercise an ever increasing influence on the government, the Chambers show a disposition to raise the low salaries and to lower the principal ones. Thus the Minister of Finance, who received 160,000 fr. under the Empire, receives 80,000 fr. in 1835; the Directors-General of Finance, who then received 50,000 fr. , now receive only 20,000 fr.

处于同一水平,而另一些人却高高居于这个水平之上。前者或许能因此激起他们的同情,而后者则会让他们产生嫉妒。

在薪俸看似是随着公务人员的权力的增加而减少的美国,这种情形也清晰可见。[①]

在贵族统治的帝国,情况则与此相反,高级官员都会获得极高的薪金,而小官员的收入只够维持基本生活,其原因可以很容易地从我们上面指出的类似原因中找到。如果说在民主体制下,不允许只有富人享乐而穷人应对富人嫉妒,那么贵族体制则无法了解到穷人的困苦,或者说它根本不知穷困是什么。确切地说,穷人与富人并不是同一类人,穷人是另一种类人。因此,在贵族体制下,下级官员的命运很少被关心;只有当下级官员因为薪金过少而拒绝为贵族服务的时候,它才会稍微增加他们的薪金。

民主制度虽然不提倡节约,但对它们的高级公共官员却采取

[①]　为了使这种说法变得更有力,我将对联邦政府官员的薪俸进行考察并对比。下面我增加了法国官员的薪俸来使对比完整。

美国	法国
(财政部官员)	(财政部官员)
传达员⋯⋯⋯⋯⋯700 美金	大臣的传达员⋯⋯⋯1500 法郎
低级科员⋯⋯⋯⋯1000 美金	低级科员⋯⋯⋯⋯1000 ~ 1800 法郎
高级科员⋯⋯⋯⋯1600 美金	高级科员⋯⋯⋯3200 ~ 3600 法郎
科长⋯⋯⋯⋯⋯⋯2000 美金	科长⋯⋯⋯⋯⋯⋯20000 法郎
部长(国务卿)⋯⋯ 6000 美金	大臣⋯⋯⋯⋯⋯⋯80000 法郎
政府首脑(总统)⋯ 25000 美金	政府首脑(国王)⋯ 12000000 法郎

我拿法国作为比较的标准或许存在着不妥之处。在法国,民主的本能已经逐渐深入到政府中,已经出现国会要求提高低额薪金和普遍降低高额薪金的强硬趋势。因此,在第一帝国时期,法国财政大臣的年薪已为 16 万法郎,而在 1835 年已降低为 8 万法郎;而财政部各司长的年薪则由以前的 5 万法郎,而现在已降低为 2 万法郎。

to it than it really possesses. It is true that it scarcely allows the means of decent maintenance to those who conduct its affairs; but it lavishes enormous sums to succor the wants or facilitate the enjoyments of the people. ① The money raised by taxation may be better employed, but it is not economically used. In general, democracy gives largely to the people and very sparingly to those who govern them. The reverse is the case in aristocratic countries, where the money of the state profits the persons who are at the head of affairs.

Difflculty Of Distinguishing The Causes That Incline The American Government To Economy

We Are liable to frequent errors in seeking among facts for the real influence that laws exercise upon the fate of mankind, since nothing is more difficult to appreciate than a fact. One nation is naturally fickle and enthusiastic; another is sober and calculating; and these characteristics originate in their physical constitution or in remote causes with which we are unacquainted.

There are nations which are fond of parade, bustle, and festivity, and which do not regret millions spent upon the gayeties of an hour. Others, on the contrary, are attached to more quiet enjoyments and seem almost ashamed of appearing to be pleased. In some countries high value is set upon the beauty of public edifices; in others the productions of art are treated with indifference, and everything that is unproductive is regarded with contempt. In some, renown, in others, money, is the ruling passion.

---

① See the American budgets for the support of paupers and for publicinstruction. In 1831 over $250,000 or 1,290,000 francs were spent in the state of New York for the maintenance of the poor; and at least $1,000,000 or 5,240,000 francs were devoted to public instruction. (Williams's *New York Annual Register*, 1832, pp. 205 and 243.) The state of New York contained only 1,900,000 inhabitants in the year 1830, which is not more than double the amount of population in the Département du Nord in France.

了节省开支的态度,以至于要亏待他们或有吝啬的倾向。不错,民主制度也使主政者能够过上勉强舒适的生活,但它为了使人民的需要得到满足和使人人都过上舒适的生活,却能以耗费巨资为代价。[①] 税收是这些开支的主要来源,但没有被很好地利用。一般说来,在民主体制中,用于统治者方面的开支较少,而用于被治者方面的开支相对较多。贵族制度则与此不同,它把国家的收入主要用于统领国家事务的阶级身上了。

在识别促使美国政府实行节约的原因时的困难

那些寻找法律对人类命运产生真正的影响事实的人,很可能犯过很多错误,因为再没有什么会比识别这种事实更加困难的了。一个民族天生活泼并充满热情,而另一个民族则善于冷静思考和精打细算;这些特点来源于他们的身体状况或一些我们并不清楚的古老原因。

有些民族喜欢游行、热闹和欢庆,他们不惜花费万金求一时之乐。而另一些民族则相反,他们喜欢享受宁静,羞于表现自己富有。有些国家对建筑之美情有独钟;而另一些国家则从不对艺术加以重视,对一切没有实效的东西表示轻视。最后,一些国家爱好名誉地位,另一些国家则崇尚拜金主义。这都是这些国家所固有的喜好。

---

① 考察一下美国的预算,就可知道美国为了维持穷人的生活和免费教育的开支是多少了。1831 年,纽约州为维持穷人的生活共支出了 25 万美金或 129 万法郎,而国民教育费至少高达 100 万美金或 524 万法郎。(见威廉斯:《纽约年报》,1832 年,第 205、243 页。)1830 年,纽约州的人口为 190 万,约等于法国诺尔省人口的两倍。

Independently of the laws, all these causes exercise a powerful influence upon the conduct of the finances of the state. If the Americans never spend the money of the people in public festivi ties, it is not merely because the taxes are under the control of the people, but because the people take no delight on festivities. If they repudiate all ornament from their architecture and set no store on any but practical and homely advantages, it is not because they live under democratic institutions, but because they are a commercial nation. The habits of private life are continued in public; and we ought carefully to distinguish that economy which depends upon their institutions from that which is the natural result of their habits and customs.

Whether The Expenditure Of The United States Can Be Compared With That Of France

Two points to be established in order to estimate the extent of the public charges: *viz.* , *the national wealth and the rate of taxation—The wealth and the charges of France not accurately known—Why the wealth and charges of the Union cannot be accurately known—Researches of the author to discover the amount of taxation of Pennsylvania—General symptoms that may serve to indicate the amount of the public charges in a given nation—Result of this investigation for the Union.*

Many attempts have recently been made in France to compare the public expenditure of that country with the expenditure of the United States. All these attempts have been fruitless, however, and a few words will suffice to show that they could not have a satisfactory result. In order to estimate the amount of the public charges of a people, two preliminaries are indispensable: it is necessary, in the first place, to know the wealth of that people; and, in the second, to learn what portion of that wealth is devoted to the expenditure of the state. To show the amount of taxation without showing the resources which are destined to meet it would be a futile task; for it is not the expenditure, but the relation of the expenditure to the revenue that it is desirable to know. The same rate of taxation which may easily be supported by a wealthy contributor will reduce a poor one to extreme

除了法律以外,所有这一切表现都深深地影响着各自国家的财政体系。如果美国人从来不会把人民的钱浪费在公共庆典上,这不仅是因为美国的税收在人民的控制之下,而是因为美国人民不喜欢场面宏大的庆典。如果美国人拒绝建筑物上的华丽装饰,除了有实用性的东西,它们并不重视虚有的外表,这不仅是因为他们生活在民主制度下,而是因为他们是一个商业民族。私人生活的习惯也被公共生活所认可;但是我们不应该把来自美国制度本身的节约,与来自人们的习惯和社会风气的节约混淆在一起。

是否可将美国的公共开支与法国的进行相比

要衡量公共开支的范围,必须确定两点:国家财产和税收比率——我们无法确切地了解到法国的财富和开支——为什么也不能准确地了解美国的财富和开支——作者在研究宾夕法尼亚州的税收总额方面所做的调查——可以表示一个国家的开支多少的总指标——对美国进行的这项调查的结果。

最近,人们试图对美国和法国的公共开支进行了大量的对比研究,但最终都以失败而告终,而且我认为用几句话就足以说明他们为什么会失败。为了能够清楚地了解一个国家的公共开支有多少,必须先做好两项预备工作:首先,必须知道这个国家的财富是多少;其次,必须知道它用于公共开支方面的财富又是多少。只调查税收的总额而不研究应当征税的源头,将会使这项工作变得毫无意义;因为我们想要知道的并不仅仅是开支,而且还有开支与收入之间的关系。一笔同样的税款,如果由一个富人缴纳,则是很容易的事,但如果由穷人去支

misery.

The wealth of nations is composed of several elements; real property is the first of these, and personal property the second. It is difficult to know precisely the amount of cultivable land in a country and its natural or acquired value; and it is still more difficult to estimate the whole personal property which is at the disposal of a nation, and which eludes the strictest analysis because of the diversity and the number of shapes under which it may occur. And, indeed, we find that the nations of Europe which have been the longest civilized, including even those in which the administration is most centralized, have not succeeded as yet in determining the exact amount of their wealth.

In America the attempt has never been made; for how would such an investigation be possible in a new country, where society has not yet settled into fixed and tranquil habits, where the national government is not assisted by a multitude of agents whose exertions it can command and direct to one end, and where statistics are not studied because no one is able to collect the necessary documents or find time to peruse them? Thus the primary elements of the calculations that have been made in France cannot be obtained in the Union; the relative wealth of the two countries is unknown: the property of the former is not yet accurately determined, and no means exist of computing that of the latter.

I consent therefore, for the moment, to abandon this necessary term of the comparison, and I confine myself to a computation of the actual amount of taxation, without investigating the ratio of the taxation to the revenue. But the reader will perceive that my task has not been facilitated by thus narrowing the circle of my researches.

It cannot be doubted that the central administration of France, assisted by all the public officers who are at its disposal, might determine precisely the amount of the direct and indirect taxes levied upon the citizens. But this investigation, which no private individual can undertake, has not hitherto been completed by the French government, or at least its results have not been made public. We are acquainted with the sum total of the charges of the state; we know the amount of the departmental expenditure; but the expenses of the

付,则可使这个穷人一无所有。

人民的财富由许多因素构成;其中最主要的是不动产,其次才是动产。我们很难精确地计算出一个国家的可耕地面积及其天然价值和可增值价值;但要是想计算出人民拥有的动产的价值,则会是件更困难的事。由于财产一般都有很多种,且数量相当巨大,所以即使你能计算出总数,你也根本无法进行正确的分析。因此,我们发现,在欧洲的一些文明悠久的国家,甚至在一些行政集权的国家,至今都未能精确地计算出它们的财富总额。

美国人就从来没有进行过这样的尝试;在这个新兴的国家,社会还没有完全稳定下来,全国政府还没有像我国政府这样,拥有大批量的可供随时调动的下属人员,统计资料由于没有人收集或没有时间进行研究而变得残缺不全,在这种情况下,我们又怎能计算出正确结果呢? 因此,我们在计算法国的财富时的重要因素是不适用于美国的;我们无法将法国的财富与美国的财富进行比较:没有精确计算出法国的财富,而更无法用这种计算得出美国的财富。

因此,在此时,我宁愿先放弃这种对比,先不去考察税收与税源的关系,而只想计算税收的实际金额。读者将会发现,虽然我的研究范围变小了,但我的任务并没有减轻。

我从来没有怀疑过,虽有大批官员在协助着法国的中央集权行政管理制度,也还是无法精确算出征收公民的直接税和间接税的总额。而且,这项由个人无法承担的工作,迄今为止,也没有被法国政府本身完成,或至少尚未对外公布其结果。现在,我们虽然对国家的支出总额以及各省的支出总额都有所了解,但还是不清楚乡镇的开支情况,所以还不能说我们已经知道了法国的

communes have not been computed, and the total of the public expenses of France is consequently unknown.

If we now turn to America, we perceive that the difficulties are multiplied and enhanced. The Union publishes an exact return of the amount of its expenditure; the budgets of the four-and-twenty states publish similar returns; but the expenses of the counties and the townships are unknown. [1]

The Federal authority cannot oblige the state governments to throw any light upon this point; and even if these governments were inclined to give their simultaneous aid, it may be doubted whether they are able to furnish a satisfactory answer. Independently of the natural difficulties of the task, the political organization of the country would hinder the success of their efforts. The country and town magistrates are not appointed by the authorities of the state and are not subjected to their control. It is therefore allowable to suppose that even if the state was desirous of obtaining the returns which we require, its design would be counteracted by the neglect of those

---

[1] The Americans, as we have seen, have four separate budgets: the Union, the states, the counties, and the townships having each its own. During my stay in America, I made every endeavor to discover the amount of the public expenditure in the townships and counties of the principal states of the Union; and I readily obtained the budget of the larger townships, but found it quite impossible to procure that of the smaller ones. Hence for these latter I have no exact figures. I possess, however, some documents relating to county expenses which, although incomplete, may still interest the reader. I have to thank Mr. Richards, former Mayor of Philadelphia, for the budgets of thirteen of the counties of Pennsylvania: viz., Lebanon, Centre, Franklin, Fayette, Montgomery, Luzerne, Dauphin, Butler, Allegheny, Columbia, Northampton, Northumberland, and Philadelphia, for the year 1830. Their population at the time consisted of 495,207 inhabitants. On looking at the map of Pennsylvania it will be seen that these thirteen counties are scattered in every direction, and so generally affected by the causes which usually influence the condition of a country that they may fairly be supposed to furnish a correct average of the financial state of the counties of Pennsylvahia in general. The expenses of these counties amounted in the year 1830 to about 1,800, 221, or nearly 3 fr. 64 cent for each inhabitant; and, calculating that each of them contributed in the same year about 12 fr. 70 cent. towards the Union, and about 3 fr. 80 cent. to the state of Pennsylvania, it appears that they each contributed, as their share of all the public expenses (except those of the townships), the sum of 20 fr. 14 cent. This calculation is doubly incomplete, as it applies only to a single year and to one part of the public expenditure; but it has at least the merit of being exact.

整个公共开支情况。

如果我们现在回过头来研究美国的公共收支,则会发现困难将变得更多和更大。美国的出版社使我知道了它的开支总额的确切数字;总共有 24 个州的预算;但是我无法知道美国公民向他们所在的县和乡镇提供了多少行政开支。[①]

联邦政府没有权力强迫各州政府为我提供研究这方面的资料;而且就算各州政府愿意尽全力帮助我,我也怀疑它们能否提供给我一个满意的答案。先抛开这项工作的自然困难,国家的政治结构也在阻碍着各州政府为成功所做的努力。各州的州长既不会对乡镇和县的行政委员进行任命,也不会对这些官员进行控制。由此可以断定,即使各州政府愿意全力协助我,为我提供研究所需的资料,也还是存在着很大的困难,本应当向州政府服务

---

① 像我们所看到的一样,美国有四个独立的预算:它们是联邦、州、县和乡镇。在我留美期间,我努力研究了美国花费在主要县和乡镇上的公共开支;并已经获得了一些较大乡镇的预算,但我发现对于一些小乡镇的预算则是很难得到的。因此,我并没有小乡镇的预算的精确数据。但是,我有一些关于县的公共开支的材料,尽管很不完整,但我确定仍能引起读者的兴趣。我要感谢费城的前任市长查德先生,他为我提供了在 1830 年宾夕法尼亚州的 13 个县的预算:其中有黎巴嫩、森特、富兰克林、菲耶特、蒙哥马利、卢参、道芬、巴特勒、阿勒格尼、哥伦比亚、北安普顿、诺森伯兰和宾夕法尼亚。到 1830 年,它们的人口数为 495207。纵观宾夕法尼亚州的地图,你会发现这 13 个县分布在四面八方,并且希望它们能完成一个正确的关于宾夕法尼亚州国家财政平均数,而且这个数字经常影响着各国的财政状况。在 1830 年这些县的花销达到 1800221 法郎,平均每人的消费量在 3 法郎 64 分;估计他们每人在同年贡献给联邦的将近 12 法郎 70 分,而贡献给宾夕法尼亚州的则为 3 法郎 80 分,表面上看来,他们贡献的总量达到 20 法郎 14 分,就如同他们一起分享所有公共开支一样(除了一些乡镇的)。这种计算结果肯定是不完整的,它只适用于在一年中对某一公共开支的部分预算;但他至少可以作为一种存在适应了某些人的要求。

subordinate officers whom it would be obliged to employ. ① It is in fact useless to inquire what the Americans might do to forward this inquiry, since it is certain that they have hitherto done nothing. There does not exist a single individual at the present day, in America or in Europe, who can inform us what each citizen of the Union annually contributes to the public charges of the nation. ②Hence we must conclude

---

① Those who have attempted to demonstrate a similarity between the expenses of France and America have at once perceived that no such comparison could be drawn between the total expenditures of the two countries; but they have endeavored to compare detached portions of this expenditure. It may readily be shown that this second system is not at all less defective than the first.

If I attempt to compare the French budget with the budget of the Union, it must be remembered that the latter embraces far fewer objects than the centralized government of the former country, and that the American expenditure must consequently be much smaller. If I contrast the budgets of our departments with those of the states that constitute the Union, it must be observed that as the states have the supervision of more numerous and important interests than the departments, their expenditure is naturally more considerable. As for the budgets of the counties, nothing of the kind occurs in the French system of finances; and it is doubtful whether the corresponding expenses in France should be referred to the budget of the state or to those of the municipal divisions.

Municipal expenses exist in both countries, but they are not always analogous. In America the townships discharge a variety of offices which are reservedin France to the departments or to the state. Moreover, it may be asked what is to be understood by the municipal expenses of America. The organization of the municipal bodies or townships differs in the several states. Are we to be guided by what occurs in New England or in Georgia, in Pennsylvania or in Illinois?

A kind of analogy may very readily be perceived between certain budgets in the two countries; but as the elements of which they are composed always differ more or less, no fair comparison can be drawn between them.

② Even if we knew the exact pecuniary contributions of every French and American citizen to the coffers of the state, we should only arrive at a portion of the truth. Governments not only demand supplies of money, but call for personal services, which may be looked upon as equivalent to a given sum. When a state raises an army, besides the pay of the troops, which is furnished by the entire nation, each soldier must give up his time, the value of which depends on the use he might make of it if he were not in the service. The same remark applies to the militia; the citizen who is in the militia devotes a certain portion of valuable time to the maintenance of the public security, and in reality surrenders to the state those earnings that he is prevented from gaining. Many other instances might be cited. The governments of France and America both levy taxes of this kind, which weigh upon the citizens; but who can estimate with accuracy their relative amount in the two countries?

This, however, is not the last of the difficulties which prevent us from comparing the expenditure of the Union with that of France. The French government contracts certain obligations which are not assumed by the state in America, and vice versa. The French government pays the clergy; in America the voluntary principle prevails. In America the state provides for the poor; in France they are

的下级官员可能敷衍了事。① 事实上,想从美国人口中寻求答案
是无用的,因为,迄今为止,美国人什么也没做。今天,无论是在
美国还是在法国,都不会有人能确切的告诉我们联邦的每一位公
民每年为国家贡献的公共开支是多少。② 总之,比较美国和法国

---

① 那些试图证明法国与美国开支的相似处的人,会立刻发现这两个国
家的公共开支并没有任何可比性;但他们曾试图努力比较这种开支。并且
可以证明,第一种制度比第二种制度的缺陷更大。

如果我试图比较法国的预算和美国的预算,我应清楚地记得美国比法
国的中央集权政府拥有更少的目标,因此美国的公共开支必定少于法国。
如果我又试图对比美国州的预算和我们法国各部门的预算,又会发现美国
的州拥有比法国的部门更多和更重要的利益,它们的公共开支自然比法国
大。而法国的财政系统里永远也不会有像美国各个县的那种预算;并且我
怀疑法国的相一致的开支是否与美国各州的开支或市政的开支有关?

法国和美国都存在市政开支,但两国的开支并不总是相似的。在美国,
乡镇会分出各个职能的办公室,而法国则将其职能保留给部门或国家。也
许有人会问,应该怎样理解美国的市政开支? 在一些国家,市政组织与乡镇
组织存在着很大的差别。我们是否能以在新英格兰或佐治亚州,在宾夕法
尼亚州或伊利诺伊州所发生的作为依据呢?

在这两个国家之间,我们会观察到对一些特定预算的分析;但是构成这
种分析的因素或多或少会存在着差异,因此我们永远无法得到一个公平的
对比。

② 即使我们能准确地知道每个法国公民和美国公民在金钱上为国家
的贡献是多少,我们也只能获得真相的一部分。政府不仅需要金钱,同样也
需要被看作和金钱处于同等地位的能为政府服务的官员。当一个国家准备
作战时,除了需要整个国家供养的军队以外,每个士兵必须放弃自己的时
间,以及如果他在不服军役时可能在这些时间里创造的价值。同样的情况
也适用于民兵;为了维持社会的公共安全,参与民兵组织的公民必定会牺牲
自己的宝贵时间。以及在实际中为了国家自己被迫所放弃的那部分收入还
有许多可以用来引证例子。法国政府与美国政府用同样的方式向公民征
税;但是在这两个国家里又有谁能估算出一个准确的金额呢?

当然,这并不是阻碍我们比较美国公共开支和法国公共开支的最后一个困
难。法国政府规定了很多义务,而美国政府则没有。法国政府为神职人员付薪
俸;而美国则盛行神职人员为自愿的原则。美国政府会救济穷人;而法国则把这类

that it is no less difficult to compare the social expenditure than it is to estimate the relative wealth of France and America. I will even add that it would be dangerous to attempt this comparison; for when statistics are not based upon computations that are strictly accurate, they mislead instead of guiding aright. The mind is easily imposed upon by the affectation of exactitude which marks even the misstatements of statistics; and it adopts with confidence the errors which are appareled in the forms of mathematical truth.

We abandon, therefore, the numerical investigation, with the hope of meeting with data of another kind. In the absence of posi tive documents, we may form an opinion as to the proportion that the taxation of a people bears to its real wealth, by observing whether its external appearance is flourishing; whether, after having paid the dues of the state, the poor man retains the means of subsistence, and the rich the means of enjoyment; and whether both classes seem contented with their position, seeking, however, to ameliorate it by perpetual exertions, so that industry is never in want of capital, nor capital unemployed by industry. The observer who draws his inferences from these signs will undoubtedly be led to the conclusion that the American of the United States contributes a much smaller portion of his income to the state than the citizen of France. Nor, indeed, can the result be otherwise.

A portion of the French debt is the consequence of two invasions; and the Union has no similar calamity to fear. The position of France obliges it to maintain a large standing army; the isolation of the Union enables it to have only six thousand soldiers. The French

---

abandoned to the charity of the public. All French public officers are paid a fixed salary; in America they are allowed certain perquisites. In France contributions in labor take place on very few roads, in America upon almost all the thoroughfares: in the former country the roads are free to all travelers; in the latter toll roads abound. All these differences in the manner in which taxes are levied in the two countries enhance the difficulty of comparing their expenditure; for there are certain expenses which the citizens would not be subject to, or which would at any rate be less considerable, if the state did not undertake to act in their name.

的社会开支是很难有结果的,而比较两国的财富也是如此。我再补充一句,试图这样做也同样存在着危险;当统计资料不是以真实可信的计算为基础时,不但不能协助我们的工作,反而会把你引向一条弯路。人们的头脑容易被表面上正确而实际上却不准确的事物所迷惑;对在数学真理掩盖下的错误深信不疑。

因此,让我们放弃对数字的调查而设法找其他可靠的证明吧。在缺乏真实可靠的资料的情况下,我们要想彻底的知道是否人民的公共开支负担与他们的财富成比例,那就只能通过观察这个国家是否拥有繁荣的物质生活;观察人民在向国家缴纳税款之后穷人是否还能勉强度日,富人是否拥有更多所得财产;双方是否满意于自己的命运,双方是否每天又在继续改善自己的生活,因此资本是否没有合适的投资场所,而需要投资的产业是否又缺少资本。通过这些作为观察基础的人,无疑会断定美国人民交给国家的那部分收入远远低于法国人民交给国家的那一部分。但是,用什么方式才能断定这两者之间存在的差别呢?

法国的一部分债务,是因为它曾受到过两次侵略;而美国不必为类似的灾难担忧。法国的地理位置,使它不得不维持一支庞大的军队;而美国被隔离于大西洋彼岸的地理优势,使它只拥

事情扔给公共慈善事业。所有的法国公共官员拥有固定的薪水;而美国则给公共官员进行一定的额外补贴。在法国,无偿劳动者们只愿意对很少的公路进行修复,而在美国,几乎对所有大道的修复都有劳动者的贡献:法国的公路向所有旅行者开放;美国的公路则向旅行者收取通行费。所有这些关于两国税则方面的不同将加大我们对它们公共开支的对比;因为对于一部分开支,如果连国家都不愿以自己的名义来承担,那么公民也不会去承受,或者说这部分开支的数目是非常小的。

have a fleet of three hundred sail; the Americans have only fifty-two vessels. ①How, then, can the inhabitant of the Union be taxed as heavily as the inhabitant of France? No parallel can be drawn between the finances of two countries so differently situated.

It is by examining what actually takes place in the Union, and not by comparing the Union with France, that we can judge whether the American government is really economical. On casting my eyes over the different republics which form the confederation, I perceive that their governments often lack perseverance in their undertakings, and that they exercise no steady control over the men whom they employ. I naturally infer that they must often spend the money of the people to no purpose, or consume more of it than is really necessary for their enterprises. Faithful to its popular origin, the government makes great efforts to satisfy the wants of the lower classes, to open to them the road to power, and to diffuse knowledge and comfort among them. The poor are maintained, immense sums are annually devoted to public instruction, all services are remunerated, and the humblest agents are liberally paid. This kind of government appears to be useful and rational, but I am bound to admit that it is expensive.

Wherever the poor direct public affairs and dispose of the national resources, it appears certain that, as they profit by the expenditure of the state, they will often augment that expenditure. I conclude, therefore, without having recourse to inaccurate statistics, and without hazarding a comparison which might prove incorrect, that the democratic government of the Americans is not a cheap government, as is sometimes asserted; and I do not fear to predict that, if the United States is ever involved in serious difficulties, taxation will speedily be raised as high there as in most of the aristocracies or the monarchies of Europe.

---

① See the budget of the Ministry of Marine for France and, for America, the *National Calendar* (1833), p. 228.

有 6000 名士兵就可以了。法国有 300 艘军舰;而美国只有 52 艘。① 因此,怎么能说美国居民的负担比法国居民的还要多呢? 由此可见,对存在着如此差异的两国的财政进行对比是不正确的。

我们对美国政府是否是真正节俭的政府所做出的判断,是通过对美国的实际情况的考察,而并非出自对美国同法国的对比。在对联邦的各个州进行考察后,我发现各州政府在其事业中常常缺乏首尾连贯性,对雇佣的人员也不进行固定的检查。因此,我自然得出一个结论:认为它们必然要经常漫无目的的浪费人民的金钱,或在一些事业上花费了本不需要的金钱。可是我看到,对选民忠诚的政府,却在以极大的努力去满足社会下层阶级的需要,将权力之门大大地向他们打开,并把幸福和知识带给他们。穷人在它的帮助下维持生活,它每年还会拨付巨款创办学校,它的每项服务都是有报酬的,使小人物也能得到良好的待遇。这样的治国方式听起来是合乎情理的,但我又不得不承认它的成本是昂贵的。

每当穷人在管理公共事务和掌握国家的财源时,可以肯定的是这里的国家支出是对穷人有利的,所以国家从不吝啬增加新的开支。因此,我不去以那些不完整的统计数字为基础,也不想再进行任何没有意义的对比,便敢肯定地说,美国人的民主政府绝不是像人们有时想象的那样是一个极其吝啬的政府;我也敢说,一旦当美国人民遇到严重的灾难,美国的税收也将会与大多数欧洲贵族国家或君主国家的税收一样高。

----

① 见 1833 年《国家年历》,第 228 页,对法国和美国海军部门的预算。

Corruption And The Vices Of The Rulers In a Democracy, And Consequent Effects Upon Public Morality

In aristocracies, rulers sometimes endeavor to corrupt the people—In democracies, rulers frequently show themselves to be corrupt—In the former, their vices are directly prejudicial to the morality of the people—In the latter, their indirect influence is still more pernicious.

A distinction must be made when aristocracies and democracies accuse each other of facilitating corruption. In aristocratic governments, those who are placed at the head of affairs are rich men, who are desirous only of power. In democracies, statesmen are poor and have their fortunes to make. The consequence is that in aristocratic states the rulers are rarely accessible to corruption and have little craving for money, while the reverse is the case in democratic nations.

But in aristocracies, as those who wish to attain the head of affairs possess considerable wealth, and as the number of persons by whose assistance they may rise is comparatively small, the government is, if I may so speak, put up at auction. In democracies, on the contrary, those who are covetous of power are seldom wealthy, and the number of those who confer power is extremely great. Perhaps in democracies the number of men who might be bought is not smaller, but buyers are rarely to be found; and, besides, it would be necessary to buy so many persons at once that the attempt would be useless.

Many of the men who have governed France during the last forty years have been accused of making their fortunes at the expense of the state or its allies, a reproach which was rarely addressed to the public men of the old monarchy. But in France the practice of bribing electors is almost unknown, while it is notoriously and publicly carried on in England. In the United States I never heard anyone accused of spending his wealth in buying votes, but I have often heard the probity of public officers questioned; still more frequently have I heard their success attributed to low intrigues and immoral practices.

民主国家统治者的贪污腐化
及其对公共道德的影响

在贵族政体下,统治者有时会试图腐化人民——在民主政体下,统治者经常自己被腐化——前者的腐化行为对人民道德产生直接的影响——后者虽然对人民道德产生了间接的影响,但其危害却更大。

贵族政体和民主政体互相指责对方容易贪污腐化。对此问题要进行分析。在贵族政府,都是由富人来担任政务工作人员,他们只看重权势。在民主政府,国家工作人员都由穷人担当,而他们只关心自己的前途。结果,在贵族国家,统治者很少贪污,因为他们对金钱没有太多的奢求;而在民主国家,情况与此相反。

但在贵族制度下,那些想当统治者的人都拥有很多金钱,而能够当上统治者的人,又因为有限的职位而人数很少,所以可以说政府是等待拍卖的政府。相反的,在民主制度下,那些贪心于权势的人很少拥有财富,而竞争当权的人又为数甚多。或许在民主制度下,卖主可能很多,但几乎找不到买主;而且,必须一次就收买很多人才能达到目的,否则,一切尝试都是无用的。

四十年来独揽法国大权的人,有许多被指控曾经为了发财而出卖了本国和盟国的利益,而在旧君主体制下的官员却很少受到这样的指控。但在法国,几乎没有贿赂选举者的事件,而在英国,这种事情则是屡见不鲜的。我在美国从未听说有人用钱去买选票,但我总是质疑于公务人员的廉政性;甚至我还常常听到有人说他们是凭借阴谋手段和对人民不利的手段取得成功的。

If, then, the men who conduct an aristocracy sometimes endeavor to corrupt the people, the heads of a democracy are themselves corrupt. In the former case the morality of the people is directly assailed; in the latter an indirect influence is exercised which is still more to be dreaded.

As the rulers of democratic nations are almost always suspected of dishonorable conduct, they in some measure lend the authority of the government to the base practices of which they are accused. They thus afford dangerous examples, which discourage the struggles of virtuous independence and cloak with authority the secret designs of wickedness. If it be asserted that evil passions are found in all ranks of society, that they ascend the throne by hereditary right, and that we may find despicable characters at the head of aristocratic nations as well as in the bosom of a democracy, the plea has but little weight in my estimation. The corruption of men who have casually risen to power has a coarse and vulgar infection in it that renders it dangerous to the multitude. On the contrary, there is a kind of aristocratic refinement and an air of grandeur in the depravity of the great, which frequently prevent it from spreading abroad.

The people can never penetrate into the dark labyrinth of court intrigue, and will always have difficulty in detecting the turpitude that lurks under elegant manners, refined tastes, and graceful language. But to pillage the public purse and to sell the favors of the state are arts that the meanest villain can understand and hope to practice in his turn.

Besides, what is to be feared is not so much the immorality of the great as the fact that immorality may lead to greatness. In a democracy private citizens see a man of their own rank in life who rises from that obscure position in a few years to riches and power; the spectacle excites their surprise and their envy, and they are led to inquire how the person who was yesterday their equal is today their ruler. To attribute his rise to his talents or his virtues is unpleasant, for it is tacitly to acknowledge that they are themselves less virtuous or less talented than he was. They are therefore led, and often rightly,

因此,如果说贵族政体的统治者们偶尔试图腐化人民,那么民主政府的首脑则腐化自己。在前一种情况下,人民的道德会直接受到学坏的官员的打击;在后一种情况下,变坏的官员在人民的思想意识方面产生的影响将更为可怕。

民主国家的统治者们几乎总要受到各种各样使他感到痛苦的怀疑,所以他会利用某种办法借助政府的权威来保护他被指控的罪行。这样,他就为在同恶势力进行斗争的友善行为提供了危险的榜样,使恶被掩盖在光荣的外衣下。也许有人会说,邪恶的感情存在于社会的各个阶层,王位往往是依靠与生俱来的权力而获得的,比如在贵族国家的统治者中和民主国家的领导者中,我们都会发现非常卑鄙的人物。但是,这种解释也是毫无用处的。这种答辩不会让我觉得满意,因为在偶然取得权利的人物中,有一种俗不可耐的东西将这些人的腐败行为传染给人民大众。而在一些有钱人的堕落的生活中,反而有某种气质不会使他们的堕落生活被公开,这种气质就是贵族的文雅风度和高大气派。

人民永远无法理解宫廷内部斗争的秘密,而且往往很难揭露出掩盖在高雅的行为、崇高的情趣和虚伪的言词下的邪恶行为。但是,掠夺人民的财产或出卖国家利益的行为,就是最微不足道的小人物也能看得出来,而且他们自己也很想加入这一勾当。

另外,值得害怕的倒不是大人物的不道德,而是不道德成就了大人物。在民主制度下,一些普通公民看到与他们同水平中的一个人在没几年的时间里,就从不知名的小辈爬到有钱有势的地位后,必定会产生惊讶与嫉妒的心情,并奇怪为什么在昨天还与自己地位一样的人而今天就成了自己的统治者了。要把这个人的晋升归因于他的才能或道德,是让人感到不痛快的,因为这等于承认自己的能

to impute his success mainly to some of his vices; and an odious connection is thus formed between the ideas of turpitude and power, unworthiness and success, utility and dishonor.

Efforts Of Which A Democracy Is Capable

The Union has only had one struggle hitherto for its existence—Enthusiasm at the commencement of the war—Indifference towards its close—Difficulty of establishing military conscription or impressment of seamen in America—Why a democratic people is less capable than any other of sustained effort.

I warn the reader that I here speak of a government that follows the real will of the people, and not of a government that simply commands in their name. Nothing is so irresistible as a tyrannical power commanding in the name of the people, because, while wielding the moral power which belongs to the will of the greater number, it acts at the same time with the quickness and persistence of a single man.

It is difficult to say what degree of effort a democratic government may be capable of making on the occurrence of a national crisis. No great democratic republic has hitherto existed in the world. To style the oligarchy which ruled over France in 1793 by that name would be an insult to the republican form of government. The United States affords the first example of the kind.

The American Union has now subsisted for half a century, and its existence has only once been attacked; namely, during the War of Independence. At the commencement of that long war, extraordinary efforts were made with enthusiasm for the service of the country.①But as the contest was prolonged, private selfishness began to reappear. No money was brought

---

① One of the most singular, in my opinion, was the resolution that the Americans took of temporarily abandoning the use of tea. Those who know that men usually cling more to their habits than to their life will doubtless admire this great though obscure sacrifice, which was made by a whole people.

力不如别人。因此,他们便把这个人的成功归结到他的缺点当中;并且经常认为这样做是对的。结果,在卑鄙和权势之间,在低微和成功之间,在羞耻和实惠之间,便出现了概念混乱的可悲局面。

民主可能做出的努力

迄今为止,联邦只为自己的生存做过一次斗争——战争开始时的热情——战争即将结束时热情的减退——在美国建立征兵制和海员强迫服役制的困难——为什么民主国家不如任何其他国家那样可以做出不懈地努力。

我要唤起读者的注意,我在这里讲的政府是以人民的真正意愿为己任的政府,而不是仅在人民的名义下发号施令的政府。没有比以人民的名义发号施令的政府更让人难以抗拒的了,因为它可以在凭借多数的意志所形成的道德权力的同时迅速地并坚定地去实现独夫的意志。

我们很难判断一个民主政府在国家发生危机时所做的努力究竟有多大。迄今为止,还没有一个伟大的民主共和国存在过。把曾经在 1793 年统治过法国的民主共和国称为寡头政治,是对共和政体的一种侮辱。美国的共和政体就是一个典型的事例。

联邦政府至今已经存在了半个世纪,但它的生存只受到过一次威胁;那就是在独立战争时期。在这场长期战争开始时,人们曾以极度的热情为祖国卖命。① 但是,随着战争的日益持久,以往的自

---

① 在我看来,一个最显著的特征就是美国人决定暂时放弃喝茶。那些注重于自己的习惯胜过自己的生活的人,对全国人民的这种牺牲佩服得五体投地。

into the public treasury; few recruits could be raised for the army; the people still wished to acquire independence, but would not employ the only means by which it could be obtained. "Tax laws," says Hamilton, in *The Federalist* (No. 12), "have in vain been multiplied; new methods to enforce the collection have in vain been tried; the public expectation has been uniformly disappointed; and the treasuries of the States have remained empty. The popular system of administration inherent in the nature of popular government, coinciding with the real scarcity of money incident to a languid and mutilated state of trade, has hitherto defeated every experiment for extensive collections, and has at length taught the different legislatures the folly of attempting them."

Since that period the United States has not had a single serious war to carry on. In order, therefore, to know what sacrifices democratic nations may impose upon themselves, we must wait until the American people are obliged to put half their entire income at the disposal of the government, as was done by the English; or to send forth a twentieth part of its population to the field of battle, as was done by France. In America conscription is unknown and men are induced to enlist by bounties. The notions and habits of the people of the United States are so opposed to compulsory recruiting that I do not think it can ever be sanctioned by the laws. What is termed conscription in France is assuredly the heaviest tax upon the people; yet how could a great Continental war be carried on without it? The Americans have not adopted the British practice of impressing seamen, and they have nothing that corresponds to the French system of maritime conscription; the navy as well as the merchant service is supplied by volunteers. But it is not easy to conceive how a people can sustain a great maritime war without having recourse to one or the other of these two systems. Indeed, the Union, which has already fought with honor upon the seas, has never had a numerous fleet, and the equipment of its few vessels has always been very expensive.

私自利心理又重新出现。人们不再向国库交款;不去应征军队;人民仍想渴望拥有独立,但在争取独立的手段面前却停下了脚步。汉密尔顿在《联邦党人文集》(第12篇)中写道:"我们突然增加了许多赋税,我们又突然试行了一些新的征税办法。人民大众的希望已经全部变成失望,国库也已经亏空。我们的民主政府的性质所固有的民主行政制度,面临着通货短缺的困境,而这种局面又导致贸易陷入前所未有的不景气中。迄今为止,民主行政当局虽然一次次的试图努力扩大税收,但仍然是徒劳无益,以至于使各州的立法机构也终于认识到这种做法的愚蠢性。"

从此以后,美国再没有遇到过一次需要斗争到底的严重灾难。因此,要想知道民主制度能够忍受的牺牲是些什么,必须等到美国人民也像英国人民那样不得不把收入的一半交给政府处理的时候,或者等到也像法国人民那样必须把全国人口的二十分之一送去征兵的时候。在美国,征兵制向来得不到人民的认可,想让我去参军就得付给我报酬。美国人民的思想和习惯严重反对强制征兵的办法,以至于使我不敢相信有人可以把征兵制写进法律里去。法国意义上的征兵制,无疑就像一把沉重的枷锁,无情地压在人民身上;但是,如果没有征兵制,我们国家又怎么能完成一场陆地大战呢? 美国人对英国的那种强制海员服役的办法也不承认,他们也没有法国那样的海军征兵制;美国的海军同商船的海员一样,都是采取自愿的原则。但是,很难想象如果不是依靠上述两种办法之一,一个国家还能够支持一场大型海战。因此,曾在海上进行过光荣战斗的联邦共和国,就不曾拥有过一支庞大的舰队,可是它装备里为数不多的几只舰艇,也是极其昂贵的。

I have heard American statesmen confess that the Union will with difficulty maintain its power on the seas without adopting the system of impressment or maritime conscription; but the difficulty is to induce the people, who exercise the supreme authority, to submit to such measures.

It is incontestable that, in times of danger, a free people display far more energy than any other. But I incline to believe that this is especially true of those free nations in which the aristocratic element preponderates. Democracy appears to me better adapted for the conduct of society in times of peace, or for a sudden effort of remarkable vigor, than for the prolonged endurance of the great storms that beset the political existence of nations. The reason is very evident; enthusiasm prompts men to expose themselves to dangers and privations; but without reflection they will not support them long. There is more calculation even in the impulses of bravery than is generally supposed; and although the first efforts are made by passion alone, perseverance is maintained only by a distinct view of what one is fighting for. A portion of what is dear to us is hazarded in order to save the remainder.

But it is this clear perception of the future, founded upon judgment and experience, that is frequently wanting in democracies. The people are more apt to feel than to reason; and if their present sufferings are great, it is to be feared that the still greater sufferings attendant upon defeat will be forgotten.

Another cause tends to render the efforts of a democratic government less persevering than those of an aristocracy. Not only are the lower less awake than the higher orders to the good or evil chances of the future, but they suffer more acutely from present privations. The noble exposes his life, indeed, but the chance of glory is equal to the chance of harm. If he sacrifices a large portion of his income to the state, he deprives himself for a time of some of the pleasures of affluence; but to the poor man death has no glory, and the imposts that are merely irksome to the rich often deprive him of the necessaries of life.

This relative weakness of democratic republics in critical times is

我曾听到美国的国务活动家们承认,如果美国不采用海员强制服役制或海军征兵制,将很难维持它在海上的地位;但是要是对行使国家主权的人民采用这种制度无疑是困难的。

无需证明,自由国家在危机时期一般能比非自由国家发挥出更多的能量。但我更相信,这种情况在贵族成分占优势的自由国家更为真实。在我看来,民主制度更适用于在和平时期治理社会,或在必要时用它作为鼓舞人心的强烈的力量,要比用它去长期抵制威胁国家政治生活的大灾难更为合适。这个理由很明显:热情虽能促使人们克服艰险和贫困;但如果不加以深思熟虑,人们难以长期顶住艰险。所谓天生的不畏艰险,也比在毫无思考下的行动更有成效;虽然最初的努力只靠激情就能达到,但最终结果的成功与否全凭是否能坚持最初的热情。人们用一部分珍贵的东西去冒险,是为了拯救其余的部分。

但是,民主所经常缺乏的,正是这种建立在判断和经验的基础上,对未来所做的一个清楚的判别。人们更多的是相信感情,而不是相信理智;眼前虽然有很大的苦难,但更可怕的是,不去考虑因为无法忍受苦难而带来的更大苦难。

使民主政府的努力不如贵族政府的持久的另外一个原因。不仅是因为人民不如高层阶级那样能够看清未来的旦夕祸福,而且还要比高层阶级更多地忍受目前的灾祸。贵族的生命被危险重重包围,但他们赢得名誉与遭受痛苦的机会是相等的。当贵族将其大部分收入交由国家支配时,他们所失去的对某些富裕的享受也只是暂时的;但是,对穷人来说,死并不代表什么光荣,而连富人都极其厌烦的赋税负担,却经常使他们的生活来源受到威胁。

民主共和国在危机时期所表现出来的这种相对弱点,也许是

perhaps the greatest obstacle to the foundation of such a republic in Europe. In order that one such state should exist in the European world, it would be necessary that similar institutions should be simultaneously introduced into all the other nations.

I am of opinion that a democratic government tends, in the long run, to increase the real strength of society; but it can never combine, upon a single point and at a given time, so much power as an aristocracy or an absolute monarchy. If a democratic country remained during a whole century subject to a republican government, it would probably at the end of that period be richer, more populous, and more prosperous than the neighboring despotic states. But during that century it would often have incurred the risk of being conquered by them.

Self-Control Of The American Democracy

The American people acquiesce slowly, and sometimes do not acquiesce, in what is beneficial to their interests—The faults of the American democracy are, for the most part, reparable.

The difficulty that a democracy finds in conquering the passions and subduing the desires of the moment with a view to the future is observable in the United States in the most trivial things. The people, surrounded by flatterers, find great difficulty in surmounting their inclinations; whenever they are required to undergo a privation or any inconvenience, even to attain an end sanctioned by their own rational conviction, they almost always refuse at first to comply. The deference of the Americans to the laws has been justly applauded; but it must be added that in America legislation is made by the people and for the people. Consequently, in the United States the law favors those classes that elsewhere are most interested in evading it. It may therefore be supposed that an offensive law of which the majority should not see the immediate utility would either not be enacted or not be obeyed.

In America there is no law against fraudulent bankruptcies, not because they are few, but because they are many. The dread of being prosecuted as a bankrupt is greater in the minds of the majority than the fear of being ruined by the bankruptcy of others; and a sort of

阻止在欧洲建立这样的共和国的最大障碍。要使民主共和国能轻易地在欧洲的一个国家生存下去，就必须同时在其他所有国家建立这种制度。

我相信，随着时间地流逝，民主政府一定能增加社会的实力；但它不能像贵族政府或专制君主国那样立即把力量集中到某一点上和某一个时刻上。如果由共和政府对一个民主国家管理了一个世纪，那么在这个世纪即将结束的时候，我相信它一定会比相邻的专制国家更加富有，更加兴旺，更加繁荣富强。但在这一个世纪内，它也会多次受到这些专制国家入侵的威胁。

美国民主的自制能力

美国人民需要用很长的时间才能对有利于他们幸福生活的东西加以认可，有时还曾拒绝这些东西——美国人能够补救他们的失误。

为了未来的利益，而使民主克服激情并压制欲望的困难，会很明显的在美国的一些小事情上被表现出来。喜欢被别人奉承的人，自我克制力很差；每当有人请求他们解决困难或寻求支援时，即使他们自己很理性的相信这种做法是合理的，但在最初他们也几乎总是加以拒绝。美国人对法律的遵从，赢得了人们公正的赞许；但必须补充一句，美国的法律是由人民制造并服从于人民的。因此，美国的法律是有利于那些处处都想躲避法律的人。由此可以认为，一项在大多数人看来对自己没有实际利用价值的令人讨厌的法律，不是很难被通过，就是通过以后也没人会服从。

在美国，没有惩治欺诈破产行为的法律，这并不是因为美国没有破产者，而是因为破产者太多了。大多数人害怕被指控为破

guilty tolerance is extended by the public conscience to an offense which everyone condemns in his individual capacity. In the new states of the Southwest the citizens generally take justice into their own hands, and murders are of frequent occurrence. This arises from the rude manners and the ignorance of the inhabitants of those deserts, who do not perceive the utility of strengthening the law, and who prefer duels to prosecutions. Someone observed to me one day in Philadelphia that almost all crimes in America are caused by the abuse of intoxicating liquors, which the lower classes can procure in great abundance because of their cheapness. "How comes it," said I, "that you do not put a duty upon brandy?" "Our legislators," rejoined my informant, "have frequently thought of this expedient; but the task is difficult: a revolt might be anticipated; and the members who should vote for such a law would be sure of losing their seats." "Whence I am to infer," replied I, "that drunkards are the majority in your country, and that temperance is unpopular."

When these things are pointed out to the American statesmen, they answer: "Leave it to time, and experience of the evil will teach the people their true interests." This is frequently true: though a democracy is more liable to error than a monarch or a body of nobles, the chances of its regaining the right path when once it has acknowledged its mistake are greater also; because it is rarely embarrassed by interests that conflict with those of the majority and resist the authority of reason. But a democracy can obtain truth only as the result of experience; and many nations may perish while they are awaiting the consequences of their errors. The great privilege of the Americans does not consist in being more enlightened than other nations, but in being able to repair the faults they may commit.

It must be added that a democracy cannot profit by past experience unless it has arrived at a certain pitch of knowledge and civilization. There are nations whose first education has been so vicious and whose character presents so strange a mixture of passion, ignorance, and erroneous notions upon all subjects that they are unable to discern the causes of their own wretchedness, and they fall a sacrifice to ills of which they are ignorant.

产者,多于害怕因他人破产而使自己受牵连;而且对于私人告发的犯罪,大众总是持有一种宽容态度,而这种态度往往是错误的。在新成立的西南各州,公民几乎将司法权全都掌握在自己手里,谋杀案件不断发生。这种现象产生的原因,是居住在那片荒漠上的居民的粗野的作风和思想的无知,他们并没有意识到诉讼法律的重要性,而是喜欢彼此进行斗争。有一天,在费城有人对我说,美国的几乎所有犯罪全是由酗酒造成的,下层人民可以开怀畅饮,因为酒很便宜。我问他:"你们为什么不对酒征税呢?"他回答说:"我们的立法者倒是常想这样做;但是恐怕很难做到;因为人民会极力反对;而且投票赞成这项法律的议员,肯定没有再次当选的机会了。"我接着说:"这样看来,嗜酒者在你们国家是多数,而禁酒在你们国家就不得人心了。"

当你向美国的国务活动家提到这个问题时,他们只会这样回答:"让时间去冲淡一切吧;痛苦的经历迟早会让人民清醒,让他们彻底明白什么才是真正的需要。"事实往往就是这样:民主制度虽然比一个君主或一群贵族更容易犯错误,但它一旦察觉到错误,回头改正的机会也多;因为民主制度本身一般不会与大多数人对抗,并抵制理性的利益。但是,只有通过实践才能使民主制度达到真知;而且可能有许多国家在还没有来得及看到失误的恶果后就已经灭亡了。因此,美国人的巨大优越性,不仅体现在他们比其他民族明智,而且还体现在他们犯了错误之后能够立即改正。

我还要补充一点:除非民主制度已经达到一定的文明和教育水平,否则它就不能从过去的经验吸取教训。有些国家的初等教育水平很落后,人民的性格混杂着对激情、无知和对一切事物的错误认识,以致它们自己都找不到错误的根源,为自己的无知作出牺牲。

I have crossed vast tracts of country formerly inhabited by powerful Indian nations who are now extinct; I have passed some time a-
mong remnants of tribes, which witness the daily decline of their
numbers and of the glory of their independence; and I have heard
these Indians themselves anticipate the impending doom of their race.
Every European can perceive means that would rescue these unfortunate beings from the destruction otherwise inevitable. They alone are
insensible to the remedy; they feel the woes which year after year
heaps upon their heads, but they will perish to a man without accepting the cure. Force would have to be employed to compel them to
live.

The incessant revolutions that have convulsed the South American states for the last quarter of a century are regarded with astonishment, and we are constantly hoping that before long, they will return
to what is called their *natural state*. But who can affirm that revolutions are not, at the present time, the most natural state of the South
American Spaniards? In that country society is struggling in the depths
of an abyss whence its own efforts are insufficient to rescue it. The inhabitants of that fair portion of the Western hemisphere seem obstinately bent on the work of destroying one another. If they fall into momentary quiet, from exhaustion, that repose soon prepares them for a
new frenzy. When I consider their condition, alternating between misery and crime, I am tempted to believe that despotism itself would be
a blessing to them, if it were possible that the words "despotism" and
"blessing" could ever be united ;in my mind.

Conduct Of Foreign Affairs By The American Democracy

*Direction given to the foreign policy of the United States by Wash-
ington and Jefferson—Almost all the defects inherent in democratic institutions are brought to light in the conduct of foreign affairs; their advantages are less perceptible.*

We have seen that the Federal Constitution entrusts the permanent

我曾路过了几处曾经是强大的印第安人的家乡,而现已不见他们踪影的地方;并在这里住过几日,这已经完全没有了昔日的众多的人口和光辉的形象,只有少数的印第安部落在勉强度日;我还听到这些印第安人预测他们自己的种族即将消失。每个欧洲人都认为应当设法保护这些不幸的人,使他们免于灭亡。但是,他们自己又完全不知道该怎么补救;他们感到灾难年复一年地加在他们的头上,直到毁灭到只剩下一个人,他们也不肯接受救助。而只有采取强制办法,才能让他们生存下去。

人们被南美的一些新兴国家在 25 年来一直处于革命的战火之中而震惊。我们每天都在等待,希望这些国家能早日回到所谓的自然状态。但是,谁又敢说目前的革命不是南美西班牙人的最自然状态呢? 在这一地区,社会正挣扎在一个深渊的底部,而社会却无法通过自身的努力而摆脱这个束缚。住在占西半球二分之一的美丽土地上的这些人民,好像一直都把心思放在怎样歼灭对方上,毫无悔改的迹象。疲惫了,他们放下战刀休息片刻;但没过多久,他们又陷入再次的拼杀。当我看到他们不是在受苦受辗转于灾难和犯罪之间时,我不得不相信专制对他们或许还是一种恩惠。但是,专制和恩惠这两个词却无法在我的思想中统一起来。

美国民主在国家对外事务上的处理方法

华盛顿和杰斐逊对美国对外政策的指导——民主制度的固有缺陷在指导对外事务时几乎全部表现出来;而其进步性则很少能被人察觉。

我们可以看到,联邦宪法把经常指导对外事务的责任交给了

direction of the external interests of the nation to the President and the Senate,① which tends in some degree to detach the general foreign policy of the Union from the direct control of the people. It cannot, therefore, be asserted with truth that the foreign affairs of the state are conducted by the democracy.

There are two men who have imparted to American foreign policy a tendency that is still being followed today; the first is Washington and the second Jefferson. Washington said, in the admirable Farewell Address which he made to his fellow citizens, and which may be regarded as his political testament: "The great rule of conduct for us in regard to foreign nations is, in extending our commercial relations, to have with them as little *political* connection as possible. So far as we have already formed engagements, let them be fulfilled with perfect good faith. Here let us stop." "Europe has a set of primary interests, which to us have none, or a very remote relation. Hence she must be engaged in frequent controversies, the causes of which are essentially foreign to our concerns. Hence, therefore, it must be unwise in us to implicate ourselves, by artificial ties, in the ordinary vicissitudes of her politics, or the ordinary combinations and collisions of her friendships or enmities."

"Our detached and distant situation invites and enables us to pursue a different course. If we remain one people, under an efficient government, the period is not far off when we may defy material injury from external annoyance; when we may take such an attitude as will cause the neutrality we may at any time resolve upon to be scrupulously respected; when belligerent nations, under the impossibility of making acquisitions upon us, will not lightly hazard the giving us provocation; when we may choose peace or war, as our interest,

---

① "The President," says the Constitution, Article II, Section 2, § 2, "shall have power, by and with the advice and consent of the Senate, to make treaties, provided two thirds of the Senators present concur." The reader is reminded that the Senators are returned for a term of six years, and that they are chosen by the legislature of each state.

总统和参议院,①而总统和参议院却在一定程度上能使总的对外政策摆脱人民直接的和日常的监督。因此,绝对不可以说美国在管理对外事务方面是民主的。

有两个人至今还在对美国对外政策的指导发生影响;第一个人是华盛顿,第二个人是杰斐逊。华盛顿在一封致其同胞的值得赞美的告别信中,我们可以把它看作是这位伟人的政治遗嘱。他在信里这样写道:"在对外政策方面,我们主要的原则是,尽量大的增加我们与外国的贸易往来,但也要尽可能少的与它们发生政治关系。就我们已经签订的条约来说,我们要尽量真诚地履行它们。但是,这里也就到此为止了。""欧洲各国有一系列最基本利益,这些利益不是与我们根本无关,就是关系极为疏远。因此,它们必然要陷入经常性的争论之中,而争论的根源本质上与我们无关。因此,今后要用人为的纽带来连接我们与欧洲的日常政治变动,或是连接我们与欧洲各国的时而友好和时而破裂的关系,将是很不明智的。"

"我们的远离他国的独立的地理位置,促使和允许我们能够采取与众不同的路线。假如我们作为一个民族存在于一个高效的政府的统治下,那么在不远的未来, 我们就可以摆脱由外国侵略而遭受物质损失;可以采取使我们在任何时候都能保持的中立受到尊重的立场;可以使各交战国由于不能从我们这里得到什么好处而不敢轻易地挑衅于我们;可以根据我们的利益和正义的原则来选择是迎战还是求和。" 为什么要抛弃这种独特的地理位置

---

① 宪法第二篇第二部分的第二句写道,"总统应有权,并同时结合参议院的意见和同意,使条约规定的三分之二议员同意提出;"读者应当知道,参议员的任期为六年,并由各个州的立法机构选举。

guided by justice, shall counsel. "Why forego the advantages of so peculiar a situation? Why quit our own to stand upon foreign ground? Why, by interweaving our destiny with that of any part of Europe, entangle our peace and prosperity in the toils of European ambition, rivalship, interest, humor, or caprice?

"It is our true policy to steer clear of permanent alliances with any portion of the foreign world, so far, I mean, as we are now at liberty to do it; for let me not be understood as capable of patronizing infidelity to existing engagements. I hold the maxim no less applicable to public than to private affairs, that honesty is always the best policy. I repeat it, therefore, let those engagements be observed in their genuine sense; but in my opinion it is unnecessary, and would be unwise, to extend them. Taking care always to keep ourselves, by suitable establishments, in a respectable defensive posture, we may safely trust to temporary alliances for extraordinary emergencies." In a previous part of the same address Washington makes this admirable and just remark: "The nation which indulges towards another an habitual hatred, or an habitual fondness, is in some degree a slave. It is a slave to its animosity or to its affection, either of which is sufficient to lead it astray from its duty and its interest." The political conduct of Washington was always guided by these maxims. He succeeded in maintaining his country in a state of peace while all the other nations of the globe were at war; and he laid it down as a fundamental doctrine that the true interest of the Americans consisted in a perfect neutrality with regard to the internal dissensions of the European powers. Jefferson went still further and introduced this other maxim into the policy of the Union, that "the Americans ought never to solicit any privileges from foreign nations, in order not to be obliged to grant similar privileges themselves."

" These two principles, so plain and just as to be easily understood by the people, have greatly simplified the foreign policy of the United States. As the Union takes no part in the affairs of Europe, it has, properly speaking, no foreign interests to discuss, since it has, as yet, no powerful neighbors on the American continent. The country is as much removed from the passions of the old World by its

为我们带来的好处呢？为什么要离开自己的地盘而跑到外国的地盘去呢？为什么要把我们的命运同欧洲的某一部分的命运联系起来，从而使我们的和平与繁荣同欧洲人的野心、对抗、利益、任性或狂妄纠缠在一起呢？

"我们真正的政策，是要躲避与任何外国永远保持同盟，也就是说，我们要像现在这样自由地行动下去；请千万不要把我的意思误解为主张不遵守现有的条约。诚实守信向来是最好的策略，我在公务上对这个箴言的信守决不亚于我在个人私事上对它的信守。因此，我再重复一遍，我们要按条约的本义信守条约。但在我看来，扩充原来的条约或重新签订新的条约是没有必要的，同时也是不明智的。要始终注意确保我们在适当的情况下，使自己保持受人尊重的防御姿态，在遇到意外的危险时也用暂时的联盟当挡箭牌。"在这段话的前面，华盛顿说过一句值得钦佩的至理名言："一个国家总是喜欢仇恨或是仰慕另一个国家，它便如同一个奴隶，也就是成为自己的爱和憎的奴隶，这样就足够使他违背自己的职责和利益。"华盛顿的政治活动，始终是以这些箴言为指导的。当世界上的其他所有国家都陷入战争中时，他成功地使自己的国家保持在和平的状态下；他认为美国人的根本利益，是卷入到欧洲内部的纷争中，永远处于中立状态，并把这一点作为他的行动准则。杰斐逊走得更远，他在对外政策上信守的箴言是："美国人决不向外国索取任何特权，以免自己被迫向外国出让特权。"

这两项原则表示得很清楚，容易被群众理解，它们大大地简化了美国的对外政策。由于联邦政府不参与欧洲事务，所以严格说来，它就没有什么需要争夺的对外利益，因为美国还没有强有力的邻国。美国的地理位置和它的本身愿望，使它摆脱了旧大陆

position as by its wishes, and it is called upon neither to repudiate nor to espouse them; while the dissensions of the New World are still concealed within the bosom of the future.

The Union is free from all pre-existing obligations; it can profit by the experience of the old nations of Europe, without being obliged, as they are, to make the best of the past and to adapt it to their present circumstances. It is not, like them, compelled to accept an immense inheritance bequeathed by their forefathers, an inheritance of glory mingled with calamities, and of alliances conflicting with national antipathies. The foreign policy of the United States is eminently expectant; it consists more in abstaining than in acting.

It is therefore very difficult to ascertain, at present, what degree of sagacity the American democracy will display in the conduct of the foreign policy of the country; upon this point its adversaries as well as its friends must suspend their judgment. As for myself, I do not hesitate to say that it is especially in the conduct of their foreign relations that democracies appear to me decidedly inferior to other governments. Experience, instruction, and habit almost always succeed in creating in a democracy a homely species of practical wisdom and that science of the petty occurrences of life which is called good sense. Good sense may suffice to direct the ordinary course of society; and among a people whose education is completed, the advantages of democratic liberty in the internal affairs of the country may more than compensate for the evils inherent in a democratic government. But it is not always so in the relations with foreign nations. Foreign politics demand scarcely any of those qualities which are peculiar to a democracy; they require, on the contrary, the perfect use of almost all those in which it is deficient. Democracy is favorable to the increase of the internal resources of a state; it diffuses wealth and comfort, promotes public spirit, and fortifies the respect for law in all classes of society: all these are advantages which have only an indirect influence over the relations which one people bears to another. But a democracy can only with great difficulty regulate the details of an important undertaking, persevere in a fixed design, and work out its execution in spite of serious obstacles. It cannot combine its measures with secrecy or await their consequences with patience. These are qualities which more especially belong to an individual or an aristocracy; and they are precisely the qualities by which a nation,

的那种狂乱的激情,它既不拒绝动乱,也不支持动乱;至于新大陆的动乱,还隐藏在未来之中。

联邦政府完全不用服从旧的义务;因此,它既从欧洲的一些旧国家的经验中受益,但又不像它们那样要被迫利用过去并努力使过去适应现在。这样,它也就可以不像它们那样不得不接受祖先遗留下来的一大堆遗产。在这堆遗产里,既有荣誉,也有灾难,既有国家间的相互友好,又有国家间的相互仇视。美国的对外政策,是一种执行得非常有效的观望政策;这种政策的要求是逃避,而不是实行。

因此,目前人们还很难断定,美国的民主将会以如何成熟的方式处理国家的对外事务;关于这一点,无论是它的敌人,还是它的朋友,都只能暂缓它们的决定。至于我自己,我会毫不犹豫地说:在我看来,在指导国家的对外关系方面,民主政府绝对不如其他政府优秀。但是,经验、知识和习惯,总是能成功地为民主制度提供一些日常的实用技巧,以及一些关于生活小事的被称之为常识的学问。常识足以指导社会的一般进程;一个有着完整教育体系的国家,在将民主自由应用到国内事务方面,通常要比民主政府由于失误而造成灾难而好很多。但在处理与外国的关系时,情况就不是这样了。对外政策几乎不需要民主的一些所特有的素质;恰恰相反,它所需要的却是民主几乎完全不曾有过的那些素质。民主对增加国内资源是非常有益的;为人民创造财富,并使人民生活舒适,促进公共精神,促进社会各阶级尊重法律:所有的这些优点,只会对一个国家的对外关系发生间接的影响。但是,让民主去调整一项艰巨事业的细枝末节,无疑是很困难的。它只能草拟大体计划,然后排除万难去监督执行。民主很少能够秘密地拟定措施并耐心地等待这项措施产生的结果。而这种精神却常常可以体现在单个的人或一个贵族身上;但是,一个有着长期

like an individual, attains a dominant position.

If, on the contrary, we observe the natural defects of aristocracy, we shall find that, comparatively speaking, they do not injure the direction of the external affairs of the state. The capital fault of which aristocracies may be accused is that they work for themselves and not for the people. In foreign politics it is rare for the interest of the aristocracy to be distinct from that of the people.

The propensity that induces democracies to obey impulse rather than prudence, and to abandon a mature design for the gratification of a momentary passion, was clearly seen in America on the breaking out of the French Revolution. It was then as evident to the simplest capacity as it is at the present time that the interest of the Americans forbade them to take any part in the contest which was about to deluge Europe with blood, but which could not injure their own country. But the sympathies of the people declared themselves with so much violence in favor of France that nothing but the inflexible character of Washington and the immense popularity which he enjoyed could have prevented the Americans from declaring war against England. And even then the exertions which the austere reason of that great man made to repress the generous but imprudent passions of his fellow citizens nearly deprived him of the sole recompense which he ever claimed, that of his country's love. The majority reprobated his policy, but it was afterwards approved by the whole nation. ①

---

① See the fifth volume of Marshall's Life of Washington. "In a government constituted like that of the United States," he says, at p. 314, "it is impossible for the chief magistrate, however firm he may be, to oppose for any length of time the torrent of popular opinion; and the prevalent opinion of that day seemed to incline to war. In fact, in the session of Congress held at the time, it was frequently seen that Washington had lost the majority in the House of Representatives." The violence of the language used against him in public was extreme, and, in a political meeting, they did not scruple to compare him indirectly with the traitor Arnold (p. 265). "By the opposition," says Marshall (p. 355), "the friends of the administration were declared to be an aristocratic and corrupt faction, who, from a desire to introduce monarchy, were hostile to France, and under the influence of Britain; that they were a paper nobility, whose extreme sensibility at every measure which threatened the funds induced a tame submission to injuries and insults which the interests and honor of the nation required them to resist."

管理经验的国家,也能像一个个人那样达到这种状态。

反之,如果我们考察一下贵族制度的天然缺陷,就会发现这些缺陷可能造成的后果几乎不会对指导国家的对外事务方面产生直接影响。贵族制度的主要缺点就是,它只为自己工作,而不为人民大众工作。在对外政策方面,贵族制度很少将自己的利益与人民的利益区别开来,它认为自己就代表着人民的利益。

促使民主在政治方面服从冲动而不服从谨慎,为满足一时的激情而抛弃成熟的长期计划的那种倾向,在法国爆发革命时期也曾在美国产生。当时,就和现在一样,只有那些头脑清晰的人会去说服美国人,让他们相信不参与正爆发在欧洲的战争,避免美国受到任何损害才是他们真正的利益所在。但是,人民对法国的同情之心也极为热烈,若不是华盛顿具有不屈不挠的坚定性格和为人民所爱戴的精神,恐怕将无法抵制美国向英国宣战。但是,这位伟人以其缜密的思想去阻止人民为自己慷慨然而草率的激情所做的努力,还差点使他对唯一希望得到的奖赏也化为灰烬:那就是他的国家对他的尊重与爱戴。曾经有大多数人责备过他的政策,但现在全国人民都支持这个政策。[①] 假如宪法和人民并

---

① 见马歇尔:《华盛顿生平》第 5 卷,第 314 页。他讲到:"在像美国政府这种组织形式的政府里,一个行政首脑都不可能去反对公共舆论的洪流,不管他有多么严厉;尽管当时的舆论可能引发战争。实际上,在那时举办的国会中,华盛顿已经失去了他在众议员的多数的支持。"在公共场合中,用于反对华盛顿的过激语言非常猛烈,在政治会议中,人们毫不顾忌地将他和叛国贼阿诺得间接的作比较(第 265 页)。马歇尔还讲到(第 355 页):"通过这种反对,管理部门的支持者被宣告成贵族阶级和腐败阶级,他们在英国的影响下,想要实行君主制,并被看作是法国的敌人;他们是图有虚表的贵族,他们对每一项威胁到基金的措施都极度敏感,但这种基金会引发对侮辱和伤害的顺从的屈服,而这正是国家的利益和尊严要求他们去忍受的。"

If the Constitution and the favor of the public had not entrusted the direction of the foreign affairs of the country to Washington, it is certain that the American nation would at that time have adopted the very measures which it now condemns.

Almost all the nations that have exercised a powerful influence upon the destinies of the world, by conceiving, following out, and executing vast designs, from the Romans to the English, have been governed by aristocratic institutions. Nor will this be a subject of wonder when we recollect that nothing in the world is so conservative in its views as an aristocracy. The mass of the people may be led astray by ignorance or passion; the mind of a king may be biased and made to vacillate in his designs, and, besides, a king is not immortal. But an aristocratic body is too numerous to be led astray by intrigue, and yet not numerous enough to yield readily to the intoxication of unreflecting passion. An aristocracy is a firm and enlightened body that never dies.

没有把指导国家对外事务的责任交给华盛顿，并且也不支持他。那么美国当时一定和被迫采取在今天会招来一片骂声的措施。

从古罗马到大英帝国，几乎所有的民族都对世界的命运产生过影响，它们拟定、遵循并执行过伟大的计划，而这些民族几乎都是用贵族制度治理自己的国家。对此怎么能感到惊奇呢？其实，在这些国家看来，世界上最牢不可破的制度就是贵族制度。人民大众可能因思想上无知或行为上冲动而混淆是非；国王可能因意志不坚而被执行计划所困扰。另外，国王也不是不朽的。但是，一个贵族集体的人数太多，以至不会使它们陷入迷途，又可因为人强而不容易被轻率的激情所驱使。一个贵族集体，就像一个长生不老的坚定而明智的个人。

CHAPTER XIV
What Are The Real Advantages
Which American Society Derives From
A Democratic Government

Before entering upon the present chapter I must remind the reader of what I have more than once observed in this book. The political Constitution of the United States appears to me to be one of the forms of government that a democracy may adopt; but I do not regard the American Constitution as the best, or as the only one, that a democratic people may establish. In showing the advantages which the Americans derive from the government of democracy, I am therefore very far from affirming, or believing, that similar advantages can be obtained only from the same laws.

General Tendency Of The Laws Under
American Democracy, And Instincts Of
Those Who Apply Them

Defects of a democratic government easy to be discovered—Its advantages discerned only by long observation—Democracy in America often inexpert, but the general tendency of the laws is advantageous—In the American democracy public officers have no permanent interests distinct from those of the majority—Results of this state of things.

The defects and weaknesses of a democratic government may readily be discovered; they can be proved by obvious facts, whereas their healthy influence becomes evident in ways which are not obvious and are, so to speak, hidden. A glance suffices to detect its faults, but its good qualities can be discerned only by long observation. The laws of the American democracy are frequently defective or incomplete;

第十四章　美国社会从民主政府获得的真正好处

在进入本章的正文之前，我认为应当请读者回想一下我在前面已经重复过多次的观点。美国的政治结构，在我看来只是民主国家想要建立政府所采取的形式之一；但我并不认为它是民主国家应当建立政府的最好的和唯一的形式。因此，在说明美国人可从民主政府获得什么利益时，我决不会妄言、也不相信类似利益的获取就只能凭借同样的一些法律。

美国民主制度下法律的总趋势以及使用者的本能

民主政府的缺陷很容易被察觉——而其优点却要经过长时间的观察才能被发现——美国的民主往往不够成熟，但法制的总趋势是进步的——在美国民主制度下，公共官员的长远利益不会与大多数人不同——由此产生的结果。

民主政府的缺点和弱点很容易就会被发现；并为一些明显的事实所证明，但它的正面影响只能以不够明显的形式，甚至可以说是通过秘密的形式表现出来。轻轻地瞥一眼就足够发现民主政府的缺点，而其优点却要经过长时间的观察才能被发现。美国的民主法制，经常是有缺陷的或不完整的；

they sometimes attack vested rights, or sanction others which are dangerous to the community; and even if they were good, their frequency would still be a great evil. How comes it, then, that the American republics prosper and continue?

In the consideration of laws a distinction must be carefully observed between the end at which they aim and the means by which they pursue that end; between their absolute and their relative excellence. If it be the intention of the legislator to favor the interests of the minority at the expense of the majority, and if the measures he takes are so combined as to accomplish the object he has in view with the least possible expense of time and exertion, the law may be well drawn up although its purpose is bad; and the more efficacious it is, the more dangerous it will be.

Democratic laws generally tend to promote the welfare of the greatest possible number; for they emanate from the majority of the citizens, who are subject to error, but who cannot have an interest opposed to their own advantage. The laws of an aristocracy tend, on the contrary, to concentrate wealth and power in the hands of the minority; because an aristocracy, by its very nature, constitutes a minority. It may therefore be asserted, as a general proposition, that the purpose of a democracy in its legislation is more useful to humanity than that of an aristocracy. This, however, is the sum total of its advantages.

Aristocracies are infinitely more expert in the science of legislation than democracies ever can be. They are possessed of a selfcontrol that protects them from the errors of temporary excitement; and they form far-reaching designs, which they know how to mature till a favorable opportunity arrives. Aristocratic government proceeds with the dexterity of art; it understands how to make the collective force of all its laws converge at the same time to a given point. Such is not the case with democracies, whose laws are almost always ineffective or inopportune. The means of democracy are therefore more imperfect than those of aristocracy, and the measures that it unwittingly adopts are frequently opposed to its own cause; but the object it has in view is more useful.

美国的法律有时会对既得权益有所侵犯,或认可一些对社会有害的危险行为;即使承认美国的法律都是好的,但法律的频繁改变性仍然是它的一个重大的缺点。所有这一切,都是非常明显的事实。那么,美国的共和制度怎么又能够长久地存在下去并保持繁荣呢?

在研究法律时,首先应当认真地辨别清楚,什么是法律想要达到的目的,而什么又是法律为达到此目的而采取的手段;把法律的绝对好处与相对好处认真区分开来。假如立法者此刻的目的是要以少数人的利益为主而牺牲多数人的利益,并定出了既最省时又最省力的达到目的的方法,那么法律虽然被制定得很细致,但其目的并不是很好;而且,它的效力越大,其危险性就越高。

民主的法制一般趋向于以大多数人的利益为主;因为它来自公民之中的多数。公民中的多数虽然也可能会犯错误,但它不会和自己的利益相抗衡。而如此不同的,贵族的法制则倾向于将财富和权力控制在少数人手中;因为贵族向来总是少数。因此,一般可以认为民主立法的目的比贵族立法的目的更对人类有利。但是,民主立法的好处也就这么多了。

贵族制度比民主制度更精通于立法科学。贵族制度有很好的自我控制的能力,这会保护它们不被一时的冲动所驱使。它有长远的计划,并懂得在有利的时机很好地实现它。贵族政府有一套很好的办事技巧;懂得如何把法律的合力同时会聚于一点。而民主制度就不能做到,它的法制几乎总是会有残缺或不合时宜。因此,民主制度的手段比贵族制度的手段更不完善,民主制度在行动时往往不注重手段,甚至违背自己的意愿,但它的目的却是对人民有利的。

Let us now imagine a community so organized by nature or by its constitution that it can support the transitory action of bad laws, and that it can await, without destruction, the general tendency of its legislation: we shall then conceive how a democratic government, notwithstanding its faults, may be best fitted to produce the prosperity of this community. This is precisely what has occurred in the United States; and I repeat, what I have before remarked, that the great advantage of the Americans consists in their being able to commit faults which they may afterwards repair.

An analogous observation may be made respecting public officers. It is easy to perceive that American democracy frequently errs in the choice of the individuals to whom it entrusts the power of the administration; but it is more difficult to say why the state prospers under their rule. In the first place, it is to be remarked that if, in a democratic state, the governors have less honesty and less capacity than elsewhere, the governed are more enlightened and more attentive to their interests. As the people in democracies are more constantly vigilant in their affairs and more jealous of their rights, they prevent their representatives from abandoning that general line of conduct which their own interest prescribes. In the second place, it must be remembered that if the democratic magistrate is more apt to misuse his power, he possesses it for a shorter time. But there is yet another reason which is still more general and conclusive. It is no doubt of importance to the welfare of nations that they should be governed by men of talents and virtue; but it is perhaps still more important for them that the interests of those men should not differ from the interests of the community at large; for if such were the case, their virtues might become almost useless and their talents might be turned to a bad account. I have said that it is important that the interests of the persons in authority should not differ from or oppose the interests of the community at large; but I do not insist upon their having the same interests as the *whole* population, because I am not aware that such a state of things ever existed in any country.

No political form has hitherto been discovered that is equally favorable to the prosperity and the development of all the classes into which society is divided. These classes continue to form, as it were, so many distinct communities in the same nation; and experience has

现在让我们设想有这样一个社会,不良的法律在它的自然条件和政治体制的纵容下可以暂时通行,并在这种法律的总趋势即将瓦解的时候社会还能依旧存在;而尽管它的民主政府还存在着许多缺点,但它仍是最能使社会繁荣的政府。这正是美国所发生的情景;我再重复一遍我在前面说过的话,美国人的巨大优点,在于他们允许错误的发生,而事后又能及时的纠正错误。

而在选举公共官员时,情况也是如此。不难发现,美国的民主在选择负责行政权力的人员方面常常会犯错误;但很难解释为什么美国在这种制度下还会如此繁荣。首先,我们可以看到,一个民主国家的统治者虽然不如其他地方的忠诚或能干,但它们在对待自己的利益方面却很聪明和认真。因为民主国家的人民在不断担心于自己的事业和对自己已得的权利非常重视,并防止他们的代表违背他们根据自己的利益为代表规定的总路线。其次,我们应该知道,如果民主国家的行政官员比其他国家的更易于滥用职权,则人民一般不会再让他们任职。但是,还有一个很重要的理由,比这个理由更具有普遍性和说服力。毫无疑问,统治者的才能与道德,对于国家的繁荣富强是十分重要的;但更重要的或许是统治者没有同被统治者相背离的利益;如果出现这样的情况,道德就变得几乎没有用了,而其才能也将被用于干坏事。我已经讲过,统治者没有同被统治者相背离或不同的利益是非常重要的;但我也决不认为,统治者同全体被统治者拥有同样的利益也很重要,因为迄今为止,我还不曾见到哪里出现过这样的利益。

我至今还从未见过对社会各阶级都平等,并积极地促进它们兴旺和繁荣的政治形势。这些社会阶级在同一个国家里,会形成不同的社会群体;而且经验也已证明,把其他阶级的命运完全交

shown that it is no less dangerous to place the fate of these classes exclusively in the hands of any one of them than it is to make one people the arbiter of the destiny of another. When the rich alone govern, the interest of the poor is always endangered; and when the poor make the laws, that of the rich incurs very serious risks. The advantage of democracy does not consist, therefore, as has sometimes been asserted, in favoring the prosperity of all, but simply in contributing to the well-being of the greatest number.

The men who are entrusted with the direction of public affairs in the United States are frequently inferior, in both capacity and morality, to those whom an aristocracy would raise to power. But their interest is identified and mingled with that of the majority of their fellow citizens. They may frequently be faithless and frequently mistaken, but they will never systematically adopt a line of conduct hostile to the majority; and they cannot give a dangerous or exclusive tendency to the government. The maladministration of a democratic magistrate, moreover, is an isolated fact, which has influence only during the short period for which he is elected. Corruption and incapacity do not act as common interests which may connect men permanently with one another. A corrupt or incapable magistrate will not combine his measures with another magistrate simply because the latter is as corrupt and incapable as himself; and these two men will never unite their endeavors to promote the corruption and inaptitude of their remote posterity. The ambition and the maneuvers of the one will serve, on the contrary, to unmask the other. The vices of a magistrate in democratic states are usually wholly personal.

But under aristocratic governments public men are swayed by the interest of their order, which, if it is sometimes confused with the interests of the majority, is very frequently distinct from them. This interest is the common and lasting bond that unites them; it induces them to coalesce and combine their efforts to attain an end which is not always the happiness of the greatest number; and it serves not only to connect the persons in authority with one another, but to unite them with a considerable portion of the community, since a numerous body of citizens belong to the aristocracy without being invested with official functions. The aristocratic magistrate is therefore constantly supported by a portion of the community as well as by the government of which he is a member.

给一个阶级去掌控,其危险并不会比让国家中的一个民族充当另些民族的仲裁者要少。当只由富人统治国家时,穷人的利益会受到威胁;而当穷人独揽制定法律的大权时,富人的利益要受到严重的威胁。因此,民主的真正好处,并非像人们所说的能够促进所有阶级的发展,而只是以最大多数人的利益为主。

在美国,负责领导公共事务的人,不论是在德才方面还是在品德方面都不如贵族国家的执政者。但他们的利益却是与大多数同胞的利益相一致的。因此,他们可能常常玩忽职守并犯下重大过错,但他们决不会采用这个敌视大多数的方针;他们也无法使政府具有危险的且专断的形象。而且,在民主制度下,一个行政首脑的不良政绩只不过是个孤立的事实,并只能在其短暂的任期内产生影响。腐败和无能,决不能被作为可以永久连接人们的共同纽带。一个腐败或无能的行政官员,不能将自己的行为措施与另一个与他同样的腐败与无能的官员联系在一起;并尽他们所有的努力去促进腐败和无能的繁衍。相反,一个行政官员的野心和阴谋,还会促使他去揭露另一个行政官员的丑恶嘴脸。在民主制度下,行政官员的所有卑劣行为,通常都是完全属于他们个人的。

但是,在贵族国家的政府中,公共官员就受他们自己的利益支配了,他们的阶级利益只是偶尔才与多数人的利益相一致,而在一般情况下都与多数人的利益相背离的。这个阶级利益就像是连接官员之间的一条共同而持久的纽带;促使他们把力量联合起来,以向着一个总是不让绝大多数人幸福的目标前进;它不仅使统治者之间彼此相互勾结,而且还使统治者与相当数量被统治者联合起来,因为很多没有担当任何公职的公民也属于贵族。因此,贵族政体的行政官员既受到社会的不断支持,又得到政府的一致支持。

The common purpose which in aristocracies connects the interest of the magistrates with that of a portion of their contemporaries identifies it also with that of future generations; they labor for the future as well as for the present. The aristocratic magistrate is urged at the same time towards the same point by the passions of the community, by his own, and, I may almost add, by those of his posterity. Is it, then, wonderful that he does not resist such repeated impulses? And, indeed, aristocracies are often carried away by their class spirit without being corrupted by it; and they unconsciously fashion society to their own ends and prepare it for their own descendants.

The English aristocracy is perhaps the most liberal that has ever existed, and no body of men has ever, uninterruptedly, furnished so many honorable and enlightened individuals to the government of a country. It cannot escape observation, however, that in the legislation of England the interests of the poor have often been sacrificed to the advantages of the rich, and the rights of the majority to the privileges of a few. The result is that England at the present day combines the extremes of good and evil fortune in the bosom of her society; and the miseries and privations of her poor almost equal her power and renown.

In the United States, where public officers have no class interests to promote, the general and constant influence of the government is beneficial, although the individuals who conduct it are frequently unskillful and sometimes contemptible. There is, indeed, a secret tendency in democratic institutions that makes the exertions of the citizens subservient to the prosperity of the community in spite of their vices and mistakes; while in aristocratic institutions there is a secret bias which, notwithstanding the talents and virtues of those who conduct the government, leads them to contribute to the evils that oppress their fellow creatures. In aristocratic governments public men may frequently do harm without intending it; and in democratic states they bring about good results of which they have never thought.

贵族阶级的共同目的,是先联合行政官员的和与他们的一部分同代人的利益,然后再进一步将他们未来子孙的利益统一起来,甚至是完全遵循于子孙的利益;在贵族阶级中,行政官员的工作既是为了现在,又是为了将来。而贵族行政官员,同时被自己的激情和被统治者的激情驱向同一目标,甚至在我看来,这种激情可以说是他们后代的激情。因此,它们有什么理由不去坚持这种激情呢? 实际上,贵族阶级的属性总是指引行政官员免于腐化,让他们不知不觉地使社会逐渐按照自己的意志前进,并做好随时把这个社会传给他们的后代的准备。

英国的贵族阶级或许是迄今为止所存在的最自由的一个阶级,没有一个国家的阶级能像贵族阶级那样对政府不断提供如此高尚和如此贤明的人才。但是,也不难看到,英国的立法常常是以富人的利益为主而牺牲穷人的利益,使大多数权力被控制在少数几个人手中。结果,今天的英国结合极富与极穷于一身;在其穷人的悲惨处境和其繁荣的国力之间形成一个鲜明的对比。

在美国,公共官员没有可以促进的属于自己的阶级利益,尽管统治者常是一些无能无德无才的人,有时甚至是一些卑鄙之徒,但政府的日常工作仍然是对人民有力的。因此,在民主制度中,有一种秘密的源泉在不断引导人们从改正错误与缺点之中走向共同繁荣;而在贵族制度中,则存在着一股隐秘的力量会时不时地引诱官员们滥用他们的才能与品德去带给同胞灾难。可见,在贵族政府中,官员可能是在无心之下做了坏事;而在民主政府中,公务人员做了好事可能并非有意。

Public Spirit In The United States

Instinctive patriotism—Patriotism of reflection—Their different characteristics—Nations ought to strive to acquire the second when the first has disappeared—Efforts of the Americans to acquire it—Interest of the individual intimately connected with that of the country.

There is one sort of patriotic attachment which principally arises from that instinctive, disinterested, and undefinable feeling which connects the affections of man with his birthplace. This natural fondness is united with a taste for ancient customs and a reverence for traditions of the past; those who cherish it love their country as they love the mansion of their fathers. They love the tranquillity that it affords them; they cling to the peaceful habits that they have contracted within its bosom; they are attached to the reminiscences that it awakens; and they are even pleased by living there in a state of obedience. This patriotism is sometimes stimulated by religious enthusiasm, and then it is capable of making prodigious efforts. It is in itself a kind of religion: it does not reason, but it acts from the impulse of faith and sentiment. In some nations the monarch is regarded as a personification of the country; and, the fervor of patriotism being converted into the fervor of loyalty, they take a sympathetic pride in his conquests, and glory in his power. There was a time under the ancient monarchy when the French felt a sort of satisfaction in the sense of their dependence upon the arbitrary will of their king; and they were wont to say with pride: "We live under the most powerful king in the world. "

But, like all instinctive passions, this kind of patriotism incites great transient exertions, but no continuity of effort. It may save the state in critical circumstances, but often allows it to decline in times of peace. While the manners of a people are simple and its faith unshaken, while society is steadily based upon traditional institutions

美国的公共精神

　　本能的爱国主义——理智的爱国主义——两者的不同特点——为什么各国都纷纷在前者即将消失时要全力去发展后者——美国人在发展理智的爱国主义方面所做的努力——个人利益与国家利益紧密联系在一起。

　　有一种爱国心，主要来自于那种把人们同其出生地联系起来的本能的、无私的和很难说清楚的感情。这种本能的喜好由很多复杂的成分构成，其中既有对古老习惯的依恋，又有对祖先的尊敬和对过去的不舍；这些人在珍爱自己国家的人就像心疼父辈留下的房产。他们喜爱家乡为他们带来的安宁；遵守在祖国养成的良好的习惯；依恋回荡在脑中的记忆；甚至觉得生活于服从之中也是很快乐的。这种爱国心有时会被宗教热情所鼓舞，于是便会产生巨大的效果。这种爱国心本身就是一种宗教：它不具有任何理性的思考，完全凭借信仰和感情行事。在一些国家，人们把君主看作是国家的完美化身；因此，他们把爱国主义的热忱转化为忠诚的热情，他们骄傲于君主的胜利，自豪于君主的强大。在法国旧的贵族统治时期，人民就曾有一段时间因此而感到快乐与安慰，而并不为国王对自己的专制统治而感到痛心。他们大声地赞叹："我们生活在世界上最强大的国王的统治之下。"

　　但是，同所有本能的激情一样，这种爱国心虽能暂时地激起强大的干劲，但并不能使之长久。它或许可以把国家从危机中拯救出来，但常常又会使其灭亡在安宁之中。当人民还持有朴素的生活习惯和坚定宗教的信仰时；当社会还牢牢地抓着事物的旧秩

whose legitimacy has never been contested, this instinctive patriotism is wont to endure.

But there is another species of attachment to country which is more rational than the one I have been describing. It is perhaps less generous and less ardent, but it is more fruitful and more lasting: it springs from knowledge; it is nurtured by the laws; it grows by the exercise of civil rights; and, in the end, it is confounded with the personal interests of the citizen. A man comprehends the influence which the well-being of his country has upon his own; he is aware that the laws permit him to contribute to that prosperity, and he labors to promote it, first because it benefits him, and secondly because it is in part his own work.

But epochs sometimes occur in the life of a nation when the old customs of a people are changed, public morality is destroyed, religious belief shaken, and the spell of tradition broken, while the diffusion of knowledge is yet imperfect and the civil rights of the community are ill secured or confined within narrow limits. The country then assumes a dim and dubiour shape in the eyes of the citizens; they no longer behold it in the soil which they inhabit, for that soil is to them an inanimate clod; nor in the usages of their forefathers, which they have learned to regard as a debasing yoke; nor in religion, for of that they doubt; nor in the laws, which do not originate in their own authority; nor in the legislator, whom they fear and despise. The country is lost to their senses; they can discover it neither under its own nor under borrowed features, and they retire into a narrow and unenlightened selfishness. They are emancipated from prejudice without having acknowledged the empire of reason; they have neither the instinctive patriotism of a monarchy nor the reflecting patriotism of a republic; but they have stopped between the two in the midst of confusion and distress.

序不放,而这种秩序的合法性尚未遭到质疑的时候,这种本能的
爱国心也习惯于忍受。

　　然而,还存在另外一种爱国心,这种爱国心比我刚才讲的这
种爱国心更富有理智。它虽然可能不够爽快并富有热情,但却非
常地坚定和非常地持久:它是出于对真知的理解;并在法律的保
护下成长;它随着权利的运用而逐渐扩大;但在混合了私人利益
之后便会消减。一个人应当理解到国家的福利会影响到他个人
的福利;应当意识到法律要求他对国家的福利做出贡献,他之所
以关心本国的繁荣,首先是因为这是一件对他自己有利的事情,
其次才是因为这里面也饱含着他的一份辛劳。

　　当一个国家的人民的旧的习惯改变了,社会道德遭到了破
坏,宗教信仰动摇了,昔日的荣誉不见了,而知识普及还不够完
善,政治权利得不到保证或受到限制时,国家的发展有时也会出
现停滞时期。这时,国家在人们的眼中只是一个模糊而虚弱的影
子;他们不再从国土的角度去看待国家,因为这片国土在他们看
来已经变成一片废墟;他们不再用祖宗的习惯去看待国家,因为
他们把这些习惯看成是沉重的枷锁;他们不再从宗教的立场去看
待国家,因为宗教已变得不可信;他们不再以法律为基础去看待
国家,因为他们自己已不是法律的制定者;他们也不再以立法机
构去看待国家,因为立法机构使他们恐惧并遭到他们的鄙视。这
时,国家已从他们的意义中消失;他们只认为自己对,而其他都是
错的,最后,他们便完全陷入狭隘而又封闭的自我利益中。这种
人虽然排斥原先的偏见,但不承认理性的王国;他们既没有君主
的爱国主义的本能,又没有共和国的理智的爱国主义;他们在这
两者之间停下了脚步,陷入困惑和忧虑之中。

In this predicament to retreat is impossible, for a people cannot recover the sentiments of their youth any more than a man can return to the innocent tastes of childhood; such things may be re gretted, but they cannot be renewed. They must go forward and accelerate the union of private with public interests, since the period of disinterested patriotism is gone by forever.

I am certainly far from affirming that in order to obtain this result the exercise of political rights should be immediately granted to all men. But I maintain that the most powerful and perhaps the only means that we still possess of interesting men in the welfare of their country is to make them partakers in the government. At the present time civic zeal seems to me to be inseparable from the exercise of political rights; and I think that the number of citizens will be found to augment or decrease in Europe in proportion as those rights are extended. How does it happen that in the United States, where the inhabitants have only recently immigrated to the land which they now occupy, and brought neither customs nor traditions with them there; where they met one another for the first time with no previous acquaintance; where, in short, the instinctive love of country can scarcely exist; how does it happen that everyone takes as zealous an interest in the affairs of his township, his county, and the whole state as if they were his own? It is because everyone, in his sphere, takes an active part in the government of society.

The lower orders in the United States understand the influence exercised by the general prosperity upon their own welfare; simple as this observation is, it is too rarely made by the people. Be sides, they are accustomed to regard this prosperity as the fruit of their own exertions. The citizen looks upon the fortune of the public as his own, and he labors for the good of the state, not merely from a sense of pride or duty, but from what I venture to term cupidity. It is unnecessary to study the institutions and the history of the Americans in order to know the truth of this remark, for their manners render it sufficiently evident. As the American participates in

从这种尴尬的境地中脱身是很不可能的。一个民族如果不能恢复其青春的锐气,正如一个人不能恢复其童年的稚气一样。这种事情也许会让人觉得惋惜,但谁也无法重新开始。他们必须继续前进,在人民面前将个人与国家的利益完美地结合起来,因为公正无私的爱国心已经一去不复返了。

我当然不会认为,为了获得这一结果,就必须立即让人人行使政治权利。但我坚持认为,使人人都参加政府的管理工作,则是我们可以使人人都能关心自己祖国命运的最强有力手段,甚至可以说是唯一的手段。在现今这个时代,公民的精神对我来说是与政治权利的行使不可分的;而在我看来,对于将来的欧洲,公民人数的增加或减少,将与这项权利的扩大和缩小成正比。而在被不久以前移来的居民开发的美国又是怎样的呢? 移民们既没有把他们从前必须遵守的习惯带进来,也没有把他们难忘的回忆带进来;他们彼此在这里都是初次相见,以前不曾相识;简单地讲,要想在这里产生本能的爱国心是非常困难的;那么,为什么每个人还会像关心自己的事业那样去关心本乡、本县甚至是本州的事业呢? 这是因为每个人都在自己的能力范围内,通过积极的活动参加了对社会的管理。

在美国,人民都知道社会的普遍繁荣对他们本身的幸福会产生一定的影响。这个看法虽然如此简单,但却很少被人提出。而且,美国人民向来喜欢把这种繁荣看作是自己辛勤劳动的果实。所以他们认为公共的财富也理应有属于他们的一份,并愿为国家的富强而卖力,他们这样做不仅出于责任感和自豪感,而且还有一种自私心理的驱使,也可以大胆地将它称之为贪婪之心。为了了解这个说法的真实性,我们没有必要去研究美国的制度和历史,因为美国的民情已经很有力地向我们证明了这一点。因为美

all that is done in his country, he thinks himself obliged to defend whatever may be censured in it; for it is not only his country that is then attacked, it is himself. The consequence is that his national pride resorts to a thousand artifices and descends to all the petty tricks of personal vanity.

Nothing is more embarrassing in the ordinary intercourse of life than this irritable patriotism of the Americans. A stranger may be well inclined to praise many of the institutions of their country, but he begs permission to blame some things in it, a permission that is inexorably refused. America is therefore a free country in which, lest anybody should be hurt by your remarks, you are not allowed to speak freely of private individuals or of the state, of the citizens or of the authorities, of public or of private undertakings, or, in short, of anything at all except, perhaps, the climate and the soil; and even then Americans will be found ready to defend both as if they had co-operated in producing them. In our times we must choose between the patriotism of all and the government of a few; for the social force and activity which the first confers are irreconcilable with the pledges of tranquillity which are given by the second.

The Idea Of Rights In The United States

No great people without an idea of right—How the idea of right can be given to a people—Respect for right in the United States—Whence it arises.

After the general idea of virtue, I know no higher principle than that of right; or rather these two ideas are united in one. The idea of right is simply that of virtue introduced into the political world. It was

国人参加了国家所有事业的建设,他们认为自己有义务保护所有被人莫名痛斥的事情;因为这时不仅仅是他们的国家遭到了无端攻击,甚至还有他们自己。因此,他们要利用各种各样的方法来维护国家的荣誉,有时甚至玩弄出于自己小聪明的阴谋诡计。

在日常的交往中,再没有比美国人的这种急躁的爱国主义更使人觉得尴尬的了。一个陌生者也许都愿意赞扬美国的许多制度,但在乞求美国人对他们的某件事情进行谴责时,那他们一定会拒绝。因此,美国虽然是一个自由国家,但外国人在那里为了不使自己的言论伤害到别人,既不能自由地谈论个人私事,又不能自由地谈论国家大事,既不能自由地谈论公民,又不能自由地谈论统治者,既不能自由地谈论公共事业,又不能自由地谈论私人事业,总之一句话,或许除了气候与土地,再没有什么东西可以在那里被自由地谈论;而且,即使在谈论气候和土地的时候,美国人也随时准备好了为两者辩护,好像他们曾经参与过制造天气和土地一样。在现代,我们必须勇敢地在全体人民的爱国主义和少数人的政府之间进行选择;因为不能同时把前者产生的社会力量和社会积极性与后者提供的社会安宁的保证结合起来。

美国的权利观念

任何一个伟大民族都具有权利的观念——怎样使一个民族产生权利观念——在美国,人们尊重权利——这种尊重是怎么产生的。

除了一般道德观念之外,我不知道再有什么观念高于权利观念了;或者说两者是成一体的。权利观念无非是将道德观念运用

the idea of right that enabled men to define anarchy and tyranny, and that taught them how to be independent without arrogance and to obey without servility. The man who submits to violence is debased by his compliance; but when he submits to that right of authority which he acknowledges in a fellow creature, he rises in some measure above the person who gives the command. There are no great men without virtue; and there are no great nations—it may almost be added, there would be no society—without respect for right; for what is a union of rational and intelligent beings who are held together only by the bond of force?

I am persuaded that the only means which we possess at the present time of inculcating the idea of right and of rendering it, as it were, palpable to the senses is to endow all with the peaceful exercloe of certain rights; this is very clearly seen in children, who are men without the strength and the experience of manhood. When a child begins to move in the midst of the objects that surround him, he is instinctively led to appropriate to himself everything that he can lay his hands upon; he has no notion of the property of others; but as he gradually learns the value of things and begins to perceive that he may in his turn be despoiled, he becomes more circumspect, and he ends by respecting those rights in others which he wishes to have respected in himself. The principle which the child derives from the possession of his toys is taught to the man by the objects which he may call his own. In America, the most democratic of nations, those complaints against property in general, which are so frequent in Europe, are never heard, because in America there are no paupers. As everyone has property of his own to defend, everyone recognizes the principle upon which he holds it.

The same thing occurs in the political world. In America, the lowest classes have conceived a very high notion of political rights, because they exercise those rights; and they refrain from attacking the rights of others in order that their own may not be violated. While in Europe the same classes sometimes resist even the supreme power,

到政界中。正是这种权利观念使人们能够确定什么是混乱的和暴政的。对权利观念很清楚的人，可以谦虚而独立地表现自己的意志，正直地表示服从而从不屈从。向暴力低头的人，只会自取其辱和自惭形秽；但是，当让他听命于一个和他同水平的人的指令时，他在某些程度上却表现好像有些高于那个指挥者一样。伟大的人物都有很好的德行；任何一个伟大民族都尊重权利，甚至可以说，任何一个社会都尊重权利；因为怎能仅仅依靠强迫就使理性与良知结合起来呢？

我曾想过，在我们这个时代，用什么办法可以培养人们的权利观念，并使人们牢牢地记住这种方法。结果发现，唯一的办法是让所有的人都和平地行使一定的权利；大家都知道，儿童的能力和经验都是在后天中逐渐获得的，当一个婴儿刚刚学会移动自己身体的时候，凡是在他周围能够被他碰到的东西，他都会本能地将它抓住不放；他还没有这个财产是属于谁的意识，更不会明白财产为何物；但是，随着他逐渐长大，对物品的价值有所了解，发现别人也会抢走他手中的物品时，便会变得小心，并通过对他人的尊重而最后得到他所期望于他人的尊重。儿童希望获得玩具的心理，发展到后来就变成大人渴望获得财物的心理。在美国这个极度民主的国家，人们从来不会听到一般产生于欧洲各地的那种为苦于没有财产而发出的抱怨声，因为美国没有无产者。由于人人都有需要保护的属于自己的财产，所以在原则上，人人都承认其财产权。

同样的情况也发生在政界。在美国，底层阶级都把政治权利看得很高，因为他们都有政治权利；为使自己的政治权利不受侵犯，他们从来不会去攻击别人的政治权利。在欧洲，同样拥有政治权利的社会阶级，甚至连国家主权都不放在眼里，而美国人却

the American submits without a murmur to the authority of the pettiest magistrate.

This truth appears even in the trivial details of national life. In France few pleasures are exclusively reserved for the higher classes; the poor are generally admitted wherever the rich are received; and they consequently behave with propriety, and respect whatever promotes the enjoyments that they themselves share. In England, where wealth has a monopoly of amusement as well as of power, complaints are made that whenever the poor happen to enter the places reserved for the pleasures of the rich, they do wanton mischief;. can this be wondered at, since care has been taken that they should have nothing to lose?

The government of a democracy brings the notion of political rights to the level of the humblest citizens, just as the dissemination of wealth brings the notion of property within the reach of all men; to my mind, this is one of its greatest advantages. I do not say it is easy to teach men how to exercise political rights, but I maintain that, when it is possible, the effects which result from it are highly important; and I add that, if there ever was a time at which such an attempt ought to be made, that time is now. Do you not see that religious belief is shaken and the divine notion of right is declining, that morality is debased and the notion of moral right is therefore fading away? Argument is substituted for faith, and calculation for the impulses of sentiment. If, in the midst of this general disruption, you do not succeed in connecting the notion of right with that of private interest, which is the only immutable point in the human heart, what means will you have of governing the world except by fear? When I am told that the laws are weak and the people are turbulent, that passions are excited and the authority of virtue is paralyzed, and therefore no measures must be taken to increase the rights of the democracy, I reply that for these very reasons some measures of the kind ought to be taken; and I believe that governments are still more interested in taking them than society at large, for governments may perish, but society cannot die.

能对行政官员的微小的权力认真地服从。

这个真理,也表现在人民日常生活的细枝末节上。在法国,专供社会高层阶级享乐的东西只占很少一部分的;凡是富人可以去的地方,穷人几乎都可以去;因此,人们的行为举止都表现得很有礼貌,并对他们参与的一切享乐表示尊重。在英国,富人既对享乐主义进行垄断,同时还霸占了权力,因此,每当穷人溜进专为富人设立的娱乐场所,并在里面肆意的恶作剧时,抱怨声就此起彼伏。这有什么奇怪的呢?

他们准知道这对自己无所损害。正如财产的分配使所有成年人都具有财产观念一样,民主政府使每个公民都具有了政治权利的观念;我认为这也是民主政府的最大优点之一。我并不是说,让教会所有的人行使政治权利将会变得很容易,我的意思是,如果可以的话,这件事所产生的影响是很重要的;我需要补充一句,如果说曾经有哪个时代试图产生这种想法,那就是现今这个时代。你难道没有看到宗教信仰已经被动摇,上帝赋予我们权利的观念也已经消失? 社会道德已经变坏,道义的权利观念也随之衰弱? 诡辩已经取替了一切信仰,而阴谋则替代了一切感情。假如在这场大变革中,你没能把权利观念与人们心中根深蒂固的私人利益结合起来,那么除了胆怯,你又能有什么方法敢于去治理社会呢? 因此,如果有人对我说,法律已经变得软弱无力,人民也更加骚动起来,激情使人变得兴奋,而德行已经毫无用处,在这种情况下已没有什么方法可以被用来主张扩大民主权利,那么,我的回答是,正是由于这些事实,才让我觉得应当扩大民主权利;而且我相信,政府对扩大民主权利的关心远远比社会要大,因为政府也许会消失,而社会是不会灭亡的。

But I do not wish to exaggerate the example that America furnishes. There the people were invested with political rights at a time when they could not be abused, for the inhabitants were few in number and simple in their manners. As they have increased, the Americans have not augmented the power of the democracy; they have rather extended its domain.

It cannot be doubted that the moment at which political rights are granted to a people that had before been without them is a very critical one, that the measure, though often necessary, is always dangerous. A child may kill before he is aware of the value of life; and he may deprive another person of his property before he is aware that his own may be taken from him. The lower orders, when they are first invested with political rights, stand in relation to those rights in the same position as the child does to the whole of nature; and the celebrated adage may then be applied to them: *Homo puer robustus*. This truth may be perceived even in America. The states in which the citizens have enjoyed their rights longest are those in which they make the best use of them. It cannot be repeated too often that nothing is more fertile in prodigies than the art of being free; but there is nothing more arduous than the apprenticeship of liberty. It is not so with despotism: despotism often promises to make amends for a thousand previous ills; it supports the right, it protects the oppressed, and it maintains public order. The nation is lulled by the temporary prosperity that it produces, until it is roused to a sense of its misery. Liberty, on the contrary, is generally established with difficulty in the midst of storms; it is perfected by civil discord; and its benefits cannot be appreciated until it is already old.

Respect For Law In The United States

Respect of the Americans for law—Parental affection which they entertain for it—Personal interest of everyone to increase the power of

但是,我决不想滥用美国提供的范例。美国的公民早在一个时期就被赋予了这种政治权利,而这正是在他们人数不多和社会习惯简朴而不能很好地行使政治权利的时期。随着美国人数的增多,美国人也并没有增加民主的权力,而只是将民主的范围扩大了。

毋庸置疑,赋予一个从未享有过政治权利的民族以政治权利的时刻,是一个关键性的时刻,这种现象虽然往往是必要的,但总是伴随着危险。一个儿童在尚不清楚生命的宝贵价值时可能会去杀人;在知道别人会随时抢走自己的财物后也会去抢走别人的财物。成年人在最初被赋予政治权利的时候,他对这种权利所持的态度,就如同儿童在尚不懂事时对自然所持的态度;而后面这句名言用在此处最为合适,那就是:年富力强之士。这个真理也同样见于美国。在那些公民们长期享有政治权利的州里,也正是公民们将政治权利行使到最好的地方。下述的说法也不为过:任何才能的收获都没有比保持自由的技巧的收获更丰富了;但任何事情也不会苦于对运用自由的学习。专制并非如此。专制往往表现为成千上万的罪恶的惩罚者;它支持正当的权利,保护被压迫者并维持公共秩序。国家被它制造出来的暂时繁荣所蒙蔽,进入梦乡,但一觉醒来以后,便会感到难以忍受的痛苦。自由与专制不同,它通常在暴风骤雨中诞生;在内乱的艰难环境中成长,只有在它已经长大成熟的时候,人们才能了解到它的益处。

美国对法律的尊重

美国人尊重法律——美国人爱法律如同爱自己的父母——

law.

It is not always feasible to consult the whole people, either directly or indirectly, in the formation of law; but it cannot be denied that, when this is possible, the authority of law is much augmented. This popular origin, which impairs the excellence and the wisdom of legislation, contributes much to increase its power. There is an amazing strength in the expression of the will of a whole people; and when it declares itself, even the imagination of those who would wish to contest it is overawed. The truth of this fact is well known by parties, and they consequently strive to make out a majority whenever they can. If they have not the greater number of voters on their side, they assert that the true majority abstained from voting; and if they are foiled even there, they have recourse to those persons who had no right to vote.

In the United States, except slaves, servants, and paupers supported by the townships, there is no class of persons who do not exercise the elective franchise and who do not indirectly contribute to make the laws. Those who wish to attack the laws must consequently either change the opinion of the nation or trample upon its decision. A second reason, which is still more direct and weighty, may be adduced: in the United States everyone is personally interested in enforcing the obedience of the whole community to the law; for as the minority may shortly rally the majority to its principles, it is interested in professing that respect for the decrees of the legislator which it may soon have occasion to claim for its own. However irksome an enactment may be, the citizen of the United States complies with it, not only because it is the work of the majority, but because it is his own, and he regards it as a contract to which he is himself a party. In the United States, then, that numerous and turbulent multitude does not exist who, regarding the law as their natural enemy, look upon it with fear and distrust. It is impossible, on the contrary, not to perceive that all classes display the utmost reliance upon the legislation of their country and are attached to it by a kind of parental affection.

每个人可从加强法律力量中看到自己利益的增加。

号召全体人民去制定法律，不管是直接的还是间接的，并不总是可行的；但也不能否认，当这种情况可行时，法律就将拥有巨大的权威。这个群众基础虽然常常会损害立法者的才能和智慧，但它却能使立法者的力量大大地增强。在全民的意志表现当中，有一种力量是相当强大的；这种力量一旦爆发，本想与它对抗的人也会消失的无影无踪。各个党派清楚地知道这种情况的真实性。因此，各党派都尽最大努力去争取多数。如果已经投票的人并没有构成多数，各党派便到弃权投票的人中去寻找希望；而当这些人还不能凑成多数时，各党派便到没有投票权的人中去找多数。

在美国，除了奴隶、仆人和依靠乡镇救济的穷人以外，任何社会阶级都有选举特权，并由此间接的对立法产生了影响。因此，那些想要攻击法律的人，就必须设法改变全国的舆论，或是对人民的意志进行毁灭性攻击。除了这项重要的理由之外，我还可以举出另一项更加直接和更加有力的理由。那就是：在美国，每个人对法律的服从都与他的私人利益有关；因为少数派在很短的时间里可能进入多数的行列，而现在口口声声说要尊重立法者意志的人在不久以后又会要求别人屈从于他的意志。不管一项法律让人感到多么窝火，美国的居民都会服从它，这不仅因为这项立法是为大多数人服务的，而且因为这项立法也是他本人的作品，在他们眼中，这项立法就如同是一份契约，而自己也参与过契约的制定。因此，在美国没有为数众多的暴徒将法律看作是天生的敌人，对法律怀有恐惧的心理和持有怀疑的态度。因此经常集聚起来闹事。相反，你却一定可以察觉到所有的阶级都对国家的现行法律投以信任的目光，用自己对父母的爱去爱现行的法律。

I am wrong, however, in saying all classes; for as in America the European scale of authority is inverted, there the wealthy are placed in a position analogous to that of the poor in the Old World, and it is the opulent classes who frequently look upon law with suspicion. I have already observed that the advantage of democracy is not, as has been sometimes asserted, that it protects the interests of all, but simply that it protects those of the majority. In the United States, where the poor rule, the rich have always something to fear from the abuse of their power. This natural anxiety of the rich may produce a secret dissatisfaction; but society is not disturbed by it, for the same reason that withholds the confidence of the rich from the legislative authority makes them obey its mandates: their wealth, which prevents them from making the law, prevents them from withstanding it.

Among civilized nations, only those who have nothing to lose ever revolt; and if the laws of a democracy are not always worthy of respect, they are always respected; for those who usually infringe the laws cannot fail to obey those which they have themselves made and by which they are benefited; while the citizens who might be interested in their infraction are induced, by their character and station, to submit to the decisions of the legislature, whatever they may be. Besides, the people in America obey the law, not only because it is their own work, but because it may be changed if it is harmful; a law is observed because, first, it is a self-imposed evil, and, secondly, it is an evil of transient duration.

Activity That Pervades All Parts Of The Body Politic In The United States; Influence That It Exercises Upon Society

More difficult to conceive the political activity that pervades the United States than the freedom and equality that reign there—The great activity that perpetually agitates the legislative bodies is only an episode, a prolongation of the general activity—Difficult for an American

我在这里讲到所有的阶级也许是错的;在美国,人们把欧洲人的权力阶梯倒置过来,在那里,富人的地位与旧世界穷人的地位一样,而经常怀疑法律的反而是富人。我在本章的前面说过,民主政府的益处,并不像人们有时所声称的那样要以保护所有人的利益为准则,而仅仅只是维持大多数人的利益。在美国,穷人居于统治地位,富人总是害怕穷人滥用自己的权力。富人的这种自然的忧虑,可能在内心产生不满;但社会并不会因此而被扰乱,因为让富人不相信立法者的那个理由,也同时让他们不会去反对立法者的命令。是富人的身份阻止他们享有立法权,而且还阻止他们不敢违法。

在文明国家,只有那些没有什么可以失去的人才会起来造反;可见,如果民主的法律并不总是值得尊重的,但却几乎总是受到尊重的;因为一般说来,有违法打算的人,还不能不遵守他自己制定的有利于他的法律,而且即使有些公民可能从违法当中获利,也会因为自己的人格和地位而不得不去服从立法者的任何一项决定。再者说,美国人之所以对法律言听计从,不仅因为法律是他们自己制定的,而且因为当法律损害到他们时他们可以对法律进行修订。这就是说,首先法律是他们加在自己身上的一种灾难,其次法律是可以随时解除的灾难。

美国各党派在政界的活动及其对社会的影响

考虑盛行在美国的政治活动将比考虑支配美国的自由或平等还要困难——立法机构不断发起的巨大活动,仅仅是全国的普遍政治活动的插曲和延续——很难让美国人察觉到自己整日都

to confine himself to his own business—Political agitation extends to all social intercourse—Commercial activity of the Americans partly attributable to this cause—Indirect advantages which society derives from a democratic government.

On passing from a free country into one which is not free the traveler is struck by the change; in the former all is bustle and activity; in the latter everything seems calm and motionless. In the one, amelioration and progress are the topics of inquiry; in the other, it seems as if the community wished only to repose in the enjoyment of advantages already acquired. Nevertheless, the country which exerts itself so strenuously to become happy is generally more wealthy and prosperous than that which appears so contented with its lot; and when we compare them, we can scarcely conceive how so many new wants are daily felt in the former, while so few seem to exist in the latter.

If this remark is applicable to those free countries which have preserved monarchical forms and aristocratic institutions, it is still more so to democratic republics. In these states it is not a portion only of the people who endeavor to improve the state of society, but the whole community is engaged in the task; and it is not the exigencies and convenience of a single class for which provision is to be made, but the exigencies and convenience of all classes at once. It is not impossible to conceive the surprising liberty that the Americans enjoy; some idea may likewise be formed of their extreme equality; but the political activity that pervades the United States must be seen in order to be understood. No sooner do you set foot upon American ground than you are stunned by a kind of tumult; a confused clamor is heard on every side, and a thousand simultaneous voices demand the satisfaction of their social wants. Everything is in motion around you; here the people of one quarter of a town are met to decide upon the building of a church; there the election of a representative is going on; a little farther, the delegates of a district are hastening to the town in order to consult upon some local improvements; in

在忙于私事——政治鼓动扩展到社会的方方面面——美国人的商业活动部分地归因于这种鼓动——社会从民主政府中取得的间接好处。

当你从一个自由国家步入到一个没有自由的国家,你会震惊于这些巨大的变化;在前一个国家,人们匆忙地并积极地忙于各种活动;而在后一个国家,一切都看似很平静和很安稳,社会好像处在停滞的状态。在一个当中,人们谈论的问题是改革和进步;而在另一个当中,社会好像沉寂在对已得财产的享受中,整日陷于享乐中,不在创造新的财富。但是,一个奋发的努力想使自己变得更幸福的国家,一般总是比满足于自己现状的国家更加富有和繁荣;当我们对比这两种国家时,我们简直不能理解为什么前者每天都会产生那么多需要革新的思想,而后者却好像根本就不需要新东西。

如果说这种说法可以适用于仍然保留君主政体的或仍在采用贵族制度的自由国家,那么,它将更适用于民主共和国。在民主共和国,已经不仅仅是一部分人民想要努力去改善社会的状况,而且是整个社会都忙于这项任务;这时,不只是向一个阶级,而且是同时向所有阶级提供生活的必需品和舒适。想象美国人享有的广泛自由,并很有可能的;人们也能对美国人的极端平等形成一个初步的理解;但是,对于流行于美国各处的政治鼓动,除非亲眼见到,否则根本不能理解。当你刚刚进入美国境内,就会觉得置身于一片纷闹的海洋中;嘈杂的喊叫来自四面八方,成千上万的代表一些社会要求呼声同时传到你的耳膜里。每个人都在你周围活动;这里,一伙人正在开会讨论怎样建立一座教堂;那里,人们在忙于对一名议员的选举;再远一点,一个选区的代表们正匆忙赶赴乡镇,去商讨某些地方的改革措施;在另一处,一群劳

another place, the laborers of a village quit their plows to deliberate upon the project of a road or a public school. Meetings are called for the sole purpose of declaring their disapprobation of the conduct of the government; while in other assemblies citizens salute the authorities of the day as the fathers of their country. Societies are formed which regard drunkenness as the principal cause of the evils of the state, and solemnly bind themselves to give an example of temperance. ①

The great political agitation of American legislative bodies. which is the only one that attracts the attention of foreigners, is a mere episode, or a sort of continuation, of that universal movement which originates in the lowest classes of the people and extends successively to all the ranks of society. It is impossible to spend more effort in the pursuit of happiness.

It is difficult to say what place is taken up in the life of an inhabitant of the United States by his concern for politics. To take a hand in the regulation of society and to discuss it is his biggest concern and, so to speak, the only pleasure an American knows. This feeling pervades the most trifling habits of life; even the women frequently attend public meetings and listen to political harangues as a recreation from their household labors. Debating clubs are, to a certain extent, a substitute for theatrical entertainments: an American cannot converse, but he can discuss, and his talk falls into a dissertation. He speaks to you as if he was address ing a meeting; and if he should chance to become warm in the discussion, he will say "Gentlemen" to the person with whom he is conversing.

In some countries the inhabitants seem unwilling to avail themselves of the political privileges which the law gives them; it would seem that they set too high a value upon their time to spend it on the interests of the community; and they shut themselves up in a narrow selfishness, marked out by four sunk fences and a quickset hedge.

---

① At the time of my stay in the United States the temperance societies already consisted of more than 270,000 members; and their effect had been to diminish the consumption of strong liquors by 500,000 gallons per annum in Pennsylvania alone. Temperance societies are organizations the members of which undertake to abstain from strong liquors.

动者放下了田间的工作,纷纷前来讨论在他们这里修路或建立学校的计划。有些集会的主要目的是专为宣布他们反对政府对政策的实施;而有的则是为了公布某一官员为本地的父母官。在美国,还有人将酗酒看作是国家的主要祸源,他们集合起来开会,庄严地宣布要从自身出发,为禁酒起表率作用。[①]

美国立法机构不断进行的巨大政治活动,是唯一吸引外国人注意的运动,这个运动,不过是在人民的最底阶层中开始,而后又逐步扩展到公民的所有阶级的全国运动的一个插曲,或是它的一种延续而已。要想在追求幸福上花费比这项活动更多的精力是不可能的了。

很难说美国成年人的政治生活所关心的是哪些职位。而美国人的头等大事是参与社会的管理并讨论管理的问题,这也可以被称为他们所了解的唯一乐趣了。这种情感渗透到美国人生活习惯的细微之处;甚至是妇女,也经常参加公共集会,以倾听政治辩论来解除家务带来的烦恼。对于妇女来说,辩论俱乐部在一定程度上已经代替了娱乐场所:一个美国人,虽然不善言词,但却会辩论,他的谈话会变成一个学术演讲。他对你讲话,就好像是在大会上发言一样;如果他的演讲被热烈的气氛所包围,还会对他的对话者说上一句:"先生们"。

在某些国家,居民们似乎总是很不情愿来对待法律授予他们的政治权利;他们认为,用自己最宝贵的时间为公共利益活动简直是种浪费;他们把自己封闭在狭隘的自私自利的圈子里,四周

---

① 我在留美的这段时间里,临时禁酒社团的人数已达到 27 万人;只在宾夕法尼亚州,他们的目标是要每年减少 50 万加仑的酒精消耗量。临时社团由那些强烈要求禁止酒精的人们组成。

But if an American were condemned to confine his activity to his own affairs, he would be robbed of one half of his existence; he would feel an immense void in the life which he is accustomed to lead, and his wretchedness would be unbearable,①I am persuaded that if ever a despotism should be established in America, it will be more difficult to overcome the habits that freedom has formed than to conquer the love of freedom itself.

This ceaseless agitation which democratic government has introduced into the political world influences all social intercourse. I am not sure that, on the whole, this is not the greatest advantage of democracy; and I am less inclined to applaud it for what it does than for what it causes to be done.

It is incontestable that the people frequently conduct public business very badly; but it is impossible that the lower orders should take a part in public business without extending the circle of their ideas and quitting the ordinary routine of their thoughts. The humblest individual who co-operates in the government of society acquires a certain degree of self-respect; and as he possesses authority, he can command the services of minds more enlightened than his own. He is canvassed by a multitude of applicants, and in seeking to deceive him in a thousand ways, they really enlighten him. He takes a part in political undertakings which he did not originate, but which give him a taste for undertakings of the kind. New improvements are daily pointed out to him in the common property, and this gives him the desire of improving that property which is his own. He is perhaps neither happier nor better than those who came before him, but he is

---

① The same remark was made at Rome under the first Cæsars. Montespuieu somewhere alludes to the excessive despondency of certain Roman citizens who, after the excitement of political life, were all at once flung back into the ntagnation of private life.

围着高高的墙壁和坚固的栅栏，完全将自己与外界隔离开来。但美国人却与此相反，如果只限制他们为自己的私事活动，那将会剥夺他们生存的一半乐趣；他们将会陷入日常生活中的无限空虚，并觉得无法忍受，①我深信，假如总有一天，美国会建立专制制度，它在克服自由所形成的习惯方面，将要比压制人们对自由本身的热爱更加困难。

由民主政府引入政界的这种永无停止的狂热鼓动，会扩及整个市民社会。我不知道这究竟是不是民主政府的最大优点；但我希望民主政府的将来会比现在更好。毋庸置疑，人民经常参与公共事务，往往会把事情搞得很糟；但是，如果不扩大人民的思想境界和停止他们循规蹈矩的老观念，他们就不可能参与公共事务。

让一个身份卑微的人去参与社会管理，就必须提高他对自我的尊敬程度；这样，如果他手中有权，就能命令非常有知识的人为他服务。人们纷纷求助于他，而在面对着这些人的各式各样欺骗方式时，他也从中接受了教训。他所参与的政治方面的事业，并非他的本行，但却使他对此项活动产生了强烈的兴趣。人们每天都在向他提出关于改进公共财产的新建议，于是，这就使他产生了想增进自己的私人财产的愿望。他也许不比他的前任更受人尊敬和幸福，但却比前任拥有更渊博的知识和更加积极。毋庸置疑，结合美国的民主制度与其国家的物质条件，虽然不像人们所认为

---

① 这种说法也适用于恺撒大帝统治时期的罗马。孟德斯鸠在某处就提及到了一些罗马公民的这种过度的沮丧，这些公民在经历了兴奋的政治生活后，会为自己立刻陷入私人生活中而沮丧。

better informed and more active. I have no doubt that the democratic institutions of the United States, joined to the physical constitution of the country, are the cause (not the direct, as is so often asserted, but the indirect cause) of the prodigious commercial activity of the inhabitants. It is not created by the laws, but the people learn how to promote it by the experience derived from legislation.

When the opponents of democracy assert that a single man performs what he undertakes better than the government of all, it appears to me that they are right. The government of an individual, supposing an equality of knowledge on either side, is more consistent, more persevering, more uniform, and more accurate in details than that of a multitude, and it selects with more discrim ination the men whom it employs. If any deny this, they have never seen a democratic government, or have judged upon partial evidence. It is true that, even when local circumstances and the dispositions of the people allow democratic institutions to exist, they do not display a regular and methodical system of government. Democratic liberty is far from accomplishing all its projects with the skill of an adroit despotism. It frequently abandons them before they have borne their fruits, or risks them when the consequences may be dangerous; but in the end it produces more than any absolute government; if it does fewer things well, it does a greater number of things. Under its sway the grandeur is not in what the public administration does, but in what is done without it or outside of it. Democracy does not give the people the most skillful government, but it produces what the ablest governments are frequently unable to create: namely, an all-pervading and restless activity, a superabundant force, and an energy which is inseparable from it and which may, however unfavorable circumstances may be, produce wonders. These are the true advantages of democracy.

In the present age, when the destinies of Christendom seem to be in suspense, some hasten to assail democracy as a hostile power while it is yet growing; and others already adore this new deity which is springing forth from chaos. But both parties are imperfectly acquainted with the object of their hatred or their worship; they strike in the dark and distribute their blows at random.

的是直接来源于其巨大的实业活动,但却有些间接的原因。这种实业活动并非由法律创造,而是人民在立法过程中学会怎样创建它。

当反对民主的人们宣称道,一个人单独去做他所承担的工作要比由多人管理的政府去做它所承担的工作好很多,我认为他们的话很有道理。假如双方的才力相等,则一个人主持的政府会比多人主持的政府更具有首尾统一性,更坚定不移,更思想一致,更精确于细节,更能准确的选举官员。如果有人否认这一点,那么不是因为他从来没有见过民主共和国,就是只在少数例证的基础上做的判断。即使当地方环境和人民的习性允许民主制度存在,民主制度也不能立刻显示出一套关于政府的有规则的和管理有序的方案,这一点尤为真实。民主的自由不能使它的每项事业都像开明的专制所做的那样完善。它往往在一项事业获得成功以前就夭折了,或拿事业去冒风险;但是最终它举办的事业将比专制政府举办的多很多;虽然它办成的事业很少,但它创办事业的数量却很多。在民主制度下,公家并不可能完成无比宏大的壮举,而是由私人以靠自己的力量完成的。民主制度并不能给予人民最精明能干的政府,但它所提供给人民的东西往往是最精明能干的政府所无法创造的:而到底什么才是民主的真正好处,那就是要使整个社会保持永久的积极性,整日精力充沛,形成一股离开它就无法存在和不论环境多么不利都能创造出奇迹的激情。

在现今这个时代,当基督教世界的命运似乎还悬而未决的时候,有些人则成为敌视的力量在民主尚在成长的时候,便急于对民主进行攻击;而另一些人,则把它作为在混乱之中出生的新神加以崇拜。但是,双方还都不能很全面地认识他们所仇恨或崇拜的对象;他们在黑暗中互相厮打,也许偶尔能击中对方一下。首

We must first understand what is wanted of society and its government. Do you wish to give a certain elevation to the human mind and teach it to regard the things of this world with generous feelings, to inspire men with a scorn of mere temporal advantages, to form and nourish strong convictions and keep alive the spirit of honorable devotedness? Is it your object to refine the habits, embellish the manners, and cultivate the arts, to promote the love of poetry, beauty, and glory? Would you constitute a people fitted to act powerfully upon all other nations, and prepared for those high enterprises which, whatever be their results, will leave a name forever famous in history? If you believe such to be the principal object of society, avoid the government of the democracy, for it would not lead you with certainty to the goal.

But if you hold it expedient to divert the moral and intellectual activity of man to the production of comfort and the promotion of general well-being; if a clear understanding be more profitable to man than genius; if your object is not to stimulate the virtues of heroism, but the habits of peace; if you had rather witness vices than crimes, and are content to meet with fewer noble deeds, provided offenses be diminished in the same proportion; if, instead of living in the midst of a brilliant society, you are contented to have prosperity around you; if, in short, you are of the opinion that the principal object of a government is not to confer the greatest possible power and glory upon the body of the nation, but to ensure the greatest enjoyment and to avoid the most misery to each of the individuals who compose it—if such be your desire, then equalize the conditions of men and establish democratic institutions. But if the time is past at which such a choice was possible, and if some power superior to that of man already hurries us, without consulting our wishes, towards one or the other of these two governments, let us endeavor to make the best of that which is allotted to us and, by finding out both its good and its evil tendencies, be able to foster the former and repress the latter to the utmost.

先,我们必须了解社会需要什么,而政府又需要什么。对此,是需要花时间解释的。你想使人的思想达到一定的境界,让它以慷慨的胸怀去接受这个世界上的各种事物吗?你想让人们用鄙视的眼光去对待物质财富吗?你要养成并保持坚强的信念吗?你要使高雅的形象、文明的举止和灿烂的艺术大放光芒吗?你向往诗歌、美好的事物和崇高的荣誉吗?你试图组织一个民族对其他一切民族采取强力措施吗?你打算创办伟大的事业,而且不管是成还是败,都让你的名字被历史所记载吗?假如你认为人生在世的主要目的就在于此,你就得回避民主政府,因为民主政府肯定不会让你达到这个特定的目的。

但是,如果你认为把人在道德和智力方面的活动转向于对物质生活需要的满足和创造福利是有利的;如果你觉得清楚地理解比天才对人们更有利;如果你的目的不是创造崇高的品德,而是培养一种温和的习惯;如果你宁愿看到弊端而不愿看到罪恶,而且只要没有重大犯罪,你觉得少一些高尚的行为也无所谓;如果你安逸于在一个繁荣社会里的生活,而不认为出入于一个时尚华丽的社会是一种光荣;最后,如果在你眼中,政府的主要目的并不是想使整个国家拥有更强大的力量或更崇高的荣誉,而是使国内的每一个人享有更多的福利和免遭苦难;那么,你就得使人们具有平等的身份和建立民主政府。但是如果你已经失去了可以选择的机会,而且一个居于芸芸众生之上的最高权力在没经过你的同意下就已把你推进这两种政府中之一种,那你就要努力从你被推进的那个政府中吸取到最好的营养,并在发现那个政府的善与恶的倾向后极力地抑制后者而促进前者。

CHAPTER XV

Unlimited Power Of The Majority In The
United States, And Its Consequences

*Natural Strength of the majority in democracies—Most of the A-
merican constitutions have increased this strength by artificial means—
How this has been done—Pledged delegates—Moral power of the majority—Opinion as to its infallibility—Respect for its rights, how augmented in the United States.*

The very essence of democratic government consists in the absolute sovereignty of the majority; for there is nothing in democratic
states that is capable of resisting it. Most of the American constitutions have sought to increase this natural strength of the majority by
artificial means. ①

Of all political institutions, the legislature is the one that is most
easily swayed by the will of the majority. The Americans determined
that the members of the legislature should be elected by the people *directly*, and for a *very brief term*, in order to subject them, not only to
the general convictions, but even to the daily passions, of their constituents. The members of both houses are taken from the same classes in society and nominated in the same manner; so that the
movements of the legislative bodies are almost as rapid, and quite as
irresistible, as those of a single assembly. It is to a legislature thus
constituted that almost all the authority of the government has been
entrusted.

---

① We have seen, in examining the Federal Constitution, that the efforts of
the legislators of the Union were directed against this absolute power. The consequence has been that the Federal government is more independent in its sphere
than that of the states. But the Federal government scarcely ever interferes in any
but foreign affairs; and the governments of the states in reality direct society in A-
merica.

第十五章　美国多数的无限权威及其后果

多数在民主政体中的自然力量——这种力量在美国大部分州的宪法中都人为地得到了加强——它们是怎样做到的——强制性委托——多数的道德影响——关于无错论——对权利的尊重,及其在美国的推广。

民主政府的本质,在于多数对政府的绝对统治;因为在民主制度下,任何事情都无法与多数对抗。在美国大部分州的宪法中,这种天然力量还被人为地加强了。[①]

在所有的政权机构中,最受多数意志左右的是立法机构。美国人规定由人民直接任命立法机构的成员,其成员任期也被定得很短,这样使他们不仅服从选民的长远观点,而且服从选民的临时决议。两院的议员是从同样的一些阶级中选出,并用同样的方法任命的;因此,由两院构成的立法机构,其行动的迅速和不可抗拒几乎与单一的立法机构相当。立法机构通过这样的方式被立法者们建立之后,立法机构几乎控制了政府的所有权力。

[①]　在考察联邦宪法时,我们已经看到联邦立法者努力的成果直接反对专制权利。其结果是联邦政府在其范围内比州政府拥有更多的独立权。但是联邦政府几乎不参与任何事务,除了在同外国的关系上;而州政府则直接指导着美国社会的一切事务。

At the same time that the law increased the strength of those authorities which of themselves were strong, it enfeebled more and more those which were naturally weak. It deprived the representatives of the executive power of all stability and independence; and by subjecting them completely to the caprices of the legislature, it robbed them of the slender influence that the nature of a democratic government might have allowed them to exercise. In several states the judicial power was also submitted to the election of the majority; and in all of them its existence was made to depend on the pleasure of the legislative authority, since the representatives were empowered annually to regulate the stipend of the judges.

Custom has done even more than law. A proceeding is becoming more and more general in the United States which will, in the end, do away with the guarantees of representative government: it frequently happens that the voters, in electing a delegate, point out a certain line of conduct to him and impose upon him certain positive obligations that he is pledged to fulfill. With the exception of the tumult, this comes to the same thing as if the majority itself held its deliberations in the market-place. Several particular circumstances combine to render the power of the majority in America not only preponderant, but irresistible. The moral authority of the majority is partly based upon the notion that there is more intelligence and wisdom in a number of men united than in a single individual, and that the number of the legislators is more important than their quality. The theory of equality is thus applied to the intellects of men; and human pride is thus assailed in its last retreat by a doctrine which the minority hesitate to admit, and to which they will but slowly assent. Like all other powers, and perhaps more than any other, the authority of the many requires the sanction of time in order to appear legitimate. At first it enforces obedience by constraint; and its laws are not *respected* until they have been long maintained.

The right of governing society, which the majority supposes itself to derive from its superior intelligence, was introduced into the United States by the first settlers; and this idea, which of itself would

对于本来就很弱的权力当局,当立法者在增加本来就有很强的权力当局的力量同时,其力量就会逐步减小。行政权的代表们的稳定性和独立性,都未被立法者赋予;而且,行政权的代表们被立法者驱使着完全服从于立法机构的任性,同时,他们为民主政府所容许可以行使的少许权力也被剥夺走了。在某些州,立法者把对司法权的表决也交给多数;而在所有的州,立法者甚至使立法机构为司法人员的生存所依,因为立法机构的代表享有规定每年法官薪金的权限。

习惯比法律有时更有效应。在美国,有一种习惯变得越来越流行,那就是一定要把代议制政府的种种保证推翻,否则就不善罢甘休。比如,常常会发生这样的事情:选民们在选举一名议员时,除了会为他拟出行动计划外,还为他定出一定数量的必须去执行的硬性义务。这样的多数表决,就像市场上的小贩,一边叫卖,一边讨价还价。在美国,一些特殊的环境联合起来可以促使多数的力量不仅居于压倒一切的地位,而且促使它成为无法抗拒的力量。多数的道义影响,一部分来源于下述这样一种思想:多数人联合起来的智慧和才能总比一个人的大,所以立法的人数比立法人的品质还重要。这种平等理论被应用到人的智能上;这个理论反对个人骄傲自大,对此穷追不舍,所以不容易为少数所接受,但久而久之会被少数慢慢地接受。因此,多数的权利就如同其他一切权利一样,也需要经过时间的考验才能显出它的合法性,也许它比任何权利还更需要如此。起初,多数的权利依靠强制使人服从;只有在它的法制下长期生活以后,人们才会开始对它表示尊重。

多数以为自己有可以管理社会的优越才能,是由最初的移民带到美国来的;这个只凭本身的力量就足以创造一个自由国家的

be sufficient to create a free nation, has now been amalgamated with the customs of the people and the minor incidents of social life.

The French under the old monarchy held it for a maxim that the king could do no wrong; and if he did do wrong, the blame was imputed to his advisers. This notion made obedience very easy; it enabled the subject to complain of the law without ceasing to love and honor the lawgiver. The Americans entertain the same opinion with respect to the majority.

The moral power of the majority is founded upon yet another principle, which is that the interests of the many are to be preferred to those of the few. It will readily be perceived that the respect here professed for the rights of the greater number must naturally increase or diminish according to the state of parties. When a nation is divided into several great irreconcilable interests, the privilege of the majority is often overlooked, because it is intolerable to comply with its demands.

If there existed in America a class of citizens whom the legislating majority sought to deprive of exclusive privileges which they had possessed for ages and to bring down from an elevated station to the level of the multitude, it is probable that the minority would be less ready to submit to its laws. But as the United States was colonized by men holding equal rank, there is as yet no natural or permanent disagreement between the interests of its different inhabitants. There are communities in which the members of the minority can never hope to draw the majority over to their side, because they must then give up the very point that is at issue between them. Thus an aristocracy can never become a majority while it retains its exclusive privileges, and it cannot cede its privileges without ceasing to be an aristocracy.

In the United States, political questions cannot be taken up in so general and absolute a manner; and all parties are willing to recognize the rights of the majority, because they all hope at some time to be able to exercise them to their own advantage. The majority in that country, therefore, exercise a prodigious actual authority, and a power

观念,今天已经普遍流行于社会中,深入到日常生活的一切细枝末节。

在旧的君主政体统治时期的法国人,坚定不移地认为国王的存在是无可厚非的;而当国王犯错的时候,他们却责备国王的顾问们。这种想法极大地方便了统治;使人民在抱怨法律的同时却继续拥戴和尊重立法的人。对于多数美国人也持有这种看法。

多数的道义影响,还依赖于多数人的利益应当优先于少数人的利益的原则。因此,不难理解,随着政党情况的变化,对大多数人的这种权利表示尊重,会相应地自然增加或减少的。当数个不可调和的利益集团共存于一个国家时,多数的特权往往会被忽略,因为人们将难以忍受服从于这种特权。

在美国,如果存在一个特权公民阶层,他们居于少数地位,而立法者试图剥夺他们长期独享的某些特权,想把他们从高高在上的地位上拉下来,使他们降到和大众一样的水平,那么,立法者的立法也许不会轻易地被这个少数服从。但是,由于一些彼此完全平等的人开发建立了美国,所以在那里不同居民之间还没有自然产生的利益的长期对立。有些国家的社会体制,使少数派永远不想让多数站到自己这一边,因为如果他们要这样做,就必须放弃他们最初想要反对多数的斗争目的本身。因此当一个贵族体制还保留其贵族特权时,它就永远不可能成为多数,而如果叫贵族让出特权,它自己就不再是贵族体制了。

在美国,不能以这样一般的和这样绝对的方式提出政治问题;而且所有党派都愿意认可多数的权利,因为它们都希望有朝一日能通过控制多数的权利而为自己谋利。因此,强大的管理国家的实权和几乎相当强大的影响舆论的实力都为美国的多数同时拥有;

of opinion which is nearly as great; no obstacles exist which can impede or even retard its progress, so as to make it heed the complaints of those whom it crushes upon its path. This state of things is harmful in itself and dangerous for the future.

How The Omnipotence Of The Majority Increases, In America, The Instability Of Legislation And Administration Inherent In Democracy

The Americans increase the mutability of law that is inherent in a democracy by changing the legislature every year, and investing it with almost unbounded authority—The same effect is produced upon the administration—In America the pressure for social improvements is vastly greater, but less continuous, than in Europe.

I have already spoken of the natural defects of democratic institutions; each one of them increases in the same ratio as the power of the majority. To begin with the most evident of them all, the mutability of the laws is an evil inherent in a democratic government, because it is natural to democracies to raise new men to power. But this evil is more or less perceptible in proportion to the authority and the means of action which the legislature possesses.

In America the authority exercised by the legislatures is supreme; nothing prevents them from accomplishing their wishes with celerity and with irresistible power, and they are supplied with new representatives every year. That is to say, the circumstances which contribute most powerfully to democratic instability, and which admit of the free application of caprice to the most important objects, are here in full operation. Hence America is, at the present day, the country beyond all others where laws last the shortest time. Almost all the American constitutions have been amended within thirty years; there is therefore not one American state which has not modified the principles of its legislation in that time. As for the laws themselves, a

多数一旦提出一项动议,可以说任何障碍都不会存在。这不仅仅包括阻止通过动议的阻碍,甚至包括推迟表决动议的阻碍,以及在表决的过程中留出点时间来听一听反对者的呼声的阻碍。这样处理问题的结果,有损于未来而且潜伏危险。

在美国多数的无限权威是如何
增加民主所固有的立法
与行政的不稳定性的

通过每年改选立法者和授予立法者以几乎无限的权力,美国人增加了民主所固有的立法的不稳定性——同样的影响发生在行政方面——社会改革的压力,在美国远比在欧洲强大,但不如在欧洲持久。

我已叙述过民主政府所固有的缺点;这些缺点全都随着多数的权力增加而扩大的。让我们先从最明显的缺点开始,立法的不稳定性,是民主政府固有的一个弊端,因为它来自民主制度要求不断改换新人执政的本性。但是,这个弊端或多或少是随着授予立法者的权限和行动手段而改变的。

在美国,立法当局享有最高的权力;任何事情都不能阻止它迅速地和一路通畅地提出自己的每一议项的权力,而且每年它都有新议员补缺。也就是说,凡是能滋长民主的不稳定性和迫使民主政府采纳议员对一些重大问题的反复无常意见的手段,它都一应俱全。这样,在现今,美国成了世界上法律寿命最短的国家。30 年期间,美国各州的宪法几乎全都被修改过;因此,在此当中,美国每一个州的立法原则都被修改过。至于法律本身,只要看一眼联邦各个州的档案,就足以使

single glance at the archives of the different states of the Union suffices to convince one that in America the activity of the legislator never slackens. Not that the American democracy is naturally less stable than any other, but it is allowed to follow, in the formation of the laws, the natural instability of its desires. ①

The omnipotence of the majority and the rapid as well as absolute manner in which its decisions are executed in the United States not only render the law unstable, but exercise the same influence upon the execution of the law and the conduct of the administration. As the majority is the only power that it is important to court, all its projects are taken up with the greatest ardor; but no sooner is its attention distracted than all this ardor ceases; while in the free states of Europe, where the administration is at once independent and secure, the projects of the legislature continue to be executed even when its attention is directed to other objects.

In America certain improvements are prosecuted with much more zeal and activity than elsewhere; in Europe the same ends are promoted by much less social effort more continuously applied.

Some years ago several pious individuals undertook to ameliorate the condition of the prisons. The public were moved by their statements, and the reform of criminals became a popular undertaking. New prisons were built; and for the first time the idea of reforming aswell as punishing the delinquent formed a part of prison discipline.

But this happy change, in which the public had taken so hearty an interest and which the simultaneous exertions of the citizens rendered irresistible, could not be completed in a moment. While the new penitentiaries were being erected and the will of the majority was hastening the work, the old prisons still existed

---

① The legislative acts promulgated by the state of Massachusetts alone from the year 1780 to the present time already fill three stout volumes; and it must not be forgotten that the collection to which I allude was revised in 1823, when many old laws which had fallen into disuse were omitted. The state of Massachusetts, which is not more populous than a department of France, may be considered as the most stable, the most consistent, and the most sagacious in its undertakings of the whole Union.

你确信美国的立法者一直在进行立法活动,他们不断颁布或修订法律。这不能说是美国的民主在本性上比其他国家不稳定,而是说美国人民使民主拥有允许将其意愿的天然不稳性带进立法工作的手段。①

多数的无限权威及其快速坚定地执行其决定的方式,致使法律在美国不仅趋于不稳定,并且对法律的执行和国家的行政活动发生了同样的影响。多数是至关重要的唯一力量,所以人们都付诸了极大的热情竞相完成它的所有工作;但当多数的注意力转到别处时,人们也就不会在原来的工作上花费更多的努力了;而在欧洲的一些自由国家,由于行政具有独立性并受到人们的保护,所以当立法机构的注意力转到另一项事业时,立法机构原来的决定仍将被行政机构继续执行。

在美国,人们对一些改革事业要比其他国家更加热心和更加积极;在欧洲,人们为这种事业投入的力量虽然不是太瞩目,但却很持久。

多年以来,一些虔诚的宗教信徒,一直在努力想改善监狱的状况。公众被他们的宣传所打动,因而帮助犯人新生的工作也成为事业而日益流行起来。于是,一批新的监狱建成了;对罪犯进行革新的观点,第一次与对罪犯进行惩罚的观点同时成了监狱纪律的一部分。

但是,这场有公众热心参加的和通过公民一致努力的不可抗拒的可喜改革,并未能在瞬间完成。当新的感化院正在兴建,而多数的意愿也急于促成这项事业的时候,旧的监狱依然

———————

①　一个马萨诸塞州自 1780 年至今对立法的颁布就已达到整整三大卷;并且应当注意的是,当一些陷入争议的旧法律被废除时,我所讲的这部立法著作在 1823 年已被修改。马萨诸塞州的人口不如法国稠密,但它却被看作是联邦里最稳定、最具有一贯性和最能顺利完成其事业的州。

and contained a great number of offenders. These jails became more unwholesome and corrupt in proportion as the new establishments were reformed and improved, forming a contrast that may readily be understood. The majority was so eagerly employed in founding the new prisons that those which already existed were forgotten; and as the general attention was diverted to a novel object, the care which had hitherto been bestowed upon the others ceased. The salutary regulations of discipline were first relaxed and after wards broken; so that in the immediate neighborhood of a prison that bore witness to the mild and enlightened spirit of our times, dungeons existed that reminded one of the barbarism of the Middle Ages.

Tyranny Of The Majority

How the principle of the sovereignty of the people is to be understood—Impossibility of conceiving a mixed government—The sovereign power must exist somewhere—Precautions to be taken to control its action—These precautions have not been taken in the United States—Consequences. I hold it to be an impious and detestable maxim that, politically speaking, the people have a right to do anything; and yet I have asserted that all authority originates in the will of the majority. Am I, then, in contradiction with myself?

A general law, which bears the name of justice, has been made and sanctioned, not only by a majority of this or that people, but by a majority of mankind. The rights of every people are therefore confined within the limits of what is just. A nation may be considered as a jury which is empowered to represent society at large and to apply justice, which is its law. Ought such a jury, which represents society, to have more power than the society itself whose laws it executes?

When I refuse to obey an unjust law, I do not contest the right of the majority to command, but I simply appeal from the sovereignty of

存在,并关押着大批的罪犯。这些旧的监狱,随着新感化院的日益完善和健全,而使人感到更加有害健康和更加腐败。这种鲜明的对比很容易被人所理解。而大多数都在渴望建立新的监狱,竟把早已存在的旧监狱忘得一干二净;于是,大众的注意力都被转向了新兴事物,对旧监狱的监督停止了。这先是使一系列有益的管教制度变得松弛,随后这些制度又遭到破坏;因此,在建有足以表现当代的艺术和文明的宏伟建筑物的监狱中,还有会使人想起存在于中世纪的野蛮的地牢。

多数的暴政

人民主权原则应被如何理解——设想建立一个混合政府是不可能的——最高主权必须存在于某处——必须采取预防措施,以控制最高主权的行动——在美国这种预防措施未被采纳——造成的后果。我认为有一句格言,它严重地亵渎了神灵并令人讨厌,它是这样讲的,"人民有权做任何事情";然而我又宣称,一切权力都根源于多数的意志。那么,我是不是自相矛盾呢?

一项被允许的法律,如果在一个国家需要由人民的多数来制定并进行最后表决,那么在整个世界,则要由全人类的多数来制定并进行最后表决,只有这样的法律才是公正的法律。因此,公正实际上就是对各个国家的权利进行了限定。一个国家就像一个大陪审团,它被授权代表整个社会并成为公正的仲裁者,而公正就体现在国家的法律中。代表社会的这个大陪审团的权力,是不是比社会本身在实施法律时还具有更大的权力呢?

当我拒绝对一项不公正法律的屈从时,我并不是否认多数的发布施令的权力,而仅仅是从最开始的对人民主权的依赖

the people to the sovereignty of mankind. Some have not feared to assert that a people can never outstep the boundaries of justice and reason in those affairs which are peculiarly its own; and that consequently full power may be given to the majority by which it is represented. But this is the language of a slave.

A majority taken collectively is only an individual, whose opinions, and frequently whose interests, are opposed to those of an other individual, who is styled a minority. If it be admitted that a man possessing absolute power may misuse that power by wronging his adversaries, why should not a majority be liable to the same reproach? Men do not change their characters by uniting with one another; nor does their patience in the presence of obstacles increase with their strength. ①For my own part, I cannot believe it; the power to do everything, which I should refuse to one of my equals, I will never grant to any number of them.

I do not think that, for the sake of preserving liberty, it is possible to combine several principles in the same government so as really to oppose them to one another. The form of government that is usually termed *mixed* has always appeared to me a mere chimera. Accurately speaking, there is no such thing as a *mixed government*, in the sense usually given to that word, because in all communities some one principle of action may be discovered which preponderates over the others. England in the last century, which has been especially cited as an example of this sort of government, was essentially an aristocratic state, although it comprised some great elements of democracy; for the laws and customs of the country were such that the aristocracy could not but preponderate in the long run and direct public affairs according to its own will. The error arose

---

① No one will assert that a people cannot forcibly wrong another people; but parties may be looked upon as lesser nations within a great one, and they are aliens to each other. If, therefore, one admits that a nation can act tyrannically towards another nation, can it be denied that a party may do the same towards another party?

转化为对全人类的主权。有些人曾经敢于宣称,只与其自身利益有关的问题上,人民绝对不能超越公正和理性的鸿沟,而且也不必为授予代表他们的多数以全部的权力而感到恐惧。但是,这是奴隶的语言。

如果多数不能团结得如同一个人一样,而这个人在意见上甚至常常是在利益上反对另一个人的所谓少数,那又算是什么多数呢? 但是,如果我们承认一个拥有无限权威的人可以滥用他的权力去反对他的对手,那你有什么理由不承认多数也可以这样做呢? 当大家团结在一起的时候,人们就会改变他们性格吗? 在面对种种障碍的时候,他们的耐力就不会因其力量强大而强大吗?①总之我是不相信这一点的;我反对赋予我的任何一位同胞可以决定一切的权利,并且也决不授予某几个同胞以这种权力。

我并不认为,为了维护自由,就可以联合一些不同的原则在同一政府之中,以便能真正反对另一个。我一直认为,建立所谓的混合政府,不过是一种想象。老实说,从这个词的本意来理解,从来就没有存在过混合政府,因为在所有社会,最终只能保留一个基本行动原则,它支配其他一切行动原则。18 世纪的英国是作为这种政府的例子而最常被人引证的,尽管其中包含了许多重要的民主因素;但国家的法制和习惯实质上是一个贵族国家,因为它向来是按照贵族的要求建立起来的,并随着时间的推移而逐渐占居了统治地位并按照其自身意志去指导公共事务。这种引证

---

① 没有人能断言一个人不会对另一个人犯错误;但在一个大民族里,政党通常会被看作是较小的民族,他们彼此间的性质是完全不同的。因此,如果有人承认一个民族可以对另一个民族实行暴政,那么又有谁能反对,一个政党不会对另一个政党实行暴政呢?

from seeing the interests of the nobles perpetually contending with those of the people, without considering the issue of the contest, which was really the important point. When a community actually has a mixed government—that is to say, when it is equally divided between adverse principles—it must either experience a revolution or fall into anarchy.

I am therefore of the opinion that social power superior to all others must always be placed somewhere; but I think that liberty is endangered when this power finds no obstacle which can retard its course and give it time to moderate its own vehemence.

Unlimited power is in itself a bad and dangerous thing. Human beings are not competent to exercise it with discretion. God alone can be omnipotent, because his wisdom and his justice are always equal to his power. There is no power on earth so worthy of honor in itself or clothed with rights so sacred that I would admit its uncontrolled and all-predominant authority. When I see that the right and the means of absolute command are conferred on any power whatever, be it called a people or a king, an aristocracy or a democracy, a monarchy or a republic, I say there is the germ of tyranny, and I seek to live elsewhere, under other laws. In my opinion, the main evil of the present democratic institutions of the United States does not arise, as is often asserted in Europe, from their weakness, but from their irresistible strength. I am not so much alarmed at the excessive liberty which reigns in that country as at the inadequate securities which one finds there against tyranny.

When an individual or a party is wronged in the United States, to whom can he apply for redress? If to public opinion, public opinion constitutes the majority; if to the legislature, it represents the majority and implicitly obeys it; if to the executive power, it is appointed by the majority and serves as a passive tool in its hands. The public

之所以错误,是因为引证人在持续观察贵族利益与人民利益的相互斗争时,仅仅看到了斗争本身,而没有注意这一斗争的结果,但斗争的结果恰恰是最重要的问题。如果一个社会真正建立一个混合政府,也就是说,它以平等的态度处理一些相互对立的原则时,它不是正在酝酿一场革命,就是将会陷入混乱之中。

因此,我认为有一个社会权力必然会高于其他一切权力;但我又相信,当这个权力的面前没有任何可以阻止它前进和使它延迟前进的障碍时,自由就会受到危害。

无限权威本身是一个恐怖而危险的东西。而人类不可能以明辨的态度很好的行使这个权威。我只承认上帝可以拥有这种无限权威,因为上帝的智慧和公正始终是与它的权力相等的。人世间没有一个权威因其本身的荣誉值得尊重或因其拥有不可侵犯的权利,而使我愿意承认它可以不受监督而任意行动,和随便发号施令而无人抵制。当我看到任何一个权威被授予决定一切的权利和能力时,不管人们把这个权威称做人民还是国王,或者称做民主政府还是贵族政府,或者这个权威是在君主国行使还是在共和国行使,我都要说:这是给暴政埋下了种子,而且我将设法寻找别的适合生活的地方,不再留在这里。在我看来,现今美国民主政府的最大缺陷,并不像大多数欧洲人所指责的那样在于它软弱无力,而恰恰相反,在于它拥有不可抗拒的力量。我最担心于美国的,并不在于它所拥有的极端自由的权力,而在于它反对暴政的措施太少。

当一个人或一个党在美国受到不公正的待遇时,他又能向谁去得到补偿呢?如果是向公共舆论,但舆论是由多数组成的;如果是向立法机构,但立法机构代表多数,并盲目服从多数;如果是向行政当局,但行政首脑是由多数选任的,是服从于多数的被动

force consists of the majority under arms; the jury is the majority invested with the right of hearing judicial cases; and in certain states even the judges are elected by the majority. However iniquitous or absurd the measure of which you complain, you must submit to it as well as you can. ①

If, on the other hand, a legislative power could be so constituted as to represent the majority without necessarily being the slave of its passions, an executive so as to retain a proper share of authority, and a judiciary so as to remain independent of the other two powers, a government would be formed which would still be democratic while incurring scarcely any risk of tyranny.

I do not say that there is a frequent use of tyranny in America

---

① A striking instance of the excesses that may be occasioned by the despotism of the majority occurred at Baltimore during the War of 1812. At that time the war was very popular in Baltimore. A newspaper that had taken the other side excited, by its opposition, the indignation of the inhabitants. The mob assembled, broke the printing-presses, and attacked the house of the editors. The militia was called out, but did not obey the call; and the only means of saving the wretches who were threatened by the frenzy of the mob was to throw them into prison as common malefactors. But even this precaution was ineffectual; the mob collected again during the night; the magistrates again made a vain attempt to call out the militia; the prison was forced, one of the newspaper editors was killed upon the spot, and the others were left for dead. The guilty parties, when they were brought to trial, were acquitted by the jury.

I said one day to an inhabitant of Pennsylvania: "Be so good as to explain to me how it happens that in a state founded by Quakers, and celebrated for its toleration, free blacks are not allowed to exercise civil rights. They pay taxes; is it not fair that they should vote?"

"You insult us," replied my informant, "if you imagine that our legislators could have committed so gross an act of injustice and intolerance." "Then the blacks possess the right of voting in this country?" "Without doubt."

"How comes it, then, that at the polling-booth this morning I did not perceive a single Negro?"

"That is not the fault of the law. The Negroes have an undisputed right of voting, but they voluntarily abstain from making their appearance." "A very pretty piece of modesty on their part!" rejoined I. "Why, the truth is that they are not disinclined to vote, but they are afraid of being maltreated; in this country the law is sometimes unable to maintain its authority without the support of the majority. But in this case the majority entertains very strong prejudices against the blacks, and the magistrates are unable to protect them in the exercise of their legal rights."

"Then the majority claims the right not only of making the laws, but of breaking the laws it has made?"

的工具。如果是向公安机关,但警察不外乎是多数掌握的军队;如果是向陪审团,但陪审团就是拥有宣判权的多数;而且在某些州,甚至连法官都是由多数选派的。因此,不管你所告发的事情如何地不公正和荒唐,你还得照样忍受。①

相反,假如把立法权力组织得既能代表多数,又不需要成为多数的激情的奴隶,要使行政权保留适当的权力行使权,让司法当局仍然独立于两大权力之外,那就可以建立起一个民主的政府,而又使它很少有机会受到暴政的威胁。

我并不是说,在今天的美国,暴政的手段经常被使用;而是说,

---

①　有一个可以证明多数的专制权的很好的例子,那是在 1812 年巴尔的摩的战争期间。那时战争在巴尔的摩非常流行。一家报社提出了战争的负面影响,由此就引发了居民的强烈不满。群众立即自发组织集会并闹事,破坏了印刷机,并袭击了编辑部。武装组织被调集过来,但也没能抑制住人民的亢奋;只有一个方法可以解救这些受人民威胁的可怜人,那就是以罪犯的名义将他们送入大牢。但即使这样做也没有用;群众再次集合于晚上;行政长官也再次集合军队,但仍旧已无用而告终;监狱被迫将一名编辑斩首示众,并将剩下的全部杀害。这时,即使把这些群众告上法庭,他们最终也会被宣告无罪而释放。

一天,我对宾夕法尼亚州的一个居民说:"请你好心地解释一下,为什么会在引起忍受能力而著名的贵格会会员建立的州会发生如此的事? 就是自由黑人不被允许执行其公民权利。他们缴税;难道让他们参加选举是不公平的吗?"他回答道,"如果你认为我们的立法者所制定的法案是如此的不公平和让人无法忍受,那么你就侮辱了我们。"

"那么黑人在此享有选举权了?""当然有。"

"怎么会这样? 今早,我在投票站怎么没有看到一个黑人呢?"

"那不是法律的问题。黑人毫无疑问地享有选举权,但是他们可以自愿选择弃权。""他们都很谦虚嘛!"我补充道。"为什么,事实上他们不是不愿意来投票,而是害怕遭受虐待;有时在没有多数支持下,这个国家的法律就不能维持其权威性。然而多数对黑人怀有强烈的偏见,以至于地方执行官也无法保护他们行使其合法权力。"

"也就是说,多数既要求制定法律,又要求破坏自己制定的法律?"

at the present day; but I maintain that there is no sure barrier against it, and that the causes which mitigate the government there are to be found in the circumstances and the manners of the country more than in its laws.

Effects Of The Omnipotence Of The Majority Upon The Arbitrary Authority Of American Public Officers

Liberty left by the American laws to public officers within a certain sphere—Their power.

A distinction must be drawn between tyranny and arbitrary power. Tyranny may be exercised by means of the law itself, and in that case it is not arbitrary; arbitrary power may be exercised for the public good, in which case it is not tyrannical. Tyranny usually employs arbitrary means, but if necessary it can do without them.

In the United States the omnipotence of the majority, which is favorable to the legal despotism of the legislature, likewise favors the arbitrary authority of the magistrate. The majority has absolute power both to make the laws and to watch over their execution; and as it has equal authority over those who are in power and the community at large, it considers public officers as its passive agents and readily confides to them the task of carrying out its designs. The details of their office and the privileges that they are to enjoy are rarely defined beforehand. It treats them as a master does his servants, since they are always at work in his sight and he can direct or reprimand them at any instant.

In general, the American functionaries are far more independent within the sphere that is prescribed to them than the French civil officers. Sometimes, even, they are allowed by the popular authority to exceed those bounds; and as they are protected by the opinion and backed by the power of the majority, they dare do things that even a European, accustomed as he is to arbitrary power, is astonished at. By this means habits are formed in the heart of a free country which may some day prove fatal to its liberties.

那里没有防范暴政的保证措施,而要想寻找缓和美国政府态度的原因,与其到美国的法律中去寻找,不如到它的地理环境和民俗中去寻找。

多数的无限权威对美国公共官员的专断权的影响

美国法律赋予公共官员的自由是在一定范围内的——他们的权力。

必须清楚地把专断权与暴政分开。暴政可能通过法律本身来实施,而专断权则与此不同;专断权可以为大众的利益所行使,这时它决不是暴政。暴政也常常使用专断权,但如果可以,暴政也可以不依靠专断权。

在美国,多数的无限权威有利于立法者的合法专制,同时它也有利于行政官员的专断权。多数在立法和监督执行方面有着绝对权力;它既控制着统治者,又控制着整个社会,它认为公共官员是服从于自己的下属,而且也愿意托付他们去执行自己的计划。因此,多数决不用操心公共官员的职责的细节,以及他所享受的权利。它对待他们,犹如主人对待仆人,因为他们总是在它的监视下工作,所以它能随时指导或修正他们的行动。

一般说来,赋予美国公共官员在其一定范围内的自由,要比法国公务人员享有的这种自由更大。有时,多数甚至准许公共官员越过为其规定的界限;并且,他们受舆论的保护,并有多数力量的支持,所以他们的胆识连看惯了专断权的欧洲人见了也会大吃一惊。一些习惯就以这样的方式在自由国度的中心产生,而这些习惯对于自由来说终有一天会是致命的。

Power Exercised By The Majority
In America Upon Opinion

In America, when the majority has once irrevocably decided a question, all discussion ceases—Reason for this—Moral power exercised by the majority upon opinion—Democratic republics have applied despotism to the minds of men.

IT is in the examination of the exercise of thought in the United States that we clearly perceive how far the power of the majority surpasses all the powers with which we are acquainted in Europe. Thought is an invisible and subtle power that mocks all the efforts of tyranny. At the present time the most absolute monarchs in Europe cannot prevent certain opinions hostile to their authority from circulating in secret through their dominions and even in their courts. It is not so in America; as long as the majority is still undecided, discussion is carried on; but as soon as its decision is irrevocably pronounced, everyone is silent, and the friends as well as the opponents of the measure unite in assenting to its propriety. The reason for this is perfectly clear: no monarch is so absolute as to combine all the powers of society in his own hands and to conquer all opposition, as a majority is able to do, which has the right both of making and of executing the laws.

The authority of a king is physical and controls the actions of men without subduing their will. But the majority possesses a power that is physical and moral at the same time, which acts upon the will as much as upon the actions and represses not only all contest, but all controversy.

I know of no country in which there is so little independence of mind and real freedom of discussion as in America. In any constitutional state in Europe every sort of religious and political the ory may be freely preached and disseminated; for there is no country in Europe so subdued by any single authority as not to protect the man

美国多数在行使权力时对舆论的影响

在美国,当多数一旦对一个问题做出不可更改的决定时,那么所有的讨论都会停止——原因是什么——多数行使道德权力时对舆论的影响——民主共和制度已将专制应用到人们的思想里。

当考察美国是怎样控制人们的思想时,我们就会立刻清晰地认识到多数的权威是怎样超过我们在欧洲所熟知的一切权威的。思想是一种看不见的并且很微妙的力量,它敢于对一切暴政的成果表示轻视。在现今这个时代,欧洲的一些最专制的君主,也不能阻止某些敌视他们的权威的思想在国内和甚至在宫内秘密传播。美国就不会发生这种现象;在美国,只要多数仍然没有达成最后的决定,讨论就得继续下去;但是,一旦多数做出不可更改的决定,所有的人便保持沉默,不管是决定的支持者,还是决定的反对者,都会联合在一起,表现拥护决定。这种现象的理由很清楚:那就是没有一个君主能像既有权立法又有权执法的多数这样可以专制到把一切社会权力都集结到自己手中,并征服所有反对者。

而且,国王只拥有一种物质力量,这种力量只能控制人民的行动,并不能影响人民的意志。但是,多数则同时拥有物质力量和精神力量,这两种力量结合起来既能影响人民的行动,又能改变人民的意志,它不但能镇压反抗,而且能消除内乱。

据我所知,还没有哪个国家能在思想的独立性和讨论的真正自由方面超过美国。在任何一个欧洲立宪国家,每一种宗教和政治理论都可以自由的传播,并可以向外国传播;因为没有一个欧洲国家曾被一个单独的权威统治得使敢说真话的人都得不到支

who raises his voice in the cause of truth from the consequences of his hardihood. If he is unfortunate enough to live under an absolute government, the people are often on his side; if he inhabits a free country, he can, if necessary, find a shelter behind the throne. The aristocratic part of society supports him in some countries, and the democracy in others. But in a nation where democratic institutions exist, organized like those of the United States, there is but one authority, one element of strength and success, with nothing beyond it.

In America the majority raises formidable barriers around the liberty of opinion; within these barriers an author may write what he pleases, but woe to him if he goes beyond them. Not that he is in danger of an auto-da-fé , but he is exposed to continued obloquy and persecution. His political career is closed forever, since he has offended the only authority that is able to open it. Every sort of compensation, even that of celebrity, is refused to him. Before making public his opinions he thought he had sympathizers; now it seems to him that he has none any more since he has revealed himself to everyone; then those who blame him criticize loudly and those who think as he does keep quiet and move away without courage. He yields at length, overcome by the daily effort which he has to make, and subsides into silence, as if he felt remorse for having spoken the truth.

Fetters and headsmen were the coarse instruments that tyranny formerly employed; but the civilization of our age has perfected despotism itself, though it seemed to have nothing to learn. Monarchs had, so to speak, materialized oppression; the democratic republics of the present day have rendered it as entirely an affair of the mind as the will which it is intended to coerce. Under the absolute sway of one man the body was attacked in order to subdue the soul; but the soul escaped the blows which were directed against it and rose proudly

持,从而无法维护自己的独立的成果的地步。如果很不幸的,敢说真话的人生活在一个专制政府的统治之下,则人民往往都会站在他一边;如果他幸运的生活在一个自由国度,则在有必要时他可以在王权的背后寻找庇护。如果在民主国家,一些国家的社会的贵族阶层会支持他,而相反,另一些国家的民主势力又会站在他这边。但是,在民主制度组织得像美国这样的国家,却只有一个权威,即只有一个力量和成功的根源,没有任何事物可以超越这个。

在美国,多数在舆论自由的周围筑起一座难以抗拒的屏障;在这座屏障内,作家可以写他喜欢写的东西,但如果他越过这个界限,痛苦就会随之而来。这不是说他有被宗教裁判所烧死的危险,而是说他将要受到众人的不断谴责和迫害。他的政治生涯从此便关上了大门,因为他冒犯了唯一能为他开启这个大门的权威。任何一种补偿,甚至是名分都将他拒之门外。在向公众发表自己的观点之前,他本以为会有人支持;而现在对他来说似乎什么都没有,因为他已把自己完全暴露于众人的面前;于是,责骂他的人呼声震耳,而与他想法相同的人,则失去勇气,不敢做声,躲避起来。他只好表示让步,直到最后完全屈服,保持沉默,好像为自己说出真话而后悔。

镣铐和刽子手,是昔日的暴政使用的野蛮工具;而在现今这个时代,文明也使本来觉得自己没有什么可学的专制得到了改进。可以说,昔日的君主是靠物质力量进行镇压;而今天的民主共和国则靠精神力量进行镇压,以至于连人们的意志它都想征服。在独夫统治的专制政府下,专制专门攻击身体,以便更好的压制意志;但意志却能逃脱专制直接砸向它的拳头,使自己更加高尚。这并不是暴政在民主共和国所采用的方法;它让身体保持

superior. Such is not the course adopted by tyranny in democratic republics; there the body is left free, and the soul is enslaved. The master no longer says: "You shall think as I do or you shall die"; but he says: "You are free to think differ ently from me and to retain your life, your property, and all that you possess; but you are henceforth a stranger among your people. You may retain your civil rights, but they will be useless to you, for you will never be chosen by your fellow citizens if you solicit their votes; and they will affect to scorn you if you ask for their esteem. You will remain among men, but you will be deprived of the rights of mankind. Your fellow creatures will shun you like an impure being; and even those who believe in your innocence will abandon you, lest they should be shunned in their turn. Go in peace! I have given you your life, but it is an existence worse than death."

Absolute monarchies had dishonored despotism; let us beware lest democratic republics should reinstate it and render it less odious and degrading in the eyes of the many by making it still more onerous to the few.

Works have been published in the proudest nations of the Old World expressly intended to censure the vices and the follies of the times: Labruy re inhabited the palace of Louis XIV when he composed his chapter upon the Great, and Moli re criticized the courtiers in the plays that were acted before the court. But the ruling power in the United States is not to be made game of. The smallest reproach irritates its sensibility, and the slightest joke that has any foundation in truth renders it indignant; from the forms of its language up to the solid virtues of its character, everything must be made the subject of encomium. No writer, whatever be his eminence, can escape paying this tribute of adulation to his fellow citizens. The majority lives in the perpetual utterance of self-applause, and there are certain truths which the Americans can learn only from strangers or from experience.

If America has not as yet had any great writers, the reason is given in these facts; there can be no literary genius without freedom of opinion, and freedom of opinion does not exist in America. The

自由，而直接奴役其意志。这时，国家的首脑已不再说："你得按我的思想去想，否则你就得死。"而是说："你的思想是自由的，不必跟着我思想；你的生活，你的财产，你的一切，都属于你；但从今以后，你在我们当中将是一个陌生者。你可以保留你在社会上的特权，但这些特权对你将是无用的，因为如果你恳求你的同胞选举你，他们也不会选举你；而如果你想让他们尊重你，他们将假装尊重你。你虽然仍是我们当中的一员，但你将被剥夺了做人的权利。在你接近你的同胞时，他们将像躲避脏东西一样远远离开你；即使有些人认为你是干净的，他们也一样会抛弃你，因为他们也怕别人躲避他们。你在和平中继续吧！我已经给过你生命，但你的存在将比死还难受。"

专制的君主政体已彻底使专制到了受人耻辱的地步。我们可要警惕，别让民主共和制度使专制死灰复燃，使专制只成为少数人的沉重负担，而在大多数人眼中并不那么可恨和堕落。

在旧大陆的一些骄傲自大的国家，还曾有人发表作品想要公开谴责时代的弊端和愚蠢：比如，拉布吕耶尔住在路易十四宫内期间，完成了其巨著中的《论伟大》一章，莫里哀在演给朝臣们看的戏剧里批判宫廷。但是，统治整个美国的权威，是不能被拿来戏弄的。最轻微的指责，都会激怒权威，稍微带点责备的语言，都会使权威勃然大怒；从它的语言形式到其性格的固有特点，都得加以称赞。任何一个作家，不管他多么出名，都不能逃避对其同胞的献媚。因此，多数永远生活在自我喝彩声当中，关于国内的一些真实情况，美国人只能从外国人口中听到，或从经验中感知。

如果美国至今还没出现过伟大作家，那原因只会来自这些方面；如果没有自由的舆论，就不会有文学天才，而美国恰恰就没有

Inquisition has never been able to prevent a vast number of anti-religious books from circulating in Spain. The empire of the majority succeeds much better in the United States, since it actually removes any wish to publish them. Unbelievers are to be met with in America, but there is no public organ of infidelity. Attempts have been made by some governments to protect morality by prohibiting licentious books. In the United States no one is punished for this sort of books, but no one is induced to write them; not because all the citizens are immaculate in conduct, but because the majority of the community is decent and orderly. In this case the use of the power is unquestionably good; and I am discussing the nature of the power itself. This irresistible authority is a constant fact, and its judicious exercise is only an accident.

Effects Of The Tyranny Of The Majority Upon The National Character Of The Americans— The Courtier Spirit In The United States

Effects of the tyranny of the majority more sensibly felt hitherto on the manners than on the conduct of society—They check the development of great characters —Democratic republics, organized like the United States, infuse the courtier spirit into the mass of the people— Proofs of this spirit in the United States—Why there is more patriotism in the people than in those who govern in their name.

The tendencies that I have just mentioned are as yet but slightly perceptible in political society, but they already exercise an unfavorable influence upon the national character of the Americans. I attribute the small number of distinguished men in political life to the ever increasing despotism of the majority in the United States.

When the American Revolution broke out, they arose in great numbers; for public opinion then served, not to tyrannize over, but to direct the exertions of individuals. Those celebrated men, sharing the agitation of mind common at that period, had a grandeur peculiar

这种舆论的自由。宗教裁判所始终不能阻止大量反对宗教的书籍在西班牙肆意传播。在美国,多数的统治在这方面比西班牙做得要好,因为它确实剥夺了人们打算出版这种书籍的愿望。美国虽有不信宗教的人,但他们没有自己的公共期刊。有些政府曾试图以维护公共道德来禁止淫秽书刊的发行。在美国,没有人因为出版这类书刊而受到谴责,但也没有人想去写这种书;这并不是因为每个公民都具有崇高的精神,而是因为多数公民是正派的并严肃的。在这种情况下,权力的行使无疑是好的;但我目前只是谈论权力的本身。这种不可抗拒的权力,是一个永恒的事实,而它的正确行使,却只是偶然的现象。

多数的暴政对美国人民族特性的影响及谦恭精神在美国的表现

迄今为止,多数的暴政在对社会民情方面的影响远远要比它对社会行动方面的影响大得多——这种影响抑制了伟大人物的发展——像美国建立的这种民主共和制度,容易使大多数人产生谦恭的精神——这种思想在美国的表现——人民自身的爱国主义为什么比那些以人民的名义进行统治的人的爱国主义更加强烈。

我刚才提到的那种趋势,虽然只在政界有轻微的表现,但已对美国人的民族特性产生了一些不良的影响。我甚至觉得活动于政治舞台上的为数不多的杰出人物就来自于美国多数逐渐增强其专制作用。

在美国爆发独立战争时,涌现出大批杰出的人物;当时,他们的公共舆论曾激发了人们的斗志,而没有压制人民的斗志。这个时期的那些有名的人士,在分享人民大众的鼓舞之情时,表现出了他们各自特有的伟大性格,这种伟大性格的光辉

to themselves, which was reflected back upon the nation, but was by no means borrowed from it.

In absolute governments the great nobles who are nearest to the throne flatter the passions of the sovereign and voluntarily truckle to his caprices. But the mass of the nation does not degrade itself by servitude; it often submits from weakness, from habit, or from ignorance, and sometimes from loyalty. Some nations have been known to sacrifice their own desires to those of the sovereign with pleasure and pride, thus exhibiting a sort of independence of mind in the very act of submission. These nations are miserable, but they are not degraded. There is a great difference between doing what one does not approve, and feigning to approve what one does; the one is the weakness of a feeble person, the other befits the temper of a lackey.

In free countries, where everyone is more or less called upon to give his opinion on affairs of state, in democratic republics, where public life is incessantly mingled with domestic affairs, where the sovereign authority is accessible on every side, and where its at tention can always be attracted by vociferation, more persons are to be met with who speculate upon its weaknesses and live upon ministering to its passions than in absolute monarchies. Not because men are naturally worse in these states than elsewhere, but the temptation is stronger and at the same time of easier access. The result is a more extensive debasement of character.

Democratic republics extend the practice of currying favor with the many and introduce it into all classes at once; this is the most serious reproach that can be addressed to them. This is especially true in democratic states organized like the American republics, where the power of the majority is so absolute and irresistible that one must give up one's rights as a citizen and almost abjure one's qualities as a man if one intends to stray from the track which it prescribes.

In that immense crowd which throngs the avenues to power in the United States, I found very few men who displayed that manly candor and masculine independence of opinion which frequently distinguished the Americans in former times, and which constitutes the leading

照遍全国,并且不曾依靠全国的力量来使自己的光辉添彩。

在专制政府中,那些最接近王权的高官贵族,献媚于君主的感情,并心甘情愿的屈从权威的任性。但是,全国的人民大众并不想把自己视为奴役;他们由于自己的软弱,习惯或无知,有时甚至是忠诚而常常服从于权威。有些民族将牺牲自己的意志而满足君主的意志视为是一种快乐和骄傲,以至于在每次服从中仍然使其思想独立。这样的民族虽然痛苦,但并没有堕落。而且,在做自己不情愿的事与做自己假装情愿的事之间是有很大差别的;前者是一个人的软弱无能的表现,而后者是来自一种被奴役的本性。

在自由国家里,每个人多多少少都能在处理国家的事务上发表自己的看法,在民主共和国里,公共生活与私人生活混合在一起,从而使各个方面都容易接近主权,主权也总是通过人民的叫喊声才能引起注意,因此,在这两种国家里,企图在主权的弱点下投机取巧和靠献媚主权而生活的人,一般都比专制君主国里的多。这不是因为这些国家的人天生就比别处的坏,而是因为这些国家的诱惑人的东西要比别的地方多,同时又很容易达到。结果,人们的性格就变得更加堕落。

民主共和国普遍扩大了大多数阿谀奉承的思想,并立即使这个思想立即渗入各个阶层;这是主要指责民主共和国的因素之一。这种指责在特别是在像美国这样的民主共和国更为确切。在这里,多数的权力是如此的专制和不可抗拒,以至于一个人要想摆脱多数规定的路线,就必须放弃自己作为公民的某些权利,甚至要放弃自己做人的本质。

在挤进美国权力大道的拥挤人群中,现已很少有人具有豪爽的个性和坚定不屈的精神了,而这正是美国人曾经骄傲的和

feature in distinguished characters wherever they may be found. It seems at first sight as if all the minds of the Americans were formed upon one model, so accurately do they follow the same route. A stranger does, indeed, sometimes meet with Americans who dissent from the rigor of these formulas, with men who deplore the defects of the laws, the mutability and the ignorance of democracy, who even go so far as to observe the evil tendencies that impair the national character, and to point out such remedies as it might be possible to apply; but no one is there to hear them except yourself, and you, to whom these secret reflections are confided, are a stranger and a bird of passage. They are very ready to communicate truths which are useless to you, but they hold a different language in public. If these lines are ever read in America, I am well assured of two things: in the first place, that all who peruse them will raise their voices to condemn me; and, in the second place, that many of them will acquit me at the bottom of their conscience.

I have heard of patriotism in the United States, and I have found true patriotism among the people, but never among the leaders of the people. This may be explained by analogy: despotism debases the oppressed much more than the oppressor: in absolute monarchies the king often has great virtues, but the courtiers are invariably servile. It is true that American courtiers do not say "Sire," or "Your Majesty," a distinction without a difference. They are forever talking of the natural intelligence of the people whom they serve; they do not debate the question which of the virtues of their master is pre-eminently worthy of admiration, for they assure him that he possesses all the virtues without having acquired them, or without caring to acquire them; they do not give him their daughters and their wives to be raised at his pleasure to the rank of his concubines; but by sacrificing their opinions they prostitute themselves. Moralists and philosophers in America are not obliged to conceal their opinions under the veil of allegory;

随时随地都作为伟大人物的显著特性。第一眼看过去,似乎所有美国人的头脑都是出于同一个模式,才会使他们能够如此精确地沿着同样道路前进。不错,陌生者有时会遇到一些离经叛道的美国人,还会遇到一些痛斥法律的弊端和激愤于民主任性多变的人。这些人常常会讲到那些使国民性遭到破坏的缺陷,并指出对这些错误进行补救的方法;但是,除了你以外,没有人会听他们的言词,而能让他们诉说其隐秘思想的你,却是一个外国人,一个匆匆的过客。他们愿意对你讲真心话,即使这对你毫无用处,他们到了公共场所,便用另一种说词了。如果有一天被美国人看到了上面这些被我转述的话,我猜会出现两种情况:第一,读者们将提高嗓子放声指责我;第二,其中大多数人将在内心深处默默原谅我。

我在美国曾听到人们谈论爱国主义,并且我也在人民中间发现了真正的爱国主义,但却从来没有在国家的领导者身上找到爱国主义的表现。用类推方法将很好解释这个现象:为什么专制主义对其所治人民的败坏作用,会远远超过对其执行者的败坏作用:在专制君主国,国王的品德总是高尚的,但他的朝臣多是卑鄙之人。不错,美国的官员们从来不称他们的君主为"大人"或"陛下",这似乎与君主国的朝臣有很大不同。但是,他们永远都会称赞他们的主人富有才智;从不为他们的主人到底有什么值得称赞的高尚道德而争执不休,因为他们深信主人是将一切美德都兼顾于其身的,就算现在没有或不想有,将来也一定会有;他们并不把自己的妻子和女儿送给主人,让其纳为妻妾并倍加宠爱;但他们却因为牺牲自己的观点而出卖了自己。美国的道德家们和哲学家们,虽然不必将自己的观点掩盖在寓言的面纱下;但是在他们

but before they venture upon a harsh truth, they say: "We are aware that the people whom we are addressing are too superior to the weaknesses of human nature to lose the command of their temper for an instant. We should not hold this language if we were not speaking to men whom their virtues and their intelligence render more worthy of freedom than all the rest of the world. " The sycophants of Louis XIV could not flatter more dexterously.

For my part, I am persuaded that in all governments, whatever their nature may be, servility will cower to force, and adulation will follow power. The only means of preventing men from degrading themselves is to invest no one with that unlimited authority which is the sure method of debasing them.

The Greatest Dangers Of The American Republics Proceed From The Omnipotence Of The Majority

Democratic republics liable to perish from a misuse of their power, and not from impotence—The governments of the American republics are more centralized and more energetic than those of the monarchies of Europe—Dangers resulting from this—Opinions of Madison and Jefferson upon this point.

Governments usually perish from impotence or from tyranny. In the former case, their power escapes from them; it is wrested from their grasp in the latter. Many observers who have witnessed the anarchy of democratic states have imagined that the government of those states was naturally weak and impotent. The truth is that when war is once begun between parties, the government loses its control over society. But I do not think that a democratic power is naturally without force or resources; say, rather, that it is almost always by the abuse of its force and the misemployment of its resources that it becomes a failure. Anarchy is almost always produced by its tyranny or its mistakes, but not by its want of strength.

It is important not to confuse stability with force, or the greatness of a thing with its duration. In democratic republics the power

敢于讲述一项让人痛苦的真理之前,总是先这样说:"我们知道,听我们讲话的人民都是具有高尚品德的人民,决没有有失自己主人身份的那些缺陷。我们对那些其德行和学问不是好得使他们比其他人更有权享有自由的人就不说这样的话了。"巴结路易十四的人,能够比这还会献媚吗?

在我看来,我确信在一切政府中,不管其性质如何,下贱者一定会畏惧权势,并献媚于权势。而且我认为,只有一种方法可防止人们自取其辱,那就是不对任何人赋予无限权威,这种无限权威就是确信会使其他人堕落的最高权力。

美国共和政体的最大威胁就是多数的无限权威

民主共和政体可能由于滥用其权力而导致破灭,而并非由于政府无能——美国的共和政府比欧洲的君主政府更集权和更强大——由此产生的危险——麦迪逊和杰斐逊对这个问题的看法。

政府通常不是在无能中灭亡,就是在暴政中灭亡。在前种情况下,是权力自己摆脱了政府束缚;在后种情况下,是有人抢走权力。许多人都见证过民主国家的无政府状态,并认为这是这些国家的政府天生的软弱无能而导致的。而实际上,这些国家的政党之间一旦开始了战争,政府就失去了对社会的控制力。但在我看来,一个民主政权不可能生来就缺乏人力和物力;恰恰相反,我却相信一个民主政府之所以会失败,几乎总是由于对人力和物力的滥用。无政府状态总是来源于暴政或管理不当,而不是由于政府无能。

不要把稳定与力量混在一起,或把一件事情的伟大性与其持

that directs① society is not stable, for it often changes hands and assumes a new direction. But whichever way it turns, its force is almost irresistible. The governments of the American republics appear to me to be as much centralized as those of the absolute monarchies of Europe, and more energetic than they are. I do not, therefore, imagine that they will perish from weakness. ②

If ever the free institutions of America are destroyed, that event may be attributed to the omnipotence of the majority, which may at some future time urge the minorities to desperation and oblige them to have recourse to physical force. Anarchy will then be the result, but it will have been brought about by despotism.

Mr. Madison expresses the same opinion in *The Federalist*, No. 51. "It is of great importance in a republic, not only to guard the society against the oppression of its rulers, but to guard one part of the society against the injustice of the other part. Justice is the end of government. It is the end of civil society. It ever has been, and ever will be, pursued until it be obtained, or until liberty be lost in the pursuit. In a society, under the forms of which the stronger faction can readily unite and oppress the weaker, anarchy may as truly be said to reign as in a state of nature, where the weaker individual is not secured against the violence of the stronger: and as, in the latter state, even the stronger individuals are prompted by the uncertainty of their condition to submit to a government which may protect the weak as well as themselves, so, in the former state, will the more powerful factions be gradually induced by a like motive to wish for a government which will protect all parties, the weaker as well as the more powerful. It can be little doubted, that, if the State of Rhode Island was separated from the Confederacy and left to itself, the insecurity of right under the popular

---

① This power may be centralized in an assembly, in which case it will be strong without being stable; or it may be centralized in an individual, in which case it will be less strong, but more stable.

② I presume that it is scarcely necessary to remind the reader here, as well as throughout this chapter, that I am speaking, not of the Federal government, but of the governments of the individual states, which the majority controls at its pleasure.

久性混在一起。在民主共和国,指导社会的权力一直不稳定,①因为它经常换手并指定一个新的方向。但是,每当在改变权力的控制者及其方向时,权力的力量也几乎是不可抗拒的。对我来说,美国的共和制政府也如欧洲专制君主国政府那样集权,并且比它的力量更强大。因此,我不认为它会因为软弱无力而被毁灭。②

假使有一天美国的自由事业都被毁坏了,那也一定是因为多数的无限权威,因为这种权威将会使少数忍无可忍,不得不动用武力。那么结果就是无政府状态的出现,但却是专制引发了这种状态。

麦迪逊总统在《联邦党人文集》第51篇就表达过同样的看法,他说:"对于共和政体来说,最为重要的是:不仅要保护整个社会不受统治者的压迫,而且要保护社会上的一部分弱者不会受到另一部分强者的不公平待遇。政府向来把公正作为自己的目的,而这也正是公民社会的目的。人们曾一直追求,并将赋予全力地永远追求这个目的,直到获得成功为止,或直到在追求中失去自由而被迫停止。在一个社会中,较强的派别能够联合起来镇压较弱的派别,那么可以断言,这个社会必将自然地陷入无政府状态,使软弱的个人失去了任何可以抵抗较强的个人的暴力的任何保障:在后种情况下,即使是原来较强的人也会出于对社会动荡的不满,而愿意对一个既能保护弱者又能保护自己的政府表示投降;而一旦产生了这种愿望,较强的一派和较弱的一派又在同样目的的驱使下,自愿联合起来组织一个能够保护一切强派和一切

---

① 这种权力可以在集会中被集权,这样,他在不稳定的情况下也可以变得强壮;或者以个人的形式被集中,这样,他就会不很强壮,但很稳定。

② 这里我几乎不用在提醒读者,在整个这一章中,我一直在讲多数按照自己意愿控制的是各个州的政府,而不是联邦政府。

form of government within such narrow limits would be displayed by such reiterated oppressions of the factious majorities, that some power altogether independent of the people would soon be called for by the voice of the very factions whose misrule had proved the necessity of it. "

Jefferson also said: "The executive power in our government is not the only, perhaps not even the principal, object of my solicitude. The tyranny of the legislature is really the danger most to be feared, and will continue to be so for many years to come. The tyranny of the executive power will come in its turn, but at a more distant period. "①

I am glad to cite the opinion of Jefferson upon this subject rather than that of any other, because I consider him the most powerful advocate democracy has ever had.

---

① *Letter from Jefferson to Madison*, March 15, 1789.

弱派的政府。毋庸置疑,如果罗德岛州脱离联邦而独立,那么权力的不稳定性在受到限定的政府的普遍形式下,将会对多数政党呈现出反复的压迫性,而那些所有的不依靠于人民的权力,正是由那个需要这种暴政的多数迫不及待地弄出来的。"

杰斐逊也说:"我国政府的行政权,并不是我唯一担心的问题,或许可以说不是我主要担心的问题。立法机构的暴政才真正是最可怕的危险,而且在今后许多年中仍会继续。行政权的暴政虽然也会出现,但那是很久以后的事了。"①

我很愿意在这个问题上引用杰斐逊的观点,而不愿引用其他人的话,因为我认为他是迄今为止最有力量的宣传民主的人。

---

① 1789 年 3 月 15 日,杰斐逊给麦迪逊的信中。

CHAPTER XVI

Causes Which Mitigate The Tyranny Of The Majority In The United States

Absence Of Centralized Administration. The national majority does not pretend to do everything—Is obliged to employ the town and county magistrates to execute its sovereign will.

I have already pointed out the distinction between a centralized government and a centralized administration. The former exists in America, but the latter is nearly unknown there. If the directing power of the American communities had both these instruments of government at is disposal and united the habit of executing its commands to the right of commanding; if, after having established the general principles of government, it descended to the details of their application; and if, having regulated the great interests of the country, it could descend to the circle of individual interests, freedom would soon be banished from the New World.

But in the United States the majority, which so frequently displays the tastes and the propensities of a despot, is still destitute of the most perfect instruments of tyranny.

In the American republics the central government has never as yet busied itself except with a small number of objects, sufficiently prominent to attract its attention. The secondary affairs of society have never been regulated by its authority; and nothing has hitherto betrayed its desire of even interfering in them. The majority prerogatives of the central government; those great prerogatives have been confined to a certain sphere; and although the despotism of the majority may be galling upon one point, it cannot be said to extend to all. However the predominant party in the nation may be carried away by its passions, however ardent it may be in the pursuit of its projects, it cannot oblige all the citizens to comply with its desires in the same manner

第十六章　美国怎样减轻多数的暴政

行政集权的缺乏。国家的多数没有想要总揽一切思想——是不是必须要利用乡镇和县的行政委员去执行其主权的意愿。

我在前面曾指出过政府集权和行政集权的区别。在美国，只有第一种集权，而另一种集权几乎不被人所知。假如指导美国社会的权力同时也拥有管理国家的手段，并兼有包办一切的能力和习惯以及发号施令的大权；假如它在建立了管理国家的一般原则之后，还要研究其应用的细节；假如它在规定国家的重大利益之后，还能去关心私人利益，那么，自由在新大陆早就不复存在了。

在美国，多数虽然经常流露出暴君的喜好和倾向，但还一直没有施行暴政的最完美的手段。

在美国的共和制度里，中央政府从来不会因公务而繁忙，它只管理少数值得它特别注意的事务。它从不参与管理社会的次要事务；迄今为止，它甚至没有参与管理这些事物的想法。多数变得越来越专制，但没有增加中央政府的特权；而那些特权通常被限制在一定的范围内；因此，专制在一个点上可能是大大加强了，但并未扩及到全部。尽管国内占主要地位的团体群情激奋，但无论他们追求目标的热情如何高涨，但它也无法在全国范围内

and at the same time throughout the country. When the central government which represents that majority has issued a decree, it must entrust the execution of its will to agents over whom it frequently has no control and whom it cannot perpetually direct. The townships, municipal bodies, and counties form so many concealed breakwaters, which check or part the tide of popular determination. If an oppressive law were passed, liberty would still be protected by the mode of executing that law; the majority cannot descend to the details and what may be called the puerilities of administrative tyranny. It does not even imagine that it can do so, for it has not a full consciousness of its authority. It knows only the extent of its natural powers, but is unacquainted with the art of increasing them.

This point deserves attention; for if a democratic republic, similar to that of the United States, were ever founded in a country where the power of one man had previously established a centralized administration and had sunk it deep into the habits and the laws of the people, I do not hesitate to assert that in such a republic a more insufferable despotism would prevail than in any of the absolute monarchies of Europe; or, indeed, than any that could be found on this side of Asia.

The Temper Of The Legal Profession In The United States, And How It Serves As A Counterpoise To Democracy

Utility of ascertaining what are the natural instincts of the legal profession—These men are to act a prominent part in future society—How the peculiar pursuits of lawyers give an aristocratic turn to their ideas—Accidental causes that may check this tendency—Ease with which the aristocracy coalesces with legal men—Use of lawyers to a despot—The profession of the law constitutes the only aristocratic element with which the natural elements of democracy will combine—Peculiar causes which tend to give an aristocratic turn of mind to English and American lawyers—The aristocracy of America is on the bench and at the bar—Influence of lawyers upon American society—

让人们同时用它的方法附和它的意志。当代表多数的中央政府发布国家命令时,必须命令一些官员去执行它的旨意,但这些官员并不总是受它控制,它也不能永远监督他们。因此,乡镇、市政和县形成了如此众多的隐形的障碍,这些障碍或阻碍或错导了人民意志的洪流。假如法令是令人难以忍受的,自由也会在法令的实施当中找到保护;而且多数也无法管到事情的细枝末节,甚至我敢说管不住行政专制的敷衍了事。其实,他们甚至根本没有意识到自己能够这么做,因为它们根本还没能充分认识自己的权力。它只知道自己的自然力量,但并不熟悉扩大这个力量范围的技巧。

这一点很值得注意;假如将来有一天在某一个国家建立了类似美国这样的民主共和制度,而这个国家原先就是寡头执政并完全按照习惯法和成文法行使职权,那么,我会毫不犹豫地说在这样一个新建的共和国里,一种新的令人难以忍受的专政制度将超过在欧洲的任何君主国家;而只有到亚洲,才会找到能与这种专横相媲美的某些事实。

美国的法学家精神以及它是如何平衡民主力量的

探讨法学家精神的本性的实用性——这些法学家在未来社会中扮演了重要的角色——法学家从事的工作怎样使他们的思想具有了贵族气质——可以抑制这种思想发展的偶然原因——贵族发现自己容易与法学家联合——暴君对法学家的利用——法学家是如何成为与民主因素自然结合起来的唯一的贵族因素的——使英国和美国的法学家精神易于具有贵族气质的特殊原因——美国的贵族是律师和法官——法学家对美国社会的影

Their peculiar magisterial spirit affects the legislature, the administration, and even the people.

In visiting the Americans and studying their laws, we perceive that the authority they have entrusted to members of the legal profession, and the influence that these individuals exercise in the government, are the most powerful existing security against the excesses of democracy. This.effect seems to me to result from a general cause, which it is useful to investigate, as it may be reproduced elsewhere.

The members of the legal profession have taken a part in all the movements of political society in Europe for the last five hundred years. At one time they have been the instruments of the political authorities, and at another they have succeeded in converting the political authorities into their instruments. In the Middle Ages they afforded a powerful support to the crown; and since that period they have exerted themselves effectively to limit the royal prerogative. In England they have contracted a close alliance with the aristocracy; in France they have shown themselves its most dangerous enemies. Under all these circumstances have the members of the legal profession been swayed by sudden and fleeting impulses, or have they been more or less impelled by instincts which are natural to them and which will always recur in history? I am incited to this investigation, for perhaps this particular class of men will play a prominent part in the political society that is soon to be created.

Men who have made a special study of the laws derive from this occupation certain habits of order, a taste for formalities, and a kind of instinctive regard for the regular connection of ideas, which naturally render them very hostile to the revolutionary spirit and the unreflecting passions of the multitude.

The special information that lawyers derive from their studies ensures them a separate rank in society, and they constitute a sort of privileged body in the scale of intellect. This notion of their superiority perpetually recurs to them in the practice of their profession: they are the masters of a science which is necessary, but which is not very generally known; they serve as arbiters between the citizens; and the habit of directing to their purpose the blind passions of parties in litigation inspires them with a certain contempt for the judgment of the multitude. Add to this that they naturally constitute *a body*; not by any previous understanding, or by an agreement that directs them to a

响——他们的特殊的思想是如何深入到立法机构和行政机构的，甚至是人民身上的。

在走访了一些美国人和研究了美国法律之后，我发现美国人赋予法学家的权威和其个人对政府施加的影响，美国今天防止对民主的滥用的最有力的保障。在我看来，这个效果来自一个一般原因，而研究这个原因是非常有益的，因为它在别处可能再现。

500 多年以来，法学家在欧洲一直参加政治社会的各种运动。有时，他们是政治权威的工具，又有时，它们能成功地把政权变为自己的工具。在中世纪，他们曾大力地支持过王权；从那以后，他们却坚定不移地致力于限制这个权力。在英国，他们同贵族结成了亲密的联盟；在法国，他们视贵族为自己最危险的敌人。因此，在所有这些环境下，法学家是不是被这些偶然的和暂时的冲动左右过呢？或者是不是因为本能而被他们天生的和经常重复出现的天性驱使过呢？我之所以急于探究这个问题，因为也许这个阶级的人们将会在不久即将建立起来的政治社会中占据的地位。

对法律做过特别研究的人，养成了在工作中按部就班的习惯，喜欢讲究规范，对观念之间的有规律联系有一种本能的爱好。这一切，自然使他们将多数的革命精神和民主的轻率激情视为敌人。

法学家从研究法律当中获得的特殊经验，使他们在社会中形成一个独立的阶级，并且在知识领域有着一种特殊的权力。他们在进行自己的专业时总会感到一种优越感：他们是一门虽然还未普及的但又不可缺少的科学的大师；他们是公民之间的仲裁者；把诉讼人的盲目激情引向正轨的习惯，又使他们对人民群众的判断产生一种鄙视的情绪。此外，他们自然地形成一个团体；这个团体的形成，并没有什么预先的沟通或者彼此达成一致希望借此

common end; but the analogy of their studies and the uniformity of their methods connect their minds as a common interest might unite their endeavors. Some of the tastes and the habits of the aristocracy may consequently be discovered in the characters of lawyers. They participate in the same instinctive love of order and formalities; and they entertain the same repugnance to the actions of the multitude, and the same secret contempt of the government of the people. I do not mean to say that the natural propensities of lawyers are sufficiently strong to sway them irresistibly; for they, like most other men, are governed by their private interests, and especially by the interests of the moment.

In a state of society in which the members of the legal profession cannot hold that rank in the political world which they enjoy in private life, we may rest assured that they will be the foremost agents of revolution. But it must then be asked whether the cause that then induces them to innovate and destroy results from a permanent disposition or from an accident. It is true that lawyers mainly contributed to the overthrow of the French monarchy in 1789; but it remains to be seen whether they acted thus because they had studied the laws or because they were prohibited from making them.

Five hundred years ago the English nobles headed the people and spoke in their name; at the present time the aristocracy supports the throne and defends the royal prerogative. But notwithstanding this, aristocracy has its peculiar instincts and propensides. We must be careful not to confound isolated members of a body with the body itself. In all free governments, of whatever form they may be, members of the legal profession will be found in the front ranks of all parties. The same remark is also applicable to the aristocracy; almost all the democratic movements that have agitated the world have been directed by nobles. A privileged body can never satisfy the ambition of all its members: it has always more talents and more passions than it can find places to employ, so that a considerable number of individuals are usually to be met with who are inclined to attack those very privileges which they cannot soon enough turn to their own account.

I do not, then, assert that *all* the members of the legal profession are at *all* times the friends of order and the opponents of innovation,

实现某一目的,而是与他们所做的类似的研究和所采用的几乎相同的方法将他们的思想连接起来,犹如共同的利益可以激发人们携手共进一般。因此,我们在法学家的心灵深处,可以发现与贵族相似的部分兴趣和习惯。他们的本性和贵族一样,喜欢按部就班,并拘泥于形式;他们也和贵族一样,对群众的行动极为反感,并对人民政府心怀不满。我并不是说法学家的这些本性已经强壮到使他们到了无法抵抗的地步;他们也和大多数人民一样,被自己私人的利益支配着,特别是眼前的利益。

有一种社会,其法律界人士在政界不能得到他们在民间所拥有的地位,在这种社会体制下,我们可以肯定法学家必将成为革命的先驱。但是,有人会问,引诱他们走上破坏或改造现实的原因是出于他们的固有本性还是出于偶然? 不错,1789 年推翻法国的君主政体,主要应当归功于法学家;但是,他们之所以能够这样,是因为他们研究了法律还是因为他们被禁止制定法律。

500 多年以来,英国的贵族曾经不止一次的领导着人民,并代表人民发言;但在今天,他们却拥护王权,并誓死捍卫皇家特权。但是,贵族仍保持其特有的本性和癖好。因此我们必须注意,不要把团体中的个别成员和团体本身混淆。在所有的自由政府中,不管其形式如何,法学家总是在各党派中占居首要地位。这种看法也同样适用于贵族政体;几乎所有能激起群众的民主运动都是由贵族控制的。一个拥有特权的团体,永远满足不了它的全体成员的各种野心:他们的成员满怀着满溢的天才和激情却无处释放,以至于很多个体常常就会倾向于攻击这些特权,以便能够升到上层或重建新的团体。

因此,我不认为所有法学家在任何时候都能表现出自己是秩

but merely that most of them are usually so. In a community in which lawyers are allowed to occupy without opposition that high station which naturally belongs to them, their general spirit will be eminently conservative and antidemocratic. When an aristocracy excludes the leaders of that profession from its ranks, it excites enemies who are the more formidable as they are independent of the nobility by their labors and feel themselves to be their equals in intelligence though inferior in opulence and power. But whenever an aristocracy consents to impart some of its privileges to these same individuals, the two classes coalesce very readily and assume, as it were, family interests.

I am in like manner inclined to believe that a monarch will always be able to convert legal practitioners into the most serviceable instruments of his authority. There is a far greater affinity between this class of persons and the executive power than there is between them and the people, though they have often aided to overturn the former; just as there is a greater natural affinity between the nobles and the monarch than between the nobles and the people, although the higher orders of society have often, in concert with the lower classes, resisted the prerogative of the crown.

Lawyers are attached to public order beyond every other consideration, and the best security of public order is authority. It must not be forgotten, also, that if they prize freedom much, they generally value legality still more: they are less afraid of tyranny than of arbitrary power; and, provided the legislature undertakes of itself to deprive men of their independence, they are not dissatisfied.

I am therefore convinced that the prince who, in presence of an encroaching democracy, should endeavor to impair the judicial authority in his dominions, and to diminish the political influence of lawyers, would commit a great mistake: he would let slip the substance of authority to grasp the shadow. He would act more wisely in introducing lawyers into the government; and if he entrusted despotism to them under the form of violence, perhaps he would find it again in their hands under the external features of justice and law.

The government of democracy is favorable to the political power of lawyers; for when the wealthy, the noble, and the prince are excluded

序的友人和改革的敌人,只是他们中的大多数人会这样。在一个
社会里,如果法学家安居本应属于他们的高位而无人反对,那他
们的思想将是极其保守的,并将是完全反民主的。当贵族政体把
法学家排斥在外时,法学家就会变成它的最危险的敌人,这个敌
人在财力和权力上虽然不如贵族,但在行为上却可以独立于贵
族,并认为自己的智力与贵族不相上下。但是,每当贵族愿意将
其某些特权让给法学家时,这两个阶级便会欣然地与对方结合,
甚至可以说能够成为一家人。

　　我也愿意相信,一个国王总是能够使法学家成为给自己政权
服务的最有用工具。尽管法学家往往与人民联合起来打击行政
权,但法学家与行政权之间的自然亲和力,却远远大于法学家与
人民之间的这种亲和力;同样的,尽管经常看到社会的高层阶级
与其他阶级联合起来反对王权,但贵族与国王之间的自然亲和
力,却大于贵族与人民之间的这种亲和力。

　　法学家对秩序的热爱胜过爱其他一切事物,而公共秩序的最
好保障是权威。另外,也不应当忘记,即使法学家崇尚自由,他们
一般也会更重视法制:他们害怕暴政不如害怕专断;而且,如果立
法机构以立法剥夺人们的自由,并对此承担责任,法学家也不会
对此感到不满。

　　因此我深深地相信,一个国王面临逐渐高涨的民主而欲削弱国
家的司法权和减弱法学家的政治影响,那将是大错特错。他将会使
权威的实质从它指尖溜走。他在介绍法学家参与政府时也变得更
加理智;如果政府的专制是以暴力进行的,或许在把政府交给法学
家管理以后,专制在法学家手里又会具有公正和法律的外貌。

　　民主政府有利于加强法学家的政治权力;当政府把富人、贵

from the government, the lawyers take possession of it, in their own right, as it were, since they are the only men of information and sagacity, beyond the sphere of the people, who can be the object of the popular choice. If, then, they are led by their tastes towards the aristocracy and the prince, they are brought in contact with the people by their interests. They like the government of democracy without participating in its propensities and without imitating its weaknesses; whence they derive a twofold authority from it and over it. The people in democratic states do not mistrust the members of the legal profession, because it is known that they are interested to serve the popular cause; and the people listen to them without irritation, because they do not attribute to them any sinister designs. The lawyers do not, indeed, wish to overthrow the institutions of democracy, but they constantly endeavor to turn it away from its real direction by means that are foreign to its nature. Lawyers belong to the people by birth and interest, and to the aristocracy by habit and taste; they may be looked upon as the connecting link between the two great classes of society.

The profession of the law is the only aristocratic element that can be amalgamated without violence with the natural elements of democracy and be advantageously and permanently combined with them. I am not ignorant of the defects inherent in the character of this body of men; but without this admixture of lawyer-like sobriety with the democratic principle, I question whether democratic institutions could long be maintained; and I cannot believe that a republic could hope to exist at the present time if the influence of lawyers in public business did not increase in proportion to the power of the people.

This aristocratic character, which I hold to be common to the legal profession, is much more distinctly marked in the United States and in England than in any other country. This proceeds not only from the legal studies of the English and American lawyers, but from the nature of the law and the position which these interpreters of it occupy in the two countries. The English and the Americans have retained the law of precedents; that is to say, they continue to found their legal opinions and the decisions of their courts upon the opinions and decisions of their predecessors. In the mind of an English or American lawyer a taste and a reverence for what is old is almost always

族和君主撵出大门,法学家在政府里就将总揽大权,因为他们是人民所能找到的唯一的有能力并聪明的人了。如果法学家一方面因其爱好而自然倾向贵族和君主,另一方面又因其利益而自然倾向人民。因此,法学家虽然也喜欢民主政府,但他们没有参与民主的偏好,没有被染上民主的弱点;从而能通过民主并超过民主使自己加倍强大。民主政体下的人民非常相信法学家,因为人民知道法学家的利益在于对人民的事业服务;人民听法学家的话而不气恼,因为人民预料法学家不会有什么邪恶的想法。事实上,法学家根本不想推翻民主创造的政府,而是想不断设法按照非民主所固有的倾向,以非民主所具有的手段去领导政府。法学家,从利益和出身上来说,属于人民,而从习惯和爱好上来说,又属于贵族;法学家被视为是人民和贵族之间地自然链接。

法学家的行业,是唯一容易与民主的自然因素在非暴力的情况下混合,并以有利于己的方式与其永久结合的贵族因素。我并没有忽视法学家精神的固有缺点;但民主原则如果不与法学家思想相结合,我就很怀疑民主机构是否能够长久维持下去;而且,我也不相信,如果法学家在社会事务中的干预产生的影响不随着人民权力的增加而加强,共和政体仍旧有望可以在今天存在下去。

我从法学家精神中见到的这个贵族特点,在美国和英国的表现比在其他任何国家都更明显。其原因不仅在于英国和美国的法学家参与了立法工作,而且在于法律的自然本性及法律解释者在这两个国家所处的地位。英国人和美国人保留了立法的先例;也就是说,他们继续依据祖先的法学观点和法律定则来建立自己在法律方面应持的观点和应守的规则。一个英国或美国的法学家,几乎总是把对古老东西的尊敬和热爱与对正规的和合法的东

united with a love of regular and lawful proceedings.

This predisposition has another effect upon the character of the legal profession and upon the general course of society. The English and American lawyers investigate what has been done; the French advocate inquires what should have been done; the former produce precedents, the latter reasons. A French observer is surprised to hear how often an English or an American lawyer quotes the opinions of others and how little he alludes to his own, while the reverse occurs in France. There the most trifling litigation is never conducted without the introduction of an entire system of ideas peculiar to the counsel employed; and the fundamental principles of law are discussed in order to obtain a rod of land by the decision of the court. This abnegation of his own opinion and this implicit deference to the opinion of his forefathers, which are common to the English and American lawyer, this servitude of thought which he is obliged to profess, necessarily give him more timid habits and more conservative inclinations in England and America than in France.

The French codes are often difficult to comprehend, but they can be read by everyone; nothing, on the other hand, can be more obscure and strange to the uninitiated than a legislation founded upon precedents. The absolute need of legal aid that is felt in England and the United States, and the high opinion that is entertained of the ability of the legal profession, tend to separate it more and more from the people and to erect it into a distinct class. The French lawyer is simply a man extensively acquainted with the statutes of his country; but the English or American lawyer resembles the hierophants of Egypt, for like them he is the sole interpreter of an occult science.

The position that lawyers occupy in England and America exercises no less influence upon their habits and opinions. The English aristocracy, which has taken care to attract to its sphere whatever is at all analogous to itself, has conferred a high degree of importance and authority upon the members of the legal profession. In English society, lawyers do not occupy the first rank, but they are contented with the station assigned to them: they constitute, as it were, the younger branch of the English aristocracy; and they are attached to

西的爱好结合起来。

这种习性对法学家的精神面貌和社会的动向,还起着另一种影响。英国或美国的法学家喜欢研究已完成的事实;法国的法学家拥护事实出现的原因;即前者注重判决的文本,后者注重判决的理由。当一个法国人听到英国或美国的法学家会常常引用他人的观点,而极少发表自己的见解时,他会因此感到非常吃惊,因为法国的情况就完全与此不同。法国的律师即使在处理一个很小的案件时,也不能只是进行一般的陈述而不引证他所持的成套法学思想;他将滔滔不绝地引述法律的基本原则,以劝说法庭能灵活变通并采取让步的原则。英国和美国的法学家,习惯于放弃自己的意见并百依百顺地遵从其祖先的思想,这种对祖先思想的盲目的顺从,必然使法学家精神产生胆小猥琐的习性,使其在英国和美国养成的惰性比在法国严重。

法国的成文法往往很难理解,但人人都可以对其进行研究;相反的,对于普通人来说,再也没有比以先例为基础的法律更使他糊涂和感到奇怪的了。英国和美国的法学家非常尊重这种先例,他们在教育中逐渐形成了这种尚古思想,并使他们渐渐脱离人民,并最终成为一个与众不同的阶级。法国的法学家是对自己国家状况熟知的简单的人;而英国或美国的法律界人士,则好像是埃及的祭司,并像埃及的祭司一样,是这种玄秘科学的解释者。

法律界人士在英国和美国所处的地位,对他们的习惯和思想产生了一种不小的影响。一心想把一切在本性上与己有某些类似的东西拉到自己方面来的英国贵族,对法学家很是尊重,并赋予他们以极大的权力。在英国的社会里,法学家虽然不曾占有最高等级,但他们却对现在所在的等级很满意:他们构成了英国贵

their elder brothers, although they do not enjoy all their privileges. The English lawyers consequently mingle the aristocratic tastes and ideas of the circles in which they move with the aristocratic interests of their profession.

And, indeed, the lawyer-like character that I am endeavoring to depict is most distinctly to be met with in England: there laws are esteemed not so much because they are good as because they are old; and if it is necessary to modify them in any respect, to adapt them to the changes that time operates in society, recourse is had to the most inconceivable subtleties in order to uphold the traditionary fabric and to maintain that nothing has been done which does not square with the intentions and complete the labors of former generations. The very individuals who conduct these changes disclaim any desire for innovation and had rather resort to absurd expedients than plead guilty to so great a crime. This spirit appertains more especially to the English lawyers; they appear indifferent to the real meaning of what they treat, and they direct all their attention to the letter, seeming inclined to abandon reason and humanity rather than to swerve one tittle from the law. English legislation may be compared to the stock of an old tree upon which lawyers have engrafted the most dissimilar shoots in the hope that, although their fruits may differ, their foliage at least will be confused with the venerable trunk that supports them all.

In America there are no nobles or literary men, and the people are apt to mistrust the wealthy; lawyers consequently form the highest political class and the most cultivated portion of society. They have therefore nothing to gain by innovation, which adds a conservative interest to their natural taste for public order. If I were asked where I place the American aristocracy, I should reply without hesitation that it is not among the rich, who are united by no common tie, but that it occupies the judicial bench and the bar.

The more we reflect upon all that occurs in the United States, the more we shall be persuaded that the lawyers, as a body, form the most powerful, if not the only, counterpoise to the democratic element. In that country we easily perceive how the legal profession is

族中比较年轻的队伍;他们爱戴和尊敬他们的大哥,虽然他们不能享有全部特权,他们也从不计较。这样,英国的法学家便把他们活动圈子里的贵族喜好和思想,与他们职业的贵族利益结合起来。

实际上,我努力描绘的这种法学家的形象,在英国表现得最为明显:这些法律之所以会受到尊重,并不是因为它们良好,而是因为它们古老;如果有必要对法律的某些方面进行修改,使其适应时代的变革,他们也不会脱离其根本,只是对祖先留下的东西进行修修补补,只对祖先的思想进行发展,只对祖先的业绩进行提升。不要奢望他们会以革新者的面貌出现,他们宁愿被人指为荒谬无比谴责和嘲笑,也不愿承担冒犯老祖宗遗训的大罪。这种精神特别适用于英国的法学家;他们似乎从不关心事物的实质,他们把所有的注意力集中到文本上,宁肯违反理性和人情,也不改动法律上的一文一字。我们可以把英国的立法工作比作修饰一棵古树,立法者向这棵树上嫁接各式各样的枝条,希望这样会结出千奇百怪的果实,或至少让繁茂的枝叶簇拥着它们的树干。

在美国,既没有贵族也没有文学家,人民不信任富人;因此,法学家形成了一个最高政治阶级,并且是社会上最有知识的部分。因此,他们并没有需要改革而获得的利益,使自己的爱好秩序的本性增添了保守的兴趣。假如有人问我将把美国的贵族放在何处,我将毫不迟疑地回答:他们不属于富人,富人没有把他们联合在一起的共同纽带,美国的贵族是那些大律师和大法官。

我们越是深思美国发生的一切,就越是确信法学界是能够协调美国民主的最强有力的力量,甚至可以说是能够协调美国民主的唯一力量。在这个国家,我们会很容易发现,法学家精神是如

qualified by its attributes, and even by its faults, to neutralize the vices inherent in popular government. When the American people are intoxicated by passion or carried away by the impetuosity of their ideas, they are checked and stopped by the almost invisible influence of their legal counselors. These secretly oppose their aristocratic propensities to the nation's democratic instincts, their superstitious attachment to what is old to its love of novelty, their narrow views to its immense designs, and their habitual procrastination to its ardent impatience.

The courts of justice are the visible organs by which the legal profession is enabled to control the democracy. The judge is a lawyer who, independently of the taste for regularity and order that he has contracted in the study of law; derives an additional love of stability from the inalienability of his own functions. His legal attainments have already raised him to a distinguished rank among his fellows; his political power completes the distinction of his station and gives him the instincts of the privileged classes.

Armed with the power of declaring the laws to be unconstitutitonal,[1] the American magistrate perpetually interferes in political affairs. He cannot force the people to make laws, but at least he can oblige them not to disobey their own enactments and not to be inconsistent with themselves. I am aware that a secret tendency to diminish the judicial power exists in the United States; and by most of the constitutions of the several states the government can, upon the demand of the two houses of the legislature, remove judges from their station. Some other state constitutions make the members of the judiciary elective, and they are even subjected to frequent re-elections. I venture to predict that these innovations will sooner or later be attended with fatal consequences; and that it will be found out at some future period that by thus lessening the independence of the judiciary they have attacked not only the judicial power, but the democratic republic itself.

It must not be supposed, moreover, that the legal spirit is confined in the United States to the courts of justice; it extends far beyond them. As the lawyers form the only enlightened class whom the people do not

---

[1] See Chapter VI, on "The Judicial Power in the United States."

何利用其优点,甚至还可以说如何利用其缺点,来协调平民政府所固有的缺点的。当美国人民陶醉于自己的激情中,并因自己的理想而忘形时,他们会受到法学家的一种几乎是看不见的影响而打击,甚至会停止下来。法学家秘密地用他们的贵族习性去对抗民主的本能,用他们对古老事物的崇敬去对抗民主对新鲜事物的热爱,用他们的狭窄的观点去对抗民主广泛的原则,用他们喜欢深思熟虑的处事习惯去对抗民主的急躁。

法院是法学界对付民主的最有效的工具。法官都是法学家,他们除了喜欢独立研究法律过程中的规则和秩序以外;还因其职位的终身性而酷爱安宁。他们的法学知识,早已使他们在同胞中处于杰出的地位;他们的政治权力,可以使他们占据高于他人的地位,并养成特权阶级的习惯。

有权宣布法律违宪的美国司法官员,①经常参与政治事务。他们不能强迫人民制定法律,但至少可以强迫人民服从他们自己制定的法律,并要求他们言行一致。我已经意识到,在美国存在着一种驱使人民削弱司法权的潜在趋势;大部分州的宪法,都规定州政府可以在两院的要求下撤换法官。而另一些州的宪法,规定法庭的成员由选举产生,甚至准许多次连选连任。我敢大胆预言,这项改革迟早要产生极坏的后果;而且在未来的某一天将被发现,这样削弱司法官员的独立性,不仅使司法权受到打击,而且使民主共和制度本身也受到了打击。

此外,千万不要以为,只有美国的法院才具有法学家精神;这种精神早已超出法院的界限以外。由于法学家是人民唯一能够

---

① 见第六章,《美国的司法权》。

mistrust, they are naturally called upon to occupy most of the public stations. They fill the legislative assemblies and are at the head of the administration; they consequently exercise a powerful influence upon the formation of the law and upon its execution. The lawyers are o-bliged, however, to yield to the current of public opinion, which is too strong for them to resist; but it is easy to find indications of what they would do if they were free to act. The Americans, who have made so many innovations in their political laws, have introduced very sparing alterations in their civil laws, and that with great difficulty, al though many of these laws are repugnant to their social condition. The reason for this is that in matters of civil law the majority are obliged to defer to the authority of the legal profession, and the American law-yers are disinclined to innovate when they are left to their own choice. It is curious for a Frenchman to hear the complaints that are made in the United States against the stationary spirit of legalmen and their prejudices in favor of existing institutions.

The influence of legal habits extends beyond the precise limits I have pointed out. Scarcely any political question arises in the United States that is not resolved, sooner or later, into a judicial question. Hence all parties are obliged to borrow, in their daily controversies, the ideas, and even the language, peculiar to judicial proceedings. As most public men are or have been legal practitioners, they intro-duce the customs and technicalities of their profession into the man-agement of public affairs. The jury extends this habit to all classes. The language of the law thus becomes, in some measure, a vulgar tongue; the spirit of the law, which is produced in the schools and courts of justice, gradually penetrates beyond their walls into the bos-om of society, where it descends to the lowest classes, so that at last the whole people contract the habits and the tastes of the judicial mag-istrate. The lawyers of the United States form a party which is but lit-tle feared and scarcely perceived, which has no badge peculiar to it-self, which adapts itself with great flexibility to the exigencies of the time and accommodates itself without resistance to all the movements of the social body. But this party extends over the whole community and penetrates into all the classes which compose it; it acts upon the country imperceptibly, but finally fashions it to suit its own purposes.

信任的有知识的阶级,因此他们自然会占领很多公共职位。他们既是立法机构的成员,又是行政机构的首领;因此,他们对法律的制定和行使都具有极大的影响。但是,他们必须服从对他们发生强烈的抑制作用的公共舆论;即使他们可以自由的行动,人民也不难发现它们行动的目的。在政治法方面做了很多改革的美国人,却在民法方面只做了微小的改革,而且这一小点改革还费了很大的困难,尽管民法中的许多规定与美国的社会情况是极端不符的,但他们还会依旧这么做。造成这种情况的原因是,在民法的问题上,多数往往被迫交给法学家去处理,而美国法学家却不肯改革,依旧按照自己的决定办事。一个法国人,在听到美国人民抱怨法学家有惰性和偏爱已存在的现状时,确实非常吃惊。

法学家精神的影响,大大超过了我已确切指出的范围。在美国,几乎所有政治问题最终都会与司法挂钩。因此,所有的党派在它们的日常论辩中,都要借用司法程序的思想和语言。大多数公务员都是或曾经是法学家,所以他们把自己专业的习惯和思维方式都应用到公共事务的管理上。陪审制度则把这一习惯扩展到所有阶级。因此,法律的语言在某种程度上几乎变成了普通语言;法学家精神本来产生于学校和法院,但现在也逐渐超越学校和法院的范围,并扩展到整个社会,深入到社会最底层,最终使全民都沾染了司法官们的习惯和爱好。美国的法学家形成一个派别,这个派别不足以畏惧但却几乎难以察觉,它没有属于自己的旗帜,却能够极其灵活地迎合时代的要求,不加抵抗地顺应社会的一切运动。但是,这个派别却扩展到整个社会,并深入到社会上的所有阶级;在暗中推动社会,最终使社会的发展顺应自己的目的。

Trial By Jury In The United States Considered As A Political Institution

Trial by jury, which is one of the forms of the sovereignty of the people, ought to be compared with the other laws which establish that sovereignty—Composition of the jury in the United States—Effect of trial by jury upon the national character—It educates the people— How it tends to establish the influence of the magistrates and to extend the legal spirit among the people.

Since my subject has led me to speak of the administration of justice in the United States, I will not pass over it without referring to the institution of the jury. Trial by jury may be considered in two separate points of view: as a judicial, and as a political institution. If it was my purpose to inquire how far trial by jury, especially in civil cases, ensures a good administration of justice, I admit that its utility might be contested. As the jury was first established when society was in its infancy and when courts of justice merely decided simple questions of fact, it is not an easy task to adapt it to the wants of a highly civilized community when the mutual relations of men are multiplied to a surprising extent and have assumed an enlightened and intellectual character. [1]

---

[1]   The consideration of trial by jury as a judicial institution, and the appraisal of its effects in the United States, together with an inquiry into the manner in which the Americans have used it, would suffice to form a book, and a book very interesting to France. One might trace therein, for example, what parts of the American system pertaining to the jury might be introduced among us, and by what steps. The state of Louisiana would throw the most light upon the subject, as it has a mingled population of French and English. The two systems of law, as well as the two nations, are there found side by side and are gradually combining with each other. The most useful books to consult would be the *Digeste des Lois de la Louisiane*; and the *Traité sur les Règles des Actions civiles*, printed in French and English at New Orleans, in 1830, by Buisson. This book has a special advantage; it presents, for Frenchmen, an exact and an authentic glossary of English legal terms. The language of law is everywhere different from that of the people, a fact particularly true of the English.

陪审团在美国被视为是一种政治机构

　　作为人民主权的表现形式之一的陪审团,必须与其他建立这个主权的法律协调一致——美国陪审团的结构——陪审制度在国民性方面的影响——陪审制度在人民的教育方面产生的作用——陪审制度是如何建立司法官员的影响并扩大法学家精神在人民中的影响的。

　　由于我的讲题引导我要去叙述美国的司法制度,我在这里就不能不谈陪审制度。我们可以用两个独立的观点来审视陪审制度:第一,它是作为司法制度而存在的;第二,它是作为政治制度而起作用的。如果要问陪审制度在哪一方面对司法制度有利,特别是在民事方面,我承认陪审制度的实用性会引起争论。陪审制度在社会尚不发达的时候就已存在,那时法院只受理一些简单的诉讼,但是,要想使陪审制度适应高度发展的文明社会的需要,任务就变得很艰巨,因为这时人与人之间的关系已经超乎寻常的复杂,并具有需要用科学和理智加以判断的性质。①

---

　　① 要考察陪审制度的司法方面和评价它对美国发生的效用,以及询问美国人使用陪审制度的方式,这些问题足够出一本让法国人非常感兴趣的书了。有人也许会调查,例如,美国制度中有哪些是为陪审制度服务的,并采取了哪些措施。在这里,路易斯安那州将给我们很大的启示,因为在那里既存在法国人,也存在英国人。但是我们会发现这两个国家以及它们各自不同的法律制度在逐步与对方结合,肩并肩地向前进。可供查阅的最有用的书籍是"Digeste des Lois de la Louisiane";和"Traité sur les Règles des Actions civiles",于1830年以法文和英文的形式在新奥尔良的布恩森出版。这本书有个特别的优点,那就是,对于法国人,它是一本精确地汇集了英国法律术语的权威书籍。法律术语会因地方的差异而有所不同,这一点对英国人尤为真实。

My present purpose is to consider the jury as a political institution; any other course would divert me from my subject. Of trial by jury considered as a judicial institution I shall here say but little. When the English adopted trial by jury, they were a semi-barbarous people; they have since become one of the most enlightened nations of the earth, and their attachment to this institution seems to have increased with their increasing cultivation. They have emigrated and colonized every part of the habitable globe; some have formed colonies, others independent states; the mother country has maintained its monarchical constitution; many of its offspring have founded powerful republics; but everywhere they have boasted of the privilege of trial by jury. ①They have established it, or hastened to reestablish it, in all their settlements. A judicial institution which thus obtains the suffrages of a great people for so long a series of ages, which is zealously reproduced at every stage of civilization, in all the climates of the earth, and under every form of human government, cannot be contrary to the spirit of justice. ②

---

① All the English and American jurists are unanimous on this point. Mr. Story, Justice of the Supreme Court of the United States, speaks, in his *Commentaries on the Constitution*, of the advantages of trial by jury in civil cases: "The inestimable privilege of a trial by jury in civil cases," says he, "a privi-lege scarcely inferior to that in criminal cases, which is counted by all per-sons to be essential to political and civil liberty. " (Story, Book III, Ch. 38.)

② If it were our object to establish the utility of the jury as a judicial institution, many arguments might be brought forward, and among others the following: In proportion as you introduce the jury into the business of the courts, you are enabled to diminish the number of judges, which is a great advantage. When judges are very numerous, death is perpetually thinning the ranks of the judicial functionaries and leaving places vacant for new-comers. The ambition of the magistrates is therefore continually excited, and they are naturally made dependent upon the majority or the person who nominates to vacant offices; the officers of the courts then advance as do the officers of an army. This state of things is entirely contrary to the sound administration of justice and to the intentions of the legislator. The office of a judge is made inalienable in order that he may remain independent; but of what advantage is it that his independence should be protected if he be tempted to sacrifice it of his own accord? When judges are very numerous, many of them must necessarily be incapable; for a great magistrate is a man of no common powers: I do not know if. a half-enlightened tribunal is not the worst of all combinations for attaining those ends which underlie the establishment of courts of justice. For my own part, I had rather submit the decision of a case to ignorant jurors directed by a skillful judge than to judges a majority of whom are imperfectly acquainted with jurisprudence and with the laws.

现在,我的主要目标是考察陪审制度的政治方面;其他的都会使我偏题。对于作为司法手段陪审制度,我在这里只能简单提一下。当年英国人采用陪审制度的时候,他们还处于半野蛮状态;从那时起,他们逐渐发展成为世界上最文明的民族之一,而随着受教育程度增长,他们对这种制度的喜爱也日益加深。他们逐步向别的国家扩展,并垄断了一些地方;结果,有些地方成了他们的殖民地,而另一些地方则建立了独立的国家;他们的母国仍旧维持着君主制度;他们的后裔虽大都建立起了强大的共和政体;但他们仍旧四处鼓吹陪审制度的优越性。① 他们在自己的领地建立起了陪审制度,或者加紧建立着。这个伟大民族所提倡的司法制度,后来便长期存在下来,并在文明的各个阶段,在没有遭到司法界反对的情况下,被各个地区和各种政府所采用。②

---

① 在这个问题上,英国与美国的所有法学家的态度都是一致的。美国最高法院的法官约瑟夫先生,在他的著作《对美国宪法的评论》中,谈到陪审制度在民事案件中的优点:他说"陪审制度在民事案件中有着不可估量的特权","并被所有人民认为是对政治自由和文明自由的一种重要特权。"(《评论》第三卷,第38章。)

② 如果我们的目标是建立陪审制度在司法方面的实用性,那将会引起很多争论,如下所示:当你把陪审制度引介到法庭中,你必须要按比例的减少法官的数量,这是陪审制度一个很大的优势。当法官的人数众多时,司法官员这一职能在不断地走向死亡,并为后来者留出一个空缺的职位。因此,野心家们依旧存在着,他们自然会去依靠多数或者是有任命权力的掌权者;于是,法庭的官员犹如军队的士兵进步着。这种事态完全违背了司法制度和立法者的用心。为了让法官保持独立,法院赋予他不可剥夺的权力;但是如果法官自愿去牺牲这种权利时,那么法官这种独立性的优势在哪里呢?当法官人数众多时,他们中的许多将变成是无用的;因为伟大的官员都是有着特殊权力的人:我不知道是否一个半开明的法庭在要达到建立正义法庭的环节里是最糟糕的。在我看来,对于一宗案件,我宁愿承认一群无知的陪审员在一个有技巧的法官的指导下所做的决定,而不是一些熟悉法学和精通法律的多数所做的判决。

But to leave this part of the subject. It would be a very narrow view to look upon the jury as a mere judicial institution; for however great its influence may be upon the decisions of the courts, it is still greater on the destinies of society at large. The jury is, above all, a political institution, and it must be regarded in this light in order to be duly appreciated.

By the jury I mean a certain number of citizens chosen by lot and invested with a temporary right of judging. Trial by jury, as applied to the repression of crime, appears to me an eminently republican element in the government, for the following reasons.

The institution of the jury may be aristocratic or democratic, according to the class from which the jurors are taken; but it always preserves its republican character, in that it places the real direction of society in the hands of the governed, or of a portion of the governed, and not in that of the government. Force is never more than a transient element of success, and after force comes the notion of right. A government able to reach its enemies only upon a field of battle would soon be destroyed. The true sanction of political laws is to be found in penal legislation; and if that sanction is wanting, the law will sooner or later lose its cogency. He who punishes the criminal is therefore the real master of society. Now, the institution of the jury raises the people itself, or at least a class of citizens, to the bench of judges. The institution of the jury consequently invests the people, or that class of citizens, with the direction of society. ①

In England the jury is selected from the aristocratic portion of the nation; the aristocracy makes the laws, applies the laws, and punishes

① An important remark must, however, be made. Trial by jury does unquestionably invest the people with a general control over the actions of the citizens, but it does not furnish means of exercising this control in all cases or with an absolute authority. When an absolute monarch has the right of trying offenses by his representatives, the fate of the prisoner is, as it were, decided beforehand. But even if the people were predisposed to convict, the composition and the nonresponsibility of the jury would still afford some chances favorable to the protection of innocence.

但是,先抛下这个问题不谈。只把陪审制度看作是一种司法制度,这是十分狭窄的看法;因为不论它对法庭的最终判决会产生多么大的影响,它由此也要对诉讼当事人的命运发生更大的影响。因此,陪审制度首先是一种政治制度。应当始终从这个观点去评价陪审制度。

我意义上的陪审制度,就是随时请来几位公民,组成一个陪审团,暂时赋予他们以参加审判的权利。在我看来,作为惩治犯罪行为方面的陪审制度,是建立共和制度的一个重要因素,其理由如下:

陪审制度既可能是贵族性质的,也可能是民主性质的,这要取决于陪审员所在的阶级;但是,只要它不把这项工作的实际控制权交给统治者,或使其掌握在一部分被统治者手里,它始终可以保持共和性质。强制不过就是转瞬即逝的成功因素,而被强制之后紧接着就会产生权利的观念。一个只能在战场上击败敌人的政府,很快也会被人推翻。因此,对政治法的真实处罚,必须体现在刑法里面;如果没有处罚,法律迟早会失去其强制作用。因此,那些惩治社会罪犯的人,才是社会真正的主人。实行陪审制度,就可把人民本身,或至少把整个一个阶级的公民提到法官的席位。因此,陪审制度在实质上就是把领导社会的权力置于人民或一个阶级的公民的手中。①

在英国,陪审团由国家的贵族中选出;贵族既制定法律,又执

---

① 有一个值得注意的理论就是,陪审制度无疑是赋予给人民指导社会的权力,但这种权力的行使并没有以专制权的形势发展到所有阶级。当一个专制君主有权通过他的亲信审判罪犯时,犯人的命运已经事先被决定了。即使人民倾向于宣判犯人有罪,陪审团中的没有责任感的成员依旧有能力提供一些保护无辜者的机会。

infractions of the laws; ① everything is established upon a consistent footing, and England may with truth be said to constitute an aristocratic republic. In the United States the same system is applied to the whole people. Every American citizen is both an eligible and a legally qualified voter. ② The jury system as it is understood in America appears to me to be as direct and as extreme a consequence of the sovereignty of the people as universal suffrage. They are two instruments of equal power, which contribute to the supremacy of the majority. All the sovereigns who have chosen to govern by their own authority, and to direct society instead of obeying its directions, have destroyed or enfeebled the institution of the jury. The Tudor monarchs sent to prison jurors who refused to convict, and Napoleon caused them to be selected by his agents.

However clear most of these truths may seem to be, they do not command universal assent; and in France, at least, trial by jury is still but imperfectly understood. If the question arises as to the proper qualification of jurors, it is confined to a discussion of the intelligence and knowledge of the citizens who may be returned, as if the jury was merely a judicial institution. This appears to me the least important part of the subject. The jury is preeminently a political institution; it should be regarded as one form of the sovereignty of the people: when that sovereignty is repudiated, it must be rejected, or it must be adapted to the laws by which that sovereignty is established. The jury is that portion of the nation to which the execution of the laws is entrusted, as the legislature is that part of the nation which makes the laws; and in order that society may be governed in a fixed and uniform manner, the list of citizens qualified to serve on juries must increase and diminish with the list of electors. This I hold to be the point of view most worthy of the attention of the legislator; all that remains is merely accessory.

---

① See Appendix Q.
② See Appendix R.

行法律和惩治违法行为。① 所有事务都要建立在立场一致的基础上,所以英国可以说就是一个贵族的共和国。而在美国,这一个制度则应用于全体人民。每一个美国公民都有选举权,都有资格参加竞选。② 在我看来,美国人意义上的陪审制度,像普选权一样,都是人民主权学说的直接结果,并且是最终结果。陪审制度和普选权,是使多数拥有至高无上权力的两个力量相等的手段。那些曾经想以自己的权威作为统治力量的统治者,并以控制社会来取代社会对他的领导的统治者,都曾破坏或是削弱过陪审制度。像在都铎王朝,就曾把不愿做有罪判决的陪审员关进监狱,拿破仑曾让自己的亲信挑选陪审员。

尽管大部分真理看上去都十分有利,但并没有得到所有人的赞成;在法国,陪审制度最终还是没有被人们很好的理解。如果有人问到,什么样的人才有资格当选陪审员,那就好像仅仅把陪审制度看作是一种司法制度,讨论参与审判工作的陪审员应当具备什么知识和能力就可以了。其实,我认为这并不是问题的关键所在。因为陪审制度是一种卓越的政治制度;它应当被看成是一种人民主权的形式:当人民的主权被推翻时,就要把陪审抛弃掉,而当人民主权存在时,就得使陪审制度与建立这个主权的各项法律协调一致。就像立法机构是负责国家法律的制定一样,陪审团是负责国家法律的执行;为了使社会得到稳定的和统一的管理,就必须使陪审员的名单随着选民的名单变化而变化。依我看,这一点最能引起立法机构的注意力。其余的一切,都无关紧要。

---

① 　见附录 Q。
② 　见附录 R。

I am so entirely convinced that the jury is preeminently a political institution that I still consider it in this light when it is applied in civil causes. Laws are always unstable unless they are founded upon the customs of a nation: customs are the only durable and resisting power in a people. When the jury is reserved for criminal offenses, the people witness only its occasional action in particular cases; they become accustomed to do without it in the ordinary course of life, and it is considered as an instrument, but not as the only instrument, of obtaining justice. ①

When, on the contrary, the jury acts also on civil causes, its application is constantly visible; it affects all the interests of the community; everyone co-operates in its work: it thus penetrates into all the usages of life, it fashions the human mind to its peculiar forms, and is gradually associated with the idea of justice itself.

The institution of the jury, if confined to criminal causes, is always in danger; but when once it is introduced into civil proceedings, it defies the aggressions of time and man. If it had been as easy to remove the jury from the customs as from the laws of England, it would have perished under the Tudors; and the civil jury did in reality at that period save the liberties of England. In whatever manner the jury be applied, it cannot fail to exercise a powerful influence upon the national character; but this influence is prodigiously increased when it is introduced into civil causes. The jury, and more especially the civil jury, serves to communicate the spirit of the judges to the minds of all the citizens; and this spirit, with the habits which attend it, is the soundest preparation for free institutions. It imbues all classes with a respect for the

---

① This is unequivocally true since the jury is employed only in certain criminal cases.

我完全相信陪审制度首先是一种政治制度，所以在把这一制度应用于民事诉讼时，我依然用这样的观点审视它。法律总要处于不稳定的状态，除非它是建立在民情的基础上：民情是一个民族的唯一的坚强耐久的力量。当陪审团参与刑事案件的审理时，人民只能从个别的案件中偶尔发现它的作用；人民已经习惯在日常生活中不应用陪审制度，只把它看作是获得公理的一种手段，而没有把它视为获得公理的唯一手段。①

相反的，当陪审团参加民事案件的审理时，它的作用总是非常明显的；这时，它影响着社会的所有利益；每个人都来请它帮助：于是，它深入到生活的一切习惯，让人们的头脑去迎合它的特殊形式，并逐渐把它自己与道德联系在一起。

因此，只用于刑事案件的陪审制度，将一直处于危险之中；而一旦把它用于民事案件，它就经得起时间的考验和人类的反抗。假如能像从英国的法律中那样容易地排除陪审制度而从英国人的民情中排除陪审制度，英国的陪审制度早在都铎王朝时期就不复存在了；因此，事实上在那个时期拯救英国自由的，正是民事陪审制度。不管以什么方式应用陪审制度，它都无疑会对国民性发生重大影响；但是，当把陪审制度应用于民事案件时，这种影响便会无限加强。陪审制度，特别是民事陪审制度，能将法官的一部分思想精神与全体公民的联合起来；而这种思想精神，正是人民为使自己自由而要养成的习惯。这种制度让所有的阶级对判决的事实要充满尊敬，并养成权利观念。假如这两种因素没有达到其应

---

①　无疑这一点是真实的，因为陪审制度仅仅应用到一些特定的案件中。

thing judged and with the notion of right. If these two elements be removed, the love of independence becomes a mere destructive passion. It teaches men to practice equity; every man learns to judge his neighbor as he would himself be judged. And this is especially true of the jury in civil causes; for while the number of persons who have reason to apprehend a criminal prosecution is small, everyone is liable to have a lawsuit. The jury teaches every man not to recoil before the responsibility of his own actions and impresses him with that manly confidence without which no political virtue can exist. It invests each citizen with a kind of magistracy; it makes them all feel the duties which they are bound to discharge towards society and the part which they take in its government. By obliging men to turn their attention to other affairs than their own, it rubs off that private selfishness which is the rust of society.

The jury contributes powerfully to form the judgment and to increase the natural intelligence of a people; and this, in my opinion, is its greatest advantage. It may be regarded as a gratuitous public school, ever open, in which every juror learns his rights, enters into daily communication with the most learned and enlightened members of the upper classes, and becomes practically acquainted with the laws, which are brought within the reach of his capacity by the efforts of the bar, the advice of the judge, and even the passions of the parties. I think that the practical intelligence and political good sense of the Americans are mainly attributable to the long use that they have made of the jury in civil causes.

I do not know whether the jury is useful to those who have lawsuits, but I am certain it is highly beneficial to those who judge them; and I look upon it as one of the most efficacious means for the education of the people which society can employ.

What I have said applies to all nations, but the remark I am about to make is peculiar to the Americans and to democratic com munities. I have already observed that in democracies the members of the legal profession and the judicial magistrates constitute the only aristocratic body which can moderate the movements of the people. This aristocracy is invested with no physical power; it exercises its conservative influence upon the minds of men; and the most abundant

有的效果,那么人们对独立的喜爱就只能变成一种破坏性的激情。这种制度教导人们做事要公平公正;每个人在审判他人的时候,总会想到有一天他们自己也会被审判。这种情况在民事案件中更为真实;几乎没有人不害怕有朝一日自己成为刑事诉讼的对象,而且每个人都有可能成为诉讼的对象。陪审制度教导每个人不能在需要对自己的行为负责时就退缩,这是男子汉的气魄,没有这种气魄,任何政治道德都将不复存在。陪审制度赋予每个公民一种地方行政官员的地位;使人人感到自己对社会负有责任和参与了自己的政府。陪审制度迫使人们把眼光从只做自己的事情转变为去关心他人的事情,而这种自私自利则是社会的锈病。

陪审团对于判决的形成和人们自然智慧的提高做出了有力的帮助;而且我认为,这也正是它的最大的优点。我们甚至可以把陪审团看成是一所常设的免费学校,陪审员们在这里学会运用自己的权利,经常接触上层阶级的最有教养和最有知识的人群,并在律师的帮助和法官的指点,甚至是党派的激情下,使自己在实践中精通了法律。我认为,美国人的政治常识和实践知识,主要是在长期运用民事陪审制度当中获得的。

我不知道陪审制度对诉讼者是否有利,但我确信它对判决者们绝对有利;我认为陪审团是社会能够用来教育人民的最有效手段之一。

我刚才所讲的是适用于一切国家的,但我下面将要叙述的,则是专门针对于美国和一般民主国家的。我在前面已经说过,在民主共和国,法学家和司法人员,构成了唯一能够缓和人民运动的贵族政体。这种贵族政体并没有被赋予任何物质力量;只对人们的思想产生保守的影响;但是,他们的权威的主要根源,就存在

source of its authority is the institution of the civil jury. In criminal causes, when society is contending against a single man, the jury is apt to look upon the judge as the passive instrument of social power and to mistrust his advice. Moreover, criminal causes turn entirely upon simple facts, which common sense can readily appreciate; upon this ground the judge and the jury are equal. Such is not the case, however, in civil causes; then the judge appears as a disinterested arbiter between the conflicting passions of the parties. The jurors look up to him with confidence and listen to him with respect, for in this instance, his intellect entirely governs theirs. It is the judge who sums up the various arguments which have wearied their memory, and who guides them through the devious course of the proceedings; he points their attention to the exact question of fact that they are called upon to decide and tells them how to answer the question of law. His influence over them is almost unlimited.

If I am called upon to explain why I am but little moved by the arguments derived from the ignorance of jurors in civil causes, I reply that in these proceedings, whenever the question to be solved is not a mere question of fact, the jury has only the semblance of a judicial body. The jury only sanctions the decision of the judge; they sanction this decision by the authority of society which they represent, and he by that of reason and of law. [1]

In England and in America the judges exercise an influence upon criminal trials that the French judges have never possessed. The reason for this difference may easily be discovered; the English and A-merican magistrates have established their authority in civil causes and only transfer it afterwards to tribunals of another kind, where it was not first acquired. In some cases, and they are frequently the most important ones, the American judges have the right of deciding causes alone. [2] On these occasions they are accidentally placed in the

---

[1]　See Appendix S.

[2]　The Federal judges decide almost always only such questions as touch directly the government of the country.

于民事陪审制度之中。在刑事诉讼中，当社会反对某个人时，陪审团都喜欢把法官视为社会权威的消极力量，对法官的意见持怀疑态度。甚至，刑事诉讼要完全以常识容易辨认的简单事实为依据；在这一点上，法官和陪审员是平等的。在民事诉讼上，情况就不一样了；这时，法官是激烈争论的两派之间的公正的仲裁者。陪审员要对法官完全信任，并以敬重的态度接受法官的仲裁，因为法官的法律知识远远高于陪审员。正是法官，将陪审员们已经混沌不清的各项法律加以总结并当庭陈述，并在情况复杂的诉讼过程中对陪审团加以引导；法官会提醒陪审团注意一些事件的详情情况和告诉他们这些法律方面的问题的解决方法。法官对陪审员的影响几乎可以说是无限的。

如果有人问我为什么对于陪审员在民事案件中没有能力引证论据而无动于衷？我的回答是在民事诉讼中，凡是不涉及事实的问题，陪审团司法审理的一个形式，他们并没有实际的发言权。陪审员只是宣布法官所做的判决；一般来说，他们都是以他们所代表的社会权威，以理性和法律的权威认定法官的判决。[①]

在英国和美国，法官对于刑事诉讼的影响是法国的法官从来不曾拥有过的。这种差别的产生原因是不难理解的；英国和美国的法官已经在民事诉讼中确立了自己的权威，然后又仅仅把这种权威转移到另一种他们不曾熟悉的法庭上。对某些案件，而且往往是重大案件，美国的法官有权独自进行判决。[②] 这时，他们的地位偶尔会与

---

① 　见附录 S。
② 　联邦法官几乎总是直接对国家政府的问题进行判决。

position that the French judges habitually occupy, but their moral power is much greater; they are still surrounded by the recollection of the jury, and their judgment has almost as much authority as the voice of the community represented by that institution. Their influence extends far beyond the limits of the courts; in the recreations of private life, as well as in the turmoil of public business, in public, and in the legislative assemblies, the American judge is constantly surrounded by men who are accustomed to regard his intelligence as superior to their own; and after having exercised his power in the decision of causes, he continues to influence the habits of thought, and even the characters, of those who acted with him in his official capacity.

The jury, then, which seems to restrict the rights of the judiciary, does in reality consolidate its power; and in no country are the judges so powerful as where the people share their privileges. It is especially by means of the jury in civil causes that the American magistrates imbue even the lower classes of society with the spirit of their profession. Thus the jury, which is the most energetic means of making the people rule, is also the most efficacious means of teaching it how to rule well.

法国法官的通常所占有地位一样,但他们的道德力量却更大;因为他们还在受陪审团的影响,他们的声音几乎与陪审团所代表的社会的声音同样具有权威性。他们的影响大大超过法院本身的影响;这是因为美国的法官在私人的娱乐中和在混乱的政治活动中,以及在公共场所和在立法机构内部,都不断遇到一些惯于认为自己的智慧总有些不如法官的人向他们致敬;而且在他们处理完案件以后,他们的权力还在影响着与他一起行使官员权利的那些人的思维习惯,甚至影响着这些人的特性。

　　陪审制度在表面上看来似乎限制了司法权,而实际上却巩固了司法权的力量;而且,任何一个国家的法官的权力都不如有人民分享法官权力的国家的法官的权力强大。美国的司法人员之所以能把我所说的法治精神渗透到社会的最底阶层,是特别借助了实行民事陪审制度。因此,陪审制度作为使人民实施统治的最有力的手段,也同样是教会人民如何很好地统治的最有效手段。

CHAPTER XVII
Principal Causes Which Tend
To Maintain The Democratic Republic
In The United States

A democratic republic exists in the United States; and the principal object of this book has been to explain the causes of its existence. Several of these causes have been involuntarily passed by, or only hinted at, as I was borne along by my subject. Others I have been unable to discuss at all; and those on which I have dwelt most are, as it were, buried in the details of this work. I think, therefore, that before I proceed to speak of the future, I ought to collect within a small compass the reasons that explain the present. In this retrospective chapter I shall be brief, for I shall take care to remind the reader only very summarily of what he already knows and shall select only the most prominent of those facts that I have not yet pointed out.

All the causes which contribute to the maintenance of the democratic republic in the United States are reducible to three heads:

I. The peculiar and accidental situation in which Providence has placed the Americans.

II. The laws.

III. The manners and customs of the people.

Accidental Or Providential Causes Which
Contribute To Main Tain The Democratic
Republic In The United States

The Union has no neighbors—No metropolis—The Americans have had the chance of birth in their favor—America an empty country—How this circumstance contributes powerfully to maintain the democratic republic in America—How the American wilds are peopled—Avidity of the Anglo-Americans in taking possession of the solitudes of the New World—Influence of physical prosperity upon the political opinions of the Americans.

第十七章　美国主张民主共和
制度的主要起因

美国实行民主共和政体；而本书的主要目的就是解释它存在的起因。在我讲述的过程中，对于一些原因我轻描淡写而过，或者点到即止；有一些原因我根本就没来得及讨论；有一些原因虽然我已提及，但大多数，还是被埋没在长篇累牍的描述中而被遗忘。因此，我认为，在我继续往下进行讨论美国的未来之前，我应该先集中对现在的状况作一解释。在这个总结性的章节中，我会简明扼要，因为我要让读者回忆起一些他所知道了的知识的梗概，而对那些我所没有提及的问题中的具有显著特点的部分加以说明。

所有导致美国维持民主共和政体的原因可以归结为三点：

1. 上帝赐予美国的独特的偶然造成的地理位置。

2. 法律。

3. 人们的生活习惯和民情。

有助于维护美国民主共和政体的
偶然的和幸运的原因

这个联邦没有邻居——没有大都会——美国人生存的环境很有利——美国资源贫瘠——这样的环境是如何有利的帮助维护美国的民主共和政体的——美国这块荒地何以有了人烟——英裔美国人对于拥有荒凉的新大陆的渴望——物质繁荣对于美国人民政治观念的影响。

A thousand circumstances independent of the will of man facilitate the maintenance of a democratic republic in the United States. Some of these are known, the others may easily be pointed out; but I shall confine myself to the principal ones.

The Americans have no neighbors and consequently they have no great wars, or financial crises, or inroads, or conquest, to dread; they require neither great taxes, nor large armies, nor greatgen erals; and they have nothing to fear from a scourge which is more formidable to republics than all these evils combined: namely, military glory. It is impossible to deny the inconceivable influence that military glory exercises upon the spirit of a nation. General Jackson, whom the Americans have twice elected to be the head of their government, is a man of violent temper and very moderate talents; nothing in his whole career ever proved him qualified to govern a free people; and, indeed, the majority of the enlightened classes of the Union has always opposed him. But he was raised to the Presidency, and has been maintained there, solely by the recollection of a victory which he gained, twenty years ago, under the walls of New Orleans; a victory which was, however, a very ordinary achievement and which could only be remembered in a country where battles are rare. Now the people who are thus carried away by the illusions of glory are unquestionably the most cold and calculating, the most unmilitary, if I may so speak, and the most prosaic of all the nations of the earth. America has no great capital ① city, whose direct or indirect influence

---

① The United States has no metropolis, but it already contains several very large cities. Philadelphia reckoned 161,000 inhabitants, and New York 202,000, in the year 1830. The lower ranks which inhabit these cities constitute a rabble even more formidable than the populace of European towns. They consist of freed blacks, in the first place, who are condemned by the laws and by public opinion to a hereditary state of misery and degradation. They also contain a multitude of Europeans who have been driven to the shores of the New World by their misfortunes or their misconduct; and they bring to the United States all our greatest vices, without any of those interests which counteract their baneful influence. As inhabitants of a country where they have no civil rights, they are ready to turn all the passions which agitate the community to their own advantage; thus, within the last few months, serious riots have broken out in Philadelphia and New York. Disturbances of this kind are unknown in the rest of the country, which is not alarmed by them, because the population of the cities has hitherto exercised neither power nor influence over the rural districts. Nevertheless, I look

许多不以人们的意志为转移的自然环境,促进了民主共和政体在美国得以维持。其中一些因素是大家已知的,而另一些则很容易指出;但是我要说的只是其中一些主要的因素。

美国因为没有邻国,所以就少了战争、金融危机、袭击、征战或者还有畏惧的苦恼;他们既不需要大量的税收,也不需要庞大的军队和伟大的将军;因此他们就不用担心所谓的军队的荣耀,这是所有苦难的源泉,对共和政体来说,比所有一切不幸加起来还要令人生畏的多。不可否认,军队的荣耀会给一个民族的精神带来难以想象的影响。杰克逊将军,曾两次被推选为美国政府的首领,是一个脾气暴躁智力中等的人;在他的政治生涯中,没有任何事情可以证明他适合做一位自由人民的领袖;并且,实际上,他遭到了联邦中大多数开明阶层的人们的反对。但是他却当上了总统,并且一直保持了总统的地位,仅仅是因为人们怀念起他20年前在新奥尔良取得的胜利;尽管这一胜利只是一次很平常的战绩,仅仅在这个战事极少的国家才会被怀念。而今天被虚荣心蒙蔽的民族,无疑是世界上最冷酷、最斤斤计较、最不懂得军情,如果我可以这么说的话,最平凡的民族。美国没有可以对整个国家产生直接或间接影响的大的首都①;这就是我所

——————

① 美国虽没有大都会,但已经出现了几个很大的城市。1830年费城居民人口达16.1万,纽约20.2万。这些城市中下等阶层聚集的乌合之众的势力比欧洲乡镇中的更强大。这群人包括一些被法律和舆论谴责永远处于悲惨境地的下流社会被释放的黑人;还有一部分为灾难和罪行而流放到新大陆的欧洲人;他们给美国带去的只有极度的罪恶,而没有带去任何利益可以用以抵消这些邪恶的所产生的危害影响。作为国家的公民,他们却没享受到公民的权利。他们要将搅乱社会的这些激情转化为自己的优势;因此,在最后的几个月中,费城和纽约爆发了动乱。这样的暴动在其他国家从未发生过,也没给他们以警觉,因为这些城市的人口既没权利也没影响力强大到足以涉及那些偏远的地区。

is felt over the whole extent of the country; this I hold to be one of the first causes of the maintenance of republican in stitutions in the United States. In cities men cannot be prevented from concerting together and awakening a mutual excitement that prompts sudden and passionate resolutions. Cities may be looked upon as large assemblies, of which all the inhabitants are members; their populace exercise a prodigious influence upon the magistrates, and frequently execute their own wishes without the intervention of public officers.

To subject the provinces to the metropolis is therefore to place the destiny of the empire not only in the hands of a portion of the community, which is unjust, but in the hands of a populace carrying out its own impulses, which is very dangerous. The preponderance of capital cities is therefore a serious injury to the repre-sentative system; and it exposes modern republics to the same defect as the republics of antiquity, which all perished from not having known this system.

It would be easy for me to enumerate many secondary causes that have contributed to establish, and now concur to maintain, the democratic republic of the United States. But among these favorable circumstances I discern two principal ones, which I hasten to point out. I have already observed that the origin of the Americans, or what I have called their point of departure, may be looked upon as the first and most efficacious cause to which the present prosperity of the United States may be attributed. The Americans had the chances of birth in their favor; and their forefathers imported that equality of condition and of intellect into the country whence the democratic republic has very naturally taken its rise. Nor was this all; for besides this republican condition of society, the early settlers bequeathed to their descendants the customs, manners, and opinions that contribute most to the success of a republic. When I reflect upon the consequences of

---

upon the size of certain American cities, and especially on the nature of their population, as a real danger which threatens the future security of the democratic republics of the New World; and I venture to predict that they will perish from this circumstance, unless the government succeeds in creating an armed force which, while it remains under the control of the majority of the nation, will be independent of the town population and able to repress its excesses.

认为得以维持美国民主共和政体的首要原因之一。在城市中,很
难避免人们聚众议事,突发暴动或者集体采取过激的行为。城市
可以被看作是一个大的集会,每位城市的居民都是集会的成员;
他们的活动对地方官员的影响很大,并且常常会自己裁决他们的
意愿,不需要政府的参与。

使地方服从于大都会,就等于不仅把全国的命运不公平地放
在了一部分人的手中,也危险地放在一些为自己的观念驱动的人
们的手中。于是,作为大都会的城市所具有的优势因此也变成了
对代议制的损害;而且它将现代共和政体置于与陈旧的共和政体
一样错误的境地,而这一陈旧的共和政体就是因为对此不了解而
消亡的。

我很容易就能列举出一些有助于美国民主共和政体的建立,
如今同时又起到保护其作用的次要因素。但是在这些有利的情
况当中,我发现了两个我急于指出的最主要的因素。我已经说过
美国的本源,或者我称之为他们的出发点,应该是首要的并且最
有效地促成美国现今的繁荣的原因。美国人有幸生在有利的环
境下;他们的父辈引入了平等的环境和资质,使得民主共和政体
自然的滋生。不仅仅是这些;除了社会的共和体制,早期的定居
者还将自己的习俗、民情和观念传给了子孙,这些都最大的造就
了共和政体的胜利。当我反省这一重要事实产生的结果时,我仿

然而,在我看来,一些美国城市的规模,尤其是它们的人口的本性,却对未
来新大陆的民主和政体的安全具有极大的威胁;并且我斗胆预测,它们
将在这样的环境下灭亡,除非政府能建立起一支独立于乡镇人口之外的武
装力量,在它滥用职权的时候可以实施镇压,而且这支力量要控制在国家
大多数人手中。

this primary fact, I think I see the destiny of America embodied in the first Puritan who landed on those shores, just as the whole human race was represented by the first man.

The chief circumstance which has favored the establishment and the maintenance of a democratic republic in the United States is the nature of the territory that the Americans inhabit. Their ancestors gave them the love of equality and of freedom; but God himself gave them the means of remaining equal and free, by placing them upon a boundless continent. General prosperity is favorable to the stability of all governments, but more particularly of a democratic one, which depends upon the will of the majority, and especially upon the will of that portion of the community which is most exposed to want. When the people rule, they must be rendered happy or they will overturn the state; and misery stimulates them to those excesses to which ambition rouses kings. The physical causes, independent of the laws, which promote general prosperity are more numerous in America than they ever have been in any other country in the world, at any other period of history. In the United States not only is legislation democratic, but Nature herself favors the cause of the people.

In what part of human history can be found anything similar to what is passing before our eyes in North America? The celebrated communities of antiquity were all founded in the midst of hostile nations, which they were obliged to subjugate before they could flourish in their place. Even the moderns have found, in some parts of South America, vast regions inhabited by a people of inferior civilization, who nevertheless had already occupied and cultivated the soil. To found their new states it was necessary to extirpate or subdue a numerous population, and they made civilization blush for its own succese. But North America was in habited only by wandering tribes, who had no thought of profiting by the natural riches of the soil; that vast country was still, properly speaking, an empty continent, a desert land awaiting its inhabitants.

Everything is extraordinary in America, the social condition of the inhabitants as well as the laws; but the soil upon which these institutions are founded is more extraordinary than all the rest. When the earth was given to men by the Creator, the earth was inexhaustible; but men were weak and ignorant, and when they had learned to take advantage of the treasures which it contained, they already covered its surface and were soon obliged to earn by the sword an asylum

佛在首批登陆这些海岸的清教徒身上看到了美国人的命运,就仿佛在第一个人身上看到人类的命运一样。

有利于美国民主共和政体的建立和维护的主要环境,是他们所居住的那片土地。祖先留给他们对平等和自由的热爱;而上帝则将他们安置在这片广袤的大地上,赐予他们维护平等和自由的手段。社会的普遍繁荣是所有政府稳定的有利条件,但尤其对民主的社会有利,因为它依赖于大多数人的意志,尤其是那些最贫困的社会群体。如果人民掌权,他们必然会幸福否则就会颠覆政权;而只有怀有野心想当皇帝的人,才会希望国家动荡不安。独立于促进普遍繁荣的法律之外的物质因素,与任何时期任何其他国家相比,在美国都存在更多。在美国,不仅立法民主,而且大自然本身也有利于人的因素。

在人类历史上哪一时期是目前北美洲正在发生的情形与之类似的?古老的杰出的民族,都是在征服的周围的敌人之后,才能得到自身的繁荣。当现代社会发现,在南美洲大片的土地上还居住着一些未开化的人们,他们仅仅只是占有并耕种着那片土地。为了建立他们的新统治就必须消灭或者征服大量的人口,他们用自己的胜利玷污了文明。但北美洲还只是被一些不定居的民族占领。这些不定居的民族还没有意识到要用天然的土地资源为自己谋利;辽阔的国家依然,应该说,是一片一无所有的陆地和荒漠等待着人们来居住。

美国所有的事情都很特别,居民的社会状况和法律;但是最奇特的还是这些制度建立在其上的土地。上帝赐予人们土地的时候,土地是无穷无尽的;但是由于人们的软弱和无知,并没能加以利用,当他们开始学会利用它的资源的时候,已经到处都是人,不久后人们就开始武力相见以争夺生存和自由的空间。就在这

for repose and freedom. Just then North America was discovered, as if it had been kept in reserve by the Deity and had just risen from beneath the waters of the Deluge. That continent still presents, as it did in the primeval time, rivers that rise from never failing sources, green and moist solitudes, and limitless fields which the plowshare of the husbandman has never turned. In this state it is offered to man, not barbarous, ignorant, and isolated, as he was in the early ages, but already in possession of the most important secrets of nature, united to his fellow men, and instructed by the experience of fifty centuries. At this very time thirteen millions of civilized Europeans are peaceably spreading over those fertile plains, with whose resources and extent they are not yet themselves accurately acquainted. Three or four thousand soldiers drive before them the wandering races of the aborigines; these are followed by the pioneers, who pierce the woods, scare off the beasts of prey, explore the courses of the inland streams, and make ready the triumphal march of civilization across the desert.

Often, in the course of this work, I have alluded to the favorable influence of the material prosperity of America upon the institutions of that country. This reason had already been given by many others before me, and is the only one which, being palpable to the senses, as it were, is familiar to Europeans. I shall not, then, enlarge upon a subject so often handled and so well understood, beyond the addition of a few facts. An erroneous notion is generally entertained that the deserts of America are peopled by European emigrants who annually disembark upon the coasts of the New World, while the American population increase and multiplyupon the soil which their forefathers tilled. The European settler usually arrives in the United States without friends and often without resources; in order to subsist, he is obliged to work for hire, and he rarely proceeds beyond that belt of industrious population which adjoins the ocean. The desert cannot be ex plored without capital or credit; and the body must be accustomed to the rigors of a new climate before it can be exposed in the midst of the forest. It is the Americans themselves who daily quit the spots which gave them birth, to acquire extensive domains in a remote region. Thus the European leaves his cottage for the transatlantic shores, and the American, who is born on that very coast, plunges in his turn into the wilds of central America. This double emigration is incessant; it begins in the middle of Europe, it crosses the Atlantic Ocean, and it

个时候,人们发现了北美,仿佛一直为神储备着,刚从洪水淹没的地方冒了出来。这块大陆一直存在着,就像它最初时一样,河水源源不断,绿色湿润的草地和广袤无垠的土地是农夫们从未耕种过的模样。北美洲以这样的形态展现在人们面前,但是人们已经不再像最初那样野蛮、无知和孤陋寡闻,他们已经了解了自然界最重要的秘密,联合自己的同胞,并且有15个世纪所积累的经验加以指导。在这一时期,13000000文明的欧洲人以和平的方式占据着那片肥沃的草原,而对这片草原的面积和资源,他们自己都不清楚。在他们前面,三四千战士驱逐着那些不定居的土著;他们后面是先锋,披荆斩棘,驱逐捕食的野兽,开拓内陆的河流,在荒漠中开拓文明的胜利进程。

在这部作品中,我常常会提到建立在美国社会制度之上的物质繁荣对其产生的有利的影响。在我之前的很多人已经解释过这个原因,也是唯一一个为欧洲所熟悉和接受的原因。我不需要再扩展这个被提及多次大家已很了解的题目,只就它提供几个事例。大家普遍都有一个错误的观念,美洲荒漠上所居住的居民都是来自欧洲的移民。他们每年都有一批人从新大陆的海岸线登陆,而美国的人口数量上升并且依旧在他们的祖先的这块土地上繁衍生殖。从欧洲来美国定居的人们通常都没有朋友和来历;为了生存,他不得不受雇于人,而且也很少有机会能跨越沿海到内地去开发。没有资金和贷款是很难开发这块荒漠的;而要想到森林里去,还得先让身体适应严酷的气候。是美国人自己,离开自己出生的地方,到偏僻的地方占领更广阔的土地。因此,欧洲人离开家园远渡重洋到大西洋沿岸定居,而生长在大西洋海岸的美

advances over the solitudes of the New World. Millions of men are marching at once towards the same horizon; their language, their religion, their manners differ; their object is the same. Fortune has been promised to them somewhere in the West, and to the West they go to find it.

No event can be compared with this continuous removal of the human race, except perhaps those irruptions which caused the fall of the Roman Empire. Then, as well as now, crowds of men were impelled in the same direction, to meet and struggle on the same spot; but the designs of Providence were not the same. Then every newcomer brought with him destruction and death; now each one brings the elements of prosperity and life. The future still conceals from us the remote consequences of this migration of the Americans towards the West; but we can readily apprehend its immediate results. As a portion of the inhabitants annually leave the states in which they were born, the population of these states increases very slowly, although they have long been established. Thus in Connecticut, which yet contains only fifty-nine inhabitants to the square mile, the population has not been increased by more than one quarter in forty years, while that of England has been augmented by one third in the same period. The European emigrant always lands, therefore, in a country that is but half full, and where hands are in demand; he becomes a workman in easy circumstances, his son goes to seek his fortune in unpeopled regions and becomes a rich landowner. The former amasses the capital which the latter invests; and the stranger as well as the native is unacquainted with want.

The laws of the United States are extremely favorable to the division of property; but a cause more powerful than the laws prevents property from being divided to excess. ①This is very perceptible in the states which are at last beginning to be thickly peopled. Massachusetts is the most populous part of the Union, but it contains only eighty inhabitants to the square mile, which is much less than in

---

① In New England estates are very small, but they are rarely divided further.

国人,却投身到美国的内陆创业。这两方移民都在不断进行;从
欧洲中部开始,跨越大西洋,到达荒芜的新大陆。成千上万的人
们涌向同一目的地,操着不同的语言、宗教信仰和习俗;但他们的
目的一致。西部对他们来说意味着财富,他们要到那里寻找
财富。

　　也许除了导致罗马帝国灭亡的那些剧增的人口以外,没有其
他事件可以与这次持续不断的人口迁徙相媲美。像现在这样,人
们被驱使着朝同一方向前进,在那里相遇争斗,但是上帝对他们
的安排却不尽相同。那时候,等待着每一个新来的人们的是毁灭
和死亡;而如今人们却带来了繁荣和生命的种子。未来虽对我们
掩盖了美国人向西部移民的一些微妙的影响,但是我们能了解其
直接的结果。随着每年都有一部分居民离开自己出生的州,尽管
这些州已建立很久,但其人口数量增长就会很慢。因此在康涅狄
格每平方英里只有 59 人,40 年内人口数量增长还不到四分之一,
而在英格兰同一时期人口增长了三分之一。欧洲移民都集中到
一个国家,这里人口不足而且缺乏劳动力;在这样舒适的环境中,
他做了工人,而他的儿子在人烟稀少的地方寻找财富,变成了富
裕的地主。前人聚积财富,后人拿来投资,外来的人口和当地的
居民都生活富足。

　　美国的法律极其有利于分散财产;但有一个比法律更强大的
因素抑制着财产的过度分散。[①] 这一点在这个人口开始日益密集
的地区越发明显。马萨诸塞州是联邦中人口最稠密的地区,但是其
每平方英里也只有 80 个居民,比法国少很多,那里每平方英里大约

---

　　① 新英格兰的地产虽然都很小,但是也没有再进一步被分化。

France, where one hundred and sixty-two are reckoned to the same extent of country. But in Massachusetts estates are very rarely divided; the eldest son generally takes the land, and the others go to seek their fortune in the wilderness. The law has abolished the right of primogeniture, but circumstances have concurred to re-establish it under a form of which none can complain and by which no just rights are impaired.

A single fact will suffice to show the prodigious number of individuals who thus leave New England to settle in the wilds. We were assured in 1830 that thirty-six of the members of Congress were born in the little state of Connecticut. The population of Connecticut, which constitutes only one forty-third part of that of the United States, thus furnished one eighth of the whole body of representatives. The state of Connecticut of itself, however, sends only five delegates to Congress; and the thirty-one others sit for the new Western states. If these thirty-one individuals had remained in Connecticut, it is probable that, instead of becoming rich landowners, they would have remained humble laborers, that they would have lived in obscurity without being able to rise into public life, and that, far from becoming useful legislators, they might have been unruly citizens.

These reflections do not escape the observation of the Americans any more than of ourselves. "It cannot be doubted," says Chancellor Kent, in his Treatise on American Law (Vol. IV, p. 580), "that the division of landed estates must produce great evils, when it is carried to such excess as that each parcel of land is insufficient to support a family; but these disadvantages have never been felt in the United States, and many generations must elapse before they can be felt. The extent of our inhabited territory, the abundance of adjacent land, and the continual stream of emigration flowing from the shores of the Atlantic towards the interior of the country, suffice as yet, and will long suffice, to prevent the parcelling out of estates."

It would be difficult to describe the avidity with which the American rushes forward to secure this immense booty that for tune offers. In the pursuit he fearlessly braves the arrow of the Indian and the diseases of the forest; he is unimpressed by the silence of the woods; the

有 162 人。但在马萨诸塞州,地产几乎不会被分化,因为他们只有年长的子女才能继承地产,其他人都必须到荒野中寻找自己财富。这条法律虽破坏了年长子女继承的权利,但是环境赋予了它新的形式,而这一形式没有人会抱怨,因为它并没有削弱任何公正的权利。

一个简单的事实就足以证明当年离开新英格兰定居荒野的人数的庞大。我们确定的是,1830 年,有 36 个国会议员诞生在康涅狄格这个小州上。只占美国总人口四十三分之一的康涅狄格的人口,就占据了整个议员代表的八分之一。而康涅狄格只有 5 位代表参加国会,其余 31 人作为西部各州的议员参加国会。如果这 31 位代表仍然留在康涅狄格,那么就不会成为富有的地主,而仍旧是卑微的劳动者,生活在艰苦的环境中,没有机会晋升到政界,更不会成为立法者,也许还会成为难以管理的公民。

美国人关于这一现象的评论并不比我们少。"无须怀疑,"前衡平法院首席法官肯特在其著作《关于美国法律的论述》(第四卷第 580 页)中说,"如果这种地产分化的情况一直继续的话,那么每块土地将不能满足一个家庭的需要,就必然导致严重的灾难;但是美国不存在这样的情况,一代又一代人也都没有遇到这种情况。我们居住的广阔的国土,周边富裕的土地,还有从大西洋沿岸不断涌入内陆的移民人流,现在以至将来很久都能够避免土地的过于分化。"

很难描述美国人带着什么样的贪欲冲向前去保护命运为他们提供的无尽的猎物。在追逐过程中,不畏艰险勇敢地与印第安人的弓箭和森林中的疾病斗争;他们不顾森林的寂静;捕食动物

approach of beasts of prey does not dis turb him, for he is goaded onwards by a passion stronger than the love of life. Before him lies a
boundless continent, and he urges onward as if time pressed and he
was afraid of finding no room for his exertions. I have spoken of the
emigration from the older states, but how shall I describe that which
takes place from the more recent ones? Fifty years have scarcely e-
lapsed since Ohio was founded; the greater part of its inhabitants were
not born within its confines; its capital has been built only thirty
years, and its territory is still covered by an immense extent of uncultivated fields; yet already the population of Ohio is proceeding westward, and most of the settlers who descend to the fertile prairies of Illinois are citizens of Ohio. These men left their first country to improve their condition; they quit their second to ameliorate it still
more; fortune awaits them everywhere, but not happiness. The desire
of prosperity has become an ardent and restless passion in their
minds, which grows by what it feeds on. They early broke the ties
that bound them to their natal earth, and they have contracted no
fresh ones on their way. Emigration was at first necessary to them;
and it soon becomes a sort of game of chance, which they pursue for
the emotions it excites as much as for the gain it procures.

Sometimes the progress of man is so rapid that the desert reap
pears behind him. The woods stoop to give him a passage, and spring
up again when he is past. It is not uncommon, in crossing the new
states of the West, to meet with deserted dwellings in the midst of the
wilds; the traveler frequently discovers the vestiges of a log house in
the most solitary retreat, which bear witness to the power, and no less
to the inconstancy, of man. In these abandoned fields and over these
ruins of a day the primeval forest soon scatters a fresh vegetation; the
beasts resume the haunts which were once their own; and Nature
comes smiling to cover the traces of man with green branches and
flowers, which obliterate his ephemeral track.

的掠夺也没能影响到他们,因为驱动他们奔向目标的激情远比对
生命的热爱之情更强烈。在他们的前方,是一望无垠的大陆,仿
佛受到时间限制的敦促,他们迫切地想要向前进唯恐去的晚了就
没有了他们的空地。我所说的是那些从古老的州迁来的移民们,
但是我该如何描述这些来自较新的州的人们呢? 自俄亥俄州成
立到现在已经过去 50 年了;它的大部分居民都不是出生在那里;
它的州府建立仅仅 30 年,那大片的土地都未开垦,而俄亥俄州的
居民却开始西进,大多数俄亥俄州的居民都迁入了土地肥沃的伊
利诺伊州大草原。这些人离开自己的家园寻找更好的生活环境;
接着又离开第二个居住地转向更好的;到处都有的财富等着他
们,但幸福不是处处都有的。对繁荣的渴望成为他们脑海中最渴
盼最活跃的激情,而这种渴望随着进一步的满足变得越来越强
烈。他们打破了将他们与自己的出生地紧系在一起的纽带,并且
在新的地方也没有再结成这种纽带。开始时移民对他们来说是
必需的;然后就变成了一种他们想赢多少就能赢多少的赌博游
戏。

　　有时人们的迁徙的进程很快,以至于其身后重又是一片荒
漠。树木屈服于他们的刀下而留下通道,而在他们经过后又茂密
生长起来。在穿越西部各个新开辟的州的途中,常常会遇到一些
被遗弃在荒野中的住所,在森林深处常常会发现一些木屋的痕
迹。这一切既见证了人的力量,也显示了人们的反复无常。在这
些被遗弃的土地和新近的废墟上,原始森林很快就铺开了新的植
被;野兽重新出没在它们的属地;大自然也微笑着用绿色的枝叶
和各种花朵覆盖了人们留下的足迹,抹去了他们留下不久的
车辙。

I remember that in crossing one of the woodland districts which still cover the state of New York, I reached the shores of a lake which was embosomed in forests coeval with the world. A small island, covered with woods whose thick foliage concealed its banks, rose from the center of the waters. Upon the shores of the lake no object attested the presence of man except a column of smoke which might be seen on the horizon rising from the tops of the trees to the clouds and seeming to hang from heaven rather than to be mounting to it. An Indian canoe was hauled up on the sand, which tempted me to visit the islet that had first attracted my attention, and in a few minutes I set foot upon its banks. The whole island formed one of those delightful solitudes of the New World, which almost led civilized man to regret the haunts of the savage. A luxuriant vegetation bore witness to the incomparable fruitfulness of the soil. The deep silence, which is common to the wilds of North America, was broken only by the monotonous cooing of the wood-pigeons and the tapping of the woodpecker on the bark of trees. I was far from supposing that this spot had ever been inhabited, so completely did Nature seem to be left to herself; but when I reached the center of the isle, I thought that I discovered some traces of man. I then proceeded to examine the surrounding objects with care, and I soon perceived that a European had undoubtedly been led to seek a refuge in this place. Yet what changes had taken place in the scene of his labors! The logs which he had hastily hewn to build himself a shed had sprouted afresh; the very props were intertwined with living verdure, and his cabin was transformed into a bower. In the midst of these shrubs a few stones were to be seen, blackened with fire and sprinkled with thin ashes; here the hearth had no doubt been, and the chimney in falling had covered it with rubbish. I stood for some time in silent admiration of the resources of Nature and the littleness of man; and when I was obliged to leave that enchanting solitude, I exclaimed with sadness: "Are ruins, then, already here?"

In Europe we are wont to look upon a restless disposition, an unbounded desire of riches, and an excessive love of independence as propensities very dangerous to society. Yet these are the very elements that ensure a long and peaceful future to the republics of America. Without these unquiet passions the population would collect in certain spots and would soon experience wants like those of the old

我记得在穿越仍然被森林覆盖的纽约州的一块林地的时候，曾到过一个被原始森林包围着的湖的岸边。一个小岛，立于水中，被树木覆盖着，厚密的树叶遮盖了它的岸沿。从湖的岸边看不出有任何迹象可以证明这里曾有人迹，除了一个烟柱，在天边树林的上空升起，直上云霄，看起来仿佛从天空降下来而不是升上去的。一艘停泊在沙滩上的印第安独木舟引诱着我到这个第一个吸引我的小岛上去看一看。没过一会儿，我就登上了小岛。小岛呈现出一派令人愉悦的幽静，而在新大陆的这种幽静，几乎让文明的人们面对野人的生活时感到羞愧。茂盛的植被见证了无与伦比的肥沃土地。北美荒野处处可见的寂静，偶尔被单调的斑鸠咕咕的叫声和树干上啄木鸟笃笃的声音打破。我从未想过这里会有人居住，因为它完全是一幅大自然本来的面貌；但是当我到达小岛的中心的时候，我想我发现了人的痕迹。于是我小心地观察着周围的事物，果然很快就发现曾有一个欧洲人确实在这里居住过。可这个他劳动过的地方发生了多么大的变化啊！那些他匆匆砍伐下来搭建小屋的圆木又发出了新芽；篱笆与一些活的植物纠缠在一起，小屋也变成了凉亭。灌木丛中几个被火烧成了黑色的石块，粘着薄薄的灰烬，壁炉当时肯定在这里，倒塌的烟囱将其碎片覆盖在灶台上。我站在那里，默默地对大自然的能力表示钦佩，并感叹着人的渺小。当我不得不离开这迷人的寂静时，我伤感地呼喊："这么快就成了废墟吗？"

在欧洲我们习惯于把人心的激荡，对财富的无止境的追求，对独立的过度的热爱当作对社会具有危害的倾向。然而，这些正是确保美国共和制度长久和平的未来的因素。没有了这些动荡的激情，人口就会相对的集中在一个地方，接着就会像欧洲那样，

World, which it is difficult to satisfy; for such is the present good fortune of the New World that the vices of its inhabitants are scarcely less favorable to society than their virtues. These circumstances exercise a great influence on the estimation in which human actions are held in the two hemispheres. What we should call cupidity, the Americans frequently term a laudable industry; and they blame as faintheartedness what we consider to be the virtue of moderate desires.

In France simple tastes, orderly manners, domestic affections, and the attachment that men feel to the place of their birth are looked upon as great guarantees of the tranquillity and happiness of the state. But in America nothing seems to be more prejudicial to society than such virtues. The French Canadians, who have faithfully preserved the traditions of their ancient customs, are already embarrassed for room in their small territory; and this little community, which has so recently begun to exist, will shortly be a prey to the calamities incident to old nations. In Canada the most enlightened, patriotic, and humane inhabitants make extraordinary efforts to render the people dissatisfied with those simple enjoyments which still content them. There the seductions of wealth are vaunted with as much zeal as the charms of a moderate competency in the Old World; and more exertions are made to excite the passions of the citizens there than to calm them elsewhere. If we listen to their accounts, we shall hear that nothing is more praiseworthy than to exchange the pure and tranquil pleasures which even the poor man tastes in his own country for the sterile delights of prosperity under a foreign sky; to leave the patrimonial hearth and the turf beneath which one's forefathers sleep-in short, to abandon the living and the dead, in quest of fortune.

At the present time America presents a field for human effort far more extensive than any sum of labor that can be applied to work it. In America too much knowledge cannot be diffused; for all knowledge, while it may serve him who possesses it, turns also to the advantage of those who are without it. New wants are not to be feared there, since they can be satisfied without difficulty; the growth of human passions need not be dreaded, since all passions may find an easy and a legitimate object; nor can men there be made too free, since they are scarcely ever tempted to misuse their liberties.

The American republics of the present day are like companies of adventurers, formed to explore in common the wastelands of the New World and busied in a flourishing trade. The passions that agitate the Americans most deeply are not their political, but their commercial passions; or, rather, they introduce the habits of busi ness into their political life. They love order, without which affairs do not prosper;

因不满而产生难以得到满足的需求。新大陆所表现的好运气，实际上其居民的恶性对社会起到的有益的作用，并不比他们所具有美德作出的贡献少。这些对两半球人类行为的评价影响很大。我们口中所说的贪婪，美国人常常将其定义为一种值得赞誉的勤勉；而我们认为淡泊名利的美德在他们眼中则被视为懦弱。

在法国，人们把趣味单纯、行为有序、家庭情感和重乡情结视为国家安宁幸福的保证。而在美国却认为这些德行对社会最有害。仍然信守着他们古老的传统的加拿大法国人，已经为他们生存的小国土上的空间感到困窘；这一刚刚成立不久的小团体，不久就会变成古老民族顽疾的牺牲品。加拿大最有知识、最有爱国心和最仁慈的居民都作出极大的努力，企图使人们不要满足于使他们感到富足的生活。他们对财富魅力的鼓吹引发人们如同在欧洲对平庸同样的热情；他们用以激发人们激情所作出的努力比使他们心境平和的努力更多。如果让他们解释原因，他们就会说，最值得称赞，不是人们在自己原来的国家所崇尚的单纯、平静的幸福，而是在这异国他乡致富享乐；是离开父辈们的壁灶和他们睡过的草席——总之一句话，抛弃一切去外面追求幸福。

今天，美国提供出一片无比广袤的土地供人们劳作。美国有很多知识无法广泛的传播；为某些人服务的知识，也会是那些没有知识的人们的优势。在那里不怕有新需求，任何需求都能轻易地满足；不必担心人们激情的膨胀，所有的激情都能找到有益的合理的发泄对象；这里也不会使人过于自由，因为他们从未想要滥用自由。

今天美国共和制度就像是冒险家的公司一样，就是为了共同开发新大陆荒废的土地，经营繁荣的商业。挑起美国人的最深层激情的并不是他们对政治的激情，而是商业激情。或者说，他们

and they set an especial value upon regular conduct, which is the foundation of a solid business. They prefer the good sense which a-masses large fortunes to that enterprising genius which frequently dissipates them; general ideas alarm their minds, which are accustomed to positive calculations; and they hold practice in more honor than theory.

It is in America that one learns to understand the influence which physical prosperity exercises over political actions, and even over o-pinions which ought to acknowledge no sway but that of reason; and it is more especially among strangers that this truth is perceptible. Most of the European emigrants to the New World carry with them that wild love of independence and change which our calamities are so apt to produce. I sometimes met with Europeans in the United States who had been obliged to leave their country on account of their political o-pinions. They all astonished me by the language they held, but one of them surprised me more than all the rest. As I was crossing one of the most remote districts of Pennsylvania, I was benighted and obliged to beg for hospitality at the gate of a wealthy planter, who was a French-man by birth. He bade me sit down beside his fire, and we began to talk with that freedom which befits persons who meet in the back woods, two thousand leagues from their native country. I was aware that my host had been a great leveler and an ardent demagogue forty years ago, and that his name was in history. I was therefore not a lit-tle surprised to hear him discuss the rights of property as an economist or a landowner might have done: he spoke of the necessary gradations that fortune establishes among men, of obedience to established laws, of the influence of good morals in commonwealths, and of the support that religious opinions give to order and to freedom; he even went so far as to quote the authority of our Saviour in support of one of his po-litical opinions.

I listened, and marveled at the feebleness of human reason. How can we discover whether a proposition is true or false in the midst of the uncertainties of science and the conflicting lessons of experience? A new fact disperses all my doubts. I was poor, I have become rich; and I am not to expect that prosperity will act upon my conduct and

把商业习惯引入了政治领域。他们热爱秩序,没有了它事业就不会兴隆;他们很重视信誉,这同时也是稳固商业的基础。他们习惯凭借自己的认识积累巨额财富,而不要商业天才冒险获利;按常规办事的思想随时使他们保持警惕,并坚持切合实际的考虑;他们重视实践更甚于理论。

在美国,就要了解物质繁荣对政治行为带来的影响,甚至对合理的舆论造成的影响;尤其外国人对此的了解尤为重要。大多数到新大陆的欧洲移民都怀揣着对独立狂热追求、希望能改变困境的心愿。我常常会碰到一些在美国的欧洲人,他们都是因为政见不一致而被迫离开祖国的。他们的语言使我震惊,尤其是其中的一位。那是我在穿越宾夕法尼亚州最偏僻的地区发生的,那天天色已晚,我不得不到一位富裕的庄园主门前乞求帮助,这位庄园主是法裔美国人。他让我坐在炉火旁,于是两个在远离法国两千里远的荒地上相遇的人开始自由地交谈。我知道了这家的主人原来40年前就是一位伟大的平等派活动家和激进的政治鼓吹者,他的名字甚至被载入史册。我也就毫不惊奇地听着他以一位经济学家的身份讨论对财产权利的看法,与大地主的言论如出一辙:他讲到财富所带来的人们之间必然的等级分化,讲到对已建立的法律的服从,讲到共和制度对良好的道德在国民整体中的影响以及宗教信念对秩序和自由的支持;他甚至引用上帝的权威来支持自己的政治观点。

我一面倾听,一面感叹于人类理性的脆弱。我们如何才能在这些科学的不确定中和经验的互相矛盾中发现某种主张的真伪呢?他后面的言论化解了我所有的疑惑:我从前很穷,然而现在变得富裕了;但在财富对我的行为发生作用的时候,我就能够自

leave my judgment free. In truth, my opinions change with my fortune; and the happy circumstances which I turn to my advantage furnish me with that decisive argument which before was wanting.

The influence of prosperity acts still more freely upon Americans than upon strangers. The American has always seen public order and public prosperity intimately united and proceeding side by side before his eyes; he cannot even imagine that one can exist without the other; he has therefore nothing to forget, nor has he, like so many Europeans, to unlearn the lessons of his early education.

Influence Of The Laws Upon The Maintenance Of The Demoeratic Republic In The United States

Three principal causes of the maintenance of the democratic republic—Federal union—Township institutions—Judicial power.

THE principal aim of this book has been to make known the laws of the United States; if this purpose has been accomplished, the reader is already enabled to judge for himself which are the laws that really tend to maintain the democratic republic, and which endanger its existence. If I have not succeeded in explaining this in the whole course of my work, I cannot hope to do so in a single chapter. It is not my intention to retrace the path I have already pursued, and a few lines will suffice to recapitulate what I have said. Three circumstances seem to me to contribute more than all others to the maintenance of the democratic republic in the United States

The first is that federal form of government which the Americans have adopted, and which enables the Union to combine the power of a great republic with the security of a small one.

The second consists in those township institutions which limit the despotism of the majority and at the same time impart to the people a taste for freedom and the art of being free.

The third is to be found in the constitution of the judicial power. I have shown how the courts of justice serve to repress the excesses of democracy, and how they check and direct the impulses of the majority without stopping its activity.

由的作出判断。事实上,我的观念是随着我的财富的增长而改变的;而在一切有利于我的环境当中,我才发现了我以前所没有的决定性的论据。

富裕的生活对美国人的影响仍旧远远大于对其他国家人们的影响。美国人始终认为,公共秩序和公共繁荣紧密结合并肩前进;他们甚至不能想象其中一个可以单独存在;因此,他们既没什么好忘却的,也不会像许多欧洲人那样,忘掉了早期学校里教的知识。

法律对维护美国民主共和制度的影响

民主共和制度得以维护的三大原因——联邦形式——乡镇制度——司法权力。

这本书的主旨就是为了使读者了解美国的法律。如果这一任务已经完成,那么读者就能够自己判断哪些法律真正起到了维护民主共和制度的作用,而哪些法律对其存在产生威胁。如果我没能在这部书已完成的行文当中成功地说明这一原委,那么在这一章中我也不能完成这一任务。我并不想再折回我已经叙述过的问题,而以下几行文字就能对我前面所讲的内容作一总结。维护美国民主共和制度有三个因素在我看来是超越其他所有因素最重要的。

首先是美国采用的联邦式政府,这样的形式保证了联邦中的大共和国的权利与小共和国的安全的统一。

第二是其乡镇制度,限制了大多数的专政并同时使人们得到了自由的品性和自由的艺术。

第三在于司法权的构成。我已经讲述过法庭是如何纠正民主的过度运用,以及如何抑制和引导大多数人的冲动而并不阻止其行为。

Influence Of Customs Upon The Mainteance Of A Democratic Republic In The United States

I have previously remarked that the manners of the people may be considered as one of the great general causes to which the maintenance of a democratic republic in the United States is attributable. I here use the word customs with the meaning which the ancients attached to the word mores; for I apply it not only to manners properly so called—that is, to what might be termed the habits of the heart—but to the various notions and opinions current among men and to the mass of those ideas which constitute their character of mind. I comprise under this term, therefore, the whole moral and intellectual condition of a people. My intention is not to draw a picture of American customs, but simply to point out such features of them as are favorable to the maintenance of their political institutions.

Religion Considered As A Political Institution Which Power Fully Contributes To The Maintenance Of A Democratic Republic Among The Americans

North America peopled by men who professed a democratic and republican Christianity—Arrival of the Catholics—Why the Catholics now form the most democratic and most republican class.

BY the side of every religion is to be found a political opinion, which is connected with it by affinity. If the human mind be left to follow its own bent, it will regulate the temporal and spiritual institutions of society in a uniform manner, and man will endeavor, if I may so speak, to harmonize earth with heaven. The greatest part of British America was peopled by men who, after having shaken off the authority of the Pope, acknowledged no other religious supremacy: they brought with them into the New World a form of Christianity which I cannot better describe than by styling it a democratic and republican religion. This contributed powerfully to the establishment of a republic and a democracy in public affairs; and from the beginning, politics and religion contracted an alliance which has never been dissolved. About fifty years ago Ireland began to pour a Catholic population into the United States; and on their part, the Catholics of America made proselytes, so that, at the present moment more than a million Christians professing the truths of the Church of Rome

民情对于维护美国民主共和制度的影响

我在前面已经指出民情应该作为影响维护美国民主制度最主要的因素之一。这里我所用的民情一词,更多的带有古人对这个词所下的定义。不仅指通常所说的心理习惯方面的东西,而且包括人们拥有的各种见解和社会上流行的不同观念,以及人们的生活习惯所遵循的全部思想。因此,我认为其包含了一个民族全部的道德和精神状态。我的目的并不是为了描绘出美国民情的画面,而只是简单地指出他们所具有的有利于维护他们政治体制的特征。

宗教作为政治设施的一种极大的助力于维护美国的民主共和制度

北美到处都是信仰民主和共和的基督教的人们——天主教徒的到来——为什么今天天主教形成了最民主最共和的阶级。

每一种宗教都伴有一种政见,二者因意见一致而结合。如果人类的思想可以因循着自己的喜好发展,它就会将社会现实制度和精神世界加以规范成为统一的模式,如果可以这么说的话,它还会努力使人世和天堂和谐一致。英属美国大部分地区的居民,在摆脱了罗马教皇的统治之后,也不相信其他宗教至高无上的权力:他们自有一套基督教的形式带入新大陆,对这一基督教,我认为只能说它是一种民主的共和的宗教。这一宗教形式极大地促进了社会事务民主和共和性质的建立;而且从最初开始,政教合一就一直存在着。早在五十年前,爱尔兰就有大批的天主教徒的居民迁入美国;随着他们的到来,美国的天主教徒增加了很多,所

are to be found in the Union. These Catholics are faithful to the observances of their religion; they are fervent and zealous in the belief of their doctrines. Yet they constitute the most republican and the most democratic class in the United States. This fact may surprise the observer at first, but the causes of it may easily be discovered upon reflection.

I think that the Catholic religion has erroneously been regarded as the natural enemy of democracy. Among the various sects of Christians, Catholicism seems to me, on the contrary, to be one of the most favorable to equality of condition among men. In the Catholic Church the religious community is composed of only two elements: the priest and the people. The priest alone rises above the rank of his flock, and all below him are equal.

On doctrinal points the Catholic faith places all human capacities upon the same level; it subjects the wise and ignorant, the man of genius and the vulgar crowd, to the details of the same creed; it imposes the same observances upon the rich and the needy, it inflicts the same austerities upon the strong and the weak; it listens to no compromise with mortal man, but, reducing all the human race to the same standard, it confounds all the distinctions of society at the foot of the same altar, even as they are confounded in the sight of God. If Catholicism predisposes the faithful to obedience, it certainly does not prepare them for inequality; but the contrary may be said of Protestantism, which generally tends to make men independent more than to render them equal. Catholicism is like an absolute monarchy; if the sovereign be removed, all the other classes of society are more equal than in republics. It has not infrequently occurred that the Catholic priest has left the service of the altar to mix with the governing powers of society and to take his place among the civil ranks of men. This religious influence has sometimes been used to secure the duration of that political state of things to which he belonged. Thus we have seen Catholics taking the side of aristocracy from a religious motive. But no sooner is the priesthood entirely separated from the gov ernment, as is the case in the United States, than it is found that no class of men is more naturally disposed than the Catholics to transfer the doctrine of the equality of condition into the political world.

If, then, the Catholic citizens of the United States are not forcibly led by the nature of their tenets to adopt democratic and republican

以，直到现在有一百多万基督教徒信奉罗马教会真谛。这些天主教徒诚心地遵守它们的宗教仪式；狂热地追随他们信仰的教义。但是，他们却建成了美国最民主最共和的阶层。可能这一事实会使读者最初感到惊奇，但是仔细想想就很容易发现它的起因。

我认为，把天主教认为是民主天生的敌人是错误的。在基督教的众多教派中，天主教对我来说，相反的，是最有利于人们的地位平等的建立的。在天主教会中，宗教集团有两部分组成：神职人员和普通教徒。神职人员单独位居其他人之上，而在其下的所有信徒一律平等。

按教义来说，天主教的宗教信仰将人类资质置于平等地位；它要求智者和愚者、天才和庸夫都必须按照统一的信条的规则行事；它在穷人和富人间推行相同的仪式，它使强者和弱者都履行同样的苦修；它绝不向任何人妥协，并将所有的种族归为一类，它使所有社会的阶级都站在神坛前，正如将所有的人都领到神的面前。如果说天主教预先要求信徒服从，那么它一定没有让他们不平等；但是新教恰恰相反，它更提倡人们的自由却不那么要求大家地位平等。天主教就像一个专制君主政体；去掉君主皇权不说，则社会中各民族的地位比在共和制下更加平等。天主教的神职人员也会辞去其教会中的职位，参与到社会统治阶层中而进入社会等级行列，这样的事情也不是没有发生过。有时他也用这样的宗教影响来保护他所归属的政治状态的持久。因此我们看到，天主教徒往往从自己的宗教立场出发来维护贵族统治。但是，像美国发生的那样，神职人员一旦完全脱离了政府统治，就会发现再没有人像天主教徒那样将其地位平等的教义在政治统治中传播。

如果说，美国天主教徒并不是遵从其教义的本性而接受民主

principles, at least they are not necessarily opposed to them; and their social position, as well as their limited number, obliges them to adopt these opinions. Most of the Catholics are poor, and they have no chance of taking a part in the government unless it is open to all the citizens. They constitute a minority, and all rights must be respected in order to ensure to them the free exercise of their own privileges. These two causes induce them, even unconsciously, to adopt political doctrines which they would perhaps support with less zeal if they were rich and preponderant. The Catholic clergy of the United States have never attempted to oppose this political tendency; but they seek rather to justify it. The Catholic priests in America have divided the intellectual world into two parts: in the one they place the doctrines of revealed religion, which they assent to without discussion; in the other they leave those political truths which they believe the De ity has left open to free inquiry. Thus the Catholics of the United States are at the same time the most submissive believers and the most independent citizens.

It may be asserted, then, that in the United States no religious doctrine displays the slightest hostility to democratic and republican institutions. The clergy of all the different sects there hold the same language; their opinions are in agreement with the laws, and the human mind flows onwards, so to speak, in one undivided current.

I happened to be staying in one of the largest cities in the Union when I was invited to attend a public meeting in favor of the Poles and of sending them supplies of arms and money. I found two or three thousand persons collected in a vast hall which had been prepared to receive them. In a short time a priest in his ecclesiastical robes advanced to the front of the platform. The spectators rose and stood uncovered in silence while he spoke in the following terms:

"Almighty God! the God of armies! Thou who didst strengthen the hearts and guide the arms of our fathers when they were fighting for the sacred rights of their national independence! Thou who didst make them triumph over a hateful oppression, and hast granted to our people the benefits of liberty and peace! turn, O Lord, a favorable eye upon the other hemisphere; pitifully look down upon an heroic nation which is even now struggling as we did in the former time, and

和共和原则,但至少也不是天生就持反对意见的;并且,他们的社会地位和有限的人数,迫使他们接受这些观念。大多数天主教徒都生活贫困,他们没有机会进入统治阶层,除非这一阶层向全民开放。他们是少数,所以他们尊敬所有的权力,为了确保能够自由的行使自己的权利。这两个原因,不知不觉地使他接受了这一政治教条,而对这一教条,如果他们生活富裕或在某方宁愿跟从当前的政治体制,而不想去验证其对错。如果有优势的话,就不会有这么大的热情去支持其实施。美国的天主教徒从未想去反对这种政治倾向;反而设法证明其合理。美国的天主教徒将知识分为两类:一类用来揭示他们的宗教教义,这一点毫无疑问;另一类他们认为神让人们自由探索的政治真理。因此,美国的天主教徒同时是最顺从的追随者也是最独立的公民。

那么,就可以宣称,在美国,没有任何宗教教义含有丝毫的对民主和共和制度的敌意。不同教派的神职人员有共同的语言;他们的观点也不违背法律,可以说,人们的思想都追随同一种信念。

我凑巧在美国最大的城市之一中待过,并被邀请去参加支持波兰人并讨论给与武器和金钱支持的公共集会。有两三千人集中在一个开阔的接待大厅内。不一会儿,一个神职人员穿着教袍走到了讲台前。所有听众都站起来,摘掉帽子,安静地听他以下的演讲:

全能的神啊!万军的首领!当我们的父辈为民族独立的神圣权利而斗争的时候,是您坚定了他们的信心,指引了他们的方向!是您使他们推翻了残酷的压迫取得胜利并使他们承认我们人民自由和和平的利益!主啊,请您将恩慈的目光转向另一个半球;请您怜悯那个英勇的民族,他们甚至到现在还在为争取我们

for the same rights. Thou, who didst create man in the same image, let not tyranny mar thy work and establish inequality upon the earth. Almighty God! do thou watch over the destiny of the Poles, and make them worthy to be free. May thy wisdom direct their councils, may thy strength sustain their arms! Shed forth *thy* terror over their enemies; scatter the powers which take counsel against them; and permit not the injustice which the world has witnessed for fifty years to be consummated in our time. O Lord, who holdest alike the hearts of nations and of men in thy powerful hand, raise up allies to the sacred cause of right; arouse the French nation from the apathy in which its rulers retain it, that it may go forth again to fight for the liberties of the world.

"Lord, turn not thou thy face from us, and grant that we may always be the most religious, as well as the freest, people of the earth. Almighty God, hear our supplications this day. Save the Poles, we beseech thee, in the name of thy well-beloved Son, our Lord Jesus Christ, who died upon the cross for the salvation of all men. Amen."

The whole meeting responded: "Amen!" with devotion.

Indirect Influence Of Religious Opinions Upon Political Society In The United States

Christian morality common to all sects—Influence of religion upon the manners of the Americans—Respect for the marriage tie—How religion confines the im agination of the Americans within certain limits and checks the passion for innovation—Opinion of the Americans on the po litical utility of religion—Their exertions to extend and secure its authority.

I have just shown what the direct influence of religion upon politics is in the United States; but its indirect influence appears to me to be still more considerable, and it never instructs the Americans more fully in the art of being free than when it says nothing of freedom.

The sects that exist in the United States are innumerable. They all differ in respect to the worship which is due to the Creator; but they all agree in respect to the duties which are due from man to man. Each sect adores the Deity in its own peculiar manner, but all sects

曾为之奋战过的权利而战斗。您既以同样的模式创造了相同的我们,就不要让暴政再损害您的成果,不要让不平等在世上得以建立。全能的神啊！请您看顾波兰人的命运,使他们获得自由。让您的智慧引导他们决策,让您的力量支持他们的行动！让他们的敌人感到恐惧;使企图敌对他们的力量分散;决不允许过去五十年存在的不公平现象再在我们的时代出现。主啊,人类和各民族的情感全部掌握在您的手中,愿你唤起同盟者为正义的神圣事业而奋斗;唤起法国的民族在其领袖统治维护下的冷漠的状态,使他们再次前进为世界的自由而战。

"主啊,请您不要从我们这里转移视线,请您准予我们永远成为世上最虔诚、最自由的人民。全能的神啊,请倾听我们今天的祷告:我们恳求您拯救波兰。以您爱子,为拯救苍生而钉死在十字架上的我们的主耶稣基督的名义。阿门。"

集会的人们虔诚地回答:"阿门!"

宗教观念对美国政治社会的间接影响各教派一致的基督教精神

各教派一致主张的基督教道德——宗教对美国民情的影响——对婚姻关系的尊重——宗教是如何将美国人的想象力限制在一定的范围内并遏制其创造激情的——美国人在宗教对政治的作用方面的观点——他们为扩大和保护其权力作出的努力。

我在前面已经谈到了美国宗教对政治的直接影响;但是它的间接影响我认为更多,并且它虽从未谈起自由,但却很好地指引美国走向自由。

美国的宗教派系有很多。因为他们所认同的造物主不同,所以他们敬拜神的方式也不同。但是他们对人与人之间的道义观点一致。每一个教派都以自己独特的方式敬拜上帝,但所有的教

preach the same moral law in the name of God. If it be of the highest importance to man, as an individual, that his religion should be true, it is not so to society. Society has no future life to hope for or to fear; and provided the citizens profess a religion, the peculiar tenets of that religion are of little importance to its interests. Moreover, all the sects of the United States are comprised within the great unity of Christianity, and Christian morality is everywhere the same.

It may fairly be believed that a certain number of Americans pursue a peculiar form of worship from habit more than from conviction. In the United States the sovereign authority is religious, and consequently hypocrisy must be common; but there is no country in the world where the Christian religion retains a greater influence over the souls of men than in America; and there can be no greater proof of its utility and of its conformity to human nature than that its influence is powerfully felt over the most enlightened and free nation of the earth.

I have remarked that the American clergy in general, without even excepting those who do not admit religious liberty, are all in favor of civil freedom; but they do not support any particular political system. They keep aloof from parties and from public af fairs. In the United States religion exercises but little influence upon the laws and upon the details of public opinion; but it directs the customs of the community, and, by regulating domestic life, it regulates the state.

I do not question that the great austerity of manners that is observable in the United States arises, in the first instance, from religious faith. Religion is often unable to restrain man from the numberless temptations which chance offers; nor can it check that passion for gain which everything contributes to arouse; but its influence over the mind of woman is supreme, and women are the protectors of morals. There is certainly no country in the world where the tie of marriage is more respected than in America or where conjugal happiness is more highly or worthily appreciated.

In Europe almost all the disturbances of society arise from the irregularities of domestic life. To despise the natural bonds and le gitimate

派都以上帝的名义推崇相同的道德规则。如果对于一个人来说，他所信仰的教派对他来说至关重要的话，而对社会来说则不尽然。社会并不会为自己的将来的命运的好坏而担心；对社会来说，人们信什么教派并不重要。此外，美国所有的教派都包含在基督教的大一统下，基督教的道德也都完全一致。

可以确信的是，一些美国人所进行的宗教崇拜的独特形式更多的因为习惯而非信仰。在美国，掌权者必须信教，因此伪装信教的现象也很普遍；但是世界上没有哪个国家基督教势力对人们思想造成的影响可以超过美国；并且，也没有任何东西可以表明它比宗教更有用更合乎人情，因为在它的影响下已造就了世上最开明最自由的民族。

我已笼统地描述过美国的神职人员都支持公民自由，甚至那些不主张宗教信仰自由的人们也不例外；但是他们不支持某一具体的政治派系。他们远离党派和公众事务。在美国，宗教对法律和政见的细节的影响微乎其微；但是它可以指导民情，并通过规范家庭生活治理整个州。

我毫不怀疑，存在于美国的民情的极端严苛性首先来自宗教信仰。宗教往往并不能阻止人们免于被各种机遇带来的种种诱惑的吸引。宗教也不能制止人们对于各种事物的热切的追求之心。但宗教带来的影响，在控制妇女思想方面却有着至高无上的力量，而妇女恰恰是人们精神守护者。确实，世界上再没有哪个国家比美国更尊重婚姻关系，而且美国人对夫妻的幸福也持有高尚的和正确的看法。

在欧洲，社会上的一切混乱现象，几乎都来因于无规律的家庭生活。对家庭的天然纽带和合法乐趣的轻视，也就是对混乱生

pleasures of home is to contract a taste for excesses, a restlessness of heart, and fluctuating desires. Agitated by the tumultuous passions that frequently disturb his dwelling, the European is galled by the o-bedience which the legislative powers of the state exact. But when the American retires from the turmoil of public life to the bosom of his family, he finds in it the image of order and of peace. There his pleasures are simple and natural, his joys are innocent and calm; and as he finds that an orderly life is the surest path to happiness, he ac-customs himself easily to moderate his opinions as well as his tastes. While the European endeavors to forget his domestic troubles by agita-ting society, the American derives from his own home that love of or-der which he afterwards carries with him into public affairs.

In the United States the influence of religion is not confined to the manners, but it extends to the intelligence of the people. Among the Anglo-Americans some profess the doctrines of Christianity from a sincere belief in them, and others do the same because they fear to be suspected of unbelief. Christianity, therefore, reigns without obsta-cle, by universal consent; the consequence is, as I have before ob-served, that every principle of the moral world is fixed and determi-nate, although the political world is abandoned to the debates and the experiments of men. Thus the human mind is never left to wander o-ver a boundless field; and whatever may be its pretensions, it is checked from time to time by barriers that it cannot surmount. Before it can innovate, certain primary principles are laid down, and the boldest conceptions are subjected to certain forms which retard and stop their completion.

The imagination of the Americans, even in its greatest flights, is circumspect and undecided; its impulses are checked and its works unfinished. These habits of restraint recur in political society and are singularly favorable both to the tranquillity of the people and to the durability of the institutions they have established. Nature and cir-cumstances have made the inhabitants of the United States bold, as is sufficiently attested by the enterprising spirit with which they seek for fortune. If the mind of the Americans were free from all hindrances, they would shortly become the most daring innovators and the most persistent disputants in the world. But the revolutionists of America

活的喜爱。他们心里不能保持平静,愿望总是在变。一个欧洲人,在这些往往会扰乱其家庭生活的起伏不定的激情影响下,很难服从国家的立法权。而一个美国人,从政界的激烈斗争中退出而回到家里后,立刻会产生秩序安定和生活宁静的感觉。在家里,他的一切享乐简朴而自然,他的兴致纯真而淡泊。他好像因为生活有了秩序而获得幸福,而且容易习惯于调整自己的观点和爱好。欧洲人喜欢用扰乱社会的办法来忘却其家庭忧伤,而美国人则从家庭中汲取对秩序的爱好,然后再把这种爱好带到公务中去。

宗教在美国的影响不仅局限在民情方面,而且还影响民智。在英裔美国人中,对某些人来说信奉基督教教条源于虔诚的信仰,而另一些人遵守教条则是因为担心被怀疑没有信仰。因此,基督教的统治没有受到任何阻碍而得到了所有人的承认;就像我前面描述的结果一样,道德世界的每一项原则都是既定的不可更改的,而政治世界责任由人们讨论和研究。因此人类的思想从未被遗弃使之毫无限制的漫游;并且,无论它持有什么主张,都总是会被一次次不可逾越的障碍阻止。在人们的思想革新前,一些主要的原则已经先规定下来,因此即使是最大胆的设想也都要服从那些可以延缓和阻止他们思想革新完成的规定。

美国人的想象力,即使飞得再高,也表现得谨慎而犹豫不决;它的激情总是被遏制,而其目标也难以实现。这些谨小慎微的习惯被带入政治社会并对人民的安宁和他们所建立的制度的持久产生了显著的有利作用。自然环境使居住在这里的美国人变得果敢,他们借以追求财富的魄力已充分的证实了这一点。如果说美国人的思想可以完全不受任何限制,他们将会很快地成就最大胆的创新者和最有逻辑头脑的理论家。但是,美国的革命家必须

are obliged to profess an ostensible respect for Christian morality and equity, which does not permit them to violate wantonly the laws that oppose their designs; nor would they find it easy to surmount the scruples of their partisans even if they were able to get over their own. Hitherto no one in the United States has dared to advance the maxim that everything is permissible for the interests of society, an impious adage which seems to have been invented in an age of freedom to shelter all future tyrants. Thus, while the law permits the Americans to do what they please, religion prevents them from conceiving, and forbids them to commit, what is rash or unjust.

Religion in America takes no direct part in the government of society, but it must be regarded as the first of their political institutions; for if it does not impart a taste for freedom, it facilitates the use of it. Indeed, it is in this same point of view that the inhabitants of the United States themselves look upon religious belief. I do not know whether all Americans have a sincere faith in their religion—for who can search the human heart? —but I am certain that they hold it to be indispensable to the maintenance of republican institutions. This opinion is not peculiar to a class of citizens or to a party, but it belongs to the whole nation and to every rank of society.

In the United States, if a politician attacks a sect, this may not prevent the partisans of that very sect from supporting him; but if he attacks all the sects together, everyone abandons him, and he remains alone.

While I was in America, a witness who happened to be called at the Sessions of the county of Chester (state of New York) declared that he did not believe in the existence of God or in the immortality of the soul. The judge refused to admit his evidence, on the ground that the witness had destroyed beforehand all the confidence of the court in what he was about to say. ①The newspapers related the fact without any further comment.

---

① The New York *Spectat* or of August 23, 1831 relates the fact in the following terms: "The Court of Common Pleas of Chester County (New York) a few days since rejected a witness who declared his disbelief in the existence of God. The presiding judge remarked, that he had not before been aware that there was a man living who did not believe in the existence of God; that this belief constituted the sanction of all testimony in a court of justice; and that he knew of no cause in a Christian country where a witness had been permitted to testify without such belief."

公开承认对基督教道德和公理的尊重,而这不允许他们违反所执行的法律,即使那些法律与他们的初衷完全相反;即使他们能够不顾自己的良心谴责而违法,也会由于同党人的谴责而动摇。迄今为止美国还没有哪一个人敢于提出诸如凡事都要有利于社会这样的格言,这种有点蔑视宗教的格言,似乎在某个自由的时代已经提出过,以此来庇护后来所有的暴政。因此,当法律允许美国人去任由自己的喜好做事时,而宗教会阻止他们想入非非,并且禁止他们做出一些鲁莽和不公的事来。

美国的宗教从不直接参与社会统治,但是却被人们置于政治制度之首;因为宗教即使没有传播自由的思想,却利于自由的实施。事实上,美国居民自己正是以这种观点看待宗教信仰的。我不知道是否所有的美国人都真诚的信仰他们的宗教——谁又能钻到别人心里呢? ——但是我可以确信的是他们把宗教当作维护共和制度不可或缺的东西。这一观点并非是某一阶层的民众和政党所专有,而是存在于整个民族和社会的各个阶层之中的。

在美国,如果一个政客攻击某一教派,不能阻止其同教派人支持他;但是如果这一政客攻击所有的教派,那么人人都会抛弃他,使他成为孤家寡人。

当我在美国期间,得知一个证人被传唤到切斯特县(属纽约州)法庭出庭作证,他在法庭上宣称不相信任何真神的存在或者灵魂不死之说。于是法官拒绝承认他的证词,称证人在他作出陈词之前就已失去了法庭对他的信任。[①] 新闻报道也只引据事实,

---

① 1831 年 8 月 23 日《纽约观察》刊载了这样一件事情:"切斯特郡的一般法庭几天前驳回了一位目击证人的申诉,因为他宣称不信仰上帝。大法官陈述,他还从未见过有人竟然不相信上帝的存在。而这一信仰构成了对法庭上所有证词的裁断。因为他认为在一个基督教国家中,没有任何理由允许一位没有基督信仰的人成为目击证人。"

The Americans combine the notions of Christianity and of liberty so intimately in their minds that it is impossible to make them conceive the one without the other; and with them this conviction does not spring from that barren, traditionary faith which seems to vegetate rather than to live in the soul.

I have known of societies formed by Americans to send out ministers of the Gospel into the new Western states, to found schools and churches there, lest religion should be allowed to die away in those remote settlements, and the rising states be less fitted to enjoy free institutions than the people from whom they came. I met with wealthy New Englanders who abandoned the country in which they were born in order to lay the foundations of Christianity and of freedom on the banks of the Missouri or in the prairies of Illinois. Thus religious zeal is perpetually warmed in the United States by the fires of patriotism. These men do not act exclusively from a consideration of a future life; eternity is only one motive of their devotion to the cause. If you converse with these missionaries of Christian civilization, you will be surprised to hear them speak so often of the goods of this world, and to meet a politician where you expected to find a priest. They will tell you that "all the American republics are collectively involved with each other; if the republics of the West were to fall into anarchy, or to be mastered by a despot, the republican institutions which now flourish upon the shores of the Atlantic Ocean would be in great peril. It is therefore our interest that the new states should be religious, in order that they may permit us to remain free. "

Such are the opinions of the Americans; and if any hold that the religious spirit which I admire is the very thing most amiss in America, and that the only element wanting to the freedom and happiness of the human race on the other side of the ocean is to believe with Spinoza in the eternity of the world, or with Cabanis that thought is secreted by the brain, I can only reply that those who hold this language have never been in America and that they have never seen a religious or a

并未作任何评论。

在美国人的思想中，基督教教义和自由两者是密不可分的，不可能使人们只相信其一而抛弃另一方；但是他们的这种信念并不是源自那种看上去就要灭顶但却又生存于人民灵魂深处的贫乏的、传统的信仰。

我曾看到美国人初建新的西部各州时向那里派遣神职人员，建造学校和教堂，唯恐宗教会在这些偏远的地区失去了威严，担心这些新增的州的人们会比在原籍时享有较少的自由制度。我遇到过一些富裕的新英格兰人，他们离开了自己的出生地，想要到密苏里州海岸和伊利诺伊州大草原建立起基督教和自由的基石。由于这样的爱国激情，使得人们对于宗教的热情在美国永久的保持。这些人这样做并不完全是基于对未来生活的考虑；来世只是他们关心的事情之一。如果你与这些基督教文明的传播者交谈，你会很惊讶他们总是将现世的种种好处挂在嘴边，而你本来约见的是一位教士，而他却展示给你以政客的形象。他们会告诉你"所有的美国政客都互相纠缠不清；如果西部的共和制陷入无政府主义的混乱，或者被暴君所掌控，则现在在大西洋沿岸昌盛的共和制度将会陷入极大的危机。因此，新建的州应当是信仰宗教的才是我们关心的所在，只有这样他们才会允许我们维持自由。"

这些才是美国的见解；并且如果任何对我所推崇的宗教精神认为是极其错误的人，认为希望像大洋彼岸的民族那样拥有自由和幸福的想法，就像与斯宾诺莎一样相信世界永恒，像卡巴尼斯那样主张思想是头脑的分泌物，那我只能回答说，那些持有这些言论的人从未去过美国，也从未见过有宗教信仰和自由的民族。

free nation. When they return from a visit to that country, we shall hear what they have to say. There are persons in France who look upon republican institutions only as a means of obtaining grandeur; they measure the immense space that separates their vices and misery from power and riches, and they aim to fill up this gulf with ruins, that they may pass over it. These men are the condottieri of liberty, and fight for their own advantage, whatever the colors they wear. The republic will stand long enough, they think, to draw them up out of their present degradation. It is not to these that I address myself. But there are others who look forward to a republican form of government as a tranquil and lasting state, towards which modern society is daily impelled by the ideas and manners of the time, and who sincerely desire to prepare men to be free. When these men attack religious opinions, they obey the dictates of their passions and not of their interests. Despotism may govern without faith, but liberty cannot. Religion is much more necessary in the republic which they set forth in glowing colors than in the monarchy which they attack; it is more needed in democratic republics than in any others. How is it possible that society should escape destruction if the moral tie is not strengthened in proportion as the political tie is relaxed? And what can be done with a people who are their own masters if they are not submissive to the Deity?

Principal Causes Which Render Religion Powerful In America

Care taken by the Americans to separate the church from the state—The laws, public opinion, and even the exertions of the clergy concur to promote this end—Influence of religion upon the mind in the United States attributable to this cause—Reason for this—What is the natural state of men with regard to religion at the present time—What are the peculiar and incidental causes which prevent men, in certain countries, from arriving at this state.

在他们去过美国以后,我们才有必要再听听他的说法。法国有这样一些人,他们仅仅将共和制度当作显示自己伟大的手段;他们估算着邪恶和贫穷的阶层与掌握权势和财富的人们之间的无穷的差距,他们打算通过破坏以填补这块空缺,直到可以忽略之间的差距。这些人是自由的卫士,他们为自己的利益而战,不论穿着什么颜色的衣服。他们认为,共和制将会持久地站立,足以维持到将他们从目前的低卑状态中解救出来。这些人与我所描述的人不一样。但是还有另一些人,他们视共和制度为稳定持久统治的制度,是理想和民情每天都在迫使现代社会必须追求的目标。他们衷心地渴望把人教育为自由的人。当这些人攻击宗教的时候,他们是出于自己的激情,而不是出于自己的利益。专制统治可以抛却信仰,而自由的国家不行。宗教在他们宣扬的共和制下,比在他们攻击的君主制下更需要;而在民主共和制下比在其他任何制度下更需要。当政治纽带松弛而道德纽带没有加强的时候,社会如何才能避免毁灭呢?并且,如果人们不归从上帝,这些自己做主的民族又可以做什么呢?

宗教在美国发生强大影响的主要原因

美国人注重政教分离——法律、政治见解以及神职人员都在为达到这一目的而努力——宗教对美国人民思想的影响,可归于这一原因——为什么——目前跟宗教有关的人们的自然状态是怎样的——在一些国家,阻碍人们适应这一特殊的和偶然的原因是什么。

The philosophers of the eighteenth century explained in a very simple manner the gradual decay of religious faith. Religious zeal, said they, must necessarily fail the more generally liberty is established and knowledge diffused. Unfortunately, the facts by no means accord with their theory. There are certain populations in Europe whose unbelief is only equaled by their ignorance and debasement; while in America, one of the freest and most enlightened nations in the world, the people fulfill with fervor all the out ward duties of religion.

On my arrival in the United States the religious aspect of the country was the first thing that struck my attention; and the longer I stayed there, the more I perceived the great political consequences, resulting from this new state of things. In France I had almost always seen the spirit of religion and the spirit of freedom marching in opposite directions. But in America I found they were intimately united and that they reigned in common over the same country. My desire to discover the causes of this phenomenon in creased from day to day. In order to satisfy it I questioned the members of all the different sects; I sought especially the society of the clergy, who are the depositaries of the different creeds and are especially interested in their duration. As a member of the Roman Catholic Church, I was more particularly brought into contact with several of its priests, with whom I became intimately acquainted. To each of these men I expressed my astonishment and explained my doubts. I found that they differed upon matters of detail alone, and that they all attributed the peaceful dominion of religion in their country mainly to the separation of church and state. I do not hesitate to affirm that during my stay in America I did not meet a single individual, of the clergy or the laity, who was not of the same opinion on this point.

This led me to examine more attentively than I had hitherto done the station which the American clergy occupy in political society. I learned with surprise that they filled no public appoint ments; ① I did not see one of them in the administration, and they are not even represented

---

① Unless this term is applied to the functions which many of them fill in the schools. Almost all education is entrusted to the clergy.

十八世纪的哲学家们以简单的方法解释了宗教信仰逐渐消退的原因。他们说,宗教热情,必然随着自由思想的确立和知识的广泛传播而逐渐消失。不幸的是,这个理论与事实完全不符。欧洲有一些无信仰的居民,这只是由于他们的无知和愚昧;而在美国,这个世界上最自由最开化的民族,人民都以极大的热情履行宗教赋予的职责。

我刚到美国,首先引起我注意的就是这个国家宗教方面的事务;我在这里呆得越久,就越感到这个新鲜的事物对政治的极大的影响。在法国,我总是见到宗教精神和自由主义背道而驰,而在美国,二者紧密结合并共同统治着这个国家。我希望能找到产生这种现象的原因的渴望一天比一天强烈。为了满足我的好奇心,我询问了各个教派的信徒;尤其是一些不同教派和终身献身于宗教事业的教士们的团体。作为一名罗马天主教会的信徒,我尤其愿意与天主教徒们接触,与他们亲密的交谈。对他们我都表示了自己的惊讶并提出了我的疑问。我发现他们只是在一些细节上略有不同,并且他们都把宗教在国内的和平统治归功于政教分离。我可以断定,在我在美国期间,我没有见过任何一个人,不论是神职人员还是普通人,在这一问题上都持有不同意见。

这使我比以前更加专心地研究美国神职人员在政界占据的地位。我惊奇地发现他们没有担任公职。① 我在管理层中没有发现他们中的任何一人,在参议院和众议院也没有他们的代表。在

---

① 除非这个条款大多数适用于学校。几乎所有的教育都由神职人员担任。

in the legislative assemblies. In several states① the law excludes them from political life; public opinion excludes them in all. And when I came to inquire into the prevailing spirit of the clergy, I found that most of its members seemed to retire of their own accord from the exercise of power, and that they made it the pride of their profession to abstain from politics. I heard them inveigh against ambition and deceit, under what ever political opinions these vices might chance to lurk; but I learned from their discourses that men are not guilty in the eye of God for any opinions concerning political government which they may profess with sincerity, any more than they are for their mistakes in building a house or in driving a furrow. I perceived that these ministers of the Gospel eschewed all parties, with the anxiety attendant upon personal interest. These facts convinced me that what I had been told was true; and it then became my object to investigate their causes and to inquire how it happened that the real authority of religion was increased by a state of things which diminished its apparent force. These causes did not long escape my researches.

The short space of threescore years can never content the imagination of man; nor can the imperfect joys of this world satisfy his heart. Man alone, of all created beings, displays a natural contempt of existence, and yet a boundless desire to exist; he scorns life, but he dreads annihilation. These different feelings incessantly urge his soul to the contemplation of a future state, and religion directs his musings thither. Religion, then, is simply another form of hope, and it is no less natural to the human heart than hope itself. Men cannot abandon their religious faith without a kind of aberration of intellect

---

① See the Constitution of New York, Art. VII,4:

"And whereas the ministers of the Gospel are, by their profession, dedicated to the service of God and the care of souls, and ought not to be diverted from the great duties of their functions; therefore no minister of the Gospel, or priest of any denomination whatsoever, shall at any time here after, under any pretence or description whatever, be eligible to, or capable of holding, any civil or military office or place within this State. "See also the Constitutions of North Carolina, Art. XXXI; Virginia; South Carolina, Art. I,23; Kentucky, Art. II,26; Tennessee, Art. VIII,1; Louisiana, Art. II,22.

一些州①法律将他们排除在政治生活之外。而所有州的公众舆论都不同意他们从政。当我询问神职人员对于此事的看法时,我发现大多数人脱离政界之外与他们的初衷是一致的,他们认为与政治划清界限正是他们的职业值得骄傲之处。我听到他们猛烈地抨击野心和谎言,而无论这些恶习隐藏在何种政治言论下;但我从他们的谈话中了解到,在上帝眼中,持有任何政治统治观点的人都是无罪的,只要他们是真诚的,他们所犯的错误并不比出现在建造房屋和犁地时出现的失误更严重。我看到这些宗教的神职人员总是避开其他党派,唯恐损失自己利益。这些事实使我相信,之前人们告诉我的都是事实;之后这也变成了我研究他们的起因,寻求宗教的真实地权威在表面上被削弱而实际上得以增强的原因。这些原因从未脱离过我的研究。

短暂的 60 年并没能使人们充分的发挥其想象;现实生活的不完美也没能使他们感到满足。世上所有的生物,只有人类,表现出了对生存的本能的追求和无尽的渴望;他蔑视生命但又惧怕死亡。这些不同的情感不断地促使他的灵魂沉思未来,而宗教指引着他对未来的沉思。宗教,于是成了另一种形式存在的希望,他并不比人们内心的希望更不自然。人们只要不是精神失常或者为暴力扭曲了自己的真实本愿,就不能丢掉自己的宗教信仰;

---

① 见纽约州宪法第七章。"然而就传教士的职业来说,他们应该专心致力于为上帝服务和照顾人们的灵魂,不应该丢开他们神圣的职责。因此,没有任何传教士或者任何名义命名的牧师,在任何时间,通过任何托词或者掩饰,符合条件或能够参与本州的任何政务和军事。"见美国北卡罗来纳州宪法第三十一章;弗吉尼亚州;南卡罗来纳州宪法第一章第 23 条;肯塔基州宪法第二章第 26 条;田纳西州宪法第八章第 1 条;路易斯安那州宪法第二章第 22 条。

and a sort of violent distortion of their true nature; they are invincibly brought back to more pious sentiments. Unbelief is an accident, and faith is the only permanent state of mankind. If we consider religious institutions merely in a human point of view, they may be said to derive an inexhaustible element of strength from man himself, since they belong to one of the constituent principles of human nature.

I am aware that at certain times religion may strengthen this influence, which originates in itself, by the artificial power of the laws and by the support of those temporal institutions that direct society. Religions intimately united with the governments of the earth have been known to exercise sovereign power founded on terror and faith; but when a religion contracts an alliance of this nature, I do not hesitate to affirm that it commits the same error as a man who should sacrifice his future to his present welfare; and in obtaining a power to which it has no claim, it risks that authority which is rightfully its own. When a religion founds its empire only upon the desire of immortality that lives in every human heart, it may aspire to universal dominion; but when it connects itself with a government, it must adopt maxims which are applicable only to certain nations. Thus, informing an alliance with a political power, religion augments its authority over a few and forfeits the hope of reigning over all.

As long as a religion rests only upon those sentiments which are the consolation of all affliction, it may attract the affections of all mankind. But if it be mixed up with the bitter passions of the world, it may be constrained to defend allies whom its interests, and not the principle of love, have given to it; or to repel as an tagonists men who are still attached to it, however opposed they may be to the powers with which it is allied. The church cannot share the temporal power of the state without being the object of a portion of that animosity which the latter excites.

The political powers which seem to be most firmly established have frequently no better guarantee for their duration than the opinions of a generation, the interests of the time, or the life of an individual. A law may modify the social condition which seems to be most fixed and determinate; and with the social condition everything else must change. The powers of society are more or less fugitive, like the years that we spend upon earth; they succeed each other with rapidity, like the fleeting cares of life; and no government has ever yet been founded

但是有一种不可战胜的力量,在使人恢复宗教信仰。没有宗教信仰是偶然的,有信仰才是人类的正常状态。如果我们以人类的出发点考虑宗教制度,可以说制度从人本身汲取了用之不竭的力量因素,因为这些因素也是人类本性的构成原则。

我知道,在过去某些时候,宗教除了自身固有的影响之外,还可能通过法律的力量和那些指导社会的现实制度的支持加强这种影响。宗教曾与人世的政府紧密结合,行使建造在恐怖和信仰上的统治权力;但是当宗教与人世的政府建立这样的联盟时,我毫无疑问地认定它会像人一样犯错误,用未来换取现世的幸福,为取得不应属于它的权力,而威胁到自己合法的权益。当宗教将它的统治建造在人人心中都梦想着的永生的渴望上时,它就有望取得普遍的统治,但是当它与政府结合,那么它就必然的采用适合某些民族的准则。因此,在与政治力量结成同盟的时候,宗教实际上只在某些人中增强了其权威,而失去了统治一切人的希望。

宗教只有依靠使所有人得到安慰的情感时,他才能得到全人类的爱戴。但是,如果宗教与世上苦难的情感混合在一起的时候,则可能会被迫去帮助一些不是为了爱而是为了利的盟友,或者抵制一些仍旧依恋它但是全力反对它的盟友。宗教只要不变成统治者煽动的仇恨的一部分目标就不能分享现世的权力。

表面上看起来建立的很稳固的政治统治,却常常并不比一辈人的观念、时代的利益甚至个人的生命有更持久地保障。法律可以改变看起来似乎十分牢固稳定的社会状态;而随着社会状态的变化,所有的事情都随之改变。社会的权利总是多少有些变化无常,宛若人生在世;权力之间迅速更替,犹如人生飞逝而过的情

upon an invariable disposition of the human heart or upon an imperishable interest.

As long as a religion is sustained by those feelings, propensities, and passions which are found to occur under the same forms at all periods of history, it may defy the efforts of time; or at least it can be destroyed only by another religion. But when religion clings to the interests of the world, it becomes almost as fragile a thing as the powers of earth. It is the only one of them all which can hope for immortality; but if it be connected with their ephemeral power, it shares their fortunes and may fall with those transient passions which alone supported them. The alliance which religion contracts with political powers must needs be onerous to itself, since it does not require their assistance to live, and by giving them its assistance it may be exposed to decay.

The danger which I have just pointed out always exists, but it is not always equally visible. In some ages governments seem to be imperishable; in others the existence of society appears to be more precarious than the life of man. Some constitutions plunge the citizens into a lethargic somnolence, and others rouse them to feverish excitement. When governments seem so strong and laws so stable, men do not perceive the dangers that may accrue from a union of church and state. When governments appear weak and laws inconstant, the danger is self-evident, but it is no longer possible to avoid it. We must therefore learn how to perceive it from afar.

In proportion as a nation assumes a democratic condition of society and as communities display democratic propensities, it becomes more and more dangerous to connect religion with political institutions; for the time is coming when authority will be bandied from hand to hand, when political theories will succeed one an other, and when men, laws, and constitutions will disappear or be modified from day to day, and this not for a season only, but unceasingly. Agitation and mutability are inherent in the nature of democratic republics, just as stagnation and sleepiness are the law of absolute monarchies.

If the Americans, who change the head of the government once in four years, who elect new legislators every two years, and renew

感;之间还没有哪个政府建立在恒一的民心的支持或者永不磨灭的利益之上。

人们的情感、喜好和激情,在人类历史上总是出现在相同的模式下,在宗教依赖着这些时就能称霸一时,至少只能是被另一种宗教模式所取代而不是其他任何事物。但是当宗教与人世的利益结合在一起的时候,就变得和人世的权利一样不堪一击。宗教本是他们中间唯一可能永恒的事物,而其一旦与短暂的权力结合在一起,就会和这些权利的命运一样,与那些曾支持他们的短暂激情一同消亡。因此,宗教与政治权利结盟必然给自己添加责任,因为宗教不需要他们的帮助求得生存,而如果宗教帮助政治权利,则会导致自己的灭亡。

我方才所指出的危险总是存在的,但却不总是表现得那么明显。在一些时期,政府看起来是永不会灭亡的;而在有些时期,社会的存在显得比人们的生命更微弱。一些制度将公民引入了浑浑噩噩的状态,而有些则激起他们的亢奋和激情。当政府的势力显得强大法制稳定的时候,人们看不到政教结合带来的危险;当政府的势力显得微弱法制变化无常的时候,危险就显而易见了,可是想要避开它已经来不及了。因此,我们一定要防患于未然。

随着一个国家社会情况日益趋向民主,社会表现出向民主发展的倾向,政教结合就会变得越来越危险;这一时期,政权从一方转到另一方,政治理论迭出不穷,人们、法律和制度每天都在消亡或更改,而所有这些现象并不是暂时的存在,而是永无止境的。民主共和制度固有的兴奋和多变,就像君主专制下的法律那样停滞不前昏昏欲睡。

美国人每四年换一届政府首脑,每两年选举一次新的立法官

the state officers every twelve months; if the Americans, who have given up the political world to the attempts of innovators, had not placed religion beyond their reach, where could it take firm hold in the ebb and flow of human opinions? Where would be that respect which belongs to it, amid the struggles of faction? And what would become of its immortality, in the midst of universal decay? The American clergy were the first to perceive this truth and to act in conformity with it. They saw that they must renounce their religious influence if they were to strive for political power, and they chose to give up the support of the state rather than to share its vicissitudes.

In America religion is perhaps less powerful than it has been at certain periods and among certain nations; but its influence is more lasting. It restricts itself to its own resources, but of these none can deprive it; its circle is limited, but it pervades it and holds it under undisputed control.

On every side in Europe we hear voices complaining of the absence of religious faith and inquiring the means of restoring to re ligion some remnant of its former authority. It seems to me that we must first attentively consider what ought to be the natural state of men with regard to religion at the present time; and when we know what we have to hope and to fear, we may discern the end to which our efforts ought to be directed.

The two great dangers which threaten the existence of religion are schism and indifference. In ages of fervent devotion men sometimes abandon their religion, but they only shake one off in order to adopt another. Their faith changes its objects, but suffers no decline. The old religion then excites enthusiastic attachment or bitter enmity in either party; some leave it with anger, others cling to it with increased devotedness, and although persuasions differ, irreligion is unknown. Such, however, is not the case when a religious belief is secretly undermined by doctrines which may be termed negative, since they deny the truth of one religion without affirming that of any other. Prodigious revolutions then take place in the human mind, without the apparent co-operation of the passions of man, and almost without his

员,而每年都更换一次地方官员;他们将政治交给一些新手按照自己的意愿创新,使宗教与政治毫无干系,那么,宗教如何在此消彼长的舆论中站稳脚跟呢? 在党派之间的斗争中,人们对它应有的敬重又在哪里? 在这万物萧条的环境中他又能凭借什么永垂不朽呢? 美国的神职人员最先认识到这一事实并且努力与其行动一致。他们认识到,如果想得到政治权利,必须与宗教势力断绝关系,他们宁愿放弃州的支持也不愿牵扯到它的兴衰之中。

在美国,宗教也许不如从前在一些国家的某些时期那样拥有强大的权力,但是它的影响却更持久。宗教局限在自己的园囿内,任何事物都不能剥夺它的权力;它的范围虽然很有限,但是一切都处于它绝对的掌控之中。

欧洲各个层面都传来大家对宗教信仰迷失的怨言,人们希望能够重新拾起宗教昔日的权威,哪怕只剩一些残片。在我看来,我们首先应该做的,是认真思考当今人类与宗教的自然的状态到底应该是怎样的;只有当我们了解了我们希望和害怕的是什么以后,我们才能看清我们应该努力的方向。

威胁着宗教存亡的两大因素是教派的分裂和人们的漠视。在那些热心献身的年代,人们常常会放弃自己的宗教,但也只是放弃一个选择另一个。他们的信仰虽改变了目标,但却并没有消退。旧的宗教既激发着人们的激情也同时增强着人们的仇恨;一些人愤怒地将之抛弃,而另一些人以更大的热情投向它,尽管有不同的说词,但是没有无信仰的存在。无论如何,这样的情形并不会是一些反面的教条暗地破坏宗教信仰,因为它在否认一个宗教的同时并没有树立起另一个新的宗教形象。人们的思想旋即发生了巨大的革命,这些变革显然不是人们激情的主动配合,它

knowledge. Men lose the objects of their fondest hopes as if through forgetfulness. They are carried away by an imperceptible current, which they have not the courage to stem, but which they follow with regret, since it bears them away from a faith they love to a skepticism that plunges them into despair.

In ages which answer to this description men desert their religious opinions from lukewarmness rather than from dislike; they are not rejected, but they fall away. But if the unbeliever does not admit religion to be true, he still considers it useful. Regarding religious institutions in a human point of view, he acknowledges their influence upon manners and legislation. He admits that they may serve to make men live in peace and prepare them gently for the hour of death. He regrets the faith that he has lost; and as he is deprived of a treasure of which he knows the value, he fears to take it away from those who still possess it.

On the other hand, those who continue to believe are not afraid openly to avow their faith. They look upon those who do not share their persuasion as more worthy of pity than of opposition; and they are aware that to acquire the esteem of the unbelieving, they are not obliged to follow their example. They are not hostile, then, to anyone in the world; and as they do not consider the society in which they live as an arena in which religion is bound to face its thousand deadly foes, they love their contemporaries while they condemn their weaknesses and lament their errors.

As those who do not believe conceal their incredulity, and as those who believe display their faith, public opinion pronounces itself in favor of religion: love, support, and honor are bestowed upon it, and it is only by searching the human soul that we can detect the wounds which it has received. The mass of mankind, who are never without the feeling of religion, do not perceive anything at variance with the established faith. The instinctive desire of a future life brings the crowd about the altar and opens the hearts of men to the precepts and consolations of religion.

甚至不为人知。人们就这样失去了自己最喜爱的希望对象,就像被遗忘掉了一样。他们被暗暗涌动的潮流带动着,而这潮流他们没有勇气去阻止,只好心怀愧疚的跟随其后,因为这股潮流将他们带离了他们喜爱的信仰,走向将他们陷入绝望的疑惑。

在这样的年代中,人们放弃宗教的原因更多的是因为淡漠而不是厌烦。他们没有遭到宗教的拒绝,而是自己推出了。但是如果不信仰宗教的人也不承认宗教的真实性的话,他至少仍然相信其具有实用性。从人类的角度看待宗教制度,他承认他们在民情和立法方面产生的影响。他承认宗教使人们生活和平并使他们平静地面对死亡。因为他很遗憾自己丢失这样的信仰,仿佛丢失了自己明明知道其珍贵价值的珠宝,因此他担心那些还拥有的人也会失去它。

相反的,那些拥有信仰的人不怕大声地说出他们的信仰。他们认为那些不听从他们劝服的人们甚至比那些反对者更可怜,他们也明白,自己没有必要去学他们的样来获得这些没有信仰的人们的尊重。他们对世上的人并不怀着敌对的情绪。就如同他们并不认为他们生活的社会就像竞技场一样,宗教必须去面对数以千计的死敌,他们热爱自己的同胞,但同时也苛责他们的软弱,为他们所犯的错误感到悲伤。

像那些不相信的人们隐藏自己的怀疑,而相信的人宣扬自己的信仰一样,公众的意见表明了它支持宗教的心意:爱、支持和尊敬都给与它,只有通过探求人们的灵魂深处,才能找到灵魂所受的创伤。那些从未想过放弃宗教的人们,没有使这种情感与已建立的信仰脱离。向往来世的本能愿望,将人们引到圣坛前接受洗礼,敞开他们的心扉来接受信仰的劝诫和安慰。

But this picture is not applicable to us, for there are men among us who have ceased to believe in Christianity, without adopting any other religion; others are in the perplexities of doubt and already affect not to believe; and others, again, are afraid to avow that Christian faith which they still cherish in secret.

Amid these lukewarm partisans and ardent antagonists a small number of believers exists who are ready to brave all obstacles and to scorn all dangers in defense of their faith. They have done violence to human weakness in order to rise superior to public opinion. Excited by the effort they have made, they scarcely know where to stop; and as they know that the first use which the French made of independence was to attack religion, they look upon their contemporaries with dread, and recoil in alarm from the liberty which their fellow citizens are seeking to obtain. As unbelief appears to them to be a novelty, they comprise all that is new in one indiscriminate animosity. They are at war with their age and country, and they look upon every opinion that is put forth there as the necessary enemy of faith.

Such is not the natural state of men with regard to religion at the present day, and some extraordinary or incidental cause must be at work in France to prevent the human mind from following its natural inclination and to drive it beyond the limits at which it ought naturally to stop.

I am fully convinced that this extraordinary and incidental cause is the close connection of politics and religion. The unbelievers of Europe attack the Christians as their political opponents rather than as their religious adversaries; they hate the Christian religion as the opinion of a party much more than as an error of belief; and they reject the clergy less because they are the repre sentatives of the Deity than because they are the allies of government.

In Europe, Christianity has been intimately united to the powers of the earth. Those powers are now in decay, and it is, as it were, buried under their ruins. The living body of religion has been bound down to the dead corpse of superannuated polity; cut but the bonds that restrain it, and it will rise once more. I do not know what could

　　但是这样的描述并不适合我们，因为我们中的一些人已经不再信仰基督教，也不信仰其他的教派；另一些人则处于混乱迷惑中，或者宣称不再信教；还有一些人，则因为害怕而隐瞒自己信仰基督教的事实。

　　置身于情绪冷淡的同教中人和激烈的反对者中，一些信徒时刻准备着为保卫他们的信仰而英勇地扫除一切障碍，蔑视一切危险。他们不顾舆论用暴力打击人们的弱处。他们为自己的努力鼓舞着，不知休止；当他们了解到法国人取得的独立首先就被用来攻击宗教的时候，他们用恐惧的眼神注视着这个时代，惊慌地在他们的同胞们奋力争夺自由的行列里退缩。他们认为不信仰宗教是很新奇的事情，凡是新的东西，他们都一律仇视。他们那个年代和所在的国家处于战乱之中，他们将每一个提出的观点都当作信仰的死敌。

　　这不是目前人类在宗教方面所处的正常状态。在法国还存在着一些特殊的偶然的原因用于防止人们的思想按照其本性发展并驱使它超越自己的本能要求停止的界限。

　　我深信政教紧密结合就是这一特殊的和偶然的原因。欧洲不信教的人将基督教当作他们的政治敌人，而不是当作宗教敌人加以攻击；他们憎恨基督教的原因更多的是从党派的观点出发而不是信仰的错误；他们不反对神职人员，认为他们是上帝的代表，而不是因为他们是政府的同盟。

　　在欧洲，基督教曾与人世的权力紧密地结合。这些权力如今已经衰退，而基督教也仿佛被深埋在这些废墟下。宗教的躯体还没死，但被死去的政权压在身下；一旦禁锢着它的势力被劈开，它就会再一次站起来。我不知道怎样做才能恢复欧洲基督教会早

restore the Christian church of Europe to the energy of its earlier days; that power belongs to God alone; but it may be for human policy to leave to faith the full exercise of the strength which it still retains.

How The Education, The Habits, And The Practical Experience Of The Americans Promote The Success Of Their Democratic Institutions

What is to be understood by the education of the American people—The human mind more superficially in structed in the United States than in Europe—No one completely uninstructed—Reason for this—Rapidity with which opinions are diffused even in the half-cultivated states of the West—Practical experience more serviceable to the Americans than book-learning.

I have but little to add to what I have already said concerning the influence that the instruction and the habits of the Americans exercise upon the maintenance of their political institutions. America has hitherto produced very few writers of distinction; it possesses no great historians and not a single eminent poet. The inhabitants of that country look upon literature properly so called with a kind of disapprobation; and there are towns of second-rate importance in Europe in which more literary works are annually published than in the twenty-four states of the Union put together.

The spirit of the Americans is averse to general ideas; it does not seek theoretical discoveries. Neither politics nor manufactures direct them to such speculations; and although new laws are perpetually enacted in the United States, no great writers there have hitherto inquired into the general principles of legislation. The Americans have lawyers and commentators, but no jurists; and they furnish examples rather than lessons to the world. The same observation applies to the mechanical arts. In America the inventions of Europe are adopted with sagacity; they are perfected, and adapted with admirable skill to the wants of the country. Manufactures exist, but the science of manufacture is not cultivated; and they have good workmen, but very few inventors. Fulton was obliged to proffer his services to foreign nations for a long time before he was able to devote them to his own country.

The observer who is desirous of forming an opinion on the state of instruction among the Anglo-Americans must consider the same object from two different points of view. If he singles out only the learned,

先的活力;只有上帝有这样的能力;但是无论如何,也得有赖于人们相信它仍然保留的全部力量是有用的。

美国人的教育、习惯和实践经验是
如何促进民主制度获得成功的

美国人民的教育应当如何理解——美国对人们的思想的指引比起欧洲来显得更浮于表面——所有的人都受过教导——为什么——各种见解迅速地在西部半开化的地区传播开来——实践经验比书本知识更有助于美国人民。

我现在此就前面提到的对于美国人的教育和习惯在维护其政治制度方面的影响做一点补充:美国迄今很少有声名显赫的作家,没有伟大的历史学家和著名的诗人。整个国家的人民都带着一种不赞成的眼光看待文学。欧洲一个二流城镇每年文学作品的出版量相比其他 24 个州出版的总量还多。

美国人的思想与一般的概念相反,他们不追求理论的发现。政治和实业都没能引导他们进行这样的思索,尽管美国永远都在颁布新的法律,却没有一个学者深入地探讨过立法的普遍原则。美国有法官评论家,但是没有法理学家。而这些人只向世界提供了实例而没有教训。技术方面也是如此。在美国,对欧洲的发明创造利用得很好,并在加以改善之后,极好地满足了国内的需要。实业虽然存在,然而有关实业的科学还没出现;优秀的工人虽已有,但是却缺少发明家。富尔顿长久以来一直为外国人服务,才得以将自己的才能在自己的国家施展。

凡欲考察英裔美国人的智力水平的人,都应当从两个不同的方面去研究这个问题。如果他选择的都是受过教育的人们,他会

he will be astonished to find how few they are; but if he counts the ignorant, the American people will appear to be the most enlightened in the world. The whole population, as I observed in another place, is situated between these two extremes. In New England every citizen receives the elementary notions of human knowledge; he is taught, moreover, the doctrines and the evidences of his religion, the history of his country, and the leading features of its Constitution. In the states of Connecticut and Massachusetts, it is extremely rare to find a man imperfectly acquainted with all these things, and a person wholly ignorant of them is a sort of phenomenon.

When I compare the Greek and Roman republics with these American states; the manuscript libraries of the former, and their rude population, with the innumerable journals and the enlight ened people of the latter; when I remember all the attempts that are made to judge the modern republics by the aid of those of antiquity, and to infer what will happen in our time from what took place two thousand years ago, I am tempted to burn my books in order to apply none but novel ideas to so novel a condition of society.

What I have said of New England must not, however, be applied to the whole Union without distinction; as we advance to wards the West or the South, the instruction of the people diminishes. In the states that border on the Gulf of Mexico a certain number of individuals may be found, as in France, who are devoid even of the rudiments of instruction. But there is not a single district in the United States sunk in complete ignorance, and for a very simple reason. The nations of Europe started from the darkness of a barbarous condition, to advance towards the light of civilization; their progress has been unequal; some of them have improved rapidly, while others have loitered in their course, and some have stopped and are still sleeping upon the way.

Such has not been the case in the United States. The AngloAmericans, already civilized, settled upon that territory which their descendants occupy; they did not have to begin to learn, and it was sufficient for them not to forget. Now the children of these same Americans are the persons who, year by year, transport their dwellings into the wilds, and, with their dwellings, their acquired information and their esteem for knowledge. Education has taught them the utility of instruction and has enabled them to transmit that instruction to their

惊讶地发现他们的数量竟然是这么地少;而如果在调查的时候将一些无知的人也算在内的话,美国人民就会成为世界上最文明开化的国家。这如我在另一处提到的,全体美国人民的受教育程度处于最高和最低者之间。在新英格兰,每一位公民都有机会接受初等教育;他们可以学习宗教教条和论证,学习关于自己国家的历史和宪法的要点。在康涅狄格州和马萨诸塞州,很难找到不了解这些知识的人,而对这些一无所知者简直就是怪物。

当我把希腊和罗马共和制与美国的共和制度,把前者手抄本的珍贵图书以及他们无知的群众和后者无数的报刊杂志和有知识的人们进行比较的时候,当我回顾我们依靠古代的遗物来判断当今的共和政体所作的努力,和根据两千年前的经验来推断我们今后的未来而仍在进行的一切努力时,我真想把我的书全部烧掉,以便用全新的观点来考察这一全新的社会状况。

但是,我所说的新英格兰的情形并不能不加区别地套在整个联邦身上。越往西或越往南,人们的知识水平就越低。在濒临墨西哥湾的各州,像法国一样,有些人甚至没有接受过初等教育。但是,在美国,没有任何一个地区的居民完全没有受过教育。理由很简单:欧洲各国都起源于野蛮黑暗的环境,然后一步步走向文明,他们之间的进程并不平等,一些提高的快一点,一些缓慢地前进着,还有一些甚至已经停止了脚步蒙头大睡。

这些状况在美国都不曾出现过。英裔美国人在定居在这块后来为子孙继承的土地上时本就已开化;他们不用从头学起,只要不忘记已有的知识就可以了。如今,这些人的子孙年年都会向内地的荒野迁移一部分人。随着他们迁移的还有他们已有的知识和对知识的尊敬。教育使他们知道了知识的功用,并使得他们

posterity. In the United States society has no infancy, but it is born in man's estate.

The Americans never use the word peasant, because they have no idea of the class which that term denotes; the ignorance of more remote ages, the simplicity of rural life, and the rusticity of the villager have not been preserved among them; and they are alike unacquainted with the virtues, the vices, the coarse habits, and the simple graces of an early stage of civilization. At the extreme borders of the confederated states, upon the confines of society and the wilderness, a population of bold adventurers have taken up their abode, who pierce the solitudes of the American woods and seek a country there in order to escape the poverty that awaited them in their native home. As soon as the pioneer reaches the place which is to serve him for a retreat, he fells a few trees and builds a log house. Nothing can offer a more miserable aspect than these isolated dwellings. The traveler who approaches one of them towards nightfall sees the flicker of the hearth flame through the chinks in the walls; and at night, if the wind rises, he hears the roof of boughs shake to and fro in the midst of the great forest trees. Who would not suppose that this poor hut is the asy lum of rudeness and ignorance? Yet no sort of comparison can be drawn between the pioneer and the dwelling that shelters him. Everything about him is primitive and wild, but he is himself the result of the labor and experience of eighteen centuries. He wears the dress and speaks the language of cities; he is acquainted with the past, curious about the future, and ready for argument about the present; he is, in short, a highly civilized being, who consents for a time to inhabit the backwoods, and who penetrates into the wilds of the New World with the Bible, an axe, and some newspapers. It is difficult to imagine the incredible rapidity with which thought circulates in the midst of these deserts. ① I do not think that so much intellectual

---

① I traveled along a portion of the frontier of the United States in a sort of cart, which was termed the mail. Day and night we passed with great rapidity along the roads, which were scarcely marked out through immense forests. When the gloom of the woods became impenetrable, the driver lighted branches of pine, and we journeyed along by the light they cast. From time to time we came to a hut in the midst of the forest; this was a post-office. The mail dropped an enormous bundle of letters at the door of this isolated dwelling, and we pursued our way at full gallop, leaving the inhabitants of the neighboring log houses to send for their share of the treasure.

能够将自己的知识传给后人。因此,在美国社会没有摇篮时期,
它在建立时就已是成年。

美国人从来不使用农民这个词,他们从不知道这个词代表着
什么含义;在他们中,没有人生活在无知的初民年代,过着简单的
田园生活,伴着粗野的村民。他们好像也并不了解什么是文明开
化早期所有的德行、恶习、鄙俗和粗犷。在联邦的边缘地带,或在
人群与荒野交接的地方,一群大胆的冒险家在这里占据了他们的
居所,打破了美国森林的孤寂,在那里寻找能够免于在自己的祖
国遭受贫穷的国度。拓荒者一旦找到了栖息之所,就砍伐树木搭
建木屋。再没有什么比这些偏僻的木屋更让人感到凄惨的了。
在傍晚时分走近这样木屋的旅人,远远地就可以看到透过墙壁的
裂缝闪耀着壁炉的火光。夜晚起风的时候,可以听到原木的屋顶
随着风在森林中摇来晃去发出的声音。有谁会不认为这是一间
粗鄙无知的人儿寻求庇护的贫穷小屋呢? 但是,拓荒者本身却与
他所居住的小屋毫无可比之处。他周围的一切都那么原始粗野,
而他自身却是十八世纪劳动和经验的体现。他的衣着和语言都
是城市里的方式;他了解过去、憧憬未来、正视现状。简而言之,
他是一位很文明的人,很快就适应了森林里的生活。他进入新大
陆荒野的时候,随身只有一本圣经、一把斧子和几张报纸。思想
在这片荒野中传播的速度迅速地匪夷所思。① 我想像这样文明的

---

① 我坐在一辆邮车中沿着美国的边界前行。我们沿着很难被辨别出
的林间小路没日没夜地快速前进着。当走到树林茂密昏暗的地方,赶车人
就削薄树木的枝叶,我们就沿着透过它们投射下来的光线前进。我们在森
林中碰到很多小木屋。这都是邮局。邮递员将成捆的信件放在这些荒弃的
房前,然后我们接着赶路,让周围木屋的居民们去拿自己的一份。

activity exists in the most enlightened and populous districts of France. ①

It cannot be doubted that in the United States the instruction of the people powerfully contributes to the support of the democratic republic; and such must always be the case, I believe, where the instruction which enlightens the understanding is not separated from the moral education which amends the heart. But I would not exaggerate this advantage, and I am still further from thinking, as so many people do think in Europe, that men can be instantaneously made citizens by teaching them to read and write. True information is mainly derived from experience; and if the Americans had not been gradually accustomed to govern them selves, their book-learning would not help them much at the present day.

I have lived much with the people in the United States, and I cannot express how much I admire their experience and their good sense. An American should never be led to speak of Europe, for he will then probably display much presumption and very foolish pride. He will take up with those crude and vague notions which are so useful to the ignorant all over the world. But if you question him respecting his own country, the cloud that dimmed his intel ligence will immediately disperse; his language will become as clear and precise as his thoughts. He will inform you what his rights are and by what means he exercises them; he will be able to point out the customs which obtain in the political world. You will find that he is well acquainted with the rules of the adminis tration, and that he is familiar with the mechanism of the laws. The citizen of the United States does not acquire his practical science and his positive notions from books; the instruction he has acquired may have prepared him for receiving those ideas, but it did not furnish them. The American learns to know the laws by participating in the act of legislation; and he takes a lesson in the forms of government from governing. The great work of society is ever going on before his eyes and, as it were, under his hands.

In the United States politics are the end and aim of education; in

---

① In 1832 each inhabitant of Michigan paid 1 fr. 22 cent. to the post-office revenue; and each inhabitant of the Floridas paid 1 fr. 5 cent. (See National Calendar [1833], p. 244.) In the same year each inhabitant of the Dé parte-ment du Nord paid not quite 1 fr. 4 cent. to the revenue of the French postoffice. (See the Compte g énéral de 'Administration des Finances [1833], p. 623.) Now, the state of Michigan contained at that time only 7 inhabitants per square league, and Florida only 5. Instruction was less universal, and the commercial activity of these districts inferior to those of most of the states in the Union; while the Département du Nord, which contains 3,400 in habitants per square league, is one of the most enlightened and most industrial parts of France.

行为,即使在法国最文明最繁华的地区也不可能发生。①

　　毫无疑问,美国的国民教育对帮助民主共和制极其有利。我相信,在启发智力和对道德的教育永不被分离的地方,情况更是如此。但是我并不想夸大这个优势,而且我也不像欧洲很多其他人那样,认为只要教会人们读书写字,他们就立刻可以成为公民。真正的知识主要来自经验;如果美国人没有慢慢地适应来管理自己,他们的书本知识也不会对他们今天的状况有很大地帮助。

　　我和美国人一起生活了一段时间,很难表达我对他们的经验和广博的见识的崇拜。绝不能让一个美国人谈起欧洲,否则他很快就会表现出自负和愚蠢的骄傲。他会引用一些粗俗含混的论调糊弄一下那些无知的人们。但是,当你把话题转向他自己的国家时,笼罩着他的愁云立即烟消云散;他的言语和思维变得清晰准确。他会告诉你,他的权力以及运用权力的方式;他会指出政界的惯例。你会发现他对管理规则很熟悉,而且深知法律的机制。美国的居民不从书本去汲取实际知识和实证思想;书本知识只能帮助他接受这些思想,但并不能直接提供给他。美国人通过参加立法学习法律,从参加管理工作掌握政府的组织形式。社会的主要工作在他眼前运作,甚至通过他们亲手完成。

　　在美国,政治是教育的终点和目标;在欧洲,它的核心目标则

---

　　① 1832年密歇根州的居民每人需要支付给邮局的费用约1.22法郎,而每个佛罗里达的居民需要支付1.5法郎。同一年,北部的居民每人只要给法国的邮局支付不到1.4法郎。(见1833年财政部报告第623页。)如今密歇根州每平方里约只有7个居民,佛罗里达有5个。教育还没有普及,这些地区的商业活动也不如联邦的其他地区。而北部地区每平方里约人口数量为3400,是法国最文明开化工业最发达的地区之一。

Europe its principal object is to fit men for private life. The in terference of the citizens in public affairs is too rare an occurrence to be provided for beforehand. Upon casting a glance over society in the two hemispheres, these differences are indicated even by their external aspect.

In Europe we frequently introduce the ideas and habits of private life into public affairs; and as we pass at once from the do mesticcircle to the government of the state, we may frequently be heard to discuss the great interests of society in the same manner in which we converse with our friends. The Americans, on the other hand, transport the habits of public life into their manners in private; in their country the jury is introduced into the games of schoolboys, and parliamentary forms are observed in the order of a feast.

The Laws Contribute More To The Maintenance Of The Democratic Republic In The United States Than The Physical CirCumstances Of The Country, And The Customs More Than The Laws

All the nations of America have a democratic state of society—Yet democratic institutions are supported only among the Anglo-Americans— The Spaniards of South America, as much favored by physical causes as the Anglo-Americans, unable to maintain a democratic republic— Mexico, which has adopted the Constitution of the United States, in the same predicament—The Anglo-Americans of the West less able to maintain it than those of the East—Reason for these differences.

I have remarked that the maintenance of democratic institutions in the United States is attributable to the circumstances, the laws, and the customs of that country. ①Most Europeans are acquainted with only the first of these three causes, and they are apt to give it a preponderant importance that it does not really possess. It is true that the Anglo-Americans settled in the New World in a state of social equality; the low-born and the noble were not to be found among them;

---

① I remind the reader of the general signification which I give to the word customs: namely, the moral and intellectual characteristics of men in society.

是帮助人们协调自己的私生活。公民参加公务活动,很少需要预先学习。随便瞥一眼两半球,它们之间的区别甚至可以从其外表辨认得出。

在欧洲,我们常常把一些私人生活的习惯和想法带到公共事务中;而当我们忽然从家庭的圈子进入政府的统治,我们常常会听到人们用我们与朋友之间交谈的方式来讨论社会的重要利益。而美国人,相反的,将公共生活的习惯带入家庭;在他们的国家,陪审团的理念被传入学生们的游戏中,而代议制则被用于组织宴会。

法制比自然环境更有助于美国维护民主共和制度,而民情比法制的贡献更大

美洲的所有民族都有民主的社会情况——而只有在英裔美国人中民主制才得到人们的支持——南美洲的西班牙人,虽然和英裔美国人一样占据了地理的优势,但是没能维持民主共和制——墨西哥,虽采用了美国的宪法,但是也没有实现民主共和制——西部的英裔美国人没能像东部的英裔美国人那样好的维护这种制度——出现这些差异的原因。

我前面已经提过,民主制度在美国得以维持应归功于其地理环境、法律和民情。[①] 大多数欧洲人都只知道其中第一个原因,并且都倾向于赋予其并不具备的重大作用。英裔美国人确实在新大陆建立起了平等地位的社会形态,在人们中间没有出身低微和

---

① 我还要提醒读者我对民情的定义:就是指社会中的人们的道德和智力特征。

and professional prejudices were always as unknown as the prejudices of birth. Thus, as the condition of society was democratic, the rule of democracy was established with out difficulty. But this circumstance is not peculiar to the United States; almost all the American colonies were founded by men equal among themselves, or who became so by inhabiting them. In no one part of the New World have Europeans been able to create an aristocracy. Nevertheless, democratic institutions prosper nowhere but in the United States.

The American Union has no enemies to contend with; it stands in the wilds like an island in the ocean. But the Spaniards of South America were no less isolated by nature; yet their position has not relieved them from the charge of standing armies. They make war upon one another when they have no foreign enemies to oppose; and the Anglo-American democracy is the only one that has hitherto been able to maintain itself in peace.

The territory of the Union presents a boundless field to human activity, and inexhaustible materials for labor. The passion for wealth takes the place of ambition, and the heat of faction is mitigated by a consciousness of prosperity. But in what portion of the globe shall we find more fertile plains, mightier rivers, or more unexplored and inexhaustible riches than in South America? Yet South America has been unable to maintain democratic institutions. If the welfare of nations depended on their being placed in a remote position, with an unbounded space of habitable territory before them, the Spaniards of South America would have no reason to complain of their fate. And although they might enjoy less prosperity than the inhabitants of the United States, their lot might still be such as to excite the envy of some nations in Europe. There are no nations upon the face of the earth, however, more miserable than those of South America.

Thus not only are physical causes inadequate to produce results analogous to those which occur in North America, but they cannot raise the population of South America above the level of European states, where they act in a contrary direction. Physical causes do not therefore affect the destiny of nations so much as has been supposed.

I have met with men in New England who were on the point of leaving a country where they might have remained in easy circumstances,

贵族的区别,出身的贵贱和行业的偏见都不存在。因此,由于社会的民主,就很容易建立起民主原则。但是这样的环境并不是美国所特有的,几乎美洲所有的殖民地都由一些彼此平等的人或者迁来后变得平等的人建立的。在新大陆欧洲人没能建立起君主制。尽管如此,民主制还是只在美国得以繁荣。

美利坚合众国地处偏僻,如同大洋中的小岛,所以没有对抗的敌人。但美洲南部的西班牙虽也同样地处偏僻,但是他们仍然储备了常备军。在没有外敌入侵的时候,他们就打内战。因此,只有英裔美国人的民主在和平中得以维持。

美国的领土为人类的活动展现了一片广袤的天地,为人们的劳动提供了用之不竭的资源。人们对财富的激情取代了他们争权夺利的野心,社会繁荣的意识减低了派系斗争的热度。但是在地球的哪一部分我们才会找到比南美洲更肥沃的草原、更湍急的河流或者更原始更富足的资源呢? 但是南美洲却没能维持民主制。如果说民族的幸福取决于人们定居在一处偏远的地方,在他们面前有着没有尽头的可供居住的土地,那么南美洲的西班牙人也就没有抱怨自己命运不济的原因了。而且尽管他们也许没有像居住在美国的居民那样的繁荣景象,也仍然遭到欧洲一些民族的嫉妒。无论如何,世界上再没有哪个国家比南美洲的国家更悲惨了。

因此,并不是因为地理原因使南美洲难以取得像北美洲的成果,而且使南美洲在许多方面还不如欧洲各国的水平。因此,自然环境对一个国家的命运的影响并不如我们想象得那么大。

我曾见过一些新英格兰人准备离开他们安居乐业的故乡,到荒野中寻找财富。在离他们不远,我见到了一批加拿大的法国移

to seek their fortune in the wilds. Not far from that region I found a French population in Canada, closely crowded on a narrow territory, although the same wilds were at hand; and while the emigrant from the United States purchased an extensive estate with the earnings of a short term of labor, the Canadian paid as much for land as he would have done in France. Thus Nature offers the solitudes of the New World to Europeans also; but they do not always know how to make use of her gifts. Other in habitants of America have the same physical conditions of prosperity as the Anglo-Americans, but without their laws and their customs; and these people are miserable. The laws and customs of the Anglo-Americans are therefore that special and pre-dominant cause of their greatness which is the object of my inquiry. I am far from supposing that the American laws are pre-eminently good in themselves: I do not hold them to be applicable to all democratic nations; and several of them seem to me to be dangerous, even in the United States. But it cannot be denied that American legislation, taken as a whole, is extremely well adapted to the genius of the peo-ple and the nature of the country which it is intended to govern. A-merican laws are therefore good, and to them must be attributed a large portion of the success that at tends the government of democracy in America; but I do not be lieve them to be the principal cause of that success; and if they seem to me to have more influence than the nature of the country upon the social happiness of the Americans, there is still reason to believe that their effect is inferior to that pro-duced by the customs of the people.

The Federal laws undoubtedly constitute the most important part of the legislation of the United States. Mexico, which is not less fortu-nately situated than the Anglo-American Union, has adopted these same laws, but is unable to accustom itself to the government of de-mocracy. Some other cause is therefore at work, independently of physical circumstances and peculiar laws, which enables the democ-racy to rule in the United States.

Another still more striking proof may be adduced. Almost all the in-habitants of the territory of the Union are the descendants of a common

民,密集的居住在一个狭小的地方,而不愿开辟附近的荒野;而从美国迁徙来的移民用不长时间的劳动收入,就在荒地里购进大片的地产;而加拿大的法国移民,却甘愿以比在法国还要高的价格去购买人口稠密地区的土地。可见,大自然同样也给了欧洲与新大陆的荒地,但是他们却不知道怎么运用上帝的恩赐。除此之外,美洲其他国家居民的繁荣昌盛的自然环境与英裔美国人的相同,唯一缺乏的就是他们的法律和民情;这些人民现在都很贫苦。英裔美国人的法律和民情因此就成为他们强大起来的特殊的先决条件,这也正是我所要探求的因素。我并不认为美国的法律本身有多么卓越:因为我不认为它能够适用于所有的民主国家,甚至是美洲的民主国家;而且他们中的一些条款我甚至觉得在美洲运用也是很危险的。但是,我们不能否认美国的立法,总的来说,是极其适用它所治理的人民的天才和国家的性质的。因此,美国的法制是优秀的,而美国民主所取得的成就,也有很大一部分已归功于法制;但是我并不认为法制是美国民主获得成功的主要原因;并且,如果说法制对美国人民社会幸福的影响更甚于自然环境所起的作用的话,那么它所产生的影响又比民情在这方面的影响略逊一筹。

联邦法律毫无疑问地构成了美国立法最主要的部分。莫斯科与英裔美国人的居住环境不相上下,并且也采用了相同的法律,可是却难以适应民主的统治。所以,独立在自然环境和特殊的法律之外,应该还有一些其他的因素在起作用并使得民主得以在美国实施统治。

但是,对这一因素还须进一步加以证明。几乎所有联邦领土内的居民都是同一祖先的后裔;他们的语言相同,信仰一致,受到

stock; they speak the same language, they worship God in the same manner, they are affected by the same physical causes, and they obey the same laws. Whence, then, do their characteristic differences arise? Why, in the Eastern states of the Union, does the republican government display vigor and regularity and proceed with mature deliberation? Whence does it derive the wisdom and the durability which mark its acts, while in the Western states, on the contrary, society seems to be ruled by chance? There public business is conducted with an irregularity and a passionate, almost feverish excitement which do not announce a long or sure duration.

I am no longer comparing the Anglo-Americans with foreign nations; I am contrasting them with each other and endeavoring to discover why they are so unlike. The arguments that are derived from the nature of the country and the difference of legislation are here all set aside. Recourse must be had to some other cause; and what other cause can there be, except the customs of the people?

It is in the Eastern states that the Anglo-Americans have been longest accustomed to the government of democracy and have adopted the habits and conceived the opinions most favorable to its maintenance. Democracy has gradually penetrated into their customs, their opinions, and their forms of social intercourse; it is to be found in all the details of daily life as well as in the laws. In the Eastern states the book instruction and practical education of the people have been most perfected and religion has been most thoroughly amalgamated with liberty. What are these habits, opinions, usages, and beliefs if not what I have called customs? In the Western states, on the contrary, a portion of the same advantages is still wanting. Many of the Americans of the West were born in the woods, and they mix the ideas and customs of savage life with the civilization of their fathers. Their passions are more intense, their religious morality less authoritative, and their convictions less firm. The inhabitants exercise no sort of control over their fellows, for they are scarcely acquainted with one an other. The nations of the West display, to a certain extent, the in experience and the rude habits of a people in their infancy; for although they are composed of old elements, their assemblage is of recent date.

The customs of the Americans of the United States are, then, the

同样的自然环境的影响,遵守同样的法律。那么,我们所要考察的他们之间的差异又是从何而来的呢？又为什么在联邦东部,共和统治可以显得很有活力并有条不紊,成熟稳健？又是什么原因使政府的一切活动具有了明智性和持久性呢？而与之相反的,在西部社会的管理为什么显得很混乱？为什么在西部,支配公众活动的是一些并不确定的东西或仅凭人们的激情,而且几乎可以说有点发狂,以致不考虑长远的未来呢？

我不再拿英裔美国人和国外的民族加以比较；转而在他们之间互相对比,并努力发现他们为什么如此不同。得自自然环境和立法区别的论据,在这里都没用。我需要其他一些原因；可是除了民情外,还能有什么其他的原因存在呢？

东部的英裔美国人长久以来已习惯于民主的统治并接受了一些最有利于维护民主统治的习惯和言论。民主的思想逐渐渗入了他们民俗、他们的观点和他们在社会中的生活方式。在人们的日常生活的细节和法律中,民主无处不在。也是在东部,人民的书本教育和社会实践教育最完善,宗教最富有自由的色彩。如果这些习惯、意见、习俗和信仰不是我所说的民情,那它们还能被称作什么？相反的,在西部各州,这些长处在这里还未出现。西部的一些美国人生在荒野丛林中,于是他们就将父辈们文明与其野蛮的习性集为一身。他们的激情更强烈、宗教道德对他们并不那么至高无上,他们的信仰也不够坚定。在那里他们谁也管不了谁,因为大家彼此之间也是刚刚认识。从某种程度来说,西部各族表现得像婴儿时期的民族那样,缺乏经验,行为粗鲁。尽管他们是由旧社会的人组成的,但是对于整个集体来说,还是全新的。

因此,美国的民情的特殊性使得其得以维护民主的统治；而

peculiar cause which renders that people the only one of the American nations that is able to support a democratic government; and it is the influence of customs that produces the differ ent degrees of order and prosperity which may be distinguished in the several Anglo-American democracies. Thus the effect which the geographical position of a country may have upon the duration of democratic institutions is exaggerated in Europe. Too much im portance is attributed to legislation, too little to customs. These three great causes serve, no doubt, to regulate and direct American democracy; but if they were to be classed in their proper order, I should say that physical circumstances are less efficient than the laws, and the laws infinitely less so than the customs of the people. I am convinced that the most advantageous situation and the best possible laws cannot maintain a constitution in spite of the customs of a country; while the latter may turn to some advantage the most unfavorable positions and the worst laws. The importance of customs is a common truth to which study and experience incessantly direct our attention. It may be regarded as a central point in the range of observation, and the common termination of all my inquiries. So seriously do I insist upon this head that, if I have hitherto failed in making the reader feel the important influence of the practical experience, the habits, the opinions, in short, of the customs of the Americans upon the maintenance of their institutions, I have failed in the principal object of my work.

Whether Laws And Customs Are Sufficient To Maintain Democratic Institutions In Other Countries Besides America

The Anglo-Americans, if transported into Europe, would be obliged to modify their laws—Distinction to be made between democratic institutions and American institutions—Democratic laws may be conceived better than, or at least different from, those which the American democracy has adopted—The example of America only proves that it is possible, by the aid of customs and legislation, to regulate democracy.

I have asserted that the success of democratic institutions in the United States is more attributable to the laws themselves and the customs of the people than to the nature of the country. But does it follow that the same causes would of themselves produce the same results if they were put in operation elsewhere; and if the country is no adequate substitute for laws and customs, can laws and manners in their

正是因为受到民情的影响,使得英裔美国人在各州建立的民主制度在细节和发展程度上有所区别。因此,一个国家的地理位置在对民主制度持续的作用方面在欧洲被扩大了。人们对法制的重要性评价过高,而对民情的作用认识较低。毋庸置疑,这三个主要因素都对规范和指导民主制度有所作为;但是,如果它们能按照适当的顺序排列的话,我认为自然环境的作用应小于法制、而法制的作用又远远低于民情。我确信,最佳的地理位置和最好的法制,如果没有民情的支持,也不能维护一个政体;而民情却有可能减轻劣势的地理位置和最坏的法律的影响。民情的重要性,经过不断的研究和实践的证明并提醒我们注意的普遍真理。在整个观察中,民情应该说是我的中心所在,也是我全部想法的终点。我如此真诚地坚持这一观点,如果我没能使读者认识到实践经验、习惯、意见,总而言之就是美国民情在维护他们的制度方面的重要性,我就没能达到我写作这部书的主要目的。

法制和民情在其他国家能否比在美国更足以维护民主制度

如果英裔美国人到了欧洲,也许就不得不修改其法律了——应当分开一般的民主制度和美国的民主制度的区别——民主法律也许容易被接受,或者至少不同于,美国民主所采取的法制——美国的例子仅能证明,在民情和立法的帮助下,有助于规范民主制度。

我已经说过,美国民主制度的成功,更多的是有赖于其法律和民情而不是其自然环境。但是,是否由此可以认为同样的这些因素放在别处也能发生同样的作用;或者如果自然环境无法取代

turn take the place of a country? It will readily be understood that the elements of a reply to this question are wanting: other inhabitants are to be found in the New World be sides the Anglo-Americans, and, as these are affected by the same physical circumstances as the latter, they may fairly be compared with them. But there are no nations out of America which have adopted the same laws and customs, though destitute of the physical advantages peculiar to the Anglo-Americans. No standard of comparison therefore exists, and we can only hazard an opinion.

It appears to me, in the first place, that a careful distinction must be made between the institutions of the United States and demo cratic institutions in general. When I reflect upon the state of Europe, its mighty nations, its populous cities, its formidable armies, and the complex nature of its politics, I cannot suppose that even the Anglo-Americans, if they were transported to our hemisphere, with their ideas, their religion, and their customs, could exist without considerably altering their laws. But a democratic na tion may be imagined organized differently from the American people. Is it, then, impossible to conceive a government really es tablished upon the will of the majority, but in which the majority, repressing its natural instinct of equality, should consent, with a view to the order and the stability of the state, to invest a family or an individual with all the attributes of executive power? Might not a democratic society be imagined in which the forces of the nation would be more centralized than they are in the United States; where the people would exercise a less direct and less ir resistible influence upon public affairs, and yet every citizen, invested with certain rights, would participate, within. his sphere, in the conduct of the government? What I have seen among the Anglo-Americans induces me to believe that democratic institutions of this kind, prudently introduced into society so as gradually to mix with the habits and to be interfused with the opinions of the people, might exist in other countries besides America. If the laws of the United States were the only imaginable democratic laws or the most perfect which it is possible to conceive, I should admit that their success in America affords no proof of the success of democratic institutions in general in a country less favored by nature. But as the laws of America appear to me to be defective in several respects, and as I can readily imagine

法律和民情,则法律和民情就可以取代自然环境吗? 这很容易理解为问题答案的因素还不存在:新大陆除了英裔美国人外还有其他的居民,因为对两者产生影响的自然环境都是相同的,所以两者之间可以进行比较。但是除了美国之外,没有其他国家在自己的环境并没有英裔美国人那样优越的情况下,采用与他们相同的法律和民情。所以,两者并不存在可比性,我们只能随便谈谈自己的看法。

对我来说,首先,美国的民主制度和一般的民主制度之间是存在着细小的差别的。当我回想起欧洲的环境,强大的民族、人口密集的城市、坚不可摧的军队和政治的复杂性,我不能想象即使是英裔美国人,如果他们移居到我们这个半球,带着他们的思想、宗教和习俗,有没有可能在对他们的法律大肆修改而存活下去。但是,可以设想一个不像美国那样的民主国家,在这个国家中,大多数人都压抑住自己要求平等的天性,为了国家的秩序和稳定,赋予一个家族或个人以所有的行政权力呢? 能否设想一个其国家权力比美国更集中的民主国家,人民对公众事务的参与不那么直接或不可抗拒,但拥有一定权力的每个公民都可以依靠这些权力参加国家的管理呢? 我在英裔美国人的国家中所见到的一切,使我相信这种民主制度,如果能谨慎地移植到社会,逐渐地与其习惯相融合,深入人们的思想,也许就可以在美国以外的国家存在。如果美国的法律才是唯一人们可以想象得出的民主的法律或者能否持有的最有可能的完美的法律,那么我必须承认,美国的胜利除了证明一般的民主法制可在自然条件较差的国家获得成功以外,什么也不能证明。但是,如果我认为美国的法律在一些方面还有缺陷,而且我还能想出其他一些好的法律,那么

others, the peculiar advantages of that country do not prove to me that democratic institutions cannot succeed in a nation less favored by circum stances if ruled by better laws.

If human nature were different in America from what it is else where, or if the social condition of the Americans created habits and opinions among them different from those which originate in the same social condition in the Old World, the American democracies would afford no means of predicting what may occur in other democracies. If the Americans displayed the same propen sities as all other democratic nations, and if their legislators had relied upon the nature of the country and the favor of circumstances to restrain those propensities within due limits, the pros perity of the United States, being attributable to purely physical causes, would afford no encouragement to a people inclined to imitate their example without sharing their natural advantages. But neither of these suppositions is borne out by facts.

In America the same passions are to be met with as in Europe, some originating in human nature, others in the democratic condition of society. Thus, in the United States I found that restless ness of heart which is natural to men when all ranks are nearly equal and the chances of elevation are the same to all. I found there the democratic feeling of envy expressed under a thousand different forms. I remarked that the people there frequently displayed in the conduct of affairs a mixture of ignorance and presumption; and I inferred that in America men are liable to the same failings and exposed to the same evils as among ourselves. But upon examining the state of society more attentively, I speedily discovered that the Americans had made great and successful efforts to counteract these imperfections of human nature and to correct the natural defects of democracy. Their divers municipal laws appeared to me so many means of restraining the restless ambition of the citizens within a narrow sphere and of turning those same passions which might have worked havoc in the state to the good of the township or the parish. The American legislators seem to have succeeded to some extent in opposing the idea of right to the feelings of envy; the permanence of religious morality to the continual shifting of politics; the experience of the people to their theoretical ignorance; and their practical knowledge of business to the impatience of their desires.

美国特殊的优越性也不能向我们证明民主制度不能在一个自然
环境恶劣但法制良好的国家取得成功。

　　如果人们的本性在美国与在其他国家表现不同,又或者美国
人的社会地位与欧洲同样的社会地位下人们产生的习惯和思想
不同,则美国的民主就无法预测其他国家民主制度的状况。如果
美国人的爱好表现得与其他民主国家的人们一样,并且他们的立
法者又能够依靠国家的自然条件和有利的环境把他们的爱好约
束在合理的范围内,则完全归功于环境因素的美国的繁荣,对于
希望以美国为榜样但没有美国的自然优势的国家,并非没有借鉴
作用。但是,这些如果都不存在。

　　美国的这种激情在欧洲同样可以见到,它们一些源自人的本
性,另一些存在于社会的民主性。因此,在美国我发现,当人们之
间地位接近平等的时候,当机遇对每个人来说都是公平的时候,
人心的焦虑对人们来说就是自然产生的情绪。我发现民主嫉妒
感有很多种表现形式。我曾说过,美国人在处理工作的过程,经
常有自以为是和不懂装懂的表现;并且我推断,在美国,也和法国
一样,人们很容易犯相同的错误,容易暴露在相同的罪恶下。但
是,随着对社会状态的进一步的研究,我很快发现美国人曾付出
巨大而可贵努力去克服人性的缺点,纠正民主天然的不足。对我
来说,美国的种种地方性法律,就是以多种途径将公众长久不能
满足的野心限制在狭小的范围内,并将那些可能对社会造成伤害
的激情转化为对地方造福的激情。美国的立法者在一定程度上
来说,在以权力观反对嫉妒感上,在以宗教道德的持久性反对政
见的不断变化上,在人们丰富的经验弥补理论的缺乏上,在他们
处事的熟练习惯抵消急躁的欲望上,取得了一定的成功。

The Americans, then, have not relied upon the nature of their country to counterpoise those dangers which originate in their Constitution and their political laws. To evils that are common to all democratic nations they have applied remedies that none but themselves had ever thought of; and, although they were the first to make the experiment, they have succeeded in it. The manners and laws of the Americans are not the only ones which may suit a democratic people, but the Americans have shown that it would be wrong to despair of regulating democracy by the aid of customs and laws. If other nations should borrow this general and pregnant idea from the Americans, without, however, intending to imitate them in the peculiar application which they have made of it; if they should attempt to fit themselves for that social condition which it seems to be the will of Providence to impose upon the generations of this age, and so to escape from the despotism or the anarchy which threatens them, what reason is there to suppose that their efforts would not be crowned with success? The or ganization and the establishment of democracy in Christendom is the great political problem of our times. The Americans, unquestionably, have not resolved this problem, but they furnish useful data to those who undertake to resolve it. ·

Importance Of What Precedes With Respect To The State Of Europe

It may readily be discovered with what intention I undertook the foregoing inquiries. The question here discussed is interesting not only to the United States, but to the whole world; it concerns, not a nation only, but all mankind. If those nations whose social condition is democratic could remain free only while they inhabit uncultivated regions, we must despair of the future destiny of the human race; for democracy is rapidly acquiring a more extended sway, and the wilds are gradually peopled with men. If it were true that laws and customs are insufficient to maintain democratic institutions, what refuge would remain open to the nations, except the despotism of one man? I am aware that there are many worthy persons at the present time who are not alarmed at this alternative and who are so tired of liberty as to be glad of repose far from its storms. But these persons are ill acquainted

　　因此,美国人并没有依靠其自身的自然环境的优势缓解他们的制度和政治法律带来的危险。对于所有的民主国家共有的弊端,他们采取的补救措施其他人从未想到过;并且,尽管他们是第一个吃螃蟹的人,可也获得了成功。美国的民情和法制,并不是只对民主国家适用,而且美国人也已证明,存在放弃以民情和法律来调节民主的念头是不正确的。如果其他国家能够从美国得来这一全面的成熟的思想,而不想模仿他们在实际操作中独特的方法,而是试图将自己融入上帝为这一代人所安排的社会环境中,以此来避开给他们造成威胁的专制或混乱的状态。那么,有什么理由认为他们的努力不会取得成功呢? 基督教世界民主的组织和建立是我们这一时代最重要的政治问题。美国人毫无疑问并没有解决这一问题,但是他们为那些试图解决这些问题的人们提供了有利的经验。

已发生的事情对欧洲的重要性

　　读者不难发现我对前面所提到的问题讨论的意图。前面所讨论的问题,不仅仅跟美国有关,跟整个世界都有关系;它不仅仅关系到一个国家,还关系到全人类。如果那些民主国家的社会状况只有当他们居住在未开垦的地区的时候才可以保持自由,我们一定会对人类将来的命运感到绝望;因为民主正迅速占领了更大范围,荒野也逐渐为人们所占据。如果法律和民情真的不足以维护民主制度,那么除了个人的专政,还有什么样的制度可以用以维护各个民族呢? 我意识到,现今还有一些杰出人士,他们并未被这样的局面惊慌,他们厌恶自由,希望远离这场风暴以寻求安

with the haven towards which they are bound. Preoccupied by their remembrances, they judge of absolute power by what it has been and not by what it might become in our times.

If absolute power were re-established among the democratic nations of Europe, I am persuaded that it would assume a new form and appear under features unknown to our fathers. There was a time in Europe when the laws and the consent of the people had invested princes with almost unlimited authority, but they scarcely ever availed themselves of it. I do not speak of the prerogatives of the nobility, of the authority of high courts of justice, of corporations and their chartered rights, or of provincial privileges, which served to break the blows of sovereign authority and to keep up a spirit of resistance in the nation. Independently of these political institutions, which, however opposed they might be to personal liberty, served to keep alive the love of freedom in the mind and which may be esteemed useful in this respect, the manners and opinions of the nation confined the royal authority within barriers that were not less powerful because less conspicuous. Religion, the affections of the people, the benevolence of the prince, the sense of honor, family pride, provincial prejudices, custom, and public opinion limited the power of kings and re strained their authority within an invisible circle. The constitution of nations was despotic at that time, but their customs were free. Princes had the right, but they had neither the means nor the desire of doing whatever they pleased.

But what now remains of those barriers which formerly arrested tyranny? Since religion has lost its empire over the souls of men, the most prominent boundary that divided good from evil is overthrown; everything seems doubtful and indeterminate in the moral world; kings and nations are guided by chance, and none can say where are the natural limits of despotism and the bounds of license. Long revolutions have forever destroyed the respect which surrounded the rulers of the state; and since they have been relieved from the burden of public esteem, princes may henceforward surrender themselves without fear to the intoxication of ar bitrary power.

When kings find that the hearts of their subjects are turned to wards them, they are lenient, because they are conscious of their strength; and they are careful of the affection of their people because

宁。但是这些人对他们将要驶往的避风港并不了解。他们凭借着自己的经验,通过绝对的权利的过往行为来判断它,而不考虑它有可能在我们今天的表现来评价。

如果绝对的权利在欧洲民主的国家重新建立,那么我猜测,他将会展示以全新的、不为我们父辈所知的形式。在欧洲,有一段时间,法律和人们的认同,曾使国王拥有无限的权利,但是他们却几乎没有加以利用。我不打算讨论贵族的特权,或高级法院的职权,或行会的特权,或地方的优惠权等等这些打破君主皇权并在国家中保持着反抗情绪的权利。除了这些尽管反对个人自由,但却有利于保持人们热爱自由的思想的政治制度,民情和社会舆论还起到限制皇室的权利的作用,虽然不那么显著却能起到作用。宗教、人民的爱戴、国王的善行、荣耀感、家族的骄傲、地方偏见、习俗和公共舆论将国王的权利和权威限制在一个肉眼看不见的圈子里。那个时候还是国王专政,但是民情却还是自由的。国王拥有权力,但是他们既缺乏途径也没有欲望去做任何自己想做的事情。

但是,从前禁锢着暴政的樊篱如今靠什么来维持呢?自从宗教失去了其在人们心中的权利,也同时推翻了区分善与恶最显著的界限;人类道德世界的所有事情都充满了值得怀疑和不确定的因素;国王和国家的命运都不确定,没有人能够说出专制的自然的界限和特权的范围在何处。长时间的革命永久地毁灭了人们对统治者的尊敬;并且,他们从公众尊敬的负担中解脱出来之后,就可以肆无忌惮的滥用自己的权利了。

当国王们发现,他们的国民心意转向他的时候,他们就显得宽宏大量,因为他们感觉到了自己的权利;同时,他们对国民很爱

the affection of their people is the bulwark of the throne. A mutual interchange of goodwill then takes place between the prince and the people, which resembles the gracious intercourse of domestic life. The subjects may murmur at the sovereign's decree, but they are grieved to displease him; and the sovereign chastises his subjects with the light hand of parental affection.

But when once the spell of royalty is broken in the tumult of revolution, when successive monarchs have crossed the throne, so as alternately to display to the people the weakness of their right and the harshness of their power, the sovereign is no longer regarded by any as the father of the state, and he is feared by all as its master. If he is weak, he is despised; if he is strong, he is detested. He is himself full of animosity and alarm; he finds that he is a stranger in his own country, and he treats his subjects like conquered enemies.

When the provinces and the towns formed so many different nations in the midst of their common country, each of them had a will of its own, which was opposed to the general spirit of subjection; but now that all the parts of the same empire, after having lost their immunities, their customs, their prejudices, their traditions, and even their names, have become accustomed to obey the same laws, it is not more difficult to oppress them all together than it was formerly to oppress one of them separately.

While the nobles enjoyed their power, and indeed long after that power was lost, the honor of aristocracy conferred an extraordinary degree of force upon their personal opposition. Men could then be found who, notwithstanding their weakness, still entertained a high opinion of their personal value, and dared to cope single-handed with the public authority. But at the present day, when all ranks are more and more undifferentiated, when the in dividual disappears in the throng and is easily lost in the midst of a common obscurity, when the honor of monarchy has almost lost its power, without being succeeded by virtue, and when nothing can enable man to rise above himself, who shall say at what point the exigencies of power and the servility of weakness will stop?

As long as family feeling was kept alive, the opponent of oppression was never alone; he looked about him and found his clients, his hereditary friends, and his kinsfolk. If this support was wanting, he

戴又很爱惜,因为这些爱戴是保护皇权的壁垒。双方之间友好感情的互换,就像家庭生活中亲切感情的交流。人们也许会对国王的权利产生抱怨,但是他们如果发现国王不愉快就会感到后悔;同时,国王在惩罚他的国民的时候,满怀着父母般的情感而只用手轻轻拍打他的臣民。

但是,一旦皇权的威严在混乱的革命中被破坏之后,当相继的君主一代不如一代,要么表现得很软弱,要么就实行暴政,君主统治不再被人们视为国父,而因为其权力而被所有人所畏惧。那么,当他软弱的时候,就会遭到人们的轻视;而当他变得强壮,就会遭到人们的憎恶。他本身充满了仇恨和恐慌,他发现在自己的国家他像一个陌生人,并像对待已征服的敌人那样对待自己的人民。

当一个国家中的各个省和乡镇形成了一个个不同的国家,他们各有自己的意志,而这一意志又与国家一般的意志完全相反;而如今,同一领袖下的所有部分,在失去他们的特性、民情、偏见、习俗甚至他们的名字之后,就会变得遵从同一法律,这样的话,将他们作为一个整体实施统治并不比从前将他们分别统治时困难。

当贵族享受他们拥有的权利,并在失去权利之后很久一段时间,贵族的荣誉给予了个人莫大的力量对抗他们的敌人。有些人虽然还很软弱,但仍然拥有高尚的人格,并敢于单独对抗政府当局。但是,如今,当阶级之间的差别渐趋消失,当个人都隐于群体之中并很快迷失在大众中时,当君主的荣耀几乎失去了其权威的同时却没有良好的德行相继,当没有什么可以敦促人们上进的时候,谁又能说清强者的要求和弱者的服从将会在何处停止呢?

随着家庭观念的维持,对镇压的反抗就决不会孤独;他看着自己,发现了他的追随者,世交和近亲。如果缺少这些人的支持,

felt himself sustained by his ancestors and animated by his posterity. But when patrimonial estates are divided, and when a few years suffice to confound the distinctions of race, where can family feeling be found? What force can there be in the customs of a country which has changed, and is still perpetually changing, its aspect, in which every act of tyranny already has a precedent and every crime an example, in which there is nothing so old that its antiquity can save it from destruction, and nothing so unparalleled that its novelty can prevent it from being done? What resistance can be offered by customs of so pliant a make that they have already often yielded? What strength can even public opinion have retained when no twenty persons are connected by a common tie, when not a man, nor a family, nor chartered corporation, nor class, nor free institution, has the power of representing or exerting that opinion, and when every citizen, being equally weak, equally poor, and equally isolated, has only his personal impotence to oppose to the organized force of the government?

The annals of France furnish nothing analogous to the condition in which that country might then be thrown. But it may more aptly be assimilated to the times of old, and to those hideous eras of Roman oppression when the manners of the people were corrupted, their traditions obliterated, their habits destroyed, their opinions shaken, and freedom, expelled from the laws, could find no refuge in the land; when nothing protected the citizens, and the citizens no longer protected themselves; when human nature was the sport of man, and princes wearied out the clemency of Heaven before they exhausted the patience of their subjects.

Those who hope to revive the monarchy of Henry IV or of Louis XIV appear to me to be afflicted with mental blindness; and when I consider the present condition of several European nations, a condition to which all the others tend, I am led to believe that they will soon be left with no other alternative than democratic liberty or the tyranny of the Cæsars.

Is not this deserving of consideration? If men must really come to this point, that they are to be entirely emancipated or entirely enslaved, all their rights to be made equal or all to be taken away from them; if the rulers of society were compelled either gradually to raise

他也会感到自己的先辈们的支持和后代们的鼓舞。但是,当祖传的地产被划分,而种族之间的差异也随着时间的流逝而逐渐消失,哪里还能留存家族的情感? 在已经变化了或正在变化着的国家的民情中,它的暴政的一切行为都已有了先例,每一个罪行都有例可循,没有什么事物久远到无法保存,也没有什么事物是空前的以至于其新奇的特性使人们不敢去尝试它,那么还有什么力量存在在这样的环境中呢? 如此顺从屡遭践踏的民情可以提供怎样的抵抗力呢? 而当人们的意见都不能为一条共同的纽带维系,当没有任何人、任何家庭、任何团体、任何阶级、任何自由的体制都没有权力代表或提出任何一条意见,当所有的公民都同样软弱、同样贫穷、同样孤立,只有个人的软弱对抗政府有组织的力量的时候,公众舆论又能有什么作用呢?

至于法国在某些方面是否会出现类似的局面,这不是我们这一代人所能预见到的。但是也许吸收古代的例证、那个可怕的罗马时代的暴政,人们的道德沦丧,习俗被抹灭,他们的习惯遭到破坏,意见动摇,自由被法律放逐,那个人们没有容身之地的时代更合适。当人民无所保护,他们也无法自保;当人性成为人们的玩物,国王在耗尽对臣民的耐性之前就已厌倦了上帝的仁慈。

那些希望复兴亨利四世或者路易十四世君主专制的人们,在我看来,都是头脑发昏的举止;而当我想起一些欧洲国家的现状,以及其他国家将要达到的状况,我相信他们不久就会陷入民主自由或专制统治的抉择之中。

难道这不值得深思吗? 如果人们必须到这样的境地,要么完全自由,要么全部被束缚,要么所有他们的权利都趋于平等,要么就剥夺他们所有的权利;如果社会统治者被迫逐渐将人们的地位

the crowd to their own level or to allow all the citizens to fall below that of humanity, would not the doubts of many be resolved, the consciences of many be confirmed, and the community prepared to make great sacrifices with little difficulty? In that case the gradual growth of democratic manners and institutions should be regarded, not as the best, but as the only means of preserving freedom; and, without caring for the democratic form of government, it might be adopted as the most applicable, and the fairest remedy for the present ills of society.

It is difficult to make the people participate in the government, but it is still more difficult to supply them with experience and to inspire them with the feelings which they need in order to govern well. I grant that the wishes of the democracy are capricious, its instruments rude, its laws imperfect. But if it were true that soon no just medium would exist between the rule of democracy and the dominion of a single man, should we not rather incline towards the former than submit voluntarily to the latter? And if complete equality be our fate, is it not better to be leveled by free institutions than by a despot?

Those who, after having read this book, should imagine that my intention in writing it was to propose the laws and customs of the Anglo-Americans for the imitation of all democratic communities would make a great mistake; they must have paid more attention to the form than to the substance of my thought. My aim has been to show, by the example of America, that laws, and especially customs, may allow a democratic people to remain free. But I am very far from thinking that we ought to follow the example of the American democracy and copy the means that it has employed to attain this end; for I am well aware of the in fluence which the nature of a country and-its political antecedents exercise upon its political constitution; and I should regard it as a great misfortune for mankind if liberty were to exist all over the world under the same features.

But I am of the opinion that if we do not succeed in gradually in troducing democratic institutions into France, if we despair of imparting to all the citizens those ideas and sentiments which first prepare them for freedom and afterwards allow them to enjoy it, there will be no independence at all, either for the middle classes or for the nobility,

提升到与他们相同,或者使所有人都低于人的水平,那么,如果没有了怀疑、坚定了人们的信心,使人们甘愿作出巨大的牺牲不就行了吗？在那种情况下,民主化的民情和制度的逐步成长,不仅仅是最优异的,也是唯一保持自由的途径。同时,如果不考虑民主的统治形势,就应当算是补救现时社会弊端最实用、最公正的方式。

虽然使人民参与政府统治很困难,但是要他们积累相关的经验或者使他们充满激情以更好的实行政府统治更困难。我承认,民主的意愿是反复无常的,实行的手段很不成熟,法制也不完备,但是如果不久后在民主规则和专制统治之间真的不存在什么公正的途径,那么我们难道不该投向民主而不是自动屈服于专制统治吗？如果我们命中注定要实行完全的平等,那么难道让我们被自由制度带入平等不比被专制统治更好吗？

读完此书的读者应该会想象得到,我写作这部书的目的,是主张所有民主国家模仿英裔美国人的法律和民情的话,那就大错特错了。他们一定是只注意到我表达的形式,而没有注意到我思想的实质。通过美国人的例证,我已经阐述了我的观点,我认为法律,尤其是民情能使民主的人民保持自由。但是我从未想过我们应该效仿美国的民主,并照搬美国实现民主的途径,因为我非常了解一个国家的自然环境和它的政治经历对政治制度所产生的影响。我认为,如果自由在全世界都以相同的模式出现,那将是人类的灾难。

但是,我认为如果我们不能逐渐将民主制度引入法国,如果我们没能给每个公民灌输对他们来说完全陌生的自由的思想和情感,并允许他们享用它们,那么无论对中层阶级还是那些贵族,

for the poor or for the rich, but an equal tyranny over all; and I foresee that if the peaceable dominion of the majority is not founded a-
mong us in time, we shall sooner or later fall under the unlimited authority of a single man.

都不存在独立之说。我预测,如果大多数专政的和平统治不能在我们中间及时建立,我们迟早会陷入个人专制的无限权利统治之下。

【英汉对照全译本】

DEMOCRACY IN AMERICA

论 美 国 民 主

—— [法]托克维尔　著 ——

朱尾声　译

马高霞　译校

（三）

中国社会科学出版社

CHAPTER XVIII

The Present And Probable Future Condition

Of The Three Races That Inhabit

The Territory Of The United States

The principal task that I had imposed upon myself is now performed: I have shown, as far as I was able, the laws and the customs of the American democracy. Here I might stop; but the reader would perhaps feel that I had not satisfied his expectations.

An absolute and immense democracy is not all that we find in America; the inhabitants of the New World may be considered from more than one point of view. In the course of this work my subject has often led me to speak of the Indians and the Negroes, but I have never had time to stop in order to show what place these two races occupy in the midst of the democratic people whom I was engaged in describing. I have shown in what spirit and according to what laws the Anglo-American Union was formed; but I could give only a hurried and imperfect glance at the dangers which menace that confederation and could not furnish a detailed account of its chances of survival independently of its laws and manners. When speaking of the united republics, I hazarded no conjectures upon the permanence of republican forms in the New World; and when making frequent allusions to the commercial activity that reigns in the Union, I was unable to inquire into the future of the Americans as a commercial people. These topics are collaterally connected with my subject without forming a part of it; they are American without being democratic, and to portray democracy has been my principal aim. It was therefore necessary to postpone these questions, which I now take up as the proper termination of my work.

第十八章 居住在美国疆土上的三个种族 的现状及其可能出现的未来

　　我为自己定的主要任务如今已经完成：我已尽可能地向大家说明了美国民主的法律和民情。如果我现在不再将文章继续下去，也许我的读者觉得我并没有达到他们期望的目的。

　　一个完整的广泛的民主决不是我们从美国发现的唯一的东西，我们还可以从其他角度思考居住在新大陆的居民。在写这部书的过程中，我所著述的对象常常需要涉及印第安人和黑人，但是我行文中没有机会停下来说明生活在我所描述的民主的人民中间的这两个种族所处的地位。我已经讲述了英裔美国联邦是凭借着什么样的法制和精神建立起来的，但是我只在匆忙间对威胁着联邦的危险作了粗略地一瞥，并且除了它的法律和民情，也没能详尽地叙述它得以存活的条件。谈到合众国的共和制时，我从未大胆地猜测新大陆民主制度长期存在的问题；并且即使频繁地提及支配着合众国的经济活动，我仍然很难探讨美国作为商业民族的未来。这些话题都与我的主题有关，但我在文中并没有谈及；他们虽与美国有关，但却与民主无关，而我的主要目的在于对民主的描述。因此在一开始就需要暂且将这些问题搁置，而现在将它们重新拾起给本书作一合适的终结。

The territory now occupied or claimed by the American Union spreads from the shores of the Atlantic to those of the Pacific Ocean. On the east and west its limits are those of the continent itself. On the south it advances nearly to the tropics, and it extends upward to the icy regions of the north.

The human beings who are scattered over this space do not form, as in Europe, so many branches of the same stock. Three races, naturally distinct, and, I might almost say, hostile to each other, are discoverable among them at the first glance. Almost insurmountable barriers had been raised between them by education and law, as well as by their origin and outward characteristics; but fortune has brought them together on the same soil, where, although they are mixed, they do not amalgamate, and each race fulfills its destiny apart.

Among these widely differing families of men, the first that attracts attention, the superior in intelligence, in power, and in enjoyment, is the white, or European, the man pre-eminently so called; below him appear the Negro and the Indian. These two unhappy races have nothing in common, neither birth, nor features, nor language, nor habits. Their only resemblance lies in their misfortunes. Both of them occupy an equally inferior position in the country they inhabit; both suffer from tyranny; and if their wrongs are not the same, they originate from the same authors.

If we reason from what passes in the world, we should almost say that the European is to the other races of mankind what man himself is to the lower animals: he makes them subservient to his use, and when he cannot subdue he destroys them. Oppression has, at one stroke, deprived the descendants of the Africans of almost all the privileges of humanity. The Negro of the United States has lost even the remembrance of his country; the language which his forefathers spoke is never heard around him; he abjured their religion and forgot their customs when he ceased to belong to Africa, without acquiring any claim to European privileges. But he remains half-way between the two communities, isolated between two races; sold by the one,

美国联邦所占据或宣称的国土,从大西洋沿岸一直延伸到太平洋海域。它的疆界往西或往东都是大陆本身的边界,往南几乎深入了热带地区,往北则到达冰原。

散布在这块地域的人们,不像在欧洲那样,形成同一种族下的各个分支。几乎可以认为,他们是三个自然划分的彼此敌视的种族,人们只要看一眼就能发现。他们之间由于教育、法律,以及他们的本源和外貌特征筑起了几乎无法跨越的栏障;但是命运将他们带到了同一块土地上,然而他们虽然混居在这里,但是并没有彼此融合,每一个民族都独立地完成着自己的使命。

存在于人们中间的巨大差异,最引人注目的,要数无论在智力、权力还是生活享受方面都高人一等的白人,或者叫欧洲人,人们称之为卓越的人种;在其下的是黑人和印第安人。这两个悲惨的种族没有任何一方面是相同的,无论本源、外貌特征,还是语言和习性。然而他们都遭受了悲惨的命运。他们在自己居住的国家中遭受到了不公平的劣等公民的待遇;他们忍受暴政;即使它们所受到的待遇不尽相同,然而这样的待遇的提供者却出自同样的人。

如果我们从历史中寻找原因,我们几乎可以说欧洲人对待其他种族的方式,就同人们对待动物的态度如出一辙:他使他们屈从于自己的淫威之下,而当他无法征服的时候就毁灭他们。欧洲人的镇压一下子就剥夺了美洲人后裔几乎所有作为人的特权。美国的黑人甚至失去了对自己国家的记忆;他们的父辈使用的语言在他们的生活中从未听到过;当他们不再属于美洲后,他们放弃了自己的宗教信仰,遗忘了自己的民情却没能获得任何欧洲人们的特权。但是他仍然停留在这两种社会之间的道路上,隔绝在这两个民族之外;他们被一方卖掉,又遭到另一方的排斥;他们找

repulsed by the other; finding not a spot in the universe to call by the name of country, except the faint image of a home which the shelter of his master's roof affords.

The Negro has no family: woman is merely the temporary companion of his pleasures, and his children are on an equality with himself from the moment of their birth. Am I to call it a proof of God's mercy, or a visitation of his wrath, that man, in certain states, appears to be insensible to his extreme wretchedness and almost obtains a depraved taste for the cause of his misfortunes? The Negro, plunged in this abyss of evils, scarcely feels his own calamitous situation. Violence made him a slave, and the habit of servitude gives him the thoughts and desires of a slave; he admires his tyrants more than he hates them, and finds his joy and his pride in the servile imitation of those who oppress him. His understanding is degraded to the level of his soul.

The Negro enters upon slavery as soon as he is born; nay, he may have been purchased in the womb, and have begun his slavery before he began his existence. Equally devoid of wants and of enjoyment, and useless to himself, he learns, with his first notions of existence, that he is the property of another, who has an interest in preserving his life, and that the care of it does not devolve upon himself; even the power of thought appears to him a useless gift of Providence, and he quietly enjoys all the privileges of his debasement.

If he becomes free, independence is often felt by him to be a heavier burden than slavery; for, having learned in the course of his life to submit to everything except reason, he is too unacquainted with her dictates to obey them. A thousand new desires beset him, and he has not the knowledge and energy necessary to Tesist them: these are masters which it is necessary to contend with, and he has learned only to submit and obey. In short, he is sunk to such a depth

不到可以被称为自己的祖国的地方,只除了他的主人为他们提供的庇护之所,可以勾起对家的模糊记忆。

黑人是没有家庭的:女人对他们来说只是临时为他们提供快乐的工具,他的孩子一出生就具有与他们平等的地位。从某种程度上说,人们对他们遭遇的极度的痛苦表现得无动于衷,甚至对引起这些不幸的原因表现出堕落的神情,我应当将之称作是上帝仁慈的证明,抑或是上帝愤懑的发泄呢?陷入罪恶深渊的黑人们却从未感到他们自身所处的不幸的境地。暴力将他们驯成了奴隶,受人奴役的习惯逐渐养成了他们奴隶的思想和渴望;对于奴役自己的暴君,他们更多的是羡慕而不是仇恨,他们在卑鄙的模仿那些压迫他们的人们的行为中寻找自己的快乐并引以为荣。他们的智力已下降到与他们的灵魂相同的水平。

黑人们一出生就沦为了奴隶;甚至,他们还未出生时就已被贩卖,于是身为奴隶的时间更要早于他出生的时间。被剥夺了希望和享乐的权利,这些对他也丝毫没用。他意识到,在他一出生时就知道了,他是属于另一个人的财产,是这个人保留了他的生命,而保护自己生命的权利也不掌握在自己的手中。甚至对他来说连上帝赐予的思想的权利也毫无用处。他安静地置身于自己所有的卑贱的地位。

即使他获得了自由,而这种独立对他来说常常比奴役的生活给他造成更大的压力;因为在他的一生中,他学习的都是毫无缘由的顺从他人,他对其他的教谕太过陌生而不敢听从。尽管有上千种新的欲望困扰着他,可是他没有必要的知识和能力抵抗它们。这些要求来自他们本应当反对的主人,可是他们只知道屈从和顺服。总之,他陷入了一种悲惨的境地:奴役的生活使他丧失

of wretchedness that while servitude brutalizes, liberty destroys him.

Oppression has been no less fatal to the Indian than to the Negro race, but its effects are different. Before the arrival of white men in the New World, the inhabitants of North America lived quietly in their woods, enduring the vicissitudes and practicing the virtues and vices common to savage nations. The Europeans, having dispersed the Indian tribes and driven them into the deserts, condemned them to a wandering life, full of inexpressible sufferings.

Savage nations are only controlled by opinion and custom. When the North American Indians had lost the sentiment of attachment to their country; when their families were dispersed, their traditions obscured, and the chain of their recollections broken; when all their habits were changed, and their wants increased beyond measure, European tyranny rendered them more disorderly and less civilized than they were before. The moral and physical condition of these tribes continually grew worse, and they became more barbarous as they became more wretched. Nevertheless, the Europeans have not been able to change the character of the Indians; and though they have had power to destroy, they have never been able to subdue and civilize them. The lot of the Negro is placed on the extreme limit of servitude, while that of the Indian lies on the uttermost verge of liberty; and slavery does not produce more fatal effects upon the first than independence upon the second. The Negro has lost all property in his own person, and he cannot dispose of his existence without committing a sort of fraud. But the savage is his own master as soon as he is able to act; parental authority is scarcely known to him; he has never bent his will to that of any of his kind, nor learned the difference between voluntary obedience and a shameful subjection; and the very name of law is unknown to him. To be free, with him, signifies to escape from all the shackles of society. As he delights in this barbarous independence and would rather perish than sacrifice the least part of it, civilization has little hold over him.

The Negro makes a thousand fruitless efforts to insinuate himself among men who repulse him; he conforms to the tastes of his

了理性,而放任自由又使他走向毁灭。

对印第安人压迫的失败并不亚于对黑人压迫的失败,但是产生的作用不同。在白人抵达新大陆之前,北美洲的居民在森林中过着平静的生活,持续地迁徙,有着像野蛮民族般的品行。是欧洲人使印第安民族消失在原野,将他们赶入荒漠,使他们过着流浪的生活,饱经沧桑。

野蛮的民族只受到习惯和舆论的控制。当北美印第安人没有了对祖国的眷恋,当他们的家庭分崩离析,他们的传统被遗忘,当记忆的链锁被割断,当他们所有的习惯都已改变,欲望极度膨胀,欧洲人的暴政带给他们比以前更加混乱更不文明的生活。这些民族的道德物质状况越来越差,而人们也随着不断恶化的生活环境变得越来越粗野。尽管如此,欧洲人也没能改变印第安人的性格特征,他们曾利用自己的权力摧残印第安人,但他们却从未能使它们变得驯服和文明起来。当印第安人享受着最广泛的自由的权利的时候,黑人则遭受到最大限度的奴役,然而奴役对黑人造成的严重影响并不比独立给印第安人带来的影响更大。黑人们失去了自身本应拥有的所有的财产,他们不能自行转让自己否则就是一种欺诈行为。但是他只要一开始行为,野蛮就成了他的主人。他们几乎不知道什么是家长权。他从未使自己的意志屈从于族长权,也从不知道自愿的服从和屈辱的遵从之间的区别,甚至法律这个名词他也从未听说过。对他来说,自由就意味着避开所有社会的枷锁。就仿佛他享受着原始的自由一样,他宁愿在这种自由中毁灭也不愿有丝毫的放弃,文明并不能对他造成什么影响。

为使自己能够挤进那个排斥他的人群,黑人作了无数次的努

oppressors, adopts their opinions, and hopes by imitating them to form a part of their community. Having been told from infancy that his race is naturally inferior to that of the whites, he assents to the proposition and is ashamed of his own nature. In each of his features he discovers a trace of slavery, and if it were in his power, he would willingly rid himself of everything that makes him what he is.

The Indian, on the contrary, has his imagination inflated with the pretended nobility of his origin, and lives and dies in the midst of these dreams of pride. Far from desiring to conform his habits to ours, he loves his savage life as the distinguishing mark of his race and repels every advance to civilization, less, perhaps, from hatred of it than from a dread of resembling the Europeans. ①

While he has nothing to oppose to our perfection in the arts but the resources of the wilderness, to our tactics nothing but undisciplined courage, while our well-digested plans are met only by the

---

① The native of North America retains his opinions and the most insignifi cant of his habits with a degree of tenacity that has no parallel in history. For more than two hundred years the wandering tribes of North America have had daily intercourse with the whites, and they have never derived from them a custom or an idea. Yet the Europeans have exercised a powerful influence over the savages: they have made them more licentious, but not more European. In the summer of 1831 I happened to be beyond Lake Michi gan, at a place called Green Bay, which serves as the extreme frontier be tween the United States and the Indians of the Northwest. Here I became acquainted with an American officer, Major H., who, after talking to me at length about the inflexibility of the Indian character, related the following fact: "I formerly knew a young Indian," said he, who had been educated at a college in New England, where he had greatly distinguished himself and had acquired the external appearance of a civilized man. When the war broke out between ourselves and the English in 1812, I saw this young man a-gain; he was serving in our army, at the head of the warriors of his tribe; for the Indians were admitted among the ranks of the Americans, on condition only that they would abstain from their horrible custom of scalping their victims. On the evening of the battle of - - - , C. came and sat himself down by the fire of our bivouac. I asked him what had been his fortune that day. He related his exploits, and growing warm and animated by the recollection of them, he concluded by suddenly opening the breast of his coat, saying:"You must not betray me; see here! And I actually beheld,"said the major, "between his body and his shirt, the skin and hair of an English head, still dripping with blood."

力,但都没有成功。他服从于自己的压迫者的喜好,接受他们的观念,以希通过模仿他们来成为他们中的一员。从年幼时起,他们就被告知自己的民族天生就低于白人种族,他接受了这种观念并对自己的本性感到羞耻。从自己的每一个特性中,他都能找到奴隶的影子,如果他有这个权力,他就希望能摆脱使他成为今天这种样子的所有的一切。

相反的,印第安人的脑海中满都是自己高贵的出身,他们的生死都寄予自以为是的梦幻中。他们并不希望遵从我们的习惯,他们热爱自己蛮夷的生活方式,以为自己与其他民族的独特区别,他们排斥文明,而这种排斥的原因更多的不是因为与欧洲人的相似,而是由于自己的厌恶。①

他们只能以原始的弓箭来抵御我们精良的武器,以毫无章法的勇气对抗我们的战术,以自发的野蛮人的本能对抗我们策划已

① 北美本地人以之前少有的坚韧的态度保留了他们的主张和他们没有任何显著特色的习俗。在过去的两百多年中,北美的流浪民族整天与白人混迹在一起,但是却从没从白人那里沾染任何他们的民情和思想。欧洲人对蛮夷人实施了强大的影响:只是使他们变得更加肆无忌惮而没有更欧洲化。1831年的夏天,我碰巧到密歇根湖一个叫绿色海湾的地方,这里是美国和印第安西北方的边界地带。在这我认识了一位美国官员H,他向我详细地描述了印第安人顽强不屈的性格特征,他说到:我从前认识一位年轻的印第安人,他在新英格兰接受了高等教育。他在那里表现优异并拥有了文明人的外表。当1812年我们与英国开战的时候,我又一次见到了这位年轻人。他在我们的部队服役并且是他们部族战士的首领。只要印第安人愿意抛弃自己剥掉死人头皮这样令人恐怖的习惯,他们就可以被列入美国人的行列。在一场战争快结束的时候,C来到我们的营地。我问他那天的运气怎样。他谈起了他的冒险,说着说着逐渐熟悉起来,渐渐变得很活跃。他突然解开胸口的衣扣,说:"你不能背叛我,看这里! 我看到了,"这位官员说,"在他的身体和衬衣之间,一个英国人头颅上的皮肤和头发仍在滴着鲜血。"

spontaneous instincts of savage life, who can wonder if he fails in this unequal contest?

The Negro, who earnestly desires to mingle his race with that of the European, cannot do so; while the Indian, who might succeed to a certain extent, disdains to make the attempt. The servility of the one dooms him to slavery, the pride of the other to death.

I remember that while I was traveling through the forests which still cover the state of Alabama, I arrived one day at the log house of a pioneer. I did not wish to penetrate into the dwelling of the American, but retired to rest myself for a while on the margin of a spring, which was not far off, in the woods. While I was in this place (which was in the neighborhood of the Creek territory), an Indian woman appeared, followed by a Negress, and holding by the hand a little white girl of five or six years, whom I took to be the daughter of the pioneer. A sort of barbarous luxury set off the costume of the Indian; rings of metal were hanging from her nostrils and ears, her hair, which was adorned with glass beads, fell loosely upon her shoulders; and I saw that she was not married, for she still wore that necklace of shells which the bride always deposits on the nuptial couch. The Negress was clad in squalid European garments. All three came and seated them selves upon the banks of the spring; and the young Indian, taking the child in her arms, lavished upon her such fond caresses as mothers give, while the Negress endeavored, by various little artifices, to attract the attention of the young Creole. The child displayed in her slightest gestures a consciousness of superiority that formed a strange contrast with her infantine weakness; as if she received the attentions of her companions with a sort of condescension. The Negress was seated on the ground before her mistress, watching her smallest desires and apparently divided between an almost maternal affection for the child and servile fear; while the savage, in the midst of her tenderness, displayed an air of freedom and pride which was almost ferocious. I had approached the group and was contemplating them in silence, but my curiosity was probably displeasing to the Indian woman, for she suddenly rose, pushed the child roughly from her, and, giving me an angry look, plunged into the thicket.

久的计划,在这样的情况下,谁会怀疑他是否会在这场不公平的斗争中失败呢?

黑人希望混入欧洲人的群体而不能;而印第安人在一定程度上可以做到这一点,但他们又不屑于这样做。黑人的奴性使他们注定沦入奴隶身份,而另一方的骄傲则将其置于死地。

我记得当我旅途中横穿那片仍旧覆盖着阿拉巴马州的大森林的时候,有一天,我到了一个拓荒人的小木屋。当时我并不想进一个美国人的房子,所以在它附近的一个泉边休息了一会儿。就在我在那里休息的时候(那个地方靠近克里克联盟的印第安人的疆域),一个印第安妇女出现在我面前,后面跟着黑人妇女,怀里抱着一个五六岁大的女孩。我想这个女孩一定是那个拓荒人的孩子。那个印第安女人的穿着,极尽野蛮人华贵之能事:戴着金属的鼻环和耳环,头发上装饰着玻璃珠链披散到肩头。我看得出她应该还没有结婚,因为她仍然带着贝壳项链,而如果结过婚的话,这条链子应该放在她的新婚的床上。黑人妇女穿着破破烂烂的欧洲人的服装。她们三人来到泉水边坐下。年轻的印第安人将孩子搂在怀里,像母亲一样宠溺着小女孩,而黑人妇女则使出浑身解数以期吸引小女孩的注意。小女孩则从她微小的动作中表现出一种与她幼小的年纪所应体现的弱小相比令人诧异的优越感,仿佛她是用一种谦逊的态度接受其同伴对她的关心。黑人妇女坐在主人前面的地上,看着她的小主人并表现出一种近似母爱和奴婢的担心心理的神态。而那个印第安女人,在她的温柔的神态中,表现得自由自在以及极度的骄傲。我默默地向她们走去,但也许我的好奇心引起了这个印第安妇女的不满,因为她忽然站了起来,将孩子从身边猛地推开,狠狠地瞪了我一眼,就走进森林深处去了。

In the same place I had often chanced to see individuals together who belonged to the three races that people North America. I had perceived from many different traits the preponderance of the whites. But in the picture that I have just been describing there was something peculiarly touching; a bond of affection here united the oppressors with the oppressed, and the effort of Nature to bring them together rendered still more striking the immense distance placed between them by prejudice and the laws.

The Present And Probable Future Condition Of The Indian Tribes That Inhabit The Territory Possessed By The Union

Gradual disappearance of the native tribes—Manner in which it takes place—Miseries accompanying the forced migrations of the Indians—The savages of North America had only two ways of escaping destruction, war or civilization—They are no longer able to make war—Reasons why they refused to become civilized when it was in their power, and why they cannot become so now that they desire it—Instance of the Creeks and Cherokees—Policy of the particular states towards these Indians—Policy of the Federal government.

None of the Indian tribes which formerly inhabited the territory of New England, the Narragansetts, the Mohicans, the Pequots, have any existence but in the recollection of man. The Lenapes, who received William Penn a hundred and fifty years ago upon the banks of the Delaware, have disappeared; and I myself met with the last of the Iroquois, who were begging alms. The nations I have mentioned formerly covered the country to the seacoast; but a traveler at the present day must penetrate more than a hundred leagues into the interior of the continent to find an Indian. Not only have these wild tribes receded, but they are destroyed;[①]and as they give way or perish, an immense and increasing people fill their place. There is no instance upon record of so prodigious a growth or so rapid a destruction; the

---

① In the thirteen original states there are only 6,273 Indians remaining. (See Legislative Documents, 20th Congress, No. 117, p. 20.)

　　我常常可以见到北美这三个种族的人们居住在同一个地方
的场景。而且从种种迹象中我看出身为白人的优越。但是在我
刚才描述的场景中,有一些特别感人的地方:在这里亲情将压迫
者和被压迫者紧紧地联系在一起,而大自然想要将他们联系在一
起的努力,却被偏见和法制划出令人侧目的无尽距离。

居住在联邦境内的印第安部 落的现状及其可能出现的未来

　　土著部落的逐渐消失——进行的方式——伴随着印第安人
被迫迁徙而来的不幸——北美的原始人只有两种方法逃避灭亡,
要么战争,要么接受文明——他们已不再有能力发动战争——当
他们强大时为何拒绝接受文明的原因,以及在他们渴求文明的时
候却又无能为力的原因——克里克部和柴罗基部的例子——个
别州对待印第安人的政策——联邦政府的政策。

　　那些曾经居住在新英格兰土地上的印第安部落,像纳拉干
族、莫希干族和佩科特族,除了留存在人们的记忆中以外,都已不
复存在。而早在150年前在特拉华州湾迎接威廉佩恩的德拉瓦
族也灭亡了。我见到的最后几位易洛魁族人正在沿街乞讨。我
在前面提及的几个部落,他们曾遍布北美各地,一直延伸到海岸,
而到了现在,要想找到一个印第安人,就要深入大陆内部一百多
里格。这些野蛮的部落不仅已向内陆撤离,他们也逐渐走向灭
亡;[1]随着印第安人的迁徙和消亡,大量的人口迅速地占据了他们
的土地。这是史上有记载以来从未有过的发展地如此迅速而又如

---

　　[1]　在最初的十三个州中,只有6273个印第安人。(见《立法文件》第
20次会议第117号,第20页。)

manner in which the latter change takes place is not difficult to describe.

When the Indians were the sole inhabitants of the wilds whence they have since been expelled, their wants were few. Their arms were of their own manufacture, their only drink was the water of the brook, and their clothes consisted of the skins of animals, whose flesh furnished them with food.

The Europeans introduced among the savages of North America firearms, ardent spirits, and iron; they taught them to exchange for manufactured stuffs the rough garments that had previously satisfied their untutored simplicity. Having acquired new tastes, without the arts by which they could be gratified, the Indians were obliged to have recourse to the workmanship of the whites; but in return for their productions the savage had nothing to offer except the rich furs that still abounded in his woods. Hence the chase became necessary, not merely to provide for his subsistence, but to satisfy the frivolous desires of Europeans. He no longer hunted merely to obtain food, but to procure the only ob jects of barter which he could offer. ①While the wants of the natives were thus increasing, their resources continued

---

① Messrs. Clarke and Cass, in their *Report to Congress*, of February 4, 1829, p. 23, remarked: "The time when the Indians generally could supply themselves with food and clothing, without any of the articles of civilized life, has long since passed away. The more remote tribes, beyond the Mississippi, who live where immense herds of buffalo are yet to be found, and who follow those animals in their periodical migrations, could more easily than any others recur to the habits of their ancestors, and live without the white man or any of his manufactures. But the buffalo is constantly receding. The smaller animals, the bear, the deer, the beaver, the otter, the musk-rat, etc. , principally minister to the comfort and support of the Indians; and these cannot be taken without guns, ammunition, and traps. Among the Northwestern Indians, particularly, the labor of supplying a family with food is exces sive. Day after day is spent by the hunter without success, and during this interval his family must exist upon bark or roots, or perish. Want and misery are around them and among them. Many die every winter from actual starvation. " The Indians will not live as Europeans live; and yet they can neither exist without them nor live exactly after the fashion of their fathers. This is dem onstrated by a fact which I likewise give upon official authority. Some In dians of a tribe on the banks of Lake Superior had killed a European; the American government prohibited all traffic with the tribe to which the guilty parties belonged until they were delivered up to justice. This measure had the desired effect.

此迅速地消亡的民族。这一消亡发生的原因并不难解释。

当印第安人还是他们后来被逐出的荒野的唯一的居民的时候,他们没什么需求。他们自己制造武器,小溪里的水是他们唯一的饮品,他们穿着兽皮做的衣服,而把野兽的肉当作食物。

欧洲人为野蛮的北美人带来了火器、烈酒和钢铁,他们教印第安人改穿纺织制成的衣服,替换掉那些粗糙的只能满足未开化人们的简单的需求的衣服。印第安人尝试了这些新的体验,却没能学会满足他们这种需要的技能,因此他们不得不依赖白人的技术,而为了换取这些自己无法制造的东西,这些野蛮人除了可以用森林中遍布的富足的野兽的兽皮外,他们没有任何其他东西。因此,捕猎就成了必需,这不仅仅是为了用以交换,也为了满足欧洲人无尽的欲望。人们的捕猎不再是仅仅为了获取食物,也为了获取他们需要支付的以物易物的物资。① 就这样随着土著人需求

---

① 1829 年 2 月 4 日,克拉克先生和卡斯先生在他们对国会的报告第 23 页中提到:"不考虑对精神文明需求的满足,印第安人能够在衣食方面自给自足的时代已经过去了。在密西西比河上游更加偏远的部落,他们生活在一片连成群的水牛都还没有足迹的地方,随着这些动物周期性的迁徙,他们的生活比起那些遵循着祖辈们习俗的部落轻松得多,没有白人和他们的手工制品的侵扰。但是水牛群不断地向内地撤退。而那些体积小些的动物,像熊、鹿、海狸、水獭、麝香鹿等,主要为印第安人提供日常所需,使他们的生活更舒适。捕获这些动物离不开猎枪、炸药和陷阱。在这些西北部的印第安人中,尤其充沛的就是提供一个家庭食物的劳力。一天天过去了,猎人们却一无所获。在他们没有收获的时期,一个家庭的人就要靠树皮河草根为生,甚至饿死。贫穷和苦难伴随着他们。很多人在冬天被活活饿死。"印第安人不会像欧洲人那样生活。并且他们既不会完全摆脱父辈们的生活模式又无法完全按照他们的模式生存下去。通过一个我提供给政府的事实可以说明这件事。居住在苏必利尔湖边的一个部落的一些印第安人杀了一个欧洲人。然后美国政府就封锁了所有通往这个犯事的部落领地的交通,直到他们被遣送法院接受审判。这一方法得到了预期的效果。

to diminish. From the moment when a European settlement is formed in the neighborhood of the territory occupied by the Indians, the beasts of chase take the alarm. ①Thousands of savages, wandering in the forests and destitute of any fixed dwelling, did not disturb them; but as soon as the continuous sounds of European labor are heard in their neighborhood, they begin to flee away and retire to the West, where their instinct teaches them that they will still find deserts of immeasurable extent. "The buffalo is constantly receding," say Messrs. Clarke and Cass in their Report of the year 1829; "a few years since they approached the base of the Allegheny; and a few years hence they may even be rare upon the immense plains which extend to the base of the Rocky Mountains." I have been assured that this effect of the approach of the whites is often felt at two hundred leagues' distance from their frontier. Their influence is thus exerted over tribes whose name is unknown to them, and who suffer the evils of usurpation long before they are acquainted with the authors of their distress. ②

Bold adventurers soon penetrate into the country the Indians have deserted, and when they have advanced about fifteen or twenty leagues from the extreme frontiers of the whites, they begin to build habitations for civilized beings in the midst of the wilderness. This is done without difficulty, as the territory of a hunting nation is ill defined; it is the common property of the tribe and belongs to no one in particular, so that individual interests are not concerned in protecting any part of it.

---

① "Five years ago," says Volney in his *Tableau des Etats-Unis*, p. 370, "in going from Vincennes to Kaskaskia, a territory which now forms part of the state of Illinois, but which at the time I mention was completely wild (1797), you could not cross a prairie without seeing herds of from four to five hundred buffaloes. There is now none remaining; they swam across the Mississippi, to escape from the hunters, and more particularly from the bells of the American cows."

② The truth of what I here advance may be easily proved by consulting the tabular statement of Indian tribes inhabiting the United States and their territories. (Legislative Documents, 20th Congress, No. 117, pp. 90 – 105.) It is there shown that the tribes in the center of America are rapidly decreas ing, although the Europeans are still at a considerable distance from them.

的增加,他们的资源越来越少。终于,当欧洲人在印第安人居住的领地邻近的地方形成了一个定居的群落之后,捕猎就成为了一件引起人们关注的事件了。[1] 大量在森林中流浪居无定所的野蛮人并不能影响他们,但是一旦有欧洲人的声音从它们周围传来,他们就立刻向西部逃窜,他们的直觉告诉自己他们将在那里找到广阔的荒漠。"水牛不断地撤退,"卡斯先生和克拉克先生在1829年的报告中写到"几年前它们还在阿勒格尼山麓出没过,而几年之后他们也许在一直延伸到落基山脉的广袤的原野上也难以见到。"有人曾坚信,白人来临的这种影响,常常影响到他们周围方圆 200 里约的地方。他们的影响力甚至渗透了那些他们根本不知道名字的部落,而这些部落的人们在认识他们的苦难的制造者之前,早就尝到掠夺的痛苦。[2]

　　一些勇敢的探险家很快就深入了印第安人遗弃的土地,他们在越过白人的边界大约十五里格到二十里格的地方,在荒野中建造起文明人的住所。这一切都很容易,因为狩猎民族的领土是不确定的。它是所有民族的领土但却又不属于任何人,因此没有人的利益与保护领地的任何部分相关。

―――――――――――

[1] "五年前,"俄尔尼在他的《美国面貌》一书中第 370 页中说道,"在从文森斯到卡斯卡斯基亚的一片土地,如今已成为伊利诺伊州的一部分,但在我所提到的这个时期还是一片荒野(1797 年),穿过这片草地,你会看到成群的野牛估计有四五百头。现在一头也没有了。它们为了躲避猎人的追捕,都游过密西西比河到了另一边,并且多是被那边的母牛吸引过去的。"

[2] 我在此所说的事实,很容易通过计算居住在美国和他们的疆土上的印第安人部落得到证实。(立法文档,第 20 次会议第 117 号,第 90 ~ 105 页。)上面记载了居住在美国中心地带的部落迅速地减少,尽管当时欧洲人仍然居住在距他们很远的地方。

A few European families, occupying points very remote from one another, soon drive away the wild animals that remain be tween their places of abode. The Indians, who had previously lived in a sort of a-bundance, then find it difficult to subsist, and still more difficult to procure the articles of barter that they stand in need of. To drive away their game has the same effect as to render sterile the fields of our agriculturists; deprived of the means of subsistence, they are reduced, like famished wolves, to prowl through the forsaken woods in quest of prey. Their instinctive love of country attaches them to the soil that gave them birth, ①even after it has ceased to yield anything but misery and death. At length they are compelled to acquiesce and depart; they follow the traces of the elk, the buffalo, and the beaver and are guided by these wild animals in the choice of their future country. Properly speaking, therefore, it is not the Europeans who drive away the natives of America; it is famine, a happy distinction which had escaped the casuists of former times and for which we are indebted to modern discovery!

It is impossible to conceive the frightful sufferings that attend these forced migrations. They are undertaken by a people already exhausted and reduced; and the countries to which the new comers betake themselves are inhabited by other tribes, which re ceive them with jealous hostility. Hunger is in the rear, war awaits them, and misery besets them on all sides. To escape from so many enemies, they separate, and each individual endeavors to procure secretly the

---

① "The Indians," say Messrs. Clarke and Cass, in their *Report to Congress*, p. 15, "are attached to their country by the same feelings which bind us to ours; and, besides, there are certain superstitious notions connected with the alienation of what the Great Spirit gave to their ancestors, which operate strongly upon the tribes which have made few or no cessions, but which are gradually weakened as our intercourse with them is extended. We will not sell the spot which contains the bones of our fathers, is almost always the first answer to a proposal to buy their land."

一些欧洲人全家搬到了印第安人居住的地方并相隔很远各占一角,不久在他们居住点之间的动物就都四散逃窜。之前居住在土地肥沃的地方的印第安人开始发现生活的艰难,他们越来越难以用自己的东西换取到他们必需的用品。赶走他们的猎物,其后果跟我们的农民的土地变得贫瘠不毛一样。因为没有赖以生存的食物,他们的人数减少,大家就像极度饥饿的狼一样,在这片被遗弃的森林中逡巡着期望能捕获到猎物。他们本能的对自己国家的热爱使他们紧紧的与这片哺育了他们的土地联系在一起,即使这片土地在生育了他们之后就只带给了他们苦难和死亡。[①] 最后,他们只好被迫分散逃离,追随着麋鹿、野牛、海狸等动物的足迹,由这些野兽引导着他们选择未来的国界。因此,有人认为应当说,美洲土著并不是被欧洲人赶走的,而是被饥荒赶走的。这真是以往的诡辩家都没有找到而为现代人所发明的高论!

被迫迁徙的同时,人们忍受着难以想象的可怕苦难。而这些承受着苦难的人们早已被折磨的筋疲力尽、衰败不堪;而他们选择落脚的这片土地,早已被其他部落的人们占据着,那里的人们对新来的人们心存敌意。前面等待他们的是战争,饥饿在他们身后虎视眈眈,围绕在他们身边的只有悲惨。为了躲避这么多的敌

---

① 克拉克先生和卡斯先生在他们对国会的报告第 15 页中写道:"印第安人对他们的国家有着和我们一样的感情。并且,除此之外,他们的感情中还带有一定的宗教情感,这种情感与伟大的神灵给与他们的祖先的那种距离感联系在一起,这些感情强烈的作用于那些决不退让的部落之上,而那些我们与之交往渐趋广阔的部落却逐渐衰落下去。'我们不会将埋藏着父辈们的土地卖掉',当我们试图买他们的土地的时候,他们就会冲口而出这句话。"

means of supporting his existence by isolating himself, living in the immensity of the desert like an outcast in civilized society. The social tie, which distress had long since weakened, is then dissolved; they have no longer a country, and soon they will not be a people; their very families are obliterated; their common name is forgotten; their language perishes; and all traces of their origin disappear. Their nation has ceased to exist except in the recollection of the antiquaries of America and a few of the learned of Europe.

I should be sorry to have my reader suppose that I am coloring the picture too highly; I saw with my own eyes many of the miseries that I have just described, and was the witness of sufferings that I have not the power to portray.

At the end of the year 1831, while I was on the left bank of the Mississippi, at a place named by Europeans Memphis, there arrived a numerous band of Choctaws (or Chactas, as they are called by the French in Louisiana). These savages had left their country and were endeavoring to gain the right bank of the Mississippi, where they hoped to find an asylum that had been prom ised them by the American government. It was then the middle of winter, and the cold was unusually severe; the snow had frozen hard upon the ground, and the river was drifting huge masses of ice. The Indians had their families with them, and they brought in their train the wounded and the sick, with children newly born and old men upon the verge of death. They possessed neither tents nor wagons, but only their arms and some provisions. I saw them embark to pass the mighty river, and never will that solemn spectacle fade from my remembrance. No cry, no sob, was heard among the assembled crowd; all were silent. Their calamities were of ancient date, and they knew them to be irremediable. The Indians had all stepped into the bark that was to carry them across, but their dogs remained upon the bank. As soon as these animals perceived that their masters were finally leaving the shore, they set up a dismal howl and, plunging all together into the icy waters of the Mississippi, swam after the boat.

The expulsion of the Indians often takes place at the present day in a regular and, as it were, a legal manner. When the European population begins to approach the limit of the desert inhabited by a savage tribe, the government of the United States usually sends forward

人,他们只有分散开来。个人独自在茫茫的荒漠谋生,仿佛被文明社会遗弃的人们。久经削弱地维系着社会的纽带,如今已完全断裂。他们已不再有国家,不久他们也不复有部落。他们的家庭观念已渐淹没,共同拥有的族名也逐渐消失。他们的语言以及所有原始的痕迹都将不复存在。他们的民族只有一些美国的考古学家和欧洲一些学识渊博的学者才会记得。

如果我的描述使读者产生怀疑,认为我过于夸张,那么我很抱歉。我只是把我所亲眼看到的一切悲惨的状况描述给大家,把我所看到的苦难尽可能地再现。

1831 年底,我来到密西西比河左岸一个欧洲人称做孟菲斯的地方。我在这里停留期间,来了一帮巧克陶部人。路易斯安那的法裔美国人称他们为夏克塔部。这些野蛮人离开自己的土地,想到密西西比河右岸去,自以为在那里可以找到一处美国政府准许他们栖身的地方。那时还是冬天,而且那一年异常的冷。雪在地面上冻成厚厚的一层。河里漂浮着巨大的冰块。印第安人迁徙的队伍里,有家眷和一批伤患病人,还有刚出生的婴儿和行将朽木的老人。他们既没有帐篷也没有马车,有的只是一点点粮食和他们的双臂。可是,在他们密密麻麻的人群中,既听不到哭声也没有抽泣声,所有的人都很安静。他们的灾难由来已久,他们知道自己无法摆脱。他们登上了那艘搭载他们的大船,把狗留在了岸边。但这些动物预感到它们的主人将离它们而去的时候,就一起狂吠起来,纷纷跳进了冰冷的河水中,跟着大船泅水过河。

现在,对印第安人的驱逐,常常是以一种有序而合法的方式实施的。当欧洲人开始进驻被一个野蛮部族占据的荒野时,美国

envoys who assemble the Indians in a large plain and, having first eaten and drunk with them, address them thus: "What have you to do in the land of your fathers? Before long, you must dig up their bones in order to live. In what respect is the country you inhabit better than another? Are there no woods, marshes, or prairies except where you dwell? And can you live no where but under your own sun? Beyond those mountains which you see at the horizon, beyond the lake which bounds your territory on the west, there lie vast countries where beasts of chase are yet found in great abundance; sell us your lands, then, and go to live happily in those solitudes. " After holding this language, they spread before the eyes of the Indians firearms, woolen garments, kegs of brandy, glass necklaces, bracelets of tinsel, ear-rings, and looking-glasses. ① If, when they have beheld all these riches, they still hesitate, it is insinuated that they cannot refuse the required consent and that the government itself will not long have the power of protecting them in their rights. What are they to do? Half convinced and half compelled, they go to inhabit new deserts, where the importunate whites will not let them remain ten years in peace. In this manner do the Americans obtain, at a very low price,

---

① See in the *Legislative Documents of Congress* (Doc. 117) the narrative of what takes place on these occasions. This curious passage is from the formerly mentioned Report made to Congress by Messrs. Clarke and Cass, February 4, 1829.

"The Indians," says the Report, "reach the treaty-ground poor, and almost naked. Large quantities of goods are taken there by the traders, and are seen and examined by the Indians. The women and children become importunate to have their wants supplied, and their influence is soon exerted to induce a sale. Their improvidence is habitual and unconquerable. The gratification of his immediate wants and desires is the ruling passion of an Indian. The expectation of future advantages seldom produces much effect. The experience of the past is lost, and the prospects of the future disregarded. It would be utterly hopeless to demand a cession of land, unless the means were at hand of gratifying their immediate wants; and when their condition and circumstances are fairly considered, it ought not to surprise us that they are so anxious to relieve themselves. "

政府一般都先向这个部族派去几个官方信使,他们将印第安人召集到平地上,同他们大吃大喝一通,然后对他们说:"你们在你们祖先的这块土地上能干出来什么? 过不了多久,你们就得靠挖他们的骨头为生。这块土地哪里比别的地方好? 难道除了你们住的这个地方,别处就没有森林、沼泽和草原吗? 难道除了这里,在别的地方你们就没法活了吗? 在你们看见的天边那些大山后面,在你们的土地西面尽头的那个湖的对岸,有一大片还奔驰着许多野兽的土地。把你们的土地卖给我们吧,然后到那片土地上去过幸福生活。"讲完这一番话后,他们就在印第安人面前,摆出一堆东西:火枪、呢绒服装、成桶的酒、玻璃项链、金手镯、耳环和镜子。① 假如印第安人看到这些贵重物品后还不动心,可以慢慢说服他们不要拒绝对他们提出的要求,并向他们暗示将来政府也不能保证他们行使自己的权利。结果呢? 印第安人在胁迫之下,半推半就地来到新的荒凉地区。但那些可恶的白人也不会让他们在那里太太平平地住上十年。就这样,美国人以非常低廉的价

---

① 见议会的《立法文件》第 117 卷,在这些时期所发生的时间的陈述。这一令人好奇的篇节是来自之前提到的 1829 年 2 月 4 日克拉克先生和卡斯先生向国会提出的报告中摘取的。

报告中提到,"印第安人来到了他们协商中提到的这片贫瘠的、近乎荒凉的土地。商人们带来了大量的商品摆在印第安人面前供他们检查。女人和孩子们为了得到他们想要的东西而纠缠不清,在他们的影响下很快就成就了一笔买卖。他们目光短浅早已养成习惯并且难以克服。印第安人主要的志趣就在于对自己突发起来的需求和渴望的满足。而很少考虑到对未来的影响。他们失去了以往的经验,对未来也漠不关心。一旦土地被割让,再想要回来是完全不可能的事情,除非这一途径也成为他们急需满足的渴望。如果我们公正地考虑过他们所处的环境和条件之后,就不会惊讶他们为何为解脱自己而如此担忧。"

whole provinces, which the richest sovereigns of Europe could not purchase. ①

These are great evils; and it must be added that they appear to me to be irremediable. I believe that the Indian nations of North America are doomed to perish, and that whenever the Europeans shall be established on the shores of the Pacific Ocean, that race of men will have ceased to exist. The Indians had only the alter native of war or civilization; in other words, they must either de stroy the Europeans or become their equals.

At the first settlement of the colonies they might have found it possible, by uniting their forces, to deliver themselves from the small bodies of strangers who landed on their continent. ② They several times attempted to do it, and were on the point of succeeding; but the disproportion of their resources at the present day, when compared with those of the whites, is too great to allow such an enterprise to be thought of. But from time to time among the Indians men of sagacity

---

① On May 19, 1830 Mr. Edward Everett affirmed before the House of Representatives that the Americans had already acquired by *treaty*, to the east and west of the Mississippi, 230,000,000 acres. In 808 the Osages gave up 48,000,000 acres for an annual payment of 1,000 dollars. In 1818 the Quapaws yielded up 20,000,000 acres for 4,000 dollars. They reserved for themselves a territory of 1,000,000 acres for a hunting-ground. A solemn oath was taken that it should be respected, but before long it was invaded like the rest.

Mr. Bell, in his *Report of the Committee on Indian Affairs*, February 24, 1830, has these words: "To pay an Indian tribe what their ancient huntinggrounds are worth to them after the game is fled or destroyed, as a mode of appropriating wild lands claimed by Indians, has been found more convenient, and certainly it is more agreeable to the forms of justice, as well as more merciful, than to assert the possession of them by the sword. Thus the practice of buying Indian titles is only the substitute which humanity and expediency have imposed, in place of the sword, in arriving at the actual enjoyment of property claimed by the right of discovery, and sanctioned by the natural superiority allowed to the claims of civilized communities over those of savage tribes. Up to the present time, so invariable has been the operation of certain causes, first in diminishing the value of forest lands to the Indians, and secondly, in disposing them to sell readily, that the plan of buying their right of occupancy has never threatened to retard, in any perceptible degree, the prosperity of any of the States." (*Legislative Documents*, 21st Congress, No. 227, p. 6.)

② This seems, indeed, to be the opinion of almost all American statesmen. "Judging of the future by the past,"says Mr. Cass, "we cannot err in anticipating a progressive diminution of their numbers, and their eventual extinction, unless our border should become stationary, and they be removed beyond it, or unless some radical change should take place in the principles of our intercourse with them, which it is easier to hope for than to expect."

格,买到了欧洲最富有的君主也买不起的大片的土地。①

　　这就是我所描述的深重苦难,但我还得补充一句:在我看来,这些灾难是无以弥补的。我相信,北美的印第安人注定要灭亡,而且一旦欧洲人在太平洋海岸立足,那里的印第安人亦将不复存在。北美的印第安人只有两条出路:不是对白人开战,就是自己接受文明的洗礼。换句话说,不是消灭欧洲人,就是变成同欧洲人一样的人。

　　在白人建立殖民地之初,他们本来可以联合起来赶走刚刚登上这个大陆海岸的一小撮外来人。② 而且他们曾不止一次地试图这样做过并几乎成功。但是如今,与白人相比,双方力量的对比悬殊,他们甚至已不敢有这样的念头了。但在印第安人中间,仍

---

　　① 1830 年 5 月 19 日,爱德华埃弗雷特先生在众议院前断言,美国已经通过协议获得,从密西西比州东部到西部共 230000000 英亩。808 年,奥色治人为了每年 1000 美元的报酬就放弃了 48000000 英亩土地。1818 年另一个地方(Quapaws)20000000 英亩的土地以 4000 美元的报酬就被放弃。他们只为自己保留了 1000000 英亩的土地以供捕猎之用。人们本当尊重的严肃的誓言,然而不久之后剩下的也被侵略殆尽。

　　1830 年 2 月 24 日,贝尔先生就印第安事务对国会的报告中说道:"对印第安人所作出的对他们的祖先捕猎过的土地的赔偿,在这场规则被破坏之后,就如同印第安人所要求的那些可怜的荒野一样,变得更加容易得手。并且,也变得越来越公正,越来越充满同情,好过用武器逼着他们就范。在见者有份的意识的驱动下而产生的对财富的渴望以及喜悦中,在文明社会对蛮夷种族天生的优越感的驱动下,剥夺印第安人的手段,不再以武力相逼,而取而代之以用一种人性和私利的手段。到目前为止,这样的定数是由一些原因造成的。首先,印第安人从森林土地中得到的价值不断减少。其次,不论他们占有哪块土地,那些为了使他们同意出卖土地的计划总是层出不穷。"(立法文件,第 21 次国会,227 号,第 6 页。)

　　② 事实上,这几乎代表了所有美国政客的观点。"以过去判断将来,"卡斯先生说,"我们不能错误的期望他们的人数巨减或最终会走向消亡,除非我们的疆域一直保持不变,而他们则迁离这里,或者除非我们之间的交流会发生一些本质性的改变,而这都是梦想大于希望。"

and energy foresee the final destiny that awaits the native population and exert themselves to unite all the tribes in common hostility to the Europeans; but their efforts are unavailing. The tribes which are in the neighborhood of the whites are too much weakened to offer an effectual resistance; while the others, giving way to that childish carelessness of the morrow which characterizes savage life, wait for the near approach of danger before they prepare to meet it; some are unable, others are unwilling, to act.

It is easy to foresee that the Indians will never civilize themselves, or that it will be too late when they may be inclined to make the experiment. Civilization is the result of a long social process, which takes place in the same spot and is handed down from one generation to another, each one profiting by the experience of the last. Of all nations, those submit to civilization with the most difficulty who habitually live by the chase. Pastoral tribes, indeed, often change their place of abode; but they follow a regular order in their mi grations and often return to their old stations, while the dwelling of the hunter varies with that of the animals he pursues.

Several attempts have been made to diffuse knowledge among the Indians, leaving unchecked their wandering propensities, by the Jesuits in Canada and by the Puritans in New England; ①but none of these endeavors have been crowned by any lasting success. Civilization began in the cabin, but soon retired to expire in the woods. The great error of these legislators for the Indians was their failure to understand that in order to succeed in civilizing a people it is first necessary to settle them permanently which can not be done without inducing them to cultivate the soil; the Indians ought in the first place to have been accustomed to agriculture. But not only are they destitute of this indispensable preliminary to civilization, they would even have great difficulty in acquiring it.

---

① See the historians of New England, the *Histoire de la Nouvelle France*, by Charlevoix, and the work entitled *Lettres difiantes*.

有些睿智的人士预见到蛮族未来的厄运,而试图把所有的部落联合起来,共同对付欧洲人。然而,他们的努力无济于事。邻近白人的部落已经衰弱得无力进行有效的抵抗;而其他一些部落,则出于野蛮人的天性,对于明天抱着听天由命的心理。他们只等待厄运来临,而不采取任何对策。有些部落是无力采取对策,有的部落则根本不想采取对策。[1]

不难预见,印第安人不是永不会接受文明,就是在想开始这样做的时候已经为时甚晚。文明是社会长期发展的结果。文明在一个地方发生并代代相传,每一代都得益于上一代。使文明最难在其中建立统治地位的民族,是狩猎民族。事实上,游牧部落虽然经常改换驻地,但在迁徙的过程中总是依照一定的路线,最后常常又回到原处。而狩猎部落的驻地,则随着他们所追捕的动物的栖息场所而改变。

有人曾多次试图在印第安人地区传播知识,并任其保持漂泊流动的习性。耶稣会士在加拿大试图这样做过,清教徒在新英格兰也试图这样做过。① 但是他们都未能取得长久的胜利。文明在猎人的茅屋里开了花,但却枯死在森林里。这些在印第安人中间传播文明的人所犯的最大错误,在于他们不懂:要想使一个民族接受文明,首先必须先让它永久的定居下来,而要使它定居下来,就得叫它耕作。因此,印第安人应该首先学会耕作。印第安人不仅被剥夺了迈向文明不可或缺的第一步,而且他们也很难获得迈向这一步的权利。

---

① 　见新英格兰史,法国史。作者夏洛瓦。

〔1〕在一些好战派中,有万帕诺亚格部落之一,以及 1675 年梅塔克姆下面反对新英格兰殖民者的其他一些同盟部落。1622 年英国人也在弗吉尼亚与他们陷入了战事。

Men who have once abandoned themselves to the restless and adventurous life of the hunter feel an insurmountable disgust for the constant and regular labor that tillage requires. We see this proved even in our own societies; but it is far more visible among races whose partiality for the chase is a part of their national character.

Independently of this general difficulty, there is another, which applies peculiarly to the Indians. They consider labor not merely as an evil, but as a disgrace; so that their pride contends against civilization as obstinately as their indolence. ①

There is no Indian so wretched as not to retain under his hut of bark a lofty idea of his personal worth; he considers the cares of industry as degrading occupations; he compares the plowman to the ox that traces the furrow; and in each of our handicrafts he can see only the labor of slaves. Not that he is devoid of admira tion for the power and intellectual greatness of the whites; but although the result of our efforts surprises him, he despises the means by which we obtain it; and while he acknowledges our ascendancy, he still believes in his own superiority. War and hunting are the only pursuits that appear to him worthy of a man. ②The Indian, in the dreary solitudes of his woods, cherishes the same ideas, the same opinions, as the noble of the Middle Ages in his castle; and he only needs to become a conqueror

---

① "In all the tribes," says Volney, in his Tableau des Etats-Unis (p. 423), "there still exists a generation of old warriors who cannot forbear, when they see their countrymen using the hoe, from exclaiming against the degradation of ancient manners and asserting that the savages owe their decline to these innovations; adding that they have only to return to their primitive habits in order to recover their power and glory."

② The following description occurs in an official document: "Until a young man has been engaged with an enemy, and has performed some acts of valor, he gains no consideration, but is regarded nearly as a woman. In their great war-dances, all the warriors in succession strike the post, as it is called, and recount their exploits. On these occasions, their audience consists of the kinsmen, friends, and comrades of the narrator. The profound impression which his discourse produces on them is manifested by the silent attention it receives, and by the loud shouts which hail its termination. The young man who finds himself at such a meeting without anything to recount is very unhappy; and instances have sometimes occurred of young warriors whose passions had been thus inflamed, quitting the war-dance suddenly, and going off alone to seek for trophies which they might exhibit and ad ventures by which they might be allowed to glorify themselves."

人们一旦沉迷于猎人的到处游荡的冒险生活,就对农耕所需的持续而有规律的劳动产生一种不可克服的厌恶感。事实证明在我们的文明社会中这种情况也会发生;但在狩猎的习惯已变成全民的习惯的民族中,表现得尤为明显。

除了这个普遍存在的困难之外,还有一个原因,但只适用于印第安人。他们把劳动视为邪恶,认为劳动是一件不光彩的事。他们的傲慢之对抗文明,与他们的懒惰之对抗文明,几乎同样顽固。①

没有一个印第安人认为在自己的树皮盖的小屋里生活就失去了个人的尊严并因而觉得可悲。他们认为辛苦的劳动是下贱的活动。他们将农夫比做耕田的牛,并把每一种手艺都看成是奴隶的劳作。他们对白人的能力和高超智慧充满钦佩,但他们在惊讶于这些勤劳的成果时,却又瞧不起我们获得这种成果的手段;在承认我们的高超时,同时也感觉着自己的优越。在他们看来,只有打猎和打仗是值得男人们去做的。② 印第安人在他们沉寂荒凉的森林里生活着,他们的思想和观点同中世纪在古堡里生活的

① 俄尔尼在他的《美国面貌》一书中(第423页)说,"在所有的部落中,还存在着一代古老的武士,当他们看到自己的同胞手举着锄头,呼喊着反抗古老的习俗的衰退并叫嚣着是野蛮使他们衰退然后发生这些变革的时候,他们不能克制。他们为了恢复往日的权势和荣耀,必须恢复他们最初的习俗。"

② 以下的描述出自一份官方的资料:"一位年轻人在遭遇了敌人,并且表现出一定的勇猛以前,都会被一概认为像女人一般懦弱。在他们伟大的战阵舞中,所有的战士前仆后继的打击中间的一个叫柱子的东西,并同时叙述自己的战绩。在这些时候,他们的观众有同族的人、朋友和叙述者的伙伴。他的演讲给他们带来的深刻的影响通过他们默默的关注和人们高兴的欢呼它的结束表露无遗。如果一个年轻人在这样的情况下没有一点可以夸耀陈述的东西就会觉得很丢脸。而一些年轻人的激情就这样被激发出来,他们会立刻退出战阵舞的队伍,独自出发去寻找他们可以用来展示的战绩或者通过一些冒险的活动为自己争得荣耀。"

to complete the resemblance. Thus, however strange it may seem, it is in the forests of the New World, and not among the Europeans who people its coasts, that the ancient prejudices of Europe still exist.

More than once in the course of this work I have endeavored to explain the prodigious influence that the social condition appears to exercise upon the laws and the manners of men, and I beg to add a few words on the same subject.

When I perceive the resemblance that exists between the political institutions of our ancestors, the Germans, and the wandering tribes of North America, between the customs described by Tacitus and those of which I have sometimes been a witness, I cannot help thinking that the same cause has brought about the same results in both hemispheres; and that in the midst of the apparent diversity of human affairs certain primary facts may be discovered from which all the others are derived. In what we usually call the German institutions, then, I am inclined to perceive only barbarian habits, and the opinions of savages in what we style feudal principles.

However strongly the vices and prejudices of the North American Indians may be opposed to their becoming agricultural and civilized, necessity sometimes drives them to it. Several of the Southern tribes, considerably numerous, and among others the Cherokees and the Creeks,①found themselves, as it were, sur rounded by Europeans, who had landed on the shores of the Atlantic and, either descending the Ohio or proceeding up the Mississippi, arrived simultaneously upon their borders. These tribes had not been driven from place to place like their Northern brethren; but they had been gradually shut up within narrow limits, like game driven into an enclosure before

---

① These nations are now swallowed up in the states of Georgia, Tennessee, Alabama, and Mississippi. There were formerly in the South four great nations (remnants of which still exist), the Choctaws, the Chickasaws, the Creeks, and the Cherokees. The remnants of these four nations amounted in 1830 to about 75, 000 individuals. It is computed that there are now remaining in the territory occupied or claimed by the Anglo-American Union about 300,000 Indians. (See *Proceedings of the Indian Board in the City of New York.*) The official documents supplied to Congress make the number amount to 313,130. The reader who is curious to know the names and nu merical strength of all the tribes that inhabit the Anglo-American territory should consult the documents I have just referred to. (Legislative Documents, 20th Congress, No. 117, pp. 90 – 105.)

贵族丝毫无异。他们只要变成征服者,便与中世纪的贵族一般无二了。因此,尽管看起来很奇怪,可是今天竟在新大陆的森林中,而不是在欧洲人居住的海岸,重现欧洲古老偏见。

我在本书的叙述当中,曾不止一次试图说明:在我看来,社会情况对于法制和民情具有重大的影响。在这个问题上,请允许我再补充几句。

当我认识到我们的祖先日耳曼人和北美的游猎部落在政治制度上存在的相似之处,看到塔西佗当年描写的日耳曼人和我常常亲眼目睹的印第安人在生活习惯上存在的相似之处时,我不禁在想:同样的原因竟使两个半球产生了同样的结果。那么,是不是在纷繁不一的人类活动中,那些促成事物的个别的主要起因,也是促使其他事实产生的主要事实。因此,我倾向于认为能在我们所称的日耳曼人的政治制度中找到野蛮人的习惯,在我们所说的封建思想中找到野蛮人的观点。

尽管北美的印第安人的恶习和偏见会妨碍他们从事农耕和接受文明,但现实的需要常常会驱使他们不得不这么做。南部的几个相当大的部落,特别是其中的柴罗基部和克里克部,①现已被欧洲人包围。这些欧洲人有的来自大西洋沿岸,有的顺俄亥俄河而下,有的溯密西西比河而上,同时来到他们的周边。这些部落没有像北部的部落那样被从一个地方撵到另一个地方,而是在各自

① 这些民族如今在佐治亚州、田纳西州、阿拉巴马州和密西西比州已不复存在。之前在南部有四个伟大的民族(这些民族的残留至今仍存在),乔克托族、契卡索族、克里克族和切罗基族。这四个部落在 1830 年人数总计达约75000 人。经计算如今这块被英裔美国联盟占据的土地上有大约30000 印第安人。提供给国会的官方文件显示,这一人数已达到 313130。想知道所有居住在英裔美国领土上的民族的名称和数量,需要参考我前面提到的资料。(《立法文档》,第 20 次国会第 117 号,第 90～105 页。)

the huntsmen plunge among them. The Indians, who were thus placed between civilization and death, found themselves obliged to live ignominiously by labor, like the whites. They took to agriculture and, without entirely forsaking their old habits or manners, sacrificed only as much as was necessary to their existence.

The Cherokees went further; they created a written language, established a permanent form of government, and, as everything proceeds rapidly in the New World, before they all of them had clothes they set up a newspaper. [1]

The development of European habits has been much accelerated among these Indians by the mixed race which has sprung up[2] Deriving intelligence from the father's side without entirely losing the savage customs of the mother, the half-blood forms the natural link between civilization and barbarism. Wherever this race has multiplied, the savage state has become modified and a great change has taken place in the manners of the people. [3]

---

[1] I brought back with me to France one or two copies of this singular publication.

[2] See, in the *Report of the Committee on Indian Affairs*, 21st Congress, No. 227, p. 23, the reasons for the multiplication of Indians of mixed blood among the Cherokees. The principal cause dates from the War of Independence. Many Anglo-Americans of Georgia, having taken the side of England, were obliged to retreat among the Indians, where they married.

[3] Unhappily, the mixed race has been less numerous and less influential in North America than in any other country. The American continent was peopled by two great nations of Europe, the French and the English. The former were not slow in connecting themselves with the daughters of the natives, but there was an unfortunate affinity between the Indian character and their own: instead of giving the tastes and habits of civilized life to the savages, the French too often grew passionately fond of Indian life. They became the most dangerous inhabitants of the wilderness, and won the friend ship of the Indian by exaggerating his vices and his virtues. M. de Senonville, the Governor of Canada, wrote thus to Louis XIV in 1685: "It has long been believed that in order to civilize the savages we ought to draw them nearer to us. But there is every reason to suppose we have been mistaken. Those that have been brought into contact with us have not become French, and the French who have lived among them are changed into savages, affecting

所在地区,被逐渐围缩在一块很小的土地上,就像猎物被猎人围住,只待就擒了。这样被置于文明和死亡之间的印第安人,只好依靠白人那样的劳动糊口了。于是,他们开始种田,但并没有完全放弃他们原有的习惯和民情,只是为了生存而做了不可不做的牺牲。

柴罗基部比其他部落进步一些。他们创造了文字,建立了相当稳定的管理组织。同时,由于新大陆里的一切都是发展得很快的,所以他们在还没能使所有人都不过着裸体生活的时候,就出了一份报纸。[1]

混血儿的出现,明显地加速了欧洲人的生活习惯在印第安人中间的传播。[2] 混血儿从父方学来了知识,但又没有完全放弃母方种族的野蛮人习惯,他们是文明和野蛮之间的天然纽带。凡是混血儿多的地方,野蛮人就逐渐在改变他们的社会情况和民情。[3]

---

① 我把这套单行本的副本带回法国一两套。

② 见委员会就印第安诸事的报告,第 21 次国会第 227 号,第 23 页。切罗基族中混血印第安人数量剧增的原因。求其主要原因就要追述到独立战争了。一些占据了英格兰周边地区的乔治亚州的英裔美国人,也被迫随着印第安人一起撤退并在那里结婚。

③ 不幸的是,这些混杂的种族在其他国家不如在北美洲那样数量庞大影响深远。美洲大陆被欧洲两个大的民族,法国和英国占据着。前者与当地人结亲的事情上行动毫不缓慢,但是他们自身与印第安人的性格的结合并不合适:法国人并没有将自己的文明生活的趣味和习惯带给这些野蛮民族,相反的却迅速地滋生了对印第安人生活方式的热爱之情。他们成了这片荒野上最危险的居民,并通过夸大自己的恶行和美德赢得了与印第安人的友谊。加拿大政府官员 M. 赛努维拉 1685 年写信给路易十四世说:"很久以来,人们都认为为了消除野蛮的品行,我们必须将文明拉得离我们更近。但是所有的事实都证明我们的理解是错误的。那些与我们接触的野蛮人并没有因此变成法国人,相反生活在他们中间的法国人却变得野蛮起来,从穿

The success of the Cherokees proves that the Indians are capable of civilization, but it does not prove that they will succeed in it. This difficulty that the Indians find in submitting to civilization proceeds from a general cause, the influence of which it is almost impossible for them to escape. An attentive survey of history demonstrates that, in general, barbarous nations have raised themselves to civilization by degrees and by their own efforts. When ever they derived knowledge from a foreign people, they stood towards them in the relation of conquerors, and not of a conquered nation. When the conquered nation is enlightened and the conquerors are half-savage, as in the invasion of the Roman Empire by the northern nations, or that of China by the Mongols, the power that victory bestows upon the barbarian is sufficient to keep up his importance among civilized men and permit him to rank as their equal until he becomes their rival. The one has might on his side, the other has intelligence; the former admires the knowledge and the arts of the conquered, the latter envies the power of the conquerors. The barbarians at length admit civilized man into their palaces, and he in turn opens his schools to the barbarians. But when the side on which the physical force lies also possesses an intellectual superiority, the conquered party seldom becomes civilized; it retreats or is destroyed. It may therefore be said, in a general way, that savages go forth in arms to seek knowledge, but do not receive it when it comes to them. [1]

---

to dress and live like them. " (*History of New France*, by Charlevoix, Vol. II, p. 345.) The Englishman, on the contrary, continuing obstinately attached to the customs and the most insignificant habits of his forefathers, has re mained in the midst of the American solitudes just what he was in the heart of European cities; he would not establish any communication with savages whom he despised, and a-voided with care the union of his race with theirs. Thus, while the French exercised no salutary influence over the Indians, the English have always remained alien from them.

[1] There is in the adventurous life of the hunter a certain irresistible charm, which seizes the heart of man and carries him away in spite of reason and experience. This is plainly shown by the *Memoirs of Tanner*. Tanner was a European who was carried away at the age of six by the Indians and remained thirty years with them in the woods. Nothing can be conceived more appalling than the miseries that he describes. He tells us of tribes with out a chief, families without a nation to call their own, men in a state of isolation, wrecks of powerful tribes wandering at random amid the ice andsnow and desolate solitudes of Canada. Hunger

因此,柴罗基部的成就证明印第安人有能力接受文明,但决不代表他们能够成功。印第安人发现他们难于接受文明,主要来自一个他们无法摆脱的普遍原因。仔细地阅读一下历史,就可以发现:一般说来,野蛮民族都是依靠自己的努力,逐渐地自行文明起来的。当他们主动从外族汲取知识的时候,他们在这个外族面前,总是处于征服者的位置,而不是站在被征服者的地位。当被征服的民族是开化的民族,而征服者的民族还处于半开化的时候,就如同罗马帝国被北方民族入侵时,或像中国被蒙古人入侵时,胜利赋予蛮族的权力足以使他们达到文明人的水平,并能把他们的平等地位保持到文明人变成他们的对手的时候。一方凭借武力,另一方依靠智力,而前者钦佩被征服者的知识和文化,后者羡慕征服者的权力。最终,野蛮人把文明人请进他们的宫殿,而文明人则对野蛮人开放他们的学校。但是,当拥有物质力量的一方也同时具有智力的优势时,则被征服的一方很少能够走向文明,他们不是后退便是灭亡。总之,可以说野蛮人是手持武器去寻找知识,而不是凭自己的资质去接受知识。①

着到生活方式都像他们。"(《新法国历史》,夏林伏克著,第二卷第 345 页。)相反的,英国人由于顽强地保持了自己祖辈们遗留下来的传统和一些微小的习俗,因而得以保持原来的风貌。他们不屑与那些野蛮的民族交流,也尽量避免与他们有任何关系。因此,法国人并没有给印第安人以任何有益的影响,而英国人也一直与他们保持距离。

　① 猎人们的冒险生活带有一丝难以抵抗的诱惑力,这种诱惑紧紧地抓住了人们的心并使人们不顾一切。泰纳的论文集很清晰地描述了这一情形。泰纳是欧洲人,但在他六岁的时候被一个印第安人带走并与他们在丛林中生活了 30 年。在没有什么事情比他所描述的更悲惨。他告诉我们,一个没有首领的部落,没有国家的家庭,应该说一些完全孤立的人们,在冰天

If the Indian tribes that now inhabit the heart of the continent could summon up energy enough to attempt to civilize themselves, they might possibly succeed. Superior already to the barbarous nations that surround them, they would gradually gain strength and experience, and when the Europeans appear upon their borders, they would be in a state, if not to maintain their independence, at least to assert their right to the soil and to incorporate themselves with the conquerors. But it is the misfortune of Indians to be brought into contact with a civilized people, who are also (it must be owned) the most grasping nation on the globe, while they are still semi-barbarian; to find their masters in their instructors, and to receive knowledge and oppression at the same time. Living in the freedom of the woods, the North American Indian was destitute, but he had no feeling of inferiority towards anyone; as soon, however, as he desires to penetrate into the

---

and cold pursue them; every day their life is in jeopardy. Among these men manners have lost their empire, traditions are without power. They become more and more savage. Tanner shared in all these miseries; he was aware of his European origin; he was not kept away from the whites by force; on the contrary, he came every year to trade with them, entered their dwellings, and witnessed their enjoyments; he knew that whenever he chose to return to civilized life, he was perfectly able to do so, and he remained thirty years in the wilderness. When he came into civilized society, he declared that the rude existence, the miseries of which he described, had a secret charm for him which he could not define; he returned to it again and again, at length he abandoned it with poignant regret; and when he was at length settled among the whites, several of his children refused to share his tranquil and easy situation. I saw Tanner myself at the lower end of Lake Superior: he seemed to me more like a savage than a civilized being. His book is written without either taste or order; but he gives, even unconsciously, a lively picture of the prejudices, the passions, the vices, and, above all, the destitution in the midst of which he lived. The Viscount Ernest de Blosseville, author of an excellent treatise on the penal colonies of England, has translated the *Memoirs of Tanner*. M. de Blosseville has added to his translation some very interesting notes which will enable the reader to compare the facts related by Tanner with those already recorded by a great number of observers, ancient and modern.

All those who desire to know the present status of the Indians of North America and would foresee their destiny should consult M. de Blosseville's work.

　　现今住在大陆中部的印第安部落,当初如果凭借自己的力量,发愤图强使自己开化,它们也许可以成功。当时,它们已比周围的部族优越,本可以逐步发展自己的力量并取得经验;这样,后来当欧洲人出现于它们的边疆时,它们即使不能保持独立,至少也能让欧洲人承认它们的土地所有权或融入征服者的行列。但是,不幸的是,印第安人被卷入了与地球上最贪婪的开化民族打交道的厄运中,而可悲的是它自己还处在半野蛮的状态。也就是说,印第安人不仅找了个教员做他们的主人,而且在接受文明的同时就接受了压迫。在北美的森林里,印第安人虽然生活贫困,但他们自由自在,在任何人面前都没有自卑感。然而,一旦他们试图进入白人的社会阶层后,他们就只能位于最底层,因为他们

雪地的加拿大的荒野中到处流浪的强大的部落的毁灭。饥饿和寒冷紧紧地抓着他们。每一天,他们的生命都危在旦夕。在这些人中间,道德已不复存在,传统也失去了力量。他们变得越来越野蛮。泰纳品尝了所有这些苦难。他知道自己是欧洲人。他并没有脱离白人的习性。相反的,他每年都在与他们交易,进出于他们的住所,眼见着他们的享乐。他知道如果他能够选择重回文明社会,他也能把这些做得很好,尽管他在丛林中呆了30年。当他重返文明社会的时候,他信誓旦旦地说那些存在着的粗鲁,他所描述的悲惨的生活都给了他一种难以名状的神秘的吸引力。他一次又一次重返,而最终只能抱憾终身。而当他最终与白人居住在一起的时候,他的几个孩子都不愿与他分享宁静和简易环境。我有次亲眼看到泰纳湖的下游,在我看来,他看起来更像一个野人。他的书写没有风格也没有次序;但是他无意中给与了我们一幅生动的画面,里面有偏见、有激情、有邪恶以及他所经历的贫困。一位写过一部优秀的关于英格兰殖民地刑法论文集的作者,翻译了泰纳的论文集。在他的翻译作品中,他补充了一些有趣的注释,是读者可以将泰纳描写的事实与其他一些包括从古到今的已经描述过的类似的情景加以对照。

　　如果你想了解北美印第安人的现状,并希望预见他们的未来,即可以看看他的这部著作。

social scale of the whites, he can take only the lowest rank in society, for he enters ignorant and poor within the pale of science and wealth. After having led a life of agitation, beset with evils and dangers, but at the same time filled with proud emotions, he is obliged to submit to a wearisome, obscure, and degraded state. To gain by hard and ignoble labor the bread that nourishes him is in his eyes the only result of which civilization can boast; and even this he is not always sure to obtain.

When the Indians undertake to imitate their European neighbors, and to till the earth as they do, they are immediately exposed to a formidable competition. The white man is skilled in the craft of agriculture; the Indian is a rough beginner in an art with which he is unacquainted. The former reaps abundant crops without difficulty, the latter meets with a thousand obstacles in raising the fruits of the earth.

The European is placed among a population whose wants he knows and shares. The savage is isolated in the midst of a hostile people, with whose customs, language, and laws he is imperfectly acquainted, but without whose assistance he cannot live. He can procure only the materials of comfort by bartering his commodities for the goods of the European, for the assistance of his countrymen is wholly insufficient to supply his wants. Thus, when the Indian wishes to sell the produce of his labor, he cannot al ways find a purchaser, while the European readily obtains a market; the former can produce only at considerable cost what the latter sells at a low rate. Thus the Indian has no sooner escaped those evils to which barbarous nations are exposed than he is subjected to the still greater miseries of civilized communities; and he finds it scarcely less difficult to live in the midst of our abundance than in the depth of his own forest.

He has not yet lost the habits of his erratic life; the traditions of his fathers and his passion for the chase are still alive within him. The wild enjoyments that formerly animated him in the woods painfully excite his troubled imagination; the privations that he endured there appear less keen, his former perils less appalling. He contrasts the independence that he possessed among his equals with the servile position

在走进一个被知识和财富所统治的社会时,而他们自己既没有知识也没有财富。他们在经历了一段动荡不安、充满灾难和危险、但又觉得高兴和自豪的生活以后,就只好去煎熬单调无味的和浑浑噩噩的一生。在他们看来,通过卑贱艰辛的劳动赚钱养家糊口,就是他们所赞扬的文明的唯一成果! 而且,就连这一点点成果,他们也不是总有把握拿得到的。

当印第安人开始模仿他们周边的欧洲人,学着他们的样种田的时候,他们立即遭到了激烈的竞争。白人的农业技术娴熟,而印第安人作为生手才刚刚开始这一他们完全没有接触过的手艺。所以白人们很容易就获得丰收,而印第安人却在种植方面碰到了重重障碍。

欧洲人对与他们生活在一起的人群的需求了如指掌,并且也拥有跟他们相同的需求,而野蛮人孤立于与他们为敌的白人中间,他们不十分了解白人的习俗、语言和法律,可离开了白人他们又没法活。他们只有与白人交换自己的产品,才能获得生活所需的物品,因为他们的族人不能完全提供他们生活所需。因此,印第安人在打算出售自己的劳动果实时,并不是总能像白人农户那样找到买主。而且,他们只有付出高额的费用,才能生产出白人以低价出售的产品。这样,印第安人刚刚走出野蛮民族的生活苦海,又陷入了走向开化的民族的更加悲痛的深渊。他们觉得在我们的富裕环境中生活,其困难并不亚于他们在森林里生活。

他们还没有丢掉居无定所的生活习惯。他们父辈们的传统和他们自身对狩猎的爱好仍然存在他们的心中。昔日在森林里享受的欢乐痛苦勾起了他们纷乱的思绪。这样一来,从前在森林里忍受的贫苦变得不那么可怕了,而以前在森林里面临的危险

that he occupies in civilized society. On the other hand, the solitudes which were so long his free home are still at hand; a few hours' march will bring him back to them once more. The whites offer him a sum which seems to him considerable for the half-cleared ground whence he obtains sustenance with difficulty. This money of the Europeans may possibly enable him to live a happy and tranquil life far away from them; and he quits the plow, resumes his native arms, and returns to the wilderness forever. ①The condition of the Creeks and Cherokees, to which I have already alluded, sufficiently corroborates the truth of this sad picture.

The Indians, in the little which they have done, have unquestionably displayed as much natural genius as the peoples of Europe in

---

① This destructive influence of highly civilized nations upon others which are less so has been observed among the Europeans themselves. About a century ago the French founded the town of Vincennes on the Wabash, in the middle of the wilderness; and they lived there in great plenty until the arrival of the American settlers, who first ruined the previous inhabitants by their competition and afterwards purchased their lands at a very low rate. At the time when M. de Volney, from whom I borrow these details, passed through Vincennes, the number of the French was reduced to a hundred individuals, most of whom were about to migrate to Louisiana or to Canada. These French settlers were worthy people, but idle and uninstructed; they had contracted many of the habits of savages. The Americans, who were perhaps their inferiors from a moral point of view, were immeasurably superior to them in intelligence: they were industrious, well informed, well off, and accustomed to govern their own community.

I myself saw in Canada, where the intellectual difference between the two races is less striking, that the English are the masters of commerce and manufacture in the Canadian country, that they spread on all sides and confine the French within limits which scarcely suffice to contain them. In like manner in Louisiana almost all activity in commerce and manufacture centers in the hands of the AngloAmericans.

But the case of Texas is still more striking: the state of Texas is a part of Mexico and is on the frontier between that country and the United States. In the course of the last few years the Anglo-Americans have penetrated into this province, which is still thinly peopled; they purchase land, they produce the commodities of the country, and supplant the original population. It may easily be foreseen that if Mexico takes no steps to check this change, the province of Texas will very shortly cease to belong to that government. If the differences, comparatively less obvious, which exist in European civilization lead to similar results, it is easy to understand what must happen when the most perfect European civilization comes in contact with Indian barbarism.

也不算大了。他们以前在彼此平等的人们中间享有的独立,与他们现今在文明社会所处的奴隶地位形成了鲜明的对照。另一方面,他们曾长期自由生活的荒野仍唾手可得;只消走几个小时的路程,他们就能重回旧地。如果他们的那块赖以勉强糊口的半荒土,被他们的邻居白人用一笔在他们看来是相当不小的款项买去,而欧洲人给他们的这笔钱可使他们远离白人而去过幸福安宁的生活,那么,他们便要放下犁头,重新拿起武器,永远回到荒野中去。[①] 我已提到的克里克部和柴罗基部的情况,足以证明这幅悲惨的图景的真实性。

这些印第安人在他们所做小事上表现的天才,与那些欧洲人

---

① 高度文明的社会给那些不如它们的国家带来的破坏性的影响在欧洲人中间已显现出来。一个世纪前,法国人在荒野中发现了凡仙。于是他们大批人一直居住在那里,直到那些最先通过竞争瓦解了其先前的居民的美国定居者到来后,接着利用低价购买了他们的土地。借给我这些资料的俄尔尼先生,当他到达凡仙的时候,发现那里的法国人口数量已经减少到100多人且其中大多数人打算迁离。这些法国定居者都是一些富有的人,只是没有受过教育。他们已经养成了许多野蛮人的生活习惯。而美国人,从道德意义上来说,也许比他们更低级,但是在智力方面却超越他们太多,因为他们都很努力,受过良好的教育,富有而且知道如何去管理他们的社会。

我自己在加拿大,这里人种之间智力的差别不明显,就见到英国人支配着这里的制造业和商业。他们的范围涉及各个行业,将法国人局限在很小的范围内,勉强能维持温饱。路易斯安那州的情况也相似,也是英裔美国人处于支配地位。

但是,在得克萨斯州,这种现象更明显:得克萨斯只占墨西哥的一部分,而且位于其与美国交界的地方。在过去的一些年中,英国人已在这里居住,尽管这里现在人口依然很稀少。他们购买土地,生产这个国家所用的商品,排挤当地人。我们几乎可以预见,如果莫斯科不采取措施制止这种现象,得克萨斯将很快就不属于他们了。如果这种差别,与欧洲人民情况相比,相对来说不那么明显,那么我们就很容易理解,当优异的欧洲文明与印第安蛮夷交往的时候,会发生什么样的结果。

their greatest undertakings; but nations as well as men require time to learn, whatever may be their intelligence and their zeal. While the savages were endeavoring to civilize themselves, the Europeans continued to surround them on every side and to confine them within narrower limits; the two races gradually met, and they are now in immediate contact with each other. The Indian is already superior to his barbarous parent, but he is still far below his white neighbor. With their resources and acquired knowledge, the Europeans soon appropriated to themselves most of the advantages that the natives might have derived from the possession of the soil: they have settled among them, have purchased land at a low rate, or have occupied it by force, and the Indians have been ruined by a competition which they had not the means of sustaining. They were isolated in their own country, and their race constituted only a little colony of troublesome strangers in the midst of a numerous and dominant people. ①

Washington said in one of his messages to Congress: "We are more enlightened and more powerful than the Indian nations; we are therefore bound in honor to treat them with kindness, and even with generosity." But this virtuous and high-minded policy has not been followed. The rapacity of the settlers is usually backed by the tyranny of the government. Although the Cherokees and the Creeks are established upon territory which they in habited before the arrival of the

---

① See in the *Legislative Documents* (21st Congress, No. 89) instances of excesses of every kind committed by the whites upon the territory of the Indians, either in taking possession of a part of their lands, until compelled to retire by federal troops, or carrying off their cattle, burning their houses, cutting down their corn, and doing violence to their persons. The Union has a representative agent continually employed to reside among the Indians; and the report of the Cherokee agent, which is among the documents I have referred to, is almost always favorable to the Indians. "The intrusion of whites," he says, "upon the lands of the Cherokees will cause ruin to the poor, helpless, and inoffensive inhabitants." And he further remarks upon the attempt of the state of Georgia to establish a boundary line for the country of the Cherokees that the line, having been made by the whites alone, and entirely upon exparte evidence of their several rights, was of no validity whatever.

在他们的大事业上表现出的天才毫无二致。但是,民族同个人一样,无关乎其智力和热情,都需要时间来学习。在野蛮人努力学习文明开化的时候,欧洲人则继续从四面八方包围他们,并逐渐缩小范围。这两个民族终于相会,并直接接触了。印第安人比起他们的蛮夷祖先已进步很多,但他们与他们的白人邻居比起来就逊色多了。欧洲人凭借自己的资源和学习的知识,很快就夺取了大部分土著因占有土地才能得到的好处:他们定居在土著人之中,用低价购买土著的土地,或者干脆用武力强占。土著人在这场根本毫无招架之力的竞争中一败涂地。印第安人在自己的土地上被孤立了起来。他们生活在一个人数众多并占有统治地位的民族之中,而这个民族认为他们构成了一个不够安分守己的异族殖民地。①

华盛顿在他给国会的一份报告中说过:"我们远比印第安诸部更文明、更强大;因此,为了我们的荣誉,我们必须对他们友善,甚至宽容。"但是,这一高尚而合乎道德的政策,并没有被遵守。殖民者的贪婪,常常以政府的专制为庇护。尽管早在欧洲人没有到来以前,柴罗基部和克里克部就在这片土地上定居,而且美国

---

① 见《立法文件》(第21次国会第89号),白人允许在印第安人的领土上实施的各种行径,包括在联邦部队强迫他们撤退之前,占有他们的部分土地,抢夺他们的牲畜、烧毁他们的房屋、收割他们的粮食并且对他们的人民施以暴政。联邦设有代表机构,长期居住在印第安人之中。柴罗基部代表处的报告,也就是我说的其中之一,其内容几乎总是有利于印第安人的。其中写道"白人侵入柴罗基部,就会对穷人、无依无靠和那些毫无危害性的居民带来伤害。"并且,他进一步说明,乔治亚州企图对柴罗基部划定疆域,而这一界限仅由白人规定,并且他们完全没有任何合法效力或者任何有权这么作的证明。

Europeans, and although the Americans have frequently treated with them as with foreign nations, the surrounding states have not been willing to acknowledge them as an independent people and have undertaken to subject these children of the woods to Anglo-American magistrates, laws, and customs. ①Destitution had driven these unfortunate Indians to civilization, and oppression now drives them back to barbarism: many of them abandon the soil which they had begun to clear and return to the habits of savage life.

If we consider the tyrannical measures that have been adopted by the legislatures of the Southern states, the conduct of their governors, and the decrees of their courts of justice, we shall be convinced that the entire expulsion of the Indians is the final result to which all the efforts of their policy are directed. The Americans of that part of the Union look with jealousy upon the lands which the natives still possess; ②they are aware that these tribes have not yet lost the traditions of savage life, and before civilization has permanently fixed them to the soil it is intended to force them to depart by reducing them to despair. The Creeks and Cherokees, oppressed by the several states, have appealed to the central government, which is by no means insensible to their misfortunes and is sincerely desirous of saving the remnant of the natives and of maintaining them in the free possession of that territory which the Union has guaranteed to them. ③But when it seeks to carry out this plan, the several states set up a tremendous

---

① In 1829 the state of Alabama divided the Creek territory into counties and subjected the Indian population to European magistrates.

In 1830 the state of Mississippi assimilated the Choctaws and Chickasaws to the white population and declared that any of them who should take the title of chief would be punished by a fine of 1,000 dollars and a year's imprisonment. When these laws were announced to the Choctaws who inhab ited that district, the tribe assembled, their chief communicated to them the intentions of the whites and read to them some of the laws to which it was intended that they should submit, and they unanimously declared that it was better at once to retreat again into the wilds. (Mississippi *Papers.*)

② The Georgians, who are so much troubled by the proximity of the Indians, inhabit a territory that does not at present contain more than seven inhabitants to the square mile. In France there are one hundred and sixtytwo inhabitants in the same extent of country.

③ In 1818 Congress appointed commissioners to visit the Arkansas territory, accompanied by a deputation of Creeks, Choctaws, and Chickasaws. This expedition was commanded by Messrs. Kennerly, M'Coy, Wash Hood, and John Bell. See the different reports of the commissioners and their journal in the *Documents of Congress*, No. 87, House of Representatives.

人也总是把他们当外族人对待,但他们周边的各州都一直不愿意承认他们是独立的民族,并强迫这些刚从森林里走出来定居的人服从本州的管理、法律和民情。① 贫困曾使这些不幸的印第安人走向文明,而压迫现在又把他们往回赶。许多人于是放弃了已开始开垦的土地,而重回其野蛮人的生活。

如果我们对南部各州的立法机构采取的暴虐措施稍加思考,对那些州的政府官员的行径和法院的判例稍加考虑,我们就会确信:这些州的所有政策的一致指向,就是将印第安人完全驱逐出境。住在联邦这一地区的美国人,②贪婪地注视着仍被土著们占据着的土地。他们认识到这些土著人还没有放弃野蛮人的生活习惯,所以,他们想在文明使这些人安心于耕种之前,就迫使他们因绝望而远离这里。被这几个州压迫的克里克族和柴罗基族向中央政府申诉。中央政府并没有对他们的不幸置若罔闻,并且衷心希望拯救这些残存的土著,使他们获得联邦曾允诺他们的土地的自由拥有权力。③ 但当

---

① 1829 年,阿拉巴马州将克里克族的领土分为了几个县,并且将印第安人口划归欧洲行政管辖。

1830 年,密西西比州将巧克陶族和契卡索人纳入白人人口,并宣称他们如果自立酋长便罚款 1000 美元,并监禁 1 年。当这些法律公布于居住在那里的巧克陶族时,这些部落聚集在了一起,他们的首领向大家讲明了白人的企图,并且读了一些他们今后要遵守的有关法律,当即他们全体一致通过,认为这样好过把他们再次推回到蛮夷之地。(《密西西比报》。)

② 因为与印第安人的亲密接触而惹来众多麻烦的乔治亚人,如今居住的地方,每平方里只有 7 个居民。在法国,同样面积的土地上居住着 162 个居民。

③ 1818 年,国会派遣代表团前去阿肯色州视察,同去的还有由克里克族、乔克托族和契卡索族人组成的代表团。这支代表团是受肯纳利先生、科伊先生、沃什胡德先生和琼贝尔先生的指派前去的。见国会中不同的专员报告和他们的日记,第 87 号,众议院。

resistance, and so it makes up its mind not to take the easier way, and to let a few savage tribes perish, since they are already half-decimated, in order not to endanger the safety of the American Union.

But the Federal government, which is not able to protect the Indians, would fain mitigate the hardships of their lot; and with this intention it has undertaken to transport them into remote regions at the public cost.

Between the 33rd and 37th degrees of north latitude lies a vast tract of country that has taken the name of Arkansas, from the principal river that waters it. It is bounded on one side by the confines of Mexico, on the other by the Mississippi. Numberless streams cross it in every direction; the climate is mild and the soil productive, and it is inhabited only by a few wandering hordes of savages. The government of the Union wishes to transport the broken remnants of the indigenous population of the South to the portion of this country that is nearest to Mexico and at a great distance from the American settlements.

We were assured, towards the end of the year 1831, that 10,000 Indians had already gone to the shores of the Arkansas, and fresh detachments were constantly following them. But Congress has been unable to create a unanimous determination in those whom it is disposed to protect. Some, indeed, joyfully consent to quit the seat of oppression; but the most enlightened members of the community refuse to abandon their recent dwellings and their growing crops; they are of opinion that the work of civilization, once interrupted, will never be resumed; they fear that those domestic habits which have been so recently contracted may be irrevocably lost in the midst of a country that is still barbarous and where nothing is prepared for the subsistence of an agricultural people; they know that their entrance into those wilds will be opposed by hostile hordes, and that they have lost the energy of barbarians without having yet acquired the resources of civilization to resist their attacks. Moreover, the Indians readily discover that the settlement which is proposed to them is merely temporary. Who can

开始着手实施这项计划时,那几个州却坚决地抵制。于是,中央政府为了不使美国联邦陷入危机,就想,既然那几个部落已几乎毁灭,不如就任由他们灭亡。

但是,没能保护印第安人的联邦政府,后来也曾企图减轻他们的苦难。怀着这样的意图,他们决定由政府出钱把这些印第安人迁往偏远的地方。

在北纬33°和37°之间,有一片广阔的土地,因流经域内的一条大河的名字,而被称为阿肯色。它一侧与墨西哥接壤,另一侧濒临密西西比河。其境内河流纵横交错,气候温和,土壤肥沃,只有几个野蛮的游牧部落居住在那里。联邦政府就想把南部土著的残余,迁到这个毗邻墨西哥并且远离美国白人居住地的地方。

接近1831年底,已有一万多名印第安人来到阿肯色河两岸,并且陆续有新人前来。但是,对于这些需要得到保护的人们,国会对他们的处置意见并不一致。于是,一部分印第安人很高兴离开被白人欺压的地方;但是,一些已经接受开化的印第安人,却不愿放弃他们的新居和种在地里的庄稼。因为他们认为,接受文明的进程一旦中断,便永远无法恢复。他们担心,到了那片仍旧荒夷的地方后,会使他们永远遗失刚刚养成的定居生活习惯,因为那里还没有任何农夫生活所需的必须条件。他们知道,他们到了新的荒凉地区,将会遇到一些敌对部落,而他们已丧失了野蛮人的体力,又还没能有文明人的智力。他们无力抵抗。然而,到了新地点后,印第安人很快就发现,为他们所做的一切安排也只是临时性的。谁能担保他们在这次新的迁徙后可以平平安安地生

assure them that they will at length be allowed to dwell in peace in their new retreat? The United States pledges itself to maintain them there, but the territory which they now occupy was formerly secured to them by the most solemn oaths. ①The American gov ernment does not indeed now rob them of their lands, but it al lows perpetual encroachments on them. In a few years the same white population that now flocks around them will doubtless track them anew to the solitudes of the Arkansas; they will then be exposed to the same evils, without the same remedies; and as the limits of the earth will at last fail them, their only refuge is the grave. The Union treats the Indians with less cupidity and violence than the several states, but the two governments are alike deficient in good faith. The states extend what they call the benefits of their laws to the Indians, believing that the tribes will re-cede rather than submit to them; and the central government, which promises a permanent refuge to these unhappy beings in the West, is well aware of its inability to secure it to them. ②Thus the tyranny of the states obliges the savages to retire; the Union, by its

---

① One finds in the treaty made with the Creeks in 1790 this clause: "The United States solemnly guarantee to the Creek nation all their land within the limits of the United States. "

The treaty concluded in 1791 with the Cherokees states: "The United States solemnly guarantee to the Cherokee nation all their lands not hereby ceded. If any citizen of the United States, or other settler not of the Indian race, establishes himself upon the territory of the Cherokees, the United States declare that they will withdraw their protection from that individual, and give him up to be punished as the Cherokee nation thinks fit. " (Art. 8.)

② This does not prevent them from promising in the most solemn manner to do so. See the letter of the President addressed to the Creek Indians, March 23, 1829 (*Proceedings of the Indian Board in the City of New York*, p. 5): "Beyond the great river Mississippi, where a part of your nation has gone, your father has provided a country large enough for all of you, and he advises you to remove to it. There your white brothers will not trouble you; they will have no claim to the land, and you can live upon it, you and all your children, as long as the grass grows, or the water runs, in peace and plenty. It will be yours forever. "

The Secretary of War in a letter written to the Cherokees, April 18, 1829, declares to them that they cannot expect to retain possession of the lands at that time occupied by them, but gives them the most positive assurance of uninterrupted peace if they would remove beyond the Mississippi (ibid. , p. 6); as if the power which could not grant them protection then would be able to afford it to them hereafter!

活下去呢？美国政府答应到那里后保护他们，①但美国政府也曾信誓旦旦地对他们现在所在的地区做过同样的保证。美国政府现在的确没有抢夺他们的土地，但它却听任别人去侵占。再过几年，现在聚集在他们周围的这伙白人，毫无疑问又会追随着他们的脚印，再次侵占阿肯色的荒原。那时，他们将会遭到同样的苦难，却再没有新的土地供他们迁徙。土地迟早要从他们手中夺走，而他们唯一的避难所只有自己的墓冢。联邦政府不像其他一些州那样贪婪和暴虐地对待印第安人。但是，联邦政府和州政府却都不怎么守信用。这些州在把它们所谓的法律恩典施于印第安人时，就已预料到印第安人宁愿远走他乡，也不愿意受这些法律的束缚；而中央政府在给这些不幸的人在西部安排永久住所时，也很清楚它并不能保证他们永久住下去。② 因此，可以说各州全是暴政迫使野蛮人远离；而联邦政府则利用它的诺言和土地，

---

① 有人在 1790 年与克里克族签订的协议中找到这样的条款：“美国允诺克里克族，所有在美国范围内属于他们的土地。”

这一协议签订于 1791 年，克里克族宣称：“美国向克里克族保证，所有他们的土地决不放弃。如果美国任何公民，或者其他非印第安种族的居民在属于克里克族的土地上定居，美国须公开声明，放弃对任何人的保护措施，交由克里克族酌情处置。”（第八章。）

② 这并没有阻止他们用最庄严的形势允诺会这样去做。见 1829 年 3 月 23 日总统对克里克族印第安人信中写道：“在密西西比河上游，克拉克族的一部分居民已经离去，你们父辈们建造了一座足够容纳你们所有人的国家，并且建议你们搬迁到那里去。在那里，你们的白人伙伴不会去打扰你们；他们也不会去索要你们的这块土地，你们和你们的子孙可以在上面尽情地、和平并富足地居住。这块土地将永远属于你们。”

1829 年 4 月 18 日，陆军部长又给克里克族写了一封信，信中声称他们不希望拥有那块他们曾经居住的土地的所有权，但同时又肯定地允诺他们，如果他们愿意迁移到密西西比州上游的地区，就会得到不受侵扰的和平。如果他们的力量不能给他们以保护，则会对他们给予偿付。

promises and resources, facilitates their retreat; and these measures tend to precisely the same end. [1]

"By the will of our Father in heaven, the Governor of the whole world," said the Cherokees in their petition to Congress, [2]" the red man of America has become small, and the white man great and renowned. When the ancestors of the people of these United States first came to the shores of America, they found the red man strong: though he was ignorant and savage, yet he received them kindly and gave them dry land to rest their weary feet. They met in peace and shook hands in token of friendship. Whatever the white man wanted and asked of the Indian, the latter willingly gave. At that time the Indian was the lord, and the white man the suppliant. But now the scene has changed. The strength of the red man has become weakness. As his neighbors increased in numbers, his power became less and less; and now, of the many and powerful tribes who once covered these United States, only a few are to be seen—a few whom a sweeping pestilence has left. The Northern tribes, who were once so numerous and powerful, are now nearly extinct. Thus it has happened to the red man in America. Shall we, who are remnants, share the same fate?

"The land on which we stand we have received as an inheritance from our fathers, who possessed it from time immemorial, as a gift from our common Father in heaven. They bequeathed it to us as their children, and we have sacredly kept it, as containing the remains of our beloved men. This right of inheritance we have never ceded nor ever forfeited. Permit us to ask what better right can the people have to a country than the right of in heritance and immemorial peaceable

---

① To obtain a correct idea of the policy pursued by the several states and the Union with respect to the Indians, it is necessary to consult: (1) "The Laws of the Colonial and State Governments relating to the Indian Inhabitants" (see Legislative Documents, 21st Congress, No. 319); (2) "The Laws of the Union on the same subject, and especially that of March 30th, 1802" (these laws will be found in the work of Mr. Story entitled Laws of the United States); (3) "The Report of Mr. Cass, Secretary of War, relative to Indian Affairs, November 29th, 1823."

② November 19, 1829. This item is literally translated.

促使这些土著不得不退缩。他们所采取的措施,其目的都是一致的。① 柴罗基部在它提交国会的请愿书中说道:②

"奉我们的天父,宇宙的统治者的旨意,美洲的红色人种越来越少,而白色人种则变得强大并盛名远负。当美国人的祖先首次登上美洲的海岸时,红色人种是强大的;尽管红色人当时野蛮无知,但却友善地接待了他们,并让出陆地供他们疲劳的双脚休息。我们的先人和土著的先人当时和平相处。无论白人提出什么要求,印第安人都欣然允诺。当时,印第安人是施主,而白人是乞者。而如今局面变了:红色人种的力量削弱了。随着邻人数量的增加,红色人的权力越来越小了。昔日布满你们称谓的合众国各地的许多强大部落,而今幸存的已屈指可数——许多已如肆虐的瘟疫般消失殆尽。往昔在我们当中曾以强大著称的北方诸部落,如今已几尽灭绝。这就是美洲红色人种至今的遭遇。我们这些幸免于难的红色人种,也会遭遇同样的境地吗?

"从无法追忆的远古起,我们共同的祖先就拥有了我们现在占据的这块土地,然后他把这块土地给了我们的先人,我们先人又把它作为遗产传给了我们。我们怀着尊敬的心情保有着这块土地,因为这里埋藏着先人的遗骨。我们从未放弃或丧失这一继承的权力。请允许我们冒昧地问一句:还有什么权力比继承权和自古以来和平占有的权力具有更充分的理由,可使一个民族拥有

---

① 为了得到这些州和联邦对待印第安人所采用的政策的正确思想,很有必要参考以下条款:(1)"殖民地和州政府对于印第安居民的法律条款";(2)"联邦在这一主题上的法律,尤其是 1802 年 3 月 30 日的";(3)"卡斯先生,印第安诸事,1823 年 11 月 29 日"。

② 1829 年 11 月 19 日,这一条款被逐字翻译。

possession? We know it is said of late by the state of Georgia and by the Executive of the United States that we have forfeited this right; but we think this is said gratuitously. At what time have we made the forfeit? What great crime have we committed whereby we must forever be di vested of our country and rights? Was it when we were hostile to the United States and took part with the King of Great Britain during the struggle for independence? If so, why was not this forfeiture declared in the first treaty of peace between the United States and our beloved men? Why was not such an article as the following inserted in the treaty: "The United States give peace to the Cherokees, but, for the part they took in the late war, declare them to be but tenants at will, to be removed when the convenience of the states within whose chartered limits they live shall require it? That was the proper time to assume such a possession. But it was not thought of; nor would our forefathers have agreed to any treaty whose tendency was to deprive them of their rights and their country. "

Such is the language of the Indians: what they say is true; what they foresee seems inevitable. From whichever side we consider the destinies of the aborigines of North America, their calamities appear irremediable: if they continue barbarous, they are forced to retire; if they attempt to civilize themselves, the contact of a more civilized community subjects them to oppression and destitution. They perish if they continue to wander from waste to waste, and if they attempt to settle they still must perish. The assistance of Europeans is necessary to instruct them, but the approach of Europeans corrupts and repels them into savage life. They refuse to change their habits as long as their solitudes are their own, and it is too late to change them when at last they are forced to submit.

The Spaniards pursued the Indians with bloodhounds, like wild beasts; they sacked the New World like a city taken by storm, with no discernment or compassion; but destruction must cease at last and

一片国土呢？我们知道后来佐治亚州和合众国总统说我们已经丧失了这项权利。但我们认为这种说法毫无根据。我们在什么时候丧失了它？我们犯了什么可使我们丧失这项权利的罪行？是因为我们在独立战争时期曾站在联合大不列颠国王一边与你们兵戎相见吗？假如你们说这就是罪行，那么，为什么在这次战争后签订的第一个条约中，你们没有指出我们已经丧失对我们土地的所有权呢？你们当时为什么没有在这项条约中加进'合众国愿意同柴罗基部讲和，但为了惩罚它曾在战争即将结束时参入，现郑重宣布：今后只把柴罗基部视为土地的出租户，当与柴罗基部接壤的州要求它撤走时，它必须服从而离开'这样的条款呢？那时你们原可以这样说，但当时你们谁也没有想到这一点，况且，我们的先人也未曾同意过任何会使他们丧失最神圣的权利和失去他们的土地的条约。"

这就是印第安人所说的话：他们所说的都是实话；而他们所预见的事也仿佛不可避免。无论我们从哪一方面去考虑北美土著人的命运，他们的灭顶之灾都似乎无法弥补：如果他们继续保持野蛮，则会被步步紧逼；如果他们想要变得文明开化，而与比他们更加文明的人打交道，就只有使自己受压迫变得更贫困；而继续从一块荒野飘泊到另一块荒野，结果只会灭亡；可是即使想定居下来，也难逃灭亡。他们需要欧洲人的指引，但欧洲人的来临，却使他们的处境恶化，又把他们赶回到野蛮生活中去。他们拒绝改变他们的习俗，只要他们的荒野还在自己的掌握之中。而最终，当他们不得不屈服的时候来了，要改变他们又太迟了。

西班牙人曾用猎犬像追捕野兽那样去追赶印第安人。他们像摧毁一座城市那样洗劫了新大陆，没有任何分辨，不带任何怜

frenzy has a limit: the remnant of the Indian population which had escaped the massacre mixed with its conquerors and adopted in the end their religion and their manners. ①The conduct of the Americans of the United States towards the aborigines is characterized, on the other hand, by a singular attachment to the formalities of law. Provided that the Indians retain their barbarous condition, the Americans take no part in their affairs; they treat them as independent nations and do not possess themselves of their hunting-grounds without a treaty of purchase; and if an Indian nation happens to be so encroached upon as to be unable to subsist upon their territory, they kindly take them by the hand and transport them to a grave far from the land of their fathers.

The Spaniards were unable to exterminate the Indian race by those unparalleled atrocities which brand them with indelible shame, nor did they succeed even in wholly depriving it of its rights; but the Americans of the United States have accomplished this twofold purpose with singular felicity, tranquilly, legally, philanthropically, without shedding blood, and without violating a single great principle of morality in the eyes of the world. ②It is impossible to destroy men with more respect for the laws of humanity.

---

① The honor of this result, however, is by no means due to the Spaniards. If the Indian tribes had not been tillers of the ground at the time of the arrival of the Europeans, they would unquestionably have been destroyed in South as well as in North America.

② See, among other documents, the Report made by Mr. Bell in the name of the Committee on Indian Affairs, February 24, 1830, in which it is most logically established and most learnedly proved that "the fundamental principle; that the Indians had no right, by virtue of their ancient possession, either r of soil or sovereignty, has never been abandoned either expressly or by implication. "

In perusing this Report, which is evidently drawn up by a skillful hand, one is astonished at the facility with which the author gets rid of all argu ments founded upon reason and natural right, which he designates as abstract and theoretical principles. The more I contemplate the difference between civilized and uncivilized man with regard to the principles of justice, the more I observe that the former contests the foundation of those rights, which the latter simply violates.

悯;但摧残总有结束的一天,疯狂也有限度:在大屠杀中幸存的印第安人残余,与他们的征服者融为一体,并最终接受了他们的宗教和生活方式。[①] 而另一方面,美国人对待土著的态度,有些受到法律的约束。只要印第安人愿意保持他们的野蛮状态,美国人决不干预他们的事务。他们像对待独立的民族那样对待他们,在按照条约中规定的手续购买以前,决不允许任何人占有印第安人的土地。当某一印第安部落因被侵占无以生存时,美国人会把他们送到远离故土的地方,让他们在那里自消自灭。

西班牙甘冒天下之大不韪,使自己臭名昭著,以史无前例的残酷手段,也未能灭绝印第安种族,甚至未能完全剥夺印第安人的权利。而美国人用十分巧妙的手段,不慌不忙,合情合理,慈善为怀,没有战争,不被世人认为是违反伟大的道德原则的情况下,[②]达到了双重目的。再无可能以尊重人道的法律的办法消灭人。

----

①　尽管如此,这一结果的荣耀决不能归功于西班牙人。如果印第安部落在欧洲人入侵的时候并没有在这片土地上耕种过,他们必然像在北美洲一样早已灭亡了。

②　见其他文件中,贝尔先生以国会委员的身份于 1830 年 2 月 24 日就印第安诸事的报告,这件事得以符合逻辑最清楚地证实"基础的原则,凭借他们的祖先拥有的美德,印第安人没有得到任何权利,无论是土地或主权,都没有很清楚明确或含混的被放弃过。"

在获取这份很明显出自一位很老练的人之手的报告的过程中,人们惊讶地发现,作者摆脱掉了所有建立在合理和自然权利的基础之上的一切以抽象理性为原则的争论。我越是公正地思索文明国家和不文明国家的人们之间的差别,就越是发现,前者争夺这些权利的基础,而后者只是简单的对其加以违犯。

Situation Of The Black Population In The United States, And Dangers With Which It's Presence Threatens The Whites[①]

Why it is more difficult to abolish slavery, and to efface all vestiges of it among the moderns than it was among the ancients—In the United States the prejudices of the whites against the blacks seem to increase in proportion as slavery is abolished-Situation of the Negroes in the Northern and Southern states—Why the Americans abolish slavery—Servitude, which de bases the slave, impoverishes the master—Contrast between the left and the right bank of the Ohio—To what attributable-The black race, as well as slavery, recedes towards the South—Explanation of this fact – – Difficulties attendant upon the abolition of slavery in the South—Dangers to come—General anxiety—Foundation of a black colony in Africa—Why the Americans of the South increase the hardships of slavery while they are distressed at its continuance.

The Indians will perish in the same isolated condition in which they have lived, but the destiny of the Negroes is in some measure interwoven with that of the Europeans. These two races are fastened to each other without intermingling; and they are alike unable to separate entirely or to combine. The most formidable of all the ills that threaten the future of the Union arises from the presence of a black

---

① Before treating of this matter, I would call the reader's attention to a book of which I spoke at the beginning of this work, and which is about to be published. The chief aim of M. Gustave de Beaumont, my traveling-companion, was to inform Frenchmen of the position of the Negroes among the white population in the United States. M. de Beaumont has plumbed the depths of a question which my subject has allowed me merely to touch upon.

His book, the notes to which contain a great number of legislative and historical documents, extremely valuable and heretofore unpublished, furthermore presents pictures the vividness of which is ample proof of their verity. M. de Beaumont's book should be read by all those who would know into what excesses men may be driven when once they attempt to go against natural and human laws.

黑色人种在美国的处境和
他们的存在给白人带来的危险[①]

　　为什么废除蓄奴制和消除其存在过的一切痕迹在现代比古代更为困难——在美国，白人对黑人的偏见似乎是随着蓄奴制的废除而日益加深的——黑人在北方和南方各州的地位——美国人为什么要废除蓄奴制——使奴隶致蠢的奴役不再能使奴隶主发财致富——俄亥俄河左岸和右岸之间出现的差异——这种差异应归因于什么——随黑色人种向南方退却蓄奴制也向南方转移——怎样解释这一现象——在南方废除蓄奴制时所遇到的困难——将来的危险——人们的普遍忧虑——在非洲建立一个黑人殖民地——为什么南方的美国人在厌恶蓄奴制的同时反而加剧了这种制度的残酷性。

　　印第安人将在孤立状态中灭亡，如同他们在孤立中生存一样。但是，黑人的命运却从某种意义上，总与白人的命运交织在一起。这两个种族互相联系却不相混合。它们似乎既不能完全分开，也不会完全结合。在威胁美国未来的一切灾难中，最可怕的灾难起因于黑人在他们的国土上的出现。在考察美国目前困

————————

　　① 处理这件事之前，我想先提醒读者注意我在这本书最初提到的一本书，这本书即将出版发行。波蒙特的主要目的，我对旅游的热情，都是为了告诉法国人民黑人在美国白人中的地位。波蒙特曾探测过我的主题允许我在这个问题上探究的深度。

　　他的书，注释中包含了很多立法和历史的文献资料，更重要的是，运用大量的例证生动地展示了事实的真相。波蒙特的书适合那些希望了解一旦人们想要违反自然惯例和人类的法律的时候，人们将会被带入什么样的境地的读者。

population upon its territory; and in contem plating the cause of the present embarrassments, or the future dangers of the United States, the observer is invariably led to this as a primary fact.

Generally speaking, men must make great and unceasing efforts before permanent evils are created; but there is one calamity which penetrated furtively into the world, and which was at first scarcely distinguishable amid the ordinary abuses of power: it originated with an individual whose name history has not preserved; it was wafted like some accursed germ upon a portion of the soil; but it afterwards nurtured itself, grew without effort, and spread naturally with the society to which it belonged. This calamity is slavery. Christianity suppressed slavery, but the Christians of the sixteenth century re-established it, as an exception, indeed, to their social system, and restricted to one of the races of mankind; but the wound thus inflicted upon humanity, though less extensive, was far more difficult to cure.

It is important to make an accurate distinction between slavery itself and its consequences. The immediate evils produced by slavery were very nearly the same in antiquity as they are among the moderns, but the consequences of these evils were different. The slave among the ancients belonged to the same race as his master, and was often the superior of the two in education①and intelligence. Freedom was the only distinction between them; and when freedom was conferred, they were easily confounded together. The ancients, then, had a very simple means of ridding themselves of slavery and its consequences: that of enfranchisement; and they succeeded as soon as they adopted this measure generally. Not but that in ancient states the vestiges of servitude subsisted for some time after servitude itself was abolished. There is a natural prejudice that prompts men to despise whoever has been their inferior long after he has become their equal; and the real inequality that is produced by fortune or by law is always succeeded by an imaginary inequality that is implanted in the

---

① It is well known that several of the most distinguished authors of antiquity, and among them sop and Terence, were, or had been, slaves. Slaves were not always taken from barbarous nations; the chances of war reduced highly civilized men to servitude.

境和未来危险的原因时,观察家们最后总是一致地引出这一主要
事实。

一般说来,那些永久性的灾难的出现,总是人们拼命追求所
导致的结果。但是,有一种灾难却是悄悄地降临于世界上的:最
初,它出现于日常的滥用权力之中,微不可觉,源起于一个历史上
没有留下名字的人之手;仿佛被诅咒的病菌一般,在大地的一点
上滋生出并四处蔓延。经过自身的繁殖,毫不费力地四外蔓延,
并随着它所在社会的发展自然地成长起来。这个灾难就是蓄奴
制。基督教起初禁止了奴役,而到了 16 世纪的基督教徒又把它
恢复了。他们仅仅是作为对于他们的社会体系一种例外,而将其
限制在了全人类的这一种族之中。但是,这种创伤却涉及了全人
类,尽管不如以前广泛,但却更难以治愈。

准确的区分蓄奴制本身和蓄奴制所造成的后果是很重要的。
蓄奴制造成的直接灾难,在古代和现代大致一样;但这些灾难的
后果却不尽相同。在古代,奴隶与其主人属于同一种族,而且奴
隶的教育和知识水平往往高于他的主人。① 他们之间的唯一差别
在于有无自由。一旦给与奴隶自由,二者就会很容易融为一体。
因此,在古代,要消除奴隶制以及其产生的影响很容易,那就是解
放奴隶。而且,他们一旦普遍采取这个办法,就会获得成功。但
在古代,取消奴役以后,奴役的痕迹还继续存在一个时期。人们
看不起比自己地位低的人,即使这些人已与自己平等,有很长一
段时间,他们还是会看不起这些人。这是人天生的习性。由财富

---

① 大家都知道,古代一些最著名的作家都是或曾经是奴隶。奴隶并不
都是来自蛮夷之地。战争使一些受过教育的人们也沦为了奴隶。

manners of the people. But among the ancients this secondary consequence of slavery had a natural limit; for the freedman bore so entire a resemblance to those born free that it soon became impossible to distinguish him from them.

The greatest difficulty in antiquity was that of altering the law; among the moderns it is that of altering the customs, and as far as we are concerned, the real obstacles begin where those of the ancients left off. This arises from the circumstance that among the moderns the abstract and transient fact of slavery is fatally united with the physical and permanent fact of color. The tradition of slavery dishonors the race, and the peculiarity of the race perpetuates the tradition of slavery. No African has ever voluntarily emigrated to the shores of the New World, whence it follows that all the blacks who are now found there are either slaves or freedmen. Thus the Negro transmits the eternal mark of his ignominy to all his descendants; and although the law may abolish slavery, God alone can obliterate the traces of its existence.

The modern slave differs from his master not only in his condition but in his origin. You may set the Negro free, but you cannot make him otherwise than an alien to the European. Nor is this all; we scarcely acknowledge the common features of humanity in this stranger whom slavery has brought among us. His physiognomy is to our eyes hideous, his understanding weak, his tastes low; and we are almost inclined to look upon him as a being inter mediate between man and the brutes. ①The moderns, then, after they have abolished slavery, have three prejudices to contend against, which are less easy to attack and far less easy to conquer than the mere fact of servitude: the prejudice of the master, the prejudice of the race, and the prejudice of color.

It is difficult for us, who have had the good fortune to be born among men like ourselves by nature and our equals by law, to conceive

① To induce the whites to abandon the opinion they have conceived of the moral and intellectual inferiority of their former slaves, the Negroes must change; but as long as this opinion persists, they cannot change.

或法律造成的不平等,总是伴随着一种假想的不平等存在于民情之中。但在古代,奴役的这种附加影响是有限制的。奴隶一旦获得自由,就将与生来自由的人完全一样,无法再将二者加以区分。

在古代,最大困难在于改变法律,放在现代就在于改变民情;而就我们所知,我们现代人存在的困难都起因于古代人遗留的问题。这是因为,在现代,蓄奴制的抽象性和短暂性被不幸地与有形的和长期的种族压迫结合在了一起。蓄奴制使一些种族遭受耻辱,而这些种族又无法摆脱他们的这一特质。没有一个非洲人是自愿迁徙到新大陆的海岸的,并且他们要么是奴隶,要么是被解放了的奴隶。因此,黑人将其永恒的耻辱传给了他们的后代。尽管法律可以废除奴役,而只有上帝才能够抹去奴役存在过的痕迹。

现代奴隶与奴隶主的区别,不仅在于他们所处的环境,而且在于他们的本源。你可以使黑人获得自由,但你无法使白人不把他们当做异族。不仅如此;我们几乎不会认为这些异族具有人类一般的特性,因为他们是以奴隶身份进入我们之间的。我们会觉得他们的面貌丑陋,智力低下,品味庸俗,我们几乎把他们视为介于人兽之间的生物。① 因此,现代人在废除蓄奴制以后,还有三个比蓄奴制还难对付更难克服的顽固偏见,这就是奴隶主的偏见、种族的偏见和肤色的偏见。

我们有幸出生在与自己同族的人群中并在出生时就被赋予

---

① 为了促使被人放弃他们持有的认为他们先前的奴隶在道德和智力方面低下的观念,黑人必须有所变化,但是这种观念一旦形成,就很难被改变。

the irreconcilable differences that separate the Negro from the European in America. But we may derive some faint notion of them from analogy. France was formerly a country in which numerous inequalities existed that had been created by law. Nothing can be more fictitious than a purely legal inferiority, nothing more contrary to the instinct of mankind than these permanent divisions establlished between beings evidently similar. Yet these divisions existed for ages; they still exist in many places; and everywhere they have left imaginary vestiges, which time alone can efface. If it be so difficult to root out an inequality that originates solely in the law, how are those distinctions to be destroyed which seem to be based upon the immutable laws of Nature herself? When I remember the extreme difficulty with which aristocratic bodies, of whatever nature they may be, are commingled with the mass of the people, and the exceeding care which they take to preserve for ages the ideal boundaries of their caste inviolate, I despair of seeing an aristocracy disappear which is founded upon visible and indelible signs. Those who hope that the Europeans will ever be amalgamated with the Negroes appear to me to delude themselves. I am not led to any such conclusion by my reason or by the evidence of facts. Hitherto wherever the whites have been the most powerful, they have held the blacks in degradation or in slavery; wherever the Negroes have been strongest, they have destroyed the whites: this has been the only balance that has ever taken place between the two races.

I see that in a certain portion of the territory of the United States at the present day the legal barrier which separated the two races is falling away, but not that which exists in the manners of the country; slavery recedes, but the prejudice to which it hasgiven birth is immovable. Whoever has inhabited the United States must have perceived that in those parts of the Union in which the Negroes are no longer slaves they have in no wise drawn nearer to the whites. On the contrary, the prejudice of race appears to be stronger in the states that have abolished slavery than in those where it still exists; and nowhere is it so intolerant as in those states where servitude has never been known.

了和其他人一样的平等地位,这就是我们很难理解美国黑人与欧洲人之间不可调和的矛盾。但是,我们可以用类比推理的办法,得出一个大致不会离谱的看法。在我们国家,曾经有过一些由于立法而所造成的较大的不平等。再没有任何东西比完全由法律规定的尊卑更荒诞。再没有比在同类人之间建立的永恒差别更大的对人性的违反。但是,这些区别却存在了许多世纪,而且现在许多地方仍然存在,而那些假象在各处遗留的痕迹,唯有时间可以抹去。如果纯由法律规定的不平等都如此难于根除,那么,怎样才能消除那种似乎是由永恒的自然规律造成的差别呢?当我想起一些贵族团体,不管它们具有哪种性质,在与人民大众融合方面存在极大困难的时候;当我想起这些贵族团体,苦心经营几个世纪就为了保护它们的特权不被侵犯的完美屏障的时候,我觉得要想看到一个举着鲜明而光辉的旗帜的贵族制度自消自灭,恐怕是没有希望的。那些希望欧洲人有一天会与黑人融合的人们,我认为都是在自欺欺人。我的理性和我所观察到的事实无不告诉我,这一天不会到来。即使是现在,凡是白人拥有最强大势力的地方,他们都把黑人置于低等或被奴役的地位;而凡是黑人势力强大的地方,他们就消灭白人。这才是两个种族之间保持平衡的唯一途径。

我清楚地看到,在今天美国的一些地方,把两个种族隔开的法律屏障正在消除,但民情方面的屏障并未消除。蓄奴制衰弱了,但它所造成的偏见却仍然存在。那些生活在美国的人们必须认识到,在美国一些黑人已经不再是奴隶地位的地区,他们与白人的距离是否在一步步接近。情况恰恰相反,种族偏见在已经废除蓄奴制的州,比在还保存着蓄奴制的州更强烈;而且,没有一个地方的种族偏见比在从未有过蓄奴制存在的州那样令人难以容忍。

It is true that in the North of the Union marriages may be legally contracted between Negroes and whites; but public opinion would stigmatize as infamous a man who should connect himself with a Negress, and it would be difficult to cite a single instance of such a union. The electoral franchise has been conferred upon the Negroes in almost all the states in which slavery has been abolished, but if they come forward to vote, their lives are in danger. If oppressed, they may bring an action at law, but they will find none but whites among their judges; and although they may legally serve as jurors, prejudice repels them from that office. The same schools do not receive the children of the black and of the European. In the theaters gold cannot procure a seat for the servile race beside their former masters; in the hospitals they lie apart; and although they are allowed to invoke the same God as the whites, it must be at a different altar and in their own churches, with their own clergy. The gates of heaven are not closed against them, but their inferiority is continued to the very confines of the other world. When the Negro dies, his bones are cast aside, and the distinction of condition prevails even in the equality of death. Thus the Negro is free, but he can share neither the rights, nor the pleasures, nor the labor, nor the afflictions, nor the tomb of him whose equal he has been declared to be; and he cannot meet him upon fair terms in life or in death.

In the South, where slavery still exists, the Negroes are less carefully kept apart; they sometimes share the labors and the recreations of the whites; the whites consent to intermix with them to a certain extent, and although legislation treats them more harshly, the habits of the people are more tolerant and compassionate. In the South the master is not afraid to raise his slave to his own standing, because he knows that he can in a moment reduce him to the dust at pleasure. In the North the white no longer distinctly perceives the barrier that separates him from the degraded race, and he shuns the Negro with the more pertinacity since he fears lest they should some day be confounded together.

Among the Americans of the South, Nature sometimes reasserts her rights and restores a transient equality between the blacks and the

北部联邦的法律的确准许黑人与白人合法结婚,但社会舆论会贬斥与黑人女人结婚的白人男人,而且也难以见到这种婚配的例子。几乎所有废除了蓄奴制的州的黑人都被授予了选举权;但他们如果胆敢去投票就会受到生命危险。他们受到迫害时可以去告状,但当法官的都是白人。法律准许黑人充当陪审员,但偏见使他们被判出局。黑人的子女不能与白人的小孩在同一所学校读书。在剧院里,黑人有钱也买不到座位是同他们曾经的白人主人在一起的票。在医院里,黑人与白人是分区的。虽然黑人被允许与白人信仰同一个上帝,但黑人也只能在自己的教堂自己的圣坛前进行礼拜。在那里,黑人有自己的教士。天堂的大门虽然未对他们关闭,但不平等的地位只能使他们停在来世的墙外。当黑人死去时,他们的骨头被消除,甚至在毫无差别的死亡面前也存在身份的差别。可见,黑人虽然获得了自由,但他们并未分享向他们宣布大家都已平等的那些人享有的同样的权利、快乐、劳动机会和痛苦的感情,甚至死后都进不了同一墓地。无论是在生前,还是在死后,他们都不能与那些人平等地在一起。

在南方,蓄奴制仍旧存在,黑人也并不那么严格地被排斥在外。他们有时还能与白人一起劳动和娱乐,白人也同意在一定限度内与黑人混在一起。尽管立法对待黑人比白人更严厉一些,但人们的习性相对来说更宽容并富于同情。在南方,奴隶主不怕把奴隶的能力提高到与自己相等的水平,因为他们知道,只要自己乐意,他们可以随时把奴隶踩在脚下。在北方,白人虽然不再把自己与劣等种族之间的壁垒看得那样森严,但他们总是小心翼翼地避免同黑人接触,唯恐有一天会同黑人混为一体。

在南方的美国人中间,造物主有时会重新施展他的力量,使

whites; but in the North pride restrains the most imperious of human passions. The American of the Northern states would perhaps allow the Negress to share his licentious pleasures if the laws of his country did not declare that she may aspire to be the legitimate partner of his bed, but he recoils with horror from her who might become his wife.

Thus it is in the United States that the prejudice which repels the Negroes seems to increase in proportion as they are emancipated, and inequality is sanctioned by the manners while it is ef faced from the laws of the country. But if the relative position of the two races that inhabit the United States is such as I have described, why have the Americans abolished slavery in the North of the Union, why do they maintain it in the South, and why do they aggravate its hardships? The answer is easily given. It is not for the good of the Negroes, but for that of the whites, that measures are taken to abolish slavery in the United States.

The first Negroes were imported into Virginia about the year 16z1. [1] In America, therefore, as well as in the rest of the globe, slavery originated in the South. Thence it spread from one settlement to another; but the number of slaves diminished towards the Northern states, and the Negro population was always very limited in New England. [2]

A century had scarcely elapsed since the foundation of the colonies when the attention of the planters was struck by the extraordinary fact that the provinces which were comparatively destitute of slaves

---

[1]　See Beverley's *History of Virginia*. See also, in Jefferson's Memoirs, some curious details concerning the introduction of Negroes into Virginia, and the first Act that prohibited the importation of them, in 1778.

[2]　The number of slaves was less considerable in the North, but the advantages resulting from slavery were not more contested there than in the South. In 1740 the legislature of the state of New York declared that the direct importation of slaves ought to be encouraged as much as possible, and smuggling severely punished, in order not to discourage the fair trader. (Kent's *Commentaries*, Vol. II, p. 206.) Curious researches by Belknap upon slavery in New England are to be found in the *Historical Collections of Massachusetts*, Vol. IV, p. 193. It appears that Negroes were introduced there in 1630, but that the legislation and manners of the people were opposed to slavery from the first. See also, in the same work, the manner in which public opinion, and afterwards the laws, finally put an end to slavery.

白人与黑人之间短暂的平等。但是在北方,自尊心已经使人达到不敢流露真实感情的地步。如果他们的法律不允许黑人女人可以与白人男人同床共枕,北方的白人男人倒可能找一个黑人女人作为临时伴侣行乐;但在北方,法律允许她可以成为他的妻子,所以他出于一种害怕的心理而不敢接近她。

因此在美国,对黑人的偏见仿佛随着废奴制的增长而加深,并且日常生活中的不平等也随着法律废除不平等而加强。但是,既然居住在美国的这两个种族的地位如同我所说的这样,为什么美国人在北方废除了蓄奴制,而在南方却保留着它呢?而他们又为什么加剧了其残酷性呢?答案很简单。因为这并不是从黑人方面考虑的,而是出于白人的利益才在美国废除蓄奴制的。

第一批黑人被输入弗吉尼亚是在 1621 年左右。[①] 因此,像在世界其他地方一样,在美国,蓄奴制始于南方。然后,从一个聚集点向另一个聚集点移动。但是,奴隶的人数是越往北越少。因此,黑人在新英格兰的人数极其有限。[②]

自那些殖民地建立的时间已有 100 多年了,这时一个奇怪的现象开始引起所有人的注意:几乎完全没有奴隶的地区,在人口、

---

① 见贝弗利的《弗吉尼亚史》。见杰斐逊论文集中一些关于黑人进入维吉尼亚的介绍的细节,以及 1778 年颁布的禁止输入黑人的第一法案。

② 东部奴隶的数量没有那么多,但是因奴隶而带来的好处并不比南部少。1740 年,纽约州的立法机关宣布,奴隶的直接输入应该被尽可能的得到鼓励,但为了鼓励公平贸易,走私应该受到严厉的惩罚。因为对奴隶制度的好奇而在新英格兰进行的调查可以在马萨诸塞州的《历史文献集锦》的第四卷第 193 页中找到。看起来似乎黑人是在 1630 年被引入那里的,但是当时的立法和民情最初很反对奴役。在这本著作中也能查到这样的观点,公众的民情和随后的法律,最终结束了奴役制度。

increased in population, in wealth, and in prosperity more rapidly than those which contained many of them. In the former, however, the inhabitants were obliged to cultivate the soil themselves or by hired laborers; in the latter they were furnished with hands for which they paid no wages. Yet though labor and expense were on the one side and ease with economy on the other, the former had the more advantageous system. This result seemed the more difficult to explain since the settlers, who all belonged to the same European race, had the same habits, the same civilization, the same laws, and their shades of difference were extremely slight.

Time, however, continued to advance, and the Anglo-Americans, spreading beyond the coasts of the Atlantic Ocean, penetrated farther and farther into the solitudes of the West. They met there with a new soil and an unwonted climate; they had to over come obstacles of the most various character; their races intermingled, the inhabitants of the South going up towards the North, those of the North descending to the South. But in the midst of all these causes the same result occurred at every step; in general, the colonies in which there were no slaves became more populous and more prosperous than those in which slavery flourished. The farther they went, the more was it shown that slavery, which is so cruel to the slave, is prejudicial to the master.

But this truth was most satisfactorily demonstrated when civilization reached the banks of the Ohio. The stream that the Indians had distinguished by the name of Ohio, or the Beautiful River, waters one of the most magnificent valleys which have ever been made the abode of man. Undulating lands extend upon both shores of the Ohio, whose soil affords inexhaustible treasures to the laborer; on either bank the air is equally wholesome and the climate mild; and each of them forms the extreme frontier of a vast state: that which follows the numerous windings of the Ohio upon the left is called Kentucky; that upon the right bears the name of the river. These two states differ only in a single respect: Kentucky has admitted slavery, but the state of Ohio has prohibited the existence of slaves within its borders. [①]

---

① Not only is slavery prohibited in Ohio, but no free Negroes are allowed to enter the territory of that state or to hold property in it. See the statutes of Ohio.

财富和福利方面,都比拥有奴隶的地区发展迅速。在前者中,人们要自己种地或雇人耕种;而后者中,居民不必付薪水便有人为自己耕田。虽然前者既要出力又要出钱,而另一方却可以安闲自在又不用花钱,但前者却得到了更有力的体系。因为既然他们都是欧洲人,拥有同样的习俗、文明和法制,而仅仅在一些很不显眼的地方存在差别,所以产生这样的结果似乎很难解释。

时间继续,英裔美国人离开大西洋沿岸,越来越多地向西部的荒野开进。在那里,他们找到了新的土地,同时也碰到了罕见的气候。他们不得不克服各种各样的困难。各个民族的人们融合在一起:有从南往北的,有从北南下的。但是在所有这些因素的影响下,却同步地产生了相同的结果。一般而言,没有奴隶的殖民地,要比盛行蓄奴制的殖民地人口更多更繁荣。随着各殖民地的发展,就更多地显示出:奴隶制正在如此残酷地奴役着奴隶,也在对奴隶主产生着严重的影响。

但是,当文明到达俄亥俄州两岸的时候,这一真理得到了完美的论证。被印第安人称为俄亥俄的这条河,或者叫美丽的河,流经了人们居住过的最好河谷之一。俄亥俄河的两岸起伏不平的土地向四处延伸,为人们提供用之不竭的资源。在河的两岸,都有宜人的空气和温和的气候。河的两岸,各是一个土地辽阔的大州的边界。在左岸的,以蜿蜒曲折的俄亥俄河水为界,名为肯塔基州;而在另一岸的州与河同名。这两个州的唯一差别在于:肯塔基州允许蓄奴,而俄亥俄州境内不准有奴隶。[①]

---

① 俄亥俄州不仅禁止奴役黑人,而且也不许任何自由黑人进入该州领域或者在其境内拥有财产。见俄亥俄州法令。

Thus the traveler who floats down the current of the Ohio to the spot where that river falls into the Mississippi may be said to sail between liberty and servitude; and a transient inspection of surrounding objects will convince him which of the two is more favorable to humanity. Upon the left bank of the stream the population is sparse; from time to time one descries a troop of slaves loitering in the halfdesert fields; the primeval forest reappears at every turn; society seems to be asleep, man to be idle, and nature alone offers a scene of activity and life.

From the right bank, on the contrary, a confused hum is heard, which proclaims afar the presence of industry; the fields are covered with abundant harvests; the elegance of the dwellings announces the taste and activity of the laborers; and man appears to be in the enjoyment of that wealth and contentment which is the reward of labor. ①

The state of Kentucky was founded in 1775, the state of Ohio only twelve years later; but twelve years are more in America than half a century in Europe; and at the present day the population of Ohio exceeds that of Kentucky by two hundred and fifty thousand souls. ② These different effects of slavery and freedom may readily be understood; and they suffice to explain many of the differences which we notice between the civilization of antiquity and that of our own time.

Upon the left bank of the Ohio labor is confounded with the idea of slavery, while upon the right bank it is identified with that of prosperity and improvement; on the one side it is degraded, on the other it is honored. On the former territory no white laborers can be found, for they would be afraid of assimilating themselves to the Negroes; all the work is done by slaves; on the latter no one is idle, for the white population extend their activity and intelligence to every kind of employment. Thus the men whose task it is to cultivate the rich soil of

---

① The activity of Ohio is not confined to individuals, but the undertakings of the state are surprisingly great: a canal has been established between Lake Erie and the Ohio, by means of which the valley of the Mississippi communicates with the river of the North, and the European commodities which arrive at New York may be forwarded by water to New Orleans across five hundred leagues of continent.

② The exact numbers given by the census of 1830 were: Kentucky, 688, 844; Ohio, 937,679.

因此,一个人乘船顺俄亥俄河而下,到了河流引入密西西比河的地方,就刚好处身于自由和奴役之间。这时,他只要看一眼周围的环境,就立刻可以断定哪一岸对人类更为有利。因为,在河的左岸人烟稀少,偶尔会见到一群奴隶懒散地在半荒的土地上游荡,被砍伐的原始树木季节交替时发出新芽。整个社会好像已经入睡,人们看起来懒懒散散,只有大自然还显现出一丝生机和活力。

相反,河的右岸,充入耳中的净是机器的轰鸣,那说明远方有工厂在运作。田里到处长着茂盛的庄稼,优雅的房屋处处显示着主人的喜好和活力。这里的人们享受着劳动给他们带来的财富和满足感。①

肯塔基州建于 1775 年,俄亥俄州比它晚建 12 年。但是,美洲的 12 年胜过欧洲的 50 年。现在,俄亥俄州的人口已比肯塔基州多 25 万人。② 蓄奴制和自由造成的这种不同后果是不难理解的,并足以说明古代文明与现代文明之差异。

在俄亥俄河的左岸,人们认为劳动与奴役不可分割;而右岸的人们却认为劳动与致富和进步密不可分。一方认为劳动是下贱的而另一方承认劳动光荣。在河的左岸,绝没有白人劳力,因为白人担心自己与黑人混为一谈,他们认为一切劳力都应由奴隶去做。而在河的右岸,找不到懒散的人,白人把他们的精力和智慧用于各种劳动。因此,在肯塔基州肩负开垦肥沃土地任务的

---

① 俄亥俄州的活跃不仅仅局限在个人,该州领土上的企业都惊人的巨大:他们曾在伊利湖和俄亥俄州之间建造了一条运河,这样密西西比大峡谷就与北部的河流联系在了一起,而抵达纽约的欧洲人的日用品也可以通过水运抵达新奥尔良,跨越了整整 500 里约的路程。

② 1830 年人口普查的确切数字:肯塔基州,688844;俄亥俄州,937679。

Kentucky are ignorant and apathetic, while those who are active and enlightened either do nothing or pass over into Ohio, where they may work without shame.

It is true that in Kentucky the planters are not obliged to pay the slaves whom they employ, but they derive small profits from their labor, while the wages paid to free workmen would be returned with interest in the value of their services. The free workman is paid, but he does his work quicker than the slave; and rapidity of execution is one of the great elements of economy. The white sells his services, but they are purchased only when they may be useful; the black can claim no remuneration for his toil, but the expense of his maintenance is perpetual; he must be supported in his old age as well as in manhood, in his profitless infancy as well as in the productive years of youth, in sickness as well as in health. Payment must equally be made in order to obtain the services of either class of men: the free workman receives his wages in money; the slave in education, in food, in care, and in clothing. The money which a master spends in the maintenance of his slaves goes gradually and in detail, so that it is scarcely perceived; the salary of the free workman is paid in a round sum and appears to enrich only him who receives it; but in the end the slave has cost more than the free servant, and his labor is less productive. [1]

---

[1] Independently of these causes, which, wherever free workmen abound, render their labor more productive and more economical than that of slaves, another cause may be pointed out which is peculiar to the United States: sugar-cane has hitherto been cultivated with success only upon the banks of the Mississippi, near the mouth of that river in the Gulf of Mexico. In Louisiana the cultivation of sugar-cane is exceedingly lucrative; nowhere does a laborer earn so much by his work; and as there is always a certain relation between the cost of production and the value of the produce, the price of slaves is very high in Louisiana. But Louisiana is one of the federal states, and slaves may be carried thither from all parts of the Union; the price given for slaves in New Orleans consequently raises the value of slaves in all the other markets. The consequence of this is that in the regions where the land is less productive, the cost of slave labor is still very considerable, which gives an additional advantage to the competition of free labor.

人,既无知也缺乏兴趣;而拥有这两种东西的人,要么什么也不干,要么已渡过俄亥俄河,到那边去发挥自己的才智了。

在肯塔基州,种植园主不必为他们雇用的奴隶支付报酬,但他们从奴隶中获得的劳动的成果也不大;而如果他们付给自由工人工钱,他们就可以得到远远高于工人劳动价值的收益。虽然用自由工人要付酬,但他们的劳动效率比奴隶高,而工作迅速则是经济效益的主要因素之一。白人出卖他们的劳动力.但只有当他们的劳动力有用时才有人购买。黑人虽然不要求支付劳动报酬,但奴隶主对他们的赡养是无止境的,无论在他们老年或年轻的时候,或是在他们不能创造收益的童年和多产的青年时期,在他们生病和健康时期,都得同样地养活他们。因此,要让这两种人付出劳动,都得同样付薪水:自由工人得到的是钱,而奴隶呢,则耗费在对他们的教育、生活、抚育和服装上面。奴隶主为维持奴役所支付的费用,是逐渐而繁琐的,所以不容易被人察觉。而自由工人的工资因为是整笔付出,所以得到钱的人好像会变得富有一样。但最后算起来,奴隶花费的开销要远远高于雇用自由工人的薪酬,而且奴隶劳动的效率却远远低于自由工人。①

---

①　这些原因之外,无论在什么情况下,自由工人的充足,使得他们的劳力更加多产并且与奴隶相比更经济,另一个原因,则是美国比较特殊的一个情况:迄今为止,只由密西西比河两岸,靠近墨西哥湾河口的地方才能成功地种植出甘蔗。在路易斯安那州,甘蔗的种植极其有利,再没有其他地方的农民付出的劳动能够赚取这么多的回报。并且,这里一直维持着一定的生产成本与产品价值的关系,而路易斯安那州奴隶的成本很高。但是路易斯安那州是联邦州之一,那里的奴隶来自联邦的各个地方。新奥尔良奴隶的价格因此也就提升了所有其他市场奴隶的价格。这一结果直接导致了在那些物产不丰富的地方,奴隶的价格却仍旧很高,因此就给自由劳动力创造了更大的优势。

The influence of slavery extends still further: it affects the character of the master and imparts a peculiar tendency to his ideas and tastes. Upon both banks of the Ohio the character of the inhabitants is enterprising and energetic, but this vigor is very differently exercised in the two states. The white inhabitant of Ohio, obliged to subsist by his own exertions, regards temporal prosperity as the chief aim of his existence; and as the country which he occupies presents inexhaustible resources to his industry, and ever varying lures to his activity, his acquisitive ardor surpasses the ordinary limits of human cupidity: he is tormented by the desire of wealth, and he boldly enters upon every path that fortune opens to him; he becomes a sailor, a pioneer, an artisan, or a cultivator with the same indifference, and supports with equal constancy the fatigues and the dangers incidental to these various professions; the resources of his intelligence are astonishing, and his avidity in the pursuit of gain amounts to a species of heroism. But the Kentuckian scorns not only labor but all the undertakings that labor promotes; as he lives in an idle independence, his tastes are those of an idle man; money has lost a portion of its value in his eyes; he covets wealth much less than pleasure and excitement; and the energy which his neighbor devotes to gain turns with him to a passionate love of field sports and military exercises; he delights in violent bodily exertion, he is familiar with the use of arms, and is accustomed from a very early age to expose his life in single combat. Thus slavery prevents the whites not only from becoming opulent, but even from desiring to become so.

As the same causes have been continually producing opposite effects for the last two centuries in the British colonies of North America, they have at last established a striking difference between the commercial capacity of the inhabitants of the South and those of the North. At the present day it is only the Northern states that are in possession of shipping, manufactures, railroads, and canals. This difference is perceptible not only in comparing the North with the South, but in comparing the several Southern states. Almost all those who carry on commercial operations or endeavor to turn slave labor to account in the most southern districts of the Union have emigrated from the North. The natives of the Northern states are constantly spreading over that portion of the American territory where they have less to fear from competition; they discover resources there which

蓄奴制的影响更大。它甚至影响了奴隶主的性格,对他们的思想和爱好施加了极大的影响。在俄亥俄河两岸,人们都很有魄力充满激情,但这一相同性格在河两岸的发挥却得到了不同的结果。俄亥俄州的白人必须依靠自己的努力生活,并以追求物质为人生的主要目的。由于他们居住的土地为他们的工业发展提供了取之不尽的资源,并且总是不断有各种诱惑激发他们的活力,所以他们的进取精神远远超过了人类贪婪的界限;他们渴望致富的欲望使他们勇于踏入财富为他们指引的每一条道路。无论是当水手还是去拓荒,或者是作艺人或农夫,他们都有坚忍不拔的毅力支持着去克服不同行业可能遭到的风险。他们智慧的源泉令人赞叹,他们对物欲追求的渴望有一种英雄主义的气概。但是,肯塔基人不仅轻视劳动本身,而且看不起劳动所成就的一切事业。他们的生活悠闲自在,他们的志趣也是懒汉的志趣。金钱在他们眼中失去了其应有的价值;他们对于财富的追求,远远不如他们追求享乐寻求刺激;而且他们用于追求享乐的精力,不亚于他们的邻居用于其他方面的精力。他们热爱打猎和打仗,喜欢体力透支。他们沉湎于武力。从很小的年纪开始就会不顾生命的与人格斗。因此,蓄奴制不但未使白人发财致富,反而使他们没有了发财致富的愿望。

200年来这些同样的原因一直在北美的英国殖民地发生着各种不同的作用。最后,南北方人的经商能力出现了令人诧异的差别。如今,只有北方各州有航运业、制造业、铁路和运河。这些差别,不仅在对比南北方时可以见到,而且也存在于南方各地。在联邦最南的几个地区,几乎所有致力于商业或试图从蓄奴制中得到好处的人,都来自北方。现在,北方的土著不断地涌向这里,因为在美国的这块地方,他们不必担心竞争。他们发现,当地人

escaped the notice of the inhabitants; and as they comply with a system which they do not approve, they succeed in turning it to better advantage than those who first founded and who still maintain it.

Were I inclined to continue this parallel, I could easily prove that almost all the differences which may be noticed between the characters of the Americans in the Southern and in the Northern states have originated in slavery; but this would divert me from my subject, and my present intention is not to point out all the consequences of servitude, but those effects which it has produced upon the material prosperity of the countries that have admitted it.

The influence of slavery upon the production of wealth must have been very imperfectly known in antiquity, as slavery then obtained throughout the civilized world, and the nations that were unacquainted with it were barbarians. And, indeed, Christianity abolished slavery only by advocating the claims of the slave; at the present time it may be attacked in the name of the master, and upon this point interest is reconciled with morality.

As these truths became apparent in the United States, slavery receded before the progress of experience. Servitude had begun in the South and had thence spread towards the North, but it now retires again. Freedom, which started from the North, now descends uninterruptedly towards the South. Among the great states, Pennsylvania now constitutes the extreme limit of slavery to the North; but even within those limits the slave system is shaken: Maryland, which is immediately below Pennsylvania, is preparing for its abolition; and Virginia, which comes next to Maryland, is already discussing its utility and its dangers. ①

No great change takes place in human institutions without

---

① A peculiar reason contributes to detach the two last-mentioned states from the cause of slavery. The former wealth of this part of the Union was principally derived from the cultivation of tobacco. This cultivation is specially suited to slave labor; but within the last few years the market price of tobacco has diminished, while the value of the slaves remains the same. Thus the ratio between the cost of production and the value of the produce is changed. The inhabitants of Maryland and Virginia are therefore more disposed than they were thirty years ago to give up slave labor in the cultivation of tobacco, or to give up slavery and tobacco at the same time.

还没注意发现这里的资源,于是利用他们本来并不赞成的制度,他们成功地得到了比最初建立这个制度后仍在维护这个制度的人们所得到的更多的好处。

如果我愿意再继续将这两条平行线继续下去,我可以很容易证明:几乎所有美国南北方人在性格上表现出的差异,都源于蓄奴制。但这并不是我所要讨论的话题,因为我的目的,并不在于指出奴役造成的所有后果,而是奴役将对赞同奴役的那些人或地区产生的物质方面的影响。

在古代人们并不能完全理解蓄奴制对财富制造方式的影响。因为当时,奴隶普遍存在于整个文明世界,不知道奴隶为何物的民族都是蛮族。而且,基督教所谓的废除蓄奴制,也不过是替奴隶讨回自己的权利而已。现在,人们可以用奴隶主的名义去攻击蓄奴制,而且在这一点上,利益与道德也是一致的。

随着真相在美国变得日益明显,蓄奴制在经验的逼近下步步退后。蓄奴制始于南方,随后又发展到北方,而今开始节节败退。而起于北方的自由,如今不断向南方推进。在一些大州当中,蓄奴制存在的最北边是宾夕法尼亚州;但即使在这个州里,蓄奴制也开始不稳定。马里兰州,紧挨着宾夕法尼亚州,也在准备着废除蓄奴制。马里兰州下面是弗吉尼亚州,也已在权衡蓄奴制的利弊。①

人类的任何一项制度发生重大变化,都会涉及继承法。

① 作用于将以上提到的两个州与奴隶制脱离的原因很奇特。联邦初期的财富主要来源于烟草种植。这一种植尤其需要奴隶作为劳动力,但是,在过去的一些年中,烟草的价格降低了,而奴隶的价格保持不变。因此,商品成本和价值的比率发生了变化。因此马里兰岛和维吉尼亚的居民比他们在30年前更愿意放弃使用奴隶耕种烟草,或者甚至将两者都放弃。

in volving among its causes the law of inheritance. When the law of primogeniture obtained in the South, each family was represented by a wealthy individual, who was neither compelled nor induced to labor; and he was surrounded, as by parasitic plants, by the other members of his family, who were then excluded by law from sharing the common inheritance, and who led the same kind of life as himself. The same thing then occurred in all the families of the South which still happens in the noble families of some countries in Europe: namely, that the younger sons remain in the same state of idleness as their elder brother, without being as rich as he is. This identical result seems to be produced in Europe and in America by wholly analogous causes. In the South of the United States the whole race of whites formed an aristocratic body, headed by a certain number of privileged individuals, whose wealth was permanent and whose leisure was hereditary. These leaders of the American nobility kept alive the traditional prejudices of the white race, in the body of which they were the representatives, and maintained idleness in honor. This aristocracy contained many who were poor, but none who would work; its members preferred want to labor; consequently Negro laborers and slaves met with no competition; and, whatever opinion might be entertained as to the utility of their industry, it was necessary to employ them, since there was no one else to work.

No sooner was the law of primogeniture abolished than fortunes began to diminish and all the families of the country were simultaneously reduced to a state in which labor became necessary to existence; several of them have since entirely disappeared, and all of them learned to look forward to the time when it would be necessary for everyone to provide for his own wants. Wealthy individuals are still to be met with, but they no longer constitute a compact and hereditary body, nor have they been able to adopt a line of conduct in which they could persevere and which they could infuse into all ranks of society. The prejudice that stigmatized labor was, in the first place, abandoned by common consent, the number of needy men was increased, and the needy were allowed to gain a subsistence by labor without blushing for their toil. Thus one of the most immediate consequences of the equal division of estates has been to create a class of free laborers. As soon as competition began between the free laborer and the slave, the inferiority of the latter became manifest and slavery

当长子继承制通行于南方时,每个家庭都会有一个代表人物,他既不需劳动而且其本身也没有劳动的欲望。他的那些依法不能与他平等继承遗产的亲眷,依靠他与他过着同样的生活。从前美国南方一切富裕家庭中的情景,在今天欧洲某些国家的贵族家庭仍在上演:弟弟妹妹虽然不如哥哥姐姐富有,但与哥哥姐姐同样游手好闲。在美洲和欧洲产生的这一相同的后果,仿佛是由于一些完全类似的原因引起的。在美国南方,全体白人形成了一个贵族集团,并由一定数目的特权人物领导。这些特权人物拥有世袭的财产和祖辈相传的悠闲生活的习惯。美国贵族的这些领袖,保留着白色人种的传统偏见,使这种偏见继续存在在他们所代表的集团之中,并骄傲地维持着这种生活。在这个贵族集团内部也可见到一些穷人,但他们并不劳动。他们宁可受穷,也不愿劳动。因此,黑人劳力和奴隶不会面临任何竞争,而且不管白人对他们的劳动效果持有什么看法,都非得雇用他们不可,因为只有他们才会付出劳力。

长子继承法废除后不久,各种财产便开始分散减少,而所有的家庭的处境,也变得不得不依靠劳动维持生计。一些家庭已完全消失,但所有的家庭都预感到,必须自食其力的日子就要来了。虽然还能见到一些富人,但他们已经不再是紧密结合的世袭团体,也无法通过一系列的行为再重获使自己强大和影响社会各阶层的精神力量了。于是,首先大家开始一致放弃对劳动的偏见。穷人的数目虽增加了,但他们不再因通过劳动获得生存而感到脸红了。因此,财产分配平等的最直接成果之一,就是创造了一个自由劳动阶级。而一旦自由工人同奴隶之间开始竞争以后,奴隶的劣势便暴露出来,而蓄奴制也在它的本质的原则上遭受到了打

was attacked in its fundamental principle, which is the interest of the master.

As slavery recedes, the black population follows its retrograde course and returns with it towards those tropical regions whence it originally came. However singular this fact may at first appear to be, it may readily be explained. Although the Americans abolish the principle of slavery, they do not set their slaves free, To illustrate this remark, I will quote the example of the state of New York. In 1788 this state prohibited the sale of slaves within its limits, which was an indirect method of prohibiting the importation of them. Thenceforward the number of Negroes could only increase according to the ratio of the natural increase of population. But eight years later, a more decisive measure was taken, and it was enacted that all children born of slave parents after the 4th of July 1799 should be free. No increase could then take place, and although slaves still existed, slavery might be said to be abolished. As soon as a Northern state thus prohibited the importation, no slaves were brought from the South to be sold in its markets. On the other hand, as the sale of slaves was forbidden in that state, an owner could no longer get rid of his slave (who thus became a burdensome possession) otherwise than by transporting him to the South. But when a Northern state declared that the son of the slave should be born free, the slave lost a large portion of his market value, since his posterity was no longer included in the bargain, and the owner had then a strong interest in transporting him to the South. Thus the same law prevents the slaves of the South from coming North and drives those of the North to the South.

But there is another cause more powerful than any that I have described. The want of free hands is felt in a state in proportion as the number of slaves decreases. But in proportion as labor is performed by free hands, slave labor becomes less productive; and the slave is then a useless or onerous possession, whom it is important to export to the South, where the same competition is not to be feared. Thus the abolition of slavery does not set the slave free, but merely transfers him to another master, and from the North to the South.

击,那就是维护奴隶主利益。

随着蓄奴制的败退,黑人便沿着其的退路,同蓄奴制一起回到他们当初离开的热带地区。如果单看这个现象,乍一看来似乎令人觉得奇怪,但不久就被人们理解了。因为尽管美国人废除了奴隶制度,但并没有给奴隶自由。为了说明这一理论,我举一个纽约州的例子来解释一下。1788 年,纽约州禁止在境内买卖奴隶。这其实是间接地禁止输入奴隶。从那以后,黑人的人数只是依靠自然繁殖而增加。8 年以后,该州采取了一项更具有决定性意义的措施,即以法令宣布:自 1799 年 7 月 4 日以后出生的,凡父母均为奴隶的新生婴儿,一律自由。于是,使奴隶人数增加的一切途径都没了。虽然还有奴隶,但可以说蓄奴制已不复存在。在北方的一个州这样禁止输入奴隶以后,便没有人再从南方向北方贩卖黑人了。从另一方面来说,因为奴隶买卖已在这个州被禁止,奴隶主除非到南方去贩卖奴隶而别无他途。但是,当北方的一个州宣布奴隶的子女出生后即获得自由的时候,奴隶就失去了大部分的市场价值,因为他们的子孙已无法包含在内了。但把他们输往南方,还能赚一笔大钱。因此,同样的一条法令,虽防止了南方的奴隶来到北方,但却把北方的奴隶赶到了南方。

但是,这里还有一个原因比我说过其他原因还要有说服力。那就是,随着一个州的奴隶人数的减少,人们便更加感到对自由劳力的需求。但是,随着自由劳力的推广,奴隶劳动的生产效益便日益降低。于是,奴隶便成了没有利用价值或用处不大的财产。但在南方使用奴隶就不必担心同样的竞争。因此,废除蓄奴制并未能使奴隶都自由了,而只是给他们换了新主人,并把他们从北方送到了南方。

The emancipated Negroes and those born after the abolition of slavery do not, indeed, migrate from the North to the South; but their situation with regard to the Europeans is not unlike that of the Indians; they remain half civilized and deprived of their rights in the midst of a population that is far superior to them in wealth and knowledge, where they are exposed to the tyranny of the laws[1] and the intolerance of the people. On some accounts they are still more to be pitied than the Indians, since they are haunted by the reminiscence of slavery, and they cannot claim possession of any part of the soil. Many of them perish miserably,[2] and the rest congregate in the great towns, where they perform the meanest offices and lead a wretched and precarious existence.

If, moreover, the number of Negroes were to continue to grow in the same proportion during the period when they did not have their liberty, yet, with the number of the whites increasing at a double rate after the abolition of slavery, the Negroes would soon be swallowed up in the midst of an alien population.

A district which is cultivated by slaves is in general less populous than a district cultivated by free labor; moreover, America is still a new country, and a state is therefore not half peopled when it abolishes slavery. No sooner is an end put to slavery than the want of free labor is felt, and a crowd of enterprising adventurers immediately arrives from all parts of the country, who hasten to profit by the fresh resources which are then opened to industry. The soil is soon divided among them, and a family of white settlers takes possession of each portion. Besides, European immigration is exclusively directed to the free states; for what would a poor immigrant do who crosses the Atlantic

---

[1] The states in which slavery is abolished usually do what they can to render their territory disagreeable to the Negroes as a place of residence; and as a kind of emulation exists between the different states in this respect, the unhappy blacks can only choose the least of the evils that beset them.

[2] There is a great difference between the mortality of the blacks and of the whites in the states in which slavery is abolished; from 1820 to 1831 only one out of forty-two individuals of the white population died in Philadelphia; but one out of twenty-one of the black population died in the same time. The mortality is by no means so great among the Negroes who are still slaves. (See Emerson's *Medical Statistics*, p. 28.)

已经被解放的黑人以及在废除蓄奴制后出生的黑人,事实上,并没有从北方迁去南方,但考虑到他们在欧洲人中间的处境,与土著的印第安人是一样的。在远比他们更有钱有知识的白人中间,他们仍旧未完全开化也没有权利。他们既是法律的压迫的对象①,也不容于人民。在某些方面,他们比印第安人还值得可怜,因为他们常常受到从前奴隶生活的回忆的困扰,但他们却不能说出哪块土地原本是他们的。许多人在饥寒交迫中死去,②而其余的人则聚集在一些大的城镇里,靠做一些下贱的活计,过着悲惨动荡的生活。

而且,即使黑人的人数仍按照他们未获自由时期的速度增长,但白人的人数却在废除蓄奴制后以两倍于前的速度增长,所以不久之后,黑人就将被淹没在异族人的人海之中。

奴隶耕种的地区一般来说比白人聚居的农业地区人口稀少。而且,美国仍旧是一个新兴国家,因此一个州在废除蓄奴制的时候,尚有一半的土地没有人居住。一个州刚刚取消掉奴隶身份,便立即感到自由劳力的匮乏,于是一群怀有野心的冒险家从四面八方涌进来,企图从刚刚对实业开放的新资源中牟取暴利。他们很快瓜分了土地,并在分得的每块土地上建立起白人的家园。除此之外,欧洲的移民就这样无一例外地进驻了这片自由之州。如

---

① 奴隶制被废止的那些州通常都尽其可能说明他们的领土不适于黑人成长;而在这方面各个州的情况都相似,因此不幸的黑人只能选择那些相对来说最少的邪恶。

② 黑人和白人的死亡率在同一个被废止奴役制度的州中是有很大差别的。从 1820 年到 1831 年,费城白人每 42 个人中只有一个人死亡,而在同一时间,每 21 个黑人中就有一个死亡。而在黑人还处于奴役地位的时候,他们的死亡率绝没有这么高。(见爱默生:《医用统计学》第 28 页。)

in search of ease and happiness if he were to land in a country where labor is stigmatized as degrading?

Thus the white population grows by its natural increase, and at the same time by the immense influx of immigrants; while the black population receives no immigrants and is upon its decline. The proportion that existed between the two races is soon inverted. The Negroes constitute a scanty remnant, a poor tribe of vagrants, lost in the midst of an immense people who own the land; and the presence of the blacks is only marked by the injustice and the hardships of which they are the victims.

In several of the Western states the Negro race never made its appearance, and in all the Northern states it is rapidly declining. Thus the great question of its future condition is confined within a narrow circle, where it becomes less formidable, though not more easy of solution. The more we descend towards the South, the more difficult it becomes to abolish slavery with advantage; and this arises from several physical causes which it is important to point out.

The first of these causes is the climate: it is well known that, in proportion as Europeans approach the tropics, labor becomes more difficult to them. Many of the Americans even assert that within a certain latitude it is fatal to them, while the Negroes can work there without danger; ①but I do not think that this opinion, which is so favorable to the indolence of the inhabitants of the South, is confirmed by experience. The southern parts of the Union are not hotter than the south of Italy and of Spain; ②and it may be asked why the European

---

① This is true of the places in which rice is cultivated; rice-fields, which are unhealthful in all countries, are particularly dangerous in those regions which are exposed to the rays of a tropical sun. Europeans would not find it easy to cultivate the soil in that part of the New World if they insisted on making it produce rice; but may they not exist without growing rice?

② These states are nearer to the equator than Italy and Spain, but the temperature of the continent of America is much lower than that of Europe.

果那些漂洋过海到新大陆来寻找安乐和幸福的欧洲穷人来到了一个视劳动为下贱的地区,他们能有什么样的作为呢?

因此,白种人通过自然繁殖和大量移民,而迅速增加起来;而黑人的人口没有移民来补充,于是每况愈下。于是不久,两种人口之间的比例就颠倒过来了。黑人变成了一群可怜的穷人,成了一群到处流浪的游民,淹没在人口众多且拥有土地的白种人群之中。如今的黑人只有忍受不公正的对待,过着悲惨的生活。

在西部一些州里,至今尚无黑人;而在北方的所有州里,黑人数量正迅速减少。因此,黑人的未来面临的重大问题,是他们将要被挤到一个日益狭小的地区。虽然这个问题不怎么令人担忧,但也并不容易解决。随着越来越多黑人的南下,有效地废除蓄奴制就会变得越困难。造成这一结果的几个物质因素,很有必要在此指出。

第一个原因是气候。大家都知道,欧洲人越靠近热带,劳动对他们就越显得困难。许多美国人甚至断言,在一定的纬度下干活会导致死亡。而黑人却能在这种环境下劳作而毫无危险。[①] 但是,我不认为这个如此有利于南方人偷懒的想法是经验之谈。因为,南部联邦并不比西班牙和意大利的南方更热。[②] 那么,我们就

---

① 水稻种植在这些地方,这是事实。所有国家的稻田都对人的健康都是不利的,尤其是那些热带地区直接面对太阳辐射的地方更危险。欧洲人发现自己很难在新大陆开垦土地,如果他们仍旧坚持要种植水稻的话。但是他们不种植水稻的话,要靠什么生活呢?

② 这些国家比西班牙和意大利更靠近赤道地区,但是在美国大陆这些地区的温度要比欧洲低很多。

cannot work as well there as in the latter two countries. If slavery has been abolished in Italy and in Spain without causing the destruction of the masters, why should not the same thing take place in the Union? I cannot believe that nature has prohibited the Europeans in Georgia and the Floridas, under pain of death, from raising the means of subsistence from the soil; but their labor would unquestionably be more irksome and less productive①to them than to the inhabitants of New England. As the free workman thus loses a portion of his superiority over the slave in the Southern states, there are fewer inducements to abolish slavery.

All the plants of Europe grow in the northern parts of the Union; the South has special products of its own. It has been observed that slave labor is a very expensive method of cultivating cereal grain. The farmer of grainland in a country where slavery is un known habitually retains only a small number of laborers in his service, and at seed-time and harvest he hires additional hands, who live at his cost for only a short period. But the agriculturist in a slave state is obliged to keep a large number of slaves the whole year round in order to sow his fields and to gather in his crops, although their services are required only for a few weeks; for slaves are unable to wait till they are hired and to subsist by their own labor in the meantime, like free laborers; in order to have their services, they must be bought. Slavery, independently of its general disadvantages, is therefore still more inapplicable to countries in which grain is cultivated than to those which produce crops of a different kind. The cultivation of tobacco, of cotton, and especially of sugar-cane demands, on the other hand, unremitting attention; and women and children are employed in it, whose services are of little use in the cultivation of wheat. Thus slavery is naturally more fitted to the countries from which these productions are derived.

---

① The Spanish government formerly caused a certain number of peasants from the Azores to be transported into a district of Louisiana called Attakapas. Slavery was not introduced among them; it was an experiment. These settlers still cultivate the soil without the assistance of slaves, but their industry is so sluggish as scarcely to supply their most necessary wants.

要问了,为什么欧洲人不能像其他两个国家的人那样劳动呢?既然意大利和西班牙废除奴隶制度后并没有使奴隶主跟着毁灭,那么,联邦为什么就不能这样呢?我不相信大自然由于怕佐治亚和佛罗里达的欧洲人累死而不让他们在那里靠自己的土地谋生,但他们在那里劳动肯定要比新英格兰的居民辛苦,而且收益不如人家。[1] 因为自由劳动者在南方失去他们与奴隶相比的一些优势,所以也就延缓了蓄奴制的废除。

欧洲所有的农作物都能在联邦的北部生长,但在联邦南方有其特有的产物。人们发现,利用奴隶种植谷物的方式支出的费用太高。在没有蓄奴制地区种植小麦的农户,习惯于雇用少数劳力,并且只在播种和收割季节多雇几个短期工,临时供给他们食宿。但是在实行蓄奴制的州经营农业的人,就不得不全年保留着大量的奴隶,就为了播种和收割庄稼,尽管这些奴隶提供的劳动可能需要短短地几个礼拜时间。但是因为奴隶不像自由人那样,无法等到有人雇用他们而在其他时间依靠自己的劳力过活。所以,为了得到他们的劳力,就得把他们买下。除了这些不利因素以外,蓄奴制在种植谷物的地方也不如在种植其他作物的地方适用。种植烟草、棉花,特别是甘蔗,需要不断地照顾。这时,妇女儿童都用得上,而种植小麦就不需要这样的劳力。因此,从自然规律来说,蓄奴制更适于种植我方才提到的那几种作物的地区。

---

[1] 西班牙政府曾派遣过一批农民进入路易斯安那州的一个地方。他们中间没有奴隶,他们以此来做实验。这些人不用奴隶自己耕种,但是他们的工业发展的速度太缓慢而无法支撑他们的生活。

Tobacco, cotton, and sugar-cane are exclusively grown in the South, and they form the principal sources of the wealth of those states. If slavery were abolished, the inhabitants of the South would be driven to this alternative: they must either change their system of cultivation, and then they would come into competition with the more active and more experienced inhabitants of the North; or, if they continued to cultivate the same produce without slave labor, they would have to support the competition of the other states of the South, which might still retain their slaves. Thus peculiar reasons for maintaining slavery exist in the South which do not operate in the North.

But there is yet another motive, which is more cogent than all the others: the South might, indeed, rigorously speaking, abolish slavery; but how should it rid its territory of the black population? Slaves and slavery are driven from the North by the same law; but this twofold result cannot be hoped for in the South.

In proving that slavery is more natural and more advantageous in the South than in the North, I have shown that the number of slaves must be far greater in the former. It was to the Southern settlements that the first Africans were brought, and it is there that the greatest number of them have always been imported. As we advance towards the South, the prejudice that sanctions idleness increases in power. In the states nearest to the tropics there is not a single white laborer; the Negroes are consequently much more numerous in the South than in the North. And, as I have already observed, this disproportion increases daily, since the Negroes are transferred to one part of the Union as soon as slavery is abolished in the other. Thus the black population augments in the South, not only by its natural fecundity, but by the compulsory emigration of the Negroes from the North; and the African race has causes of increase in the South very analogous to those which accelerate the growth of the European race in the North.

In the state of Maine there is one Negro in three hundred inhabitants; in Massachusetts, one in one hundred; in New York, two in one hundred; in Pennsylvania, three in the same number; in Maryland, thirty-four; in Virginia, forty-two; and lastly, in South

烟草、棉花和甘蔗只适于在南方生长,它们是当地的主要经济来源。如果蓄奴制被废除,南部的居民就只有两种选择:要么改变原来的耕种体系,这样就不得不同更富有激情和经验的北方人展开激烈的竞争;要么就仍然种植原来的作物而不使用奴隶,同仍然保留蓄奴制的南方其他州展开竞争。因此,在南方保留奴隶制的特殊原因,在北方并不适用。

但还有一个比其他理由都更有说服力的动机,那就是:事实上,严厉地说,南方也可以废除蓄奴制。但是,那将怎样安置那些居住其上的黑人呢?在北方,奴隶和奴隶制是受到同一法律驱动的。在南方就不会取得这样的双重效果。

为了证明蓄奴制在南方比北方更合乎自然规律更有利,我只需指出,南方的奴隶人数远远多于后者。第一批非洲人正是输入到南方,而且也正是南方使奴隶人数日益增加的。我们越往南去,越觉得推崇悠闲自在的偏见势力的强大。在离热带最近的几个州里没有一个白人劳力的存在。而南方黑人人数远多于北方。正如我在前面已经说过的,这一不平衡现象还在日益严重,因为黑人在不断地输往联邦的同一地区,而同时,另一地区的奴隶正在不断地减少。因此,南方黑人的增加原因,不仅有人口的自然繁殖的原因,而且有北方黑人地被迫南迁的原因。非洲人种在美国南方的激增原因,与欧洲人种在北方的迅速增加原因类似。

在缅因州,每300个居民中有一个黑人。在马萨诸塞州,这个比例数为100∶1。在纽约州为100∶2,在宾夕法尼亚州为100∶3,在马里兰州为100∶34,在弗吉尼亚州为100∶42,而在南卡

Carolina,① fifty-five per cent of the inhabitants are black. Such was the proportion of the black population to the whites in the year 1830. But this proportion is perpetually changing, as it constantly decreases in the North and augments in the South.

It is evident that the most southern states of the Union cannot a-bolish slavery without incurring great dangers, which the North had no reason to apprehend when it emancipated its black population. I have already shown how the Northern states made the transition from slaver-y to freedom, by keeping the present generation in chains and setting their descendants free; by this means the Negroes are only gradually introduced into society; and while the men who might abuse their freedom are kept in servitude, those who are emancipated may learn the art of being free before they become their own masters. But it would be difficult to apply this method in the South. To declare that all the Negroes born after a certain period shall be free is to introduce the principle and the notion of liberty into the heart of slavery; the blacks whom the law thus maintains in a state of slavery from which their children are delivered are astonished at so unequal a fate, and their astonishment is only the prelude to their impatience and irrita-tion. Thenceforward slavery loses, in their eyes, that kind of moral power which it derived from time and habit; it is reduced to a mere palpable abuse of force. The Northern states had nothing to fear from the contrast, because in them the blacks were few in number, and the

---

① We find it asserted in an American work entitled *Letters on the Coloniza-tion Society*, by Mr. Carey (1833): "That for the last forty years, the black race has increased more rapidly than the white race in the State of South Carolina; and that, if we take the average population of the five States of the South into which slaves were first introduced, viz. Maryland, Virginia, South Carolina, North Carolina, and Georgia, we shall find that from 1790 to 1830 the whites have aug-mented in the proportion of 80 to 100, and the blacks in that of 100 to 112."

In the United States in 1830 the population of the two races stood as follows: States where slavery is abolished, 6,565,434 whites; 120,520 blacks. Slave States, 3,960,814 whites; 2,208,102 blacks.

罗来纳竟达 100:55。① 这是 1830 年黑人人口与白人人口的比例。但是,这个比例仍在不断地变化:北方黑人所占的比例越来越小,而南方的数目则越来越大。

显而易见,联邦南部大多数州中,要废除奴隶制就必然引起极大的危险,是居住在北方各州解放了奴隶的人们所不能理解的。我已经说明了北方各州废除蓄奴制和解放奴隶的大转变,是以当时活着的黑人奴隶为纽带,来解放他们的新出生子女的;通过这一方法将黑人逐渐吸收到社会里来;同时,使那些有可能会滥用自己的自由的人们仍旧保留奴役状态,而那些解放了的奴隶,则有机会在他们成为自己的主人之前,以自由之身学习文化。但是,在南方,使用这种办法就有困难。当南方宣布从某一时段开始准许黑人的新出生子女获得自由时,自由的原则和思想就会进入奴隶们的心里,那些按立法规定身为奴隶的黑人,在看到自己的子女获得自由后,会惊讶于他们之间出现的不平等命运,并随之而来就是急躁和愤怒。于是,蓄奴制在他们的眼中便失去了历史和习惯使其造就的道德的力量,摇身一变成了一种一目了然对暴力的滥用。北方各州就不必担心发生这样的对比,因为北

---

① 我们发现在一个美国人凯里先生的著作,名为《关于殖民地社会的描述》(1833 年)中写道:"在过去的四十年中,在卡罗来纳州南部的地区,黑人的数量增长的比白人更快。如果我们以最先引进黑人奴隶的南方五个州的平均人数来计,像马里兰、弗吉尼亚、南卡罗来纳州、北卡罗来纳州和乔治亚,我们会发现,1790 年到 1830 年间白人所占的比例已扩大到 80:100,而黑人则有 100:112。"

1830 年,美国两个种族人口数量如下:废除奴隶制的各州,白人 6565434;黑人 120520。奴隶制各州白人有 3960814;黑人数目则为 2208102。

white population was very considerable. But if this faint dawn of freedom were to show two millions of men their true position, the oppressors would have reason to tremble. After having enfranchised the children of their slaves, the Europeans of the Southern states would very
shortly be obliged to extend the same benefit to the whole black population.

In the North, as I have already remarked, a twofold migration
ensues upon the abolition of slavery, or even precedes that event
when circumstances have rendered it probable: the slaves quit the
country to be transported southwards; and the whites of the Northern
states, as well as the immigrants from Europe, hasten to fill their
place. But these two causes cannot operate in the same manner in the
Southern states. On the one hand, the mass of slaves is too great to
allow any expectation of their being removed from the country; and on
the other hand, the Europeans and Anglo-Americans of the North are
afraid to come to inhabit a country in which labor has not yet been re-
instated in its rightful honors. Besides, they very justly look upon the
states in which the number of the Negroes equals or exceeds that of
the whites as exposed to very great dangers; and they refrain from
turning their activity in that direction.

Thus the inhabitants of the South, while abolishing slavery,
would not be able, like their Northern countrymen, to initiate the
slaves gradually into a state of freedom; they have no means of per-
ceptibly diminishing the black population, and they would remain unsupported to repress its excesses. Thus in the course of a few years a
great people of free Negroes would exist in the heart of a white nation
of equal size.

The same abuses of power that now maintain slavery would then
become the source of the most alarming perils to the white population
of the South. At the present time the descendants of the Europeans
are the sole owners of the land and the absolute masters of all labor;
they alone possess wealth, knowledge, and arms. The black is destitute of all these advantages, but can subsist without them because he
is a slave. If he were free, and obliged to provide for his own subsistence, would it be possible for him to remain without these things and
to support life? Or would not the very instruments of the present superiority of the white while slavery exists expose him to a thousand dangers if it were abolished?

方的黑人数量极少,而白人人数庞大。但在南方,一旦自由微弱的光芒显露于 200 多万黑人面前,压迫者必然坐立不安。而且,南方的白人如果胆敢把奴隶的子女解放,那么他们很快就将被迫将之施于全部黑人。

就像我已经说过的,在北方,随着蓄奴制的废除,或者甚至还在预计即将废除蓄奴制的时候,就开始了一种双重迁徙:奴隶们被运往南方;而北方各州的白人和欧洲的移民则迅速地补充了他们的位置。这两种情况不能以同样的方式出现于南方的几个州。一方面,奴隶人数太多,使人们无法设想能把他们迁走;另一方面,欧洲人和北方的英裔美国人,也不肯到劳动尚未恢复其应有的荣耀的地区去定居。除此之外,他们也有理由认为,在黑人的人数超过或等于白人的州里,容易遇到极大的危险,所以他们不敢到那里去创业。

因此,南部居民随着蓄奴制的废除,无法像他们北方同胞那样逐渐使黑人获得自由。他们没有采取措施使黑人数量减少,并对其数量的过度增长置之不理。因此,只消几年工夫,便将在白人国家中出现几乎与之数量平等的庞大的自由黑人。

现在的这种通过滥用权力维持蓄奴制的办法,那时就是使南部白人胆战心惊的严重危险的根源。现在,欧洲人的后裔是土地唯一的主人,他们是一切劳力的绝对主人,而且只有他们既有钱又有知识和军队。黑人在他们的这些优势方面一无所有,但因为他们是奴隶,所以他们没有这些东西也能活下去。如果他们自由了,就需要自食其力,但他们没有这些东西还能维持生活吗? 又或者难道不恰恰是白人在奴隶制度存在时所有的优势使白人在废除蓄奴制后面临了许多危险的吗?

As long as the Negro remains a slave, he may be kept in a condition not far removed from that of the brutes; but with his liberty he cannot but acquire a degree of instruction that will enable him to appreciate his misfortunes and to discern a remedy for them. Moreover, there exists a singular principle of relative justice which is firmly implanted in the human heart. Men are much more forcibly struck by those inequalities which exist within the same class than by those which may be noted between different classes. One can understand slavery, but how allow several millions of citizens to exist under a load of eternal infamy and hereditary wretchedness? In the North the population of freed Negroes feels these hardships and indignities, but its numbers and its powers are small, while in the South it would be numerous and strong. As soon as it is admitted that the whites and the emancipated blacks are placed upon the same territory in the situation of two foreign communities, it will readily be understood that there are but two chances for the future: the Negroes and the whites must either wholly part or wholly mingle. I have already expressed my conviction as to the latter event. ①I do not believe that the white and black race? will ever live in any country upon an equal footing. But I believe the difficulty to be still greater in the United States than elsewhere. An isolated individual may surmount the prejudices of religion, of his country, or of his race; and if this individual is a king, he may effect surprising changes in society; but a whole people cannot rise, as it were, above itself. A despot who should subject the Americans and their former slaves to the same yoke might perhaps succeed in commingling their races; but as long as the American democracy remains at the head of affairs, no one will undertake so difficult a task; and it

---

① This opinion is sanctioned by authorities infinitely weightier than anything that I can say. Thus, for instance, it is stated in the *Memoirs of Jefferson*: "Nothing is more clearly written in the book of destiny than the emancipation of the blacks; and it is equally certain, that the two races will never live in a state of equal freedom under the same government, so insurmountable are the barriers which nature, habit; and opinion have established between them." (See *Extracts from the Memoirs of Jefferson*, by M. Conseil.)

　　如果黑人继续处于奴隶地位,也许他们会一直保持在接近野蛮的状态。但如果让他们自由了,就不能阻止他们增长知识,而知识会使他们了解自己的不幸并且会寻求解决不幸的途径。除此之外,还有一个相对公正的重要原则牢固地扎根于人们的心中。人们对于同一阶级内部存在的不平等的强烈感应,远远大于不同阶级之间出现的不平等。人们可以看到蓄奴制的存在,但到底是什么才能使几百万公民背负着这一永恒的耻辱和世世代代遭到的苦难呢? 在北方,已经获得解放的黑人,虽然忍受这种苦难和遭到不公正待遇,但他们的力量很小,而且人数日渐减少。而在南方,黑人的人数很多,而且力量也大。如使白人与被解放的黑人同住在一块土地上,并彼此视为异族,则不难预见将来会出现两种可能:不是黑人与白人将要完全混为一体,就是两者将要永远分离。我已经在前面表述过我对后者的看法。[①] 我不认为白人和黑人将来会在任何一个国家得到平等的生存待遇。但是我相信,在美国这种困难的程度将比在其他地方大的多。一个孤立的个体可能会放弃宗教的偏见、国家的偏见或种族的偏见。但是如果这一个体的身份是国王,他有可能还会对整个社会造成惊人的影响。但是一个民族恐怕很难超越自己。一个专制的君主可能会将美国人民和他们先前的奴隶置于同一轭下,也许会使他们彼此融合起来。但是只要美国的民主处

---

　　①　这一建议没有得到很强烈的认同。因此,比如说,就像《杰弗逊回忆录》中记载的那样:"命运之书说得最清楚的事情,莫过于黑人的解放。同样的,在同一政府统治下生活的两个民族,将永不会处于平等自由的状态,习惯就像不可跨越的横栏,他们至今永远存在着矛盾。"(见《杰弗逊论文集节选》。)

may be foreseen that the freer the white population of the United States becomes, the more isolated will it remain. ①

I have previously observed that the mixed race is the true bond of union between the Europeans and the Indians; just so, the mulattoes are the true means of transition between the white and the Negro; so that wherever mulattoes abound, the intermixture of the two races is not impossible. In some parts of America the European and the Negro races are so crossed with one another that it is rare to meet with a man who is entirely black or entirely white; when they have arrived at this point, the two races may really be said to be combined, or, rather, to have been absorbed in a third race, which is connected with both without being identical with either.

Of all Europeans, the English are those who have mixed least with the Negroes. More mulattoes are to be seen in the South of the Union than in the North, but infinitely fewer than in any other European colony. Mulattoes are by no means numerous in the United States; they have no force peculiar to themselves, and when quarrels originating in differences of color take place, they generally side with the whites, just as the lackeys of the great in Europe assume the contemptuous airs of nobility towards the lower orders.

The pride of origin, which is natural to the English, is singularly augmented by the personal pride that democratic liberty fosters among the Americans: the white citizen of the United States is proud of his race and proud of himself. But if the whites and the Negroes do not intermingle in the North of the Union, how should they mix in the South? Can it be supposed for an instant that an American of the

---

① If the British West India planters had governed themselves, they would assuredly not have passed the Slave Emancipation Bill which the mother country has recently imposed upon them.

于所有的事物的首位,就没有人能完成此重任了。可以预见,美国的白人越自由,他们就会越孤立。[①]

我在前面说过,混血儿是欧洲人和印第安人之间真正的纽带。同样的,白人和黑人生出的混血儿才是这两个种族之间的真正桥梁。因此,凡是黑白人混血儿大量生存的地方,两个种族的混合就不是不可能的。在美洲的一些地区,白人与黑人种族之间的交叉混合,对于一个纯粹白人或纯粹黑人来说,是极其罕见的。如果两个种族之间到了这种程度,那就可以说是达到两个种族混合的地步,或者不如说是被另一个第三种族所吸收,这一种族与其他两个种族有关联,但又不同于其中的任何一个种族。

英国人是在所有的欧洲人中最少与黑人结婚的。联邦南方的混血儿多于北方,但与其他欧洲殖民地相比则少之又少。美国的黑白人混血儿很少,他们本身毫无力量,并且他们在种族纠纷中一般都站在白人一边。如同在欧洲常见的那些大贵族的奴仆以贵族自居而蔑视一般人民的情况一般无二。

产生这种骄傲的根源,对英国人来说是再自然不过,而在美国人身上又因民主自由所造成的个人骄傲而得到特别地加强。美国的白人既以其民族感到自负,又因为自己是美国人而感到骄傲。但是,如果白人和黑人未在联邦的北方混合,他们怎么在南方混合呢? 我们能否设想一个案例,比如说一位一直生活在身心均占有优势的白人和黑人之间的南方白人,会想与黑人结合吗?

---

① 　如果英国西部的印第安耕种者可以自己管理自己的事务,他们肯定不会同意他们的祖国在他们身上颁布的《奴隶解放法案》。

Southern states, placed, as he must forever be, between the white man, with all his physical and moral superiority, and the Negro, will ever think of being confounded with the latter? The Americans of the Southern states have two powerful passions which will always keep them aloof: the first is the fear of being assimilated to the Negroes, their former slaves; and the second, the dread of sinking below the whites, their neighbors.

If I were called upon to predict the future, I should say that the abolition of slavery in the South will, in the common course of things, increase the repugnance of the white population for the blacks. I base this opinion upon the analogous observation I have already made in the North. J have remarked that the white inhabitants of the North avoid the Negroes with increasing care in proportion as the legal barriers of separation are removed by the legislature; and why should not the same result take place in the South? In the North the whites are deterred from intermingling with the blacks by an imaginary danger; in the South, where the danger would be real, I cannot believe that the fear would be less.

If, on the one hand, it be admitted (and the fact is unquestionable) that the colored population perpetually accumulate in the extreme South and increase more rapidly than the whites; and if, on the other hand, it be allowed that it is impossible to foresee a time at which the whites and the blacks will be so intermingled as to derive the same benefits from society, must it not be inferred that the blacks and the whites will, sooner or later, come to open strife in the Southern states? But if it be asked what the issue of the struggle is likely to be, it will readily be understood that we are here left to vague conjectures. The human mind may succeed in tracing a wide circle, as it were, which includes the future; but within that circle chance rules, and eludes all our foresight. In every picture of the future there is a dim spot which the eye of the understanding cannot penetrate. It appears, however, extremely probable that in the West Indies islands the white race is destined to be subdued, and upon the continent the blacks.

In the West Indies the white planters are isolated amid an immense black population; on the continent the blacks are placed between the ocean and an innumerable people, who already extend above them, in a compact mass, from the icy confines of Canada to the frontiers of Virginia, and from the banks of the Missouri to the shores of the Atlantic. If the white citizens of North America remain

南方各州的美国人有两种强烈的情感使他们永远保持孤立的状态:第一,担心自己与原来的奴隶黑人平等;第二,害怕自己处于邻居白人之下。

如果让我对未来做预测,我会说:从事物发展的一般规律来看,在南方废除蓄奴制后,会加深白人对黑人的反感。我的这个看法的产生源于我以前对北方做过的类似论断。我曾说过,随着立法机构逐渐废除种族之间的法律屏障,北方的白人会越来越小心不与黑人接触。为什么这种情况不会发生于南方呢?因为,在北方,白人不敢与黑人混合,是出于害怕假想的危险。而在南方,这个危险可能是真实存在的,所以我不认为害怕的程度会降低。

如果,一方面已经承认(事实也无可怀疑)黑人日益向南聚集,而且其人口增长的速度快于白人;而如果另一方面又确信不能预见黑人何时可与白人混合并从中获得同样的好处,难道就不能由此推论出,黑人和白人迟早要在南方各州发生冲突吗?而如果被问及这场冲突的最终结果,不难理解,我们只能做个大致的推测。人的思想对于未来勉强只能画出一个大致的轮廓,但在这个轮廓内,机会决定一切,可能会推翻我们的预测。在为未来勾画出的所有蓝图上,总有一些人们智慧之眼也无法辨别的黑点。尽管如此,有一点是可以预见的,即在安的列斯群岛,白人注定要屈服;而在大陆,黑人注定要屈服。

在安的列斯群岛,白人耕作者被孤立于不计其数的黑人之中。在大陆上,黑人被夹在两个大洋之间陷入茫茫的人海之中。这众多的人们,从加拿大的冰原到弗吉尼亚的南缘,从密西西比河岸边到大西洋海岸,已结成一个紧密的团体凌驾于黑人之上。

united, it is difficult to believe that the Negroes. will escape the destruction which menaces them; they must be subdued by want or by the sword. But the black population accumulated along the coast of the Gulf of Mexico have a chance of success if the American Union should be dissolved when the struggle between the two races begins. The Federal tie once broken, the people of the South could not rely upon any lasting succor from their Northern countrymen. The latter are well aware that the danger can never reach them; and unless they are constrained to march to the assistance of the South by a positive obligation, it may be foreseen that the sympathy of race will be powerless.

Yet, at whatever period the strife may break out, the whites of the South, even if they are abandoned to their own resources, will enter the lists with an immense superiority of knowledge and the means of warfare; but the blacks will have numerical strength and the energy of despair upon their side, and these are powerful resources to men who have taken up arms. The fate of the white population of the Southern states will perhaps be similar to that of the Moors in Spain. After having occupied the land for centuries, it will perhaps retire by degrees to the country whence its ancestors came and abandon to the Negroes the possession of a territory which Providence seems to have destined for them, since they can subsist and labor in it more easily than the whites.

The danger of a conflict between the white and the black inhabitants of the Southern states of the Union (a danger which, however remote it may be, is inevitable) perpetually haunts the imagination of the Americans, like a painful dream. The inhabitants of the North make it a common topic of conversation, although directly they have nothing to fear from it; but they vainly endeavor to devise some means of obviating the misfortunes which they foresee. In the Southern states the subject is not discussed: the planter does not allude to the future in conversing with strangers; he does not communicate his apprehensions to his friends; he seeks to conceal them from himself. But there is something more alarming in the tacit forebodings of the South than in the clamorous fears of the North.

This all-pervading disquietude has given birth to an undertaking as yet but little known, which, however, may change the fate

如果北美的白人仍旧能保持团结,我们很难相信黑人能够逃脱危及他们的毁灭性灾难:他们不是屈服于枪炮,就是屈服于贫穷。但是,如果在两个种族间的斗争开始的时候,美国联邦能够解体,那么,聚居在墨西哥湾一带的黑人就有机会取胜。一旦联邦的纽带断裂,南方的白人就没法依靠北方同胞给予他们的持久支援。因为北方的白人十分清楚,危险永远不会临到他们的头上。即使抱着积极地承担义务的心态远征前去施以援助,我们也可以预见种族之间的同情所产生的威力是微乎其微的。

但是,不管在任何情况下爆发战争,南方白人即使被北方同胞抛弃,仍可以依靠知识的优势和武器投入战场,而黑人则全凭人多势众和不怕死的精神同他们斗争。但是,一旦黑人手中掌握了武器,这种精神就会变成巨大的战斗力。那样的话,南方的白人也许会遭遇到与西班牙摩尔人同样的命运。在那里占据数个世纪之后,他们也许被迫逐步退回到祖先迁来前的地点,把上苍似乎注定要给黑人的这块土地还给黑人,因为黑人在这里的生活和劳动比白人显得轻松容易得多。

联邦南方各州的白人与黑人发生冲突的危险尽管看起来还很遥远,但是不可避免的。它总是像梦魇般萦绕于美国人的脑际。北方居民常常会谈论这一话题,尽管这种危险对他们并无直接威胁。他们企图找到办法来防止他们所预料的不幸,但始终徒劳无功。在南方各州,人们从不谈论这个话题。南方人向来不对外来人谈论未来,即使对亲友也从不谈及自己对此的感受,每个人都把话藏在自己的心里。但是。事实上,南方人的这种沉默的预示,比北方人的四处喊叫更令人可怕。

他们的这种普遍忧虑导致了一项可能改变人类一部分人的

of a portion of the human race. From apprehension of the dangers that I have just described, some American citizens have formed a society for the purpose of exporting to the coast of Guinea, at their own expense, such free Negroes as may be willing to escape from the oppression to which they are subject. ①

In 1820 the society to which I allude formed a settlement in Africa, on the seventh degree of north latitude, which bears the name of Liberia. The most recent intelligence informs us that two thousand five hundred Negroes are collected there. They have introduced the democratic institutions of America into the country of their forefathers. Liberia has a representative system of government, Negro jurymen, Negro magistrates, and Negro priests; churches have been built, newspapers established, and, by a sin gular turn in the vicissitudes of the world, white men are prohibited from establishing themselves within the settlement. ②

This is indeed a strange caprice of fortune. Two hundred years have now elapsed since the inhabitants of Europe undertook to tear the Negro from his family and his home in order to transport him to the shores of North America. Now the European settlers are engaged in sending back the descendants of those very Negroes to the continent whence they were originally taken: the barbarous Africans have learned civilization in the midst of bondage and have become acquainted with free political institutions in slavery. Up to the present time Africa has been closed against the arts and sciences of the whites, but the inventions of Europe will perhaps penetrate into those regions now that they are introduced by Africans themselves. The settlement of Liberia is founded upon a lofty and fruitful idea; but, whatever may be its results with regard to Africa, it can afford no remedy to the New World.

---

① This society assumed the name of "The Society for the Colonization of the Blacks." See its Annual Reports and more particularly the fifteenth. See also the pamphlet, to which allusion has already been made, entitled: *Letters on the Colonization Society, and on Its Probable Results*, by Mr. Carey (Philadelphia, April 1833).

② This last regulation was laid down by the founders of the settlement; they believed that a state of things might arise in Africa similar to that which exists on the frontiers of the United States, and that if the Negroes, like the Indians, were brought into collision with a people more enlightened than themselves, they would be destroyed before they could be civilized.

命运的事业的发生,尽管迄今为止鲜为人知。由于对我方才谈到的危险感到害怕和担心,一些美国人组织了一个协会,目的就是由他们自己出资,将愿意摆脱暴政压迫的自由黑人,送到几内亚海岸去居住。①

1820 年,我所说的这个协会在非洲北纬 7°附近建立了一个据点,取名为利比里亚。据最新消息,已有 2500 多名黑人聚居于此处。他们把美国的民主制度带回到自己祖先的土地上。利比里亚实行代议制,有黑人陪审员、黑人行政官和黑人教士,也建有教堂和出版报纸。这些历经沧桑的人回到故地后,不准白人到他们那里定居。②

这真是一个奇迹!自从欧洲人开始强迫黑人背井离乡把他们运到北美海岸出卖以来,已经过去 200 多年了。现在,欧洲人又把这些黑人的后代送回他们祖先被掠走的地方。这些野蛮人已在被奴役时期学会了文明人的知识,并在实行蓄奴制的地方学到了享用自由的办法。直到现在非洲还对白人的技术和科学采取全面抵制的态度。被这些非洲人带回来的欧洲发明,也许能够渗入这些地区。因此,利比里亚是人们怀着美好而崇高的理想建造起来的。但是,这种在旧大陆可能产生丰硕成果的理想,对新世界并无助益。

---

① 这个社会采用了一个名称"黑人殖民地化的社会"。见第十五次年报。以及凯里著的题名为《殖民地社会的论述以及可能出现的结果》的小册子中所提及的暗示。(1833 年四月于费城。)

② 最后一条规则已被殖民地的开拓者们所遗弃。他们认为在美洲国家的所有事情都要和美国的相似,并且,如果黑人像印第安人一样陷入了与比他们文明的人们之间的冲突之中的话,他们就会在还没有被文明开化之前就已经消亡。

In twelve years the Colonization Society has transported two thousand five hundred Negroes to Africa; in the same space of time about seven hundred thousand blacks were born in the United States. If the colony of Liberia were able to receive thousands of new inhabitants every year, and if the Negroes were in a state to be sent thither with advantage; if the Union were to supply the society with annual subsidies, [1] and to transport the Negroes to Africa in government vessels, it would still be unable to counterpoise the natural increase of population among the blacks; and as it could not remove as many men in a year as are born upon its territory within that time, it could not prevent the growth of the evil which is daily increasing in the states[2] The Negro race will never leave those shores of the American continent to which it was brought by the passions and the vices of Europeans; and it will not disappear from the New World as long as it continues to exist. The inhabitants of the United States may retard the calamities which they apprehend; but they cannot now destroy their efficient cause.

I am obliged to confess that I do not regard the abolition of slavery as a means of warding off the struggle of the two races in the Southern states. The Negroes may long remain slaves without complaining; but if they are once raised to the level of freemen, they will soon revolt at being deprived of almost all their civil rights; and as they cannot become the equals of the whites, they will speedily show themselves as enemies. In the North everything facilitated the emancipation of the slaves, and slavery was abolished without rendering the free Negroes formidable, since their number was too small for them

---

[1] Nor would these be the only difficulties attendant upon the undertaking; if the Union undertook to buy up the Negroes now in America in order to transport them to Africa, the price of slaves, increasing with their scarcity, would soon become enormous; and the states of the North would never consent to expend such great sums for a purpose that would profit them but little. If the Union took possession of the slaves in the Southern states by force, or at a rate determined by law, an insurmountable resistance would arise in that part of the country. Both courses are equally impossible.

[2] In 1830 there were in the United States 2,010,327 slaves and 319,439 free blacks, in all 2,329,766 Negroes, who formed about one fifth of the total population of the United States at that time.

12 年来,黑人移民协会向非洲输送了共 2500 名黑人。在同一时期,美国约有 70 万黑人婴儿出世。即使利比里亚殖民地每年能够接纳几千名新居民;即使新居民能在那里过上好日子;即使联邦政府包办协会的一切,年年由国库出钱支援协会,①用国家的船向非洲运送黑人,也无法抵消美国黑人自然繁殖人数的增加。于是,由于每年新出世的黑人人数多于每年运出的黑人人数,所以也就阻止不了每天都在加深的黑人苦难的加剧。② 黑色人种永远不会从美洲大陆的海岸消失,只要有新大陆存在,就会有黑色人种,并在那里受欧洲人的贪欲和恶习的影响而堕落。美国的居民可以推迟他们所担心的灾难的来临,但他们现在还没能消除造成灾难的根源。

我必须承认,我并不认为废除蓄奴制是在南方各州避免两个种族斗争的方法。黑人可以长期为奴而没有怨言;但一旦他们进入自由人的行列以后,很快就会对被剥夺了几乎所有的权利而产生怨恨,而且由于不能成为与白人平等的人,所以他们很快就会以敌对的姿态站在白人面前。北方的一切条件都有利于解放奴隶,废除蓄奴制后不必担心自由黑人闹事。他们的人数很少,永远不会去要求自己的权利。而在南方,情况却非如此。蓄奴制对

---

① 这些并不是唯一存在的困难。如果联邦开始实施购买所有美国黑人然后运往非洲的话,奴隶的价格将会随着他们的减少而上升,并且很快就会上升到很高的价格。而在北部州则绝不会同意扩大到这么大的数量,只为了牟取暴利。如果联邦在南部州用武力可以对奴隶拥有所有权,或者在一定程度上依靠法律的力量,而在州的北部则会发起一股不可抵抗的反对力量。两种途径都是不可行的。

② 1830 年,美国有 2030327 个奴隶和 319439 个自由黑人,总共有 2329766 个黑人,这些人占据了美国当时人口总数的五分之一。

ever to claim their rights. But such is not the case in the South. The question of slavery was a commercial and manufacturing question for the slave-owners in the North; for those of the South it is a question of life and death. God forbid that I should seek to justify the principle of Negro slavery, as has been done by some American writers! I say only that all the countries which formerly adopted that execrable principle are not equally able to abandon it at the present time.

When I contemplate the condition of the South, I can discover only two modes of action for the white inhabitants of those States: namely, either to emancipate the Negroes and to intermingle with them, or, remaining isolated from them, to keep them in slavery as long as possible. All intermediate measures seem to me likely to terminate, and that shortly, in the most horrible of civil wars and perhaps in the extirpation of one or the other of the two races. Such is the view that the Americans of the South take of the question, and they act consistently with it. As they are determined not to mingle with the Negroes, they refuse to emancipate them.

Not that the inhabitants of the South regard slavery as necessary to the wealth of the planter; on this point many of them agree with their Northern countrymen, in freely admitting that slavery is prejudicial to their interests; but they are convinced that the removal of this evil would imperil their own existence. The instruction which is now diffused in the South has convinced the inhabitants that slavery is injurious to the slave-owner, but it has also shown them, more clearly than before, that it is almost an impossibility to get rid of it. Hence arises a singular contrast: the more the utility of slavery is contested, the more firmly is it established in the laws; and while its principle is gradually abolished in the North, that selfsame principle gives rise to more and more rigorous consequences in the South.

The legislation of the Southern states with regard to slaves presents at the present day such unparalleled atrocities as suffice to show that the laws of humanity have been totally perverted, and to betray the desperate position of the community in which that legislation has been promulgated. The Americans of this portion of the union have not, indeed, augmented the hardships of slavery; on the contrary,

北方的奴隶主来说，只是一个涉及商业和工业的问题；而在南方则事关生死。上帝不允许我像某些美国作者那样为奴役黑人的原则辩护。我只是说，凡曾经赞同这个罪恶制度的人，现在也不会轻易放弃它。

我坦白承认，在我考察南方诸州时，我发现这个地区的白色人种只有两条出路：不是解放黑人并与他们融合，就是仍让他们孤立并尽可能使其处于奴隶地位。所有折衷的办法，在我看来，都只有终结。在不久即将上演的可怕的内战，两个种族必有一个由此毁灭。南方的美国白人就是从这个观点来看待问题的，并且据此而行动。他们不想与黑人融合，所以就不让黑人自由。

这并不是说南方的居民认为蓄奴制是奴隶主获得致富的必要手段。在这一点上，他们当中的大多数人与其北方同胞的见解一致，愿意承认奴役黑人有损他们的利益。但他们又认为，终结这种罪恶就会使自己处于危险境地。随着教育在南方的散播，这一地区的居民日益认识到蓄奴制对奴隶主是有害处的。但是，这种教育也比从前更清楚地向他们表明，暂时还无法废除它。于是，出现了一种鲜明的对比：蓄奴制越是受到质疑，它在法律上就越是得到加强；在北方，蓄奴制的原则逐渐被废除，而同样的原则在南方产生越来越严酷的后果。

南方各州对奴隶的立法，在如今，具有一种前所未有的残酷性，简直可以说是对人类法律的不正当的运用，暴露了立法被公布的那个社会所处的绝望的状态。居住在联邦这些地方的美国人，事实上，夸大了奴隶制带来的苦难。另一方面，他们也改善了奴隶的物质生活条件。古代人只知道用铁链和死亡来维护奴隶制度；联邦南方的美国人，发现了一些更聪明的方法以保证他们

they have bettered the physical condition of the slaves. The only means by which the ancients maintained slavery were fetters and death; the Americans of the South of the Union have discovered more intellectual securities for the duration of their power. They have employed their despotism and their violence against the human mind. In antiquity precautions were taken to prevent the slave from breaking his chains; at the present day measures are adopted to deprive him even of the desire for freedom. The ancients kept the bodies of their slaves in bondage, but placed no restraint upon the mind and no check upon education; and they acted consistently with their established principle, since a natural termination of slavery then existed, and one day or other the slave might be set free and become the equal of his master. But the Americans of the South, who do not admit that the Negroes can ever be commingled with themselves, have forbidden them, under severe penalties, to be taught to read or write; and as they will not raise them to their own level, they sink them as nearly as possible to that of the brutes.

The hope of liberty had always been allowed to the slave, to cheer the hardships of his condition. But the Americans of the South are well aware that emancipation cannot but be dangerous when the freed man can never be assimilated to his former master. To give a man his freedom and to leave him in wretchedness and ignominy is nothing less than to prepare a future chief for a revolt of the slaves. Moreover, it has long been remarked that the presence of a free Negro vaguely agitates the minds of his less fortunate brethren, and conveys to them a dim notion of their rights. The Americans of the South have consequently taken away from slave-owners the right of emancipating their slaves in most cases. [1]

I happened to meet an old man, in the South of the Union, who had lived in illicit intercourse with one of his Negresses and had had several children by her, who were born the slaves of their father. He had, indeed, frequently thought of bequeathing to them at least their liberty; but years had elapsed before he could surmount the legal obstacles to their emancipation, and meanwhile his old age had come

---

[1] Emancipation is not prohibited, but surrounded with such formalities as to render it difficult.

的权力持久。他们已经把他们的专制和虐行深植于人们的头脑中。在古代,奴隶主是想办法防止奴隶打碎枷锁;而现代,奴隶主是设法剥夺奴隶产生这种欲望的能力。古代人给奴隶身上戴上链子,但让他们思想自由,允许他们学习知识。并且,奴隶主严格按照制度办事,遵守他们所定的原则。在古代,受奴役的期限不是固定不变的,奴隶随时都可能获得自由而与主人平等。但联邦南方的美国人,从来没有想过黑人会有一天与他们融为一体。他们禁止奴隶识字和写字。他们不希望把黑人提高到与自己相等的水平,并且尽可能使奴隶保持其原始生活状态。

奴隶从来都向往自由,并借此给自己的悲惨生活增添一丝欢乐。但是,联邦南方的美国人十分清楚,解放黑奴的运动如果不能使获得解放的奴隶达到与其原来的主人相互融合的地步,就终究是要带来危险的。给予奴隶自由,同时又让他处于苦难和屈辱之中,就是在为奴隶的造反提供一个主因。除此之外,很早就有人指出,只要出现一个自由黑人,就会在还没有获得自由的不幸的黑人心中埋下隐患,使他们感受到他们的权力闪烁的荧光。因此,联邦南方的美国人,在大多数情况下,剥夺了奴隶主解放自己的奴隶的权利。①

我在联邦的南方曾遇见过一位老人,他曾同他的一个女黑奴长期非法同居并且生了几个孩子,这些孩子一出世就成了自己父亲的奴隶。这位老人曾多次想把自己的权利传给他的孩子,至少让他们获得自由,但是经过多年的努力,他最终还是不能克服立

---

① 奴隶解放虽然没有受到限制,但是围绕在它周边的种种形式为它设置了重重困难。

and he was about to die. He pictured to himself his sons dragged from market to market and passing from the authority of a parent to the rod of the stranger, until these horrid anticipations worked his expiring imagination into frenzy. When I saw him, he was a prey to all the anguish of despair; and I then understood how awful is the retribution of Nature upon those who have broken her laws.

These evils are unquestionably great, but they are the necessary and foreseen consequences of the very principle of modern slavery. When the Europeans chose their slaves from a race differing from their own, which many of them considered as inferior to the other races of mankind, and any notion of intimate union with which they all repelled with horror, they must have believed that slavery would last forever, since there is no intermediate state that can be durable between the excessive inequality produced by servitude and the complete equality that originates in independence. The Europeans did imperfectly feel this truth, but without acknowledging it even to themselves. Whenever they have had to do with Negroes, their conduct has been dictated either by their interest and their pride or by their compassion. They first violated every right of humanity by their treatment of the Negro, and they afterwards informed him that those rights were precious and inviolable. They opened their ranks to their slaves, arid when the latter tried to come in, they drove them forth in scorn. Desiring slavery, they have allowed themselves unconsciously to be swayed in spite of themselves towards liberty, without having the courage to be either completely iniquitous or completely just.

If it is impossible to anticipate a period at which the Americans of the South will mingle their blood with that of the Negroes, can they allow their slaves to become free without compromising their own security? And if they are obliged to keep that race in bondage in order to save their own families, may they not be excused for availing themselves of the means best adapted to that end? The events that are taking place in the Southern states appear to me to be at once the most

法机构为解放黑奴所设的障碍。而这时他也已经年老,将不久于人世。当时,他向我描述了他的儿子被从一个市场拖到另一个市场,最终离开父母的关爱被送到一个陌生人手下鞭笞。这些可怕的情景终于使老人的已经枯竭的想象变得激愤。当我看着他的时候,他正在饱受着绝望的痛苦的煎熬,而我也领悟了自然规律对破坏其规律的人们的可怕惩罚。

这种灾难无疑是巨大的,但这也是现代蓄奴制原则注定要产生的必然结果。当欧洲人从一个与他们自己不同的种族中掠夺奴隶的时候,多数人都会认为这个种族比人类的其他种族低劣,所以任何一种与它融合在一起的设想都使人感到不安而产生排斥。他们预想蓄奴制可以永久长存,因为他们认为,在奴役所制造的极端不平等与独立在人们当中所自然产生的完全平等之间,决不会有能够持久存在的中间状态。虽然并不彻底的相信,但是欧洲人还是认为这就是真理,但又始终未能使自己确信。因此,当他们与黑人不得不发生关系的时候,其行为时而受到他们的利益和高傲偏见的支配,时而又受到他们的同情心的影响。他们先在对待黑人上侵犯了人权,然后他们又告诉黑人明白这些权利的珍贵性和不可侵犯性。他们对自己的奴隶敞开了他们的社会,然而当奴隶试图进入这个社会时,又对他们嗤之以鼻。他们一方面希望奴役黑人,另一方面又身不由己地或不知不觉地使自己受自由思想的支配。他们既不想丧尽天良,又没有勇气完全伸张正义。

既然无法预测何时南方的美国人会使自己与黑人真正融合起来,他们怎么能够冒着给自己带来的危险而允许黑人自由呢?而且,既然他们为了拯救自己的种族不得不将黑人奴役起来,那么他们现在为了达到这个目的而采取一些更有效的手段就不可

horrible and the most natural results of slavery. When I see the order of nature overthrown, and when I hear the cry of humanity in its vain struggle against the laws, my indignation does not light upon the men of our own time who are the instruments of these outrages; but I reserve my execration for those who, after a thousand years of freedom, brought back slavery into the world once more.

Whatever may be the efforts of the Americans of the South to maintain slavery, they will not always succeed. Slavery, now confined to a single tract of the civilized earth, attacked by Christianity as unjust and by political economy as prejudicial, and now contrasted with democratic liberty and the intelligence of our age, cannot survive. By the act of the master, or by the will of the slave, it will cease; and in either case great calamities may be expected to ensue. If liberty be refused to the Negroes of the South, they will in the end forcibly seize it for themselves; if it be given, they will before long abuse it.

What Are The Chances Of Duration Of The American Union, And What Dangers Threaten It

What makes the preponderant force lie in the states rather than in the Union—The Union will last only as long as all the states choose to belong to it—Causes that tend to keep them united—Utility of the Union to resist foreign enemies and to exclude foreigners from America—No natural barriers between the several states—No conflicting interests to divide them—Reciprocal interests of the Northern, Southern, and Western states—Intellectualties of Union-Uniformity of opinions—Dangers of the Union resulting from the different characters and the passions of its citizens—Character of the citizens in the South and in the North—The rapid growth of the Union one of its greatest dangers—Progress of the population to the northwest—Power gravitates in the same direction—Passions originating from sudden turns of fortune Whether the existing government of the Union tends to gain

原谅吗？在我看来,联邦南方所发生的一切,虽是蓄奴制的最可怕结果,却也是蓄奴制发展的必然结果。当我看到自然秩序被颠覆,听到人性在与法律做徒劳的斗争的呼喊,我不会怒斥制造这些罪恶的我们这一代人,我要憎恨的,是那些享受了1000多年的平等之后又使奴隶制度重返世界的人。

不管南方的美国人尽了多大努力去维护蓄奴制,他们永远也不会达到目的。而今仅存在于文明世界一角的蓄奴制,曾被基督教斥为不义、被政治经济学视为偏颇,在现代的民主自由和文明的对比下难于存活。它要么将被奴隶推翻,要么被奴隶主取消。但无论在哪一种情况下,都可预见一场巨大的灾难的发生。如果拒绝给予南方黑人自由,他们终将通过暴力为自己争取获得;但是如果同意给他们自由,他们很快又要滥用自由。

美国联邦持久存在的机缘是什么 和威胁着它存在的危险是什么

为什么优越权力的来源存在于各州,而不存在于联邦——构成联邦的各州愿意属于联邦一天,联邦就会存在一天——促使各州继续联合下去的原因——联邦的存在对于抵抗外敌和不使外敌入侵美洲的功用——各州之间不存在天然屏障——没有使各州分裂的物质利益冲突——北部、西部、南部的互惠——联邦的精神纽带——舆论的一致——联邦的危险来自联邦各地居民的性格和感情的不同——南方人和北方人的性格——联邦的迅速扩大是其主要危险之一——人口向西北移动——势力倾向——形势的这种快速发展引起的激情——联邦这样存在下去会使它的

strength or to lose it—Various signs of its decrease—Internal improvements—Wastelands—Indians—The bank—The tariff—General Jackson.

The maintenance of the existing institutions of the several states depends in part upon the maintenance of the Union itself. We must therefore first inquire into the probable fate of the Union. One point may be assumed at once: if the present confederation were dissolved, it appears to me to be incontestable that the states of which it is now composed would not return to their original iso lated condition, but that several unions would then be formed in the place of one. It is not my intention to inquire into the principles upon which these new unions would probably be established, but merely to show what the causes are which may effect the dismemberment of the existing confederation.

With this object, I shall be obliged to retrace some of the steps that I have already taken and to revert to topics that I have before discussed. I am aware that the reader may accuse me of repetition, but the importance of the matter which still remains to be treated is my excuse: I had rather say too much than not be thoroughly understood; and I prefer injuring the author to slighting the subject.

The legislators who formed the Constitution of 1789 endeavored to confer a separate existence and superior strength upon the Federal power. But they were confined by the conditions of the task which they had undertaken to perform. They were not appointed to constitute the government of a single people, but to regulate the association of several states; and, whatever their inclinations might be, they could not but divide the exercise of sovereignty.

In order to understand the consequences of this division it is necessary to make a short distinction between the functions of government. There are some objects which are national by their very nature; that is to say, which affect the nation as a whole, and can be entrusted only to the man or the assembly of men who most completely represent the entire nation. Among these may be reckoned war and diplomacy. There are other objects which are provincial by their very nature; that is to say, which affect only certain localities and which can be properly treated only in that locality. Such, for instance, is the budget of a municipality. Lastly, there are objects of a mixed nature, which are national inasmuch as they affect all the citizens who

政府强大还是软弱——联邦政府软弱的各种迹象——政府内部的改革——荒地——印第安人——银行业——关税——杰克逊将军。

联邦各州现存制度之所以得以维持,部分原因是由于依赖联邦的存在。因此,我们首先探讨的,必然是联邦的未来命运。首先要确认一点:如果现存的联邦解体,我认为可以肯定的是,现在组成联邦的各州也不会恢复其最初各自独立的状态。而将会出现几个联邦取而代之。对这些新联邦建立的基础的研究,并不是我的目的,而我想指出的是可能导致现存联邦解体的一些原因。

为了达到这一目的,我不得不回过头去再谈一下已经叙述过的几个问题。读者也许会指责我重复。但是,我有我的理由,因为问题的重要性尚有待于研究。我宁愿多说几次,也不让读者读后不解其意。我宁愿让自己挨骂,也不放过一个问题。

制定1789年宪法的立法者们,曾一再努力使联邦政权具有独立性和优越权力。但是,他们受到的局限,在于他们所要解决的问题本身。当时,他们的任务不是组建一个单一国家的政府,而是要规范几个各自享有主权的州的联合体。另外,不管他们意愿如何,他们都得使这些州分享国家的主权。

为了使读者更好地了解这种对国家主权的分享所造成的后果,必须简略地区分一下政府的功用。其中有些事务究其本身性质来说是属于全国性的,也就是说,会对整个国家产生影响,只能委托全权代表整个国家的某几个人或某个集体行使。比如说战争和外交都属于这类事务。另有一些事务究其本身的性质来说是地方性的,只归各地方政府管辖,只能由该地方政府作相应处理,像编制地方的预算。最后,还有一些事务究其本身的性质来

compose the nation, and which are provincial inasmuch as it is not necessary that the nation itself should provide for them all. Such are the rights that regulate the civil and political condition of the citizens. No society can exist without civil and political rights. These rights, therefore, interest all the citizens alike; but it is not always necessary to the existence and the prosperity of the nation that these rights should be uniform, nor, consequently, that they should be regulated by the central authority.

There are, then, two distinct categories of objects which are submitted to the sovereign power; and these are found in all well constituted communities, whatever may be the basis of the political constitution. Between these two extremes the objects which I have termed mixed may be considered to lie. As these are neither exclusively national nor entirely provincial, the care of them may be given to a national or a provincial government, according to the agreement of the contracting parties, without in any way impairing the object of association.

The sovereign power is usually formed by the union of individuals, who compose a people; and individual powers or collective forces, each representing a small fraction of the sovereign, are the only elements that are found under the general government. In this case the general government is more naturally called upon to regulate not only those affairs which are essentially national, but most of those which I have called mixed; and the local governments are reduced to that small share of sovereign authority which is indispensable to their well-being.

But sometimes the sovereign authority is composed of preorganized political bodies, by virtue of circumstances anterior to their union; and in this case the state governments assume the control not only of those affairs which more peculiarly belong to them, but of all or a part of the mixed objects in question. For the confederate nations, which were independent sovereignties before their union, and which still represent a considerable share of the sovereign power, have consented to cede to the general government the exercise only of those rights which are indispensable to the Union.

说是混合性的,从它们涉及国家所有人民方面来说,它们是全国性的,而因为可以不必由国家出面的方面来说,它们又属地方性。例如,规范公民的民事活动权利和政治活动权利的问题。任何社会体制都存在着公民权利和政治权利。因此,这些权利关乎全国公民共有的利害,但对于国家的生存和繁荣并不必需,因此,这些事务不是非由中央政府规定不可。

于是,有两种不同范畴的事务共同属于国家主权的管辖范围。并且,它们都建立在机构健全的国家,无论其政治契约是建立在什么样的基础之上。在这两个极端之间,就存在着我所描述的这种混合性质的事务。这些事务既不完全属于国家的,又不完全属于地方的管辖,而是根据联邦各国达成的协议,在不损害联邦共同目的的前提下,交由全国政府或地方政府去处理。

最高权力通常是由一些个体的联合形成的,而这些个体又形成国家。分别代表国家主权的一小部分的个体权利和集体权利,是存在于中央政府直辖的唯一权力。因此,全国政府也就更加理所当然地不仅要主管本质上属于全国的事务,而且要主管大部分我方才提到的混合性事务。而地方政府只拥有一小部分主权,这部分主权仅是为维护本地方的福利所不可缺少的。

但是有时候,由于联合之前的实际情况使然,最高权力当局由几个已存在的政治团体所组成。在这种情况下,州政府就不仅要管辖在性质上完全属于地方的事务,而且要管理全部或部分尚不明确的混合性事务。这是因为在联合之前,这几个国家或地区都是独立于联邦之外的国家,至今也还代表着联合前的自己主权,而只是同意让联合的总政府行使联合政府所不可缺少的职权。

When the national government, independently of the prerogatives inherent in its nature, is invested with the right of regulating the mixed objects of sovereignty, it possesses a preponderant influence. Not only are its own rights extensive, but all the rights which it does not possess exist by its sufferance; and it is to be feared that the provincial governments may be deprived by it of their natural and necessary prerogatives.

When, on the other hand, the provincial governments are invested with the power of regulating those same affairs of mixed interest, an opposite tendency prevails in society. The preponderant force resides in the province, not in the nation; and it may be apprehended that the national government may, in the end, be stripped of the privileges that are necessary to its existence. Single nations have therefore a natural tendency to centralization, and confederations to dismemberment.

It now remains to apply these general principles to the American Union. The several states necessarily retained the right of regulating all purely local affairs. Moreover, these same states kept the rights of determining the civil and political competency of the citizens, of regulating the reciprocal relations of the members of the community, and of dispensing justice—rights which are general in their nature, but do not necessarily appertain to the national government. We have seen that the government of the Union is invested with the power of acting in the name of the whole nation in those cases in which the nation has to appear as a single and undivided power; as, for instance, in foreign relations, and in offering a common resistance to a common enemy; in short, in conducting those affairs which I have styled exclusively national.

In this division of the rights of sovereignty the share of the Union seems at first sight more considerable than that of the states, but a more attentive investigation shows it to be less so. The undertakings of the government of the Union are more vast, but it has less frequent occasion to act at all. Those of the state governments are comparatively small, but they are incessant and they keep alive the authority which they represent. The government of the Union watches over the general interests of the country; but the general interests of a people have but a questionable influence upon individual happiness, while state interests produce an immediate effect upon the welfare of the

当全国政府,除了本身性质所固有的特权外,还被授予规定主权中的混合性事务的权限的时候,它就具有了一种占有优势的影响力。它不仅有广泛的权力,而且可以使本非它所有的权力受到其影响。所以,这时候,人们就会担心地方政府固有的必须的特权会被它剥夺。

反之,如果授予地方政府以规定混合性事务的权力,则在社会上会出现一种反对中央政府的趋势。这样,优先权便成了地方政府的,而不存在于全国政府,所以人们害怕,全国政府最终会因失去维持其存在所必要的特权而垮台。因此,单一的国家便有天然走向集权的趋势,而联邦国家的趋势则必然走向分裂。

现在,我们就用这些通行的原则评述美国的联邦。美联邦各州必然保留那些纯属地方事务的权力。除此之外,各州还保留了规定公民的民事和政治行为能力的权力,规范公民之间关系的权力以及对公民进行审判的权力。这些权力,按其性质来说属全国性的,但不一定非属于全国政府。前面已经说过,联邦政府在国家以一个单一的不可分割体行动时,才被授予以全国的名义发号施令的权力。比如说,在处理外交关系的时候,或领导全国力量共同对敌的时候。总之,执行我所说的纯属全国性的事务。

对于主权的这种划分,粗略一看的话,会觉得联邦分享的主权大于各州分享的主权。但稍加留心考察就会发现:事实上,联邦分得的主权是较少的一方。联邦政府主管的工作虽然非常广泛,但它根本就很少会去办理。地方政府办理的事务虽然很小,但它从来没停止过工作,使人每时每刻都感到它所代表的权利的存在。联邦政府关心全国的普遍利益,但一个国家的普遍利益,对个人的幸福只能产生很模糊的影响。反之,地方政府对本地居

inhabitants. The Union secures the independence and the greatness of the nation, which do not immediately affect private citizens; but the several states maintain the liberty, regulate the rights, protect the fortune, and secure the life and the whole future prosperity of every citizen.

The Federal government is far removed from its subjects, while the state governments are within the reach of them all and are ready to attend to the smallest appeal. The central government has on its side the passions of a few superior men who aspire to conduct it; but on the side of the state governments are the interests of all those second-rate individuals who can only hope to obtain power within their own state, and who nevertheless exercise more authority over the people because they are nearer to them.

The Americans have, therefore, much more to hope and to fear from the states than from the Union; and, according to the natural tendency of the human mind, they are more likely to attach themselves strongly to the former than to the latter. In this respect their habits and feelings harmonize with their interests.

When a compact nation divides its sovereignty and adopts a confederate form of government, the traditions, the customs, and the usages of the people for a long time struggle against the laws and give an influence to the central government which the laws forbid. But when a number of confederate states unite to form a single nation, the same causes operate in an opposite direction. I have no doubt that if France were to become a confederate republic like that of the United States, the government would at first be more energetic than that of the Union; and if the Union were to alter its constitution to a monarchy like that of France, I think that the American government would long remain weaker than the French. When the national existence of the Anglo-Americans began, their colonial existence was already of long standing: necessary relations were established between the townships and the individual citizens of the same states; and they were accustomed to consider some objects as common to them all, and to conduct other affairs as exclusively relating to their own special interests.

The Union is a vast body, which presents no definite object to patriotic feeling. The forms and limits of the state are distinct and circumscribed, since it represents a certain number of objects that are

民的福利,会发生直接的效应。联邦政府负责保障国家的独立和强大,这与个人没有直接影响。各州负责维护本州人民的自由,规范他们的权利,保护他们的财产还要保障对他们生命和未来繁荣。

联邦政府远离它的百姓,而地方政府与人民亲密接触并随时准备接受人民的请愿。中央政府依靠少数几个希望领导它的优秀人物的热情,而地方政府则依靠一些二级人物的关心。这些人只希望在本州掌权并且他们接近人民,对人民有很大的权威性影响。

因此,美国人对于州的期待和担心远比对联邦多得多;并且,从人心的自然趋势来看,美国人对前者依附显然多过后者。在这方面,他们的习俗和感情与他们的利益是一致的。

当一个紧密团结的国家实行主权分制和联邦制度时,其人民所形成的传统、习俗和惯例将会在很长一段时期内与法律进行斗争,并给中央政府造成极大地影响,这些是法律不允许的。而当联邦各州联合起来组成一个单一的主权国家时,这些因素就会作用于完全发生相反的方向。我毫不怀疑,假如法国变成像美国那样的联邦共和国,它的政府在一开始就会比美国的联邦政府更强大有力;而如果美国把它的政体改成君主政体,那么,我认为美国政府将会在很长一段时间内比法国政府更疲软。当英裔美国人开始建立国家时,他们的殖民地已存在很久了,乡镇和所在州之间也已建立起必要的关系,人民已经习惯于用共同的观点去考察一些问题,而且也只会前去处理那些与己有关的特殊事务。

美国联邦是一个庞大联合体,它无法给爱国主义提供明确的目标;而各州的组织形式和范围都是被明确规定的,负责执行居

familiar to the citizens and dear to them all. It is identified with the soil; with the right of property and the domestic affections; with the recollections of the past, the labors of the present, and the hopes of the future. Patriotism, then, which is frequently a mere extension of individual selfishness, is still directed to the state and has not passed over to the Union. Thus the tendency of the interests, the habits, and the feelings of the people is to center political activity in the states in preference to the Union.

It is easy to estimate the different strength of the two governments by noting the manner in which they exercise their respective powers. Whenever the government of a state addresses an individual or an assembly of individuals, its language is clear and imperative, and such is also the tone of the Federal government when it speaks to individuals; but no sooner has it anything to do with a state than it begins to parley, to explain its motives and justify its conduct, to argue, to advise, and, in short, anything but to command. If doubts are raised as to the limits of the constitutional powers of either government, the state government prefers its claim with boldness and takes prompt and energetic steps to support it. Meanwhile the government of the Union reasons; it appeals to the interests, the good sense, the glory of the nation; it temporizes, it negotiates, and does not consent to act until it is reduced to the last extremity. At first sight it might readily be imagined that it is the state government which is armed with the authority of the nation and that Congress represents a single state.

The Federal government is, therefore, notwithstanding the precautions of those who founded it, naturally so weak that, more than any other, it requires the free consent of the governed to enable it to exist. It is easy to perceive that its object is to enable the states to realize with facility their determination of remaining united; and as long as this preliminary condition exists, it is wise, strong, and active. The Constitution fits the government to control individuals and easily to surmount such obstacles as they may be inclined to offer, but it was by no means established with a view to the possible voluntary separation of one or more of the states from the Union.

If the sovereignty of the Union were to engage in a struggle with that of the states at the present day, its defeat may be confidently predicted; and it is not probable that such a struggle would be seriously

民们都知道和重视的一些工作。州的限定范围就是那块土地,它负有财产的权力和对内部事务的热爱之情,它必须珍惜过去的历史遗留、现在的工作和未来的理想。因此,爱国主义往往不过是个人私心延伸的结果。它只存在于州,而不会及于联邦。因此,人们的利益、习惯和感情,都趋于将真正的政治生活集中于州,而不集中于联邦。

只要观察一下州政府和联邦政府是如何行使自己的职权的,就可以很容易对这两种权利加以区别。每当州政府与一个人或一群人对话时,它所使用的语言明确且含有命令口吻。联邦政府与个体对话时也是如此。但是一旦它与一个州交涉时,就得改用谈判的口气,解释它的动机、辩解它的做法,要用争辩、建议的口吻,总之不能下命令。如果是两个政府在宪法规定的权限上产生质疑,州政府总是敢于提出自己的权利要求,并立刻采取积极的措施维护自己的权利。而联邦政府则要晓之以理,并求助于全国人民的良知、国家的利益和荣誉。它见风使舵,采用谈判的途径,不到迫不得已,决不采取行动。乍看上去,人们可能以为掌握国家大权的是州政府,而国会只是代表一个州了。

因此,尽管建立联邦的立法者们采取了种种预防措施,但由于其本身的性质的软弱,它比其他任何政府都需要被统治者的主动支持来维护它的存在。不难看出,联邦政府的目的,是要顺利实现各州继续联合的愿望。只要这一先决条件存在,就表明联邦政府是明智的、有力的和活跃的。政府利用宪法统治个体,又能容易战胜人们对公共决定的有意抵制,但他们决不期望看到联邦可能解体或几个州可能自愿退出联邦。

如果联邦的主权在于与各州分享的主权发生纠纷,则不难预

undertaken. As often as a steady resistance is offered to the Federal government, it will be found to yield. Experience has hitherto shown that whenever a state has demanded anything with perseverance and resolution, it has invariably succeeded; and that if it has distinctly refused to act, it was left to do as it thought fit. [1]

But even if the government of the Union had any strength inherent in itself, the physical situation of the country would render the exercise of that strength very difficult. [2] The United States covers an immense territory, the individual states are separated from each other by great distances, and the population is disseminated over the surface of a country which is still half a wilderness. If the Union were to undertake to enforce by arms the allegiance of the federated states, it would be in a position very analogous to that of England at the time of the War of Independence.

However strong a government may be, it cannot easily escape from the consequences of a principle which it has once admitted as the foundation of its constitution. The Union was formed by the voluntary agreement of the states; and these, in uniting together, have not forfeited their sovereignty, nor have they been reduced to the condition of one and the same people. If one of the states chose to withdraw its name from the contract, it would be difficult to disprove its right of doing so, and the Federal government would have no means of maintaining its claims directly, either by force or by right. In order to enable the Federal government easily to conquer the resistance that may be offered to it by any of its subjects, it would be necessary that one or more of them should be specially interested in the existence of the Union, as has frequently been the case in the history of confederations.

If it be supposed that among the states that are united by the federal tie there are some which exclusively enjoy the principal advantages

---

① See the conduct of the Northern states in the War of 1812. "During that war," says Jefferson in a letter of March 17, 1817, to General Lafayette, "four of the Eastern States were only attached to the Union like so many inanimate bodies to living men." (*Correspondence of Jefferson*, published by M. Conseil.)

② The state of peace of the Union affords no pretext for a standing army, and without a standing army a government is not prepared to profit by a favorable opportunity to conquer resistance and seize the sovereign power by surprise.

见联邦终会遭遇失败。我甚至认为,两者的斗争很可能会以激烈的形式进行。每逢联邦政府受到顽强的抵制时,总是联邦政府作出让步。经验已经表明:迄今为止,只要一个州下定决心坚持一项主张,就没有不成功的;而它要完全拒绝执行联邦的命令,也只好听之任之。[1]

但是,虽然联邦政府拥有自己的权力,但国家的物质条件却使它对自己权力行使变得异常困难。[2] 美国的幅员辽阔,州与州之间距离又很远,而其人口散布在仍有一半是荒野的国土上。如果联邦政府打算用武力使加盟的各州臣服,它就会陷于类似英国在美国独立战争时期所处的境地。

再说,一个政府无论多么强大,它也难以逃避它所同意的原则对它的约束,所以它必须服从公权。联邦是根据各州的自愿原则建立起来的,各州的联合并没有使他们放弃自己的主权,也没有组成一个单一社会环境或民族相同的国家。如果有一个州现在要想把自己的名字从盟约中取消,那也很难驳回他这样做的权利。联邦政府既缺乏武力也没有权利去制止。为了使联邦政府容易战胜某个从属州对它的反抗,它就必须像世界联邦制度史上常见的那样,使一个州或几个州的利益同联邦的存在紧密地联系起来。

假如在由联邦纽带联合在一起的各州中,有一些州要独享联

---

① 见 1812 年北部州人民在战争中的行为。"在这场战争中,"杰斐逊在 1817 年 3 月 17 日给三刺光鲲将军的一封信中写道"东部有四个州死气沉沉地依附着联邦。"(法院公布的杰弗逊的信件。)

② 联邦中和平的州都没有常备军,而没有常备军一个政府就不可能利用有利时机战胜反抗或者夺取主权。

of union, or whose prosperity entirely depends on the duration of that union, it is unquestionable that they will always be ready to support the central government in enforcing the obedience of the others. But the government would then be exerting a force not derived from itself, but from a principle contrary to its nature. States form confederations in order to derive equal advantages from their union; and in the case just alluded to, the Federal government would derive its power from the unequal distribution of those benefits among the states.

If one of the federated states acquires a preponderance sufficiently great to enable it to take exclusive possession of the central authority, it will consider the other states as subject provinces and will cause its own supremacy to be respected under the borrowed name of the sovereignty of the Union. Great things may then be done in the name of the Federal government, but in reality that government will have ceased to exist. ①In both these cases the power that acts in the name of the confederation becomes stronger the more it abandons the natural state and the acknowledged principles of confederations.

In America the existing Union is advantageous to all the states, but it is not indispensable to any one of them. Several of them might break the Federal tie without compromising the welfare of the others, although the sum of their joint prosperity would be less. As the existence and the happiness of none of the states are wholly dependent on the present Constitution, none of them would be disposed to make great personal sacrifices to maintain it. On the other hand, there is no state which seems hitherto to have been by its ambition much interested in the maintenance of the existing Union. They certainly do not all exercise the same influence in the Federal councils; but no one can hope to domineer over the rest or to treat them as its inferiors or as its subjects.

It appears to me unquestionable that if any portion of the Union seriously desired to separate itself from the other states, they would not be able, nor indeed would they attempt, to prevent it; and

---

① Thus the province of Holland, in the republic of the Low Countries, and the Emperor in the Germanic Confederation, have sometimes put themselves in the place of the Union and have employed the federal authority to their own advantage.

邦的主要好处,或者它的繁荣完全依赖于联邦的存在,则显而易见,它们就会一直支持中央政权去迫使其他州服从。但是,这样的话,中央政权力量并非来自本身,而是源自一项与它的本性相反的原则。联邦各州之所以要结成联邦,目的是为了从联邦中获得同等的好处;而在方才所说的那种情况上,却是在联合起来的各州之间制造不平等,而使联邦政府强大的。

如果联邦各州中有一个州所占的优势,使其拥有大到足以垄断中央政权的权力,它就会把其他的州视为从属州,并借助联邦主权的名义,企图得到其他州对它的尊重。这时,虽然名义上还是由联邦政府出面处理一些大事,但这个政府事实上早已不存在了。① 在这两种情况下,以联邦名义行事的政权变得越强,它就越不会考虑联邦的原来政体和公认原则。

在美国,现存联邦虽然对所有的州都有利,但却并非必不可少。即使有几个州断绝与联邦的联系,也不会危害其他州的继续联合,当然,由它们联合创造的繁荣富强的总成果会有所减少。正是因为没有哪个州的存在和繁荣需要完全依靠现存的联邦,所以也就没有一个州会为维护联邦而甘愿付出重大的牺牲。另一方面,就目前的情况来看,还没有哪个州怀有想控制现存的联邦的野心。当然,各州对联邦在立法、司法、行政上的影响并不完全一样,但没有一个州能够居于其他州之上,把它们当做不如自己的州或从属来对待。

所以我确信,如果真要有联邦的某一部分想与其他州脱离关系,它们不仅不可能阻止得了,而且也没有谁想去阻止。因此,只

---

① 因此,荷兰的各省以及德国联邦的君主就不时地加入联邦以借助联邦政府的力量为己用。

that the present Union will last only as long as the states which compose it choose to continue members of the confederation. If this point be admitted, the question becomes less difficult; and our object is, not to inquire whether the states of the existing Union are capable of separating, but whether they will choose to remain united.

Among the various reasons that tend to render the existing Union useful to the Americans, two principal ones are especially evident to the observer. Although the Americans are, as it were, alone upon their continent, commerce gives them for neighbors all the nations with which they trade. Notwithstanding their apparent isolation, then, the Americans need to be strong, and they can be strong only by remaining united. If the states were to split, not only would they diminish the strength that they now have against foreigners, but they would soon create foreign powers upon their own territory. A system of inland custom-houses would then be established; the valleys would be divided by imaginary boundary lines; the courses of the rivers would be impeded, and a multitude of hindrances would prevent the Americans from using that vast continent which Providence has given them for a dominion. At present they have no invasion to fear, and consequently no standing armies to maintain, no taxes to levy. If the Union were dissolved, all these burdensome things would before long be required. The Americans are, then, most deeply interested in the maintenance of their Union. On the other hand, it is almost impossible to discover any private interest that might now tempt a portion of the Union to separate from the other states.

When we cast our eyes on the map of the United States, we perceive the chain of the Allegheny Mountains, running from the northeast to the southwest, and crossing nearly one thousand miles of country; and we are led to imagine that the design of Providence was to raise between the valley of the Mississippi and the coasts of the Atlantic Ocean one of those natural barriers which break the mutual intercourse of men and form the necessary limits of different states. But the average height of the Alleghenies does not exceed 800 meters. [1] Their rounded summits, and the spacious valleys which they enclose

---

[1]   Average height of the Alleghenies, following Volney (*Atlas of the United States*, p. 33), 700 – 800 meters; following Derby, 500 – 6,000 feet. The highest point of the Vosges is 1,400 meters above sea level.

要组成联邦的各州愿意联合下去,现存的联邦就能存在下去。只要大家承认这一点,问题就变得简单多了。因为我们的目的不是研究是否目前结成联邦的各州能够分离,而是要研究是否它们愿意维持联合的状态。

在所有能使目前的联邦给美国人带来好处的原因当中,有两个原因最容易为所有的观察者注意到。尽管美国人仿佛独居于他们的大陆,但商业却使同他们有往来的一切国家都成为他们的邻国。因此,尽管它们地处偏远,但他们却必须强大,而他们要强大,就必须依靠维持联邦。如果各州分裂,自成一派,它们现有的一致对敌的力量就会被削弱,有可能招致外敌入侵。如果各州分裂,就要另建一套内陆关税制度,山谷将会被一些假象的界限分割,河流会被改道,以及其他无数的障碍阻碍美国人享有上帝赐予的这片土地。如今,美国人没有外敌入侵之忧,所以他们不必配备常备军,也不必为此征税;而一旦联邦解体,这一切很快就会需要。因此,美国人民从维持联邦中获得了重大的利益。另一方面,也没有什么个体私利驱使联邦的某一部分脱离其他部分而独立。

当我们的目光投向美国的地图的时候,我们看到阿勒格尼山脉,从东北走向西南需要横跨 400 里格〔1000 英里〕国土时,我们禁不住会想,上帝这样安排的意图,也许是要在密西西比河流域和大西洋海岸之间建立一道天然屏障,以隔断人们的往来,为不同的民族划出必要的界限。但是,阿勒格尼山脉的平均高度不超过 800 米。[①] 它的一些圆形山巅,以及山间的宽敞谷地,便于人们

---

① 阿勒格尼山脉的平均高度,紧追俄尔尼,达到 700～800 米,接着是德贝,500～6000 英尺。佛日山脉的最高点在海平面 1400 米以上。

within their passes, are of easy access in several directions. Besides, the principal rivers that fall into the Atlantic Ocean, the Hudson, the Susquehanna, and the Potomac, take their rise beyond the Alleghenies, in an open elevated plain, which borders on the valley of the Mississippi. These streams quit this region, [1] make their way through the barrier which would seem to turn them westward, and, as they wind through the mountains, open an easy and natural passage to man.

No natural barrier divides the regions that are now inhabited by the Anglo-Americans; the Alleghenies are so far from separating nations that they do not even divide different states. New York, Pennsylvania, and Virginia comprise them within their borders and extend as much to the west as to the east of these mountains. [2]

The territory now occupied by the twenty-four states of the Union, and the three great districts which have not yet acquired the rank of states, although they already contain inhabitants, cover a surface of 131,144 square leagues, [3] which is about equal to five times the extent of France. Within these limits the quality of the soil, the temperature, and the produce of the country are extremely various. The vast extent of territory occupied by the Anglo-American republics has given rise to doubts as to the maintenance of their Union. Here a distinction must be made; contrary interests sometimes arise in the different provinces of a vast empire, which often terminate in open dissensions; and the extent of the country is then most prejudicial to the duration of the state. But if the inhabitants of these vast regions are not divided by contrary interests, the extent of the territory is favorable to their prosperity; for the unity of the government promotes the interchange of the different products of the soil and increases their value by facilitating their sale.

It is indeed easy to discover different interests in the different parts of the Union, but I am unacquainted with any that are hostile

---

[1] See View of the United States, by Darby, pp. 64 and 79.

[2] The chain of the Alleghenies is not so high as that of the Vosges and does not offer as many obstacles as the latter to the efforts of human industry. The regions lying on the eastern slopes of the Alleghenies are as naturally attached to the Mississippi Valley as Franche-Comt , Upper Burgundy, and Alsace are to France.

[3] 1,002,600 square miles. See Darby's *View of the United States*, p. 435.

从任何方向进入。而且，注入大西洋的几条主要的河流：赫德森河、萨斯奎哈纳河、波托马克河，都发源于阿勒格尼山脉上的一片与密西西比河流域接壤的高原。这些河流从这个地区流出后，[①]穿过那些迫使它们向西流的层层屏障，而在它们蜿蜒的山路上，为人们开辟出数条容易通行的天然小径。

因此，在现今英裔美国人居住的地区之间，没有任何天然屏障将它们加以区分。阿勒格尼山脉不仅没有把他们隔离开，更没隔开各州的通道。纽约州、宾夕法尼亚州和弗吉尼亚州把这条山脉围了起来，并向它的西面和东面延展。[②]

现在，美国疆域内占据着 24 个州以及虽已住有居民但尚未取得州的地位的三大区域，共拥有领土 131144 平方里格，[③]大约相当于法国领土面积的五倍。在它的领土范围内，地质不同，气候条件各异，物产也多种多样。英裔美国人所建各州的土地是如此的辽阔，以致人们不得不对其维持产生怀疑。在这里必须要指出一个差别。在一个领土辽阔的帝国内，各省或州之间的利益对立，最后可能导致彼此冲突。这时，国土的辽阔可能对国家的维持产生影响。但是，如果居住在这样广大国土的人民彼此间的利益并不冲突，国土的辽阔就会有利于国家的繁荣，因为政府的统一，对国内不同产品的交换相当有益，便于产品的流通和增殖。

的确，我见到美国的不同地区各有自己的不同利益，但我从

---

① 见《美国见闻》，达贝著，第 64、79 页。

② 阿勒格尼山脉不如佛山高，而且也不像佛山那样对人类工业建设有很多的阻碍。这块地区坐落在阿勒格尼山脉东面的山坡上，与密西西比大峡谷自然接壤。

③ 1002600 平方英里。见达贝：《美国见闻》，第 435 页。

to one another. The Southern states are almost exclusively agricultural. The Northern states are more peculiarly commercial and manufacturing. The states of the West are at the same time agricultural and manufacturing. In the South the crops consist of tobacco, rice, cotton, and sugar; in the North and the West, of wheat and corn. These are different sources of wealth, but union is the means by which these sources are opened and rendered equally advantageous to all.

The North, which ships the produce of the Anglo-Americans to all parts of the world and brings back the produce of the globe to the Union, is evidently interested in maintaining the confederation in its present condition, in order that the number of American producers and consumers may remain as large as possible. The North is the most natural agent of communication between the South and the West of the Union on the one hand, and the rest of the world on the other; the North is therefore interested in the union and prosperity of the South and the West, in order that they may continue to furnish raw materials for its manufactures, and cargoes for its shipping.

The South and the West, on their side, are still more directly interested in the preservation of the Union and the prosperity of the North. The produce of the South is, for the most part, exported beyond seas; the South and the West consequently stand in need of the commercial resources of the North. They are likewise interested in the maintenance of a powerful fleet by the Union, to protect them efficaciously. The South and the West have no vessels, but willingly contribute to the expense of a navy, for if the fleets of Europe were to blockade the ports of the South and the delta of the Mississippi, what would become of the rice of the Carolinas, the tobacco of Virginia, and the sugar and cotton that grow in the valley of the Mississippi? Every portion of the Federal budget does, therefore, contribute to the maintenance of material interests that are common to all the federated states.

Independently of this commercial utility, the South and the West derive great political advantages from their union with each other and with the North. The South contains an enormous slave population, a population which is already alarming and still more formidable for the future. The states of the West occupy a single valley; the rivers that

未发现这些利益之间互有冲突。联邦各州几乎都以农业为主,北方各州专门从事制造业和商业,西部各州则兼营制造业和农业。在南方,人们种植烟草、水稻、棉花和甘蔗。在北方和西部,种植玉米和小麦。这些财富的来源虽然不同,但联邦却能为人人提供取得这些机会的均等条件。

北方的人们把英裔美国人的产品运到世界各地,又把世界其他地方的产品运回联邦;很明显,为使美国的生产者和消费者保持较高的人数,它最希望使联邦按目前状况维持下去。北方是联邦南方与西部最天然的联络员,另一方面又是联邦与世界其余各地的中间人。因此,北方必然希望南方和西部继续留在联邦里使得联邦进一步繁荣,以便向它的制造业提供原料和租用它的船舶。

南部和西部,从他们的角度来说,仍然愿意保留联邦和使北方繁荣的意图也各有其直接的利益的原因。南部的农产品大都要通过海上出口运输,所以南部和西部需要北方商业资源的支援。它们必然希望联邦拥有一支强大的舰队,以便对它们实施有效地保护。南方和西部虽然自己没有船舶,但也一定愿意出钱建设海上力量,因为欧洲的舰队一旦封锁南方的港口和密西西比河三角洲,那时,他们该如何处理南、北卡罗来纳两州出产的大米,弗吉尼亚州的烟草,以及密西西比河流域生产的糖和棉花呢?因此,联邦预算的每一部分,都是为了保护联邦所有州的共同物质利益。

除了这种商业效用之外,南部和西部联邦还能从它们彼此结盟和与北方继续结盟当中获得的政治方面的益处。因为南方境内有大量的奴隶,这部分人口已造成了威胁,而且他们对未来的

intersect their territory rise in the Rocky Mountains or in the Alleghenies, and fall into the Mississippi, which bears them onwards to the
Gulf of Mexico. The Western states are consequently entirely cut off,
by. their position, from the traditions of Europe and the civilization of
the Old World. The inhabitants of the South, then, are induced to
support the Union in order to avail themselves of its protection against
the blacks; and the inhabitants of the West, in order not to be excluded from a free communication with the rest of the globe and shut up
in the wilds of central America. The North cannot but desire the maintenance of the Union in order to remain, as it now is, the connecting link between that vast body and the other parts of the world.

The material interests of all the parts of the Union are, then, intimately connected; and the same assertion holds true respecting those
opinions and sentiments that may be termed the immaterial interests of
men.

The inhabitants of the United States talk much of their attachment to their country; but I confess that I do not rely upon that calculating patriotism which is founded upon interest and which a change in
the interests may destroy. Nor do I attach much importance to the language of the Americans when they manifest, in their daily conversation, the intention of maintaining the Federal system adopted by their
forefathers. A government retains its sway over a great number of citizens far less by the voluntary and rational consent of the multitude
than by that instinctive, and to a certain extent involuntary, agreement which results from similarity of feelings and resemblances of o-
pinion. I will never admit that men constitute a social body simply because they obey the same head and the same laws. Society can exist
only when a great number of men consider a great number of things
under the same as pect, when they hold the same opinions upon many
subjects, and when the same occurrences suggest the same thoughts
and impressions to their minds.

威胁更大。西部各州共有着一条大河的流域。流经这些州的河流,发源于落基山脉和阿勒格尼山脉,汇入密西西比河后流入墨西哥湾。由于地理位置的原因,西部各州隔离于欧洲的传统和旧大陆的文明之外。所以说,南方居民之所以愿意保持联邦,也是为了使自己在敌对的黑人面前得到有益的保护;而西部居民之所以愿意保持联邦,则是为了使自己不被闭塞在美国的中部,不与世界其他各地断绝自由来往。而北方之所以不希望联邦分裂,是因为它要把联邦作为纽带,使这片广大的国土与世界其余部分保持联系。

因此,联邦各部分之间紧密的物质利益迅速地被联系在一起。并且,通过其产生的观点和感情,也能形成人们之间的非物质利益的联系。

美国的居民对他们的爱国精神谈得很多;但我承认,我并不认为这种爱国主义精神是理智的,因为它是建立在利害关系之上的。一旦情况发生变化,利害关系也将变化。美国人经常表示他们要把祖先采用的联邦制度维护下去,并提出他们的论点,我对于这些观点并不怎样看重。他们的那种要把人数众多的公民置于同一政府的保护之下的论点,主要的不是出于人民自愿联合的理智,而是出于本能的同意,或者从某种程度上说,是出于一种非自愿的同意。这种同意是感情上的类似和看法上的接近产生的结果。我决不承认,人们只是由于承认同一个首领或服从同样的法律而就组成了社会。而只有当人们用同一个观点去考虑绝大多数问题时,并且对绝大多数问题具有同样看法,或只有同样的事件会给他们留下同样的印象、使他们产生同样的思想时,社会才能存在。

The observer who examines what is passing in the United States upon this principle will readily discover that their inhabitants, though divided into twenty-four distinct sovereignties, still constitute a single people; and he may perhaps be led to think that the Anglo-American Union is more truly a united society than some nations of Europe which live under the same legislation and the same prince.

Although the Anglo-Americans have several religious sects, they all regard religion in the same manner. They are not always agreed upon the measures that are most conducive to good government, and they vary upon some of the forms of government which it is expedient to adopt; but they are unanimous upon the general principles that ought to rule human society. From Maine to the Floridas, and from the Missouri to the Atlantic Ocean, the people are held to be the source of all legitimate power. The same notions are entertained respecting liberty and equality, the liberty of the press, the right of association, the jury, and the responsibility of the agents of government.

If we turn from their political and religious opinions to the moral and philosophical principles that regulate the daily actions of life and govern their conduct, we still find the same uniformity. The Anglo-Americans[①] acknowledge the moral authority of the reason of the community as they acknowledge the political authority of the mass of citizens; and they hold that public opinion is the surest arbiter of what is lawful or forbidden, true or false. The majority of them believe that a man by following his own interest, rightly understood, will be led to do what is just and good. They hold that every man is born in possession of the right of self-government, and that no one has the right of constraining his fellow creatures to be happy. They have all a lively

---

① It is scarcely necessary for me to observe that by the expression Anglo Americans I mean to designate only the great majority of the nation. Some isolatedindividuals, of course, hold very different opinions.

以这一原则为基础观察美国发生的事情的观察者，很容易就会发现，美国的居民，尽管分别居住在 24 个不同主权的州，但仍旧团结得仿佛一个民族一样。而且，他也许会考虑，英裔美国人的联邦欧洲那些生活在同一立法机构和受控于同一国王下的一些国家，更像是一个联合在一起的社会。

尽管英裔美国人有好几个教派，但对所有教派都一视同仁。他们并不总是采用一直通过的最有利的方法治理国家，他们时常改变统治方式使其适应政府的工作，但他们对待治理人类社会所必要的普遍原则的意见一致。从缅因州到佛罗里达州，从密苏里州到大西洋沿岸，人民是一切依法成立的机关的权利来源。在所有的州，对自由、平等、出版、结社权、陪审制和公务人员的职责，都有一致的看法。

如果我们转而从政治和宗教观点看制约他们的日常生活行为和指导他们的全部活动的哲学和道德思想，我们仍旧会发现同样的一致性。他们不仅认为全体公民是政治权威，英裔美国人也承认公认的理论是道德权威。[①] 而且他们认为，公众的意愿是判断合法的、被禁止的、真实的、虚假的最准确的判官。他们中的大多数都相信，一个人只要能够正确地理解和服从自己的利益，就能使自己走向公正和至善。他们认为，每个人生下来就有自己管理自己的权利，任何人都无权阻止他的同胞去追求幸福。他们都坚信人的至善。他们认定知识的传播必然会产生有益的结果，而无知将导致致命后果。他们把社会视为一个不断进步的机体，

[①] 我几乎不需要观察英裔美国人的表情就可以指出这个民族的大多数。一些偏远的人们，肯定会持有一些不同的观点。

faith in the perfectibility of man, they judge that the diffusion of knowledge must necessarily be advantageous, and the consequences of ignorance fatal; they all consider society as a body in a state of improvement, humanity as a changing scene, in which nothing is, or ought to be, permanent; and they admit that what appears to them today to be good, may be superseded by something better tomorrow. I do not give all these opinions as true, but as American opinions. Not only are the Anglo-Americans united by these common opinions, but they are separated from all other nations by a feeling of pride. For the last fifty years no pains have been spared to convince the inhabitants of the United States that they are the only religious, enlightened, and free people. They perceive that, for the present, their own democratic institutions prosper, while those of other countries fail; hence they conceive a high opinion of their superiority and are not very remote from believing themselves to be a distinct species of mankind.

Thus the dangers that threaten the American Union do not originate in diversity of interests or of opinions, but in the various characters and passions of the Americans. The men who inhabit the vast territory of the United States are almost all the issue of a common stock; but climate, and more especially slavery, have gradually introduced marked differences between the British settler of the Southern states and the British settler of the North. In Europe it is generally believed that slavery has rendered the interests of one part of the Union contrary to those of the other, but I have not found this to be the case. Slavery has not created interests in the South contrary to those of the North, but it has modified the character and changed the habits of the natives of the South. I have already explained the influence of slavery upon the commercial ability of the Americans in the South; and this same influence equally extends to their manners. The slave is a servant who never remonstrates and who submits to everything without complaint. He may sometimes assassinate his master, but he never withstands him. In the South there are no families so poor as not to have slaves. The citizen of the Southern states becomes a sort of domestic dictator from infancy; the first notion he acquires in life is that he is born to command, and the first habit which he contracts is that of ruling without resistance. His education tends, then, to give him the character of a haughty and hasty man, irascible, violent, ardent in

认为人生是一幅不断变换的图画,没有任何一件东西是永久不变的或应当永久不变的。他们承认,今天在他们看来是好的东西,明天有可能被其他更好的东西取代。我并不能说这所有的观点都是正确的,而只是说美国人就是那样想的。一方面因这些共同的观点使英裔美国人互相团结起来,另一方面又因骄傲而使自己与其他民族隔离开。过去的 50 多年来,美国人一直被说成是世界上最虔信宗教、最有知识和最自由的民族。他们认为,目前,民主制度只在他们那里得到蓬勃发展,而在其他地方都失败了。因此,他们把自己看得很高,甚至几乎确信他们就是人类中的杰出人种。

因此美国联邦面临的危险,不是来自他们的意见分歧或利害冲突,而是存在于美国人多变的性格和激情。居住在美国广大领土上的人,几乎都是属于同一种族。但是,久而久之,气候,尤其是蓄奴制,造成了美国南方和北方的英裔在性格上的显著差别。一些人认为,蓄奴制使美国地区之间出现了对立的利益。我还没有发现这种情况。蓄奴制并没有在南方产生与北方对立的利益,但它改变了南方居民的性格,并使生活在南部的人们养成了与北方不同的习惯。我在前面已经指出蓄奴制对南方美国人的经商能力发生的影响。南方的民情也受到这种影响。奴隶是百依百顺和默不敢言的仆人。他们虽然可以暗杀他们的主人,但他们从来不公开反抗主人。在南方,没有一个家庭穷得养不起奴隶。南方的美国人,从小就养成了家庭专制的习惯。他们有生以来最先获得的观念就是他们是发号施令者。他们养成的第一个习惯,就是叫奴隶百依百顺地听他们指挥。因此,南方人所受到的教育把他们培养成高傲、狂暴、易怒、急躁的人。他们穷奢极欲,遇到困

his desires, impatient of obstacles, but easily discouraged if he cannot succeed upon his first attempt.

The American of the North sees no slaves around him in his childhood; he is even unattended by free servants, for he is usually obliged to provide for his own wants. As soon as he enters the world, the idea of necessity assails him on every side; he soon learns to know exactly the natural limits of his power; he never expects to subdue by force those who withstand him; and he knows that the surest means of obtaining the support of his fellow creatures is to win their favor. He therefore becomes patient, reflecting, tolerant, slow to act, and persevering in his designs.

In the Southern states the more pressing wants of life are always supplied; the inhabitants, therefore, are not occupied with the material cares of life, from which they are relieved by others; and their imagination is diverted to more captivating and less defi nite objects. The American of the South is fond of grandeur, luxury, and renown; of gayety, pleasure, and, above all, of idleness; nothing obliges him to exert himself in order to subsist; and as he has no necessary occupations, he gives way to indolence and does not even attempt what would be useful.

But the equality of fortunes and the absence of slavery in the North plunge the inhabitants in those material cares which are disdained by the white population of the South. They are taught from infancy to combat want and to place wealth above all the pleasures of the intellect or the heart. The imagination is extinguished by the trivial details of life, and the ideas become less numerous and less general, but far more practical, clearer, and more precise. As prosperity is the sole aim of exertion, it is excellently well attained; nature and men are turned to the best pecuniary advantage; and society is dexterously made to contribute to the welfare of each of its members, while individual selfishness is the source of general happiness.

The American of the North has not only experience but knowledge; yet he values science not as an enjoyment, but as a means,

难就不耐烦,一遇到失败就心生气馁。

北方的美国人从未见过奴隶服侍在他们左右。他们甚至没有被临时雇用的仆人服侍过,他们通常都得自食其力。一进入社会,各种观念从四面八方向他们的脑际袭来。因此,他们很早就得学会准确地判断天赋权利的有限,并进行自力更生。他们决不愿屈服于强加于他们身上的指令;而且他们知道,要想得到他人的支持,就得赢得他人的信任。因此,他们办事有耐心,思维缜密,对人宽容,行为从容不迫,定出计划就坚持到底。

在南方的各州,人们的那些迫切需要总能得到满足。因此,那里的居民从不为物质生活担心,因为有另一些人在替他们操心。由于在生计方面可以无忧无虑,所以他们的想象力便用于另一些花哨但无实用价值的活动方面。南方的美国人生活奢侈、喜欢讲究排场,追逐名利、高谈阔论和寻欢作乐,尤其是愿意闲散自在。没有什么事情迫使他们去为生活操劳,由于他们不必亲自劳动,所以整天懒懒散散,根本不去想什么事情是有益的。

但是,财富的平等和奴隶制度的消除,促使北方的人们为了物质而奋斗,而他们的这种奋斗在南方是被白人们所瞧不起的。他们在少年时期就开始学着为生存拼搏,学着把财富置于其他一切精神和心灵的享乐之上。他们的想象力都在生活的琐事中耗尽,他们的思想不够丰富不够广泛,但却更切合实际并清晰明确。由于财富是他们的唯一目标,所以人人都全力以赴,欲尽早达到目的。令人钦佩和赞叹的是,他们知道如何利用自然和人力去创造财富,并了解使社会走向人人幸福和从个人奋斗中去汲取一切好东西的方法。

北方人不仅有实际经验,而且有知识。但他们并未把科学作

and is only anxious to seize its useful applications. The American of the South is more given to act upon impulse; he is more clever, more frank, more generous, more intellectual, and more brilliant. The former, with a greater degree of activity, common sense, information, and general aptitude, has the characteristic good and evil qualities of the middle classes. The latter has the tastes, the prejudices, the weaknesses, and the magnanimity of all aristocracies.

If two men are united in society, who have the same interests, and, to a certain extent, the same opinions, but different characters, different acquirements, and a different style of civilization, it is most probable that these men will not agree. The same remark is applicable to a society of nations.

Slavery, then, does not attack the American Union directly in its interests, but indirectly in its manners.

The states that gave their assent to the Federal contract in 1790 were thirteen in number; the Union now consists of twenty-four members. The population, which amounted to nearly four millions in 1790, had more than tripled in the space of forty years; in 1830 it amounted to nearly thirteen millions. ①Changes of such magnitude cannot take place without danger.

A society of nations, as well as a society of individuals, has three principal chances of duration: namely, the wisdom of its members, their individual weakness, and their limited number. The Americans who quit the coasts of the Atlantic Ocean to plunge into the Western wilderness are adventurers, impatient of restraint, greedy of wealth, and frequently men expelled from the states in which they were born. When they arrive in the wilderness, they are unknown to one another; they have neither traditions, family feeling, nor the force of example to check their excesses. The authority of the laws is feeble among them; that of morality is still weaker. The settlers who are constantly peopling the valley of the Mississippi are, then, in every respect, inferior to the Americans who inhabit the older parts of the Union. But they already exercise a great influence in its councils;

---

① Census of 1790 3,929,328; Census of 1830 12,856,165

为消遣,而把它看作是一种手段,对科学唯一的要求就是早日得到有效的应用。南方的美国人易于冲动,幽默,性格坦率,大方,也很有才华。北方的美国人积极主动,办事依照理智,比南方人更具才干。前者性格中的优缺点都是中产阶级的特点。而后者的兴趣、偏见、弱点和优点都是属于贵族阶级的。

假如让两个人联合起来,假使他们的利益和见解一致,而性格、知识水平和文明程度保持不同,则他们十之八九不会同意联合。这个观念也适用于国家或民族的联合。

因此,蓄奴制并未直接损害美国联邦的利益,而是破坏了它的民情。

1790 年在联邦公约上签字的州共有 13 个。今天,联邦已有 24 个州。1790 年人口将近 400 万,经过 40 年增加了两倍多,即在 1830 年已达 1300 万人。[①] 这样的巨大变化,不可能不伴随危险。

由数个国家或地方组成的社会,同由一些个人组成的团体一样,存在三个使它能够持久存在的主要原因:成员的理智,每个个体力量弱小,成员的数目有限。离开大西洋海岸深入西部荒野地区的美国人,都是冒险家。他们对束缚缺乏耐性,对财富的欲望强烈,而且往往被他们出生的州驱逐出境。他们到达荒地时,彼此都是初次见面,以前互不相识。在这里既无传统和家庭感情的束缚,又没有范例仿效。他们对法制的作用淡薄,民情的作用就更小。因此,不断迁往密西西比河流域落户的人,在各个方面都不如居住在原来各个旧州内的美国人。但是,他们却对所在西部

---

① 1790 年人口普查结果 3929328。1830 年任口普查结果 12856165。

and they arrive at the government of the commonwealth before they have learned to govern themselves. ①②③

The greater the individual weakness of the contracting parties, the greater are the chances of the duration of the contract; for their safety is then dependent upon their union. When, in 1790, the most populous of the American republics did not contain 500,000 inhabitants, each of them felt its own insignificance as an independent people, and this feeling rendered compliance with the Federal authority more easy. But when one of the federated states reckons, like the state of New York, two million inhabitants and covers an extent of territory equal to a quarter of France, it feels its own strength; and although it may still support the Union as useful to its prosperity, it no longer regards it as necessary to its existence; and while consenting to continue in it, it aims at preponderance in the federal councils. The mere increase in number of the states weakens the tie that holds them together. All men who are placed at the same point of view do not look at the same objects in the same manner. Still less do they do so when the point of view is different. In proportion, then, as the American republics become more numerous, there is less chance of their unanimity in matters of legislation. At present the interests of the different parts of the Union are not at variance, but who can foresee the various changes of the future in a country in which new towns are founded every day and new states almost every year?

Since the first settlement of the British colonies the number of inhabitants has about doubled every twenty-two years. I perceive no causes that are likely to check this ratio of increase of the Anglo

---

① This indeed is only a temporary danger. I have no doubt that in time society will assume as much stability and regularity in the West as it has already done upon the Atlantic coast.

② Pennsylvania contained 431,373 inhabitants in 1790.

③ The area of the state of New York is about 6,213 square leagues (500 [sic; actually about 50,000] square miles). See *View of the United States*, by Darby, p. 435.

乡镇发生了重大的影响。他们早在学会自己管理自己之前,就已建立起了管理公共事务的政府。①

联邦各成员的力量越小,联邦持久存在的可能性就越强。因为这时各个成员的安全都依赖于它们的联合体。1790年,美国各州的人口,没有一个超过50万人。② 当时,每个州都认为自己没有资格成为独立的国家,这种思想便使它们更轻易地听从联邦当局。但联邦的某个州,比如纽约州的面积相当于四分之一的法国。③ 当它的人口数量达到200万时,就会自以为足以强大;而如果它想要继续留在联邦里是出于自身发展的考虑的话,就不再会认为联邦的存在有其必要了。并且,即使它同意留在联邦里,也很快会要求居于优势地位。而如果单单在数量上增加美国联邦成员,则会破坏其之间联合的纽带。即使是持有同样观点的人,也并不一定用同样的方法去观察同样的问题。如果观点不同,当然就更难达到一致了。因此,随着美国联邦成员数目的增加,成员之间在立法上达成一致的机会就更少了。如今,美国各州之间的利益虽然不是彼此对立;但是,对一个每天都有新的城市建立,每五年就有一个新州加入的国家,谁能预见到它未来的各种变化呢?

从英国人的第一批殖民地建立至今,其居民数量大约每22年就翻一倍。我至今还没有发现有什么因素会阻止在今后100

---

① 这确实只是一个暂时的危险。我毫不怀疑西部社会会被设想的尽可能的稳定和有规律,就像大西洋岸边的情形一样。

② 1790年宾夕法尼亚州有431373居民。

③ 纽约州的面积大约有6213平方里格。见达贝:《美国见闻》。

American population for the next hundred years; and before that time has elapsed, I believe that the territories and dependencies of the U-nited States will be covered by more than a hundred millions of inhab-itants and divided into forty states. [1] I admit that these hundred millions of men have no different interests. I suppose, on the contrary, that they are all equally interested in the maintenance of the Union; but I still say that, for the very reason that they are a hundred millions, forming forty distinct nations unequally strong, the continuance of the Federal government can be only a fortunate accident.

Whatever faith I may have in the perfectibility of man, until human nature is altered and men wholly transformed I shall refuse to believe in the duration of a government that is called upon to hold together forty different nations spread over a territory equal to one half of Europe, [2] to avoid all rivalry, ambition, and struggles between them, and to direct their independent activity to the accomplishment of the same designs.

But the greatest peril to which the Union is exposed by its increase arises from the continual displacement of its internal forces. The distance from Lake Superior to the Gulf of Mexico is more than twelve hundred miles as the crow flies. The frontier of the United States winds along the whole of this immense line; sometimes falling within its limits, but more frequently extending far beyond it, into the waste. It has been calculated that the whites, advance every year a mean distance of seventeen miles along the whole of this vast boundary. [3] Obstacles such as an unproductive district, a lake, or an Indian nation are from time to time encountered. The advancing column then

---

[1] If the population continues to double every twenty-two years, as it has done for the last two hundred years, the number of inhabitants in the United States in 1852 will be twenty-four million; in 1874, forty-eight million; and in 1896, ninety-six million. This may still be the case even if the lands on the eastern slope of the Rocky Mountains should be found unfit for cultivation. The territory that is already occupied can easily contain this number of inhabitants. One hundred million men spread over the surface of the twentyfour states and the three dependencies which now constitute the Union would give only 762 inhabitants to the square league; this would be far below the mean population of France, which is 1,006 to the square league; or of England, which is 1,457; and it would even be below the population of Switzerland, for that country, notwithstanding its lakes and mountains, contains 783 inhabitants to the square league. See Malte-Brun, Vol. VI, p. 92.

[2] The area of the United States is 295,000 square leagues, that of Europe, following Malte-Brun (Vol. VI, p. 4), is 500,000.

[3] See Legislative Documents, 20th Congress, No. 117, p. 105.

年内英裔美国人数量的增长。① 我认为,在未来的 100 年之内,美国的领土或属地上将会住有一亿多居民,并且被划分为 40 多个州。而且我认为这些人会有共同的利益。另一方面,我认为他们继续联合会使它们得到同等的好处。但我还要说,正是因为这个拥有上亿的人口的原因,会使它被划分为 40 多个情况不同和力量不等的州,所以联邦政府的继续存在,只能作为一个幸运的偶然事件。

我虽然一再强调我坚信人的向善性,但直到人类的本性被改变,人们被彻底转变,我才会拒绝承认一个以管理面积相当于大半个欧洲的 40 多个州为己任的政府能够长期存在下去。② 这个政府会设法避免州与州之间出现对抗、斗争和野心,并指引他们各自的独立行动,共同去完成相同的目标。

对联邦来说,因日益扩大而面临的最大危险,却起因于其内部势力的不断转移。从苏必利尔湖畔到墨西哥湾,直线距离约有 400 里格。美国的疆界就沿着这条长线为轴蜿蜒;尽管在有些地方缩回一点,但在更多的地方远远越过这条线而深入到荒地。有人统计过,白人每年平均向这片荒地沿线挺进 17 里格。③他们常常碰到一些障碍,诸如不毛之地、湖泊和突然出现在途中的印第

---

① 如果每 22 年人口就翻倍的情况依然像之前的 200 年间一样继续,则 1852 年美国的居民将达到 2400000。1896 年达到 9600000。即使洛矶山脉东部斜坡不适宜耕种也仍然会这样。已经占据的疆域已足以包容这些数量的居民。一百万居民分散在 24 个州和 3 个如今已属于联邦的殖民地将会使每平方里约有 772 个居民。这个数字远远低于法国的平均数每平方里约 1006 人,也低于英格兰的每平方里约 1457 人,甚至低于瑞士的每平方里约 783 人。见《马特－布伦》第六卷,第 92 页。

② 美国的面积是 295000 平方里约,欧洲则为 500000 平方里约,根据《马特－布伦》(第六卷第 4 页)。

③ 见《立法文件》第 20 次国会第 117 号,第 105 页。

halts for a while; its two extremities curve round upon themselves, and as soon as they are reunited, they proceed onwards. This gradual and continuous progress of the European race towards the Rocky Mountains has the solemnity of a providential event; it is like a deluge of men rising unabatedly, and daily driven onwards by the hand of God.

Within this front line of conquering settlers, towns are built and vast states founded. In 1790 there were only a few thousand pioneers sprinkled along the valleys of the Mississippi; at the present day these valleys contain as many inhabitants as were to be found in the whole Union in 1790. Their population amounts to nearly four million. [1] The city of Washington was founded in 1800, in the very center of the U-nion; but such are the changes which have taken place that it now stands at one of the extremities; and the delegates of the most remote Western states, in order to take their seats in Congress, are already o-bliged to perform a journey as long as that from Vienna to Paris. [2]

All the states of the Union are carried forward at the same time towards prosperity, but all cannot grow and prosper at the same rate. In the North of the Union the detached branches of the Allegheny chain, extending as far as the Atlantic Ocean, form spacious roads and ports, constantly accessible to the largest vessels. But from the Potomac, following the shore, to the mouth of the Mississippi, the coast is sandy and flat. In this part of the Union the mouths of almost all the rivers are obstructed; and the few harbors that exist among these inlets do not offer the same depth to vessels and present, for commerce, facilities less extensive than those of the North.

The first and natural cause of inferiority is united to another cause proceeding from the laws. We have seen that slavery, which is abolished in the North, still exists in the South; and I have pointed out its fatal consequences upon the prosperity of the planter himself.

---

[1] 3,672,317, census of 1830.

[2] The distance from Jefferson, the capital of the state of Missouri, to Washington is 1,019 miles or 420 leagues. (*American Almanac*, 1831, p. 48.)

安人等。这时,前进中的人马暂时停下来,等到后续的人马跟上来聚拢以后,又开始前进。欧洲人种向落基山的这种连续不断地节节推进,好像是在奉诏神谕:人们像潮水般层叠而来,在神的引导下不断前进。

在征服者占领的边界以内,相继建立起一座座城镇和几个规模巨大的州。1790 年,在密西西比河流域还只有几千名拓荒者散布其上;而在今天,这个流域的居民人数,已与 1790 年全联邦的人口接近,即将达到 400 万人。① 华盛顿市建于 1800 年,当时它还算是处于美国联邦的中心地带;而现在,它已位属联邦四极之中的一极了。西部最远几个州的议员,为了出席国会,不得不经过一段相当于由维也纳到巴黎这样长的旅程。②

联邦的所有各州都在同时走向繁荣,但他们成长和繁荣的速度却各不相同。在北部联邦,阿勒格尼山脉的几个支脉伸进大西洋,形成多处宽敞的停泊所和港口可以容纳巨大的船舶。但是,从波托马克河口开始,顺美洲沿岸南下,一直到密西西比河河口,海岸都是平坦的沙地。在联邦的这一区域,几乎所有河流的河口都被泥沙堵塞,而稀稀拉拉分布在这条浅水海岸线上的港口,又不能为船舶提供北方港口那样的深度,所以为商业提供的便利条件也就大大不如北方。

除了这一由于自然环境造成的主要的劣势,还有一个因法制原因而造成的缺憾。那就是我们已提及的已在北方废除但还存在于南方的蓄奴制。我也已经在前面指出过它对于种植园主带来的致命的危害。

---

① 1830 年人口普查结果为 3672317。
② 杰斐逊,密苏里州的首都到华盛顿约有 1019 英里或 420 里约。

The North is therefore superior to the South both in comMerce①
and in manufacture, the natural consequence of which is the more
rapid increase of population and wealth within its borders. The states
on the shores of the Atlantic Ocean are already half peopled. Most of
the land is held by an owner, and they cannot therefore receive so
many immigrants as the Western states, where a boundless field is
still open to industry. The valley of the Mississippi is far more fertile
than the coast of the Atlantic Ocean. This reason, added to all the
others, contributes to drive the Europeans westward, a fact which may
be rigorously demonstrated by figures. It is found that the sum total of
the population of all the United States has about tripled in the course
of forty years. But in the new states adjacent to the Mississippi the
population② has increased thirty-one-fold within the same time. ③

The center of the federal power is continually displaced. Forty
years ago the majority of the citizens of the Union were established upon the coast of the Atlantic, in the environs of the spot where Washington

---

① The following statements will show the difference between the commercial activity of the South and of the North.

In 1829 the tonnage of all the merchant vessels belonging to Virginia, the
two Carolinas, and Georgia (the four great Southern states) amounted to only 5,
243 tons. In the same year the tonnage of the vessels of the state of Massachusetts
alone amounted to 17,322 tons. (See *Legislative Documents*, 21st Congress, 2nd
Session, No. 140, p. 244.) Thus Massachusetts alone had three times as much
shipping as the four above-mentioned states. Neverthe less, the area of the state
of Massachusetts is only 959 square leagues (7,335 square miles), and its population amounts to 610,014 inhabitants; while the area of the four other states I
have quoted is 27,204 square leagues (210,000 square miles), and their population 3,047,767. Thus the area of the state of Massachusetts forms only one thirti-
eth part of the area of the four states, and its population is but one fifth of theirs.
(*View of the United States*, by Darby.) Slavery is prejudicial to the commercial
prosperity of the South in several dif erent ways, by diminishing the spirit of enterprise among the whites and by preventing them from obtaining the sailors whom
they require. Sailors are usually taken only from the lowest ranks of the population; but in the Southern states, these lowest ranks are composed of slaves, and it
is very difficult to employ them at sea. They are unable to serve as well as a white
crew, and fears would always be entertained of their mutinying in the middle of
the ocean or of their escaping in the foreign countries at which they might touch.

② *View of the United States*, by Darby, p. 444.

③ Note that when I speak of the basin of the Mississippi, I do not include
that portion of the states of New York, Pennsylvania, and Virginia situated west of
the Alleghenies, which should, however, be considered as also com prising a part
of it.

因此,北方无论在商业上或在工业上,^①都必定比南方强大;而其在人口和财富方面比南方增长迅速,也在情理之中。在大西洋沿岸的各州人口已居住过半。大部分土地都已有了主人。因此,它们不能像西部各州那样接纳大量移民,因为西部各州还有无尽的土地等待着开发。密西西比河流域的土地也远比大西洋沿岸肥沃。把这项理由再入其他理由之中的话,对促使欧洲人西迁就很有说服力了。这个事实可以通过一些数据加以证实。以全美人口计算,40 年来人口数量增加了两倍多。而只算密西西比河流域附近的土地上,^②其人口数量在同期却增加了 30 倍。^③

联邦权力中心一直在不停地变化。40 年前,联邦的大部分居民都居住在沿海地区,即在今天的华盛顿郊区。如今,大部分居民向内

---

① 以下的描述将会向我们揭示南部和北部商业行为的区别。

1829 年,所有商人船舶的吨位登记,弗吉尼亚、两个卡罗来纳州和乔治亚(南部四大州)总量为 5243 吨。在同一年,马萨诸塞州一个州的吨位登记就达到 17322 吨。(见《立法文件》,第 21 次国会,第二次会议,第 140 号,第 244 页。)因此,马萨诸塞州一个州就相当于以上提到的四个州的总量。然而,马萨诸塞的面积只有 959 平方里格(7335 平方英里),人口总数为 610014。而另外提到的四个州的面积约 27204 平方里格(210000 平方英里),人口总数达 3047767。因此,马萨诸塞的面积只有其他四个州总面积的三十分之一,人口也只有他们的五分之一。奴隶制度给南部商业繁荣在各个方面带来了损害,通过削减白人的士气,阻碍他们获得需要的水手。而水手一般都来自社会的最底层,但是在南部各州,奴隶构成了社会的最底层,所以在船运时很难雇佣到他们。他们不能像白人水手那样工作,在海中航行的时候,他们总会发生暴动以摆脱他们的恐惧,要么他们就会在任何他们到达的国家潜逃。

② 见《美国见闻》,达贝著,第 444 页。

③ 请注意,当我谈及密西西比盆地的时候,我并没有把纽约州、宾夕法尼亚和坐落在阿勒格尼山脉西部的弗吉尼亚州的那一部分包括在内,这些地方也应该包括在密西西比盆地范围之内。

now stands; but the great body of the people is now advancing inland and to the North, so that in twenty years the majority will unquestionably be on the western side of the Alleghenies. If the Union continues, the basin of the Mississippi is evidently marked out, by its fertility and its extent, to be the permanent center of the Federal government. In thirty or forty years that tract of country will have assumed its natural rank. It is easy to calculate that its population, compared with that of the coast of the Atlantic, will then be, in round numbers, as 40 to 11. In a few years the states that founded the Union will lose the direction of its policy, and the population of the valley of the Mississippi will preponderate in the Federal assemblies.

This constant gravitation of the Federal power and influence towards the northwest is shown every ten years, when a general census of the population is made and the number of delegates that each state sends to Congress is settled anew. ① In 1790 Virginia had nineteen representatives in Congress. This number continued to increase until 1813, when it reached twenty-three; from that time it began to decrease, and in 1833 Virginia elected only twenty-one. ② During the

---

① It may be seen that in the course of the last ten years the population of one district, as, for instance, the state of Delaware, has increased in the proportion of 5 percent; while that of another, like the territory of Michigan, has increased 250 per cent. Thus the population of Virginia had augmented 13 per cent, and that of the border state of Ohio 61 per cent, in the same time. The general table of these changes, which is given in the National Calendar, is a striking picture of the unequal fortunes of the different states.

② It has been said that in the course of the last period the population of Virginia has increased 13 per cent; and it is necessary to explain how the number of representatives for a state may decrease when the population of that state, far from diminishing, is actually increasing. I take the state of Virginia, to which I have already alluded, as the basis of my comparison. The number of representatives of Virginia in 1823 was proportionate to the total number of the representatives of the Union and to the relation which its population bore to that of the whole Union; in 1833 the number of representatives of Virginia was likewise proportionate to the total number of the representatives of the Union and to the relation which its population, increased in the course of ten years, bore to the increased population of the Union in the same space of time. The new number of Virginian representatives will then be to the old number, on the one hand, as the new number of all the representatives is to the old number; and, on the other hand, as the increase of the population of Virginia is to that of the whole population of the country. Thus if the increase of the population of the lesser region be to that of the greater in an exact inverse ratio of the proportion between the new and the old numbers of all the representatives, the number of the representatives of Virginia will remain stationary; and if the increase of the Virginia population be to that of the whole Union in a smaller ratio than the new number of the representatives of the Union to the old number, the number of the representatives of Virginia must decrease.

地或北方移动。所以 20 年后,大部分居民都将迁往阿勒格尼山的西侧。只要联邦继续存在,密西西比河盆地就必然会因其肥沃而辽阔的土地而胜出,将会成为联邦政府永恒的中心。在今后三四十年内,这个国家的广阔疆域必将取得其应有的地位。不难推算出来,到那时候,这里的人口与大西洋沿岸各州的人口数量的比例,将接近 40∶11。因此,再过几年,早先建起联邦的各州,将会失去其政策导向能力,而密西西比河流域的人口数则将对联邦议会发生重要的影响。

联邦的力量和影响的这种逐渐向西北移动的趋势,每隔 10 年就可显现一次,因为在每 10 年进行一次的全国人口普查之后,要重新规定各州应选入国会的众议员人数。[①] 1790 年,弗吉尼亚州有 19 名众议员。这个名额后来有所增加,1813 年达到 23 名。从此以后,名额开始下降,1833 年只有 21 名了。[②] 但在同期,纽约州

———————

① 也许人们会认为,在过去 10 年中,像特拉华州的人口数量应该会按照 5% 的比例增长。而同时,像密歇根州则按照 250% 的比例增长。因此,弗吉尼亚的人口数量增长了 13%,拥有更大面积的新奥尔良则增长了 61%。这些变化的综合表格,显示了各个不同州不同的际运。

② 据说过去弗吉尼亚的人口数量增长速度为 13%,我们有必要解释一下,一个州的代表人数如何才会随着该州的人口数量的增加而减少。我以弗吉尼亚为例,我已经提及,作为我参照的基础。弗吉尼亚代表人数在 1823 年与联邦中代表的人数成正比,也与该州的人数与整个联邦人数的比例有关。1833 年,弗吉尼亚代表的人数同样与联邦代表的人数成正比,而其双方的人数在这十年中都有所增长。而弗吉尼亚新的代表数量与旧的人数,从一方面来说,是所有新代表的数量与旧代表的人数的比例相同。而从另一方面来说,弗吉尼亚人口数量的增长比之于整个国家增长的人口数量相同。因此,如果一个人口较少的地区的人数的增加,与人口较多的地区之间在新旧代表数量的比例上刚好成反比。而弗吉尼亚代表的数量将会一直保持不变。如果弗吉尼亚恩口数量的增长数与这个联邦的数量的比率小于联邦代表新旧人数的比率,则弗吉尼亚代表的数量必然减少。

same period the state of New York followed the contrary direction: in 1790 it had ten representatives in Congress; in 1813, twenty-seven; in 1823, thirty-four; and in 1833, forty. The state of Ohio had only one representative in 1803; and in 1833 it already had nineteen.

It is difficult to imagine a durable union of a nation that is rich and strong with one that is poor and weak, even if it were proved that the strength and wealth of the one are not the causes of the weakness and poverty of the other. But union is still more difficult to maintain at a time when one party is losing strength and the other is gaining it. This rapid and disproportionate increase of certain states threatens the independence of the others. New York might perhaps succeed, with its two million inhabitants and its forty representatives, in dictating to the other states in Congress. But even if the more powerful states make no attempt to oppress the smaller ones, the danger still exists; for there is almost as much in the possibility of the act as in the act itself. The weak generally mistrust the justice and the reason of the strong. The states that increase less rapidly than the others look upon those that are more favored by fortune with envy and suspicion. Hence arise the deepseated uneasiness and ill-defined agitation which are observable in the South and which form so striking a contrast to the confidence and prosperity which are common to other parts of the Union. I am inclined to think that the hostile attitude taken by the South recently is attributable to no other cause. The inhabitants of the Southern states are, of all the Americans, those who are most interested in the maintenance of the Union; they would assuredly suffer most from being left to themselves; and yet they are the only ones who threaten to break the tie of confederation. It is easy to perceive that the South, which has given four Presidents to the Union, ①which perceives that it is losing its federal influence and that the number of its representatives in Congress is diminishing from year to year, while those of the Northern and Western states are increasing, the South, which is peopled with ardent and irascible men, is becoming more and more irritated and alarmed. Its inhabitants reflect upon their present position and remember their past influence, with the melancholy uneasiness of men who suspect oppression. If they discover a law of the union that is not unequivocally favorable to their

①　Washington, Jefferson, Madison, and Monroe.

的众议员人数一直在增加:1790 年为 10 人,1813 年为 27 人,1823年为 34 人,1833 年为 40 人。俄亥俄州 1803 年只有一名众议员,1833 年达到 19 人。

很难想象一个持久存在的富强国家与贫穷国家结成的联盟。即使我们已经得到证实,其中一个富强并不是另一方贫穷弱小的原因。但是,当其中的一方逐渐丧失其实力而另一方却不断强大的时期,联盟就更难维持了。一些州迅速地不成比例的增长,威胁着另一些州的独立地位。拥有 200 万人口和 40 名众议员纽约州,也许就可以成功地使国会中的其他州不得不听命于它的旨意。但即使是强大的州没有压迫企图其他比它小的州的企图,但这种危险仍不可避免,因为压迫的可能性和其真实发生的可能性几乎是同等的。弱小的一方通常不相信强者的公正和理论。那些发展较慢的州,总以猜忌的眼神看待那些走运的国家。由此在南方产生的强烈的不安和难过,与联邦另一些州显示的自信和繁荣形成了强烈的对比。我倾向于认为,南部最近所采取的敌对的态度,其原因就在于此。南部各州的居民,在全体美国人中,是最需要联盟的。因为任其自由发展,他们必然会吃亏最大。而他们也是唯一有可能破坏联邦纽带的因素。这个原因很简单,因为南方已出过四届联邦总统,[①]而现在南方在联邦中已不再有威信而其在国会中众议员的数量也在减少,同时北方和西部的众议员人数却逐年增加;而且南方人性格急躁,容易发怒,不够冷静。他们正以忧虑的眼光看待自己现在的状况,缅怀着自己的过去。他们每天都在自问自己是否受到了压迫。如果他们发现联邦的某

---

① 华盛顿、杰弗逊、麦迪逊和门罗。

interests, they protest against it as an abuse of force; and if their ardent remonstrances are not listened to, they threaten to quit an association that loads them with burdens while it deprives them of the profits. "The Tariff," said the inhabitants of Carolina in 1832, "enriches the North and ruins the South; for, if this were not the case, to what can we attribute the continually increasing power and wealth of the North, with its inclement skies and arid soil; while the South, which may be styled the garden of America, is rapidly declining. " ①

If the changes which I have described were gradual, so that each generation at least might have time to disappear with the order of things under which it had lived, the danger would be less; but the progress of society in America is precipitate and almost revolutionary. The same citizen may have lived to see his state take the lead in the Union and afterwards become powerless in the Federal assemblies; and an Anglo-American republic has been known to grow as rapidly as a man, passing from birth and infancy to maturity in the course of thirty years. It must not be imagined, however, that the states that lose their preponderance also lose their population or their riches; no stop is put to their prosperity, and they even go on to increase more rapidly than any kingdom in Europe. ②But they believe themselves to be impoverished because their wealth does not augment as rapidly as that of their neighbors; and they think that their power is lost because

---

① See the report of its committee to the convention that proclaimed nullification in South Carolina.

② The population of a country assuredly constitutes the first element of its wealth. During this same period, from 1820 to 1832, in which Virginia lost two of its representatives in Congress, its population increased in the proportion of 13. 7 per cent; that of Carolina in the proportion of 15 percent; and that of Georgia 15. 5 per cent. (See *American Almanac*, 1832, p. 162.) But the population of Russia, which increases more rapidly than that of any other European country, only augments in ten years at the rate of 9. 5 per cent; of France at the rate of 7 per cent; and of Europe all together at the rate of 4. 7 per cent. (See Malte-Brun, Vol. VI, p. 95.)

项法令不是很明显地对他们有利,马上就会大声叫嚣着抗议,说他们是滥用职权。如果他们的意见不被采纳,就会大发雷霆,以退出联邦相威胁,说联邦只让他们承担义务,不给他们好处。卡罗来纳的居民们在 1832 年声称:"关税法使北方得以致富,使南方沦落破产,因为如果不是这样,怎么能想象气候寒冷、土地瘠薄的北方的财富和权势会不断增涨,而堪称美洲花园的南方会衰落如此迅速?"①

如果我所描述的变化是缓慢而逐渐地进行着的,以至于每一代人看不出他们目睹的现实秩序对他们有多大影响,这样的话,危险是会少一些。但是,在美国社会进步是显而易见的,并且几乎是革命性的。一个公民在他的一生中,就有可能看到自己居住的州在联邦中领先,后又在联邦的议会中失势。英裔美国的共和国的增长速度像一个人的成长那样迅速,经历从出生,到青年到成年,整个过程只需要三十几年时间。但是,千万不要认为一个州失去了其在国会中的优势,就等于同时丧失了人口数量或者其富裕程度。它们繁荣的脚步不会停止,甚至有可能其发展的速度会高于欧洲的所有王国。② 但是,它们自己却会觉得自己变穷了,因为它们的财富增长速度低于其邻州;它们会感到自己失势了,因

---

① 见委员会向大会提交的关于要求在南卡罗来纳州废奴的请求。

② 一个国家的人口数量确实是决定其财富的首要因素。在 1820 年到 1832 年这段时间,弗吉尼亚在国会中少了两名代表,而其人口数按照 13.7% 的比例增长。卡罗来纳州 15%,乔治亚 15.5%。(见《美国年鉴》,1832,第 162 页。)而俄罗斯的人口增长速度比欧洲所有国家都快。在十年中按照 9. 5% 的比例增长,法国 7%,而欧洲平均值 4.7%。(见《马特 – 布伦》第六卷,第 95 页。)

they suddenly come in contact with a power greater than their own. ①
Thus they are more hurt in their feelings and their passions than in
their interests. But this is amply sufficient to endanger the maintenance of the Union. If kings and peoples had only had their true interests in view ever since the beginning of the world, war would
scarcely be known among mankind.

Thus the prosperity of the United States is the source of their
most serious dangers, since it tends to create in some of the federated
states that intoxication which accompanies a rapid increase of fortune,
and to awaken in others those feelings of envy, mistrust, and regret
which usually attend the loss of it. The Americans contemplate this
extraordinary progress with exultation; but they would be wiser to consider it with sorrow and alarm. The Americans of the United States
must inevitably become one of the greatest nations in the world; their
offspring will cover almost the whole of North America; the continent
that they inhabit is their dominion, and it cannot escape them. What
urges them to take possession of it so soon? Riches, power, and renown cannot fail to be theirs at some future time, but they rush upon
this immense fortune as if but a moment remained for them to make it
their own.

I think that I have demonstrated that the existence of the present
confederation depends entirely on the continued assent of all the confederates; and, starting from this principle, I have inquired into the
causes that may induce some of the states to separate from the others.
The Union may, however, perish in two different ways: one of the
federated states may choose to retire from the compact, and so forcibly
to sever the Federal tie; and it is to this supposition that most of the
remarks that I have made apply; or the authority of the Federal government may be gradually lost by the simultaneous tendency of the

---

① It must be admitted, however, that the depreciation that has taken place
in the value of tobacco during the last fifty years has notably diminished the opulence of the Southern planters: but this circumstance is as independent of the will
of their Northern brethren as it is of their own.

为它们突然碰到一个比自己更强大的力量。① 这样,它们在感情和欲望上所受的挫伤,要比在利益上受到的损失更大。但是,这足以对联邦的存在产生威胁。如果各国的国王和人民在世界的最初时候开始就只注重真正的利益,那么人类几乎是可以避免战争的。

可见,美国的繁荣是其最大危机的来源,因为联邦某些州的繁荣会使他们沉醉在自己财富迅速增长的大好形势之下,同时引起另一些州对它们心怀嫉妒和猜疑,他们还会因自己的财富不断减少而觉得难堪。美国人对这一奇异的变动保持沉默并且感到欣慰;但他们其实应当以遗憾和警惕的心情来看待它。因为不管将来发生什么事情,美国人终将成为世界上最伟大民族之一,他们的后代会遍布几乎整个北美。他们现在所居住的陆地已是他们的领土,而且将来也不会从他们的手中丢掉。那么,将来会是什么东西促使他们继续占有这块土地呢? 财富、权势和声望,在他们看来是一刻也不能少的;他们争先恐后地扑向这无尽的宝藏,好像去晚了就抢不到似的。

我想我已证实了一点,目前联邦的存在完全依存于各州都同意继续留在联邦里。而且,从这一点延伸开来,我还探讨了可能导致某些州要求脱离联邦的一些因素。破坏联邦的方式有两种。第一,联邦某一州可能要求退出联邦,这样便强制割断共同的纽带;我在这以前所指出的,大部分属于这种情况。第二,联邦政府

---

① 我们必须承认,尽管如此,在过去50年间烟草价格的降低严重缩减了南部种植园主的财富。但是这一境况既不是北部同胞们的意愿也与他们自己的意志无关。

united republics to resume their independence. The central power, successively stripped of all its prerogatives and reduced to impotence by tacit consent, would become incompetent to fulfill its purpose, and the second union would perish, like the first, by a sort of senile imbecility. The gradual weakening of the Federal tie, which may finally lead to the dissolution of the Union, is a distinct circumstance that may produce a variety of minor consequences before it operates so violerlt a change. The confederation might still exist although its government were reduced to such a degree of inanition as to paralyze the nation, to cause internal anarchy, and to check the general prosperity of the country.

After having investigated the causes that may induce the AngloAmericans to disunite, it is important to inquire whether, if the Union continues to survive, their government will extend or contract its sphere of action, and whether it will become more energetic or more weak.

The Americans are evidently disposed to look upon their condition with alarm. They perceive that in most of the nations of the world the exercise of the rights of sovereignty tends to fall into a few hands, and they are dismayed by the idea that it may be so in their own country. Even the statesmen feel, or affect to feel, these fears; for in America centralization is by no means popular, and there is no surer means of courting the majority than by inveighing against the encroachments of the central power. The Americans do not perceive that the countries in which this alarming tendency to centralization exists are inhabited by a single people, while the Union is composed of different communities, a fact that is sufficient to baffle all the inferences which might be drawn from analogy. I confess that I am inclined to consider these fears of a great number of Americans as purely imaginary. Far from participating in their dread of the consolidation of power in the hands of the Union, I think that the Federal government is visibly losing strength. To prove this assertion, I shall not have recourse to any remote occurrences, but to circumstances which I have myself witnessed and which belong to our own time.

可能因联邦各州同时要求恢复原来的独立地位而失去其权力。联邦政府逐渐失去其所有的特权,并最终默认无力去实现自己的目的。于是,这第二次联盟也将像第一次联盟那样,由于衰败无力而灭亡。逐渐被削弱的联邦纽带,最后可能导致联邦解体。并且在如此猛烈的变革发生之前,还可能造成许多其他的次要结果。即使联邦政府的软弱无力已使国家形同虚设,完全瘫痪,造成内部混乱的状态,阻碍全国的普遍繁荣,联邦也依然可以存在。

在研究了可能引起英裔美国人分裂的各种原因以后,寻求联邦政府是否能继续存在下去,以及其是会扩大还是会缩小其活动范围,是会变得更加强大有力还是会更加软弱的种种原因,就显得异常重要了。

很明显,美国人对他们的未来感到紧张。他们看到,世界上大部分国家最高主权的行使,都容易陷入被少数几个人的垄断之中。他们一想到自己的国家也难免如此,便感到不安。甚至一些政客也有这种紧张感,或者至少装作有此紧张感。他们之所以要如此,是因为在美国,中央集权不得民心,而出面攻击中央政府而拿权,是向多数讨好的最佳手法。美国人没有察觉,凡是出现他们所害怕的中央集权趋势的国家,其国内都是同一民族的人们,而美国则是由多个不同民族组成的联邦。这一事实,足以推翻以此做出的一切推测。我承认,我认为许多美国人的这种紧张感纯粹来自假想。我不仅不像美国人那样害怕联邦的主权会被加强,而事实上我认为联邦政府的权力分明在减弱。我不必寻找那些古代的事例,而只用我亲眼目睹的事例或当代发生的事例就可以证明我的这个论断。

An attentive examination of what is going on in the United States will easily convince us that two opposite tendencies exist there, like two currents flowing in contrary directions in the same channel. The Union has now existed for forty-five years, and time has done away with many provincial prejudices which were at first hostile to its power. The patriotic feeling that attached each of the Americans to his own state has become less exclusive, and the different parts of the Union have become more amicable as they have become better acquainted with each other. The post, that great instrument of intercourse, now reaches into the backwoods;[1] and steamboats have established daily means of communication between the different points of the coast. An inland navigation of unexampled rapidity conveys commodities up and down the rivers of the country. [2]And to these facilities of nature and art may be added those restless cravings, that busy-mindedness and love of pelf, which are constantly urging the American into active life and bringing him into contact with his fellow citizens. He crosses the country in every direction; he visits all the various populations of the land. There is not a province in France in which the natives are so well known to one another as the thirteen millions of men who cover the territory of the United States. While the Americans intermingle, they assimilate; the differences resulting from their climate, their origin, and their institutions diminish; and they all draw nearer and nearer to the common type. Every year thousands of men leave the North to settle in different parts of the Union; they bring with them their faith, their opinions, and their manners, and as they are more enlightened than the men among whom they are about to dwell, they soon rise to the head of affairs and adapt society to their own advantage. This continual emigration of the North to the South is peculiarly favorable to the fusion of all the different provincial characters into one national character. The civilization of the North

---

[1] In 1832 the district of Michigan, which had only 31,639 inhabitants and was hardly more than a wilderness, had developed 940 miles of post roads. The almost entirely unsettled territory of Arkansas was already covered by 1,938 miles of post roads. See the *Report of the Postmaster General*, November 30, 1833. The carriage of newspapers alone throughout the Union brought in $254,796 annually.

[2] In the course of ten years, from 1821 to 1831, 271 steamboats were launched on the rivers flowing through the Mississippi Valley. In 1829 there were 256 steamboats in the United States. See *Legislative Documents*, No. 140, p. 274.

留心观察美国所发生的一切,我们不难发现这个国家的发展有两个彼此相反的趋势,仿佛一个河道中有了两条逆向的水流。联邦现已存在 45 年,时间使最初反对联邦的许多地方偏见逐渐消失。美国人热爱所在州的情愫中已抹去了大多原有的排外性。联邦的不同地区,也随着彼此日益熟悉,变得更加亲密。邮政是人们用来彼此联系的有力工具,它现已深入到荒漠的腹地。[①] 每天往返于各口岸之间轮船,各种货物也以空前的速度被运到内河上下游。[②] 除了自然和人工提供的这些便利条件,还有人们孜孜不息地追求、急于实现的愿望和热爱发财的心理,也在不断驱使美国人形成积极的生活态度,并促使他们与其同胞们之间的广泛交流。他们走遍了全国各地,接触到国内居住的各种居民。在法国,没有哪一个省的居民,能像美国 1300 万居民那样彼此了解。美国人一边融合一边同化。因气候、本源和制度的不同而造成的差异,正在逐渐减少。他们都变得越来越接近于同一类型。每年都有成千上万人,从北方迁往联邦的其他各地定居。这些北方人带来了他们的信仰、观点和民情,并由于他们的文化高于新落户地区的居民,而很快担当起主管当地的事务的差使,并根据自己的利益改造着社会。这种居民连续不断从北向南迁徙的行为,对于把不同的地方特点融合为全国普遍存在的特点,起了重大的促

---

① 1832 年,密歇根州地区只有 31639 居民,只比荒野上的居住人数稍多一些,却修建了 940 英里邮递通路。几乎完全没有人迹的阿肯色州也覆盖了 1938 英里邮递通路。见邮政部长 1833 年 11 月 30 日的报告。而在联邦内报纸的邮费每年就有 254796 美元。

② 在从 1821 年到 1831 年十年间,共有 271 艘轮船停泊在流经密西西比大峡谷的河内。1829 年,美国有 256 艘。见《立法文件》第 140 号,第 274 页。

appears to be the common standard, to which the whole nation will one day be assimilated.

The commercial ties that unite the federated states are strengthened by the increasing manufactures of the Americans, and the union which began in their opinions gradually forms a part of their habits; the course of time has swept away the bugbear thoughts that haunted the imaginations of the citizens in 1789. The Federal power has not become oppressive; it has not destroyed the independence of the states; it has not subjected the confederates to monarchical institutions; and the Union has not rendered the lesser states dependent upon the larger ones. The confederation has continued to increase in population, in wealth, and in power. I am therefore convinced that the natural obstacles to the continuance of the American Union are not so powerful as they were in 1789, and that the enemies of the Union are not so numerous.

And yet a careful examination of the history of the United States for the last forty-five years will readily convince us that the Federal power is declining; nor is it difficult to explain the causes of this phenomenon. When the Constitution of 1789 was promulgated, the nation was a prey to anarchy; the Union which succeeded this confusion excited much dread and hatred, but it was warmly supported because it satisfied an imperious want. Although it was then more attacked than it is now, the Federal power soon reached the maximum of its authority, as is usually the case with a government that triumphs after having braced its strength by the struggle. At that time the interpretation of the Constitution seemed to extend rather than to repress the Federal sovereignty; and the Union offered, in several respects, the appearance of a single and undivided people, directed in its foreign and internal policy by a single government. But to attain this point the people had risen, to some extent, above itself.

The Constitution had not destroyed the individuality of the states, and all communities, of whatever nature they may be, are impelled by a secret instinct towards independence. This propensity is still more decided in a country like America, in which every village forms a sort of republic, accustomed to govern itself. It therefore cost the states an effort to submit to the Federal supremacy; and all efforts, however

进作用。因此,北方的文明将会被所有民族吸收。

联结联邦各州的商业纽带随着美国工业的发展也日益增强,而最初由见解一致而联合在一起的联邦而今已将这种联合变成一种习惯。时间的长河洗去了 1789 年盘亘在人们心中对假想的恐惧。联邦政府没有变成压迫者,没有损害各州的独立,没有使联合的各州屈于君主制度之下。小州参加联邦后,也没有扮演着依附于大州的小角色。联邦在人口、财富和势力方面得到不断地增加。因此我认为,阻碍美国人结成联邦的天然障碍,已不如 1789 年时那样强大,而且联邦的敌人也没有那时多了。

然而,美国 45 年来的历史的仔细研究使我们确信,联邦的权力在不断地下降。产生这种现象的原因,也不难找到。当公布 1789 年宪法时,全国正处于无政府状态。这种情况下,联邦的成立,激起了很大的恐惧和憎恨,但因为联邦同时也满足了一种巨大的需要,所以也得到了热心的支持。尽管联邦政权那时受到的打击比今天更猛烈,但它很快就像一个政府因奋力斗争而获胜时通常所做的那样,使自己的权力达到了高峰。在这一时期,对宪法的解释似乎更多是扩大而不是约束联邦主权,所以联邦在许多方面都表现出是一个对内对外均由一个政府领导的单一国家的样子。但是,为了达到这一点,从某些方面来说,也把人民抬高到凌驾于联邦之上的地位。

宪法并没有销毁各州的个性,而且所有的共同体,不管其性质如何,都有一种趋向独立的潜在本能。这种倾向在美国这样的国家表现得更坚决,因为在美国,每个乡镇都像一个习惯于自己管理自己的共和国。因此,各州都不得不花费一番努力服从联邦的统治地位。然而,尽管这种努力能够取得巨大的成功,也必

successful, necessarily subside with the causes in which they originated.

As the Federal government consolidated its authority, America resumed its rank among the nations, peace returned to its frontiers, and public credit was restored; confusion was succeeded by a fixed state of things, which permitted the full and free exercise of industrious enterprise. It was this very prosperity that made the Americans forget the cause which had produced it; and when once the danger was passed, the energy and the patriotism that had enabled them to brave it disappeared from among them. Delivered from the cares that oppressed them, they easily returned to their ordinary habits and gave themselves up without resistance to their natural inclinations. When a powerful government no longer appeared to be necessary, they once more began to think it irksome. Everything prospered under the Union, and the states were not inclined to abandon the Union; but they desired to render the action of the power which represented it as light as possible. The general principle of union was adopted, but in every minor detail there was a tendency to independence. The principle of confederation was every day more easily admitted and more rarely applied, so that the Federal government, by creating order and peace, brought about its own decline.

As soon as this tendency of public opinion began to be manifested externally, the leaders of parties, who live by the passions of the people, began to work it to their own advantage. The position of the Federal government then became exceedingly critical. Its enemies were in possession of the popular favor, and they obtained the right of conducting its policy by pledging themselves to lessen its influence. From that time forwards the government of the Union, as often as it has entered the lists with the governments of the states, has almost invariably been obliged to recede. And whenever an interpretation of the terms of the Federal Constitution has been pronounced, that interpretation has generally been opposed to the Union and favorable to the states.

The Constitution gave to the Federal government the right of providing for the national interests; and it had been held that no other authority was so fit to superintend the internal improvements that affected the prosperity of the whole Union, such, for instance, as the

然会随着产生这种努力的原因的消逝而衰退。

联邦政府既巩固了自己的权力,美国也便恢复了它的国际地位,美国边界再现和平局面并获得了公众的信任。于是,稳定的秩序取代了混乱,个人勤奋也走上了正常轨道获得自由发展。然而,使人们开始忘却繁荣来因的,也正是繁荣本身。危险一旦过去,美国人便把当初帮助他们克服危险的那种毅力和爱国精神抛掷脑后。一旦摆脱了使他们困惑的恐惧之后,他们轻易地就回到自己的老路子上去了,放任自己的喜好儿丝毫不加以约束。一旦一个强大的政府被人们认为不再需要时,人们对它的厌恶感就油然而生。当大家跟着联邦一起繁荣的时候,没人愿意放弃联邦,只是希望代表联邦的当局尽量少管事情。各州都接受了一般意义上的联合,但在有关本州的每项事务上,又都倾向于处于原来的独立地位。任何时候联邦的原则都容易为人接受,但却很少被人采用。因此,联邦政府在建立秩序与和平的同时,也在走向衰落。

一旦公众的情绪开始外露,依靠人民激情而存的政党领袖们,便开始利用他们为自己谋利。联邦政府的地位就变得岌岌可危了;而它的对手们却得到了人民的好感,并且正期望它垮台,以取得推行己方政策的权利。进入这样的时期后,一旦联邦政府与联邦各州发生争执时,几乎总是被迫退让。而一旦问题涉及对联邦宪法的解释时,解释的结果通常都是不利于联邦,而有利于州的。

宪法授权联邦政府关心全国性利益。并且认为,政府最适合去管理这类增进联邦内部繁荣的事务,比如开凿运河。而当各州看到另一个权力当局因此而支配它们自身的一部分领土时,心中

cutting of canals. But the states were alarmed at a power that could thus dispose of a portion of their territory; they were afraid that the central government would by this means acquire a formidable patronage within their own limits, and exercise influence which they wished to reserve exclusively to their own agents. The Democratic Party, which has constantly opposed the increase of the Federal authority, accused Congress of usurpation, and the chief magistrate of ambition. The central government was intimidated by these clamors, and it finally acknowledged its error, promising to confine its influence for the future within the circle that was prescribed to it.

The Constitution confers upon the Union the right of treating with foreign nations. The Indian tribes which border upon the frontiers of the United States had usually been regarded in this light. As long as these savages consented to retire before the civilized settlers, the Federal right was not contested; but as soon as an Indian tribe attempted to fix its residence upon a given spot, the adjacent states claimed possession of the lands and a right of sovereignty over the natives. The central government soon recognized both these claims; and after it had concluded treaties with the Indians as independent nations, it gave them up as subjects to the legislative tyranny of the states. [1]

Some of the states which had been founded on the Atlantic coast extended indefinitely to the West, into wild regions where no European had yet penetrated. The states whose confines were irrevocably fixed looked with a jealous eye upon the unbounded regions that were thus opened to their neighbors. The latter, with a view to conciliate the others and to facilitate the act of union, then agreed to lay down their own boundaries and to abandon all the territory that lay beyond them to the confederation at large. [2] Thenceforward the Federal government became the owner of all the uncultivated lands that lie beyond the borders of the thirteen states first confederated. It had the right of parceling and selling them, and the sums derived from this source were paid into the public treasury to

[1] See, in the legislative documents already quoted in speaking of the Indians, the letter of the President of the United States to the Cherokees, his correspondence on this subject with his agents, and his messages to Congress.

[2] The first act of cession was made by the state of New York in 1780; Virginia, Massachusetts, Connecticut, South and North Carolina followed this example at different times, Georgia making the last; its act of cession was not completed till 1802.

不免惶惶不安。它们害怕中央政府通过这种办法在自己领土内发号施令,并把它们专为本州人员保留的权力抢走。因此,一直反对扩大联邦政府权力的民主党开始指责国会滥用职权,说国家元首怀有野心。中央政府在这种阵势的胁迫下,终于承认其错误,并允诺将来把自己的影响力限制在一定的范围之内。

宪法授予联邦政府同外国交涉的特权。与联邦毗邻的印第安部落,也通常会遭遇这样的对待。只要这些野蛮部落同意从文明人的区域撤退,联邦政权就不表示异议;但当印第安部落试图定居于某个指定地点时,紧靠着这个地点的州便会宣称自己对这块土地拥有所有权,并对居住其上的人行使主权。中央政府不久就会认可该州的这种做法,并在把印第安部落当作一个独立国家同它签订条约之后,就听任该州的立法机构对他们实施暴政。①

建立在大西洋沿岸的一些州一直向西部无限扩张,延伸到欧洲人从未深入的荒野。那些边界已经定好无法更改的州,只好用嫉妒的双眼,盯着这片无垠的荒漠对他们的领州敞开自己的胸怀。于是,这些得到好处的邻州,出于和解的目的,同时也为了便于联邦行事,同意划定自己的州界,把本州以外的土地全部交给联邦。② 从此以后,联邦政府便成了最初组成联邦的 13 个州境外的全部未开发土地的主人。这意味着,联邦政府有权分配和出售这些土地,并将所得收入全部纳入国库。联邦政还利用这笔收入

---

① 《立法文件》中已引述,在谈及印第安人时,有一封美国总统给切罗基族的信,他与自己的代表,与国会就此事的信件。

② 1780 年在纽约制定了割让的第一份法案。弗吉尼亚、马萨诸塞州、康涅狄格、南部和北部卡罗莱纳州先后采用了这一先例,乔治亚是最后采用该法案的州。这一割让法案直至 1802 年才补充完整。

furnish the means of purchasing tracts of land from the Indians, opening roads to the remote settlements, and accelerating the advance of
civilization. New states have been formed in the course of time in the
midst of those wilds which were formerly ceded by the Atlantic states.
Congress has gone on to sell, for the profit of the nation at large, the
uncultivated lands which those new states contained. But the latter at
length asserted that, as they were now fully constituted, they ought to
have the right of converting the produce of these sales exclusively to
their own use. As their remonstrances became more and more threatening, Congress thought fit to deprive the Union of a portion of the
privileges that it had hitherto enjoyed; and at the end of 1832 it passed a law by which the greatest part of the revenue derived from the
sale of lands was made over to the new Western republics, although
the lands themselves were not ceded to them. ①

The slightest observation in the United States enables one to appreciate the advantages that the country derives from the Bank of the
United States. These advantages are of several kinds, but one of them
is peculiarly striking to the stranger. The notes of the bank are taken
upon the borders of the wilderness for the same value as at Philadelphia, where the bank conducts its operations. ②

But the Bank of the United States is the object of great animosity. Its directors proclaimed their hostility to the President,
and they were accused, not without probability, of having abused
their influence to thwart his election. The President therefore attacked the establishment with all the warmth of personal enmity;
and he was encouraged in the pursuit of his revenge by the conviction that he was supported by the secret inclinations of the majority. The bank may be regarded as the great monetary tie of the U-
nion,
just as Congress is the great legislative tie ; and the same passions
that tend to render the states independent of the central power

---

① It is true that the President refused his assent to this law; but he completely adopted it in principle. See Message of December 8, 1883.

② The Bank of the United States was established in 1816, with a capital of
35,000,000 dollars (185,500,000 fr.); its charter expired in 1836. In 1832
Congress passed a law to renew it, but the President vetoed the bill. The struggle
continues with great violence on either side, and it is easy to fore cast the speedy
fall of the bank.

购买印第安人的土地,修建通向新荒地的道路,加速发展社会文明。在各州让出的荒地上住进由大西洋沿岸迁来的居民以后,便随着时间的推移相继成立了几个新州。国会为了全国的利益,仍继续出售已被划入新州界内的荒地。但这时那些新州宣称,既然它们自己的政体已经趋于成熟,它们要求独享出售土地的收入,以供自己使用。由于它们的这些要求日益具有威胁性,国会便考虑让联邦政府放弃它现在享有的这项特权。于是,在1832年末通过一项法案,①规定西部新成立的各州境内的未开垦荒地所卖得的收入的大半,由各该州扣留供自己使用,虽然这些土地仍不属各该州所有。

只要对美国稍加观察过的人,就可以看出银行制度给这些国家带来的好处。在这些众多的好处当中,有一项最引人注目,即国家银行的纸币可以在全国流通,并且这些纸币在边远地区的价值与银行所在地的费城完全相同②

但是,国家银行却是人们憎恨的主要目标。它的董事们表示了对总统的不友善态度,而他们也被不无根据地指控曾滥用自己的影响阻挠过总统当选。因此,总统出于个人仇恨全力攻击这些人所代表的银行。总统在复仇过程中从自己得到的大多数人的秘密支持中受到鼓舞。犹如国会是最大的立法纽带,银行就是最大的金融纽带。而人们积极地建立拥有中央政权机能的独立

---

① 总统否决了自己对该法律的认同一事属实,但是他还是在原则上完全的采用了该法律。

② 美国银行建于1816年,注册资金35000000美元(185500000法郎)。它的章程截止日期为1836年。在1832年,国会通过一则法案对它加以更新,但是总统否决了该提议。这一斗争在双方引起了严重的混乱,而且也不难预测银行倒闭的迅速。

contributed to the overthrow of the bank.

The Bank of the United States always held a great number of the notes issued by the state banks, which it can at any time oblige them to convert into cash. It has itself nothing to fear from a similar demand, as the extent of its resources enables it to meet all claims. But the existence of the provincial banks is thus threatened and their operations are restricted, since they are able to issue only a quantity of notes duly proportioned to their capital. They submitted with impatience to this salutary control. The newspapers that they bought over, and the President, whose interest rendered him their instrument, attacked the bank with the greatest vehemence. They roused the local passions and the blind democratic instinct of the country to aid their cause; and they asserted that the bank directors formed a permanent aristocratic body, whose influence would ultimately be felt in the government and affect those principles of equality upon which society rests in America.

The contest between the bank and its opponents was only an incident in the great struggle which is going on in America between the states and the central power, between the spirit of democratic independence and that of a proper distribution and subordination of power. I do not mean that the enemies of the bank were identically the same individuals who on other points attacked the Federal government, but I assert that the attacks directed against the Bank of the United States originated in the same propensities that militate against the Federal government, and that the very numerous opponents of the former afford a deplorable symptom of the decreasing strength of the latter.

But the Union has never shown so much weakness as on the celebrated question of the tariff. ① The wars of the French Revolution and of 1812 had created manufacturing establishments in the North of the Union, by cutting off free communication between America and Europe. When peace was concluded and the channel of intercourse reopened by which the produce of Europe was transmitted to the New

---

① See principally, for the details of this affair, *Legislative Documents*, 22nd Congress, 2nd Session, No. 30.

州的激情,也同样用在了促使银行垮台上面。

国家银行经常持有各地方银行发行的大量债券,可以随时拿它们去逼使地方银行兑换现金。对国家银行自己来说,并不害怕这样的威胁。它的巨额流动资金,使它可以应付一切提款要求。而地方银行在受到这样的威胁之后,就不能自由地使用自己的存款余额,而只能按其资本的一定比例发行债券了。地方银行只好不耐烦地忍受这种有益于货币流通而实施的控制。因此,被地方银行所收买的报刊,以及由于自身利益而变成它们工具的总统,便猛烈地攻击国家银行。这些报刊在全国各地煽动地方激情和盲目的民主本能去反对国家银行已达成自己的目的。在它们看来,该行的董事们就是一个持久存在的贵族集团,不断对政府施加影响,迟早要破坏美国社会平等原则的基础。

银行与其对手的争斗,不过是美国上演的各州与中央政府之间、民主独立精神与等级服从精神之间展开的大规模斗争中的一件小事。我不是说国家银行的敌人,同那些在另一些问题上攻击中央政府的人完全一样;但我承认对国家银行施行的攻击,与对联邦政府产生的不良影响,都出于同样的本性,而且正是合众国银行的众多反对者,为联邦政府的力量衰落提供了一个可悲征兆。

但是,联邦从未像在著名的关税问题上表现出的那样软弱。[①]法国大革命和 1812 年的美英战争,促使联邦北方建立起制造业,切断了美国与欧洲的自由贸易往来。当恢复和平,而使欧洲产品得以运往新大陆的航路再次开启时,美国人基于两个原因觉得应

---

① 详细内容请参阅《立法文件》第 22 次国会第二次会议第 30 号。

World, the Americans thought fit to establish a system of import duties for the twofold purpose of protecting their incipient manufactures and of paying off the amount of the debt contracted during the war. The Southern states, which have no manufactures to encourage and which are exclusively agricultural, soon complained of this measure. I do not pretend to examine here whether their complaints were well or ill founded, but only to recite the facts.

As early as 1820 South Carolina declared in a petition to Congress that the tariff was "unconstitutional, oppressive, and unjust." And the states of Georgia, Virginia, North Carolina, Alabama, and Mississippi subsequently remonstrated against it with more or less vigor. But Congress, far from lending an ear to these complaints, raised the scale of tariff duties in the years 1824 and 1828 and recognized anew the principle on which it was founded. A doctrine was then proclaimed, or rather revived, in the South, which took the name of Nullification.

I have shown in the proper place that the object of the Federal Constitution was not to form a league, but to create a national government. The Americans of the United States form one and the same people, in all the cases which are specified by that Constitution; and upon these points the will of the nation is expressed, as it is in all constitutional nations, by the voice of the majority. When the majority has once spoken, it is the duty of the minority to submit. Such is the sound legal doctrine, and the only one that agrees with the text of the Constitution and the known intention of those who framed it.

The partisans of Nullification in the South maintain, on the contrary, that the intention of the Americans in uniting was not to combine themselves into one and the same people, but that they meant only to form a league of independent states; and that each state, consequently, retains its entire sovereignty, if not de facto, at least de jure, and has the right of putting its own construction upon the laws of Congress and of suspending their execution within the limits of its own territory if they seem unconstitutional and unjust.

The entire doctrine of Nullification is comprised in a sentence uttered by Vice President Calhoun, the head of that party in the South, before the Senate of the United States, in 1833: "The Constitution is

当建立进口关税制度,其一是能保护本国刚刚发展起来的制造业,再就是可以以关税收入偿还在战争时期举借的债款。没有可以发展的制造业,而只有农业的南方各州,很快对这项措施怨声载道。我并不想在这里研究它们的抱怨是出于想象还是有真凭实据,而只想说明事实。

早在 1820 年,南卡罗来纳州就在给国会的一份请愿书中声称,关税法案是"违宪的、具有压迫性而且不公正"。接着,佐治亚州、弗吉尼亚州、北卡罗来纳州、亚拉巴马州和密西西比州,也相继对关税法案提出不同程度的抗议。但是,国会对这些抱怨置若罔闻,在 1824 和 1828 年又提高了税率,并再次肯定征收关税的原则。于是,在南方提出了或者毋宁说是唤醒了一个名为"拒绝执行联邦法令"的主张。

我已经指出,联邦宪法的目的不在于建立一个联盟,而是要创造一个国家政府。根据美国宪法,美国只是在一定的条件下算是一个单一的民族。也只是在这些条件下,才像在一切立宪国家里那样,通过多数来表达全国的意志。一旦多数的意见获得通过,少数就只有服从的义务。这是法律健全的学说,只有这个学说才符合宪法的条文和宪法制定者们的初衷。

南方主张的"拒绝执行联邦法令派",与此相反,他们声称美国联合起来的用意不在于建立单一民族的国家,而在于结成几个独立州的联盟,因此,每个州即使不是在实际中,但至少在原则上应保持其完整的主权,有权解释国会颁布的法令,并且有权在本州领域内叫停任何在它看来是违宪和不公正的国会法令。

"拒绝执行联邦法令派"的整个主张,可用这一派在南部的公认领袖卡尔霍恩 1833 年向参议院发表的演说中的一段话来概

a compact to which the States were parties in their sovereign capacity: now, whenever a compact is entered into by parties which acknowledge no common arbiter to decide in the last resort, each of them has a right to judge for itself in relation to the nature, extent, and obligations of the instrument." It is evident that such a doctrine destroys the very basis of the Federal Constitution and brings back the anarchy from which the Americans were delivered by the act of 1789.

When South Carolina perceived that Congress turned a deaf ear to its remonstrances, it threatened to apply the doctrine of Nullification to the Federal tariff law. Congress persisted in its system, and at length the storm broke out. In the course of 1832 the people of South Carolina[1] named a national convention to consult upon the extraordinary measures that remained to be taken; and on the 24th of November of the same year this convention promulgated a law, under the form of a decree, which annulled the Federal tariff law, forbade the levy of the duties which that law commands, and refused to recognize the appeal that might be made to the Federal courts of law. [2] This decree was only to be put in execution in the ensuing month of February; and it was intimated that if Congress modified the tariff before that period, South Carolina might be induced to proceed no further with

---

[1]　That is to say, the majority of the people; for the opposite party, called the Union Party, always formed a very strong and active minority. Carolina may contain about 47,000 voters; 80,000 were in favor of nullification, and 17,000 opposed to it.

[2]　This decree was preceded by a *Report* of the committee by which it was framed, containing the explanation of the motives and object of the law. The following passage occurs in it (p. 34): "When the rights reserved by the Constitution to the different States are deliberately violated, it is the duty and the right of those States to interfere, in order to check the-progress of the evil; to resist usurpation, and to maintain, within their respective limits, those powers and privileges which belong to them as *independent, sovereign States*. If they were destitute of this right, they would not be sovereign. South Carolina declares that she acknowledges no tribunal upon earth above her authority. She has indeed entered into a solemn compact of union with the other States; but she demands, and will exercise, the right of putting her own construction upon it; and when this compact is violated by her sister States, and by the government which they have created, she is determined to avail herself of the unquestionable right of judging what is the extent of the infraction, and what are the measures best fitted to obtain justice."

括。他说:"宪法是一项合约,各州在其中均以独立主权者的身份
出现。而一旦缔约的各方对合约的解释发生分歧时,每一方均有
权自行判断其履约的范围。"这项主张很显然从原则上破坏了联
邦宪法的基础,使美国人依靠 1789 年宪法而摆脱的无政府状态
又将再现。

当南卡罗来纳州看到国会对它的抗议不予理睬以后,便以对
关税法实施"拒绝执行联邦法令派"的主张来威胁。国会坚持自
己规定的制度,最终一场风暴终于袭来。1832 年间,南卡罗来纳
州的人民成立了国民代表会议,①商讨他们保留采用的非常措施
的权利;同年 11 月 24 日,这个国民代表会议以法令形式颁布了一
项法律,其中规定联邦的关税法无效,反对征收该法规定的税款,
拒绝接受任何可能向联邦法院提出的诉讼。② 这项法令定于次年
二月正式生效,并且声称:如国会在此期限之前修改关税制度,则南卡
罗来纳同意不再予以追究。不久,南卡罗来纳州又以含糊其词的口

---

① 也就是说,大多数人。反对派被称为联邦派,是由一些具有强壮活
跃的少数人组成。卡罗莱纳州有 47000 位投票者,80000 人支持"拒绝执行
联邦法令派",而 17000 人投反对票。

② 这则法令还包括先前的一个委员会报告。报告中包含了对这条法
律动机和目的的解释。以下短文如下(第 34 页):"当宪法对各州保留的权
利遭到故意破坏时,为了阻止罪恶的发生,各州有责任和权利对其加以干
涉;为了防止他们在独立以及对州行使的主权方面所拥有的权利和特权被
篡夺,或为了保留这些权利。如果他们被剥夺了这些权利,他们将不复有主
权。南卡罗来纳州宣称,没有任何法官高于其主权。事实上,她加入了一个
与其他州的严肃的联盟之中。但是她要求,并且将按照自己的解释加以实
施。如果这一合约被与她一起联盟的各州破坏,并且遭到了他们所创建的
州的破坏,她坚决会按照自己的利益,赋予自己权利来判断受到侵害的范
围,并且会算出怎样才算公平。"

her menaces; and a vague desire was afterwards expressed of submitting the question to an extraordinary assembly of all the federated states. In the meantime South Carolina armed her militia and prepared for war.

But Congress, which had slighted its suppliant subjects, listened to their complaints as soon as they appeared with arms in their hands. ① A law was passed② by which the tariff duties were to be gradually reduced for ten years, until they were brought so low as not to exceed the supplies necessary to the government. Thus Congress completely abandoned the principle of the tariff and substituted a mere fiscal impost for a system of protective duties. ③ The government of the Union, to conceal its defeat, had recourse to an expedient that is much in vogue with feeble governments. It yielded the point de facto, but remained inflexible upon the principles; and while it was altering the tariff law, it passed another bill by which the President was invested with extraordinary powers enabling him to overcome by force a resistance which was then no longer to be feared.

But South Carolina did not consent to leave the Union in the enjoyment of these scanty appearances of success: the same national convention that had annulled the tariff bill met again and accepted the proffered concession; but at the same time it declared its unabated perseverance in the doctrine of Nullification; and to prove what it said, it annulled the law investing the President with extraordinary powers, although it was very certain that the law would never be carried into effect.

Almost all the controversies of which I have been speaking have taken place under the Presidency of General Jackson; and it cannot

---

① Congress was finally persuaded to take this step by the conduct of the powerful state of Virginia, whose legislature offered to serve as a mediator between the Union and South Carolina. Hitherto the latter state had appeared to be entirely abandoned, even by the states that had joined in her remonstrances.

② Law of March 2, 1833.

③ This bill was brought in by Mr. Clay, and it passed, in four days, through both houses of Congress, by an immense majority.

气表示希望,说它愿意将问题提交由联邦的所有州组成的特别委员会处理。在等待国会答复期间,南卡罗来纳武装民兵,积极备战。

一直对苦苦哀求的老百姓采取置之不理态度的国会,直到看到老百姓拿起了武器,①才开始对他们的意见加以关注。于是,国会通过一项法令,②规定税率在十年内递减,一直减到关税收入不超过政府开支所需的程度。由此,国会完全放弃了最初的关税原则,以一种纯财政措施取代了保护关税制度。③ 联邦政府为了掩饰失败,采用了一项为软弱的政府所常用的权宜之计:即在事实上表示让步,而在原则上坚持己见。国会在修改关税立法的同时,又通过了另一项授予总统以特别权力的法案,使总统可以使用武力去制服当时已无须担心的反抗。

但是,南卡罗来纳州并未让联邦得到这个可怜的胜利表相。废除了关税法的那个国民代表会议再次召开会议,会上接受了联邦的让步;但它同时宣布,它并不因此不再坚持"拒绝执行联邦法令派"的主张。而且,为了证实它所说的,它声明授予总统特别权力的那项法案对南卡罗来纳州无效,尽管它也知道这项权力永远也不会被付诸实施。

我所说的这些争端几乎都发生在杰克逊将军总统任期期间。

---

① 在强大的弗吉尼亚政府的作用下,其立法机关出面在联邦和南卡罗来纳州之间调停,国会最终被说服采取行动。因此,南卡罗来纳州就仿佛被抛弃了,甚至包括那些曾经加入到他的抗议的国家们。

② 1833 年 3 月 2 日法律。

③ 这一法案由克莱先生引入,并于四天后,在两大议会中已占大多数的优势通过执行。

be denied that in the question of the tariff he has supported the rights of the Union with energy and skill. I think, however, that the conduct of this President of the Federal government may be reckoned as one of the dangers that threaten its continuance.

Some persons in Europe have formed an opinion of the influence of General Jackson upon the affairs of his country which appears highly extravagant to those who have seen the subject nearer at hand. We have been told that General Jackson has won battles; that he is an energetic man, prone by nature and habit to the use of force, covetous of power, and a despot by inclination. All this may be true; but the inferences which have been drawn from these truths are very erroneous. It has been imagined that General Jackson is bent on establishing a dictatorship in America, introducing a military spirit, and giving a degree of influence to the central authority that cannot but be dangerous to provincial liberties. But in America the time for similar undertakings, and the age for men of this kind, has not yet come; if General Jackson had thought of exercising his authority in this manner, he would infallibly have forfeited his political station and compromised his life; he has not been so imprudent as to attempt anything of the kind.

Far from wishing to extend the Federal power, the President belongs to the party which is desirous of limiting that power to the clear and precise letter of the Constitution, and which never puts a construction upon that act favorable to the government of the Union; far from standing forth as the champion of centralization, General Jackson is the agent of the state jealousies; and he was placed in his lofty station by the passions that are most opposed to the central government. It is by perpetually flattering these passions that he maintains his station and his popularity. General Jackson is the slave of the majority: he yields to its wishes, its propensities, and its demands—say, rather, anticipates and forestalls them.

Whenever the governments of the states come into collision with that of the Union, the President is generally the first to question his own rights; he almost always outstrips the legislature; and when the extent of the Federal power is controverted, he takes part, as it were, against himself; he conceals his official interests, and labors to diminish

不可否认,在关税问题上,他曾用巧妙的方法大力维护了联邦的权力。但我认为,他也为联邦政府留下一个隐患,使得今天的联邦政府不得不按照他采取的那种办法处理类似的问题。

一些没有走出欧洲到美国考察的人,对于杰克逊将军的政绩持有的看法,使那些在美国考察过的人看来有些荒谬。据他们说,杰克逊将军打过许多胜仗,精力充沛,生性惯用武力,贪图权势,天生是个暴君。这些说法也许是实情,但从这些实情所做的一切推论极端错误。有人推测,杰克逊将军想在美国建立独裁统治,推崇尚武精神,并将扩大中央政权的权力,使其壮大到足以威胁地方自由。然而在美国,出现这样的人物发生这样的事情的时代还没有到来。假如杰克逊将军果真想以这种方式实行统治,他无疑会丧失他的政治地位并危及生命。他从不这样轻率,也不会试图去干这类蠢事的。

现任总统杰克逊从未想过扩大联邦政府的权力,相反的,他所代表的党希望把联邦政府的权力限制在宪法明确规定的范围之内,而且从未对宪法做过有利于联邦政府的解释。杰克逊将军绝不是支持中央集权制度的战士,而是一个时刻觊觎着地方政府权利的代表。是地方分权的激情,把他推上了代表国家主权的地位。而他之所以保住了自己的地位和声望,全靠不断地谄媚这种激情。杰克逊将军是大多数人的奴仆;他是应多数人的愿望、倾向和需求应运而生的产物,或者也可以说他自己就有这种激情和带头鼓动这种激情。

一旦州政府与联邦政府发生纠纷,总统总是站在州政府一方来反对自己的权力,并且几乎总是走在立法机构的前面。当出现辩论联邦职权范围的问题时,他总是站在反对自己的那一边。他隐藏自己的政治利益,尽量不表现自己。事实上,

his own dignity. Not, indeed, that he is naturally weak or hostile to the Union; for when the majority decided against the claims of Nullification, he put himself at their head, asserted distinctly and energetically the doctrines which the nation held, and was the first to recommend force; but General Jackson appears to me, if I may use the American expression, to be a Federalist by taste and a Republican by calculation.

General Jackson stoops to gain the favor of the majority; but when he feels that his popularity is secure, he overthrows all obstacles in the pursuit of the objects which the community approves or of those which it does not regard with jealousy. Supported by a power that his predecessors never had, he tramples on his personal enemies, whenever they cross his path, with a facility without example; he takes upon himself the responsibility of measures that no one before him would have ventured to attempt. He even treats the national representatives with a disdain approaching to insult; he puts his veto on the laws of Congress and frequently neglects even to reply to that powerful body. He is a favorite who sometimes treats his master roughly. The power of General Jackson perpetually increases, but that of the President declines; in his hands the Federal government is strong, but it will pass enfeebled into the hands of his successor.

I am strangely mistaken if the Federal government of the United States is not constantly losing strength, retiring gradually from public affairs, and narrowing its circle of action. It is naturally feeble, but it now abandons even the appearance of strength. On the other hand, I thought that I noticed a more lively sense of independence and a more decided attachment to their separate governments in the states. The Union is desired, but only as a shadow; they wish it to be strong in certain cases and weak in all others; in time of warfare it is to be

这一切并不表明他天生懦弱或敌视联邦。当多数出来反对南方的"拒绝执行联邦法令派"的无理主张时,他立即站到多数的队首,明确而坚决地表达多数所持的主张,并首先提议诉诸武力。如果允许我用美国人的表达方式说一句,我认为杰克逊将军有着作为一个联邦主义者的所有的兴趣爱好,但在务实上却是一个共和主义者。

杰克逊将军通过如此卑躬屈膝的方式获得了大多数人的支持。但是,当他觉得自己的地位稳固之后,便开始排除一切障碍,奋力向多数所追求的或多数尚且表示怀疑的目标前进。他的前任们从来没有得到过像他所得到这样强大的支持,并到处利用任何一位总统没有过的便利条件把自己的敌人打翻在地。他担当起自己所采取的一些以前没有人敢实行的措施的责任,甚至用一种近乎侮辱的轻蔑态度对待全国的议员;他拒绝批准国会的法案,而且常常根本不理会这个强大立法机构的质问。他就像一个常常对主人很粗暴的宠仆。因此,杰克逊将军的权威在不断加强,而其作为总统的威信却日益削弱。虽然在他执政期间联邦政府很强大的;但当权利转交到他的继任者手中的时候,联邦政府就变得软弱无力了。

如果我说的这些错的不会很离谱的话,我认为美国的联邦政府将会不断地被削弱下去。它将从一些公务抽身而出,尽量把自己的活动局限在一个越来越小的范围之内。而这个天生软弱的联邦政府,甚至会失去其强大的表相。另一方面,我认为,在美国,人们的独立感在各州表现得日益明显,对地方政府的爱护也显得日益强烈。人们想要联邦,但只把它作为幌子。人们在某些情况下希望联邦强大,而在另些情况下又希望它软弱。人们主张

able to concentrate all the forces of the nation and all the resources of the country in its hands, and in time of peace its existence is to be scarcely perceptible, as if this alternate debility and vigor were natural or possible.

I do not see anything for the present that can check this general tendency of opinion; the causes in which it originated do not cease to operate in the same direction. The change will therefore go on, and it may be predicted that unless some extraordinary event occurs, the government of the Union will grow weaker and weaker every day.

I think, however, that the period is still remote at which the Federal power will be entirely extinguished by its inability to protect itself and to maintain peace in the country. The Union is sanctioned by the manners and desires of the people; its results are palpable, its benefits visible. When it is perceived that the weakness of the Federal government compromises the existence of the Union, I do not doubt that a reaction will take place with a view to increase its strength.

The government of the United States is, of all the federal governments which have hitherto been established, the one that is most naturally destined to act. As long as it is only indirectly assailed by the interpretation of its laws and as long as its substance is not seriously impaired, a change of opinion, an internal crisis, or a war may restore all the vigor that it requires. What I have been most anxious to establish is simply this: Many people in France imagine that a change of opinion is going on in the United States which is favorable to a centralization of power in the hands of the President and the Congress. I hold that a contrary tendency may distinctly be observed. So far is the Federal government, as it grows old, from acquiring strength and from threatening the sovereignty of the states that I maintain it to be growing weaker and the sovereignty of the Union alone to be in danger. Such are the facts that the present time discloses. The future conceals the final result of this tendency and the events which may check, retard, or accelerate the changes I have described; I do not pretend to be able to remove the veil that hides them.

在战争时期联邦要把全国的人力和物力集中于自己手里,而在和平时期联邦就可以被忽略。这种一会儿软弱一会儿强大的交替现象,是由于联邦的本性造成的。

我不认为有什么东西现在可以阻止人们思想的这一普遍趋势。造成这一趋势的原因,也在不停地照旧发生作用。因此,变化将继续进行下去,并且可以预言,除非发生某种特别的情况,联邦政府必将日益衰弱下去。

尽管如此,我认为,对于联邦当局无力维护自己的生存、不能保持国内和平、从而自消自灭的说法,还为时尚远。联邦已为民情和人们所接受。联邦的成就是显而易见的,联邦的好处是人所共知的。但是,当人们察觉联邦政府的弱点足以危害联邦的存在时,我坚信那时就会出现一种反作用,以增强联邦的力量。

合众国政府是所有联邦政府中行为最符合联邦性质的一个。只要不受到法律解释的直接攻击,或者没有严重削弱联邦的本质,舆论的变化、内部的危机或战争,都可以立刻恢复联邦应当具有的活力。我最热切希望的一点,就是在我们法国,有许多人都希望像在美国一样,舆论趋向中央集权,主张将一切权力都交给总统和国会。但我认为,美国显然正存在着一种与此相反的舆论。我不是说联邦政府因为日益老化而失去权力并威胁各州的主权,而是说它正在不断趋向软弱,而且我认为只有联邦的主权遭到了破坏。这就是目前存在的实际情况。隐藏在这一趋势下的最终结果是什么。有什么事件可能阻止、推迟或加速我所指出的变化? 这种都藏而不为人知,我也不自以为能够揭开遮盖着它们的面纱。

Of The Republican Institutions Of The United States, And What Their Chances Of Duration Are

The Union is only an accident—Republican institutions have more permanence—Arepublic for the present is the natural state of the Anglo-Americans—Reason for this—In order to destroy it, all the laws must be changed at the same time, and a great alteration take place in manners—Difficulties which the Americans would experience in creating an aristocracy.

The dismemberment of the Union, by introducing war into the heart of those states which are now federated, with standing armies, a dictatorship, and heavy taxation, might eventually compromise the fate of republican institutions. But we ought not to confound the future prospects of the republic with those of the Union. The Union is an accident, which will last only as long as circumstances favor it; but a republican form of government seems to me the natural state of the A-mericans, which nothing but the continued action of hostile causes, always acting in the same direction, could change into a monarchy. The Union exists principally in the law which formed it; one revolution, one change in public opinion, might destroy it forever; but the republic has a deeper foundation to rest upon.

What is understood by a republican government in the United States is the slow and quiet action of society upon itself. It is a regular state of things really founded upon the enlightened will of the people. It is a conciliatory government, under which resolutions are allowed time to ripen, and in which they are deliberately discussed, and are executed only when mature. The republicans in the United States set a high value upon morality, respect religious belief, and acknowledge the existence of rights. They profess to think that a people ought to be moral, religious, and temperate in proportion as it is free. What is called the republic in the United States is the tranquil rule of the majority, which, after having had time to examine itself and to give proof of its existence, is the common source of all the powers of the state. But the power of the majority itself is not unlimited. Above it in

论美国的共和制度及其持久存在的机缘是什么。

联邦只是一个偶然——共和制度更持久——就目前来说,共和适应于英裔美国人的自然状态——原因——要破坏共和,就得同时改变所有法律,整个民情也将发生翻天覆地的变化——在建立贵族制度时美国人将要遭遇的困难。

如果现在的联邦各州之间发生战争,以及随之而拥有的常备军,实行独裁和加重税负,都会导致联邦解体,而最终危害共和制度的命运。但决不能把共和的前途与联邦的前途混为一谈。联邦只是一个偶然的存在,只有在环境有利于它时,才能存活下去;而在我看来,共和制是适应美国人的自然状态的体制。除非敌对的因素继续不断地向同一方向发生作用,否则没有任何东西能够使贵族制度取代共和制度。联邦主要依靠组建联邦的法律而存在。一旦革命爆发,或舆论一有改变,联邦就可能不复存在。而共和却有根深蒂固的基础。

美国人所理解的共和就是社会对自身进行的缓慢而和平的运动。它是一种真正建立在人民的开明意愿之上的合理状态。在这种管理体制下,每一项决定都要经过长期酝酿,审慎讨论,待到完全成熟后方可付诸实施。美国的共和主义者重视民情,尊重宗教信仰,承认各种权利。他们认为,一个民族越是享有自由,就越是应该讲究道德,信仰宗教并温文尔雅。美国人所谓的共和,是指多数人的和平统治。多数,是指经过长时间对其研究并证实自己的存在以后,成为一切国家权力的共同来源。但是,多数本身并不是指他们拥有无限权力。在道德界,还有

the moral world are humanity, justice, and reason; and in the political world, vested rights. The majority recognizes these two barriers; and if it now and then oversteps them, it is because, like individuals, it has passions and, like them, it is prone to do what is wrong, while it discerns what is right.

But the demagogues of Europe have made strange discoveries.

According to them, a republic is not the rule of the majority, as has hitherto been thought, but the rule of those who are strenuous partisans of the majority. It is not the people who preponderate in this kind of government, but those who know what is good for the people, a happy distinction which allows men to act in the name of nations without consulting them and to claim their gratitude while their rights are trampled underfoot. A republican government, they hold, moreover, is the only one that has the right of doing whatever it chooses and despising what men have hitherto respected, from the highest moral laws to the vulgar rules of common sense. Until our time it had been supposed that despotism was odious, under whatever form it appeared. But it is a discovery of modern days that there are such things as legitimate tyranny and holy injustice, provided they are exercised in the name of the people.

The ideas that the Americans have adopted respecting the republic render it easy for them to live under it and ensure its duration. With them, if the republic is often bad practically, at least it is good theoretically; and in the end the people always act in conformity to it.

It was impossible at the foundation of the states, and it would still be difficult, to establish a central administration in America. The inhabitants are dispersed over too great a space and separated by too many natural obstacles for one man to undertake to direct the details of their existence. America is therefore preeminently the country of state and municipal government. To this cause, which was plainly felt by all the Europeans of the New World, the Anglo-Americans added several others peculiar to themselves.

人道、正义和理性居于其上;在政界,有各种既得权利高于其上。多数承认它在这两方面所受的限制。如果它逾越了这两项限制,那也像人一样是出于激情,并且像人那样,激动时可能把好事办坏。

但是,欧洲具有煽动性的政治家们却有了新的发现。

据他们说,共和并非像大家现在所想的那样是多数的统治,而是多数得势的几个人的统治;在这种统治中起领导作用的不是人民,而是那些知道什么对人民最有效的人;这些人经过自己的独特判断,可以不与人民商量而以人民的名义行事,把人民的利益踩在脚下还要人民对他们感恩戴德;而且,他们所坚持的共和政府是要求人民承认它有权任意行事,敢于蔑视人们所尊重的一切,即从最高的道德规范到初浅的公认准则都一概敢于蔑视的政府。至今他们一直认为,专制不论以什么形式出现,都令人厌恶。而如今,他们又有了新的发现:在这个世界上,只要以人民的名义来实行暴政也会变得合法,以人民的名义实施不公正的行为也会变得神圣不可侵犯。

美国人认为他们最便于采用共和,而且可以保证共和持久存在下去。在他们看来,即使共和政府的运作常常出差错,但至少在理论上还是好的。因此,人民最后总是遵照其原则行事。

美国从最初就不可能建立集权政权,而且将来也很难建立。居民被分布在一片辽阔的国土上,加上许多天然障碍的阻隔,所以他们只能各自去管理自己的生活细节。因此,美国是一个地地道道由州政府和乡镇政府管理的国家。英裔美国人除了置身在新大陆的所有欧洲人都感知到的这个原因之外,还添加了另外几个他们所特有的原因。

At the time of the settlement of the North American colonies municipal liberty had already penetrated into the laws as well as the customs of the English, and the immigrants adopted it, not only as a necessary thing, but as a benefit which they knew how to appreciate. We have already seen how the colonies were founded: every colony and almost every district was peopled separately by men who were strangers to one another or were associated with very different purposes. The English settlers in the United States, therefore, early perceived that they were divided into a great number of small and distinct communities, which belonged to no common center; and that each of these little communities must take care of its own affairs, since there was not any central authority that was naturally bound and easily enabled to provide for them. Thus the nature of the country, the manner in which the British colonies were founded, the habits of the first immigrants—in short, everything—united to promote in an extraordinary degree municipal and state liberties.

In the United States, therefore, the mass of the institutions of the country is essentially republican; and in order permanently to destroy the laws which form the basis of the republic, it would be necessary to abolish all the laws at once. At the present day it would be even more difficult for a party to found a monarchy in the United States than for a set of men to convert France into a republic. Royalty would not find a system of legislation prepared for it beforehand; and a monarchy would then really exist surrounded by republican institutions. The monarchical principle would likewise have great difficulty in penetrating into the customs of the Americans.

In the United States the sovereignty of the people is not an isolated doctrine, bearing no relation to the prevailing habits and ideas of the people; it may, on the contrary, be regarded as the last link of a chain of opinions which binds the whole Anglo-American world. That Providence has given to every human being the degree of reason necessary to direct himself in the affairs that interest him exclusively is the grand maxim upon which civil and political society rests in the United States. The father of a family applies it to his children, the master to his servants, the township to its officers, the county to its townships, the state to the counties, the Union to the states; and when extended to the nation, it becomes the doctrine of the sovereignty of the people.

在北美的各殖民地建立之初,英国人就融入了他们的法制和民情中的乡镇自由精神;英国的移民们不仅认为乡镇自由非常必要,而且还把他们认为最有价值的东西继承了下来。我们已经讲过各殖民地是如何建立起来的。当时,每个地方,甚至每个教区,都分别由一些彼此陌生或因不同目的而聚集在一起的人各自占据。因此,美国的英裔移民一开始就形成许许多多不属于任何统一核心管辖的小社区,而且每个小社区都自行管理各自的事务,因为它们既不属于任何一个理应管理它们或者可以轻易提供给它们的中央当局。因此,国家的自然条件,英国各殖民地的建立的方式,初期移民们的生活习惯——所有这一切——结合起来,就使乡镇自由和各州自由得到极大的发展。

由于这个缘故,美国的全部国家制度实质上都是共和性质的;而要想在美国彻底破坏构成共和的一切基础法律,就必须同时废除一切法律。今天,如果一个政党试图在美国建立君主政体,那它的处境要比现在就想在法国建立起共和政党更加困难。法国的王权没能在建立之前为自己拟定一套立法体系,所以就只能存在一个被共和制度包围的君主政体。而君主政体的原则要想渗入美国的民情,也会遇到同样巨大的困难。

在美国,人民的主权并不是一个孤立存在的学说,与其他主流民情和思想不相融和。相反地,它应该被认为是全美国人的观念链条中的最后一环。上帝赋予每个人一定的理性,用以指导他们在于自己有关的事务,这是美国的市民社会和政治社会据以建立的伟大箴言;父亲将之用于自己的子女,主人将之用于自己的仆人,乡镇将之用于自己的官员,州将之用于自己的乡镇,而国家将之用于自己的民族。当它被扩展到民族的时候,就便成了统治人民的学说

Thus in the United States the fundamenta principle of the republic is the same which governs the greater part of human actions; republican notions insinuate themselves into all the ideas, opinions, and habits of the Americans and are formally recognized by the laws; and before the laws could be altered, the whole community must be revolutionized. In the United States even the religion of most of the citizens is republican, since it submits the truths of the other world to private judgment, as in politics the care of their temporal interests is abandoned to the good sense of the people. Thus every man is allowed freely to take that road which he thinks will lead him to heaven, just as the law permits every citizen to have the right of choosing his own government.

It is evident that nothing but a long series of events, all having the same tendency, could substitute for this combination of laws, opinions, and manners a mass of opposite opinions, manners, and laws.

If republican principles are to perish in America, they can yield only after a laborious social process, often interrupted and as of ten resumed; they will have many apparent revivals and will not become totally extinct until an entirely new people have succeeded to those who now exist. There is no symptom or presage of the approach of such a revolution. There is nothing more striking to a person newly arrived in the United States than the kind of tumultuous agitation in which he finds political society. The laws are incessantly changing, and at first sight it seems impossible that a people so fickle in its desires should avoid adopting, within a short space of time, a completely new form of government. But such apprehensions are premature; the instability that affects political institutions is of two kinds, which ought not to be confounded. The first, which modifies secondary laws, is not incompatible with a very settled state of society. The other shakes the very foundations of the constitution and attacks the fundamental principles of legislation; this species of instability is always followed by troubles and revolutions, and the nation that suffers under it is in a violent and transitory state.

Experience shows that these two kinds of legislative instability have no necessary connection, for they have been found united or separate, according to times and circumstances. The first is common

因此在美国,共和的根本原则,是与制约人类的大部分行为的原则一致的。共和在建立起法制的同时,就深入到了美国人的思想、观点和一切习惯之中,并通过法律将其牢牢地固定。而在改变其法律之前,整个共和体制必须加以变革。在美国,甚至大多数人所信仰的宗教也是共和的,因为宗教使来世的真理服从于个人的理性,就如同政治让个人对私人利益的关心服从于人之常情;因此,宗教允许每个人可以自由选择引导自己走向天堂之路,如同法律承认每个公民都有权选择自己的政府。

显而易见,只有发生一连串向同一趋势迈进的事件,才能使一套法制、观点和民情为另一套法制、观点和民情完全取代。

如果共和的原则在美国消灭,也只有经过长期、艰苦、时断时续的社会进程之后才有可能;而在一个全新的民族取代现代的民族之前,有些共和原则将在表面上复兴,但不会完全消灭。然而,这样的革命发生之前,没有任何征兆在表明其即将来临。让一个初到美国的人最感到吃惊的,是政治社会令人眼花缭乱的运动。他们的法律不断地在改变,猛一看,你会认为很快就会有一个全新的政府取代她这个信念如此不稳定的民族现存的政府。但是,你的这种担心根本不必要。政治制度存在两种不稳定情况,两者不可混淆。其一,常常改变次要的法律,但不影响已确定的社会状态的继续存在;其二,是动摇制度的基础本身,攻击法制的基本原则。这样的不稳定之后,随之而来的就是动乱和革命,而身受迫害的国家则处于激烈的变幻莫测的状态。

经验显示,立法方面的这两种不稳定情况并无必然的联系,因为随着时间和环境的不同,它们可能结合也可能分离。在美国见到的不稳定情况属于第一种,而不是第二种。美国人虽然常常

in the United States, but not the second: the Americans often change their laws, but the foundations of the Constitution are respected.

In our days the republican principle rules in America, as the monarchical principle did in France under Louis XIV. The French of that period not only were friends of the monarchy, but thought it impossible to put anything in its place; they received it as we receive the rays of the sun and the return of the seasons. Among them the royal power had neither advocates nor opponents. In like manner the republican government exists in America, without contention or opposition, without proofs or arguments, by a tacit agreement, a sort of consensus universalis.

It is my opinion, however, that by changing their administrative forms as often as they do, the inhabitants of the United States compromise the stability of their government. It may be apprehended that men perpetually thwarted in their designs by the mutability of legislation will learn to look on the republic as an inconvenient form of society; the evil resulting from the instability of the secondary enactments might then raise a doubt as to the nature of the fundamental principles of the Constitution and indirectly bring about a revolution; but this epoch is still very remote. It may be foreseen even now that when the Americans lose their republican institutions they will speedily arrive at a despotic government, without a long interval of limited monarchy. Montesquieu remarked that nothing is more absolute than the authority of a prince who immediately succeeds a republic, since the indefinite powers that had fearlessly been entrusted to an elected magistrate are then transferred to a hereditary sovereign. This is true in general, but it is more peculiarly applicable to a democratic republic. In the United States the magistrates are not elected by a particular class of citizens, but by the majority of the nation; as they are the immediate representatives of the passions of the multitude and are wholly dependent upon its pleasure, they excite neither hatred nor fear; hence, as I have already shown, very little care has been taken to limit their authority, and they are left in possession of a vast amount of arbitrary power. This state of things has created habits that would outlive itself; the American magistrate would retain his indefinite power, but would cease to be responsible for it; and it is impossible to say what bounds

改变其法律,但宪法的基础却一直受到尊重。

今天,共和主义对美国的统治,犹如路易十四时期君主主义对法国的统治。当时,法国人不仅热爱君主政体,而且觉得没有什么东西能够取代它。他们接受君主政体,犹如人们接受阳光的照射和四季的更迭。那时的法国人,既没有王权的积极拥护者,又没有王权的强烈反对者。共和在美国是基于默认或一种一致同意的情况下建立的,并且无须争辩、反驳和证明。

可是,我认为,美国居民如果总是更改他们的行政制度的话,必将危害共和政府的稳定。立法方面的经常变更,使人们的计划总是受挫。这就使人们认为共和制度是一种不方便的社会方式。次要法律的不稳定性最终导致不良后果的产生,使人们对宪法的基本原则产生怀疑,并可能间接地引起一场革命。不过,这个时代的到来还十分遥远。尽管这样我们仍可以预见,美国人一旦放弃共和,君主政体很快就会进入专制的桎梏。孟德斯鸠说过,再没有比继共和而建立的君主权力更专制的权力了,因为原本勇敢地交给人民选举的首脑的无限权力,这时便落到了一个世袭君主的手中。这个说法一般而言是正确的,并特别适用于民主共和国。美国的行政官员,不是由公民中的一个特殊阶级,而是由全国的多数选举产生的。因为他们直接代表人民大众的意志,并完全依靠人民大众的激情,所以他们才不会被人怀恨,也不会引起人们的担心。因此如同我所说的,人民在规定他们的职权时很少关心他们权力界限的划分,而将很大一部分权力交给他们自行专断。这种行为形成了一些比它本身还有生命力的影响。美国的立法行政官员,在国会休会期间或去职后,虽仍旧保留着无限的权力,却不

could then be set to tyranny.

Some of our European politicians expect to see an aristocracy a-
rise in America, and already predict the exact period at which it will
assume the reins of government. I have previously observed, and I repeat it, that the present tendency of American society appears to me
to become more and more democratic. Nevertheless, I do not assert
that the Americans will not at some future time restrict the circle of
political rights, or confiscate those rights to the advantage of a single
man; but I cannot believe that they will ever give the exclusive use of
them to a privileged class of citizens or, in other words, that they will
ever found an aristocracy.

An aristocratic body is composed of a certain number of citizens
who, without being very far removed from the mass of the people, are
nevertheless permanently stationed above them; a body which it is
easy to touch, and difficult to strike, with which the people are in
daily contact, but with which they can never combine. Nothing can
be imagined more contrary to nature and to the secret instincts of the
human heart than a subjection of this kind; and men who are left to
follow their own bent will always prefer the arbitrary power of a king to
the regular administration of an aristocracy. Aristocratic institutions
cannot exist without laying down the inequality of men as a fundamental principle, legalizing it beforehand and introducing it into the family as well as into society; but these are things so repugnant to natural
equity that they can only be extorted from men by force.

I do not think a single people can be quoted, since human society began to exist, which has, by its own free will and its own exertions, created an aristocracy within its own bosom. All the aristocracies of the Middle Ages were founded by military con quest; the conqueror was the noble, the vanquished became the serf. Inequality was
then imposed by force; and after it had once been introduced into the
manners of the country, it maintained itself and passed naturally into
the laws. Communities have existed which were aristocratic from their
earliest origin, owing to circumstances anterior to that event, and
which became more democratic in each succeeding age. Such was the
lot of the Romans, and of the barbarians after them. But a people,
having taken its rise in civilization and democracy, which should
gradually establish inequality of condition, until it arrived at inviolable

再对其负责。所以说，很难说暴政将止于何时何处。

一些欧洲人希望美国出现贵族政体，甚至已经预言贵族政体得势的确切时期。我已经说过，现在再重复一遍，目前美国社会的动向，是越来越趋向民主。但是，我决不敢断言美国人将来会在某一天限制政治权利的范围，或者没收这些权利而让某一个人独享；不过，我也无法相信他们将来有一天会让公民中的某个特殊阶级独占这些权利，或者说，在某一天建立贵族政体。

贵族集团是由一定数目的公民组成，他们虽与人民大众离得不远，但却永远凌驾于人民之上。我们可以与这个集团接近，却无法推翻它；可以天天与它来往，但休想与它融合。无法想象还有什么服从比这种服从更违反人的天性和人心的隐秘本能了。一个依靠自己生存的人，总是宁愿受一个国王的专断统治，也不愿受贵族的正规行政管理。贵族制度没有不平等原则为基础，就无法长期存在下去。事先使不平等合法化，并使这种不平等存在于社会和家庭生活。凡与合情合理的公平截然相反的东西，只有依靠压制的办法强加于人。

我不相信，自从人类社会开始存在以来，没有一个民族，通过自己的意志和努力，在其内部建立起贵族制度。中世纪所有的贵族阶级，都是通过武力征服获得的。征服者于是成了贵族，被征服者沦为奴隶。不平等通过武力得到保障；在其原则被引入民情后，便保持住独立的姿态并逐渐渗入法律条文之中。存在着的社会，由于其最初的贵族化的本源，以及一些在它之前存在的事件，在之后的时代中变得更加民主。罗马人和继他们之后的蛮族的命运就是如此。但是，一个已经文明开化实行民主的民族，随着不平等的社会地位的逐渐确立，通过在自己的内部建立不可侵犯

privileges and exclusive castes, would be a novelty in the world; and nothing indicates that America is likely to be the first to furnish such an example.

Some Considerations On The Causes Of The Commercial Prosperity Of The United States

The Americans destined by nature to be a great maritime people— Extent of their coasts—Depth of their ports—Size of their rivers—The commercial superiority of the Anglo-Americans less attributable, however, to physical circumstances than to moral and intellectual causes— Reason for this opinion—Future of the Anglo-Americans as a commercial nation—The dissolution of the Union would not check the maritime vigor of the states—Reason for this—Anglo-Americans will naturally supply the wants of the inhabitants of South America—They will become, like the English, the commercial ´agents of a great portion of the world.

The coast of the United States, from the Bay of Fundy to the Sabine River in the Gulf of Mexico, is more than two thousand miles in extent. These shores form an unbroken line, and are all subject to the same government. No nation in the world possesses vaster, deeper, or more secure ports for commerce than the Americans.

The inhabitants of the United States constitute a great civilized people, which fortune has placed in the midst of an uncultivated country, at a distance of three thousand miles from the central point of civilization. America consequently stands in daily need of Europe. The Americans will no doubt ultimately succeed in producing or manufacturing at home most of the articles that they require; but the two continents can never be independent of each other, so numerous are the natural ties between their wants, their ideas, their habits, and their manners.

The Union has peculiar commodities which have now become necessary to us, as they cannot be cultivated or can be raised only at an enormous expense upon the soil of Europe. The Americans consume only a small portion of this produce, and they are willing to sell us the rest. Europe is therefore the market of America, as America is the market of Europe; and maritime commerce is no less necessary to enable the inhabitants of the United States to transport their raw materials to the ports of Europe than it is to enable us to supply them with our manufactured produce. The United States must therefore either

的特权和唯我独尊的等级而获得成功,倒是世所罕见的。没有任何迹象表明,美国似乎会在这方面提供第一个范例。

略述美国商业兴盛的原因。

美国人的本性决定他们要成为一个伟大的海洋民族——海岸线长——港口水深——河流长——英裔美国人的商业优势应归功于这些自然原因之处,远少于应归功于他们的智力和道德原因之处——英裔美国人作为一个商业民族的未来——联邦的解体也阻止不了原来组成联邦的人民的海上跃进——原因——英裔美国人生来就是要供养南美居民的——他们将像英国人一样成为世界大部分地区的商业代理人。

美国的海岸线,从芬迪湾起,到墨西哥湾的萨宾河,全长近2000英里。美国的海岸连成一条毫无间断的线,并且归属于同一政府管理。世界上没有其他国家能为商业提供比美国所提供的更深、更阔和更安全的港口。

美国的居民构成一个伟大的文明民族,命运又将他们置于一片从未开垦过的土地上。于是,美国人的日常生活都需要得到欧洲人的帮助。毫无疑问,美国人最终既能生产又能制造他们所需要的部分物品。但这两大洲从未离开过彼此,他们的需求、观念、习惯和习俗有着那么多的相似之处,使二者不可分离。

联邦的一些产品已成为我们的必需,因为我们的土地完全不出产这些东西,或者只能用很高的成本去生产它们。美国人只能消费这些产品中的一小部分,他们很乐意把其余的卖给我们。因此,欧洲是美国的市场,就像美国是欧洲的市场一样;海上贸易也使得美国人得以将他们的原材料运到欧洲的港口,再把欧洲的制

furnish much business to other maritime nations, even if they should themselves renounce commerce, as the Spaniards of Mexico have hitherto done, or they must become one of the foremost maritime powers of the globe.

The Anglo-Americans have always displayed a decided taste for the sea. The Declaration of Independence, by breaking the commercial bonds that united them to England, gave a fresh and powerful stimulus to their maritime genius. Ever since that time the shipping of the Union has increased almost as rapidly as the number of its inhabitants. The Americans themselves now transport to their own shores nine tenths of the European produce which they consume. [1] And they also bring three quarters of the exports of the New World to the European consumer. [2] The ships of the United States fill the docks of Havre and of Liverpool, while the number of English and French vessels at New York is comparatively small. [3]

Thus not only does the American merchant brave competition on his own ground, but he even successfully supports that of foreign nations in their own ports. This is readily explained by the fact that the vessels of the United States cross the seas at a cheaper rate. As long as the mercantile shipping of the United States preserves this superiority, it will not only retain what it has acquired, but will constantly increase in prosperity.

It is difficult to say for what reason the Americans can navigate at a lower rate than other nations; one is at first led to attribute this

---

[1] The total value of imports for the year ending September 30, 1832 was $101,129,266. The imports carried in foreign vessels amounted to only $10,731,039, or approximately one tenth.

[2] The total value of exports during the same year was $87,176,945. The exports carried in foreign vessels was $21,036,183, or approximately one fourth. (Williams's *Register*, 1833, p. 398.)

[3] During the years 1829, 1830, and 1831, vessels of the tonnage of 3,307,719 entered the ports of the Union. Foreign vessels accounted for a total of only 544,571 tons. The latter were approximately in the proportion of 16 to 100. (*National Calendar*, 1833, p. 304.) During the years 1820, 1826, and 1831 the English vessels entering the ports of London, Liverpool, and Hull amounted to a tonnage of 443,800. Foreign vessels entering the same ports during the same years amounted to a tonnage of 159,431. The relation between the two was approximately 36 to 100. (*Companion to the Almanac*, 1834, p. 169.) In 1832, the proportion of foreign to English vessels enter ing British ports was 29 to 100.

成品运回美国,美国的居民也同样需要海上贸易。因此,美国不是像墨西哥的西班牙人迄今所做的那样放弃贸易而专向海洋国家的工业供应大量原材料,就是要使自己成为地球上的第一流海洋强国。

英裔美国人对于海洋的喜爱不言而喻。独立宣言在打断了把他们与英国联系起来的商业纽带的同时,却使他们的航海天赋得到了全新的有力的飞跃。独立以后,联邦的船数递增的速度几乎与居民人数的增加速度持平。美国人如今消费的欧洲产品,十分之九都是用自己的船只运输的。[1] 并且他们还用自己的船把新大陆的四分之三出口货物运给欧洲的消费者。[2] 美国的船舶塞满了哈佛和利物浦的码头;而英国和法国的船舶在纽约港里则为数甚少。[3]

由此可见,美国的商人不仅在本土敢于同外国商人竞争,而且能在外国的港口同国外的商人进行有利的斗争。这一点很容易解释:因为在海上运输中,美国船只的运费较低。而且只要美国的商船继续保持这个优势,它将不仅保有已经取得的成就,而且会日益增多。

很难回答为什么美国人能以比他人低得多的成本经营航运。

---

[1] 截至 1832 年 9 月 30 日,进口总值为 101129266 美元。通过国外船舶运送总量只占 10731039 美元,仅十分之一。

[2] 在同一年出口总值为 87176945 美元。国外船舶运载总值占 21036183 美元,占四分之一。(威廉姆的纪录,1833,第 398 页。)

[3] 1829 年、1830 年和 1831 年间,进入联邦海港的船舶运载吨位达 3307719 吨。国外船舶运载量为 544571 吨。比例为 16:100(国家日志,1833,第 304 页)1820 年、1826 年和 1831 年间英国船只进入伦敦港口,利物浦和赫尔的总吨量为 443800 吨。同一时间国外船只进入同一港口的总吨量为 159431 吨。二者比率为 36:100。(年鉴,1834,第 169 页。)1832 年,国外船只与英国本土船只进入英国港口的比率为 29:100。

superiority to the physical advantages that nature gives them; but it is not so. The American vessels cost almost as much to build as our own;[1] they are not better built, and they generally last a shorter time. The pay of the American sailor is higher than the pay on board European ships, as is proved by the great number of Europeans who are to be found in the merchant vessels of the United States. How does it happen, then, that the Americans sail their vessels at a cheaper rate than we can ours? I am of the opinion that the true cause of their superiority must not be sought for in physical advantages, but that it is wholly attributable to moral and intellectual qualities.

The following comparison will illustrate my meaning. During the campaigns of the Revolution the French introduced a new system of tactics into the art of war, which perplexed the oldest generals and very nearly destroyed the most ancient monarchies of Europe. They first undertook to make shift without a number of things that had always been held to be indispensable in warfare; they required novel exertions of their troops which no civilized nations had ever thought of; they achieved great actions in an incredibly short time and risked human life without hesitation to obtain the object in view. The French had less money and fewer men than their enemies; their resources were infinitely inferior; nevertheless, they were constantly victorious until their adver saries chose to imitate their example.

The. Americans have introduced a similar system into commerce: they do for cheapness what the French did for conquest. The European sailor navigates with prudence; he sets sail only when the weather is favorable; if an unforeseen accident befalls him, he puts into port; at night he furls a portion of his canvas; and when the whitening billows intimate the vicinity of land, he checks his course and takes an observation of the sun. The American neglects these precautions and braves these dangers. He weighs anchor before the tempest is over; by night and by day he spreads his sails to the wind; such damage as his vessel may have sustained from the storm, he repairs as he goes along; and when he at last approaches the end of his voyage,

---

① Materials are, generally speaking, less expensive in America than in Europe, but the price of labor is much higher.

有人认为,这首先应当归功于美国人得天独厚的优越物质条件。但是,事实并非如此。美国船的造价与我们的一样,[①]但船质量并不好,而且一般使用寿命也不长。美国海员的工资比欧洲海员高。有很多欧洲人在美国商船上工作就证明了这一点。那么,美国人的航运成本为什么还比我们的低呢? 我认为,从实物的优势去寻找原因是徒劳的,我们应该要到道德和精神方面去寻找。

下面进行的对比可以解释我的意思。在大革命战争中,法国人引进了一种新的战术,使那些老将军们困惑不解,几乎推翻了欧洲最古老的君主国家。他们首先替换掉了很多从前战争中必不可少的东西,他们重新编制了军队,而这些都是文明国家从未想到可以去运用的。他们用很短的时间就完成了伟大的行动,士兵们都冒着生命危险盯紧目标奋勇前进。法国人在那场战争中的兵力和财力都远远少于其敌对势力,而且他们的装备也很差。但是,他们不断获得胜利,直到他们的敌人也开始模仿他们的战术。

美国人在商业中也引入了类似的办法。法国人的目的是获得胜利,而美国人的目的就是节约成本。欧洲的航运公司办事谨慎。它们只在天气好的时候扬帆出海,一预测到会有不可预见的危险,便收船回港。夜里,船员们收起部分船帆;当海上的白色的浪花标明陆地临近的时候,船员会立即降低航速,根据太阳的方位调整航向。而美国人对这些防范措施无所顾忌,并且勇于与危险挑战。风暴还未停歇,他们就拔锚起航了。无论白天还是夜里,他们都拉起风帆。他们一边航行,一边修复船舶遭遇风暴而

[①] 一般来说,美国的原料比欧洲的便宜,但是劳力价格比欧洲高。

he darts onward to the shore as if he already descried a port. The A-
mericans are often shipwrecked, but no trader crosses the seas so rapidly. And as they perform the same distance in a shorter time, they
can perform it at a cheaper rate.

The European navigator touches at different ports in the course of
a long voyage; he loses precious time in making the harbor or in wait-
ing for a favorable wind to leave it; and he pays daily dues to be allowed to remain there. The American starts from Boston to purchase
tea in China; he arrives at Canton, stays there a few days, and then
returns. In less than two years he has sailed as far as the entire circumference of the globe and has seen land but once. It is true that during a voyage of eight or ten months he has drunk brackish water and
lived on salt meat; that he has been in a continual contest with the
sea, with disease, and with weariness; but upon his return he can
sell a pound of his tea for a halfpenny less than the English merchant,
and his purpose is accomplished.

I cannot better explain my meaning than by saying that the A-
mericans show a sort of heroism in their manner of trading. The European merchant will always find it difficult to imitate his American
competitor, who, in adopting the system that I have just described,
does not follow calculation, but an impulse of his nature.

The inhabitants of the United States experience all the wants
and all the desires that result from an advanced civilization; and as
they are not surrounded, as in Europe, by a community skillfully organized to satisfy them, they are often obliged to procure for themselves the various articles that education and habit have rendered
necessaries. In America it sometimes happens that the same person
tills his field, builds his dwelling, fashions his tools, makes his
shoes, and weaves the coarse stuff of which his clothes are composed. This is prejudicial to the excellence of the work, but it powerfully contributes to awaken the intelligence of the workman. Nothing tends to materialize man and to deprive his work of the faintest
trace of mind more than the extreme division of labor. In a country like
America, where men devoted to special occupations are rare, a long apprenticeship cannot be required from anyone who embraces a profession.
The Americans therefore change their means of gaining a livelihood very

受到的损伤。即使最后当他们接近航程的终点时,他们仍旧飞速前行,仿佛已经看到港口似地急于靠岸。因此,美国的船舶常在海上失事,但却没有哪一个国家的船舶可以像他们的船舶航行得那么迅速。而正是由于他们用较短的时间走完同样的航程,所以他们的船价才会比别人低。

欧洲的商船在长途航行中会多次靠岸休整。它们在寻找靠岸的港口和等待最佳的离岸的时机的同时,浪费了宝贵的时间,而且还要支付停泊费。美国的商船,如果从波士顿出发,到中国去购买茶叶。船到广州后,停留数日便起航回国。在不到两年的时间内,船便航行了相当于绕地球一圈的距离,在往返途中只各靠岸一次。但是,在历时 8 个月或 10 个月的单程航行中,船员们喝的是咸水,吃的是腌肉,这也是事实。他们要不断同海洋、疾病和疲劳抗争。但一旦回来,他们每磅茶叶的售价就可以比英国商人的便宜0.5 便士。他们达到了目的。

我除了说美国人在经商方面表现出了一种英雄气概,实在无法更好地表达我的想法。欧洲的商人永远无法赶超他们的美国同行。美国人在经商中采用的上述战略,并非完全出于精打细算,也是出于他们的本性。

美国的居民经历了先进的文明所带来的一切苦难和快乐。并且,他们不像欧洲人那样,生活在一个能满足他们各种欲望的国家中。他们总是得依靠自己的努力,去创造和学习生活中的各种必需。在美国,一个人常常需要自己耕种、自己盖房、自己更新工具、自己做鞋、自己编织衣物。这不利于工艺的进步,但是对启发艺人的智慧很有帮助。再没有比过细的分工,更容易使人变得愚钝和使产品毫无特色的了。在像美国这样的国家中,人们很少完全地投入某一项工作中去,没有人会长时间地从事同一项工作

readily, and they suit their occupations to the exigencies of the moment. Men are to be met with who have successively been lawyers, farmers, merchants, ministers of the Gospel, and physicians. If the American is less perfect in each craft than the European, at least there is scarcely any trade with which he is utterly unacquainted. His capacity is more general, and the circle of his intelligence is greater.

The inhabitants of the United States are never fettered by the axioms of their profession; they escape from all the prejudices of their present station; they are not more attached to one line of operation than to another; they are not more prone to employ an old method than a new one; they have no rooted habits, and they easily shake off the influence that the habits of other nations might exercise upon them, from a conviction that their country is unlike any other and that its situation is without a precedent in the world. America is a land of wonders, in which everything is in constant motion and every change seems an improvement. The idea of novelty is there indissolubly connected with the idea of amelioration. No natural boundary seems to be set to the efforts of man; and in his eyes what is not yet done is only what he has not yet attempted to do.

This perpetual change which goes on in the United States, these frequent vicissitudes of fortune, these unforeseen fluctuations in private and public wealth, serve to keep the minds of the people in a perpetual feverish agitation, which admirably invigorates their exertions and keeps them, so to speak, above the ordinary level of humanity. The whole life of an American is passed like a game of chance, a revolutionary crisis, or a battle. As the same causes are continually in operation throughout the country, they ultimately impart an irresistible impulse to the national character. The American, taken as a chance specimen of his countrymen, must then be a man of singular warmth in his desires, enterprising, fond of adventure and, above all, of novelty. The same bent is manifest in all that he does: he introduces it into his political laws, his religious doctrines, his theories of social economy, and his domestic occupations; he bears it with him in the depth of the backwoods as well as in the business of the city. It is this same passion, applied to maritime commerce, that

的学徒。因此美国人要改变自己谋生的手段很方便。而且随时找有利于自己的工作去做。有人一生中曾当过律师、农夫、商人、牧师和医师。如果说美国人在各项工艺中都不如欧洲人作得完美,至少可以说对美国人来说,没有什么行业是完全陌生的。他的能力变得更全面,知识范围也就越广。

美国的居民在行业上没有什么定数,也没有形成任何职业偏见,不会重此轻彼或轻此重彼。而且他们更倾向于创新而不拘泥于传统的方法。他们没有固定的习惯,也很容易摆脱在其他民族的习俗的影响下形成的习惯,因为他们确信自己的国家不同于其他,而且他们的社会状况也史无前例。美国是一个神奇的地方,其上的所有东西无时无刻不在运动,每一次变化都标志着一次进步。新奇的思想总是和改进的目标紧密联系。看起来似乎没有任何天然的界限限制着他们的努力,在美国人的眼中,只有想不到的,没有做不到的。

美国发生的这种永无止境的变化,这种运气好坏的经常反复,这种公共财富和私人财富的变化莫测的起落,使人们的精神完全处于一种奋发图强和不甘人后的狂热状态。一个美国人的一生就像一场赌博,一次革命,一个战役。这些同样的原因在对每一个国人发生作用的同时,也给民族性格打下了不可遏止的冲动的烙印。因此,美国人,以他的国民的机遇为榜样,随时随地都必然是热心于追求、勇于进取、敢于冒险、尤其是善于创新的人。这种精神都完全地体现在他们的一切工作当中。他们把这种精神带进了他们的政治条例、宗教教义、社会经济学理论和他们的个人实业活动。他们带着这种精神开拓荒野,带着这种精神在城市中创业。在他们的海运事业中也正是由于精神,才使美国商船

makes him the cheapest and the quickest trader in the world.

As long as the sailors of the United States retain these mental advantages, and the practical superiority which they derive from them, they not only will continue to supply the wants of the producers and consumers of their own country, but will tend more and more to become, like the English, ①the commercial agents of other nations. This prediction has already begun to be realized; we perceive that the American traders are introducing themselves as intermediate agents in the commerce of several European nations, ② and America will offer a still wider field to their enterprise. The great colonies that were founded in South America by the Spaniards and the Portuguese have since become empires. Civil war and oppression now lay waste those extensive regions. Population does not increase, and the thinly scattered inhabitants are too much absorbed in the cares of self-defense even to attempt any amelioration of their condition. But it will not always be so. Europe has succeeded by her own efforts in piercing the gloom of the Middle Ages. South America has the same Christian laws and usages as we have; she contains all the germs of civilization that have grown amid the nations of Europe or their offshoots added to the advantages to be derived from our example: why, then, should she always remain uncivilized? It is clear that the question is simply one of time; at some future period, which may be more or less remote, the inhabitants of South America will form flourishing and enlightened nations.

But when the Spaniards and Portuguese of South America begin to feel the wants common to all civilized nations, they will still be unable to satisfy those wants for themselves; as the youngest children of civilization they must perforce admit the superiority of their elder brothers.

---

① It must not be supposed that English vessels are exclusively employed in transporting foreign produce into England, or British produce to foreign countries; at the present day the merchant shipping of England may be regarded in the light of a vast system of public conveyances, ready to serve all the producers of the world, and to open communications between all nations. The maritime genius of the Americans prompts them to enter into competition with the English.

② Part of the commerce of the Mediterranean is already carried on by American vessels.

比其他一切国家商船的运费低廉且航行迅速。

　　只要美国的海员保持这种精神优势，以及从中产生的实践优势，他们将不仅能够保障本国生产者和消费者的需求，而且会越来越多地成为其他国家的商务代理，比如英国。① 他们已经开始并正在将这样的宏图付诸实施。我们发现，一些美国的海运企业正在充当几个欧洲国家商业的中间代理商，并且他们还打算扩大商业领域。② 西班牙人和葡萄牙人在南美建立的一些大殖民地，都已各自称帝。内战和专制，目前正在损毁这些辽阔的区域。那里的人口数量没有增加，散居在这里的为数不多的居民，每天都只顾着自卫，根本无从谈起改善自己命运的打算。但是，情况不会一直如此。欧洲人曾全凭自己的努力冲破了中世纪的枷锁。南美在基督教信仰和法制、生活习惯方面同我们的一样。它拥有在欧洲各族人民和他们的子孙中成长起来的文明的一切萌芽以及我们先进的榜样可供借鉴：为什么，它还一直处于未开化状态？显而易见，这都只是时间问题。在不久的将来，南美人民就会建成一个富饶文明的国家。

　　但是，当南美的西班牙人和葡萄牙人自身开始感到与文明国家同样的需求时，他们还远远不能完全凭借自己满足这些需求。作为向文明学习的小学生，他们必须承认那些学龄更早的人们已经

---

　　①　我们必须设想，英国的船只全部都被雇来运输送达英格兰国外的商品，或者是英国运往其他国家的商品。今天，英格兰货物运输也许会被认为属于公共运输体系的一部分，为了提供给全世界的制造商并打开了所有国家互相交流的窗口。美国人的海上运输的天赋使他们得以与英国相抗衡。

　　②　地中海上的一部分商业已由美国的船只运载。

They will be agriculturists long before they succeed in manufactures or commerce; and they will require the mediation of strangers to exchange their produce beyond seas for those articles for which a demand will begin to be felt.

It is unquestionable that the North Americans will one day be called upon to supply the wants of the South Americans. Nature has placed them in contiguity and has furnished the former with every means of knowing and appreciating those demands, of establishing permanent relations with those states and gradually filling their markets. The merchant of the United States could only forfeit these natural advantages if he were very inferior to the European merchant; but he is superior to him in several respects. The Americans of the United States already exercise a great moral influence upon all the nations of the New World. They are the source of intelligence, and all those who inhabit the same continent are already accustomed to consider them as the most enlightened, the most powerful, and the most wealthy members of the great American family. All eyes are therefore turned towards the United States: these are the models which the other communities try to imitate to the best of their power; it is from the Union that they borrow their political principles and their laws.

The Americans of the United States stand in precisely the same position with regard to the South Americans as their fathers, the English, occupy with regard to the Italians, the Spaniards, the Portuguese, and all those nations of Europe that receive their articles of daily consumption from England because they are less advanced in civilization and trade. England is at this time the natural emporium of almost all the nations that are within its reach; the American Union will perform the same part in the other hemisphere, and every community which is founded or which prospers in the New World is founded and prospers to the advantage of the Anglo-Americans.

If the Union were to be dissolved, the commerce of the states that now compose it would undoubtedly be checked for a time, but less than one would think. It is evident that, whatever may happen, the commercial states will remain united. They are contiguous, they have the same opinions, interests, and manners, and they alone form a great maritime power. Even if the South of the union were to become

取得的优势。他们要先学会耕作,其次再学会制造业和经商。他们将暂时需要外国人作为中介,把他们的产品运到海外,再换回外国的产品来满足他们新产生的需求。

毫无疑问,北美的美国人总有一天被要求去满足南美人的需求。大自然已使他们彼此为邻,并将为北美人提供极大方便去了解和调查后者的需求,与后者建立永久关系,并逐渐进驻他们的市场。除非美国的商人不如欧洲的商人,否则他们是不会丧失这种天赐良机的,何况他们在某些方面还比欧洲商人优越。美国人早已对新大陆的各个民族进行了精神上的影响。他们是智慧的源泉,所有居住在同一大陆上的各族人民,早已习惯于把他们看作是美洲大家庭中的最有知识、最强大和最富有的成员。因此,所有的视线都盯着美国各州,因为他们是其他民族模仿的最好的榜样。他们所有的政治理论和法制都是从美国照搬来的。

美国人在南美人面前所处的地位,恰好是他们的祖先英国人当年在意大利人、西班牙人、葡萄牙人和欧洲其他一些国家面前所处的同样的地位。这些国家当年在文化与工业上均不如英国先进而且大部分消费要仰仗英国。今天,英国是同它往来的几乎所有国家自然的贸易中心,而美国将要在另一半球产生同样的作用。每个在新大陆建立或繁荣起来的国家,其建立和成长对英裔美国人都有利。

假如联邦解体,那么构成联邦商业的各州的商业发展无疑在一段时间内要被迫受到阻碍,但这个时间决不会像人们想象的那样长久。显而易见,不管将来出现什么情况,各州的商业仍需联合。它们相互为邻,彼此在观点、利益和民情上也完全一致,而且它们可以组成一个极大的海洋强国。即使联邦的南方独立于北

independent of the North, it would still require the services of those states. I have already observed that the South is not a commercial country, and nothing indicates that it will become so. The Americans of the South of the United States will therefore long be obliged to have recourse to strangers to export their produce and supply them with the commodities which satisfy their wants. But the Northern states are undoubtedly able to act as their intermediate agents more cheaply than any other merchants. They will therefore retain that employment, for cheap ness is the sovereign law of commerce. Sovereign will and national prejudices cannot long resist the influence of cheapness. Nothing can be more virulent than the hatred that exists between the Americans of the United States and the English. But in spite of these hostile feelings the Americans derive most of their manufactured commodities from England, because England supplies them at a cheaper rate than any other nation. Thus the increasing prosperity of America turns, notwithstanding the grudge of the Americans, to the advantage of British manufactures.

Reason and experience prove that no commercial prosperity can be durable if it cannot be united, in case of need, to naval force. This truth is as well understood in the United States as anywhere else: the Americans are already able to make their flag respected; in a few years they will make it feared. I am convinced that the dismemberment of the Union would not have the effect of diminishing the naval power of the Americans, but would powerfully contribute to increase it. At present the commercial states are connected with others that are not commercial and that unwillingly see the increase of a maritime power by which they are only indirectly benefited. If, on the contrary, the commercial states of the Union formed one and the same nation, commerce would become the foremost of their national interests; they would consequently be willing to make great sacrifices to protect their shipping, and nothing would prevent them from pursuing their desires on this point.

Nations as well as men almost always betray the prominent features of their future destiny in their earliest years. When I contemplate the ardor with which the Anglo-Americans prosecute commerce, the advantages which aid them, and the success of their

方之外,它也仍旧需要其他州的帮助。我已经说过,南方不是经商的地区,而且也没有任何迹象表明它会成为这样的地区。因此,南部的美国人不得不长期求助外力把他们的产品运出去,并向他们供应一些生活必需品。而他们所能找到的中介人中,只有北方人能够保证为他们提供物美价廉的市场。他们当然也会自己去找北方人,因为廉价才是经商的最高法则。主权意志和民族偏见,都不能长期抵制廉价的影响力。但是,如果说仇恨,恐怕再没有什么仇恨能比得过美国人与英国人之间的仇恨。尽管有这种敌对情绪,英国的商人仍能让美国人购买他们的大部分产品;而美国人之所以会买英国的货物,只因为他们购买英国的货物比购买其他国家的货物价格低。因此,不管美国人愿意与否,美国正在发展中的繁荣,并不能给英国的制造业带来不利。

理性和经验向我们证明,在必要的时候得不到武力的支援,商业上的强大是不可能持久的。美国同其他国家一样明白这个道理。美国人已能使他们的船舶受人尊重,而且再过几年,可能会让人害怕。我确信,即使联邦解散,北美的海上力量也不会被削弱,而只能被大大增强。如今经商的州与不经商的州联合在一起。而不经商的州对增强与它并无直接利益的海上力量并不喜闻乐见。反之,如果联邦中的所有经商州组成一个单一国家,商业便将成为它们最主要的国家利益,因此它们便会同意为保护航运作出巨大的牺牲,而且任何东西也阻止不了它们实现这一目的的愿望。

国家同人一样,几乎总是在其青年时代就显露出它未来命运的主要特征。当我看到英裔美国人的那种经商干劲、它们的便利条件和所获得的成就时,就不禁地相信,他们总有一天会成为全

undertakings, I cannot help believing that they will one day become the foremost maritime power of the globe. They are born to rule the seas, as the Romans were to conquer the world.

球第一海上强国。因为他们生来就是来统治海洋的,就像罗马人生来就是来统治世界的一样。

CONCLUSION

I am approaching the close of my inquiry; hitherto, in speaking of the future destiny of the United States, I have endeavored to divide my subject into distinct portions in order to study each of them with more attention. My present object is to embrace the whole from one point of view; the remarks I shall make will be less detailed, but they will be more sure. I shall perceive each object less distinctly, but I shall descry the principal facts with more certainty. A traveler who has just left a vast city climbs the neighboring hill; as he goes farther off, he loses sight of the men whom he has just quitted; their dwellings are confused in a dense mass; he can no longer distinguish the public squares and can scarcely trace out the great thoroughfares; but his eye has less difficulty in following the boundaries of the city, and for the first time he sees the shape of the whole. Such is the future destiny of the British race in North America to my eye; the details of the immense picture are lost in the shade, but I conceive a clear idea of the entire subject.

The territory now occupied or possessed by the United States of America forms about one twentieth of the habitable earth. But extensive as these bounds are, it must not be supposed that the Anglo-American race will always remain within them; indeed, it has already gone far beyond them.

There was a time when we also might have created a great French nation in the American wilds, to counterbalance the influence of the English on the destinies of the New World. France formerly possessed a territory in North America scarcely less extensive than the whole of Europe. The three greatest rivers of that continent then flowed within her dominions. The Indian tribes that dwelt between the mouth of the St. Lawrence and the delta of the Mississippi were unaccustomed to any other tongue than ours; and all the European settlements scattered over that immense region recalled the traditions of our country. Louisburg, Montmorency, Duquesne, St. Louis, Vincennes, New Orleans (for such were the names they bore) are words dear to - France

结 论

我的叙述已接近尾声。我在上面探讨美国未来命运的时候，总是竭力把题目分成几块，以便专心研究每个部分。现在，我要把这些部分集合起来，进行统一的论述。我所做的统一的论述可能不够详尽，但会更加简明扼要。在我分析每个问题时也可能不如以前清晰，但我能更准确地掌握全局。仿佛一个从大都市出来到近郊小山上去的旅游者一样，他出城一直往前走，行人越来越稀少，当他回顾城市，房屋已经模糊不清，他已看不见任何公共建筑，街道也难以分辨，但他却能容易的分清整个城市的轮廓了。于是，他才第一次看到了这个城市的整体面貌。这也是我眼中新大陆上的英裔人的未来。虽然这幅大图的细节还很模糊，但我已看到了它的全景，对它的整体有了清晰的概念。

美利坚合众国如今拥有或占据的领土，约为全世界可居住人口土地的二十分之一。尽管土地如此辽阔，但如果你以为英裔美国人种会永远停在那里不动，那你就错了。因为事实上，他们现在就已经远远越出了这个范围。

我们也曾有可能在美洲的荒野上建立一个可以同英国人在新大陆上平分秋色的法兰西帝国。从前法国在北美拥有的领土，几乎有整个欧洲那么大。北美大陆上的三条最大的河流，当时都流经其管辖的区域。住在从圣劳伦斯河口至密西西比河三角洲之间的印第安各部，除了法语，对其他语言都闻所未闻。分布在这片辽阔土地上的一些欧洲人居民点都延续着我们的传统。如，路易堡、蒙莫朗西、迪凯纳、圣路易、万森、新奥尔良等，这些名称

and familiar to our ears.

But a course of circumstances which it would be tedious to enumerate[①] has deprived us of this magnificent inheritance. Wherever the French settlers were numerically weak and partially established, they have disappeared; those who remain are collected on a small extent of country and are now subject to other laws. The 400,000 French inhabitants of Lower Canada constitute at the present time the remnant of an old nation lost in the midst of a new people. A foreign population is increasing around them unceasingly and on all sides, who already penetrate among the former masters of the country, predominate in their cities, and corrupt their language. This population is identical with that of the United States; it is therefore with truth that I asserted that the British race is not confined within the frontiers of the Union, since it already extends to the northeast.

To the northwest nothing is to be met with but a few insignifi cantRussian settlements; but to the southwest Mexico presents a barrier to the Anglo-Americans. Thus the Spaniards and the Anglo-Americans are, properly speaking, the two races that divide the possession of the New World. The limits of separation between them have been settled by treaty; but although the conditions of that treaty are favorable to the Anglo-Americans, I do not doubt that they will shortly infringe it. Vast provinces extending beyond the frontiers of the Union towards Mexico are still destitute of inhabitants. The natives of the United States will people these solitary regions before their rightful occupants. They will take possession of the soil and establish social institutions, so that when the legal owner at length arrives, he will find

---

① The foremost of these circumstances is that nations which are accustomed to township institutions and municipal government are better able than any others to establish prosperous colonies. The habit of thinking and governing for oneself is indispensable in a new country, where success necessarily depends in a great measure upon the individual exertions of the settlers.

对法国人来说都是亲切而熟悉。

但是,一连串的单调乏味原因使我们失去了这笔可观的遗产。[①] 法国人口数量本来就不多,而且这些居民也没能很好的建设这里,现在人们都不见了。那些仍旧居住在这里的人们,也都聚集在一块土地上,甚至还生存在别国法律的管辖之下。加拿大居住着的40多万法国人,如今就像一个古老民族的孑遗,迷失在新民族人群之中。他们周边的异族居民不断地向四面延伸并逐渐强大,最终深入了这个地区原来主人的势力范围,甚至后来者居上,取代了这块土地的原来主人。他们统治了原来主人建设的城市,破坏他们的语言。这批人口原本就是美国的居民。因此,我有理由断言英裔美国人不会留在联邦的范围里不动,既然它已向东北方面推进。

在西北方面,除了一些普通的俄国人居民点别无其他;但在西南方面,墨西哥就像一块屏障挡在了英裔美国人的面前。因此,严格说来,今天在分占着新大陆的,只有两个互相竞争的种族,即西班牙人和英国人。人们通过条约规定了这两个种族的分界线。尽管这项条约对英裔美国人有利,但我确信英裔美国人过不了多久就会违约。在联邦南部边界之外的墨西哥境内尚有一大片无人居住土地。美国人早在没有任何权力占据的时候就已占有了这片荒野。他们拥有土地的所有权,并将建立起自己的乡镇。而当合法的所有者姗姗而来时,将会发现这块荒地已被人开

---

① 这些环境中最重要的是,那些习惯于乡镇制度和地方自治统治的国家,与其他国家相比,能够更好的建立繁荣的殖民地。自身善于思考和管理的习惯是一个新的国家所不可缺少的。而一个新的国家的成功很大程度上都建立在开拓者们的个人努力的基础之上。

the wilderness under cultivation, and strangers quietly settled in the midst of his inheritance.

The lands of the New World belong to the first occupant; they are the natural reward of the swiftest pioneer. Even the countries that are already peopled will have some difficulty in securing themselves from this invasion. I have already alluded to what is taking place in the province of Texas. The inhabitants of the United States are perpetually migrating to Texas, where they purchase land; and although they conform to the laws of the country, they are gradually founding the empire of their own language and their own manners. The province of Texas is still part of the Mexican dominions, but it will soon contain no Mexicans; the same thing has occurred wherever the Anglo-Americans have come in contact with a people of a different origin.

It cannot be denied that the British race has acquired an amazing preponderance over all other European races in the New World; and it is very superior to them in civilization, industry, and power. As long as it is surrounded only by wilderness or thinly peopled countries, as long as it encounters on its route no dense population through which it cannot work its way, it will assuredly continue to spread. The lines marked out by treaties will not stop it, but it will everywhere overleap these imaginary barriers.

The geographical position of the British race in the New World is peculiarly favorable to its rapid increase. Above its northern frontiers the icy regions of the Pole extend; and a few degrees below its southern confines lies the burning climate of the Equator. The Anglo-Americans are therefore placed in the most temperate and habitable zone of the continent.

It is generally supposed that the prodigious increase of population in the United States is posterior to their Declaration of Independence, but this is an error. The population increased as rapidly under the colonial system as at the present day; that is to say, it doubled in about twenty-two years. But this proportion, which is now applied to millions of inhabitants, was then applied to thousands; and the same fact which was scarcely noticeable a century ago is now evident to every observer.

发,并且早已有外来人在他们的遗产上悄悄地定居下来了。

新大陆的土地总是谁先到就归谁,所以占有土地是上天赐给捷足先登者的报酬。要想保护自己已居住的土地不受这样的侵犯也得付出很大的努力。我前面已经说过得克萨斯境内发生的情况:美国的居民不断向得克萨斯迁移并在那里购置土地。虽然他们也服从当地的法律,但却逐渐使自己的语言和民情占据了统治地位。得克萨斯州目前仍属墨西哥管辖范围,但不久便会没有墨西哥人的踪影。因为凡是英裔美国人与其他不同种族接触的地方,都会出现类似现象。

无可否认,对居住在新大陆的其他一切欧裔人来说,英裔人占有巨大的优势。在文明、实业和武力上,他们都远比其他欧裔人优越。只要他们周围有荒野或人烟稀少的地方,或是他们在前进途中没有遇到使他们无法穿越的人口稠密地区,他们就不会停止扩张。条约规定的边界线对他们根本不发生效力,他们必然会排除阻碍继续前进。

英裔人在新大陆所处的地理位置,对加速他们的这种发展中所起的有利作用令人惊叹。他们北部边界以外是北极的冰原;他们南部边界往下只要再过几纬度,就到了热带。因此,英裔美国人所处的位置正是新大陆的气候最温和、最适合人们居住的地区。

人们大都错误地认为,美国人口的飞速增长始于独立以后。其实,在殖民体系下的人口增长,与现在同样迅速,大约每22年就翻了一番。只是现在人口增长的比例是以几百万计,而当时只是以几十万计而已。这种现象在一个世纪前几乎不被人察觉,而现在清楚地摆在观察者的面前。

The English in Canada, who are dependent on a king, augment and spread almost as rapidly as the British settlers of the United States, who live under a republican government. During the War of Independence, which lasted eight years, the population continued to increase without intermission in the same ratio. Although powerful Indian nations allied with the English existed at that time on the western frontiers, the emigration westward was never checked. While the enemy laid waste the shores of the Atlantic, Kentucky, the western parts of Pennsylvania, and the states of Vermont and of Maine were filing with inhabitants. Nor did the unsettled state of things which succeeded the war prevent the increase of the population or stop its progress across the wilds. Thus the difference of laws, the various conditions of peace and war, of order or anarchy, have exercised no perceptible influence upon the continued development of the Anglo-Americans. This may be readily understood, for no causes are sufficiently general to exercise a simultaneous influence over the whole of so extensive a territory. One portion of the country always offers a sure retreat from the calamities that afflict another part; and however great may be the evil, the remedy that is at hand is greater still.

It must not, then, be imagined that the impulse of the British race in the New World can be arrested. The dismemberment of the Union and the hostilities that might ensue, the abolition of republican institutions and the tyrannical government that might succeed, may retard this impulse, but they cannot prevent the people from ultimately fulfilling their destinies. No power on earth can shut out the immigrants from that fertile wilderness which offers resources to all industry and a refuge from all want Future events, whatever they may be, will not deprive the Americans of their climate or their inland seas, their great rivers or their exuberant soil. Nor will bad laws, revolutions, and anarchy be able to obliterate that love of prosperity and spirit of enterprise which seem to be the distinctive characteristics of their race or extinguish altogether the knowledge that guides them on their way.

Thus in the midst of the uncertain future one event at least is sure. At a period that may be said to be near, for we are speaking

　　加拿大的英国人受国王管辖,其人口数目的增长和扩散的速度几乎与生活在共和政府下的英裔美国人口数目同步。即使在 8 年独立战争期间,人口的增长比例也没有受到影响,仍然按照相同的比率增长。尽管当时在西部边界上有同英国人结盟的强大的印第安部落,但人口的西进运动可以说从来没有放慢过脚步。在敌人将大西洋沿岸洗劫一空的时候,肯塔基州、宾夕法尼亚的西部地区、佛蒙特州和缅因州住满了人。战后的混乱局面丝毫也没有妨碍人口增加和阻止继续向荒地进军。可见,法制的差异,和平和战争环境的不同,秩序的好坏,仅对英裔美国人的继续发展产生了微弱的影响。这一点并不难理解,因为没有任何因素足以对如此辽阔的国土的各个地方都产生影响。因此,无论哪一部分发生了灾难,国内总有很大的回旋余地,为遭灾地区的人民提供避难的场所,而且不管灾难多大,总能被成功挽救。

　　绝不能认为英裔人在新大陆上的飞跃发展会受到任何阻碍。联邦的解体以及因此引发的人们之间的仇恨,共和的废除和继而出现的暴政,也许会延缓其发展,但最终仍旧阻止不了他们完成既定的使命。世界上没有任何力量能将移民阻止在能够为各种工业提供发展资源的肥沃的荒野之外,也没有任何力量能够将人们阻止在一片充满生机的、为受苦难的人们提供庇护的荒野之外。不管未来发生什么事情,都夺不走美国人的气候、内海、河流和他们肥沃的土地。法制的败坏、革命和无政府状态,既无法消灭人们对于财富的热爱,也无法抹去人们勇于进取的精神,又不能完全摧毁指引他们前进的知识,因为这一切仿佛已经成为这个民族的特性。

　　因此,在充满众多无法确知因素的未来中,至少有一件事是

of the life of a nation, the Anglo-Americans alone will cover the immense space contained between the polar regions and the tropics, extending from the coasts of the Atlantic to those of the Pacific Ocean. The territory that will probably be occupied by the Anglo – Americans may perhaps equal three quarters of Europe in extent. [1] The climate of the Union is, on the whole, preferable to that of Europe, and its natural advantages are as great; it is therefore evident that its population will at some future time be proportionate to our own. Europe, divided as it is between so many nations and torn as it has been by incessant wars growing out of the barbarous manners of the Middle Ages, has yet attained a pop ulation of 410 inhabitants to the square league. [2]What cause can prevent the United States from having as numerous a population in time?

Many ages must elapse before the different offshoots of the British race in America will cease to present the same physiognomy; and the time cannot be foreseen at which a permanent inequality of condition can be established in the New World. Whatever differences may arise, from peace or war, freedom or oppression, prosperity or want, between the destinies of the different descendants of the great Anglo-American family, they will all preserve at least a similar social condition and will hold in common the customs and opinions to which that social condition has given birth.

In the Middle Ages the tie of religion was sufficiently powerful to unite all the different populations of Europe in the same civilization. The British of the New World have a thousand other reciprocal ties; and they live at a time when the tendency to equality is general among mankind. The Middle Ages were a period when everything was broken up, when each people, each province, each city, and each family

---

[1] The United States alone cover an area equal to one half of Europe. The area of Europe is 500,000 square leagues; its population is 205,000,000. (Malte-Brun, Vol. VI, Bk. 114, p. 4.)

[2] See *Malte-Brun*, Vol. VI, Bk. 116, p. 92.

可以肯定的。那就是,在我们所说的那个即将到来的时代,(我们这里指的是一个民族的范畴,)英裔美国人将散布从北极的冰原到热带之间的整个辽阔大地,并从大西洋沿岸一直扩散到太平洋之滨。他们占据的领土,终将达到整个欧面积的四分之三。[①] 总的来说,联邦的气候比欧洲的气候好。联邦自然条件的优势也远远大于欧洲。因此,很明显他们的人口,终有一天会可以与欧洲抗衡。欧洲,被划分成如此众多国家,并在中世纪的野蛮统治下经历了连续不断的战争被不断瓜分,现在每平方里格的居民人数还不到 410 人。[②] 又有什么原因能够阻止联邦人口不会这么多呢?

美洲英裔人的几个分支只有再过几个世纪才会出现差别,失去其共同的外貌。我们无法预见新大陆何时将会建起永久的不平等制度。因此,不管由于战争或和平、自由或暴政、繁荣或匮乏会在英裔美国人的后裔的各个分支的大家庭的命运之间产生什么样的差别,他们至少将仍能保持类似的社会情况,并在这种条件下持有共同的习俗和观念。

在中世纪,宗教的纽带就足以强大到把居住在欧洲的所有不同种族联合在同一文明之下。新大陆的英裔人之间有着各种互惠的关系纽带,并且他们生活的这一时期,全人类中正有一种全体趋于平等的趋势。

中世纪是一个四分五裂的时代,每个民族,每个地方,每个城

---

① 仅美国就占据了将近欧洲 1.5 倍的面积。欧洲的面积有 500000 平方里格,人口数量为 205000000。(见《马特－布伦》第六卷,第 114 册第 4 页。)

② 见《马特－布伦》第六卷,bk 116,第 92 页。

tended strongly to maintain its distinct individuality. At the present time an opposite tendency seems to prevail, and the nations seem to be advancing to unity. Our means of intellectual intercourse unite the remotest parts of the earth; and men cannot remain strangers to one another or be ignorant of what is taking place in any corner of the globe. The consequence is that there is less difference at the present day between the Europeans and their descendants in the New World, in spite of the ocean that divides them, than there was in the thirteenth century between certain towns that were separated only by a river. If this tendency to assimilation brings foreign nations closer to each other, it must a fortiori prevent the descendants of the same people from becoming aliens to one another.

The time will therefore come when one hundred and fifty million men will be living in North America, [1] equal in condition, all belonging to one family, owing their origin to the same cause, and preserving the same civilization, the same language, the same religion, the same habits, the same manners, and imbued with the same opinions, propagated under the same forms. The rest is uncertain, but this is certain; and it is a fact new to the world, a fact that the imagination strives in vain to grasp.

There are at the present time two great nations in the world, which started from different points, but seem to tend towards the same end. I allude to the Russians and the Americans. Both of them have grown up unnoticed; and while the attention of mankind was directed elsewhere, they have suddenly placed themselves in the front rank among the nations, and the world learned their existence and their greatness at almost the same time.

All other nations seem to have nearly reached their natural limits, and they have only to maintain their power; but these are still in the act of growth. [2] All the others have stopped, or continue to advance with extreme difficulty; these alone are proceeding with ease

---

[1] This would be a population proportionate to that of Europe, taken at a mean rate of 410 inhabitants to the square league.

[2] The population of Russia increases proportionately more rapidly than that of any other country in the Old World.

市,每个家庭,都只求自保和独立。但在今天,却出现了一种相反的趋势,各国仿佛都在走向统一。各国之间的文化联系,正把世界上最遥远的地区都联合到一起。人们之间不能继续孤立而不互通往来,也不能继续对地球上任何角落发生的事情一无所知。我们现在已经看到,在欧洲人与他们在新大陆的后裔之间尽管隔着汪洋大海,但他们之间的差别还不如 13 世纪某些只有一河之隔的城市之间的差别大。既然这种同化趋势正在使异国人民之间相互接近,那它也将更会有力地阻止同一民族的后代互为异族。

北美人口达到 1.5 亿的这一天终将到来。[①] 他们之间互相平等,同属于一个大家庭,有相同的族源,具有同样的文明、语言、宗教、习惯、民情、思想方法和肤色。其他方面还不确定,但有一点是肯定的,而且对世界来说是全新,那就是世界上将出现一个我们的想象无法企及的全新局面。

当今世界上存在着两大民族,它们虽从不同的起点出发,但又仿佛走向同一目标。这就是俄国人和英裔美国人。这两个民族悄悄地壮大起来。当人们的视线还停留在别处的时候,它们突然就出现在了各国的前列,而几乎在同一时间,全世界就认识到了它们的存在和他们国家的强大。

其他民族都好像已接近它们发展的自然极限,他们只需要保持原状即可,但这两个民族仍在成长。[②] 其他民族都已停止前进,或者为了前进要付出千辛万苦,只有这两个民族,正沿着一条还

---

① 这将是欧洲的人口比例,平均比例在每平方里格 410 位居民。
② 俄国的人口数量比欧洲其他国家的人口数量增长的速度更快。

and celerity along a path to which no limit can be perceived. The A-
merican struggles against the obstacles that nature opposes to him; the
adversaries of the Russian are men. The former combats the wilderness and savage life; the latter, civilization with all its arms. The
conquests of the American are therefore gained by the plowshare;
those of the Russian by the sword. The Anglo-American relies upon
personal interest to accomplish his ends and gives free scope to the
unguided strength and common sense of the people; the Russian centers all the authority of society in a single arm. The principal instrument of the former is freedom; of the latter, servitude. Their starting-
point is different and their courses are not the same; yet each of them
seems marked out by the will of Heaven to sway the destinies of half
the globe.

看不到尽头的道路轻松而迅速地前进。美国人在与自然为他们
设置的障碍进行斗争,俄国人在与人搏斗。一个在与荒野和野蛮
战斗,另一个在与全副武装的文明作战。因此,美国人的征服是
用劳动者的犁,而俄国人的征服则是靠士兵的剑。为了达到目
的,美国人以个人利益为动力,任凭个人去发挥自己的力量和智
慧,而不加以限制。而俄国人则差不多把社会的一切权力都集中
在一个人手中。前者以自由为行为准则,而后者则利用以奴役。
他们的起点不同,道路各异。然而,它们两个民族都好像接受到
上天的意志,终有一天要各主世界一半的。

SECOND PART

Author's Preface

To The Second Part

The Americans have a democratic state of society, which has naturally suggested to them certain laws and certain political manners. It has also created in their minds many feelings and opinions which were unknown in the old aristocratic societies of Europe. It has destroyed or modified the old relations of men to one another and has established new ones. The aspect of civil society has been as much altered as the face of the political world.

I have treated of the former subject in the work which I published, five years ago, on American Democracy; the latter is the object of the present book. These two Parts complete each other and form but a single work.

But I must warn the reader immediately against an error that would be very prejudicial to me. Because I attribute so many different effects to the principle of equality, it might be inferred that I consider this principle as the only cause of everything that takes place in our day. This would be attributing to me a very narrow view of things.

A multitude of the opinions, sentiments, and instincts that belong to our times owe their origin to circumstances that have nothing to do with the principle of equality or are even hostile to it Thus, taking the United States for example, I could easily prove that the nature of the country, the origin of its inhabitants, the religion of the early settlers, their acquired knowledge, their previous habits, have exercised, and still do exercise, independently of democracy, an immense influence upon their modes of thought and feeling. Other causes, equally independent of the principle of equality, would be found in Europe and would explain much of what is passing there.

下　卷

作者下卷序

美国人居住的民主的社会,天生就为他们提供了相应的法律和政治民情。并且使人们的思想产生了很多在旧的贵族制度下的欧洲不可能产生的感情和观念。它彻底的打破和修正了过去人们之间的联系。民主社会的各个方面的改变并不比政治社会面貌的变化更小。

五年前我已出版了这部书的上卷,题为《论美国民主》;下卷在这部书中加以描述。这两部分互为补充但又独立成卷。

但是,我还是要立即提醒读者注意不要受这部容易引起误解的书的诱导而产生错误的认识。因为在书中我给平等的原则赋予了很多不同的意义,这就可能使人们觉得我认为平等的原则是当今所有事件的起因。这样的话我的视角未免太狭窄了。

当代人们的意见、情感和本性不是由于平等原则或者甚至是与平等原则对立的环境造成的。因此,以美国为例,很容易就可以得出,国家的本性,其居民的本源,早期定居者的宗教信仰,他们所掌握的知识,他们从前的习惯,这些独立与民之外的东西,不仅曾经而且现在仍然对他们的思想和情感产生了巨大的影响。欧洲发生的其他一些与平等原则无关的事情的原因,这些原因也可以用来解释很多发生在这里的事情。

I recognize the existence and the efficiency of all these various causes; but my subject does not lead me to speak of them. I have not undertaken to point out the origin and nature of all our inclinations and all our ideas; I have only endeavored to show how far both of them are affected by the equality of men's conditions.

As I am firmly convinced that the democratic revolution which we are now beholding is an irresistible fact, against which it would be neither desirable nor prudent to contend, some persons perhaps may be surprised that, in the course of this book, I have often applied language of strong censure to the democratic communities which this revolution has created. The simple reason is, that precisely because I was not an opponent of democracy I wished to speak of it with all sincerity. Men will not receive the truth from their enemies, and it is very seldom offered to them by their friends; on this very account I have frankly uttered it. I believed that many persons would take it upon themselves to inform men of the benefits which they might hope to receive from the establishment of equality, while very few would venture to point out from afar the dangers with which it would be attended. It is principally towards these dangers, therefore, that I directed my gaze; and, believing that I had clearly discerned what they are, it would have been cowardice to say nothing about them.

I hope the same impartiality will be found in this second work which people seemed to observe in its predecessor. Placed between the conflicting opinions that divide my countrymen, I have endeavored for the time to stifle in my own bosom the sympathy or the aversion that I felt for either. If the readers of my book find in it a single phrase intended to flatter either of the great parties that have agitated our country, or any one of the petty factions that in our day harass and weaken it, let them raise their voices and accuse me.

The subject that I wished to cover by my investigations is immense, for it includes most of the feelings and opinions produced by the new condition of the world's affairs. Such a subject certainly exceeds my strength, and in the treatment of it I have not been able to satisfy myself. But even if I could not attain the goal towards which I strove, my readers will at least do me this justice, that I conceived and pursued my enterprise in a spirit which could make me worthy of succeeding.

　　我承认这些不同的起因的存在和效果;但是我的话题并没有涉及它们。我并没想指出人们的所有情感和思想的起因和本性,而只是想展示一下人们地位的平等对他们的影响。

　　我确信我们现在坚持的民主革命是一场不可抵挡的事实,并认为对它的抵抗即无希望又有失谨慎。一些人也许就会觉得奇怪,在这部书中,我还是常常用一些严厉的言语指责这场革命造就的民主社会。这个原因很简单,正是因为我并不是民主的对立者,所以我希望当我谈到它的时候能够满怀诚挚。人们不会从自己的敌人口中得到事情的真相,而朋友往往又很少谈到。正是由于这样,我才坦诚地将它说出来。我相信,很多人都勇于告诉人们,他们希望平等原则的建立为人们带来的益处,而极少数人会冒险指出其带来的危险。而我关注的正是这些存在的危险,并且一旦我清楚的分辨这些危险后,我就会勇敢地将它们指出。

　　我希望读者在这部书的下卷,依旧可以发现与上卷一样的公正评述。置身于将我的同胞们分裂的相互对立的意见中,我努力抑制自己满怀的同情或对一方的厌恶。如果我的读者在阅读这本书的过程中,发现有哪怕一句对那些搅乱了我们国家的伟大的政党中任何一方的赞誉,或者对我们今天存在的任何一个正在搅乱和削弱国力的派别的奉承,就请他们大声地指责我吧。

　　我在研究中希望能涵盖的方面有很多,因为它包含了大多数在新的社会事务条件下产生的感情和观点。这个主题超越了我的能力,在研究它的过程中,我自己也感到很不满意。但是,即使我没能实现我为之努力的目的,相信我的读者也会认为我怀着能够使自己的构思和追求值得别人去继续努力的精神是正确的。

FIRST BOOK
Influence Of Democracy On The Action
Of Intellect In The United States

CHAPTER I
Philosophical Method Of The Americans

I think that in no country in the civilized world is less attention paid to philosophy than in the United States. The Americans have no philosophical school of their own, and they care but little for all the schools into which Europe is divided, the very names of which are scarcely known to them.

Yet it is easy to perceive that almost all the inhabitants of the United States use their minds in the same manner, and direct them according to the same rules; that is to say, without ever having taken the trouble to define the rules, they have a philosophical method common to the whole people.

To evade the bondage of system and habit, of family maxims, class opinions, and, in some degree, of national prejudices; to accept tradition only as a means of information, and existing facts only as a lesson to be used in doing otherwise and doing better; to seek the reason of things for oneself, and in oneself alone; to tend to results without being bound to means, and to strike through the form to the substance—such are the principal characteristics of what I shall call the philosophical method of the Americans.

But if I go further and seek among these characteristics the principal one, which includes almost all the rest, I discover that in most of the operations of the mind each American appeals only to the individual effort of his own understanding.

America is therefore one of the countries where the precepts of Descartes are least studied and are best applied. Nor is this surprising. The Americans do not read the works of Descartes, because their social condition deters them from speculative studies; but they

第一部　民主对美国民智行为的影响

第一章　美国人的哲学方法

我认为在文明社会中没有任何一个国家对哲学的关注比美国少。美国人没有自己的哲学学派，他们也不太关心那些使欧洲分裂对立的各种学派，他们甚至很少知道这些派别的名称。

但是，很容易发现，几乎所有的美国居民思考问题的方式都是一样的，他们都根据相同的规则行事。也就是说，甚至没有人想要去定义这些规则，而所有人民都拥有相同的哲学方法。

为了摆脱体制和习惯的约束，家规的限制、阶级观念和一定程度上的民族偏见的束缚，为了只把传统视为习得的知识，将存在的事实在其他事件中引以为鉴以做得更好，为了凭借自己的力量寻找事件的起因，为了得到结果不择手段，为了抛开现象认识本质——这就是我所说的美国人的哲学方法的主要特征。

但是，如果我进一步深入在这些特征中寻找可以囊括其他所有的一个主要特征，我发现在大多数人的思想活动中每个人都表现的只执著于一己的理解。

因此美国是一个几乎没有接受过笛卡儿的思想但却将他的思想运用得最好的国家之一。这并不奇怪。美国人不读笛卡儿

follow his maxims, because this same social condition naturally disposes their minds to adopt them.

In the midst of the continual movement that agitates a democratic
community, the tie that unites one generation to another is relaxed or
broken; every man there readily loses all trace of the ideas of his forefathers or takes no care about them.

Men living in this state of society cannot derive their belief from
the opinions of the class to which they belong; for, so to speak, there
are no longer any classes, or those which still exist are composed of
such mobile elements that the body can never exercise any real control
over its members.

As to the influence which the intellect of one man may have on
that of another, it must necessarily be very limited in a country where
the citizens, placed on an equal footing, are all closely seen by one
another; and where, as no signs of incontestable greatness or superiority are perceived in any one of them, they are constantly brought
back to their own reason as the most obvious and proximate source of
truth. It is not only confidence in this or that man which is destroyed,
but the disposition to trust the authority of any man whatsoever. Everyone shuts himself up tightly within himself and insists upon judging
the world from there.

The practice of Americans leads their minds to other habits, to fixing the standard of their judgment in themselves alone. As they perceive
that they succeed in resolving without assistance all the little difficulties
which their practical life presents, they readily conclude that everything
in the world may be explained, and that nothing in it transcends the limits of the understanding. Thus they fall to denying what they cannot comprehend; which leaves them but little faith for whatever is extraordinary
and an almost insurmountable distaste for whatever is supernatural. As it
is on their own testimony that they are accustomed to rely, they like to
discern the object which engages their attention with extreme clearness;
they therefore strip off as much as possible all that covers it; they rid themselves of whatever separates them from it, they remove whatever conceals it

的著作,因为他们的社会环境阻碍了他们阅读投机者的著作,但是他们遵循了他的规则,因为相同的社会环境使他们很自然地接受了这些规则。

在搅动了民主社会的连续不断的运动中,一代人与一代人之间联系的纽带变得松弛或遭到破坏。人们很容易抛弃自己前辈们思想的痕迹,或者对这些根本不关心。

生活在这种社会环境下的人们不再相信他们所处的地位形成的阶级观念而造就的信仰。也就是说,不再有什么阶级,即使那些仍旧存在的阶级,也是由这些机动的因素构成的,以致他们的团体再也无法控制其成员。

至于一个人的智力对其他人造成的影响,就必然限制在这样的一个国家中,在这里,所有的公民都处于相等的地位,因为大家彼此的能力都很接近,任何人都不被认为具有无可争辩的强大和优势,人们总是按照他们自己的理智作为最明显最便捷的判断事实的来源。这不仅仅是不相信某一种人,而且也表示不相信任何其他人的权威。每个人都禁锢在自己的世界里,并坚持根据自己的理念对世界作出判断。

美国人的习惯将他们的思想引入了其他的思维习惯,将他们判定的标准固定于依靠自己本身。当他发现他们可以不依靠任何帮助解决他们日常生活中的所有的小困难,他们就很容易得出结论,认为世界上所有的事情都是可以解释的,世界上没有任何事物是不可理解的。因此,他们就开始否定所有他们没法理解的东西。这就使得他们很少相信那些特别的事物和对超自然的东西几乎不可抑制的厌恶。由于他们习惯于相信自己找到证据,他们喜欢把自己研究的对象搞得一清二楚。因此他们尽可能多地

from sight, in order to view it more closely and in the broad light of day. This disposition of mind soon leads them to condemn forms, which they regard as useless and inconvenient veils placed between them and the truth.

The Americans, then, have found no need of drawing philosophical method out of books; they have found it in themselves. The same thing may be remarked in what has taken place in Europe. This same method has only been established and made popular in Europe in proportion as the condition of society has become more equal and men have grown more like one another. Let us consider for a moment the connection of the periods in which this change may be traced.

In the sixteenth century reformers subjected some of the dogmas of the ancient faith to the scrutiny of private judgment; but they still withheld it from the discussion of all the rest. In the seventeenth century Bacon in the natural sciences and Descartes in philosophy properly so called abolished received formulas, destroyed the empire of tradition, and overthrew the authority of the schools. The philosophers of the eighteenth century, generalizing at length on the same principle, undertook to submit to the private judgment of each man all the objects of his belief.

Who does not perceive that Luther, Descartes, and Voltaire employed the same method, and that they differed only in the greater or less use which they professed should be made of it? Why did the reformers confine themselves so closely within the circle of religious ideas? Why did Descartes, choosing to apply his method only to certain matters, though he had made it fit to be applied to all, declare that men might judge for themselves in matters philosophical, but not in matters political? How did it happen that in the eighteenth century those general applications were all at once drawn from this same method, which Descartes and his predecessors either had not perceived or had rejected? To what, lastly, is the fact to be attributed that at this period the method we are speaking of suddenly emerged from the schools, to penetrate into society and become the common standard of intelligence; and that after it had become popular among the French, it was ostensibly adopted or secretly followed by all the nations of Europe?

The philosophical method here designated may have been born

剥去覆盖在事实上的外衣,排除任何将他们与事物隔开的东西,移开任何妨碍他们视线的东西,就是为了能够更近地在光天化日之下看到它。这样的思维方式很快就使他们谴责他们认为毫无用处并且使他们与事实形成隔膜的形式。

然后,美国人认为从书本中学习哲学的方法根本就没有用。他们自己就能发现事实。欧洲也出现过这样的现象。随着欧洲人们的社会地位越来越平等,人们之间变得越来越相似,与美国相同的方法才得以在欧洲建立并逐渐流行起来。让我们思考一下这些变化发生的时间联系。

16 世纪改革家们遵从于个人的判断来论证一些古老信仰的某些教条,但对其他的教义则避而不谈。17 世纪培根在自然科学领域,笛卡儿在哲学领域可以说都放弃了已有的规则,打破了传统的统治,推翻了教派至高无上的权力。18 世纪的哲学家们进一步推广了这一原理,试图用个人的体会去论证他所信仰的一切。

路德、笛卡儿和伏尔泰都采用了相同的方法,他们之间的区别只在于采用的多少的差别,这是大家有目共睹的。为什么这些改革家将自己局限在如此局促的宗教思想的园囿内呢?为什么笛卡儿只选择在特定的事物上实行自己的方法,尽管他使其哲学方法可以使用在所有的领域。他宣称人们可以在哲学的问题上自行判断正误,但是不能将之用于政治事务?在 18 世纪,那些方法却以笛卡儿和他的先驱未曾想到或者表示反对的形式得到了普遍的应用?最终,在这一时期,我们所谈到的这一方法突然走出了学术界并渗入了社会变成了衡量人们智商的一般标准,接着这一方法在法国盛行,并为欧洲所有国家公开采用或者暗中实行呢,这是如何发生的?

这一哲学方法虽然在 16 世纪就得以出现,但对其更其更精

in the sixteenth century; it may have been more accurately defined
and more extensively applied in the seventeenth; but neither in the
one nor in the other could it be commonly adopted. Political laws, the
condition of society, and the habits of mind that are derived from
these causes were as yet opposed to it.

It was discovered at a time when men were beginning to equalize
and assimilate their conditions. It could be generally followed only in
ages when those conditions had at length become nearly equal and
men nearly alike.

The philosophical method of the eighteenth century, then, is not
only French, but democratic; and this explains why it was so readily
admitted throughout Europe, where it has contributed so powerfully to
change the face of society. It is not because the French have changed
their former opinions and altered their former manners that they have
convulsed the world, but because they were the first to generalize and
bring to light a philosophical method by the aid of which it became
easy to attack all that was old and to open a path to all that was new.

If it be asked why at the present day this same method is more
rigorously followed and more frequently applied by the French than by
the Americans, although the principle of equality is no less complete
and of more ancient date among the latter people, the fact may be attributed to two circumstances, which it is first essential to have clearly
understood.

It must never be forgotten that religion gave birth to AngloAmeri-
can society. In the United States, religion is therefore mingled with
all the habits of the nation and all the feelings of patriotism, whence it
derives a peculiar force. To this reason another of no less power may
be added: in America religion has, as it were, laid down its own limits. Religious institutions have remained wholly distinct from political
institutions, so that former laws have been easily changed while former belief has remained unshaken. Christianity has therefore retained
a strong hold on the public mind in America; and I would more particularly remark that its sway is not only that of a philosophical doctrine which has been adopted upon inquiry, but of a religion which is
believed without discussion. In the United States, Christian sects are
infinitely diversified and perpetually modified; but Christianity itself
is an established and irresistible fact, which no one undertakes

确的定义更广泛的应用却应该是在 17 世纪了。但是这两者都没能得到大家普遍的接受。政治法律、社会状况和由这些原因造成的人们思想习性都在阻止它的推广。

这种方法曾出现在人们开始追求地位平等和彼此相差无几的时期,而只是到了人们的社会地位完全平等和人们几乎完全一样的时代,这一方法才得以普遍的实行。

18 世纪的哲学方法并非只在法国盛行,而且具有民主的特性,这就说明了为什么它很容易为欧洲的人们所接受,而为社会面貌的改变做出了巨大的贡献。法国人之所以能撼动世界,这并不是因为改变了其旧的观念和民情,而是因为他们是首先借助提出和引入哲学的方法来摧毁所有的旧的世界并开启新的道路。

如果被问及为什么现在法国人比美国人更严格地遵守更广泛地应用了这一方法,而美国人民的地位平等原则并不比法国弱,他们的人民地位平等的原则实施的时期也更早一些。这一事实也许是由两个我们首先应该掌握了解的原因造成的。

宗教创造了英裔美国人的社会这一事实决不能忘记。在美国,宗教与民族所有的习惯和爱国情结相融合,从而产生了一种特殊的力量。除了这一力量,还要加上另一个作用也不小的力量:在美国,宗教只局限在自己的圈内起作用。宗教制度一直以来都与政治制度相分离,所以,旧的信仰即使不受到动摇,旧的法律也可以很轻易地被改变。因此,基督教可以根深蒂固地坚守在美国人民的观念中。我还要特别指出的一点就是,基督教不仅仅是作为一门经过人们论证而被接受的哲学在发生支配作用,而且也作为人们坚信不疑的宗教信仰在发生支配作用。在美国,基督

either to attack or to defend. The Americans, having admitted the principal doctrines of the Christian religion without inquiry, are obliged to accept in like manner a great number of moral truths originating in it and connected with it. Hence the activity of individual analysis is restrained within narrow limits, and many of the most important of human opinions are removed from its influence.

The second circumstance to which I have alluded is that the social condition and the Constitution of the Americans are democratic, but they have not had a democratic revolution. They arrived on the soil they occupy in nearly the condition in which we see them at the present day; and this is of considerable importance.

There are no revolutions that do not shake existing belief, enervate authority, and throw doubts over commonly received ideas. Every revolution has more or less the effect of releasing men to their own conduct and of opening before the mind of each one of them an almost limitless perspective. When equality of conditions succeeds a protracted conflict between the different classes of which the elder society was composed, envy, hatred, and uncharitableness, pride and exaggerated self-confidence seize upon the human heart, and plant their sway in it for a time. This, independently of equality itself, tends powerfully to divide men, to lead them to mistrust the judgment of one another, and to seek the light of truth nowhere but in themselves. Everyone then attempts to be his own sufficient guide and makes it his boast to form his own opinions on all subjects. Men are no longer bound together by ideas, but by interests; and it would seem as if human opinions were reduced to a sort of intellectual dust, scattered on every side, unable to collect, unable to cohere.

Thus that independence of mind which equality supposes to exist is never so great, never appears so excessive, as at the time when equality is beginning to establish itself and in the course of that painful labor by which it is established. That sort of intellectual freedom

教派样式繁多并且总在不停地变化其形式,但是基督教本身是作为一个已确立的、不可抵抗的事实存在的,没有任何人会对它进行攻击,也没有人会去防御。美国人毫不怀疑地承认了基督教的主要教义后,就承担起接受它所提出和支持的大量的道德真理任务了。因此,个人的分析活动被限制在狭小的范围内,一些最重要的人们的观念也脱离了个人分析的影响。

我在前面提及的另一种情况,就是社会情况和美国的宪法的民主性质,但是他们并没有经历过民主的革命。他们来到这块他们占据的土地上的时候,就如同我们现在所看到的情形,这一点非常重要。

任何一场革命都会撼动已存的信仰,削弱其权威,并引起人们对常规思想的猜疑。任何一场革命都或多或少会起到将人们引向自己本性行为的作用,在每个人的思想面前展开一片广阔的空间。当地位平等战胜了拖延已久的在旧社会中存在的各个不同阶级之间的矛盾的时候,嫉妒、仇恨、凶残、骄傲和膨胀的自信就牢牢地抓住了人们的心思,并在一段时期内在人们的心中扎根。这种独立的平等,有力的分化了人们,使人们不相信其他人的判断,而只依靠自己寻找真理。每个人因此相信自己足以成了他自己的向导,这使他信心大增,也促使了他根据自己的观念对所有的事物作出判断。人们不再因为思想而结合在一起,而是因为利益。而人们的见解也仿佛变成了智力的垃圾,遍地都是,无法收集、无法聚集。

因此,随着平等而来的思想的独立,从没有像在平等最初开始建立时和为巩固其尽力而付出艰辛努力时那样强大,表现得那样过分。平等所提供的这种智力的自由,因此就应该小心地从

which equality may give ought, therefore, to be very carefully distinguished from the anarchy which revolution brings. Each of these two things must be separately considered in order not to conceive exaggerated hopes or fears of the future.

I believe that the men who will live under the new forms of society will make frequent use of their private judgment, but I am far from thinking that they will often abuse it. This is attributable to a cause which is more generally applicable to democratic countries, and which, in the long run, must restrain, within fixed and sometimes narrow limits, individual freedom of thought.

I shall proceed to point out this cause in the next chapter.

革命带来的混乱中区分出来。这两样中的任何一种都应该单独予以考虑,以免怀有过高的期望或对未来过于担心。

我相信,生活在新的社会模式下的人们,将会更多地根据自己的意见作出判断,但是我并不是认为,他们可以滥用自己的个人理性。这都是因为一个在民主的国家中能得以广泛的应用的原因。并且最终必须在限定的,有时甚至是狭窄的范围内,对个人的思想的自由加以限制。

我将在下一章节中对这一原因进一步加以说明。

CHAPTER II

Of The Principal Source Of Belief
Among Democratic Nations

At different periods dogmatic belief is more or less common. It a-rises in different ways, and it may change its object and its form; but under no circumstances will dogmatic belief cease to exist, or, in oth-er words, men will never cease to entertain some opinions on trust and without discussion. If everyone undertook to form all his own opinions and to seek for truth by isolated paths struck out by himself alone, it would follow that no considerable number of men would ever unite in any common belief.

But obviously without such common belief no society can pros-per; say, rather, no society can exist; for without ideas held in com-mon there is no common action, and without common action there may still be men, but there is no social body. In order that society should exist and, *a fortiori*, that a society should prosper, it is neces-sary that the minds of all the citizens should be rallied and held to-gether by certain predominant ideas; and this cannot be the case un-less each of them sometimes draws his opinions from the common source and consents to accept certain matters of belief already formed.

If I now consider man in his isolated capacity, I find that dog-matic belief is not less indispensable to him in order to live alone than it is to enable him to co-operate with his fellows. If man were forced to demonstrate for himself all the truths of which he makes daily use, his task would never end. He would exhaust his strength in preparatory

第二章　民主国家信仰的主要来源

　　在各个不同时期教条主义的信仰都或多或少有相同之处。这种信仰的兴起有很多不同的方式,但是随后可能会改变其目的和形式。但是教条主义的信仰在任何环境下都不会消亡,或者说,人们永远不会停止由于完全的信任而持有一些观点并无须争论。如果每个人都力图形成自己的观点,并独辟蹊径寻求真理,就不会有许多人愿团结在同一信仰之下。

　　但是很显然,没有了这些普遍的信仰,没有哪个社会可以获得繁荣。或者不如说,社会就不存在。因为缺少了这些思想的普遍存在,人们就没有统一的行为,可是没有了统一的行为,人虽然仍为人,但是就不存在社会的人。为了使社会存在,并使其欣欣向荣,那就必须使人们的思想集中并统一领导在某种主要的思想之下。但是这很难实现,除非他们中的每个人都时时会从同一根源去汲取自己的思想并同意接受一些既定的信仰中的一定数量的信仰。

　　现在,如果我考虑一个人单独存在的情况,会发现他单独生活也和他与其他同胞们一起生活一样对教条的信仰不可或缺。如果人们都要证明他每天运用的所有真理,那他的求证工作就没有尽头了。他将会将自己的精力都耗费在对前面所遇到的真理

demonstrations without ever advancing beyond them. As, from the shortness of his life, he has not the time, nor, from the limits of his intelligence, the capacity, to act in this way, he is reduced to take on trust a host of facts and opinions which he has not had either the time or the power to verify for himself, but which men of greater ability have found out, or which the crowd adopts. On this groundwork he raises for himself the structure of his own thoughts; he is not led to proceed in this manner by choice, but is constrained by the inflexible law of his condition. There is no philosopher in the world so great but that he believes a million things on the faith of other people and accepts a great many more truths than he demonstrates.

This is not only necessary but desirable. A man who should undertake to inquire into everything for himself could devote to each thing but little time and attention. His task would keep his mind in perpetual unrest, which would prevent him from penetrating to the depth of any truth or of making his mind adhere firmly to any conviction. His intellect would be at once independent and powerless. He must therefore make his choice from among the various objects of human belief and adopt many opinions without discussion in order to search the better into that smaller number which he sets apart for investigation. It is true that whoever receives an opinion on the word of another does so far enslave his mind, but it is a salutary servitude, which allows him to make a good use of freedom.

A principle of authority must then always occur, under all circumstances, in some part or other of the moral and intellectual world. Its place is variable, but a place it necessarily has. The independence of individual minds may be greater or it may be less; it cannot be unbounded. Thus the question is, not to know whether any intellectual authority exists in an age of democracy, but simply where it resides and by what standard it is to be measured. I have shown in the preceding chapter how equality of conditions leads men to entertain a sort of instinctive incredulity of the supernatural and a very lofty and often exaggerated opinion of human understanding.

加以说明,而无法在此基础上继续求证下去。然而,就人短暂的生命来说,他既没有时间,倾其智力和能力,也无法这样做下去。因此,他还是要相信一些他没有时间或没有精力去自己取证的事实和观点,这些事实和观点由其他一些伟人发现,或为大众接受的。在此基础上,他建造起自己的思想框架。他并不是自己选择以这样的方式,而是由他所处的环境中的特定的法律所限定的。世界上还没有哪个伟大的哲学家不是通过相信其他人的论断而认识许多事物或者接受大量没有经过他所论证的事实。

这不仅仅是必需的也是他所渴望的。一个人如果想要对每一件事都亲力亲为,那么他投入每件事的时间和精力必然很少。他的任务将会使他的头脑永无休息,这就会妨碍他对每件事实进行深入的分析或妨碍他的思想牢牢的集中在某一确定的事实上面。他的智力虽然得到独立但却威力大减。因此他不得不从人类已相信的各种事实中进行选择并不经论证的接受一些已存在的信仰,以便于从留待研究的问题中挑出优秀的部分进行进一步的论证。事实上,一个人接受了别人的观点后确实会极大地禁锢了自己的思想,但是这个禁锢是有益的,它使得人们可以更好地运用自由。

因此,不管在什么情况下,道德和智力世界中都必须有某种权威存在。权威的所在处可以不定,但必须有。个人思想的独立可能变大也可能变小,但不能没有限制。因此,问题就在于我们无从知道在一个民主时代是否存在智力方面的权威,只知道权威的所在和判断的标准。我在上一章节中已经说明了地位的平等如何使人们产生了一种本能的对超自然的能力的怀疑和对人的

The men who live at a period of social equality are not therefore easily led to place that intellectual authority to which they bow either beyond or above humanity. They commonly seek for the sources of truth in themselves or in those who are like themselves. This would be enough to prove that at such periods no new religion could be established, and that all schemes for such a purpose would be not only impious, but absurd and irrational. It may be foreseen that a democratic people will not easily give credence to divine missions; that they will laugh at modern prophets; and that they will seek to discover the chief arbiter of their belief within, and not beyond, the limits of their kind.

When the ranks of society are unequal, and men unlike one another in condition, there are some individuals wielding the power of superior intelligence, learning, and enlightenment, while the multitude are sunk in ignorance and prejudice. Men living at these aristocratic periods are therefore naturally induced to shape their opinions by the standard of a superior person, or a superior class of persons, while they are averse to recognizing the infallibility of the mass of the people.

The contrary takes place in ages of equality. The nearer the people are drawn to the common level of an equal and similar condition, the less prone does each man become to place implicit faith in a certain man or a certain class of men. But his readiness to believe the multitude increases, and opinion is more than ever mistress of the world. Not only is common opinion the only guide which private judgment retains among a democratic people, but among such a people it possesses a power infinitely beyond what it has elsewhere. At periods of equality men have no faith in one another, by reason of their common resemblance; but this very resemblance gives them almost unbounded confidence in the judgment of the public; for it would seem probable that, as they are all endowed with equal means of judging, the greater truth should go with the greater number.

When the inhabitant of a democratic country compares himself individually with all those about him, he feels with pride that he is the equal of any one of them; but when he comes to survey the totality of his fellows and to

理性高高在上的夸大的评价。生活在社会地位平等时期的人们很难将自己信服的智力权威置于人性之上。他们一般都是依靠自身或者与自己相似的人寻找事实的真相。这就足以证明,在这种情况下,新的宗教不可能建立,而所有以这一目的安排的计划不仅仅得不到人们的尊敬,反而显得很荒谬而缺乏理智。这也许预示着一个民主的民族很难信任那些天赋的使者,他们嘲笑那些新近的先知的预言,他们寻找以期发现人类本身而不是超越人类的信仰的主宰。

当社会阶级的不平等,人们之间的地位产生差异的时候,一些人因为有高超的智慧、知识而获得权利,而大多数人则显得无知而偏颇。生活在贵族制度统治时期的人们很自然地被一些高水平或者拥有较高地位的人们的带动而形成他们的意见,而不愿承认人民大众是永不会犯错的。

在人们地位平等的时期,情况与此相反。随着人们逐渐变得平等并且差别越来越小,人们对于某个人或者某一个阶级的盲目的信仰就会变得越来越淡。而同时他对于大众的信任感会上升,并逐渐成为支配社会的观点。在民主社会中,大众的意见不仅仅是个人判断的唯一导向,而且在这些人中它拥有超越了其他地方的无穷力量。身处平等时期的人们,因为大家拥有相同的地位,所以就没有了对他人的信仰。但是这种彼此之间的相似性又使他们对公众的判断产生了几乎无穷的信任。于是事情看起来就发展成了,因为人人都被赋予了公平的判断的能力,于是真理就往往站在大多数一边。

民主国家的人民将自己与周围的人们进行比较的时候,他很骄傲地发现自己与其他人拥有等同的身份;而当他深入到全体同

place himself in contrast with so huge a body, he is instantly over-whelmed by the sense of his own insignificance and weakness. The same equality that renders him independent of each of his fellow citizens, taken severally, exposes him alone and unprotected to the influence of the greater number. The public, therefore, among a democratic people, has a singular power, which aristocratic nations cannot conceive; for it does not persuade others to its beliefs, but it imposes them and makes them permeate the thinking of everyone by a sort of enormous pressure of the mind of all upon the individual intelligence.

In the United States the majority undertakes to supply a multitude of ready-made opinions for the use of individuals, who are thus relieved from the necessity of forming opinions of their own. Everybody there adopts great numbers of theories, on philosophy, morals, and politics, without inquiry, upon public trust; and if we examine it very closely, it will be perceived that religion itself holds sway there much less as a doctrine of revelation than as a commonly received opinion.

The fact that the political laws of the Americans are such that the majority rules the community with sovereign sway materially increases the power which that majority naturally exercises over the mind. For nothing is more customary in man than to recognize superior wisdom in the person of his oppressor. This political omnipotence of the majority in the United States doubtless augments the influence that public opinion would obtain without it over the minds of each member of the community; but the foundations of that influence do not rest upon it. They must be sought for in the principle of equality itself, not in the more or less popular institutions which men living under that condition may give themselves. The intellectual dominion of the greater number would probably be less absolute among a democratic people governed by a king than in the sphere of a pure democracy, but it will always be extremely absolute; and by whatever political laws men are governed in the ages of equality, it may be foreseen that faith in public opinion will become for them a species of religion, and the majority its ministering prophet.

Thus intellectual authority will be different, but it will not be diminished; and far from thinking that it will disappear, I augur that it may readily acquire too much preponderance and confine the action of private judgment within narrower limits

胞中去,他将自己与那些伟人们相比,就立刻为自己的默默无闻和弱小而遭受打击。这种平等的地位使他在同胞面前具有独立的地位,但也将他孤立并且对大多数人带来的影响毫无抵抗能力。因此,民主国家的公众具有的非凡力量是贵族制统治下的国家不可比拟的;因为它不是通过说服个人来相信它的信仰,而是通过大众思想的无穷压力作用于个人智力,将他们的信仰强加并渗透于每个人的思想中。

在美国,多数人都承担着向大众提供现成的观点的责任,而人们也从必须形成自己的观点的压力中解脱出来。人们毫不犹豫地采纳了大量对待公共事务的哲学理念、道德观念和政治意见方面的理论。而如果仔细研究一下,就会发现宗教所发挥的作用更多的是作为一种被普遍接受的见解而不是神启的教条。

美国的政治法制就是让多数人对社会实行统治权,这一事实极大地增强了大多数对智力的自然作用能力的极大增强。因为人们都已习惯认为自己的统治者一定在智商方面比自己更高明。多数在美国的这种无限政治权威,确实在加强舆论原本就对每个人的精神发生的影响,但它并非这种影响的基础。应该到平等的原则中,而不是在人们生活的环境下或多或少得到人们支持的制度中去寻找这种影响的根源。大多数对智力的统治在君主统治下的民主性质的国家中比在完全的民主国家不那么绝对,但它能一直保持着这种绝对;然而在平等的时代中,人们无论是被何种政治法制统治,都可以预言对于舆论的信仰将会变成人们的一种宗教并且是以多数为先知的一种宗教。

因此,智力的权威会不同,但绝不会减弱。我认为它非但不会消失,反而将会在各方面占尽优势,并将个人的行为判断限制

than are suited to either the greatness or the happiness of the human race. In the principle of equality I very clearly discern two tendencies; one leading the mind of every man to untried thoughts, the other prohibiting him from thinking at all. And I perceive how, under the dominion of certain laws, democracy would extinguish that liberty of the mind to which a democratic social condition is favorable; so that, after having broken all the bondage once imposed on it by ranks or by men, the human mind would be closely fettered to the general will of the greatest number.

If the absolute power of a majority were to be substituted by democratic nations for all the different powers that checked or retarded overmuch the energy of individual minds, the evil would only have changed character. Men would not have found the means of independent life; they would simply have discovered (no easy task) a new physiognomy of servitude. There is, and I cannot repeat it too often, there is here matter for profound reflection to those who look on freedom of thought as a holy thing and who hate not only the despot, but despotism. For myself, when I feel the hand of power lie heavy on my brow, I care but little to know who oppresses me; and I am not the more disposed to pass beneath the yoke because it is held out to me by the arms of a million men.

在与人类的伟大和幸福不相称的狭窄的范围内。在平等的原理中，我认清了两点趋势：一是将每个人的思想都引向一个全新的领域；一是禁止人们有思想。我也认识到，在一定的法律统治下，民主也会压制对民主的社会环境有利的自由思想。因此，一旦打破了曾一度被人们或某个阶级强加在身的束缚之后，人们的思想将会更紧密地为大多数人的意愿所束缚。

假如大多数的绝对权利因为所有过多地限制或延迟个人思想的能力的各种力量而为民主国家所取代，那么，也只是改变了邪恶的特性。人们不会找到独立生活的途径。他们仅仅是发现了一种新的奴隶的形式。因此，我在这里再次重复，凡是将思想自由作为一件神圣的事件的人们，凡是仇恨专制君主和君主专制的人们，都应当三思而行。对我自己来说，当我感到权利的大手重重地在我面前挥舞的时候，我不必去关心是谁在压迫我，而是将头伸进这枷锁，因为这是千万双臂膀为我举着的枷锁。

CHAPTER III

Why The Americans Show More Aptitude And Taste For General Ideas Than Their Forefathers, The English

The Deity does not regard the human race collectively. He surveys at one glance and severally all the beings of whom mankind is composed; and he discerns in each man the resemblances that assimilate him to all his fellows, and the differences that distinguish him from them. God, therefore, stands in no need of general ideas; that is to say, he never feels the necessity of collecting a considerable number of analogous objects under the same form for greater convenience in thinking.

Such, however, is not the case with man. If the human mind were to attempt to examine and pass a judgment on all the individual cases before it, the immensity of detail would soon lead it astray and it would no longer see anything. In this strait, man has recourse to an imperfect but necessary expedient, which at the same time assists and demonstrates his weakness.

Having superficially considered a certain number of objects and noticed their resemblance, he assigns to them a common name, sets them apart, and proceeds onwards.

General ideas are no proof of the strength, but rather of the insufficiency of the human intellect; for there are in nature no beings exactly alike, no things precisely identical, no rules indiscriminately and alike applicable to several objects at once. The chief merit of general ideas is that they enable the human mind to pass a rapid judgment

第三章 为什么美国人表现出比他们的祖先英国人更倾向和喜爱一般观念

神并不笼统地看待人类。他匆匆一瞥，就知道了人性中包含的所有东西，就知道每个人之所以与其同伴相似的共同之处，也知道他们之间的区别何在。因此，上帝不需要笼统地概念。也就是说，他从未感到有必要收集大量类似的东西至于同一形式之下，以便于对他们进行更有益的思考。

然而人类的情形就与此不同了。如果人们的头脑欲对所有映入个人眼中的事物都独自进行研究做出判断的话，那么无尽的细节将会使人们的头脑产生混乱而不再能看到任何东西。在这样窘迫的情况下，人们不得不采用一些不够完美但有必要的权宜之计，这既暴露了他的弱点但同时也帮助了他的弱点。

人们在表面上观察一定数量事物并注意到它们的相似之处，给它们冠上一个相同的名字，然后就将它们放在一边开始考察别的事物。

一般思想的得出并不能证明人智的强大，而毋宁说成是人智不足的体现。因为在自然界中，没有哪种生物与其他生物是完全相似的，也没有任何生物是完全相同的，也没有任何规则可以不加选择地适用于或相似的同时适用于某一部分生物。一般概念

on a great many objects at once; but, on the other hand, the notions they convey are never other than incomplete, and they always cause the mind to lose as much in accuracy as it gains in comprehensiveness.

As social bodies advance in civilization, they acquire the knowledge of new facts and they daily lay hold almost unconsciously of some particular truths. The more truths of this kind a man ap-prehends, the more general ideas he is naturally led to conceive. A multitude of particular facts cannot be seen separately without at last discovering the common tie that connects them. Several individuals lead to the notion of the species, several species to that of the genus. Hence the habit and the taste for general ideas will always be greatest among a people of ancient culture and extensive knowledge.

But there are other reasons which impel men to generalize their ideas or which restrain them from doing so.

The Americans are much more addicted to the use of general ideas than the English and entertain a much greater relish for them. This appears very singular at first, when it is remembered that the two nations have the same origin, that they lived for centuries under the same laws, and that they still incessantly interchange their opinions and their manners. This contrast becomes much more striking still if we fix our eyes on our own part of the world and compare together the two most enlightened nations that inhabit it. It would seem as if the mind of the English could tear itself only reluctantly and painfully away from the observation of particular facts, to rise from them to their causes, and that it only generalizes in spite of itself. Among the French, on the contrary, the taste for general ideas would seem to have grown to so ardent a passion that it must be satisfied on every occasion. I am informed every morning when I wake that some general and eternal law has just been discovered which I never heard mentioned before. There is not a mediocre scribbler who does not try his hand at discovering truths applicable to a great kingdom and who is not very ill pleased with himself if he does not succeed in compressing

的好处就是能够使人们的头脑迅速地对大量的事物作出判断,但是,从另一方面说,这样所传递的概念永远都是不完整的,它总会是人们在得到一些理解的同时也遗漏掉一些事实。

随着社会文明的进步,人们也在获取新的知识并且几乎每天都在不知不觉中获取一些个别的真理。人们掌握了越多这样的真理,他就会越多地获得一般概念。大量特殊的事实,如果不从将这一类事物连接起来的一般纽带来看,就不能单独被发现。几个个体可以形成关于这一种的概念,而对几个种的理解就可以形成关于这一类的概念。因此,一个民族越是拥有悠久的文化和广博的知识,它的一般概念的习惯和爱好也将会达到最大。

但是,还有其他一些原因促使人们的思想趋向一般化或者阻止他们向这方面发展。

美国人与英国人相比更多的沉溺于对一般概念的使用,并且对他们来说具有更大的意义。当注意到这两个民族拥有相同的本源、几百年来生活在相同的法律约束下,并仍旧互相交换着彼此的观点和民情,则这种情况在最初出现时人们感到很异常。如果我们把视线锁定欧洲,然后对比居住其上的这两个世界上最伟大的国家,这种差异会更使我们感到惊讶。我们会看到,英国人的思想只能不情愿并痛苦地放弃对某些个别原则的观察,以便从观察中寻找事实的起因。而且英国人之接受事件的起因,也并非出于自愿。相反的在法国人中,他们对一般概念的喜好迅速的长成为需要在各个方面都得到满足的火热的激情。每天清晨醒来之后,总会有一些之前从未听说过的新发现的一般的永恒的规则。即使是平庸的小作家都会努力去发现一些适用于伟大的王国的真理,而且他要是不在一篇文章中阐述全人类是绝不会感到

the human race into the compass of an article.

So great a dissimilarity between two very enlightened nations surprises me. If I again turn my attention to England and observe the events which have occurred there in the last half-century, I think I may affirm that a taste for general ideas increases in that county in proportion as its ancient constitution is weakened.

The state of civilization is therefore insufficient by itself to explain what suggests to the human mind the love of general ideas or diverts it from them.

When the conditions of men are very unequal and the inequalities are permanent, individual men gradually become so dissimilar that each class assumes the aspect of a distinct race. Only one of these classes is ever in view at the same instant; and, losing sight of that general tie which binds them all within the vast bosom of mankind, the observation invariably rests, not on man, but on certain men. Those who live in this aristocratic state of society never, therefore, conceive very general ideas respecting themselves; and that is enough to imbue them with a habitual distrust of such ideas and an instinctive aversion for them.

He, on the contrary, who inhabits a democratic country sees around him on every hand men differing but little from one another; he cannot turn his mind to any one portion of mankind without expanding and dilating his thought till it embraces the whole. All the truths that are applicable to himself appear to him equally and similarly applicable to each of his fellow citizens and fellow men. Having contracted the habit of generalizing his ideas in the study which engages him most and interests him most, he transfers the same habit to all his pursuits; and thus it is that the craving to discover general laws in everything, to include a great number of objects under the same formula, and to explain a mass of facts by a single cause becomes an ardent and sometimes an undiscerning passion in the human mind.

心满意足的。

存在于两个伟大的文明国家的巨大差异使我感到惊奇。如果我再次将视线转向英格兰,并考察它在过去 50 年中的种种变化,那么我就可以得出肯定的结论,那就是,英国人逐渐上升的对于一般观念的爱好,与其古老制度的衰退成正比发展。

因此,人们对文明的喜好本身并不足以说明人们是否应该热爱一般观念还是应该排斥它们。

当人们的社会地位变得极不平等,并且这种不平等的现象永久存在的时候,人与人之间将越来越不同,以至于有多少种不同的人,就会有多少个阶级。但是,在同一时间,人们总是只注意到其中的一个阶级,而看不到将所有的阶级联系在人类的广阔胸怀下的一般纽带,人们的观察的对象的范围都不同,可是都不是在于人类而只在于一部分人。因此,那些生活在贵族制度下的人们,从未考虑过关于自身的一般性的观念,而这又足以使他们在习惯上不相信一般观念,在本能上厌恶一般观念。

相反,一个生活在民主环境下的人,就会看到他周围的人们几乎没有差别。一个人只要将自己的思想不断扩大并一直扩展直到全世界,他就不会再将自己的思维锁定在某一部分人们的身上。所有对自己适用的真理必然也同样适用于其他的市民和同胞。他们一旦在自己从事的领域和研究中对一般概念感到浓厚的兴趣,那么就会将同样的习惯带到他所从事的其他领域中去。因而就会形成对所有领域的追求一般概念的渴望,形成为众多的事物总结规律的渴望,以及渴望用同样的原因来解释大量事实起因的渴望,这一渴望变得激烈并常常成为人们思想中一份盲目的激情。

Nothing shows the truth of this proposition more clearly than the opinions of the ancients respecting their slaves. The most profound and capacious minds of Rome and Greece were never able to reach the idea, at once so general and so simple, of the common likeness of men and of the common birthright of each to freedom; they tried to prove that slavery was in the order of nature and that it would always exist. Nay, more, everything shows that those of the ancients who had been slaves before they became free, many of whom have left us excellent writings, themselves regarded servitude in no other light.

All the great writers of antiquity belonged to the aristocracy of masters, or at least they saw that aristocracy established and uncontested before their eyes. Their mind, after it had expanded itself in several directions, was barred from further progress in this one; and the advent of Jesus Christ upon earth was required to teach that all the members of the human race are by nature equal and alike.

In the ages of equality all men are independent of each other, isolated, and weak. The movements of the multitude are not permanently guided by the will of any individuals; at such times humanity seems always to advance of itself. In order, therefore, to explain what is passing in the world, man is driven to seek for some great causes, which, acting in the same manner on all our fellow creatures, thus induce them all voluntarily to pursue the same track. This again naturally leads the human mind to conceive general ideas and superinduces a taste for them.

I have already shown in what way the equality of conditions leads every man to investigate truth for himself. It may readily be perceived that a method of this kind must insensibly beget a tendency to general ideas in the human mind. When I repudiate the traditions of rank, professions, and birth, when I escape from the authority of example to seek out, by the single effort of my reason, the path to be followed, I am inclined to derive the motives of my opinions from human nature itself, and this leads me necessarily, and almost unconsciously, to adopt a great number of very general notions.

All that I have here said explains why the English display much less aptitude and taste for the generalization of ideas than their American

古代人对于奴隶的看法最能证明我上述观点的正确性。即使是罗马和希腊最广阔最博学的思想也从未想到过人类的一般相似性和人们与生俱来的自由这个曾经是如此一般如此简单的观念。他们曾试图证明，奴隶存在于大自然的规律之中，并将永远存在。然而，所有的事实都向我们展示了，那些古代的人们，在他们成为自由之身之前都曾是奴隶，许多人还为我们留下了伟大的著作。他们虽然也曾目睹今天这样的奴役现象，但他们当时仍然认为奴隶制度是合乎自然的。

古代所有伟大的作家都是贵族或至少见证了贵族制度的建立并没有加以反对。他们的思想向四面八方扩展之后，最终被贵族的思想范畴所阻隔。只是基督教的出现，才教导人们，所有的人类都天生平等，彼此相似。

在平等的时代，人人都是各自独立的，孤单并虚弱。单个人的意志不能长久的引导大众的行为。在这样的时期，人们仿佛一直是自主前进的。因此，为了解释世界上到底发生过什么，人们就不得不去寻找一些以同样的方式作用于所有人类并使人们自愿地走上同一道路的伟大的借口。这又再次自然的引导人们的思想去考虑一般观念并引导人们喜爱使用一般观念。

我在前面已经指出人们地位的平等是如何导致人们喜爱亲自寻找真理的。不难发现，这种方法必然逐渐地使人的精神倾向于一般观念。当我批判阶级、职业和家世的传统时，当我摆脱榜样的力量，单凭个人的理性寻找前进的道路时，我倾向于到人的本性中去汲取自己观点的起因。这一思想必然地，不知不觉地使我得到了许多非常一般的概念。

我所描述的一切，都揭示了为什么英国人表现得不如他的后

progeny, and still less again than their neighbors the French; and likewise why the English of the present day display more than their forefathers did.

The English have long been a very enlightened and a very aristocratic nation; their enlightened condition urged them constantly to generalize, and their aristocratic habits confined them to the particular. Hence arose that philosophy, at once bold and timid, broad and narrow, which has hitherto prevailed in England and which still obstructs and stagnates so many minds in that country. Independently of the causes I have pointed out in what goes before, others may be discerned less apparent, but no less efficacious, which produce among almost every democratic people a taste, and frequently a passion, for general ideas. A distinction must be made between ideas of this kind. Some of them are the result of slow, minute, and conscientious labor of the mind, and these extend the sphere of human knowledge; others spring up at once from the first rapid exercise of the wits and beget none but very superficial and uncertain notions.

Men who live in ages of equality have a great deal of curiosity and little leisure; their life is so practical, so confused, so excited, so active, that but little time remains to them for thought. Such men are prone to general ideas because they are thereby spared the trouble of studying particulars; they contain, if I may so speak, a great deal in a little compass, and give, in a little time, a great return. If, then, on a brief and inattentive investigation, they think they discern a common relation between certain objects, inquiry is not pushed any further; and without examining in detail how far these several objects agree or differ, they are hastily arranged under one formula, in order to pass to another subject.

One of the distinguishing characteristics of a democratic period is the taste that all men then have for easy success and present enjoyment. This occurs in the pursuits of the intellect as well as in all others. Most of those who live in a time of equality are full of an ambition

裔美国人和他的近邻法国人一般喜爱一般概念，以及为什么今天的英国人就表现得比他的祖先在这方面走得更远。

英国长期以来一直是一个非常文明又非常贵族化的民族。他们的开明文化，促使他们不断地追求一般概念，而他们的贵族习惯又将他们局限在一些个别的观念中。因此，他们所引发的哲学，既大胆又懦弱，既广阔又狭隘，这一哲学广泛的流行在英格兰境内直到现在仍然支配并限制着人们的思想。除了我上述描述的原因之外，还有其他一些不大明显的但并非无力的原因，来解释为什么几乎在所有民主的国家中都会产生的一种对一般观念的热爱和激情。我们必须对这一类观念加以区别。有些一般观念是长期的，细致的，精心的智力劳动的结果，这些观念扩展了人们的知识范围。而另一些一般观念，则来自一刹那的智慧的火花，这些观念就造成一些肤浅的不确定的观念。

生活在平等时期的人们总是拥有很多的好奇心，而很少有悠闲的心境。他们的生活是那么的实际、复杂和活跃，几乎没有时间让他们去思考。这样的人倾向于接受一般观念因为这样他们就免除了去研究每一个特例的麻烦。如果我可以这么说的话，他们在小小的罗盘中容纳很多东西，并在短暂的时间内获得丰厚的回报。因此，这个时代的人们在一次简短而不够细致的调查之后，他们就认定自己发现了某些事物之间的共同关系，不再进一步深入研究这些事物，也不详细考察这些纷纭的事物在哪些方面相似或有别，而是匆匆忙忙把他们归类，随后便不去做深入考察。

民主时期的一个显著的特点就是，人们都追求轻易地获得成功并享受现时的快乐。这一现象表现在人们对知识的追求和其他方面的追求上面。大多数生活在平等时期的人们都怀有勃勃

equally alert and indolent: they want to obtain great success immediately, but they would prefer to avoid great effort. These conflicting tendencies lead straight to the search for general ideas, by the aid of which they flatter themselves that they can delineate vast objects with little pains and draw the attention of the public without much trouble.

And I do not know that they are wrong in thinking so. For their readers are as much averse to investigating anything to the bottom as they are; and what is generally sought in the productions of mind is easy pleasure and information without labor.

If aristocratic nations do not make sufficient use of general ideas, and frequently treat them with inconsiderate disdain, it is true, on the other hand, that a democratic people is always ready to carry ideas of this kind to excess and to espouse them with injudicious warmth.

的野心但却又显得懒惰:他们急功近利但却又不愿努力。这些矛盾的倾向将他们引向探求一般概念,并且夸下海口,认为凭借这些一般概念,可以不费力气就能绘出广袤世界并且可以轻而易举的引起公众的注意。

我本身并不认为他们这样想有什么错误。因为他们的读者也像他们一样,不愿对任何事情进行深入的调查研究。他们不愿用大脑思考问题而希望不经努力就获得知识和痛快地享乐。

如果说贵族制国家没有充分运用一般概念,而是常常轻率的蔑视一般概念,那么,从另一方面来说,民主国家的人们就一直在滥用这种一般观念,时时准备积极的应用这种观念。

CHAPTER IV

Why The Americans Have Never
Been So Eager As The French For
General Ideas In Political Affairs

I have observed that the Americans show a less decided taste for general ideas than the French. This is especially true in politics.

Although the Americans infuse into their legislation far more general ideas than the English, and although they strive more than the latter to adjust the practice of affairs to theory, no political bodies in the United States have ever shown so much love for general ideas as the Constituent Assembly and the Convention in France. At no time has the American people laid hold on ideas of this kind with the passionate energy of the French people in the eighteenth century, or displayed the same blind confidence in the value and absolute truth of any theory.

This difference between the Americans and the French originates in several causes, but principally in the following one. The Americans are a democratic people who have always directed public affairs themselves. The French are a democratic people who for a long time could only speculate on the best manner of conducting them. The social condition of the French led them to conceive very general ideas on the subject of government, while their political constitution prevented them from correcting those ideas by experiment and from gradually detecting their insufficiency; whereas in America the two things constantly balance and correct each other.

It may seem at first sight that this is very much opposed to what I have said before, that democratic nations derive their love of theory

第四章　为什么美国人从不会像法国人那样热心于在政治事务中运用一般观念

我在前面已经说过,美国人对于一般概念的喜好表现出的决心不如法国人。这句话在政治方面尤其适用。

尽管美国人在立法方面采用的一般观念比英国人多得多,并且在用实践调整理论方面也比英国多,然而美国却没有一个政治机构曾像法国制宪会议和国民公会那样热爱一般观念。美国人民也从未像18世纪的法国人那样对持有这种观念表现出任何激情,或者对任何理论的价值和绝对性表现出与法国人相同的盲目的信任。

美国人和法国人之间的不同源于一些原因,但是最主要的还是下面提到的这个。美国是一个民主的民族,它的人民总是自主的引导社会事务。而法国虽然也是一个民主的民族,在很长一段时间内,只能口头上讨论最适用的管理社会事务的方法。法国人民的社会状况引导他们认识到一些政府管理的一般观念,而同时他们的政治体制却又阻止他们通过实验对这些认识加以更正并且使他们只能逐渐发现其不足之处。然而,在美国,一般观念和政治制度却总是互为平衡,从而得以彼此修正。

乍一看来,这与我前面所说的民主的民族是从他们的现实生

from the very excitement of their active life. A more attentive examination will show that there is nothing contradictory in the proposition.

Men living in democratic countries eagerly lay hold of general ideas because they have but little leisure and because these ideas spare them the trouble of studying particulars. This is true, but it is only to be understood of those matters which are not the necessary and habitual subjects of their thoughts. Mercantile men will take up very eagerly, and without any close scrutiny, all the general ideas on philosophy, politics, science, or the arts which may be presented to them; but for such as relate to commerce, they will not receive them without inquiry or adopt them without reserve. The same thing applies to statesmen with regard to general ideas in politics.

If, then, there is a subject upon which a democratic people is peculiarly liable to abandon itself, blindly and extravagantly, to general ideas, the best corrective that can be used will be to make that subject a part of their daily practical occupation. They will then be compelled to enter into details, and the details will teach them the weak points of the theory. This remedy may frequently be a painful one, but its effect is certain.

Thus it happens that the democratic institutions which compel every citizen to take a practical part in the government moderate that excessive taste for general theories in politics which the principle of equality suggests.

活中获得对理论的热爱恰好相反。如果进一步仔细观察的话，就会发现这种说法并不存在互相矛盾的地方。

生活在民主国家的人们都渴望一般观念。因为他们几乎没有空暇而且这些观念使得他们得以逃脱对个别事物进行研究的麻烦。这固然是事实，但只限于不是他们常想的或必想的问题。比如，商人急切地希望不用仔细研究就可以获得展现在他们面前的哲学、政治、科学以及艺术方面的一般概念。而对于这些与商业有关的东西，他们不会毫无怀疑不经调查的全盘接受或者只是有保留地接受。政治家当涉及有关政治的一般观念时，情形也是如此。

如果民主国家的人们在某个问题上盲目过分的追求一般概念从而有迷失自己的倾向，那么最好的补救办法就是使这个问题成为他们每天实践调查的对象。这样一来，他们就不得不深入到问题的细节，这些细节将教会他们明白理论的薄弱环节。这一补救工作将会长期成为让人头痛的东西，但是它的效果是肯定的。

因此，强迫每一个公民实际加入政府管理工作的民主制度，可以节制人们对于平等原则所造成的政治方面的一般概念的过多爱好。

CHAPTER V

How Religion In The United States
Avails Itself Of Democratic Tendencies

I have shown in a preceding chapter that men cannot do without dogmatic belief, and even that it is much to be desired that such belief should exist among them. I now add that, of all the kinds of dogmatic belief, the most desirable appears to me to be dogmatic belief in matters of religion; and this is a clear inference, even from no higher consideration than the interests of this world.

There is hardly any human action, however particular it may be, that does not originate in some very general idea men have conceived of the Deity, of his relation to mankind, of the nature of their own souls, and of their duties to their fellow creatures. Nor can anything prevent these ideas from being the common spring from which all the rest emanates.

Men are therefore immeasurably interested in acquiring fixed ideas of God, of the soul, and of their general duties to their Creator and their fellow men; for doubt on these first principles would abandon all their actions to chance and would condemn them in some way to disorder and impotence.

This, then, is the subject on which it is most important for each of us to have fixed ideas; and unhappily it is also the subject on which it is most difficult for each of us, left to himself, to settle his opinions by the sole force of his reason. None but minds singularly free from the ordinary cares of life, minds at once penetrating, subtle, and trained by thinking, can, even with much time and care,

第五章　在美国宗教是如何
利用民主的特性的

　　我在前一章中已经说明,人们离不开教条式的信仰,甚至人们也渴望这样的信仰存在于他们中间。在这里我再加上一句:这所有这些教条式的信仰中,在我看来人们最渴望的还是关于宗教的信仰。即使人们只考虑现世的利益,这也是完全符合条理的推论。

　　人的任何行为,不管被认为有何特殊性,几乎都源于他对上帝、对他与人类的关系、对他灵魂的本性、对他的同胞应负的责任所持的一般概念。谁也无法阻止这些一般观念成为其余所有事物发生的共同的源泉。

　　因此,人们对上帝、灵魂和他们对于获取自己的创造者和自己的同胞所负有的责任的固定的思维富有无限的兴趣。因为对这些基本原则的怀疑会使他们的行为迷失在偶然因素的支配下,也可以说使他们陷入某种意义上的混乱和无能之中。

　　可见,我们每个人都应当有确定不移的观念,乃是一个非常重要的问题。但不幸的是,对我们每个人来说,仅靠个人的理性努力去取得这种观念,使它成为一项最艰巨的任务。只有摆脱日常生活的琐事,人们的头脑只有经过深入、细致和训练有素的思考,再加上大量的时间和关心,才能深入的了解这些必不可少的

sound the depths of these truths that are so necessary. And, indeed, we see that philosophers are themselves almost always surrounded with uncertainties; that at every step the natural light which illuminates their path grows dimmer and less secure; and that, in spite of all their efforts, they have discovered as yet only a few conflicting notions, on which the mind of man has been tossed about for thousands of years without every firmly grasping the truth or finding novelty even in its errors. Studies of this nature are far above the average capacity of men; and, even if the majority of mankind were capable of such pursuits, it is evident that leisure to cultivate them would still be wanting.

Fixed ideas about God and human nature are indispensable to the daily practice of men's lives; but the practice of their lives prevents them from acquiring such ideas.

The difficulty appears to be without a parallel. Among the sciences there are some that are useful to the mass of mankind and are within its reach; others can be approached only by the few and are not cultivated by the many, who require nothing beyond their more remote applications; but the daily practice of the science I speak of is indispensable to all, although the study of it is inaccessible to the greater number.

General ideas respecting God and human nature are therefore the ideas above all others which it is most suitable to withdraw from the habitual action of private judgment and in which there is most to gain and least to lose by recognizing a principle of authority.

The first object and one of the principal advantages of religion is to furnish to each of these fundamental questions a solution that is at once clear, precise, intelligible, and lasting, to the mass of mankind. There are religions that are false and very absurd, but it may be

真理。事实上,我们看到哲学家们本身也总是被一些不确定的因素所包围,照亮他们前进道路的自然的光芒随着每一次前进的脚步变得越来越暗淡越来越使人不安。我们看到,尽管他们很努力,可是到目前为止也只是发现了一些存在争议的概念,在这些问题上,人们的思想已斗争了上千年的时间,却从未发现过一些确定的事实或者说有一些更新的发现,即使是错误的也没有。对这个自然的研究已远远超出了人们的能力。并且,即使大多数的人类还是可以胜任这样的研究,显然他们也没有这种闲心和余暇。

有关上帝和人性的确定不移的观念,虽然是人的日常生活所不可缺少的,但是他们的生活实践却阻止人们去掌握这些思想。

这是一个绝无仅有的困难。在社会中,存在着一些对人类有利的并且是人们有能力掌握的知识。另一些知识则只能为少数人所掌握而大多数人是无法获取的,对大多数人来说,对后一类知识的应用是相对来说比较间接的。但是,我所说的每日的社会实践对所有人来说都是必不可少的,尽管多数人并没有去研究它。

因此,关系到上帝和人类自然的一般观念是远远高于其他思想之上的。这一思想最适于去除习惯性行为对个人理性判断的影响,并且对于个人理性来说,承认一个权威的存在,就可以有最大的收获和最小的损失。

宗教的首要目的和最主要的优势之一在于,对这些重要问题中的每个问题,都能够为人民大众提供一个清晰、准确、容易理解和恒久的解决方法。有些宗教是虚假的甚至非常荒谬,但是可以断言任何一个包含在我所描述的范围内的宗教,只要它不脱离这

affirmed that any religion which remains within the circle I have just traced, without pretending to go beyond it (as many religions have attempted to do, for the purpose of restraining on every side the free movement of the human mind), imposes a salutary restraint on the intellect; and it must be admitted that, if it does not save men in another world, it is at least very conducive to their happiness and their greatness in this.

This is especially true of men living in free countries. When the religion of a people is destroyed, doubt gets hold of the higher powers of the intellect and half paralyzes all the others. Every man accustoms himself to having only confused and changing notions on the subjects most interesting to his fellow creatures and himself. His opinions are ill-defended and easily abandoned; and, in despair of ever solving by himself the hard problems respecting the destiny of man, he ignobly submits to think no more about them.

Such a condition cannot but enervate the soul, relax the springs of the will, and prepare a people for servitude. Not only does it happen in such a case that they allow their freedom to be taken from them; they frequently surrender it themselves. When there is no longer any principle of authority in religion any more than in politics, men are speedily frightened at the aspect of this unbounded independence. The constant agitation of all surrounding things alarms and exhausts them. As everything is at sea in the sphere of the mind, they determine at least that the mechanism of society shall be firm and fixed; and as they cannot resume their ancient belief, they assume a master.

For my own part, I doubt whether man can ever support at the same time complete religious independence and entire political freedom. And I am inclined to think that if faith be wanting in him, he must be subject; and if he be free, he must believe. Perhaps, however, this great utility of religions is still more obvious among nations where equality of conditions prevails than among others. It must be acknowledged that equality, which brings great benefits into the world, nevertheless suggests to men (as will be shown hereafter) some very dangerous propensities. It tends to isolate them from one another, to concentrate every man's attention upon himself; and it lays open the soul to an inordinate love of material gratification.

个范围,都能使智力活动加以有益的限制(就像一些宗教试图去限制人们的思想在所有方面自由发展的企图一样)。并且,我们必须承认,即使这样做并不能在另一个世界拯救人类,至少在现世有益于他们获得幸福和高尚。

这对生活在自由国家的人们尤为真实。当宗教在一个国家遭到破坏的时候,怀疑就会在智者中产生优势力量,并将其他人陷于麻痹状态。每一个人都习惯于使自己对有利于自己和同胞的事物持有困惑和不断变化的观念。他的观点并不牢靠随时都可以遗弃。于是,他们因为无力解决人生提出的一些重大问题而陷入绝望状态,以致自暴自弃,干脆不再去想它。

这样的环境只能削弱人的精力,松懈人们的意志然后培养出一批奴隶。在这样的环境中,人们不仅仅使得自己被剥夺了自由的权利,他们常常自己就会交出自己的自由。当宗教的威严也像在政治领域那样不复存在,人们立刻会对由此产生的无限独立感到恐慌。一切事物的这种经常动荡状态,将使人们心神不安,筋疲力尽。因为在精神世界一切已经陷于迷茫,他们就决定至少物质的社会需要保持坚固稳定。但是,他们已无力再寻回过去的信仰,就只能要求一个统治者。

至于我,我怀疑人们是否能既支持宗教的完全独立,又保持完全的政治自由。我一向认为,人要是没有信仰,就必然受人奴役;而要想有自由,就必须信奉宗教。尽管如此,也许宗教的这一伟大效用,在地位平等的国家比在任何其他国家都明显。我们必须承认,平等虽然给世界带来了巨大的好处,但也给人们带来了一些危险的倾向(就像我随后指出的那样)。平等使人们相互独立,使人们只关心自己。平等为人们敞开对物质的欲望的大门。

The greatest advantage of religion is to inspire diametrically contrary principles. There is no religion that does not place the object of man's desires above and beyond the treasures of earth and that does not naturally raise his soul to regions far above those of the senses. Nor is there any which does not impose on man some duties towards his kind and thus draw him at times from the contemplation of himself. This is found in the most false and dangerous religions.

Religious nations are therefore naturally strong on the very point on which democratic nations are weak; this shows of what importance it is for men to preserve their religion as their conditions become more equal.

I have neither the right nor the intention of examining the supernatural means that God employs to infuse religious belief into the heart of man. I am at this moment considering religions in a purely human point of view; my object is to inquire by what means they may most easily retain their sway in the democratic ages upon which we are entering.

It has been shown that at times of general culture and equality the human mind consents only with reluctance to adopt dogmatic opinions and feels their necessity acutely only in spiritual matters. This proves, in the first place, that at such times religions ought more cautiously than at any other to confine themselves within their own precincts; for in seeking to extend their power beyond religious matters, they incur a risk of not being believed at all. The circle within which they seek to restrict the human intellect ought therefore to be carefully traced, and beyond its verge the mind should be left entirely free to its own guidance.

Mohammed professed to derive from Heaven, and has inserted in the Koran, not only religious doctrines, but political maxims, civil and criminal laws, and theories of science. The Gospel, on the contrary, speaks only of the general relations of men to God and to each other, beyond which it inculcates and imposes no point of faith. This alone, besides a thousand other reasons, would suffice to prove that

　　宗教的最大优势,就是直接激发人们与此相反的秉性。所有的宗教都让人追求的目标远远高于和超于现世享乐之外,它们迫使人们的灵魂上升到一个他们的感知无法触摸的高度。所有的宗教都叫一定的人对人类承担某种特定的义务,并常常将人们拽出自顾自的小圈子。即使是最虚伪的和最危险的宗教,也都采用这样的手法。

　　因此,宗教国家的长处,自然正是民主国家的弱处。这就表明,在人们的地位变得越来越平等的同时得以维护他们的宗教,对人们来说是多么重要。

　　我既没有权利也没有欲望去研究这些超自然的,上帝以此使宗教信仰完全的灌注人心的方法。我现在只是纯粹从人的观点来考察宗教的。我的目的,就是通过什么途径,他们可以在自己即将进入的民主社会里轻易地保持自己的影响力。

　　前面已经讲过,在普遍文明和平等的时代,人们的理性思想不愿接受教条式的说教,而只在人们的精神世界中,才认为有其存在的必要性。这首先说明了在这样的时代宗教要比在其他任何时代都更加谨慎,固守自己的范围,因为如果宗教要想把自己的权力扩展到宗教事务以外,就会冒着全盘失信的危险。因此,宗教应当非常小心地规定自己的活动范围,并在这个范围内对人的精神施加影响,而在这个范围之外,人们的思想就要完全自由。

　　穆罕默德声称自己从天上来,并把宗教教条、政治原则、民法和刑法都融入了《可兰经》中。与之相反,《圣经》仅囊括了人们与上帝,和人们彼此之间的一般联系,他并不强加任何东西或者对人们淳淳诱导。除了其他众多理由之外,只这一条,就足以证明这两种宗教的前一种宗教将难以在一个民主文明的时代长久处

the former of these religions will never long predominate in a cultivated and democratic age, while the latter is destined to retain its sway at these as at all other periods.

In continuation of this same inquiry I find that for religions to maintain their authority, humanly speaking, in democratic ages, not only must they confine themselves strictly within the circle of spiritual matters, but their power also will depend very much on the nature of the belief they inculcate, on the external forms they assume, and on the obligations they impose.

The preceding observation, that equality leads men to very general and very vast ideas, is principally to be understood in respect to religion. Men who are similar and equal in the world readily conceive the idea of the one God, governing every man by the same laws and granting to every man future happiness on the same conditions. The idea of the unity of mankind constantly leads them back to the idea of the unity of the Creator; while on the contrary in a state of society where men are broken up into very unequal ranks, they are apt to devise as many deities as there are nations, castes, classes, or families, and to trace a thousand private roads to heaven.

It cannot be denied that Christianity itself has felt, to some extent, the influence that social and political conditions exercise on religious opinions.

When the Christian religion first appeared upon earth, Providence, by whom the world was doubtless prepared for its coming, had gathered a large portion of the human race, like an immense flock, under the scepter of the Caesars. The men of whom this multitude was composed were distinguished by numerous differences, but they had this much in common: that they all obeyed the same laws, and that every subject was so weak and insignificant in respect to the Emperor that all appeared equal when their condition was contrasted with his. This novel and peculiar state of mankind necessarily predisposed men to listen to the general truths that Christianity teaches, and may serve to explain the facility and rapidity with which they then penetrated into the human mind. The counterpart of this state of things was exhibited after the destruction of the Empire. The Roman world being then, as it were, shattered into a thousand fragments, each nation resumed its former

于领先地位,而后者则注定要在这个或者其他任何时代保持其影响力。

在对这个问题继续进行探究的同时,我发现,作为一个宗教,如果想保持自己的影响力,人性化地说,尤其是在民主时期保持其影响力,就不仅仅要把自己的活动范围严守在精神领域的范围之内,他们的力量来源的很大因素也在于他们所劝导的信仰的性质:它的外部表象和它所要求人们应尽的义务。

前面有关平等如何引导人们具备一般的、广泛的思想的论述,主要是考虑到宗教的层面。人们在一个可能接受同一上帝的观念的世界中,是彼此相似和平等的,所有的人都约束在同一种法律之下,人们所追求的幸福也指向同一目标。人类统一的观念不断地将人们拉回到同一造物主的思想,而相反的,与此同时在人们被划分为许多不平等阶级的社会情况下,他们就倾向于按照民族、阶级、等级或者家族的数量来划分神的数量,这样就造就了无数条通往天堂的小径。

我们不能否认,从某种程度上说,基督教本身就已感觉到的社会和政治条件施加在它们身上的影响力。

当基督教最初出现的时候,毫无疑问,上帝早已在世上为它的来临准备好了一切,上帝集聚了一大批人类,就像数不尽的羊群,都统治在罗马皇帝的麾下。这一大群人虽然彼此之间有很多不同,但他们有一点是相同的:都遵守同样的法则,而所有的事物在皇权的威严下都显得那么的弱小和平庸以至于所有的东西在他面前都变得平等。这一新奇独特的状况使得人们都倾向于倾听基督所宣讲的一般真理,而基督教之所以在当时能够顺利迅速的深入人心,也正是源于此。罗马帝国崩溃以后,事情就向着完全相反的方向发展了。罗马帝国也随之像从前一样分崩离析,各

individuality. A scale of ranks soon grew up in the bosom of these nations; the different races were more sharply defined, and each nation
was divided by castes into several peoples. In the midst of this common effort, which seemed to be dividing human society into as many
fragments as possible, Christianity did not lose sight of the leading
general ideas that it had brought into the world. But it appeared, nevertheless, to lend itself as much as possible to the new tendencies created by this distribution of mankind into fractions. Men continue to
worship one God, the Creator and Preserver of all things; but every
people, every city, and, so to speak, every man thought to obtain
some distinct privilege and win the favor of an especial protector near
the throne of grace. Unable to subdivide the Deity, they multiplied
and unduly enhanced the importance of his agents. The homage due
to saints and angels became an almost idolatrous worship for most
Christians; and it might be feared for a moment that the religion of
Christ would retrograde towards the superstitions which it had overcome.

It seems evident that the more the barriers are removed which
separate one nation from another and one citizen from another, the
stronger is the bent of the human mind, as if by its own impulse, towards the idea of a single and all-powerful Being, dispensing equal
laws in the same manner to every man. In democratic ages, then, it
is particularly important not to allow the homage paid to secondary a-
gents to be confused with the worship due to the Creator alone.

Another truth is no less clear, that religions ought to have fewer
external observances in democratic periods than at any others.

In speaking of philosophical method among the Americans I have
shown that nothing is more repugnant to the human mind in an age of
equality than the idea of subjection to forms. Men living at such times
are impatient of figures; to their eyes, symbols appear to be puerile
artifices used to conceal or to set off truths that should more naturally
be bared to the light of day; they are unmoved by ceremonial observances and are disposed to attach only a secondary importance to the
details of public worship.

Those who have to regulate the external forms of religion in a

个民族都纷纷恢复了昔日的独立。很快在这些民族内部就出现了大批阶级,并对不同的阶级进行了更细的划分,每一个民族都被分为不同等级的许多集团。在这些共有的似乎要将人类社会尽可能分裂成无数小块的共同的努力中,基督教并没有丢弃它曾带给世界的主要一般观念。不过,它表现得尽量使自己准备适用人类分裂后出现的新趋势。人们仍旧信仰创造和庇护万物的唯一的上帝。但是所有的民族、所有的城市甚至可以说所有人,又都相信自己能够得到某种特权,使至高无上的上帝成为自己的保护者。因为不能把上帝进行划分,他们就增加神的使者的数量并不负责任地提高其重要性。因为人们对圣徒和天使的敬意已近乎一种盲目的偶像崇拜,以致人们一时不得不担心,基督教是否也会退回到它所推翻的那些宗教的状态。

很明显,如果能把每个民族与其他民族之间、每个公民与其他公民之间的隔阂消除得越多,人类思想联结的纽带就会变得越强健,就会在自身的推动下,转向单一的思想和万能的存在的观念,就会用平等的法律和同样的方式施于每个人。在民主时期,最重要的事情就是不能把人对神的使者的崇敬与对造物主的崇拜混为一谈。

另一个事实也很清楚,那就是,在民主时期,应使宗教的表面仪式带给信徒的负担轻于在其他时期。

在谈及美国的哲学方法时,我已经说过,在平等时代,人的精神最厌恶的,莫过于使自己的观念服从于形式。生活在这个时期的人们厌恶图像。在他们看来,象征的手法就像儿戏般,就是为了掩藏或者抵消事实,而这些事实本来就应该暴露在光天化日之下。他们对宗教仪式漠然视之,认为礼拜的细节只是次要。

在民主时期,那些对宗教的外在仪式加以规范的人们,

democratic age should pay a close attention to these natural propensities of the human mind in order not to run counter to them unnecessarily.

I firmly believe in the necessity of forms, which fix the human mind in the contemplation of abstract truths and aid it in embracing them warmly and holding them with firmness. Nor do I suppose that it is possible to maintain a religion without external observances; but, on the other hand, I am persuaded that in the ages upon which we are entering it would be peculiarly dangerous to multiply them beyond measure, and that they ought rather to be limited to as much as is absolutely necessary to perpetuate the doctrine itself, which is the substance of religion, of which the ritual is only the form. ①A religion which became more insistent in details, more inflexible, and more burdened with small observances during the time that men became more equal would soon find itself limited to a band of fanatic zealots in the midst of a skeptical multitude.

I anticipate the objection that, as all religions have general and eternal truths for their object, they cannot thus shape themselves to the shifting inclinations of every age without forfeiting their claim to certainty in the eyes of mankind. To this I reply again that the principal opinions which constitute a creed, and which theologians call articles of faith, must be very carefully distinguished from the accessories connected with them. Religions are obliged to hold fast to the former, whatever be the peculiar spirit of the age; but they should take good care not to bind themselves in the same manner to the latter at a time when everything is in transition and when the mind, accustomed to the moving pageant of human affairs, reluctantly allows itself to be fixed on any point. The permanence of external and secondary things seems to me

---

① In all religions there are some ceremonies that are inherent in the substance of the faith itself, and in these nothing should on any account be changed. This is especially the case with Roman Catholicism, in which the doctrine and the form are frequently so closely united as to form but one point of belief.

必须审慎考虑人们智力的这种自然本性,以免与其发生不必要的冲突。

我坚决相信形式的必要性,正是形式将人们的思想与对抽象的事实的思考紧密地联系在一起,帮助其坚定地坚持真理,使其热烈地追求真理。我决不认为一种宗教能够在没有外在的仪式情况下保持下去。但是,另一方面,我又觉得:在我们正在踏入的时代,过分地讲究宗教的外在仪式是极其危险的;而应当只保留一些必要的仪式,以延续教义本身所绝对需要者为限,因为教义才是宗教的本质,而礼拜只是它的形式。① 在人们越来越平等的时代,拘泥于细节、顽固死板、迫使信徒遵守一大堆清规戒律的宗教,很快就会只剩下一群狂热的信徒,而大多数人将放弃对它的信仰。

我知道一定会有人反驳我说:宗教都是以一般的、永恒的真理为其追求的目标,所以它不能随波逐流,跟着每个时代的特点的变化而改变其目标,从而不会在人们面前失去其可信性。对此我仍旧会回答:必须把构成一种信仰的和神学家们所说的信条所包含的主要观点,同由这些观点派生出来的从属概念小心地区开来。不管时代的精神有什么特点,宗教都必须牢牢地坚持前者;但当万事都在变化,当人们的思想已经习惯于人世间的千变万化而不愿意墨守陈规的时候,宗教也要小心,不要让自己的墨守陈规蒙蔽了双眼,要慎重地注意自己与后者的联系。我认为,

---

① 在任何综教中,仪式都与信仰的本质本身有密切联系,而且最好不加任何改变。在形式与内容永远密切联系的像一个整体的天主教中,更是如此。

to have a chance of enduring only when civil society is itself static; under any other circumstances I am inclined to regard it as dangerous.

We shall see that of all the passions which originate in or are fostered by equality, there is one which it renders peculiarly intense, and which it also infuses into the heart of every man; I mean the love of well-being. The taste for well-being is the prominent and indelible feature of democratic times.

It may be believed that a religion which should undertake to destroy so deep-seated a passion would in the end be destroyed by it, and if it attempted to wean men entirely from the contemplation of the good things of this world in order to devote their faculties exclusively to the thought of another, it may be foreseen that the minds of men would at length escape its grasp, to plunge into the exclusive enjoyment of present and material pleasures.

The chief concern of religion is to purify, to regulate, and to restrain the excessive and exclusive taste for well-being that men feel in periods of equality; but it would be an error to attempt to overcome it completely or to eradicate it. Men cannot be cured of the love of riches, but they may be persuaded to enrich themselves by none but honest means.

This brings me to a final consideration, which comprises, as it were, all the others. The more the conditions of men are equalized and assimilated to each other, the more important is it for religion, while it carefully abstains from the daily turmoil of secular affairs, not needlessly to run counter to the ideas that generally prevail or to the permanent interests that exist in the mass of the people. For as public opinion grows to be more and more the first and most irresistible of existing powers, the religious principle has no external support strong enough to enable it long to resist its attacks. This is not less true of a democratic people ruled by a despot than of a republic. In ages of equality kings may often command obedience, but the majority always commands belief; to the majority, therefore, deference is to be paid in whatever is not

表面的和次要的事物要想得到永恒,只有让市民社会本身也停滞不前。否则,在其他任何情况下,我都认为僵化是一种危险。

我们应当看到,在所有植根于平等或者在平等的环境下成长起来的激情当中,有一种激情显得特别的强烈并且深入人心。那就是人们对于享乐的热爱之情。而这种热爱之情是民族时期卓著而不可磨灭的特性。

可以相信,如果宗教企图去破坏这一根深蒂固的激情,最终可能反而会被这一激情所毁灭。而如果宗教企图让人们完全放弃对世界美好事物的幻想,而将他们的精力完全投入另一个方面,我们可以预见,人们的思想最终就会逃离宗教的束缚,而将自己完全投入到现世享乐和物欲的洪流之中。

宗教主要应该考虑的是如何净化、规范和抑制人们在平等时期对于享乐的过多地和排他地追求。但是,如果说将这种追求完全抑制或者彻底泯灭也是不正确的。人们无法控制自己对于财富的热爱之情,但是宗教可以劝服他们通过正当的途径获取财富。

最后,我还有一项考察,这项考察不仅仅是其本身,它也包含了对其他各项考察的综合。随着人们的社会地位趋于平等,人们在各方面趋于相似,这种现象对有意远离人们日常琐事的宗教来说,使其愈加不需求与在人们中间普遍流行的观念和他们永久存在的利益进行无谓的抗争,因为大众舆论越来越成为不可小觑的首要的和主要的存在力量,而宗教原则也没有任何其他外在力量足以使其长期抵御其所受到的抨击。这种现象在君主专制统治下的民主国家或在共和政体下的民主国家都同样真实。在平等时代,国王也许常常也能使其臣民服从其旨意,但在人们信服的还是人民中的大多数。因此,对大多数来说,为了不违背自己

contrary to the faith.

I showed in the first Part of this work how the American clergy stand aloof from secular affairs. This is the most obvious but not the only example of their self-restraint. In America religion is a distinct sphere, in which the priest is sovereign, but out of which he takes care never to go. Within its limits he is master of the mind; beyond them he leaves men to themselves and surrenders them to the independence and instability that belong to their nature and their age. I have seen no country in which Christianity is clothed with fewer forms, figures, and observances than in the United States, or where it presents more distinct, simple, and general notions to the mind. Although the Christians of America are divided into a multitude of sects, they all look upon their religion in the same light. This applies to Roman Catholicism as well as to the other forms of belief. There are no Roman Catholic priests who show less taste for the minute individual observances, for extraordinary or peculiar means of salvation, or who cling more to the spirit and less to the letter of the law than the Roman Catholic priests of the United States. Nowhere is that doctrine of the church which prohibits the worship reserved to God alone from being offered to the saints more clearly inculcated or more generally followed. Yet the Roman Catholics of America are very submissive and very sincere.

Another remark is applicable to the clergy of every communion. The American ministers of the Gospel do not attempt to draw or to fix all the thoughts of man upon the life to come; they are willing to surrender a portion of his heart to the cares of the present, seeming to consider the goods of this world as important, though secondary, objects. If they take no part themselves in productive labor, they are at least interested in its progress and they applaud its results; and while they never cease to point to the other world as the great object of the hopes and fears of the believer, they do not forbid him honestly to court prosperity in this. Far from attempting to show that these things

的信仰，就必须选择服从。

　　我在本书的上卷中已经说过美国的神职人员是如何不问政治的。这是他们自我约束的最明显例子，但还不是唯一的例子。在美国，宗教有其明确的界限，在这个范围内，牧师拥有至高无上的权力，而且他们从来不想走出这个天地；牧师在这个界限内统治着人们的思想，而在这个天地外，人们就不再受它的约束。人们可以拥有自己的本性和时代的特性赋予他们的独立和不稳定性。我从来没有见过哪个国家的基督教像在美国那样不讲究形式和不重视繁文缛节，也从未见过像美国人民那样拥有最清晰、最简明和最普遍的观念。尽管美国的基督徒分成许多宗派，但他们对各宗派都一视同仁，无论是对天主教，还是对其他教派。任何地方的天主教神职人员都没有像美国的天主教神职人员那样，他们不重视教徒的礼拜琐事，也不采取格外的和特殊的礼拜方法；他们不拘泥于教义的法则字句而重视教义的精神。天主教的只对上帝礼拜而禁止对圣徒礼拜的教义，在美国的宣讲比其他地方更为清晰，在美国人们对其的遵守也比其他地方更好。然而，美国的天主教徒却是最驯服和最虔诚的。

　　美国各个的教派的神职人员还有另一个特点。美国的神职人员从不企图把所有人类的思想都引向或者固定在来世；他们宁愿腾出一部分精力放在最现世的各个方面。在他们看来，他们认为现世的幸福很重要，虽然只是人们追求的次要的目标。所以，如果说他们不从事实业活动，但至少可以说他们还是关心实业发展并对其成果加以赞扬。而另一方面，他们从未停止宣扬来世才是信徒们应当追求的目标和害怕的对象，但他们并不禁止信徒以正当的方法去追求现世的幸福。他们不仅不想要说明这些事物

are distinct and contrary to one another, they study rather to find out on what point they are most nearly and closely connected.

All the American clergy know and respect the intellectual supremacy exercised by the majority; they never sustain any but necessary conflicts with it. They take no share in the altercations of parties, but they readily adopt the general opinions of their country and their age, and they allow themselves to be borne away without opposition in the current of feeling and opinion by which everything around them is carried along. They endeavor to amend their contemporaries, but they do not quit fellowship with them. Public opinion is therefore never hostile to them; it rather supports and protects them, and their belief owes its authority at the same time to the strength which is its own and to that which it borrows from the opinions of the majority.

Thus it is that by respecting all democratic tendencies not absolutely contrary to herself and by making use of several of them for her own purposes, religion sustains a successful struggle with that spirit of individual independence which is her most dangerous opponent.

之间的差别和矛盾，反而致力于寻找二者之间的共同点和相似之处。

所有美国的神职人员都承认多数对人们思想的支配作用，并尊重这种作用。除非逼不得已，他们决不会反对多数。他们从不参加党派之间的争论，但他们随时准备接受国家和他们所处的时代中大多数的意见，他们使自己符合当代流行的思想和观念并随着潮流前进而不是加以抵触。他们努力修正同时代的人们，却决不与他们决裂。因此，舆论从来不以他们为敌，反而支持和庇护他们。并且，他们宣扬的信仰，通过其本身的努力，再加上多数的力量而同时发挥作用。

因此，宗教通过尊重不与它完全对立的一切民主倾向，并利用其中的一部分，成功地抵制了它最危险的敌人，个体的独立意志。

CHAPTER VI
The Progress Of Roman Catholicism
In The United States

America is the most democratic country in the world, and it is at the same time (according to reports worthy of belief) the country in which the Roman Catholic religion makes most progress. At first sight this is surprising.

Two things must here be accurately distinguished: equality makes men want to form their own opinions; but, on the other hand, it imbues them with the taste and the idea of unity, simplicity, and impartiality in the power that governs society. Men living in democratic times are therefore very prone to shake off all religious authority; but if they consent to subject themselves to any authority of this kind, they choose at least that it should be single and uniform. Religious powers not radiating from a common center are naturally repugnant to their minds; and they almost as readily conceive that there should be no religion as that there should be several.

At the present time, more than in any preceding age, Roman Catholics are seen to lapse into infidelity, and Protestants to be converted to Roman Catholicism. If you consider Catholicism within its own organization, it seems to be losing; if you consider it from outside, it seems to be gaining. Nor is this difficult to explain. The men of our days are naturally little disposed to believe; but as soon as they have any religion, they immediately find in themselves a latent instinct that urges them unconsciously towards Catholicism. Many of the doctrines and practices of the Roman Catholic Church astonish them, but they feel a secret admiration for its discipline, and its

第六章　天主教在美国的发展

美国是世界上最民主的国家,同时也是天主教发展最强盛的国家(根据可靠报道)。乍一看来人们会觉得惊讶。

有两件事必须明确地加以区分:平等虽使得人们勇于形成个人的观点,但是,从另一方面说,这也给人们的思想渗透了一些对于统一、单一和平等的统治社会的权力的喜爱和向往。因此,生活在民主时期的人们都倾向于不受任何宗教权威的束缚,但是如果他们自愿顺从于某种这类的权威之下的话,他们会选择至少这个权力必须是单一的统一的。不是从一个中心传播开来的宗教力量对人们思想的影响也不一致。所以他们就倾向于认为,与其有好多个宗教一起存在那就不如没有宗教。

在当前时代比在之前任何时代,都更使我们认为天主教徒已陷入了罪恶的境地,而基督教新教教徒却开始转信天主教。如果从天主教自身的组织来看,它好像是衰退了;而如果以旁观者的角度去看它,它是处于壮大的进程。这些都不难解释。我们这个时代的人们的天性,注定我们不会有虔诚的信仰,但如果这些人一旦下定决心,立刻就会觉得自身有一种潜在的本能在不知不觉地把他们推向天主教。罗马天主教会的很多教义和教规使他们

great unity attracts them. If Catholicism could at length withdraw itself from the political animosities to which it has given rise, I have hardly any doubt but that the same spirit of the age which appears to be so opposed to it would become so favorable as to admit of its great and sudden advancement.

One of the most ordinary weaknesses of the human intellect is to seek to reconcile contrary principles and to purchase peace at the expense of logic. Thus there have ever been and will ever be men who, after having submitted some portion of their religious belief to the principle of authority, will seek to exempt several other parts of their faith from it and to keep their minds floating at random between liberty and obedience. But I am inclined to believe that the number of these thinkers will be less in democratic than in other ages, and that our posterity will tend more and more to a division into only two parts, some relinquishing Christianity entirely and others returning to the Church of Rome.

吃惊,但在他们的内心却由衷地钦佩它的纪律,并且为教会的高度团结所吸引。如果最终天主教义能从自身引起的政治恩怨中全身而退,那么,我几乎可以肯定,这个似乎与它相抵触的时代精神,将会成为其伟大和进步的有力支持。

人类智商最常见的弱点之一,就是一直希望寻找途径调和互相对立的原则,不惜牺牲逻辑原则以求和解。因此,过去和现在以及将来总会有人在使自己的宗教信仰在某种程度上屈从于权威理论之下,然后又企图使自己的信仰在另一种程度上获得独立,于是,任思想在服从和自由之间随意摇摆。但是,我还是相信这样的人在民主时代会比在其他时代数量少些,而我们的后代将来必然会被两极分化:一些人会完全脱离基督教,而另一些人则皈依罗马教会。

CHAPTER VII

What Causes Democratic Nations
To Incline Towards Pantheism

I shall show hereafter how the preponderant taste of a democratic people for very general ideas manifests itself in politics, but I wish to point out at present its principal effect on philosophy.

It cannot be denied that pantheism has made great progress in our age. The writings of a part of Europe bear visible marks of it: the Germans introduce it into philosophy, and the French into literature. Most of the works of imagination published in France contain some opinions or some tinge caught from pantheistic doctrines or they disclose some tendency to such doctrines in their authors. This appears to me not to proceed only from an accidental, but from a permanent cause.

When the conditions of society are becoming more equal and each individual man becomes more like all the rest, more weak and insignificant, a habit grows up of ceasing to notice the citizens and considering only the people, of overlooking individuals to think only of their kind. At such times the human mind seeks to embrace a multitude of different objects at once, and it constantly strives to connect a variety of consequences with a single cause. The idea of unity so possesses man and is sought by him so generally that if he thinks he has found it, he readily yields himself to repose in that belief. Not content with the discovery that there is nothing in the world but a creation and a Creator, he is still embarrassed by

第七章　是什么原因使民主
国家倾向于泛神论

　　本来我想在后面谈谈民主国家的人民对一般观念的突出爱好是如何在政治方面表现的,但我现在就要指出它在哲学方面的主要作用。

　　不可否认,泛神论在我们的时代中取得了极大的发展。欧洲一些国家的作品中就有着明显的泛神论的色彩:德国人最先将其引入了哲学,接着法国人又将它带入了文学。法国出版的大部分虚构作品,就包含了一些泛神论的某些观点或蛛丝马迹,或者使人感到他们的作者有一种趋于这方面的倾向。在我看来,这种情况的出现并不是偶然现象,而有其久远的原因。

　　随着人们的社会地位趋于平等,个人与其他人的差别越来越小,个人变得很弱小而无力的时候,人们就逐渐变得不再关心单个公民而只注重全体人民了,考虑问题时也只考虑人类全体而不再关心个体。在这样的时期,人们的思想喜欢同时包含各种不同的事物,而且总是致力于将所有的结论都归结到一个单一的起因中去。统一的观念支配着人们,他们到处去寻找它。当人们认为自己找到这一观念的时候,就打算停下自己探索的脚步依靠它的信念过活了。然而,人们并不满足于发现世界只有一个造物主,并且世界万物都是由他所创造出来的。他们对自己的这种初

this primary division of things and seeks to expand and simplify his conception by including God and the universe in one great whole.

If there is a philosophical system which teaches that all things material and immaterial, visible and invisible, which the world contains are to be considered only as the several parts of an immense Being, who alone remains eternal amidst the continual change and ceaseless transformation of all that constitutes him, we may readily infer that such a system, although it destroy the individuality of man, or rather because it destroys that individuality, will have secret charms for men living in democracies. All their habits of thought prepare them to conceive it and predispose them to adopt it. It naturally attracts and fixes their imagination; it fosters the pride while it soothes the indolence of their minds.

Among the different systems by whose aid philosophy endeavors to explain the universe I believe pantheism to be one of those most fitted to seduce the human mind in democratic times. Against it all who abide in their attachment to the true greatness of man should combine and struggle.

步的发现感到不安,于是他们又试图扩展并简化自己的想法,即把神和宇宙融为一个单一的整体。

假如有一个哲学体系能把世界上的万物,不管是物质的还是非物质的,可见的还是无形的,均视为一个巨大载体的许多组成部分,而只有这个巨大载体能在其组成部分的不断变化和持续的转换当中永远存在下去,那么,我们就可以很容易得出:这个哲学体系,虽然它破坏了人的个性,但是也正因为它破坏了这种个性,而使生活在民主制度下的人具有神秘的魅力。人们的一切智力活动习惯都在引导人们去理解这一哲学体系,把人们领上接受这一体系的道路。这一哲学体系自然地吸引并锁定了人们的想象力,并提高人的精神自豪感和满足人的精神愉快感。

在帮助哲学致力于寻找解释宇宙万物的各种体系当中,我相信泛神论是最适于诱使笼络民主时代人心的。凡是坚信人类真正伟大的人们,都应当团结起来反对它。

CHAPTER VIII

How Equality Suggests To The Americans The Idea Of The Indefinite Perfectibility Of Man

Equality suggests to the human mind several ideas that would not have originated from any other source, and it modifies almost all those previously entertained. I take as an example the idea of human perfectibility, because it is one of the principal notions that the intellect can conceive and because it constitutes of itself a great philosophical theory, which is everywhere to be traced by its consequences in the conduct of human affairs.

Although man has many points of resemblance with the brutes, one trait is peculiar to himself: he improves; they are incapable of improvement. Mankind could not fail to discover this difference from the beginning. The idea of perfectibility is therefore as old as the world; equality did not give birth to it, but has imparted to it a new character.

When the citizens of a community are classed according to rank, profession, or birth and when all men are forced to follow the ca reer which chance has opened before them, everyone thinks that the utmost limits of human power are to be discerned in proximity to himself, and no one seeks any longer to resist the inevitable law of his destiny. Not, indeed, that an aristocratic people absolutely deny man's faculty of self-improvement, but they do not hold it to be indefinite; they can conceive amelioration, but not change: they imagine that the future condition of society may be better, but not essentially different; and, while they admit that humanity has made progress and may still have some to make, they assign to it beforehand certain impassable limits.

第八章　平等是怎样唤起美国人产生人可无限完善的观念的

平等带给人们一些想法，他们认为这些想法在其他时代不会产生，并且平等纠正了几乎之前所有时代的观念。我以人可完善性为例，因为这是人类智慧产生的重要的观念之一，同时它自身也有一套完整的伟大的哲学体系，并且处处都有其指导人类事物的痕迹。

尽管人们与动物在许多地方都有相似之处，但有一点却是人类所独具的，那就是，人类能够自我完善。人类在最初的时期，就发现了这一差别。因此，自我完善的观念存在于世界初始。平等并没有生出自我完善，但却赋予了自我完善以新的意义。

当公民被按照等级、职业和出身而分类的时候，所有人都不得不沿着机遇为他们提供的道路前进时，人人都会认为人类能力的最高界限几乎与自己同步，再没有人想去对抗不可抗拒的命运。事实上，贵族制国家的人民，并非完全否定自我完善能力，他们只是不认为这种完善能力是可以无限的。他们只想改进，不想变革。他们期望未来的社会条件会越变越好，但从不奢望发生根本性的变化。他们虽然承认人类至今已经取得了很大进步，而且今后也会有进步，但他们已预先把人类置于一个不可逾越的界限之内。

Thus they do not presume that they have arrived at the supreme good or at absolute truth (what people or what man was ever wild enough to imagine it?), but they cherish an opinion that they have pretty nearly reached that degree of greatness and knowledge which our imperfect nature admits of; and as nothing moves about them, they are willing to fancy that everything is in its fit place. Then it is that the legislator affects to lay down eternal laws; that kings and nations will raise none but imperishable monuments; and that the present generation undertakes to spare generations to come the care of regulating their destinies.

In proportion as castes disappear and the classes of society draw together, as manners, customs, and laws vary, because of the tumultuous intercourse of men, as new facts arise, as new truths are brought to light, as ancient opinions are dissipated and others take their place, the image of an ideal but always fugitive perfection presents itself to the human mind. Continual changes are then every instant occurring under the observation of every man; the position of some is rendered worse, and he learns but too well that no people and no individual, however enlightened they may be, can lay claim to infallibility; the condition of others is improved, whence he infers that man is endowed with an indefinite faculty for improve ment. His reverses teach him that none have discovered absolute good; his success stimulates him to the never ending pursuit of it. Thus, forever seeking, forever falling to rise again, often disappointed, but not discouraged, he tends unceasingly towards that unmeasured greatness so indistinctly visible at the end of the long track which humanity has yet to tread. It can hardly be believed how many facts naturally flow from the philosophical theory of the indefinite perfectibility of man or how strong an influence it exercises even on those who, living entirely for the purposes of action and not of thought, seem to conform their actions to it without knowing anything about it. I accost an American sailor and inquire why the ships of his country are built so as to last for only a short time; he answers without hesitation that the art of navigation is every day making such rapid

　　因此,他们并不认为自己已经达到至善或获得绝对真理(又有哪个民族或哪个人敢有如此妄想呢?),但他们怀有一个理念,那就是他们已经距离人类本身不够完善的本性所能达到的伟大和明智的最高程度很近了。同时,由于他们看到周围的一切都没有变动,所以就很自然地认为一切都各得其位。于是,立法者们喜欢颁布永久性的法律,国王和民族都只建造不朽的建筑物,当代人为后代承担着规划他们自己命运的责任。

　　随着等级的消失和社会各阶层的日益融合,仪礼、民情和法律也在变化;由于人们之间日益密切的交流,随着新事物的出现、新真理的发现、旧观点的消失和新观点的接替,人们思想中就会出现一个完美的形象,虽然它并不完美且多变。于是人们发现周围的事物无时无刻不在变化中。有些人的处境变坏了,于是他们开始清晰地认识到,一个民族或一个个体,无论多么有智慧,都不能永远不犯错误。虽然他们的这种认识过于偏激。还有人的处境变好了,于是他们由此断言,一般说来,人是有能力无限完善自己的。他的反面例证告诉他,没有人能达到尽善;而成功者本身的实例敦促自己,决不放弃追求新的成功。因此,人人都在不断追求,跌倒后再爬起来,虽然时时感到失望,但却从不绝望,于是人们向着人类企及的目标不断地前进着,虽然这一漫长道路的尽头是那么的渺茫而不可见。很难想象,这种认为人可无限完善的哲学理论,曾使人们心甘情愿地付出了多少,以及它对那些只在行动上与它有关而在思想上与它无涉,但在活动中又好像不知不觉地与它吻合的人发生了多么奇妙而巨大的影响。我曾问过一位美国船员,为什么美国的船不造得更结实一点。他不假思索地

progress that the finest vessel would become almost useless if it lasted beyond a few years. In these words, which fell accidentally, and on a particular subject, from an uninstructed man, I recognize the general and systematic idea upon which a great people direct all their concerns.

Aristocratic nations are naturally too liable to narrow the scope of human perfectibility; democratic nations, to expand it beyond reason.

回答说:航海技术的进步日新月异,再好的船用上几年之后也不能再用了。从这个并非专业人员就一个专业问题脱口而出的答话中,我看到了一个伟大民族凡事都遵循的一般的和有体系的观念。

贵族制国家从本性上会易于过多地限制人可完善的范围,而民主国家又有些扩大了这个范围。

CHAPTER IX

The Example Of The Americans Does Not Prove That A Democratic People Can Have No Aptitude And No Taste For Science, Literature, Or Art

It must be acknowledged that in few of the civilized nations of our time have the higher sciences made less progress than in the United States; and in few have great artists, distinguished poets, or celebrated writers been more rare. Many Europeans, struck by this fact, have looked upon it as a natural and inevitable result of equality; and they have thought that if a democratic state of society and democratic institutions were ever to prevail over the whole earth, the human mind would gradually find its beacon lights grow dim, and men would relapse into a period of darkness.

To reason thus is, I think, to confound several ideas that it is important to divide and examine separately; it is to mingle, unintentionally, what is democratic with what is only American.

The religion professed by the first immigrants and bequeathed by them to their descendants, simple in its forms, austere and almost harsh in its principles, and hostile to external symbols and to ceremonial pomp, is naturally unfavorable to the fine arts and yields only reluctantly to the pleasures of literature. The Americans are a very old and a very enlightened people, who have fallen upon a new and unbounded country, where they may extend themselves at pleasure and which they may fertilize without difficulty. This state of things is without a parallel in the history of the world. In America everyone finds facilities unknown elsewhere for making or increasing his fortune. The spirit of gain is always eager, and the human mind, constantly diverted from the pleasures of imagination and the labors of the intellect, is there swayed by no impulse but the pursuit of wealth. Not only are manufacturing and commercial classes to be found in the

第九章　美国人的例子并不能证明民主国家的人民对科学、文学和艺术没有天赋也不喜好

必须承认,在我们的时代,美国在高科技方面进步不大,而大艺术家、杰出的诗人和作家也很少。一些对此表示惊奇的欧洲人,就把它当作习以为常了,认为这是平等的必然结果,他们认为如果一个社会的民主政府和体制马上席卷全球,那么指引着人们的思想的灯塔也会逐渐暗淡,人们又将陷入黑暗之中。

我认为,推论这一切的人将几点重要的必须加以区别并单独进行考虑的观念混淆起来了。他们无意中把民主的东西和美国人独有的东西混在一起了。

初期移民信奉并传给他们后代的宗教,虽然在仪式上简单,但在教义上却严肃得近乎苛刻。它反对外在的浮夸,反对繁文缛节。这样的宗教,自然不利于艺术的发展,只能衍生出消遣性文艺。美国是一个非常古老而又开化的民族。美国人后来迁到一个使他们可以任意开发的有肥沃土地的地方。这对一个国家来说在世界史上是绝无仅有的。在美国,每个人都在利用其他地方根本不知道的便利条件创造和增长着自己的财富。他们的欲求总是很强烈,同时,不断地从对于幸福的想象和理性的劳动中开溜的人类的思想,在不受任何影响的情况下,总是为财富所吸引。

United States, as they are in all other countries, but, what never occurred elsewhere, the whole community is simultaneously engaged in productive industry and commerce.

I am convinced, however, that if the Americans had been alone in the world, with the freedom and the knowledge acquired by their forefathers and the passions which are their own, they would not have been slow to discover that progress cannot long be made in the application of the sciences without cultivating the theory of them; that all the arts are perfected by one another: and, however absorbed they might have been by the pursuit of the principal object of their desires, they would speedily have admitted that it is necessary to turn aside from it occasionally in order the better to attain it in the end.

The taste for the pleasures of mind, moreover, is so natural to the heart of civilized man that among the highly civilized nations, which are least disposed to give themselves up to these pursuits, a certain number of persons is always to be found who take part in them. This intellectual craving, once felt, would very soon have been satisfied.

But at the very time when the Americans were naturally inclined to require nothing of science but its special applications to the useful arts and the means of rendering life comfortable, learned and literary Europe was engaged in exploring the common sources of truth and in improving at the same time all that can minister to the pleasures or satisfy the wants of man.

At the head of the enlightened nations of the Old World the inhabitants of the United States more particularly identified one to which they were closely united by a common origin and by kindred habits. Among this people they found distinguished men of science, able artists, writers of eminence; and they were enabled to enjoy the treasures of the intellect without laboring to amass them. In spite of the ocean that intervenes, I cannot consent to separate America from Europe. I consider the people of the United States as that portion of the English people who are commissioned to explore the forests of the New World, while the rest of the nation, enjoying more leisure and less harassed by the drudgery of life, may devote their energies to thought

在美国,不仅仅有制造业和商业阶层的人们,而且还存在其他国家所没有的现象,即美国整个社会都沉浸在工业生产和商业制造之中。

但是,我敢肯定,假如世界上只剩美国人了,而他们仍然保留着祖先遗留的自由和知识,同时拥有他们自有的激情,那么,他们很快就会发现:不研究理论,科学的实用性是无法长足发展的,而一切艺术也只有互相影响才能得到完善。并且,不论如何全神贯注,在他们欲望驱使下对主要的目标追求中,他们很快就会承认,有时从这种追求中脱离出来,也是为了更好地实现这种追求。

除此之外,对于文明的人们,他们很自然就会有在精神上的享受,因此在高度文明的国家中,他们拒绝放弃对精神享受的追求,而且总有一些人在致力于此。这种对智力的追求,一旦被人们感知,就会很快得到满足。

但是,当美国人完全不顾科学的实际运用而只注重追求实用的艺术和使生活变得舒适的途径的时候,重视学术和文化的欧洲人已经在致力于探求真理共同的源泉并同时完善一切人们可以得到的享乐和人们应当得到满足的需要。

在旧大陆所有开化民族中最突出的,美国居民多倾向于承认一个民族。他们与这个民族依靠共同的起源和相似的习俗而紧密地联系在一起。在这些人中,他们发现了杰出的科学家、才华横溢的艺术家和伟大的作家;他们也能够从中汲取知识财富而免除了为积累这些财富而付出的辛劳。除了两者之间的大洋,我不认为还有什么可以将美国从欧洲隔离开。我认为,美国人民作为来新大陆的那一部分英国人,他们致力于开发新大陆的荒野丛林,而另一部分英国人则相对来说享受了更多的悠闲而少了一些疲于奔命的辛劳,才因此能

and enlarge in all directions the empire of mind.

The position of the Americans is therefore quite exceptional, and it may be believed that no democratic people will ever be placed in a similar one. Their strictly Puritanical origin, their exclusively commercial habits, even the country they inhabit, which seems to divert their minds from the pursuit of science, literature, and the arts, the proximity of Europe, which allows them to neglect these pursuits without relapsing into barbarism, a thousand special causes, of which I have only been able to point out the most important, have singularly concurred to fix the mind of the American upon purely practical objects. His passions, his wants, his education, and everything about him seem to unite in drawing the native of the United States earthward; his religion alone bids him turn, from time to time, a transient and distracted glance to heaven. Let us cease, then, to view all democratic nations under the example of the American people, and attempt to survey them at length with their own features.

It is possible to conceive a people not subdivided into any castes or scale of ranks, among whom the law, recognizing no privileges, should divide inherited property into equal shares, but which at the same time should be without knowledge and without freedom. Nor is this an empty hypothesis: a despot may find that it is his interest to render his subjects equal and to leave them ignorant, in order more easily to keep them slaves. Not only would a democratic people of this kind show neither aptitude nor taste for science, literature, or art, but it would probably never arrive at the possession of them. The law of descent would of itself provide for the destruction of large fortunes at each succeeding generation, and no new fortunes would be acquired. The poor man, without either knowledge or freedom, would not so much as conceive the idea of raising himself to wealth; and the rich man would allow himself to be degraded to poverty, without a notion of selfdefense. Between these two members of the community complete and invincible equality would soon be established. No one

有机会投入更多的精力去思考和在各个方面扩展思维。

因此，美国人所处的位置相当特殊，也许我们也可以相信，没有哪个民主国家能被置于与他们相同的处境。他们严厉的清教徒渊源，他们独一无二的商业习俗，甚至他们居住的国家也似乎将他们的思想转离了对科学、文学和艺术的追求，而他们的欧洲邻居使他们即使放弃了对这些的追求也不至于重返野蛮状态。有很多的原因一起作用使美国人的思想牢牢地锁定纯物质方面的东西，而对这些原因，我只能就其最重要的加以指出。人们的激情、需求、教育和他所处的环境都仿佛联合起来迫使美国人民面对现实。他所信仰的宗教也只能使其偶尔仰头心烦意乱的向着天堂的方向匆忙一瞥。所以，让我们停止再在美国人民影响下去推断其他的民主国家，而尝试着根据他们自己的特点去研究他们。

我们可以假想一个没有被等级划分的民族，在这样的民族中，所有的法律中都不存在特权，并且法律规定将遗产平均分配，但同时，人们也就没有了知识和自由。这并不是凭空构想的。因为对一位专制君主来说，他会发现自己很有兴趣使自己的臣民处于平等的地位，并使他们变得愚昧无知，因为这样做可以使他的臣民更加容易处于被奴役状态。不仅仅是这类民主的人民没有倾向也没有兴趣研究科学、文化或者艺术，而且他们永远也不会有这样的才能。继承法本身就是将大量集中的财产在继承者的一代划分为更小的部分，没有谁去攫取新的财富。那些贫穷的人们，既没有知识，也没有自由，因此根本就不会产生任何希望增加自己财富的想法。而富人们则使自己的财富越来越少，却没有任何防范意识。在社会这两种成员之间，很快就建立起了一种完全

would then have time or taste to devote himself to the pursuits or pleasures of the intellect, but all men would remain paralyzed in a state of common ignorance and equal servitude.

When I conceive a democratic society of this kind, I fancy myself in one of those low, close, and gloomy abodes where the light which breaks in from without soon faints and fades away. A sudden heaviness overpowers me, and I grope through the surrounding darkness to find an opening that will restore me to the air and the light of day. But all this is not applicable to men already enlightened who retain their freedom after having abolished those peculiar and hereditary rights which perpetuated the tenure of property in the hands of certain individuals or certain classes.

When men living in a democratic state of society are enlightened, they readily discover that they are not confined and fixed by any limits which force them to accept their present fortune. They all, therefore, conceive the idea of increasing it. If they are free, they all attempt it, but all do not succeed in the same manner. The legislature, it is true, no longer grants privileges, but nature grants them. As natural inequality is very great, fortunes become unequal as soon as every man exerts all his faculties to get rich.

The law of descent prevents the establishment of wealthy families, but it does not prevent the existence of wealthy individuals. It constantly brings back the members of the community to a common level, from which they as constantly escape; and the inequality of fortunes augments in proportion as their knowledge is diffused and their liberty increased.

A sect which arose in our time and was celebrated for its talents and its extravagance proposed to concentrate all property in the hands of a central power, whose function it should afterwards be to parcel it out to individuals according to their merits. This would have been a method of escaping from that complete and eternal equality which seems to threaten democratic society. But it would be a simpler and

的无法抗拒的平等。没有人有时间或者兴趣投入到对智力的追求和享受之中，但是所有的人却都在一种普遍的无知和平等地受到奴役的状态下麻木地生活着。

我一想到这样的民主社会，就会觉得自己好像置身于一所低矮、封闭和阴暗的小房子里，外面有时射进一道光线，很快就变得微弱而终于消失。想到这，我突然觉得心中沉闷得喘不过气来；我在黑暗中四下摸索，希望找到一个出口可以到外面吸点空气和见到阳光。但是，这些假想，并不适用于开化已久，在废除规定财产永久归于某些个人或某些团体的特殊法令和继承法以后仍然保有自由的民族。

当生活在民主社会里的人民是受到过教育的时候，他们不难明白没有任何东西限制和迫使他们接受现状。因此，他们每个人都要想方设法去改进现状。而如果他们都是自由的，则每个人都将努力尝试，虽然不一定获得同样的成果。当然，立法机构不会再给予人们特权，但天赋会给予人们以这种特权。天生的不平等带来的差距很大，所以财富也将因每个人运用其才智去致富的情况而不均。

继承法虽然阻碍了富裕家族的建立，但它并没有阻止富人存在。继承法在不断使公民们趋于相同的水平，而公民们也在不断使自己逃避这一趋势。随着公民的知识日益提高和他们的自由日益扩大，他们的财富也愈加不平等。

有一派崛起在我们这个时代并因其才华和狂妄而出名的人士主张，先将一切财富集中于一个中央当局之手。而这个中央当局的职责就是，将这些财富按照每个人的贡献分配给所有的人。这也许是个方法，可以帮助逃离那种似乎威胁到民主社会的完全

less dangerous remedy to grant no privilege to any, giving to all equal cultivation and equal independence and leaving everyone to determine his own position. Natural inequality will soon make way for itself, and wealth will spontaneously pass into the hands of the most capable.

Free and democratic communities, then, will always contain a multitude of people enjoying opulence or a competency. The wealthy will not be so closely linked to one another as the members of the former aristocratic class of society; their inclinations will be different, and they will scarcely ever enjoy leisure as secure or complete; but they will be far more numerous than those who belonged to that class of society could ever be. These persons will not be strictly confined to the cares of practical life, and they will still be able, though in different degrees, to indulge in the pursuits and pleasures of the intellect. In those pleasures they will indulge, for if it is true that the human mind leans on one side to the limited, the material, and the useful, it naturally rises on the other to the infinite, the spiritual, and the beautiful. Physical wants confine it to the earth, but as soon as the tie is loosened, it will rise of itself.

Not only will the number of those who can take an interest in the productions of mind be greater, but the taste for intellectual enjoyment will descend step by step even to those who in aristocratic societies seem to have neither time nor ability to indulge in them. When hereditary wealth, the privileges of rank, and the prerogatives of birth have ceased to be and when every man derives his strength from himself alone, it becomes evident that the chief cause of disparity between the fortunes of men is the mind. Whatever tends to invigorate, to extend, or to adorn the mind rises instantly to a high value. The utility of knowledge becomes singularly conspicuous even to the eyes of the multitude; those who have no taste for its charms set store upon its results and make some efforts to acquire it.

In free and enlightened democratic times there is nothing to separate men from one another or to retain them in their place; they rise

的和永恒的平等。但是应该还有一种更简单和危险性小的补救措施:这就是不让任何人享有特权,给予每个人以同等的受教育权利和平等的独立地位,让每个人自己决定自己的地位。天生的不平等很快就会为自己创造机会,而这时财富也自然将落入那些最有能力的人们的手中。

因此,自由而民主的社会里总会有一批富裕或有能力的人。这些富人之间,不会像之前的贵族制度下那样联系紧密。他们的本性也有区别,他们没有时间去享乐,但他们的人数将比之前任何富有阶级的人数都多得多。这些人不会整天局限于对物质生活的奔波之中,他们也会不同程度地进行一些精神生活方面的追求和享受。在他们所沉溺的这种享乐中,如果人们的精神在某一方面倾向于限定某一物质的和实用的极限,另一方面还当需要有一个无限精神的和美好的目标。对于物质的需要使人的精神限定在现世,但一旦物质的需要的纽带与人的精神松懈的时候,人的精神需求就会自发而生。

不仅仅是注重精神享受的人数将要大大增加,而且对于智力活动的爱好也将会被逐步延续到贵族时代那些既没有时间也没有能力从事这种活动的人们当中去。当不再存在世袭财产、阶级特权和门第优越感,而每个人只能依靠自己的努力的时候,造成财富差距的原因很明显就只能取决于人的智力。无论什么,只要它可以激发、扩大或者提升智力就立即会升值。对于知识的运用即使是在大众的眼中,也会变得异常显著。那些没有感受到知识的魅力的人们,也将尊重知识所作出的成绩并努力去获取知识创造的成果。

在自由、开明的民主时代,没有任何力量可以把人们分开,或

or sink with extreme rapidity. All classes mingle together because they live so close together. They communicate and intermingle every day; they imitate and emulate one another. This suggests to the people many ideas, notions, and desires that they would never have entertained if the distinctions of rank had been fixed and society at rest. In such nations the servant never considers himself as an entire stranger to the pleasures and toils of his master, nor the poor man to those of the rich; the farmer tries to resemble the townsman, and the provinces to take after the metropolis. No one easily allows himself to be reduced to the mere material cares of life; and the humblest artisan casts at times an eager and a furtive glance into the higher regions of the intellect. People do not read with the same notions or in the same manner as they do in aristocratic communities, but the circle of readers is unceasingly expanded, till it includes all the people.

As soon as the multitude begins to take an interest in the labors of the mind, it finds out that to excel in some of them is a powerful means of acquiring fame, power, or wealth. The restless ambition that equality begets instantly takes this direction, as it does all others. The number of those who cultivate science, letters, and the arts, becomes immense. The intellectual world starts into prodigious activity; everyone endeavors to open for himself a path there and to draw the eyes of the public after him. Something analogous occurs to what happens in society in the United States politically considered. What is done is often imperfect, but the attempts are innumerable; and although the results of individual effort are commonly very small, the total amount is always very large.

It is therefore not true to assert that men living in democratic times are naturally indifferent to science, literature, and the arts; only it must be acknowledged that they cultivate them after their own fashion and bring to the task their own peculiar qualifications and deficiencies.

使人们固定不变。人们发迹或破产的速度异常得迅速。各个阶级因为集中居住在一起而相互融合。他们每天都不断地进行交流和相互融合，彼此模仿。这激发了很多想法、观念和思想，而这在等级制度森严或社会停滞的时代是不可产生的。在这样的民族里，无论仆人和主人，或是穷人和富人，都可以共同享乐和劳动；乡下人努力学习城里人，地方尝试着学习首都。这样一来，没有人会使自己局限在物质生活方面的关心，即使是最卑微的手艺人也会贪婪地偷偷地窥视智慧成就的高一级的世界。人们不再带着贵族制国家采用的那种观点和方法去学习；但是，读书人的范围会不断地扩大，直到囊括了全人类。

一旦人们开始关心精神劳动，他们就会发现只有在某些方面胜过其他人，才能取得荣誉、权力和财富。基于平等的基础，人们产生的在其他方面的跃跃欲试的野心也立刻会转到这一方面来。研究科学、文学和艺术的人数越来越多。知识界开始变得生机勃勃。每个人都想要为自己打开通往知识界的大门，并吸引公众跟随着自己。一些类似于在美国政界所发生的事情正在上演。他们所作的工作虽称不上完美，但是数量众多。尽管个人努力的结果一般来说都微不足道，但是合起来的总成果却总是不容小觑的。

因此，声称生活在民主时代的人天生就不关心科学、文学与艺术是不正确的；唯一值得人们承认的是，他们按照自己的方法发展自己，并且给这一工作赋予了他们特有的品质和缺憾。

CHAPTER X

Why The Americans Are More Addicted
To Practical Than To Theoretical Science

If a democratic state of society and democratic institutions do not retard the onward course of the human mind, they incontestably guide it in one direction in preference to another. Their efforts, thus circumscribed, are still exceedingly great, and I may be pardoned if I pause for a moment to contemplate them.

I had occasion, in speaking of the philosophical method of the American people, to make several remarks that it is necessary to make use of here.

Equality begets in man the desire of judging of everything for himself; it gives him in all things a taste for the tangible and the real, a contempt for tradition and for forms. These general tendencies are principally discernible in the peculiar subject of this chapter.

Those who cultivate the sciences among a democratic people are always afraid of losing their way in visionary speculation. They mistrust systems; they adhere closely to facts and study facts with their own senses. As they do not easily defer to the mere name of any fellow man, they are never inclined to rest upon any man's authority; but, on the contrary, they are unremitting in their efforts to find out the weaker points of their neighbors' doctrine.

Scientific precedents have little weight with them; they are never long detained by the subtlety of the schools nor ready to accept big words for sterling coin; they penetrate, as far as they can, into the

第十章　美国人在科学方面关注实践多于理论的原因

如果说民主的社会情况和制度没有抑制人类精神的发展,则它们必然不是从这一方面就是从另一方面推动了它。它们的作用虽然有限,却仍然十分强大。请允许我稍停片刻,先来谈一谈它们的作用。

我曾在讲述美国人的哲学方法时提出的几个论点,在这里也一定有用。

平等使每个人都希望凡事自己判断,对一切事物都抱着务实的态度,不注重传统和形式。民主的这些一般本性将会在这一章节中加以单独讨论。

在民主国家研究科学的人,总害怕自己陷入空想而迷失方向。他们不信任制度,而是凭自己的感觉紧抓事实进行研究。他们既不会仅凭某一同行的名气就轻易地加以相信,也从不依附于某一权威的论断。与此相反,他们不断地去寻找这些人或权威教义的弱点。

学术先例对他们的作用很小,他们从未长久地被一些学派的繁琐理论所牵绊,也不会不假思索地全盘接受某位伟人的经典论述。他们总是尽可能地深入研究那些研究对象的主要部分,并尽量用大众的语言加以说明。这样一来,科学的探索的过

principal parts of the subject that occupies them, and they like to expound them in the popular language. Scientific pursuits then follow a freer and safer course, but a less lofty one.

The mind, it appears to me, may divide science into three parts.

The first comprises the most theoretical principles and those more abstract notions whose application is either unknown or very remote.

The second is composed of those general truths that still belong to pure theory, but lead nevertheless by a straight and short road to practical results.

Methods of application and means of execution make up the third.

Each of these different portions of science may be separately cultivated, although reason and experience prove that no one of them can prosper long if it is absolutely cut off from the two others.

In America the purely practical part of science is admirably understood, and careful attention is paid to the theoretical portion which is immediately requisite to application. On this head the Americans always display a clear, free, original, and inventive power of mind. But hardly anyone in the United States devotes himself to the essentially theoretical and abstract portion of human knowledge. In this respect the Americans carry to excess a tendency that is, I think, discernible, though in a less degree, among all democratic nations.

Nothing is more necessary to the culture of the higher sciences or of the more elevated departments of science than meditation; and nothing is less suited to meditation than the structure of democratic society. We do not find there, as among an aristocratic people, one class that keeps quiet because it is well off; and another that does not venture to stir because it despairs of improving its condition. Everyone is in motion, some in quest of power, others of gain. In the midst of this universal tumult, this incessant conflict of jarring interests, this continual striving of men after fortune, where is that calm to be found which is necessary for the deeper combinations of the intellect? How

程虽不如以前高大,但却遵循着一条比以前更自由更准确的道路前进着。

在我看来,如果依照人的精神来划分,科学可以被分为三个部分。

第一部分包括一些最纯粹的理论原理和一些更为抽象的概念,尽管对于它们的应用目前还不了解或者以后很久也不会被知道。

第二部分包括那些还属于纯理论范围但通过直接便捷的途径就可以应用的一般真理。

第三部分包括应用的方法和执行的方式。

科学的这三个不同部分的每一部分都可以被单独地进行研究,尽管人们的推论和经验证明,如果其中任何一个部分与其余两者完全隔离,它就不可能长期地存在下去。

在美国,科学的纯应用部分已为人们完全接受,而在科学的理论方面,人们只注重研究那些急需付诸实践的部分。而在这方面,美国人经常表现出求真、自由、大胆和创新的精神。但是在美国,却很难有人能够专心研究人类知识在本质上属于理论和抽象的那一部分。在这方面,我认为美国人把一种倾向表现得非常明显,尽管这种倾向在所有的民主国家都存在,但却不如在美国那么明显。

对高等科学或科学的高级部分的研究,沉思是最关键的。而在民主社会内部,沉思则成了最不需要的部分。在民主社会,既没有贵族制国家中的那种因为生活富足而从容淡定的阶级,也没有那种因为无望改善处境而不思进取的阶级。每个人都在积极活动:有的希望获得权力,有的希望获得财富。在这种全民的混乱环境中,尖锐的利益矛盾造成不断的冲突,人们不断追求财富,

can the mind dwell upon any single point when everything whirls a-round it, and man himself is swept and beaten onwards by the heady current that rolls all things in its course?

You must make the distinction between the sort of permanent agitation that is characteristic of a peaceful democracy and the tumultuous and revolutionary movements that almost always attend the birth and growth of democratic society. When a violent revolution occurs among a highly civilized people, it cannot fail to give a sudden impulse to their feelings and ideas. This is more particularly true of democratic revolutions, which stir up at once all the classes of which a people is composed and beget at the same time inordinate ambition in the breast of every member of the community. The French made surprising advances in the exact sciences at the very time at which they were finishing the destruction of the remains of their former feudal society; yet this sudden fecundity is not to be attributed to democracy, but to the unexampled revolution that attended its growth. What happened at that period was a special incident, and it would be unwise to regard it as the test of a general principle.

Great revolutions are not more common among democratic than among other nations; I am even inclined to believe that they are less so. But there prevails among those populations a small, distressing motion, a sort of incessant jostling of men, which annoys and disturbs the mind without exciting or elevating it.

Men who live in democratic communities not only seldom indulge in meditation, but they naturally entertain very little esteem for it. A democratic state of society and democratic institutions keep the greater part of men in constant activity; and the habits of mind that are suited to an active life are not always suited to a contemplative one. The man of action is frequently obliged to content himself with the best he can get because he would never accomplish his purpose if he chose to carry every detail to perfection. He has occasion perpetually to rely on ideas that he has not had leisure to search to the bottom;

哪有智者深思所必需的安静处所呢？当你周围的一切都在活动，而你本身已被卷入席卷万物的激流，并且每天都被迫随着激流前进的时候，你怎么能停下来思考高级科学呢？

你必须把建立已久的和平的民主社会中发生的经常性运动，与几乎是伴随民主社会的诞生和发展而发生的骚乱性和革命性的运动加以区分。当一个高度文明的国家发生暴力革命时，人们的情感和思想会突然受到刺激。而在发生民主革命时，情况亦是如此。因为这个革命不仅把民族的所有阶级都发动起来了，而且会同时使每个公民的心中产生巨大的野心。如果说法国人在消灭旧封建社会残余的同时，使精密科学获得了骄人发展的话，那么，这个意外成果的来因并不在于民主，而应当把它归功于这场前所未有的革命。在这样的情况下取得的成果是一个偶然现象，而如果把它视为遵循一般规律的事件，则是不明智的想法。

我认为大革命的发生在民主国家不会比在其他国家多，我甚至倾向于认为只会比其他国家少。但是，在民主国家里，却充满了一些轻微的令人厌烦的运动，比如人们之间产生的不断地互相排斥。这种运动起不到激发和振奋的作用，只会扰乱和涣散人心。

生活在民主社会的人们不仅很少沉思，而且对这种思维活动也天生不够重视。民主的社会情况和制度，使大部分人总是保持运动的状态。而这种适于动态的习惯，并不总是适于静静地沉思。处于不断运动状态的人，就得常常迫使自己满足于所能获得的一切，因为如果他们想使自己追求的一切细节都达到完美，就永远也无法实现自己预期的目的。因此，他们经常需要借助一些合时宜的思考，因此这种思想的正确性本身就显得不那么

for he is much more frequently aided by the seasonableness of an idea than by its strict accuracy; and in the long run he risks less in making use of some false principles than in spending his time in establishing all his principles on the basis of truth. The world is not led by long or learned demonstrations; a rapid glance at particular incidents, the daily study of the fleeting passions of the multitude, the accidents of the moment, and the art of turning them to account decide all its affairs. In the ages in which active life is the condition of almost everyone, men are generally led to attach an excessive value to the rapid bursts and superficial conceptions of the intellect, and on the other hand to undervalue unduly its slower and deeper labors. This opinion of the public influences the judgment of the men who cultivate the sciences; they are persuaded that they may succeed in those pursuits without meditation, or are deterred from such pursuits as demand it.

There are several methods of studying the sciences. Among a multitude of men you will find a selfish, mercantile, and trading taste for the discoveries of the mind, which must not be confounded with that disinterested passion which is kindled in the heart of a few. A desire to utilize knowledge is one thing; the pure desire to know is another. I do not doubt that in a few minds and at long intervals an ardent, inexhaustible love of truth springs up, self-supported and living in ceaseless fruition, without ever attaining full satisfaction. It is this ardent love, this proud, disinterested love of what is true, that raises men to the abstract sources of truth, to draw their mother knowledge thence.

If Pascal had had nothing in view but some large gain, or even if he had been stimulated by the love of fame alone, I cannot conceive that he would ever have been able to rally all the powers of his mind, as he did, for the better discovery of the most hidden things of the Creator. When I see him, as it were, tear his soul from all the cares of life to devote it wholly to these researches and, prematurely snapping the links that bind the body to life, die of old age before forty, I stand amazed and perceive that no ordinary cause is at work to produce efforts so extraordinary.

重要了。总的说来,他使用一些错误的原理而冒的风险远比费时使一切原理正确无误所冒的风险更小些。何况这个世界也不是依据长久不变的和学术理论而运动的。对某一特殊现象的粗略了解,对大众千变万化的激情和对大事件的经常研究,以及利用这些情况的技术决定着世界上的一切事情。在这个几乎社会上所有的人都富有激情的时代,人们一般都高估了智力的快速成果和一些肤浅的论证,而另一方面则错误地轻视缓进而深刻的智力劳动的成果。这样的公众舆论影响着进行科学研究的人们的判断,并使他们相信:不用沉思也可以在研究当中获得成果,或者在对那些需要沉思的科学进行研究的时候受到阻碍。

研究科学的方法有很多。许多人对于智力活动得出的发明,有一种利己主义的,即把它们用于工商业的爱好。不应当把这种爱好同少数人心中燃起的无私的激情混为一谈。前者是为了一己的利益而利用知识,而后者纯粹的对知识的追求的渴望则是完全另一回事。我毫不怀疑,经过很长一段时间后,在一些人们的思想中就会产生一种强烈的、永不衰竭的对真理的热爱之情。这种热爱之情只靠自己成长起来并不断壮大,并且永远不会感到自满。正是因为这种激情、这种骄傲和对真理的无私的热爱使人们接触到了真理的抽象的源泉并从那里汲取到最初的知识。

如果帕斯卡的眼中只有某种名利,或者甚至他只为了名誉而行为,那么我不相信他会像他所作的那样,倾尽自己所有的力量只为了揭开造物主深藏的秘密。当我想到他仿佛抛开了人生的一切杂念,全神专注于这项研究,以致过早地耗尽心力,不到40岁就离开人世时,不禁感佩不已。而且我认为,绝不是任何一种平常的原因能使他付出如此非凡的努力。

The future will prove whether these passions, at once so rare and so productive, come into being and into growth as easily in the midst of democratic as in aristocratic communities. For myself, I confess that I am slow to believe it.

In aristocratic societies the class that gives the tone to opinion and has the guidance of affairs, being permanently and hereditarily placed above the multitude, naturally conceives a lofty idea of itself and of man. It loves to invent for him noble pleasures, to carve out splendid objects for his ambition. Aristocracies often commit very tyrannical and inhuman actions, but they rarely entertain groveling thoughts; and they show a kind of haughty contempt of little pleasures, even while they indulge in them. The effect is to raise greatly the general pitch of society. In aristocratic ages vast ideas are commonly entertained of the dignity, the power, and the greatness of man. These opinions exert their influence on those who cultivate the sciences as well as on the rest of the community. They facilitate the natural impulse of the mind to the highest regions of thought, and they naturally prepare it to conceive a sublime, almost a divine love of truth.

Men of science at such periods are consequently carried away towards theory; and it even happens that they frequently conceive an inconsiderate contempt for practice. "Archimedes," says Plutarch, "was of so lofty a spirit that he never condescended to write any treatise on the manner of constructing all these engines of war. And as he held this science of inventing and putting together engines, and all arts generally speaking which tended to any useful end in practice, to be vile, low, and mercenary, he spent his talents and his studious hours in writing only of those things whose beauty and subtlety had in them no admixture of necessity." Such is the aristocratic aim of science; it cannot be the same in democratic nations.

The greater part of the men who constitute these nations are extremely eager in the pursuit of actual and physical gratification. As they

在贵族制社会出现的如此罕见和如此丰产的求知热情,将来是否也会出现于民主社会。我坦白承认,对于我,我还难于相信这一点。

在贵族制社会中,那些拥有话语权并有权指导社会事务的阶级,总是永久性的或者通过继承权居于大众之上的。这些人天生对自己的阶层和人类抱着一种高高在上的观念。这个阶级热爱发明出各种手段使自己享受贵族的荣誉,为自己的远大抱负定出宏伟的目标。贵族虽然常常会作出极其残暴和不人道的行为,但很少会产生低级下流的想法。即使他们会沉迷于一些小型娱乐,但对它们却抱着一种轻视的心态。他们的这种表现,却也间接地提高了一般人的思想境界。在贵族时代,人们对大多数事物的看法都充满敬意,像权力和人类的伟大。这些观念不仅将其影响力威及那些进行科学研究的人们,并且威及其余的大众群体。促使人们的观念自然地趋向更高的层面,并使人们自然产生一种更严肃,近乎神圣地对真理的热爱之情。

因此在这些时期研究科学的人都倾向于对理论的研究,并且常常甚至产生了对实践的轻视心理。希腊的历史学家曾说过:"阿基米得的治学精神,崇高到不肯自贬身价去撰写一部制造兵器的著作的地步。在他看来,关于发明和组装机器的一切科学,以及一般与应用有某种实利关系的一切技艺,都是没有价值的、卑贱的和向钱看的。他把自己的精力和研究全部用于撰写其美处和妙处跟实际需要毫无关系的著作方面。"这就是贵族阶级对研究科学的目的,与民主国家的目的不可能相同。

在这些国家中生活的大部分人们都处于极度的追求现实和

are always dissatisfied with the position that they occupy and are always free to leave it, they think of nothing but the means of changing their fortune or increasing it. To minds thus predisposed, every new method that leads by a shorter road to wealth, every machine that spares labor, every instrument that diminishes the cost of production, every discovery that facilitates pleasures or augments them, seems to be the grandest effort of the human intellect. It is chiefly from these motives that a democratic people addicts itself to scientific pursuits, that it understands and respects them. In aristocratic ages science is more particularly called upon to furnish gratification to the mind; in democracies, to the body.

You may be sure that the more democratic, enlightened, and free a nation is, the greater will be the number of these interested promoters of scientific genius and the more will discoveries immediately applicable to productive industry confer on their authors gain, fame, and even power. For in democracies the working class take a part in public affairs; and public honors as well as pecuniary remuneration may be awarded to those who deserve them.

In a community thus organized, it may easily be conceived that the human mind may be led insensibly to the neglect of theory; and that it is urged, on the contrary, with unparalleled energy, to the applications of science, or at least to that portion of theoretical science which is necessary to those who make such applications. In vain will some instinctive inclination raise the mind towards the loftier spheres of the intellect; interest draws it down to the middle zone. There it may develop all its energy and restless activity and bring forth wonders. These very Americans who have not discovered one of the general laws of mechanics have introduced into navigation an instrument that changes the aspect of the world.

Assuredly I do not contend that the democratic nations of our time are destined to witness the extinction of the great luminaries of man's intelligence, or even that they will never bring new lights into

物质满足的欲望之中。因为他们总是对他们所处的地位心怀不满并随时可以脱离这种处境,所以他们除了考虑改变命运或增加财富的途径之外,其余的什么都不想。对于倾向于保有这样的思想的人,每一种通往财富的捷径的新方法,任何一种节约劳力的机器,每一种减少生产费用的设备,每一种有利于或者可以提升享乐的发现,都是人类智慧最伟大的努力成果。民主国家的人民主要是从这些动机出发沉溺于对它所理解和尊重的科学的追求的。在贵族制时期,科学更多的是用来满足人们精神上的需求的;在民主社会,则主要是用于肉体上的享受。

你可以想象,一个越是民主、开明和自由的国家中,对这些感兴趣的具备科学天赋的推进者的人数就越多,而能够直接应用于生产型工业的发明,也越能使其发明者得到更多的名利,甚至权力。因为在民主社会,劳动阶级参加政务,而为政府服务的那些人,则要从那里获得声望和报酬。

不难想象,以这种方式组织起来的社会,人的思想会被一种不知不觉的意识导向对理论的忽视。这反而要求人们要以无比的精力去追求科学的应用,至少也要去追求对于应用不可缺少的那一部分科学理论。即使本能的求知欲使人的精神上升到高层次的智力活动领域,也不起任何作用,因为现实的利益会将人们拉回平庸的领域。在这个平庸的领域,人的精神才能发挥它的力量和持久的活跃状态,展示出其神奇的力量。正是这些连机械力学的一个普通定理都没有发现的美国人,为航运业引进了一部足以改变世界海运面貌的新机器。

当然,我并不是说,当代的民主国家注定要见证人类智慧之光逐渐暗淡,更不是说它们不能再发出新的光芒。世界如今发展

existence. At the age at which the world has now arrived, and among so many cultivated nations perpetually excited by the fever of productive industry, the bonds that connect the different parts of science cannot fail to strike the observer; and the taste for practical science itself, if it is enlightened, ought to lead men not to neglect theory. In the midst of so many attempted applications of so many experiments repeated every day, it is almost impossible that general laws should not frequently be brought to light; so that great discoveries would be frequent, though great inventors may be few.

I believe, moreover, in high scientific vocations. If the democratic principle does not, on the one hand, induce men to cultivate science for its own sake, on the other it enormously increases the number of those who do cultivate it. Nor is it credible that among so great a multitude a speculative genius should not from time to time arise inflamed by the love of truth alone. Such a one, we may be sure, would dive into the deepest mysteries of nature, whatever the spirit of his country and his age. He requires no assistance in his course; it is enough that he is not checked in it. All that I mean to say is this: permanent inequality of conditions leads men to confine themselves to the arrogant and sterile research for abstract truths, while the social condition and the institutions of democracy prepare them to seek the immediate and useful practical results of the sciences. This tendency is natural and inevitable; it is curious to be acquainted with it, and it may be necessary to point it out.

If those who are called upon to guide the nations of our time clearly discerned from afar off these new tendencies, which will soon be irresistible, they would understand that, possessing education and freedom, men living in democratic ages cannot fail to improve the industrial part of science, and that henceforward all the efforts of the constituted authorities ought to be directed to support the highest branches of learning and to foster the nobler passion for science itself. In the present age the human mind must be coerced into theoretical studies; it runs of its own accord to practical applications; and, instead of perpetually referring it to the minute examination of secondary effects, it is well to divert it from them sometimes, in order to raise it up

到了今天这样的时代,有很多开化的国家都一直依靠多元化工业生产,所以把科学的各个不同领域联结起来的各种纽带,引起人们的注意;甚至对于应用科学本身的爱好,当它是合理的时候,也应当敦促人们不要忽略理论。每天都在重复如此众多的对实验结果的反复试用,几乎不可能不常常窥探到一些一般规律。因此,即使伟大的发明家不多,伟大的发现却定不会少。

除此之外,我相信科学的崇高使命。从一方面来说,如果说民主原则没能引导人们从科学本身出发去研究它,但是另一方面,民主原则却使研究科学的人数大量增加。在这样一群伟大的研究人员当中,定会常常产生出一位秉承着真理而生的卓著的天才。这样的天才,我们几乎可以肯定,将一定会深入到大自然最深奥的奥妙之中。这一切的发生,与他所存在社会的或者时代的精神无关。他的研究过程不需要外界的帮助,只要不给他设置障碍,他就知足了。我想说的是:永久存在的地位的不平等,会把人们限定在对抽象理论的华而不实的研究之中。而民主的社会情况和制度,又要人们只追求科学所能达到的直接而有利现实作用。这种趋势是自然而不可避免的。对这一趋势的了解是有趣的,而且我们有必要将这一趋势指明。

如今的国家领导人如能从长远的角度认清这种不可抗拒的特性,就会知道生活在民主时代的人有了知识和自由之后,就会对科学的工业应用加以改进,而今后政府当局的力量,也应当全力支持高级科学的研究并且营造科学研究的高尚情操。在我们这个时代,人的思想必须重视理论研究,然后通过其自身的运转与实践融合。我们不应当让它总是追求一些次要效用的琐碎的研究。我们应该让人的思想常常从此类研究中解脱出来,把它转

to the contemplation of primary causes.

Because the civilization of ancient Rome perished in consequence of the invasion of the Barbarians, we are perhaps too apt to think that civilization cannot perish in any other manner. If the light by which we are guided is ever extinguished, it will dwindle by degrees and expire of itself. By dint of close adherence to mere applications, principles would be lost sight of; and when the principles were wholly forgotten, the methods derived from them would be ill pursued. New methods could no longer be invented, and men would continue, without intelligence and without art, to apply scientific processes no longer understood.

When Europeans first arrived in China, three hundred years ago, they found that almost all the arts had reached a certain degree of perfection there, and they were surprised that a people which had attained this point should not have gone beyond it. At a later period they discovered traces of some higher branches of science that had been lost. The nation was absorbed in productive industry; the greater part of its scientific processes had been preserved, but science itself no longer existed there. This served to explain the strange immobility in which they found the minds of this people. The Chinese, in following the track of their forefathers, had forgotten the reasons by which the latter had been guided. They still used the formula without asking for its meaning; they retained the instrument, but they no longer possessed the art of altering or renewing it. The Chinese, then, had lost the power of change; for them improvement was impossible. They were compelled at all times and in all points to imitate their predecessors lest they should stray into utter darkness by deviating for an instant from the path already laid down for them. The source of human knowledge was all but dry; and though the stream still ran on, it could neither swell its waters nor alter its course.

Notwithstanding this, China had existed peaceably for centuries. The invaders who had conquered the country assumed the manners of the inhabitants, and order prevailed there. A sort of physical prosperity was everywhere discernible; revolutions were rare, and war was, so to speak, unknown.

换到为了最原始的原因而进行沉思的阶段。

正是因为古罗马的文明是随蛮族的入侵而灭亡的,所以我们也许过于倾向于相信,文明灭亡的方式仅此一种。如果指引我们前进的光芒有一天熄灭,它也会是一点一点地黯淡下去,最终自消自灭。如果人们仅仅借助实践应用,就会丢掉原理;而一旦原理被完全遗忘,须由原理产生的方法也就被引入歧途。结果,不再有新的方法被发现,而人们也只能在无知并缺乏技术的情况下糊里糊涂地使用他们并不理解其原理的工作方法。

300 年前,当欧洲人第一次抵达中国时,他们发现那里几乎所有的工艺都在一定程度上趋于完美。他们感到很惊讶,他们认为一个获得这样成就的国家是不会再被超越的。很快,他们才发现其实中国人只剩下了一些高级技术的残迹,而其技术本身已不复存在。中国实业发达,大部分科学的方法还在那里保留下来,但是科学本身已不复存在。这使人们相信,他们找到了这个国家的人民的思想为什么处于一种奇怪的固定模式的原因。善于遵循其祖辈遗迹的中国人,早已忘记了指引他们的父辈前进的向导。他们仍旧套用古老的公式,而从不询问这些套式的来因。他们保留使用父辈们创造的工具,但是却永远地失去了改进或者更新这些工具的工艺原理。因为他们已失去了变革的能力。他们为了一刻也不偏离祖先的足迹,尽量不踏入不可知的歧途,时时刻刻在所有方面都竭力仿效祖先。人类智慧的源泉已经枯竭。因此,尽管溪水仍在流动,但它已无法扩充水量重获水源。

尽管如此,中国还是平安地度过了许多个世纪。征服了中国的入侵者,仍旧采用了当地的习俗,一切都井然有序。物质繁荣随处可见。但是,变革却是罕见,而由变革引发的战争可以说闻所未闻。

It is then a fallacy to flatter ourselves with the reflection that the barbarians are still far from us; for it there are some nations that allow civilization to be torn from their grasp, there are others who themselves trample it underfoot.

因此,如果自以为是地认为蛮族离我们还远,那就错了。因为如果说有些民族的文明火把是被人夺走的,那么还有些民族曾将文明的火把践踏在自己脚下。

CHAPTER XI

In What Spirit The Americans
Cultivate The Arts

It would be to waste the time of my readers and my own if I strove to demonstrate how the general mediocrity of fortunes, the absence of superfluous wealth, the universal desire for comfort, and the constant efforts by which everyone attempts to procure it make the taste for the useful predominate over the love of the beautiful in the heart of man. Democratic nations, among whom all these things exist, will therefore cultivate the arts that serve to render life easy in preference to those whose object is to adorn it. They will habitually prefer the useful to the beautiful, and they will require that the beautiful should be useful.

But I propose to go further, and, after having pointed out this first feature, to sketch several others.

It commonly happens that in the ages of privilege the practice of almost all the arts becomes a privilege, and that every profession is a separate sphere of action, into which it is not allowable for everyone to enter. Even when productive industry is free, the fixed character that belongs to aristocratic nations gradually segregates all the persons who practice the same art till they form a distinct class, always composed of the same families, whose members are all known to each other and among whom a public opinion of their own and a species of corporate pride soon spring up. In a class or guild of this kind each artisan has not only his fortune to make, but his reputation to preserve. He is not exclusively swayed by his own interest or even by that of his customer, but by that

第十一章　美国人对艺术有着怎样的精神

　　如果我费劲去解释：谁也没有多余的财富，人们对舒适的追求以及人人为此付出的努力，这使人们对于实用的追求更高于人们的爱美之心，那无疑是浪费我们大家的时间。所有这些事情在民主国家都存在，并且人们在艺术方面的耕作，更多的是为了追求生活上的简易方便，而不是单纯的因为热爱而研究。人们都习惯于更多的追求其实用性多过对其美感的追求，而且他们认为，他们所追求的美必须具有实用价值。

　　但是我想要更进一步说，在指出这一最基础的特征之后，也能将其他特征加以说明。

　　一般来说，在特权存在的时期，对于几乎所有艺术的实践都变成了一种特权的表现，每一种职业都自有其相对独立的圈子，并不是所有人都能踏入这个特权的圈子。即使是在生产行业都处于自由状态的时期，属于贵族社会的那种固有的特性也逐渐将从事同一技术的所有的人们彼此分开，直到各自形成一个独立的阶级。这个独立的阶级总是由一些相同的成员组成，他们彼此熟悉，因此很快就会在他们中间产生一种共有的舆论观念和行业骄傲感。在这样的一个阶层或者说这样一种行业之中，每一个工匠不仅仅要创造自己的财富，而且还要维护自己的声誉。他们的行为

of the body to which he belongs; and the interest of that body is that each artisan should produce the best possible workmanship. In aristocratic ages the object of the arts is therefore to manufacture as well as possible, not with the greatest speed or at the lowest cost.

When, on the contrary, every profession is open to all, when a multitude of persons are constantly embracing and abandoning it, and when its several members are strangers, indifferent to and because of their numbers hardly seen by each other, the social tie is destroyed, and each workman, standing alone, endeavors simply to gain the most money at the least cost. The will of the customer is then his only limit. But at the same time a corresponding change takes place in the customer also. In countries in which riches as well as power are concentrated and retained in the hands of a few, the use of the greater part of this world's goods belongs to a small number of individuals, who are always the same. Necessity, public opinion, or moderate desires exclude all others from the enjoyment of them. As this aristocratic class remains fixed at the pinnacle of greatness on which it stands, without diminution or increase, it is always acted upon by the same wants and affected by them in the same manner. The men of whom it is composed naturally derive from their superior and hereditary position a taste for what is extremely well made and lasting. This affects the general way of thinking of the nation in relation to the arts. It often occurs among such a people that even the peasant will rather go without the objects he covets than procure them in a state of imperfection. In aristocracies, then, the handicraftsmen work for only a limited number of fastidious customers; the profit they hope to make depends principally on the perfection of their workmanship.

Such is no longer the case when, all privileges being abolished, ranks are intermingled and men are forever rising or sinking in the social scale. Among a democratic people a number of citizens always

既不是完全由自己的利益驱使,也不是完全受到顾客的影响,而是由所从属的这个行业决定的。行业的利益就是要求每个工匠必须创造出最好的工艺品。在贵族时期,艺术的终极目标就因此变成了尽可能做出精美的制品,而不是讲求用最快的速度或者最低的成本。

相反,当每一种职业都对所有人开放的时候,当人民大众可以随时介入或者退出某一种职业的时候,当任一种行业的部分成员可以彼此陌生,互不关心或者其行业成员之间很少碰面的时候,社会的纽带就被破坏了。同时,每个工人都独立存在,并致力于用最低的成本获得最大的收益。这时候,顾客的要求就成了他们唯一的准则。但,同时,在消费者之中也在发生一种相应的变化。在财富也像权力那样集中在少数人手中的时候,那么,对于世界上大部分商品的使用也就集中在了少数个体身上,而这些人也总是同一拨人。而其他人则由于生活所迫、公众舆论或者自我节制而被排除在这些享受之外。因为贵族阶级总是固定在它所居于的顶尖位置,既不缩小也不扩大,所以他们总是遵循着相同的欲求,受着同样的行为约束。像这样组成的一些人,他们天生就因为其高贵和世袭的地位,秉承着一种追求精致和耐用的品性。这一品性影响着人们有关艺术的思维方式。在这样民族中常常会发生这样的情形,即使是一位农夫,也宁愿垂涎一件他买不起的工艺品,也不愿屈就一件不完美的物件。在贵族制国家中,手艺人工作的对象只是一些有限的挑剔的顾客。他们只能通过制作出完美的工艺品来获取利益。

当所有贵族不复存在、所有的阶级都消失,人们总是在社会各阶层之间彼沉此浮的时候,这一现象也随之消失了。在民主国

exists whose patrimony is divided and decreasing. They have contracted, under more prosperous circumstances, certain wants, which remain after the means of satisfying such wants are gone; and they are anxiously looking out for some surreptitious method of providing for them. On the other hand, there is always in democracies a large number of men whose fortune is on the increase, but whose desires grow much faster than their fortunes, and who gloat upon the gifts of wealth in anticipation, long before they have means to obtain them. Such men are eager to find some short cut to these gratifications, already almost within their reach. From the combination of these two causes the result is that in democracies there is always a multitude of persons whose wants are above their means and who are very willing to take up with imperfect satisfaction rather than abandon the object of their desires altogether.

The artisan readily understands these passions, for he himself partakes in them. In an aristocracy he would seek to sell his workmanship at a high price to the few; he now conceives that the more expeditious way of getting rich is to sell them at a low price to all. But there are only two ways of lowering the price of commodities. The first is to discover some better, shorter, and more ingenious method of producing them; the second is to manufacture a larger quantity of goods, nearly similar, but of less value. Among a democratic population all the intellectual faculties of the workman are directed to these two objects: he strives to invent methods that may enable him not only to work better, but more quickly and more cheaply; or if he cannot succeed in that, to diminish the intrinsic quality of the thing he makes, without rendering it wholly unfit for the use for which it is intended. When none but the wealthy had watches, they were almost all very good ones; few are now made that are worth much, but everybody has one in his pocket. Thus the democratic principle not only tends to direct the human mind to the useful arts, but it induces the artisan to produce with great rapidity many imperfect commodities, and the consumer to content himself with these commodities.

家中总有一部分公民,他们的财产被划分或者缩小。他们在以前比较富裕的环境中,养成了一些需求,而当满足这些需求的途径消失之后,他们仍没有放弃这些需求的习惯。他们焦躁不安,不断地向外探索一些秘密的途径可以帮助他们满足这些需求。另一方面,在民主国家中,总有一大帮人,他们的财富在不断地上升,但是他们的欲望总是比自己的财富增长的速度快那么一点。他们满足于可以预见获得的财富,因为不久后他们就能得到满足。这些人总是急于寻找捷径更快地满足自己几乎要得到的欲求。因为这两种原因相互混合,结果就在民主国家中,总是存在着一群人,他们的需求总是高于他们的能力范围,而且这些人愿意用一些并不完美的替代品来满足自己的需求,而不愿完全放弃他们的欲求。

工匠们容易理解这种感情,因为他们自己也有同样的感受。在贵族制国家中,他可以把自己的工艺品高价卖给少数人群,现在,他发现了一条更便捷的致富之路,那就是把它低价卖给更多的大众群体。但是,要想使商品降价,只有两种途径。第一种,就是发现更好的、时间更短的、更富于创造性的方法生产商品;其次就是大量生产近乎类似但是价值低廉的商品。在民主国家中,所有工匠的智慧都指向这两个目标:他致力于发明一种方法,可以不仅使自己的工艺品更精致,而且时间更短成本更低。如果他不能在这方面取胜,他就设法既保证其实用功能,又降低其质量。当只有富人才能拥有手表的年代,几乎每一块表都是精品。如今很少有人制造价值昂贵的手表了,因为几乎每一个人兜里都揣着一块。因此,民主原则不仅使人们的思想趋于实用工艺,也使得手艺人迅速地生产大量不完美的制品,又使得消费者满足于这样的商品。

Not that in democracies the arts are incapable, in case of need, of producing wonders. This may occasionally be so if customers appear who are ready to pay for time and trouble. In this rivalry of every kind of industry, in the midst of this immense competition and these countless experiments, some excellent workmen are formed who reach the utmost limits of their craft. But they rarely have an opportunity of showing what they can do; they are scrupulously sparing of their powers; they remain in a state of accomplished mediocrity, which judges itself, and, though well able to shoot beyond the mark before it, aims only at what it hits. In aristocracies, on the contrary, workmen always do all they can; and when they stop, it is because they have reached the limit of their art.

When I arrive in a country where I find some of the finest productions of the arts, I learn from this fact nothing of the social condition or of the political constitution of the country. But if I perceive that the productions of the arts are generally of an inferior quality, very abundant, and very cheap, I am convinced that among the people where this occurs privilege is on the decline and that ranks are beginning to intermingle and will soon become one.

The handicraftsmen of democratic ages not only endeavor to bring their useful productions within the reach of the whole community, but strive to give to all their commodities attractive qualities that they do not in reality possess. In the confusion of all ranks everyone hopes to appear what he is not, and makes great exertions to succeed in this object. This sentiment, indeed, which is only too natural to the heart of man, does not originate in the democratic principle; but that principle applies it to material objects. The hypocrisy of virtue is of every age, but the hypocrisy of luxury belongs more particularly to the ages of democracy.

To satisfy these new cravings of human vanity the arts have recourse to every species of imposture; and these devices sometimes

这并不是说，在民主制度下，在需要的时候也无法制造出优质商品。如果买主肯出钱支付手艺人的时间和劳动所应付的报酬，偶尔也会造出品质优秀的产品。在这种各种行业相互竞争的情况下，处身于这些无尽的竞争和无以计数的试验中，一些优异的手艺人出现了，他们的技艺已达到了本行业的顶峰。但是他们却鲜有机会向大家展示自己的技艺，他们小心翼翼地守护着自己的手艺。他们停留在简单地完成制品的阶段，即使他们完全可以做出超过市场需求的水平，但却仅仅停留在市场指向的目标水平阶段。在贵族制国家中，与此相反，手艺人总是竭尽全力。他们只会在达到了顶峰的水平时才会停下来。

当我到达一个国家，发现一些精美的作品时，我并不能从中理解该国的社会情况和政治制度。但是，只要我发现该国的工艺品大都不够完美，但数量很多而且价格便宜，我就可以肯定：这个国家处于特权正在消失的阶段，各阶级正在相互混合而且不久即将融为一体。

生活在民主时代的手艺人，不仅要使全体公民都购买到有实用价值的制品，而且要设法使其全部制品具有它们实际上并不具备的诱人之处。在各阶级互相混杂的社会里，人人都想掩饰自己的真实模样，并为达到目的大费周章。事实上，民主制度不是这种感情的成因，因为这种感情完全自然出于人心。但是，民主制度以物质为目的指向。道德伪善存在于各个时代，但奢侈方面的伪善则更多地为民主时代所特有。

为了满足人类虚荣心的新的渴望，在工艺上便出现了种种欺骗手段，有时这些手法做得过了头甚至损害了其工艺本身。如

go so far as to defeat their own purpose. Imitation diamonds are now made which may be easily mistaken for real ones; as soon as the art of fabricating false diamonds becomes so perfect that they cannot be distinguished from real ones, it is probable that both will be abandoned and become mere pebbles again.

This leads me to speak of those arts which are called, by way of distinction, the fine arts. I do not believe that it is a necessary effect of a democratic social condition and of democratic institutions to diminish the number of those who cultivate the fine arts, but these causes exert a powerful influence on the manner in which these arts are cultivated. Many of those who had already contracted a taste for the fine arts are impoverished; on the other hand, many of those who are not yet rich begin to conceive that taste, at least by imitation; the number of consumers increases, but opulent and fastidious consumers become more scarce. Something analogous to what I have already pointed out in the useful arts then takes place in the fine arts; the productions of artists are more numerous, but the merit of each production is diminished. No longer able to soar to what is great, they cultivate what is pretty and elegant, and appearance is more attended to than reality.

In aristocracies a few great pictures are produced; in democratic countries a vast number of insignificant ones. In the former statues are raised of bronze; in the latter, they are modeled in plaster.

When I arrived for the first time at New York, by that part of the Atlantic Ocean which is called the East River, I was surprised to perceive along the shore, at some distance from the city, a number of little palaces of white marble, several of which were of classic architecture. When I went the next day to inspect more closely one which had particularly attracted my notice, I found that its walls were of whitewashed brick, and its columns of painted wood. All the edifices that I had admired the night before were of the same kind.

The social condition and the institutions of democracy impart, moreover, certain peculiar tendencies to all the imitative arts, which

今,假冒的钻石已经几乎可以达到以假乱真的地步。一旦制造假冒钻石的工艺趋于完善,人们就很难再区分真假钻石的区别了,那时候,也许不管是真的还是假的钻石,都会被人们抛弃,钻石就会重新回归普通的小石子的身份了。

这使我想起了一种艺术,为了加以区分,我们称之为"美术"。我不认为,民主的社会情况和制度必然导致从事美术的人数减少,但它将对美术工作者的造就方式方面产生巨大的影响。一方面,许多原来爱好美术的人都变得很穷;另一方面,许多还不富裕的人们会开始养成这种爱好,至少会模仿别人的这种喜好。消费者的人数不断增长,但是那些富有并且挑剔的顾客则变得越来越少。于是,我之前在讲实用艺术时提到过的现象就会在美术中发生了。艺术家的作品的数量变得越来越多,但是每件艺术品的价值却大大降低了。人们不再追求伟大,而只注意优雅和美观,对他们来说,外表远比实质关键。

在贵族制社会中,出现了一些伟大的绘画作品;而在民主国家,绘画作品的数量虽多但多为平庸之作。在贵族制社会条件下,建造了许多青铜像,而在民主时期只塑造了一些石膏像。

当我从大西洋的支流伊斯特河第一次抵达纽约的时候,我惊奇地看到离市区不远的地方,沿着河两岸建造了许多白色大理石的小宫殿,其中有几座建筑很是经典。但是,第二天当我特意到特别引起我注意的一座宫殿近前去观看的时候,发现它的墙是砖砌的,表面抹上了白石灰,而它的柱廊也是涂了油漆的木柱。前一天使我赞叹不已的那些伟大建筑,原来都是这样的质地。

民主的社会情况和制度,赋予了所有模仿艺术品一些特有的品质,而这些特性又特别容易为人们看穿。这一特性使艺术往往

it is easy to point out. They frequently withdraw them from the delineation of the soul to fix them exclusively on that of the body, and they substitute the representation of motion and sensation for that of sentiment and thought; in a word, they put the real in the place of the ideal.

I doubt whether Raphael studied the minute intricacies of the mechanism of the human body as thoroughly as the draftsmen of our own time. He did not attach the same importance as they do to rigorous accuracy on this point because he aspired to surpass nature. He sought to make of man something which should be superior to man and to embellish beauty itself. David and his pupils, on the contrary, were as good anatomists as they were painters. They wonderfully depicted the models that they had before their eyes, but they rarely imagined anything beyond them; they followed nature with fidelity, while Raphael sought for something better than nature. They have left us an exact portraiture of man; but he discloses in his works a glimpse of the Divinity.

This remark as to the manner of treating a subject is no less applicable to its choice. The painters of the Renaissance generally sought far above themselves, and away from their own time, for mighty subjects, which left to their imagination an unbounded range. Our painters often employ their talents in the exact imitation of the details of private life, which they have always before their eyes; and they are forever copying trivial objects, the originals of which are only too abundant in nature.

只专注于描绘形象,而不重视刻画灵魂,他们通过描绘行为和感触代替了对情感和思想的描绘。总之,他们用现实的需求代替了理想的位置。

我怀疑是否拉斐尔对人体构造的繁琐细节的研究,能像我们时代的画家那样彻底。他所关注的重点与那些画家对待人体构造时所关注的严格的精确性不同,他追求的是超越自然。他既要把人画得像人,但又要高于人本身,而且要把美画得更完美。刚好相反,大卫和他的学生们既是著名的画家又是有名的解剖学家。所以,虽然他们能够真实地再现他们的模特儿,但却很难利用想象超越模特本身。他们完美地再现了他们眼前的模特的模样,而拉斐尔则在追求一些超越自然的东西。他们留给我们精确的肖像画,但拉斐尔却能使我们从他的作品中窥到神韵。

以上关于绘画方法所述的一切,也可适用于题材的选择。文艺复兴时期的画家大都选取一些超越自我的伟大题材并远离他们所处的时代,这使他们得以发挥无限的想象力。而当代的画家,则经常把自己的天才用于精确地再现他们眼前的个人生活的细节,并只根据自然界到处可见的原物去复制琐碎的细节。

【英汉对照全译本】

DEMOCRACY IN AMERICA

—— 论 美 国 民 主 ——

———— [法]托克维尔　著 ————

朱尾声　译

马高霞　译校

（四）

中国社会科学出版社

CHAPTER XII

Why The Americans Raise Some Insignificant Monuments And Others That Are Very Grand

I have just observed that in democratic ages monuments of the arts tend to become more numerous and less important. I now hasten to point out the exception to this rule.

In a democratic community individuals are very weak, but the state, which represents them all and contains them all in its grasp, is very powerful. Nowhere do citizens appear so insignificant as in a democratic nation; nowhere does the nation itself appear greater or does the mind more easily take in a wide survey of it. In democratic communities the imagination is compressed when men consider themselves; it expands indefinitely when they think of the state. Hence it is that the same men who live on a small scale in cramped dwellings frequently aspire to gigantic splendor in the erection of their public monuments.

The Americans have traced out the circuit of an immense city on the site which they intend to make their capital, but which up to the present time is hardly more densely peopled than Pontoise, though, according to them, it will one day contain a million inhabitants. They have already rooted up trees for ten miles around lest they should interfere with the future citizens of this imaginary metropolis. They have erected a magnificent palace for Congress in the center of the city and

第十二章　为什么美国人既建造了一些无名的建筑物又建有那些宏大的建筑物

我刚才已经提到,在民主时代,艺术作品的数量越来越多,但也变得越来越没有价值。现在我急于指出例外于这一规律的实例。

在民主国家,每个个体的力量都很弱小,但代表众人实施统治的国家的权力非常强大。任何国家的公民都不会比民主国家的公民显得更弱小,而也没有哪个国家自身像民主国家那样强大,任何一个国家的精神都不会像民主国家的精神那样具有广阔的视野。在民主国家中,当人们考虑自己的时候,他们的想象力就会缩小,而当他们以国家为考虑对象的时候,想象力就会被无限的扩大。因此,正是同样的这批居住在狭促的空间的人们,常常期望将公共场所的建筑物搞得气势恢宏。

美国人已在他们准备建造首都的地方划出一座巨大的城市的轮廓,但是目前这个地方的人口密集程度还很难超过蓬图瓦兹多,尽管如此,根据他们的意志,终有一天这里会有百万人口聚集。他们早已清除了方圆十里约的树木,以免给这个想象中未来的首都的居民带来麻烦。他们还在这座城市的中心建起一座宏

have given it the pompous name of the Capitol.

The several states of the Union are every day planning and erecting for themselves prodigious undertakings which would astonish the engineers of the great European nations.

Thus democracy not only leads men to a vast number of inconsiderable productions; it also leads them to raise some monuments on the largest scale; but between these two extremes there is a blank. A few scattered specimens of enormous buildings can therefore teach us nothing of the social condition and the institutions of the people by whom they were raised. I may add, though the remark is outside my subject, that they do not make us better acquainted with its greatness, its civilization, and its real prosperity. Whenever a power of any kind is able to make a whole people cooperate in a single undertaking, that power, with a little knowledge and a great deal of time, will succeed in obtaining something enormous from efforts so multiplied. But this does not lead to the conclusion that the people are very happy, very enlightened, or even very strong.

The Spaniards found the city of Mexico full of magnificent temples and vast palaces, but that did not prevent Cortes from conquering the Mexican Empire with six hundred foot-soldiers and sixteen horses.

If the Romans had been better acquainted with the laws of hydraulics, they would not have constructed all the aqueducts that surround the ruins of their cities; they would have made a better use of their power and their wealth. If they had invented the steam-engine, perhaps they would not have extended to the extremities of their empire those long artificial ways which are called Roman roads. These things are the splendid memorials at the same time of their ignorance and of their greatness.

A people that left no other vestige than a few leaden pipes in the earth and a few iron rods on its surface might have been more the master of nature than the Romans.

伟大厦供国会使用,并给它起了个响亮的名字:国会大厦。

美国的一些州每天都在计划着并为自己兴建着巨大的建筑,这些建筑即使是最伟大的欧洲国家的工程师们见到了也会感到吃惊的。

因此,民主不但引导人们去生产大量毫不起眼的建筑,同时也促使他们去兴建一些宏大的建筑物。但在这两个极端之间却是空缺。因此,散布于各地的几座巨大建筑物,并不能使我们了解建造这些建筑物的民族的社会状态和制度。尽管有点跑题,我还要补充一句,这样的建筑物也并不能使我们更好地理解这个民族的伟大、文明和其真正的繁荣。无论何时,任何一种政权都能使全民同时参与一项工程建设。即使在科学水平不高,或者还需要大量的时间的情况下,它也会通过巨大的努力去实现一项宏伟的事业。但这样并不足以得出结论说这个民族非常幸福、很文明,甚至是强大有力。

当年,西班牙人发现墨西哥城到处都是宏伟的庙宇和巨大的宫殿。可这些并没有阻止只有 600 名步兵和 16 匹马的西班牙人征服墨西哥帝国。

如果罗马人再稍微懂得一些水力学原理,就根本不会在如今已变成废墟的城市的周围构筑那些沟渠,而会使他们的人力和物力发挥更好的作用。假如他们那时已经发明了蒸汽机,也许就不会修筑伸向帝国四面八方的长长的被称为“罗马大道”的石头大道。这些宏伟的遗迹,既昭显了他们的伟大,也暴露了他们的无知。

一个民族,除了一些铺设在地下的铅质管道和一些地上搭建的铁架之外,再没有任何遗迹遗留人世,但它也许比罗马人更应称为是大自然的征服者。

CHAPTER XIII
Literary Characteristics
Of Democratic Times

When a traveler goes into a bookseller's shop in the United States and examines the American books on the shelves, the number of works appears very great, while that of known authors seems, on the contrary, extremely small. He will first find a multitude of elementary treatises, destined to teach the rudiments of human knowledge. Most of these books were written in Europe; the Americans reprint them, adapting them to their own use. Next comes an enormous quantity of religious works, Bibles, sermons, edifying anecdotes, controversial divinity, and reports of charitable societies; lastly appears the long catalogue of political pamphlets. In America parties do not write books to combat each other's opinions, but pamphlets, which are circulated. for a day with incredible rapidity and then expire.

In the midst of all these obscure productions of the human brain appear the more remarkable works of a small number of authors whose names are, or ought to be, known to Europeans.

Although America is perhaps in our days the civilized country in which literature is least attended to, still a large number of persons there take an interest in the productions of the mind and make them, if not the study of their lives, at least the charm of their leisure hours. But England supplies these readers with most of the books that they require. Almost all important English books are republished in the United States. The literary genius of Great Britain still darts its rays into the recesses of the forests of the New World, There is hardly a pioneer's hut that does not contain a few odd volumes of Shakespeare.

第十三章 民主时期的文学特征

当一位旅行者走进美国的书店，看一看书架上摆着的美国出版的图书，会觉得书籍的数量倒是很多，但知名作家的人数却少得可怜。首先跃入你眼帘的，是一大堆介绍人类基础知识的初级读物。而其中大部分是先在欧洲出版，后美国人将其翻印出版并加以利用。其次，是多得数不胜数的宗教书籍，像圣经、布道集、醒世故事集、教义辩论书和慈善团体报告等。还有名单能列一长串的政治小册子。在美国，各党派并不出版互相驳斥的书籍，但却代之以用难以置信的速度印发小册子，而这些小册子在出版的当天就被人们遗忘了。

在所有这些晦涩的人类思想产物当中，也会见到极少的一些较优秀的作品，这些作品的作者为欧洲人所知的或应当为欧洲人所知。

尽管美国可能是当代文明国家中最不关心文学的一个，但也还有很多美国人对精神方面的产物有很大的兴趣。并且即使他们并非终生致力于这方面的研究，也至少是他们业余时间的一大爱好。不过，却是英国供给着这些人阅读的大部分书籍。几乎所有重要的英国书籍都在美国被翻印。大不列颠的文学天才还将他们的光芒射入了新大陆的原始森林中。在那里，几乎每个拓荒

I remember that I read the feudal drama of *Henry V* for the first time in a log cabin.

Not only do the Americans constantly draw upon the treasures of English literature, but it may be said with truth that they find the literature of England growing on their own soil. The larger part of that small number of men in the United States who are engaged in the composition of literary works are English in substance and still more so in form. Thus they transport into the midst of democracy the ideas and literary fashions that are current among the aristocratic nation they have taken for their model. They paint with colors borrowed from foreign manners; and as they hardly ever represent the country they were born in as it really is, they are seldom popular there.

The citizens of the United States are themselves so convinced that it is not for them that books are published, that before they can make up their minds upon the merit of one of their authors, they generally wait till his fame has been ratified in England; just as in pictures the author of an original is held entitled to judge of the merit of a copy.

The inhabitants of the United States have, then, at present, properly speaking, no literature. The only authors whom I acknowledge as American are the journalists. They indeed are not great writers, but they speak the language of their country and make themselves heard. Other authors are aliens; they are to the Americans what the imitators of the Greeks and Romans were to us at the revival of learning, an object of curiosity, not of general sympathy. They amuse the mind, but they do not act upon the manners of the people.

I have already said that this state of things is far from originating in democracy alone, and that the causes of it must be sought for in several peculiar circumstances independent of the democratic principle. If the Americans, retaining the same laws and social condition, had had a different origin and had been transported into another country, I do not question that they would have had a literature. Even

者的小茅屋中,都会有一些莎士比亚的剧著。我记得我第一次阅读封建时代的戏剧《亨利五世》,就是在一间小圆木屋中。

美国人不仅常常从英国的文学宝藏中汲取精华,而且也许应该说他们还在自己的国土上发展了英国文学。在美国从事文学创作的人数本来就不多,而其中的大部分人原本就是英国人,于是也往往采用英国式的表现手法。因此,他们把贵族制国家当前流行的奉为楷模的文学思潮和风格,也移入自己的民主制度里来。他们借用其他国家的方式粉饰自己的作品。并因此难以真实再现他们所生活着的这个国度,故而他们的作品很少会受到大家的欢迎。

美国居民自身十分确信的是,那些出版的书籍并不是给他们准备的,并且,他们对自己国家的某位作者的美德进行高度评价之前,通常都会等到这位作家在英国得到认可之后。这种情形,就像在绘画界,画的原作者被授权对一件赝品高度评价一般。

因此,确切地说,美国目前还没有文学。在我看来称得上美国作家的就只有新闻记者。这些人虽然不是大作家,但他们说的是自己国家的语言,而且说出来的话是给美国人民听的。至于其余的作家则都是外国人。美国人对这类作家的看法,跟我们对文艺复兴时期模仿希腊罗马文学的作家的看法一样,只会感到不可思议,而不会引起普遍的共鸣。这些作家虽然愉悦了人们的精神,但对民情却没有任何作用。

我已经说过,这种状况的发生并不是仅仅起因于民主制度,而应该在民主原则之外的一些特殊的社会环境中寻找原因。假如美国人保留着与现今相同的社会情况和法制,而其本源却完全不同,并被移植到另一个国家之中,那我不会怀疑他们也将会有

as they are, I am convinced that they will ultimately have one; but its character will be different from that which marks the American literary productions of our time, and that character will be peculiarly its own. Nor is it impossible to trace this character beforehand.

In an aristocratic people, among whom letters are cultivated, I suppose that intellectual occupations, as well as the affairs of government, are concentrated in a ruling class. The literary as well as the political career is almost entirely confined to this class, or to those nearest to it in rank. These premises suffice for a key to all the rest.

When a small number of the same men are engaged at the same time upon the same objects, they easily concert with one another and agree upon certain leading rules that are to govern them each and all. If the object that attracts the attention of these men is literature, the productions of the mind will soon be subjected by them to precise canons, from which it will no longer be allowable to depart. If these men occupy a hereditary position in the country, they will be naturally inclined, not only to adopt a certain number of fixed rules for themselves, but to follow those which their forefathers laid down for their own guidance; their code will be at once strict and traditional. As they are not necessarily engrossed by the cares of daily life, as they have never been so, any more than their fathers were before them, they have learned to take an interest, for several generations back, in the labors of mind. They have learned to understand literature as an art, to love it in the end for its own sake, and to feel a scholar-like satisfaction in seeing men conform to its rules. Nor is this all: the men of whom I speak began and will end their lives in easy or affluent circumstances; hence they have naturally conceived a taste for carefully chosen gratifications and a love of refined and delicate pleasures. Moreover, a kind of softness of mind and heart, which they frequently contract in the midst of this long and peaceful enjoyment of so much welfare, leads them to put aside, even from their pleasures,

自己的文学。即使他们实在这种状况,我也相信他们终有一天总会有自己的文学的。但是,这一文学的特点将与当代美国文学的特点不同,并且这一特点将会是他们所特有的。要对这一特点预先加以描绘也不是不可能的。

假如在一个文学繁荣的贵族制国家中,智力劳动跟政务工作一样,都掌握在同一个统治阶级手中;文学活动跟政治事务一样,几乎完全被集中在这个阶级或与它最密切的几个阶级手中。这样,就足以找到解决所有其余问题的答案。

当少数一些相同的人们在同一时间从事同一劳动的时候,他们很容易就会彼此达成一致,并统一在某一固定的指导性规则之下,这个原则统领着这个群体的每个个体和整体。如果这群人所关注的同一对象变成了文学,人类精神的产物将很快被这些人置于某种规范之下,而这种规范是不允许违反的。如果这些人都在社会中占据着世袭的地位,那么他们很自然地就会倾向于不仅采纳一些固有的规则,还可能会遵从祖辈遗留下来的他们为自己制定的规范。他们的规则将会很严格且遵循传统。因为他们不必为日常琐事而费心,也因为他们从未这样做过,他们的父辈们也从未这样做过,因此,他们能够一连好几代人都专心地从事智力劳动。他们学会了将文学看作一门艺术,学会了因为文学本身而热爱文学,学会了以学者的角度感受人们与这些规则相吻合的满足感。这还不是全部:我所说的这些人们过去已经开始,而且将来还会在简单或者富裕的环境中最终结束自己的生命。因此,他们自然会精心挑选享乐并且热爱精致优雅的消遣。除此之外,在这种长期而平静的富裕生活中享乐,使他们的身心都变得温和起来,从而使他们即使在享受方面也会避开那些过于突然或

whatever might be too startling or too acute. They had rather be a-mused than intensely excited; they wish to be interested, but not to be carried away.

Now let us fancy a great number of literary performances executed by the men, or for the men, whom I have just described, and we shall readily conceive a style of literature in which everything will be regular and prearranged. The slightest work will be carefully wrought in its least details; art and labor will be conspicuous in everything; each kind of writing will have rules of its own, from which it will not be allowed to swerve and which distinguish it from all others. Style will be thought of almost as much importance as thought, and the form will be no less considered than the matter; the diction will be polished, measured, and uniform. The tone of the mind will be always dignified, seldom very animated, and writers will care more to perfect what they produce than to multiply their productions. It will sometimes happen that the members of the literary class, always living among themselves and writing for themselves alone, will entirely lose sight of the rest of the world, which will infect them with a false and labored style; they will lay down minute literary rules for their exclusive use, which will insensibly lead them to deviate from common sense and finally to transgress the bounds of nature. By dint of striving after a mode of parlance different from the popular, they will arrive at a sort of aristocratic jargon which is hardly less remote from pure language than is the coarse dialect of the people. Such are the natural perils of literature among aristocracies. Every aristocracy that keeps itself entirely aloof from the people becomes impotent, a fact which is as true in literature as it is in politics. ①

---

① All this is especially true of the aristocratic countries that have been long and peacefully subject to a monarchical government. When liberty pre vails in an aristocracy, the higher ranks are constantly obliged to make use of the lower classes; and when they use, they approach them. This frequently introduces something of a democratic spirit into an aristocratic community. There springs up, moreover, in a governing privileged body an energy and habitually bold policy, a taste for stir and excitement, which must infallibly affect all literary performances.

令人激动的方面。他们要的是安享，而不是刺激。他们愿意从享乐中感到乐趣，但不会为享乐疯狂。

现在让我们想想这些人写了或为这些人写的大量的文学著作，我们很容易发现这种文学仿佛预先安排好的按照一个调子写成的。即使是最不起眼的作品，也要在微小的细节上费力加以润色。这种文学在所有方面都要显示作者的技巧和功力。每一种体裁都有自己独特的写作规则。这些规则不允许被改变并与其他题材相区别。在这种文学中，文体与思想、形式与内容几乎同样重要，而措辞必须文雅、规律和一致。语气必须有威信，极少采用欢快的笔调。作家考虑更多的是作品的完美程度，而不是作品的数量。在文学界常常会发生这样一种情况，其中的成员都生活在自己的这个圈子中间，他们写作都是只考虑自己，所以常常把外界因素忘得一干二净，写作风格变得虚假而枯燥。他们把自己限定在只有他们自己使用的烦琐的写作规则中，不知不觉脱离了人们的一般思维模式，最终也将脱离现实。他们尽量避免使用通俗的语言，使用那些与通俗语言相去甚远的贵族化的语言。这一切便是文学在贵族制社会天然的坟墓。任何一个与人民保持距离的贵族阶级都会变得软弱无力，这一事实既发生在文学界，也存在于政治界。①

----

① 这些在长久以来都和平地从属于君主统治之下的贵族制国家内显得尤其真实可信。当自由在贵族政府中广泛传播时，高等阶级就常常利用低等阶级。而当他们实施利用手段的时候，他们就要与低等阶级接触，这就常常使得民主的精神得以进入贵族群体。除此之外，在拥有特权占统治地位的人群中还滋生出一种力量和一种习惯性的大胆的原则，对混乱和刺激的喜好，这一原则准确地作用于所有的文学行为。

Let us now turn the picture and consider the other side of it: let us transport ourselves into the midst of a democracy not unprepared by ancient traditions and present culture to partake in the pleasures of mind. Ranks are there intermingled and identified; knowledge and power are both infinitely subdivided and, if I may use the expression, scattered on every side. Here, then, is a motley multitude whose intellectual wants are to be supplied. These new votaries of the pleasures of mind have not all received the same education; they do not resemble their fathers; nay, they perpetually differ from themselves, for they live in a state of incessant change of place, feelings, and fortunes. The mind of each is therefore unattached to that of his fellows by tradition or common habits; and they have never had the power, the inclination, or the time to act together. It is from the bosom of this heterogeneous and agitated mass, however, that authors spring; and from the same source their profits and their fame are distributed.

I can without difficulty understand that under these circumstances I must expect to meet in the literature of such a people with but few of those strict conventional rules which are admitted by readers and writers in aristocratic times. If it should happen that the men of some one period were agreed upon any such rules, that would prove nothing for the following period; for among democratic nations each new generation is a new people. Among such nations, then, literature will not easily be subjected to strict rules, and it is impossible that any such rules should ever be permanent.

In democracies it is by no means the case that all who cultivate literature have received a literary education; and most of those who have some tinge of belles-lettres are engaged either in politics or in a profession that only allows them to taste occasionally and by stealth the pleasures of mind. These pleasures, therefore, do not constitute the principal charm of their lives, but they are considered as a transient and necessary recreation amid the serious labors of life. Such men can never acquire a sufficiently intimate knowledge of the art of literature to appreciate its more delicate beauties; and the minor shades

现在,我们把图翻过来,考察一下民主社会的另一面。让我们转至其传统风俗和当代文明都使人们获得精神愉悦的民主社会。在这样的民主社会中,各个阶层的人们混合在一起并形成一个整体。知识和力量已被无限分割,用我的话来说,已经被分得七零八落。在这里,各种各样的人物都要求满足他们在智力活动方面的愿望。对于这种新的精神喜好的信奉者,他们的知识构成水平并不一样。他们与自己的父辈们不同。不仅如此,因为他们的住所、情感和财富的不断变动,他们本身也时时刻刻处于变化之中。因此他们彼此的思想并没有因为传统或者共同的习俗而联系在一起。他们也从来没有权利、意向或者时间去彼此联系。作家们就是从这样一些不同的、容易激动的人们当中产生的,并且因着同样的因素获利得名。

我可以很容易理解,在这样的环境下,我如果期望在这样的民族文学中找到一些与贵族时期的读者和作者们都认可的那些严格的传统规则,哪怕只是几个,也不会有结果。如果某一时期这些人们对某些规则达成一致,那也不能保证之后也会继续下去。因为在民主国家中,每一代人都是一些全新的民族组成的。因此在这样的国家中,文学不会被轻易地约束在某些严苛的规则之下,而且这些规则也不会被永久地保持下去。

在民主时期,绝不会使所有从事文学事业的人都接受专业的教育。事实上,他们中的大多数人都要么从事政治要么从事其他行业,他们只是偶尔抽空来感受一下精神上的享受。因此这些愉悦并不构成他们生活的主线,而只是作为他们在繁重的生活中短暂而必要的消遣。这样的人永远也不会拥有足够的艺术鉴赏

of expression must escape them. As the time they can devote to letters is very short, they seek to make the best use of the whole of it. They prefer books which may be easily procured, quickly read, and which require no learned researches to be understood. They ask for beauties selfproffered and easily enjoyed; above all, they must have what is unexpected and new. Accustomed to the struggle, the crosses, and the monotony of practical life, they require strong and rapid emotions, startling passages, truths or errors brilliant enough to rouse them up and to plunge them at once, as if by violence, into the midst of the subject.

Why should I say more, or who does not understand what is about to follow before I have expressed it? Taken as a whole, literature in democratic ages can never present, as it does in the periods of aristocracy, an aspect of order, regularity, science, and art; its form, on the contrary, will ordinarily be slighted, sometimes despised. Style will frequently be fantastic, incorrect, overburdened, and loose, almost always vehement and bold. Authors will aim at rapidity of execution more than at perfection of detail. Small productions will be more common than bulky books; there will be more wit than erudition, more imagination than profundity; and literary performances will bear marks of an untutored and rude vigor of thought, frequently of great variety and singular fecundity. The object of authors will be to astonish rather than to please, and to stir the passions more than to charm the taste. Here and there, indeed, writers will doubtless occur who will choose a different track and who, if they are gifted with superior abilities, will succeed in finding readers in spite of their defects or their better qualities; but these exceptions will be rare, and even the authors who so depart from the received practice in the main subject of their works will always relapse into it in some lesser details.

I have just depicted two extreme conditions, but nations never leap from the first to the second; they reach it only by stages and through infinite gradation. In the progress that an educated people makes from the one to the other, there is almost always a moment

力去欣赏艺术更细致之处的美感。他们也感受不出文学的细微差别。因为他们投入到文字推敲的时间少得有限，他们就希望能够充分地利用这段时间。他们更喜欢那些方便获取、能够快速阅读，不需要花费精力去研究的浅显易懂的作品。他们要求那种直接的显而易见的美，除此之外，更要求有新奇感。习惯了面对冲突、漫长而单调的现实生活，他们需要强烈的迅速的情感，令人惊异的作品，以及那些真伪明显、足以激发他们使他们仿佛在一种力量的驱使下马上进入状态的故事情节。

我为什么还要多说？还有谁不明白我即将说的这些吗？总之，民主时期的文学永远不会像贵族时期的文学一样，描述一些秩序井然、有规律的事物，科学和艺术。相反的，它的形式并不受人们的重视甚至被忽略。它的文体常常表现得很荒诞、不正确，过于繁琐或者松散，而且几乎总是强烈而大胆。作家们都更注重出版作品的数量而不注重其质量。短篇作品远远多于长篇大著。作品中卖弄智慧多于博学多才，富于想象却缺乏深度。这种文学作品充满了未受教育和粗野的思想的痕迹，种类众多且数量庞大。作者的目的就是要引起人们的诧异而不是想要带给大家愉悦，为了激起人们的激情更甚于吸引人们对美的享受。当然，偶尔也会有一些打算走另一条道路的作家，如果他们才华横溢，不管作品好坏还会赢得一批读者。但是这样的例外总是少的，而且脱离了常轨的这些作家，在次要细节方面又总是要回到常轨上去的。

我刚才描述是两个极端的情况，但是作为国家来说，永不会从一个跳跃到另一个的。他们在这两个极端之间的转换，总是要经历一个渐近的过程，穿过无数的阶段。在引导一个有文明的

when the literary genius of democratic nations coinciding with that of aristocratic nations, both seek to establish their sway jointly over the human mind. Such epochs are transient, but very brilliant; they are fertile without exuberance, and animated without confusion. The French literature of the eighteenth century may serve as an example.

I should say more than I mean if I were to assert that the literature of a nation is always subordinate to its social state and its political constitution. I am aware that, independently of these causes, there are several others which confer certain characteristics on literary productions; but these appear to me to be the chief. The relations that exist between the social and political condition of a people and the genius of its authors are always numerous; whoever knows the one is never completely ignorant of the other.

民族由一个极端向另一个极端转换的过程中,几乎总是要经过一段使民主民族的文学天才与贵族民族的文学天才相遇和两者一致表示愿意去共同影响人的精神的时间。这一时期虽然转瞬即逝,但是却异常卓著。这一时期成果众多而不会有滥竽充数之众,活泼而不混乱。18 世纪的法国文学如同此例。

我想说的绝不是如我所断言的,一个民族的文学总是附属于它的社会状态和政治制度而生的。我明白,除了这些原因之外,还有一些其他的因素赋予文学一些特质。但我认为,这两个原因是起决定性作用的。一个国家的社会和政治情况,同它的作家天才们之间有千丝万缕的关系;了解了其一就不会完全忽略其二。

CHAPTER XIV
The Trade Of Literature

Democracy not only infuses a taste for letters among the trading classes, but introduces a trading spirit into literature.

In aristocracies readers are fastidious and few in number; in democracies they are far more numerous and far less difficult to please. The consequence is that among aristocratic nations no one can hope to succeed without great exertion, and this exertion may earn great fame, but can never procure much money; while among democratic nations a writer may flatter himself that he will obtain at a cheap rate a moderate reputation and a large fortune. For this purpose he need not be admired; it is enough that he is liked.

The ever increasing crowd of readers and their continual craving for something new ensure the sale of books that nobody much esteems.

In democratic times the public frequently treat authors as kings do their courtiers; they enrich and despise them. What more is needed by the venal souls who are born in courts or are worthy to live there?

Democratic literature is always infested with a tribe of writers who look upon letters as a mere trade; and for some few great authors who adorn it, you may reckon thousands of idea-mongers.

第十四章　文学的贸易

　　民主不仅仅为商人注入了对文学的爱好,而且也将商业引入了文学。

　　属于贵族阶级的读者要求很苛刻并且数量极少,而民主国家中,读者的数量众多而且比较容易得到满足。因此,在贵族制国家中,文人要想获得成功就要付出艰辛的努力,而他们付出的努力只能为他们赢得名誉不能给他们带来金钱。而在民主国家中,作家却可以通过以低廉的价格获取一点名声并敛得财富。为了达到这个目的,他不需要得到大家的尊敬,只要受到大家的欢迎他就心满意足了。

　　数量不断增长的读者群以及他们对新事物的不断追求,保证了书的销售量即使这本书本身并不受到人们的尊重。

　　在民主时期,公众对待作者的态度就像是国王对待他的子民一般。他们从他们中获利却轻视他们。对于那些出生在宫廷或者应当生活在那里的贪婪的心灵们,除了这样还需要什么呢?

　　民主国家的文学界,总是充斥着这样一批视文学为商业的作家群体,而且那里出现的某些大作家周围总有几千位思想商贩加以点缀。

CHAPTER XV

The Study Of Greek And Latin Literature Is Peculiarly Useful In Democratic Communities

What was called the People in the most democratic republics of antiquity was very unlike what we designate by that term. In Athens all the citizens took part in public affairs; but there were only twenty thousand citizens to more than three hundred and fifty thousand inhabitants. All the rest were slaves, and discharged the greater part of those duties which belong at the present day to the lower or even to the middle classes. Athens, then, with her universal suffrage, was, after all, merely an aristocratic republic, in which all the nobles had an equal right to the government.

The struggle between the patricians and plebeians of Rome must be considered in the same light: it was simply an internal feud between the elder and younger branches of the same family. All belonged to the aristocracy and all had the aristocratic spirit.

It is to be remarked, moreover, that, among the ancients books were always scarce and dear, and that very great difficulties impeded their publication and circulation. These circumstances concentrated literary tastes and habits among a small number of men, who formed a small literary aristocracy out of the choicer spirits of the great political aristocracy. Accordingly, nothing goes to prove that literature was ever treated as a trade among the Greeks and Romans.

These communities, which were not only aristocracies, but very polished and free nations, of course imparted to their literary productions the special defects and merits that characterize the literature of aristocratic times. And indeed a very superficial survey of the works

第十五章　对希腊和拉丁文学的研究在民主国家尤其有用

那些古代的民主共和国的人民，与我们今天所指的人民完全不同。所有的雅典公民都参加政治事务管理，但是雅典城内的35万居民中只有2万公民。其余的人全是奴隶，他们所做的工作大部分如今是我们的人民中的低级或中产阶级所做的工作。因此，虽然雅典实行普选制，但它毕竟仍是贵族共和国，其中的全体贵族平等行使参政权。

对古罗马的贵族和平民之间的斗争，也要用这种观点进行分析，只能把这种斗争看成是同一家族的长辈与后辈之间的内部矛盾。实际上，古罗马的平民也属于贵族阶级，具有贵族阶级的精神。

还应当指出，在整个古代，书籍的数量少而价格昂贵，不论是出版还是发行都存在着很大的困难。这种情况，使得人们对文学的爱好和享用集中在少数人身上，这些少数人在一个大的政治贵族精神世界之内形成一个小的贵族文学集团。因此，没人能证明在古希腊和罗马，文学曾被当作一种买卖关系来对待。

这些国家虽是贵族统治，但是却都是非常文明自由的国度，所以自然也赋予了他们的文学产物以贵族时代文学性质特有的优缺点。事实上，只要粗略地浏览一下古代作家的作品，我们就

of ancient authors will suffice to convince us that if those writers were sometimes deficient in variety and fertility in their subjects, or in boldness, vivacity, and power of generalization in their thoughts, they always displayed exquisite care and skill in their details. Nothing in their works seems to be done hastily or at random; every line is written for the eye of the connoisseur and is shaped after some conception of ideal beauty. No literature places those fine qualities in which the writers of democracies are naturally deficient in bolder relief than that of the ancients; no literature, therefore, ought to be more studied in democratic times. This study is better suited than any other to combat the literary defects inherent in those times; as for their natural literary qualities, these will spring up of their own accord without its being necessary to learn to acquire them.

It is important that this point should be clearly understood. A particular study may be useful to the literature of a people without being appropriate to its social and political wants. If men were to persist in teaching nothing but the literature of the dead languages in a community where everyone is habitually led to make vehement exertions to augment or to maintain his fortune, the result would be a very polished, but a very dangerous set of citizens. For as their social and political condition would give them every day a sense of wants, which their education would never teach them to supply, they would perturb the state, in the name of the Greeks and Romans, instead of enriching it by their productive industry.

It is evident that in democratic communities the interest of individuals as well as the security of the commonwealth demands that the education of the greater number should be scientific, commercial, and industrial rather than literary. Greek and Latin should not be taught in all the schools; but it is important that those who, by their natural disposition or their fortune, are destined to cultivate letters or prepared to relish them should find schools where a complete knowledge of ancient literature may be acquired and where the true scholar may be formed. A few excellent universities would do more towards the attainment of this object than a multitude of bad grammar-schools, where superfluous matters, badly learned, stand in the way of sound instruction in necessary studies.

足以发现,它们的作者虽然在题材上穷于变化,在思想上不够大胆、活泼和具有纵览性,但在情节的描写上却有着令人钦佩的技巧和匠心。他们的作品没有任何匆忙赶工或随意下笔的痕迹,每一处细节都写得很内行,对每一处的推敲都是出于对美的追求。民主国家作家们的作品都没有达到这样的水平,他们天生不像古代的作家们那样显著地表露这些特点。因此,在民主时代除了研究古代文学,也没有什么更好的文学以供研究。这种研究比任何一种都更能克服那些时期文学内在的缺憾。至于文学的自然特质,则完全是不用依靠任何学习就自发产生的。

认清这点很重要。这项研究也许对一个民族的文学很有帮助,但对其社会和政治需要则无一补益。如果人们坚持在一个人人都习惯于采取过激行为来增加或保护自己的财产的社会中只教授纯语言类的文学,结果就会造就一个非常开化但也异常危险的公民群体。因为,如果他们所处的社会和政治环境,总是时时都使他们充满欲望,他们的教育没教过他们如何供给这些需求。那么,他们就会打着古希腊和古罗马的旗号,扰乱国家,而不会去用工业生产使国家变得富裕起来。

很明显,在民主社会里,个人的利益和社会安全都需要对大多数人受到科学、商业和工业方面的教育,然后才是文学教育。并不需要所有的学校都开设教授希腊文和拉丁文的专业,重要的是,对那些由于出身或命运而注定要学习文学或对文学感兴趣的人,也应开设一些使他们能够完全掌握古代文学或培养真正意义上的学者的学校。为了达到这个目的,办几所好的大学胜于一大批劣等专科学校,因为在劣等学校中传授的都是一些质量不高的肤浅教育,反而会影响以后一些必需的学习。

All who aspire to literary excellence in democratic nations ought frequently to refresh themselves at the springs of ancient literature; there is no more wholesome medicine for the mind. Not that I hold the literary productions of the ancients to be irreproachable, but I think that they have some special merits, admirably calculated to counter-balance our peculiar defects. They are a prop on the side on which we are in most danger of falling.

所有期望在文学方面获得杰出成就的民主国家的人们，都必须常常从古代的文学源泉中汲取新的知识。这是充实大脑最有益的方法。我并不是说古代的作品都是没有缺点的，而是认为古代的作品中有一些可以有效地抵消我们缺点的特殊优点。它们使我们处于危险境地的救命稻草。

CHAPTER XVI

How American Democracy Has Modified
The English Language

If the reader has rightly understood what I have already said on the subject of literature in general, he will have no difficulty in understanding that species of influence which a democratic social condition and democratic institutions may exercise over language itself, which is the chief instrument of thought.

American authors may truly be said to live rather in England than in their own country, since they constantly study the English writers and take them every day for their models. But it is not so with the bulk of the population, which is more immediately subjected to the peculiar causes acting upon the United States. It is not, then, to the written, but to the spoken language that attention must be paid if we would detect the changes which the idiom of an aristocratic people may undergo when it becomes the language of a democracy.

Englishmen of education, and more competent judges than I can be of the nicer shades of expression, have frequently assured me that the language of the educated classes in the United States is notably different from that of the educated classes in Great Britain. They complain, not only that the Americans have brought into use a number of new words (the difference and the distance between the two countries might suffice to explain that much), but that these new words are more especially taken from the jargon of parties, the mechanical arts, or the language of trade. In addition to this, they assert that old English words are often used by the Americans in new acceptations; and lastly, that the inhabitants of the United States frequently intermingle phraseology in the strangest manner, and sometimes place words together which are always kept apart in the language of the mother country. These remarks, which were made to me at various times by

第十六章 美国的民主是如何改善英语语言的

如果读者对我刚才所述的文学的概况了解得很透彻,那么他就很容易理解,民主的社会和制度,对语言这一主要的思想工具本身产生了什么样的影响。

美国的作者事实上更应该被称作是生活在英国而不是他们自己的国家,因为他们一直坚持不懈地向英国的作家们学习并每天将之作为自己的模范。但是对于人民大众来说,他们更容易受到美国发生的一些特殊的原因的直接影响。因此,如果我们想要发现贵族制国家人民的习惯用语和民主国家所用语言之间的变化,我们就应该更注重口语而不是书面语言。

有教养的英国人,和一些比我更有能力辨别这些细微差别的人,都常常说服我使我相信:美国受教育阶级同大不列颠受教育阶级在语言上有显著的差别。他们解释说,不仅仅只有美国人引进了一些新的词汇(两国之间的差异和地理位置上的距离也许足以解释这一现象),这些新的词汇更多地来源于各政党专业术语、机械美术或者商业语言。除此之外,一些旧的英语词汇,往往被美国人拿去用以别的含义。最后,他们说,美国的居民常常会混杂一些莫名其妙的措辞,而且有时他们连在一起用的词汇,在母

persons who appeared to be worthy of credit, led me to reflect upon the subject; and my reflections brought me, by theoretical reasoning, to the same point at which my informants had arrived by practical observation.

In aristocracies language must naturally partake of that state of repose in which everything remains. Few new words are coined because few new things are made; and even if new things were made, they would be designated by known words, whose meaning had been determined by tradition. If it happens that the human mind bestirs itself at length or is roused by light breaking in from without, the novel expressions that are introduced have a learned, intellectual, and philosophical character, showing that they do not originate in a democracy. After the fall of Constantinople had turned the tide of science and letters towards the west, the French language was almost immediately invaded by a multitude of new words, which all had Greek and Latin roots. An erudite neologism then sprang up in France, which was confined to the educated classes, and which produced no sensible effect, or at least a very gradual one, upon the people.

All the nations of Europe successively exhibited the same change. Milton alone introduced more than six hundred words into the English language, almost all derived from the Latin, the Greek, or the Hebrew. The constant agitation that prevails in a democratic community tends unceasingly, on the contrary, to change the character of the language, as it does the aspect of affairs. In the midst of this general stir and competition of minds, many new ideas are formed, old ideas are lost, or reappear, or are subdivided into an infinite variety of minor shades. The consequence is that many words must fall into desuetude, and others must be brought into use.

Besides, democratic nations love change for its own sake, and this is seen in their language as much as in their politics. Even when they have no need to change words, they sometimes have the desire.

The genius of a democratic people is not only shown by the great number of words they bring into use, but also by the nature of the ideas these new words represent. Among such a people the majority lays

语中往往是不能连用的。一些值得我相信的人多次向我说的这些话，使我不得不对这个问题进行思考。并且，我通过理性的思维得出的结论，与在实践调查中得出的结论相吻合。

在贵族制社会，语言必然带有与社会其他一切事物相同的特性。因为新事物不多，所以这种社会创造的新词也不多。即使出现新的事物，也会代之以传统中既定的已知词汇。如果碰巧人类的思想最后终于自发崛起或者被一些从未有过的光芒唤醒，它所创造的新词也要显得博学、聪慧并富含哲理，以表明它并非源自民主社会。君士坦丁的陷落使科学和文学向西部转移，因此法语立即受到了大量新词的冲击，这些词都源自希腊语和拉丁语。于是，在法国出现了流行新词的风气，但使用新词的都是有教养阶级，这种流行并未造成任何影响，或者说，是经过很长时期才在人民群众中间传播开来。

所有欧洲的国家都成功地展示了这一变化。仅弥尔顿一人就为英语引进了 600 多个新词，几乎所有的新词都源于拉丁文、希腊语或者希伯来语。而民主社会内部连续不断发生的运动，不断改变语言和事物的面貌。这种普遍存在的思想混乱和竞争中，新观念层出不穷，而一些旧的观念则逐渐消失或重现，但更多的是发生一些小的变化。因此，常常是有些词被废止不用，而另一些词又开始使用。

而且，民主国家本性喜欢变动。这种情况既见于其语言，又见于其政治。因此，民主国家即使没有必要也会常常产生这样的念头。

民主国家人民的天赋，不仅表现在他们引进的大量的词汇方面，也表现在这些新词汇所赋予的意义上。在这样的民族中，语

down the law in language as well as in everything else; its prevailing spirit is as manifest in this as in other respects. But the majority is more engaged in business than in study, in political and commercial interests than in philosophical speculation or literary pursuits. Most of the words coined or adopted for its use will bear the mark of these habits; they will mainly serve to express the wants of business, the passions of party, or the details of the public administration. In these departments the language will constantly grow, while it will gradually lose ground in metaphysics and theology.

As to the source from which democratic nations are accustomed to derive their new expressions and the manner in which they coin them, both may easily be described. Men living in democratic countries know but little of the language that was spoken at Athens or at Rome, and they do not care to dive into the lore of antiquity to find the expression that they want. If they sometimes have recourse to learned etymologies, vanity will induce them to search for roots from the dead languages; but erudition does not naturally furnish them its resources. The most ignorant, it sometimes happens, will use them most. The eminently democratic desire to get above their own sphere will often lead them to seek to dignify a vulgar profession by a Greek or Latin name. The lower the calling is and the more remote from learning, the more pompous and erudite is its appellation. Thus the French rope-dancers have transformed themselves into *acrobates* and *funambules*.

Having little knowledge of the dead languages, democratic nations are apt to borrow words from living tongues, for they have constant mutual intercourse, and the inhabitants of different countries imitate each other the more readily as they grow more like each other every day.

But it is principally upon their own languages that democratic nations attempt to make innovations. From time to time they resume and restore to use forgotten expressions in their vocabulary, or they borrow from some particular class of the community a term peculiar to it, which they introduce with a figurative meaning into the language of daily life. Many expressions which originally belonged to the technical

言规则与其他规则制定方法相同,也要由多数决定;其主流意志在所有方面都得到充分的体现。但是,占绝对优势的多数中从事实业的比从事研究的人多,从事政务和商业的比从事哲学研究或者文学追求的人多。多数所创造或采用的词汇的含义都带有由此所产生的习惯特质。这些词汇将主要应用于表达商业需求、政治激情或者公共事务管理方面。语言的这些方面将会持续地增长,而其在哲学和神学方面的语言则逐渐失去了立足之处。

对于民主国家新词的来源和创造方法的问题是很容易描述的。生活在民主国家的人,对于罗马人和雅典人所用的语言知之甚少,而且他们也不必到古代语言中去挖掘他们所缺乏的词汇。如果他们偶尔需要求助于高深的语源学,他们的自傲感也会将他们引到从一些已经腐朽的语言中寻找根源。但是博学并不是天生就赋予了他们这些知识。所以最无知的人,反而是最经常使用这些词汇的人。期望高于他们自身的领域的民主的愿望,常常使他们用希腊或者拉丁语的名字来显示他们平庸的职业。他们认为,职业越是低下也就越没知识,而名称越好听,就越显得自己学识渊博。比如,法国的走索演员,就用希腊语的"杂技"和拉丁文的"走绳索的人"来称谓自己。

由于对那些已经腐朽的语言知之甚少,民主国家倾向于从一些活着的语言中借用词汇,因为这些词汇常常被他们拿来彼此交流,不同国家的人民相互模仿并一天天变得越来越相似。

但是,民主国家的人民主要还是试图从他们自己的语言中寻找革新。他们一次又一次地重新启用一些在他们的词汇中早已被遗忘的表达方式,或者借用社会中一些特殊阶层人民的术语,赋予其比喻的意义并将之用于日常生活中的语言。许多用于日

language of a profession or a party are thus drawn into general circulation.

The most common expedient employed by democratic nations to make an innovation in language consists in giving an unwonted meaning to an expression already in use. This method is very simple, prompt, and convenient; no learning is required to use it correctly and ignorance itself rather facilitates the practice; but that practice is most dangerous to the language. When a democratic people double the meaning of a word in this way, they sometimes render the meaning which it retains as ambiguous as that which it acquires. An author begins by a slight deflection of a known expression from its primitive meaning, and he adapts it, thus modified, as well as he can to his subject. A second writer twists the sense of the expression in another way; a third takes possession of it for another purpose; and as there is no common appeal to the sentence of a permanent tribunal that may definitively settle the meaning of the word, it remains in an unsettled condition. The consequence is that writers hardly ever appear to dwell upon a single thought, but they always seem to aim at a group of ideas, leaving the reader to judge which of them has been hit.

This is a deplorable consequence of democracy. I had rather that the language should be made hideous with words imported from the Chinese, the Tatars, or the Hurons than that the meaning of a word in our own language should become indeterminate. Harmony and uniformity are only secondary beauties in composition: many of these things are conventional, and, strictly speaking, it is possible to do without them; but without clear phraseology there is no good language.

The principle of equality necessarily introduces several other changes into language.

In aristocratic ages, when each nation tends to stand aloof from all others and likes to have a physiognomy of its own, it often happens that several communities which have a common origin become nevertheless strangers to each other; so that, without ceasing to understand the same language, they no longer all speak it in the same manner. In these ages each nation is divided into a certain number

常生活的表达词汇都是源于一些行业或政党的专业术语。

民主国家对语言的革新,最常用的权宜之计,就是给一些旧的词汇赋予全新的含义。这种方法简单方便快捷。人们并不需要学习就可以正确地加以运用,而且对于一无所知的人更方便运用,但是这种操作方法对语言本身来说存在着很大的危险。当民主国家的人民通过这种方法赋予一个词汇多种含义的时候,也常常难免使其本身的含义和新赋予的词义都变得含混不清。一个作者开始用这个词的时候,与其原始的词义稍有偏差,他这样用了,然后又根据自己的需要对其加以修饰。第二位作者将这两种含义用另一种方法混合起来使用。然后另一位作者又将其含义用作他途。结果,因为并没有一个公正的判决可以对这个词的含义下一定论,于是它的含义就变得模棱两可。结果就是,作者们所表达的含义往往各有不同,而他们对于其含义也仿佛有多种想法,最终只能让读者去猜测作家们的本意了。

这是民主造成的一个可叹的结果。我宁愿我们的语言因为加入了一些从汉语,鞑靼语或者休伦语中引进的单词而变得丑陋不堪,也不愿我们的词义变得含混不清。毕竟,谐声和押韵只是写作的次要方面:在这方面,许多规则都是既定的,严格地说,完全可以没有它们。但是,如果缺少了清晰的措辞,就不能成为优秀的语言了。

平等的原则有必要在语言方面引入一些变化。

在贵族时期,各个民族都彼此隔绝,有着自己的特点。所以几个本是同源的民族,却终于形同陌路。最后,他们虽然还使用着同一种语言,可他们使用的方式却大相径庭。在这样的时代

of classes, which see but little of each other and do not intermingle. Each of these classes contracts and invariably retains habits of mind peculiar to itself and adopts by choice certain terms which afterwards pass from generation to generation, like their estates. The same idiom then comprises a language of the poor and a language of the rich, a language of the commoner and a language of the nobility, a learned language and a colloquial one. The deeper the divisions and the more impassable the barriers of society become, the more must this be the case. I would lay a wager that among the castes of India there are a-mazing variations of language, and that there is almost as much differ-ence between the language of a pariah and that of a Brahmin as there is in their dress.

When, on the contrary, men, being no longer restrained by ranks, meet on terms of constant intercourse, when castes are de-stroyed and the classes of society are recruited from and intermixed with each other, all the words of a language are mingled. Those which are unsuitable to the greater number perish; the remainder form a common store, whence everyone chooses pretty nearly at random. Almost all the different dialects that divided the idioms of European nations are manifestly declining; there is no patois in the New World, and it is disappearing every day from the old countries.

The influence of this revolution in social condition is as much felt in style as it is in language. Not only does everyone use the same words, but a habit springs up of using them without discrimination. The rules which style had set up are almost abolished: the line ceases to be drawn between expressions which seem by their very nature vul-gar and others which appear to be refined. Persons springing from dif-ferent ranks of society carry with them the terms and expressions they are accustomed to use into whatever circumstances they may enter; thus the origin of words is lost like the origin of individuals, and there is as much confusion in language as there is in society.

I am aware that in the classification of words there are rules which do not belong to one form of society any more than to another, but which are derived from the nature of things. Some expressions and phrases are vulgar because the ideas they are meant to express

中,每个民族都被分为一定数目的阶级,这些阶级之间彼此很少往来,不相融合。每个阶级都固守着自己特有的思维习惯,采用一些经过选择而来的固定词组,同他们的遗产一样,世代相传。因此在同一种方言中,既包含有穷人用的语言,也有富人用的语言,既有有学识的人用的语言,也有口语化的语言。社会之间的分化越深,彼此间的隔阂越难以跨越,这种现象就越严重。我敢打赌,在印度的世袭阶级中,存在着多种不同的语言,如同他们所穿戴的服装一样,在最下层人民之间所用的语言必然与婆罗门的语言存在着显著的差别。

相反地,当人们不再受到阶级限制,彼此之间可以进行频繁的交流的时候,当等级制度被破坏,社会阶层复原并重新融合的时候,所有的语言就会相互融合。那些对大多数不适用的语言将会被取消。而剩余的词汇将会形成公用的词汇总库,人们可以任意选取。将欧洲分化为几大语言区域的一切方言,都明显地衰退。新大陆上将不再有方言,即使是在旧大陆上,方言也在一天天消失。

社会变革带来的影响,不但涉及了语言,而且影响了文体。每个人不仅仅使用相同的词汇,而且养成了一种习惯,对所有的词汇都有同样的理解。文体方面树立的规则几乎全部废除:例如,粗俗的语言和精致的语言表达之间不再有界限。社会不同阶级的人们,带着他们所熟悉惯用的短语和词汇,可以进入到任何他们需要打入的环境之中。因此,单词的原始含义如果个体的出身一样消失不见,语言将同社会一样浑然一体。

我明白,区别单词的规则,并不是隶属于哪一种社会形式,而是来源于事物的本性。有些表达方式和句子显得粗俗,是因为它

are low in themselves; others are of a higher character because the objects they are intended to designate are naturally lofty. No intermixture of ranks will ever efface these differences. But the principle of equality cannot fail to root out whatever is merely conventional and arbitrary in the forms of thought. Perhaps the necessary classification that I have just pointed out will always be less respected by a democratic people than by any other, because among such a people there are no men who are permanently disposed, by education, culture, and leisure, to study the natural laws of language and who cause those laws to be respected by their own observance of them.

I shall not leave this topic without touching on a feature of democratic languages that is, perhaps, more characteristic of them than any other. It has already been shown that democratic nations have a taste and sometimes a passion for general ideas, and that this arises from their peculiar merits and defects. This liking for general ideas is displayed in democratic languages by the continual use of generic terms or abstract expressions and by the manner in which they are employed. This is the great merit and the great imperfection of these languages.

Democratic nations are passionately addicted to generic terms and abstract expressions because these modes of speech enlarge thought and assist the operations of the mind by enabling it to include many objects in a small compass. A democratic writer will be apt to speak of *capacities* in the abstract for men of capacity and without specifying the objects to which their capacity is applied; he will talk about *actualities* to designate in one word the things passing before his eyes at the moment; and, in French, he will comprehend under the term *éventualits* whatever may happen in the universe, dating from the moment at which he speaks. Democratic writers are perpetually coining abstract words of this kind, in which they sublimate into further abstraction the abstract terms of the language. Moreover, to render their mode of speech more succinct, they personify the object of these abstract terms and make it act like a real person. Thus they would say in French: *La force des choses veut que les capacités gouvernent.*

们所要表达的含义本身的低下的性质,而另一些显得高贵则是由于它们所指的对象本身的性质高贵。没有任何一种等级之间的融合,能永远消除这些差异。但是平等的原则可以根除无论是思想中的传统因素或者武断因素产生的结果。也许,我前面所指出的阶级划分的必要性在民主社会将永远不会比在其他社会受到更多的重视,因为在民主国家中,没有人会因为教育、文化和消遣的原因而倾向于研究语言的自然规律,也没有人能自己考察这些规律并使它受到人们的重视。

我不能不讲民主国家与其他国家的语言的最后一个差别。这一差别也许比其他特性更突出。前面已经说过,民主国家人民爱好或者说热爱一般观念。这源自他们固有的特性。他们的这种对一般观念的爱好在民主的语言中的表现,是通过长期使用专业术语和抽象概念,以及他们所运用的方法的结果。这就是这些语言最大的优缺点所在。

民主国家对于通用术语和抽象表达有着极大的热情,因为这种语言表达方式扩展了他们的思想,通过把大量的对象囊括在一个小范围内帮助思想活动。一位民主国家的作者倾向于用"有才干"一词抽象地表示某人有能力,而不会去赘述具体在哪些方面具有能力。他会用一个词"现状"来表示此刻他眼前所发生的事物。在法语中,人们会用"偶然性"一词概括从他说话起的那个时刻在宇宙中可能发生的事情。民主国家的作者不断地创造这类抽象的词汇,或者是语言中抽象的名词进一步抽象化。除此之外,为了使他们的讲话更简洁,他们给这些抽象的短语赋予人性化的含义,使它们具有像人一样的行为反应。这样,在法语中,他们就会说,物力喜欢人才支配它。

I cannot better illustrate what I mean than by my own example. I have frequently used the word *equality* in an absolute sense; nay, I have personified equality in several places; thus I have said that e- quality does such and such things or refrains from doing others. It may be affirmed that the writers of the age of Louis XIV would not have spoken in this manner; they would never have thought of using the word *equality* without applying it to some particular thing; and they would rather have renounced the term altogether than have con- sented to make it a living personage. These abstract terms which a- bound in democratic languages, and which are used on every occasion without attaching them to any particular fact, enlarge and obscure the thoughts they are intended to convey; they render the mode of speech more succinct and the idea contained in it less clear. But with regard to language, democratic nations prefer obscurity to labor.

I do not know, indeed, whether this loose style has not some se- cret charm for those who speak and write among these nations. As the men who live there are frequently left to the efforts of their individual powers of mind, they are almost always a prey to doubt; and as their situation in life is forever changing, they are never held fast to any of their opinions by the immobility of their fortunes. Men living in demo- cratic countries, then, are apt to entertain unsettled ideas, and they require loose expressions to convey them. As they never know whether the idea they express today will be appropriate to the new position they may occupy tomorrow, they naturally acquire a liking for abstract terms. An abstract term is like a box with a false bottom; you may put in it what ideas you please, and take them out again without being ob- served.

Among all nations generic and abstract terms form the basis of language. I do not, therefore, pretend that these terms are found only in democratic languages; I say only that men have a special tendency in

　　我用我自己的例子来证明这一说法是再合适不过了。我以前常常习惯于使用"平等"这个词表达一种绝对的意义。不仅如此，我还在许多地方将这个词人格化。因此，我说过，平等使得怎样怎样或者平等禁止什么什么。可以确信的是，路易十四时期的作家们，不会用这样的语气写作。他们也许根本不会想到在使用"平等"一词时，不用它去明确地指出某一事物。他们也许宁愿完全不用这个词组也不会同意将之人格化。这种抽象用法在民主国家的语言中比比皆是，并且总是被用于不明确地与特定的事物联系起来，这也就在扩大人的思想的同时，模糊了人的概念。虽然它们使语言的表达方式更加简洁，但是其所包含的意思就变得不那么清晰了。但是，考虑到语言本身，民主国家宁愿使其意思含糊也不愿对其加以详细分析。

　　事实上，我不知道是否这种松散的形式对于那些在这些国家中生活的在读写方面使用这些语言的人们有某种隐秘的魅力。由于这些生活在那些国家中的人们，经常需要依靠它们自己的脑力劳动做出判断，所以他们总是犹豫不决。而且，由于他们的生活环境总是处于不断地变化之中，所以即使他们的财产固定不变，他们的思想观念也不会持久不变。生活在民主国家的人们的思想极易变化，他们需要用一些笼统的语言表达他们的思想。由于他们永远也无法确定自己今天的观点是否还会适用于明天新的立场，所以他们很自然地就会选择将之抽象化。一个抽象化的短语就像一个有两层底的箱子，你可以随意地把自己的想法放进去，而再次把他们取出来的时候又可以不引起人们的注意。

　　笼统的和抽象的短语组成了所有国家的语言基础。因此，我并不认为只有民主国家的语言才存在这种短语。我只说明，在民

the ages of democracy to multiply words of this kind, to take them always by themselves in their most abstract acceptation, and to use them on all occasions, even when the nature of the discourse does not require them.

主国家生活的人们，对这类词汇有一种特殊的喜好，他们总是选取一些最抽象的意思，并将之运用到各个方面，即使有时候根本没有必要。

CHAPTER XVII
Of Some Sources Of Poetry
Among Democratic Nations

Many different meanings have been given to the word *poetry*. It would weary my readers if I were to discuss which of these definitions ought to be selected; I prefer telling them at once that which I have chosen. In my opinion, Poetry is the search after, and the delineation of, the Ideal.

The Poet is he who, by suppressing a part of what exists, by adding some imaginary touches to the picture, and by combining certain real circumstances that do not in fact happen together, completes and extends the work of nature. Thus the object of poetry is not to represent what is true, but to adorn it and to present to the mind some loftier image. Verse, regarded as the ideal beauty of language, may be eminently poetical; but verse does not of itself constitute poetry.

I now proceed to inquire whether among the actions, the sentiments, and the opinions of democratic nations there are any which lead to a conception of the ideal, and which may for this reason be considered as natural sources of poetry.

It must, in the first place, be acknowledged that the taste for ideal beauty, and the pleasure derived from the expression of it, are never so intense or so diffused among a democratic as among an aristocratic people. In aristocratic nations it sometimes happens that the body acts as it were spontaneously, while the higher faculties are bound and burdened by repose. Among these nations the people will often display poetic tastes, and their fancy sometimes ranges beyond and above what surrounds them.

第十七章　民主国家诗的某些来源

诗这个单词被赋予了许多不同的意义。如果我开始讨论应该选择这些当中哪一个含义势必会使我的读者感到厌烦。我宁肯直接告诉他们答案。我认为,诗是对理想的追求和描绘。

诗人是通过在描写的过程中剔除一部分现实的东西,加进一些想象的成分,融入若干并非同时发生的真实存在的手法而使自然更完美更广阔的人。因此,诗的目的并不在于再现真实,而在于将之美化并在人的思想中形成一种美好的影像。韵,作为语言的一种理想的完美,也许还饱含诗意,但是韵其自身并不能称之为诗。

我在这里要探讨的是,是否在民主国家人们的行为、情感和观念中存在着某些使人们趋于完美的观念,还有哪些可以因此被认为是诗的自然的源泉。

首先,必须承认,对于理想中的完美的喜好,以及来源于对其表述的愉悦,在民主国家从未像在贵族制国家中一样,显得如此强烈而广泛。在贵族制国家,肉体的活动有时好像是自发的,而精神的活动则离不开宁静。在这些国家中的人民,常常表现出一种对于诗的爱好,他们的想象也常常远远高于或超越了他们周遭的一切。

But in democracies the love of physical gratification, the notion of bettering one's condition, the excitement of competition, the charm of anticipated success, are so many spurs to urge men onward in the active professions they have embraced, without allowing them to deviate for an instant from the track. The main stress of the faculties is to this point. The imagination is not extinct, but its chief function is to devise what may be useful and to represent what is real. The principle of equality not only diverts men from the description of ideal beauty; it also diminishes the number of objects to be described.

Aristocracy, by maintaining society in a fixed position, is favorable to the solidity and duration of positive religions as well as to the stability of political institutions. Not only does it keep the human mind within a certain sphere of belief, but it predisposes the mind to adopt one faith rather than another. An aristocratic people will always be prone to place intermediate powers between God and man. In this respect it may be said that the aristocratic element is favorable to poetry. When the universe is peopled with supernatural beings, not palpable to sense, but discovered by the mind, the imagination ranges freely; and poets, finding a thousand subjects to delineate, also find a countless audience to take an interest in their productions.

In democratic ages it sometimes happens, on the contrary, that men are as much afloat in matters of faith as they are in their laws. Skepticism then draws the imagination of poets back to earth and confines them to the real and visible world. Even when the principle of equality does not disturb religious conviction, it tends to simplify it and to divert attention from secondary agents, to fix it principally on the Supreme Power.

Aristocracy naturally leads the human mind to the contemplation of the past and fixes it there. Democracy, on the contrary, gives men a sort of instinctive distaste for what is ancient. In this respect aristocracy is far more favorable to poetry; for things commonly grow larger and more obscure as they are more remote, and for this twofold reason

但在民主国家中,对于物质享受的热爱,改善人们环境的观念,竞争的刺激,渴望成功的魅力像许多锥子似的刺激着人们在自己的事业中前进,一刻也不允许它们从自己的轨道中脱离。人们的主要精力都用在了这一方面。人们的想象力还没有枯竭,但是其主要作用已经是为了构思哪些是有利用价值的,或者只是再现一些真实存在的东西。平等的主要原则不仅仅使人们放弃了对美好事物的描述,也使得可以描述的对象越来越少。

贵族制度在将社会维持在一个固定状态的同时,也有利于政治制度的稳定和正统宗教的可靠持续发展。它不仅仅将人类的思想局限在一定信仰范围之内,而且它还使人们的思想在选择一种信仰的同时放弃另一种信仰。一个贵族制国家的人民总是倾向于在上帝与人之间放置一个中间力量。在这方面,可以说贵族化的因素有利于诗的创作。当宇宙间充满感官无法感知,只有精神才能察觉的超自然存在时,想象力就可以自由驰骋,可以供诗人描写的对象数以千计,而且也会找到无数欣赏诗人作品的读者。

在民主时期,事情的发生常常刚好相反。人们在信仰上和他们对在法律时一样飘忽不定。怀疑论把诗人的想象力硬生生拉回现实,并将他们局限在真实可见的世界中。即使当平等的原则不再扰乱宗教信念,它也趋向于将其简化或者将注意力从一些次要的方面引开,将其锁定在对最高上帝的崇拜方面。

贵族制天生使人们的思想趋于对过去的沉思,并把它固定在这种沉思之中。民主则相反,它给予人们一种天生的对古老的事物的反感心理。在这一方面,贵族制对诗的创作更有利。因为事物越是离我们遥远,就越显得高大而宏伟,在这种双重作用的影

they are better suited to the delineation of the ideal.

After having deprived poetry of the past, the principle of equality robs it in part of the present. Among aristocratic nations there is a certain number of privileged personages whose situation is, as it were, without and above the condition of man; to these, power, wealth, fame, wit, refinement, and distinction in all things appear peculiarly to belong. The crowd never sees them very closely or does not watch them in minute details, and little is needed to make the description of such men poetical. On the other hand, among the same people you will meet with classes so ignorant, low, and enslaved that they are no less fit objects for poetry, from the excess of their rudeness and wretchedness, than the former are from their greatness and refinement. Besides, as the different classes of which an aristocratic community is composed are widely separated and imperfectly acquainted with each other, the imagination may always represent them with some addition to, or some subtraction from, what they really are.

In democratic communities, where men are all insignificant and very much alike, each man instantly sees all his fellows when he surveys himself. The poets of democratic ages, therefore, can never take any man in particular as the subject of a piece; for an object of slender importance, which is distinctly seen on all sides, will never lend itself to an ideal conception.

Thus the principle of equality, in proportion as it has established itself in the world, has dried up most of the old springs of poetry. Let us now attempt to see what new ones it may disclose.

When skepticism had depopulated heaven, and the progress of equality had reduced each individual to smaller and better-known proportions, the poets, not yet aware of what they could substitute for the great themes that were departing together with the aristocracy, turned their eyes to inanimate nature. As they lost sight of gods and heroes, they set themselves to describe streams and mountains. Thence originated, in the last century, that kind of poetry which has been called, by way of distinction, *descriptive*. Some have thought that this embellished delineation of all the physical and inanimate objects which cover the earth was the kind of poetry peculiar to democratic ages; but I believe this to be an error,

响下,他们就变得更趋于完美化。

在剥夺了诗的古老过去之后,平等原则又夺取了它现在的一部分。在贵族制国家中,有一定数量的有特权的人们,他们的地位独立于或者说高于一般人之外。对这些人来说,一切好的东西:权力、财富、名誉、智慧、优雅和卓越都是他们的。群众从来没有近距离接触过他们或者仔细地观察过他们,使这些在他们心目中诗化很容易。另一方面,在同一个民族中,你还会见到另一些无名阶层的人们,他们地位低下,被人奴役,他们由于自身的极度粗俗和悲惨不同于前者的伟大优雅,也被纳入了诗人描写的对象。除此之外,贵族制国家的不同阶级是彼此隔离不相了解的,于是,凭借想象力再现他们的时候,总是会对他们的实际情况添油加醋或者舍弃一些东西。

在民主社会里,所有人都平凡而相似,所以每个人在观察自己的时候,就等于看到了他的同类的情况。民主时期的诗人不能仅用某个个体来代替某个主题。因为一个平凡的,清楚地显现在人们面前的个体,绝不能抽象成为一个完美的概念。

因此,随着平等的原则的出现,便使得古老的诗的源泉逐渐枯竭。让我们试着寻找它所展现的新的源泉。

当怀疑论使人们不再相信天堂的存在,当平等的进程使人们越来越相似、越来越渺小的时候,诗人还没有意识到什么可以替代这一随着贵族制度消亡的伟大的旋律,于是他们把目光转向了枯燥的大自然。诗人的眼睛里没有了英雄和诸神以后,他们便开始描写山水。于是,在上一世纪,便诞生了被人们为了加以区分而称为"田园诗"的诗。有些人觉得这种对世上存在的物质性的和枯燥的对象加以修饰性的描述,是民主时期特有的一种诗的表现形式。我认为这

and that it belongs only to a period of transition.

I am persuaded that in the end democracy diverts the imagination from all that is external to man and fixes it on man alone. Democratic nations may amuse themselves for a while with considering the productions of nature, but they are excited in reality only by a survey of themselves. Here, and here alone, the true sources of poetry among such nations are to be found; and it may be believed that the poets who neglect to draw their inspirations hence will lose all sway over the minds which they would enchant, and will be left in the end with none but unimpassioned spectators of their transports.

I have shown how the ideas of progress and of the indefinite perfectibility of the human race belong to democratic ages. Democratic nations care but little for what has been, but they are haunted by visions of what will be; in this direction their unbounded imagination grows and dilates beyond all measure. Here, then, is the widest range open to the genius of poets, which allows them to remove their performances to a sufficient distance from the eye. Democracy, which shuts the past against the poet, opens the future before him.

As all the citizens who compose a democratic community are nearly equal and alike, the poet cannot dwell upon any one of them; but the nation itself invites the exercise of his powers. The general similitude of individuals, which renders any one of them taken separately an improper subject of poetry, allows poets to include them all in the same imagery and to take a general survey of the people itself. Democratic nations have a clearer perception than any others of their own aspect; and an aspect so imposing is admirably fitted to the delineation of the ideal.

I readily admit that the Americans have no poets; I cannot allow that they have no poetic ideas. In Europe people talk a great deal of the wilds of America, but the Americans themselves never think about them; they are insensible to the wonders of inanimate nature and they may be said not to perceive the mighty forests that surround them till they fall beneath the hatchet. Their eyes are fixed upon another sight:

种看法是错误的。我以为这种诗只是过渡时期的代表。

我相信,民主最终必使想象力从身外之物转向人本身,并使想象力只专注于人。民主国家可能会在一段时间内对这种自然界的生物产生兴趣,但是在现实生活中,他们感兴趣的只有对他们自身的研究。也只有在这里,这些国家的诗的真实的源泉才会被发现。也许我们应该相信,那些忽略掉去挖掘着这一源泉的诗人,就会失去对于他们想打动的那帮人的影响力,最终只会落得使人们在看完他们的作品之后面无表情。

我已经说过专属于民主时期的人类希望进步和无限完善的思想。民主国家的人民从不关心已经发生过的一切,而只关心他们如野马般的思想未来前进的方向,并逐渐扩大和升高。因此,在这里,诗人们的天赋有了广阔的发挥空间,为他们的才能提供了广阔的视野。对诗人们关闭了过往的民主社会,同时为他们开启了面向未来的大门。

由于民主社会的公民彼此大致是平等相同的,所以诗人不会去专门描写其中的某个人,但民族本身却可以入诗。个人之间的彼此相似,使某一个人不宜单独入诗,但容许诗人把所有的个人合成为一个形象,对整个民族进行描绘。民主的民族对于本身的形象,比其他任何民族都有更清晰的认识,而这个伟大的形象则为理想的塑造提供了最好的素材。

我乐意承认美国是没有诗人的,但我不能苟同他们没有诗化的思想。欧洲国家的人民谈论的最多的,是美国的荒凉,但是美国人民自己并不那么认为。他们对死气沉沉的大自然的事物没有感觉,可以这么说,如果不是森林被砍伐殆尽的话,他们根本就不会意识到有森林的存在。他们被另一种现象吸引了注意力,那

the American people views its own march across these wilds, draining swamps, turning the course of rivers, peopling solitudes, arid subduing nature. This magnificent image of themselves does not meet the gaze of the Americans at intervals only; it may be said to haunt every one of them in his least as well as in his most important actions and to be always flitting before his mind.

Nothing conceivable is so petty, so insipid, so crowded with paltry interests—in one word, so antipoetic—as the life of a man in the United States. But among the thoughts which it suggests, there is always one that is full of poetry, and this is the hidden nerve which gives vigor to the whole frame.

In aristocratic ages each people as well as each individual is prone to stand separate and aloof from all others. In democratic ages the extreme fluctuations of men and the impatience of their desires keep them perpetually on the move, so that the inhabitants of different countries intermingle, see, listen to, and borrow from each other. It is not only the members of the same community, then, who grow more alike; communities themselves are assimilated to one another, and the whole assemblage presents to the eye of the spectator one vast democracy, each citizen of which is a nation. This displays the aspect of mankind for the first time in the broadest light. All that belongs to the existence of the human race taken as a whole, to its vicissitudes and its future, becomes an abundant mine of poetry.

The poets who lived in aristocratic ages have been eminently successful in their delineations of certain incidents in the life of a people or a man; but none of them ever ventured to include within his performances the destinies of mankind, a task which poets writing in democratic ages may attempt.

At that same time at which every man, raising his eyes above his country, begins at length to discern mankind at large, the Deity is more and more manifest to the human mind in full and entire majesty. If in democratic ages faith in positive religion be often shaken and the belief in intermediate agents, by whatever name they are called, be overcast, on the other hand men are disposed to conceive a far broader idea of Providence itself, and its interference in human affairs assumes a new and more imposing appearance to their eyes. Looking at the human race as one great whole, they easily conceive that its destinies are regulated by the same design; and in the actions of every

就是,他们当时一心一意要穿越这片荒野,排干沼泽,改变河道,开发荒野,征服这片贫瘠的大自然产物。他们的这一伟大梦想从未须臾逃离过他们的眼睛。可以说这一梦想牵引着每个人,融入了每个人的行为并一直在他们脑海中闪耀。

我们所能想象到的任何东西,都不会显得如此渺小、平淡、充满了琐碎的欲望,总之,如此没有诗意,就像美国人民的生活。但是,在指引生活前进的所有思想中,总有一个是富于诗意的。她就像一根隐秘的神经,为整个机体提供活力。

在贵族时期,每个民族和一个个单个个体一样,都彼此隔离互不往来。在民主时期,人们极端的波动和他们急躁的欲求使他们总是处于前进的状态,导致不同国家的居民相互融合,彼此学习、倾听,取长补短。不仅仅是同一个社会中的成员如此,社会本身也趋于彼此相似,于是在人们眼前呈现出一片广袤的民主,每一个公民都是一个民族。这是首次如此清晰地展示了人类的面貌。所有人类存在都成为一个整体,它的兴衰和它的未来,便成了诗人无限的源泉。

生活在贵族时期的诗人,在他们对一个民族或个人一生发生的事件的描绘方面取得了不同寻常的成就。但是却没有一个人敢于将人类的命运加以描述,而这一任务则可能由民主时期的诗人作出尝试。

在每个人都能超越自己的国家限制,放眼纵观人类的这一时期,神谕在人们的思想中也越来越多地显示出了它最强大最彻底的权威。如果说在民主时期,人们常常会动摇对正统宗教的信心,而对他们所称呼的一些居间权威的信任也逐渐消失的时候,在另一方面,人们展示了人们对于神意本身的认识已变得更广泛了,而神意对人类事务的干预也以一种全新的更显著的效果出现在他们眼前。把人类民族当作一个整体纵览,就会轻易地发现,

individual they are led to acknowledge a trace of that universal and e-
ternal plan by which God rules our race. This consideration may be
taken as another prolific source of poetry which is opened in democratic times.

Democratic poets will always appear trivial and frigid if they seek
to invest gods, demons, or angels with corporeal forms and if they attempt to draw them down from heaven to dispute the supremacy of
earth. But if they strive to connect the great events they commemorate
with the general providential designs that govern the universe and,
without showing the finger of the Supreme Governor, reveal the
thoughts of the Supreme Mind, their works will be admired and understood, for the imagination of their contemporaries takes this direction of its own accord.

It may be foreseen in like manner that poets living in democratic
times will prefer the delineation of passions and ideas to that of persons and achievements. The language, the dress, and the daily actions of men in democracies are repugnant to conceptions of the ideal.
These things are not poetical in themselves; and if it were otherwise,
they would cease to be so, because they are too familiar to all those to
whom the poet would speak of them. This forces the poet constantly to
search below the external surface which is palpable to the senses, in
order to read the inner soul; and nothing lends itself more to the delineation of the ideal than the scrutiny of the hidden depths in the immaterial nature of man. I need not traverse earth and sky to discover a
wondrous object woven of contrasts, of in finite greatness and littleness, of intense gloom and amazing brightness, capable at once of exciting pity, admiration, terror, contempt. I have only to look at myself. Man springs out of nothing, crosses time, and disappears forever
in the bosom of God; he is seen but for a moment, wandering on the
verge of the two abysses, and there he is lost.

If man were wholly ignorant of himself, he would have no poetry
in him; for it is impossible to describe what the mind does not conceive. If man clearly discerned his own nature, his imagination
would remain idle and would have nothing to add to the picture. But

其命运都是受控于同一旨意的。每个个体的行为中，都能看出受到一种普遍的和不灭的神的指引的痕迹。这样的认识，也可以被看作是民主时期另一个丰富的诗源。

民主时期的诗人总是试图赋予上帝、撒旦或者天使以血肉之躯，或者期望是他们降临人世推翻在地上的一切统治，所以他们总是表现得很琐碎无力。但是，如果他们致力于将他们纪念的这些伟大的事件与统治宇宙的普遍神谕联系起来的时候，并且不向人们显示至高无上的神的肉身，而仅仅展示神的思想，他们的作品就会受到大家的尊敬并获得共鸣。因为这也是他们同时代的人的想象力发展的方向。

同样的方法，我们也可以预料到，生活在民主时期的诗人更喜欢描绘人们的激情和思想，而不仅限于人物本身或者他们获得的成就。民主国家人们的语言、穿着和日常行为，与人们的理想观念完全不同。这些东西本身没有任何诗意，而且即使不是这样，他们也不会把它们写进诗里，因为人们对诗人所要说的这些都太熟悉了。这就使诗人不断地要到感官所能触碰的表面现象的里面去探索内在的灵魂。于是能深入自己的灵魂深处，就越是能帮助他塑造理想的形象。我不必上天入地到处去寻找矛盾纠结的物体，它兼具伟大和弱小、黑暗和光明，能够立即激起人们的怜悯、崇敬、恐惧和蔑视。我只要观察自己就行了。人从无处来，穿越时间的隧道，最终消失在上帝的怀抱之中。他停留的时间短暂，在生与死的边缘徘徊，最终消失殆尽。

人如果对自己一无所知，那他永远不会心怀诗意。因为如果人的思想如果想象不出，那他就无法描述诗境。如果人对自己认识得很清晰，他的想象力极度空虚，也无法为描述的图画增添内

the nature of man is sufficiently disclosed for him to know something of himself, and sufficiently obscure for all the rest to be plunged in thick darkness, in which he gropes forever, and forever in vain, to lay hold on some completer notion of his being.

Among a democratic people poetry will not be fed with legends or the memorials of old traditions. The poet will not attempt to people the universe with supernatural beings, in whom his readers and his own fancy have ceased to believe; nor will he coldly personify virtues and vices, which are better received under their own features. All these resources fail him; but Man remains, and the poet needs no more. The destinies of mankind, man himself taken aloof from his country and his age and standing in the presence of Nature and of God, with his passions, his doubts, his rare prosperities and inconceivable wretchedness, will become the chief, if not the sole, theme of poetry among these nations.

Experience may confirm this assertion if we consider the productions of the greatest poets who have appeared since the world has been turned to democracy. The authors of our age who have so admirably delineated the features of Faust, Childe Harold, Ren, and Jocelyn did not seek to record the actions of an individual, but to enlarge and to throw light on some of the obscurer recesses of the human heart.

Such are the poems of democracy. The principle of equality does not, then, destroy all the subjects of poetry: it renders them less numerous, but more vast.

容。但是，人的天性使得他能清楚地认识自己，但是糊涂的一面也使得他在其他方面的认识处于一片混沌。在这片混沌中，他摸索着有关人类的完整概念，却总是徒劳无功。

民主国家的诗不会以传奇或者用传统和古代传闻为题材。诗人们也不会试图让宇宙间到处都充满超自然的力量的痕迹，因为这些在读者和他自己的想象中都已不复相信。他也不会冷漠地将人性的美德和恶习人格化地表现出来，因为这些都显而易见。所有这些都不是他们取材的来源。只要人类存在，对诗来说就足够了。人类的命运，呈现在大自然和神面前的国家和时代，以及他们的激情、疑问、鲜有的繁荣和难以想象的苦难，都将成为，即使不是唯一的，也是这些国家中诗的主要旋律。

如果我们对那些自世界转入民主时期后的最伟大的诗人的作品加以考虑，就知道此言不差。当代作家们在生动地刻画出卡尔德·哈罗德、勒内、若斯兰等人的容貌的时候，并没有力求记录每个人的行为，而是对人心的隐藏的一面加以夸大和照亮。

这就是民主时期的诗。平等的原则并没有毁掉诗所有的题材，只是使它们的数量减少，范围变广了。

CHAPTER XVIII

Why American Writers And Orators
Often Use An Inflated Style

I have frequently noticed that the Americans, who generally treat of business in clear, plain language, devoid of all ornament and so extremely simple as to be often coarse, are apt to become inflated as soon as they attempt a more poetical diction. They then vent their pomposity from one end of a harangue to the other; and to hear them lavish imagery on every occasion, one might fancy that they never spoke of anything with simplicity.

The English less frequently commit a similar fault. The cause of this may be pointed out without much difficulty. In democratic communities, each citizen is habitually engaged in the contemplation of a very puny object: namely, himself. If he ever raises his looks higher, he perceives only the immense form of society at large or the still more imposing aspect of mankind. His ideas are all either extremely minute and clear or extremely general and vague; what lies between is a void. When he has been drawn out of his own sphere, therefore, he always expects that some amazing object will be offered to his attention; and it is on these terms alone that he consents to tear himself for a moment from the petty, complicated cares that form the charm and the excitement of his life.

This appears to me sufficiently to explain why men in democracies, whose concerns are in general so paltry, call upon their poets for conceptions so vast and descriptions so unlimited.

第十八章　为什么美国的作家和演说家总爱夸张

我常常会注意到,美国人总是用清楚简洁的言语对待所有事物,避免一切修饰,并且这种极度的简洁常常会显得有些言语粗俗,但是,一旦他们开始某种富于诗意的言辞,他们就变得夸张起来。他们通篇都是华丽的词藻,在任何方面都用想象大加渲染,这时候,人们会觉得他们从来说话都不会简洁。

英国人就很少犯这样的错误。这个原因并不难指出。在民主国家中,每个公民都习惯于对微小的事物冥思苦想,或者说对于自己有关的事物冥思苦想煞费苦心。如果他们一旦拓宽眼界,他们就会总揽社会无穷的形态,或者说人类更为显著的方面。这样,他的思想就要么变得极度的琐碎清晰,要么就变得宽广笼统。而在这两种极端之间确实存在一个空档。当他脱离自己的小氛围后,他就总是期望见到一些令人惊异的事物,而且也只有在这些事件上,他才会允许自己偶尔从那些构成他独具魅力和活力的生活的琐碎、复杂的事情中脱离出来。

对我来说,这足以说明为什么民族国家人民所关心的问题总体来说是如此的琐碎,却要求他们的诗人的作品题材广泛、描述夸张。

The authors, on their part, do not fail to obey a propensity of which they themselves partake; they perpetually inflate their imaginations, and, expanding them beyond all bounds, they not infrequently abandon the great in order to reach the gigantic. By these means they hope to attract the observation of the multitude and to fix it easily upon themselves; nor are their hopes disappointed, for as the multitude seeks for nothing in poetry but objects of vast dimensions, it has neither the time to measure with accuracy the proportions of all the objects set before it nor a taste sufficiently correct to perceive at once in what respect they are out of proportion. The author and the public at once vitiate one another.

We have also seen that among democratic nations the sources of poetry are grand, but not abundant. They are soon exhausted; and poets, not finding the elements of the ideal in what is real and true, abandon them entirely and create monsters. I do not fear that the poetry of democratic nations will prove insipid or that it will fly too near the ground; I rather apprehend that it will be forever losing itself in the clouds and that it will range at last to purely imaginary regions. I fear that the productions of democratic poets may often be surcharged with immense and incoherent imagery, with exaggerated descriptions and strange creations; and that the fantastic beings of their brain may sometimes make us regret the world of reality.

从作者的角度出发,他们本身也有这种本性。他们总是无限地夸大其想象,跨越一切的束缚,他们为了达到宏伟的目的不愿放弃任何对伟大事物的描述。他们希望通过这种方法吸引人们的注意力,让他们的视线锁定在自己的作品上面。他们的期望没有破灭,因为人民大众也正想从他们的诗中寻找一些伟大的东西。他们没有时间去衡量眼前的主体是否适合,他们也没有能力一眼就看出来那些地方不对。结果,这给作家和读者双方都带来损害。

我们已看出,民主国家的诗的来源还是好的,只是不特别富足。源泉不久会枯竭。诗人们因为在真实的生活中找不到理想的素材,就完全将之抛弃并创造出一些奇怪的东西。我并不担心民主国家的诗会变得平淡无奇或者过于接近现实生活。我反而觉得它将会迷失自己最终陷入纯想象的境地。我害怕民主国家诗人的作品常常充斥着过多的不和谐的想象,夸张的言词和奇怪的描写。我害怕他们的头脑里满是幻想,而终使我们觉得现实的可叹。

CHAPTER XIX

Some Observations On The Drama
Among Democratic Nations

When the revolution that has changed the social and political state of an aristocratic people begins to penetrate into literature, it generally first manifests itself in the drama, and it always remains conspicuous there.

The spectator of a dramatic piece is, to a certain extent, taken by surprise by the impression it conveys. He has no time to refer to his memory or to consult those more able to judge than himself. It does not occur to him to resist the new literary tendencies that begin to be felt by him; he yields to them before he knows what they are.

Authors are very prompt in discovering which way the taste of the public is thus secretly inclined. They shape their productions accordingly; and the literature of the stage, after having served to indicate the approaching literary revolution, speedily completes it altogether. If you would judge beforehand of the literature of a people that is lapsing into democracy, study its dramatic productions.

The literature of the stage, moreover, even among aristocratic nations, constitutes the most democratic part of their literature. No kind of literary gratification is so much within the reach of the multitude as that which is derived from theatrical representations. Neither preparation nor study is required to enjoy them; they lay hold on you in the midst of your prejudices and your ignorance.

第十九章　略谈民主国家的戏剧

当改变了贵族制国家社会和政治情况的革命开始进入文艺界的时候,首先受到影响的一般是戏剧,而且戏剧所受的影响总是很显著。

戏剧的观众,从一定程度上来说,都是随着演出情节的变化而感情起伏。他们在观剧的过程中既没有时间仔细玩味剧情,也没有时间同比自己高明的人讨论剧情。他们对自己身上开始产生的新的文学兴趣根本没想加以压抑。他们还没有弄清楚这种新兴趣之前,便先向它低头了。

作家们很快就会发现大众的爱好在暗中倾向何方并依此修饰自己的作品。而他们所写的剧本,在通过上演来预示文学革命行将来临之前,就已起了推动革命的作用。如果你想预测一个逐步走向民主制度的国家的文学发展,你就研究研究它的戏剧好了。

除此之外,戏剧文学即使在贵族制国家中,也构成了他们的文学最具民主性的部分。没有任何其他一种文学比戏剧的表现形式带来的满足感可以更充分地满足人民大众的需求。而且你不需要任何学习和准备就能够欣赏戏剧。不管观众具备什么样的素质或者多么无知,戏剧都可以把他紧紧吸引住。

When the yet untutored love of the pleasures of mind begins to affect a class of the community, it immediately draws them to the stage. The theaters of aristocratic nations have always been filled with spectators not belonging to the aristocracy. At the theater alone, the higher ranks mix with the middle and the lower classes; there alone do the former consent to listen to the opinion of the latter, or at least to allow them to give an opinion at all. At the theater men of cultivation and of literary attainments have always had more difficulty than elsewhere in making their taste prevail over that of the people and in preventing themselves from being carried away by the latter. The pit has frequently made laws for the boxes.

If it be difficult for an aristocracy to prevent the people from getting the upper hand in the theater, it will readily be understood that the people will be supreme there when democratic principles have crept into the laws and customs, when ranks are intermixed, when minds as well as fortunes are brought more nearly together, and when the upper class has lost, with its hereditary wealth, its power, its traditions, and its leisure. The tastes and propensities natural to democratic nations in respect to literature will therefore first be discernible in the drama, and it may be foreseen that they will break out there with vehemence. In written productions the literary canons of aristocracy will be gently, gradually, and, so to speak, legally modified; at the theater they will be riotously overthrown.

The drama brings out most of the good qualities and almost all the defects inherent in democratic literature. Democratic communities hold erudition very cheap and care but little for what occurred at Rome and Athens; they want to hear something that concerns themselves, and the delineation of the present age is what they demand. When the heroes and the manners of antiquity are frequently brought upon the stage and dramatic authors faithfully observe the rules of antiquated precedent, that is enough to warrant a conclusion that the democratic classes have not yet got the upper hand in the theaters.

Racine makes a very humble apology in the preface to the *Britannicus* for having disposed of Junia among the Vestals, who, according

当人们未接受教育的思想培育起来的享乐喜好开始在社会的一部分当中发生影响力的时候,它迅速将人们拉向了戏剧舞台前。贵族制国家的戏剧的观众常常是一些不属于贵族阶层的人们。只有在剧院,上流社会的人们才会和一些中等和低等阶级的人们混合在一起。只有在那里,上流社会的人们才会听取下层人们的意见,或者说至少允许他们发表意见。在剧院,接受过教育的人们和那些有文学修养的人们很难不让人民大众追随他们的喜好,也很难防止他们追随下层人民的喜好。因此,上层阶级往往在剧院里订包厢。

如果对于贵族制国家来说,很难阻止人们进入剧院的话,我们就很容易理解,但民主原则进入法律和习俗的时候,当各个阶级相互融合的时候,当人们的思想和财富变得越来越相等的时候,当上层阶级和随之产生的特权财富、权力、传统和享乐逐渐消失的时候,人们就会在剧院占据统治地位。民族国家人民在文学方面的喜好和从事文艺活动的本性就因此首先表现在戏剧中,而且可以预见,这种喜好和本性将会以一种激烈的方式进入戏剧。贵族国家的文学规则在文字作品中温和地、缓慢地,或者说合法地加以改善。但在剧院中,将会遭到猛烈的推翻。

戏剧将民主的文学中大多数的优点和几乎所有的缺点都暴露出来。民主国家的人们对于才智看得很低,他们也很少关心罗马和雅典的历史。他们只关心与自己有关的事情,只希望看到对现在生活的描写。因此,当古代的英雄和故事经常出现在舞台上的时候,戏剧作家们十分忠诚地遵守古代传统的规则的现象,就足以说明民主阶级尚未对戏剧发生支配作用。

拉辛在《布里塔尼居斯》一书的序言中为他把儒尼叶作为侍

to Aulus Gellius, he says, "admitted no one below six years of age, nor above ten." We may be sure that he would neither have accused nor defended himself for such an offense if he had written for our contemporaries.

A fact of this kind illustrates not only the state of literature at the time when it occurred, but also that of society itself. A democratic stage does not prove that the nation is in a state of democracy, for, as we have just seen, it may happen even in aristocracies that democratic tastes affect the drama; but when the spirit of aristocracy reigns exclusively on the stage, the fact irrefragably demonstrates that the whole of society is aristocratic; and it may be boldly inferred that the same lettered and learned class that sways the dramatic writers commands the people and governs the country.

The refined tastes and the arrogant bearing of an aristocracy, when it manages the stage, will rarely fail to lead it to make a kind of selection in human nature. Some of the conditions of society claim its chief interest, and the scenes that delineate their manners are preferred upon the stage. Certain virtues, and even certain vices, are thought more particularly to deserve to figure there; and they are applauded while all others are excluded. On the stage, as well as elsewhere, an aristocratic audience wishes to meet only persons of quality and to be moved only by the misfortunes of kings. The same remark applies to style; an aristocracy is apt to impose upon dramatic authors certain modes of expression that give the key in which everything is to be delivered. By these means the stage frequently comes to delineate only one side of man, or sometimes even to represent what is not to be met with in human nature at all, to rise above nature and to go beyond it.

In democratic communities the spectators have no such preferences, and they rarely display any such antipathies: they like to see on the stage that medley of conditions, feelings, and opinions that occurs

奉女灶神维斯塔的一名贞女进行艺术加工一事,谦虚地做出了道歉。他根据格利乌斯的记述,说:"决不收 6 岁以下 10 岁以上的女孩。"我们也许可以确认,如果他在我们这个时代这样写,决不会受到这样的攻击,也就无所谓受到这样的苛责和为自己辩护了。

这一事实不仅说明了那个时代文学所处的地位,也说明了那个时代的社会情况。民族的舞台并没有证明一个国家处于民主时代,正如我们所看到的,也有可能是发生在贵族制国家中的民主爱好对戏剧产生了影响。但是当贵族精神完全统治了舞台,则必然证明整个社会都是贵族化的。而且可以大胆地推测,这一左右着戏剧作家的有学识有教养的阶级也可以施令于人民并统治整个国家。

当贵族阶级的高雅的爱好和傲慢的气质统治整个戏剧舞台的时候,他们就会依此去判断人的本性。他们对有一定社会地位的人们最感兴趣,并且喜欢描述这些人的场景出现在舞台上面。他们认为,有些善甚至恶最值得再现于戏剧。至于其余的一切,他们觉得最好不要出现才好。他们进入剧院,也像到其他地方一样,只愿意同有身份的人交谈,在演出当中看到王公们的悲欢离合才有所感动。对于剧本的体裁,他们也持这种态度。他们随意给剧作家规定某些台词,希望一切都合乎他们的腔调。因此,戏剧经常是只描写人的一个侧面,有时甚至演出了人的本性中根本不存在的东西,这些东西既超越了人的本性也完全不符合人的本性。

在民主社会中,观众并没有这样的偏好,他们也很好表现出这种需求:他们希望在舞台上看到各种各样的场景、各种不同的

before their eyes. The drama becomes more striking, more vulgar, and more true. Sometimes, however, those who write for the stage in democracies also transgress the bounds of human nature; but it is on a different side from their predecessors. By seeking to represent in minute detail the little singularities of the present moment and the peculiar characteristics of certain personages, they forget to portray the general features of the race.

When the democratic classes rule the stage, they introduce as much license in the manner of treating subjects as in the choice of them. As the love of the drama is, of all literary tastes, that which is most natural to democratic nations, the number of authors and of spectators, as well as of theatrical representations, is constantly increasing among these communities. Such a multitude, composed of elements so different and scattered in so many different places. Cannot acknowledge the same rules or submit to the same laws. No agreement is possible among judges so numerous, who do not know when they may meet again, and therefore each pronounces his own separate opinion on the piece. If the effect of democracy is generally to question the authority of all literary rules and conventions, on the stage it abolishes them altogether and puts in their place nothing but the caprice of each author and each public.

The drama also displays in a special manner the truth of what I have before said in speaking more generally of style and art in democratic literature. In reading the criticisms that were occasioned by the dramatic productions of the age of Louis XIV one is surprised to notice the great stress which the public laid on the probability of the plot, and the importance that was attached to the perfect consistency of the characters and to their doing nothing that could not be easily explained and understood. The value which was set upon the forms of language at that period, and the paltry strife about words with which dramatic authors were assailed, are no less surprising. It would seem that the men of the age of Louis XIV attached very exaggerated importance to those details which may be perceived in the study, but which escape attention on the stage; for, after all, the principal object of a dramatic piece is to be performed, and its chief merit is to affect the audience. But the audience and the readers in that age were the same:

感情和各种不同的观念。戏剧变得越来越动人、越来越通俗也越来越真实。不错,民主国家的作者们有时也会进行脱离人的本性的描写,但是他们的出发点与其先辈们不同。通过再现当今一些琐碎事件的细节方面,以及一些特殊的人物特性,他们就忽略了对整个民族特性的刻画。

当民主阶级统治戏剧舞台的时候,他们无论在题材的表达方式上还是在题材的选择上都有充分的选择权。在所有文学爱好中,对于戏剧的爱好在民主国家最普遍,无论是戏剧作家还是观众,或是戏院的演出次数,都一路攀升。这样的一些公众,组成了一个具有如此众多元素,居住如此分散的观众群。对于他们,要实行相同的规则或者服从相同的法律都是很难的。如此众多的戏剧评论,评论者互不认识,各抒己见,因此要他们达成一致是根本不可能的。如果说民主制度所起的作用只是使人们对文学方面的普遍规则和章法提出疑问,那么在戏剧方面,可以说民主制度把这些规则和章法全部废除,取而代之以听凭每个作家和每个观众去各行其是。

我在上面就民主文艺的体裁和技巧所作的论述,也特别适用于戏剧。在阅读路易十四时期剧评家对当时的戏剧作品所作的评论时,我们感到惊奇的是:观众对于情节的真实性特别重视,要求剧中人物性格的连贯性,他们的行为不能出现使人无法解释和难于理解的情况。另外,当时人们对于语言的表达形式也十分重视,台词上有一点细小的矛盾,剧作家就得遭受责难。这一现象也使我们感到很惊讶。看来,路易十四时期的人,对于那些在舞台上表现不出来的,经过仔细研究后才能发现的细节是有些过度重视。要知道,戏剧作品的主要目的在于表现,而它的主要作用在于感动观众。但在路易十四时期,观众和读者都是同样一些

on leaving the theater they called up the author for judgment at their own firesides.

In democracies dramatic pieces are listened to, but not read. Most of those who frequent the amusements of the stage do not go there to seek the pleasures of mind, but the keen emotions of the heart. They do not expect to hear a fine literary work, but to see a play; and provided the author writes the language of his country correctly enough to be understood, and his characters excite curiosity and awaken sympathy, the audience are satisfied. They ask no more of fiction and immediately return to real life. Accuracy of style is therefore less required, because the attentive observance of its rules is less perceptible on the stage.

As for the probability of the plot, it is incompatible with perpetual novelty, surprise, and rapidity of invention. It is therefore neglected, and the public excuses the neglect. You may be sure that if you succeed in bringing your audience into the presence of something that affects them, they will not care by what road you brought them there, and they will never reproach you for having excited their emotions in spite of dramatic rules.

The Americans, when they go to the theater, very broadly display all the different propensities that I have here described; but it must be acknowledged that as yet very few of them go to the theater at all. Although playgoers and plays have prodigiously increased in the United States in the last forty years, the population indulge in this kind of amusement only with the greatest reserve. This is attributable to peculiar causes, which the reader is already acquainted with and of which a few words will suffice to remind him.

The Puritans who founded the American republics not only were enemies to amusements, but they professed an especial abhorrence for the stage. They considered it as an abominable pastime; and as long as their principles prevailed with undivided sway, scenic performances were wholly unknown among them. These opinions of the first fathers of the colonies have left very deep traces on the minds of their descendants.

The extreme regularity of habits and the great strictness of morals that are observable in the United States have as yet little favored the growth of dramatic art. There are no dramatic subjects in a country

人,他们看完演出后,便把剧作者请到家里,当面加以评论。

在民主时代,人们只听戏,不看剧本。经常坐在剧院里看戏的人,大部分不是去追求精神的享乐,而是去追求情感的刺激。他们不期望听到华丽的词藻,只希望看一场表演。只要剧作家能够正确地运用本国语言让大家都理解,他笔下的人物能够引起观众的兴趣,唤起人们的共鸣,就可以了。观众不问戏的真假,看完戏后马上又回到现实。因此,戏剧的文体并不太重要,因为在舞台上你很难发现它是否遵守了这方面的规则。

至于剧情的真实性问题,如果让剧情完全合乎事实,那就与新奇、突然和急转直下的剧情相矛盾了。因此,剧作家忽略其真实性,而观众也理解。只要你写出的戏能打动他们的心,他们是不会追究你使用了什么方法的。即使你违背了戏剧的规则,但只要让观众感动,他们就不会责备你。

当美国人进入剧院,就会暴露出我前面提到的种种特性。但是我们必须知道,至今也只有极少数的人到剧院去。尽管在过去的四十年中,美国喜欢戏剧的人数和戏剧的数量越来越多,人们对这种娱乐方式的欢迎程度也还是有所保留。造成这种情况的特殊原因,读者在上文中已经了解。为了唤起大家的记忆,我还是要补充几句。

创建了美国共和的清教徒们,不仅仇视娱乐,而且对戏剧怀有一种特别的恐怖感。他们认为这是一种令人憎恶的消遣方式。所以只要清教徒的原则占据主流地位的地方,戏剧就不会在人们中间出现。

这些最早的殖民地居民的观点对他们的后代产生了极其深远的影响。而且,美国人的极度有规律的生活习惯和循规蹈矩的

which has witnessed no great political catastrophes and in which love invariably leads by a straight and easy road to matrimony. People who spend every day in the week in making money, and Sunday in going to church, have nothing to invite the Muse of Comedy.

A single fact suffices to show that the stage is not very popular in the United States. The Americans, whose laws allow of the utmost freedom, and even license of language in all other respects, have nevertheless subjected their dramatic authors to a sort of censorship. Theatrical performances can take place only by permission of the municipal authorities. This may serve to show how much communities are like individuals; they surrender themselves unscrupulously to their ruling passions and afterwards take the greatest care not to yield too much to the vehemence of tastes that they do not possess.

No portion of literature is connected by closer or more numerous ties with the present condition of society than the drama. The drama of one period can never be suited to the following age if in the interval an important revolution has affected the manners and laws of the nation.

The great authors of a preceding age may be read, but pieces written for a different public will not attract an audience. The dramatic authors of the past live only in books. The traditional taste of certain individuals, vanity, fashion, or the genius of an actor may sustain or resuscitate for a time the aristocratic drama among a democracy; but it will speedily fall away of itself, not overthrown, but abandoned.

民情。至今对戏剧艺术的成长没有助益。在没有巨大的政治变动发生的国家中,以及那些爱情无一例外最终都直接简单地走向婚姻的国家中,是没有什么戏剧题材可写的。人们天天都为了赚钱疲于奔波,周日去教堂礼拜,根本就与戏剧无缘。

只要一个事实就足以证明,戏剧在美国并不那么受欢迎。法律允许获得极大的自由的美国人民,甚至在其他所有方面都有言论自由,但戏剧作家们却要接受审查制度。只有经过市政机构的认可,戏剧才能上演。这也让我们看清了,社会和个人对待戏剧的态度是一致的。人们对于他们关心的对象无不热心对待,而对于他们不喜欢的对象则强烈地反对。

没有任何其他一种文学能像戏剧这样,与现实社会结合得这么紧密,有如此错综复杂的联系。如果在两个时代之间发生的一场重要的变革,对一个国家的民情和法律发生了影响的话,一个时代的戏剧,将永不能适用于下一个时代。

前一个时代的伟大的作家也许会有人阅读,但是如果一段文字描述的是另一个不同的公众对象,就不会吸引人们的关注。上一个时代的戏剧作者,只存活在书中。一些具有传统爱好的个体,他们的好奇心、虚荣心和某位演员的天分,也许会使贵族时代的戏剧在民主时期上演或者复兴一段时间,但很快就会自然消灭,并不是被什么推翻的,而是被人们遗弃的。

CHAPTER XX

Some Characteristics Of Historians
In Democratic Times

Historians who write in aristocratic ages are inclined to refer all occurrences to the particular will and character of certain individuals; and they are apt to attribute the most important revolutions to slight accidents. They trace out the smallest causes with sagacity, and frequently leave the greatest unperceived.

Historians who live in democratic ages exhibit precisely opposite characteristics. Most of them attribute hardly any influence to the individual over the destiny of the race, or to citizens over the fate of a people; but, on the other hand, they assign great general causes to all petty incidents. These contrary tendencies explain each other.

When the historian of aristocratic ages surveys the theater of the world, he at once perceives a very small number of prominent actors who manage the whole piece. These great personages, who occupy the front of the stage, arrest attention and fix it on themselves; and while the historian is bent on penetrating the secret motives which make these persons speak and act, the others escape his memory. The importance of the things that some men are seen to do gives him an exaggerated estimate of the influence that one man may possess, and naturally leads him to think that in order to explain the impulses of the multitude, it is necessary to refer them to the particular influence of some one individual.

When, on the contrary, all the citizens are independent of one another, and each of them is individually weak, no one is seen to exert a great or still less a lasting power over the community. At first sight individuals appear to be absolutely devoid of any influence over it, and society would seem to advance alone by the free and voluntary action of all the men who compose it. This naturally prompts the mind

第二十章　民主时期历史学家的某些特性

　　贵族时期的历史学家，通常都把所有事件同某些个人的特殊意志和性格联系起来，喜欢将重大的革命归因于一些并不重要的偶然事件。他们的智慧帮助其找到一些最细小的原因，但往往忽略那些重大的原因。

　　生活在民主时期的历史学家的性格恰恰相反。他们大多数都认为，个人对于整个民族的命运，公民对人民整体的命运的影响是微乎其微的。但是，从另一方面来说，他们用一些普遍的原因去解释所有细小的事件。这两种完全相反的倾向互为佐证。

　　当贵族时代的历史学家纵览世界上的戏剧的时候，他立刻就发现有少数一些卓著的人，他们掌控了整个舞台。这些伟人们占据了舞台的前沿，将所有的注意力都锁定在他们几个人身上。当历史学家们全力研究这几个人的一言一行的隐秘动机的时候，其他人就避开了他的注意力。由于他们重视某些个人的重要性，于是就夸大了个人所能发挥的影响力，并自然地使他认为，为了解释人民大众的推动力，就必然需要考察某些个人的特殊影响力。

　　相反地，当所有的公民都相互独立的时候，则每个个体都势单力薄的。没有人对全体公民有着巨大的或者持久地影响。乍一看来，每个个体都仿佛对社会没有任何影响力，社会也仿佛

to search for that general reason which operates upon so many men's faculties at once and turns them simultaneously in the same direction.

I am very well convinced that even among democratic nations the genius, the vices, or the virtues of certain individuals retard or accelerate the natural current of a people's history; but causes of this secondary and fortuitous nature are infinitely more various, more concealed, more complex, less powerful, and consequently less easy to trace, in periods of equality than in ages of aristocracy, when the task of the historian is simply to detach from the mass of general events the particular influence of one man or of a few men. In the former case the historian is soon wearied by the toil, his mind loses itself in this labyrinth, and, in his inability clearly to discern or conspicuously to point out the influence of individuals, he denies that they have any. He prefers talking about the characteristics of race, the physical conformation of the country, or the genius of civilization, and thus abridges his own labors and satisfies his reader better at less cost.

M. de Lafayette says somewhere in his *Memoirs* that the exaggerated system of general causes affords surprising consolations to second-rate statesmen. I will add that its effects are not less consolatory to second-rate historians; it can always furnish a few mighty reasons to extricate them from the most difficult part of their work, and it indulges the indolence or incapacity of their minds while it confers upon them the honors of deep thinking.

For myself, I am of the opinion that, at all times, one great portion of the events of this world are attributable to very general facts and another to special influences. These two kinds of cause are always in operation; only their proportion varies. General facts serve to explain more things in democratic than in aristocratic ages, and fewer things are then assignable to individual influences. During periods of

是由组成它的人们的不受约束的自发的行为推动着独立前进。这种情况,自发的催促着人们的思想探寻作用在全体人民才智之上的,使他们向着同一方向前进的一般原理。

我十分确信,即使是在民主国家中,个人的天赋、恶习或者美德都会拖延或加速民族历史发展的自然潮流。但是这些次要的和偶然的原因总是多变的,隐蔽和复杂的,他们力量弱小,因此就很难追踪其痕迹,在平等时期比贵族时期更是如此。在贵族时期,历史学家们的任务只是简单地从众多的一般事件中摘取某些个人的特殊影响力加以分析。在历史学家进行这样的研究后不久,就会对这种单调的工作感到厌烦。他的思想完全迷失了方向,他们没办法清楚的辨别或者明显地指出个人的影响力,于是就否认这些力量的存在。他宁愿选择去谈论有关民族的个性,国家的自然环境或者文明时期的精神。这样,他既减少了自己的劳力,也用更少的代价满足了人们的需求。

拉法耶特先生在其《回忆录》中说过,夸大一般原因的研究方法,对二流政治家起到了极大的慰藉作用。我还认为,其对二流历史学家的慰藉作用也不小。这种方法总能提供一些极大的原因,从而使这些人从他们著作的一些难以解决的问题中解脱出来,而且,也纵容这些人好逸恶劳和无能的思想,同时使他们获得深入思考的荣誉。

对于我来说,我认为在所有的时代中,世界上发生的事件中的大部分都归因于非常一般的事实,而另一些则归因于一些特殊的影响。这两种原因常常是共同作用的,只是彼此所占的比例不同。一般的事实更多地用来解释民主国家发生的事件多于贵族制度下的事实,而可以用个别影响解释的事件还远远少于贵族时

aristocracy the reverse takes place: special influences are stronger, general causes weaker; unless, indeed, we consider as a general cause the fact itself of the inequality of condition, which allows some individuals to baffle the natural tendencies of all the rest.

The historians who seek to describe what occurs in democratic societies are right, therefore, in assigning much to general causes and in devoting their chief attention to discover them; but they are wrong in wholly denying the special influence of individuals because they cannot easily trace or follow it.

The historians who live in democratic ages not only are prone to assign a great cause to every incitent, but are also given to connect incidents together so as to deduce a system from them. In aristocratic ages, as the attention of historians is constantly drawn to individuals, the connection of events escapes them; or rather they do not believe in any such connection. To them, the thread of history seems constantly to be broken by the course of one man's life. In democratic ages, on the contrary, as the historian sees much more of actions than of actors, he may easily establish some kind of sequence and methodical order among the former.

Ancient literature, which is so rich in fine historical compositions, does not contain a single great historical system, while the poorest of modern literatures abound with them. It would appear that the ancient historians did not make sufficient use of those general theories which our historical writers are ever ready to carry to excess.

Those who write in democratic ages have another more dangerous tendency. When the traces of individual action upon nations are lost, it often happens that you see the world move without the impelling force being evident. As it becomes extremely difficult to discern and analyze the reasons that, acting separately on the will of each member of the community, concur in the end to produce movement in the whole mass, men are led to believe that this movement is involuntary and that societies unconsciously obey some superior force ruling

代。在贵族时期,则恰恰相反:个别的影响变得强大,而一般原因则作用很小。事实上,除非我们认为身份不平等是准许某些个人阻碍其余人的天赋意愿的一般原因。

寻求描述在民主社会中发生的事件的正确性的历史学家们,因此,有很多理由运用一般的原因去说明大部分问题并用他们主要的精力去发现这些原因。但是他们错在了只是因为他们无法发现个人的影响力而将这种影响力全盘否定了。

生活在民主时期的历史学家们不仅倾向于用一般的原因去解释每件事实,而且还努力寻找事件之间的联系,为自己推演出一套体系。在贵族时期,历史学家的注意力始终放在个人的作用上而忽视了事件之间的联系,或者说他们根本不相信它们之间的联系。对他们来说,历史的线圈仿佛常常会因为个人生命的终结而断裂。在民主时代,与之相反,因为历史学家更看重的是戏剧的情节而不是演员本身,所以他就可以很容易地在前者中建立起一种次序和有系统的秩序。

古代文学曾有过如此丰富的美丽史诗,却没能形成一个伟大的历史体系;而现代如此贫瘠的文学却充满了这样的秩序。看起来似乎,古代的历史学家们并没有充分的利用这些我们如今的历史学家们频繁照搬的一般原因。

那些在民主时期的作家,有另一种更危险的倾向。当个人的行为对国家的影响力消失的时候,你就常常会觉得世界虽然在运动,但是你却看不到明显的事件推动其动作。当它变得极度的难以察觉或者难以分辨其之所以作用在每个单个社会成员身上的原因的时候,最后就会在社会中引起全民运动,人们就不得不相信,这种运动是自发产生的,并且社会也会不知不觉地受到某一

over them. But even when the general fact that governs the private vo-lition of all individuals is supposed to be discovered upon the earth, the principle of human free-will is not made certain. A cause suffi-ciently extensive to affect millions of men at once and sufficiently strong to bend them all together in the same direction may well seem irresistible, having seen that mankind do yield to it, the mind is close upon the inference that mankind cannot resist it.

Historians who live in democratic ages, then, not only deny that the few have any power of acting upon the destiny of a people, but deprive the people themselves of the power of modifying their own condition, and they subject them either to an inflexible Providence or to some blind necessity. According to them, each nation is indissolu-bly bound by its position, its origin, its antecedents, and its character to a certain lot that no efforts can ever change. They involve genera-tion in generation, and thus, going back from age to age, and from necessity to necessity, up to the origin of the world, they forge a close and enormous chain, which girds and binds the human race. To their minds it is not enough to show what events have occurred: they wish to show that events could not have occurred otherwise. They take a nation arrived at a certain stage of its history and affirm that it could not but follow the track that brought it thither. It is easier to make such an assertion than to show how the nation might have adopted a better course.

In reading the historians of aristocratic ages, and especially those of antiquity, it would seem that, to be master of his lot and to govern his fellow creatures, man requires only to be master of himself. In pe-rusing the historical volumes which our age has produced, it would seem that man is utterly powerless over himself and over all around him. The historians of antiquity taught how to command; those of our time teach only how to obey; in their writings the author often appears great, but humanity is always diminutive.

If this doctrine of necessity, which is so attractive to those who write history in democratic ages, passes from authors to their readers

高高在上的力量的支配。但是即使是当统治着所有个体的意志的一般事实终于可能在世界上被发现，人类自由的原则也不会得到保证。一个广泛的、可以同时影响上百万人们的、足以强大到使所有的人们的意志指向同一目标的原因，是难以抵抗的。人们一旦服从它，人们的思想就接近于一个结论，人类无法抵抗它。

因此，生活在民主时期的历史学家们，不仅否认个人具有对整个民族命运的影响力，并且剥夺了人们改善自己处境的能力。他们认为人民既受一意孤行的天意的摆布，也受到盲目的宿命的支配。在他们看来，每个民族都不可逾越地受到它的地理位置、出身、历史原因和特性的影响，而与它无法改变的某种命运绑定在一起。他们逐一考察每一代人，每一个年代，每一个必然事件，一直上溯到世界的起源，然后铸出一条密封的大锁链，把整个人类用锁链联系起来。他们不满足于知道发生了什么样的事件，而喜欢叫人知道事件的必然发展。他们研究一个已经走到了一定历史阶段的国家，然后确定说它是不得不按着至今走过的道路前进的。也许做出这样的论断比说明一个国家为何有可能有更好的发展道路更简便。

在阅读贵族时期的历史学家的作品时，尤其是那些古代的作品，我们会发现，要想成为自己命运的主人和统治他们的同胞，人们只需要先成为自己的主人即可。细读我们这个时代的历史著作时，我们会发现，人是无法掌控自己或者他周围人们的命运的。古代的历史学家们教人们如何下达命令，而我们这一时代的历史学家们则只教会我们如何服从。在现代的著作中，作者常常形象高大，而人类则很渺小。

使民主时期的历史学家如此醉心的这个教条，如果从作者传

till it infects the whole mass of the community and gets possession of the public mind, it will soon paralyze the activity of modern society and reduce Christians to the level of the Turks.

Moreover, I would observe that such doctrines are peculiarly dangerous at the period at which we have arrived. Our contemporaries are only too prone to doubt of human free-will, because each of them feels himself confined on every side by his own weakness; but they are still willing to acknowledge the strength and independence of men united in society. Do not let this principle be lost sight of, for the great object in our time is to raise the faculties of men, not to complete their prostration.

到读者,并深入到全体公民和控制了舆论,那么,我们可以预言:用不了多少时间,这个学说就将使现代社会的运动瘫痪,使基督教徒退回到土耳其人的水平。

我还要指出,这样的学说对于我们现在所处的时代来说特别危险。当代的人十分怀疑意志自由,因为每个人都觉得自己在各方面都是很虚弱的;但是,他们仍然承认大家结成团体就会有力量并且独立。我们应当发扬这个思想,因为我们的时代需要振奋人的精神,而不应当压抑人的精神。

CHAPTER XXI

Of Parliamentary Eloquence

In The United States

Among aristocratic nations all the members of the community are connected with and dependent upon each other; the graduated scale of different ranks acts as a tie which keeps everyone in his proper place and the whole body in subordination. Something of the same kind always occurs in the political assemblies of these nations. Parties naturally range themselves under certain leaders, whom they obey by a sort of instinct, which is only the result of habits contracted elsewhere. They carry the manners of general society into the lesser assemblage.

In democratic countries it often happens that a great number of citizens are tending to the same point; but each one moves thither, or at least flatters himself that he moves, only of his own accord. Accustomed to regulate his doings by personal impulse alone, he does not willingly submit to dictation from without. This taste and habit of independence accompany him into the councils of the nation. If he consents to connect himself with other men in the prosecution of the same purpose, at least he chooses to remain free to contribute to the common success after his own fashion. Hence it is that in democratic countries parties are so impatient of control and are never manageable except in moments of great public danger. Even then the authority of leaders, which under such circumstances may be able to make men act or speak, hardly ever reaches the extent of making them keep silence.

Among aristocratic nations the members of political assemblies are at the same time members of the aristocracy. Each of them enjoys high established rank in his own right, and the position that he occupies in the assembly is often less important in his eyes than that which he fills in the country. This consoles him for playing no part in the discussion of public affairs and restrains him from too eagerly attempting to play an insignificant one.

第二十一章　美国的议会

在贵族制国家中,所有社会成员都互有联系相互依靠。等级制度像一条纽带,使每个人都处于自己合适的位置,使整个社会井然有序。贵族制国家中的政治集团的情况也大同小异。各个党派自然受到某个领袖的指挥,其党员出于本能服从政党领袖。他们将社会的这套做法搬到了小集团里。

在民主国家大多数公民都朝着同一目标前进,但每个公民都是独立前行的,或至少他们自认为是自行前进。习惯于根据个人意志指挥行动的人们,不愿意服从外来的指导。人们的对这种自主行为的习惯和爱好,也被带进国民会议里去。即使他同意与其他人联合实现同一目的,他至少会选择保留自由的权利按照他的意志去完成目标。因此,在民主国家,其政党难于容忍受制于人从不服从管理,除非国家遇到严重危机,在这种情况下,国家首脑虽然有权命令政党怎样行动和怎样发表意见,但其权威也还不能使政党保持缄默。

在贵族制国家,各种政治性会议的成员都来自贵族。他们本就享有很高的和固定阶级待遇。在他们眼中在议会中所占的地位,往往还不如他们在国家机关中的地位重要。这就是使他们不肯在议会中积极讨论议案,也不热切的希望在议会中争辩一些无足轻重的问题。

In America it generally happens that a representative becomes somebody only from his position in the assembly. He is therefore perpetually haunted by a craving to acquire importance there, and he feels a petulant desire to be constantly obtruding his opinions upon his fellow members. His own vanity is not the only stimulant which urges him on in this course, but also that of his constituents and the continual necessity of propitiating them. Among aristocratic nations a member of the legislature is rarely in strict dependence upon his constituents: he is frequently to them a sort of unavoidable representative; sometimes they are themselves strictly dependent upon him, and if, at length, they reject him, he may easily get elected elsewhere or, retiring from public life, he may still enjoy the pleasures of splendid idleness. In a democratic country, like the United States, a representative has hardly ever a lasting hold on the minds of his constituents. However small an electoral body may be, the fluctuations of democracy are constantly changing its aspect; it must therefore be courted unceasingly. A representative is never sure of his supporters, and, if they forsake him, he is left without a resource; for his natural position is not sufficiently elevated for him to be easily known to those not close to him; and, with the complete state of independence prevailing among the people, he cannot hope that his friends or the government will send him down to be returned by an electoral body unacquainted with him. The seeds of his fortune, therefore, are sown in his own neighborhood; from that nook of earth he must start, to raise himself to command the people and to influence the destinies of the world. Thus it is natural that in democratic countries the members of political assemblies should think more of their constituents than of their party, while in aristocracies they think more of their party than of their constituents.

But what ought to be said to gratify constituents is not always what ought to be said in order to serve the party to which representatives profess to belong. The general interest of a party frequently demands that members belonging to it should not speak on great questions which they understand imperfectly; that they should speak but little on those minor questions which impede the great ones; lastly, and for the most part, that they should not speak at all. To keep silence

在美国,通常议员都是依据其在议会中的地位而施加其影响力的。因此,他就总是渴望在议会中获得重要的地位,并且急于在议会中用自己的观点干预他的同僚们的行为。他这样做的目的不仅仅是为了一己的虚荣心,也是为自己的选民做事,以期获得他们继续的支持。在贵族制国家中,立法机构的成员很少严格地依靠他的选民:他对他的选民来说常常是一种不可或缺的代表。有时甚至是选民完全依靠着他。最后,如果他们对他投反对票的话,他也很容易在其他地方获得选票,或者退出议员生活,他仍旧可以享受悠闲生活带来的享乐。在像美国这样的民主国家中,任何一个代表都很难长时间地在选民心中保持其地位。无论多么小的一个选区,民主的不稳定性总是改变着这个选取的各个方面。因此,议员必须时时讨好选民。一个代表永远不会对他的支持率有确定的信心,如果他们放弃了他,他就一无所有了。因为他的地位本来就没有高到远近皆知的地步。何况在公民完全自主的条件下,他不能希望他的朋友或者政府会把他丢到一个对他不熟悉的地方重新进行选举。他好运的善意因此只能长在他周遭的地区。他必须先从这个小地方开始,逐步使自己可以对他人施加命令,从而影响世界的命运。因此,很自然的在民主国家中,政治团体的成员必须更多的考虑他的选民的利益,而不是他的政党的利益,而在贵族制国家中,他们考虑的刚好相反。

但是,为使选民满意而发表的言论,并不总是对自己信奉的政党有利。一个政党的一般利益常常需要其成员对他们不了解的大问题保持沉默。他们应该尽可能地少谈或者不谈那些可能对大问题造成影响的小问题。最后也是最重要的就是,什么都不

is the most useful service that an indifferent spokesman can render to the commonwealth.

Constituents, however, do not think so. The population of a district send a representative to take a part in the government of a country because they entertain a very high notion of his merits. As men appear greater in proportion to the littleness of the objects by which they are surrounded, it may be assumed that the opinion entertained of the delegate will be so much the higher as talents are more rare among his constituents. It will therefore frequently happen that the less constituents ought to expect from their representative, the more they anticipate from him; and however incompetent he may be, they will not fail to call upon him for signal exertions, corresponding to the rank they have conferred upon him.

Independently of his position as a legislator of the state, electors also regard their representative as the natural patron of the constituency in the legislature; they almost consider him as the proxy of each of his supporters, and they flatter themselves that he will not be less zealous in defense of their private interests than of those of the country. Thus electors are well assured beforehand that the representative of their choice will be an orator, that he will speak often if he can, and that, in case he is forced to refrain, he will strive at any rate to compress into his less frequent orations an inquiry into all the great questions of state, combined with a statement of all the petty grievances they have themselves to complain of; so that, even though he is not able to come forward frequently, he should on each occasion prove what he is capable of doing; and that, instead of perpetually lavishing his powers, he should occasionally condense them in a small compass, so as to furnish a sort of complete arid brilliant epitome of his constituents and of himself. On these terms they will vote for him at the next election.

These conditions drive worthy men of humble abilities to despair; who, knowing their own powers, would never voluntarily have come forward. But thus urged on, the representative begins to speak, to the great alarm of his friends; and rushing imprudently into the midst of the most celebrated orators, he perplexes the debate and wearies the House.

谈。保持沉默,是一个普通的议员能够为其共和国作贡献的最有用的办法。

但是,选民们并不这么认为。一个地区的人民选送一位代表参加国家管理,是因为他们对他的优点有着清晰的认识。人的形象在与其周遭的一些小人物相比较的时候,就会显得异常高大。所以我们可以设想,要求当选代表的能力越高,则这样的天才人物越是难以寻觅。因此常常就会发生这样的情况,代表对他的选民要求得越少,选民对他的期望就越高。而如果选出一个不称职的人当选代表,又得要求他付出与他们所给予他的地位相称的努力。

一个议员除了是国家的立法者外,选民们还认为他们的代表是他们在本选区内立法方面天然的保护人。他们几乎认为把他当作每个支持者的代理人,他们使自己相信,他永远会在保护他们的私人利益方面与保护国家的利益一样,保有同样的热情。因此,选举者早就预先使自己确信,他们选举出的代表是一位雄辩家,他会尽可能地说啊说,即使遭到制止,也会力争在简短的发言中,询问到所有国家大事方面的疑问,并且穿插着所有他们抱怨过的琐碎不平。因此,即使他不能再继续下去了,他也要抓住每个时机证明,他有能力做得到。在他不能长篇大论的时候,他也要常常把他们聚集在一起,提出他与其选民对问题的卓越而完整的见解。只有这样,他们才会在下一次的选举中继续投他的票。

这种情形,使那些虽有才华但是谦逊的人感到失望。他们知道自己的能力,但是不愿自我表现。但是如果这样的人当选,他可以在他的朋友面前侃侃而谈;但是,一旦他进入到满是优秀的演说家的人群中,就必然把辩论弄得一塌糊涂,使国会的议员感到厌烦。

All laws that tend to make the representative more dependent on the elector affect not only the conduct of the legislators, as I have remarked elsewhere, but also their language. They exercise a simultaneous influence on affairs themselves and on the manner in which affairs are discussed.

There is hardly a member of Congress who can make up his mind to go home without having dispatched at least one speech to his constituents, or who will endure any interruption until he has introduced into his harangue whatever useful suggestions may be made touching the four-and-twenty states of which the Union is composed, and especially the district that he represents. He therefore presents to the mind of his auditors a succession of great general truths (which he himself comprehends and expresses only confusedly) and of petty minutiæ, which he is but too able to discover and to point out. The consequence is that the debates of that great assembly are frequently vague and perplexed and that they seem to drag their slow length along rather than to advance towards a distinct object. Some such state of things will, I believe, always arise in the public assemblies of democracies.

Propitious circumstances and good laws might succeed in drawing to the legislature of a democratic people men very superior to those who are returned by the Americans to Congress; but nothing will ever prevent the men of slender abilities who sit there from obtruding themselves with complacency, and in all ways, upon the public. The evil does not appear to me to be susceptible of entire cure, because it originates not only in the tactics of that assembly, but in its constitution and in that of the country. The inhabitants of the United States seem themselves to consider the matter in this light; and they show their long experience of parliamentary life, not by abstaining from making bad speeches, but by courageously submitting to hear them made. They are resigned to it as to an evil that they know to be inevitable.

I have shown the petty side of political debates in democratic assemblies; let me now exhibit the imposing one. The proceedings within the Parliament of England for the last one hundred and fifty years have never occasioned any great sensation outside that country;

　　所有倾向于将当选的代表越来越依附于选民的法律,不仅仅影响到了立法者们的行为,如同我在前面谈到的,而且还使他们的语言发生变化。他们既对自身事务产生了影响,也给他们讨论国事方式带来了变化。

　　几乎没有一个国会的议员不在面对其选民的时候,实现准备好至少一份演讲稿的。他会在他的长篇大论中说明他对联邦24个州所做出的有效的建议,尤其是他对其所代表的地区的杰出贡献。因此,他向他的听众展示了一连串的大道理(这些道理连他自己都说不清道不明)以及琐碎的小事,而这些琐事也都是一些鸡毛蒜皮丁点大的事情。结果就是,这样的集会演讲常常是内容含混不清,错综复杂,仿佛只是想拖延时间,不愿去接近显而易见的目标。我相信,民主国家的议会都会发生这样的情况。

　　良好的环境和法律有利于把美国议会中的杰出人才吸引到民主人民的立法机构中去。但是没有什么能阻止那些没什么能力的人们在议会中心满意足地对所有方面都高谈阔论。对我来说,我认为这一病患已无可根治,因为它不仅植根于议会的组织中,而且存在于其宪法和整个国家之中。美国的居民自己似乎也是这么认为的。他们对国会很有经验,遇到差劲的演讲也不回避,而是勇于坚持听完。他们对其顺从的态度,就像对待一场明知不可救药的疾患。

　　我已说明了民主国家政治辩论的细节,现在让我们再看看它的重要方面。英国下院在过去150多年来的议事程序,从未听说有什么重大的事情引起国外的关注。议员们的意见和感情,即使是在离伟大的大不列颠最近的一些国家,也没能唤起他们的共

the opinions and feelings expressed by the speakers have never awakened much sympathy even among the nations placed nearest to the great arena of British liberty; whereas Europe was excited by the very first debates that took place in the small colonial assemblies of America at the time of the Revolution.

This was attributable not only to particular and fortuitous circumstances, but to general and lasting causes. I can conceive nothing more admirable or more powerful than a great orator debating great questions of state in a democratic assembly. As no particular class is ever represented there by men commissioned to defend its own interests, it is always to the whole nation, and in the name of the whole nation, that the orator speaks. This expands his thoughts and heightens his power of language. As precedents have there but little weight, as there are no longer any privileges attached to certain property, nor any rights inherent in certain individuals, the mind must have recourse to general truths derived from human nature to solve the particular question under discussion. Hence the political debates of a democratic people, however small it may be, have a degree of breadth that frequently renders them attractive to mankind. All men are interested by them because they treat of *man*, who is everywhere the same.

Among the greatest aristocratic nations, on the contrary, the most general questions are almost always argued on some special grounds derived from the practice of a particular time or the rights of a particular class, which interest that class alone, or at most the people among whom that class happens to exist.

It is owing to this as much as to the greatness of the French people and the favorable disposition of the nations who listen to them that the great effect which the French political debates sometimes produce in the world must be attributed. The orators of France frequently speak to mankind even when they are addressing their countrymen only.

鸣。然而,欧洲却因为美国大革命期间发生在一个小的殖民地议会的首次辩论,而发生了骚动。

这不仅有其特殊的和偶然的环境因素,而且还因为一些一般的和持久的原因。我认为,没有什么比一个伟大的辩论家在一场民主集会中对国家的重要问题进行辩论更值得人尊敬,更具有权威。因为没有一个特殊的阶级曾在那里上演一场由自己任命的代表进行捍卫自己阶级利益的辩论,议员们总是为了整个国家,或者举着整个民族的名义进行演讲。这有利于扩展他的思想,加重了他言语的分量。在这里,前例没有什么威慑力,因为再没有任何特权绑定在一定的财产之上,再没有任何权力掌握在某些个人手中,人们的思想必须求助于从人性本身得来的一般原理来解决讨论中的特殊问题。因此,民主人民之间的政治辩论,尽管规模小,但却具有一种关系到人类命运的广泛意义。所有的人都对它感兴趣,因为辩论中涉及的人,在各处都是相同的。

相反的,在伟大的贵族制国家中,最普遍的问题几乎总是根据一些从某一特殊的时期或者拥有特权的阶级中衍生出的特殊的原理来处理的。这些利益总是只与这些特定的阶级有关,或者最多还与这些阶级得以存在的群体有关系。

正是基于这个原因,以及因为法国人民的伟大和其他国家的愿意倾听,才使法国的政治辩论在世界上引起了巨大的反响。法国的辩论家们即使只是在国内发表演讲,也常常面对的是全世界的观众。

SECOND BOOK
Influence Of Democracy On The Feelings
Of The Americans

CHAPTER I
Why Democratic Nations Show
A More Ardent And Enduring Love
Of Equality Than Of Liberty

The First and most intense passion that is produced by equality of condition is, I need hardly say, the love of that equality. My readers will therefore not be surprised that I speak of this feeling before all others.

Everybody has remarked that in our time, and especially in France, this passion for equality is every day gaining ground in the human heart. It has been said a hundred times that our contemporaries are far more ardently and tenaciously attached to equality than to freedom; but as I do not find that the causes of the fact have been sufficiently analyzed, I shall endeavor to point them out.

It is possible to imagine an extreme point at which freedom and equality would meet and blend. Let us suppose that all the people take a part in the government, and that each one of them has an equal right to take a part in it. As no one is different from his fellows, none can exercise a tyrannical power; men will be perfectly free because they are all entirely equal; and they will all be perfectly equal because they are entirely free. To this ideal state democratic nations tend. This is the only complete form that equality can assume upon earth; but there are a thousand others which, without being equally perfect, are not less cherished by those nations.

第二部　民主对美国民情的影响

第一章　为什么民主国家对待平等比对待自由的热爱更热烈更持久

身份平等带来的首要的和最强烈的激情,不必说,当然是对于平等本身的热爱。因此,我在这里先把它提出来讨论,就不会使读者感到奇怪。

大家都已经看到,在我们这个时代,尤其是在法国,热爱平等的激情,日益在人们的心中扎下了根基。人们一而再、再而三地指出,当代人对于平等的热爱比对自由更炽烈和更强大。但是,我还没有见到有人将其原因分析得很透彻。现在,我斗胆对它们加以探讨。

我们可以想象一个极端,在那里自由和平等同时存在且相互融合。让我们想象,那里所有的公民都参加政府管理,人人都拥有平等的管理权。因为大家都彼此相似,所以没人能行使专制。人们获得完全的自由,因为大家全部都平等。因为大家都平等,所以每个人都拥有完全的自由。民主国家的目标就是这一完美状态。这也是平等在世上所能要求的唯一的完美形式。但是,还有许多其他的形式,虽然并不是完美,但是也同样受到这些国家的珍视。

The principle of equality may be established in civil society without prevailing in the political world. There may be equal rights of indulging in the same pleasures, of entering the same professions, of frequenting the same places; in a word, of living in the same manner and seeking wealth by the same means, although all men do not take an equal share in the government. A kind of equality may even be established in the political world though there should be no political freedom there. A man may be the equal of all his countrymen save one, who is the master of all without distinction and who selects equally from among them all the agents of his power. Several other combinations might be easily imagined by which very great equality would be united to institutions more or less free or even to institutions wholly without freedom.

Although men cannot become absolutely equal unless they are entirely free, and consequently equality, pushed to its furthest extent, may be confounded with freedom, yet there is good reason for distinguishing the one from the other. The taste which men have for liberty and that which they feel for equality are, in fact, two different things; and I am not afraid to add that among democratic nations they are two unequal things.

Upon close inspection it will be seen that there is in every age some peculiar and preponderant fact with which all others are connected; this fact almost always gives birth to some pregnant idea or some ruling passion, which attracts to itself and bears away in its course all the feelings and opinions of the time; it is like a great stream towards which each of the neighboring rivulets seems to flow.

Freedom has appeared in the world at different times and under various forms; it has not been exclusively bound to any social condition, and it is not confined to democracies. Freedom cannot, therefore, form the distinguishing characteristic of democratic ages. The peculiar and preponderant fact that marks those ages as its own is the equality of condition; the ruling passion of men in those periods is the love of this equality. Do not ask what singular charm the men of democratic ages find in being equal, or what special reasons they may

平等原则也许可以在公民社会中建立,但是无法在政治社会中推广。人们也许有平等的权利享受相同的享乐,从事相同的行业,居住在相同的地方。总之,尽管人们在政府中不能享有平等的权利,但是他们生活的方式和追求财富的方法都一样。尽管不存在政治自由,但是还是可以在政治世界中建立起某种形式的平等。人们也许和其他所有的国民一样,处于平等的地位,除了一个人。这个人是他们无可厚非的统治者,并从所有人中平等地选拔出他的代理人。我们还可以设想出其他一些组合方式,比如高度平等与一种或多或少拥有自由的制度的联合,或者完全没有自由的制度与平等的联合。

尽管如果人们没有完全的自由就不能实现绝对平等,而当平等达到其极限时又会与自由融合,但我们还是有理由把两者区分开来。人对自由的爱好和对平等的爱好,实际上是两件完全不同的事情。我甚至敢说:在民主国家,这两件事也完全不同。

我们只要仔细考察一下,就会发现任何时代都有一个占有支配地位的与其他事实相联系的独特事实。那个时代一些富有意义的思想,或由此引起并将人人的感情和思想汇集起来的主要激情,几乎都是由这个事实造成的。这就像小溪总会归于大河一样。

自由曾在不同的时期以不同的形式出现过。它并不是完全依附于某一种社会形态,也并不局限于民主国家之中。因此,自由不能构成民主时期的显著特点。那一时期的奇特的占有统治地位的事实是平等的社会地位。那一时期统领着人们的主要情感是对平等的热爱之情。不要问民主国家的人民从地位的平等

have for clinging so tenaciously to equality rather than to the other advantages that society holds out to them: equality is the distinguishing characteristic of the age they live in; that of itself is enough to explain that they prefer it to all the rest.

But independently of this reason there are several others which will at all times habitually lead men to prefer equality to freedom.

If a people could ever succeed in destroying, or even in diminishing, the equality that prevails in its own body, they could do so only by long and laborious efforts. Their social condition must be modified, their laws abolished, their opinions superseded, their habits changed, their manners corrupted. But political liberty is more easily lost; to neglect to hold it fast is to allow it to escape. Therefore not only do men cling to equality because it is dear to them; they also adhere to it because they think it will last forever.

That political freedom in its excesses may compromise the tranquillity, the property, the lives of individuals is obvious even to narrow and unthinking minds. On the contrary, none but attentive and clear-sighted men perceive the perils with which equality threatens us, and they commonly avoid pointing them out. They know that the calamities they apprehend are remote and flatter themselves that they will only fall upon future generations, for which the present generation takes but little thought. The evils that freedom sometimes brings with it are immediate; they are apparent to all, and all are more or less affected by them. The evils that extreme equality may produce are slowly disclosed; they creep gradually into the social frame; they are seen only at intervals; and at the moment at which they become most violent, habit already causes them to be no longer felt.

The advantages that freedom brings are shown only by the lapse of time, and it is always easy to mistake the cause in which they originate. The advantages of equality are immediate, and they may always

中发现了什么样的神奇魅力,或者说是什么样的特殊原因使他们顽强地抓紧平等不放,而不去掌握社会提供给他们的其他有利条件。平等是他们生活的时代的显著的特点,仅仅是这一点,就足以说明为什么他们热爱平等更甚于其余的一切。

但是,除了这个原因以外,还有几个原因使人们在各个时代习惯性的爱平等甚于爱自由。

如果一个民族能够将存在于其内部的平等毁灭,或者甚至缩小,他们也只有经过长期而艰苦的努力才能实现。他们的社会条件必然会加以改变,他们的法律被废除,他们的意见被取代,他们的习惯被改变,他们的民情被破坏。但是政治自由更容易丢失。忽视它抓紧它都会使它被遗忘。因此,人们不仅因为懂得平等的可贵而将其紧紧依附,更因为他们认为平等将会永存。

对于政治自由的滥用,就有可能危及人们的宁静生活、财富和个体的生命,这即使是那些思想狭隘没有思考能力的人们也显而易见的。相反地,只有那些头脑清晰观察力强的人们,才会发现平等给他们带来的威胁,他们也尽量避免不指出这些危险。他们知道,他们了解的灾难还很遥远,他们自欺欺人地认为,这只会降临在后代人的身上,所以现代的人们就很少考虑这个方面。然而自由有时带来的罪恶却近在眼前。人人都很明显地可以看到。而且都或多或少的与己有关。极度平等造成的灾难是缓慢地被发现的。它们悄悄地深入了社会机体之中。只有在偶然的机会下才能被发现。当他们变得异常猛烈的时候,习惯早已使人们对它们无所察觉。

自由带来的好处只有经过时间的流逝才能被人们发现,并且人们常常会对其来源的起因产生误解。平等带来的好处很直接,

be traced from their source.

Political liberty bestows exalted pleasures from time to time upon a certain number of citizens. Equality every day confers a number of small enjoyments on every man. The charms of equality are every instant felt and are within the reach of all; the noblest hearts are not insensible to them, and the most vulgar souls exult in them. The passion that equality creates must therefore be at once strong and general. Men cannot enjoy political liberty unpurchased by some sacrifices, and they never obtain it without great exertions. But the pleasures of equality are self-proffered; each of the petty incidents of life seems to occasion them, and in order to taste them, nothing is required but to live.

Democratic nations are at all times fond of equality, but there are certain epochs at which the passion they entertain for it swells to the height of fury. This occurs at the moment when the old social system, long menaced, is overthrown after a severe internal struggle, and the barriers of rank are at length thrown down. At such times men pounce upon equality as their booty, and they cling to it as to some precious treasure which they fear to lose. The passion for equality penetrates on every side into men's hearts, expands there, and fills them entirely. Tell them not that by this blind surrender of themselves to an exclusive passion they risk their dearest interests; they are deaf. Show them not freedom escaping from their grasp while they are looking another way; they are blind, or rather they can discern but one object to be desired in the universe.

What I have said is applicable to all democratic nations; what I am about to say concerns the French alone. Among most modern nations, and especially among all those of the continent of Europe, the taste and the idea of freedom began to exist and to be developed only at the time when social conditions were tending to equality and as a consequence of that very equality. Absolute kings were the most efficient levelers of ranks among their subjects. Among these nations equality preceded freedom; equality was therefore a fact of some standing when freedom was still a novelty; the one had already created customs, opinions, and laws belonging to it when the other, alone and

而且很容易被发现其来龙去脉。

政治自由时不时使一部分人享得崇高的快乐。平等则每天给所有人提供大量的小小慰藉。平等的美好处时时刻刻都能使人感到，并传递给每一个人：高贵的人不能无所感，普通老百姓皆大欢喜。因此，平等引发的激情既是强烈的，又是普遍的。不付出一定的代价，人是享受不到政治自由的；而要获得政治自由，就得付出巨大的努力。但是，平等带来的快乐是自动产生的，生活中的每一件小事上都能感到，人只要活着就能尝到。

民主国家在所有时候都热爱平等，但是在一些特定的时代，人们的激情已经达到了狂热的高度。这种现象发生在当长久以来一直处于危险境地的旧的社会体系被推翻在一场剧烈的内部争斗之后，并且阶级间的隔阂最终消失殆尽的时候。在这样的时期，人们仿佛获得战利品似的获得了平等的地位，并且像对待珍贵的财富般的珍稀它，唯恐将其丢失。平等的激情渗入了人心的各个方面，并逐渐扩展，完全地充斥其中。但是，不能告诉他们，像他们这样盲目地一门心思地追求平等最终会威胁他们的利益。因为他们已经听不进去了。也不要向他们说明当他们追逐平等的时候，自由会从他们身边溜走。他们已经看不到别的了，或者毋宁说他们眼中最值得追求的东西只有平等。

我所说的一切对所有的民主国家都适用。下面我将要单独谈谈法国。在大部分现代国家中，尤其是在欧洲大陆的那些国家中，对于自由的喜好和思想将只在社会环境向着平等方向发展的时候开始产生和发展并作为平等的结果存在。绝对的王权是其臣民阶级的最有效的持平者。在这些国家中，平等先于自由诞生。因此，在平等已经作为存在的事实时，自由还只是新生儿。

for the first time, came into actual existence. Thus the latter was still only an affair of opinion and of taste while the former had already crept into the habits of the people, possessed itself of their manners, and given a particular turn to the smallest actions in their lives. Can it be wondered at that the men of our own time prefer the one to the other?

I think that democratic communities have a natural taste for freedom; left to themselves, they will seek it, cherish it, and view any privation of it with regret. But for equality their passion is ardent, insatiable, incessant, invincible; they call for equality in freedom; and if they cannot obtain that, they still call for equality in slavery. They will endure poverty, servitude, barbarism, but they will not endure aristocracy.

This is true at all times, and especially in our own day. All men and all powers seeking to cope with this irresistible passion will be overthrown and destroyed by it. In our age freedom cannot be established without it, and despotism itself cannot reign without its support.

平等已经为自己创造了民情、观念和法律,而自由还是孤身一个,并且首次来到现实存在之中。因此,自由还只是一种意见或者想法的时候,平等已经逐渐形成了人们的习惯,掌控了人们的民情,使人们的细微生活具有了某种倾向。如果当代的人们更喜欢二者中的一个,那又有什么奇怪的呢?

我认为,民主国家对自由有一种天生的喜好。放任他们自由,他们也会去寻找它,珍视它,失去一点就会觉得惋惜。但是,他们对于平等的激情显得更炙热、更贪求无厌,更不可抗拒。他们希望在自由之中享受平等,如果这个不能如愿的话,就希望在奴役之中享受平等。他们可以忍受贫困、奴役和野蛮,但不能忍受贵族制度。

这在所有的时代都是事实,在我们这个时代尤其如是。凡是想与这种不可抗拒的激情相抗衡的人和权力,都必将被它推翻和摧毁。在我们这个时代,没有它就不可能实现自由,而专制制度本身没有它的支持也难于统治下去。

CHAPTER II

Of Individualism

In Democratic Countries

I have shown how it is that in ages of equality every man seeks for his opinions within himself; I am now to show how it is that in the same ages all his feelings are turned towards himself alone. *Individualism* is a novel expression, to which a novel idea has given birth. Our fathers were only acquainted with *égoïsme* (selfishness). Selfishness is a passionate and exaggerated love of self, which leads a man to connect everything with himself and to prefer himself to everything in the world. Individualism is a mature and calm feeling, which disposes each member of the community to sever himself from the mass of his fellows and to draw apart with his family and his friends, so that after he has thus formed a little circle of his own, he willingly leaves society at large to itself. Selfishness originates in blind instinct; individualism proceeds from erroneous judgment more than from depraved feelings; it originates as much in deficiencies of mind as in perversity of heart.

Selfishness blights the germ of all virtue; individualism, at first, only saps the virtues of public life; but in the long run it attacks and destroys all others and is at length absorbed in downright selfishness. Selfishness is a vice as old as the world, which does not belong to one form of society more than to another; individualism is of democratic origin, and it threatens to spread in the same ratio as the equality of condition.

Among aristocratic nations, as families remain for centuries in the same condition, often on the same spot , all generations become, as it were, contemporaneous. A man almost always knows his forefathers

第二章 民主国家中的个人主义

　　我在前面讲过,在平等的时代,每个人是怎样依靠自己寻找到自己的观念的。现在,我要指明的是,在相同的时代,人们所有的感情都是指向自己的。个人主义是对刚诞生的观念的一种全新的称呼。我们的父辈们只知道利己主义。利己主义是对自身的一种热情的和夸大的爱,它使人们只关心自己和爱自己高于一切。个人主义是一种成熟的平静的情感,它使社会中的每个公民与其他同胞大众隔离,同亲属和朋友疏远。因此,当每个公民都这样各自建立了自己的小圈子之后,他们就对社会的发展放任自由了。利己主义源自一种盲目的本能,而个人主义与其说来自颓废的感情,不如说来自错误的判断。个人主义的起源既有理性缺失的因素,又有心地不善的因素。

　　利己主义使一切美德的萌芽枯萎,而个人主义首先吸干的则是公德。但是长久以后,个人主义也会攻击和破坏其他一切美德,并最后沦为利己主义。利己主义是跟世界同样古老的一种恶习,它不属于任何一种社会形态。个人主义是民主的结果,它有可能随着平等地位的扩展而四处蔓延。

　　在贵族制国家,家庭的情况几百年不变,常年居于同一地点,数代同堂。每个人几乎始终都知道祖辈们的身世,并对其表示敬

and respects them; he thinks he already sees his remote descendants and he loves them. He willingly imposes duties on himself towards the former and the latter, and he will frequently sacrifice his personal gratifications to those who went before and to those who will come after him. Aristocratic institutions, moreover, have the effect of closely binding every man to several of his fellow citizens. As the classes of an aristocratic people are strongly marked and permanent, each of them is regarded by its own members as a sort of lesser country, more tangible and more cherished than the country at large. As in aristocratic communities all the citizens occupy fixed positions, one above another, the result is that each of them always sees a man above himself whose patronage is necessary to him, and below himself another man whose co-operation he may claim. Men living in aristocratic ages are therefore almost always closely attached to something placed out of their own sphere, and they are often disposed to forget themselves. It is true that in these ages the notion of human fellowship is faint and that men seldom think of sacrificing themselves for mankind; but they often sacrifice themselves for other men. In democratic times, on the contrary, when the duties of each individual to the race are much more clear, devoted service to any one man becomes more rare; the bond of human affection is extended, but it is relaxed.

Among democratic nations new families are constantly springing up, others are constantly falling away, and all that remain change their condition; the woof of time is every instant broken and the track of generations effaced. Those who went before are soon forgotten; of those who will come after, no one has any idea: the interest of man is confined to those in close propinquity to himself. As each class gradually approaches others and mingles with them, its members become undifferentiated and lose their class identity for each other. Aristocracy had made a chain of all the members of the community, from the peasant to the king; democracy breaks that chain and severs every link of it.

As social conditions become more equal, the number of persons increases who, although they are neither rich nor powerful enough to

仰。他们在活着的时候,就能够亲眼看到自己喜爱的曾孙的出世。他们愿意为自己的父辈或者晚辈承担责任。原意为已经死去的或为尚未出生的牺牲自己的享乐。除此之外,贵族制度还可以把每个人同其他多数同胞紧密地联系起来。在贵族制国家,阶级之间的差别极为明显并持久存在,它们中间的每个阶层都被其成员认为是其中更小的一个国家,并且比他们的大国还值得亲近和爱护。在贵族制社会,每个公民都有其固定不变的位置,等级层次分明,所以每个公民都经常意识到在自己之上有一个一定能够庇护他的人,在自己之下又有一个他有义务扶助的人。因此,生活在贵族时代的人,几乎总是跟本身以外的某些事物有密切的联系,并常常为了处理这些事情而忘了自己。在这些时代中,人类友情的观念淡漠,人们也很少想到要为了人类牺牲自己的利益,但是他们却常常为了其他人而牺牲自己的利益。在民主时期,刚好相反,当每个个体对国家民族的有义务变得更清晰的时候,牺牲精神在每个个体之中反而变得罕见了。联系着人们之间友情的纽带被拓宽了,但是却变得松弛了。

在民主国家,新的家庭不断出现,同时另外一些家庭衰落,所有的家庭都处于兴衰无定的状态;时代的联系随时都有断开的危险,一代代人的足迹被淹没;前人很快被人们遗忘,而根本就没人去想后来的人。人们所关心的,都是与自己最亲近的人。但在各个阶级互相接近而融为一体之后,大家便彼此漠不关心,互为陌路。贵族制度把所有的公民,从农民到国王,结成一条长长的锁链;而民主制度打断了这条锁链,使其环环脱节。

随着社会环境变得越来越平等,那些通过努力获得或原本就持有知识和财富来满足自己需要的人们的数量不断地增长。尽

exercise any great influence over their fellows, have nevertheless acquired or retained sufficient education and fortune to satisfy their own wants. They owe nothing to any man, they expect nothing from any man; they acquire the habit of always considering themselves as standing alone, and they are apt to imagine that their whole destiny is in their own hands.

Thus not only does democracy make every man forget his ancestors, but it hides his descendants and separates his contemporaries from him; it throws him back forever upon himself alone and threatens in the end to confine him entirely within the solitude of his own heart.

管他们既不富裕也没有足够的权力对他们的同胞施加影响。他们不欠任何人,也不企图从任何人那里获利。他们习惯独立思考,认为他们的命运是掌握在自己手中的。

因此,民主不仅使每个人都忘记了他的先辈,也隐藏了他的子孙后代,并与同代人相隔离。它使人们只考虑自己,最终可能会使人们完全局限在他自己内心的完全孤寂之中。

CHAPTER III

Individualism Stronger At
The Close Of A Democratic Revolution
Than At Other Periods

The Period when the construction of democratic society upon the ruins of an aristocracy has just been completed is especially that at which this isolation of men from one another and the selfishness resulting from it most forcibly strike the observer. Democratic communities not only contain a large number of independent citizens, but are constantly filled with men who, having entered but yesterday upon their independent condition, are intoxicated with their new power. They entertain a presumptuous confidence in their own strength, and as they do not suppose that they can henceforward ever have occasion to claim the assistance of their fellow creatures, they do not scruple to show that they care for nobody but themselves.

An aristocracy seldom yields without a protracted struggle, in the course of which implacable animosities are kindled between the different classes of society. These passions survive the victory, and traces of them may be observed in the midst of the democratic confusion that ensues. Those members of the community who were at the top of the late gradations of rank cannot immediately forget their former greatness; they will long regard themselves as aliens in the midst of the newly composed society. They look upon all those whom this state of society has made their equals as oppressors, whose destiny can excite no sympathy; they have lost sight of their former equals and feel no longer bound to their fate by a common interest; each of them, standing aloof, thinks that he is reduced to care for himself alone. Those, on the contrary, who were formerly at the foot of the social scale and

第三章　个人主义为什么在民主革命结束后比在其他时期显得更强烈

当民主社会在贵族社会的废墟上的建立刚刚完成的时期,也正是人们彼此孤立和随之而来的利己主义引起人们的关注的时期。民主社会不仅包含了大量的独立公民,并且总是充斥着一些对他们昨天刚刚获得的独立的地位的新权力感到极度兴奋的人们。他们相信自己的实力并且自负起来,认为从今往后他们不再需要求助于邻人。他们的一言一行无不证明他们眼中只有自己。

贵族制度只有经历了艰苦的斗争后才肯屈服。在这个斗争的过程中,各个阶级之间的矛盾变得不可调和。即使在民主获得胜利之后,这种激情也不会消失,仍可能在继之而来的民主混乱时期窥见其踪。社会中的这些在上一个时代居于阶级首位的人们,无法立刻忘怀他们从前的辉煌。他们会在今后很长一段时间内都把自己当作新社会的外来人口。他们看待所有由于新社会而获得平等地位的人们都是命运未卜不值得同情的压迫者。他们不再去看那些昔日与他们同等地位的人们,也不再认为需要因为共同的利益而与这些人的命运绑在一起。每个人都自成一隅,独善其身。相反

who have been brought up to the common level by a sudden revolution cannot enjoy their newly acquired independene without secret uneasiness; and if they meet with some of their former superiors on the same footing as themselves, they stand aloof from them with an expression of triumph and fear.

It is, then, commonly at the outset of democratic society that citizens are most disposed to live apart. Democracy leads men not to draw near to their fellow creatures; but democratic revolutions lead them to shun each other and perpetuate in a state of equality the animosities that the state of inequality created.

The great advantage of the Americans is that they have arrived at a state of democracy without having to endure a democratic revolution, and that they are born equal instead of becoming so.

的,那些从前居于社会最底层的人们以及那些因为一场突然的革命而获得平等地位的人们,毫不掩饰的享受着他们新获得的独立地位。如果他们碰到了如今与他们平等而从前是他们的上司的人,他们就离得远远的,怀着胜利的喜悦和害怕的神情望着他们。

因此,在民主社会初始,人们大多倾向于各自独立生活。民主制度教会人们不要与其他人过于接近。但是民主革命却使人们彼此远离,并使得之前在不平等时期产生的仇恨,永久地保留在了新建立的平等关系之中。

美国的巨大优势,就是他们没有经历民主革命而直接进入了民主社会,因此他们生而平等,而不是后天得到了平等的地位。

CHAPTER IV

That The Americans Combat The Effects Of Individualism By Free Institutions

Despotism, which by its nature is suspicious, sees in the separation among men the surest guarantee of its continuance, and it usually makes every effort to keep them separate. No vice of the human heart is so acceptable to it as selfishness: a despot easily forgives his subjects for not loving him, provided they do not love one another. He does not ask them to assist him in governing the state; it is enough that they do not aspire to govern it themselves. He stigmatizes as turbulent and unruly spirits those who would combine their exertions to promote the prosperity of the community; and, perverting the natural meaning of words, he applauds as good citizens those who have no sympathy for any but themselves.

Thus the vices which despotism produces are precisely those which equality fosters. These two things perniciously complete and assist each other. Equality places men side by side, unconnected by any common tie; despotism raises barriers to keep them asunder; the former predisposes them not to consider their fellow creatures, the latter makes general indifference a sort of public virtue.

Despotism, then, which is at all times dangerous, is more particularly to be feared in democratic ages. It is easy to see that in those same ages men stand most in need of freedom. When the members of a community are forced to attend to public affairs, they are necessarily drawn from the circle of their own interests and snatched at times from self-observation. As soon as a man begins to treat of public affairs in public, he begins to perceive that he is not so independent of his fellow men as he had at first imagined, and that in order to obtain their

第四章　美国人是怎样用自由制度对抗个人主义的

专制的本质是多疑的,它认为只有人们之间的互相分离才是其永远继续的保证,所以它总是努力使人们相互分离。在人心的所有恶之中,专制最欢迎利己主义。如果人们彼此不热爱的话,专制就会很轻易谅解它的臣民也不热爱它。它不会要求它的臣民协助它管理国家。只要他们不想自己执行统治就足够了。它诬蔑那些想要联合起来促进社会繁荣的人们为不安分守己。它扭曲词汇的本来含义,它所表扬的优秀公民就是除了自己,对任何事物都没有怜悯之心的人们。

因此,专制所产生的恶正是平等所要助长的。这两者以一种有害的方式结合并相辅相成。平等是人们肩并肩,不受任何共同纽带的联系,专制则制造隔阂使人们分离。前者教导人们不要考虑其他人,而后者则在公民中视普遍的冷漠为公德。

因此,在任何时代都充满危险的专制,在民主时代尤其可怕,我们不难看到,在这样的时代,人们最需要的是自由。当社会成员被迫参与公共事务的时候,他们就必然会跳出自己的利益范围,有时还会放弃自己的观点。一旦人们都去参加公共的工作,每个人都会发现自己不能像最初以为的那样可以离开他人

support he must often lend them his co-operation.

When the public govern, there is no man who does not feel the value of public goodwill or who does not endeavor to court it by drawing to himself the esteem and affection of those among whom he is to live. Many of the passions which congeal and keep asunder human hearts are then obliged to retire and hide below the surface. Pride must be dissembled; disdain dares not break out; selfishness fears its own self. Under a free government, as most public offices are elective, the men whose elevated minds or aspiring hopes are too closely circumscribed in private life constantly feel that they cannot do without the people who surround them. Men learn at such times to think of their fellow men from ambitious motives; and they frequently find it, in a manner, their interest to forget themselves.

I may here be met by an objection derived from electioneering intrigues, the meanness of candidates, and the calumnies of their opponents. These are occasions of enmity which occur the oftener the more frequent elections become. Such evils are doubtless great, but they are transient; whereas the benefits that attend them remain. The desire of being elected may lead some men for a time to violent hostility; but this same desire leads all men in the long run to support each other; and if it happens that an election accidentally severs two friends, the electoral system brings a multitude of citizens permanently together who would otherwise always have remained unknown to one another. Freedom produces private animosities, but despotism gives birth to general indifference.

The Americans have combated by free institutions the tendency of equality to keep men asunder, and they have subdued it. The legislators of America did not suppose that a general representation of the whole nation would suffice to ward off a disorder at once so natural to the frame of democratic society and so fatal; they also thought that it would be well to infuse political life into each portion of the territory

而独立,而为了得到他人的帮助,自己就必须经常帮助他人。

当公众实施管理的时候,所有的人都感受到了公共善意的价值,并且都努力通过表达这种善意,为自己赢得周围的人们的尊敬和喜爱。于是,一些使人们的情感冻结和分裂人心的感情就不得不被抛弃或者掩藏在表面之下。骄傲之心不再彰显,轻蔑之情也不敢再流露,利己主义本身也感到了害怕。在自由的政府统治之下,由于大部分的公职是选举产生的,那些将自己紧密地封闭在私人生活圈子里的具有学识的和有进取精神的人们常常会感到,他们失去了周围人们的帮助是无法存活下去的。这一时期的人们开始出于一种野心对周围的人们表示关心。并且他们常常发现有时忘记自己反而会给自己带来利益。

在这里,我可能会遭遇源自选举阴谋、候选人的卑鄙手法以及对手之间的中伤之类的反对意见。这种敌意的发生,是随着选举次数的频繁而增强的。这种弊端毫无疑问危害极大,但这种现象也只是暂时的。但是选举所带来的好处却是一直保留的。希望被选中的欲望促使一些人有一段时间矛盾激烈。但是相同的欲望也使所有的人长期相互支持。而且,如果一场选举使得原本的两位朋友反目,但是选举体系也同时使一大批原本永远也不会有机会彼此结识的公民走到了一起。自由产生了个人仇恨,但是专制则滋生了广泛的冷漠。

美国人已经利用自由制度抵抗使人们保持孤立的平等的趋势,并且成功地使其屈服。美国的立法者们不认为,只在全国实行代议制就可以治愈社会机体在民主时期自然产生的致命的疾患。他们还认为,使国内的各个构成部分享有自己的独立政治生活权利,以无限增加公民们能够共同行动并时时感到必须互相信

in order to multiply to an infinite extent opportunities of acting in concert for all the members of the community and to make them constantly feel their mutual dependence. The plan was a wise one. The general affairs of a country engage the attention only of leading politicians, who assemble from time to time in the same places; and as they often lose sight of each other afterwards, no lasting ties are established between them. But if the object be to have the local affairs of a district conducted by the men who reside there, the same persons are always in contact, and they are, in a manner, forced to be acquainted and to adapt themselves to one another.

It is difficult to draw a man out of his own circle to interest him in the destiny of the state, because he does not clearly understand what influence the destiny of the state can have upon his own lot. But if it is proposed to make a road cross the end of his estate, he will see at a glance that there is a connection between this small public affair and his greatest private affairs; and he will discover, without its being shown to him, the close tie that unites private to general interest. Thus far more may be done by entrusting to the citizens the administration of minor affairs than by surrendering to them in the control of important ones, towards interesting them in the public welfare and convincing them that they constantly stand in need of one another in order to provide for it. A brilliant achievement may win for you the favor of a people at one stroke; but to earn the love and respect of the population that surrounds you, a long succession of little services rendered and of obscure good deeds, a constant habit of kindness, and an established reputation for disinterestedness will be required. Local freedom, then, which leads a great number of citizens to value the affection of their neighbors and of their kindred, perpetually brings men together and forces them to help one another in spite of the propensities that sever them.

In the United States the more opulent citizens take great care not to stand aloof from the people; on the contrary, they constantly keep on easy terms with the lower classes: they listen to them, they speak to them every day. They know that the rich in democracies always stand in need of the poor, and that in democratic times you attach a poor man to you more by your manner than by benefits conferred. The magnitude of such benefits, which sets off the difference of condition, causes a secret irritation to those who reap advantage from them, but the charm of simplicity of manners is almost irresistible; affability carries men away, and even want of polish is not always displeasing.

赖的机会,是应该的。这个计划很明智。国家大事仅有一些主要的政治家操持,这些人也只是偶尔聚在一起开个会。由于他们彼此之间常常不能见面,所以就没有什么固定的纽带维系。但是,如果让本地的居民管理本地区的地方事务,这些居民可以常常接触,而且,从某种意义上说,不得不彼此了解相互讨好。

人们很难使一个人放弃自我去关心整个国家的命运,因为他并不十分了解国家的命运会对他个人的境遇发生的影响。但是,如要说要修筑一条公路通到他的家园,他马上会知道这件小小的公共事宜与他的个人的大事之间的关系,而且不必告诉他,他就会发现个人利益和全体利益之间存在紧密的联系。因此,让公民多管小事少管大事,反而会使他们更关心社会福利事业,并且使他们觉得为了实现福利事业他们必须一直依靠彼此的帮助。一次光荣的作为可能会使一个人赢得大家的好感,但是要赢得周围人们的尊敬和爱戴,就必须要长期的提供微小方面的服务,做一些不引人注意的好事,具备善于助人的习惯和无私助人的声誉。所以,地方性的自由引导着一大批人重视邻人和家人的友情,将他们联系起来使他们无论具有怎样的分离倾向都要互相帮助。

在美国,越是富有的人就越是注意不远离别人,相反的,他们总是不断地同不如他们的人接近:倾听那些人的意见,经常与之交谈。他们知道,在民主制度下,富人经常需要穷人的支持,在民主时期,要使穷人与自己更亲近,你对他们的态度往往比给他们施与恩惠更有效。这种恩惠给与的越大,就越显得地位的差异巨大,反而会引起从他们那里获得好处的人们的仇富心理,但是礼

This truth does not take root at once in the minds of the rich. They generally resist it as long as the democratic revolution lasts, and they do not acknowledge it immediately after that revolution is accomplished. They are very ready to do good to the people, but they still choose to keep them at arm's length; they think that is sufficient, but they are mistaken. They might spend fortunes thus without warming the hearts of the population around them; that population does not ask them for the sacrifice of their money, but of their pride.

It would seem as if every imagination in the United States were upon the stretch to invent means of increasing the wealth and satisfying the wants of the public. The best-informed inhabitants of each district constantly use their information to discover new truths that may augment the general prosperity; and if they have made any such discoveries, they eagerly surrender them to the mass of the people.

When the vices and weaknesses frequently exhibited by those who govern in America are closely examined, the prosperity of the people occasions, but improperly occasions, surprise. Elected magistrates do not make the American democracy flourish; it flourishes because the magistrates are elective.

It would be unjust to suppose that the patriotism and the zeal that every American displays for the welfare of his fellow citizens are wholly insincere. Although private interest directs the greater part of human actions in the United States as well as elsewhere, it does not regulate them all. I must say that I have often seen Americans make great and real sacrifices to the public welfare; and I have noticed a hundred instances in which they hardly ever failed to lend faithful support to one another. The free institutions which the inhabitants of the United States possess, and the political rights of which they make so much use, remind every citizen, and in a thousand ways, that he lives in society. They every instant impress upon his mind the notion that it is the duty as well as the interest of men to make themselves

貌带来的魅力却使人难以抗拒。和蔼的态度让人难以拒绝,缺乏风度让人不悦。这种观念并不是一下子就扎根在富人们的头脑中的。只要民主革命还未完成,他们就总是抗拒这种观念。革命结束后,他们也不是立刻就持有这种看法的。他们时刻准备着对人民做好事,但是他们仍旧和这些人保持着一定的距离。他们认为这样就够了,但是其实他们错了。因此,他们可能既花费了钱财,却没能温暖周围人们的心。那些人需要的不是他们的钱财施舍,而是他们的谦逊。

仿佛美国人民的每一种想象都致力于寻找增加财富和满足公众需求的途径上面。每个地区最有学识的居民都努力用自己的才学发现促进地区繁荣的新的真理。并且如果他们在这方面有所发现,也都会迫切地将它在人民中推广。

当我们近距离仔细考察那些美国当政者时,他们的优缺点便会暴露无遗。而人们也会对美国的繁荣感到惊讶,尽管他们的这种惊讶之情表现得并不合时宜。当选的行政官员并没有使美国变得繁荣昌盛,其繁荣的产生却正是由于它的官员们都是由于选举产生。

如果我们认为美国人民对其同胞们的公益事业所表现出的那种爱国情绪和热情不是发自内心的,那也许也不完全公正。尽管在美国也像在其他国家一样,私人的利益指导着大多数人们的行动,但在美国它并不能支配人们的所有行为。我必须说明,我就常常看到一些美国人热心于为福利事业做出很大的牺牲。我也注意到很多次,只要人们需要,他们都能为彼此提供真诚的支持。美国居民的自由制度,通过各种途径,提醒着每个公民他是生活在社会中的人。这些制度使他们的脑海中常常会浮现一种

useful to their fellow creatures; and as he sees no particular ground of animosity to them, since he is never either their master or their slave, his heart readilyleans to the side of kindness. Men attend to the interests of the public, first by necessity, afterwards by choice; what was intentional becomes an instinct, and by dint of working for the good of one's fellow citizens, the habit and the taste for serving them are at length acquired.

Many people in France consider equality of condition as one evil and political freedom as a second. When they are obliged to yield to the former, they strive at least to escape from the latter. But I contend that in order to combat the evils which equality may produce, there is only one effectual remedy: namely, political freedom.

观念,那就是,为同胞们效力,不仅是每个人的职责所在,也对自己有利。而且,因为美国人从来也不是某人的主人或者某人的奴隶,所以他对任何人都没有任何仇恨的情绪,他们的心总是向善的。人们参加社会福利事业最初是因为必须,后来就是自愿的了。有目的的行为会变成人们的本能反应,而为同胞们的幸福做出的劳动,最后会变成他们的习惯和兴趣。

法国的一部分人,认为平等的地位是一大恶,而政治自由是第二恶。但他们不得不向平等屈服的时候,他们就努力避开政治自由。但是我认为,为了对抗平等有可能带来的恶,只有一个有效的补救方法,那就是,实现政治自由。

CHAPTER V

Of The Use Which The Americans Make
Of Public Associations In Civil Life

I do not propose to speak of those political associations by the aid of which men endeavor to defend themselves against the despotic action of a majority or against the aggressions of regal power. That subject I have already treated. If each citizen did not learn, in proportion as he individually becomes more feeble and consequently more incapable of preserving his freedom singlehanded, to combine with his fellow citizens for the purpose of defending it, it is clear that tyranny would unavoidably increase together with equality.

Only those associations that are formed in civil life without reference to political objects are here referred to. The political associations that exist in the United States are only a single feature in the midst of the immense assemblage of associations in that country. Americans of all ages, all conditions, and all dispositions constantly form associations. They have not only commercial and manufacturing companies, in which all take part, but associations of a thousand other kinds, religious, moral, serious, futile, general or restricted, enormous or diminutive. The Americans make associations to give entertainments, to found seminaries, to build inns, to construct churches, to diffuse books, to send missionaries to the antipodes; in this manner they found hospitals, prisons, and schools. If it is proposed to inculcate some truth or to foster some feeling by the encouragement of a great example, they form a society. Wherever at the head of some new undertaking you see the government in France, or a man of rank in England, in the United States you will be sure to find an association.

I met with several kinds of associations in America of which I confess I had no previous notion; and I have often admired the extreme

第五章 美国人在市民生活中对结社的运用

我不想谈人们为了抵御多数的专制或反对王权的侵犯而组织的政治结社。关于政治结社的问题，我已经讲过了。显而易见，如果每个公民随着个人的日益软弱无力和最后无力独自保住自己的自由，或无法联合同胞去保护自由，那么，暴政必将随着平等的扩大而增强。

在这里，我只说一说那些没有任何政治目的的市民生活中形成的结社。美国的政治结社仅仅是那个国家无数结社中的一种。美国人，不论年龄、社会地位和兴趣所在，都喜欢结社。他们不仅仅有人人都可以参加的商业和实业公司，还有其他数千种的社团：宗教的、道德的、严肃的、散漫的、一般的、有限制条件的、人数众多的和小型的各种社团。美国人结社可以为了娱乐、为了建立学院、开旅店、创教堂、销售图书、向边远地区派送教士等。他们通过这种方式创建了医院、监狱和学校。如果有人建议需要传播某一真理，或者鼓励某种情绪树立典范的时候，他们就要组织一个团体。在法国，你见到的任何新事业的领袖都是政府；在英国则是一个阶级；而在美国，就变成了社团。

在美国，我遇见了一些从未听说过的社团种类。我总是感到

skill with which the inhabitants of the United States succeed in proposing a common object for the exertions of a great many men and in inducing them voluntarily to pursue it.

I have since traveled over England, from which the Americans have taken some of their laws and many of their customs; and it seemed to me that the principle of association was by no means so constantly or adroitly used in that country. The English often perform great things singly, whereas the Americans form associations for the smallest undertakings. It is evident that the former people consider association as a powerful means of action, but the latter seem to regard it as the only means they have of acting.

Thus the most democratic country on the face of the earth is that in which men have, in our time, carried to the highest perfection the art of pursuing in common the object of their common desires and have applied this new science to the greatest number of purposes. Is this the result of accident, or is there in reality any necessary connection between the principle of association and that of equality?

Aristocratic communities always contain, among a multitude of persons who by themselves are powerless, a small number of powerful and wealthy citizens, each of whom can achieve great undertakings single-handed. In aristocratic societies men do not need to combine in order to act, because they are strongly held together. Every wealthy and powerful citizen constitutes the head of a permanent and compulsory association, composed of all those who are dependent upon him or whom he makes subservient to the execution of his designs.

Among democratic nations, on the contrary, all the citizens are independent and feeble; they can do hardly anything by themselves, and none of them can oblige his fellow men to lend him their assistance. They all, therefore, become powerless if they do not learn voluntarily to help one another. If men living in democratic countries had no right and no inclination to associate for political purposes, their independence would be in great jeopardy, but they might long preserve their wealth and their cultivation: whereas if they never acquired the habit of forming associations in ordinary life, civilization itself would be endangered. A people among whom individuals lost the

很佩服美国人民为了实现共同的目的而采取的这种高超的技巧。它使得多数人致力于同一个目标并且人人都自觉推进。

我后来也到过英国，美国的很多法律和一些习俗都是从它们那里照搬来的。但是，在我看来，他们对于结社原理的运用并像美国人那么频繁和熟练。英国人只有在重大的事件上才采用结社，而美国人即使是再小的事情，也要结个社。很明显，英国人民认为结社是一种权力很大的行动。而美国人则把结社看作是他们做事情的唯一手段。

因此，在我们这个时代地球上最民主的国家采用极端的艺术来追求共同实现人们的共同目标，并将这一新科学最大程度的运用其上。这仅仅是偶然的结果，或是现实生活中结社原理和平等的必要联系？

贵族制国家总有一些人，他们自身是没有任何权力的；还有一些人则既有钱又有权，可以单独地依靠自己的力量做成大事。在贵族制社会中，人们不需要为采取行动而联合，因为它们本身就是紧密联合在一起的。在这个永恒存在和强制执行的社会团体中，其有钱有权的人都是首领。而这个社团的成员则是那些依附于他，由他驱使完成他的旨意的人们。

在民主国家中，与此相反，所有的公民都独立而软弱。他们凭借自己的力量几乎不能做事，而且他们也无法强迫自己的同胞帮助自己。因此，如果他们不学着主动帮助别人的话，就会陷入全部都软弱无力的境地。如果生活在民主国家的人们没有权力也没有意愿为某一政治目的而联合的话，他们的独立地位就会变得岌岌可危，但是他们的财富和知识却可以得到长久的维持，然而，如果他们没能在日常生活中养成结社的习惯，这个社会本身就会

power of achieving great things single-handed, without acquiring the means of producing them by united exertions, would soon relapse into barbarism.

Unhappily, the same social condition that renders associations so necessary to democratic nations renders their formation more difficult among those nations than among all others. When several members of an aristocracy agree to combine, they easily succeed in doing so; as each of them brings great strength to the partnership, the number of its members may be very limited; and when the members of an association are limited in number, they may easily become mutually acquainted, understand each other, and establish fixed regulations. The same opportunities do not occur among democratic nations, where the associated members must always be very numerous for their association to have any power.

I am aware that many of my countrymen are not in the least embarrassed by this difficulty. They contend that the more enfeebled and incompetent the citizens become, the more able and active the government ought to be rendered in order that society at large may execute what individuals can no longer accomplish. They believe this answers the whole difficulty, but I think they are mistaken.

A government might perform the part of some of the largest American companies, and several states, members of the Union, have already attempted it; but what political power could ever carry on the vast multitude of lesser undertakings which the American citizens perform every day, with the assistance of the principle of association? It is easy to foresee that the time is drawing near when man will be less and less able to produce, by himself alone, the commonest necessaries of life. The task of the governing power will therefore perpetually increase, and its very efforts will extend it every day. The more it stands in the place of associations, the more will individuals, losing the notion of combining together, require its assistance: these are causes and effects that unceasingly create each other. Will the administration of the country ultimately assume the management of all the manufactures which no single citizen is able to carry on? And if a time at length arrives when, in consequence of the extreme subdivision

陷入危险之中。一个民主,其中的每个个人如果都失去了独立完成一件大事情的能力,又没有养成联合起来共同做事的习惯,那他很快就会退回到野蛮的状态。

不幸的是,使结社在民主国家中成为必需的社会条件,却使得结社的形成在这些国家比在其他国家困难得多。当一些贵族成员达成一致要结社的时候,他们很容易就能完成。因为他们每个人都具有很大的影响力,所以他们的成员数量很少。当一个社团的成员数量很少,他们就很容易彼此了解,并且形成固定的规则。在民主国家情况就不是这样了,社团成员的数量必须很多,这样他们才能有一定的影响力。

我明白,我们的许多当代人根本不为这一点困难烦心。他们认为,公民越是软弱无力,就越是应当叫政府能干和积极,以使政府能够创办个人不能创办的事业。他们相信并且声称一切困难都能解决。但我认为,他们想错了。

政府也许可以去做美国人的一些大的社团所承担的事情,而且联邦内部的一些州已经开始这样的尝试,但是,什么样的政治力量曾经可以承担美国人民在结社原则的帮助下每天做的这些不那么重要但却数量众多的事情呢? 我们可以预见,人们越来越不能单靠自己去生产那些最常见的生活必需物了。政府权力的职责也因此变得不断地增多,而且它的努力正在每天扩展自己的职责范围。政府当局越是要取代结社的地位,完全失去了结社意识的个人就越是需要政府的支持。这一切就是因果循环永无止境。一个国家的政府当局最终会被要求管理所有个人无法维持的事业吗? 而且,如果这样的时代最终来临的那一天,几乎造成土地极度的分割的局

of landed property, the soil is split into an infinite number of parcels, so that it can be cultivated only by companies of tillers, will it be necessary that the head of the government should leave the helm of state to follow the plow? The morals and the intelligence of a democratic people would be as much endangered as its business and manufactures if the government ever wholly usurped the place of private companies.

Feelings and opinions are recruited, the heart is enlarged, and the human mind is developed only by the reciprocal influence of men upon one another. I have shown that these influences are almost null in democratic countries; they must therefore be artificially created, and this can only be accomplished by associations.

When the members of an aristocratic community adopt a new opinion or conceive a new sentiment, they give it a station, as it were, beside themselves, upon the lofty platform where they stand; and opinions or sentiments so conspicuous to the eyes of the multitude are easily introduced into the minds or hearts of all around. In democratic countries the governing power alone is naturally in a condition to act in this manner, but it is easy to see that its action is always inadequate, and often dangerous. A government can no more be competent to keep alive and to renew the circulation of opinions and feelings among a great people than to manage all the speculations of productive industry. No sooner does a government attempt to go beyond its political sphere and to enter upon this new track than it exercises, even unintentionally, an insupportable tyranny; for a government can only dictate strict rules, the opinions which it favors are rigidly enforced, and it is never easy to discriminate between its advice and its commands. Worse still will be the case if the government really believes itself interested in preventing all circulation of ideas; it will then stand motionless and oppressed by the heaviness of voluntary torpor. Governments, therefore, should not be the only active powers; associations ought, in democratic nations, to stand in lieu of those powerful private individuals whom the equality of conditions has swept away.

As soon as several of the inhabitants of the United States have taken up an opinion or a feeling which they wish to promote in the

面,土地被划分为无数的小块,以至于无法耕种,除非由耕种者来组织社团进行经营。那么,政府首脑又该何去何从呢? 如果政府完全代替了社团的作用的话,民主国家人民的道德和才智将会出现的危机,不会低于它将在工商业方面遇到的危险。

人们的感情和意见可以再生,人心可以扩大,而且人们的思想可以通过彼此间的相互作用得到进步。我已经说过,这些影响在民主国家几乎都是无用的。他们必须经过人为地创造,而且只能通过结社来实现。

当贵族制社会的成员采用了一个全新的观念或者接受了一种新的情感的时候,他们都会把它放在一个与他们自己相比高高在上的舞台上。这样,这些观念和情感就会被人民大众都清楚地看到,从而更容易地进入了他们的思想和心灵。在民主国家中,只有统治权力的本质才能以这样的方式发生作用,但是我们也很容易发现,它的行为总是不合时宜,而且经常表现得很危险。一个称职的政府,就应该保持活力,更新一大群人中间流传的思想和观念,而不是管理一切实业。如果一个政府试图超越其政治范围进入这一新的道路,那它不久就会开始不知不觉地实行让人难以忍受的暴政。对一个政府来说,只能严格照搬规则和强制执行它支持的观念,而且我们很难分辨什么是它的忠告,什么是它的建议。如果一个政府真正地相信自己的利益在于禁止人们发表意见,那事情就变得更糟了。它很快就会变得无所作为,并听任自己变得越来越迟钝。因此,政府不应该是唯一活跃的权力,在民主国家中,结社应该替换掉那些在平等的条件下失去权力的个体。

一旦美国居民中的个别人物提出一个希望得到推广的意见

world, they look out for mutual assistance; and as soon as they have found one another out, they combine. From that moment they are no longer isolated men, but a power seen from afar, whose actions serve for an example and whose language is listened to. The first time I heard in the United States that a hundred thousand men had bound themselves publicly to abstain from spirituous liquors, it appeared to me more like a joke than a serious engagement, and I did not at once perceive why these temperate citizens could not content themselves with drinking water by their own firesides. I at last understood that these hundred thousand Americans, alarmed by the progress of drunkenness around them, had made up their minds to patronize temperance. They acted in just the same way as a man of high rank who should dress very plainly in order to inspire the humbler orders with a contempt of luxury. It is probable that if these hundred thousand men had lived in France, each of them would singly have memorialized the government to watch the public houses all over the kingdom.

Nothing, in my opinion, is more deserving of our attention than the intellectual and moral associations of America. The political and industrial associations of that country strike us forcibly; but the others elude our observation, or if we discover them, we understand them imperfectly because we have hardly ever seen anything of the kind. It must be acknowledged, however, that they are as necessary to the American people as the former, and perhaps more so. In democratic countries the science of association is the mother of science; the progress of all the rest depends upon the progress it has made.

Among the laws that rule human societies there is one which seems to be more precise and clear than all others. If men are to remain civilized or to become so, the art of associating together must grow and improve in the same ratio in which the equality of conditions is increased.

或者想法的时候,他就立即回去寻找支持者。而且一旦被他们找到了,他们就结社。从结社的那一刻起,他们就不再是单独的个体,而是一个人尽皆知的行为标杆,并且他们的意见就会受到人们的重视。我第一次在美国听到上万的人们联合起来戒酒的事情,而那时这对我来说,更像是一个笑话而不是一个严肃的活动。我起初对这些有节制的公民为什么甘愿在家里喝白开水是完全无法理解的。但我最后终于明白了,这上万美国人是因为对他们周围的酒鬼越来越多的事实感到吃惊,才决心戒酒的。他们这样做,就像位居高权的人们穿上朴素的衣服以图说服一般公民戒除奢豪是一样的道理。如果这些人生活在法国,也许他们每个人都需要分别向政府申请,要求政府去监督国内的所有的公共场所了。

在我看来,最值得引起我们注意的,莫过于美国道德和智力方面的结社。美国的政治结社和实业结社很容易引起我们的关注,而其他的结社则避开了我们的观察,或者说即使我们发现了它们,我们也会因为孤陋寡闻而不能完全的理解它们。我们必须知道,尽管如此,它们和其他结社一样,对美国人民来说都很重要,也会更重要。在民主国家中,结社科学是所有其他科学的基础,所有其他科学的发展都依存在其发展之上。

在所有统治着人类社会的法律中,有一个法律与其他相比较而言,显得更明白,更清晰。如果人们想要保持文明或者想文明迈进,结社艺术就必须随着社会地位平等的进步而不断地得到发展。

CHAPTER VI

Of The Relation Between Public
Associations And The Newspapers

When men are no longer united among themselves by firm and lasting ties, it is impossible to obtain the co-operation of any great number of them unless you can persuade every man whose help you require that his private interest obliges him voluntarily to unite his exertions to the exertions of all the others. This can be habitually and conveniently effected only by means of a newspaper; nothing but a newspaper can drop the same thought into a thousand minds at the same moment. A newspaper is an adviser that does not require to be sought, but that comes of its own accord and talks to you briefly every day of the common weal, without distracting you from your private affairs.

Newspapers therefore become more necessary in proportion as men become more equal and individualism more to be feared. To suppose that they only serve to protect freedom would be to diminish their importance: they maintain civilization. I shall not deny that in democratic countries newspapers frequently lead the citizens to launch together into very ill-digested schemes; but if there were no newspapers there would be no common activity. The evil which they produce is therefore much less than that which they cure.

The effect of a newspaper is not only to suggest the same purpose to a great number of persons, but to furnish means for executing in common the designs which they may have singly conceived. The principal citizens who inhabit an aristocratic country disern each other from afar; and if they wish to unite their forces, they move towards each other, drawing a multitude of men after them. In democratic countries, on the contrary, it frequently happens that a great number of men who wish or who want to combine cannot accomplish it because

第六章　结社和报刊的关系

当人们内部不再有坚固永久的联系,除非你能说服每个你需要求得帮助的人,使他们相信是他们自己的利益在要求他们将自己的力量与其他人的力量自愿地联合起来,否则是无法使许多人携起手来共同行动的。只有通过报纸,才能常常很方便地便做到这一点。除了报纸,没有其他东西能在同一时间将同一思想灌注于无数人的头脑中。一份报纸就像一位不请自来的顾问,它每天可向你扼要地报道国家大事而又不致扰乱你的私事。

因此,当人们变得越来越平等,个人主义越来越强烈的时候,报纸就越成为了人们的必需品。如果认为报刊的作用只在于维护自由,那未免降低了它的作用:报刊维护了人类文明。我不否认,在民主国家,报刊往往引导公民去共同进行一些欠妥的活动。但是,如果没有报刊,就几乎不能有共同的行动。因此,报刊利大于弊。

报纸的作用不仅仅在于建议大多数人采取同样的计划,也在于建议使每个独自持有这种计划的人们联合起来共同实现目标。居住在贵族制国家中的大部分居民都只能彼此遥遥相望。如果他们想要彼此联合,只要能够吸引一些人追随他们的行动,就能共同前进。在民主国家中,正好相反,常常是一大帮想要

as they are very insignificant and lost amid the crowd, they cannot see and do not know where to find one another. A newspaper then takes up the notion or the feeling that had occurred simultaneously, but singly, to each of them. All are then immediately guided towards this beacon; and these wandering minds, which had long sought each other in darkness, at length meet and unite. The newspaper brought them together, and the newspaper is still necessary to keep them united.

In order that an association among a democratic people should have any power, it must be a numerous body. The persons of whom it is composed are therefore scattered over a wide extent, and each of them is detained in the place of his domicile by the narrowness of his income or by the small unremitting exertions by which he earns it. Means must then be found to converse every day without seeing one another, and to take steps in common without having met. Thus hardly any democratic association can do without newspapers.

Consequently, there is a necessary connection between public associations and newspapers: newspapers make associations, and associations make newspapers; and if it has been correctly advanced that associations will increase in number as the conditions of men become more equal, it is not less certain that the number of newspapers increases in proportion to that of associations. Thus it is in America that we find at the same time the greatest number of associations and of newspapers.

This connection between the number of newspapers and that of associations leads us to the discovery of a further connection between the state of the periodical press and the form of the administration in a country, and shows that the number of newspapers must diminish or increase among a democratic people in proportion as its administration is more or less centralized. For among democratic nations the exercise of local powers cannot be entrusted to the principal members of the community as in aristocracies. Those powers must be either abolished or placed in the hands of very large numbers of men, who then in fact constitute an association permanently established by law for the

或者希望联合的人无法联合,只因为他们个体的力量散居在人群中显得异常弱小,他们看不到别人,也不知道到哪里去找志同道合的人。报纸使人们知道了在同一时期其他个体的想法和观念。所有的人都立刻趋向这一灯塔。这些游弋不定的思想,已经在黑暗中苦苦摸索了良久,最终在这里碰面了,他们联合在了一起。是报纸将人们联合起来了,而且报纸还会保持人们之间的这种联系。

为了使民主社会中的社团具有某些力量,它就必须有大量的人。组成社团的人们因为人数过多,只能散居在各地,他们仍旧要住在自己原来的地方,靠着微薄的收入过活,为无数的琐事烦心。因此,他们必须找到一种方法使他们每天不用见面就能交流,不用碰面就能采取一致的行动。因此,民主国家的社团都离不开报纸。

结果就在公共结社和报刊之间形成了必然的联系:报刊造就了结社,而结社也制造了报刊。如果说随着人们身份越来越平等,结社的数量必然也会上升的说法被证实是正确的,那么说随着报刊数量的增长结社的数量也会上升的说法也就不为错误了。因此,美国就成了报刊和结社的数量最多的国家。

报刊的数量和结社之间的关系引导我们发现国家发行的期刊和一个国家行政管理形式之间的关系,为我们揭示了民主国家报刊的数量的减少或者增加与其行政管理集权的多少成正比的事实。因为在民主国家中,地方权力的行使不能像在贵族制国家中那样委托几个主要的公民去行使。民主国家不仅要废除这样的权力,而且要把它交到大多数人们的手中去行使。而这些人,可以依法组成一个为了管理一定区域行政事务的社团。于是他

purpose of administering the affairs of a certain extent of territory; and they require a journal to bring to them every day, in the midst of their own minor concerns, some intelligence of the state of their public weal. The more numerous local powers are, the greater is the number of men in whom they are vested by law; and as this want is hourly felt, the more profusely do newspapers abound.

The extraordinary subdivision of administrative power has much more to do with the enormous number of American newspapers than the great political freedom of the country and the absolute liberty of. the press. If all the inhabitants of the Union had the suffrage, but a suffrage which should only to the choice of their legislators in Congress, they would require but few newspapers, because they would have to act together only on very important, but very rare, occasions. But within the great national association lesser associations have been established by law in every county, every city, and indeed in every village, for the purposes of local administration. The laws of the country thus compel every American to co-operate every day of his life with some of his fellow citizens for a common purpose, and each one of them requires a newspaper to inform him what all the others are doing.

I am of the opinion that a democratic people① without any national representative assemblies but with a great number of small local powers would have in the end more newspapers than another people governed by a centralized administration and an elective legislature. What best explains to me the enormous circulation of the daily press in the United States is that among the Americans I find the utmost national freedom combined with local freedom of every kind.

There is a prevailing opinion in France and England that the circulation of newspapers would be indefinitely increased by removing the taxes which have been laid upon the press. This is a very exaggerated

---

① I say a *democratic* people: the administration of an aristocratic people may be very decentralized and yet the want of newspapers be little felt, because local powers are then vested in the hands of a very small number of men, who either act apart or know each other and can easily meet and come to an understanding.

们就需要一份天天都有的杂志,使他们每天都知道与他们有关的各种小事情,以及与他们的福利有关的国家大事。地方机构越多,合法参与行使地方权力的人数就越多。因为这种需求是时时需要的,所以就需要更多的报纸。

行政权力过于分散,对于美国报纸的数量众多起了很大的影响,其影响力远远大于国家的政治自由和出版的绝对自由产生的影响。如果所有的美国居民都有选举权,并且这种选举权只能用于选择国会的立法机构,他们就不会有对于报纸的需求了。因为他们将只能对一些非常重大的,稀少的机会采取共同行动。但是,在伟大的全国性结社中,每个州、每个城市,事实上每个村镇都会为了地方行政管理的目的而依法结社。因此,国家的法律促使每个美国人在他们的日常生活中为了某一共同的目标互相合作,而且他们中的任何一个人都需要通过报纸了解其他人的所作所为。

我认为,在没有任何全国性议会但是却有着无数地方权力机关的民主国家的人民,①最终比其他在集权统治下和经选举产生的立法机构统治下的人民拥有更多的报纸。在我看来,对美国每日出版的报纸之所以数量众多的最好的解释就是,在美国,人们享有最广泛的自由,并且拥有形式各异的地方性自由。

在法国和英国有一种流行的说法,认为一旦出版业的课税取消,那么报纸的出版将会持续上升。这是一种对这种改革所发生

---

① 我所说的民主的人民:贵族制社会的管理非常分散,人民对报刊的需求也很小的原因在于,地方权力都掌握在少数几个固定的人手中,他们之间行为分散但彼此了解,而且经常见面使得他们很容易相互达成共识。

estimate of the effects of such a reform. Newspapers increase in numbers, not according to their cheapness, but according to the more or less frequent want which a great number of men may feel for intercommunication and combination.

In like manner I should attribute the increasing influence of the daily press to causes more general than those by which it is commonly explained. A newspaper can survive only on the condition of publishing sentiments or principles common to a large number of men. A newspaper, therefore, always represents an association that is composed of its habitual readers. This association may be more or less defined, more or less restricted, more or less numerous; but the fact that the newspaper keeps alive is a proof that at least the germ of such an association exists in the minds of its readers.

This leads me to a last reflection, with which I shall conclude this chapter. The more equal the conditions of men become and the less strong men individually are, the more easily they give way to the current of the multitude and the more difficult it is for them to adhere by themselves to an opinion which the multitude discard. A newspaper represents an association; it may be said to address each of its readers in the name of all the others and to exert its influence over them in proportion to their individual weakness. The power of the newspaper press must therefore increase as the social conditions of men become more equal.

的作用的夸张的说法。报刊数量的增长，不仅与价格有关，而且或多或少跟大多数人们常常感到交际和联合的渴望有关。

同样地，我也要将持续增长的报纸带来的影响更多的归因于一些最普遍的原因，而不是一些人们常常提到的原因。一种报纸能够存活下来与否，只与其是否反映了多数人的共同思想和情感有关。因此，一份报纸总是代表其长期读者所在社团的。这个社团的定位可高可低，它的范围可大可小，人数可多可少。但是，只要一种报纸能够存活下去，就至少说明这样的一个社团的萌芽依存于它的读者的思想中。

我用下面的反思来结束这一章节。人们的身份变得越平等，个体就变得越弱小，他们就越容易向大多数的主流意识屈服，也就越难依靠自己坚持某种大多数反对的意见。一种报纸就代表了一种结社。可以说，报纸是以全体成员的名义，向它的每一位读者致词的，而且读者的能力越弱，它对其的影响力就越强。因此，报刊出版的力量的增长是随着人们社会地位的越来越平等而增长的。

CHAPTER VII

Relation Of Civil To Political Associations

There is only one country on the face of the earth where the citizens enjoy unlimited freedom of association for political purposes. This same country is the only one in the world where the continual exercise of the right of association has been introduced into civil life and where all the advantages which civilization can confer are procured by means of it.

In all the countries where political associations are prohibited, civil associations are rare. It is hardly probable. that this is the result of accident, but the inference should rather be that there is a natural and perhaps a necessary connection between these two kinds of associations.

Certain men happen to have a common interest in some concern; either a commercial undertaking is to be managed, or some speculation in manufactures to be tried: they meet, they combine, and thus, by degrees, they become familiar with the principle of association. The greater the multiplicity of small affairs, the more do men, even without knowing it, acquire facility in prosecuting great undertakings in common.

Civil associations, therefore, facilitate political association; but, on the other hand, political association singularly strengthens and improves associations for civil purposes. In civil life every man may, strictly speaking, fancy that he can provide for his own wants; in politics he can fancy no such thing. When a people, then, have any knowledge of public life, the notion of association and the wish to coalesce present themselves every day to the minds of the whole community; whatever natural repugnance may restrain men from acting in concert, they will always be ready to combine for the sake of a party. Thus political life makes the love and practice of association more general; it imparts a desire of union and teaches the means of combination

第七章　一般结社与政治结社的关系

世界上只有一个国家,它的公民享受政治结社的无限自由。也就是这个国家,结社权力的行使被引入到人民生活当中,并由此得到了文明所能给与的所有好处。

在所有禁止政治结社的国家中,一般结社也极少。这绝不是偶然的结果,而应当断言在这两种结社之间存在着一种固有的而且可能是必然的关系。

几个人由于偶然的原因可能在某一事业上有共同的利益。要么是去经商,或者去从事实业,就这样,他们碰面了并且彼此联合。因此,慢慢地,他们开始了解结社的原理。为小事情而结社的次数越多,就越使得这些人在不知不觉中,获得了共同办大事情的能力。

一般结社因此而有利于政治结社。但是,从另一方面说,政治结社能够异乎寻常地增强和提高一般结社所要实现的目的。严格地说,在日常生活中,每个人都幻想他能自己满足自己的需求。在政治方面他就不会有这样的想法了。因此,当一个人了解了公众生活之后,结社的意识和希望结合的愿望就会天天浮现在他脑海中。即使他们本身对共同行动有着天生的厌恶,考虑到政党的因素,他们也会时刻准备着与别人结社的。因此,政治生活使得人们对结社的热爱变得越来越普遍。它透露了对那些即使本来

to numbers of men who otherwise would have always lived apart.

Politics give birth not only to numerous associations, but to associations of great extent. In civil life it seldom happens that any one interest draws a very large number of men to act in concert; much skill is required to bring such an interest into existence; but in politics opportunities present themselves every day. Now, it is solely in great associations that the general value of the principle of association is displayed. Citizens who are individually powerless do not very clearly anticipate the strength that they may acquire by uniting together; it must be shown to them in order to be understood. Hence it is often easier to collect a multitude for a public purpose than a few persons; a thousand citizens do not see what interest they have in combining together; ten thousand will be perfectly aware of it. In politics men combine for great undertakings, and the use they make of the principle of association in important affairs practically teaches them that it is their interest to help one another in those of less moment. A political association draws a number of individuals at the same time out of their own circle; however they may be naturally kept asunder by age, mind, and fortune, it places them nearer together and brings them into contact. Once met, they can always meet again.

Men can embark in few civil partnerships without risking a portion of their possessions; this is the case with all manufacturing and trading companies. When men are as yet but little versed in the art of association and are unacquainted with its principal rules, they are afraid, when first they combine in this manner, of buying their experience dear. They therefore prefer depriving themselves of a powerful instrument of success to running the risks that attend the use of it. They are less reluctant, however, to join political associations, which appear to them to be without danger because they risk no money in them. But they cannot belong to these associations for any length of time without finding out how order is maintained among a large number of men and by what contrivance they are made to advance, harmoniously and methodically, to the same object. Thus they

喜好独居的人们一种渴望联合的欲望,并教会他们联合的方法。

政治不但创造了大量的社团,并创造出一些规模巨大的社团。在社会生活中,很少会出现这样的情况,一个共同的利益能使一群人共同行动。要使这样的共同利益变成现实,还需要使用一些技巧。但是在政治方面,结社的机会比比皆是。如今,只有在大型的结社中,结社原理的主要价值才会被发现。个体弱小的公民们,并不是十分清楚通过结社获得的权力。为了让他们明白,就必须展示给他们看见。因此,常常很容易纠集一群人为了一个公众的利益而联合,却很难把少数人集中在一起。比如说,1000 人联合起来的话,可能看不到任何利益。但是如果 10000 人联合起来,人们对这种利益就会看得十分透彻。在政治生活中,人们联合起来为了做大事,他们对于结社原理在重要事务上的实际运用,教会了他们在一些小事件上彼此互助可以给他们带来利益。政治结社将一群个体同时从自己的小圈子里拽出来,使他们摆脱那些因为年龄、思想、财产造成的隔离状态,使他们之间的距离缩小并相互接触。只要他们碰过一次面,他们就会策划下一次见面。

在大部分的一般结社中,人们都只投入自己的一部分财产。所有的工业公司和商业公司就是如此。人们在不十分了解结社的方法、不熟悉其基本原则的情况下,他们第一次以结社的方式进行合作,难免要担心为获得经验而付出的代价。因此,他们宁愿放弃获得成功的有力手段,也不愿承担风险。尽管如此,对于加入政治方面的结社,他们并不犹豫,因为政治结社对他们来说没有风险,因为他们不用投钱进去。但是为了使这样的社团得以长期延续,他们就必须学会在一大群人中间保有怎样的秩序,以及采取什么样的步骤才能使他们步调一致地向着同一目标前进。

learn to surrender their own will to that of all the rest and to make their own exertions subordinate to the common impulse, things which it is not less necessary to know in civil than in political associations. Political associations may therefore be considered as large free schools, where all the members of the community go to learn the general theory of association.

But even if political association did not directly contribute to the progress of civil association, to destroy the former would be to impair the latter. When citizens can meet in public only for certain purposes, they regard such meetings as a strange proceeding of rare occurrence, and they rarely think at all about it. When they are allowed to meet freely for all purposes, they ultimately look upon public association as the universal, or in a manner the sole, means that men can employ to accomplish the different purposes they may have in view. Every new want instantly revives the notion. The art of association then becomes, as I have said before, the mother of action, studied and applied by all.

When some kinds of associations are prohibited and others allowed, it is difficult to distinguish the former from the latter beforehand. In this state of doubt men abstain from them altogether, and a sort of public opinion passes current which tends to cause any association whatsoever to be regarded as a bold and almost an illicit enterprise. ①

---

① This is more especially true when the executive government has a discretionary power of allowing or prohibiting associations. When certain associations are simply prohibited by law, and the courts of justice have to punish infringements of that law, the evil is far less considerable. Then every citizen knows beforehand pretty nearly what he has to expect. He judges himself before he is judged by the law, and, abstaining from prohibited associations, he embarks on those which are legally sanctioned. It is by these restrictions that all free nations have always admitted that the right of association might be limited. But if the legislature should invest a man with a power of ascertaining beforehand which associations are dangerous and which are useful and should authorize him to destroy all associations in the bud or to allow them to be formed, as nobody would be able to foresee in what cases associations might be established and in what cases they would be put down, the spirit of association would be entirely paralyzed. The former of these laws would assail only certain associations; the latter would apply to society itself, and inflict an injury upon it. I can conceive that a government which respects the rule of law may have recourse to the former, but I do not concede that any government has the right of enacting the latter.

因此,他们学着把自己的意志从属于其他人们的意愿,使他们的个人行为与共同的行为一致。一般结社中的这些事情的重要性并不比政治结社中的事情更小。因此,政治结社被人们认为是一所免费开办的学堂,所有的社会成员都可以从中学会结社的一般原理。

但是,即使政治结社不能直接对一般结社的进步起作用,但如果它受到破坏的话,一般结社也会受到损害。当公民只能因为一些特定的目的结社时,他们就会认为这样的集会是很少发生的特殊行为,也就很少会考虑到它。当他们被允许因为各种目的自由结社的时候,他们就会彻底觉得公共结社是一种普遍存在的,或者说是人们用来实现各种目的的唯一的方法。一旦有新的欲望产生,他们就立刻会想起这一概念。因此,结社的艺术也应运而生成为行动的基础,正如我前面所说的,为人们所采用和学习。

当某种结社被禁止,而另一些被允许的时候,人们预先就很难区分二者之间的差别。在这种迟疑不决的情况下,人们就会将二者都抛弃。同时社会舆论会认为不管是哪种结社都很粗野甚至是违法的。①

---

①　当政府拥有权力可以随意的允许或禁止结社,这一切就显得越发真实了。当某些结社只是被法律所禁止,那么法院就可以判它违犯法律,这样的话危害就会很小。那么每个公民预先就很了解他应得的结果。早在法律审判他之前,他就可以预先自己定夺并会退出法律禁止的结社并参与那些法律允许的社团。通过这样的约束,所有自由的国家都会承认所有结社的权力是受到限制的。而且如果立法机关授予某人权力以预先断定哪些结社是危险的哪些是有用的,并且允许他有权在一切结社处于萌芽时期就摧毁或者允许其建立,因为如果没有人可以预见结社可能在什么情况下建立,什么情况下应该被摧毁,那么社团的精神将会处于完全瘫痪的状态。法律的创建者只能攻击某些结社,而社团也必须适应社会,否则就会产生危害。我可以想象得到,一个尊重法律的政府将会求助于其建造者,但我并不否认,所有政府都有权制定法律。

It is therefore chimerical to suppose that the spirit of association, when it is repressed on some one point, will nevertheless display the same vigor on all others; and that if men be allowed to prosecute certain undertakings in common, that is quite enough for them eagerly to set about them. When the members of a community are allowed and accustomed to combine for all purposes, they will combine as readily for the lesser as for the more important ones; but if they are allowed to combine only for small affairs, they will be neither inclined nor able to effect it. It is in vain that you will leave them entirely free to prosecute their business on joint-stock account: they will hardly care to avail themselves of the rights you have granted to them; and after having exhausted your strength in vain efforts to put down prohibited associations, you will be surprised that you cannot persuade men to form the associations you encourage.

I do not say that there can be no civil associations in a country where political association is prohibited, for men can never live in society without embarking in some common undertakings; but I maintain that in such a country civil associations will always be few in number, feebly planned, unskillfully managed, that they will never form any vast designs, or that they will fail in the execution of them.

This naturally leads me to think that freedom of association in political matters is not so dangerous to public tranquillity as is supposed, and that possibly, after having agitated society for some time, it may strengthen the state in the end. In democratic countries political associations are, so to speak, the only powerful persons who aspire to rule the state. Accordingly, the governments of our time look upon associations of this kind just as sovereigns in the Middle Ages regarded the great vassals of the crown: they entertain a sort of instinctive abhorrence of them and combat them on all occasions. They bear a natural goodwill to civil associations, on the contrary, because they readily discover that instead of directing the minds of the community to public affairs these institutions serve to divert them from such reflections, and that, by engaging them more and more in the pursuit of objects which cannot be attained without public tranquillity, they deter them from revolutions. But these governments do not attend

因此,当结社在某一点上遭到限制的时候,认为结社精神在其他方面不会受到影响的想法是不合实际的。如果人们被允许可以共同努力去实现某一特定的目的,就足以使他们迫切地希望开始共同行动的想法也是空想。当社会成员被允许或者习惯于为了各种目的彼此联合,他们就会事无巨细都采用联合的方式去实现。但是如果他们只被允许在一些小事情上结社,他们就不会也不愿去采取共同行动了。假使你在商业方面给与他们完全的结社自由也于事无补。因为他们很少关心你曾经给与过他们的权力。即使你费尽力气也还是在禁止他们组织那些不被允许的结社方面徒劳无功,而且你会吃惊地发现,你所鼓励的结社他们也不予理睬。

我不是说,一个禁止政治结社的国家也不能有一般结社的存在,因为人们不可能生活在一个没有任何需要共同行为来实现的事业的国家。但是我认为,在这样一个一般结社总是少数的、不被详细策划并且没能很好地管理的国家中,就不会有宏伟的计划,或者说即使有计划也不会被实现。

这自然使我想到,政治事件方面的结社自由对社会安定并不如人们想象的那样具有危险性,并且,也许在社会经历了一段时间的混乱之后,最终会使其得到增强。在民主社会中,政治结社可以说是唯一的希望统领国家的强有力的个体。因此,当代政府看待这种性质的结社就如同中世纪国王看待国内的大诸侯一样:他们对它有一种天生的厌恶感,一有机会就打击它们。他们对一般结社有一种天然的好感,因为他们发现,他们并不指引人们的思想关注国家大事,而是把人们的注意力从这方面拉走,通过使公民参与越来越多的需要在国家安定的前提下才能实现的

to the fact that political associations tend amazingly to multiply and facilitate those of a civil character, and that in avoiding a dangerous evil they deprive themselves of an efficacious remedy.

When you see the Americans freely and constantly forming associations for the purpose of promoting some political principle, of raising one man to the head of affairs, or of wresting power from another, you have some difficulty in understanding how men so independent do not constantly fall into the abuse of freedom. If, on the other hand, you survey the infinite number of trading companies in operation in the United States, and perceive that the Americans are on every side unceasingly engaged in the execution of important and difficult plans, which the slightest revolution would throw into confusion, you will readily comprehend why people so well employed are by no means tempted to perturb the state or to destroy that public tranquillity by which they all profit.

Is it enough to observe these things separately, or should we not discover the hidden tie that connects them? In their political associations the Americans, of all conditions, minds, and ages, daily acquire a general taste for association and grow accustomed to the use of it. There they meet together in large numbers, they converse, they listen to one another, and they are mutually stimulated to all sorts of undertakings. They afterwards transfer to civil life the notions they have thus acquired and make them subservient to a thousand purposes. Thus it is by the enjoyment of a dangerous freedom that the Americans learn the art of rendering the dangers of freedom less formidable.

If a certain moment in the existence of a nation is selected, it is easy to prove that political associations perturb the state and paralyze productive industry; but take the whole life of a people, and it may perhaps be easy to demonstrate that freedom of association in political matters is favorable to the prosperity and even to the tranquillity of the community.

I said in the former part of this work: "The unrestrained liberty of political association cannot be entirely assimilated to the liberty of the press. The one is at the same time less necessary and more dangerous than the other. A nation may confine it within certain limits without ceasing to be mistress of itself, and it may sometimes be obliged to do so in order to maintain its own authority. " And further

活动,从而阻止人们发动变革。但是,这些政府并没有意识到一个事实,那就是政治结社可以大力促进一般结社的发展,于是,为了防止危险的发生,他们自觉放弃了一种有效的补救措施。

当你看到美国人为了鼓吹一种政治原则,推捧一位政治家领袖,或企图夺权而自由结社的时候,你很难理解为什么如此独立不羁的一群人怎么会不恣意妄为。但是,另一方面,当你想到美国数不胜数的贸易公司时,看到美国人到处都在孜孜不倦地推行某些宏伟而艰巨的计划,而这些计划遇到一场小革命也会前功尽弃的时候,就不难理解这么多忙碌的人们为什么没有给国家制造麻烦,也没有破坏他们都受益的社会安定。

单独对这些事件所作的观察足够了吗? 我们可以不去寻找使他们联系在一起的隐藏的纽带吗? 通过政治结社,美国人不分地位、思想和年龄,每天都在追求结社的普遍爱好,并养成了利用结社的习惯。通过政治结社,一大群人彼此交流,相互倾听,共同完成各种事业。随后,他们将之用于日常生活的观念中,并在各个方面加以运用。因此,通过享有一种带有危险性的自由,美国人民学会了怎样减轻自由带来的危险。

如果我们只选一个民族的某个历史时期来考察,则不难证明政治结社导致国家动乱和实业瘫痪。但是,我们就这个民族的整个历史来说,或许容易证明政治结社自由不但有利于社会繁荣,也有利于社会安宁。

我在本书的上卷说过:“政治结社的无限自由,又与出版自由不完全相同:前者并不比后者更必要,却比后者更危险。一个国家能够把结社自由限制起来,并使其永远处于国家的控制之下;但是,国家有时为了维护自己的威信,也不得不这么做。”随后,我

on I added: "It cannot be denied that the unrestrained liberty of association for political purposes is the last degree of liberty which a people is fit for. If it does not throw them into anarchy, it perpetually brings them, as it were, to the verge of it." Thus I do not think that a nation is always at liberty to invest its citizens with an absolute right of association for political purposes; and I doubt whether, in any country or in any age, it is wise to set no limits to freedom of association.

A certain nation, it is said, could not maintain tranquillity in the community, cause the laws to be respected, or establish a lasting government if the right of association were not confined within narrow limits. These blessings are doubtless invaluable, and I can imagine that to acquire or to preserve them a nation may impose upon itself severe temporary restrictions: but still it is well that the nation should know at what price these blessings are purchased. I can understand that it may be advisable to cut off a man's arm in order to save his life, but it would be ridiculous to assert that he will be as dexterous as he was before he lost it.

又补充说："不可否认,为了政治目的而结社是没有限制的,这种自由也是所有自由当中最后得到人民支持的自由。如果这种自由都没能使他们陷入无政府状态,它也会一如既往地将他们引向混乱的边缘。"因此,我不认为一个国家应该总是使其公民拥有政治结社的绝对自由。并且,我怀疑,是否在任何国家任何时代,对结社放任自由都是明智的举措。

有人说,如果结社的权利不被限制在狭小的范围之内,一个国家无法保持社会的安宁,使其法律受到人们的尊重,建立起持久的统治。这些方面都毫无疑问是很珍贵的。我能想象得到,一个国家为了获得和保有这些,需要对自身暂时施加严酷的约束。但是,一个民族最好能够清楚地知道,他们为了获得这些需要付出什么样的代价。我认为,为了挽救一个人的生命而砍掉他的一条胳膊是明智之举。但是,如果我们认为他在失去了手臂之后还会和以前一样灵巧,就难免让人觉得荒谬了。

CHAPTER VIII

How The Americans Combat Individualism By The Principle Of Self-interest Rightly Understood

When the world was managed by a few rich and powerful individuals, these persons loved to entertain a lofty idea of the duties of man. They were fond of professing that it is praiseworthy to forget oneself and that good should be done without hope of reward, as it is by the Deity himself. Such were the standard opinions of that time in morals.

I doubt whether men were more virtuous in aristocratic ages than in others, but they were incessantly talking of the beauties of virtue, and its utility was only studied in secret. But since the imagination takes less lofty flights, and every man's thoughts are centered in himself, moralists are alarmed by this idea of selfsacrifice and they no longer venture to present it to the human mind. They therefore content themselves with inquiring whether the personal advantage of each member of the community does not consist in working for the good of all; and when they have hit upon some point on which private interest and public interest meet and amalgamate, they are eager to bring it into notice. Observations of this kind are gradually multiplied; what was only a single remark becomes a general principle, and it is held as a truth that man serves himself in serving his fellow creatures and that his private interest is to do good.

I have already shown, in several parts of this work, by what means the inhabitants of the United States almost always manage to combine their own advantage with that of their fellow citizens; my

第八章 美国人是怎样用个人利益的正确理解的原则同个人主义进行斗争的

当社会由少数几个有钱有势的人统治时,他们喜欢培养人们对责任的崇高思想。他们喜欢说忘我是光荣的,认为人应当像上帝本身那样做善事不求回报。这就是当时道德原则的标准。

我怀疑是否在贵族制度下的人们比在其他社会中具有更高的品质,但那个时代的人们从未停止过讨论德行之美,而这些美德的实际功用只能在下面偷偷地议论。但是,随着人们的想象力的日益衰竭,以及人们自顾自的思想,在自我牺牲的思想的影响下,人们的道德拉响了警报,他们不再冒险在人们中间持有这种思想。因此,他们开始探求是否社会的每个成员的个人利益并不在于造福于人类的共同利益。并且,一旦他们发现个人利益和公共利益相遇并融合,便急于加以说明。这类的研究逐渐多起来。而本来只是个别的观察就变成了普遍的原理,并且人们把它当作真理。人们认为,人们在为其同胞服务的过程中,也是为自己谋利的过程,并且对他个人私利也会带来好处。

我已经在这本书中多处重复说过,美国的居民是如何将个人利益与其他人结合在一起的。我在这里想要指明促使他们这样做的一般原理。在美国,几乎没有人谈论美德,但是他们都认为

present purpose is to point out the general rule that enables them to do so. In the United States hardly anybody talks of the beauty of virtue, but they maintain that virtue is useful and prove it every day. The American moralists do not profess that men ought to sacrifice themselves for their fellow creatures *because* it is noble to make such sacrifices, but they boldly aver that such sacrifices are as necessary to him who imposes them upon himself as to him for whose sake they are made.

They have found out that, in their country and their age, man is brought home to himself by an irresistible force; and, losing all hope of stopping that force, they turn all their thoughts to the direction of it. They therefore do not deny that every man may follow his own interest, but they endeavor to prove that it is the interest of every man to be virtuous. I shall not here enter into the reasons they allege, which would divert me from my subject; suffice it to say that they have convinced their fellow countrymen.

Montaigne said long ago: "Were I not to follow the straight road for its straightness, I should follow it for having found by experience that in the end it is commonly the happiest and most useful track." The doctrine of interest rightly understood is not then new, but among the Americans of our time it finds universal acceptance; it has become popular there; you may trace it at the bottom of all their actions, you will remark it in all they say. It is as often asserted by the poor man as by the rich. In Europe the principle of interest is much grosser than it is in America, but it is also less common and especially it is less avowed; among us, men still constantly feign great abnegation which they no longer feel.

The Americans, on the other hand, are fond of explaining almost all the actions of their lives by the principle of self-interest rightly understood; they show with complacency how an enlightened regard for themselves constantly prompts them to assist one another and inclines them willingly to sacrifice a portion of their time and property to the welfare of the state. In this respect I think they frequently fail to do themselves justice; for in the United States as well as elsewhere people are sometimes seen to give way to those disinterested and spontaneous

德行有用并且在每天的活动中对其加以证实。美国的道德家们不认为人因为这种行为是很高尚的,就应该牺牲自己为他人谋福利。但是他们也敢于承认,这样的牺牲是必要的,不论是对牺牲者而言,还是对受益者来说。

他们早已发现,在他们的国家和时代中,他们在一种不可抗拒的力量的驱使下,不得不注意自己。并且,在他们无望制止这种力量之后,他们就将所有的思想都指向它的方向。因此,他们承认人人都要服从自己的利益,但是他们也勇于证实,具有高尚的道德是人类共同的利益所在。我不能在这里讨论他们做出这样的判断的原因,因为这样就会使我离题太远。我只要说明一点,他们说服了自己的同胞相信其言论。

很久以前,蒙坦说过:"假使我没能沿着一条直径走,其原因不在于它是不是直的,而是因为凭借经验,我认为我走的路是一条最合适最有效地到达我的目的地的捷径。"可见,对利益的正确理解的原则,并不是一条新的概念,但是,今天,只有在美国人们普遍接受了这个原则并受到了大家的欢迎。你可以从人们行动的本源找到它,也可以从他们的话语中循到其踪迹。无论是穷人还是富人,都会常常引用这个原则。在欧洲,利益的正确理解的原则不如美国那么完善。而在我们中间,人们仍旧常常装出一副自我牺牲的样子,但其实他们心里早就不这么认为了。

从另一方面讲,美国人喜欢用利益的正确理解原则来解释他们所有的行为。他们心满意足地讲述着,他们的自爱是如何常常地促使他们互相帮助和为了国家的利益牺牲自己的部分时间和财产的。在这方面,我认为他们对自己的评价往往是不公正的。因为在美国,和在其他地方一样,人们常常会向一些出于人性本

impulses that are natural to man; but the Americans seldom admit that they yield to emotions of this kind; they are more anxious to do honor to their philosophy than to themselves.

I might here pause without attempting to pass a judgment on what I have described. The extreme difficulty of the subject would be my excuse, but I shall not avail myself of it; and I had rather that my readers, clearly perceiving my object, would refuse to follow me than that I should leave them in suspense.

The principle of self-interest rightly understood is not a lofty one, but it is clear and sure. It does not aim at mighty objects, but it attains without excessive exertion all those at which it aims. As it lies within the reach of all capacities, everyone can without difficulty learn and retain it. By its admirable conformity to human weaknesses it easily obtains great dominion; nor is that dominion precarious, since the principle checks one personal interest by another, and uses, to direct the passions, the very same instrument that excites them.

The principle of self-interest rightly understood produces no great acts of self-sacrifice, but it suggests daily small acts of selfdenial. By itself it cannot suffice to make a man virtuous; but it disciplines a number of persons in habits of regularity, temperance, moderation, foresight, self-command; and if it does not lead men straight to virtue by the will, it gradually draws them in that direction by their habits. If the principle of interest rightly understood were to sway the whole moral world, extraordinary virtues would doubtless be more rare; but I think that gross depravity would then also be less common. The principle of interest rightly understood perhaps prevents men from rising far above the level of mankind, but a great number of other men, who were falling far below it, are caught and restrained by it. Observe some few individuals, they are lowered by it; survey mankind, they are raised.

I am not afraid to say that the principle of self-interest rightly

意的无私和自发产生的激情屈服。但是美国人不会承认,他们会被这样的感情左右。对待哲学和他们自己的荣誉,他们更倾向于给哲学增光。

我本可以就此停住,不对我所做的描述加以评论。我可以借口说这个主题太难了,但我不会这么做的。我宁愿让我的读者们清楚地掌握我的主题,这样他们就可能拒绝再随着我的话题往下走,我也不愿把大家丢在疑惑里。

利益的正确理解原则并不高深莫测,而是清楚确定的。它的目的并不指向一些高大的东西,而是追求一些不需要花费很多精力就能实现的目的。因为人人都能实现它,所以大家都能不费力气学会它并保留它。由于它切合人的弱点,所以很容易掌握较大的控制权。而且,这种支配权也很容易保持,因为它是以一个个体的利益来对抗另一个个体利益的,并且通过对人们的激情加以引导而产生刺激作用。

这一原则不要求人们做出伟大的自我牺牲,但是却让人们每天都做出小小的贡献。只凭借这一原则本身是不足以使人变得品德高尚的,但是它却使一定数量的人们习惯有规律、自我克制、温和、目光远大并且自律。如果它不是让人们依靠意志来培养德行,它也会逐渐地利用习惯使他们就范。如果利益的正确理解原则对整个道德社会产生影响的话,那么一些特别的品德就不会出现了。但是我认为,堕落也将会变得更少。这一原则也许会阻碍一些人远远高于大家的一般水平,但是在这一水平线之下的大多数人,就会被这一原则紧紧抓住并限制其行为。就某几个个体来说,他们居于这一原则之下。但是对整个人类来说,他却使整体上升了。

我并不怕说,利益的正确理解原则对我来说是所有哲学理论

understood appears to me the best suited of all philosophical theories to the wants of the men of our time, and that I regard it as their chief remaining security against themselves. Towards it, therefore, the minds of the moralists of our age should turn; even should they judge it to be incomplete, it must nevertheless be adopted as necessary.

I do not think, on the whole, that there is more selfishness among us than in America; the only difference is that there it is enlightened, here it is not. Each American knows when to sacrifice some of his private interests to save the rest; we want to save everything, and often we lose it all. Everybody I see about me seems bent on teaching his contemporaries, by precept and example, that what is useful is never wrong. Will nobody undertake to make them understand how what is right may be useful?

No power on earth can prevent the increasing equality of conditions from inclining the human mind to seek out what is useful or from leading every member of the community to be wrapped up in himself. It must therefore be expected that personal interest will become more than ever the principal if not the sole spring of men's actions; but it remains to be seen how each man will understand his personal interest. If the members of a community, as they become more equal, become more ignorant and coarse, it is difficult to foresee to what pitch of stupid excesses their selfishness may lead them; and no one can foretell into what disgrace and wretchedness they would plunge themselves lest they should have to sacrifice something of their own well-being to the prosperity of their fellow creatures.

I do not think that the system of self-interest as it is professed in America is in all its parts self-evident, but it contains a great number of truths so evident that men, if they are only educated, cannot fail to see them. Educate, then, at any rate, for the age of implicit self-sacrifice and instinctive virtues is already flitting far away from us, and the time is fast approaching when freedom, public peace, and social order itself will not be able to exist without education.

中最适于我们这个时代的人们的需求的。而且我认为,这一原则是他们用以抵抗自己的最妥善的保障。因此,当代道德家们的思想应该转向对这个原则的研究。即使他们认为这个理论还不成熟,但它仍旧必须被采纳。

我不认为,总的说来,我们比美国有着更多的自私的心理。我们之间存在的唯一差别,就是美国公开主张利己主义,而我们则没有。每一位美国人都懂得何时应该牺牲自己私人利益来拯救其他人的利益。我们因为想要保护所有的利益,结果却都失去了。在我周围的每个人,仿佛都趋向于教导其同时代的人们,既有例证又有道理,追求功利不会错。难道就没有人教导人们相信正确的东西也可以是功利的吗?

世上没有任何权力能够阻止不断上升的地位的平等不去引导人们追求功利或不使人们关注自己的利益。因此,必须承认,个人利益即使不是人们行为的唯一动力,至少也是当代人们行为的主要动力来源。但是,我们还要知道一个人是如何理解他的个人利益的。如果一个社会的成员,随着他们的地位的越来越平等,变得愈加无知和粗野,我们很难预见,他们的利己主义不会使他们做出什么过激的愚蠢行为。也没有人能预料他会陷入怎样的境地,如果他们不愿为社会繁荣牺牲自己的利益。

我不认为,美国人所承认的利益的正确理解的原则的所有组成部分都已宣讲得很明白,但是它包含了大量明白的真理。如果人们受过丁点教育,那他就不会不理解。所以,教育无论如何,对绝对的自我牺牲和本能为善的年代来说,早已经距离我们很远了。而自由、公共和平和社会秩序本身只要通过简单的教育就可以实现的时代迅速地到来。

CHAPTER IX

That The Americans Apply The Principle Of Self-interest Rightly Understood To Religious Matters

If the principle of self-interest rightly understood had nothing but the present world in view, it would be very insufficient, for there are many sacrifices that can find their recompense only in another; and whatever ingenuity may be put forth to demonstrate the utility of virtue, it will never be an easy task to make that man live aright who has no thought of dying.

It is therefore necessary to ascertain whether the principle of self-interest rightly understood can be easily reconciled with religious belief. The philosophers who inculcate this system of morals tell men that to be happy in this life they must watch their own passions and steadily control their excess; that lasting happiness can be secured only by renouncing a thousand transient gratifications; and that a man must perpetually triumph over himself in order to secure his own advantage. The founders of almost all religions have held to the same language. The track they point out to man is the same, only the goal is more remote; instead of placing in this world the reward of the sacrifices they impose, they transport it to another.

Nevertheless, I cannot believe that all those who practice virtue from religious motives are actuated only by the hope of a recompense. I have known zealous Christians who constantly forgot themselves to work with greater ardor for the happiness of their fellow men, and I have heard them declare that all they did was only to earn the blessings of a future state. I cannot but think that they deceive themselves; I respect them too much to believe them. Christianity, indeed, teaches that a man must prefer his neigh-

第九章 美国人怎样在宗教上应用利益的正确理解的原则

如果利益的正确理解原则只考虑到现代的话,它就显得很不完备。因为还有许多其他种类的牺牲只有在来世才能加以回报。并且,无论你怎样去说明美德功用性,要想使一个根本没有死亡意识的人行善都是很难的。

因此,必须知道利益的正确理解的原则能够与宗教信仰和解。谆谆劝诱人们信奉这一道德体系的哲学家们告诉人们,要想在现世获得幸福,人就必须管住自己的激情,时刻把它控制在允许的范围之内。这一持续的幸福的获得,只能通过放弃多种短暂的享乐。为了维护自己的利益,人们必须时时克制自己。几乎所有宗教的创建者,都持有这样的说教。他们为人们指引的道路都是相同的,只是目标变得越来越渺茫。他们将因为自我牺牲得来的回报,都放到了来世而不是今生。

然而,我不相信,所有因着宗教的动机行使美德的人,都是为了获得回报。我认识一些虔诚的基督教徒,他们总是忘记自我,怀着极大的热忱为其同胞们的幸福辛勤的工作。我也听到过他们宣称,他们所做的一切,只是为了在来世获得好报。我不认为他们这么说是在自欺欺人。因为我非常敬重他们,所以我相信他

bor to himself in order to gain eternal life; but Christianity also teaches that men ought to benefit their fellow creatures for the love of God. A sublime expression! Man searches by his intellect into the divine conception and sees that order is the purpose of God; he freely gives his own efforts to aid in prosecuting this great design and, while he sacrifices his personal interests to this consummate order of all created things, expects no other recompense than the pleasure of contemplating it.

I do not believe that self-interest is the sole motive of religious men, but I believe that self-interest is the principal means that religions themselves employ to govern men, and I do not question that in this way they strike the multitude and become popular. I do not see clearly why the principle of interest rightly understood should undermine the religious opinions of men; it seems to me more easy to show why it should strengthen them. Let it be supposed that in order to attain happiness in this world, a man combats his instincts on all occasions and deliberately calculates every action of his life; that instead of yielding blindly to the impetuosity of first desires, he has learned the art of resisting them, and that he has accustomed himself to sacrifice without an effort the pleasure of a moment to the lasting interest of his whole life. If such a man believes in the religion that he professes, it will cost him but little to submit to the restrictions it may impose. Reason herself counsels him to obey, and habit has prepared him to endure these limitations. If he should have conceived any doubts as to the object of his hopes, still he will not easily allow himself to be stopped by them; and he will decide that it is wise to risk some of the advantages of this world in order to preserve his rights to the great inheritance promised him in another. "To be mistaken in believing that the Christian religion is true," says Pascal, "is no great loss to anyone; but how dreadful to be mistaken in believing it to be false!"

The Americans do not affect a brutal indifference to a future state; they affect no puerile pride in despising perils that they hope to escape from. They therefore profess their religion without

们所说的一切。事实上,基督教教导人们为了获得永生,人们应该屈己就人。但是基督教也教导人们,应该以上帝的名义为其同胞们谋福利。多么崇高的思想！人们凭借着自己的学识体会上帝的旨意,并认识到秩序是上帝的旨意。于是,他尽全力帮助实现这一伟大的计划。而且在实现所有生物的共同秩序这一目的时,宁愿牺牲自己的利益,除了为自己再想起它时感到愉悦之外,没有任何其他企图。

我不认为,宗教人员的唯一驱动力是自己的利益,但是我认为它是宗教本身用来支配人们的主要手段,而且我毫不怀疑,他们之所以能够打动人心并受到欢迎都是因此。我还没能清楚地认识到利益的正确理解原则是怎样破坏人们的宗教信仰的。但是我可以很轻松地指出他们可以使人们加强对宗教的信仰。让我们想象一下,为了在人世获得幸福,一个人要时时与自己的本能抗衡,并冷静地算计着人生的每一步骤。他不会盲目地听从自己一时的感情冲动,并且早已学会怎样避免这样的行为发生。他已经养成了自觉牺牲一时的利益以期获得长久的利益的习惯。如果这样的一个人皈依了他所信仰的宗教,他就会完全地顺服这一宗教可能实施的戒律。而且理智本身也会劝服他去服从,习惯也会逐渐让他适应这些规则。如果他随自己希望的目标怀有疑虑的话,他也不会轻易地放弃。而且会认为拿出一些现世的利益来换取来世的美好承诺是明智之举。帕斯卡尔曾说过:"误信宗教是真实的,对任何人都不会有损,但是,如果误信宗教是假的该是多么可怕的一件事！"

美国人并不装出一副对来世漠不关心的态度。他们也不会对自己期望躲避的危险装出一副幼稚地满不在乎的态度。因此

shame and without weakness; but even in their zeal there generally is something so indescribably tranquil, methodical, and deliberate that it would seem as if the head far more than the heart brought them to the foot of the altar.

Not only do the Americans follow their religion from interest, but they often place in this world the interest that makes them follow it. In the Middle Ages the clergy spoke of nothing but a future state; they hardly cared to prove that a sincere Christian may be a happy man here below. But the American preachers are constantly referring to the earth, and it is only with great difficulty that they can divert their attention from it. To touch their congregations, they always show them how favorable religious opinions are to freedom and public tranquillity; and it is often difficult to ascertain from their discourses whether the principal object of religion is to procure eternal felicity in the other world or prosperity in this.

他们在进行宗教活动的时候,既不觉得羞耻,也不觉得自己软弱。但是,在他们热情中,常常会感到有一种不可名状的宁静、系统化和胸有成竹的感觉,仿佛引导他们走近神坛的既有理智,但又不仅仅是理智。

美国人不仅因为自己的利益而信奉宗教,而且往往将使他们信奉宗教的利益放在现世。中世纪的牧师满嘴的来世。他们几乎不去证实一个虔诚的基督徒同时也可以是一个幸福的俗人。但是美国的传教士就会说到现世,而且只有遇到极大的困难,否则他们是不会将注意力从现世的利益身上转移开去的。为了打动大众,他们总是对信徒们说明宗教是如何可以使社会获得自由和宁静。于是,我们很难从他们的布道演讲中区分宗教的主旨到底是追求来世的永恒幸福,还是现世的繁荣。

CHAPTER X
Of The Taste For Physical Well-being In America

In America the passion for physical well-being is not always exclusive, but it is general; and if all do not feel it in the same manner, yet it is felt by all. The effort to satisfy even the least wants of the body and to provide the little conveniences of life is uppermost in every mind. Something of an analogous character is more and more apparent in Europe. Among the causes that produce these similar consequences in both hemispheres, several are so connected with my subject as to deserve notice.

When riches are hereditarily fixed in families, a great number of men enjoy the comforts of life without feeling an exclusive taste for those comforts. The heart of man is not so much caught by the undisturbed possession of anything valuable as by the desire, as yet imperfectly satisfied, of possessing it and by the incessant dread of losing it. In aristocratic communities the wealthy, never having experienced a condition different from their own, entertain no fear of changing it; the existence of such conditions hardly occurs to them. The comforts of life are not to them the end of life, but simply a way of living; they regard them as existence itself, enjoyed but scarcely thought of. As the natural and instinctive taste that all men feel for being well off is thus satisfied without trouble and without apprehension, their faculties are turned elsewhere and applied to more arduous and lofty undertakings,

第十章　美国人民对物质福利的喜好

美国人民对于物质享乐的热情并不总是个别的,而是普遍存在的。并且,虽然并不是所有的人都用同样的方式,但却是人人都有热爱之心。为了满足身体方面即使是很小的需求,或者是为生活提供哪怕一点点便利而做出努力的观念存在于每个人的思想中,并占据显要地位。类似这样的品性越来越多地见于欧洲各国。在两个半球同时产生这种相似结果的众多效应当中,有一些与我的主题有关,并且值得引起人们的关注。

但财富由于继承的关系为几个家族世代相传的时候,很多人正在享受着富足的生活,但是在他们心中却没有意识到这种差别。人心总是对于这些贵重却易得的东西不像对于企盼得到却得不到的东西,或者在得到后又时时担心失去的东西那么重视。在贵族制国家中,富人们从来不知道还有人过着与他们不同的生活,也从来没有担心过他们的生活会发生变化。而且这样的情况也很难在他们身上发生。对他们来说,富足的生活并不是生命的全部意义,而只是一种生活方式。他们对待它们就像对待生命本身,享受生活但是很少去关注生活。因为人们对于富足的生活有着这种天生的或者本能的爱好,可以很容易地得到满足,不用他们顾虑努力,他们的精力就转移到了别处,用以解决更费力更崇

which excite and engross their minds.

Hence it is that in the very midst of physical gratifications the members of an aristocracy often display a haughty contempt of these very enjoyments and exhibit singular powers of endurance under the privation of them. All the revolutions which have ever shaken or destroyed aristocracies have shown how easily men accustomed to superfluous luxuries can do without the necessaries of life; whereas men who have toiled to acquire a competency can hardly live after they have lost it.

If I turn my observation from the upper to the lower classes, I find analogous effects produced by opposite causes. Among a nation where aristocracy predominates in society and keeps it stationary, the people in the end get as much accustomed to poverty as the rich to their opulence. The latter bestow no anxiety on their physical comforts because they enjoy them without an effort; the former do not think of things which they despair of obtaining and which they hardly know enough of to desire. In communities of this kind the imagination of the poor is driven to seek another world; the miseries of real life enclose it, but it escapes from their control and flies to seek its pleasures far beyond.

When, on the contrary, the distinctions of ranks are obliterated and privileges are destroyed, when hereditary property is subdivided and education and freedom are widely diffused, the desire of acquiring the comforts of the world haunts the imagination of the poor, and the dread of losing them that of the rich. Many scanty fortunes spring up; those who possess them have a sufficient share of physical gratifications to conceive a taste for these pleasures, not enough to satisfy it. They never procure them without exertion, and they never indulge in them without apprehension. They are therefore always straining to pursue or to retain gratifications so delightful, so imperfect, so fugitive.

If I were to inquire what passion is most natural to men who are stimulated and circumscribed by the obscurity of their birth or the mediocrity of their fortune, I could discover none more peculiarly

高的事业了。并且他们也被这种工作吸引而得到激励。

因此，身处于物质享受的贵族阶级成员们常常对他们的这种享乐表现出一种高傲的轻视态度，并在物质生活匮乏的情况下，表现出一种异常的隐忍。曾经动摇或摧毁过贵族制阶级的所有革命都说明了这些曾经过着奢侈生活的人们，是如何轻易地就适应了物质匮乏的时期的生活。然而，那些从贫困的环境中奋斗出来的人们，一旦失去了富裕的条件，就变得无法忍受了。

我们如果从高层阶级向底层阶级观察，我发现两个完全相反的因素却造就了同样的效果。在贵族阶级处于统治地位并保持社会稳定的国家中，底层老百姓习惯贫困的生活，而那些富人也在奢侈的生活中安享幸福。富人们对自己富足的物质生活一点也不操心，因为他们得来容易。而穷人对他们没有希望获得的东西也不多想，而且他们几乎也没有这方面的需求。

在这样的社会中，穷人们的想象力都集中在了寻找来世。现实的悲惨生活限制了他们的思想，但是他们的思想仍旧逃脱了这种束缚，去想象在遥远的未来的幸福。相反地，当阶级间的差别湮灭特权消失的时候，当世袭的财产再次被分化而教育和自由被广泛地传播，穷人的心中也会产生享乐的念头，富人们也会开始担心失去他们所拥有的一切。于是出现了一些少量聚集的财产，那些拥有这些财产的人们的物质生活富足，他们虽能体会到这种享乐带来的快乐，但却无法从中得到满足。他们只有付出努力才能得到这些享乐，于是他们就无法放松地去尽情享受。因此他们始终在追求或竭力保持这种令人愉悦的，完美的，脆弱的满足感。

如果有人问我，对于那些被他们的出身和财富限制或者激励的人们，什么样的激情是最自然的，那么我认为，没有什

appropriate to their condition than this love of physical prosperity. The passion for physical comforts is essentially a passion of the middle classes; with those classes it grows and spreads, with them it is preponderant. From them it mounts into the higher orders of society and descends into the mass of the people.

I never met in America any citizen so poor as not to cast a glance of hope and envy on the enjoyments of the rich or whose imagination did not possess itself by anticipation of those good things that fate still obstinately withheld from him.

On the other hand, I never perceived among the wealthier inhabitants of the United States that proud contempt of physical gratifications which is sometimes to be met with even in the most opulent and dissolute aristocracies. Most of these wealthy persons were once poor; they have felt the sting of want; they were long a prey to adverse fortunes; and now that the victory is won, the passions which accompanied the contest have survived it; their minds are, as it were, intoxicated by the small enjoyments which they have pursued for forty years.

Not but that in the United States, as elsewhere, there is a certain number of wealthy persons who, having come into their property by inheritance, possess without exertion an opulence they have not earned. But even these men are not less devotedly attached to the pleasures of material life. The love of well-being has now become the predominant taste of the nation; the great current of human passions runs in that channel and sweeps everything along in its course.

么其他感情比对物质财富的热爱更适合他们的处境。因为他们是在这样的阶级的陪伴下成长和发展起来的,也正是基于这个阶级才有这样的优势。这种激情也正是从这里攀缘而上到达社会的高层并逐渐在人民中发展开去。

我在美国从未遇到过一个穷人不对富人的享乐表示想往和嫉妒的。他们的想象力预先锁定在了那些命运还顽强地拽离他们的物质财富。

另一方面,我在美国见到的富人,没有人对物质富裕表现出傲慢的轻视态度,而这种轻视态度却常常见于那些极度富裕和荒淫的贵族阶级中。这些富裕的人们中的大多数人从前都很贫穷。他们早已知道贫穷的滋味,并且长久以来一直为获得财富而努力。如今他们成功了,伴随着这种战争的激情仍旧保留在了他们思想中。他们的思想仿佛仍旧陶醉在通过 40 年的奋斗终于迎来的小小的胜利的喜悦之中。

这并不是说在美国不像在其他国家一样,有着一群富人,他们通过继承不费吹灰之力就过上了富裕的生活。但是,即使是这些人,也没有放弃对物质生活的享乐追求。对于富裕生活的热爱之情如今变成了社会的主要思潮。人们的思潮大半都流向了这股溪流并将遇到的一切冲刷殆尽。

CHAPTER XI

Peculiar Effects Of
The Love Of Physical Gratifications
In Democratic Times

It may be supposed, from what has just been said, that the love of physical gratifications must constantly urge the Americans to irregularities in morals, disturb the peace of families, and threaten the security of society at large. But it is not so: the passion for physical gratifications produces in democracies effects very different from those which it occasions in aristocratic nations.

It sometimes happens that, wearied with public affairs and sated with opulence, amid the ruin of religious belief and the decline of the state, the heart of an aristocracy may by degrees be seduced to the pursuit of sensual enjoyments alone. At other times the power of the monarch or the weakness of the people, without stripping the nobility of their fortune, compels them to stand aloof from the administration of affairs and, while the road to mighty enterprise is closed, abandons them to the disquietude of their own desires; they then fall back heavily upon themselves and seek in the pleasures of the body oblivion of their former greatness.

When the members of an aristocratic body are thus exclusively devoted to the pursuit of physical gratifications, they commonly turn in that direction all the energy which they derive from their long experience of power. Such men are not satisfied with the pursuit of comfort; they require sumptuous depravity and splendid corruption. The worship they pay the senses is a gorgeous one, and they seem to vie with one another in the art of degrading their own natures. The stronger, the more famous, and the more free an aristocracy has been, the more depraved will it then become; and however brilliant may have

第十一章　对物质享乐的热爱在民主时期产生的特殊作用

以上描述,可能会使我们认为,对于物质享乐的热爱必然会促使美国人们的道德观念陷入混乱,扰乱家庭的宁静,并且威胁到整个社会的安宁。但是事实并不如此:人们对于物质享乐的激情,在民主制度的影响下,产生了完全不同于贵族制社会的情形。

对于公众事务和奢华生活的厌倦,常常伴随着宗教信仰的破坏和国家的衰落一起发生,贵族阶级的心理也会逐渐被引向对世俗享乐的追求。在其他时代,王权的强大或者人民的弱小,会使贵族失去权力只保有财富,迫使他们远离政治事务。当通往伟大事业的道路被封锁,把他们丢在了对自己的欲望的焦躁不安里。于是,他们又回到了自己的世界,寻找物质上的快感,把过去的辉煌抛诸脑后。

当贵族阶级的成员都因此而完全投入到对物质满足的追求中去,他们通常都会把因长期掌权而积累的能量完全释放在这个方面。这样的人不会满足于对舒适生活的追求,他们追求的是奢华,穷奢无度。他们对物的无上追求,争先恐后各展其堕落之能术。一个贵族制国家越是强大、卓著和自由,它就会变得越堕落。尽管他的道德曾经光芒四射,我也敢预测,这一光

been the luster of its virtues, I dare predict that they will always be surpassed by the splendor of its vices.

The taste for physical gratifications leads a democratic people into no such excesses. The love of well-being is there displayed as a tenacious, exclusive, universal passion, but its range is confined. To build enormous palaces, to conquer or to mimic nature, to ransack the world in order to gratify the passions of a man, is not thought of, but to add a few yards of land to your field, to plant an orchard, to enlarge a dwelling, to be always making life more comfortable and convenient, to avoid trouble, and to satisfy the smallest wants without effort and almost without cost. These are small objects, but the soul clings to them; it dwells upon them closely and day by day, till they at last shut out the rest of the world and sometimes intervene between itself and heaven.

This, it may be said, can be applicable only to those members of the community who are in humble circumstances; wealthier individuals will display tastes akin to those which belonged to them in aristocratic ages. I contest the proposition: in point of physical gratifications, the most opulent members of a democracy will not display tastes very different from those of the people; whether it be that, springing from the people, they really share those tastes or that they esteem it a duty to submit to them. In democratic society the sensuality of the public has taken a moderate and tranquil course, to which all are bound to conform: it is as difficult to depart from the common rule by one's vices as by one's virtues. Rich men who live amid democratic nations are therefore more intent on providing for their smallest wants than for their extraordinary enjoyments; they gratify a number of petty desires without indulging in any great irregularities of passion; thus they are more apt to become enervated than debauched.

The special taste that the men of democratic times entertain for physical enjoyments is not naturally opposed to the principles of public order; nay, it often stands in need of order that it may be gratified. Nor is it adverse to regularity of morals, for good morals contribute

芒终有一天会被它的恶性所掩盖。

对物质生活满足的爱好不会将民主国家的人民引入极端的纵欲。对享乐的热爱在美国虽变成了一种顽强的、排他的、全民统一的激情,但是它的范围是被限制的。为了使一个人得到满足而建造庞大的宫殿、去征服或者模仿自然,去耗尽天下财富是不可想象的。人们想要的,只是再多有几亩地,有一个果园,扩建房屋,使得生活越来越舒适方便,避免麻烦并且不用费太大的力气或者根本不费力就可以满足小小的愿望。这些目标虽小,但却是人心所向。人们天天关注着这些事情,以致忘了周遭的世界,或者常常认为它们的存在仅次于上帝。

也许只有生活在不富裕的环境中的人们才会认为这些说法是合理的。富人们所表现出的爱好,仍旧与贵族制国家中的那套保持类似。我不同意这种主张。在物质享乐方面,民主国家最奢侈的人们也不会表现出与其人民不同的爱好。因为这些人不论现在如何,也始终都是来自贫民,他们也享有那些人的喜好并且认为他们有义务服从这一喜好。在民主社会中,公众的欲望享受都是在一种温和宁静的过程中进行的,而且人人都必须服从这一规律。要想从一般规则中逃脱出来做坏事,是很难的。生活在民主国家中的富人们因此更多的希望满足他们日常生活中的小小的需求,也不会去放纵欲求。他们只要求满足一些小小的需求,而不会沉浸在某种混乱的激情当中去。因此,他们只会变得弱小,而不会堕落。

民主时代的人们对物质享受表现出的这种特殊爱好,不会与公共秩序对立,而且为了满足这种需求,它还常常需要借助于社会秩序的助益。它也不会对道德秩序不利,因为好的道德有利于

to public tranquillity and are favorable to industry. It may even be frequently combined with a species of religious morality; men wish to be as well off as they can in this world without forgoing their chance of another. Some physical gratifications cannot be indulged in without crime; from such they strictly abstain. The enjoyment of others is sanctioned by religion and morality; to these the heart, the imagination, and life itself are unreservedly given up, till, in snatching at these lesser gifts, men lose sight of those more precious possessions which constitute the glory and the greatness of mankind.

The reproach I address to the principle of equality is not that it leads men away in the pursuit of forbidden enjoyments, but that it absorbs them wholly in quest of those which are allowed. By these means a kind of virtuous materialism may ultimately be established in the world, which would not corrupt, but enervate, the soul and noiselessly unbend its springs of action.

社会安宁和工业建设。它甚至会频繁地与一些宗教道德相结合。人们希望在世上越富有越好,但他们同时又不愿放弃自己在来世的权利。一些物质的满足是违法的,而对于这类欲望,他们就会尽量地加以克制。而另一些享乐则是宗教和道德所允许的。对这些来说,人心、人们的想象和生命本身都不会放弃它们,在他们争取这些较小的利益的时候,人们就会遗忘那些更加珍贵的财富,而这些财富富含着人类的荣耀和伟大。

我对于平等原则所做出的这些指责,并不在于它使人们盲目追求那些被禁止的享乐,而在于他使人们完全沉迷于被准许的享乐。这样的话,终有一天世界上会出现一种高尚的唯物主义,它不会腐蚀但却会净化人们的灵魂,并且悄无声息地缓解人们紧绷的精神。

CHAPTER XII

Why Some Americans Manifest
A Sort Of Fanatical Spiritualism

Although the desire of acquiring the good things of this world is the prevailing passion of the American people, certain momentary outbreaks occur when their souls seem suddenly to burst the bonds of matter by which they are restrained and to soar impetuously towards heaven. In all the states of the Union, but especially in the half-peopled country of the Far West, itinerant preachers may be met with who hawk about the word of God from place to place. Whole families, old men, women, and children, cross rough passes and untrodden wilds, coming from a great distance, to join a camp-meeting, where, in listening to these discourses, they totally forget for several days and nights the cares of business and even the most urgent wants of the body.

Here and there in the midst of American society you meet with men full of a fanatical and almost wild spiritualism, which hardly exists in Europe. From time to time strange sects arise which endeavor to strike out extraordinary paths to eternal happiness. Religious insanity is very common in the United States.

Nor ought these facts to surprise us. It was not man who implanted in himself the taste for what is infinite and the love of what is immortal; these lofty instincts are not the offspring of his capricious will; their steadfast foundation is fixed in human nature, and they exist in spite of his efforts. He may cross and distort them; destroy them he cannot.

The soul has wants which must be satisfied; and whatever pains are taken to divert it from itself, it soon grows weary, restless, and

第十二章　为什么有些美国人那样醉心于唯灵主义

尽管渴望获得现世的幸福是美国人民主要的激情，他们的心灵仿佛突然也会爆发一些被禁止的行为并迅速地冲入天堂。在联邦所有的州中，尤其是在那些人迹罕见的遥远西部各州，我们常常会遇到一些巡回的传教士，他们四处传播神的福祉。有些家庭，老人、妇女和儿童从遥远的地方赶来参加露营。他们跋山涉水，就为了来听这些人的布道，这些天中，他们会完全忘记他们的所关心的生意甚至是自身最紧要的需求。

在美国，到处都会见到一些狂热的唯心主义和一些近乎疯狂的唯心论，而这些现象在欧洲是不会发生的。奇怪的异族会一次次崛起，他们希望发现一些通往永久幸福的道路。宗教狂热现象在美国是很普遍的。

这些事实并不能使我们感到吃惊。因为并不是人们自身将这些无限的喜好和对永生的热爱之情植根在自己身上的。这些崇高的感情的产生与人们反复无常的意志无关。它们的基础扎根在人们的本性中，不依人的努力而存在。但是人们可以阻止它改变它，但是无法消灭它。

心灵有些必须得到满足的需求。即使你再努力想要把注意

disquieted amid the enjoyments of sense. If ever the faculties of the great majority of mankind were exclusively bent upon the pursuit of material objects, it might be anticipated that an amazing reaction would take place in the souls of some men. They would drift at large in the world of spirits, for fear of remaining shackled by the close bondage of the body.

It is not, then, wonderful if in the midst of a community whose thoughts tend earthward a small number of individuals are to be found who turn their looks to heaven. I should be surprised if mysticism did not soon make some advance among a people solely engaged in promoting their own worldly welfare.

It is said that the deserts of the Thebaid were peopled by the persecutions of the emperors and the massacres of the Circus; I should rather say that it was by the luxuries of Rome and the Epicurean philosophy of Greece.

If their social condition, their present circumstances, and their laws did not confine the minds of the Americans so closely to the pursuit of worldly welfare, it is probable that they would display more reserve and more experience whenever their attention is turned to things immaterial, and that they would check themselves without difficulty. But they feel imprisoned within bounds, which they will apparently never be allowed to pass. As soon as they have passed these bounds, their minds do not know where to fix themselves and they often rush unrestrained beyond the range of common sense.

力从它身上移开,它也会迅速地在人的感官活动中滋生出一些令人厌倦的、不安的和激动的情绪。如果大多数人的智慧被全部用在了对物质目的的追求上面,则我们可以期望,在一些人的心灵中会生出一种惊人的反应。他们会因为担心自己陷入肉体局限的苑囿之中而驰骋于人们的精神世界之上。

因此,如果在一个人们的思想趋向于现世的社会中,少数人则将自己的目光投向来世,这样不会使人诧异。我会觉得奇怪,如果神秘主义不久会在一个全心全意致力于提高社会福利的民族中提前引退的话。

人们都说,埃及的底比斯沙漠到处都是那些遭到皇权迫害和在圆形校场大屠杀的人们。我则认为,这是因为罗马的奢华和希腊的伊壁鸠鲁哲学等因素造成的。

如果他们的社会条件、地理位置和法制没有将美国人民的思想定位在对于物质福利的追求上面去,那么,我相信,他们也许会表现出更多的知识和更多的经验,只要他们的注意力放在精神方面,并且会很容易自我改进。但是,他们感到了精神上的束缚,让他们觉得似乎无法冲破这束缚。因此,一旦他们穿越了这一束缚,就会不知道该去向何处。那时,他们就会在普遍观念之上横冲直撞地行进。

CHAPTER XIII

Why The Americans Are So Restless
In The Midst Of Their Prosperity

In certain remote corners of the Old World you may still sometimes stumble upon a small district that seems to have been forgotten
amid the general tumult, and to have remained stationary while everything around it was in motion. The inhabitants, for the most part, are
extremely ignorant and poor; they take no part in the business of the
country and are frequently oppressed by the government, yet their
countenances are generally placid and their spirits light.

In America I saw the freest and most enlightened men placed in
the happiest circumstances that the world affords; it seemed to me as
if a cloud habitually hung upon their brow, and I thought them serious
and almost sad, even in their pleasures.

The chief reason for this contrast is that the former do not think
of the ills they endure, while the latter are forever brooding over advantages they do not possess. It is strange to see with what feverish
ardor the Americans pursue their own welfare, and to watch the vague
dread that constantly torments them lest they should not have chosen
the shortest path which may lead to it.

A native of the United States clings to this world's goods as if he
were certain never to die; and he is so hasty in grasping at all within
his reach that one would suppose he was constantly afraid of not living
long enough to enjoy them. He clutches everything, he holds nothing

第十三章　为什么身处繁荣时期的美国人民会感到如此心神不宁

今天,在旧大陆的一些偏僻的角落,我们仍旧会偶然发现一些小州,它们看起来似乎被人们遗忘在广袤的天地之中,并在周围一切都在发生变化的世界里静止不动。在大多数地方居住的居民,都极度的无知和贫穷。他们没有权利加入国家事务的管理工作,所以常常受到政府的镇压。但是,他们却都表情平静精神轻松。

在美国,我见到了最文明最自由的人们居住在一块幸福的土地上。但我总觉得他们眉头紧锁,即使在他们快乐的时候,我也觉得他们严肃地近乎悲伤。

造成着两种差异的主要原因在于,前者从来不多想自己承受的不幸,而后者则总是惦记着他们还没能得到的好处。这实在是令人感到奇怪,美国人民对于追求自己的福利有着如此高涨的热情,以及那些因为唯恐找不到通往致富的捷径而产生的常常折磨着他们的隐隐的忧愁。

美国本地人对于现世物质的追求,表现出一种仿佛自己可以永生的热情。他们急切地希望抓住身边的一切,以至于人们会觉得他们总在担心生命有限而他们无法尽情地享受。因此他们把

fast, but soon loosens his grasp to pursue fresh gratifications.

In the United States a man builds a house in which to spend his old age, and he sells it before the roof is on; he plants a garden and lets it just as the trees are coming into bearing; he brings a field into tillage and leaves other men to gather the crops; he embraces a profession and gives it up; he settles in a place, which he soon afterwards leaves to carry his changeable longings elsewhere. If his private affairs leave him any leisure, he instantly plunges into the vortex of politics; and if at the end of a year of unremitting labor he finds he has a few days' vacation, his eager curiosity whirls him over the vast extent of the United States, and he will travel fifteen hundred miles in a few days to shake off his happiness. Death at length overtakes him, but it is before he is weary of his bootless chase of that complete felicity which forever escapes him.

At first sight there is something surprising in this strange unrest of so many happy men, restless in the midst of abundance. The spectacle itself, however, is as old as the world; the novelty is to see a whole people furnish an exemplification of it.

Their taste for physical gratifications must be regarded as the original source of that secret disquietude which the actions of the Americans betray and of that inconstancy of which they daily afford fresh examples. He who has set his heart exclusively upon the pursuit of worldly welfare is always in a hurry, for he has but a limited time at his disposal to reach, to grasp, and to enjoy it. The recollection of the shortness of life is a constant spur to him. Besides the good things that he possesses, he every instant fancies a thousand others that death will prevent him from trying if he does not try them soon. This thought fills him with anxiety, fear, and regret and keeps his mind in ceaseless trepidation, which leads him perpetually to change his plans and his abode.

If in addition to the taste for physical well-being a social condition be added in which neither laws nor customs retain any person

握生命的一切,迅速地捕捉所有的东西,但却又很快放手去寻找新的满足。

在美国,一个人建造了一座房子打算安度晚年,但是房顶还没搭起来他就把它卖了;然后他种植了一片果园,树还没结果果园就出租了;接着他又去耕地,结果让别人尽得他的成果。他会放弃了自己的事业;他选一个地方定居,很快就会被不断变化的追求拉着离开;如果他忙完了自己的事情还有空余时间,他会不遗余力地投入到政治中去。假如他辛劳了一年,年终的时候发现还有几天假期,他的好奇心就使他对美国感到了兴趣,并在短短的几天内穿越几千里路程,到处播撒他的幸福。死亡终于来临,并在他还没有对追逐完美幸福感到厌倦的时候,就眼看着它永远地离开了自己。

乍一看来,这么多幸福的人们处于这么富裕的环境中却表现得如此好动不安,让人觉得很惊讶。尽管这一现象本身自古就有,但其新奇之处却在于整个民族都是这样。

他们对于物质享受的爱好,应当被视为是美国人的行为所透露出来的内心的不安以及他们每天对新的事物变幻莫测的追求的来源。他对物质福利的追求总是很迫切,因为他能用以追求、把握和享受这些东西的时间不多。他们对生命的短暂的思索,使他们总是感到如芒在背。除了这些他已经拥有的美好事物,他们还时时牵挂着另一些其他的东西,如果他们不尽早地享用,就有可能因为死亡的原因而无法享受得到了。这样的想法使他整天被焦虑、担心和遗憾包围着,使他的思想整天都在战战兢兢中度过,同时也使得他不得不经常改变计划和住所。

如果,社会中除了对物质享受的爱好之外,还同时存在着一

in his place, there is a great additional stimulant to this restlessness of temper. Men will then be seen continually to change their track for fear of missing the shortest cut to happiness. It may readily be conceived that if men passionately bent upon physical gratifications desire eagerly, they are also easily discouraged; as their ultimate object is to enjoy, the means to reach that object must be prompt and easy or the trouble of acquiring the gratification would be greater than the gratification itself. Their prevailing frame of mind, then, is at once ardent and relaxed, violent and enervated. Death is often less dreaded by them than perseverance in continuous efforts to one end.

The equality of conditions leads by a still straighter road to several of the effects that I have here described. When all the privileges of birth and fortune are abolished, when all professions are accessible to all, and a man's own energies may place him at the top of any one of them, an easy and unbounded career seems open to his ambition and he will readily persuade himself that he is born to no common destinies. But this is an erroneous notion, which is corrected by daily experience. The same equality that allows every citizen to conceive these lofty hopes renders all the citizens less able to realize them; it circumscribes their powers on every side, while it gives freer scope to their desires. Not only are they themselves powerless, but they are met at every step by immense obstacles, which they did not at first perceive. They have swept away the privileges of some of their fellow creatures which stood in their way, but they have opened the door to universal competition; the barrier has changed its shape rather than its position. When men are nearly alike and all follow the same track, it is very difficult for any one individual to walk quickly and cleave a way through the dense throng that surrounds and presses on

些不受法律和民情约束的人们,则对人心的这种永无休止的情绪更增添了一些刺激。我们会发现,人们因为担心失去这些短暂的幸福而变得更加频繁地改变自己的计划。我们还应该认为,如果人们过于追求物质享受,那么他们也会很容易泄气。因为他们的终极目标是享乐,通往这个目标的途径必须是简单易行的,否则人们为了获得享受而经历的困难比享受本身就大得很多。因此,人们的思想普遍都变得既激烈又轻松,既强烈又软弱。死亡对他们来说常常显得不那么令人恐怖,但坚持对享乐的追求过程却很艰难。

平等的社会条件会通过另一些直接的途径产生我所描述的效果。当所有的出身和财产的特权被废除后,当所有的职业都对所有开放的时候,当一个人依靠自己的力量就可以达到本行业的顶端的时候,他面前就会出现一条轻松而没有限制的完全对他的雄心壮志敞开的事业,他也就会觉得自己生而肩负着不平凡的任务。但是,这样的想法是不正确的,并且这一判断在每天的生活事例中都被加以证实。对于每个人都敞开的这种公平竞争某一崇高理想的方式,其实也削弱了每个人实现目标的能力。平等在各个方面削弱着人们的力量,虽然它使人们可以追求的事物的范围大大扩展。不仅仅使他们自身力量变小了,而且使他们在前进的道路上处处受阻,这是他们在最初没有意识到的。他们扫除了挡在他们路上的一些同胞们的特权,但却打开了一扇同所有人平等竞争的大门。于是,他们的障碍只是改变了形式,而没有改变其存在。当人们越来越趋于大同,所有的人都循着同一条轨迹前进的时候,就使得每个个体很难快速前进,因为他们很难从拥挤的人群中摆脱重压开辟出一条道路来。平等使人们产生了追

him. This constant strife between the inclination springing from the e-
quality of condition and the means it supplies to satisfy them harasses
and wearies the mind.

It is possible to conceive of men arrived at a degree of freedom
that should completely content them; they would then enjoy their independence without anxiety and without impatience. But men will
never establish any equality with which they can be contented. Whatever efforts a people may make, they will never succeed in reducing
all the conditions of society to a perfect level; and even if they unhappily attained that absolute and complete equality of position, the inequality of minds would still remain, which, coming directly from the
hand of God, will forever escape the laws of man. However democratic, then, the social state and the political constitution of a people may
be, it is certain that every member of the community will always find
out several points about him which overlook his own position; and we
may foresee that his looks will be doggedly fixed in that direction.
When inequality of conditions is the common law of society, the most
marked inequalities do not strike the eye; when everything is nearly
on the same level, the slightest are marked enough to hurt it. Hence
the desire of equality always becomes more insatiable in proportion as
equality is more complete.

Among democratic nations, men easily attain a certain equality
of condition, but they can never attain as much as they desire. It perpetually retires from before them, yet without hiding itself from their
sight, and in retiring draws them on. At every moment they think they
are about to grasp it; it escapes at every moment from their hold.
They are near enough to see its charms, but too far off to enjoy them;
and before they have fully tasted its delights, they die.

To these causes must be attributed that strange melancholy which
often haunts the inhabitants of democratic countries in the midst of
their abundance, and that disgust at life which sometimes seizes upon

求,但在这种追求与实现这些追求满足他们的享乐之间所要付出的努力,却一直困扰着人们的思想。

可以想象人们实现了他们满意的一定程度地平等,这时,他们就可以尽情地享受他们的独立地位,而不必再担惊受怕。但是人们将永不会建立起使他们满意的平等。不论一个国家怎样地努力,都不可能使社会中所有的阶级地位变得平行。即使有一天他们不幸地实现了这种完全绝对的平等,他们思想的差异性也仍旧存在,而这种差异却是天生的,没有任何法律可以制约。因此,尽管一个国家的社会条件和政治制度可能会是民主的,但是可以确定的是,社会中的每个成员将永远都会找出许多比他们地位更高的方面,觉得自己的处境总是受到别人的制约。而且,我们可以预见,人们的视线会一直盯在这些方面。当社会的不平等成为社会的一般法律,那么那些最明显的不平等就往往不再那么吸引人们的眼球。当所有的事物都接近于同一水平线,则最细微的差别也足以使这种平等受到伤害。因此,对于平等的渴望与平等的彻底程度比起来,总是显得很难以满足。

在民主国家中,人们更容易得到一定的平等的地位,但却永远达不到他们所想要得到的程度。它们总是在就要到你面前的时候就撤退回去,但是又不撤离你的视线,然后又前进一点。每次人们都会觉得自己就要实现平等了,可是每次都在最关键的时候被它溜掉。人们足以看清楚平等的好处,但是却享受不到。即使有幸享受到了,但却在还没有得到彻底平等的时候,就到了生命的尽头。

这些原因,也使得民主国家的居民在他们富裕的生活中经常表现出一种奇怪的忧郁感,并且常常在他们平静而又舒适的生活

them in the midst of calm and easy circumstances. Complaints are made in France that the number of suicides increases; in America suicide is rare, but insanity is said to be more common there than anywhere else. These are all different symptoms of the same disease. The Americans do not put an end to their lives, however disquieted they may be, because their religion forbids it; and among them materialism may be said hardly to exist, notwithstanding the general passion for physical gratification. The will resists, but reason frequently gives way.

In democratic times enjoyments are more intense than in the ages of aristocracy, and the number of those who partake in them is vastly larger: but, on the other hand, it must be admitted that man's hopes and desires are oftener blasted, the soul is more stricken and perturbed, and care itself more keen.

中表现出对生命的厌烦情绪。法国人抱怨自杀人数增多,美国人自杀的人数虽少,但是那里精神失常的人数却远远多于其他国家。这些都是这一病症的不同表现形式。美国人不会自杀,尽管他们也许也很厌倦生命,这是因为他们信仰的宗教不允许他们这样做。在美国人当中,唯物主义者是很难存活的,尽管人们普遍追求物质享受。美国人的意志坚强,但他们的理智却常常缴械投降。

在民主国家中,享乐的机会比在贵族制国家更多,而且追求享乐的人数也远远大于在贵族制国家中的人们。但是,从另一方面说,我们也必须承认,人们的希望和欲求也更容易被践踏,人们的灵魂也更容易激动和感到不安,而人们的顾虑也更强烈。

CHAPTER XIV

How The Taste For Physical Gratifications Is United In America To Love Of Freedom And Attention To Public Affairs

When a democratic state turns to absolute monarchy, the activity that was before directed to public and to private affairs is all at once centered on the latter. The immediate consequence is, for some time, great physical prosperity, but this impulse soon slackens and the a-mount of productive industry is checked. I do not know if a single trading or manufacturing people can be cited, from the Tyrians down to the Florentines and the English, who were not a free people also. There is therefore a close bond and necessary relation between these two elements, freedom and productive industry.

This proposition is generally true of all nations, but especially of democratic nations. I have already shown that men who live in ages of equality have a continual need of forming associations in order to pro-cure the things they desire; and, on the other hand, I have shown how great political freedom improves and diffuses the art of associa-tion. Freedom in these ages is therefore especially favorable to the production of wealth; nor is it difficult to perceive that despotism is especially adverse to the same result.

The nature of despotic power in democratic ages is not to be fierce or cruel, but minute and meddling. Despotism of this kind, though it does not trample on humanity, is directly opposed to the genius of commerce and the pursuits of industry.

Thus the men of democratic times require to be free in order to procure more readily those physical enjoyments for which they are al-ways longing. It sometimes happens, however, that the excessive

第十四章 在美国，人们是如何将对满足物质欲望的喜好与对自由的热爱和对公共事务的关心结合在一起的

当民主制国家向专制君主转变后，之前人们的社会和私人行为，就会立刻完全指向后者。这样产生的直接后果就是，在一段时间内会产生伟大的繁荣，但是这种推动力很快就会减慢，生产也会停滞不前。我不知道能否从都灵人到佛罗伦萨人和英国人那里找到一个例子证明凡是经营工商业的民族不是自由的民族。因此，在自由和制造业这两种因素之间就存在着一种紧密地必要地联系。

这一主张，对于所有的国家，尤其是对于民主国家来说，均是如此。我已经说过，生在平等时期的人们，为了实现他们的欲望，一直努力地致力于结社。并且，我已从另一方面阐述了政治自由是如何大力地推进和传播了结社艺术。在这样的时期中，自由就变得对创造财富异常有利。但是我们也不难看出，专制却只能创造出与此相反的效果。

民主国家专制的本性并不是要变得凶猛而残酷，而是要变得繁琐和啰嗦。这样的专制主义尽管并不有损于人性，但却直接压迫着人们的商业天性和在工业上的追求。

因此，民主时期的人们希望得到自由从而获得更多他们一直追求的物质享受。但是，常常却是因为他们对于这种享受的追求

taste they conceive for these same enjoyments makes them surrender to the first master who appears. The passion for worldly welfare then defeats itself and, without their perceiving it, throws the object of their desires to a greater distance.

There is, indeed, a most dangerous passage in the history of a democratic people. When the taste for physical gratifications among them has grown more rapidly than their education and their experience of free institutions, the time will come when men are carried away and lose all self-restraint at the sight of the new possessions they are about to obtain. In their intense and exclusive anxiety to make a fortune they lose sight of the close connection that exists between the private fortune of each and the prosperity of all. It is not necessary to do violence to such a people in order to strip them of the rights they enjoy; they themselves willingly loosen their hold. The discharge of political duties appears to them to be a troublesome impediment which diverts them from their occupations and business. If they are required to elect representatives, to support the government by personal service, to meet on public business, they think they have no time, they cannot waste their precious hours in useless engagements; such idle amusements are unsuited to serious men who are engaged with the more important interests of life. These people think they are following the principle of self-interest, but the idea they entertain of that principle is a very crude one; and the better to look after what they call their own business, they neglect their chief business, which is to remain their own masters.

As the citizens who labor do not care to attend to public affairs, and as the class which might devote its leisure to these duties has ceased to exist, the place of the government is, as it were, unfilled. If at that critical moment some able and ambitious man grasps the supreme power, he will find the road to every kind of usurpation open before him. If he attends for some time only to the material prosperity of the country, no more will be demanded of him. Above all, he must ensure public tranquillity: men who are possessed by the

的过多的渴望,使他们总是一遇到强大的力量就选择屈服。人们对于物质福利的激情因为没有得到满足而气馁,于是人们还没得到其追求的目标就已将之抛诸脑后。

事实上,在民主国家的历史中有过一段最危险的时期。当人们对于物质享受的爱好的增长远远快过他们在自由制度方面所接受的教育和他们的经验的时候,就会出现一个人们难以自控的时期,这时候人们一看到自己所追求的新鲜事物就完全丧失自控力。在他们强烈而紧张地攫取财富的时候,他们就完全忘掉了存在于个人财富和社会共同富裕之间的紧密纽带。我们不必用暴力去剥夺他们已有的权利,因为这样的民族,他们会自动放弃这些权利的。尽公民的政治义务在他们看来是一项讨厌的障碍,使他们无法专心于自己的工作和商业活动。如果要求他们选举代表,或者通过个人行为来支持政府的活动,或者服务于全民事业,他们就觉得自己没有时间,他们不会浪费自己宝贵的时间在无谓的事情上。这样的工作不是那些献身于更重要的人类事业的人们去做。他们相信利益的正确理解原则,但是他们对这一原则的理解还有失偏颇。而且,为了更好地完成自己的私人利益,他们就忽视了继续做自己的主人这一重要的事业。

因为有些人并不关心公共事业,而且,因为那些可能将自己多余的精力投入到这些职责的阶级已经不存在,所以政府的这类职位就好像出现了空缺。如果在这个危急时刻,一些有能力有野心的人们想要掌握统治权,他就会发现每一条通往权力的大门都是可行的。如果他坚持在一段时间内实现国家的物质繁荣,那么就没有人再对他要求更多了。除此之外,他还必须保证公共安全。因为被渴望物质享受的激情控制着的人们,常常会发现,在

passion for physical gratification generally find out that the turmoil of freedom disturbs their welfare before they discover how freedom itself serves to promote it. If the slightest rumor of public commotion intrudes into the petty pleasures of private life, they are aroused and alarmed by it. The fear of anarchy perpetually haunts them, and they are always ready to fling away their freedom at the first disturbance.

I readily admit that public tranquillity is a great good, but at the same time I cannot forget that all nations have been enslaved by being kept in good order. Certainly it is not to be inferred that nations ought to despise public tranquillity, but that state ought not to content them. A nation that asks nothing of its government but the maintenance of order is already a slave at heart, the slave of its own well-being, awaiting only the hand that will bind it. By such a nation the despotism of faction is not less to be dreaded than the despotism of an individual. When the bulk of the community are engrossed by private concerns, the smallest parties need not despair of getting the upper hand in public affairs. At such times it is not rare to see on the great stage of the world, as we see in our theaters, a multitude represented by a few players, who alone speak in the name of an absent or inattentive crowd: they alone are in action, while all others are stationary; they regulate everything by their own caprice; they change the laws and tyrannize at will over the manners of the country; and then men wonder to see into how small a number of weak and worthless hands a great people may fall.

Hitherto the Americans have fortunately escaped all the perils that I have just pointed out, and in this respect they are really deserving of admiration. Perhaps there is no country in the world where fewer idle men are to be met with than in America, or where all who work are more eager to promote their own welfare. But if the passion of the Americans for physical gratifications is vehement, at least it is

他们发现自由是如何促使他们实现目的的事实之前,总是会发现自由的滥用是如何阻碍了他们实现物质利益的。哪怕是一点点公众的激情涉入到他们的私人生活,他们都会被惊起,并感到高度警惕。而长期困扰着他们的对混乱状态的担忧,使他们总是准备着,一遇到骚动就逃离自由。

我承认,公共安宁是很好的;但我无法忘记,所有的国家在出现暴政之前都是安宁的。当然,我们并不能推断,国家无需重视社会安宁,但是国家需要的也不仅仅是安宁。一个民族对他的国家,除了要求其秩序井然,其余都不必需的话,那么它在人们的心中,就已经处于从属地位了,从属于自己的物质财富之下,只待有人来统治它。这样的民族对于党派专制统治的担心并不少于对个人专制的统治的防备。当社会集体只考虑自己的私人利益,即使是再小的派别都有可能对公共事务实施控制。在这样的时期,在世界的大舞台上,如同我们在戏院里看到的一样,一小撮人代表了全体大众的现象并不少见。他们独自站在舞台上,以未出席或者对此漠不关心的人们的名义发表演说:他们单独采取行动,而其他所有人则静止不动。他们凭借自己的奇思怪想,随意地规划着每件事。他们修改法律,对国家的民情横行霸道。然后,人们就可以想象得到,一个伟大的民族是怎样落入一小撮虚弱而无能的人们的手中的。

至今美国人已幸运地避开了我在上面指出的所有危险。在这方面,他们的确值得羡慕。也许世界上再没有一个国家能像美国那样少有游手好闲的人,也再没有什么国家像美国那样,全民都迫切地希望增加自己的财富。但是,如果说美国人民对于物质享乐的激情很强烈,但至少这种激情并不是毫无限制的。并

not indiscriminate; and reason, though unable to restrain it, still directs its course.

An American attends to his private concerns as if he were alone in the world, and the next minute he gives himself up to the common welfare as if he had forgotten them. At one time he seems animated by the most selfish cupidity; at another, by the most lively patriotism. The human heart cannot be thus divided. The inhabitants of the United States alternately display so strong and so similar a passion for their own welfare and for their freedom that it may be supposed that these passions are united and mingled in some part of their character. And indeed the Americans believe their freedom to be the best instrument and surest safeguard of their welfare; they are attached to the one by the other. They by no means think that they are not called upon to take a part in public affairs; they believe, on the contrary, that their chief business is to secure for themselves a government which will allow them to acquire the things they covet and which will not debar them from the peaceful enjoyment of those possessions which they have already acquired.

且,理性虽然不能抑制这种激情,但至少能够对它的发展加以指引。

　　一个美国人考虑自己的私人利益时,就仿佛世界上就只有他一个人存在似的,但是下一刻,当他完全投入到公益事业的时候,就仿佛将个人的利益彻底忘掉了似的。他有时仿佛被最自私的贪欲所驱使,但是有时候,又满怀崇高的爱国情义。人心不能被这样分化成两半。美国的居民却能交替地将这两种感情用于追求财富和自由。看起来,这两方面的感情似乎已经联合起来并与他的性格的一部分相融和。事实上,美国人相信自由将是他们获得财富的最佳工具,也是其最大的保障。这两者相互联系缺一不可。因此,他们从不认为自己是被迫去参加社会事务的,相反地,他们认为自己最主要的任务就是为他们自己保护将允许他们获得他们垂涎的对象的政府。而且,这个政府也不会阻止他们继续平平安安地享受他们已经获得的利益。

CHAPTER XV

How Religious Belief Sometimes Turns The Thoughts Of Americans To Immaterial Pleasures

In the United States on the seventh day of every week the trading and working life of the nation seems suspended; all noises cease; a deep tranquillity, say rather the solemn calm of meditation, succeeds the turmoil of the week, and the soul resumes possession and contemplation of itself. On this day the marts of traffic are deserted; every member of the community, accompanied by his children, goes to church, where he listens to strange language which would seem unsuited to his ear. He is told of the countless evils caused by pride and covetousness; he is reminded of the necessity of checking his desires, of the finer pleasures that belong to virtue alone, and of the true happiness that attends it. On his return home he does not turn to the ledgers of his business, but he opens the book of Holy Scripture; there he meets with sublime and affecting descriptions of the greatness and goodness of the Creator, of the infinite magnificence of the handiwork of God, and of the lofty destinies of man, his duties, and his immortal privileges.

Thus it is that the American at times steals an hour from himself, and, laying aside for a while the petty passions which agitate his life, and the ephemeral interests which engross it, he strays at once into an ideal world, where all is great, eternal, and pure.

I have endeavored to point out, in another part of this work, the

第十五章　宗教信仰是怎样常常将美国人的心灵转向非物质享乐的

在美国，每个礼拜的第七天，国家的工商业活动仿佛都是被禁止的。所有嘈杂的声音都消失殆尽。在一种深沉的宁静，或者不如说是在每个礼拜纷乱的生活后的沉思所带来的严肃的平静中，灵魂又恢复了其原有的地位和自我沉思。在这一天，繁华的商业中心被人们遗弃，社会的每个成员都带着孩子去教堂做礼拜。在那里，他们听着那些平时很少听到的布道演讲。他们听到无数由于骄傲和贪婪而引发的罪恶的例子。他被提醒抑制自己的贪欲的必要性，只有美德才能带来的快乐，以及随之而来的真正的幸福。在回家的路上，他还沉浸其中，完全没有考虑他的事业，一回家就打开《圣经》。他从中窥见了造物主的伟大和善意的一丝亮光和动人的描述，看到了造物主无穷的神奇力量以及人类的崇高使命，以及他的职责和他不朽的特权。

美国人就这样常常腾出一点时间留给自己，暂时将生活中的琐碎欲望和短暂的利益所产生的激情放置一边，而立刻进入完美世界。在那里，所有的一切都是伟大的、不朽的和纯粹的。

我还想指出，在这本书的另一部分中，我提到过美国的政治

causes to which the maintenance of the political institutions of the A-
mericans is attributable, and religion appeared to be one of the most
prominent among them. I am now treating of the Americans in an individual capacity, and I again observe that religion is not less useful
to each citizen than to the whole state. The Americans show by their
practice that they feel the high necessity of imparting morality to democratic communities by means of religion. What they think of themselves in this respect is a truth of which every democratic nation ought
to be thoroughly persuaded.

I do not doubt that the social and political constitution of a people predisposes them to adopt certain doctrines and tastes, which afterwards flourish without difficulty among them; while the same causes may divert them from certain other opinions and propensities without any voluntary effort and, as it were, without any distinct consciousness on their part. The whole art of the legislator is correctly to
discern beforehand these natural inclinations of communities of men,
in order to know whether they should be fostered or whether it may not
be necessary to check them. For the duties incumbent on the legislator differ at different times; only the goal towards which the human
race ought ever to be tending is stationary; the means of reaching it
are perpetually varied.

If I had been born in an aristocratic age, in the midst of a nation
where the hereditary wealth of some and the irremediable penury of
others equally diverted men from the idea of bettering their condition
and held the soul, as it were, in a state of torpor, fixed on the contemplation of another world, I should then wish that it were possible
for me to rouse that people to a sense of their wants; I should seek to
discover more rapid and easy means for satisfying the fresh desires
that I might have awakened; and, directing the most strenuous efforts
of the citizens to physical pursuits, I should endeavor to stimulate
them to promote their own well-being. If it happened that some men
were thus immoderately incited to the pursuit of riches and caused to
display an excessive liking for physical gratifications, I should not be
alarmed; these peculiar cases would soon disappear in the general aspect of the whole community.

The attention of the legislators of democracies is called to other
cares. Give democratic nations education and freedom and leave them
alone. They will soon learn to draw from this world all the benefits
that it can afford; they will improve each of the useful arts and will

制度的得以持久的原因而且宗教是这些原因中间最显著的一个。我现在要研究的是宗教对个人的影响，而且我再次观察到，宗教对个人的影响并不小于它对国家的影响。美国人通过他们的行为说明了，他们认为对民主国家来说，很有必要通过宗教的手段向人们输灌道德意识。在这方面，他们对自己的看法是每个民主国家都应当完全认同的事实。

我并不怀疑，一个国家的社会和政治制度必然使他们偏于接受一定的原则和喜好，而这些原则和喜好之后也将很轻易地在他们中间盛行起来。同样的原因还会使他们被动地从这样的原则和喜好转向其他爱好，而且，他们自己可能还没有任何感知。立法者的最大的才能就在于，为了了解哪些应该培养哪些需要加以遏制，他们能够预先正确地区分自己国家人民的这种自然的倾向。因为立法者的职责在不同的时期需要加以区分，所以，只有人类所追求目标指向固定不变，而人们追求的方法却各有不同。

如果我出生在一个人们因为世袭的原因而贫富差距显著的贵族时代，这样的时代使人们都放弃了改善自己的处境的企图，并且，使人们处于麻木状态，完全寄希望于来世。那么，我真的希望我能唤起人们的欲求，我会寻找一些更快速便捷的方式实现被我唤起的欲望，并且指引人们以极大的热情去追寻物质的享受，我还要努力激发他们去创造财富。如果碰巧有人因此而过度地追求财富，并且表现出一种对物质享受的过激喜爱，我也不会感到不安。因为这些特殊的事例很快就会成为社会的普遍特征而淹没其中。

民主社会立法者有他们自己的关注点。民主国家有了教育和自由以后，就可以放手让它们自己去发展了。他们很快就会学着从这个世界获得他能得到的所有对他有利的东西。他们会完

day by day render life more comfortable, more convenient, and more easy. Their social condition naturally urges them in this direction; I do not fear that they will slacken their course.

But while man takes delight in this honest and lawful pursuit of his own well-being, it is to be apprehended that in the end he may lose the use of his sublimest faculties, and that while he is busied in improving all around him, he may at length degrade himself. Here, and here only, does the peril lie. It should therefore be the unceasing object of the legislators of democracies and of all the virtuous and enlightened men who live there to raise the souls of their fellow citizens and keep them lifted up towards heaven. It is necessary that all who feel an interest in the future destinies of democratic society should unite, and that all should make joint and continual efforts to diffuse the love of the infinite, lofty aspirations, and a love of pleasures not of earth. If among the opinions of a democratic people any of those pernicious theories exist which tend to inculcate that all perishes with the body, let men by whom such theories are professed be marked as the natural foes of the whole people.

The materialists are offensive to me in many respects; their doctrines I hold to be pernicious, and I am disgusted at their arrogance. If their system could be of any utility to man, it would seem to be by giving him a modest opinion of himself; but these reasoners show that it is not so; and when they think they have said enough to prove that they are brutes, they appear as proud as if they had demonstrated that they are gods.

Materialism, among all nations, is a dangerous disease of the human mind; but it is more especially to be dreaded among a democratic people because it readily amalgamates with that vice which is most familiar to the heart under such circumstances. Democracy encourages a taste for physical gratification; this taste, if it become

善每一项有用的工艺,使自己的生活变得一天天更舒适、便捷和轻松。他们的社会地位自然会促使他们往这个方面发展。而且我也不担心他们会放慢前进的脚步。

但是,当人们醉心于以这种诚实合法的方式追求幸福的时候,我们可以了解到,他最终会使自己的非凡才能无用武之地的,而且,当他忙于改善周围的事物的时候,他最终也会使自己的地位降低。这样的话,最终受害的就只有他自己。因此,民主国家立法者永不放弃追求的目标,以及所有生活在那里的有道德有文明的人们的目标就在于不断地提升其国民的灵魂,将他们的灵魂引向天堂。所以很有必要使所有对民主国家未来命运感兴趣的人们联合起来,使他们齐心协力不懈努力,让人们心中都充满无限崇高的理想,和对非物质享乐的热爱。如果在民主国家人民的观念中,存在着一些有害的理论,说一切将随着肉体的消失而消失,那我们就应该给传播这些论点的人们打上全民自然公敌的印记。

唯物主义者在许多方面让我感到厌恶。我认为他们的学说是有害的,并且,我很反感他们高傲的态度。如果说他们的理论有些对人们有利的地方,那也只是让人们用谦卑的态度认识自己而已。但是,他们自己并不这么认为。他们认为自己已经充分地证明了他们的兽性,而且他们看起来仿佛很因此而自鸣得意,好像自己被证实是神仙了一样。

在所有的国家中,唯物主义者对人们的思想来说都是有害的。但是对民主国家的人民来说,它尤其危险,因为它最容易与民主国家人民心中的恶纠缠在一起。民主鼓励人们进行物质享受。这种爱好如果不加限制,很快就会使人们相信,一切都只是

excessive, soon disposes men to believe that all is matter only; and materialism, in its turn, hurries them on with mad impatience to these same delights; such is the fatal circle within which democratic nations are driven round. It were well that they should see the danger and hold back.

Most religions are only general, simple, and practical means of teaching men the doctrine of the immortality of the soul. That is the greatest benefit which a democratic people derives from its belief, and hence belief is more necessary to such a people than to all others. When, therefore, any religion has struck its roots deep into a democracy, beware that you do not disturb it; but rather watch it carefully, as the most precious bequest of aristocratic ages. Do not seek to supersede the old religious opinions of men by new ones, lest in the passage from one faith to another, the soul being left for a while stripped of all belief, the love of physical gratifications should grow upon it and fill it wholly.

The doctrine of metempsychosis is assuredly not more rational than that of materialism; nevertheless, if it were absolutely necessary that a democracy should choose one of the two, I should not hesitate to decide that the community would run less risk of being brutalized by believing that the soul of man will pass into the carcass of a hog than by believing that the soul of man is nothing at all. The belief in a supersensual and immortal principle, united for a time to matter is so indispensable to man's greatness that its effects are striking even when it is not united to the doctrine of future reward and punishment, or even when it teaches no more than that after death the divine principle contained in man is absorbed in the Deity or transferred to animate the frame of some other creature. Men holding so imperfect a belief will still consider the body as the secondary and inferior portion of their nature, and will despise it even while they yield to its influence; whereas they have a natural esteem and secret admiration for the immaterial part of man, even though they sometimes refuse to submit to its authority. That is enough to give a lofty cast to their opinions and their tastes, and to bid them tend, with no interested motive, and as it were by impulse, to pure feelings and elevated thoughts.

It is not certain that Socrates and his followers had any fixed

物质的。并且唯物主义这时便会开始促使人们疯狂地追求这些享乐。这些就是民主国家被驱使着循环往复的厄运。如果他们能够看到危险并谨慎对待，就好了。

大部分宗教都是普遍的、简单的和可行的教会人们通往不灭灵魂的有效途径。这也是民主国家的人民从他的信仰中获得的最大的好处，而且，信仰对民主国家的人最必需。因此，只要任何一个宗教在民主国家站稳脚跟后，你就最好不要去干涉它，你需要小心的监视着它，就如同看护着贵族时代的珍贵遗产一样。也不要想着用新的宗教信仰去取代旧的，以免在两种信念的转换间期，人们的灵魂被搁浅在一片空地上，这样的话，他们对物质享乐的热爱会迅速地成长起来，并充满人们空虚的心灵。

当然，轮回说并不比唯物主义更理性。但是，如果一个民主国家必须选择其一的话，那我会毫不犹豫地决定，社会应该选择相信人类的灵魂会转生为猪。而且我认为，这样会比使人们相信根本没灵魂的存在而最后使人们有可能生出兽性的危险小一些。处于超自然的永恒的原则的信仰，在一段时间内与物质的联合，是使人类伟大不可或缺的。因为在人们不相信因果报应的观点时，或者使人们只相信神赐予人的灵魂在死后将还给神或转到神所创造的其他生物身上时，这种信仰的作用也是很显著的。持有这种残缺的信仰的人们，仍旧认为身体是次要的、低级的，并且即使不得不受它们的影响的时候，也鄙视它们。然而，他们对人的非物质的部分又怀着一种天然的尊敬和隐秘的羡慕，即使他们常常拒绝向这一精神的东西屈服。这足以使它的观点和爱好具有某种高大的形象，并且自动地接近纯净的感情和高尚的思想。

苏格拉底及其追求者对人死后的状态的观点，我们并不能肯

opinions as to what would befall man hereafter; but the sole point of belief which they did firmly maintain, that the soul has nothing in common with the body and survives it, was enough to give the Platonic philosophy that sublime aspiration by which it is distinguished.

It is clear from the works of Plato that many philosophical writers, his predecessors or contemporaries, professed materialism. These writers have not reached us or have reached us in mere fragments. The same thing has happened in almost all ages; the greater part of the most famous minds in literature adhere to the doctrines of a spiritual philosophy. The instinct and the taste of the human race maintain those doctrines; they save them often in spite of men themselves and raise the names of their defenders above the tide of time. It must not, then, be supposed that at any period or under any political condition the passion for physical gratifications and the opinions which are superinduced by that passion can ever content a whole people. The heart of man is of a larger mold; it can at once comprise a taste for the possessions of earth and the love of those of heaven; at times it may seem to cling devotedly to the one, but it will never be long without thinking of the other.

If it be easy to see that it is more particularly important in democratic ages that spiritual opinions should prevail, it is not easy to say by what means those who govern democratic nations may make them predominate. I am no believer in the prosperity any more than in the durability of official philosophies; and as to state religions, I have always held that if they be sometimes of momentary service to the interests of political power, they always sooner or later become fatal to the church. Nor do I agree with those who think that, to raise religion in the eyes of the people and to make them do honor to her spiritual doctrines, it is desirable indirectly to give her ministers a political influence which the laws deny them. I am so much alive to the almost inevitable dangers which beset religious belief whenever the clergy take part in public affairs, and I am so convinced that Christianity must be maintained at any cost in the bosom of modern democracies, that I had rather shut up the priesthood within the sanctuary than allow them to step beyond it.

定其正确性;但是他们坚决拥护的信念,即认为灵魂与肉体毫无共同之处并且灵魂在肉体消失后仍然存在的信念,向柏拉图的哲学提供了使它变得杰出的强大支持。

从柏拉图的著作我们清楚地知道,他的先辈和与他同时代的许多哲学作家鼓吹唯物主义。这些作家的著作要么没有流传下来,要么就只有凤毛鳞爪被我们得以窥见。这样的事情几乎发生在所有时代。文学界那些最伟大的思想的最伟大的部分总与唯心主义学说有关。人类的直觉和爱好保留了这些学说,而且常常不依人的意志为转移把它从危难中救出来。并使为它们辩护的人们不被历史的洪流淹没。因此,我们万万不能以为,在任何一个时期,在任何一种政治体制下,对于物质享受的激情以及为这一激情所产成的观点都能使人民满意。人心是很宽广的,它充满了对于物质的热爱之情和对天堂的热爱。有时候,它可能表现为全心地投入其中之一,但是它也不会长久地不惦记另一个。

如果我们很容易发现,民主时代特别需要唯心主义的观点。那么,我们要发现民主国家的统治者用什么方法使这些观点占据统治地位就很难了。我不再相信官方的哲学的长久性和繁荣性。并且,对于国家的宗教,我始终认为,即使它们暂时对政治利益有利,它最终也迟早给宗教带来致命的打击。我不同意某些人的观点。他们认为,为了提升宗教在人们眼中的地位,并使人们尊重宗教的教义,最好是间接地赋予传教士依法律未给与他们的政治影响力。我认为,有宗教信仰的人一旦参与政治,就会发生几乎无可避免的信仰危机。我坚信,基督教应当在现代民主国家中不计代价地受到人们的保护。因此,我宁愿将神职人员关在教堂内,也不愿让他们走出这个保护圈。

What means then remain in the hands of constituted authorities to bring men back to spiritual opinions or to hold them fast to the religion by which those opinions are suggested?

My answer will do me harm in the eyes of politicians. I believe that the sole effectual means which governments can employ in order to have the doctrine of the immortality of the soul duly respected is always to act as if they believed in it themselves; and I think that it is only by scrupulous conformity to religious morality in great affairs that they can hope to teach the community at large to know, to love, and to observe it in the lesser concerns of life.

那么,政府手中又有什么方法将人们带回到唯心主义的观点中或使其皈依宣传唯心主义观点的宗教呢?

我的答案在政治家们看来是有害的。我相信,政府能够采用的使灵魂不灭论受到人们尊敬的唯一有效的办法,就是政府要在自己的行为中一直表现出它也相信此学说;我还认为,只有在大事情上认真遵守宗教道德,政府才能广泛地教育民众在生活琐事中了解、热爱和尊重宗教道德。

CHAPTER XVI

How Excessive Care For Worldly Welfare May Impair That Welfare

There is a closer tie than is commonly supposed between the improvement of the soul and the amelioration of what belongs to the body. Man may leave these two things apart and consider each of them alternately, but he cannot sever them entirely without at last losing sight of both.

The beasts have the same senses as ourselves, and very nearly the same appetites. We have no sensual passions which are not common to our race and theirs and which are not to be found, at least in the germ, in a dog as well as in a man. Whence is it, then, that the animals can provide only for their first and lowest wants, whereas we can infinitely vary and endlessly increase our enjoyments?

We are superior to the beasts in this, that we use our souls to find out those material benefits to which they are only led by instinct. In man the angel teaches the brute the art of satisfying its desires. It is because man is capable of rising above the things of the body, and of scorning life itself, of which the beasts have not the least notion, that he can multiply these same goods of the body to a degree of which the inferior races cannot conceive.

Whatever elevates, enlarges, and expands the soul renders it more capable of succeeding in those very undertakings which do not concern it. Whatever, on the other hand, enervates or lowers it weakens it for all purposes, the chief as well as the least, and threatens to render it almost equally impotent for both. Hence the soul must remain

第十六章 过分热爱福利为什么可能损害福利

　　心灵境界的提升和肉体享受的改善之间的密切关系比我们普遍认为的要紧密得多。人们可以随意的处理这两种完全不同的事物之间的关系,对他们轮流交替的加以重视,但是不能把两者完全分开,否则对它们都不好。

　　禽兽的感官与我们人的相同,它们的贪欲也与我们人的接近。禽兽的要求满足身体需要的激情,同我们人的没有什么不同,这种激情的萌芽在狗身上和我们人身上都可以找到。但是,为什么动物只能满足它们的最基本的需要和最低级的需求,而我们人却能无限地改变和不断地提高我们的享受呢?

　　我们在这方面优于禽兽,就在于我们是用心灵去探求物质利益的,而禽兽只能依靠本能。在人类社会,能人教导笨人学习满足自己需要的技能。正因为人能够超越肉体享受,甚至轻视生命本身,而禽兽根本不知道什么是生命,所以人才能成倍地提高肉体享受,而提高的程度又是像禽兽这样的低级生物无法想象的。

　　凡是可以提升、放大和扩展心灵的东西,都能使其变得更有利于去实现那些与心灵无关的事情。相反地,凡是削弱、降低心灵的东西,都使其变得在无论大事还是小事上面都更软弱,而且

great and strong, though it were only to devote its strength and greatness from time to time to the service of the body. If men were ever to content themselves with material objects, it is probable that they would lose by degrees the art of producing them; and they would enjoy them in the end, like the brutes, without discernment and without improvement.

还有在两方面都无能的危险。因此,灵魂必须保持强大和有力的状态,尽管它也只能将之一次次地运用到对肉体的服务中去。如果人曾满足于物质追求的享乐,也许他会逐渐丧失其生产财富的能力。而且,最终,他们就会像禽兽那样,对于物质享受既没有鉴别能力,也不能使其发展。

CHAPTER XVII

How, When Conditions Are Equal And Skepticism Is Rife, It Is Important To Direct Human Actions To Distant Objects

In ages of faith the final aim of life is placed beyond life. The men of those ages, therefore, naturally and almost involuntarily accustom themselves to fix their gaze for many years on some immovable object towards which they are constantly tending, and they learn by insensible degrees to repress a multitude of petty passing desires in order to be the better able to content that great and lasting desire which possesses them. When these same men engage in the affairs of this world, the same habits may be traced in their conduct. They are apt to set up some general and certain aim and end to their actions here below, towards which all their efforts are directed; they do not turn from day to day to chase some novel object of desire, but they have settled designs which they are never weary of pursuing.

This explains why religious nations have so often achieved such lasting results; for while they were thinking only of the other world, they had found out the great secret of success in this. Religions give men a general habit of conducting themselves with a view to eternity; in this respect they are not less useful to happiness in this life than to felicity hereafter, and this is one of their chief political characteristics.

But in proportion as the light of faith grows dim, the range of man's sight is circumscribed, as if the end and aim of human actions appeared every day to be more within his reach. When men have

第十七章 为什么在平等和怀疑
盛行时期应当把人的
行动目标放长远一些

在有信仰的时代,人生的终极目标在于生命之外。那些时代的人们因此就自然地,也可以说是几乎自觉地使自己的目光多年来锁定在某一固定不变的目标之上,并且终身致力于实现此目标。他们在随心所欲的前进过程中,学会了为了实现心中那个伟大持久的目标而自觉地压抑那些琐碎的欲望。当这些为人世的琐事纠缠时,他们的行为中无不透漏出这种习性。他们习惯于树立一个总的,明确的目标,并使他们的行为始终追随其下,使他们所有的努力都指向这一方向。他们不会常常追随一些新奇的欲望,但是他们始终毫不厌倦地追随着一个既定的目标。

有宗教信仰的民族,之所以经常能够完成目标长远的事业,就是由于这个原因。因为人们在他们追求来世的幸福时,也知道了获得现世成功的重大秘密。宗教使人养成待人处事都考虑来世的一般习惯。从这一方面来说,宗教对于现世幸福的促进作用并不亚于其对来世幸福的这种作用。这也是宗教的主要政治特征之一。

但是随着信仰之光逐渐转暗,人们的视野也变得越来越有限,仿佛人类行为的终结和目标一天天正在接近其能够探及的范

once allowed themselves to think no more of what is to befall them after life, they readily lapse into that complete and brutal indifference to futurity which is but too conformable to some propensities of mankind. As soon as they have lost the habit of placing their chief hopes upon remote events, they naturally seek to gratify without delay their smallest desires; and no sooner do they despair of living forever, than they are disposed to act as if they were to exist but for a single day. In skeptical ages it is always to be feared, therefore, that men may perpetually give way to their daily casual desires, and that, wholly renouncing whatever cannot be acquired without protracted effort, they may establish nothing great, permanent, and calm.

If the social condition of a people, under these circumstances, becomes democratic, the danger which I here point out is thereby increased. When everyone is constantly striving to change his position, when an immense field for competition is thrown open to all, when wealth is amassed or dissipated in the shortest possible space of time amid the turmoil of democracy, visions of sudden and easy fortunes, of great possessions easily won and lost, of chance under all its forms haunt the mind. The instability of society itself fosters the natural instability of man's desires. In the midst of these perpetual fluctuations of his lot, the present looms large upon his mind; it hides the future, which becomes indistinct, and men seek only to think about tomorrow.

In those countries in which, unhappily, irreligion and democracy coexist, philosophers and those in power ought to be always striving to place the objects of human actions far beyond man's immediate range. Adapting himself to the spirit of his country and his age, the moralist must learn to vindicate his principles in that position. He must constantly endeavor to show his contemporaries that even in the midst of the perpetual commotion around them it is easier than they think to conceive and to execute protracted undertakings. He must teach them that although the aspect of mankind may have changed, the methods by which men may provide for their prosperity in this world

围。当人们一旦允许自己不再思索死后的事情，他们就会陷入完全地对未来漠不关心的境地，而这又最符合人类的某些特性。当他们一旦丧失了将自己的主要希望寄托在遥远的食物上的习惯之后，他们很自然地就会寻找尽快地满足自己琐碎欲望的途径。而在他们对永生绝望后不久，他们就会表现得仿佛自己只有一天的生命可以存活。在怀疑论盛行的时期，最令人觉得害怕的事情就是人们因此而永久地屈从于自己生活琐事方面的欲求，抛弃那些必须经过长期努力才能实现的目标，这样的话，他们就不会去做出伟大的、稳妥的和长期的事业。

如果一个民族身处在这样的社会环境之下而变得民主，那么我已指出的危险就会更高。当所有的人们都不断地致力于改变自己的地位，当竞争的范围变得广阔，对所有的人都开放的时候，当财富在动荡的民主社会中积聚或者消散所需的时间极短，人们看到财富来得突然且容易，极易得到又容易失去，机会主义牵引着人们的头脑。社会的不稳定性自身揭示了社会中的人们多变的欲望。在命运起伏不定的状况下，人们就只顾眼前了。眼前的利益遮盖了未来，使其变得模糊不清，于是人们就不再梦想未来了。

在那些不幸和无宗教信仰和民主共存的国家中，哲学家和当权者应该致力于将人们的行为目标置于人们触手可及的范围之外。为了使人们适应自己国家和时代的精神，道德家应该学会在这种状态下维护自己的理论。他必须致力于向他同时代的人们展示，即使是在动荡起伏的时期，人们也可以在并不比他们想象得难的情况下，规划和实施长期的事业。他必须教会他们尽管人类的有些方面可能会发生改变，但人们要在世上实现物质繁荣的

are still the same; and that among democratic nations as well as elsewhere it is only by resisting a thousand petty selfish passions of the hour that the general and unquenchable passion for happiness can be satisfied.

The task of those in power is not less clearly marked out. At all times it is important that those who govern nations should act with a view to the future: but this is even more necessary in democratic and skeptical ages than in any others. By acting thus the leading men of democracies not only make public affairs prosperous, but also teach private individuals, by their example, the art of managing their private concerns.

Above all, they must strive as much as possible to banish chance from the sphere of politics. The sudden and undeserved promotion of a courtier produces only a transient impression in an aristocratic country, because the aggregate institutions and opinions of the nation habitually compel men to advance slowly in tracks which they cannot get out of. But nothing is more pernicious than similar instances of favor exhibited to a democratic people; they give the last impulse to the public mind in a direction where everything hurries it onwards. At times of skepticism and equality more especially, the favor of the people or of the prince, which chance may confer or chance withhold, ought never to stand in lieu of attainments or services. It is desirable that every advancement should there appear to be the result of some effort, so that no greatness should be of too easy acquirement and that ambition should be obliged to fix its gaze long upon an object before it is gratified.

Governments must apply themselves to restore to men that love of the future with which religion and the state of society no longer inspire them; and, without saying so, they must practically teach the community day by day that wealth, fame, and power are the rewards of labor, that great success stands at the utmost range of long desires, and that there is nothing lasting but what is obtained by toil.

When men have accustomed themselves to foresee from afar what is likely to befall them in the world and to feed upon hopes, they can hardly confine their minds within the precise limits of life, and they are ready to break the boundary and cast their looks beyond. I do not

途径是不会改变的。并且，在民主国家和在其他国家中一样，只有拒绝无数小的自私的激情的驱使，才能使渴望得到幸福的激情得到满足。

当权者大任务也很明确，在任何时期，统治者都应当有远见是很重要的。但是在民主国家和怀疑论盛行的国家中，这一点尤其重要。通过这种行为，民主国家的领袖们不仅可以使公众事业繁荣发展，也通过自己的实例，教会了人民管理私人事务的艺术。

最为重要的是，执政者必须尽可能地在为政当中放弃机会主义的心理。在贵族制时代，廷臣的突然得宠和无功受禄，只能在贵族国家里产生短暂的影响，因为国家的整个制度和舆论已经使人墨守陈规，在既定的道路上缓慢前行。但是，在民主国家，如果出现这样的事情，则将产生极大的恶果，因为民主国家的人民根本不关心这些事，他们忙着处理自己的私事。尤其是在怀疑主义和平等共存的时候，首先应当防止君主或人民的随心所欲，使人尽其才。应当使每一次晋升都是其努力的结果，这样，就不会有什么成就是轻易就可以获得的，而野心家不得不在未得到满足之前，紧盯着猎物，使任何目标都必须经过长期奋斗才能达到。

政府必须使自己恢复人们对于未来的热爱，而对于这些，宗教和社会情况已无法实现。即使不说，他们也必须用每天的实际行动教会人们，财富、名誉和权力都是劳动的成果，伟大的成功都是长期努力的结果，没有什么东西是持久的，除非经过了人们的辛勤劳动获得。

当人们习惯了使自己预见他们将会在世上得到的命运，并且因此而充满希望的时候，他们就不会将自己的思想限定在生活的束缚之内，并且，他们随时准备着打破这一束缚并将自己的目光

doubt that, by training the members of a community to think of their future condition in this world, they would be gradually and unconsciously brought nearer to religious convictions. Thus the means that allow men, up to a certain point, to go without religion are perhaps, after all, the only means we still possess for bringing mankind back, by a long and roundabout path, to a state of faith.

投向长远的地方。我不怀疑,通过教育一个社会的成员去思索他们在世上的未来的境遇,他们可以逐渐地不知不觉地接近宗教信仰。因此,使人们在没有宗教指引的情况下向某一目标前进的方法,也许最终也是我们仍旧拥有的唯一的方法,通过长久而迂回的道路使人们重建信仰。

CHAPTER XVIII

Why Among The Americans All Honest
Callings Are Considered Honorable

Among a democratic people, where there is no hereditary wealth, every man works to earn a living, or has worked, or is born of parents who have worked. The notion of labor is therefore presented to the mind, on every side, as the necessary, natural, and honest condition of human existence. Not only is labor not dishonorable among such a people, but it is held in honor; the prejudice is not against it, but in its favor. In the United States a wealthy man thinks that he owes it to public opinion to devote his leisure to some kind of industrial or commercial pursuit or to public business. He would think himself in bad repute if he employed his life solely in living. It is for the purpose of escaping this obligation to work that so many rich Americans come to Europe, where they find some scattered remains of aristocratic society, among whom idleness is still held in honor.

Equality of conditions not only ennobles the notion of labor, but raises the notion of labor as a source of profit.

In aristocracies it is not exactly labor that is despised, but labor with a view to profit. Labor is honorable in itself when it is undertaken at the bidding of ambition or virtue. Yet in aristocratic society it constantly happens that he who works for honor is not insensible to the attractions of profit. But these two desires intermingle only in the depths of his soul; he carefully hides from every eye the point at which they join; he would gladly conceal it from himself. In aristocratic countries there are few public

第十八章　为什么在美国人当中认为一切正当的行业都是高尚的

在民主国家的人民中，不存在世袭财产，每个人都通过劳动谋生，或者靠着劳动的积蓄谋生，或者靠着父母的劳动生存。劳动的定义对于他们来说，不论从哪个方面来说，都是人们生存所必需的、自然的和正常的条件。在这些人中间，劳动不仅不下贱，反而是光荣的。人们的偏见并不针对劳动，反而对它有利。在美国，富人认为，正是由于有舆论的支持，他们才会用自己的空闲时间从事一些工商业活动或者公共事业。他认为如果自己只是为了自己而劳动的话，就会有损于自己的名誉。因此，为了逃避这种义务，很多美国富人纷纷逃到了欧洲国家，在那里，他们发现还残存着一些贵族社会的痕迹，闲散的生活态度也是受人尊敬的。

平等的社会地位不仅使劳动变得光荣，而且使劳动变成了牟利的来源。

在贵族社会，人们轻视的不是一切劳动，而只是牟利的劳动。当劳动是因着实现个人的抱负或者某种美德的时候，劳动本身是光荣的。但是在贵族制社会中，常常却是那些为了荣誉而进行劳动的人们也并没有忽视其牟利的作用。他们只把这两种欲望在自己的心灵深处混合在一起。他小心地隐藏着两者的结合点，避

officers who do not affect to serve their country without interested motives. Their salary is an incident of which they think but little and of which they always affect not to think at all. Thus the notion of profit is kept distinct from that of labor; however they may be united in point of fact, they are not thought of together.

In democratic communities these two notions are, on the contrary, always palpably united. As the desire of well-being is universal, as fortunes are slender or fluctuating, as everyone wants either to increase his own resources or to provide fresh ones for his progeny, men clearly see that it is profit that, if not wholly, at least partially leads them to work. Even those who are principally actuated by the love of fame are necessarily made familiar with the thought that they are not exclusively actuated by that motive; and they discover that the desire of getting a living is mingled in their minds with the desire of making life illustrious.

As soon as, on the one hand, labor is held by the whole community to be an honorable necessity of man's condition, and, on the other, as soon as labor is always ostensibly performed, wholly or in part, for the purpose of earning remuneration, the immense interval that separated different callings in aristocratic societies disappears. If all are not alike, all at least have one feature in common. No profession exists in which men do not work for money; and the remuneration that is common to them all gives them all an air of resemblance.

This serves to explain the opinions that the Americans entertain with respect to different callings. In America no one is degraded because he works, for everyone about him works also; nor is anyone humiliated by the notion of receiving pay, for the President of the United States also works for pay. He is paid for commanding, other men for obeying orders. In the United States professions are more or less laborious, more or less profitable; but they are never either high or low: every honest calling is honorable.

开所有人的眼睛。他们很高兴将其掩藏。在贵族之国家中,几乎没有一个政府官员不是带着某种利益的动机为国家服务的。他们的薪酬只占了很少的一部分或者几乎不考虑在内。因此,牟利的观念就与劳动分得很开。尽管它们可能在事实上联系在一起,但是在思想上,人们还是将两者区分开来的。

反之,在民主时代,这两个观念总是明显地联系在一起的。由于大家都有追求财富的欲望,而每个人的财富都很少或不固定,而且人人都既希望增加自己的财富,也希望为自己的子女创造新的财富,所以大家都清楚:人们参加劳动即使不是全都为了牟利,至少也是部分为了牟利。即使是那些挚爱荣誉的人们,也必须承认自己并不是完全出于这个动机的。他们发现,求生的愿望在他们的脑海中总是与获得名誉的观念联系在一起的。

从另一方面说,一旦劳动为全体公民认为是人生光荣的必须,那么,从另一个角度看,劳动总是在表现上完全或者部分地表现出是为了获得报酬而进行的,则贵族制国家中区分着各个行业的鸿沟便消失了。即使所有的行业并不完全相似,至少有一个共同点。没有哪个职业的存在不是通过劳动获得钱。所以,每个人都领取的薪酬,使大家具有了相似的气息。

通过这一点可以说明一个观点,即美国人对于各个不同行业都持有尊敬的态度。在美国,没有人因为自己的职业而被看低,因为他们周围的人们也都在劳动。他们也不会为领取薪酬过活而感到羞愧,因为即使美国总统也领薪水。只是他是通过发布命令领薪,而其他人是通过服从命令获利。在美国,所有的职业都很辛苦,也比较容易赚钱。但是,它们没有高低的区分:所有正直的职业都是值得尊敬的。

CHAPTER XIX

What Causes Almost All Americans
To Follow Industrial Callings

Agriculture is perhaps, of all the useful arts, that which improves most slowly among democratic nations. Frequently, indeed, it would seem to be stationary, because other arts are making rapid strides towards perfection. On the other hand, almost all the tastes and habits that the equality of condition produces naturally lead men to commercial and industrial occupations.

Suppose an active, enlightened, and free man, enjoying a competency, but full of desires; he is too poor to live in idleness, he is rich enough to feel himself protected from the immediate fear of want, and he thinks how he can better his condition. This man has conceived a taste for physical gratifications, which thousands of his fellow men around him indulge in; he has himself begun to enjoy these pleasures, and he is eager to increase his means of satisfying these tastes more completely. But life is slipping away, time is urgent; to what is he to turn? The cultivation of the ground promises an almost certain result to his exertions, but a slow one; men are not enriched by it without patience and toil. Agriculture is therefore only suited to those who already have great superfluous wealth or to those whose penury bids them seek only a bare subsistence. The choice of such a man as we have supposed is soon made; he sells his plot of ground, leaves his dwelling, and embarks on some hazardous but lucrative calling.

Democratic communities abound in men of this kind; and in proportion as the equality of conditions becomes greater, their multitude increases. Thus, democracy not only swells the number of workingmen, but leads men to prefer one kind of labor to another; and while

第十九章 是什么使得几乎所有的 美国人都喜欢从事实业

在民主国家中,农业大概是进步得最慢的有用技术。事实上,农业常常处于停滞状态,因为其他行业好像是跑步前进。从另一方面说,平等所带来的几乎一切爱好和习惯,都自然而然地在引导人们去从事工商业。

假设有一个能干、聪明、自由、富足而充满希望的人,如果从安逸舒适的生活来说,他还很穷;而从不缺吃少穿来说,他又是够富裕的。这个人他总在想法改善自己的命运。他已经尝到物质享受的好处,而其他许多享受的好处又只是摆在他的眼前。他开始追求这些爱好,并努力增加收入来满足这些享乐。但是,人生苦短。他应当怎么办呢? 种地,则他的努力肯定能得到回报,但是速度太慢,而且只能逐渐地富裕起来,并要付出艰苦的劳动。农业只适于已经家产万贯的富人或只求糊口的穷人。我们假设的那个人做出了自己的选择:他卖了土地,离开了家乡,另谋一种虽有风险但可赚钱的行业。

民主国家到处都是这样的人。随着平等地位的日益普及,他们的人数也在不断地上升。因此,民主不仅仅使劳动者的数量增长,而且引导人们有选择地从事工作。而且还使人们从农业劳动

it diverts them from agriculture, it encourages their taste for commerce and manufactures. ①

This spirit may be observed even among the richest members of the community. In democratic countries, however opulent a man is supposed to be, he is almost always discontented with his fortune because he finds that he is less rich than his father was, and he fears that his sons will be less rich than himself. Most rich men in democracies are therefore constantly haunted by the desire of obtaining wealth, and they naturally turn their attention to trade and manufactures, which appear to offer the readiest and most efficient means of success. In this respect they share the instincts of the poor without feeling the same necessities; say, rather, they feel the most imperious of all necessities, that of not sinking in the world.

In aristocracies the rich are at the same time the governing power. The attention that they unceasingly devote to important public affairs diverts them from the lesser cares that trade and manufactures demand. But if an individual happens to turn his attention to business, the will of the body to which he belongs will immediately prevent him from pursuing it; for, however men may declaim against the rule of numbers, they cannot wholly escape it; and even among those aristocratic bodies that most obstinately refuse to acknowledge the rights of the national majority, a private majority is formed which governs the rest. ②

In democratic countries, where money does not lead those who possess it to political power, but often removes them from

---

① It has often been remarked that manufacturers and merchants are inordinately addicted to physical gratifications, and this has been attributed to commerce and manufactures; but that, I apprehend, is to take the effect for the cause. The taste for physical gratifications is not imparted to men by commerce or manufactures, but it is rather this taste that leads men to engage in commerce and manufactures, as a means by which they hope to satisfy themselves more promptly and more completely. If commerce and manufactures increase the desire of well-being, it is because every passion gathers strength in proportion as it is cultivated, and is increased by all the efforts made to satiate it. All the causes that make the love of worldly welfare predominate in the heart of man are favorable to the growth of commerce and manufactures. Equality of conditions is one of those causes; it encourages trade, not directly, by giving men a taste for business, but indirectly, by strengthening and expanding in their minds a taste for well being.

② See Appendix T.

转移到它所鼓励的工商业活动中。①

即使是在社会最富有的成员当中，也存在着这样的精神。在民主国家中，尽管人人都渴望富裕，但是他总是对自己的财富不满意，因为他发现自己没有他的父辈们的财富多，于是他担心自己的子孙的财产会更少。大多数生活在民主社会中的富人因此总是被获取财富的欲望牵着自己的鼻子，于是很自然地就将自己的注意力转移到看起来仿佛更容易获得成功的工商业方面。在这方面，虽然他们的需求不同，但他们与穷人的直觉一样，也就是说，他们也感受到了最迫切的需求。

在贵族制国家中，富人同时也掌握着权力。他们的注意力无止尽地投入到重要的公共事务，而无暇估计那些次要的工商业的需求。但是，如果一个人偶然的机会将注意力转移到商业中去，他们的阶级意志也会立刻阻止他们将注意力转移到对其的追求。因为，他们虽然反对多数人的统治，但是他们仍旧无法完全摆脱其限制。并且，即使在这些贵族机构内，也坚决地拒绝承认国家大多数的权力，就存在一个专门进行统治的多数。②

在民主国家，金钱不能使拥有它们的人得到政治权力，而是

---

① 人们常常认为，制造业者和商人极度沉溺于物质享受的满足，而这都是商业和制造业的特性使然。但是，我理解认为，这种看法是本末倒置的。对物质享受的热爱并不是商业和制造业赋予人们的，而应该说正是因为人的这种爱好使他们开始从事商业和制造业，通过这种方式来更好更完全的满足他们自己的爱好。如果说商业和制造业提高了人们的欲求，那是因为每一种激情都成比例的积累了力量，并且在所有致力于满足它们的努力下得到的增长。所有这些使对物质福利热爱控制人心的因素都是有利于商业和制造业的发展。平等地位也是这些因素之一，它促进贸易发展，虽然不是直接作用，而是间接地通过赋予人们对商业的热爱，通过增强并扩展人们对物质福利的热爱来实现的。

② 见附件 T。

it, the rich do not know how to spend their leisure. They are driven into active life by the disquietude and the greatness of their desires, by the extent of their resources, and by the taste for what is extraordinary, which is almost always felt by those who rise, by whatever means, above the crowd. Trade is the only road open to them. In democracies nothing is greater or more brilliant than commerce; it attracts the attention of the public and fills the imagination of the multitude; all energetic passions are directed towards it. Neither their own prejudices nor those of anybody else can prevent the rich from devoting themselves to it. The wealthy members of democracies never form a body which has manners and regulations of its own; the opinions peculiar to their class do not restrain them, and the common opinions of their country urge them on. Moreover, as all the large fortunes that are found in a democratic community are of commercial growth, many generations must succeed one another before their possessors can have entirely laid aside their habits of business.

Circumscribed within the narrow space that politics leaves them, rich men in democracies eagerly embark in commercial enterprise; there they can extend and employ their natural advantages, and, indeed, it is even by the boldness and the magnitude of their industrial speculations that we may measure the slight esteem in which productive industry would have been held by them if they had been born in an aristocracy.

A similar observation is likewise applicable to all men living in democracies, whether they are poor or rich. Those who live in the midst of democratic fluctuations have always before their eyes the image of chance; and they end by liking all undertakings in which chance plays a part. They are therefore all led to engage in commerce, not only for the sake of the profit it holds out to them, but for the love of the constant excitement occasioned by that pursuit.

The United States of America has only been emancipated for half a century from the state of colonial dependence in which it stood to

常常使他们远离政治,于是这些富人就不知道如何打发他们的空闲时间。于是他们被不安和他们伟大的理想所驱使,被他们的大量财富和一些几乎所有不论通过什么途径获得成功的人们的奇怪的爱好所驱使,行为活跃。经商成了他们唯一可行的道路。在民主国家中,没有什么比商业更伟大更明智。它吸引着所有公众的注意力,满足着大众的想象力。所有有活力的激情都指向经商。不论是他们自身的偏见或者任何其他人的偏见都无法阻止这些富人投身其中。民主国家的有钱人从没有形成一个有规章和约束力的团体。他们阶级中的一些独特的意见也无法限制他们,而社会舆论促使他们前进。除此之外,由于民主国家所有的巨富都是通过经商成长起来的,并要许多代人的继承经营下去,直到财富的持有人完全失去了经商的习惯。

被政见限制在狭小圈子里的民主国家的富人,迫不及待地将全部精力都投入到商业中去。在这方面,他们发挥自己得天独厚的优势开拓事业。而且,事实上,这也归功于他们的敢于创办实业的伟大精神,而如果他们出生在贵族制国家中,就很难想象他们会有着这种机会。

一种相似的表现同时适用于所有生活在民主国家的人们,不论他们是穷人还是富人。那些生活在民主动荡时期的人们,他们总是幻想各种机遇出现在眼前。他们喜欢从事所有偶然机遇在其中发挥作用的职业。因此,他们都去经商,不仅仅是为了牟利,而且喜欢在这个过程中伴随发生的不断变化的刺激。

联邦的美国人刚刚被从英国殖民地状态解放半个世纪,所以在美国很少有巨富,而且他们的资源也很少。但是他们

Great Britain; the number of large fortunes there is small, and capital is still scarce. Yet no people in the world have made such rapid progress in trade and manufactures as the Americans; they constitute at the present day the second maritime nation in the world, and although their manufactures have to struggle with almost insurmountable natural impediments, they are not prevented from making great and daily advances.

In the United States the greatest undertakings and speculations are executed without difficulty, because the whole population are engaged in productive industry, and because the poorest as well as the most opulent members of the commonwealth are ready to combine their efforts for these purposes. The consequence is that a stranger is constantly amazed by the immense public works executed by a nation which contains, so to speak, no rich men. The Americans arrived but as yesterday on the territory which they inhabit, and they have already changed the whole order of nature for their own advantage. They have joined the Hudson to the Mississippi and made the Atlantic Ocean communicate with the Gulf of Mexico, across a continent of more than five hundred leagues in extent which separates the two seas. The longest railroads that have been constructed up to the present time are in America.

But what most astonishes me in the United States is not so much the marvelous grandeur of some undertakings as the innumerable multitude of small ones. Almost all the farmers of the United States combine some trade with agriculture; most of them make agriculture itself a trade. It seldom happens that an American farmer settles for good upon the land which he occupies; especially in the districts of the Far West, he brings land into tillage in order to sell it again, and not to farm it: he builds a farmhouse on the speculation that, as the state of the country will soon be changed by the increase of population, a good price may be obtained for it.

Every year a swarm of people from the North arrive in the Southern states and settle in the parts where the cotton plant and the sugarcane grow. These men cultivate the soil in order to make it produce in a few years enough to enrich them; and they already look forward to the time when they may return home to enjoy the competency thus acquired. Thus the Americans carry their businesslike qualities into agriculture, and their trading passions are displayed in that as in their other pursuits.

却是世界上在工商业方面获得如此迅速发展的第一人。他们创造了迄今为止世界上的第二大海上强国，而且尽管他们的制造业仍旧面临着无法克服的自然缺憾，也仍旧没能阻止他们有着日新月异的巨大发展。

在美国，经营大型的工业企业没有困难，因为整个国家的人民都参与到了工业生产行业，而且，最穷的人和最富的人也随时准备着联合起来达到工业生产的目的。因此，外国人常常惊奇于这个可以说几乎没有富人的国家所创造的无数的公共设施。美国人刚刚踏上他们现在居住的国土不久，但是他们已经改变了整个自然的秩序为他们服务。他们已将哈德逊河和密西西比河沟通，并在陆上建设了五百多里格的道路使大西洋与墨西哥湾接连起来。截至目前，世界上最长的几条大铁路，也建在美国。

但是，在美国，最使我感到惊讶的，并不是这些企业的规模宏伟，而是那些数不胜数的企业。几乎所有的美国的农夫都不仅仅只从事农业劳动。他们大多数都将农业本身看作是贸易的一种。很少有美国农夫长久地居住在一片土地上。尤其是在偏远的西部，他们开垦土地只是为了以后卖掉它，而不是为了耕种。他建造一个农场，是基于早已预见这块土地上的人口数量不久就会增长，而他也可以从中获利。

每年都有大量的人们从北部来到南方，并且在这里定居种植棉花和甘蔗。这些人开垦土地的目的在于几年后用这个来致富。而且他们期盼着以后回家享受富足的生活。因此，美国人将他们用于经商的头脑用来种植庄稼，也把他们经营实业的激情带入了他们所追求的其他方面。

The Americans make immense progress in productive industry, because they all devote themselves to it at once; and for this same reason they are exposed to unexpected and formidable embarrassments. As they are all engaged in commerce, their commercial affairs are affected by such various and complex causes that it is impossible to foresee what difficulties may arise. As they are all more or less engaged in productive industry, at the least shock given to business all private fortunes are put in jeopardy at the same time, and the state is shaken. I believe that the return of these commercial panics is an endemic disease of the democratic nations of our age. It may be rendered less dangerous, but it cannot be cured, because it does not originate in accidental circumstances, but in the temperament of these nations.

美国全民都投身工业,从而使得工业有了长足的发展。因为同样的原因,他们也经常遭遇一些意想不到地强大的打击。因为他们都从事商业,所以他们的商业活动就会受到各种各样复杂的原因的影响。而这些原因却使人们难以预见将会发生什么样的困难。既然他们每个人都或多或少地与工业生产有关系,所以即使是商业方面遭受到最小的冲击,所有人的私人财产都会同时遭受损失,而引起整个国家为之动摇。我相信,这种商业恐慌的循环往复是当代民主国家无可避免的弊端。它的危险性可能会减少,但是不能被根除。因为这并不是由于偶然的原因引起的,而是民主国家的本性造成的。

CHAPTER XX
How An Aristocracy May Be Created By Manufactures

I have shown how democracy favors the growth of manufactures and increases without limit the numbers of the manufacturing classes; we shall now see by what side-road manufacturers may possibly, in their turn, bring men back to aristocracy.

It is acknowledged that when a workman is engaged every day upon the same details, the whole commodity is produced with greater ease, speed, and economy. It is likewise acknowledged that the cost of production of manufactured goods is diminished by the extent of the establishment in which they are made and by the amount of capital employed or of credit. These truths had long been imperfectly discerned, but in our time they have been demonstrated. They have been already applied to many very important kinds of manufactures, and the humblest will gradually be governed by them. I know of nothing in politics that deserves to fix the attention of the legislator more closely than these two new axioms of the science of manufactures.

When a workman is unceasingly and exclusively engaged in the fabrication of one thing, he ultimately does his work with singular dexterity; but at the same time he loses the general faculty of applying his mind to the direction of the work. He every day becomes more adroit and less industrious; so that it may be said of him that in proportion as the workman improves, the man is degraded. What can be expected of a man who has spent twenty years of his life in making heads for pins? And to what can that mighty human intelligence which has so often stirred the world be applied in him except it be to investigate the best method of making pins' heads? When a workman has spent a considerable portion of his existence in this

第二十章　实业为什么可能产生贵族制度

　　我已经说明了民主是如何有利于制造业的发展并使得制造业聚集的人数无限制地增长的。现在,我们再来看看制造业是如何把人们带回到贵族社会。

　　我们已经知道,如果一个人每天都从事相同的工作,那么所有的商品的制造就会变得更简易迅速和经济。同样地,我们知道,商品的成本的降低是随着其制造企业的规模不断扩大,其投入资本的增长和信用度的上升而发生的。这些真理早就被人们模糊地察觉,但却在我们这个时代得到最好的证实。这两项真理已被人们运用在许多重要的工业生产方面,而且一些小的工业生产也将逐渐被它们控制。我认为,在政治方面,最值得立法者仔细关注的,也正是制造业科学中的这两个公理。

　　当一个工人完全地单一地从事制作某一件东西的时候,他最终肯定会很熟练。但是同时,他就会丧失运用自己的大脑指导工作的能力。日复一日,他会变得熟练而机械。可以说,随着他手艺的提高,他本人却退化了。一个终生做了二十多年别针帽的人,你能期待他会有什么作为吗?而且,人类的智力的力量常常能够引导人们做出撼动世界的举措,对他来说,除了研究制造别针帽的最好方法外,还能有其他什么作用?

manner, his thoughts are forever set upon the object of his daily toil; his body has contracted certain fixed habits, which it can never shake off; in a word, he no longer belongs to himself, but to the calling that he has chosen. It is in vain that laws and manners have been at pains to level all the barriers round such a man and to open to him on every side a thousand different paths to fortune; a theory of manufactures more powerful than customs and laws binds him to a craft, and frequently to a spot, which he cannot leave; it assigns to him a certain place in society, beyond which he cannot go; in the midst of universal movement it has rendered him stationary.

In proportion as the principle of the division of labor is more extensively applied, the workman becomes more weak, more narrow-minded, and more dependent. The art advances, the artisan recedes. On the other hand, in proportion as it becomes more manifest that the productions of manufactures are by so much the cheaper and better as the manufacture is larger and the amount of capital employed more considerable, wealthy and educated men come forward to embark in manufactures, which were heretofore abandoned to poor or ignorant handicraftsmen. The magnitude of the efforts required and the importance of the results to be obtained attract them. Thus at the very time at which the science of manufactures lowers the class of workmen, it raises the class of masters.

While the workman concentrates his faculties more and more upon the study of a single detail, the master surveys an extensive whole, and the mind of the latter is enlarged in proportion as that of the former is narrowed. In a short time the one will require nothing but physical strength without intelligence; the other stands in need of science, and almost of genius, to ensure success. This man resembles more and more the administrator of a vast empire; that man, a brute.

The master and the workman have then here no similarity, and their differences increase every day. They are connected only like the two rings at the extremities of a long chain. Each of them fills the station which is made for him, and which he

一个工人把绝大部分时间都用在某个职业时,他的思想就永远离不开他每天所从事的领域,而他也就养成了一些永远无法摆脱的习惯。总之,他已不再是属于自己的了,而是从属于他所选择的职业。所有那些法律和民情煞费苦心地希望拿掉这些人周围的篱障,在他面前展现出无数通往财富的道路的方法都是无谓的。制造业的理论的力量远远大于法律和民情,并使他变成一个工匠,并把他绑定在一点上使其无法逃脱。这一理论还规定了他在社会中所处的地位,他也无法跨越。在千变万化的世界行为中,他却在原地踏步。

随着劳动分工的原则变得越来越普及,工人们的力量变得越来越弱小,他们的思想越来越狭隘,越来越处于从属地位。工艺是进步了,但是手艺人自身却退化了。此外,一种工业产品随着该生产部门的规模扩大和资本的增加而大量增长的时候,那些富人和有修养的人们也开始涉猎那些从前只有穷人和无知的手艺人从事的行业。大量劳动力被需求,无限的收益吸引着他们。因此,在这一时期,制造业科学在降低工人阶级的同时,抬升了有资产的阶级。

当工人日益缩小自己的智力应用范围时,工厂老板却去关注全局的工作。于是,这些工厂老板们的眼界日益开阔,而工人的视野却越来越狭隘。在很短的时间后,工人就会只从事体力劳动而不用智慧。而工厂老板们则需要依靠科学和天赋来保证成功。这样的人越来越多像一个大帝国的行政长官,而工人则越来越像牲畜。

工厂老板和工人因此变得没有任何共通之处,而且两者之间的差异越来越大。他们二者之间的联系仿佛就是一条长链的两端一样。每个人都有自己固定的位置,谁也不会离开自己的位

does not leave; the one is continually, closely, and necessarily dependent upon the other and seems as much born to obey as that other is to command. What is this but aristocracy?

As the conditions of men constituting the nation become more and more equal, the demand for manufactured commodities becomes more general and extensive, and the cheapness that places these objects within the reach of slender fortunes becomes a great element of success. Hence there are every day more men of great opulence and education who devote their wealth and knowledge to manufactures and who seek, by opening large establishments and by a strict division of labor, to meet the fresh demands which are made on all sides. Thus, in proportion as the mass of the nation turns to democracy, that particular class which is engaged in manufactures becomes more aristocratic. Men grow more alike in the one, more different in the other; and inequality increases in the less numerous class in the same ratio in which it decreases in the community. Hence it would appear, on searching to the bottom, that aristocracy should naturally spring out of the bosom of democracy.

But this kind of aristocracy by no means resembles those kinds which preceded it. It will be observed at once that, as it applies exclusively to manufactures and to some manufacturing callings, it is a monstrous exception in the general aspect of society. The small aristocratic societies that are formed by some manufacturers in the midst of the immense democracy of our age contain, like the great aristocratic societies of former ages, some men who are very opulent and a multitude who are wretchedly poor. The poor have few means of escaping from their condition and becoming rich, but the rich are constantly becoming poor, or they give up business when they have realized a fortune. Thus the elements of which the class of the poor is composed are fixed, but the elements of which the class of the rich is composed are not so. To tell the truth, though there are rich men, the class of rich men does not exist; for these rich individuals have no feelings or purposes, no traditions or hopes, in common; there are individuals, therefore, but no definite class.

置。一方对另一方的依赖性越来越强,仿佛一方生而为服从另一方,而另一方则生而指挥别人的。这样的情况除了贵族制度还会是什么呢?

因为构成一个国家的人民的社会地位越来越平等,对于工业产品的需求变得越来越广泛和普遍。于是使商品变得价格低廉就成了制胜的重要因素。因此,每天都有越来越多的富人和受过教育的人将自己的财富和天赋用于工业生产,并通过开设工厂和严格的劳动分工,来满足人们各个方面的需求。因此,随着人民大众越来越趋于民主,那些从事制造业的阶级就变得更加贵族化。人们彼此间越来越相似,而同时也与另一帮人越来越不同。不平等在少数人之间的增长速度与其在社会中的地位下降的速度一致。因此,当我们追溯到社会最底层的时候,就会发现贵族制是从民主社会的中心自然生长起来的。

但是这种贵族与之前的贵族阶级完全不同。我们会立刻发现,因为这种贵族只适用于制造业和一些生产行业,所以对整个社会层面来说属于一种奇怪的例外现象。这一小撮贵族团体是在当代广阔的民主社会里通过实业产生的,同之前的伟大的贵族制社会一样,同时存在着一帮异常富裕和非常贫穷的人们。穷人们没办法逃脱他们所处的环境变得富裕起来,而富人却常常会有可能变穷,或者他们一旦获得了一笔财富,就会放弃从商。因此,构成穷人阶级的成员是固定的,而形成富人阶级的人员却不固定。老实说,尽管有富人存在,富人阶级还是不存在的。因为这些富人既没有共同的情感,也没有共同的目标,既没有共同的传统也没有共有的希望。因此,只能说成是个体而不能称之为阶级。

Not only are the rich not compactly united among themselves, but there is no real bond between them and the poor. Their relative position is not a permanent one; they are constantly drawn together or separated by their interests. The workman is generally dependent on the master, but not on any particular master; these two men meet in the factory, but do not know each other elsewhere; and while they come into contact on one point, they stand very far apart on all others. The manufacturer asks nothing of the workman but his labor; the workman expects nothing from him but his wages. The one contracts no obligation to protect nor the other to defend, and they are not permanently connected either by habit or by duty. The aristocracy created by business rarely settles in the midst of the manufacturing population which it directs; the object is not to govern that population, but to use it. An aristocracy thus constituted can have no great hold upon those whom it employs, and even if it succeeds in retaining them at one moment, they escape the next; it knows not how to will, and it cannot act. The territorial aristocracy of former ages was either bound by law, or thought itself bound by usage, to come to the relief of its serving-men and to relieve their distresses. But the manufacturing aristocracy of our age first impoverishes and debases the men who serve it and then abandons them to be supported by the charity of the public. This is a natural consequence of what has been said before. Between the workman and the master there are frequent relations, but no real association.

I am of the opinion, on the whole, that the manufacturing aristocracy which is growing up under our eyes is one of the harshest that ever existed in the world; but at the same time it is one of the most confined and least dangerous. Nevertheless, the friends of democracy should keep their eyes anxiously fixed in this direction; for if ever a permanent inequality of conditions and aristocracy again penetrates into the world, it may be predicted that this is the gate by which they will enter.

不仅富人们内部没能紧密地团结,而且在他们与穷人之间也没有任何维系的纽带。他们之间相对的地位并不稳定,常常因为利益而分分合合。工人总是要依附于其工厂主的,但是却不依附于某一具体的人。这两类人同时存在于工厂中,但是却彼此互不相识。当他们在某一方面达成共识,但在其他方面却仍旧相隔甚远。工厂主除了要用工人的劳力外,其他并不需要。而工人要求工厂主的也只有工资。他们彼此没有义务和责任,也并不会因为习惯或者义务形成永久地联系。通过商业而形成的贵族,几乎不会在它所指引的制造业的人员中扎根。他们的目的不在于统治这些人,而是要利用他们。因此,这样组织起来的贵族的目的不在于大量控制他们所雇佣的人,即使他们有时雇佣了大量的工人,不久以后也会解雇一批。他们没有这样的想法,也无法实施。旧时代的地方贵族既受法律的约束,也自认为有义务减轻他们的侍从的痛苦。但是,当代制造业的贵族,首先把为他们服务的人变穷贬低,然后使他们被抛弃只能依靠大众的救济过活。这就是我们之前说过的事情发展的必然结果。在工厂主与工人之间虽然常有联系,但是却没有真正意义上的联合。

总之,我认为,在我们的时代成长起来的制造业的贵族,是世界上有史以来最严苛的贵族。但是同时,它也是受到最严格的制约和危险性最小的贵族。然而,民主的朋友应该谨慎地看紧这一方向。因为如果再有永久存在的不平等地位和贵族出现在这个世界的话,也许我们可以预测,他们一定是由这扇大门进来的。

THIRD BOOK
Influence Of Democracy On Manners Properly So Called

CHAPTER I
How Customs Are Softened As Social Conditions Become More Equal

We perceive that for several centuries social conditions have tended to equality, and we discover that at the same time the customs of society have been softened. Are these two things merely contemporaneous or does any secret link exist between them so that the one cannot advance without the other? Several causes may concur to render the customs of a people less rude, but of all these causes the most powerful appears to me to be the equality of conditions. Equality of conditions and greater mildness in customs are, then, in my eyes, not only contemporaneous occurrences, but correlative facts.

When the fabulists seek to interest us in the actions of beasts, they invest them with human notions and passions; the poets who sing of spirits and angels do the same; there is no wretchedness so deep nor any happiness so pure as to fill the human mind and touch the heart unless we are ourselves held up to our own eyes under other features.

This is strictly applicable to our present subject. When all men are irrevocably marshaled in an aristocratic community according to their professions, their property, and their birth, the members of each class, considering themselves as children of the same family, cherish a constant and lively sympathy towards one another, which can never be felt in an equal degree by the citizens of a democracy. But the same feeling does not exist between the several classes towards each other.

第三部　民主对民情的影响

第一章　民情是怎样随着人们社会地位的越来越平等日趋温和的

我们认识到，经过了几个世纪，人们的社会地位趋向平等，并且我们看到在同一时间，社会民情也日趋温和。这两者之间是同时发生的呢，还是存在什么神秘的联系，比如说一方的进步离不开另一方？有很多原因可以导致一个国家的民情由粗野而变得温和，但在所有这些原因当中，我认为最强有力的原因是身份的平等。因此，在我看来，身份的平等和民情的温和化不仅是同时发生的现象，而且是相关的事实。

一些寓言作家想通过对动物的描述影响我们的时候，便把人的思想和感情加于动物身上。诗人在描述鬼神的时候，也是如此。在人们的思想和心灵中，不存在根深蒂固的悲惨和纯净的幸福，除非用一些其他的手法将我们自己再现在自己的眼前。

这完全符合我们现在讨论的话题。当所有的人都依据他们的职业、财产和出身被分属于孤立组织国家中不同的阶级，每个阶级内部都将他们看作是同一个家庭的孩子一样，相互怀有一种持续的真实的同情心。而这在民主国家平等的社会状态中是不会为人们所感知的。但是，这样的感情不存在于不同的阶级之间。

Among an aristocratic people each caste has its own opinions, feelings, rights, customs, and modes of living. Thus the men who compose it do not resemble the mass of their fellow citizens; they do not think or feel in the same manner, and they scarcely believe that they belong to the same race. They cannot, therefore, thoroughly understand what others feel nor judge of others by themselves. Yet they are sometimes eager to lend one another aid; but this is not contrary to my previous observation.

These aristocratic institutions, which made the beings of one and the same race so different, nevertheless bound them to one another by close political ties. Although the serf had no natural interest in the fate of the nobles, he did not the less think himself obliged to devote his person to the service of that noble who happened to be his lord; and although the noble held himself to be of a different nature from that of his serfs, he nevertheless held that his duty and his honor required him to defend, at the risk of his own life, those who dwelt upon his domains.

It is evident that these mutual obligations did not originate in the law of nature, but in the law of society; and that the claim of social duty was more stringent than that of mere humanity. These services were not supposed to be due from man to man, but to the vassal or to the lord. Feudal institutions awakened a lively sympathy for the sufferings of certain men, but none at all for the miseries of mankind. They infused generosity rather than mildness into the customs of the time; and although they prompted men to great acts of self-devotion, they created no real sympathies, for real sympathies can exist only between those who are alike, and in aristocratic ages men acknowledge none but the members of their own caste to be like themselves.

When the chroniclers of the Middle Ages, who all belonged to the aristocracy by birth or education, relate the tragic end of a noble, their grief flows apace; whereas they tell you at a breath and without wincing of massacres and tortures inflicted on the common sort of people. Not that these writers felt habitual hatred or systematic disdain

在贵族制社会中,每个阶级都有其独特的观念、感情、权力、习俗和生活方式。因此,构成这样的国家的人们与其国家其他的人都不一样。他们的思维方式和感情都已不同,以至于很难相信他们属于同一个民族。因此,他们只凭自己是不能完全理解其他人的想法和判断。但是,他们常常乐于助人,但这也与我之前的观点不矛盾。

这些贵族制度使同一个民族的人们变得如此不同,但又用紧密的政治纽带将他们联系在一起。尽管农奴天生对贵族的命运不感兴趣,但是他仍旧认为自己有义务对使自己沦为奴隶的人们尽忠。而且,尽管贵族认为自己与他的奴隶们是完全不同的两类人,但他仍然认为自己的职责和荣誉要求他即使冒着生命危险也要保护那些居住在他领土上的人们。

很明显,这些相互的义务并不是来自自然规律,而是产生于社会法则。并且这种对社会职责的要求,要比单纯的人性的要求更严厉。这些义务并不是人与人之间应尽的职责,而是主仆之间的义务。封建制度唤醒了人们对一些贫苦人民的同情,但却不是对全人类的同情。它们给民情灌输的是温文尔雅而远非慷慨大气。尽管它鼓励人民无私奉献,但却没能产生真正的同情怜悯之心。因为发自肺腑的同情之心只能在彼此相似的人们之间产生,而在贵族社会中,人们只认为与自己属于同一阶级的人才与自己相似。

当中世纪的编年史家们,因为自己的出身和教育而被划分为贵族阶级,因而他们在描述贵族的悲惨结局的时候,显得异常悲伤。但是,当他们描述对平民百姓施加的暴行和折磨时,就显得心平气和无动于衷了。这并不表示他们这些作家惯于仇视或者

for the people; war between the several classes of the community was not yet declared. They were impelled by an instinct rather than by a passion; as they had formed no clear notion of a poor man's sufferings, they cared but little for his fate.

The same feelings animated the lower orders whenever the feudal tie was broken. The same ages that witnessed so many heroic acts of self-devotion on the part of vassals for their lords were stained with atrocious barbarities practiced from time to time by the lower classes on the higher.

It must not be supposed that this mutual insensibility arose solely from the absence of public order and education, for traces of it are to be found in the following centuries, which became tranquil and enlightened while they remained aristocratic.

In 1675 the lower classes in Brittany revolted at the imposition of a new tax. These disturbances were put down with unexampled severity. Observe the language in which Madame de Sévigné, a witness of these horrors, relates them to her daughter:

Your letter from Aix, my daughter, is droll enough. At least, read your letters over again before sending them; allow yourself to be surprised by the pretty things that you have put into them and console yourself by this pleasure for the trouble you have had in writing so many. Then you have kissed all of Provence, have you? There would be no satisfaction in kissing all Brittany, unless one liked to smell of wine. . . . Do you wish to hear the news from Rennes? A tax of a hundred thousand crowns has been imposed upon the citizens; and if this sum is not produced within four-and-twenty hours, it is to be doubled, and collected by the soldiers. They have cleared the houses and sent away the occupants of one of the great streets and forbidden anybody to receive them on pain of death; so that the poor wretches (old men, women near their confinement, and children included) may be seen wandering around and crying on their departure from this city, without knowing where to go, and without food or a place to lie in. Day before yesterday a fiddler was broken on the wheel for getting up a dance and stealing some stamped paper. He was quartered after death, and his limbs exposed at the four corners of the city. Sixty citizens have been thrown into prison, and the business of punishing

历来轻视人民大众。国内各个阶级之间尚未宣战。说他们是被一种激情所驱使，不如说他们是本能的反应。因为他们并不清楚一个贫穷的人的苦难遭遇，所以对他们的命运也毫不关心。

一旦封建的关系破除，普通老百姓也会如此。在家奴仍为主人做出自我牺牲的英雄行为的时代，也偶尔会见到下层阶级对上层阶级的残酷野蛮的行径。

我们不要以为这种互不关心的现象仅仅来因于公共秩序和文化的匮乏，因为在以后的几个秩序井然和文化发达的时代，仍然存在这种现象。

1675 年，布列塔尼地方的下层阶级，曾聚众反对新税。这次骚动被当局残酷地镇压下去。这一恐怖事件的目睹者塞文涅夫人在给她的女儿的信中这样说：

"我的亲爱的女儿：你从埃克斯寄来的信，真是太有趣了！在把信寄出之前，你至少应该再看一遍。你会对你写的那么多赞美之词表示吃惊的，但你也会因为喜欢这样不厌其烦地写了这么多而感到欣慰。可见，你已经认识了普罗旺斯地方的所有的人，是不是？不过，只要你不爱闻葡萄酒的香味，就是你吻遍了布列塔尼地方的所有的人，也不会令他们满意的。……你想听雷恩地方的消息吗？那里下令征税 10 万枚银币，如果不在 24 小时内交出，就把税额翻一番，并派兵去征收。当局已把一条大街的所有居民撵出房屋，而且不准任何人收留，违者处死。因此，一大群倒霉的人，有孕妇、老人和小孩，在恋恋不舍地离开这个城市时号啕大哭；他们不知到哪里去好，既没吃的，也没地方睡。前天，一个开舞厅的小提琴师，因为偷税被车裂。他死后尸体被分成好几块……并把他的四肢放在城市的四个角上示众。……已有 60 名

them is to begin tomorrow. This province sets a fine example to the others, teaching them above all that of respecting the governors and their wives, and of never throwing stones into their garden. ①

Yesterday, a delightful day, Madame de Tarente visited these wilds; there is no question about preparing a chamber or a collation; she comes by the gate, and returns the same way...

In another letter she adds:

You talk very pleasantly about our miseries, but we are no longer so jaded with capital punishments; only one a week now, just to keep up appearances. It is true that hanging now seems to me quite a cooling entertainment. I have got a wholly new idea of justice since I have been in this region. Your galley-slaves seem to me a society of good people who have retired from the world in order to lead a quiet life.

It would be a mistake to suppose that Madame de Sévigné, who wrote these lines, was a selfish or cruel person; she was passionately attached to her children and very ready to sympathize in the sorrows of her friends; nay, her letters show that she treated her vassals and servants with kindness and indulgence. But Madame de Sévigné had no clear notion of suffering in anyone who was not a person of quality.

In our time the harshest man, writing to the most insensible person of his acquaintance, would not venture to indulge in the cruel jocularity that I have quoted; and even if his own manners allowed him to do so, the manners of society at large would forbid it. Whence does this arise? Have we more sensibility than our fathers? I do not know that we have, but I am sure that our sensibility is extended to many more objects.

When all the ranks of a community are nearly equal, as all men think and feel in nearly the same manner, each of them may judge in a moment of the sensations of all the others; he casts a rapid glance upon himself, and that is enough. There is no wretchedness into which

---

① To understand this last pleasantry, it should be recalled that Madame de Grignan was the wife of the Governor of Provence.

市民被捕,明天开始治罪。这个地方为其他地方树立了良好的榜样,叫其他地方也尊重总督及其夫人……不能往他们的花园里投石头。①

……昨天天气很好,塔朗特夫人来到她的林园小憩。当然要为她准备住处和餐饮。她从花园走进来,又从原路回去。"

在另一封信里,她又补充说:

"你总是喜欢谈论我们这里的悲惨事件。我们这里已经不再实行车裂了。为了维护正义,每周只杀一个人。不错,我现在认为判处绞刑已经算宽大了。自从到了这里以后,我对于正义有了新的观点。在我看来,你的那些曳船奴隶,真是一伙不问世事而使生活安宁的好人。"

如果以为写出这些话的塞文涅夫人是个自私残酷的人,那就错了。她爱自己的子女,为朋友的不幸感到同情。在你读她的信的时候,甚至会发觉她对家臣和奴仆还很仁慈宽大。但是,她对贵族圈子以外的人的苦难却一无所知。

今天,最苛刻的人,向一个最没有同情心的人讲述自己的遭遇时,也不敢轻松地说出我上面引述的那些话来。而且,即使是他自身的修养允许他这样做,社会舆论也会禁止他这样的行为的。这种情况是怎么发生的呢?是我们比我们的父辈们变得更有同情心了吗?我不这么认为,但是我可以肯定的是,我们的同情心的范围扩大了。

当社会中所有的阶级都变得近乎平等的时候,当所有人的思想和感情都大致一样的时候,每个人都可以立刻判断出其他人的感情。因为他只需看看自己,就什么都知道了。再也不存在什么样的苦难是他无法体验得到的,一种内在的本能使他在苦难扩大

---

① 为了使读者了解信中最后这句话的含义,应当指出格里南就是普罗旺斯地方总督的夫人。

he cannot readily enter, and a secret instinct reveals to him its extent. It signifies not that strangers or foes are the sufferers; imagination puts him in their place; something like a personal feeling is mingled with his pity and makes himself suffer while the body of his fellow creature is in torture.

In democratic ages men rarely sacrifice themselves for one another, but they display general compassion for the members of the human race. They inflict no useless ills, and they are happy to relieve the griefs of others when they can do so without much hurting themselves; they are not disinterested, but they are humane.

Although the Americans have in a manner reduced selfishness to a social and philosophical theory, they are nevertheless extremely open to compassion. In no country is criminal justice administered with more mildness than in the United States. While the English seem disposed carefully to retain the bloody traces of the Middle Ages in their penal legislation, the Americans have almost expunged capital punishment from their codes. North America is, I think, the only country upon earth in which the life of no one citizen has been taken for a political offense in the course of the last fifty years.

The circumstance which conclusively shows that this singular mildness of the Americans arises chiefly from their social condition is the manner in which they treat their slaves. Perhaps there is not, on the whole, a single European colony in the New World in which the physical condition of the blacks is less severe than in the United States; yet the slaves still endure frightful misery there and are constantly exposed to very cruel punishments. It is easy to perceive that the lot of these unhappy beings inspires their masters with but little compassion and that they look upon slavery not only as an institution which is profitable to them, but as an evil which does not affect them. Thus the same man who is full of humanity towards his fellow creatures when they are at the same time his equals becomes insensible to their afflictions as soon as that equality ceases. His mildness should therefore be attributed to the equality of conditions rather than to

的时候,立刻就可以察觉。即使在对待陌生人和敌人的时候,他也不会加以区别,因为他的想象力可以使他与他们站在同一立场之上考虑问题。一种类似于个人感觉的东西与他的同情心混在一起,使他在看到自己的同胞们遭受痛苦的时候也感同身受。

在民主时期,人们很少牺牲自己成全别人,但是他们对人类却表现出一种广泛的同情心。他们不会让别人遭受无谓的痛苦,而且当他们自己不遭受什么损失的时候,他们很乐意减轻别人的痛苦。他们虽然不是无私的,但是他们变得人性化了。

尽管从某种意义上说,美国人已把利己主义转化成为一种社会和哲学理论,可是他们仍旧怀有同情心。没有一个国家对罪犯的审判像美国那样富有温情。当英国人小心地在刑事立法中保留着残留在他们体内的中世纪嗜血的痕迹时,美国人已经几乎从他们的法则中完全抹去了死刑。我认为,北美是地球上唯一一个在过去的五十年中,其臣民不会因为政治攻击而丧命的国家。

美国人最终表现的这种特别温和的态度主要来因于他们的社会情况,这从他们对待奴隶的态度上即可得到证明。总的说来,在新大陆的欧洲人殖民地上,没有任何一个地方的黑人的物质生活条件不比美国更艰苦。然而,那里的黑人仍然忍受着可怕的苦难,经常受到非常残酷的惩罚。不难发现,这些可怜人的命运,并没有勾起他们的主人一丝一毫的怜悯之心,他们的主人不仅认为蓄奴是有利可图的事业,而且觉得这不算什么罪恶,不会影响自己。因此,相同的一个人,对待与他平等的同类时,充满人道,而一旦平等的地位不存在,他便无所谓于他们的苦痛。由此可见,他的温和态度应是基

civilization and education.

What I have here remarked of individuals is to a certain extent applicable to nations. When each nation has its distinct opinions, belief, laws, and customs, it looks upon itself as the whole of mankind and is moved by no sorrows but its own. Should war break out between two nations animated by this feeling, it is sure to be waged with great cruelty.

At the time of their highest culture the Romans slaughtered the generals of their enemies, after having dragged them in triumph behind a car; and they flung their prisoners to the beasts of the Circus for the amusement of the people. Cicero, who declaimed so vehemently at the notion of crucifying a Roman citizen, had not a word to say against these horrible abuses of victory. It is evident that, in his eyes, a barbarian did not belong to the same human race as a Roman.

On the contrary, in proportion as nations become more like each other, they become reciprocally more compassionate, and the law of nations is mitigated.

于这种平等的社会地位,无关乎文明和教育的。

我所描述的这一切,在一定程度上,也适用于国家。一旦各个国家有了自己独特的观点、信仰、法律和习惯,它便会以整个人类自居,只关心本国的疾苦。如果两个持有这种态度的国家之间交战,则战况一定十分残酷。

在罗马文化最灿烂时期,罗马人是怎么对待他们的敌人的呢? 他们把被俘的敌人将领拖在战车后炫耀胜利,然后才把他们杀掉;他们把囚犯投进斗兽场,让犯人与野兽搏斗,以供大众娱乐。西塞罗一谈到公民被处以钉死在十字架上的刑罚,就义愤填膺,情绪激动。但他对罗马人胜利后对战俘的那种暴行,却缄口不言。可见,在他的眼目中,一个外国人和一个罗马人并不属于同一人类。

反之,随着各国之间变得越来越相似,他们开始变得更富于同情心,同时,国家的法律刑罚也减轻了。

CHAPTER II

How Democracy Renders The Habitual Intercourse Of The Americans Simple And Easy

Democracy does not attach men strongly to one another, but it places their habitual intercourse on an easier footing.

If two Englishmen chance to meet at the antipodes, where they are surrounded by strangers whose language and manners are almost unknown to them, they will first stare at each other with much curiosity and a kind of secret uneasiness; they will then turn away, or if one accosts the other, they will take care to converse only with a constrained and absent air, upon very unimportant subjects. Yet there is no enmity between these men; they have never seen each other before, and each believes the other to be a respectable person. Why, then, should they stand so cautiously apart? We must go back to England to learn the reason.

When it is birth alone, independent of wealth, that classes men in society, everyone knows exactly what his own position is in the social scale; he does not seek to rise, he does not fear to sink. In a community thus organized men of different castes communicate very little with one another; but if accident brings them together, they are ready to converse without hoping or fearing to lose their own position. Their intercourse is not on a footing of equality, but it is not constrained.

When a moneyed aristocracy succeeds to an aristocracy of birth, the case is altered. The privileges of some are still extremely great, but the possibility of acquiring those privileges is open to all; whence it follows that those who possess them are constantly haunted by the

第二章　民主怎样使美国人之间的日常关系简易化的

　　民主并不使人们之间的关系紧密，但却使他们的日常交流更简便。

　　如果有两个英国人偶然在西半球邂逅，他们对周围的外国人的民情和语言都不了解。这时候，他们两人会先以好奇的目光打量对方，同时心里暗暗感到不安；随后，便各自走开；而即使他们相遇后交谈起来，也会表现得十分拘谨，谈一些无关紧要的小事。但是，两人之间并没有什么敌意，他们虽然从来没有见过面，不过都很尊重对方。可是，他们为什么要小心翼翼地彼此回避呢？为了弄明白这个问题，就得先谈谈英国。

　　当社会中的人只靠家庭出身而不靠财产来划分等级的时候，每个人都清楚地知道他在社会阶梯中所处的地位。则他既不会想往上爬，也不担心跌落。在这样组织起来的社会里，不同等级的人之间很少往来；但是，当偶然的事件使他们接触时，他们却可以随意交谈，不会考虑有关彼此的地位。因为他们之间的关系不是建立在平等之上的，但也不是强制如此的。

　　当一个因财产而为贵族的制度，取代了一个因出身而为贵族的制度的时候，情况就变了。一些人的特权依旧很大，但是获得这种权力的机会去面向了所有人。因此，那些拥有特权的阶级总

apprehension of losing them or of other men's sharing them; those who do not yet enjoy them long to possess them at any cost or, if they fail, to appear at least to possess them, this being not impossible. As the social importance of men is no longer ostensibly and permanently fixed by blood and is infinitely varied by wealth, ranks still exist, but it is not easy clearly to distinguish at a glance those who respectively belong to them. Secret hostilities then arise in the community; one set of men endeavor by innumerable artifices to penetrate, or to appear to penetrate, among those who are above them; another set are constantly in arms against these usurpers of their rights; or, rather, the same individual does both at once, and while he seeks to raise himself into a higher circle, he is always on the defensive against the intrusion of those below him.

Such is the condition of England at the present time, and I am of the opinion that the peculiarity just adverted to must be attributed principally to this cause. As aristocratic pride is still extremely great among the English, and as the limits of aristocracy are ill-defined, everybody lives in constant dread lest advantage should be taken of his familiarity. Unable to judge at once of the social position of those he meets, an Englishman prudently avoids all contact with them. Men are afraid lest some slight service rendered should draw them into an unsuitable acquaintance; they dread civilities, and they avoid the obtrusive gratitude of a stranger quite as much as his hatred.

Many people attribute these singular antisocial propensities and the reserved and taciturn bearing of the English to purely physical causes. I may admit that there is something of it in their race, but much more of it is attributable to their social condition, as is proved by the contrast of the Americans.

In America, where the privileges of birth never existed and where riches confer no peculiar rights on their possessors, men unacquainted with one another are very ready to frequent the same places and find neither peril nor advantage in the free interchange of their thoughts. If they meet by accident, they neither seek nor avoid

是担心他们会失去这种权力或者有其他人会来分享他们的特权。而尚未取得特权的人们,则想不惜一切代价去获取。即使他们失败了,也要表现得至少拥有它们不是不可能的。因为人在社会中的重要性不再因为血缘关系而固定不变,而是随着财产的变化而变化的。阶级仍旧存在,但是已经很难从表面分辨出谁属于哪个阶级了。社会中因此产生了敌视的心理。一些人努力用尽一切办法想要进入,或者至少表面上挤入上层阶级。而另一些人则武装起来反抗那些觊觎他们权力的人们。或者也可以说,一个人腹背受敌:一方面设法爬到更高级的阶级,另一方面又在不断地防御抵抗那些入侵者。

英国当前的情况就是如此。我认为,我在前面所述的一切特性,基本上就是由于这一情况造成的。在英国人中间,贵族的傲气还很强大,但其界限已模糊不清,所以人人都时时提防别人,唯恐他人从自己的友善中得到好处。英国人由于不能一下子判断他们所遇到的人是属于哪个社会阶层,所以小心翼翼地避免与任何人接触。他们害怕因为接受别人一点小恩小惠而形成不好的关系,并对别人的多礼生疑。他们既不受陌生人的恭维,也不愿惹他人生怨。

许多人完全用个人的性格来解释英国人的这种洁身自好和冷漠寡言。我也承认这其中必然有着受他们的性格的影响的因素,但我认为他们的社会情况在发挥着更大的作用。我们可以通过与美国人对照加以证实。

在美国,无所谓家庭出身带来的特权,即使财富也不会使它的持有人享有任何独特的权利;互不相识的人可以随意见面,他们相互交换思想时既不是为了获得好处,又不怕由此带来危险。

intercourse; their manner is therefore natural, frank, and open; it is easy to see that they hardly expect or learn anything from one another, and that they do not care to display any more than to conceal their position in the world. If their demeanor is often cold and serious, it is never haughty or constrained; and if they do not converse, it is because they are not in a humor to talk, not because they think it their interest to be silent.

In a foreign country two Americans are at once friends simply because they are Americans. They are repulsed by no prejudice; they are attracted by their common country. For two Englishmen the same blood is not enough; they must be brought together by the same rank. The Americans notice this unsociable mood of the English as much as the French do and are not less astonished by it. Yet the Americans are connected with England by their origin, their religion, their language, and partially by their customs; they differ only in their social condition. It may therefore be inferred that the reserve of the English proceeds from the constitution of their country much more than from that of its inhabitants.

他们如果在某处偶遇,既不主动攀谈,也不会回避谈话。因此,他们的待人态度是自然的、坦率的和开朗的。我们还会发现,他们既不打算从对方得到什么好处,又不担心对方会加害于己;他们既不想炫耀自己的地位,也不会设法去掩饰自己的处境。虽然他们的态度往往显得冷淡而严肃,但这并不表明他们高傲或拘谨。如果他们一言不发,那只是因为他们当时的心情不好或不爱讲话,而不是因为他们认为保持沉默对他们有利。

两个美国人在异国相遇,马上就会成为朋友,只因为他们都是美国人。他们彼此没有任何成见,是他们的祖国这根纽带把他们吸引在一起。而对于两个英国人,只是同源还不够,还必须是同一阶级。美国人和法国人都看到英国人之间的这种冷漠,而且当他们如此对待我们时也都不以为奇。但是,美国人在血统、宗教、语言和一部分习俗上是与英国人一样的,他们之间的唯一差别是社会情况。因此,我们可以说英国人的谨慎态度来因于他们的国家制度,而不是来因于公民的性格。

CHAPTER III

Why The Americans Show So Little Sensitiveness In Their Own Country And Are So Sensitive In Europe

The temper of the Americans is vindictive, like that of all serious and reflecting nations. They hardly ever forget an offense, but it is not easy to offend them, and their resentment is as slow to kindle as it is to abate.

In aristocratic communities, where a small number of persons manage everything, the outward intercourse of men is subject to settled conventional rules. Everyone then thinks he knows exactly what marks of respect or of condescension he ought to display, and none are presumed to be ignorant of the science of etiquette. These usages of the first class in society afterwards serve as a model to all the others; besides this, each of the latter lays down a code of its own, to which all its members are bound to conform. Thus the rules of politeness form a complex system of legislation, which it is difficult to be perfectly master of, but from which it is dangerous for anyone to deviate; so that men are constantly exposed involuntarily to inflict or to receive bitter affronts.

But as the distinctions of rank are obliterated, as men differing in education and in birth meet and mingle in the same places of resort, it is almost impossible to agree upon the rules of good breeding. As its laws are uncertain, to disobey them is not a crime, even in the eyes of those who know what they are; men attach more importance to intentions than to forms, and they grow less civil, but at the same time less quarrelsome.

第三章　为什么美国人在本国不太爱激动而在欧洲又表现得过于激动

美国人的性格中也有报复性心理,如同所有严肃而自重的国家一样。他们很难忘记受到的攻击,但是要想攻击他们也不容易。他们的怒火既难点燃也难熄灭。

在贵族制社会,少数几个人主管所有的事情,人与人之间的对外交往都遵循着相对固定的常规。因此,每个人都认为自己确切地知道如何对人表示尊重和好意,而且认为没有人会对礼节一无所知。社会中上层阶级的这种习惯后来便成为所有其他人的典范。除此之外,其他阶级也各有其自己的规矩,本阶级所有的成员都必须遵守的这些规矩。因此,这些规矩形成了一套复杂的立法体系,一般人很难掌握,稍有违反,就会造成损失。所以,人们常常不自觉地遭受别人无意的侮辱,同时也无意地侮辱着别人。

但是,随着阶级差别消失,教育和出身不同的人在同一场所彼此交流融合,便几乎不可能定出礼节的规定。由于礼节未被明确规定,所以稍有违反也不算过失,就是那些知礼的人也认为如此。因此,人们重视行为的实质甚于行为的形式,他们变得不那么彬彬有礼,但也很少再起争执。

There are many little attentions that an American does not care a-
bout; he thinks they are not due to him, or he presumes that they are
not known to be due. He therefore either does not perceive a rudeness
or he forgives it; his manners become less courteous, and his character more plain and masculine.

The mutual indulgence that the Americans display and the manly
confidence with which they treat one another also result from another
deeper and more general cause, which I have already referred to in
the preceding chapter. In the United States the distinctions of rank in
civil society are slight, in political society they are nil; an American,
therefore, does not think himself bound to pay particular attentions to
any of his fellow citizens, nor does he require such attentions from
them towards himself. As he does not see that it is his interest eagerly
to seek the company of any of his countrymen, he is slow to fancy that
his own company is declined. Despising no one on account of his station, he does not imagine that anyone can despise him for that cause,
and until he has clearly perceived an insult, he does not suppose that
an affront was intended. The social condition of the Americans naturally accustoms them not to take offense in small matters, and, on the
other hand, the democratic freedom which they enjoy transfuses this
same mildness of temper into the character of the nation.

The political institutions of the United States constantly bring citizens of all ranks into contact and compel them to pursue great undertakings in concert. People thus engaged have scarcely time to attend
to the details of etiquette, and they are besides too strongly interested
in living harmoniously for them to stick at such things. They therefore
soon acquire a habit of considering the feelings and opinions of those
whom they meet more than their manners, and they do not allow
themselves to be annoyed by trifles.

I have often noticed in the United States that it is not easy to
make a man understand that his presence may be dispensed with;
hints will not always suffice to shake him off. I contradict an American at every word he says, to show him that his conversation bores
me; he instantly labors with fresh pertinacity to convince me; I preserve a dogged silence, and he thinks I am meditating deeply on the

　　一个美国人绝不为一些无谓的关心打动。他认为自己不该得到这些,或者装作自己不知道应当享有它们。因此,他不会觉得无理,而会选择原谅他人。在这方面,他表现得不拘小节,并且他的个性更直爽而富有男子气概。

　　美国人表现出的这种相互的宽容态度和他们对待别人时表现出的自信,都基于另外一个更深层次的、更广泛的原因,这个原因我在前一章节中已经作了描述。在美国,在民主社会中阶级之间的差别是细微的,在政界这种差别根本不存在。因此,一个美国人从不认为自己应该特别关心任何一个同胞,他也不会要求别人这样对他。因为他不认为他迫切地跟别人套近乎与他的利益有关,所以他也不以为意。他不会因为自己的身份轻视任何人,也不认为有人会因为这个原因轻视他。直到他很明确地感受到了别人的侮辱,他也不会认为人家的冒犯是故意的。美国的社会状况自然地使他们不在乎一些小事情,并且,从另一方面说,他们享受的民主的自由,又把这种温和的性情带入到民族的性格之中。

　　美国的政治制度使所有阶级的公民不断地接触,并使他们共同致力于伟大的事业。因此,人们几乎没有时间考虑礼节上的细节。并且由于对于生活环境的和谐的强烈热爱而不拘礼节。因此,他们很快就变得更重视与他们交往的人们的感情和观念,而不那么注重他们的仪表。他们不允许自己因为琐事而烦躁。

　　在美国我常常注意到,要是一个人注意到他的存在是无所谓的是多么的不容易。任何暗示都不会有用。我即使对一个美国人所说的每一个词都反驳回去,以显示我是多么的不想听他再说下去。他会立刻找出新的论据来说服我。要是我保持沉默,他会认为我在认

truths that he is uttering; at last I rush from his company, and he supposes that some urgent business hurries me elsewhere. This man will never understand that he wearies me to death unless I tell him so, and the only way to get rid of him is to make him my enemy for life.

At first sight it appears surprising that the same man, transported to Europe, suddenly becomes so sensitive and captious that I often find it as difficult to avoid offending him here as it was there to put him out of countenance. These two opposite effects proceed from the same cause. Democratic institutions generally give men a lofty notion of their country and of themselves. An American leaves his country with a heart swollen with pride; on arriving in Europe, he at once finds out that we are not so engrossed by the United States and the great people who inhabit it as he had supposed, and this begins to annoy him. He has been informed that the conditions of society are not equal in our part of the globe, and he observes that among the nations of Europe the traces of rank are not wholly obliterated, that wealth and birth still retain some indeterminate privileges, which force themselves upon his notice while they elude definition. He is therefore profoundly ignorant of the place that he ought to occupy in this halfruined scale of classes, which are sufficiently distinct to hate and despise each other, yet sufficiently alike for him to be always confounding them. He is afraid of ranking himself too high; still more is he afraid of being ranked too low. This twofold peril keeps his mind constantly on the stretch and embarrasses all he says and does.

He learns from tradition that in Europe ceremonial observances were infinitely varied according to different ranks; this recollection of former times completes his perplexity, and he is the more afraid of not obtaining those marks of respect which are due to him, as he does not exactly know in what they consist. He is like a man surrounded by traps: society is not a recreation for him, but a serious toil: he weighs your least actions, interrogates your looks, and scrutinizes all you say lest there should be some hidden allusion to affront him. I doubt whether there was ever a provincial man of quality so punctilious in breeding as he is: he endeavors to attend to the slightest rules of

真地思索他所说的事实。最后，我从他的公司冲出去,他还以为我有什么其他紧急的事情要去办理。他永远也不会了解他使我感到厌烦得要死,除非我告诉他。要想摆脱他,唯一的办法就是使他成为我终身的敌人。

乍一看来很令人惊讶,因为如果把这个人放在欧洲,他立刻就会变得敏感而挑剔,使我常常觉得要想不惹他生气和在美国使他生气同样困难。这两种现象有着相同的起因。民主制度通常使人们对他们的国家和国民充满崇高的感情。一个美国人在国外的时候,都怀着一种骄傲的心理。一到欧洲,他立刻发现我们并不像他想象的那样,对他的国家和国民充满憧憬之心,这就使他感到气恼了。因为他听人说,在我们这个半球,人们的地位并不平等,而且他发现,在欧洲国家中,阶级的痕迹并没有完全被抹去,财富和出身仍旧保留着一定的特权享受,这些是他所不能理解难于界定的。因此,他对这个行将毁灭的阶级一无所知,而在这些明显是相互仇恨和彼此轻视,却又相互接近随时准备混合的阶级中,他不知道如何自处。他怕给自己定位太高,却也担心定位过低。这样的进退两难之间使他的思想总是处于感到紧张和不安,影响着他的一言一行。

他从欧洲人的传统中了解到,欧洲人的礼仪在不同的阶级中是完全不同的。这些古老的遗风使他完全困惑了,他变得更加担心他所应得的尊重,但是他又不十分清楚人们应该在哪些方面对他表示尊敬。他仿佛是一个被套子层层裹住的人:社交对他来说不再是令人愉悦的,而是一个圈套。他必须衡量你的任何动作,研究你的表情,思索你的每一句话,以免有什么其他冒犯他的含

etiquette and does not allow one of them to be waived towards himself; he is full of scruples and at the same time of pretensions; he wishes to do enough, but fears to do too much, and as he does not very well know the limits of the one or of the other, he keeps up a haughty and embarrassed air of reserve.

But this is not all: here is yet another queer twist of the human heart. An American is forever talking of the admirable equality that prevails in the United States; aloud he makes it the boast of his country, but in secret he deplores it for himself, and he aspires to show that, for his part, he is an exception to the general state of things which he vaunts. There is hardly an American to be met with who does not claim some remote kindred with the first founders of the colonies; and as for the scions of the noble families of England, America seemed to me to be covered with them. When an opulent American arrives in Europe, his first care is to surround himself with all the luxuries of wealth; he is so afraid of being taken for the plain citizen of a democracy that he adopts a hundred distorted ways of bringing some new instance of his wealth before you every day. His house will be in the most fashionable part of the town; he will always be surrounded by a host of servants. I have heard an American complain that in the best houses of Paris the society was rather mixed; the taste which prevails there was not pure enough for him, and he ventured to hint that, in his opinion, there was a want of elegance of manner; he could not accustom himself to see wit concealed under such unpretending forms.

These contrasts ought not to surprise us. If the vestiges of former aristocratic distinctions were not so completely effaced in the United States, the Americans would be less simple and less tolerant in their own country; they would require less, and be less fond of borrowed manners, in ours.

义隐藏其中。我怀疑是否还会有比他更拘泥小节的人。他力求遵守任何一条细小的礼节，不允许任何人对他稍有失礼。他既自负又缺乏信心。他想要做得恰到好处，但是总是担心做得过多，而且因为他并不十分知道两者的界限，所以他总是保持着一副傲慢而忸怩的态度。

　　这还不是全部。人心的扭曲还体现在另一个方面。美国人总要称赞美国普遍实行的平等，大声地吹嘘着自己的国家。但是，私底下他对自己又感到很内疚，总觉得自己做得不够，说他是他所吹嘘的那种普遍现象的例外。没有一个美国人不想把自己同早期殖民着攀上关系。我觉得，所有的美国人都可以算做英国贵族家庭的后裔。一个美国富翁到了欧洲之后，他首先关心的，就是用奢侈来炫耀他的财富。他很担心别人把他当作民主国家的普通公民，因而千方百计摆阔，叫你每天都看到他挥霍的新花样。他住在全城最豪华的房屋，有许多仆人前簇后拥。我曾听到一个美国人抱怨说，巴黎的一些大沙龙也不过是中流的交际场所。在他看来，人们在这些沙龙所行的雅兴并不够高尚。他试图暗示，对他来说，人们在沙龙里的仪表也不够优雅。其实，他还没有习惯于我们的风气，看不到不加修饰的外表内隐藏的精华。

　　这样的对比不应让我们感到惊奇。如果旧的贵族等级制度不是那么彻底地在美国消失殆尽，美国人也不会在自己的国家中表现得那样简单而宽容，也不会要求甚多，并在欧洲表现得那样矫揉造作。

CHAPTER IV

Consequences Of The Three Preceding Chapters

When men feel a natural compassion for the sufferings of one another, when they are brought together by easy and frequent intercourse, and no sensitive feelings keep them asunder, it may readily be supposed that they will lend assistance to one another whenever it is needed. When an American asks for the co-operation of his fellow citizens, it is seldom refused; and I have often seen it afforded spontaneously, and with great goodwill. If an accident happens on the highway, everybody hastens to help the sufferer; if some great and sudden calamity befalls a family, the purses of a thousand strangers are at once willingly opened and small but numerous donations pour in to relieve their distress.

It often happens, among the most civilized nations of the globe, that a poor wretch is as friendless in the midst of a crowd as the savage in his wilds; this is hardly ever the case in the United States. The Americans, who are always cold and often coarse in their manners seldom show insensibility; and if they do not proffer services eagerly, yet they do not refuse to render them.

All this is not in contradiction to what I have said before on the subject of individualism. The two things are so far from combating each other that I can see how they agree. Equality of condition, while it makes men feel their independence, shows them their own weakness: they are free, but exposed to a thousand accidents; and experience soon teaches them that although they do not habitually require the assistance of others, a time almost always comes when they cannot do without it.

第四章　对前三章的总结

当人们对彼此的不幸怀有恻隐之心，当他们常常进行日常交往，当他们不会因为任何冲动而分离的时候，就不难想象在必要的时候他们会施行互助；当一个美国人请他的同胞帮忙的时候，很少有人拒绝。我就屡次见到他们满怀热情地自发助人的行为。如果公路上突然发生车祸，人们纷纷上前救护患难的人。要是某个家庭横遭大难，素昧平生的人也会慷慨解囊；每个人的捐助虽少，但积少成多，就可以让他们摆脱困难。

在世界上最文明的一些国家里，一个贫穷不幸的人往往在人群中孤立无援，就像一个野人在森林里的遭遇一样。这种现象很少会发生在美国。美国人虽然常常态度淡漠，而且往往表现得很粗野，但他们却几乎不会表现得麻木不仁。如果他们没有迫切地对别人施加援手，那也不表明他们拒绝施助。

这一切同我在前面论述个人主义时所讲的话并不矛盾。这两者不仅不会相互矛盾，我甚至发现二者极为契合。身份的平等在使人们感受独立的同时，也使他们感到自己的软弱。他们的确是自由了，但却面临着无数的意想不到的危险。而且经验教会他们，尽管他们不是经常需要别人的帮助，但总有时候需要被人帮助。

In Europe we constantly see that men of the same profession are always ready to assist one another; they are all exposed to the same ills, and that is enough to teach them to seek mutual preservation, however hard-hearted and selfish they may otherwise be. When one of them falls into danger from which the others may save him by a slight transient sacrifice or a sudden effort, they do not fail to make the attempt. Not that they are deeply interested in his fate, for if, by chance, their exertions are unavailing, they immediately forget the object of them and return to their own business; but a sort of tacit and almost involuntary agreement has been passed between them, by which each one owes to the others a temporary support, which he may claim for himself in turn.

Extend to a people the remark here applied to a class and you will understand my meaning. A similar covenant exists, in fact, between all the citizens of a democracy: they all feel themselves subject to the same weakness and the same dangers; and their interest, as well as their sympathy, makes it a rule with them to lend one another assistance when required. The more equal social conditions become, the more do men display this reciprocal disposition to oblige each other. In democracies no great benefits are conferred, but good offices are constantly rendered; a man seldom displays self-devotion, but all men are ready to be of service to one another.

在欧洲我们常常会发现,具有相同职业的人总是乐意互相帮助的。他们所遭遇的苦难相同,这就足以使他们互相寻求支持,无论在其他方面他们是如何的铁石心肠和自私。当他们其中一人陷于危难之中,如果只要别人暂时牺牲一下或者稍加努力即可,他们是不会放弃尝试的。这并不表示他们很关心这个人的命运,因为一旦他们的努力没有用,他们就会立刻放弃努力,转身投入到自己的事情当中去了。但是在他们之间有一种默契和几乎是自发的约定,根据这个约定,每个人都有义务对他人施加暂时的援手,他也可以在自己需要的时候这么要求别人。

如果把这里所说的一切运用到整个民族中去,你就会明白我的感受。事实上,在民主国家所有的人民之间,还有一种类似的契约存在。那就是,他们都认为大家有着相同的弱点和危险。他们的利益和同情心,使他们产生了在必要的时候相互施助的信念。一个社会,人们的身份越是平等,人们之间就越是会表现出这样的互助义务。在民主国家中,没有人会提供巨大的好处,但是互助的影响力却总是存在。一个人很少会表现出献身精神,但是所有的人都随时准备着对别人施加援手。

CHAPTER V

How Democracy Affects The Relations

Of Masters And Servants

An American who had traveled for a long time in Europe once said to me: "The English treat their servants with a stiffness and imperiousness of manner which surprise us; but, on the other hand, the French sometimes treat their attendants with a degree of familiarity or of politeness which we cannot understand. It looks as if they were afraid to give orders; the relative position of the superior and the inferior is poorly maintained." The remark was a just one, and I have often made it myself. I have always considered England as the country of all the world where in our time the bond of domestic service is drawn most tightly, and France as the country where it is most relaxed. Nowhere have I seen masters stand so high or so low as in these two countries. Between these two extremes the Americans are to be placed. Such is the fact as it appears upon the surface of things; to discover the causes of that fact, it is necessary to search the matter thoroughly.

No communities have ever yet existed in which social conditions have been so equal that there were neither rich nor poor, and, consequently, neither masters nor servants. Democracy does not prevent the existence of these two classes, but it changes their dispositions and modifies their mutual relations.

Among aristocratic nations servants form a distinct class, not more variously composed than that of their masters. A settled order is soon established; in the former as well as in the latter class a scale is formed, with numerous distinctions or marked gradations of rank, and generations succeed one another thus, without any change of position. These two communities are superposed one above the other,

第五章　民主怎样改善主仆的关系

一位在欧洲游历过很长时间的美国人曾对我说:"英国人对待仆人时表现的强硬专横态度,使我们感到惊讶;但是,法国人对待仆人有时过于亲昵,有时又太客气,不能理解。因为这让人感到法国人好像害怕支使仆人似的,上级和下级彼此的地位不很明晰。"他的观察是正确的,我自己也曾多次这样说过。我一向认为,在我们这个时代,英国是世界上主仆关系最严谨的国家,而法国则是主仆关系最宽松的国家。我从来没有见过哪个国家的主人地位像这两个国家那样悬殊。美国的情况处于这两种极端之间。以上事实还只是表层的。为了探明这个事实产生的原因,还要进行深入的研究。

从古至今,还没有出现过身份平等得没有贫富之分,从而也没有主仆之分的社会。民主制度并不妨碍主仆这两个阶级的存在;但是,它在改变两者的思想意识,并在调整两者之间的关系。

在贵族制国家,仆人形成为一个单独的阶级,这个阶级并不比他们的主人阶级有更多的变化。这样的国家,很快就会建立起一种固定的秩序。在下层阶级,也像在上层阶级一样,很快便出现了等级、集团和显赫人物,他们所处的地位也会随之世代相传,不会改变。主人和仆人是一个在上一个在下的两个社会,永远保

always distinct, but regulated by analogous principles. This aristocratic constitution does not exert a less powerful influence on the notions and manners of servants than on those of masters; and although the effects are different, the same cause may easily be traced.

Both classes constitute small communities in the heart of the nation, and certain permanent notions of right and wrong are ultimately established among them. The different acts of human life are viewed by one peculiar and unchanging light. In the society of servants, as in that of masters, men exercise a great influence over one another: they acknowledge settled rules, and in the absence of law they are guided by a sort of public opinion; their habits are settled, and their conduct is placed under a certain control.

These men, whose destiny it is to obey, certainly do not understand fame, virtue, honesty, and honor in the same manner as their masters; but they have a pride, a virtue, and an honesty pertaining to their condition; and they have a notion, if I may use the expression, of a sort of servile honor. ① Because a class is mean, it must not be supposed that all who belong to it are mean-hearted; to think so would be a great mistake. However lowly it may be, he who is foremost there and who has no notion of quitting it occupies an aristocratic position which inspires him with lofty feelings, pride, and self-respect, that fit him for the higher virtues and for actions above the common.

Among aristocratic nations it was by no means rare to find men of noble and vigorous minds in the service of the great, who did not feel the servitude they bore and who submitted to the will of their masters

---

① If the principal opinions by which men are guided are examined closely and in detail, the analogy appears still more striking, and one is surprised to find among them, just as much as among the haughtiest scions of a feudal race, pride of birth, respect of their ancestry and their descendants, disdain of their inferiors, a dread of contact, and a taste for etiquette, precedent, and antiquity.

持着差别,但却遵守着类似的原则。贵族制度对仆人的思想和民情的影响绝不亚于其主人受到的影响。虽然在各方产生的结果不同,但导致其发生的同一起因并不难被发现。

两个阶级在一个大国家中各自形成自己的小集团,从而对对错的判断各有其固定的看法。他们对人生的各种行为,亦各有其不变的独特观点。在仆人的社会里,也同在主人的社会里一样,人们彼此之间互相产生很大影响。他们承认既定的规则;虽然没有明文规定的法律,但是却有指导他们行为的舆论。长期形成的习惯已固定,他们的行为亦时时受到一定的约束。

命中注定受人支使的这些人,肯定理解名誉、美德、正直和光荣对他们的主人的意义。但是,他们却有一种处于他们地位所特有的名誉观、美德观和正直观;而且他们自有主张。如果用我的话来说,就是他们有一种身为仆人的光荣。① 因为这个阶级地位低下,所以一定不要以为这个阶级的所有成员都是平庸的。如果这么想,那就大错特错了。尽管这个阶级地位低下,但它的一些出类拔萃而且无意放弃高高在上地位的人物,却处于类似贵族的地位。这个地位使他们有着崇高的思想,他们感到骄傲,妄自尊大,觉得自己也有高尚的品德,也会有杰出的作为。

在贵族制国家中,很容易发现一些具有高尚思想和精力旺盛的人们为一些大人物服务。他们并没有意识到自己处于奴役状

---

① 如果对指引人们的主要原则加以近距离详细的考察的话,这一相似性就表现得更显著了。人们会惊讶于在人民中间,如同在封建社会最傲慢的子孙之中一样,存在着一种因出身而具有的骄傲之情,以及对他们的祖先和后代的尊重,对他们的仆人们的蔑视,猜疑多礼,以及对礼节、先例和遗俗的热爱。

without any fear of their displeasure.

But this was hardly ever the case among the inferior ranks of domestic servants. It may be imagined that he who occupies the lowest stage of the order of menials stands very low indeed. The French created a word on purpose to designate the servants of the aristocracy; they called them "lackeys." This word *lackey* served as the strongest expression, when all others were exhausted, to designate human meanness. Under the old French monarchy to denote by a single expression a low-spirited, contemptible fellow it was usual to say that he had the *soul of a lackey*; the term was enough to convey all that was intended.

The permanent inequality of conditions not only gives servants certain peculiar virtues and vices, but places them in a peculiar relation with respect to their masters. Among aristocratic nations the poor man is familiarized from his childhood with the notion of being commanded; to whichever side he turns his eyes, the graduated structure of society and the aspect of obedience meet his view. Hence in those countries the master readily obtains prompt, complete, respectful, and easy obedience from his servants, because they revere in him not only their master, but the class of masters. He weighs down their will by the whole weight of the aristocracy. He orders their actions; to a certain extent, he even directs their thoughts. In aristocracies the master often exercises, even without being aware of it, an amazing sway over the opinions, the habits, and the manners of those who obey him, and his influence extends even further than his authority.

The aristaratic communities not only are there hereditary families ofservants as well as of masters, but the same families of servants adherefor sereral generations to the same families of masters. (like two parallel lines, which neither meet nor separate) ; and this considerably modifies the mutual relations of these two classes of persons. Thus although in aristocratic society the master and servant have no natural resemblance, although, on the contrary, they are placed at an immense distance on the scale of human beings by their fortune, education, and opinions, yet time ultimately binds them together. They are connected by a long series of common reminiscences, and however different they may be, they grow alike; while in

态,他们服从其主人的旨意,但也不怕惹他们不高兴。

但是在仆人阶层中的下层,情况就不是这样了。我们可以想象,处于奴役阶层最底层的仆人们,他们地位是十分低下的。法国人发明了一个词,专门用来称呼为贵族们服务的奴仆们,他们称他们为"奴才"。奴才是一个很严厉的词。当人们找不到其他词的时候,就用这个词说人下贱至极。在旧法国君主专制时代,如果要骂一个卑鄙无耻的人,就说他有着奴才的劣根性。这样说就足以表达他所要表达的恶毒含义了。

身份的永恒不平等不仅使仆人养成了独特的品行和恶习,而且使他们在主人面前处于一种特殊的地位。在贵族制国家,穷人从小就惯于服从。无论他们把目光投向哪里,他们所见到的都只是等级森严的社会组织和下级服从上级的现象。结果,在身份永恒不平等的国家里,主人很容易得到仆人完全的驯服和尊敬,因为仆人对主人的尊敬之情不仅出于服从主人,而且出于服从整个上层阶级。统治阶级把贵族制度的全部压力都压在仆人的头上。主人支配仆人的行动,并在一定程度上左右他们的思想。在贵族制度下,主人对于服从于自己的人的思想、习惯和情绪,往往在不知不觉之中起着巨大的影响,而且影响的广度远远大于他们的权威产生的影响。

在贵族制社会中,不仅存在着世袭的仆人家族和世袭的统治家族,而且这一仆人家族往往一连数代为同一主人家族服务(这就像两条平行线,既不相交,也不分开)。这种情况极大的变化了两个阶级人民之间的关系。因此,尽管在这样的贵族体制下,虽然主仆之间毫无天生的共同性,而且财产、教育、观点和权利又使他们的处境有天壤之别。但是不管他们之间的差别有多大,他

democracies, where they are naturally almost alike, they always remain strangers to one another. Among an aristocratic people the master gets to look upon his servants as an inferior and secondary part of himself, and he often takes an interest in their lot by a last stretch of selfishness.

Servants, on their part, are not averse to regarding themselves in the same light; and they sometimes identify themselves with the person of the master, so that they become an appendage to him in their own eyes as well as in his. In aristocracies a servant fills a subordinate position which he cannot get out of; above him is another man, holding a superior rank, which he cannot lose. On one side are obscurity, poverty, obedience for life; on the other, and also for life, fame, wealth, and command. The two conditions are always distinct and always in propinquity; the tie that connects them is as lasting as they are themselves.

In this predicament the servant ultimately detaches his notion of interest from his own person; he deserts himself as it were, or rather he transports himself into the character of his master and thus assumes an imaginary personality. He complacently invests himself with the wealth of those who command him; he shares their fame, exalts himself by their rank, and feeds his mind with borrowed greatness, to which he attaches more importance than those who fully and really possess it. There is something touching and at the same time ridiculous in this strange confusion of two different states of being. These passions of masters, when they pass into the souls of menials, assume the natural dimensions of the place they occupy; they are contracted and lowered. What was pride in the former becomes puerile vanity and paltry ostentation in the latter. The servants of a great man are commonly most punctilious as to the marks of respect due to him, and they attach more importance to his slightest privileges than he does himself. In France a few of these old servants of the aristocracy are still to be met with here and there; they have survived their race, which will soon disappear with them altogether.

们拥有的共同岁月将他们联系在一起。尽管他们在许多方面有
所不同,但他们彼此相似。在民主社会中,主仆之间虽然几乎天
生没有差别,但他们总保持着陌生人的关系。在贵族制国家中,
主人把自己的仆人视为其附属品和自身的一部分,所以常常在利
己主义的推动下关心他们的命运。

至于仆人,也并不反对用这种观点看待自己。他们有时认为
自己属于主人的阶层,因而他们自己也像主人那样认为自己是主
人的附属物。在贵族制度下,仆人处于从属地位,而且他们自己
无法摆脱这个地位;在他们之上的是一些不会失去其高高在上地
位的人们。一方面是愚昧、贫穷和终生服从;另一方面也是终生
的荣华富贵和支配别人。这两个阶级尽管永远不同,但却经常接
近,而使两者结合起来的纽带与它们的存在共存亡。

在这种困境中,仆人最终放弃了自己的个人利益。他完全没
有了自我,将自己完全融入了他的主人的个性中,成了一个隐形
人。他为使唤他的人的财富而感到满足,以他们的荣誉为荣,以
他们的地位显示自己,靠他们的荣耀装点自己。他甚至比那些
权力和荣誉的真正的主人更重视他们的荣誉。这样的两种完
全不同的生活方式融合在一起,形成了一种令人同情却也荒
谬的现象。主人的激情转移到他们的仆人身上,限定在其本
身所有的范围内。于是就被压缩和降低了。在前者身上是那
么骄傲的东西,在后者身上就变成无聊的空虚和令人厌烦的
矫饰。大人物的仆人们通常摆出其主人应当具有的派头,他
们比其主人更重视细小的权利。在法国,到处都还存在着这
样的几个贵族的老仆。他们是这类人的残存,不久就将随着
他们的消失而消失殆尽。

In the United States I never saw anyone at all like them. The A-
mericans are not only unacquainted with the kind of man, but it is
hardly possible to make them understand that such ever existed. It is
scarcely less difficult for them to conceive it than for us to form a correct notion of what a slave was among the Romans or a serf in the
Middle Ages. All these men were, in fact, though in different degrees, results of the same cause: they are all retiring from our sight
and disappearing in the obscurity of the past, together with the social
condition to which they owed their origin. Equality of conditions turns
servants and masters into new beings, and places them in new relative
positions. When social conditions are nearly equal, men are constantly changing their situations in life; there is still a class of menials and
a class of masters, but these classes are not always composed of the
same individuals, still less of the same families; and those who command are not more secure of perpetuity than those who obey. As servants do not form a separate class, they have no habits, prejudices, or
manners peculiar to themselves; they are not remarkable for any particular turn of mind or moods of feeling. They know no vices or virtues
of their condition, but they partake of the education, the opinions,
the feelings, the virtues, and the vices of their contemporaries; and
they are honest men or scoundrels in the same way as their
masters are.

The conditions of servants are not less equal than those of masters. As no marked ranks or fixed subordination are to be found a-
mong them, they will not display either the meanness or the greatness
that characterize the aristocracy of menials, as well as all other aristocracies. I never saw a man in the United States who reminded me of
that class of confidential servants of which we still retain a reminiscence in Europe; neither did I ever meet with such a thing as *a lackey*: all traces of the one and the other have disappeared.

In democracies servants are not only equal among themselves,
but it may be said that they are, in some sort, the equals of their
masters. This requires explanation in order to be rightly understood.
At any moment a servant may become a master, and he aspires to rise
to that condition; the servant is therefore not a different man from the

在美国我从未见到过像这样的人。美国人不仅不知道这些人，而且也很难使他们理解这些人曾经的存在。要使他们相信这个，就如同让我们理解中世纪的仆人或者罗马时期的奴隶一样困难。事实上，所有这些人尽管等级不同，但是产生的原因都一样。他们全部都逐渐从我们的眼前消失，并随着时间的推移和他们所处的社会环境赋予他们地位而变得模糊不清。平等的社会地位是主人和仆人转而为新，使他们之间的关系有了新的定义。但社会环境逐渐变得平等，人们总是变换着自己的居所。虽然仍旧存在主人阶级和奴隶阶级，但是这些阶级已不再是由一些固定的人们和固定的小家庭来充当。发号施令的人们的地位也并不比奴隶们的地位稳定。因为奴隶们不再属于一个单独的阶级，他们就没有了什么习惯、偏见或者特有的民情。他们身上，既没有什么显著的精神面貌也没有什么特别的思想感情。他们并未因地位的原因而形成善恶之分，但他们与同时代的人受到一样的教育，拥有同样的思想、感情和善恶之分。他们中间也存在正直的人和卑鄙小人，同他们的主人中间也有这样的人一样。

仆人的地位并不比他们主人的社会地位低。在仆人阶级中既无优越的等级，又没有不变的从属。他们不会表现出贵族制度下和其他社会中仆人们的那种常见的尊卑。我从未见过一个美国人使我想起在欧洲仍旧常常能回忆起的那些骄傲的仆人们。我也从没见过类似的现象。所有的这种迹象在美国都不存在了。

在民主制度下，不但仆人们彼此平等，而且从某种程度可以说他们同主人也是平等的。为了正确理解这一点，还需要加以说明。仆人随时都可能变成主人，而且他希望上升到这个地位。因此，仆人与主人并没有什么不同。那么，除非他们双方达成暂时

master. Why, then, has the former a right to command, and what compels the latter to obey except the free and temporary consent of both their wills? Neither of them is by nature inferior to the other; they only become so for a time, by covenant. Within the terms of this covenant the one is a servant, the other a master; beyond it they are two citizens of the commonwealth, two men.

I beg the reader particularly to observe that this is not only the notion which servants themselves entertain of their own condition; domestic service is looked upon by masters in the same light, and the precise limits of authority and obedience are as clearly settled in the mind of the one as in that of the other.

When the greater part of the community have long attained a condition nearly alike and when equality is an old and acknowledged fact, the public mind, which is never affected by exceptions, assigns certain general limits to the value of man, above or below which no man can long remain placed. It is in vain that wealth and poverty, authority and obedience, accidentally interpose great distances between two men; public opinion, founded upon the usual order of things, draws them to a common level and creates a species of imaginary equality between them, in spite of the real inequality of their conditions. This all-powerful opinion penetrates at length even into the hearts of those whose interest might arm them to resist it; it affects their judgment while it subdues their will.

In their inmost convictions the master and the servant no longer perceive any deep-seated difference between them, and they neither hope nor fear to meet with either at any time. They are therefore subject neither to disdain nor to anger, and they discern in each other neither humility nor pride. The master holds the contract of service to be the only source of his power, and the servant regards it as the only cause of his obedience. They do not quarrel about their reciprocal situations, but each knows his own and keeps it.

的一致,主人为什么有支配权,而仆人却不得不服从呢?他们之间并非天生就有高低之分,只是根据契约暂时如此。在契约规定的范围内,一方是仆人,而另一方则为主人。在契约的范围之外,他们是两个公民,两个平等的人。

我希望读者特别注意的是,这不仅是仆人处于他们自身的地位而持有的意志。主人和仆人都有这样的看法,他们的头脑中对权威和服从的界限都很明确。

但社会中的大部分人长久地生活在一个近乎相似的环境中,而平等又已是一个陈旧而熟识的事实存在,则从未被偏见腐蚀过的人们的思想,一般都会对人的价值作出一定的限定,任何人要想长时间的超出或低于这个界限,都是不可能的。贫穷和富贵、命令和服从,虽然偶尔会在人们之间形成巨大的差距,但这都没什么。建立在一般事物规律基础之上的公共意志,将人们牵引着走向同一水平,并且在他们之间产生一种假象的平等地位,尽管他们的实际生活中的地位并不平等。这种拥有无比强大力量的观念甚至最终渗入到了那些自己的利益与之冲突的人们的心中。它在影响着他们的判断的同时,也在抑制着他们的意志。

主人和仆人在他们的内心深处不再感到彼此之间存在根深蒂固的差别。他们不再害怕在任何时候与对方相处了。因此,主人不会轻视仆人,仆人也不会记恨主人,他们对待彼此时再不怀有高高在上或卑谦的感情。主人认为他们手中的契约是他们的权力的唯一来源,而仆人也认为这是他们服从的唯一原因。他们不会因为相互的地位而起争执,因为他们都很清楚自己的位置并且自觉地遵守。

In the French army the common soldier is taken from nearly the same class as the officer and may hold the same commissions; out of the ranks he considers himself entirely equal to his military superiors, and in point of fact he is so; but when under arms, he does not hesitate to obey, and his obedience is not the less prompt, precise, and ready, for being voluntary and defined. This example may give a notion of what takes place between masters and servants in democratic communities.

It would be preposterous to suppose that those warm and deepseated affections which are sometimes kindled in the domestic service of aristocracy will ever spring up between these two men, or that they will exhibit strong instances of self-sacrifice. In aristocracies masters and servants live apart, and frequently their only intercourse is through a third person; yet they commonly stand firmly by one another. In democratic countries the master and the servant are close together: they are in daily personal contact, but their minds do not intermingle; they have common occupations, hardly ever common interests.

Among such a people the servant always considers himself as a sojourner in the dwelling of his masters. He knew nothing of their forefathers; he will see nothing of their descendants; he has nothing lasting to expect from them. Why, then, should he identify his life with theirs, and whence should so strange a surrender of himself proceed? The reciprocal position of the two men is changed; their mutual relations must be so, too.

In all that precedes I wish that I could depend upon the example of the Americans as a whole; but I cannot do this without drawing careful distinctions regarding persons and places. In the South of the Union slavery exists; all that I have just said is consequently inapplicable there. In the North the majority of servants are either freedmen or the children of freedmen; these persons occupy an uncertain position in the public estimation; by the laws they are brought up to the level of their masters; by the manners of the country they are firmly

在法国的军队中,普通士兵的出身与他们的长官平等,可能还持有着与其长官相同的任务。除了军衔之外,他们认为自己与长官是完全平等的,而且事实上也是如此。但是,在部队里,他会决不犹豫地服从命令,而且他的服从一定是非常迅速、精确和随时的,因为这种服从是他们自愿的并且有明文规定的。这个例子可以说明在民主社会中主人和仆人之间的关系。

如果你以为那种偶尔发生在贵族阶级家臣身上的热情而深切的热爱或者他们强烈的自我奉献精神也会发生在民主社会的主仆之间,那就显得很荒谬了。在贵族制度下,主仆只能偶尔相见,他们之间的对话也往往由第三者传达。但是,两者的关系是稳固的。在民主国家,主仆之间距离不远,每天都要打交道,但他们并不交流思想。他们的工作是相同的,但他们的利益绝不一致。

在这样的民族中,仆人们总是认为自己是主人家里的寄居者。他不了解主人的家世背景,也不会与主人家的子孙有任何接触。他们对主人不抱任何长远的希望。那么,是什么原因使他们要把自己与其主人的生活牵扯在一起?又是什么时候开始产生那种奇怪的牺牲精神的呢?这是因为,他们两者之间的地位发生了变化。果然这样的话,他们的关系自然也要随之变化。

以上所有的论述,我希望都能在美国人的实例中找到依据。但是,我也不能不注意人物和地点的选择。联邦南部还存在着奴隶制度。所以我以上的论述在那里并不适用。在联邦北部,那里的大多数奴隶要么是自由之身,要么其子女就是自由人。这些人在社会中的地位不明确。他们依靠法律上升到与自己的主人平等的地位。但是就民情来说,他们仍旧牢固的处于下层。他

kept below it. They do not themselves clearly know their proper place and are almost always either insolent or craven.

But in the Northern states, especially in New England, there are a certain number of whites who agree, for wages, to yield a temporary obedience to the will of their fellow citizens. I have heard that these servants commonly perform the duties of their situations with punctuality and intelligence and that, without thinking themselves naturally inferior to the person who orders them, they submit without reluctance to obey him. They appeared to me to carry into service some of those manly habits which independence and equality create. Having once selected a hard way of life, they do not seek to escape from it by indirect means; and they have sufficient respect for themselves not to refuse to their masters that obedience which they have freely promised. On their part, masters require nothing of their servants but the faithful and rigorous performance of the covenant: they do not ask for marks of respect, they do not claim their love or devoted attachment; it is enough that, as servants, they are exact and honest.

It would not, then, be true to assert that in democratic society the relation of servants and masters is disorganized; it is organized on another footing; the rule is different, but there is a rule.

It is not my purpose to inquire whether the new state of things that I have just described is inferior to that which preceded it or simply different. Enough for me that it is fixed and determined; for what is most important to meet with among men is not any given ordering, but order.

But what shall I say of those sad and troubled times at which equality is established in the midst of the tumult of revolution, when democracy, after having been introduced into the state of society, still struggles with difficulty against the prejudices and manners of the country? The laws, and partially public opinion, already declare that no natural or permanent inferiority exists between the servant and the master. But this new belief has not yet reached the innermost convictions of the latter, or rather his heart rejects it; in the secret persuasion

们自己并不十分清楚自己的位置,所以他们总是表现得近乎无理和懦弱。

但是在联邦北部,尤其是在新英格兰,有一定数目的白人,他们自愿为了薪酬而暂时服从其他同胞们的意志。我了解到,这些仆人一般遵守职责工作认真,并且他们在付出劳动的时候,并不认为自己低人一等。所以在服从主人的命令时也不会有任何的犹豫。在我看来,他们将一些独立和平等产生的有气魄的刚毅习性带进了奴役工作。他们一旦选择了这种艰苦的生活方式,就不会去想尽办法逃避。他们尊重自己,不会拒绝服从他们的主人,因为这些都是他们自愿允诺的。对他们来说,主人对仆人的要求无非是忠诚和严谨的服务。他们不要求从仆人那里获得尊敬,也不需要他们爱自己,为自己献身。只要仆人尽心工作并且忠诚,就足够了。

因此,认为民主制度下的主仆关系混乱的看法是不正确的。他们之间的关系是用另一种方式规定的。规矩虽然不同,但是还是有的。

我在这里并不想去研究我所说的这种新情况是否不如以前的情况或者只是与以前的情况不同,我只想说,这种情况是既定的,有规章可循的。因为人与人之间的最重要东西不在于任何既定的规矩,而在于秩序。

但是,对那些在令人悲伤和动乱的年代中在处于变革中的社会中建立起来的平等,并且民主在被运用到社会体制中后,仍旧艰难地与偏见和国家的民情相抗衡的情况下,我还能说什么呢?法律和一部分公共意志已经宣称,在仆人和主人之间不存在任何永恒不变的贵贱之分。但是这一新的理念还没能深入主人阶层的人们的头脑,或者说主人从心里反对它。在他们的心里,仍然认

of his mind the master thinks that he belongs to a peculiar and superior race; he dares not say so, but he shudders at allowing himself to be dragged to the same level. His authority over his servants becomes timid and at the same time harsh; he has already ceased to entertain for them the feelings of patronizing kindness which long uncontested power always produces, and he is surprised that, being changed himself, his servant changes also. He wants his attendants to form regular and permanent habits, in a condition of domestic service that is only temporary; he requires that they should appear contented with and proud of a servile condition, which they will one day shake off, that they should sacrifice themselves to a man who can neither protect nor ruin them, and, in short, that they should contract an indissoluble engagement to a being like themselves and one who will last no longer than they will.

Among aristocratic nations it often happens that the condition of domestic service does not degrade the character of those who enter upon it, because they neither know nor imagine any other; and the amazing inequality that is manifest between them and their master appears to be the necessary and unavoidable consequence of some hidden law of Providence.

In democracies the condition of domestic service does not degrade the character of those who enter upon it, because it is freely chosen and adopted for a time only, because it is not stigmatized by public opinion and creates no permanent inequality between the servant and the master.

But while the transition from one social condition to another is going on, there is almost always a time when men's minds fluctuate between the aristocratic notion of subjection and the democratic notion of obedience. Obedience then loses its moral importance in the eyes of him who obeys; he no longer considers it as a species of divine obligation, and he does not yet view it under its purely human aspect; it has to him no character of sanctity or of justice, and he submits to it as to a degrading but profitable condition.

为自己独特且高高在上。但是,他们虽不敢明说,但是对被迫平级这一趋势心含不安。他们在使唤仆人的时候,心里既胆怯又表现得很严厉。他们对自己的仆人已不再有那种因为长期稳定的权力而产生的那种想要施舍以博得别人的感激的那种感情。他感到奇怪的是,在他自己被改变的同时,他的仆人也在发生变化。他所希望自己的仆人形成的那种固定不变的有规律的习惯,在民主的环境下是不稳定的。他要求他们的仆人对自己奴役的地位感到满足,尽管迟早有一天他们会摆脱这份工作,他们希望仆人能够对主人尽忠效力,对他的主人既不能保护他,也不能损害他。最后,通过长期的联系,他们对那些与自己相同,但处境不如自己的人表示关心。

在贵族制国家里,仆人往往并不因为受人支配而感到下贱,因为他们只知道做仆人,除此之外一无所知,他们认为与主人之间存在的巨大差异,是上帝的某项神秘法律的必然的和不可避免的结果。

在民主社会中,家仆的地位并不会使从事仆人工作的人们降低自己的品格。因为这都是人们自愿选择的结果,而且这种关系也是暂时的。社会舆论并不贬低它,也不会在主人和仆人之间产生永久的不平等。

但是,当社会状态从一个向另一个转换的时候,几乎总有一段时期,人们的思想会在贵族制的臣服观念和民主社会的服从观念之间摇摆不定。服从于是就在那些需要服从的人们眼中失去了其道德价值,他也不再认为服从是某种神圣的义务,但也没能从纯粹的人的角度加以判断。对他们来说,服从既不神圣也不公正。他把服从看作是不体面的有利可图的行为。

At that period a confused and imperfect phantom of equality haunts the minds of servants; they do not at once perceive whether the equality to which they are entitled is to be found within or without the pale of domestic service, and they rebel in their hearts against a subordination to which they have subjected themselves and from which they derive actual profit. They consent to serve and they blush to obey; they like the advantages of service, but not the master; or, rather, they are not sure that they ought not themselves to be masters, and they are inclined to consider him who orders them as an unjust usurper of their own rights.

Then it is that the dwelling of every citizen offers a spectacle somewhat analogous to the gloomy aspect of political society. A secret and internal warfare is going on there between powers ever rivals and suspicious of one another: the master is ill-natured and weak, the servant ill-natured and intractable; the one constantly attempts to evade by unfair restrictions his obligation to protect and to remunerate, the other his obligation to obey. The reins of domestic government dangle between them, to be snatched at by one or the other. The lines that divide authority from oppression, liberty from license, and right from might are to their eyes so jumbled together and confused that no one knows exactly what he is or what he may be or what he ought to be. Such a condition is not democracy, but revolution.

在那个时期,仆人们的思想被一种对于平等的混乱的不完整的印象所牵引着。他们不能立刻看出是否平等对他们来说,是在摆脱奴役地位之后还是之前就能够享受得到的。而且,在他们心中存在着一种逆反心理,他们反对自己不得不服从的从属地位,虽然他们从中获得了利益。他们虽然同意去从事奴役工作,但是他们羞于自己的工作。他们只喜欢奴役工作带来的好处,但是不喜欢自己的主人。或者说,他们不知道自己为什么没有成为主人阶级的人,而总是不公正地把奴役他们的人视为剥夺了他们的权利。

这样,在每个公民的家里便出现了同政治社会中阴暗面相似的现象:一些互相猜疑的敌对势力之间不断地暗中较劲。主人阶级心怀恶意并且自身软弱,仆人也是心怀不轨而难以对付。主人希望通过不公平的制约条件推卸自己对于仆人应承担的保护和供养的义务,而仆人也设法摆脱自己服从的义务。渴望管理家政大权的激情在两者之间愈演愈烈,大家都想夺权在手。于是,权威和专横、自由和任性、权利与本分之间的界限在他们的眼中变得混乱纠缠不清。没人明确地知道自己做了什么应该去做什么。这样的一种状态不是民主的,而是属于战争的。

CHAPTER VI

How Democratic Institutions And Manners Tend To Raise Rents And Shorten The Terms Of Leases

What has been said of servants and masters is applicable to a certain extent to landowners and farming tenants, but this subject deserves to be considered by itself.

In America there are, properly speaking, no farming tenants; every man owns the ground he tills. It must be admitted that democratic laws tend greatly to increase the number of landowners and to diminish that of farming tenants. Yet what takes place in the United States is much less attributable to the institutions of the country than to the country itself. In America land is cheap and anyone may easily become a landowner; its returns are small and its produce cannot well be divided between a landowner and a farmer. America therefore stands alone in this respect, as well as in many others, and it would be a mistake to take it as an example.

I believe that in democratic as well as in aristocratic countries there will be landowners and tenants, but the connection existing between them will be of a different kind. In aristocracies the hire of a farm is paid to the landlord, not only in rent, but in respect, regard, and duty; in democracies the whole is paid in cash. When estates are divided and passed from hand to hand, and the permanent connection that existed between families and the soil is dissolved, the landowner and the tenant are only casually brought into contact. They meet for a moment to settle the conditions of the agreement and then

第六章 民主制度和民情是如何 提高租金并缩短租期的

    关于仆人和主人的论述,适用于一定意义上的地主和佃户之间的关系,但是这个主题需要单独讨论。

    在美国,确切地说,是不存在佃户的。每个人都是自己耕种的土地的主人。我们必须承认,民主的法律趋向于大力地增长地主的人数,同时减少佃户的数量。但是,美国发生的一切,主要还是归因于它所处的环境,而极少地是因为其社会制度。在美国,土地很便宜,每个人都能轻松地成为地主。但是地主的回报却很少,靠土地的收成只能勉强地使农夫和地主糊口。因此,美国人在这方面和其他国家一样。如果以他为例来讨论佃户和地主的关系的话,恐怕不合适。

    我相信,在民主国家和在贵族制国家一样,将来都会出现地主和佃户。但是他们两者的关系在这两种社会中是完全不同的。在贵族制国家中,租用土地需要付租金给地主,这不仅仅是因为租借关系,而且是出于对地主的尊敬和爱戴。在民主国家中,只要付钱就行。但土地被划分并从一个人的手中转到另一个人的手中,那种存在于家庭和土地之间的永恒的联系就被破坏了。地主和佃户只是因为偶然的原因发生关系。他们见面是为了商定

lose sight of each other; they are two strangers brought together by a common interest, who keenly talk over a matter of business, the sole object of which is to make money.

In proportion as property is subdivided and wealth distributed over the country, the community is filled with people whose former opulence is declining, and with others whose fortunes are of recent growth and whose wants increase more rapidly than their resources. For all such persons the smallest pecuniary profit is a matter of importance, and none of them feel disposed to waive any of their claims or to lose any portion of their income.

As ranks are intermingled, and as very large as well as very scanty fortunes become more rare, every day brings the social condition of the landowner nearer to that of the farmer: the one has not naturally any uncontested superiority over the other; between two men who are equal and not at ease in their circumstances, the contract of hire is exclusively an affair of money.

A man whose estate extends over a whole district and who owns a hundred farms is well aware of the importance of gaining at the same time the affections of some thousands of men. This object appears to call for his exertions, and to attain it he will readily make considerable sacrifices. But he who owns a hundred acres is insensible to similar considerations, and cares but little to win the private regard of his tenant.

An aristocracy does not expire, like a man, in a single day; the aristocratic principle is slowly undermined in men's opinion before it is attacked in their laws. Long before open war is declared against it, the tie that had hitherto united the higher classes to the lower may be seen to be gradually relaxed. Indifference and contempt are betrayed by one class, jealousy and hatred by the others. The intercourse between rich and poor becomes less frequent and less kind, and rents are raised. This is not the consequence of a democratic revolution, but its certain harbinger; for an aristocracy that has lost the affections of the people once and forever is like a tree dead at the root, which is the more easily torn up by the winds the higher its branches have spread.

协议,之后就会再见面了。他们是因为共同的利益而被带到一起的两个陌生人,大家都只是热心于谈生意,而这一行为的唯一目的就是为了钱。

随着地产的日益分割和财富日益向全国各地分散,国内到处便出现了家道中落的破落户,还有一些人一夜暴富,而另一些人总是欲求不满。对于所有这些人来说,即使是一点微薄的收入都是一件大事,没人想放弃自己的一点点好处和使自己的收入遭受损失。

随着各个阶级的相互融合,并且随着社会中巨富和赤贫的人变得罕见,地主在社会中地位一天天变得接近佃户:地主与佃户相比不再具有天生的优势。在两个地位平等和生活紧张的人们之间达成的雇佣协议,完全是一种金钱关系。

一个地产遍及整个地区并且拥有大片农场的人,就非常懂得在获得金钱的同时,赢得人们的爱戴也是很重要的。为了达到这个目的使他付出了巨大的努力,而且他愿意作出一些牺牲。但是拥有面积很小的土地的人,在面对这些的时候就显得有些麻木不仁了,而且他对赢得佃户们的热爱也不那么热心。

贵族制度不会像人那样在一天之内就会消亡。贵族制度的原则是缓慢地在人们的观念中遭到破坏之后,才受到法律的攻击。早在对抗它的战争爆发之前,链接着上层阶级和下层阶级之间的纽带就已经变得松弛起来。一个阶级暴露出他们对另一个阶级的漠不关心和蔑视,而另一个阶级对他们则充满嫉妒和仇恨。富人和穷人之间的关系变得不那么轻松友善,于是租金暴涨。这一切并不是民主革命的终结,而只是一个预示。对一个失去了人民爱戴的贵族制度来说,就仿佛一棵在根部烂掉的树,长得愈高枝叶愈茂盛,就越容易被风吹倒。

In the course of the last fifty years the rents of farms have amazingly increased, not only in France, but throughout the greater part of Europe. The remarkable improvements that have taken place in agriculture and manufactures within the same period do not suffice, in my opinion, to explain this fact; recourse must be had to another cause, more powerful and more concealed. I believe that cause is to be found in the democratic institutions which several European nations have adopted and in the democratic passions which more or less agitate all the rest.

I have frequently heard great English landowners congratulate themselves that at the present day they derive a much larger income from their estates than their fathers did. They have perhaps good reason to be glad, but most assuredly they do not know what they are glad of. They think they are making a clear gain when it is in reality only an exchange; their influence is what they are parting with for cash, and what they gain in money will before long be lost in power.

There is yet another sign by which it is easy to know that a great democratic revolution is going on or approaching. In the Middle Ages almost all lands were leased for lives or for very long terms; the domestic economy of that period shows that leases for ninety-nine years were more frequent then than leases for twelve years are now. Men then believed that families were immortal; men's conditions seemed settled forever, and the whole of society appeared to be so fixed that it was not supposed anything would ever be stirred or shaken in its structure. In ages of equality the human mind takes a different bent: the prevailing notion is that nothing abides, and man is haunted by the thought of mutability. Under this impression the landowner and the tenant himself are instinctively averse to protracted terms of obligation; they are afraid of being tied up tomorrow by the contract that benefits them today. They do not trust themselves; they are afraid that, their standards changing,

　　在过去 50 年中,不仅法国地租猛涨,而且这种现象遍及欧洲大部分国家。在这一时期在农业和制造业发生的最显著的进步,在我看来用来解释这一现象都还很不够。为了说明这一现象,必须依靠另一个更有力更隐蔽的原因。我相信,这个原因存在于民主制度中。许多欧洲国家都已采用了这一制度,并且这一制度在民主的激情中或多或少地激发了其他各国。

　　我曾经常常听到英国一些大的地主为自己庆祝,因为他们今天获得了比他们的父辈们从土地上获得的多得多的收入。他们也许有充分的理由为此感到高兴,但是我们更确定的却是他们并不知道自己为什么高兴。他们认为自己得到了一笔纯收入,但是其实这只是现实生活中的一笔交易。他们获得了金钱却失去了自己的影响力,并在得到金钱后不久就会在权力上有所损失。

　　还有一个迹象可以使人容易感到,一场民主大革命正在进行或即将来临。在中世纪,所有的土地几乎永世出租或至少是长期出租。在我们研究中世纪的家庭经济时可以见到,那时为期 99 年的租期比我们现在为期 12 年的租期还要普遍。在那个时代,人们认为家庭是永存不灭的,人们的身份似乎是永远固定不变的,整个社会也好像固若磐石,以致人们认为决不会发生任何动乱。但在平等的时代,人们的思想发生了变化。他们不难形成一种观念,认为没有什么事是永远不变的。事物无常的观念控制了人们的思想。在这种思想情绪的支配下,地主以及佃户本人就对长期的义务产生一种本能的嫌恶感。他们双方都害怕自己被眼前对他们有利的租约长期束缚下去。他们忐忑不安,不知道什么时候自己的处境就发生骤变。他们感到自身难保,唯恐自己的生

they may have trouble in ridding themselves of the thing which had been the object of their longing. And they are right to fear this, for in democratic times what is most unstable, in the midst of the instability of everything, is the heart of man.

活方式一旦有变,就可能因放弃昔日习以为常的东西而感到伤心。他们的这种担忧是有理由的,因为在民主的时代,在一切变化的事物中最容易变化的就是人心。

CHAPTER VII

Influence Of Democracy On Wages

Most of the remarks that I have already made in speaking of masters and servants may be applied to masters and workmen. As the gradations of the social scale come to be less observed, while the great sink and the humble rise and poverty as well as opulence ceases to be hereditary, the distance, both in reality and in opinion, which heretofore separated the workman from the master is lessened every day. The workman conceives a more lofty opinion of his rights, of his future, of himself; he is filled with new ambition and new desires, he is harassed by new wants. Every instant he views with longing eyes the profits of his employer; and in order to share them he strives to dispose of his labor at a higher rate, and he generally succeeds at length in the attempt.

In democratic countries as well as elsewhere most of the branches of productive industry are carried on at a small cost by men little removed by their wealth or education above the level of those whom they employ. These manufacturing speculators are extremely numerous; their interests differ; they cannot therefore easily concert or combine their exertions. On the other hand, the workmen have always some sure resources which enable them to refuse to work when they cannot get what they conceive to be the fair price of their labor. In the constant struggle for wages that is going on between these two classes, their strength is divided and success alternates from one to the other.

It is even probable that in the end the interest of the working

第七章　民主对工资的影响

在前面,我曾讲过的关于仆人和主人的叙述,大部分也可用于雇主和工人。随着社会等级的界限日益模糊,以前的大人物不断的没落,而微小的人物在不断的上升,人们的贫困和富裕已不再受祖辈的限制,工人和雇主之间存在的现实上的和观点上的差距也在逐渐缩小。工人对他们的权利、前途和自身产生了越来越崇高的理想;内心充满了新的雄心和新的希望,并不断地提出新的要求。每一秒钟,他们都把自己贪婪的目光投向其雇主的利益;为了能同雇主分享好处,他们努力争取提高劳动报酬,而且照例能够达到目的。

在民主国家也同在其他国家一样,大部分生产业的分支是由在财富和教育上都高于所雇工人的一般水平的人经营的,而且都很赚钱。这种实业家的人数很多;他们的利益各不相同;因此,他们很难联合起来,并肩努力。而在另一方面,工人当他们认为自己的劳动报酬不公平时,几乎总有把握拒绝为雇主工作。这两个阶级之间的不断的斗争,几乎都是为了工资,双方势力相当,互有胜负。

但是,可以肯定,工人阶级的利益将会越来越盛行,因为在他

class will prevail, for the high wages which they have already obtained make them every day less dependent on their masters, and as they grow more independent, they have greater facilities for obtaining a further increase of wages.

I shall take for example that branch of productive industry which is still at the present day the most generally followed in France and in almost all the countries of the world, the cultivation of the soil. In France most of those who labor for hire in agriculture are themselves owners of certain plots of ground, which just enable them to subsist without working for anyone else. When these laborers come to offer their services to a neighboring landowner or farmer, if he refuses them a certain rate of wages they retire to their own small property and await another opportunity.

I think that, on the whole, it may be asserted that a slow and gradual rise of wages is one of the general laws of democratic communities. In proportion as social conditions become more equal, wages rise; and as wages are higher, social conditions become more equal.

But a great and gloomy exception occurs in our own time. I have shown, in a preceding chapter, that aristocracy, expelled from political society, has taken refuge in certain departments of productive industry and has established its sway there under another form; this powerfully affects the rate of wages.

As a large capital is required to embark in the great manufacturing speculations to which I allude, the number of persons who enter upon them is exceedingly limited; as their number is small, they can easily concert together and fix the rate of wages as they please.

Their workmen, on the contrary, are exceedingly numerous, and the number of them is always increasing; for from time to time an extraordinary run of business takes place during which wages are inordinately high, and they attract the surrounding population to the factories. But when men have once embraced that line of life, we have already seen that they cannot quit it again, because they soon contract habits of body and mind which unfit them for any other sort of toil. These men have generally but little education and industry, with but few resources; they stand, therefore, almost at the mercy of the master.

When competition or some other fortuitous circumstance lessens

们中间,那些已经获得的高工资的人将逐渐减少对雇主的依赖,并变得越来越独立,他们会为了争取到更多工资而继续提高。

现在我将举个例子说明,那就是目前在法国和世界上的几乎所有国家还很兴盛的一种实业,即种植业。在法国,被他人雇佣种地的人,大部分也拥有自己的一小块土地,这一小块土地,可以让他们不去当雇工也可以勉强维持生活。这些人向大地主或附近农户提供劳动力时,如果对方出的工钱太低,他们可以拒绝受雇,并留在家里料理自己的那块地和等待另一个的机会。

就整体情况来看,我认为工资缓慢的和逐渐的增长是在民主社会发生作用的一般规律之一。人们的身份越来越平等,工资也越来越高;反过来,工资越来越提高,人的社会身份也越来越平等。

但是,在我们目前这个时代,却出现了一个十分令人沮丧的例外。我在前面某一章已经讲过,被逐出政治社会的贵族已经涉足到某些生产领域的特定部门,并通过另一种形式在其中建立起他们的统治地位。这个情况,对工资的水平发生了极其有力的影响。

只有拥有巨大资本的人,才能创办我所说的这种大型实业,因为有能力创办这种实业的人是少之又少;由于人数少,他们就可以轻易地彼此联合在起来,并随意规定工资。

反之,他们的工人为数众多,而且其数量在不断增加;因为有时在生意非常顺利时,工人的工资也会特别高,他们把附近的人也吸引到工厂里来。但是,人们一旦进入工厂劳动,我们可以看到他们将不能再摆脱这种劳动,因为他们在工厂里很快养成的身体和思想方面的习惯,使他们不适于再从事其他劳动。一般来讲,这些人文化水平低,手艺差,积蓄少;因此,他们几乎完全依靠雇主的怜悯才能被雇佣。

当竞争和其他意外情况使雇主的利润减少时,雇主几乎可以

his profits, he can reduce the wages of his workmen almost at pleasure and make from them what he loses by the chances of business. Should the workmen strike, the master, who is a rich man, can very well wait, without being ruined, until necessity brings them back to him; but they must work day by day or they die, for their only property is in their hands. They have long been impoverished by oppression, and the poorer they become, the more easily they may be oppressed; they can never escape from this fatal circle of cause and consequence.

It is not surprising, then, that wages, after having sometimes suddenly risen, are permanently lowered in this branch of industry; whereas in other callings the price of labor, which generally increases but little, is nevertheless constantly augmented. This state of dependence and wretchedness in which a part of the manufacturing population of our time live forms an exception to the general rule, contrary to the state of all the rest of the community; but for this very reason no circumstance is more important or more deserving of the special consideration of the legislator; for when the whole of society is in motion, it is difficult to keep any one class stationary, and when the greater number of men are opening new paths to fortune, it is no less difficult to make the few support in peace their wants and their desires.

随意降低工资,并且轻易地把损失从雇工的身上再找回来。如果工人一致起来罢工,那些富裕的雇主,在没有破产的情况下,能够静下心来等待,他们知道工人一定会再回到他们身边;而工人只能日复一日的劳动,否则他们就会饿死,因为他们唯一的财产就是他们的双手。雇主的长期压迫已使他们很贫穷,而且越穷就越容易受压迫;他们永远无法逃脱这样一个恶性循环的圈子。

因此,当一个行业的工资有时突然猛烈的上涨之后又陷入长期的谷中;而另一个行业的劳动报酬虽然一般只是缓慢地上升,但毕竟是不断增加的现象,我们不要感到奇怪。我们这个时代的产业人口所处的可悲的和依赖的地位,是一个特例,并与他们周围的人群形成了鲜明的对照;但是,正因为这个理由,任何其他情况都没有比这个情况更重要和更值得立法者的特别注意;因为当整个社会都在变动的时候,很难使一个阶级保持不变,而当大多数人都在为财富不断开拓新的道路时,也很难让某些人安然自得地去满足他们的需要和欲望。

CHAPTER VIII
Influence Of
Democracy On The Family

I have just examined the changes which the equality of conditions produces in the mutual relations of the several members of the community among democratic nations, and among the Americans in particular. I would now go deeper and inquire into the closer ties of family; my object here is not to seek for new truths, but to show in what manner facts already known are connected with my subject.

It has been universally remarked that in our time the several members of a family stand upon an entirely new footing towards each other; that the distance which formerly separated a father from his sons has been lessened; and that paternal authority, if not destroyed, is at least impaired.

Something analogous to this, but even more striking, may be observed in the United States. In America the family, in the Roman and aristocratic signification of the word, does not exist. All that remains of it are a few vestiges in the first years of childhood, when the father exercises, without opposition, that absolute domestic authority which the feebleness of his children renders necessary and which their interest, as well as his own incontestable superiority, warrants. But as soon as the young American approaches manhood, the ties of filial obedience are relaxed day by day; master of his thoughts, he is soon master of his conduct. In America there is, strictly speaking, no adolescence: at the close of boyhood the man appears and begins to trace out his own path.

第八章　民主对家庭的影响

以上，我考察了身份的平等在民主国家，尤其是在美国是怎样改变了公民之间相互关系的。现在，我要再深入一些，调查到家庭的内部；在这里，我的目的不是寻找新的真理，而是要说明那些已知的事实与我的题目有什么关系。

众所周知的，在我们这个时代，家庭的各个成员之间已经建立起一种全新的关系；父子之间在以往存在的差距已经被缩小；长辈的权威即使没有消失，至少也已经减弱。

类似的情况也见于美国，但它更使人吃惊。美国人对家庭的理解，就不像罗马人和贵族对家庭这个词的理解。美国人只是在童年时代的最初几年才隐约具有家庭的概念，在孩子的童年时期，当父亲实行绝对家庭专政时，子女不得抗拒。子女的软弱无力，使这种专政成为必要；而子女们的利益，以及父亲的无可争辩的权势，又使这种专政变得合情合理。但是，当美国人长大成年后，子女便不再重视必须服从父母意愿的做法；他们先是成为自己思想上的主人，不久又成为自己行动上的主人。严格说来，美国人没有青年时期：当少年时代刚一结束，他们便自己闯天下，开始走自己的人生道路。

— 1373 —

It would be an error to suppose that this is preceded by a domestic struggle in which the son has obtained by a sort of moral violence the liberty that his father refused him. The same habits, the same principles, which impel the one to assert his independence predispose the other to consider the use of that independence as an incontestable right. The former does not exhibit any of those rancorous or irregular passions which disturb men long after they have shaken off an established authority; the latter feels none of that bitter and angry regret which is apt to survive a bygone power. The father foresees the limits of his authority long beforehand, and when the time arrives, he surrenders it without a struggle; the son looks forward to the exact period at which he will be his own master, and he enters upon his freedom without precipitation and without effort, as a possession which is his own and which no one seeks to wrest from him. ①

It may perhaps be useful to show how these changes which take place in family relations are closely connected with the social and political revolution that is approaching its consummation under our own eyes.

There are certain great social principles that a people either introduces everywhere or tolerates nowhere. In countries which are aristocratically constituted with all the gradations of rank, the government never makes a direct appeal to the mass of the governed;

---

① The Americans, however, have not yet thought fit to strip the parent, as has been done in France, of one of the chief elements of parental authority by depriving him of the power of disposing of his property at his death. In the United States there are no restrictions on the powers of a testator.

In this respect, as in almost all others, it is easy to perceive that if the political legislation of the Americans is much more democratic than that of the French, the civil legislation of the latter is infinitely more democratic than that of the former. This may easily be accounted for. The civil legislation of France was the work of a man who saw that it was his interest to satisfy the democratic passions of his contemporaries in all that was not directly and immediately hostile to his own power. He was willing to allow some popular principles to regulate the distribution of property and the government of families, provided they were not to be introduced into the administration of public affairs. While the torrent of democracy overwhelmed the civil laws of the country, he hoped to find an easy shelter behind its political institutions. This policy was at once both adroit and selfish; but a compromise of this kind could not last, for in the end political institutions never fail to become the image and expression of civil society, and in this sense it may be said that nothing is more political in a nation than its civil legislation.

如果认为这是一场家庭的内部斗争,儿子在这场斗争中是通过暴力用违反道德的办法取得了父亲拒绝给予他的自由,那将是错误的。促使儿子宣称自己独立的那些习惯与原则,同样也适用于父亲承认儿子享有的独立权利是他所不能抗拒的。因此,前者绝对不会有那种人们在摆脱束缚他们的权势之后还将长期将怨恨埋在心中的感情;而后者也决不会产生那种在失去权势之后通常会随之而来的痛苦和气愤的遗憾感觉。也就是说,父亲早已预见到他的权威的有限性,当这个期限一到,他便毫无怨言地放弃;而儿子也已事先知道总有一天,他将成为自己的主人,他能不费吹灰之力就获得自由,就像一份财产必须归他所有,谁也不想来抢似的。①

试述一下家庭方面发生的这种变化是怎样与我们目前即将完成的社会和政治的改革密切的联系在一起的,也许会很有用的。

有一些特定的重大的社会原则,或被一个国家到处推行,或不允许它在任何地方存在。在等级森严的贵族制国家,政府从不直接向其统治下的全体臣民呼吁或求援;因为人们都是彼此连接

---

① 美国人还没有想过要像法国人一样剥夺其长辈在临死前对财产的自由处置权。美国未对立遗嘱的人有过任何限制。

在这种情况下,就像在其他所有情况下一样,我们可以很容易地发现,如果美国的政治法规比法国的政治法规更加民主,那么法国的民法一定比美国的民法民主。其原因很简单,法兰西民法是一个人的作品,这个人清楚地明白满足他同时代人的民主激情是他自己的利益所在,并且不会直接与他的权力相冲突。如果它们没有在国家的行政事务中被广泛应用,那么他宁愿有一些调整家庭财产分割的普遍原则。当民主的洪流涌进国家民法中时,他希望能在政治制度背后找到一个庇护所。这个政策是机智的,同时也是自私的;但这种妥协是不会持久的,因为最终政治制度肯定会具有民事社会的外形和内涵,因此,我们可以说,在一个国家里,再没有什么比民法更富有政治性了。

as men are united together, it is enough to lead the foremost; the rest will follow. This is applicable to the family as well as to all aristocracies that have a head. Among aristocratic nations social institutions recognize, in truth, no one in the family but the father; children are received by society at his hands; society governs him, he governs them. Thus the parent not only has a natural right but acquires a political right to command them; he is the author and the support of his family, but he is also its constituted ruler.

In democracies, where the government picks out every individual singly from the mass to make him subservient to the general laws of the community, no such intermediate person is required; a father is there, in the eye of the law, only a member of the community, older and richer than his sons.

When most of the conditions of life are extremely unequal and the inequality of these conditions is permanent, the notion of a superior grows upon the imaginations of men; if the law invested him with no privileges, custom and public opinion would concede them. When, on the contrary, men differ but little from each other and do not always remain in dissimilar conditions of life, the general notion of a superior becomes weaker and less distinct; it is vain for legislation to strive to place him who obeys very much beneath him who commands; the manners of the time bring the two men nearer to one another and draw them daily towards the same level.

Although the legislation of an aristocratic people grants no peculiar privileges to the heads of families, I shall not be the less convinced that their power is more respected and more extensive than in a democracy; for I know that, whatever the laws may be, superiors always appear higher and inferiors lower in aristocracies than among democratic nations.

When men live more for the remembrance of what has been than for the care of what is, and when they are more given to attend to what their ancestors thought than to think themselves, the father is the natural and necessary tie between the past and the present, the link by which the ends of these two chains are connected.

在一起的,所以只要上级发号施令,其余的人就一定会服从。这种情况也适用于家庭和由一个人领导的所有贵族政体。在贵族制国家,社会实际上只承认身为一家之长的父亲的存在;做儿女的只是通过父亲来认识社会;社会管束做父亲的,而父亲又管束其子女。因此,做父亲的不仅有天赋的管教子女的权力,而且被赋予对子女发号施令的政治权力;他既是家庭的创造者,又是家庭的生活维持者,并且也是家庭的统治者。

在民主制度下,政府将使人民群众中的每一个人,都服从社会的一般法律,不需要有中间调和者的存在;父亲在法律的眼中,仅仅是一个比自己子女年龄大和更有钱的社会成员而已。

当大部分人的身份极不平等,而这种不平等又将永久存在的时候,关于首长的观念就在人们的想象中成长起来;即使法律没有赋予这个首长以特权,习惯和公共舆论也会让他拥有。反之,当人们彼此之间无大差别,而且总是保持一种不同的社会身份时,关于首长的一般观念就将日益淡薄和不明显;即使立法者硬凭自己的意志强把一个人安排在首长的位置上,叫他对一个下属发号施令,也是没有用的;因为相同的民情在使这两个人彼此日益相近,逐渐走向同一水平。

尽管我从未见到一个贵族制国家的立法机构曾赋予家长以独享的特权,我也不能不确信贵族制国家的家长的权力比民主国家的更受尊重和更为广泛;因为我知道,不管是什么样的法律,首长在贵族制国家总比在民主国家地位高,而下属的地位则更为低下。

当人们的生活主要是回忆已经发生的,而不是重视现在,当人们考虑最多的是祖先的想法而不是自己的想法的时候,做父亲的便成为过去和现在之间的天然的和必然的纽带,成为联系和连

In aristocracies, then, the father is not only the civil head of the family, but the organ of its traditions, the expounder of its customs, the arbiter of its manners. He is listened to with deference, he is addressed with respect, and the love that is felt for him is always tempered with fear.

When the condition of society becomes democratic and men adopt as their general principle that it is good and lawful to judge of all things for oneself, using former points of belief not as a rule of faith, but simply as a means of information, the power which the opinions of a father exercise over those of his sons diminishes as well as his legal power.

Perhaps the subdivision of estates that democracy brings about contributes more than anything else to change the relations existing between a father and his children. When the property of the father of a family is scanty, his son and himself constantly live in the same place and share the same occupations; habit and necessity bring them together and force them to hold constant communication. The inevitable consequence is a sort of familiar intimacy, which renders authority less absolute and which can ill be reconciled with the external forms of respect.

Now, in democratic countries the class of those who are possessed of small fortunes is precisely that which gives strength to the notions and a particular direction to the manners of the community. That class makes its opinions preponderate as universally as its will, and even those who are most inclined to resist its commands are carried away in the end by its example. I have known eager opponents of democracy who allowed their children to address them with perfect colloquial equality.

Thus at the same time that the power of aristocracy is declining, the austere, the conventional, and the legal part of parental authority vanishes and a species of equality prevails around the domestic hearth. I do not know, on the whole, whether society loses by the change, but I am inclined to believe that man individually is a gainer by it. I think that in proportion as manners and laws become more democratic, the relation of father and son becomes more intimate and more affectionate; rules and authority are less talked of, confidence and tenderness are often increased, and

结上一代和下一代的锁链。因此,在贵族政体下,父亲不仅是家庭的内部首领,而且是家庭传统的继承人,是习惯的解释人,是民情的仲裁人。他发表意见时,家庭成员要认真地听,必须以尊敬的态度对待他,并且对他的爱要始终充满温和与恐惧。

当社会情况变得更加民主,而人们将自己的判断作为一切基本准则,并认为这样做是正确和合理的,只把祖传的观念作为一种参考而不再视为行为准则的时候,父亲的见解对于子女的影响力,正如他的合法权力一样,将大大降低。

或许民主制度带来的对财产的分割,比起其他任何事情都更能改变父子的关系。当一家之主的父亲财产不多时,他和儿子将长期居住在一起,并且参加同样的劳动;习惯和需要将他们联合在一起,并迫使他们不断地彼此交谈。因此,在他们之间不得不产生一种不可避免的亲密关系,这种关系可以减少做父亲的权威的绝对性,并且不很重视尊敬的外在形式。

目前,在民主国家里,拥有这样少量财产的阶级,正是能够赋予思想力量和指导民情向一定特殊方向转变的阶级。这个阶级使它的意见,同时还有它的意志,占据绝对的优势,甚至连最想抗拒它的命令的人,最后也开始将他的做法视为范例。我就看到一些强烈反对民主的人,曾允许他的子女用口语来称呼他们。

因此,随着贵族权势的消失,父母的那种严苛的、已成惯例的和合法的权威也跟着消失了,而一种平等的关系在家庭内部逐渐盛行起来。总的来说,我不知道社会是否由于这种变化而受到了损失,但我确信个人却由此得到了好处。我认为,随着民情和法制的日益民主,父子关系也会更加亲密和温和;规矩和权威在逐渐减少,而信任和容忍在不断加深,看来,父子的天然联系是紧密

it would seem that the natural bond is drawn closer in proportion as the social bond is loosened.

In a democratic family the father exercises no other power than that which is granted to the affection and the experience of age; his orders would perhaps be disobeyed, but his advice is for the most part authoritative. Though he is not hedged in with ceremonial respect, his sons at least accost him with confidence; they have no settled form of addressing him, but they speak to him constantly and are ready to consult him every day. The master and the constituted ruler have vanished; the father remains. Nothing more is needed in order to judge of the difference between the two states of society in this respect than to peruse the family correspondence of aristocratic ages. The style is always correct, ceremonious, stiff, and so cold that the natural warmth of the heart can hardly be felt in the language. In democratic countries, on the contrary, the language addressed by a son to his father is always marked by mingled freedom, familiarity, and affection, which at once show that new relations have sprung up in the bosom of the family.

A similar revolution takes place in the mutual relations of children. In aristocratic families, as well as in aristocratic society, every place is marked out beforehand. Not only does the father occupy a separate rank, in which he enjoys extensive privileges, but even the children are not equal among themselves. The age and sex of each irrevocably determine his rank and secure to him certain privileges. Most of these distinctions are abolished or diminished by democracy.

In aristocratic families the eldest son, inheriting the greater part of the property and almost all the rights of the family, becomes the chief and to a certain extent the master of his brothers. Greatness and power are for him; for them, mediocrity and dependence. But it would be wrong to suppose that among aristocratic nations the privileges of the eldest son are advantageous to himself alone, or that they excite nothing but envy and hatred around him. The eldest son commonly endeavors to procure wealth and power for his brothers, because the

了,但他们的社会联系却松弛了。

在民主的家庭里,父亲除了被赋予子女对他的爱慕之情和向子女传授经验之外,并没有任何其他权力了;他的命令可能被人违背,但他的忠告一般还很具有权威性。虽然子女们对他不是毕恭毕敬,但至少对他表示信任;子女同他交谈没有固定的礼节,而是随时可以同他谈话,并经常向他请教。在这里,主人和统治者已经消失了,但父亲还依然存在。在判明两种社会情况在这方面的差异时,我们不需要其他任何信息,只要去考察一下贵族时代留下来的一些家书就可以了。书信的文体经常是工整、死板和僵硬的,而且文字冰冷得使人心里感觉不到一点温暖。反之,在民主国家里,儿子写给父亲的信的语言中,总透露着某些随意的、熟悉的和依恋的表现,一看之下就知道与家庭建立了新的关系。

同样的变革也发生在子女的相互关系中。在贵族的家庭里就如同像在贵族社会里一样,人人的地位是早已规定好的。不只是父亲在家庭里占有独立的级别,并享有广泛的特权,就是子女之间也不平等。子女的年龄和性别,永远决定着他们每个人在家里的地位,并确保他们享有一定的特权。这些差别中的大部分已被民主制度废除或减少了。

在贵族家庭里,长子继承大部分家产和几乎家庭中的全部权力,所以他将来必定会成为家族首领,而且在一定程度上成为兄弟们的主人。他拥有最高的权力;而兄弟们则要依附于他。但是,如果认为在贵族制国家,长子的特权只能给他自己带来好处,那也是错误的,因为这样不会为长子带来任何好处,只会引起兄弟们对他忌妒和憎恨。长子一般都竭尽全力帮助他的兄弟们制造财富和获得权势,因为一个家族的显赫必然反映在它的代表身

general splendor of the house is reflected back on him who represents it; the younger sons seek to back the elder brother in all his undertakings, because the greatness and power of the head of the family better enable him to provide for all its branches. The different members of an aristocratic family are therefore very closely bound together; their interests are connected, their minds agree, but their hearts are seldom in harmony.

Democracy also binds brothers to each other, but by very different means. Under democratic laws all the children are perfectly equal and consequently independent; nothing brings them forcibly together, but nothing keeps them apart; and as they have the same origin, as they are trained under the same roof, as they are treated with the same care, and as no peculiar privilege distinguishes or divides them, the affectionate and frank intimacy of early years easily springs up between them. Scarcely anything can occur to break the tie thus formed at the outset of life, for brotherhood brings them daily together without embarrassing them. It is not, then, by interest, but by common associations and by the free sympathy of opinion and of taste that democracy unites brothers to each other. It divides their inheritance, but allows their hearts and minds to unite. Such is the charm of these democratic manners that even the partisans of aristocracy are attracted by it; and after having experienced it for some time, they are by no means tempted to revert to the respectful and frigid observances of aristocratic families. They would be glad to retain the domestic habits of democracy if they might throw off its social conditions and its laws; but these elements are indissolubly united, and it is impossible to enjoy the former without enduring the latter.

The remarks I have made on filial love and fraternal affection are applicable to all the passions that emanate spontaneously from human nature itself.

If a certain mode of thought or feeling is the result of some peculiar condition of life, when that condition is altered nothing whatever remains of the thought or feeling. Thus a law may bind two members of the community very closely to each other; but that law being abolished, they stand asunder. Nothing was more

上;而且,弟弟也设法协助长兄进行一切事业,因为家族首领的显赫和权势会使他能更好地去扶持家族的各个分支。因此,贵族家庭的各个成员间会彼此联系得非常密切;他们的利益彼此联系,他们在思想上也极为一致,但是他们的心却很少互通。

民主制度通常把兄弟以不同的方式捆绑在一起。根据民主的法制,所有子女都是平等的和自主的;没有任何东西强制他们彼此接近,也没有任何东西迫使他们互相疏远;因为他们血统相同,在同一家庭里成长,受到同样的关怀,没有任何特权能区分他们或把他们分成等级,所以他们之间从小就容易产生亲密无间的手足情感。没有任何事情能破坏他们的感情,因为兄弟的情义在使他们日益接近,而不会使他们互相憎恨。因此,在民主制度下,使兄弟们互相接近的并不是利害关系,而是一种普通的结合,以及思想和爱好的自由共鸣。民主制度虽然分割了他们的财产,但能使他们的心灵与思想融和在一起。这就是民主的民情的魅力所在,以致拥护贵族制度的人也深深被它吸引;并在经历了一段时间后,他们情愿放弃贵族家庭的那种毕恭毕敬的和严酷冷漠的规矩。只要他们能够放弃他们原来的社会情况和法制,他们随时都可以接受民主制度下的家庭习惯;但是,这些因素还牵涉另一个问题,即不忍受民主的社会情况和法制,就享用不了民主的家庭习惯。

我所叙述的关于父子之爱和手足情义的一切,也同样适用于人性本身自发产生的一切情感。

假如一种思想和一种感情的特定方式是由人们的特殊社会情况所产生出来的,当这种情况一发生变化,这种思想与感情便不复存在。因此,法律也许可以把两个公民紧紧地联系在一起;但当这项法律被废除后,他们便各奔东西了。再没有任何事物比

strict than the tie that united the vassal to the lord under the feudal system; at the present day the two men do not know each other; the fear, the gratitude, and the affection that formerly connected them have vanished and not a vestige of the tie remains.

Such, however, is not the case with those feelings which are natural to mankind. Whenever a law attempts to tutor these feelings in any particular manner, it seldom fails to weaken them; by attempting to add to their intensity it robs them of some of their elements, for they are never stronger than when left to themselves.

Democracy, which destroys or obscures almost all the old conventional rules of society and which prevents men from readily assenting to new ones, entirely effaces most of the feelings to which these conventional rules have given rise; but it only modifies some others, and frequently imparts to them a degree of energy and sweetness unknown before.

Perhaps it is not impossible to condense into a single proposition the whole purport of this chapter, and of several others that preceded it. Democracy loosens social ties, but tightens natural ones; it brings kindred more closely together, while it throws citizens more apart.

封建社会把主仆联系起来的那种民情更具有紧密的联结作用了；但在今天，这两种人已互不相识对方了；往日将他们结合起来的那种畏惧、感激、敬爱的感情，已经消失得无影无踪，而且一点痕迹也没有了。

但是，这种情况却不适用于人类的天生感情。即使法律要以某种方式驾驭这种感情，也很少能够制服或试图加剧这种感情，也很少能从中得到什么好处，因为如果这种感情只是依靠本身的力量，就永远无法强大。

民主制度几乎毁坏了旧社会的所有习俗和规则，鼓励人们去接受新的社会习惯，从而使旧社会习惯所产生的感情大部分消失；但是，民主制度只能修改其余的习惯，而且经常赋予它们原来不曾有过的活力和温和性。

我认为或许可以把本章的内容浓缩成简单的几句话。这几句话是：民主制度松弛了社会联系，但却使天然联系更加紧密了；它在使亲族接近的同时，却使公民彼此疏远了。

CHAPTER IX
Education Of Young
Women In The United States

No free communities ever existed without morals, and as I observed in the former part of this work, morals are the work of woman. Consequently, whatever affects the condition of women, their habits and their opinions, has great political importance in my eyes.

Among almost all Protestant nations young women are far more the mistresses of their own actions than they are in Catholic countries. This independence is still greater in Protestant countries like England, which have retained or acquired the right of self-government; freedom is then infused into the domestic circle by political habits and by religious opinions. In the United States the doctrines of Protestantism are combined with great political liberty and a most democratic state of society, and nowhere are young women surrendered so early or so completely to their own guidance.

Long before an American girl arrives at the marriageable age, her emancipation from maternal control begins: she has scarcely ceased to be a child when she already thinks for herself, speaks with freedom, and acts on her own impulse. The great scene of the world is constantly open to her view; far from seeking to conceal it from her, it is every day disclosed more completely and she is taught to survey it with a firm and calm gaze. Thus the vices and dangers of society are early revealed to her; as she sees them clearly, she views them without illusion and braves them without

第九章　对美国年轻女性的教育

没有一个自由社会可以在无精神道德的状态下存在,而且正如我在本书前半部分讲过的一样,社会的精神道德是由女性创造的。因此,凡是影响妇女的地位、习惯和思想的一切东西,在我看来都具有重大的政治作用。

在几乎所有的信奉新教的国家里,年轻女性对自己行动的自主性都比在信奉天主教的国家里要大得多。在像英国那样保留着或已经获得自治权利的新教国家里,这种独立自主性会表现得更加强大;因此,在这样的国家里,自由便通过政治惯例和宗教信仰进入到每个家庭。在美国,新教的教义与非常自由的政治体制和非常民主的社会互相联系,而且没有一个地方的年轻女性能像美国的年轻女性那样完全自主。

在美国的年轻女性达到结婚年龄以前,她便开始脱离母亲的监护;她们几乎还没有完全摆脱稚气,就已经开始自己独立思考,自由发表自己的见解,自己单独行动。世界的精彩不断地涌现到她们的视野里;父母从来不会试图对她们隐藏这些,而且让她们每天细致地去观察它,叫她们学会冷静正确地去正视它。因此,社会里的那些罪恶和危险早就呈现在她们的面前;当她们能清楚地认识这些罪恶和危险,她们就不会对自己的判断抱任何幻想,

fear, for she is full of reliance on her own strength, and her confidence seems to be shared by all around her.

An American girl scarcely ever displays that virginal softness in the midst of young desires or that innocent and ingenuous grace which usually attend the European woman in the transition from girlhood to youth. It is rare that an American woman, at any age, displays childish timidity or ignorance. Like the young women of Europe she seeks to please, but she knows precisely the cost of pleasing. If she does not abandon herself to evil, at least she knows that it exists; and she is remarkable rather for purity of manners than for chastity of mind.

I have been frequently surprised and almost frightened at the singular address and happy boldness with which young women in America contrive to manage their thoughts and their language amid all the difficulties of free conversation; a philosopher would have stumbled at every step along the narrow path which they trod without accident and without effort. It is easy, indeed, to perceive that even amid the independence of early youth an American woman is always mistress of herself; she indulges in all permitted pleasures without yielding herself up to any of them, and her reason never allows the reins of self-guidance to drop, though it often seems to hold them loosely.

In France, where traditions of every age are still so strangely mingled in the opinions and tastes of the people, women commonly receive a reserved, retired, and almost conventual education, as they did in aristocratic times; and then they are suddenly abandoned without out a guide and without assistance in the midst of all the irregularities inseparable from democratic society.

The Americans are more consistent. They have found out that in a democracy the independence of individuals cannot fail to be very great, youth premature, tastes ill-restrained, customs fleeting,

并且敢于面对它们,因为她们完全相信自己的力量,并认为周围的人也这么相信她。

因此,美国的年轻女孩很少会表现出少女在情窦初开时期表现出来的那种羞涩的感觉,更不可能见到欧洲女青年在从童年过渡到青年时通常伴有的那种天真无邪的优雅感。美国女性,不管年龄大小,都很少表现出孩子气的胆小和无知。同欧洲的年轻女性一样,她们也寻找快乐,但她们非常清楚这些快乐的代价。如果她们没有投身于邪恶,至少她们知道世间有邪恶;与其说她们的不平凡在于她们高尚的思想,不如说在于她们纯洁的情操。

当我看到美国女青年在所有自由的交谈中发生争执时能够巧妙地和大胆地表述自己的思想和语言时,往往使我吃惊不已,甚至被吓倒;一位哲学家在一条狭窄的道路上可能每一步都会跌倒,可是美国的年轻女性却能不费吹灰之力和不发生意外地走过去。事实上,我们可以很容易看到,美国女性在年纪很轻的时候,就已完全是自己的主人了;她们沉溺于一切被允许的快乐,但从不让自己放纵于任何一种享乐,尽管她们往往好像随随便便,但她们的理智决不会失去其控制作用。

在法国,旧习俗仍在令人不可思议地夹杂在人们的思想和喜好中,女性往往接受到的是一种像在贵族时代那样保守的、隐退的和几乎可以说是修道院式的教育;而在民主社会中,她们又在没有指导和援助的情况下,被立即抛弃在这个社会的不可抵抗的混乱中。

美国人的行为是非常一致的。他们认为,在一个民主社会里,个人的独立是一个重大原则,这不可避免地导致了年轻人的早熟、不受限制的趣味、短暂的习俗、未定的和无力的公共舆论、

public opinion often unsettled and powerless, paternal authority weak, and marital authority contested. Under these circumstances, believing that they had little chance of repressing in woman the most vehement passions of the human heart, they held that the surer way was to teach her the art of combating those passions for herself. As they could not prevent her virtue from being exposed to frequent danger, they determined that she should know how best to defend it, and more reliance was placed on the free vigor of her will than on safeguards which have been shaken or overthrown. Instead, then, of inculcating mistrust of herself, they constantly seek to enhance her confidence in her own strength of character. As it is neither possible nor desirable to keep a young woman in perpetual and complete ignorance, they hasten to give her a precocious knowledge on all subjects. Far from hiding the corruptions of the world from her, they prefer that she should see them at once and train herself to shun them, and they hold it of more importance to protect her conduct than to be over-scrupulous of the innocence of her thoughts.

Although the Americans are a very religious people, they do not rely on religion alone to defend the virtue of woman; they seek to arm her reason also. In this respect they have followed the same method as in several others: they first make vigorous efforts to cause individual independence to control itself, and they do not call in the aid of religion until they have reached the utmost limits of human strength.

I am aware that an education of this kind is not without danger; I am sensible that it tends to invigorate the judgment at the expense of the imagination and to make cold and virtuous women instead of affectionate wives and agreeable companions to man. Society may be more tranquil and better regulated, but domestic life has often fewer charms. These, however, are secondary evils, which may be braved for the sake of higher interests. At the stage at which we are now arrived, the choice is no longer left to us; a democratic education is indispensable to protect women from the dangers with which democratic institutions and manners surround them.

微弱的父权和引起争辩的婚姻权。在这种情况下,他们认为自己几乎没有权利压迫妇女发自内心的最强烈的激情,而最可靠的办法就是教会她们战胜自己这种激情的技巧。由于他们无法防止妇女的贞操常遭破坏的危险,所以他们希望女性应当懂得怎样才能更好地去保卫贞操,要更多地依靠妇女的自由意志力,而不依靠那些已经动摇的或已被推翻的措施。他们不是让妇女怀疑自己无能,而是不断设法增强妇女的自信心。由于他们不可能而且也不希望年轻女性长期处于完全无知状态,所以他们便急于传授给年轻女性以处理各种事务的初步知识。他们从来不向年轻女性隐瞒世间的腐败,相反的,他们更愿意让年轻女性了解这些,并学会如何抵制腐败,他们认为,与其特别仔细地保护年轻女性的无知的思想,不如保护她们的操行。

尽管美国人是一个非常信奉宗教的民族,他们也从不只是依靠宗教来保卫妇女的贞洁;而且也在设法寻找武装妇女理智的武器。他们在这方面采用的方法,与在其他许多方面采用的相同:首先,他们作了很大的努力,以使个人在独立自主时能很好地控制自己,其次,在用尽人为的力量之后,才求助于宗教。

我知道,这样的教育不是没有危险;我也能意识到,这样的教育可以发挥妇女的判断力而抑制她们的想象力,使妇女具有德行,且在感情上冷淡,而不能成为男人真爱的妻子和亲密伴侣。即使这样的社会会更加安定和更加有序,但家庭生活往往使人疲惫。然而,这些只是次要的缺陷,而且为了更大的利益,可以不去计较。到了现在这个地步,我们已没有选择的余地;必须实行民主教育,以保护妇女免遭民主的制度和民情所带来的危险。

【英汉对照全译本】

DEMOCRACY IN AMERICA

论 美 国 民 主

［法］托克维尔 著

朱尾声 译

马高霞 译校

（五）

中国社会科学出版社

CHAPTER X
The Young Woman
In The Character Of A Wife

In America the independence of woman is irrecoverably lost in the bonds of matrimony. If an unmarried woman is less constrained there than elsewhere, a wife is subjected to stricter obligations. The former makes her father's house an abode of freedom and of pleasure; the latter lives in the home of her husband as if it were a cloister. Yet these two different conditions of life are perhaps not so contrary as may be supposed, and it is natural that the American women should pass through the one to arrive at the other.

Religious communities and trading nations entertain peculiarly serious notions of marriage: the former consider the regularity of woman's life as the best pledge and most certain sign of the purity of her morals; the latter regard it as the highest security for the order and prosperity of the household. The Americans are at the same time a puritanical people and a commercial nation; their religious opinions as well as their trading habits consequently lead them to require much abnegation on the part of woman and a constant sacrifice of her pleasures to her duties, which is seldom demanded of her in Europe. Thus in the United States the inexorable opinion of the public carefully circumscribes woman within the narrow circle of domestic interests and duties and forbids her to step beyond it.

Upon her entrance into the world a young American woman finds these notions firmly established; she sees the rules that are derived from them; she is not slow to perceive that she cannot depart

第十章　年轻女性怎样成为别人妻子的

在美国,女性在结婚以后,便无可挽救地失去其独立自主的能力。虽然美国的未婚女性比其他国家的女性受到较少约束,但是在成为人妻后,就要承担沉重的义务。年轻的未婚女性,在出嫁前可以在自己父母家里任意享受自由和快乐;而出嫁后生活在丈夫家里就如同生活在修道院。这两种完全不同的生活状况,或许不像有些人所想象的那样矛盾,而美国妇女从前一种生活过渡到后一种生活,应该是很自然的事情。

信奉宗教的国家和贸易国家,对于婚姻持有一种严肃而特殊的观点:前者认为女性生活的规律性是道德纯朴的最好保证和最明显的标志;后者认为这是家庭稳定和繁荣的最可靠保障。美国人既是清教徒,又是商业民族;他们的宗教信仰以及他们的贸易习惯,都使他们要求女性具有自我牺牲精神,自己的快乐要永远让步于自己的职责,而这种情况在欧洲就不会发生。因此,在美国无情的公共舆论,将女性牢牢地封闭在只顾家庭的利益和责任的狭小圈子里,不准她们越出雷池一步。

美国的年轻女性一进入社会,便发现这些观念早已根深蒂固;看到从这些观念里延伸出来的责任;并很快发现自己不能有

for an instant from the established usages of her contemporaries without putting in jeopardy her peace of mind, her honor, nay, even her social existence; and she finds the energy required for such an act of submission in the firmness of her understanding and in the virile habits which her education has given her. It may be said that she has learned by the use of her independence to surrender it without a struggle and without a murmur when the time comes for making the sacrifice.

But no American woman falls into the toils of matrimony as into a snare held out to her simplicity and ignorance. She has been taught beforehand what is expected of her and voluntarily and freely enters upon this engagement. She supports her new condition with courage because she chose it. As in America paternal discipline is very relaxed and the conjugal tie very strict, a young woman does not contract the latter without considerable circumspection and apprehension. Precocious marriages are rare. American women do not marry until their understandings are exercised and ripened, whereas in other countries most women generally begin to exercise and ripen their understandings only after marriage.

I by no means suppose, however, that the great change which takes place in all the habits of women in the United States as soon as they are married ought solely to be attributed to the constraint of public opinion; it is frequently imposed upon themselves by the sole effort of their own will. When the time for choosing a husband arrives, that cold and stern reasoning power which has been educated and invigorated by the free observation of the world teaches an American woman that a spirit of levity and independence in the bonds of marriage is a constant subject of annoyance, not of pleasure; it tells her that the amusements of the girl cannot become the recreations of the wife, and that the sources of a married woman's happiness are in the home of her husband. As she clearly discerns beforehand the only road that can lead to domestic happiness, she enters upon it at once and follows it to the end without seeking to turn back.

The same strength of purpose which the young wives of America

一点点偏离已有的规则,否则她的安宁和声名,甚至她的社会存在,都有立即遭到破坏的危险;但是,由于她在理智上已有坚定的认识,她所受的教育又使她养成了刚毅的习惯,所以她有顺应社会的能力。也可以说正是由于她学会使用独立,她才在需要牺牲的时候完全服从,并且没有任何抵制也没有任何怨言。

但是,美国妇女之所以会陷进婚姻的束缚,决不是由于自己的单纯和无知。她们婚前就被教育过以后应该怎么做,并且是她们自愿把婚姻的枷锁套在脖子上的。她们勇敢地接受了新的生活条件,因为这是她们自己选择的。在美国,父母的管教是很松的,而夫妻间的关系则很严,因此一个青年女性在没有经过慎重考虑和反复衡量的情况下,是不会同意结婚的。在美国,绝没有早婚现象。因此,美国的女性只有在她们的理智达到一定成熟阶段时,才决定结婚,而其他国家的大部分妇女,通常是在结婚之后才开始锻炼她们的理智和使其成熟的。

然而,我决不认为美国女性结婚后在整个生活习惯方面所发生的这个巨大变化一定是出于公共舆论的约束;并且她们常常是依靠自己的意志力来强加给自己这个变化的。当择偶的时期一到,自由的世界观所培养和鼓舞的那个冷静而严肃的理智便教导美国女性:如果结婚后还依旧轻浮和自我独立,那就只能引来无休止的争吵,而决不会得到快乐;她们知道未婚女青年的娱乐活动不能成为已婚妇女的消遣,已婚妇女的幸福源泉是她丈夫的家。因为她们事先就已非常清楚,只有一条道路可以使其家庭得到最大幸福,所以她们一开始便沿着这条道路走下去,一直走到头而不后退。

美国少妇表现出来的这种意志力,在适应新情况的严峻考验

display in bending themselves at once and without repining to the austere duties of their new condition is no less manifest in all the great trials of their lives. In no country in the world are private fortunes more precarious than in the United States. It is not uncommon for the same man in the course of his life to rise and sink again through all the grades that lead from opulence to poverty. American women support these vicissitudes with calm and unquenchable energy; it would seem that their desires contract as easily as they expand with their fortunes.

The greater part of the adventurers who migrate every year to people the Western wilds belong, as I observed in the former part of this work, to the old Anglo-American race of the Northern states. Many of these men, who rush so boldly onwards in pursuit of wealth, were already in the enjoyment of a competency in their own part of the country. They take their wives along with them and make them share the countless perils and privations that always attend the commencement of these expeditions. I have often met, even on the verge of the wilderness, with young women who, after having been brought up amid all the comforts of the large towns of New England, had passed, almost without any intermediate stage, from the wealthy abode of their parents to a comfortless hovel in a forest. Fever, solitude, and a tedious life had not broken the springs of their courage. Their features were impaired and faded, but their looks were firm; they appeared to be at once sad and resolute. ① I do not doubt that these young American women had amassed, in the education of their early years, that inward strength which they displayed under these circumstances. The early culture of the girl may still, therefore, be traced, in the United States, under the aspect of marriage; her part is changed, her habits are different, but her character is the same.

---

① See Appendix U.

时而没有任何怨言,也在她们接受生活的一切重大考验上反映出来。世界上没有一个国家的个人命运会像美国人那样不稳定。在美国,同一个人在人生的旅程中多次的起起落落,即由富变穷,又由穷至富的现象,并不罕见。美国妇女总是以冷静而坚定的心情来对待这些巨大的变化;可以说她们的欲望是随着她们的贫富变化而变化的。

正如我在本书前半部分所讲的,每年移居西部荒凉地区的冒险家,大部分是早年定居在北部的英籍美国人。这些人中的大多数已在自己的故乡享有舒适的生活,但仍大胆地冒险前来追逐财富。他们携妻带子,让她们共同分担在干这种事业的初期总要遇到的无数艰险困苦。我甚至常常在西部荒漠的边缘地带,遇到一些在像新英格兰这样的大城市的舒适环境中成长起来的少妇,在她们从父母的豪华住宅来到森林里的简陋茅屋间,并没有任何可供她们过渡的平台。疾病、孤独和沉闷,都没有使她们丧失勇气。她们的面容憔悴并苍白,但她们的神色却是坚毅的;她们既表现出忧郁,又表现出坚决。① 我毫不怀疑,这些美国少妇在她们受教育的早期,就已养成她们在这种情况下所表现出来的内在力量。因此,美国女性早在年轻时期就已懂得怎样为人妻。她们在生活中担当的角色改变了,日常的生活习惯也不同了,但她们的思想依旧不变。

---

① 　见附录 U。

CHAPTER XI

How Equality Of Condition Contributes To Maintain Good Morals In America[①]

Some philosophers and historians have said or hinted that the strictness of female morality was increased or diminished simply by the distance of a country from the equator. This solution of the difficulty was an easy one, and nothing was required but a globe and a pair of compasses to settle in an instant one of the most difficult problems in the condition of mankind. But I am not sure that this principle of the materialists is supported by facts. The same nations have been chaste or dissolute at different periods of their history; the strictness or the laxity of their morals depended, therefore, on some variable cause and not alone on the natural qualities of their country, which were invariable. I do not deny that in certain climates the passions which are occasioned by the mutual attraction of the sexes are peculiarly intense, but I believe that this natural intensity may always be excited or restrained by the condition of society and by political institutions.

Although the travelers who have visited North America differ on many points, they all agree in remarking that morals are far

---

① See Appendix V.

第十一章　身份平等是怎样有助于维护美国的良好道德的[①]

　　有些哲学家和历史学家曾说过或暗示过,妇女的道德是随她们居住国家的地理位置离赤道的远近而变化的,即离赤道越远其精神道德就越高尚,离赤道越近其精神道德就越低俗。这是解决难题的最容易的方法,我们只需要一个地球仪和一个圆规,立刻就可解决人性方面表现出来的一个最难解决的问题。我不能确定唯物主义者的这个理论是有事实依据的。同一个民族,在历史的不同时期会有不同的表现,有时重视贞洁,有时又放荡不羁;因此,一个国家的道德是严谨的还是松弛的,是取决于一系列因素的,而不只仅仅依靠该国的不变的地理位置。我并不否认,在一定的气候下,性的相互吸引力所引起的激情是特别强烈的,但我认为这种天生的激情总是可以被社会情况和政治制度激发或抑制的。

　　尽管访问过北美的旅游者们在若干问题上意见并不一致,但他们全都承认那里的民情比其他任何地方都更加严谨。很明显,

---

① 见附录 V。

more strict there than elsewhere. It is evident that on this point the A-
mericans are very superior to their progenitors, the English. A superficial glance at the two nations will establish the fact.

In England, as in all other countries of Europe, public malice is
constantly attacking the frailties of women. Philosophers and statesmen are heard to deplore that morals are not sufficiently strict, and
the literary productions of the country constantly lead one to suppose
so. In America all books, novels not excepted, suppose women to be
chaste, and no one thinks of relating affairs of gallantry.

No doubt this great regularity of American morals is due in part
to qualities of country, race, and religion, but all these causes,
which operate elsewhere, do not suffice to account for it; recourse
must be had to some special reason. This reason appears to me to be
the principle of equality and the institutions derived from it. Equality
of condition does not of itself produce regularity of morals, but it unquestionably facilitates and increases it.

Among aristocratic nations birth and fortune frequently make two
such different beings of man and woman that they can never be united
to each other. Their passions draw them together, but the condition of
society and the notions suggested by it prevent them from contracting a
permanent and ostensible tie. The necessary consequence is a great
number of transient and clandestine connections. Nature secretly a-
venges herself for the constraint imposed upon her by the laws
of man.

This is not so much the case when the equality of conditions has
swept away all the imaginary or the real barriers that separated man
from woman. No girl then believes that she cannot become the wife of
the man who loves her, and this renders all breaches of morality before marriage very uncommon; for, whatever be the credulity of the
passions, a woman will hardly be able to persuade herself that she is
beloved when her lover is perfectly free to marry her and does not.

The same cause operates, though more indirectly, on married
life. Nothing better serves to justify an illicit passion, either to the
minds of those who have conceived it or to the world which looks

这一点上美国人比他们的祖辈英国人优越得多。只对这两个国家进行初步的观察,就可以确定事实依据。

在英国,也像在欧洲其他一切国家一样,公共的恶意总是不断地抨击着女性的弱点。人们经常听到哲学家和政治家对道德的不够严谨表示悲痛,而文学家也每天在这样虚构他们的作品。在美国,所有的书刊和小说也不例外,想把女性虚构成是冰清玉洁的,没有人敢在书中描写男女之间的事。

毫无疑问,美国的这种十分有规律的道德,部分的原因在于它的国土、种族和宗教,但是,在其他国家发生的这一切原因,还不能足够说明这个问题;因此,我们还要求助于一些特殊的理由。在我看来,这个特殊的理由就是平等的原则和由此而来的各项制度。身份的平等本身不能使道德更加正派,但它无疑能使民情容易正派和加速正派。

在贵族国家,出身和财富不同的一男一女,往往不能互相结合。激情可能让他们在一起,但是,社会情况和由此产生的观念,却阻止他们永久的结合。这样做的结果就必然会引发许多短暂的和秘密的结合。这是大自然在暗中报复法律施加给人们的限制。

当身份的平等把男女间的一切想象的和实际存在的障碍排除以后,情况就不一样了。这时,每个女孩都相信自己能够成为喜欢她的男人的好妻子,这使婚前的道德败坏的行为也将难于实现;因为不管激情会怎样使人轻信,但是一个女性很难说服自己,当他的爱人在完全可以自由同她结婚但却不同她结婚的时候,仍然相信他还在爱她。

这个原因对婚后生活也间接地发生着同样的作用。再没有比强迫婚姻或随机结合更能纠正这种不正当的激情了,无论是已

on, than marriages made by compulsion or chance. ①

In a country in which a woman is always free to exercise her choice and where education has prepared her to choose rightly, public opinion is inexorable to her faults. The rigor of the Americans arises in part from this cause. They consider marriage as a covenant which is often onerous, but every condition of which the parties are strictly bound to fulfill because they knew all those conditions beforehand and were perfectly free not to have contracted them.

The very circumstances that render matrimonial fidelity more obligatory also render it more easy.

In aristocratic countries the object of marriage is rather to unite property than persons; hence the husband is sometimes at school and the wife at nurse when they are betrothed. It cannot be wondered at if the conjugal tie which unites the fortunes of the pair allows their hearts to rove; this is the result of the nature of the contract. When, on the contrary, a man always chooses a wife for himself without any external coercion or even guidance, it is generally a conformity of tastes and opinions that brings a man and a woman together, and this same conformity keeps and fixes them in close habits of intimacy.

Our forefathers had conceived a strange opinion on the subject of marriage; as they had noticed that the small number of lovematches which occurred in their time almost always turned out badly, they

---

① The literature of Europe sufficiently corroborates this remark. When a European author wishes to depict in a work of fiction any of those great catastrophes in matrimony which so frequently occur among us, he assures himself, in advance, of the compassion of the reader by bringing before him ill-assorted or compulsory marriages. Although habitual tolerance has long since relaxed our morals, an author could hardly succeed in interesting us in the misfortunes of his characters if he did not first excuse their faults. This artifice seldom fails; the daily scenes we witness prepare us beforehand to be indulgent. But American writers could never render these excuses credible to their readers; their customs and laws are opposed to it; and as they despair of rendering levity of conduct pleasing, they cease to depict it. This is one of the causes to which must be attributed the small number of novels published in the United States.

有这种想法的人还是准备有这种想法的人,都这么认为。①

在女性永远可以自由选择而且教育使她们能够做出最佳选择的国家里,公共舆论对她们的过错是无情的。美国人的严肃精神,也部分地来因于此。他们把婚姻看作是一种沉重的负担,但契约双方又必须严格执行其中的每一项条款,因为他们事先就可以知道这一切条款,而且享有拒绝签约的自由。

使夫妇在婚后必须更加忠贞地约束自己,也使忠贞变得更加容易。

在贵族国家,结婚的目的主要是为了双方财产的结合,而不是两个相爱的人的结合;因此,有时在订婚时男方已经上学读书,而女方还在被哺乳。我们不难想象在这种以联合双方的财产为目的的婚姻中,双方的心也不在对方身上,而是漫无目的地流浪;这是契约的本质自然产生的结果。反之,当任何人都能永远自己选偶,不受外来的干涉和指使时,通常只能是喜好和观念的一致才能使男女在一起,这种一致又可以保持和巩固他们之间的亲密关系。

我们的祖辈对婚姻有过一种奇怪的看法;由于他们注意到当时刚刚出现的少数情人几乎都造成了悲剧的结局,所以他们敢断言听这类事情的当事人讲述心声是极为危险的。在他们看来,

---

① 欧洲的文学著作足以证明这个观点。当一个欧洲作家想在其著作里描述那些经常发生在我们中间的婚姻灾难,首先,他应确保自己在介绍不相配的结合和强迫的婚姻时能得到读者的同情。尽管人们习惯性的容忍已经使我们的道德观有所放松,但如果作者不先对他们的错误进行辩解,那就很难使读者对这些不幸的人物产生兴趣。这种做法很少失败过;我们目睹的日常发生的一切早已使我们麻木了。但是美国作家从来不会把这些辩解的理由写给他们的读者;他们的习俗和法律不允许他们这么做;所以他们最终在失望中结束了这样的描述。这就是为什么在美国,这类小说很少发行的原因。

resolutely inferred that it was dangerous to listen to the dictates of the heart on the subject. Accident appeared to them a better guide than choice.

Yet it was not difficult to perceive that the examples that they witnessed in fact proved nothing at all. For, in the first place, if democratic nations leave a woman at liberty to choose her husband, they take care to give her mind sufficient knowledge and her will sufficient strength to make so important a choice, whereas the young women who among aristocratic nations furtively elope from the authority of their parents to throw themselves of their own accord into the arms of men whom they have had neither time to know nor ability to judge of are totally without those securities. It is not surprising that they make a bad use of their freedom of action the first time they avail themselves of it, or that they fall into such cruel mistakes when, not having received a democratic education, they choose to marry in conformity to democratic customs. But this is not all. When a man and woman are bent upon marriage in spite of the differences of an aristocratic state of society, the difficulties to be overcome are enormous. Having broken or relaxed the bonds of filial obedience, they have then to emancipate themselves by a final effort from the sway of custom and the tyranny of opinion; and when at length they have succeeded in this arduous task, they stand estranged from their natural friends and kinsmen. The prejudice they have crossed separates them from all and places them in a situation that soon breaks their courage and sours their hearts.

If, then, a couple married in this manner are first unhappy and afterwards criminal, it ought not to be attributed to the freedom of their choice, but rather to their living in a community in which this freedom of choice is not admitted.

Moreover, it should not be forgotten that the same effort which makes a man violently shake off a prevailing error commonly impels him beyond the bounds of reason; that to dare to declare war, in however just a cause, against the opinion of one's age and country, a violent and adventurous spirit is required, and that men of this character seldom arrive at happiness or virtue, whatever be the path they follow. And this, it may be observed by the way, is

偶遇可能比选择还要好。

　　但是,要想发觉他们所见证的事例什么也不能证明,并不十分困难。因为首先:如果民主国家赋予女性可以自由择偶的权利,也要先设法使女性的头脑具备足够的进行这种选择的知识,并使她们的意志产生能够进行这种选择所需要的力量,然而贵族国家的年轻女性,摆脱父母的束缚而私奔,委屈自己嫁给一个她们根本没时间了解其情况,又没有能力辨别其善恶的男子,并且缺乏一切保障。因此,她们初次运用自由行动时就失误,她们没有受过民主教育就在结婚方面仿效民主的习惯,结果犯了如此惨痛的错误,都是不足为奇的。但是,这还不是全部。当一男一女想要打破由贵族社会所造成的各种差异而结合时,还有不计其数的困难在等着他们克服。在打破或放松父母对子女的束缚权力后,他们最后还要努力战胜习俗的势力和舆论的专横来释放自己;当他们最终在这个艰苦的旅途中取得胜利时,他们将被朋友疏远。他们虽越过了偏见,但却同一切疏远了,这种情况不久便要挫伤他们的勇气,使他们感到心里难受。

　　因此,即使在这样的结婚状态下的一对夫妻在一开始就很不幸,并且以后很可能走上犯罪的道路,那也不是由于他们的自由选择,而是由于他们生活在一个不承认他们的这种自由选择的社会里。

　　甚至,还不应该忘记,通过暴力阻止一个人不犯一般的错误,几乎总要同时驱使他失去理智;敢于让一个人合法地向他的时代和国家所流行的观念宣战,仅仅是一个原因,同时也要让他具有同暴力和冒险做斗争的精神,而凡是具有这种性格的人,不管他走到哪里,都很少能够得到幸福和很少能够有德行。在这里,顺

the reason why, in the most necessary and righteous revolutions, it is so rare to meet with virtuous or moderate revolutionary characters. There is, then, no just ground for surprise if a man who in an age of aristocracy chooses to consult nothing but his own opinion and his own taste in the choice of a wife soon finds that infractions of morality and domestic wretchedness invade his household; but when this same line of action is in the natural and ordinary course of things, when it is sanctioned by parental authority and backed by public opinion, it cannot be doubted that the internal peace of families will be increased by it and conjugal fidelity more rigidly observed.

Almost all men in democracies are engaged in public or professional life; and on the other hand the limited income obliges a wife to confine herself to the house in order to watch in person, and very closely, over the details of domestic economy. All these distinct and compulsory occupations are so many natural barriers, which by keeping the two sexes asunder render the solicitations of the one less frequent and less ardent, the resistance of the other more easy.

The equality of conditions cannot, it is true, ever succeed in making men chaste, but it may impart a less dangerous character to their breaches of morality. As no one has then either sufficient time or opportunity to assail a virtue armed in self-defense, there will be at the same time a great number of courtesans and a great number of virtuous women. This state of things causes lamentable cases of individual hardship, but it does not prevent the body of society from being strong and alert; it does not destroy family ties or enervate the morals of the nation. Society is endangered, not by the great profligacy of a few, but by laxity of morals among all. In the eyes of a legislator prostitution is less to be dreaded than intrigue.

The tumultuous and constantly harassed life that equality makes men lead not only distracts them from the passion of love by denying them time to indulge it, but diverts them from it by another more secret but more certain road. All men who live in democratic times more or less contract the ways of thinking of the manufacturing and trading classes; their minds take a serious, deliberate,

便提一下,为什么在一些最必要的和最神圣的革命中之所以很少见到温和而有道德的革命家,其原因就在于此。因此,在贵族制度时代,一个男人与一个女人素昧平生,但却因个人的意见和爱好而一见钟情,他们完全不考虑其他一切条件,就匆忙结婚,而婚后不久就见异思迁而乱搞和出现悲剧,是无须惊奇的;但是,如果这种结合能按事物的常规和自然秩序进行,受到社会情况的支持,得到父母权威的承认和公共舆论的赞扬,那么毫无疑问,家庭的内部和平将更加和睦,夫妻间的忠贞也将更好地得到遵守。

在民主国家,几乎所有的男人都参与政治生活或从事一种职业;另一方面,有限的家庭收入迫使妻子不得不将自己关在家里,操持家政和精心管理家务的一切细节。所有这些不同的和必须承担的劳动,就像许多天然障碍阻止着性生活,使一方的性冲动日益稀少和不如以前兴奋,而另一方的抵制也会更加容易。

实际上,身份的平等不一定能确保男人的贞节,但它能使男人的伤风败俗行为减少危险性。由于这时谁也没有足够的时间和机会去质问某人是否想保持贞操,所以就出现了既有大量的娼妇,又同时有许多贞节烈女的现象。这种情况虽然造成了个人的可悲不幸,但并不妨碍整个社会的强壮和发展;它既不会破坏家庭的纽带,也不会削弱民主的道德观。使整个社会陷入危险的并不是某几人的放荡不羁,而是所有人在道德上的败坏。在立法者的眼中,卖淫并不可怕,而通奸才是更可怕的。

平等所带给人们的永无止息的忙乱的生活,使人们不但无暇顾及谈情说爱,而且还通过一个比较隐秘的、但是比较可靠的办法,使人避开谈情说爱。生活在民主时代的人,或多或少都有点工商阶级的思维习惯;他们的头脑是严肃的,考虑周到的和积极

and positive turn; they are apt to relinquish the ideal in order to pursue some visible and proximate object which appears to be the natural and necessary aim of their desires. Thus the principle of equality does not destroy the imagination, but lowers its flight to the level of the earth.

No men are less addicted to reverie than the citizens of a democracy, and few of them are ever known to give way to those idle and solitary meditations which commonly precede and produce the great emotions of the heart. It is true they attach great importance to procuring for themselves that sort of deep, regular, and quiet affection which constitutes the charm and safeguard of life, but they are not apt to run after those violent and capricious sources of excitement which disturb and abridge it.

I am aware that all this is applicable in its full extent only to America and cannot at present be extended to Europe. In the course of the last half-century, while laws and customs have impelled several European nations with unexampled force towards democracy, we have not had occasion to observe that the relations of man and woman have become more orderly or more chaste. In some places the very reverse may be detected: some classes are more strict; the general morality of the people appears to be more lax. I do not hesitate to make the remark, for I am as little disposed to flatter my contemporaries as to malign them.

This fact must distress, but it ought not to surprise us. The propitious influence that a democratic state of society may exercise upon orderly habits is one of those tendencies which can be discovered only after a time. If equality of condition is favorable to purity of morals, the social commotion by which conditions are rendered equal is adverse to it. In the last fifty years, during which France has been undergoing this transformation, it has rarely had freedom, always disturbance. Amid this universal confusion of notions and this general stir of opinions, amid this incoherent mixture of the just and the unjust, of truth and falsehood, of right and might, public virtue has become doubtful and private morality wavering. But all revolutions, whatever may have been their object or their agents, have at first produced similar consequences;

向上的;他们可以随时放弃理想而寻求一些明显的和可以触摸到的目标,并把这一目标视为自己的愿望的自然的和必然的向往对象。因此,平等并没有破坏人们的想象力,但却限制了它的活动,把它的飞翔程度只限制在地球表面。

没有一个公民会比民主国家的公民还不愿意幻想,也决不喜欢让步于通常是在事前发生的并可能使心情澎湃的孤独的遐想中。不错,他们十分重视那种可以保护生活美好的那些深厚的、有规律的和恬静的感情,但他们不愿意追求那些可以干扰生活并使生命缩短的暴力的和反复无常的激情。

我知道,以上所述只适用于美国,而在目前还不能普遍地推广于欧洲。在近半个世纪,法律和习惯虽以空前的努力推动一些欧洲国家走向民主,但我们仍没有看见这些国家的男女关系变得比较正派和纯真。在某些国家,情况还恰恰相反:虽然有些阶级在这个问题上是十分严肃的;但整个国家的普遍道德是比较松懈的。我不怕指出这一点,因为我主要是想夸赞我的同时代人,而不是想诽谤他们。

这种情况是令人悲痛的,但我们也不必为此大惊小怪。民主的社会情况对有规律的习惯产生的良好影响,是只有经过一段时间才能显示出效果的现象之一。如果说身份的平等有利于道德的淳朴,那么,社会在生产这种平等时则有害于道德的淳朴。在法国不断进行改革的近50年来,他们很少获得自由,却常常发生动乱。在国家处处发生混乱、舆论处处被动摇的时候,在是非、真假、功过混淆如此难辨的时期,社会的公德遭到了怀疑,而个人的私德则处于崩溃状态。但是,法国所发生的一切革命,不管其目的是什么,或是由什么人进行的,最初都产生了同样的后果。

even those which have in the end drawn tighter the bonds of morality began by loosening them. The violations of morality which the French frequently witness do not appear to me to have a permanent character, and this is already betokened by some curious signs of the times.

Nothing is more wretchedly corrupt than an aristocracy which retains its wealth when it has lost its power and which still enjoys a vast amount of leisure after it is reduced to mere vulgar pastimes. The energetic passions and great conceptions that animated it heretofore leave it then, and nothing remains to it but a host of petty consuming vices, which cling about it like worms upon a carcass.

No one denies that the French aristocracy of the last century was extremely dissolute, yet established habits and ancient belief still preserved some respect for morality among the other classes of society. Nor will it be denied that at the present day the remnants of that same aristocracy exhibit a certain severity of morals, while laxity of morals appears to have spread among the middle and lower ranks. Thus the same families that were most profligate fifty years ago are nowadays the most exemplary, and democracy seems only to have strengthened the morality of the aristocratic classes. The French Revolution, by dividing the fortunes of the nobility, by forcing them to attend assiduously to their affairs and to their families, by making them live under the same roof with their children, and, in short, by giving a more rational and serious turn to their minds, has imparted to them, almost without their being aware of it, a reverence for religious belief, a love of order, of tranquil pleasures, of domestic endearments, and of comfort; whereas the rest of the nation, which had naturally these same tastes, was carried away into excesses by the effort that was required to overthrow the laws and political habits of the country.

The old French aristocracy has undergone the consequences of the Revolution, but it neither felt the revolutionary passions nor shared the anarchical excitement that produced it; it may easily be conceived that this aristocracy feels the salutary influence of the Revolution on its manners before those who achieved it. It may therefore be said, though at first it seems paradoxical, that at the present day the most anti-democratic classes of the nation

甚至那些以加强道德为目的革命,也开始松懈道德了。法国人经常见证的道德革命在我看来并不具有长久的特性,一些奇妙的征兆已在显示这一点。

最腐败的事情,就是贵族在失去了权力之后仍然保持着财富,因为他们享尽了庸俗的消遣之后,仍有大量的时间去享乐。曾经使他们快乐的强烈激情和伟大思想统统离他们远去,而只剩下了一大堆看来很小但腐蚀性很大的恶习,像苍蝇集聚在尸体上一样,紧紧地附着在他们身上。

没有人会否认,上一个世纪的法国贵族是极其放荡的。但是,传统的习惯和古老的信仰,仍能使社会其他阶级尊重道德。谁也不能不同意,在现今这个时代,这个贵族的残余还能在一定程度上维护道德的严肃性,而道德的松弛反而在社会的中下阶层中表现得日益明显。结果,50 年前生活上最为放纵的家庭,今日却成了最守规矩的模范家庭,而民主好像只是加强了贵族阶级的道德观。法国大革命虽然分掉了贵族的财产,强迫他们尽全力参与自己的私事和自己的家庭,规定他们必须同子女住在一起,但却使他们的头脑比以前清晰和严肃了。因此,法国大革命使贵族在不知不觉之中学会了尊重宗教信仰、爱好秩序、爱好平凡的快乐和家庭的快乐与幸福;然而本来具有同样爱好的其他阶级,却借着推翻法制和政治习惯所需的努力走上了破坏秩序的道路。

法国的旧贵族已经忍受了大革命所造成的一切后果,但他们并没有由此也产生革命激情,也没有享有在革命之前通常会有的无政府主义念头;很容易想象,他们预感这场革命将会对自己的生活方式发生健康的影响,比从事革命的那些人还早。因此可以这样说,尽管初次听来觉得有些荒谬,但在今天反而是国内最反

principally exhibit the kind of morality that may reasonably be anticipated from democracy. I cannot but think that when we shall have obtained all the effects of this democratic revolution, after having got rid
of the tumult it has caused, the observations which are now only applicable to the few will gradually become true of the whole community.

对民主的那些阶级在民主理所当然造成的道德方面表现得最好。我不能不认为,在我们已经享有民主革命的一切成果的时候,只要消除革命所造成的混乱,现在只被少数人认为是真理的一些东西,就将逐渐为所有的人所接受。

CHAPTER XII

How The Americans Understand
The Equality Of The Sexes

I Have shown how democracy destroys or modifies the different inequalities that originate in society; but is this all, or does it not ultimately affect that great inequality of man and woman which has seemed, up to the present day, to be eternally based in human nature? I believe that the social changes that bring nearer to the same level the father and son, the master and servant, and, in general, superiors and inferiors will raise woman and make her more and more the equal of man. But here, more than ever, I feel the necessity of making myself clearly understood; for there is no subject on which the coarse and lawless fancies of our age have taken a freer range.

There are people in Europe who, confounding together the different characteristics of the sexes, would make man and woman into beings not only equal but alike. They would give to both the same functions, impose on both the same duties, and grant to both the same rights; they would mix them in all things -their occupations, their pleasures, their business. It may readily be conceived that by thus attempting to make one sex equal to the other, both are degraded, and from so preposterous a medley of the works of nature nothing could ever result but weak men and disorderly women.

It is not thus that the Americans understand that species of democratic equality which may be established between the sexes. They admit that as nature has appointed such wide differences between the physical and moral constitution of man and woman, her manifest design was to give a distinct employment to their various faculties; and they hold that improvement does not consist in making beings so dissimilar do pretty nearly the same things, but in causing each of them to fulfill

第十二章　美国人是怎样理解男女平等的

　　我在前面已经讲过民主制度是怎样摧毁或改变社会所造成的各种不平等的；然而，这就是全部吗？民主是否最终能对于至今似乎始终以人性为基础的重大的男女不平等发生影响呢？我认为，是社会的变化使父与子的关系和主与仆的关系走得更近，它也提高了妇女的地位，并且必将逐渐使妇女与男人平等。但是在这里，我从来没有像以前一样有想在这详细说明我的意见的必要；因为没有一个题目比这个题目更可以使当代人信口雌黄了。

　　在欧洲，有些人混淆了男女的性别的不同，确定男女不但是平等的人，而且是完全相同的人。他们赋予男女同样的职责，给予男女同样的义务，并授予男女同样的权利；在所有事情上，他们都混淆了男女的差别——比如在职业、娱乐和商业等方面。我们很容易想象，强制两性平等，会使双方都堕落；如此荒谬的对男女工作性质的混合，必然出现一些柔弱的男人和一些粗野的女人。

　　因此，这不是美国人理解范围内的那种可以建立在男女之间的民主平等。美国人认为，既然老天爷使男女在身心和道德方面存在极大的差别，那它显然要让男女能各自发挥出他们的特点；美国人确信，进步并不是使性别不同的人去做几乎相同的工作，

their respective tasks in the best possible manner. The Americans have applied to the sexes the great principle of political economy which governs the manufacturers of our age, by carefully dividing the duties of man from those of woman in order that the great work of society may be the better carried on.

In no country has such constant care been taken as in America to trace two clearly distinct lines of action for the two sexes and to make them keep pace one with the other, but in two pathways that are always different. American women never manage the outward concerns of the family or conduct a business or take a part in political life; nor are they, on the other hand, ever compelled to perform the rough labor of the fields or to make any of those laborious efforts which demand the exertion of physical Strength. No families are so poor as to form an exception to this rule. If, on the one hand, an American woman cannot escape from the quiet circle of domestic employments, she is never forced, on the other, to go beyond it. Hence it is that the women of America, who often exhibit a masculine strength of understanding and a manly energy, generally preserve great delicacy of personal appearance and always retain the manners of women although they sometimes show that they have the hearts and minds of men.

Nor have the Americans ever supposed that one consequence of democratic principles is the subversion of marital power or the confusion of the natural authorities in families. They hold that every association must have a head in order to accomplish its object, and that the natural head of the conjugal association is man. They do not therefore deny him the right of directing his partner, and they maintain that in the smaller association of husband and wife as well as in the great social community the object of democracy is to regulate and legalize the powers that are necessary, and not to subvert all power.

This opinion is not peculiar to one sex and contested by the other; I never observed that the women of America consider conjugal authority as a fortunate usurpation of their rights, or that they thought themselves degraded by submitting to it. It appeared to me, on the contrary, that they attach a sort of pride to the voluntary surrender of their own will and make it their boast to bend themselves to the yoke, not to shake it off. Such, at least, is the feeling expressed by the most virtuous of their sex; the others are silent; and in the United States it is not the practice for a guilty

而是让男女尽最大的可能去完成自己的职责。美国人把指导当今工业的伟大政治经济学理论应用到两性方面来，即仔细划分男女的职责，以使伟大的社会劳动能被最好地完成。

没有一个国家能像美国那样如此坚持划清两性之间的行动界线，并使男女之间能和平相处，但所走的道路永远不同。美国的女性从来不会管家庭以外的事情，或去做买卖和投身政界；另一方面，也没有人会强迫妇女下田去干粗活，或做需要强壮劳力的重活。没有一个家庭会穷到要去破坏惯例。另一方面，如果美国妇女无法走出家庭这个宁静的活动小圈子，那她们也从来不会被迫被拉出来。因此，经常表现出男子般的力量和精力的美国妇女，一般仍保持着其温柔的一面，尽管她们常常表现出男子的心胸和气概，但她们的举止却永远保留着女人味。

美国人从来不曾想过民主原则的后果之一就是对婚权的颠覆和对家庭自然权威的混淆。他们认为，任何一个团体，要想完成自己的目标，必须有一个首领，而夫妻这个小团体的天然首领就是丈夫。因此，他们决不反对丈夫有权指挥自己的配偶，并且认为在夫妻的小家庭里，就好像在广大的政治界，民主的目的在于规定必要的权利并使它们合法，而不是暗中破坏所有的权利。

这种观点并非只由男性所独有而为女性所反对；我从来没有见过美国妇女将丈夫行使的婚权视为是对她们自己权利的剥夺，更没有见过美国妇女将这种服从视为是一种屈辱。恰恰相反，我好像发现她们把心甘情愿放弃自己的主见视为一种光荣，并吹嘘她们宁愿屈服而从不反抗。这至少是女性道德的很好的表现；而其他人都保持沉默。另外，在美国，你根本听不到一个有罪的妻

wife to clamor for the rights of women while she is trampling on her own holiest duties.

It has often been remarked that in Europe a certain degree of contempt lurks even in the flattery which men lavish upon women; although a European frequently affects to be the slave of woman, it may be seen that he never sincerely thinks her his equal. In the United States men seldom compliment women, but they daily show how much they esteem them. They constantly display an entire confidence in the understanding of a wife and a profound respect for her freedom; they have decided that her mind is just as fitted as that of a man to discover the plain truth, and her heart as firm to embrace it; and they have never sought to place her virtue, any more than his, under the shelter of prejudice, ignorance, and fear.

It would seem in Europe, where man so easily submits to the despotic sway of women, that they are nevertheless deprived of some of the greatest attributes of the human species and considered as seductive but imperfect beings; and (what may well provoke astonishment) women ultimately look upon themselves in the same light and almost consider it as a privilege that they are entitled to show themselves futile, feeble, and timid. The women of America claim no such privileges.

Again, it may be said that in our morals we have reserved strange immunities to man, so that there is, as it were, one virtue for his use and another for the guidance of his partner, and that, according to the opinion of the public, the very same act may be punished alternately as a crime or only as a fault. The Americans do not know this iniquitous division of duties and rights; among them the seducer is as much dishonored as his victim.

It is true that the Americans rarely lavish upon women those eager attentions which are commonly paid them in Europe, but their conduct to women always implies that they suppose them to be virtuous and refined; and such is the respect entertained for the moral freedom of the sex that in the presence of a woman the most guarded language is used lest her ear should be offended by an expression. In America a young unmarried woman may alone and without fear undertake a long journey.

子在她践踏自己的最神圣义务时会大吵大闹,要求自己的女权。

常有人说:在欧洲,即使男人对女人非常献媚,也总暗藏着一定的轻视之意;尽管欧洲男人往往表现得像女人的奴隶,但我们可以看出,他们从来不曾真诚认为女性是与他们平等的。在美国,男人很少恭维女性,但每天他们都会表现出自己对女性的尊敬。美国男人经常会表现出他们对妻子的完全信任,和对她们自由的无比尊敬;他们断定妻子的头脑也能像男人一样去发现普遍的真理,妻子的心胸也坚定得足以追随这种真理;他们从来没有想站在偏见的立场上,用妇女愚昧无知和胆小怕事来说明自己的德行比妻子的高明。

然而,在男人很容易服从女人专制的欧洲,男人却似乎剥夺女性作为人类的某些主要特性,认为女人虽然迷人,但不是完整的人;而使人更为惊奇的是,女人本身也是这么看自己的,并且一直认为表现自己无用、软弱和怯懦是她们的特权。美国妇女决不要求这种特权。

另一方面,还可以说,我们的民情实际上使男人获得了一种奇特的免疫性,以致好像有一套道德规范是专为男人使用的,而有另一套道德规范是专为其妻子使用的,而且按照舆论,同样的行为由女性来做可能是犯罪,而由男性来做可能仅仅是小错误。美国男人决不会理解权利和义务的这种不公平分配;在他们看来,诱惑者和受害者是同样不光彩的。

实际上,美国男人很少像欧洲男人那样向女性百般地献殷勤,但他们的行动常常暗示他们认为妇女是贞洁和优雅的;他们对妇女的精神自由十分尊重,以致当有女性在场时,每个人都用很规范的语言讲话,害怕让女性听到使她们感到不快的表达。在美国,一个年轻的未婚女性可以独自长途旅行而不必害怕。

The legislators of the United States, who have mitigated almost all the penalties of criminal law, still make rape a capital offense, and no crime is visited with more inexorable severity by public opinion. This may be accounted for; as the Americans can conceive nothing more precious than a woman's honor and nothing which ought so much to be respected as her independence, they hold that no punishment is too severe for the man who deprives her of them against her will. In France, where the same offense is visited with far milder penalties, it is frequently difficult to get a verdict from a jury against the prisoner. Is this a consequence of contempt of decency or contempt of women? I cannot but believe that it is a contempt of both.

Thus the Americans do not think that man and woman have either the duty or the right to perform the same offices, but they show an equal regard for both their respective parts; and though their lot is different, they consider both of them as beings of equal value. They do not give to the courage of woman the same form or the same direction as to that of man, but they never doubt her courage; and if they hold that man and his partner ought not always to exercise their intellect and understanding in the same manner, they at least believe the understanding of the one to be as sound as that of the other, and her intellect to be as clear. Thus, then, while they have allowed the social inferiority of woman to continue, they have done all they could to raise her morally and intellectually to the level of man; and in this respect they appear to me to have excellently understood the true principle of democratic improvement.

As for myself, I do not hesitate to avow that although the women of the United States are confined within the narrow circle of domestic life, and their situation is in some respects one of extreme dependence, I have nowhere seen woman occupying a loftier position; and if I were asked, now that I am drawing to the close of this work, in which I have spoken of so many important things done by the Americans, to what the singular prosperity and growing strength of that people ought mainly to be attributed, I should reply: To the superiority of their women.

美国的立法者虽然减轻了刑法典中的几乎所有的惩罚条款，但仍将强奸定为死罪，而且公共舆论也给这种罪以无情的批判。这是可以理解的；因为美国人认为没有什么东西会比女性的荣誉更宝贵，也没有什么东西会比女性的自由更让人尊敬，因此美国人认为最应该对强行使妇女失去贞节和自由的人进行严加处罚。在法国，对这种罪判得很轻，往往很难见到一个陪审团作出有罪判决。这是轻视贞节的后果还是轻视妇女的后果呢？我不能不相信，这是对两者共同的轻视。

因此，美国人虽不认为男人和女人有同样的义务和权利去履行同样的职责，但对男女的作用却做同等的估评；尽管他们的命运是不同的，但作为人来说他们却具有相等的价值。他们没有赋予女人和男人一样的坚毅的勇气，也没有让女人像男人那样去使用自己的勇气，但他们从不怀疑妇女具有勇气；如果他们认为夫妇之间不应当总是以同样的方式运用各自的智力和理解力，但至少认为女性的理智与男性的同样清晰，女性的理解力与男性的同样可靠。因此，美国人允许妇女在社会上继续处于下等地位，却在智力和道德中尽力把妇女提高到与男人相同的水平；而且在这方面，他们使我觉得他们对于民主进步的真正含义有极好的理解。

至于我，我要毫不犹豫地声明：尽管美国的妇女被限制在家庭的这个小圈子里，她们在一定程度上还具有很大的依赖性，但她们的地位处处让我觉得她们处在很高的位置；如果有人问我，在我写的这本美国人做了那么多重大事情的书的结尾的时候，我会把这个国家的惊人繁荣和国力蒸蒸日上主要归功于什么，我将回答说：应当归功于它的妇女们优秀。

CHAPTER XIII

How The Principle Of Equality
Naturally Divides The Americans Into
A Multitude Of Small Private Circles

It might be supposed that the final and necessary effect of democratic institutions would be to identify all the members of the community in private as well as in public life and to compel them all to live alike, but this would be to ascribe a very coarse and oppressive form to the equality which originates in democracy. No state of society or laws can render men so much alike but that education, fortune, and tastes will interpose some differences between them; and though different men may sometimes find it their interest to combine for the same purposes, they will never make it their pleasure. They will therefore always tend to evade the provisions of law, whatever they may be; and escaping in some respect from the circle in which the legislator sought to confine them, they will set up, close by the great political community, small private societies, united together by similitude of conditions, habits, and customs.

In the United States the citizens have no sort of pre-eminence over one another; they owe each other no mutual obedience or respect; they all meet for the administration of justice, for the government of the state, and, in general, to treat of the affairs that concern their common welfare; but I never heard that attempts have been made to bring them all to follow the same diversions or to amuse themselves promiscuously in the same places of recreation.

The Americans, who mingle so readily in their political assemblies and courts of justice, are wont carefully to separate into small distinct circles in order to indulge by themselves in the enjoyments

第十三章　平等的原则是怎样将美国人分成许多私人小团体的

人们可能认为,民主制度的最终结果和必然效果,是像确定公共生活的成员一样也确定私人生活的成员,并强迫他们过同样的生活,这样,将会对民主所产生的平等作出极其粗浅和极其蛮横的解释。没有任何一种社会或法制会赋予人们在教育、财产和爱好方面的机会如此相同,没有一点差别;即使不同的人有时候可能发现齐心协力去做同一件事对他们有利,但他们决不会从其中发现乐趣。因此,他们总是想要逃避立法者的规定;并在逃脱立法者试图限制他们的活动而为他们规定的某种范围时,他们会在大的政治团体附近,建立起一些因条件、习惯或品德相似而结成的私人小团体。

在美国,任何公民都不会比其他公民具有优越性;他们既不需要彼此服从,又不需要相互尊敬;他们共同处理政府事务,共同管理国家,总之,就是大家一起去处理与他们共同幸福相关的事务;但是,我从来没听说有人主张大家以同样方式去消遣,或使男女混杂在同一场所游乐。

经常将政治集会和司法法庭混淆在一起的美国人,习惯于将自己分成为许多不同的小团体,以便纵容自己在那里享受私人生活方

of private life. Each of them willingly acknowledges all his fellow citizens as his equals, but will only receive a very limited number of them as his friends or his guests. This appears to me to be very natural. In proportion as the circle of public society is extended, it may be anticipated that the sphere of private intercourse will be contracted; far from supposing that the members of modern society will ultimately live in common, I am afraid they will end by forming only small coteries.

Among aristocratic nations the different classes are like vast enclosures, out of which it is impossible to get, into which it is impossible to enter. These classes have no communication with each other, but within them men necessarily live in daily contact; even though they would not naturally suit, the general conformity of a similar condition brings them near together.

But when neither law nor custom professes to establish frequent and habitual relations between certain men, their intercourse originates in the accidental similarity of opinions and tastes; hence private society is infinitely varied. In democracies, where the members of the community never differ much from each other and naturally stand so near that they may all at any time be fused in one general mass, numerous artificial and arbitrary distinctions spring up by means of which every man hopes to keep himself aloof lest he should be carried away against his will in the crowd. This can never fail to be the case, for human institutions can be changed, but man cannot; whatever may be the general endeavor of a community to render its members equal and alike, the personal pride of individuals will always seek to rise above the line and to form somewhere an inequality to their own advantage.

In aristocracies men are separated from each other by lofty stationary barriers; in democracies they are divided by many small and almost invisible threads, which are constantly broken or moved from place to place. Thus whatever may be the progress of equality, in democratic nations a great number of small private associations will always be formed within the general pale of political society; but none of them will bear any resemblance in its manners to the higher class in aristocracies.

面的乐趣。每个公民都乐意承认全体同胞一律平等,但只认为其中的极少数人是他的朋友和客人。在我看来这是很自然的。公共社会的圈子越大,私人关系的范围就要缩小;我不但想象不出新社会的公民最终会在生活上相似,反而担心他们可能形成许多小圈子。

在贵族国家里,每个阶级都像一个巨大的围栏,本阶级的成员出不来,而其他阶级的成员又进不去。各个阶级之间不相往来,但在每个阶级内部,人们每天都要发生联系;即使他们的天性并不相同,但身份的基本一致使他们走得更近。

但当法律和习惯都没有表示想在某些人之间建立经常的和普遍的关系时,则观点和喜好的偶然的相似,会作用于这种关系。因此,私人小团体各有各的特点。在民主制度下,公民之间永远不会相差很大,自然感到互相接近得随时都可能融合为一体,所以便人为地和随意地制定出许多小圈子,而每个人则试图依靠这种小圈子使自己与他人保持距离,唯恐身不由己地与众人合流。这种情况将永远存在下去,因为人类自己创造的制度可以被改变,但人们自身却不能被改变;无论社会怎样竭尽全力去使公民平等和相同,个人的骄傲总会试图使自己高于平均水平线,希望在某一方面形成对己有利的局面。

在贵族制度下,人们被高高的壁垒彼此隔开;在民主制度下,人们却被许多小得几乎看不见的线所隔开,人们虽然随时都可以冲断这些线,但这些线也可以不断移动位置而重新连结起来。因此,无论平等具有多么大的进步性,在民主国家里总要形成大量的私人小团体,让它们分布在政治社会的广大范围内;但是,这些小团体的成员没有一个在仪表上跟领导贵族国家的上等阶级相同。

CHAPTER XIV
Some Reflections
On American Manners

Nothing seems at first sight less important than the outward form of human actions, yet there is nothing upon which men set more store; they grow used to everything except to living in a society which has not their own manners.

The influence of the social and political state of a country upon manners is therefore deserving of serious examination. Manners are generally the product of the very basis of character, but they are also sometimes the result of an arbitrary convention between certain men. Thus they are at once natural and acquired.

When some men perceive that they are the foremost persons in society, without contest and without effort, when they are constantly engaged on large objects, leaving the more minute details to others, and when they live in the enjoyment of wealth which they did not a-mass and do not fear to lose, it may be supposed that they feel a kind of haughty disdain of the petty interests and practical cares of life and that their thoughts assume a natural greatness which their language and their manners denote. In democratic countries manners are gener-ally devoid of dignity because private life is there extremely petty in its character; and they are frequently low because the mind has few opportunities of rising above the engrossing cares of domestic inter-ests.

True dignity in manners consists in always taking one's proper station, neither too high nor too low, and this is as much within the reach of a peasant as of a prince. In democracies all stations appear

第十四章　对美国人的礼节
上的一些反响

　　初次看来,似乎再没有什么东西会比人的外在行为更不重要的了,人们对行为外在的重视却胜过一切东西;除非人们生活在一个不讲仪表的社会里,否则人们已习惯了一切为人处世方式。

　　因此,社会情况和政治情况对仪表的影响,是很值得认真研究的。一般说来,仪表是人类基本特性的产物,但有时它也是某些人之间的随意约定的结果。因此,仪表既是天生俱有的,又是后天获得的。

　　当一些人认识到可以在不费周折和不经努力的情况下出人头地,觉得自己每天都在参与重大的工作而把一些琐碎的小事留给别人去做,感到自己在享受的不是由他们自己创造的财富且不怕失去财富的时候,你就可以想象他们对小小的利益和生活上的物质享受持有一种高傲的轻视感,他们的思想呈现出一种流露于语言和仪表上的自然伟大感。在民主国家里,人们的仪表往往缺乏尊严,因为在那里,私人的生活是很渺小的;人们的仪表往往很粗俗,因为民主国家的人只忙于家务,很少有机会提升自己的仪表。

　　仪表的真正尊严在于能找到人们适当的地位,既不高也不低,这一点,农民和王公一样都能做到。在民主国家里,所有人的

doubtful; hence it is that the manners of democracies, though often full of arrogance, are commonly wanting in dignity, and, moreover, they are never either well trained or accomplished.

The men who live in democracies are too fluctuating for a certain number of them ever to succeed in laying down a code of good breeding and in forcing people to follow it. Every man therefore behaves after his own fashion, and there is always a certain incoherence in the manners of such times, because they are molded upon the feelings and notions of each individual rather than upon an ideal model proposed for general imitation. This, however, is much more perceptible when an aristocracy has just been overthrown than after it has long been destroyed. New political institutions and new social elements then bring to the same places of resort, and frequently compel to live in common, men whose education and habits are still amazingly dissimilar, and this renders the motley composition of society peculiarly visible. The existence of a former strict code of good breeding is still remembered, but what it contained or where it is to be found is already forgotten. Men have lost the common law of manners and they have not yet made up their minds to do without it, but everyone endeavors to make to himself some sort of arbitrary and variable rule from the remnant of former usages, so that manners have neither the regularity and the dignity which they often display among aristocratic nations, nor the simplicity and freedom which they sometimes assume in democracies; they are at once constrained and without constraint.

This, however, is not the normal state of things. When the equality of conditions is long established and complete, as all men entertain nearly the same notions and do nearly the same things they do not require to agree, or to copy from one another, in order to speak or act in the same manner; their manners are constantly characterized by a number of lesser diversities, but not by any great differences. They are never perfectly alike because they do not copy from the same pattern; they are never very unlike because their social condition is the same. At first sight a traveler would say that the manners of all Americans are

地位似乎都是不确定的;所以民族社会中人们的仪表尽管充满着傲慢自大,很却缺乏尊严,甚至,民主国家的人的仪表既没有严格的规范,又不需要经过严格的训练。

生活在民主制度下的人变动性很大,以致有些人很难养成彬彬有礼的仪表,即使养成也不能长期遵守。因此,每个人根据自己的意志行动,在仪表上经常有一种互不连贯的表现,因为每个人的仪表都是根据个人的思想和感情形成的,而不是根据供所有人模仿的理想典范形成的。而且,这一点在贵族制度刚被推翻时,比在贵族制度已被推翻很久以后表现得更为明显。因此,新的政治制度和新的社会因素,便把在教育程度和生活习惯上差异很大的一些人聚集在同一地点,并常常强迫他们过共同的生活,从而使社会混杂的场景清楚可见。人们还依稀记得以前有过严格的礼仪典范,但已经忘却它的内容和出处。人们已经失去了共同的仪表准则,但还不想永远抛弃它,而是努力使用旧规矩所遗留的某种任意规定的和可以随时改变的仪表准则,结果,仪表既不像在贵族制度时期被表现的那样有规律和受人尊重,也不像在民主制度下被表现的那样简单和自由;仪表显得既受拘束又不受拘束。

当然,这不是事务的正常状态。当平等的条件实行得既长久又全面,而所有的人几乎都具有同样的观念和做同样的事情,不需要经过互相商量和彼此模仿而使他们在行动和语言上保持一致;人们便可以不断发现他们的仪表虽有很多细小的差别,但无重大的不同。仪表永远不会完全相同,因为它没有统一的模式;仪表也永远不会有极大的差别,因为它的社会条件是相同的。一个陌生者在看到美国第一眼后,可能觉得全体美国人的仪表完全

exactly similar; it is only upon close examination that the peculiarities in which they differ may be detected.

The English make game of the manners of the Americans, but it is singular that most of the writers who have drawn these ludicrous delineations belonged themselves to the middle classes in England, to whom the same delineations are exceedingly applicable, so that these pitiless censors furnish, for the most part, an example of the very thing they blame in the United States. They do not perceive that they are deriding themselves, to the great amusement of the aristocracy of their own country. Nothing is more prejudicial to democrary than its outward forms of behavior; many men would willingly endure its vices who cannot support its manners. I cannot, however, admit that there is nothing commendable in the manners of a democratic people. Among aristocratic nations, all who live within reach of the first class in society commonly strain to be like it, which gives rise to ridiculous and insipid imitations. As a democratic people do not possess any models of high breeding, at least they escape the daily necessity of seeing wretched copies of them. In democracies manners are never so refined as among aristocratic nations, but on the other hand they are never so coarse. Neither the coarse oaths of the populace nor the elegant and choice expressions of the nobility are to be heard there; the manners of such a people are often vulgar, but they are neither brutal nor mean.

I have already observed that in democracies no such thing as a regular code of good breeding can be laid down; this has some inconveniences and some advantages. In aristocracies the rules of propriety impose the same demeanor on everyone; they make all the members of the same class appear alike in spite of their private inclinations; they adorn and they conceal the natural man. Among a democratic people manners are neither so tutored nor so uniform, but they are frequently more sincere. They form, as it were, a light and loosely woven veil through which the real feelings and private opinions of each individual are easily discernible. The form and the substance of human actions, therefore, often stand there in closer relation; and if the great picture of human life is less embellished, it is more true. Thus it may be said, in one sense, that

一样;在经过仔细考察后,才能发现其中的细微差别。

英国人最爱嘲笑美国人的仪表,但很奇怪,向我们作如此可笑描述的大部分作家,自己也属于英国中产阶级,因此,这些无情的检查员,通常都是责备美国人的那些举止的行动者。他们并不认为这是在自己嘲弄自己,从而使他们本国的贵族觉得可笑。再没有什么比人们的行为的外表形式更对民主有偏见的了;许多人宁愿忍受民主的缺陷,而不愿支持其应有的仪表。但是,我并不认为民主国家人们的仪表一无可取。在贵族国家里,一般达到社会上层阶级的人,都普遍装得跟上层阶级一样,这就带给人们很多荒唐可笑的模仿行为。民主国家的人民既然没有可供高等教育的榜样,他们至少可以逃过每天履行讨厌的模仿的义务。在民主国家里,人们的仪表从来不像贵族国家的那样优雅,但另一方面,它也从来不粗俗。在那里,既没有低俗人的那种粗野的语言,也没有高贵人的那种优雅的语言;民主国家的习俗往往很平淡但决不粗野和低贱。

我曾经讲过,在民主国家里,不可能有如此正规的优雅的行为准则;这既有不便之处,又有它的好处。在贵族国家里,规章礼节使所有人的举止一致;它使同一阶级里的每个人都有相同的外表,不管这些人的私人喜好;它们修饰着并隐藏了人的本性。在民主国家里,人们的仪表既不会表现得很有教养,也不会表现得很统一,但是它们往往更真实。在这里,人们的仪表就好像是一层轻轻地并且松散的面纱,透过这层薄纱我们可以清楚地辨别出人们的真实感情和个人观点。因此,人们行动的外表和实质往往表现得很紧密;虽然它所反映出的人类的生活是不加修饰的,但却是真实的。因此,或许可以说,在某种意义上,民主的效果并不是要赋

the effect of democracy is not exactly to give men any particular manners, but to prevent them from having manners at all.

The feelings, the passions, the virtues, and the vices of an aristocracy may sometimes reappear in a democracy, but not its manners; they are lost and vanish forever as soon as the democratic revolution is completed. It would seem that nothing is more lasting than the manners of an aristocratic class, for they are preserved by that class for some time after it has lost its wealth and its power; nor so fleeting, for no sooner have they disappeared than not a trace of them is to be found, and it is scarcely possible to say what they have been as soon as they have ceased to be. A change in the state of society works this miracle, and a few generations suffice to consummate it. The principal characteristics of aristocracy are handed down by history after an aristocracy is destroyed, but the light and exquisite touches of manners are effaced from men's memories almost immediately after its fall. Men can no longer conceive what these manners were when they have ceased to witness them; they are gone and their departure was unseen, unfelt, for in order to feel that refined enjoyment which is derived from choice and distinguished manners, habit and education must have prepared the heart, and the taste for them is lost almost as easily as the practice of them. Thus, not only cannot a democratic people have aristocratic manners, but they neither comprehend nor desire them; and as they never have thought of them, it is to their minds as if such things had never been. Too much importance should not be attached to this loss, but it may well be regretted.

I am aware that it has not infrequently happened that the same men have had very high-bred manners and very low-born feelings; the interior of courts has sufficiently shown what imposing externals may conceal the meanest hearts. But though the manners of aristocracy do not constitute virtue, they sometimes embellish virtue itself. It was no ordinary sight to see a numerous and powerful class of men whose every outward action seemed constantly to be dictated by a natural elevation of thought and feeling, by delicacy and regularity of taste, and

予人们任何特殊仪表,而是阻止人们拥有一定的仪表。

　　有时在一个民主国家里可以发现贵族国家的感觉、激情、美德和恶行,但绝对不会看到贵族的仪表;在民主革命完全结束的时候,贵族的仪表便不复存在和永远消失了。表面上看,似乎任何东西都不会比贵族阶级的仪表更持久,因为这个阶级在失去了财产和权力之后,它的仪表还能保持一段时间;然而它又是如此的短暂,因为在它消失之后便一点痕迹也找不到了,因此我们几乎不可能确定它曾经存在过。社会情况的变化,创造了需要几代人的努力才能完成的奇迹。贵族制度的主要特点,在贵族制度被摧毁之后随着历史的轨迹流传下来,而贵族仪表的高雅的举止,则几乎随着贵族制度的衰落而立刻被人们遗忘。当人们见不到贵族的高雅仪表时,也就不再想象它是什么样了;它已经消逝了,它的消逝是看不见也感觉不到的,因为要想从选择和区别仪表中感觉这种有限的快乐,就必须先在习惯上和教育上有思想准备,并且对这种快乐的感觉将很容易随着停止采用选定的仪表而消失掉。因此,不仅民主国家的人民不会有贵族的仪表,而且他们也不会理解和渴望有贵族的仪表;他们从来没有想象过会有贵族的仪表,在他们看来,好像那样的仪表从来没有存在过似的。对这种损失我们不应过于重视,但要表示遗憾。

　　我知道,常常会发生一个仪表十分高雅的人,而其感情却十分低俗;法庭可以足够表现出,人们的外表往往可能隐藏其卑鄙的内心。尽管贵族的仪表不能称得上是一种美德,但有时可以修饰美德本身。但我们不能以普通的眼光去衡量一个人数众多和力量强大的阶级,他们一直都以其生活上的一切外在表现来显示其感情和思想的高尚本性,其爱好好像是高雅和合理的,其举

by urbanity of manners. Those manners threw a pleasing illusory charm over human nature; and though the picture was often a false one, it could not be viewed without a noble satisfaction.

止好像是文质彬彬的。贵族的仪表使人对人性产生了美丽的幻觉;尽管贵族的仪表往往是虚伪的,但会使人产生一种高尚的满足感。

CHAPTER XV
Of The Gravity Of The Americans, And Why It Does Not Prevent Them From Often Doing Inconsiderate Things

Men who live in democratic countries do not value the simple, turbulent, or coarse diversions in which the people in aristocratic communities indulge; such diversions are thought by them to be puerile or insipid. Nor have they a greater inclination for the intellectual and refined amusements of the aristocratic classes. They want something productive and substantial in their pleasures; they want to mix actual fruition with their joy.

In aristocratic communities the people readily give themselves up to bursts of tumultuous and boisterous gaiety, which shake off at once the recollection of their privations. The inhabitants of democracies are not fond of being thus violently broken in upon, and they never lose sight of themselves without regret. Instead of these frivolous delights they prefer those more serious and silent amusements which are like business and which do not drive business wholly out of their minds.

An American, instead of going in a leisure hour to dance merrily at some place of public resort, as the fellows of his class continue to do throughout the greater part of Europe, shuts himself up at home to drink. He thus enjoys two pleasures; he can go on thinking of his business and can get drunk decently by his own fireside.

I thought that the English constituted the most serious nation on the face of the earth, but I have since seen the Americans and have changed my opinion. I do not mean to say that temperament has not a great deal to do with the character of the inhabitants of the United States, but I think that their political institutions are a still more influential cause.

第十五章　美国人的严谨精神，和这种精神为什么没能阻止美国人经常做出草率的事情

民主国家的人民，决不喜欢贵族制度下的人民所热衷的那些简单的、喧闹的和粗俗的娱乐活动；他们认为这种娱乐是幼稚和无聊的。他们也不喜欢贵族阶级的高雅的文化娱乐。他们喜欢具有生产价值和实际物质利益的享乐；他们希望把享乐和实际联系在一起，既能享乐，也能得到实际利益。

在贵族制社会里，人们纵容自己沉湎于喧嚣和吵闹的欢乐气氛中，以暂时忘却他们生活中的苦难。民主国家的人民则不喜欢把自己放到这样激烈的环境中，他们从来不会因为自己的失控而表示后悔。相比这些轻浮的快乐，他们更喜爱那种类似于工作但又不会让他们完全忘掉工作的严肃而安静的享乐。

大部分欧洲人在工作之余喜欢到公共场所去跳舞娱乐，而与这些欧洲人职业相同的美国人则喜欢在工作之余把自己关在家里独饮。这时个人享受了两种快乐：一方面可以继续考虑自己的工作，一方面可以在自己家里喝得酩酊大醉。

我本以为英国人是世界上最严肃的民族，但当我看到美国人后便改变了我的看法。我并不是指性情未对美国人的性格产生重大作用，但我认为政治制度对他们的性格的影响更大。

I believe the seriousness of the Americans arises partly from their pride. In democratic countries even poor men entertain a lofty notion of their personal importance; they look upon themselves with complacency and are apt to suppose that others are looking at them too. With this disposition, they watch their language and their actions with care and do not lay themselves open so as to betray their deficiencies; to preserve their dignity, they think it necessary to retain their gravity.

But I detect another more deep-seated and powerful cause which instinctively produces among the Americans this astonishing gravity. Under a despotism communities give way at times to bursts of vehement joy, but they are generally gloomy and moody because they are afraid. Under absolute monarchies tempered by the customs and manners of the country, their spirits are often cheerful and even, because, as they have some freedom and a good deal of security, they are exempted from the most important cares of life; but all free nations are serious because their minds are habitually absorbed by the contemplation of some dangerous or difficult purpose. This is more especially the case among those free nations which form democratic communities. Then there is, in all classes, a large number of men constantly occupied with the serious affairs of the government; and those whose thoughts are not engaged in the matters of the commonwealth are wholly engrossed by the acquisition of a private fortune. Among such a people a serious demeanor ceases to be peculiar to certain men and becomes a habit of the nation.

We are told of small democracies in the days of antiquity in which the citizens met in the public places with garlands of roses and spent almost all their time in dancing and theatrical amusements. I do not believe in such republics any more than in that of Plato; or if the things we read of really happened, I do not hesitate to affirm that these supposed democracies were composed of very different elements from ours and that they had nothing in common with the latter except their name.

But it must not be supposed that in the midst of all their toils the people who live in democracies think themselves to be pitied; the contrary is noticed to be the case. No men are fonder of their

　　我相信美国人的严谨部分来源于他们的自傲。在民主国家里,即使是一个穷人也十分重视自身的高尚品格;他们对自己很满足,而且也以为别人也会这样看待他们。在这种情况下,他们很重视自己的言行举止,决不玩物忘形,以免暴露自己的缺点;为了保护他们的尊贵,他们认为,就必须保持其严谨的精神。

　　但我发现,使美国人产生这种使我感到吃惊的似乎是来自本能的严谨精神,还有一个更根深蒂固和更有力的原因。在专制制度下,人民有时会沉溺于激情的欢乐中,但他们总是郁郁不乐和沉默寡言的,因为他们害怕专制制度。在专制君主国家,王权会受到习惯和民情的限制,普通人民的精神往往是愉悦的,因为他们享有一定的自由和极大的安全,不必为生活过于担忧;但是,所有自由的民族都是严谨的,因为他们的思想会习惯性地想到事业的艰难险阻。而这种情况尤其适用于民主制度的自由国家的人民。因此在各个阶级,都有很多人会不断参与国家大事;而那些想法不在国家公有财产上的人,则一心专注于对个人的财富的获得。因此,严谨精神在这样的国家里就不是为某些人所特有,而成为整个民族的习惯。

　　有人告诉我们,在古代的一些小共和国里,人们戴着玫瑰花环聚集在公共场所,几乎把全部时间都花费在跳舞和观看戏剧上了。我不相信这样的共和国会更甚于不相信柏拉图的共和国;如果事实真的像他们所说的那样,我会毫不犹豫地确认,他们所设想的共和国的构成要素大大地不同于我们所说的共和国的构成要素,除了名称一样以外,两者没有任何共同之处。

　　但是我们也不应该以为,生活在民主制度下的人民总觉得自己很可怜;而情况恰恰相反。没有一个地方的人能像他们那样安

own condition. Life would have no relish for them if they were delivered from the anxieties which harass them, and they show more attachment to their cares than aristocratic nations to their pleasures.

I am next led to inquire how it is that these same democratic nations which are so serious sometimes act in so inconsiderate a manner. The Americans, who almost always preserve a staid demeanor and a frigid air, nevertheless frequently allow themselves to be borne away, far beyond the bounds of reason, by a sudden passion or a hasty opinion and sometimes gravely commit strange absurdities. This contrast ought not to surprise us. There is one sort of ignorance which originates in extreme publicity. In despotic states men do not know how to act because they are told nothing; in democratic nations they often act at random because nothing is to be left untold. The former do not know, the latter forget; and the chief features of each picture are lost to them in a bewilderment of details.

It is astonishing what imprudent language a public man may sometimes use in free countries, and especially in democratic states, without being compromised; whereas in absolute monarchies a few words dropped by accident are enough to unmask him forever and ruin him without hope of redemption. This is explained by what goes before. When a man speaks in the midst of a great crowd, many of his words are not heard or are forthwith obliterated from the memories of those who hear them; but amid the silence of a mute and motionless throng the slightest whisper strikes the ear.

In democracies men are never stationary; a thousand chances waft them to and fro, and their life is always the sport of unforeseen or (so to speak) extemporaneous circumstances. Thus they are often obliged to do things which they have imperfectly learned, to say things which they imperfectly understand, and to devote themselves to work for which they are unprepared by long apprenticeship. In aristocracies every man has one sole object, which he unceasingly pursues; but among

于自己的现状。如果不让他们为生活的烦恼而担心,那么他们反而感到人生乏味了,他们对生活的操心胜过贵族对享受的追求。

下一步,我该要询问,如此严谨的民主国家人民为什么有时候做事会那样的欠考虑。几乎总是保持冷静的风度和稳重的举止的美国人,却往往不能自我克制,在突发的激情或草率的判断之下越出了理性的限界,有时会做出一些荒唐的事情来。我们不应该对这种矛盾感到吃惊。有一种无知是由于极端的宣传引起的。在专制国家里,人们之所以不知如何行事,是因为没有人告诉他们该怎么做;而在民主国家里,人们之所以常常任意行事,是因为有人已把一切都告诉他们。前者是什么也不知道,后者是把知道的东西都忘了;双方就像两幅画,它们的特点是没有对景物细节的描绘。

让人吃惊的是,在自由国家,尤其是在民主国家,一个公共官员有时可能说出粗俗的语言,也不会对他有什么危险;而在君主专制国家,公共官员只是偶尔说出的几句话,就足以使他永远丢掉官职,并没有挽救的余地。以前发生的许多事情都可以证明这一点。当一个人在拥挤的人群里讲话时,有许多话不会被人听见,而且即使听到了,也很快被人忘掉;但当你对着安静的人群讲话时,即使是低声细语,也能被人听见。

在民主国家里,人们从来不是静止不动的;有成千上万的机会使他们来来回回,他们的生活总是受到一些未知因素的控制,或许说是被一种即兴的力量所控制。因此,他们往往会被迫去做一些他们还没有学会的事情,去说他们根本没有理解的话,去投身于他们没有经过长期学习而准备好的事业。在贵族制度下,每个人只有一个终生追求的目标;但在民主国家里,人们的生活是

democratic nations the existence of man is more complex; the same mind will almost always embrace several objects at once, and these objects are frequently wholly foreign to each other. As it cannot know them all well, the mind is readily satisfied with imperfect notions of each.

When the inhabitant of a democracy is not urged by his wants, he is so at least by his desires; for of all the possessions that he sees around him, none are wholly beyond his reach. He therefore does everything in a hurry, he is always satisfied with "pretty well," and never pauses more than an instant to consider what he has been doing. His curiosity is at once insatiable and cheaply satisfied; for he cares more to know a great deal quickly than to know anything well; he has no time and but little taste to search things to the bottom.

Thus, then, a democratic people are grave because their social and political condition constantly leads them to engage in serious occupations, and they act inconsiderately because they give but little time and attention to each of these occupations. The habit of inattention must be considered as the greatest defect of the democratic character.

极为复杂的;同一个人总是同时抱有几个目标,并且各个目标之间没有任何联系。因为他们不能对每个目的都了解得十分清楚,所以容易满足于、安于一知半解。

当民主国家的居民不再由于贫困而有强烈的欲望时,至少也要受到合理意愿的逼迫;因为他们看到周围的一切财富或福利,没有一个是超越了他们获得范围的。因此,他们急于去干一切事情,而且常常在干得差不多时就满意了,对他们的每个行动从不用一点时间去问其所以。他们的好奇心是永无止境的和容易满足的;因为他们所关心的是在最快的速度中知道更多,而不是将这些东西了解得更深刻;他们没有时间,而且主要是没有兴趣去深入研究事物。

总之,民主国家的人民之所以严谨,是因为他们的社会情况和政治情况不断地领导他们去参与需要认真办理的工作,而他们之所以有时会不假思索地办事,是因为他们只有不多的时间和精力去做其中的每一项工作。注意力不集中的习惯,应被视为民主精神的最大缺陷。

CHAPTER XVI

Why The National Vanity Of The Americans Is More Restless And Captious Than That Of The English[①]

All free nations are vainglorious, but national pride is not displayed by all in the same manner. The Americans, in their intercourse with strangers, appear impatient of the smallest censure and insatiable of praise. The most slender eulogy is acceptable to them, the most exalted seldom contents them; they unceasingly harass you to extort praise, and if you resist their entreaties, they fall to praising themselves. It would seem as if, doubting their own merit, they wished to have it constantly exhibited before their eyes. Their vanity is not only greedy, but restless and jealous; it will grant nothing, while it demands everything, but is ready to beg and to quarrel at the same time.

If I say to an American that the country he lives in is a fine one, "Ay," he replies, "there is not its equal in the world." If I applaud the freedom that its inhabitants enjoy, he answers: "Freedom is a fine thing, but few nations are worthy to enjoy it." If I remark on the purity of morals that distinguishes the United States, "I can imagine," says he, "that a stranger, who has witnessed the corruption that prevails in other nations, would be astonished at the dif-

---

① See Appendix W.

第十六章 为什么美国人的民族自负心 要比英国人轻浮和喜欢挑剔 [①]

所有自由国家的人民都是自傲的,但民族自豪感的表现形式并不一致。美国人在同外国人交往时,对很小的责难都表现出不耐烦的态度,而对赞美之词则总嫌不够。一句微不足道的赞词,都会让他们很满意,高高在上的尊贵已经不能使他们满足;他们不断骚扰你,向你索取赞美之词,如果你拒绝他们的要求,他们便会自己赞美自己。他们似乎自己都在怀疑自身的优点,所以总希望别人能在他们面前称赞他们几句。他们的自负心不仅是贪婪的,而且是无休止的和带有嫉妒之心的;这种自负心不会付出任何东西,但想索取所有东西,它既随时准备乞求,又同时准备着争吵。

如果我对一个美国人说他所生活的国家是个很好的国家,他立即回答说:"不错,世界上没有一个国家可以比得上它!"如果我继续称赞那里的人民享有自由,他回答说:"自由是一个好东西,但很少有国家能有资格享受它。"如果我指出美国人非常明显的纯朴的民情,他接着说:"我想象得出,一个曾见证过其他一切国家的贪污腐化现象的外国人,会为这种纯朴的民情大吃一惊。"最

① 见附录 W。

ference. " At length I leave him to the contemplation of himself; but he returns to the charge and does not desist till he has got me to repeat all I had just been saying. It is impossible to conceive a more troublesome or more garrulous patriotism; it wearies even those who are disposed to respect it.

Such is not the case with the English. An Englishman calmly enjoys the real or imaginary advantages which, in his opinion, his country possesses. If he grants nothing to other nations, neither does he solicit anything for his own. The censure of foreigners does not affect him, and their praise hardly flatters him; his position with regard to the rest of the world is one of disdainful and ignorant reserve: his pride requires no sustenance; it nourishes itself. It is remarkable that two nations so recently sprung from the same stock should be so opposite to each other in their manner of feeling and conversing.

In aristocratic countries the great possess immense privileges, upon which their pride rests without seeking to rely upon the lesser advantages that accrue to them. As these privileges came to them by inheritance, they regard them in some sort as a portion of themselves, or at least as a natural right inherent in their own persons. They therefore entertain a calm sense of their own superiority; they do not dream of vaunting privileges which everyone perceives and no one contests, and these things are not sufficiently new to be made topics of conversation. They stand unmoved in their solitary greatness, well assured that they are seen by all the world without any effort to show themselves off, and that no one will attempt to drive them from that position. When an aristocracy carries on the public affairs, its national pride naturally assumes this reserved, indifferent, and haughty form, which is imitated by all the other classes of the nation.

When, on the contrary, social conditions differ but little, the slightest privileges are of some importance; as every man sees around himself a million people enjoying precisely similar or analogous advantages, his pride becomes craving and jealous, he clings to mere trifles and doggedly defends them. In democracies, as the conditions of life are very fluctuating, men have almost always

后，我让他考虑一下自己都做了些什么；但他一定要回到原来的话题上来，直到让我把刚才的话重复一遍他才肯停止。我们很难想象这种令人讨厌的和做作的爱国精神；就连称赞这种精神的人也感到厌烦了。

在英国就不会发生这样的情况。英国人总是默默地享受在他们看来是自己国家所拥有的真实优点。他们既不称赞别的国家，又不要求别人称赞他们的国家。外国人的贬语责难并不会惹恼他们，而外国人的赞扬，也不会使他们得意到忘乎所以；他们对待全世界保持着一种既傲慢又无知的态度；他们的傲慢不需要别人的支持，而由自己提供营养。两个血统基本相同的民族，在举止和言谈上却如此大相径庭，实在令人惊奇。

在贵族国家里，那些高官贵族拥有得以让他们骄傲的无尽的特权，不必依靠他们本国的优点去发展这种感情。由于这些特权是由祖辈遗留给他们的，所以他们把这些特权视为自身的一部分，或者至少是他们与生俱来的权力。因此，他们对自己的优越性持有一种泰然的心理；他们从来没有想过要吹嘘这种人人都知道的和没有人想和他们争夺的权力，并且在他们看来，这些事情根本不足以构成谈话的主题。他们固若泰山，独享高贵，他们确定自己不必费力也会引起世人的注意，并且没有人企图推翻他们。当贵族处理国家事务的时候，他们的民族自豪感自然会表现出这种有所保留的、淡漠的和自傲的形式，而国内的其余一切阶级也随之效仿。

相反的，当社会身份的差别不大时，很小的特权也非常有意义；人人都见到在他周围有成千上万的人也享有与自己完全相同或类似的优势后，他们的自豪感就会变为贪婪的和嫉妒的，他们

recently acquired the advantages which they possess; the consequence is that they feel extreme pleasure in exhibiting them, to show others and convince themselves that they really enjoy them. As at any instant these same advantages may be lost, their possessors are constantly on the alert and make a point of showing that they still retain them. Men living in democracies love their country just as they love themselves, and they transfer the habits of their private vanity to their vanity as a nation.

The restless and insatiable vanity of a democratic people originates so entirely in the equality and precariousness of their social condition that the members of the haughtiest nobility display the very same passion in those lesser portions of their existence in which there is anything fluctuating or contested. An aristocratic class always differs greatly from the other classes of the nation, by the extent and perpetuity of its privileges; but it often happens that the only differences between the members who belong to it consist in small, transient advantages, which may any day be lost or acquired. The members of a powerful aristocracy, collected in a capital or a court, have been known to contest with virulence those frivolous privileges which depend on the caprice of fashion or the will of their master. These persons then displayed towards each other precisely the same puerile jealousies that animate the men of democracies, the same eagerness to snatch the smallest advantages which their equals contested, and the same desire to parade ostentatiously those of which they were in possession.

If national pride ever entered into the minds of courtiers, I do not question that they would display it in the same manner as the members of a democratic community.

为了一些细小的琐事也会竞争到底,在顽固地保护着自己的利益。在民主国家里,由于人们的生活条件是经常变动的,所以他们拥有的优势几乎总是不断更新;因此这就使他们在显示这些权势时感到无尽的快乐,以使别人相信自己是确实拥有优势。由于这种优势随时都有可能失去,所以他们总是提心吊胆的,并想极力显示自己享有优势。生活在民主国家的人,爱他们的国家就像爱他们自己,并把他们个人的自负心转变成民族自负心。

民主国家人民的永无休止和永不知足的自负心,完全来源于他们社会身份的平等和不稳定,以致一些最高尚的贵族在他们生活当中的一些小事情发生变动或引起争论时,也会显示出同样的激情。贵族阶级总是由于特权范围的扩大和永恒,而与其他阶级有所不同;至于贵族成员之间有时出现的唯一差异,则只是由于随时可以获得或失去的暂时小利益而造成的。但是,一个强大的贵族阶级的成员,聚集到首都或宫廷,为了争夺主人随心所欲赐予的很小的特权而相互争吵。这些人带着妒忌心彼此互相攻击,这使民主制度下的人感到可笑,为得到一小点利益而互不相让,并用各种理由证明他们也需要享有这种利益。

一旦阿谀逢迎的人也有了民族自豪感,我毫不怀疑,他们也会像民主国家的这号人一样来显示这种自豪感。

CHAPTER XVII

How The Aspect Of Society
In The United States Is At Once
Excited And Monotonous

It would seem that nothing could be more adapted to stimulate and to feed curiosity than the aspect of the United States. Fortunes, opinions, and laws are there in ceaseless variation; it is as if immutable Nature herself were mutable, such are the changes worked upon her by the hand of man. Yet in the end the spectacle of this excited community becomes monotonous, and after having watched the moving pageant for a time, the spectator is tired of it.

Among aristocratic nations every man is pretty nearly stationary in his own sphere, but men are astonishingly unlike each other; their passions, their notions, their habits, and their tastes are essentially different: nothing changes, but everything differs. In democracies, on the contrary, all men are alike and do things pretty nearly alike. It is true that they are subject to great and frequent vicissitudes, but as the same events of good or adverse fortune are continually recurring, only the name of the actors is changed, the piece is always the same. The aspect of American society is animated because men and things are always changing, but it is monotonous because all these changes are alike.

Men living in democratic times have many passions, but most of

第十七章　美国的社会面貌为什么
既千变万化又单调一致

看来,没有什么东西能比美国的社会面貌更适于刺激和培养人们的好奇心的。美国人的命运,观念和国家的法律在不断地变化着;由于人们每天都在改造自然,所以好像不动的自然本身也发生了变化。但是,在经过长期观察后,这个千变万化的社会会变得更加单调,而观察者对这个如此变动无常的景象观察一段时间后,还会感到厌烦。

在贵族国家,每个人几乎都固定于自己的活动范围,但人与人之间却有着惊异的差别;人们的激情、观念、习惯和喜好都有本质上的差别;看似好像任何事物都没有改变,但每件事务之间都有不同。相反的,在民主国家,所有的人都一样,并做几乎相同的工作。不错,他们受到社会的巨大和频繁的变迁的影响,但成功和失败是经常反复的,仅仅是演员的姓名改变了,剧情总是一样的。美国社会的面貌是千变万化的,因为那里的人和物都在不断地变化,但它又是单调一致的,因为那里的一切变化都是相同的。

生活在民主时代的人拥有很多激情,但他们的大部分激情都以对财富的热爱而结束,或来源于对财富的热爱。这不是因为他们的精神境界很狭隘,而是因为人们对金钱的热爱往往会产生

their passions either end in the love of riches or proceed from it. The cause of this is not that their souls are narrower, but that the importance of money is really greater at such times. When all the members of a community are independent of or indifferent to each other, the co-operation of each of them can be obtained only by paying for it: this infinitely multiplies the purposes to which wealth may be applied and increases its value. When the reverence that belonged to what is old has vanished, birth, condition, and profession no longer distinguish men, or scarcely distinguish them; hardly anything but money remains to create strongly marked differences between them and to raise some of them above the common level. The distinction originating in wealth is increased by the disappearance or diminution of all other distinctions. Among aristocratic nations money reaches only to a few points on the vast circle of man's desires; in democracies it seems to lead to all.

The love of wealth is therefore to be traced, as either a principal or an accessory motive, at the bottom of all that the Americans do; this gives to all their passions a sort of family likeness and soon renders the survey of them exceedingly wearisome. This perpetual recurrence of the same passion is monotonous; the peculiar methods by which this passion seeks its own gratification are no less so.

In an orderly and peaceable democracy like the United States, where men cannot enrich themselves by war, by public office, or by political confiscation, the love of wealth mainly drives them into business and manufactures. Although these pursuits often bring about great commotions and disasters, they cannot prosper without strictly regular habits and a long routine of petty uniform acts. The stronger the passion is, the more regular are these habits and the more uniform are these acts. It may be said that it is the vehemence of their desires that makes the Americans so methodical; it perturbs their minds, but it disciplines their lives.

The remark I here apply to America may indeed be addressed to almost all our contemporaries. Variety is disappearing from the human race; the same ways of acting, thinking, and feeling are to be met

更大的作用。当全体公民之间都是互不关心和互不依赖时，那么人与人之间的合作只有通过金钱才能达到；这就使财富的作用无限扩大，使财富的价值也随之增加。当古人的那种尊敬一旦消失，出身、地位和职业也不再能区分人类，或者说几乎不能区分人类了；而只有金钱能构成人类之间的显著差别，能使某些人高于普通大众。建立在财富之上的差别，随着其他差别的消失和缩小而增加。在贵族国家，金钱只能达到人类庞大的欲望圈的某几个点上；而在民主国家，金钱似乎能到达这个圈的所有点上。

因此，我们处处都可以见到美国人对财富的热爱，它既可以是一个主要动机，也可以是次要动机，成了美国人做事的一切基础；这使他们的所有激情都具有家庭色彩，以致在你看到这种情况之后感到讨厌。同样的热情如此相继出现，就使人感到单调了；而满足这种热情的每个具体过程，也同样是单调的。

在像美国这样稳定和和平的民主国家，人们不可能依靠战争、依靠公共事务或政治手段而使自己致富，所以对财富的热爱都使人们投身于商业和制造业。但是，由于这种追求往往会引发严重的混乱和灾难，所以如果没有严格有序的经营习惯和长期统一的经营理念，他们是无法使工商业繁荣的。经营者的激情越强，经营习惯就越严格有序，经营理念也会更加统一。可以说正是美国人的这种强烈的事业心使他们能够如此有条不紊；这种事业心虽使他们的思想感到不安，但却使他们的生活有序化。

我关于美国所述的一切，也确实适用于几乎所有当代的一切人。生活的多样性正从人类社会逐渐消失；同样的举止、同样的思想和同样的感情正在遍及世界的各个地方。这不仅是各国之

with all over the world. This is not only because nations work more upon each other and copy each other more faithfully, but as the men of each country relinquish more and more the peculiar opinions and feelings of a caste, a profession, or a family, they simultaneously arrive at something nearer to the constitution of man, which is everywhere the same. Thus they become more alike, even without having imitated each other. Like travelers scattered about some large wood, intersected by paths converging to one point, if all of them keep their eyes fixed upon that point and advance towards it, they insensibly draw nearer together, though they do not seek, though they do not see and know each other; and they will be surprised at length to find themselves all collected at the same spot. All the nations which take, not any particular man, but Man himself as the object of their researches and their imitations are tending in the end to a similar state of society, like these travelers converging at the central spot of the forest.

间的往来和相互模仿日益增加，而且是因为每个国家的人逐渐放弃了本阶级、本行业、本家族特有的观念和感情，几乎同时接近了处处都一样的人的本质。因此，他们甚至在互不模仿的情况下，也会变得越来越相似。他们就像分散在一片大森林里的旅游者，森林里的所有小路都通向同一个地点，如果他们同时将眼光聚集在同一点上，并向这一地点走去，即使他们不去互相寻找，不互相见面和彼此不认识，也会在不知不觉中向彼此靠近；而在同一地点相会之后会大吃一惊。所有国家，不以特定的人而以人本身作为学习和模仿对象的一切国家，终将像汇合在林中广场的旅游者一样，达到民情上的一致。

CHAPTER XVIII
Of Honor[1] In The United
States And In Democratic Communties

It would seem that men employ two very distinct methods in the judgment which they pass upon the actions of their fellow men; at one time they judge them by those simple notions of right and wrong which are diffused all over the world; at another they appraise them by a few very special rules which belong exclusively to some particular age and country. It often happens that these two standards differ; they sometimes conflict, but they are never either entirely identified or entirely annulled by each other. Honor at the periods of its greatest power sways the will more than the belief of men; and even while they yield without hesitation and without a murmur to its dictates, they feel notwithstanding, by a dim but mighty instinct, the existence of a more general, more ancient, and more holy law, which they sometimes disobey, although they do not cease to acknowledge it. Some actions have been held to be at the same time virtuous and dishonorable, a refusal to fight a duel is an instance.

I think these peculiarities may be otherwise explained than by

---

[1] The word *honor* is not always used in the same sense either in French or in English. (1) It first signifies the esteem, glory, or reverence that a man receives from his fellow men; and in this sense a man is said to *acquire honor*. (2) Honor signifies the aggregate of those rules by the aid of which this esteem, glory, or reverence is obtained. Thus we say that a man *has always strictly obeyed the laws of honor*; or *a man has violated his honor*. In writing the present chapter I have always used the word honor in the latter sense.

第十八章　关于美国和民主
社会中的荣誉 ①

　　人们在判断他人的行为时,似乎采用着两种完全不同的方法;有时,他们按照遍及全球的简单的对与错的观念去判断;又有时,他们则根据某些国家和时代的特有的规定去评价。这两种标准是不相同的;有时甚至会发生冲突,但是,它们永远不会被完全区别开,或者也被完全废止。荣誉,在它权力最大的时候,比人类的信仰更能左右人们的意志;而且,甚至人们会毫不犹豫和毫无怨言地服从它的命令,他们会感到一个更普遍、更古老和更神圣的法律的存在,尽管是在一种模糊但很强大的本能的驱使下,他们虽然从来没有停止去了解它,但有时还会违背它的意思。有些行为,既可被断定是体面的,又可被断定是不体面的。比如,拒绝决斗的行为,就是如此。

　　我认为,这些现象也可以被某些个人和某些国家的任性来解

---

① 荣誉在法国或英国并不总是具有相同的意义。(1)它首先强调的是一个人从同伴那里赢得的尊重、赞誉或威望;在这种情况下可以说他获得了荣誉。(2)荣誉强调规则的集合,通过这些规则可以获取尊重、赞誉或者威望。因此,我们说一个人总是严格地服从荣誉法则;或者一个人违背了他的荣誉。在写现在的这个章节时,我总是采用后者的主义。

the mere caprices of certain individuals and nations, as has hith erto been customary. Mankind is subject to general and permanent wants that have created moral laws, to the neglect of which men have ever and in all places attached the notion of censure and shame: to infringe them was *to do ill*; *to do well* was to conform to them.

Within this vast association of the human race lesser associations have been formed, which are called nations; and amid these nations further subdivisions have assumed the names of classes or castes. Each of these associations forms, as it were, a separate species of the human race; and though it has no essential difference from the mass of mankind, to a certain extent it stands apart and has certain wants peculiar to itself. To these special wants must be attributed the modifications which affect, in various degrees and in different countries, the mode of considering human actions and the estimate which is formed of them. It is the general and permanent interest of mankind that men should not kill each other; but it may happen to be the peculiar and temporary interest of a people or a class to justify, or even to honor, homicide.

Honor is simply that peculiar rule founded upon a peculiar state of society, by the application of which a people or a class allot praise or blame. Nothing is more unproductive to the mind than an abstract idea; I therefore hasten to call in the aid of facts and examples to illustrate my meaning. I select the most extraordinary kind of honor which has ever been known in the world, and that which we are best acquainted with: namely, aristocratic honor springing out of feudal society. I shall explain it by means of the principle already laid down and explain the principle by means of this illustration.

I am not here led to inquire when and how the aristocracy of the Middle Ages came into existence, why it was so deeply severed from the remainder of the nation, or what founded and consolidated its power. I take its existence as an established fact, and I am endeavoring to account for the peculiar view that it took of the greater part of human actions.

释,并且迄今为止,这已经成了惯例。人类根据自己普遍的和永远的需要制定出一套道德规范,使任何人在任何地方和任何时代都不敢违反,害怕违反时会遭到责难和羞辱;违反道德规范的行为,被称之为恶;遵守道德规范的行为,被称之为善。

在人类这个广大的团体里,要建立一些较小的团体,并把它们称之为民族;而在这个小团体之内,又要建立一些范围更小的团体,这些团体被称之为阶级或等级。每一个这样的团体,都构成了人类中的一个特殊种类;尽管它们与整个人类群体没有本质的区别,但在一定范围内又是独立存在的,并有着自己特殊的需要。这些特殊的需要归结于,在不同的国家和不同程度,对人的行为进行各自的观察,并根据这些观察进行各自的评价。人类的普遍的和永恒的利益,在于不应当互相残杀;然而,某个国家或阶级又可能有其特殊的和暂时的利益,从这个利益来说,杀人在某些情况下又是值得原谅的,甚至是值得表扬的。

简单地讲,荣誉就是建立在特殊社会基础上的特殊规则,是供一个国家或一个阶级用来赞扬或责备的特殊标准。任何事情都比抽象的概念对人类的思想具有启发性;所以我要尽快用事实和例句来证明我的观点。现在,我选择一种世界上曾经流行过的而且是众所周知的最奇特的荣誉来作例子:也就是封建社会的贵族荣誉。我一方面要用我上述的观点来说明这个例子,另一面又要用这个例子来阐述我的观点。

在这里,我不想探究中世纪的贵族是何时并且是怎样产生的,为什么它会被民族的其余部分深深地反对,而又是什么在确立和巩固它的权力。我把它的存在看成是已经被确立的事实,并努力解释它为什么要用极为特殊的眼光去看人们的大部分行为。

The first thing that strikes me is that in the feudal world actions were not always praised or blamed with reference to their intrinsic worth, but were sometimes appreciated exclusively with reference to the person who was the actor or the object of them, which is repugnant to the general conscience of mankind. Thus some of the actions which were indifferent on the part of a man in humble life dishonored a noble; others changed their whole character according as the person aggrieved by them belonged or did not belong to the aristocracy.

When these different notions first arose, the nobility formed a distinct body amid the people, which it commanded from the inaccessible heights where it was ensconced. To maintain this peculiar position, which constituted its strength, not only did it require political privileges, but it required a standard of right and wrong for its own special use. That some particular virtue or vice belonged to the nobility rather than to the humble classes, that certain actions were guiltless when they affected the villein which were criminal when they touched the noble, these were often arbitrary matters; but that honor or shame should be attached to a man's actions according to his condition was a result of the internal constitution of an aristocratic community. This has been actually the case in all the countries which have had an aristocracy; as long as a trace of the principle remains, these peculiarities will still exist. To debauch a woman of color scarcely injures the reputation of an American; to marry her dishonors him.

In some cases feudal honor enjoined revenge and stigmatized the forgiveness of insults; in others it imperiously commanded men to conquer their own passions and required forgetfulness of self. It did not make humanity or kindness its law, but it extolled generosity; it set more store on liberality than on benevolence; it allowed men to enrich themselves by gambling or by war, but not by labor; it preferred great crimes to small earnings; cupidity was less distasteful to it than avarice; violence it often sanctioned, but cunning and treachery

首先使我感到吃惊的是,在封建社会,人们的行为永远不是凭其固有的价值而受到褒贬的,而有时完全是根据行为的主体和客体来评定其好坏的,以致评定的结果与人类的普遍道德不相一致。因此,有些行为在身份低微的人看来是不高尚的,是无关紧要的;而另一些行为,则会因为行为的受害者是不是贵族而改变其性质。

当这些不同的观点一旦产生,贵族阶级就形成了与人民不同的群体,并将自己安置于不可接近的高度。而这里正是他力量所在。贵族阶级为了保住这个特殊的地位,不仅需要有政治特权,而且要按它的标准来评判对与错。有些特殊的德行和恶习是出于贵族的行为,而不是出于老百姓的行为。当一种行为受到平民的影响时,就算是有罪也会变成是无罪的;而当它发生在一个贵族身上时,即使无罪也要受到惩治,而且往往是随意惩治;但是,这些荣誉与耻辱要根据一个人的地位和他的行为联系起来,这是贵族社会的内部组织所造成的结果。这种情况真实地发生在曾经有过贵族阶级的国家;只要贵族制度的原则依然存在,这种怪现象也依旧会存在。例如,诱奸一个有色人种姑娘,很少能伤害到一个美国成年男人的名誉;而娶这个姑娘为妻,反而使他无脸见人。

在某些情况下,封建制度的荣誉倾向于复仇,轻视对侮辱的宽恕;但是,另一方面,它又专制地命令人们要战胜自己的激情,要求人们要忘我。它不要求仁慈和温存,但它提倡慷慨;它对宽大的重视远远超过它对善行的重视;它允许人们通过赌博和战争使自己富裕,而不是通过劳动;它宁愿人们犯滔天大罪,也不许他们去追求一些很小的利益;它讨厌贪婪不如讨厌吝啬;它时常鼓

it invariably reprobated as contemptible.

These fantastic notions did not proceed exclusively from the caprice of those who entertained them. A class which has succeeded in placing itself above all others, and which makes perpetual exertions to maintain this lofty position, must especially honor those virtues which are conspicuous for their dignity and splendor and which may be easily combined with pride and the love of power. Such men would not hesitate to invert the natural order of conscience in order to give these virtues precedence over all others. It may even be conceived that some of the more bold and brilliant vices would readily be set above the quiet, unpretending virtues. The very existence of such a class in society renders these things unavoidable.

The nobles of the Middle Ages placed military courage foremost among virtues and in lieu of many of them. This, again, was a peculiar opinion, which arose necessarily from the peculiar state of society. Feudal aristocracy existed by war and for war; its power had been founded by arms, and by arms that power was maintained; it therefore required nothing more than military courage, and that quality was naturally exalted above all others; whatever denoted it, even at the expense of reason and humanity, was therefore approved and frequently enjoined by the manners of the time. Such was the main principle; the caprice of man was to be traced only in minuter details. That a man should regard a tap on the cheek as an unbearable insult and should be obliged to kill in single combat the person who struck him thus lightly is an arbitrary rule; but that a noble could not tranquilly receive an insult and was dishonored if he allowed himself to take a blow without fighting were direct consequences of the fundamental principles and the wants of a military aristocracy.

Thus it was true, to a certain extent, that the laws of honor were capricious; but these caprices of honor were always confined within certain necessary limits. The peculiar rule which was called honor by our forefathers is so far from being an arbitrary law in my eyes that I would readily engage to ascribe its most incoherent and fantastic

励暴力,但却始终瞧不起诡诈和背叛。

这些稀奇古怪的想法,并非来自拥有这些思想的人的异想天开。一个成功位于其他所有阶级之上的阶级,作了永久的努力来维持它的高贵的地位,必然特别敬重使它高贵和杰出、并能容易把它的骄傲与对权力的欲望互相结合起来的德行。为了将这种德行展现给其他阶级,它会毫不犹豫地颠倒道德的自然规律。我们甚至可以想象,那些大胆的和高超的恶行会胜过、高于谦逊质朴的德行。这个阶级在社会上的存在,会使这些事情不可避免地发生。

中世纪的贵族将勇士精神视为所有美德中最高尚的,并认为它可以代替其他一切美德。这也是一种必然来自独特的社会情况的独特的观点。封建贵族是通过战争和为了战争而存在的;它把自己的权势作为武器,并用武器保持权势;因此,对于它们来说,没有什么比勇士精神更为重要的了,勇士精神比其他一切德行都更加尊贵;因此,凡是能表现勇士精神的行动,甚至是违反理性和人道,都能得到它的认可,甚至常常是出于它的命令。这是一个主要的原则;但是,人们古怪的念头,只能作用于一些小细节。一个人把挨了一记耳光看作是对他不可容忍的侮辱,并与轻轻打了他一下的那个人格斗,将其置于死地,这是出于他的自我判断;但是一个贵族不可能平静地忍受一种凌辱,并且如果在挨了一拳之后也不去反击则会使他名誉扫地,这是基本原则和贵族军事需求的直接后果。

因此,在某种程度上,可以说荣誉具有任意性;但是,荣誉的这种任意性始终被限制在一定的范围内。在我看来,被我们祖先称为荣誉的那些特殊规则决不是出于任意的,所以我可以轻易地

injunctions to a small number of fixed and invariable wants inherent in feudal society.

If I were to trace the notion of feudal honor into the domain of politics, I should not find it more difficult to explain its dictates. The state of society and the political institutions of the Middle Ages were such that the supreme power of the nation never governed the community directly. That power did not exist in the eyes of the people: every man looked up to a certain individual whom he was bound to obey; by that intermediate personage he was connected with all the others. Thus, in feudal society, the whole system of the commonwealth rested upon the sentiment of fidelity to the person of the lord; to destroy that sentiment was to fall into anarchy. Fidelity to a political superior was, moreover, a sentiment of which all the members of the aristocracy had constant opportunities of estimating the importance; for every one of them was a vassal as well as a lord and had to command as well as to obey. To remain faithful to the lord, to sacrifice oneself for him if called upon, to share his good or evil fortunes, to stand by him in his undertakings, whatever they might be, such were the first injunctions of feudal honor in relation to the political institutions of those times. The treachery of a vassal was branded with extraordinary severity by public opinion, and a name of peculiar infamy was invented for the offense; it was called *felony*.

On the contrary, few traces are to be found in the Middle Ages of the passion that constituted the life of the nations of antiquity; I mean patriotism. The word itself is not of very ancient date in the language. [1] Feudal institutions concealed the country at large from men's sight and rendered the love of it less necessary. The nation was forgotten in the passions that attached men to persons. Hence it was no part of the strict law of feudal honor to remain faithful to one's country. Not indeed that the love of their country did not exist in the hearts of our forefathers, but it constituted a dim and feeble instinct,

---

[1] Even the word *patrie* was not used by French writers until the sixteenth century.

把封建社会里一些固有的彼此之间毫无联系的离奇古怪的规定，同一些少量的固定不变的需要联系起来。

如果我从政治方面去考察封建社会的荣誉，我发现要解释它的各种政治措施也不是一件难事。中世纪的社会状况和政治制度，就是国家的最高权力从不直接治理公民。人民的眼中根本没有权力这个概念：人们只知道要去尊敬他必须服从其命令的某个人；并通过这个人同其他所有的人发生联系。因此，在封建社会里，整个国家的制度都是建立在对他们的封建领主的忠诚的情感上的；如果摧毁了这种情感，整个国家将陷入无政府状态。此外，对政治首领的忠诚，也是贵族所有成员一直用来评估其重要性的标准；因为他们每个人既是领主又是仆人，既能发号施令又得服从命令。对领主保持忠诚，必要时为他牺牲，与他有福同享，有难同当，支持他的事业，这些就是封建主义的荣誉与政治制度的首要联系。仆人的背叛将被公共舆论给予严厉的批判，人们为这种行为起了一个侮辱性极大的名字，叫做重罪。

相反地，作为构成古代社会的生命的一种激情，也就是爱国心，在中世纪已经很难看到它的痕迹了；爱国心这个名词本身，绝不是我们的古老词汇。① 封建制度在最大程度上将祖国隐瞒于人们，认为爱国没有多大的必要。国家在一个人对另一个人产生激情的同时被人们遗忘。因此，封建主义的荣誉从来没有保留对国家的忠诚。这并不是说我们的祖先心里不爱国，但他们对国家的爱只是一种微弱的和模糊的直觉，随着贵族阶级的衰败和国家最

---

① 在 1 世纪以前，法国作家从来不用爱国这个词。

which has grown more clear and strong in proportion as aristocratic classes have been abolished and the supreme power of the nation centralized.

This may be clearly seen from the contrary judgments that European nations have passed upon the various events of their histories, according to the generations by which such judgments were formed. The circumstance that most dishonored the Constable de Bourbon in the eyes of his contemporaries was that he bore arms against his King; that which most dishonors him in our eyes is that he made war against his country. We brand him as deeply as our forefathers did, but for different reasons.

I have chosen the honor of feudal times by way of illustration of my meaning because its characteristics are more distinctly marked and more familiar to us than those of any other period; but I might have taken an example elsewhere and I should have reached the same conclusion by a different road. Although we are less perfectly acquainted with the Romans than with our own ancestors, yet we know that certain peculiar notions of glory and disgrace obtained among them which were not derived solely from the general principles of right and wrong. Many human actions were judged differently according as they affected a Roman citizen or a stranger, a freeman or a slave; certain vices were blazoned abroad, certain virtues were extolled above all others. "In that age," says Plutarch, in the Life of Coriolanus, "martial prowess was more honored and prized in Rome than all the other virtues, in so much that it was called *virtus*, the name of virtue itself, by applying the name of the kind to this particular species; so that *virtue* in Latin was as much as to say *valor*." Can anyone fail to recognize the peculiar want of that singular community which was formed for the conquest of the world?

Any nation would furnish us with similar grounds of observation, for, as I have already remarked, whenever men collect together as a distinct community, the notion of honor instantly grows up among them; that is to say, a system of opinions peculiar to themselves as to what is blamable or commendable; and these peculiar rules always originate in the special habits and special interests of the community.

高权力的集中,对国家的爱才变得越来越明确和强烈。

　　这种情况,在欧洲各国,很明显地表现在根据评价人所处的时代不同而对它们的一些历史作出完全相反的评价上。在波旁王朝时代的人的眼中,波旁王朝的元帅们最不道德的行为,是他们率领军队攻打国王;但在我们眼中,他们最不道德的行为,是他们发动战争反对自己的国家。我们和我们的祖先虽然都深深地给他们加上了污名,但我们各自的原因不同。

　　我之所以选择封建时代的荣誉来说明我的观点,是因为它的特点比其他时代的荣誉的特点更明显和对我们更熟悉;我还可以举出其他例证,并且通过其他方法给出同样的结论。尽管我们对罗马人的了解不如对我们的祖先了解得多,但我们知道他们对荣誉和耻辱的特殊观念,并非来自对善与恶的一般原则。人类的许多行为由于对象不同,所以判定也会不同,比如是受罗马公民的影响还是受外国人的影响,是受自由人的影响还是受奴隶的影响;一些特定的恶行被广泛赞扬,而某些德行也被说得高于其他一切德行。普鲁塔克在《科里奥拉努斯传》中说过:"在那个时代,军事勇猛在罗马比其他一切美德都更光荣和更值得赞扬,他们把军事勇猛称为美德,使美德这个词本身的含义,就在证明这一特殊观点;于是,美德一词在拉丁语中也有勇敢的意思。"哪一个人不能从这里看出为征服世界而组成的那个奇怪的国家的特别需要呢?

　　每个国家都可以为我们提供相同的例证,正如我在前面所说的一样,每当人们集合在一起形成一个特殊的群体,立即会产生荣誉的观念;也就是说,他们对于责备或表扬会产生一套特殊的观点;这些特殊的规定总是来源于他们所在的团体的特殊习惯和特殊利益。

This is applicable to a certain extent to democratic communities as well as to others, as I shall now proceed to prove by the example of the Americans. ①

Some loose notions of the old aristocratic honor of Europe are still to be found scattered among the opinions of the Americans, but these traditional opinions are few in number, they have but little root in the country and but little power. They are like a religion which has still some temples left standing, though men have ceased to believe in it. But amid these half-obliterated notions of exotic honor some new opinions have sprung up which constitute what may be termed in our days American honor.

I have shown how the Americans are constantly driven to engage in commerce and industry. Their origin, their social condition, their political institutions, and even the region they inhabit urge them irresistibly in this direction. Their present condition, then, is that of an almost exclusively manufacturing and commercial association, placed in the midst of a new and boundless country, which their principal object is to explore for purposes of profit. This is the characteristic that most distinguishes the American people from all others at the present time.

All those quiet virtues that tend to give a regular movement to the community and to encourage business will therefore be held in peculiar honor by that people, and to neglect those virtues will be to incur public contempt. All the more turbulent virtues, which often dazzle, but more frequently disturb society, will, on the contrary, occupy a subordinate rank in the estimation of this same people; they may be neglected without forfeiting the esteem of the community; to acquire them would perhaps be to run a risk of losing it.

The Americans make a no less arbitrary classification of men's vices. There are certain propensities which appear censurable to the

---

① I speak here of the Americans inhabiting those states where slavery does not exist; they alone can be said to present a complete picture of democratic society.

　　这一点也适用于一定范围内的民主社会和其他社会,我们现在就以美国人为例来说明。①

　　在美国人的思想中,还可以零星地发现欧洲旧贵族关于荣誉的一些松散的观念,但这些传统的观念在数量上很少,它们在美国既没有根深蒂固也没有太大的力量。它们就像一种宗教,尽管已无人信仰,但它的庙宇还依然存在。在这些半隐讳的具有异国情调的观念中,出现了一些我们今天可以称之为美国人的荣誉观的新思想。

　　我在前面已经说过,美国人是怎样被不断地驱使去参与工商业的。他们的家庭出身,他们的社会情况,他们的政治制度,甚至他们习惯居住的区域,都使他们无法抗拒地朝这个方向前进。他们目前的状况,可以被看作是在一个无边无际的新国家建立的一个几乎专门搞工商业和以开发为主要目的的社会。这是目前美国人与其他各国人之间最显著的差别。

　　因此,所有能够使社会有规律地前进和促进工商业发展的安然的德行,都受到这个国家人民的特别尊重,忽略这些德行必将招来公众的轻视。所有那些激烈的德行,虽然常常使人感到目眩,但往往会扰乱社会的治安,所以反而被这个国家的人民视为是居于次等的;人们可以在不失去社会的尊重下忽略这些德行;而要求他们表现这些德行,反而会冒险失去它。

　　美国人也对人类的恶行作了任意的划分。某些特定的爱好,对于人类的普遍良心来讲似乎是该受到责备的,但却迎合了美国

---

　　①　我在这里讲的美国是没有奴隶存在的地方;可以说,它们呈现出一幅完整的民主社会的图画。

general reason and the universal conscience of mankind, but which happen to agree with the peculiar and temporary wants of the American community: these propensities are lightly reproved, sometimes even encouraged; for instance, the love of wealth and the secondary propensities connected with it may be more particularly cited. To clear, to till, and to transform the vast uninhabited continent which is his domain, the American requires the daily support of an energetic passion; that passion can only be the love of wealth; the passion for wealth is therefore not reprobated in America, and, provided it does not go beyond the bounds assigned to it for public security, it is held in honor. The American lauds as a noble and praiseworthy ambition what our own forefathers in the Middle Ages stigmatized as servile cupidity, just as he treats as a blind and barbarous frenzy that ardor of conquest and martial temper which bore them to battle.

In the United States fortunes are lost and regained without difficulty; the country is boundless and its resources inexhaustible. The people have all the wants and cravings of a growing creature; and, whatever be their efforts, they are always surrounded by more than they can appropriate. It is not the ruin of a few individuals, which may be soon repaired, but the inactivity and sloth of the community at large that would be fatal to such a people. Boldness of enterprise is the foremost cause of its rapid progress, its strength, and its greatness. Commercial business is there like a vast lottery, by which a small number of men continually lose, but the state is always a gainer; such a people ought therefore to encourage and do honor to boldness in commercial speculations. But any bold speculation risks the fortune of the speculator and of all those who put their trust in him. The Americans, who make a virtue of commercial temerity, have no right in any case to brand with disgrace those who practice it. Hence arises the strange indulgence that is shown to bankrupts in the United States; their honor does not suffer by such an accident. In this respect the Americans differ, not only from the nations of Europe, but from all the commercial nations of our time; and accordingly they resemble none of them in their position or their wants.

社会特殊的和暂时的需要；美国人对这种爱好只是轻轻指责，有时还加以鼓励；例如，可以引用美国人对财富的热爱和基于这个的一些次要爱好。为了开垦、耕耘和改造他们领域范围内的这个巨大的荒无人烟的陆地，美国人每天都要具有坚忍不拔的激情作为精神支柱；这种激情只能是对财富的热爱；因此，这种财富激情在美国并不堕落，只要它不超过国家安全机关为它规定的界限，它就是光荣的。我们中世纪祖先所轻视的那种卑鄙贪婪的欲望，被美国人赞扬为高尚的雄心，而中世纪祖先投入新的战斗的征服热情和好战精神却被美国人称为盲目的野蛮的嗜好。

在美国，财产丢失后可以很容易再得到；它的国土是广袤无垠的，它的资源又是取之不竭和用之不尽的。它的人民拥有每个成长着的人的所有需求和渴望；不管他们的努力到什么程度，周围总是围绕着他们还不能开发的财富。这样的人民所担心的并不是个别人的破落，固为还可以东山再起，他所担心的是整个民族的懒惰。在事业上的大胆精神，是他们迅速发展、国力强大和发展壮大的主要原因。商业对于他们来说就像买彩票一样，总是有少数人会不断地输钱，而国家却永远赚钱；因此，在事业上有大胆精神的这部分人，应当受到鼓舞并引以为荣。但是，所有大胆的事业都带给实业家很大的风险，他们一边担心会失去自己的财富，另一边又会担心损失合伙人的财富。把商业上的鲁莽视为一种美德的美国人，在任何时候都没有权利侮辱那些参与冒险的人。因此，美国对破产倒闭者表现出特别的放任与自由；他们的荣誉因此意外而遭受痛苦。在这方面，美国人不仅不同于欧洲各国，而且不同于同时代的所有商业国家；因此他们在地位和需要上与其他国家的人民毫无相似之处。

In America all those vices that tend to impair the purity of morals and to destroy the conjugal tie are treated with a degree of severity unknown in the rest of the world. At first sight this seems strangely at variance with the tolerance shown there on other subjects, and one is surprised to meet with a morality so relaxed and also so austere among the selfsame people. But these things are less incoherent than they seem to be. Public opinion in the United States very gently represses that love of wealth which promotes the commercial greatness and the prosperity of the nation, and it especially condemns that laxity of morals which diverts the human mind from the pursuit of well-being and disturbs the internal order of domestic life which is so necessary to success in business. To earn the esteem of their countrymen, the Americans are therefore forced to adapt themselves to orderly habits; and it may be said in this sense that they make it a matter of honor to live chastely.

On one point American honor accords with the notions of honor acknowledged in Europe; it places courage as the highest virtue and treats it as the greatest of the moral necessities of man; but the notion of courage itself assumes a different aspect. In the United States martial valor is but little prized; the courage which is best known and most esteemed is that which emboldens men to brave the dangers of the ocean in order to arrive earlier in port, to support the privations of the wilderness without complaint, and solitude more cruel than privations, the courage which renders them almost insensible to the loss of a fortune laboriously acquired and instantly prompts to fresh exertions to make another. Courage of this kind is peculiarly necessary to the maintenance and prosperity of the American communities, and it is held by them in peculiar honor and estimation; to betray a want of it is to incur certain disgrace.

I have yet another characteristic point which may serve to place the idea of this chapter in stronger relief. In a democratic society like that of the United States, where fortunes are scanty and insecure, everybody works, and work opens a way to everything; this has changed the point of honor quite around and has turned it against idleness. I have sometimes met in America with young men of wealth,

　　在美国,所有的这些试图削弱道德纯朴性和破坏婚姻的一切恶行都比世界上其他一切国家的严重。初次看来,这似乎与在其他方面表现的宽容不相吻合,我们会为同一个民族奉行既放纵又严肃的道德而感到吃惊。但是,这一切又不像人们所认为的那样互不连贯。美国的公共舆论在不断地压制能促进事业上的大胆和国家繁荣的爱财之心,而对于使人们追求财富的精神和破坏事业的成功所不可缺少的家庭内部秩序的伤风败俗行为却大力谴责。因此,为了得到同胞们的尊重,美国人不得不强迫自己服从已有的习惯;从这个意义上来说,又可以认为他们把荣誉寄托于做一个纯洁无瑕的人上了。

　　在某一点上,美国人的荣誉观与欧洲人的荣誉观是相同的;它们都认为勇敢是美德之首,并且是做人最必要的美德;但勇敢这个观念本身会表现出不同的侧面。在美国,军事上的勇猛很少会受到表扬;美国人认为最好的和最值得称赞的勇敢,是敢于冲破海洋的惊涛早日抵达港口,毫无怨言地忍受荒野中的穷困潦倒和比贫苦更难于忍受的孤寂,这种勇敢使他们费尽千辛万苦所得来的财富,在几乎不知不觉中就消失得无影无踪,然后又使他们立刻以新的努力去积累新的财富。这种勇敢对于维持和繁荣美国社会是尤其必需的,因此便受到美国人的特别尊重和赞扬;一个人如果背叛了这种需求就将引来别人的轻视。

　　我现在要说另一个能充分证明本章思想的观点。在像美国这样的民主社会里,财产是不充足的并且是不可靠的。因此,人人都要劳动,劳动可以创造一切;这使荣誉观发生了转变,并把矛头指向闲散和懒惰。有时,我在美国会见到一些有钱的年轻人,他们虽然打心眼里不愿干苦活,但也不得不被迫从事一种职业。

personally disinclined to all laborious exertion, but who had been compelled to embrace a profession. Their disposition and their fortune allowed them to remain without employment; public opinion forbade it, too imperiously to be disobeyed. In the European countries, on the contrary, where aristocracy is still struggling with the flood which overwhelms it, I have often seen men, constantly spurred on by their wants and desires, remain in idleness in order not to lose the esteem of their equals; and I have known them to submit to ennui and privations rather than to work. No one can fail to perceive that these opposite obligations are two different rules of conduct, both nevertheless originating in the notion of honor.

What our forefathers designated as honor absolutely was in reality only one of its forms; they gave a generic name to what was only a species. Honor, therefore, is to be found in democratic as well as in aristocratic ages, but it will not be difficult to show that it assumes a different aspect in the former. Not only are its injunctions different, but we shall shortly see that they are less numerous, less precise, and that its dictates are less rigorously obeyed.

The position of a caste is always much more peculiar than that of a people. Nothing is so exceptional in the world as a small community invariably composed of the same families (as was, for instance, the aristocracy of the Middle Ages) whose object is to concentrate and to retain, exclusively and hereditarily, education, wealth, and power among its own members. But the more exceptional the position of a community happens to be, the more numerous are its special wants and the more extensive are its notions of honor corresponding to those wants. The rules of honor will therefore always be less numerous among a people not divided into castes than among any other. If ever any nations are constituted in which it may even be difficult to find any peculiar classes of society, the notion of honor will be confined to a small number of precepts, which will be more and more in accordance with the moral laws adopted by the mass of mankind.

Thus the laws of honor will be less peculiar and less multifarious among a democratic people than in an aristocracy. They will also be more obscure, and this is a necessary consequence of what goes before; for as the distinguishing marks of honor are less numerous and

他们的地位和财产允许他们呆在家里不去从事任何工作；但公共舆论禁止他们这样做，他们也不得不服从公共舆论。相反地，在欧洲各国，贵族仍同冲击他们的激流进行斗争，我可以经常见到一些日益穷困潦倒的人，为了不失去与他们相同的人的尊敬，他们依旧被自己的需求与期望所鼓舞；宁愿服从这种厌倦和穷困的生活也不愿劳动。哪一个人不能从这两种截然相反的劳动观中发现两种性质完全不同但均来自荣誉观的行为规范呢？

我们祖先所指定的荣誉，实际上只是许多荣誉中的一种；他们将总概念的意义赋予给单独的种类。因此，尽管民主社会和贵族时代都有荣誉观，但不难发现荣誉在民主时代将表现出不同的侧面。这不仅是因为荣誉的规定与以前不同了，而且我们还可以发现，这方面的规定虽然为数不多和不够明确，但更能让人们顺从它们。

等级的地位总是比人民的地位要更加特殊。全世界没有一处是例外的，到处都是由同一家族组成的小团体（比如中世纪的贵族）。它们的目的，就是把教育、财富和权势都集中在自己成员的手里，并垄断地和世袭地流传下去。但是，一个团体的地位越高，它的特别需要就越多，适应它的需要的荣誉观点也会随之增加。因此，荣誉的规定，在没有等级划分的国家将总是少于其他国家。如果建成使任何阶级都难于存在的国家，则关于荣誉的观念将被限制到很少的几个规则内，而且这几条规则也会越来越与绝大多数人所采用的道德准则相一致。

因此，荣誉的规定在一个民主国家里将不会像在贵族国家那样奇特和种类繁多。它们还可能会更含糊，这是上述的原因所造成的必然结果；由于荣誉的显著特征越来越少和越来越不奇特，

less peculiar, it must often be difficult to distinguish them. To this other reasons may be added. Among the aristocratic nations of the Middle Ages generation succeeded generation in vain; each family was like a never dying, ever stationary man, and the state of opinions was hardly more changeable than that of conditions. Everyone then had the same objects always before his eyes, which he contemplated from the same point; his eyes gradually detected the smallest details, and his discernment could not fail to become in the end clear and accurate. Thus not only had the men of feudal times very extraordinary opinions in matters of honor, but each of those opinions was present to their minds under a clear and precise form.

This can never be the case in America, where all men are in constant motion and where society, transformed daily by its own operations, changes its opinions together with its wants. In such a country men have glimpses of the rules of honor, but they seldom have time to fix attention upon them. But even if society were motionless, it would still be difficult to determine the meaning that ought to be attached to the word *honor*. In the Middle Ages, as each class had its own honor, the same opinion was never received at the same time by a large number of men; and this rendered it possible to give it a determined and accurate form, which was the more easy as all those by whom it was received, having a perfectly identical and most peculiar position, were naturally disposed to agree upon the points of a law which was made for themselves alone.

Thus the code of honor became a complete and detailed system, in which everything was anticipated and provided for beforehand, and a fixed and always palpable standard was applied to human actions. Among a democratic nation, like the Americans, in which ranks are confounded and the whole of society forms one single mass, composed of elements which are all analogous though not entirely similar, it is impossible ever to agree beforehand on what shall or shall not be allowed by the laws of honor.

Among that people, indeed, some national wants exist, which

所以必然往往很难区别它们。对此我还要补充另外一些原因。在中世纪的贵族国家，人们只是一代一代相传是没有用的，上一代没有给后一代留下什么新东西；每个家族就像一个永远不会死去而又永远静止不动的人，条件变了，而思想几乎从来没有变过。在这里，每个人的目标都是一致的，头脑里所想的总是从同一个观点出发；他们的眼光逐渐深入到最微小的细节，而他们的洞察力最终将不能不变得清晰和明确。因此，封建时代的人不仅对荣誉有其独特的观点，而且在自己的脑子里印有这个观点清晰准确的形式。

在美国就永远不会发生如此情况，因为那里的所有人民都在不停地运动中，社会本身每天都在发生着变化，同时也在改变它的观点和需要。在这样的国家里，人们只能对荣誉的规则进行一些肤浅的了解，而很少有时间去仔细研究它。但即使社会是静止不动的，我们依然很难规定荣誉一词的含义。在中世纪，由于每个阶级都有自己的荣誉观，所以同一观点从来没有被大多数人在同一时间所接受；这就有可能赋予各个阶级的荣誉观以稳定和明确的形式，而且由于具有同样荣誉观的阶级的成员立场完全相同和一致排外，自然愿意接受专为他们规定的法律条款。

因此，有关荣誉的规定就变成一部完整和详细的系统，这个系统将对所有事都作预先的准备，成为衡量人的行为的固定的和明显的标准。在像美国这样的一个民主国家，由于等级已变得模糊不清，而整个社会形成了一个统一的群体，构成社会的因素虽不完全相同但很相似，所以我们不可能事先确定哪些行为是荣誉和哪些行为是耻辱。

不错，在这些人民中间存在着的某些全国性的需要使他们对

give rise to opinions common to the whole nation on points of honor: but these opinions never occur at the same time, in the same manner, or with the same intensity to the minds of the whole community; the law of honor exists, but it has no organs to promulgate it.

The confusion is far greater still in a democratic country like France, where the different classes of which the former fabric of society was composed, being brought together but not yet mingled, import day by day into each other's circles various and sometimes conflicting notions of honor, where every man, at his own will and pleasure, forsakes one portion of his forefathers' creed and retains another; so that, amid so many arbitrary measures, no common rule can ever be established, and it is almost impossible to predict which actions will be held in honor and which will be thought disgraceful. Such times are wretched, but they are of short duration.

As honor among democratic nations is imperfectly defined, its influence is of course less powerful; for it is difficult to apply with certainty and firmness a law that is not distinctly known. Public opinion, the natural and supreme interpreter of the laws of honor, not clearly discerning to which side censure or approval ought to lean, can only pronounce a hesitating judgment. Sometimes the opinion of the public may contradict itself; more frequently it does not act and lets things pass.

The weakness of the sense of honor in democracies also arises from several other causes. In aristocratic countries the same notions of honor are always ehtertained by only a few persons, always limited in number, often separated from the rest of their fellow citizens. Honor is easily mingled and identified in their minds with the idea of all that distinguishes their own position; it appears to them as the chief characteristic of their own rank; they apply its different rules with all the warmth of personal interest, and they feel (if I may use the expression) a passion for complying with its dictates. This truth is extremely obvious in the old black-letter law-books on the subject of trial by battle. The nobles in their disputes were bound to use the lance and sword, whereas the villeins among themselves used only sticks, "inasmuch as," to use the words of the old

荣誉产生了共同的观点；但这些观点并不是以同样的方式在同时产生的，或是对整个社会人民的思想的影响也不一样；存在着荣誉的有关规定，但它往往没有注释。

在像法国这样的民主国家，这种混乱更加明显。这首先是因为这里的各个不同阶级是在还不具备混合的条件下就开始互相混合起来，它们日复一日地将自己的荣誉观输入彼此的圈子里，有时这些荣誉观不但各不相同，而且还会相互抵制；其次是因为在我们国家，每个人都喜欢根据自己的意愿和喜好，抛弃了自己祖先的一部分观点和保存另一部分观点；最后是因为在众多的任意判断下，几乎无法预测哪些行为是光荣的，哪些行为是可耻的。这是一个令人痛苦的时期，但是不会持续太久。

在民主国家，荣誉并没有十分清楚的定义，其影响力当然会很弱；因为很难对一个并不明确的行为加以准确而坚定的规范。公共舆论是荣誉规范的自然的和最有权威的解释者，但由于它并不能清楚地分辨什么是应该赞扬的，而什么又是应该责难的，所以它只能对判断犹豫不决。有时公共舆论可能自相矛盾；而更多的时候是不采取措施和任由其发展。

在民主国家，荣誉的影响力的软弱还来源于另外一些原因。在贵族国家，同样的荣誉观点只被少数人持有，总是被限制在一定数量里，永远同其他人隔离。因此，他们的荣誉观容易同他们所特有的思想混合并结为一体；在他们看来，荣誉是能显示他们身份的主要标志；他们积极地利用有关荣誉的各种规定为自己的利益服务，而且如果允许我说的话，我说他们还要使自己的激情服从这些规定的支配。在中世纪的习惯法载有关于以决斗来断定是非的条款中，这一点尤为真实。这项条款写道，贵族在他们

books, "villeins have no honor." This did not mean, as it may be i-
magined at the present day, that these people were contemptible, but
simply that their actions were not to be judged by the same rules that
were applied to the actions of the aristocracy.

It is surprising, at first sight, that when the sense of honor is
most predominant, its injunctions are usually most strange; so that the
further it is removed from common reason, the better it is obeyed;
whence it has sometimes been inferred that the laws of honor were
strengthened by their own extravagance. The two things, indeed, o-
riginate from the same source, but the one is not derived from the other. Honor becomes fantastic in proportion to the peculiarity of the
wants that it denotes and the paucity of the men by whom those wants
are felt; and it is because it denotes wants of this kind that its influence is great Thus the notion of honor is not the stronger for being fantastic, but it is fantastic and strong from the selfsame cause.

Further, among aristocratic nations each rank is different, but all
ranks are fixed. Every man occupies a place in his own sphere which
he cannot relinquish, and he lives there among other men who are
bound by the same ties. Among these nations no man can either hope
or fear to escape being seen; no man is placed so low but that he has
a stage of his own, and none can avoid censure or applause by his obscurity. In democratic states, on the contrary, where all the members
of the community are mingled in the same crowd and in constant agitation, public opinion has no hold on men; they disappear at every
instant and elude its power. Consequently the dictates of honor will be
there less imperious and less stringent, for honor acts solely for the
public eye, differing in this respect from mere virtue, which lives upon itself, contented with its own approval.

If the reader has distinctly apprehended all that goes before,
he will understand that there is a close and necessary relation between the inequality of social conditions and what has here been

发生纠纷时,以长矛和剑作决斗的武器,而平民之间只能用棍棒决斗,而且习惯法补充说:"由于平民没有荣誉。"它的意思不是说,像我们今天所想象的这些人是卑贱的,而只是表示在判断贵族的行为和平民的行为时不能使用同样的标准。

初看起来令人吃惊的是:当荣誉有突出影响时,荣誉的规定也常常是最为奇特的;以致使人觉得这些规定越背离常理就越容易被人遵守;有时还可以推断荣誉的影响力因其过度的推断而变得更加强大。事实上,强大和荒谬有共同的来源,而不是一方来自于另一方。荣誉随着需求的特殊化会变得更加离奇,而这种需求是被极少数人所思慕的;而荣誉的影响力之所以强大,正是因为出现了这种特殊的和为少数人所思慕的需要。因此,荣誉的影响力的强大并非来源于荣誉观的离奇古怪,而是离奇古怪和强大都来自同一原因。

再者,在贵族国家里,所有的等级都各不相同,但所有等级固定不变;每个人都在自己的范围内占有一席之地,在他居住的地方,有同他一样的人和他生活在一起。在这样的国家里,没有人会担心或害怕生活不下去;不管一个人的地位多么低下,他都有属于自己的一片舞台,没有人会因为自己身份的低微而受到褒贬。相反地,民主国家的情况就并非如此,在那里,全体公民都混杂在一起,互相不断往来,公共舆论并不能控制人们;人们可以立即躲避起来,逃脱舆论的谴责。因此,荣誉在民主国家并不是很专横也并不是很严厉,因为荣誉只是给人看的,所以它与纯洁的德行不同,德行是依靠本身而存在,而且满足于自我承认。

如果读者对上述的一切已经完全了解,那他一定会发现在身份的不平等和我们所说的荣誉之间存在着密切的和必然的联系。

styled honor, a relation which, if I am not mistaken, had not before been clearly pointed out. I shall therefore make one more attempt to illustrate it satisfactorily.

Suppose a nation stands apart from the rest of mankind: independently of certain general wants inherent in the human race, it will also have wants and interests peculiar to itself. Certain opinions in respect to censure or approbation forthwith arise in the community which are peculiar to itself and which are styled honor by the members of that community. Now suppose that in this same nation a caste arises which, in its turn, stands apart from all the other classes, and contracts certain peculiar wants, which give rise in their turn to special opinions. The honor of this caste, composed of a medley of the peculiar notions of the nation and the still more peculiar notions of the caste, will be as remote as it is possible to conceive from the simple and general opinions of men.

Having reached this extreme point of the argument, I now return.

When ranks are commingled and privileges abolished, the men of whom a nation is composed being once more equal and alike, their interests and wants become identical, and all the peculiar notions which each caste styled honor successively disappear. The notion of honor no longer proceeds from any other source than the wants peculiar to the nation at large, and it denotes the individual character of that nation to the world.

Lastly, if it were allowable to suppose that all the races of mankind should be commingled and that all the nations of earth should ultimately come to have the same interests, the same wants, undistinguished from each other by any characteristic peculiarities, no conventional value whatever would then be attached to men's action; they would all be regarded by all in the same light; the general necessities of mankind, revealed by conscience to every man, would become the common standard. The simple and general notions of right and wrong only would then be recognized in the world, to which, by a natural and necessary tie, the idea of censure or approbation would be attached.

Thus, to comprise all my meaning in a single proposition, the dissimilarities and inequalities of men gave rise to the notion of honor; that notion is weakened in proportion as these differences are obliterated, and with them it would disappear.

如果我没有说错的话,这种关系至今还没有被人明确地指出过。因此,我要做最后的努力来说明它。

假设有一个民族与人类的其余部分隔绝:不依赖于人类所固有的某些一般需要,那它也会有自己特别的利益和需要。并且很快会在内部形成自己的关于褒贬或被它的公民称为荣辱的一定观点。现在让我们设想一下,如果在这个民族的内部形成了一个同周围的其他一切阶级隔绝并有着自己的特别利益的阶级,那么,这些特别利益又会使它产生特别观点。这个阶级的荣誉观是由本民族的特别观点和本阶级的更加特别的观点混杂而成的,与人类的简单而一般的观点相差得使人难于想象。

我的论述即将结束,现在再回过头来进行总结。

当阶级被相互混合,特权也被取消,民族的全体成员又恢复为彼此相似和平等的人,他们的利益和需求也越来越相同,而被每个阶级用来评定荣誉的一切奇特的观点也将消失了。荣誉观只能来自民族本身的需要,而不能有其他来源。每个民族的荣誉观都有自己的个性。

最后,如果可以假定所有的人类种族将融合在一起,世界上的所有国家最终将拥有同样的利益和需要,彼此之间在特性上不再有所区别,人类的行为也不再受传统观念的影响;而是要按同样的标准同样对待;用良心向每个人揭示的人类一般需要作为共同标准。这样,世界上就将产生自然和必然要富有褒贬思想的简单的共同是非观。

如果用一句简单的话来概括我的全部思想,那就是:人们之间的不同和不平等使人们产生了荣誉观;而随着这些不同和不平等的逐渐消逝,荣誉观也将逐渐变弱,最后同它们一并消失。

CHAPTER XIX

Why So Many Ambitious Men
And So Little Lofty Ambition
Are To Be Found In The United States

The First thing that strikes a traveler in the United States is the innumerable multitude of those who seek to emerge from their original condition; and the second is the rarity of lofty ambition to be observed in the midst of the universally ambitious stir of society. No Americans are devoid of a yearning desire to rise, but hardly any appear to entertain hopes of great magnitude or to pursue very lofty aims. All are constantly seeking to acquire property, power, and reputation; few contemplate these things upon a great scale; and this is the more surprising as nothing is to be discerned in the manners or laws of America to limit desire or to prevent it from spreading its impulses in every direction. It seems difficult to attribute this singular state of things to the equality of social conditions, for as soon as that same equality was established in France, the flight of ambition became unbounded. Nevertheless, I think that we may find the principal cause of this fact in the social condition and democratic manners of the Americans.

All revolutions enlarge the ambition of men. This is more peculiarly true of those revolutions which overthrow an aristocracy. When the former barriers that kept back the multitude from fame and power are suddenly thrown down, a violent and universal movement takes place towards that eminence so long coveted and at length to be enjoyed. In this first burst of triumph nothing seems impossible to anyone: not only are desires boundless, but the power of satisfying them seems almost boundless too. Amid the general and sudden

第十九章　为什么在美国可以发现很多有雄心但很少有大志的人

在美国，使旅行者吃惊的第一件事情，是那些想要改变自己的原来条件的众多的人民；而第二件让人吃惊的事，则是在这个普遍具有雄心壮志的社会中很少有胸怀大志的人。美国人都渴望前进，但很少有人能抱有远大的抱负或追求更高尚的目标。人人都在不断寻求财富、权势和名望；但很少有人能在最大程度上完成这些；这使人感到吃惊，因为美国的民情或法律没有在任何地方限制人的欲望和阻止人向各个方面发展。似乎很难将这种奇怪现象归结于社会身份的平等，因为在我们法国实现这种平等之后，人类的野心也变得没有边界。但是我认为，还是要到美国的社会情况和民主民情中去寻找上述情况的主要原因。

所有革命都在扩大人们的野心。这一点对于推翻贵族制度的革命尤其真实。当阻止广大群众得到名望和权力的障碍一旦被革除，一场激烈的普遍运动便发生了，运动的矛头指向了人们垂涎已久而最终得到的名利和权势上。在这场运动初胜的鼓舞下，人们觉得似乎没有什么事情是办不到的：不但人的欲望是无止境的，就连满足这些欲望的权力似乎也变得漫无止境。在法律和习惯的这场普遍的和突然的变革中，在使所有的人和所有的制

change of laws and customs, in this vast confusion of all men and all ordinances, the various members of the community rise and sink again with excessive rapidity, and power passes so quickly from hand to hand that none need despair of catching it in turn.

It must be recollected, moreover, that the people who destroy an aristocracy have lived under its laws; they have witnessed its splendor, and they have unconsciously imbibed the feelings and notions which it entertained. Thus, at the moment when an aristocracy is dissolved, its spirit still pervades the mass of the community, and its tendencies are retained long after it has been defeated. Ambition is therefore always extremely great as long as a democratic revolution lasts, and it will remain so for some time after the revolution is consummated.

The recollection of the extraordinary events which men have witnessed is not obliterated from their memory in a day. The passions that a revolution has roused do not disappear at its close. A sense of instability remains in the midst of re-established order; a notion of easy success survives the strange vicissitudes which gave it birth; desires still remain extremely enlarged, while the means of satisfying them are diminished day by day. The taste for large fortunes persists, though large fortunes are rare; and on every side we trace the ravages of inordinate and unsuccessful ambition kindled in hearts which it consumes in secret and in vain.

At length, however, the last vestiges of the struggle are effaced; the remains of aristocracy completely disappear; the great events by which its fall was attended are forgotten; peace succeeds to war, and the sway of order is restored in the new realm; desires are again adapted to the means by which they may be fulfilled; the wants, the opinions, and the feelings of men cohere once more; the level of the community is permanently determined, and democratic society established.

A democratic nation, arrived at this permanent and regular state of things, will present a very different spectacle from that which I have just described, and we may readily conclude that if ambition

度都改变了的这场大混乱中,社会上的不同成员都在以极快的速度升职或贬职,权力迅速地从一些人手里转到另一些人手里,以致人人都认为将会轮到自己掌权。

甚至,我们还不能忘记,那些摧毁贵族制度的人都曾经生活在贵族法制下;他们也见证过它的壮观,并且在不知不觉中吸收了贵族曾经享有的情感和观念。因此,当贵族制度一旦被瓦解,它的灵魂依旧游荡在群众之间,而在它被完全打败以后,它的趋势还将长久影响着人民。因此,民主革命持续多久,人们的野心就会持续多久,而在民主革命完成之后,这种野心还会存在一段时间。

人们一回忆他们曾经见证的那些非常事件,记忆便会涌上他们的心头。革命所带来的激情,在革命结束时并不会消失。在重新建立的秩序中仍然保持着一种不稳定性;成功来之容易的思想,依旧残存在这奇特的变迁中;欲望仍在扩大,而满足欲望的手段却在日益减少。尽管大的财富很少,但人们对财富的热爱依然如故;结果,各式各样的野心膨胀得欲裂,而失败的痛苦却隐藏在怀有野心的人的心中。

然而,斗争的最后残余最终也会消失;贵族制度的残余也会完全消失掉;人们忘记了已经灭亡的一些重大事件;和平成功地代替了战争,秩序在新的领域被重新建立起来;欲望又一次符合了实现欲望的手段;人们的需要、观念和感情互相联系起来;人们的社会水平达到了永久的平等,这样,民主社会便被建立起来。

如果有一个民主国家达到了这种永久的和规律的状态,那它将会为我们呈现出与我方才所述的情景完全不同的场景,而且我们可以断定,如果人们的野心在逐渐变大,而同时他们的社会身

becomes great while the conditions of society are growing equal, it loses that quality when they have grown so.

As wealth is subdivided and knowledge diffused, no one is entirely destitute of education or of property; the privileges and disqualifications of caste being abolished, and men having shattered the bonds that once held them fixed, the notion of advancement suggests itself to every mind, the desire to rise swells in every heart, and all men want to mount above their station; ambition is the universal feeling.

But if the equality of conditions gives some resources to all the members of the community, it also prevents any of them from having resources of great extent, which necessarily circumscribes their desires within somewhat narrow limits. Thus, among democratic nations, ambition is ardent and continual, but its aim is not habitually lofty; and life is generally spent in eagerly coveting small objects that are within reach.

What chiefly diverts the men of democracies from lofty ambition is not the scantiness of their fortunes, but the vehemence of the exertions they daily make to improve them. They strain their faculties to the utmost to achieve paltry results, and this cannot fail speedily to limit their range of view and to circumscribe their powers. They might be much poorer and still be greater.

The small number of opulent citizens who are to be found in a democracy do not constitute an exception to this rule. A man who raises himself by degrees to wealth and power contracts, in the course of this protracted labor, habits of prudence and restraint which he cannot afterwards shake off. A man cannot gradually enlarge his mind as he does his house.

The same observation is applicable to the sons of such a man: they are born, it is true, in a lofty position, but their parents were humble; they have grown up amid feelings and notions which they cannot afterwards easily get rid of; and it may be presumed that they will inherit the propensities of their father, as well as his wealth.

份也在日趋平等,则在实现平等以后,奋进之心也会失去这种趋大的性质。

因为财产已经被划分,而知识也已经被普及,所以任何人都不能独占知识和财产;一些阶级特权和没有资格享有特权的现象已经消失,人们打破了曾经禁锢他们的镣铐,进步的思想浮现在每个人的思想中,而晋升的欲望产生于每个人的心里,以致每个人都想从自己原有的地位往上爬;雄心壮志成了一种普遍的感情。

但是,如果身份的平等赋予社会上的每个公民一些财富,它也同时会阻止每个公民拥有巨额的财产,这种情况必然把人们的欲望限制在相当狭小的范围之内。因此,在民主国家,雄心是热烈的和持久的,但它的目标一般都不会很高尚;人们的一生一般只是热烈地追求可能达到的小目标。

使民主国家的人缺乏对高尚雄心追求的主要原因,不是他们在财力上的缺乏,而是使他们每天忙于提高自己的热烈的努力。他们把精力都用到一些琐碎的事情上了,这就不能不迅速地限制他们的视野和束缚他们的能力。他们可能会变的更穷,但雄心依然强大。

民主社会里的少量富裕的公民,并没有构成这个规定的例外。一个通过积累其财富和权势而提升自己的人,在他们的长期的劳动中会养成办事谨慎和自知节制的习惯,而且以后也不会丢掉这个习惯。人们不能像扩建房屋似的随心所欲依次扩大自己的胸怀。

同样的情况也适用于这个人的儿子:不错,做儿子的出生在高贵的环境中,但他们的父母曾经是卑微低下的;他们从小在父母的思想和感情的影响下长大,而且以后也难摆脱这种影响;但可以推测,他们在继承父亲的财产的同时,也继承了父亲的思想和习惯。

It may happen, on the contrary, that the poorest scion of a powerful aristocracy may display vast ambition, because the traditional opinions of his race and the general spirit of his order still buoy him up for some time above his fortune.

Another thing that prevents the men of democratic periods from easily indulging in the pursuit of lofty objects is the lapse of time which they foresee must take place before they can be ready to struggle for them. "It is a great advantage," says Pascal, "to be a man of quality, since it brings one man as forward at eighteen or twenty as another man would be at fifty, which is a clear gain of thirty years." Those thirty years are commonly wanting to the ambitious characters of democracies. The principle of equality, which allows every man to arrive at everything, prevents all men from rapid advancement.

In a democratic society, as well as elsewhere, there is only a certain number of great fortunes to be made; and as the paths that lead to them are indiscriminately open to all, the progress of all must necessarily be slackened. As the candidates appear to be nearly alike, and as it is difficult to make a selection without infringing the principle of equality, which is the supreme law of democratic societies, the first idea which suggests itself is to make them all advance at the same rate and submit to the same trials. Thus, in proportion as men become more alike and the principle of equality is more peaceably and deeply infused into the institutions and manners of the country, the rules for advancement become more inflexible, advancement itself slower, the difficulty of arriving quickly at a certain height far greater. From hatred of privilege and from the embarrassment of choosing, all men are at last forced, whatever may be their standard, to pass the same ordeal; all are indiscriminately subjected to a multitude of petty preliminary exercises, in which their youth is wasted and their imagination quenched, so that they despair of ever fully attaining what is held out to them; and when at length they are in a condition to perform any extraordinary acts, the taste for such things has forsaken them.

In China, where the equality of conditions is very great and very ancient, no man passes from one public office to another with-

相反的,曾经有权有势的贵族的子孙可能贫困潦倒,但他们可能会表现出极大的雄心壮志,因为贵族的传统观念和其阶级的共同精神只能使他们可以暂时忍受现实的处境。

能阻止民主时代的人易于沉溺于对宏伟事业的追求的另一个原因,是他们在预见了为此拼搏之前就早已错过了时间。帕斯卡尔说过:"好的家庭出身对一个人有巨大的好处,是使一个人在18岁或20岁时达到另一个人在50岁时的地位,从而可以使他少奋斗30年。"而民主国家的人通常想在30年的时间里去实现雄心壮志。平等的原则,使每个人所拥有的都一样,从而阻止了他们迅速地壮大自己。

在民主社会里也像在其他制度的社会里一样,只有少数人可以拥有巨大的财富;使他们致富的大门是无选择地向所有的公民都敞开着的,但全体公民的前进速度必然会被减慢。因为参加这样的竞选的人看来都是一样的,而且在不违反被民主社会奉为最高法律的平等原则下,很难作出选择,所以首先要解决的,就是让所有的人同步前进和全体通过同样的考验。因此,随着人们越来越相似,平等的原则也越来越温和,并日益深入到国家的整个制度和民情中,前进的规则也变得越来越死,而前进本身也变得越来越慢,迅速升到某一显赫地位的难度加大了。因为大家都憎恨特权和不愿意参加竞选,所以不管人们的能力如何,都不得不被迫通过同样残酷的考验;大家都必须遭受许许多多的这种预备性的小小的训练,从而使自己的青春被荒废掉,使自己的想象力消失,因此,他们对自己有望得到的好处充满了失望;而在他们终于有能力做一番大事业时,则已失去了兴致。

在中国,身份平等是非常重要的,并且有着悠久的历史,没有人在不经过科举考试的情况下,就可以由一个官职迁升到另一

out undergoing a competitive trial. This probation occurs afresh at every stage of his career; and the notion is now so rooted in the manners of the people that I remember to have read a Chinese novel in which the hero, after numberless vicissitudes, succeeds at length in touching the heart of his mistress by doing well on an examination. A lofty ambition breathes with difficulty in such an atmosphere.

The remark I apply to politics extends to everything: equality everywhere produces the same effects; where the laws of a country do not regulate and retard the advancement of men by positive enactment, competition attains the same end.

In a well-established democratic community great and rapid elevation is therefore rare; it forms an exception to the common rule; and it is the singularity of such occurrences that makes men forget how rarely they happen.

Men living in democracies ultimately discover these things; they find out at last that the laws of their country open a boundless field of action before them, but that no one can hope to hasten across it. Between them and the final object of their desires they perceive a multitude of small intermediate impediments, which must be slowly surmounted; this prospect wearies and discourages their ambition at once. They therefore give up hopes so doubtful and remote, to search nearer to themselves for less lofty and more easy enjoyments. Their horizon is not bounded by the laws, but narrowed by themselves.

I have remarked that lofty ambitions are more rare in the ages of democracy than in times of aristocracy; I may add that when, in spite of these natural obstacles, they do spring into existence, their character is different. In aristocracies the career of ambition is often wide, but its boundaries are determined. In democracies ambition commonly ranges in a narrower field, but if once it gets beyond that, hardly any limits can be assigned to it. As men are individually weak, as they live asunder and in constant motion, as precedents are of little authority

个官职。这样的考试发生在每一个职位上;而关于这种考试的思想,则已深深进入中国的民情。我记得,我曾经读过一本中国小说,男主人公在经历了无数的挫败后,但终于因金榜题名而赢得了女主人公的芳心。在这样的气氛中,雄心壮志很难存在下去。

我所讲的关于政治问题的这一切,也适用于其他一切问题:平等在任何地方都会产生相同的效果;凡是法律不规范和采用正面手段来延迟官职晋升的国家,实行考试也会产生这样的效果。

因此,在一个建立得很完整的民主社会里,大而快的晋升是罕见的;它相对于普通的规定只是一种例外;它的这个特点,甚至使人忘记了它是多么罕见的现象啊!

生活在民主时代的人最终会发现这一切;时间长了以后,他们发现国家的法律为他们敞开了一个不受限制的活动范围,但没有人希望去急于跨越它。在他们和他们最终的远大目标之间,他们发现有许许多多小的障碍,我们必须慢慢地克服这些小障碍;这个前景立刻使他们感到疲倦,并挫伤了他们的雄心壮志。因此,他们放弃这种既不确定而又遥远的希望,而去寻找离他们近的虽然不太高尚但容易得到的享受。他们的视野并没有受到法律的限制,而是被他们自己缩小了目标。

我曾经说过,民主时代人民的雄心壮志要比贵族时代人民的雄心壮志少很多;我需要补充一点:在民主时代,尽管有人不顾这些自然障碍,而各怀有大志,但其特征是不同的。在贵族时代,对前程的野心是远大的,但它的界限是被规定好了的。在民主国家,志向的范围通常很狭小,但是一旦当它超越了这个范围,可以说没有什么限制可以在施加于它了。由于民主国家人民的力量很薄弱、独自生活和经常变动,而且先例的权威性不大和法律的

and laws but of short duration, resistance to novelty is languid and the fabric of society never appears perfectly erect or firmly consolidated. So that, when once an ambitious man has the power in his grasp, there is nothing he may not dare; and when it is gone from him, he meditates the overthrow of the state to regain it. This gives to great political ambition a character of revolutionary violence, which it seldom exhibits to an equal degree in aristocratic communities. The common aspect of democratic nations will present a great number of small and very rational objects of ambition, from among which a few ill-controlled desires of a larger growth will at intervals break out; but no such thing as ambition conceived and regulated on a vast scale is to be met with there.

I have shown elsewhere by what secret influence the principle of equality makes the passion for physical gratification and the exclusive love of the present predominate in the human heart. These different propensities mingle with the sentiment of ambition and tinge it, as it were, with their hues.

I believe that ambitious men in democracies are less engrossed than any others with the interests and the judgment of posterity; the present moment alone engages and absorbs them. They are more apt to complete a number of undertakings with rapidity than to raise lasting monuments of their achievements, and they care much more for success than for fame. What they most ask of men is obedience, what they most covet is empire. Their manners, in almost all cases, have remained below their station; the consequence is that they frequently carry very low tastes into their extraordinary fortunes and that they seem to have acquired the supreme power only to minister to their coarse or paltry pleasures.

I think that in our time it is very necessary to purify, to regulate, and to proportion the feeling of ambition, but that it would be extremely dangerous to seek to impoverish and to repress it overmuch. We should attempt to lay down certain extreme limits which it should never be allowed to outstep; but its range within those established limits should not be too much checked.

周期很短,所以对于新鲜事物的抵制是软弱无力的,而社会结构既没有表现出很好的建造性,也没有表现出很坚实的基础。因此,当一个具有野心的人抓住了一切权力,他便无所畏惧了;而当他们失去权力的时候,他们便想推翻统治他的国家。因此,政治方面的雄心大志,便具有暴力和革命的性质,而在贵族社会却很少有这种情形。在民主国家里,通常是一个人最初有许多非常合理的小志向,然后由此爆发出一种强大的但受到不良控制的欲望;与自己的条件相适应的远大而有节制的志向,民主国家的人几乎是没有的。

我曾在本书的某个地方指出平等的原则通过某种隐秘的影响使追求物质享受的激情和只顾眼前的热情控制了人心。这种不一样的激情混合着雄心壮志,并使雄心壮志富有了激情的色彩。

我相信,民主社会的野心家们,比其他社会的人更少地集中精力关心未来的利益和规划;因为他们只顾现实,并只为现实忙碌。他们宁愿迅速地完成数量众多的小事情,而不愿去做少数几项有纪念意义的伟大事业,他们爱成功甚于爱荣誉。他们向人提出最多的是服从,而最让他们垂涎三尺的就是统治。几乎在所有情况下,他们的行为举止总是表现得在他们的社会地位之下;结果就使他们在拥有巨额财富的时候常常表现出非常低级的趣味,在握有最高权力的时候好像只是为了便于享受小小的粗俗的快乐。

我认为,在我们这个时代,很有必要去净化、规范和均衡人们的雄心壮志,但如果试图污化和过分抑制人们的奋进之心,则是极其危险的。我们应当努力为它预先规定出不得逾越的界限;但对已经确定的范围也不能过分提防。

I confess that I apprehend much less for democratic society from the boldness than from the mediocrity of desires. What appears to me most to be dreaded is that in the midst of the small, incessant occupations of private life, ambition should lose its vigor and its greatness; that the passions of man should abate, but at the same time be lowered; so that the march of society should every day become more tranquil and less aspiring.

I think, then, that the leaders of modern society would be wrong to seek to lull the community by a state of too uniform and too peaceful happiness, and that it is well to expose it from time to time to matters of difficulty and danger in order to raise ambition and to give it a field of action.

Moralists are constantly complaining that the ruling vice of the present time is pride. This is true in one sense, for indeed everyone thinks that he is better than his neighbor or refuses to obey his superior; but it is extremely false in another, for the same man who cannot endure subordination or equality has so contemptible an opinion of himself that he thinks he is born only to indulge in vulgar pleasures. He willingly takes up with low desires without daring to embark on lofty enterprises, of which he scarcely dreams.

Thus, far from thinking that humility ought to be preached to our contemporaries, I would have endeavors made to give them a more enlarged idea of themselves and of their kind. Humility is unwholesome to them; what they most want is, in my opinion, pride. I would willingly exchange several of our small virtues for this one vice.

　　我承认,我对民主社会的理解,主要不是来自于人们欲望的过大,而是它的平凡。在我看来最让人担心的:是人们在不断忙于私人生活的琐碎小事当中,会使雄心壮志失去其活力和伟大性;人们的激情会被大大地减少,同时也会跌落千丈;因此,社会一天一天地走向看来十分安宁但缺乏大志的状态。

　　因此我认为,现代社会的领袖们要想通过建立在统一和和平上的快乐使社会平静,那将是错误的,他们应当让公民们时常做一些艰巨而危险的事业,以便激发他们的雄心壮志和为他们提供展现其本领的舞台。

　　道德家们经常抱怨说,现代人的主要缺点就是自傲。这种说法在某种意义上是正确的,因为实际上任何一个人都认为自己比别人好,都不愿意服从他的上司;但从另一个意义来讲,这种说法又是错误的,因为同一个人既不愿意忍受从属的地位,又不愿意享受平等的地位,他会因此觉得受到了鄙视,以为自己生来就只能享受粗俗的乐趣。他自愿满足于平凡的欲望,不敢从事崇高的事业,而且连做梦都没敢想过。

　　因此,我不认为这种谦逊是我们的同时代人应当学习的,而希望他们以更高的标准要求自己和他人。谦逊对他们是无益的;在我看来,他们最需要的就是傲气。我宁愿拿我们的若干小小的美德,来换这个恶习。

CHAPTER XX
The Trade Of Place-hunting
In Certain Democratic Countries

In the United States, as soon as a man has acquired some education and pecuniary resources, either he endeavors to get rich by commerce or industry, or he buys land in the uncleared country and turns pioneer. All that he asks of the state is not to be disturbed in his toil and to be secure in his earnings. Among most European nations, when a man begins to feel his strength and to extend his desires, the first thing that occurs to him is to get some public employment. These opposite effects, originating in the same cause, deserve our passing notice.

When public employments are few in number, ill-paid, and precarious, while the different kinds of business are numerous and lucrative, it is to business and not to official duties that the new and eager desires created by the principle of equality turn from every side. But if, while the ranks of society are becoming more equal, the education of the people remains incomplete or their spirit the reverse of bold, if commerce and industry, checked in their growth, afford only slow and arduous means of making a fortune, the various members of the community, despairing of ameliorating their own condition, rush to the head of the state and demand its assistance. To relieve their own necessities at the cost of the public treasury appears to them the easiest and most open, if not the only way of rising above a condition which no longer contents them; place-hunting becomes the most generally followed of all trades.

第二十章 关于某些民主国家里的求官谋禄问题

在美国，只要一个公民达到了一些知识和财富之后，他就会努力通过工商业去致富，或买下一块未开发的土地，成为开拓的先锋者。他对政府的所有要求，就是不要干扰他的辛勤劳动和确保他的劳动成果。在大部分欧洲国家里，一个人开始感到自己的能力和要实现自己的愿望时，他首先会做的事是在政府找个一官半职。由同一个原因产生的这两个不同结果，值得我们在这里停留片刻加以研究。

当公共职位的数量不多、薪酬不高和不稳定，而工商业的种类繁多并且有很大的盈利时，那么，来自四面八方的平等的原则在制造着新的和热切的欲望，使人们投身于工商业，而放弃去政府当官。但是，当社会等级变得越来越平等，人们的知识水平尚不完备或有着胆小的思想，如果发展已到尽头的工商业只能向人们提供困难而缓慢的生财之道时，公民们便对改善自己的处境感到失望，而冲向政府首领那里去寻求帮助。在他们看来，用国家的财产来减缓他们自己的开支使自己的生活舒适，即使不是唯一的办法，至少也是提高他们生活质量的最容易和最可靠的办法；于是，求官谋禄就成了最常用的行业手段。

This must especially be the case in those great centralized monarchies in which the number of paid offices is immense and the tenure of them tolerably secure, so that no one despairs of obtaining a place and of enjoying it as undisturbedly as a hereditary fortune.

I shall not remark that the universal and inordinate desire for place is a great social evil; that it destroys the spirit of independence in the citizen and diffuses a venal and servile humor throughout the frame of society; that it stifles the manlier virtues; nor shall I be at the pains to demonstrate that this kind of traffic creates only an unproductive activity, which agitates the country without adding to its resources. All these things are obvious. But I would observe that a government that encourages this tendency risks its own tranquillity and places its very existence in great jeopardy. I am aware that at a time like our own, when the love and respect which formerly clung to authority are seen gradually to decline, it may appear necessary for those in power to lay a closer hold on every man by his own interest, and it may seem convenient to use his own passions to keep him in order and in silence; but this cannot long be so, and what may appear to be a source of strength for a certain time will assuredly become, in the end, a great cause of embarrassment and weakness. Among democratic nations, as well as elsewhere, the number of official appointments has, in the end, some limits; but among those nations the number of aspirants is unlimited. It perpetually increases, with a gradual and irresistible rise, in proportion as social conditions become more equal, and is checked only by the limits of the population.

Thus, when public employments afford the only outlet for ambition, the government necessarily meets with a permanent opposition at last; for it is tasked to satisfy with limited means unlimited desires. It is very certain that, of all people in the world, the most difficult to restrain and to manage are a people of office-hunters. Whatever endeavors are made by rulers, such a people can never be contented; and it is always to be apprehended that they will ultimately overturn the constitution of the country and change the aspect of the state for the sole purpose of cleaning out the present office-holders.

The sovereigns of the present age, who strive to fix upon themselves alone all those novel desires which are aroused by equality and

这种情况在实行中央集权的大君主国家尤为真实,因为在这样的国家里,领取薪俸的官员人数极多,他们的生活有充分的保证,因此没有人会不想去找个一官半职,并像享用父母的遗产那样安安稳稳地享受下去。

不用我再明确指出,这种普遍的和混乱的求官热是一大社会弊端;它摧毁了公民独立自主的精神,并在社会到处散播着贪污和腐败的风气;它抑制了光明正大的美德;更用不着我证明,这种做法只会产生不良的影响,并极严重地扰乱国家安全。所有这些都是显而易见的。但是,我要指出,鼓励这种倾向的政府会将自己的安定置于危险中,甚至会使自己的生存遭到厄运。我知道,在像我们这个时代,人民以往的那种对国家爱戴和尊敬的感情正在逐渐消失,而当权者却可能认为必须从本身的利益出发加紧控制每个人,并且看似最便利的办法是用人们的激情来使他们遵守秩序和保持沉默;但是这种局面不会持续太久,而且在一定时期内可能出现的力量源泉,最终肯定会变成阻碍和衰弱的主要原因。在民主国家也和在其他一切国家一样,公共官员的数量最终总有一个限度;而有野心去出任官职的人却没有止境。随着身份的日益平等有增无减地逐步增加,只有当公民数量减少时,它才会受到限制。

因此,当公职为人们的野心提供了唯一出路时,政府最终必然遭到长期的反对;因为政府无法用有限的手段去满足无限的欲望要求。非常清楚,在全世界的人中,最难控制和最难管理的人就是待业求职的人。不管统治者做多大的努力,也满足不了这些人的要求;因此,必须经常留意这些人只是为了使官位出缺,最终会颠覆政府的组织结构和改变国家的面貌。

因此,如果我没有弄错的话,我相信努力将精力集中于平等

to satisfy them, will repent in the end, if I am not mistaken, that ever they embarked on this policy. They will one day discover that they have hazarded their own power by making it so necessary, and that the more safe and honest course would have been to teach their subjects the art of providing for themselves.

所激发的各种新欲望并使其得到满足的现代统治者们,最后必然为采用这种办法而后悔。总有一天他们会发现,他们把自己的权力用于这样的需求是很危险的,而最安全可靠的办法应当是教会他们的被统治者自力更生的技术。

CHAPTER XXI
Why Great Revolutions
Will Become More Rare

A people that has existed for centuries under a system of castes and classes can arrive at a democratic state of society only by passing through a long series of more or less critical transformations, accomplished by violent efforts, and after numerous vicissitudes, in the course of which property, opinions, and power are rapidly transferred from one to another. Even after this great revolution is consummated, the revolutionary habits produced by it may long be traced, and it will be followed by deep commotion. As all this takes place at the very time when social conditions are becoming more equal, it is inferred that some concealed relation and secret tie exists between the principle of equality itself and revolution, in so much that the one cannot exist without giving rise to the other.

On this point reasoning may seem to lead to the same result as experience. Among a people whose ranks are nearly equal, no ostensible bond connects men together or keeps them settled in their station. None of them have either a permanent right or power to command, none are forced by their condition to obey; but every man, finding himself possessed of some education and some resources, may choose his own path and proceed apart from all his fellow men. The same causes that make the members of the community independent of each other continually impel them to new and restless desires and constantly spur them onwards. It therefore seems natural that in a democratic community men, things, and opinions should be forever changing

第二十一章 为什么大规模的革命变得越来越少

  几个世纪以来一直生活在等级制度或阶级制度下的人民,只有经过一系列长期的或多或少的艰辛改革,在暴力的帮助下,经过数次的变迁,在财产、观点和权力等相继出现多次急剧变位之后,才能达到民主的社会情况。在这场大规模的革命完成之后,它所制造的革命习惯还将长期存在下去,而且随之还会出现一些深重的动乱。因为所有这一切都是在社会身份变得越来越平等时发生的,所以人们可以由此推断出:在平等本身和革命之间存在着一种潜藏的和隐秘的联系,以致其中的一方在没有另一方的情况下就无法存在。

  关于这一点,推理和经验似乎会导致同一结果。在等级几乎接近平等的国家,没有一种公开的纽带会把人们联系在一起,并确保他们固定于自己的地位。任何人都不会拥有永久的权利和发号施令的权力,没有人会因为自己的地位而必须服从;但是,每个人都会发现,只要自己拥有知识和财富,就可以选择自己的道路,并同其他一切人分开而自己单独前进。使公民们彼此独立的同一原因,也在不断地促使他们产生新的急于实现的欲望,并在不断鞭策他们前进。因此,人们似乎可以自然地认为:在民主社

their form and place, and that democratic ages should be times of rapid and incessant transformation.

But is this really the case? Does the equality of social conditions habitually and permanently lead men to revolution? Does that state of society contain some perturbing principle which prevents the community from ever subsiding into calm and disposes the citizens to alter incessantly their laws, their principles, and their manners? I do not believe it; and as the subject is important, I beg for the reader's close attention.

Almost all the revolutions that have changed the aspect of nations have been made to consolidate or to destroy social inequality. Remove the secondary causes that have produced the great convulsions of the world and you will almost always find the principle of inequality at the bottom. Either the poor have attempted to plunder the rich, or the rich to enslave the poor. If, then, a state of society can ever be founded in which every man shall have something to keep and little to take from others, much will have been done for the peace of the world.

I am aware that among a great democratic people there will always be some members of the community in great poverty and others in great opulence; but the poor, instead of forming the immense majority of the nation, as is always the case in aristocratic communities, are comparatively few in number, and the laws do not bind them together by the ties of irremediable and hereditary penury.

The wealthy, on their side, are few and powerless; they have no privileges that attract public observation; even their wealth, as it is no longer incorporated and bound up with the soil, is impalpable and, as it were, invisible. As there is no longer a race of poor men, so there is no longer a race of rich men; the latter spring up daily from the multitude and relapse into it again. Hence they do not form a distinct class which may be easily marked out and plundered; and, moreover, as they are connected with the mass of their fellow citizens by a thousand secret ties, the people cannot assail them without inflicting an injury upon themselves.

会,人和物以及思想必将永远不断地改变其形式和地位,民主时代必将是快速的和不停的改革时代。

但是情况真的如此吗? 难道社会身份的平等会习惯性地和永远不断地促使人们去进行革命吗? 难道社会的平等中存在的某种动乱的原则在妨碍社会安定,驱使公民们不断改变他们的法律、原则和民情吗? 我认为不是这样的;这个问题很重要,我希望读者能提高注意力。

几乎所有改变国家面貌的革命,不是为了巩固社会的不平等,就是为了摧毁社会的不平等。撇开曾引起世界大动乱的次要原因不谈,你几乎总能发现不平等的原则在里面。也就是说,不是穷人想试图夺取富人的财产,就是富人要束缚穷人。因此,如果你能使一个社会处于人人都有某些东西保存在手,而很少到别人那里去取某些东西的状态,你就会对世界和平作出重大的贡献。

我知道,在一个大民主国家里,总会有一些公民处于极度贫穷,而另一些公民则拥有巨大财富;但是,民主社会的穷人并不像贵族社会的穷人那样可以构成民族的绝大多数,民主社会的穷人只占社会的很少一部分,法律也没有规定他们必须祖祖辈辈永远贫困下去。

另一方面,富人的人数不多且力量薄弱;他们没有使人看了就眼红的特权;甚至连他们的财产也不再同土地结合,而是一些不太引人注目、甚至是看不到的东西。如同不再有穷人的存在一样,富人也不复存在;每天,都会有富人从人民大众中脱颖而出,而且也不断有富人回归为普通大众。因此,他们并未形成一个容易辨认和识别的阶级;另外,由于他们与自己的同胞们被成千上万的隐秘的结联系在一起,所以人民要是攻击他们就不能不伤及自己。

Between these two extremes of democratic communities stands an innumerable multitude of men almost alike, who, without being exactly either rich or poor, possess sufficient property to desire the maintenance of order, yet not enough to excite envy. Such men are the natural enemies of violent commotions; their lack of agitation keeps all beneath them and above them still and secures the balance of the fabric of society. Not, indeed, that even these men are contented with what they have got or that they feel a natural abhorrence for a revolution in which they might share the spoil without sharing the calamity; on the contrary, they desire, with unexampled ardor, to get rich, but the difficulty is to know from whom riches can be taken. The same state of society that constantly prompts desires, restrains these desires within necessary limits; it gives men more liberty of changing, and less interest in change. Not only are the men of democracies not naturally desirous of revolutions, but they are afraid of them. All revolutions more or less threaten the tenure of property; but most of those who live in democratic countries are possessed of property; not only do they possess property, but they live in the condition where men set the greatest store upon their property.

If we attentively consider each of the classes of which society is composed, it is easy to see that the passions created by property are keenest and most tenacious among the middle classes. The poor often care but little for what they possess, because they suffer much more from the want of what they have not than they enjoy the little they have. The rich have many other passions besides that of riches to satisfy; and, besides, the long and arduous enjoyment of a great fortune sometimes makes them in the end insensible to its charms. But the men who have a competency, alike removed from opulence and from penury, attach an enormous value to their possessions. As they are still almost within the reach of poverty, they see its privations near at hand and dread them; between poverty and themselves there is nothing

在民主社会的这两个极端之间,还有无数的几乎是相同的人,这些人既不富裕也不贫穷,他们拥有足够的可以维持正常生活的财产,同时也不会引起别人的妒忌。这些人是激烈暴动的天然的敌人;他们对激情的缺乏性使激情高于他们的人和低于他们的人都保持于安静状态,并保证着社会的结构也处于安定状态。实际上,这并不是说这些人已经满足于自己现有的状况,或者说他们对能够分享到好处而又不受损失的革命有一种天然的反感;恰恰相反,他们以史无前例的热情渴望发财,但使其为难的是,他们知道这会侵夺某些人。使他们不断产生新欲望的同一社会情况,将这些欲望限制在必要的范围之内;它给人们可以改革的自由,但却减少了人们对改革的兴趣。生活在民主制度下的人,不仅不从心里渴望革命,而且从心里害怕革命。任何革命都会或多或少地威胁到已有的财产;但生活在民主国家里的大部分人都拥有财产;他们不仅仅是拥有财产,而且生活在人人都十分尊重他们财产的环境中。

如果我们仔细观察一下构成社会的每一个阶级,就会很容易发现由财富所带来的激情在中产阶级身上表现得最为热忱和坚定。穷人常常很少关心他们所拥有的财物,因为他们觉得要忍受需求所带来的痛苦远远大于他们所能享受的少量财物的快乐。而富人除了财富以外,还有许多其他需要满足的激情;但经过长期地和艰辛地经营巨额的财产之后,有时会使他们反而感觉不到财产的魅力了。但是,那些既不富裕也不贫穷的人,却对自己所拥有的财产极为重视。因为他们几乎快要到达贫困的边缘,深知贫穷的痛苦,并害怕这种痛苦;在他们和贫穷之间,只有一小部分财产,他们把自己的担心和希望随时都寄托在这点家产上。每一

but a scanty fortune, upon which they immediately fix their apprehensions and their hopes. Every day increases the interest they take in it, by the constant cares which it occasions; and they are the more attached to it by their continual exertions to increase the amount. The notion of surrendering the smallest part of it is insupportable to them, and they consider its total loss as the worst of misfortunes.

Now, these eager and apprehensive men of small property constitute the class that is constantly increased by the equality of conditions. Hence in democratic communities the majority of the people do not clearly see what they have to gain by a revolution, but they continually and in a thousand ways feel that they might lose by one.

I have shown, in another part of this work, that the equality of conditions naturally urges men to embark on commercial and industrial pursuits, and that it tends to increase and to distribute real property; I have also pointed out the means by which it inspires every man with an eager and constant desire to increase his welfare. Nothing is more opposed to revolutionary passions than these things. It may happen that the final result of a revolution is favorable to commerce and manufactures; but its first consequence will almost always be the ruin of manufactures and mercantile men, because it must always change at once the general principles of consumption and temporarily upset the existing proportion between supply and demand.

I know of nothing more opposite to revolutionary attitudes than commercial ones. Commerce is naturally adverse to all the violent passions; it loves to temporize, takes delight in compromise, and studiously avoids irritation. It is patient, insinuating, flexible, and never has recourse to extreme measures until obliged by the most absolute necessity. Commerce renders men independent of one another, gives them a lofty notion of their personal importance, leads them to seek to conduct their own affairs, and teaches how to conduct them well; it therefore prepares men for freedom, but preserves them from revolutions.

In a revolution the owners of personal property have more to fear than all others; for, on the one hand, their property is often easy to seize, and, on the other, it may totally disappear at any moment—a subject of alarm to which the owners of real property are less exposed, since, although they may lose the income of their estates, they may hope to preserve the land itself through the greatest vicissitudes. Hence the former are much more alarmed at the symptoms of

天他们都希望财产能更多一些,所以对自己所拥有的一切给予不断的关心;他们通过不断的努力使财产增加,所以对财产更加依恋。将一小部分家产让给别人的思想,在他们看来是无法忍受的,他们把财产的全部损失看作是最不幸的灾难。

但是,使这些热切的并担心自己小部分家产的阶级人数日益增加的,正是身份的平等。因此,在民主社会,公民的大多数并不能清楚地看出革命对他们会有什么好处,而是时时刻刻感到革命会从四面八方给他们带来损失。

我在本书的另一个地方说过,身份的平等会自然地激励人们去从事工商业,并使地产不断增加和不断被分配;我也曾指出,身份的平等每时每刻都在鼓励每个人热切地和不断地追求幸福。革命的最终结果可能是有利于工商业的;但它的最初结果却几乎总是使工商业者破产,因为革命一开始必须立刻改变消费的一般原则,并暂时混淆生产和需求之间的关系。

另外,我不知道再有什么东西比商业态度更反对革命态度的了。商业天生就反对所有暴力的激情;它喜爱温和,乐于妥协,并努力避免愤怒。它有耐性、柔性和灵活性,除非万不得已绝不采取极端手段。商业使人们彼此独立和非常重视自己的个人价值,使人们寻找自己处理事情的能力,并教会人们怎样才能处理得很好;因此,商业使人走向自由但远离革命。

在革命当中,个人财产的所有者比其他人都要害怕很多;因为,一方面,他们的财产往往容易被查封,另一方面又有随时全部丧失的可能。个人财产所有者就不必如此担惊受怕,因为他们即使失去了土地的收益,他们仍希望在大动荡之后至少保住土地本身。因此,在革命爆发的征兆中,前者要比后者害怕得多。由此

revolutionary commotion than the latter. Thus nations are less disposed to make revolutions in proportion as personal property is augmented and distributed among them and as the number of those possessing it is increased.

Moreover, whatever profession men may embrace and whatever species of property they may possess, one characteristic is common to them all. No one is fully contented with his present fortune; all are perpetually striving, in a thousand ways, to improve it. Consider any one of them at any period of his life and he will be found engaged with some new project for the purpose of increasing what he has. Do not talk to him of the interests and the rights of mankind; this small domestic concern absorbs for the time all his thoughts and inclines him to defer political agitations to some other season. This not only prevents men from making revolutions, but deters men from desiring them. Violent political passions have but little hold on those who have devoted all their faculties to the pursuit of their well-being. The ardor that they display in small matters calms their zeal for momentous undertakings.

From time to time, indeed, enterprising and ambitious men will arise in democratic communities whose unbounded aspirations cannot be contented by following the beaten track. Such men like revolutions and hail their approach; but they have great difficulty in bringing them about unless extraordinary events come to their assistance. No man can struggle with advantage against the spirit of his age and country; and however powerful he may be supposed to be, he will find it difficult to make his contemporaries share in feelings and opinions that are repugnant to all their feelings and desires.

It is a mistake to believe that, when once equality of condition has become the old and uncontested state of society and has imparted its characteristics to the manners of a nation, men will easily allow themselves to be thrust into perilous risks by an imprudent leader or a bold innovator. Not indeed that they will resist him openly, by well-contrived schemes, or even by a premeditated plan of resistance.

可见,一个国家的个人财产数量越大及其种类越多,就越少发生革命。

另外,不管人们操什么职业和拥有什么样的财产,所有人都具有一个共同的特点。那就是没有人会对自己现有的财产完全满意;所有人都在不断奋斗,以成千上万的办法增加财富。让我们试想一下,他们当中的任何一个人在其人生的任何一段时期,都会不断参与新的计划以增加自己现有的财富。不要对他们大讲人类的利益和权利,那都是没用的;因为他们把自己当前的全部精力都用于那些琐碎的家庭小事情上去了,希望你让他们另找时间去考虑公众共同关心的事情。这不仅阻止他们去发起革命,而且减缓了他们想要革命的念头。狂热的政治激情,很少能够打动那些将自己全部激情都用于追求幸福的人。他们对小事情的热心,使他们对大事情的热情变得平静了。

实际上,一直以来,在民主社会里也会出现一些事业心强和有雄心壮志的人,他们极大的欲望已不能满足于按照常规进行。这些人喜欢革命,并欢呼革命的到来;但是,除非有意外的事情来帮助他们,否则他们很难发起革命。没有人能在反对他的时代和他的国家的精神的斗争中得到好处;不管一个人认为自己的力量有多么强大,他会发现将很难使他的同时代人分享他们的感情和观念里所厌恶的东西。

因此,如果认为一旦身份的平等成了永久的和无可争议的社会事实,并将它的特征转嫁到民情之中,人们就会轻易地跟着一个卤莽的领袖或一位大胆的革新家走上冒险的道路,将会是完全错误的。但是,人们也不能通过深谋远虑的筹划,或者通过事先安排好的抵抗计划,去公开反对这样的领袖或革新家。人们不会

They will not struggle energetically against him, sometimes they will even applaud him; but they do not follow him. To his vehemence they secretly oppose their inertia, to his revolutionary tendencies their conservative interests, their homely tastes to his adventurous passions, their good sense to the flights of his genius, to his poetry their prose. With immense exertion he raises them for an instant, but they speedily escape from him and fall back, as it were, by their own weight. He strains himself to rouse the indifferent and distracted multitude and finds at last that he is reduced to impotence, not because he is conquered, but because he is alone.

I do not assert that men living in democratic communities are naturally stationary; I think, on the contrary, that a perpetual stir prevails in the bosom of those societies, and that rest is unknown there; but I think that men bestir themselves within certain limits, beyond which they hardly ever go. They are forever varying, altering, and restoring secondary matters; but they carefully abstain from touching what is fundamental. They love change, but they dread revolutions.

Although the Americans are constantly modifying or abrogating some of their laws, they by no means display revolutionary passions. It may be easily seen from the promptitude with which they check and calm themselves when public excitement begins to grow alarming, and at the very moment when passions seem most roused, that they dread a revolution as the worst of misfortunes and that every one of them is inwardly resolved to make great sacrifices to avoid such a catastrophe. In no country in the world is the love of property more active and more anxious than in the United States; nowhere does the majority display less inclination for those principles which threaten to alter, in whatever manner, the laws of property.

I have often remarked, that theories which are of a revolutionary nature, since they cannot be put in practice without a complete and sometimes a sudden change in the state of property and persons, are

积极地同他们进行斗争,有时甚至还会拍手称赞他们;但绝不会跟着他们走。人们秘密地以自己的惰性抵制他们的狂热,以自己的保守的利益抵制他们的革命倾向,以自己的日常爱好抵制他们冒险家的激情,以自己的强烈的判断力抵制他们的才华,以自己的散文抵制他们的诗篇。这样的领袖和革命家,在经过巨大的努力后可能会唤起人民,但人们很快又会离开他们,而他们自己就好像因体重过重而跌倒在地。他们使尽全身力气想要唤起这些态度冷淡和漫不经心的群众,但最终会发现自己无能为力,这不是因为他们已经被征服,而是因为他们很孤单。

我绝不承认生活在民主社会的人天生就是固定不动的;恰恰相反,我认为有一种永恒的运动盛行在这样的社会里,并且没人知道这种运动何时会停息;但我相信,人们总是激发自己限制在一定的范围内运动,并且从来都不曾超越。他们永远都在改变、改进或改革次要的事情;而对于主要的东西,他们则很小心地碰触。他们喜欢改革,但害怕革命。

尽管美国人不断修改或废除他们的某些法律,但他们从来不会表现出革命的激情。不难发现,当公共激情开始增长到令人担心的程度时,甚至在公共激情极其奋起的时候,他们就立即止步并冷静下来。他们害怕革命,将革命视为最大的不幸,每个人都在心里暗自决定,准备为了阻止这场大的不幸而作出重大的牺牲。世界上没有一个国家像美国那样如此积极地热爱财富而又如此担心怕失去财富;也没有一个国家像美国那样有绝大多数人反对以任何方式威胁财产制度并使其改变的学说。

我曾经常指出,最具有革命性质的理论,当它不能完整的或有时是突然改变财产和人的现状时,是无法应用到实际中的,因

much less favorably viewed in the United States than in the great monarchical countries of Europe; if some men profess them, the bulk of
the people reject them with instinctive abhorrence. I do not hesitate to
say that most of the maxims commonly called democratic in France
would be proscribed by the democracy of the United States. This may
easily be understood: in America men have the opinions and passions
of democracy; in Europe we have still the passions and opinions of
revolution.

If ever America undergoes great revolutions, they will be brought
about by the presence of the black race on the soil of the United
States; that is to say, they will owe their origin, not to the equality,
but to the inequality of condition.

When social conditions are equal, every man is apt to live apart,
centered in himself and forgetful of the public. If the rulers of democratic nations were either to neglect to correct this fatal tendency or to
encourage it from a notion that it weans men from political passions
and thus wards off revolutions, they might eventually produce the evil
they seek to avoid, and a time might come when the inordinate passions of a few men, aided by the unintelligent selfishness or the pusil-
lanimity of the greater number, would ultimately compel society to
pass through strange vicissitudes. In democratic communities revolutions are seldom desired except by a minority, but a minority may
sometimes effect them.

I do not assert that democratic nations are secure from revolutions; I merely say that the state of society in those nations does not
lead to revolutions, but rather wards them off. A democratic people
left to itself will not easily embark in great hazards; it is only led to
revolutions unawares; it may sometimes undergo them, but it does not
make them: and I will add that when such a people has been allowed
to acquire sufficient knowledge and experience, it will not allow them
to be made.

I am well aware that in this respect public institutions may themselves do much; they may encourage or repress the tendencies that o-
riginate in the state of society. I therefore do not maintain, I repeat,
that a people is secure from revolutions simply because conditions are
equal in the community; but I think that, whatever the institutions of

此它在美国就不会像在欧洲的一些大君主国那样受到无限的欢迎；即使有人主张这个理论，大多数群众也会以一种本能的反感抵制它。我敢毫不犹豫地说，被法国一贯称为民主名言的那些格言，将被美国的民主所禁止。这一点很容易理解：在美国，人们具有民主的观念和激情；而在欧洲，人们仍是具有革命的激情和思想。

如果有一天美国经历了大型的革命，那也是由美国的土地上的黑人所引起的；也就是说，造成这种革命的原因不是身份的平等，而是身份的不平等。

在社会身份平等时，每个人都想要独自生活，沉溺于自我，将公众抛到脑后。如果民主国家的统治者们不曾忽视也不去纠正这个致命的倾向或者助长它，认为它能使公民消除政治激情和远离革命，那他们将会制造出他们一直想要躲避的恶果，而且这一天总会来临，当某些人的混乱的激情，在多数愚昧自私或胆怯心虚的人的帮助下，迫使整个社会经历异常的变故。在民主社会，只有很少数的人希望革命，但有时往往是这些少数人引发了革命。

我并不是说民主国家可以免于革命；我只是说这些国家的社会情况不会导致革命，甚至可以说能避开革命。民主国家的人民凡事全靠自己，他们不会轻易投身于有重大危险的行动中；他们只是在毫无准备的情况下才被卷入革命；他们有时也经历过革命，但他们不会制造革命，我再补充一点：当这种国家的人民一旦获得足够的知识和经验，便不会允许革命出现。

我非常清楚，在这个方面国家的各项制度可能发生很大的影响；它们可能促进也可能抑制社会情况的各种习性的发展。因此，我再重复一遍，我并不认为一个国家仅仅是因为身份的平等就可以避免革命；但我确信，不管这种国家实行什么制度，在那里

such a people may be, great revolutions will always be far less violent and less frequent than is supposed, and I can easily discern a state of polity which, when combined with the principle of equality, would render society more stationary than it has ever been in our western part of the world.

The observations I have here made on events may also be applied in part to opinions. Two things are surprising in the United States: the mutability of the greater part of human actions, and the singular stability of certain principles. Men are in constant motion; the mind of man appears almost unmoved. When once an opinion has spread over the country and struck root there, it would seem that no power on earth is strong enough to eradicate it. In the United States general principles in religion, philosophy, morality, and even politics do not vary, or at least are only modified by a hidden and often an imperceptible process; even the grossest prejudices are obliterated with incredible slowness amid the continual friction of men and things.

I hear it said that it is in the nature and the habits of democracies to be constantly changing their opinions and feelings. This may be true of small democratic nations, like those of the ancient world, in which the whole community could be assembled in a public place and then excited at will by an orator. But I saw nothing of the kind among the great democratic people that dwells upon the opposite shores of the Atlantic Ocean. What struck me in the United States was the difficulty of shaking the majority in an opinion once conceived or of drawing it off from a leader once adopted. Neither speaking nor writing can accomplish it; nothing but experience will avail; and even experience must be repeated.

This is surprising at first sight, but a more attentive investigation explains the fact. I do not think that it is as easy as is supposed to uproot the prejudices of a democratic people, to change its belief, to supersede principles once established by new principles in religion, politics, and morals; in a word, to make great and frequent changes in

发生的大革命总要比想像中的缺少暴力，并少很多，于是，我不难设想，这样的政治情况一与平等结合，就会使社会达到西方世界从未有过的安定。

我在这里就事情本身所论述的一切，同样也适用于部分观点。在美国，有两件事使人感到惊奇：人们的大部分活动具有易变性，而某些特定原则的固定性很强。人们在不断的运动中；但人们的精神却似乎是不动的。一旦当某个观点在美国的土地上传播开来，并扎下了根，那就可以说世界上再没有更大的力量可以把它根除掉。在美国，宗教、哲学、道德，甚至是政治方面的普遍原则，从来不会改变，或者至少可以说，它们只是被隐秘的而且往往是人们很难发觉的方法加以改进；在人和事物的这种连续不断的摩擦中，连一些最粗野的偏见也只能以慢得令人难以想象的速度去清除。

我听说，是民主的本性和习惯在不断改变着感情和观念。这种情况在小民主国家尤为真实，像在古时候的这些小民主国家里，常常把全体公民集合于一个公共场所，然后由一位演说家任意鼓动。但是，在位于大洋彼岸的大民主共和国里，我却从没有见到过这种现象。在美国，使我感到惊奇的是，很难使多数放弃它所认定的观点和抛弃它所选定的人。无论是发表演说还是书写文章，都是没有用的。只有亲身经验才是有用的；而且这种经验有时要反复很多次。

初次看来，这会使人感到吃惊，但经过深入研究后，便可以知道它的究竟。我不认为，要根除一个民主国家的偏见，改变它的信念，在宗教、哲学、政治、道德等方面用一套新原则分别取代各自原有的原则，是像想象中的那么简单的；简单地讲，要使人们的

men's minds. Not that the human mind is there at rest, it is in constant agitation; but it is engaged in infinitely varying the consequences of known principles and in seeking for new consequences rather than in seeking for new principles. Its motion is one of rapid circumvolution rather than of straightforward impulse by rapid and direct effort; it extends its orbit by small continual and hasty movements, but it does not suddenly alter its position.

Men who are equal in rights, in education, in fortune, or, to comprise all in one word, in their social condition, have necessarily wants, habits, and tastes that are hardly dissimilar. As they look at objects under the same aspect, their minds naturally tend to similar conclusions; and though each of them may deviate from his contemporaries and form opinions of his own, they will involuntarily and unconsciously concur in a certain number of received opinions. The more attentively I consider the effects of equality upon the mind, the more am I persuaded that the intellectual anarchy which we witness about us is not, as many men suppose, the natural state of democratic nations. I think it is rather to be regarded as an accident peculiar to their youth, and that it breaks out only at that period of transition when men have already snapped the former ties which bound them together, but are still amazingly different in origin, education, and manners; so that, having retained opinions, propensities, and tastes of great diversity, nothing any longer prevents men from avowing them openly. The leading opinions of men become similar in proportion as their conditions assimilate: such appears to me to be the general and permanent law; the rest is casual and transient.

I believe that it will rarely happen to any man in a democratic community suddenly to frame a system of notions very remote from that which his contemporaries have adopted; and if some such innovator appeared, I apprehend that he would have great difficulty in finding listeners, still more in finding believers. When the conditions of men are almost equal, they do not easily allow themselves to be

思想发生巨大的和经常的改变不是那么容易的。这并不是说人类的思想是静止不动的，其实人类的思想是在不断的运动中的；但它不是在探求新的原则，而是在永无止境地改变已知原则的成果，并探求其新的结果。这种运动在快速地旋转，而不是迅速地、直接地努力冲向前去；它以连续不断的和匆忙的运动在扩大自己的活动范围，但绝不会突然改变自己的位置。

那些在权利、教育和财产上平等的人，简而言之，就是社会身份平等的人，必然有几乎相同的需要、习惯和爱好。由于他们从同一角度观察事物，他们的思想也自然会趋向相同的结论；尽管他们中的每个人都有可能背离其同时代的人，并形成自己的观点，但他们最终将在不知不觉中在一定数量的观点上达成共识。我越仔细考察平等对人们思想产生的影响，就越深信我们现今所见到的智力混乱现象，并不是像人们所想象的那样是民主国家的自然状态。我认为，还不如把这种混乱现象看成是民主国家的青年时期所特有的偶然事件，它只出现于人们已经冲破以前把他们彼此联系在一起的旧关系，而他们在出身、教育和习惯上仍有很大不同的过渡时期；因此，只要人们在过渡时期各自保留非常不同的观念、本性和爱好，就没有什么能阻止它们表现出来。但随着人们身份的逐渐相同，人们的主要见解也变得越来越相似：在我看来，这才是普遍的和永久的事实，而其余的都是偶然的和过渡的东西。

我认为，在民主时代，很难有人能够突然就形成一个与其同时代人已经采纳的思想体系相差甚远的思想体系；如果出现了这样的革新家，我能理解他将很难找到聆听者，甚至也很难找到信仰者。当人们的身份几乎平等的时候，他们是不会轻易信任他人

persuaded by one another. As they all live in close intercourse, as they have learned the same things together, and as they lead the same life, they are not naturally disposed to take one of themselves for a guide and to follow him implicitly. Men seldom take the opinion of their equal or of a man like themselves upon trust.

Not only is confidence in the superior attainments of certain individuals weakened among democratic nations, as I have elsewhere remarked, but the general notion of the intellectual superiority which any man whatsoever may acquire in relation to the rest of the community is soon overshadowed. As men grow more like each other, the doctrine of the equality of the intellect gradually infuses itself into their opinions, and it becomes more difficult for any innovator to acquire or to exert much influence over the minds of a people. In such communities sudden intellectual revolutions will therefore be rare; for if we read aright the history of the world, we shall find that great and rapid changes in human opinions have been produced far less by the force of reasoning than by the authority of a name.

Observe, too, that as the men who live in democratic societies are not connected with one another by any tie, each of them must be convinced individually, while in aristocratic society it is enough to convince a few; the rest follow. If Luther had lived in an age of equality and had not had princes and potentates for his audience, he would perhaps have found it more difficult to change the aspect of Europe.

Not, indeed, that the men of democracies are naturally strongly persuaded of the certainty of their opinions or are unwavering in belief; they frequently entertain doubts that no one, in their eyes, can remove. It sometimes happens at such times that the human mind would willingly change its position, but as nothing urges or guides it forward, it oscillates to and fro without progressive motion. ①

---

① If I inquire what state of society is most favorable to the great revolutions of the mind, I find that it occurs somewhere between the complete equality of the whole community and the absolute separation of ranks. Under a system of castes generations succeed one another without altering men's positions; some have nothing more, others nothing better, to hope for. The imagination slumbers amid this universal silence and stillness, and the very idea of change fades from the human mind.

When ranks have been abolished and social conditions are almost equalized,

的。由于大家都生活在紧密的交往中,他们一起学习同样的东西,过着同样的生活,所以自然不愿意从中选出一个人当领导并盲目追随他。人们很少会采纳与自己平等或相似的人的意见。

像我在本书的某处所讲的那样,在民主国家,不仅某些个人对于知识的信任程度降低了,而且在智力上可能优越于其他所有人的某一个人的一般观念,不久也会失去光彩。随着人们彼此之间日趋相似化,智力平等的主张便逐渐灌输到人的观念里,于是,任何一个革新家,如果想对全国人民的思想施加重大影响,将是非常困难的。因此,在这样的社会里,突发的智力革命是很少见的;因为如果正确地阅读一下世界历史,我们就会发现,使人们的观念发生迅速而巨大转变的,主要不是理论的力量,而是权威的力量。

还要注意一点,生活在民主社会的人们不会被任何束缚把大家彼此联系在一起,所以要对每个人一一进行说服,但在贵族社会里,只要对少数人进行说服就足够了;其余的人都会跟着走。如果路德生活在平等的时代,而他的听众中又没有君主和有权势者,或许他在改变欧洲面貌的活动中可能要遇到更大的困难。

这并不是说民主时代的人天生就强烈地相信自己的观点,并坚定自己的信念;他们常常产生在他们看来谁也无法解决的怀疑。在这样的时代,人们的思想有时也愿意改变自己的方位,但因为没有力量推动和指导它前进,所以仍在原地徘徊,没有任何进步。①

---

① 如果让我去探究到底是什么样的社会情况才更有利于人们思想中的大革命,我发现这种社会情况将存在于完全平等的社会与完全等级分离的社会之间。在等级制度下,人们代代相传,其地位并不会改变;人们并没有更多以及更进一步的奢求。幻想已在安静与沉寂中长眠,而改革的观念也在人们的思想中消失。

当等级制度逐渐消失,而人们的社会身份几乎趋于平等时,所有的人都处

Even when the confidence of a democratic people has been won, it is still no easy matter to gain their attention. It is extremely difficult to obtain a hearing from men living in democracies, unless it is to speak to them of themselves. They do not attend to the things said to them, because they are always fully engrossed with the things they are doing. For, indeed, few men are idle in democratic nations; life is passed in the midst of noise and excitement, and men are so engaged in acting that little time remains to them for thinking. I would especially remark, not only that they are employed, but that they are passionately devoted to their employments. They are always in action, and each of their actions absorbs their faculties; the zeal which they display in business puts out the enthusiasm they might otherwise entertain for ideas.

I think that it is extremely difficult to excite the enthusiasm of a democratic people for any theory which has not a palpable, direct, and immediate connection with the daily occupations of life; therefore they will not easily forsake their old opinions, for it is enthusiasm that flings the minds of men out of the beaten track and effects the great revolutions of the intellect as well as the great revolutions of the political world.

Thus democratic nations have neither time nor taste to go in search of novel opinions. Even when those they possess become doubtful, they still retain them because it would take too much time and inquiry to change them; they retain them, not as certain, but as established.

---

all men are in ceaseless excitement, but each of them stands alone, independent and weak. This latter state of things is excessively different from the former one; yet it has one point of analogy: great revolutions of the human mind seldom occur in it.

But between these two extremes of the history of nations is an intermediate period, a period of glory as well as of ferment, when the conditions of men are not sufficiently settled for the mind to be lulled in torpor, when they are sufficiently unequal for men to exercise a vast power on the minds of one another, and when some few may modify the convictions of all. It is at such times that great reformers arise and new ideas suddenly change the face of the world.

在赢得一个民主国家的人民的信任后,要想得到他们的注意力仍然不是件容易的事。在同生活于民主制度下的人谈话时,如果不谈到他们本身的问题,则很难使他们听你讲话。他们不是很注意听别人对他们讲的话,因为他们总是全神贯注地忙于自己所做的事情。事实上,在民主国家,很少有懒惰的人;人们的生活总是在喧闹而忙乱的环境中度过,工作紧张得连思考问题的时间都没有。我要特别指出,他们不仅仅是在工作,而且是投入了自己的所有激情在工作。他们永远在行动中,而且对每一个行动都付诸了自己的全部精力;他们用于事业上的热情,消除了他们在思想上的狂热性。

我认为,激发民主国家人们的热情同他们的日常生活实践没有明显的、直接的和迫切的关系的某一理论是极其困难的。因此,这样的人民不会轻易放弃他们的旧观念,因为能使人的思想脱离已经走习惯的老路以及完成智力大革命和政治大革命的,正是狂爱。

因此,民主国家的人民既没有时间也没有兴趣去寻求新的观念。甚至在他们对原有的见解产生怀疑的时候,也仍然要保持一段时间,因为他们要经过很长的时间和反复的思考,才能改变原来的观念;他们之所以保留原来的见解,并不是因为它是可

于无休止的兴奋中,但每个人又都独立,互不依赖且力量软弱。后者社会情况与前者完全不同;然而有一个观点与此类似:人们思想中的大革命将很少在这种情况下发生。

但是产生在人类历史的这两个极端的国家之间的时期,仅仅是一个过渡时期,这个时期既拥有荣誉,也产生过动乱,当人们的状况不在满足于思想被麻木地哄骗时,当对于人们来说,对其他人思想行使巨大权力十分不平等时,当少数人可以篡改所有人的定罪时,就在这个时候,出现了伟大的改革家,新思想突然改变了世界的面孔。

There are yet other and more cogent reasons which prevent any great change from being easily effected in the principles of a democratic people. I have already adverted to them in the nineteenth chapter.

If the influence of individuals is weak and hardly perceptible among such a people, the power exercised by the mass upon the mind of each individual is extremely great; I have already shown for what reasons. I would now observe that it is wrong to suppose that this depends solely upon the form of government and that the majority would lose its intellectual supremacy if it were to lose its political power.

In aristocracies men often have much greatness and strength of their own; when they find themselves at variance with the greater number of their fellow countrymen, they withdraw to their own circle, where they support and console themselves. Such is not the case in a democratic country; there public favor seems as necessary as the air we breathe, and to live at variance with the multitude is, as it were, not to live. The multitude require no laws to coerce those who do not think like themselves: public disapprobation is enough; a sense of their loneliness and impotence overtakes them and drives them to despair.

Whenever social conditions are equal, public opinion presses with enormous weight upon the minds of each individual; it surrounds, directs, and oppresses him; and this arises from the very constitution of society much more than from its political laws. As men grow more alike, each man feels himself weaker in regard to all the rest; as he discerns nothing by which he is considerably raised above them or distinguished from them, he mistrusts himself as soon as they assail him. Not only does he mistrust his strength, but he even doubts of his right; and he is very near acknowledging that he is in the wrong, when the greater number of his countrymen assert that he is so. The majority do not need to force him; they convince him. In whatever way the powers of a democratic community may be organized and balanced, then, it will always be extremely difficult to believe what the bulk of the people reject or to profess what they condemn.

靠的,而是因为它是早已确立的。另外,还有几个更强有力的原因阻止民主国家的人民轻易地改变原有主张。我在本书第十九章里已经说明了这些原因。

在这样的国家里,如果个人的影响力很微弱并且几乎是难以察觉的,而群众对每个人的思想的影响力却是极其巨大的;我已在其他地方讲过其原因。我现在想要指出的是,如果认为这完全取决于政府的组织形式,以为多数一旦失去其政治权力,它的智力权威也将随之消失,那将是错误的。

在贵族制度下,人们往往拥有属于自己的伟大性和力量;当他们发现自己与大多数同胞不相符合时,他们会退回到自己的小圈子里,以慰藉自己。而在民主国家里就不会有这种情况;在民主国家,公众的爱戴就像是与我们呼吸的空气那样必需,如果和群众不相符合可以说是无法生活下去的。群众不必用法律去制服那些与自己想法不同的人:公众对他们的责难就足够了;孤立感和落魄感,很快会使他们感到抑郁和失望。

每当社会身份趋于平等时,公共的舆论就会对每个人的思想产生巨大的压力;它包围、指挥和压迫每个人的思想;这主要来因于社会的组织本身,而很少来因于政治法令。随着人们彼此之间更加相似,每个人都感觉到自己在别人面前是那么的软弱;每个人看不出自己有什么高人一等或与他人不同的地方,所以在众人攻击他的时候,他会立即对自己产生怀疑。他不仅怀疑自己的力量,而且开始怀疑自己的权利;而当绝大多数人说他错了的时候,他会几乎完全认错。多数不必强迫他;他们只是说服他。因此,在一个民主社会里,不管各项权力是怎样组织和保持平衡的,要想相信群众所反对的东西和宣扬群众所谴责的东西,都是很困难的。

This circumstance is extraordinarily favorable to the stability of opinions. When an opinion has taken root among a democratic people and established itself in the minds of the bulk of the community, it afterwards persists by itself and is maintained without effort, because no one attacks it. Those who at first rejected it as false ultimately receive it as the general impression, and those who still dispute it in their hearts conceal their dissent; they are careful not to engage in a dangerous and useless conflict.

It is true that when the majority of a democratic people change their opinions, they may suddenly and arbitrarily effect strange revolutions in men's minds; but their opinions do not change without much difficulty, and it is almost as difficult to show that they are changed.

Time, events, or the unaided individual action of the mind will sometimes undermine or destroy an opinion, without any outward sign of the change. It has not been openly assailed, no conspiracy has been formed to make war on it, but its followers one by one noiselessly secede; day by day a few of them abandon it, until at last it is only professed by a minority. In this state it will still continue to prevail. As its enemies remain mute or only interchange their thoughts by stealth, they are themselves unaware for a long period that a great revolution has actually been effected; and in this state of uncertainty they take no steps; they observe one another and are silent. The majority have ceased to believe what they believed before, but they still affect to believe, and this empty phantom of public opinion is strong enough to chill innovators and to keep them silent and at a respectful distance.

We live at a time that has witnessed the most rapid changes of opinion in the minds of men; nevertheless it may be that the leading opinions of society will before long be more settled than they have been for several centuries in our history; that time has not yet come, but it

这种情况对人们观念的稳定特别有利。当一种观念已经在民主国家里扎根，并在大多数人的思想里留下深刻的烙印，它便会依靠自己的力量和不费吹灰之力地存在下去，因为没有人会再反对它。那些最初否定它是错误理论的人，最终也会因为大家都接受而接受，而在心里坚持要同它斗争到底的人，也会将这种不满埋藏在心里；他们不想卷入一场危险而又无益的斗争中。

不错，当民主国家的多数改变其观念时，他们可能在人们的思想中掀起一场突然的并且让人感到奇特的革命；但是，多数的见解是很难改变的，而要确认它的改变也是同样困难的。

有时，时间、事件，或是个人独立的思想活动，也会在没有任何表面特征变化的情况下破坏一种观念。这种变化没有被公开反对，人们无法同这种变化进行斗争，也无法为了进行斗争而集合力量，结果，这个观念的追随者都一个接着一个地静静地离开了它；每天都有一些人表示要抛弃它，直到最后，只剩少数几个人信奉它了。但在这种情况下，它仍旧发生着作用。它的敌人们仍旧保持沉默，或者只是秘密地交流思想，所以他们自己也没有意识到在很长时期内有一场大革命已在进行；他们在这种不确定中一动不动；他们彼此观察，默不作声。大多数人已经停止相信他们从前所相信过的了，但仍装作很相信的样子，而公众思想的这种虚无的幻影，便足以使革新者心灰意冷和保持沉默，被人敬而远之。

我们所生活的时代，在一个见证了人们的观念发生着急剧变化的时代；但是不久以后，人们的基本观点也许要比我们历史中过去许多世纪存在过的基本观点稳定得多；这个时间还没有到

may perhaps be approaching. As I examine more closely the natural wants and tendencies of democratic nations, I grow persuaded that if ever social equality is generally and permanently established in the world, great intellectual and political revolutions will become more difficult and less frequent than is supposed. Because the men of democracies appear always excited, uncertain, eager, changeable in their wills and in their positions, it is imagined that they are suddenly to abrogate their laws, to adopt new opinions, and to assume new manners. But if the principle of equality predisposes men to change, it also suggests to them certain interests and tastes that cannot be satisfied without a settled order of things. Equality urges them on, but at the same time it holds them back; it spurs them, but fastens them to earth; it kindles their desires, but limits their powers.

This, however, is not perceived at first; the passions that tend to sever the citizens of a democracy are obvious enough, but the hidden force that restrains and unites them is not discernible at a glance.

Amid the ruins which surround me shall I dare to say that revolutions are not what I most fear for coming generations? If men continue to shut themselves more closely within the narrow circle of domestic interests and to live on that kind of excitement, it is to be apprehended that they may ultimately become inaccessible to those great and powerful public emotions which perturb nations, but which develop them and recruit them. When property becomes so fluctuating and the love of property so restless and so ardent, I cannot but fear that men may arrive at such a state as to regard every new theory as a peril, every innovation as an irksome toil, every social improvement as a stepping-stone to revolution, and so refuse to move altogether for fear of being moved too far. I dread, and I confess it, lest they should at last so entirely give way to a cowardly love of present enjoyment as to lose sight of the interests of their future selves and those of their descendants and prefer to glide along the easy current of life rather than to

来,但它可能正在接近我们。我越深入研究民主国家人民的自然
需要和倾向,就越是相信:一旦社会平等在世界上普遍而永久地
建立起来,智力和政治上的大革命将比人们想象中的变得越来越
困难和越来越稀少。由于民主国家的人看来好像总在兴奋的、不
确定的和热情的,并且随时准备改变自己的意愿和地位,所以使
人觉得他们好像会突然废除他们的法律,并采用新的观念和新的
习惯。但是,如果平等的原则在驱使人们发生改变,它同时还会
告诉人们如果没有安定有序的环境,就没法满足自己的利益和爱
好。平等在推动人们前进,同时也在阻止他们前进;平等在鞭策
着人们,同时又紧紧地束缚着人们;平等在点燃人们的欲望,同时
又限制人们的力量。

　　但是,这种情况在最初不是一下子就可以被察觉的;因为那
些试图分散民主国家的人民的激情是非常明显的,而限制和联结
他们的隐藏的力量并不是一眼就可以分辨出来的。

　　在包围着我们的一片废墟之中,我是否敢说革命不是我对以
后几代人表示的最大担心吗? 如果人们继续将自己关在越来越
狭窄的家庭利益的小圈子里,并生活在一种无休止的追求利益的
兴奋中,我们就可以看到他们最终将难以达到那些扰乱国家的巨
大的和有力的感情,而这种感情却能使人民前进和革新。当财产
变得如此易于变动,而爱财之心又是如此永无止境和激烈时,我
不能不担心人们会将一切新的理论视为危险,将一切改革视为令人
厌恶的跋涉,将一切社会进步视为走向革命的初步,并唯恐被卷进
去而一动不动。我的心充满了恐惧,而且我承认这种恐惧,因为人
们现在完全让步于对眼前利益的追求,却遗忘了自己的将来利益和
子孙后代的利益,喜欢安然地享受命运所安排的一切,而在必要时,

make, when it is necessary, a strong and sudden effort to a higher purpose.

It is believed by some that modern society will be always changing its aspect; for myself, I fear that it will ultimately be too invariably fixed in the same institutions, the same prejudices, the same manners, so that mankind will be stopped and circumscribed; that the mind will swing backwards and forwards forever without begetting fresh ideas; that man will waste his strength in bootless and solitary trifling, and, though in continual motion, that humanity will cease to advance.

也不肯作出强烈而坚强的努力去追求更高的目标。

　　人们认为新社会每天都在改变它的面貌；至于我，则害怕新社会最终将过于固守在原来的制度、原来的偏见和原来的习俗上，结果，人类停止前进了并被限制起来；人的思想将会一直在原地反反复复，并永远创造不出新思想；每个人都把精力用于一些小而无益的独立活动之上，看来所有的人都像是在不断地活动，但整个人类却不再前进了。

CHAPTER XXII

Why Democratic Nations
Naturally Desire Peace, And
Democratic Armies, War

The same interests, the same fears, the same passions that deter democratic nations from revolutions deter them also from war; the spirit of military glory and the spirit of revolution are weakened at the same time and by the same causes. The ever increasing numbers of men of property who are lovers of peace, the growth of personal wealth which war so rapidly consumes, the mildness of manners, the gentleness of heart, those tendencies to pity which are produced by the equality of conditions, that coolness of understanding which renders men comparatively insensible to the violent and poetical excitement of arms, all these causes concur to quench the military spirit. I think it may be admitted as a general and constant rule that among civilized nations the warlike passions will become more rare and less intense in proportion as social conditions are more equal.

War is nevertheless an occurrence to which all nations are subject, democratic nations as well as others. Whatever taste they may have for peace, they must hold themselves in readiness to repel aggression, or, in other words, they must have an army. Fortune, which has conferred so many peculiar benefits upon the inhabitants of the United States, has placed them in the midst of a wilderness, where they have, so to speak, no neighbors; a few thousand soldiers are sufficient for their wants. But this is peculiar to America, not to democracy.

The equality of conditions and the manners as well as the institutions resulting from it do not exempt a democratic people from the necessity of standing armies, and their armies always exercise a powerful influence over their fate. It is therefore of singular importance to inquire what are the natural propensities of the men of whom these armies are composed.

第二十二章　为什么民主国家的人民自然希望和平而民主国家的军队希望战争

那些阻止民主国家的人民发动革命的利益、恐惧心理和激情，也同样在阻止他们发动战争；军事荣誉的精神和革命精神，在同时由于同样的原因被减弱。爱好和平的财产所有者人数的不断增加、可以迅速销毁于炮火的动产的增多、民情的纯朴、人心的温存、平等所激发的怜悯心情、很少被战时产生的诗意般的强烈激情所打动的冷静理智，这一切联合起来，便足以抑制军事精神。我认为应当承认，可以把在文明国家里随着身份的日益平等，好战的激情将越来越少和越来越不强烈，视为一个普遍的常规。

然而，战争是所有国家都会被卷入的事件，无论是民主国家或其他国家。无论它们多么热爱和平，都必须随时做好抵制侵略的准备，换句话说，就是他们必须要有一支军队。命运已经赋予美国人民很多特殊的利益，将它们置于这片广袤无垠的宽广土地上，可以说，在那里美国没有邻国；只要少数士兵就足够了。但是，这只是美国的特点，而不是民主的特点。

身份平等、民情和基于民情所建立的各项制度，并没有使民主国家的人民免于建立军队，而且它的军队还经常对它的命运起着极大的影响。因此，研究什么是军队成员的自然倾向是极其重要的。

Among aristocratic nations, especially among those in which birth is the only source of rank, the same inequality exists in the army as in the nation; the officer is noble, the soldier is a serf; the one is naturally called upon to command, the other to obey. In aristocratic armies the private soldier's ambition is therefore circumscribed within very narrow limits. Nor has the ambition of the officer an unlimited range. An aristocratic body not only forms a part of the scale of ranks in the nation, but contains a scale of ranks within itself; the members of whom it is composed are placed one above another in a particular and unvarying manner. Thus one man is born to the command of a regiment, another to that of a company. When once they have reached the utmost object of their hopes, they stop of their own accord and remain contented with their lot.

There is, besides, a strong cause that in aristocracies weakens the officer's desire of promotion. Among aristocratic nations an officer, independently of his rank in the army, also occupies an elevated rank in society; the former is almost always, in his eyes, only an appendage to the latter. A nobleman who embraces the profession of arms follows it less from motives of ambition than from a sense of the duties imposed on him by his birth. He enters the army in order to find an honorable employment for the idle years of his youth and to be able to bring back to his home and his peers some honorable recollections of military life; but his principal object is not to obtain by that profession either property, distinction, or power, for he possesses these advantages in his own right and enjoys them without leaving his home.

In democratic armies all the soldiers may become officers, which makes the desire of promotion general and immeasurably extends the bounds of military ambition. The officer, on his part, sees nothing that naturally and necessarily stops him at one grade more than at another; and each grade has immense importance in his eyes because his rank in society almost always depends on his rank in the army.

在贵族国家里,特别是在那些全凭出身来定等级的国家里,不平等既存在于军队里也存在于国家里;军官是贵族,而士兵则是奴隶;前者应征是为了发号施令,而后者应征则是为了服从命令。因此,在贵族制国家的军队里,士兵的雄心壮志被限制在很狭窄的范围内。军官的野心也并不是没有止尽的。贵族不但构成了全国等级范围内的一个等级,而且在它的内部还包括自己的一系列的等级;等级上的成员一个比一个高,而且是在一种特别的和不变的方式下。有的人生来就是要去指挥一个团,而另一个人则是要去指挥一个连。一旦当他们达到他们自己所希望的这个极限之后便自动停止,而满足于自己的现状。

另外,还有一个使贵族国家减弱军官晋升的欲望的重大原因。在贵族国家里,军官除了拥有军队的军衔以外,还在社会上占据较高的阶层;在他们眼里,前者不过是后者的附属品。贵族之所以想在军队中占有一席之地,主要的还不是因为其野心,而是出于家庭出身加于他们的一种义务。他们之所以从军,是为了光荣地打发掉他们青年时代的闲散年华,并能把军旅生活的一些光荣回忆带回家庭和自己的同伴中间;但他们的主要目的并不是打算由此发财、成名或掌权,因为他们自己已经有了这些优势,不出家门就可以享有这一切。

在民主国家的军队里,所有的士兵都可能晋升为军官,这就使晋升的念头变得既普遍又无可限制,并把军事野心的限度扩大到几乎没有止境。在军官方面,他们认为任何东西都不能自然地而又必须地使他们停于某一阶层而不上进;在他们眼里,每一个军衔都有巨大的重要性,因为他们在社会上的等级差不多总是依赖于他们在军队中的军衔。在民主国家里,军官除了薪金以外没

Among democratic nations it often happens that an officer has no property but his pay and no distinction but that of military honors; consequently, as often as his duties change, his fortune changes and he becomes, as it were, a new man. What was only an appendage to his position in aristocratic armies has thus become the main point, the basis of his whole condition.

Under the old French monarchy officers were always called by their titles of nobility; they are now always called by the title of their military rank. This little change in the forms of language suffices to show that a great revolution has taken place in the constitution of society and in that of the army.

In democratic armies the desire of advancement is almost universal: it is ardent, tenacious, perpetual; it is strengthened by all other desires and extinguished only with life itself. But it is easy to see that of all armies in the world, those in which advancement must be slowest in time of peace are the armies of democratic countries. As the number of commissions is naturally limited while the number of competitors is almost unlimited, and as the strict law of equality is over all alike, none can make rapid progress; many can make no progress at all. Thus the desire of advancement is greater and the opportunities of advancement fewer there than elsewhere. All the ambitious spirits of a democratic army are consequently ardently desirous of war, because war makes vacancies and warrants the violation of that law of seniority which is the sole privilege natural to democracy.

We thus arrive at this singular consequence, that, of all armies, those most ardently desirous of war are democratic armies, and of all nations, those most fond of peace are democratic nations; and what makes these facts still more extraordinary is that these contrary effects are produced at the same time by the principle of equality.

All the members of the community, being alike, constantly harbor the wish and discover the possibility of changing their condition and improving their welfare; this makes them fond of peace, which is

有其他收入,除了军队的荣誉以外也没有任何其他的荣誉;因此,他们经常改变职务,所以他们的命运也随之改变,好像变成了另外一个人。在贵族国家的军队里,只作为军官地位的附属品的那些东西,却变成了民主国家军队的主要东西,变成了决定军官的一切的最基本的东西。

在法国的旧君主时代,人们在称呼军官时只用他们的贵族爵位名衔;而在现代,人们在称呼军官时只用他们的军衔。这种在语言的表达形式上的小小变化,就足以说明在社会制度和军事制度当中发生了巨大的革命。

在民主国家的军队里,晋升的欲望几乎是普遍的:而且是热烈的、顽强的和永久的;它随着其他一切欲望的增加而增加,一直到人死为止。但是,也不难发现,在全世界的所有军队中,在和平时期晋升最慢的,是民主国家的军队。因为军衔的职位是很有限的,而竞争者几乎是不计其数的,但是,平等的严格的原则对每个人几乎都是相同的,所以没有人可以迅速晋升;而且有许多人根本无法晋升。因此,晋升的欲望比其他国家都要高,而晋升的机遇却比其他国家都要少。结果,民主国家军队中的那些极富野心的人,都渴望发生战争,因为战争可以使军位空缺,最后还可以违反作为民主制度所特有的按资历晋升的规定。

我们由此可以得出下面这个特殊的结论,在所有国家的军队中,最热烈地希望发生战争的军队是民主国家的军队,而在所有国家的人民中,最爱和平的则是民主国家的人民;使这种现象如此特别的原因,是平等同时产生了这两个对立的效果。

当所有公民都几乎相同的时候,便不断地觉得自己有希望并发现有可能改变自己的处境和提高自己的生活质量;这种情况使

favorable to industry and allows every man to pursue his own little undertakings to their completion. On the other hand, this same equality makes soldiers dream of fields of battle, by increasing the value of military honors in the eyes of those who follow the profession of arms and by rendering those honors accessible to all. In either case the restlessness of the heart is the same, the taste for enjoyment is insatiable, the ambition of success as great; the means of gratifying it alone are different.

These opposite tendencies of the nation and the army expose democratic communities to great dangers. When a military spirit forsakes a people, the profession of arms immediately ceases to be held in honor and military men fall to the lowest rank of the public servants; they are little esteemed and no longer understood. The reverse of what takes place in aristocratic ages then occurs; the men who enter the army are no longer those of the highest, but of the lowest class. Military ambition is indulged only when no other is possible. Hence arises a circle of cause and consequence from which it is difficult to escape: the best part of the nation shuns the military profession because that profession is not honored, and the profession is not honored because the best part of the nation has ceased to follow it.

It is then no matter of surprise that democratic armies are often restless, ill-tempered, and dissatisfied with their lot, although their physical condition is commonly far better and their discipline less strict than in other countries. The soldier feels that he occupies an inferior position, and his wounded pride either stimulates his taste for hostilities that would render his services necessary or gives him a desire for revolution, during which he may hope to win by force of arms the political influence and personal importance now denied him.

The composition of democratic armies makes this last-mentioned danger much to be feared. In democratic communities almost every man has some property to preserve; but democratic armies are generally led by men without property, most of whom have little to lose in civil broils. The bulk of the nation is naturally much more afraid of

他们热爱和平,因为和平可以繁荣工商业,允许每个人可以去追求其小小事业的目的。另一方面,这样的平等使士兵在做梦的时候都驰骋于战场,让他们更加重视军事荣誉的价值,并让所有的士兵都能容易得到这种荣誉。在这两种情况下,人们永不停止的心是相同的,对享受的喜爱是永不知足的,对成功的野心是巨大的;而满足野心的手段则有所不同。

人民和军队的这种相反的趋势,驱使民主社会走上非常危险的道路。当人民丧失军事精神时,在军队中谋求军衔便立即不再是光荣的了,而军人也将沦为等级最低的公务人员;他们不再受人尊敬,也不再被人们理解。这时,与贵族时代完全背道而行的情况发生了;从军的公民不再是那些社会等级最高的公民,而是一些社会等级最低的公民。只有当一个人在别无选择的时候才会想到从军。这就形成一个难以摆脱的恶性循环:民族的精英们躲避出任军职,因为这个职业并不光荣,而军职之所以不光荣,则是因为民族的精英不再从军。

因此,我们也不必惊讶于尽管民主国家军队的物质条件比其他国家的军队都要好很多,并且纪律也不如其他军队那样严格,但其往往情绪低落、脾气暴躁、对自己的处境很不满意。士兵们感到自己的地位很低下,他们已经受伤的自尊心,使他们越来越渴望这种离开他们就无法进行的战争,或希望在战争中能依靠自己手中的武器获得人们原来拒绝给予他们的政治权力和个人尊严。

民主国家军队的构成,使我们最后提到的这种危险变得更加可怕。在民主社会,几乎所有的公民都有需要保护的财产;但是,民主国家的军队通常都是由无产者领导的,而他们其中的大部分在国家内乱期间不会遭到重大损失。民主时代的人民自然要比

revolutions than in the ages of aristocracy, but the leaders of the army much less so.

Moreover, as among democratic nations (to repeat what I have just remarked) the wealthiest, best-educated, and ablest men seldom adopt the military profession, the army, taken collectively, eventually forms a small nation by itself, where the mind is less enlarged and habits are more rude than in the nation at large. Now, this small uncivilized nation has arms in its possession and alone knows how to use them; for, indeed, the pacific temper of the community increases the danger to which a democratic people is exposed from the military and turbulent spirit of the army. Nothing is so dangerous as an army in the midst of an unwarlike nation; the excessive love of the whole community for quiet continually puts the constitution at the mercy of the soldiery.

It may therefore be asserted, generally speaking, that if democratic nations are naturally prone to peace from their interests and their propensities, they are constantly drawn to war and revolutions by their armies. Military revolutions, which are scarcely ever to be apprehended in aristocracies, are always to be dreaded among democratic nations. These perils must be reckoned among the most formidable that beset their future fate, and the attention of statesmen should be sedulously applied to find a remedy for the evil.

When a nation perceives that it is inwardly affected by the restless ambition of its army, the first thought which occurs is to give this inconvenient ambition an object by going to war. I do not wish to speak ill of war: war almost always enlarges the mind of a people and raises their character. In some cases it is the only check to the excessive growth of certain propensities that naturally spring out of the equality of conditions, and it must be considered as a necessary corrective to certain inveterate diseases to which democratic communities are liable.

War has great advantages, but we must not flatter ourselves that it can diminish the danger I have just pointed out. That peril is only suspended by it, to return more fiercely when the war is over; for

贵族时代的人民更害怕革命,但军队的首脑们却不这样认为。

另外,正如我方才所说的,在民主国家,最有钱、最有教养和最有才干的公民,几乎都不会去出任军职,所以整个军队最后会变成一个独立的小国家,在这里,士兵的思想境界要比整个国家的低,而他们的习惯也要比整个国家的粗野。但是,这个不文明的小独立国家却掌握着军权,而且只有它知道如何使用军权;实际上,正是公民的这种和平的情绪,加剧了军队的喜欢暴动的精神给民主国家带来的危险。在一个不好战的国家里,再没有比军队更危险的东西了;而全体公民对安宁的过分喜爱,则使他们把整个社会都交给士兵去支配。

因此,在一般情况下可以这样说:如果民主国家出于自己的利益和本性而自然地爱好和平,那它终将被它的军队逐步地拖向战争和革命。贵族国家从来不会担心的军事革命,但民主国家却总对此心存畏惧。这种危险将在妨碍民主国家前进的一切可怕的危险中变得最为突出,这就使政治家必须不断地把自己的注意力放在寻找消除这种危险的办法上去。

当一个国家发现,因其军队的无休止的野心而使它的内部受到影响时,它首先想到的就是如何为这个令人讨厌的野心提供发动战争的理由。我不想说战争的坏话:战争几乎总是可以提高一个民族的思想境界,并开阔它的心胸。在某些情况下,只有战争才能遏止平等自然造成的某些倾向的过分发展,这时我们就必须认为战争是医治民主社会易于感染的某些疾病的必备良药。

战争确实有很大的好处,但我们决不能过分夸赞它,认为它可以消除我刚才指出的那些危险。战争只能暂时阻止这种危险,而在战争结束后,这种危险又会变得更加猛烈;因为军队在尝到

armies are much more impatient of peace after having tasted military exploits. War could be a remedy only for a people who were always a-thirst for military glory. ,

I foresee that all the military rulers who may rise up in great democratic nations will find it easier to conquer with their armies than to make their armies live at peace after conquest. There are two things that a democratic people will always find very difficult, to begin a war and to end it.

Again, if war has some peculiar advantages for democratic na-tions, on the other hand it exposes them to certain dangers which aris-tocracies have no cause to dread to an equal extent. I shall point out only two of these.

Although war gratifies the army, it embarrasses and often exas-perates that countless multitude of men whose minor passions every day require peace in order to be satisfied. Thus there is some risk of its causing, under another form, the very disturbance it is intended to prevent.

No protracted war can fail to endanger the freedom of a demo-cratic country. Not indeed that after every victory it is to be apprehen-ded that the victorious generals will possess themselves by force of the supreme power, after the manner of Sulla and Caesar; the danger is of another kind. War does not always give over democratic communi-ties to military government, but it must invariably and immeasurably increase the powers of civil government; it must almost compulsorily concentrate the direction of all men and the management of all things in the hands of the administration. If it does not lead to despotism by sudden violence, it prepares men for it more gently by their habits. All those who seek to destroy the liberties of a democratic nation ought to know that war is the surest and the shortest means to accomplish it. This is the first axiom of the science.

One remedy, which appears to be obvious when the ambition of soldiers and officers becomes the subject of alarm, is to augment the number of commissions to be distributed by increasing the army. This affords temporary relief, but it plunges the country into deeper difficulties at some future period. To increase the army may produce a lasting effect in an aristocratic community, because military ambi-tion is there confined to one class of men, and the ambition of each

了战争的甜头之后,便更加无法忍受和平了。战争仅仅是那些一直渴望军事荣誉的民族的补救困难的办法。

我可以预言,所有的在民主国家涌现出来的军事首领,会发现让他们率军去征战比在胜利后和平地生活下去更容易。有两件事使民主国家的人民觉得很难办:一是战争的开始,二是战争的结束。

另外,如果战争为民主国家带来了一些特殊的好处,那它就会使民主国家遭到往日的贵族国家同样不曾畏惧的某些危险。现在,我只谈一谈其中的两种危险。

战争虽然满足了军队的要求,但却阻碍了和常常激怒着每天都在嚷嚷要使自己的和平时期的需求得到满足的不可胜数的公民群众。因此,战争就有从另一方面导致它本来应当防止的动乱的危险。

没有一场长期的战争不会给民主国家的自由带来巨大的危害。这并不是说害怕在每次胜利之后看到获胜的将军们,会像罗马的苏拉和恺撒那样用武力夺取最高政权;危险是另一种。战争虽然并不总是给民主国家带来军事统治,但它总是无限制地增强民主国家的官员的权力;它差不多必定要把管理万民和处理万事的大权集中到这个政府手中。如果它不是以武力突然建立专制,而是让人们通过习惯慢慢地走向专制。那些企图消灭民主国家自由的人,应该知道达到这个目的的最可靠和最简便的办法就是战争。这是他们的第一条科学定理。

当士兵和官员的野心会明显地引起人们的恐慌时,一个看来可以进行补救的措施,就是增加军队的人数,从而扩大军官的编制。这只能暂时缓解危急,但却使国家的未来陷入了更深的危险中。在贵族社会,增加军队人数可以产生持久的影响,因为在这样的社会里,军事野心只被一个阶级的人们所特有,而且其中每

individual stops, as it were, at a certain limit, so that it may be possible to satisfy all who feel its influence. But nothing is gained by increasing the army among a democratic people, because the number of aspirants always rises in exactly the same ratio as the army itself. Those whose claims have been satisfied by the creation of new commissions are instantly succeeded by a fresh multitude beyond all power of satisfaction; and even those who were but now satisfied soon begin to crave more advancement, for the same excitement prevails in the ranks of the army as in the civil classes of democratic society, and what men want is, not to reach a certain grade, but to have constant promotion. Though these wants may not be very vast, they are perpetually recurring. Thus a democratic nation, by augmenting its army, allays only for a time the ambition of the military profession, which soon becomes even more formidable because the number of those who feel it is increased.

I am of the opinion that a restless and turbulent spirit is an evil inherent in the very constitution of democratic armies and beyond hope of cure. The legislators of democracies must not expect to devise any military organization capable by its influence of calming and restraining the military profession; their efforts would exhaust their powers before the object could be attained.

The remedy for the vices of the army is not to be found in the army itself, but in the country. Democratic nations are naturally afraid of disturbance and of despotism; the object is to turn these natural instincts into intelligent, deliberate, and lasting tastes. When men have at last learned to make a peaceful and profitable use of freedom and have felt its blessings, when they have conceived a manly love of order and have freely submitted themselves to discipline, these same men, if they follow the profession of arms, bring into it, unconsciously and almost against their will, these same habits and manners. The general spirit of the nation, being infused into the spirit peculiar to the army, tempers the opinions and desires engendered by military life, or represses them by the mighty force of public opinion. Teach the citizens to be educated, orderly, firm, and free and the soldiers will be disciplined and obedient.

Any law that, in repressing the turbulent spirit of the army, should tend to diminish the spirit of freedom in the nation and to overshadow

个人的这种野心可以停止在规定的范围之内,因此这就有可能满足所有怀有野心的人。但是,在民主国家,增加军队人数就没有任何好处,因为军队人数越多,野心家也就越多。在那些要求有空位时就职的人上任以后,又会很快出现一批欲望没有得到满足的人;而已经上任的那批人也很快又会提出更高的要求,因为盛行于民主国家公民行动的那种激动情绪也会传到军队中来,人们想得到的不是一定的军衔,而是不断的晋升。他们的需求虽然不是很大,但却持续地重复而来。因此,民主国家只能通过增加军队人数而暂时使军人的野心得到满足,但不久以后,他们的野心将会变得更为可怕,因为想晋升的人会越来越多。

至于我,则认为这种不安和躁动的情绪,是民主国家军队结构的固有缺陷,而且是不愿意根除的缺陷。民主国家的立法者们不要希望能够创造出任何军事机构,并通过这种军事机构来镇定和限制军人的激情;他们的努力只会耗尽自己的力量而最终一无所获。

能够治愈军队弊端的不是军队本身,而是国家。民主国家自然担心动乱和专制;只要使军队的那些自然本性变成有才智的、深思熟虑的和持久的爱好,问题就可以解决了。当人们最终学会如何和平地和有力地运用自由,并感觉到自由的好处时,当他们对秩序富有一种强烈的喜爱并自愿地服从纪律时,他们从军时就会不知不觉地和几乎是违背自己意愿地把这些习惯和习性带进军队。全民族的普遍精神渗入到军队所特有的精神中,就会调节军队生活所造成的观点和欲望,或者依靠公共舆论的强大力量来压制这些观点和欲望。教导公民要有知识、遵守纪律、意志坚定和爱好自由,士兵们才会纪律严明和服从命令。

任何法律,在镇压军队的暴动精神时,还会消弱国家的自由

the notion of law and right would defeat its object; it would do much more to favor than to defeat the establishment of military tyranny.

After all, and in spite of all precautions, a large army in the midst of a democratic people will always be a source of great danger. The most effectual means of diminishing that danger would be to reduce the army, but this is a remedy that all nations are not able to apply.

精神,并使国家的法律和权利观念黯然失色,那它就必然适得其
反;它不但没有消灭军人暴政,反而大大促进了军人暴政的建立。

　　不管预防措施是多么完备,一支庞大的军队在民主国家里毕
竟总是一大危险。而消除这个危险的最有效的办法就是裁军,但
这又是所有的国家都不能采用的一项解救办法。

CHAPTER XXIII
Which Is The Most Warlike
And Most Revolutionary
Class In Democratic Armies

It is of the essence of a democratic army to be very numerous in proportion to the people to which it belongs, as I shall hereafter show. On the other hand, men living in democratic times seldom choose a military life. Democratic nations are therefore soon led to give up the system of voluntary recruiting for that of compulsory enlistment. The necessity of their social condition compeis them to resort to the latter means, and it may easily be foreseen that they will all eventually a-dopt it.

When military service is compulsory, the burden is indiscriminately and equally borne by the whole community. This is another necessary consequence of the social condition of these nations and of their notions. The government may do almost whatever it pleases, provided it appeals to the whole community at once; it is the unequal distribution of the weight, not the weight itself, that commonly occasions resistance. But as military service is common to all the citizens, the evident consequence is that each of them remains for only a few years on active duty. Thus it is in the nature of things that the soldier in democracies only passes through the army, while among most aristocratic nations the military profession is one which the soldier adopts, or which is imposed upon him, for life.

This has important consequences. Among the soldiers of a democratic army some acquire a taste for military life; but the majority, being enlisted against their will and ever ready to go back to their

第二十三章　民主国家的军队里哪个是最好战和最革命的阶级

民主国家军队的本质是十分庞大的,这是按照提供兵员的人数与兵员人数的比例来说,我在后面将对这一点稍加解释。另一方面,生活在民主时代的人们,很少选择军队的生活。因此,民主国家不久就不得不放弃自愿入伍的募兵制,而采用强制入伍的征兵制。本国社会条件的必要性,要求它们采用后一种制度,而且可以不难预知,人人最终都将被征入伍。

当军队义务成为强迫性的,那么全体公民就会不加选择地和平等地承担这种义务。这也是这些国家的社会条件及其观念的必然结果。这些国家的政府,只要对全体人民提出呼吁,就几乎可以做任何它想做的事情;一般引起反抗的是负担的轻重不平等,而不是负担本身。但是,由于军队的义务已经分配到全体公民身上,因此很明显的是每个人只在军队里服役为数很少的几年。因此,民主国家的士兵仅仅是军队的过客,便成了一件很自然的事,但是,在大部分贵族国家里,军职可能是士兵所选定或被迫接受的终生职业。

这种情况会有一些很重要的后果。在民主国家军队的士兵中,有些人很希望过军人生活;但大多数人都是在违背自己意愿

— 1553 —

homes, do not consider themselves as seriously engaged in the military profession and are always thinking of quitting it. Such men do not contract the wants and only half partake in the passions which that mode of life engenders. They adapt themselves to their military duties, but their minds are still attached to the interests and the duties that engaged them in civil life. They do not therefore imbibe the spirit of the army, or rather they infuse the spirit of the community at large into the army and retain it there. Among democratic nations the private soldiers remain most like civilians; upon them the habits of the nation have the firmest hold and public opinion has most influence. It is through the private soldiers especially that it may be possible to infuse into a democratic army the love of freedom and the respect for rights, if these principles have once been successfully inculcated in the people at large. The reverse happens among aristocratic nations, where the soldiery have eventually nothing in common with their fellow citizens and where they live among them as strangers and often as enemies.

In aristocratic armies the officers are the conservative element, because the officers alone have retained a strict connection with civil society and never forgo their purpose of resuming their place in it sooner or later. In democratic armies the private soldiers stand in this position, and from the same cause.

It often happens, on the contrary, that in these same democratic armies the officers contract tastes and wants wholly distinct from those of the nation, a fact which may be thus accounted for: Among democratic nations the man who becomes an officer severs all the ties that bound him to civil life; he leaves it forever, and no interest urges him to return to it. His true country is the army, since he owes all he has to the rank he has attained in it; he therefore follows the fortunes of the army, rises or sinks with it, and henceforward directs all his hopes to that quarter only. As the wants of an officer are distinct from those of the country, he may, perhaps, ardently desire war, or labor to bring about a revolution, at the very moment when the nation is most desirous of stability and peace.

There are, nevertheless, some causes that allay this restless and warlike spirit. Though ambition is universal and continual among

的情况下而从军的,他们时刻准备返回家园,从来没认为自己会很严肃认真地从事军职,一心想着要离开军队。这些人没有什么高求,也没有染上半点这种职业所产生的激情。他们当兵只是为了履行义务,而他们心里仍旧眷恋着公民生活里的利益和职责。因此,他们不仅没有吸收军人的军队精神,反而把社会上的公民精神灌输到军队里,并在军队里保持这种精神。在民主国家的军队里,一些列兵仍然保留着很多公民的本性;全国的习惯对他们有最稳固的控制,公共舆论对他们有最大的影响。正是这些士兵把曾使人民本身受到鼓舞的爱自由和尊重权力的思想带进了民主国家的军队。贵族制国家的情形正好与此相反,在那里,士兵最终和自己的同胞没有任何共同之处,并和自己的同胞之间形同陌路,而且往往是形同敌人。

在贵族国家的军队里,军官是保守派分子,因为只有军官同市民社会保留着紧密的联系,而且从不放弃迟早会恢复他们原来地位的决心。在民主国家的军队里,只有士兵占据着这种地位,而且促使士兵如此的原因也完全相同。

相反地,在同样的民主国家军队的内部,军官们往往养成与全国人民完全不同的爱好和需求,用一个事实可以说明这种现象:在民主国家里,一个人当了军官,便切断了与市民生活的所有联系;他相当于永远离开了市民生活,而且一点回头的兴趣都没有。他的真正国家就是军队,因为他的一切都决定于他所占的军衔;因此,他必须要跟着军队的命运,同甘苦共患难,把自己以后的希望完全寄托于军队。由于军官的需要与国家的需要不同,或许他可能在全国最希望安定和和平的时候热烈地希望战争或进行革命活动。

然而,还有一些因素可以减轻军官的这种无休止的和好战的

democratic nations, we have seen that it is seldom great. A man who, being born in the lower classes of the community, has risen from the ranks to be an officer has already taken a prodigious step. He has gained a footing in a sphere above that which he filled in civil life and has acquired rights which most democratic nations will always consider as inalienable. ① He is willing to pause after so great an effort and to enjoy what he has won. The fear of risking what he has already obtained damps the desire of acquiring what he has not got. Having conquered the first and greatest impediment that opposed his advancement, he resigns himself with less impatience to the slowness of his progress. His ambition will be more and more cooled in proportion as the increasing distinction of his rank teaches him that he has more to put in jeopardy. If I am not, mistaken, the least warlike and also the least revolutionary part of a democratic army will always be its chief commanders.

But the remarks I have just made on officers and soldiers are not applicable to a numerous class which, in all armies, fills the intermediate space between them; I mean the class of non-commissioned officers. This class of non-commissioned officers, which had never acted a part in history until the present century, is henceforward destined, I think, to play one of some importance. Like the officers, non-commissioned officers have broken, in their minds, all the ties which bound them to civil life; like the former, they devote themselves permanently to the service and perhaps make it even more exclusively the object of all their desires; but non-commissioned officers are men who have not yet reached a firm and lofty post at which they may pause and breathe more freely before they can attain further promotion.

---

① The position of officers is indeed much more secure among democratic nations than elsewhere; the lower the personal standing of the man, the greater is the comparative importance of his military grade and the more just and necessary is it that the enjoyment of that rank should be secured by the laws.

情绪。如果民主国家军队里的这种野心是普遍的和持久的,我们很少能看到这种野心强大的时候。出身于社会的下等阶级的人,经过在军队内部的几次晋升,终于升到军官的地位。他已经拥有了比他在市民社会的地位高得多的地位,并且得到了被大部分民主国家经常认为是不能剥夺的权利。[①] 他在经过了巨大的努力后,愿意暂停一下,并开始享受自己已经获得的一切。由于害怕失去已经获得的东西,所以便抵制了渴望获得尚未获得的东西的心情。在克服了阻止他晋升的第一个和最大的障碍之后,他便对以后的晋升之慢不那么着急了。随着军衔级别的逐步升高,他的野心就会越来越少,并让他发现自己的危险也越来越大。如果我没有说错的话,民主国家军队中最不好战和最没有革命精神的阶层,将永远是首要的指挥官。

但是,我刚才所讲的军官和士兵的一切,并不适用于在所有军队中介乎军官和士兵之间的那些人;我在这里所指的是军士阶级。在本世纪之前还未曾在历史上扮演过角色的军士阶级,我想它今后会在历史上发生重要的作用。同军官一样,军士阶级已从思想上切断了他们同市民生活的所有关系;也同军官一样,军士阶级把自己的一生都奉献给军队,或许还把这视为在自己所有欲望之上的一个特有的目标;但是,军士阶级不能到达一个稳固的和更高一层的地位,以使他们在向更高职位晋升时都无法停下来休息一下,并深深地缓一口气。

[①] 实际上,民主国家的官员的地位比其他所有国家的都更加安全;一个人的个人身份越低,其军事级别的相对重要性就越大,其阶级快乐就更正当和更有必要受到法律的保护。

By the very nature of his duties, which are invariable, a non-commissioned officer is doomed to lead an obscure, confined, comfortless, and precarious existence. As yet he sees nothing of military life but its dangers; he knows nothing but its privations and its discipline, more difficult to support than dangers; he suffers the more from his present miseries, from knowing that the constitution of society and of the army allow him to rise above them; he may, indeed, at any time obtain his commission and enter at once upon command, honors, independence, rights, and enjoyments. Not only does this object of his hopes appear to him of immense importance, but he is never sure of reaching it till it is actually his own. The grade he fills is by no means irrevocable; he is always entirely abandoned to the arbitrary pleasure of his commanding officer, for this is imperiously required by the necessity of discipline: a slight fault, a whim, may always deprive him in an instant of the fruits of many years of toil and endeavor; until he has reached the grade to which he aspires; he has accomplished nothing; not till he reaches that grade does his career seem to begin. A desperate ambition cannot fail to be kindled in a man thus incessantly goaded on by his youth; his wants, his passions, the spirit of his age, his hopes, and his fears.

Non-commissioned officers are therefore bent on war, on war always and at any cost; but if war be denied them, then they desire revolutions, to suspend the authority of established regulations and to enable them, aided by the general confusion and the political passions of the time, to get rid of their superior officers and to take their places. Nor is it impossible for them to bring about such a crisis, because their common origin and habits give them much influence over the soldiers, however different may be their passions and their desires.

It would be an error to suppose that these various characteristics of officers, non-commissioned officers, and men belong to any articular time or country; they will always occur at all times and among all

　　由于军士阶级具有不变的性质,所以他们的存在注定是黯淡的、受限制的、不舒适的和永不稳定的。他们只看到军事生活中的危险,而没有看到任何光明;他们只知道艰苦和服从,而这比危险更难以忍受;他们更多的是去忍受眼前的痛苦,因为他们知道社会制度和军事制度总有一天能让他们从这些痛苦中解脱;实际上,在某一时刻,他们也能当上军官,这时,他们便可以发号施令了,并且得到了荣誉、独立地位、权利和享受。在他们看来,不仅他们所希望得到的东西是非常重要的,而且只有在实际拿到手后,他们才敢确信这些东西的存在。他们的军衔是决不能被擅自取消的;他们总是要完全受制于其长官的任意摆布,军队的纪律要求他们必须要这样做:一个小小的错误,或一时的稍不清醒都经常能使他们立即失去费了多年的辛苦和努力才得到的果实;在他们到达了自己所向往的军衔以前,他们什么成就都没有;只是取得了军官的军阶以后,他们好像才开始了自己的职业生涯。像他们这样不断受到自己的充沛精力、需要、激情、时代精神、希望和恐惧心情推进的人,不可能不燃起不顾一切去拼命的野心。

　　因此,军士都专注于战争,并且总是迫不及待地希望战争;如果人们反对战争,他们就希望发生革命,以延缓已经确立的规章制度的权威性,使他们在革命中利用局势混乱和群众的政治激情把高级长官撵下台,并取代这些长官的位置。他们并不是没有可能引来这样的危机,因为尽管他们的激情和欲望与士兵有很大不同,但他们的家庭出身和习惯却与士兵一样,并对士兵产生了极大的影响。

　　如果以为军官、军士和士兵的这些多种多样的性格只属于某一特定的时代或国家,那就错了;这种现象发生于一切时代和一

democratic nations. In every democratic army the noncommissioned officers will be the worst representatives of the pacific and orderly spirit of the country, and the private soldiers will be the best. The latter will carry with them into military life the strength or weakness of the manners of the nation; they will display a faithful reflection of the community. If that community is ignorant and weak, they will allow themselves to be drawn by their leaders into disturbances, either unconsciously or against their will; if it is enlightened and energetic, the community will itself keep them within the bounds of order.

切民主国家。在所有民主国家的军队里,军士永远是国家和平的
和有秩序的精神的最坏代表,而士兵则是这方面的最好代表。士
兵会把国家民情方面的优点或缺点带进军队;并在军队里忠实地
反映民族的面貌。如果一个士兵是无知的和软弱的,那他将在不
知不觉中违反本意,并被他的长官拉去搞叛乱;如果他是有知识
的和精力充沛的,那他将会约束他的长官遵守秩序。

CHAPTER XXIV

Causes Which Render Democratic Armies Weaker Than Other Armies At The Outset Of A Campaign, And More Formidable In Protracted Warfare

Any army is in danger of being conquered at the outset of a campaign, after a long peace; any army that has long been engaged in warfare has strong chances of victory: this truth is peculiarly applicable to democratic armies. In aristocracies the military profession, being a privileged career, is held in honor even in time of peace. Men of great talents, great attainments, and great ambition embrace it; the army is in all respects on a level with the nation, and frequently above it.

We have seen, on the contrary, that among a democratic people the choicer minds of the nation are gradually drawn away from the military profession, to seek by other paths distinction, power, and especially wealth. After a long peace, and in democratic times the periods of peace are long, the army is always inferior to the country itself. In this state it is called into active service, and until war has altered it, there is danger for the country as well as for the army.

I have shown that in democratic armies and in time of peace the rule of seniority is the supreme and inflexible law of promotion. This is a consequence, as I have before observed, not only of the constitution of these armies, but of the constitution of the people, and it will always occur. Again, as among these nations the officer derives his position in the country solely from his position in the army, and as he draws all the distinction and the competency he enjoys from the same source, he does not retire from his profession, or is not superannuated,

第二十四章 使民主国家军队在战争初期比其他国家军队软弱，而在战争持续时则比其他国家军队强大的原因

任何在长期和平之后开始参战的军队，都有被击败的危险；而长期作战的军队则有很大的获胜机会：这一真理特别适用于民主国家的军队。在贵族国家，军职是享有特权的职业，即使在和平时期它也拥有很高的荣誉。有才能、有成就和有雄心壮志的人都想从事军职；军队待遇在各方面都不低于国家的平均水平，甚至常常高于这一水平。

相反地，我们可以看到，在民主国家里，民族的精英都逐渐离开军职，以通过其他途径去谋求荣誉和权力，特别是财富。在长期的和平以后，再加上民主时代的和平时期会很长，军队的水平便总是次于全国的平均水平。在这种状态中的参战的军队，对于国家和军队都有危险，直到战争改变了这种状态，否则危险始终存在。

我曾经说过，在民主国家的军队里和在和平时期，资历是晋升的最高的和最不可改动的准则。正如我前面所指出的，这种结果不只是因为这种军队的制度，而且也因为这种国家的制度本身。因此，这种现象将会长期发生。另外，在这些国家里，由于军官在国家的一切地位都取决于他们在军队的地位，以及由于他们享有的所有声望和资历也全都来自这个地位，所以他们只有到死

till very near the close of life. The consequence of these two causes is that when a democratic people goes to war after a long interval of peace, all the leading officers of the army are old men. I speak not only of the generals, but of the non-commissioned officers, who have most of them been stationary or have advanced only step by step. It may be remarked with surprise that in a democratic army after a long peace all the soldiers are mere boys, and all the superior officers in declining years, so that the former are wanting in experience, the latter in vigor. This is a leading cause of defeat, for the first condition of successful generalship is youth. I should not have ventured to say so if the greatest captain of modern times had not made the observation.

These two causes do not act in the same manner upon aristocratic armies: as men are promoted in them by right of birth much more than by right of seniority, there are in all ranks a certain number of young men who bring to their profession all the early vigor of body and mind. Again, as the men who seek for military honors among an aristocratic people enjoy a settled position in civil society, they seldom continue in the army until old age overtakes them. After having devoted the most vigorous years of youth to the career of arms, they voluntarily retire, and spend the remainder of their maturer years at home.

A long peace not only fills democratic armies with elderly officers, but also gives to all the officers habits of both body and mind which render them unfit for actual service. The man who has long lived amid the calm and lukewarm atmosphere of democratic conditions can at first ill adapt himself to the harder toils and sterner duties of warfare; and if he has not absolutely lost the taste for arms, at least he has assumed a mode of life that unfits him for conquest.

Among aristocratic nations the enjoyments of civil life exercise less influence on the manners of the army, because among those

才离开或退出军界。这两个原因所带来的后果是,当一个民主国家在经过长期的和平后开始作战时,它的全部领导官员都已年迈。我讲的不仅仅是将军,还包括一些原地不动或一步一步往上爬的大部分军士。我们也许会吃惊地看到,民主国家的部队在经过很长的和平时期后,所有的士兵都是小孩子,而所有的长官均已至垂暮之年,因此,前者缺乏经验,而后者缺乏精力。这是战败的主要原因,因为使战争胜利的首要条件,就是要有年轻的将才。如果不是近代的一位最伟大的统帅指出过这一点,我是不敢这样说的。

这两个因素就不会对贵族国家的军队以同样的方式产生作用:因为在那里,人们晋升的主要依据是家庭出身而不是资历,所以在每个军阶中都有一定数量的年轻人,他们把人的身体和思想的最充沛的精力全都带进了军职。另外,由于人们都在贵族国家里谋求军事荣誉,并在市民社会里享有固有的地位,所以很少有人在快到年老的时候才离开军队。他们把精力最充沛的时间献给军事生涯,之后便自愿退休,并返回家乡去安享人生的最后几年。

长期的和平不仅使民主国家的军队充满了年迈的军官,而且使所有的军官不论是在体力还是在思想方面养成了不适于作战的习惯。长期生活在民主国家里平静和冷淡的氛围中的人,在战争的开始可能很难让自己适应战争的艰难和严厉的职责;如果他还没有完全失去对军队的喜好,那么至少他要养成一种不适于他去征服的生活方式。

在贵族国家,享乐于市民生活的作风很少能对军队的习俗产生影响,因为在这种国家里,是由贵族来指挥军队,而一个贵族,

nations the aristocracy commands the army, and an aristocracy, however plunged in luxurious pleasures, has always many other passions besides that of its own well-being, and to satisfy those passions more thoroughly its well-being will be readily sacrificed. [1]

I have shown that in democratic armies in time of peace promotion is extremely slow. The officers at first support this state of things with impatience; they grow excited, restless, exasperated, but in the end most of them make up their minds to it. Those who have the largest share of ambition and of resources quit the army; others, adapting their tastes and their desires to their scanty fortunes, ultimately look upon the military profession in a civil point of view. The quality they value most in it is the competency and security that attend it; their whole notion of the future rests upon the certainty of this little provision, and all they require is peaceably to enjoy it. Thus not only does a long peace fill an army with old men, but it frequently imparts the views of old men to those who are still in the prime of life.

I have also shown that among democratic nations in time of peace the military profession is held in little honor and practiced with little spirit. This want of public favor is a heavy discouragement to the army; it weighs down the minds of the troops, and when war breaks out at last, they cannot immediately resume their spring and vigor. No similar cause of moral weakness exists in aristocratic armies: there the officers are never lowered, either in their own eyes or in those of their countrymen; because, independently of their military greatness, they are personally great. But even if the influence of peace operated on the two kinds of armies in the same manner, the results would still be different.

When the officers of an aristocratic army have lost their warlike spirit and the desire of raising themselves by service, they still retain a

---

[1] See Appendix X.

尽管已经在享受着奢侈的幸福,但他除了追求这种幸福以外,还总是会有其他一些追求,而且为了满足这些追求,他可以自愿地暂时牺牲他的幸福。①

我曾经讲过,当民主国家处于和平时期,其军队中军职的晋升是非常慢的。起初,军官们对这种情况表示很急躁;于是,他们激动,无法安宁并且满怀愤怒,但是最终,他们中的大多数人都将适应这种情况。那些有着强烈野心和智谋的人离开了军队;其余的人不得不使自己的爱好和欲望适应这种空虚的命运,最终以市民的眼光来看待军职。他们认为军职中最有价值的地方,就是它所带来的舒适和安全;他们把对未来的全部打算都寄托在这一小点保障上,他们所有的需求就是能安安静静地享受它。因此,长期的和平不仅使民主国家的军队充满了年老的军官,而且常常把老年人的见解灌输到还年轻力壮的军官中去。

我也曾指出,当民主国家处于和平时期,军职只具有很少的荣誉和很少的高尚情操。公众的这种缺乏热情的态度,对军队来说是一个沉重的挫伤;它压低了军队的士气,并且当战争最终爆发的时候,士兵无法立即恢复他的精神和活力。相同的挫败士气的这种原因,却不会出现于贵族国家的军队:在那里,无论是从军官自己的眼中还是从同胞们的眼中,都从来没有认为军官是低人一等的;因为除了他们军队的伟大以外,他们本人也是伟大的。但是即使和平以同样的方式对这两种军队产生影响,结果仍然是不同的。

当贵族国家军队的军官失去了他们的好战精神并不愿意依靠军职提升自己的时候,他们仍会保留对本阶级的尊重和首

---

① 见附录 X。

certain respect for the honor of their class and an old habit of being foremost to set an example. But when the officers of a democratic army have no longer the love of war and the ambition of arms, nothing whatever remains to them.

I am therefore of the opinion that when a democratic people engages in a war after a long peace, it incurs much more risk of defeat than any other nation; but it ought not easily to be cast down by its reverses, for the chances of success for such an army are increased by the duration of the war. When a war has at length, by its long continuance, roused the whole community from their peaceful occupations and ruined their minor undertakings, the same passions that made them attach so much importance to the maintenance of peace will be turned to arms. War, after it has destroyed all modes of speculation, becomes itself the great and sole speculation, to which all the ardent and ambitious desires that equality engenders are exclusively directed. Hence it is that the selfsame democratic nations that are so reluctant to engage in hostilities sometimes perform prodigious achievements when once they have taken the field.

As the war attracts more and more of public attention and is seen to create high reputations and great fortunes in a short space of time, the choicest spirits of the nation enter the military profession; all the enterprising, proud, and martial minds, no longer solely of the aristocracy, but of the whole country, are drawn in this direction. As the number of competitors for military honors is immense, and war drives every man to his proper level, great generals are always sure to spring up. A long war produces upon a democratic army the same effects that a revolution produces upon a people; it breaks through regulations and allows extraordinary men to rise above the common level. Those officers whose bodies and minds have grown old in peace are removed or superannuated, or they die. In their stead a host of young men is pressing on, whose frames are already hardened, whose desires are extended and inflamed by active service. They are bent on advancement at all hazards, and perpetual advancement; they are followed by

先要树立榜样的古老习惯。但是,如果民主国家军队的军官不再爱好战争和不再拥有军事野心时,他们就什么好的东西也保存不下来。

因此,我认为当民主国家的人民在经过长期和平之后参加战争时,被打败的危险要远远大于其他国家;但是,它不会轻易因为战败而放弃,因为战争持续得越久,这种军队胜利的机会就会越大。当战争最终拖延到导致全体公民都无法和平地从事自己的职业并破坏他们的小事业时,他们就会把极力想要维持和平的激情转向支持战争。战争,在破坏了所有的事业后,使它本身变成了一个伟大的而又唯一的事业,于是,平等所产生的一切热烈的和奋进的激情,便全部集中到战争方面来。这就是为什么甚至很难发动人民奔赴战场的相同的民主国家,一旦让人民拿起武器,有时会在战场上取得惊人成就的原因。

由于战争吸引了越来越多的公众的注意力,并在短时间内为军队创造出高尚的荣誉和巨大的财富,因此全国的精英便纷纷选择军旅生涯;这时,那些有事业心、自豪感和好战思想的人,已经不像在贵族制国家那样只来自贵族,而是来自全国了。由于竞争军事荣誉的人很多,而且战争又迫使每个人找到自己适当的位置,所以不断涌现出一些伟大的将领。长期的战争对民主国家军队产生的作用,同革命对民主国家人民产生的作用是一样的;它打破常规,使一些出类拔萃的人脱颖而出。那些在和平时期身心就已经老去的军官不是离开军队,就是退休或死去。一批在战争中壮大起来的青年人接替了他们的职位,他们的体格已经足够坚实,他们的意志也非常坚定。他们不惜一切代价力求晋升,并且也在不断地晋升;在他们身后,还跟随着与他们怀有同

others with the same passions and desires, and after these are others, yet unlimited by aught but the size of the army. The principle of e-quality opens the door of ambition to all, and death provides chances for ambition. Death is constantly thinning the ranks, making vacan-cies, closing and opening the career of arms.

Moreover, there is a secret connection between the military char-acter and the character of democracies, which war brings to light. The men of democracies naturally are passionately eager to acquire what they covet and to enjoy it on easy conditions. They for the most part worship chance and are much less afraid of death than of difficul-ty. This is the spirit that they bring to commerce and manufactures; and this same spirit, carried with them to the field of battle, induces them willingly to expose their lives in order to secure in a moment the rewards of victory. No kind of greatness is more pleasing to the imagi-nation of a democratic people than military greatness, a greatness of vivid and sudden luster, obtained without toil, by nothing but the risk of life.

Thus while the interest and the tastes of the members of a demo-cratic community divert them from war, their habits of mind fit them for carrying on war well: they soon make good soldiers when they are aroused from their business and their enjoyments.

If peace is peculiarly hurtful to democratic armies, war secures to them advantages that no other armies ever possess; and these ad-vantages, however little felt at first, cannot fail in the end to give them the victory. An aristocratic nation that in a contest with a demo-cratic people does not succeed in ruining the latter at the outset of the war always runs a great risk of being conquered by it.

样激情和同样欲望的年轻人,而在这批人之后,还有另一批人,只要军队没有限制,这样的人将会不断地出现。平等的原则打开了所有人的雄心的大门,而死亡又在为各种奋进之心提供机会。死亡不断使各个军级裁军,制造空缺,既为晋升开门,又为晋升关门。

甚至,在军人的习性和民主国家人民的习性之间,还存在着一种隐秘的联系,而这种联系只有在战争中才能显露出来。民主国家的人民,会自然地有一种渴望迅速得到自己所希望的东西的热情,然后再快活地享受。他们其中的大部分人崇拜机遇,害怕困难的程度远远大于害怕死亡。正是这种精神将他们带进了工商业;也同样是这种精神被他们带到了战场,促使他们自愿冒生命的危险,以确保在瞬间取得胜利。没有一种伟大能比军事伟大更能满足民主国家人民的幻想,这种伟大拥有着大胆的和瞬时的光彩,而且不必费力,只要冒生命的危险就可得到。

因此,当民主国家人民的利益和喜好使他们偏离战争时,他们的思想习惯却使他们能打个好仗:只要他们能够从他们的事业和享受的圈子里走出来,他们便很快就能成为好士兵。

如果和平对民主国家的军队特别有害,那么,战争却可以保证它得到其他任何军队所不曾拥有过的好处;尽管这些好处在起初并不是很明显,但最终可能会使军队获得胜利。一个贵族国家在同一个民主国家交战时,如果不在战争的开始就摧毁对方,那它将有被对方打败的危险。

CHAPTER XXV
Of Discipline In Democratic Armies

It is a very common opinion, especially in aristocratic countries, that the great social equality which prevails in democracies ultimately renders the private soldier independent of the officer and thus destroys the bond of discipline. This is a mistake, for there are two kinds of discipline, which it is important not to confuse.

When the officer is noble and the soldier a serf, one rich, the other poor, the one educated and strong, the other ignorant and weak, the strictest bond of obedience may easily be established between the two men. The soldier is broken in to military discipline, as it were, before he enters the army; or rather military discipline is nothing but an enhancement of social servitude. In aristocratic armies the soldier will soon become insensible to everything but the orders of his superior officers; he acts without reflection, triumphs without enthusiasm, and dies without complaint. In this state, he is no longer a man, but he is still a most formidable animal trained for war.

A democratic people must despair of ever obtaining from soldiers that blind, minute, submissive, and invariable obedience which an aristocratic people may impose on them without difficulty. The state of society does not prepare them for it, and the nation might be in danger of losing its natural advantages if it sought artificially to acquire advantages of this particular kind. Among democratic communities military discipline ought not to attempt to annihilate the free action of the faculties; all that can be done by discipline is to direct it. The obedience thus inculcated is less exact, but it is more eager and

第二十五章　关于民主国家军队的纪律

有一个很普遍的观点,特别是在贵族国家,认为盛行于民主国家的大部分社会平等,最终将使士兵不听军官的指挥,并由此破坏纪律的约束。这种观点是不正确的,因为实际上有两种纪律,我们一定不能将它们混淆。

当军官是贵族,而士兵是农奴时,当前者富裕,而后者贫困时,当前者有教养且能干,而后者无知软弱时,很容易在两者之间建立最严格的服从关系。可以说,士兵在入伍之前就已服从军队纪律了;或者不如说,军队纪律只不过是社会奴役的增进。在贵族国家的军队里,士兵很快就会变成除了长官的命令以外对什么事都毫无感觉的人;他从来都不加思考地行动,打了胜仗也不激动,被打死了也毫无怨言。在这种状态下,他已经不再是一个人,而是一个专为战争训练的最可怕的动物。

民主国家的人民一定会失望于它的士兵也染上贵族国家可以轻易加在士兵身上的那种盲目的、服帖的和千篇一律的服从。民主国家的社会情况就不会让士兵这样,而民主国家想要人为地要求士兵养成这种习惯,则有丧失其固有优点的危险。在民主国家里,军队纪律不应当试图取消能力的自由发挥;而只能设法引导精神的自由发展。军队纪律规定的服从并不是很精确,但却很

more intelligent. It has its root in the will of him who obeys; it rests not only on his instinct, but on his reason; and consequently it will often spontaneously become more strict as danger requires. The discipline of an aristocratic army is apt to be relaxed in war, because that discipline is founded upon habits, and war disturbs those habits. The discipline of a democratic army, on the contrary, is strengthened in sight of the enemy, because every soldier then clearly perceives that he must be silent and obedient in order to conquer.

The nations that have performed the greatest warlike achievements knew no other discipline than that which I speak of. Among the ancients none were admitted into the armies but freemen and citizens, who differed but little from one another and were accustomed to treat each other as equals. In this respect it may be said that the armies of antiquity were democratic, although they came out of the bosom of aristocracy; the consequence was that in those armies a sort of fraternal familiarity prevailed between the officers and the men. Plutarch's lives of great commanders furnish convincing instances of the fact: the soldiers were in the constant habit of freely addressing their general, and the general listened to and answered whatever the soldiers had to say; they were kept in order by language and by example far more than by constraint or punishment; the general was as much their companion as their chief. I do not know whether the soldiers of Greece and Rome ever carried the minutia of military discipline to the same degree of perfection as the Russians have done, but this did not prevent Alexander from conquering Asia, and Rome the world.

热切和简明。这种服从来源于服从者的意愿；它不仅取决于服从者的本能，而且取决于他的理智；因此，危险常常要求服从变得更加严格。贵族国家军队的纪律在战争中容易松弛，因为这种纪律是建立在习惯的基础上的，而战争则打乱了这些习惯。相反，民主国家军队的纪律在面对敌人时可以自动加强，因为每个士兵都非常清楚，为了取得胜利，他必须保持沉默并无条件服从。

那些依靠战争来完成伟大事业的国家，只知道我所讲的纪律。在古代的国家里，军队只承认自由人和公民参军，他们彼此之间没有太大的不同，并习惯于平等待人。从这一方面，可以说古代国家的军队是民主的，虽然它的成员都来自贵族内部；因此，在那些军队里，盛行官员与士兵之间要拥有兄弟般的友爱。读完普鲁塔克的《名人传》，你就会相信这一点：士兵们习惯于和他们的将军们随意交谈，将军们也愿意倾听和回答士兵们的意见；而且有问必答。将军们通过谈话和示范来领导士兵，要比利用管束和惩罚好得多；将军既是士兵的伙伴，又是士兵的长官。我不知道是否希腊和罗马的士兵也曾像现在的俄国士兵那样以同样的程度遵守军队纪律的每个细节，但我知道这并没有妨碍亚历山大征服亚洲、罗马征服世界。

CHAPTER XXVI
Some Considerations On War
In Democratic Communities

When the principle of equality is spreading, not only among a single nation, but among several neighboring nations at the same time, as is now the case in Europe, the inhabitants of these different countries, notwithstanding the dissimilarity of language, of customs, and of laws, still resemble each other in their equal dread of war and their common love of peace. ① It is in vain that ambition or anger puts arms in the hands of princes; they are appeased in spite of themselves by a species of general apathy and goodwill which makes the sword drop from their grasp, and wars become more rare.

As the spread of equality, taking place in several countries at once, simultaneously impels their various inhabitants to follow manufactures and commerce, not only do their tastes become similar, but their interests are so mixed and entangled with one another that no nation can inflict evils on other nations without those evils falling back upon itself; and all nations ultimately regard war as a calamity almost as severe to the conqueror as to the conquered.

Thus, on the one hand, it is extremely difficult in democratic times to draw nations into hostilities; but, on the other, it is almost impossible that any two of them should go to war without embroiling

---

① It is scarcely necessary for me to observe that the dread of war displayed by the nations of Europe is not attributable solely to the progress made by the principle of equality among them. Independently of this permanent cause, several other accidental causes of great weight might be pointed out, and I may mention, before all the rest, the extreme lassitude that the wars of the Revolution and the Empire have left behind them.

第二十六章 对民主社会战争的一些考虑

当平等的原则不仅在一个国家散播,而且也同时在相邻的几个国家散播时,就像今天的欧洲,在这些不同国家定居的人,尽管语言、习惯和法制都不同,但彼此都一样害怕战争和热爱和平。[①]用野心和愤怒来武装各国的君主是没用的;人民普遍持有的那种漠不关心的态度,使君主们情不自愿地丢下手中的宝剑。于是,战争越来越少了。

随着平等的原则迅速地在这几个国家传播开来,同时促使这些国家的居民一起从事工商业,这不仅使他们的爱好变得相似,而且使他们的利益也逐渐混合在一起,因此,任何一个国家加于他国的危害都不能不弹回到自己身上来;从而使所有国家最终都将战争视为是一种对战胜国和战败国来说损害差不多相等的灾难。

因此,一方面是很难使民主时代的各国都卷入战争;但是,另一方面又是几乎不可能在只有两个国家交战的情况下而不牵涉到其他国家。各国的利益互相交织,它们的意见和需要也彼此相

---

① 在我看来,几乎没有必要再去讲,欧洲国家所表现出来的对战争的恐惧不仅仅要归因于这些国家里平等原则的发展。除了这些不变的因素外,我还要指出一些次要的原因,就是战争所带来的极度的疲惫以及帝国已经远离它们。

the rest. The interests of all are so interlaced, their opinions and their wants so much alike, that none can remain quiet when the others stir. Wars therefore become more rare, but when they break out, they spread over a larger field.

Neighboring democratic nations not only become alike in some respects, but eventually grow to resemble each other in almost all. ① This similitude of nations has consequences of great importance in relation to war.

If I inquire why it is that the Helvetic Confederacy made the greatest and most powerful nations of Europe tremble in the fifteenth century, while at the present day the power of that country is exactly proportioned to its population, I perceive that the Swiss have become like all the surrounding communities, and those surrounding communities like the Swiss; so that as numerical strength now forms the only difference between them, victory necessarily attends the largest army. Thus one of the consequences of the democratic revolution that is going on in Europe is to make numerical strength preponderate on all fields of battle and to constrain all small nations to incorporate themselves with large states, or at least to adopt the policy of the latter.

---

① This is not only because these nations have the same social condition, but it arises from the very nature of that social condition, which leads men to imitate and identify themselves with each other.

When the members of a community are divided into castes and classes, they not only differ from one another, but have no taste and no desire to be alike; on the contrary, everyone endeavors, more and more, to keep his own opinions undisturbed, to retain his own peculiar habits, and to remain himself. The characteristics of individuals are very strongly marked.

When the state of society among a people is democratic—that is to say, when there are no longer any castes or classes in the community, and all its members are nearly equal in education and in property—the human mind follows the opposite direction. Men are much alike, and they are annoyed, as it were, by any deviation from that likeness; far from seeking to preserve their own distinguishing singularities, they endeavor to shake them off in order to identify themselves with the general mass of the people, which is the sole representative of right and of might to their eyes. The characteristics of individuals are nearly obliterated.

In the ages of aristocracy even those who are naturally alike strive to create imaginary differences between themselves; in the ages of democracy even those who are not alike seek nothing more than to become so and to copy each other, so strongly is the mind of every man always carried away by the general impulse of mankind.

Something of the same kind may be observed between nations: two nations having the same aristocratic social condition may remain thoroughly distinct and extremely different, because the spirit of aristocracy is to retain strong individual characteristics; but if two neighboring nations have the same democratic social condition, they cannot fail to adopt similar opinions and manners, because the spirit of democracy tends to assimilate men to each other.

同,所以当一个国家稍有些动静,其他所有国家也不可能保持安宁。因此,战争越来越少,而一旦爆发战争,它所扩及的范围也会越来越大。

一些相邻的民主国家,不仅只在某些方面变得相似,而且最终达到在几乎所有方面都相同。① 因此,国家之间的这种相似,对于战争也会产生重大影响。

如果让我探究为什么在 15 世纪时,瑞士联邦曾使欧洲最强大和最有力的国家战栗,而在今天,瑞士的国力则完全与它的人口数成正比时,我发现瑞士人已变得同邻国人一样,而邻国人也变得同瑞士人一样;所以人数的不同形成了现在的瑞士与邻国的唯一差别,胜利必然归属于最强大的军队。因此,欧洲发生的民主革命的后果之一,就是人数的众多成为了所有战场上的有利因素,并强迫所有小国与大国联合,或至少采用大国的对外政策。

---

① 这不仅是因为这些国家间具有相同的社会状况,而且还来因于这些引导人们彼此相似和彼此一致的社会条件的本质。

当社会成员被分为很多阶级和等级时,他们之间不仅会有很大的不同,而且会有不一样的喜好和欲望;相反地,每个人都会很尽力使自己的观念不被干扰,保留自己特有的生活习惯,并保持自我。每个人都有很显著的个人特性。

当人们的社会状况是民主的——也就是说,当社会里不再有阶级和等级,并且所有成员都有着几乎相同的知识和财产——人们的思想境界也会向着相反的方向发展。人们彼此间是相同的,他们常常会因自己背离了这种相同性而苦恼;他们从来不会去设法保留自己突出的特性,而是努力改掉这些可以代表自己权利和见解的特性,以使自己与普通大众相同。个人特性几乎全被淹没。

在贵族时代,即使是那些本性上相同的人也会努力发挥想象使自己不同于大家;而在民主时代,即使是那些本性上有着很大差异的人,也会彼此模仿,使自己与他人变得相同,每个人的思想是如此强烈地被公众的意志所刺激着。

同样的事情也见于两个国家之间:有着相同的贵族社会背景的两个国家,可能会表现出很大的差异和完全的不同,因为贵族精神就是要保留强烈的个人特性;但是如果两个邻国具有相同的民主社会背景时,他们可以采用相同的观点和习俗,因为民主精神就是要让人们彼此之间都变得相同。

As numbers are the determining cause of victory, each people ought of course to strive by all the means in its power to bring the greatest possible number of men into the field. When it was possible to enlist a kind of troops superior to all others, such as the Swiss infantry or the French horse of the sixteenth century, it was not thought necessary to raise very large armies; but the case is altered when one soldier is as efficient as another.

The same cause that begets this new want also supplies means of satisfying it; for, as I have already observed, when men are all alike they are all weak, and the supreme power of the state is naturally much stronger among democratic nations than elsewhere. Hence, while these nations are desirous of enrolling the whole male population in the ranks of the army, they have the power of effecting this object; the consequence is that in democratic ages armies seem to grow larger in proportion as the love of war declines.

In the same ages, too, the manner of carrying on war is likewise altered by the same causes. Machiavelli observes, in *The Prince*, "that it is much more difficult to subdue a people who have a prince and his barons for their leaders than a nation that is commanded by a prince and his slaves." To avoid offense, let us read "public officials" for "slaves," and this important truth will be strictly applicable to our own time.

A great aristocratic people cannot either conquer its neighbors or be conquered by them without great difficulty. It cannot conquer them because all its forces can never be collected and held together for a considerable period; it cannot be conquered because an enemy meets at every step small centers of resistance, by which invasion is arrested. War against an aristocracy may be compared to war in a mountainous country; the defeated party has constant opportunities of rallying its forces to make a stand in a new position.

Exactly the reverse occurs among democratic nations: they easily bring their whole disposable force into the field, and when the nation is wealthy and populous it soon becomes victorious; but if it is ever

由于兵力是决定胜利的至关重要的因素,所以每个国家都尽一切办法努力把尽可能多的兵员派赴战场。当有可能征募到一支比其他军队都要出色的军队,像瑞士的步兵和16世纪法国的骑兵那样的军队,那就不需要征集如此大量的兵员;但是,到了每个士兵的力量都相差无几时,情况就会发生转变。

新需要所产生的原因,同样也为满足需要提供了手段;因为正如我前面讲过的,当人人都相同的时候,人人的力量就都会很弱。在民主国家,社会的最高权力自然大大强于其他国家。因此,当这些国家想要征募所有成年男子入伍时,它们也有能力办到;结果,在民主时代,军队的规模似乎在不断扩大,而人们的好战精神却在减弱。

在这样的时代,作战的方法也由于同样的原因而发生变化。马基雅维里在其《君主论》里写道:"征服以一个君主及其诸侯为首领的国家,要比征服由一个君主及其奴隶治理的国家困难得多。"为了避免攻击性的语言,我们可以将"奴隶"改为"公共官员"。并且,这样一个重要的真理完全可以用在我们目前讨论的问题上。

一个大的贵族国家,在征服它的邻国或被其征服时,都是非常困难的。它之所以不能征服邻国,是因为它们的所有力量不能被很好地组织起来,并长期保持下去;它之所以不能被邻国征服,是因为敌人每走一步都会遇到许多小的阻抗,阻止它前进。在贵族国家里作战犹如在山地里作战;战败者随时都有机会转入新的阵地固守。

在民主国家,情况就完全相反:民主国家可以轻易地把可用的全部兵力投入战场,当这个国家恰好很富庶并且人口稠密,它会很容易成为胜利者;但一旦当它遭到侵略,其领土也遭到破坏

conquered and its territory invaded, it has few resources at command; and if the enemy takes the capital, the nation is lost. This may very well be explained: as each member of the community is individually i-solated and extremely powerless, no one of the whole body can either defend himself or present a rallyingpoint to others. Nothing is strong in a democratic country except the state; as the military strength of the state is destroyed by the destruction of the army, and its civil power paralyzed by the capture of the chief city, all that remains is only a multitude without strength or government, unable to resist the organized power by which it is assailed. I am aware that this danger may be lessened by the creation of local liberties, and consequently of local powers; but this remedy will always be insufficient. For after such a catastrophe not only is the population unable to carry on hostilities, but it may be apprehended that they will not be inclined to attempt it.

According to the law of nations adopted in civilized countries, the object of war is not to seize the property of private individuals, but simply to get possession of political power. The destruction of private property is only occasionally resorted to, for the purpose of attaining the latter object.

When an aristocratic country is invaded after the defeat of its army, the nobles, although they are at the same time the wealthiest members of the community, will continue to defend themselves individually rather than submit; for if the conqueror remained master of the country he would deprive them of their political power, to which they cling even more closely than to their property. They therefore prefer fighting to submission, which is to them the greatest of all misfortunes; and they readily carry the people along with them, because the people have long been used to follow and obey them, and besides have but little to risk in the war.

Among a nation in which equality of condition prevails, on the contrary, each citizen has but a slender share of political power, and often has no share at all. On the other hand, all are independent, and all have something to lose; so that they are much less afraid of being conquered and much more afraid of war than an aristocratic people. It will always be very difficult to convince a democratic people to take up arms when hostilities have reached its own territory. Hence

时,它的御敌办法就不多了;如果敌人占领了它的首都,整个国家就失陷了。这个现象很好被解释:在民主国家,每个公民都是各自孤立的,并且非常软弱,谁也没有能力自我保护,或支援他人。在民主国家里,没有什么能比国家的力量更强大;国家的军事力量一旦因为军队的崩溃而消失,行政的力量由于首都被占领而瘫痪,而所剩下的只是一群没有力量和没有政府组织的人民大众,他们不能抗击这种有组织力量的入侵。我知道,使地方享有自由,并由此建立地方政权,可能使这种危险减少;但这种补救常常是作用不大的。在这种情况下,不但人民不再可能继续进行战斗,而且恐怕他们连这个想法都没有了。

根据文明国家所采用的国际法,战争的目的不是要剥夺私人的财产,而只在于占有政治权力。只是为了达到下一步目的,才偶尔破坏私人财产。

当贵族国家因军队战败而被敌军入侵时,贵族尽管是那个时代的最有钱的人,也宁愿独自继续抵抗而决不投降;因为入侵者一旦成为他们国家的主人,就会夺走他们的政治权力,而他们对政治权力的重视甚于对财产的重视。因此,他们宁愿与对他们来说是最大不幸的投降继续作战。而且,他们容易把人民组织起来,因为人民长期以来已经惯于跟随和服从他们,在战争中几乎没有什么怕损失的。

相反地,在盛行身份平等的国家,每个公民只享有很少一点政治权力,而且常常是一点也没有;另一方面,人人都是独立的,都会有一些东西可会受到损失。因此,他们不像贵族国家的人民那样害怕被征服甚于害怕战争。当战争已经蔓延到民主国家的国土时,我们将很难判断它的人民会不会拿起武器。因此,必须给予这种国家的人以政治权利和政治意识,以使每个公民觉得自

the necessity of giving to such a people the rights and the political character which may impart to every citizen some of those interests that cause the nobles to act for the public welfare in aristocratic countries.

It should never be forgotten by the princes and other leaders of democratic nations that nothing but the love and the habit of freedom can maintain an advantageous contest with the love and the habit of physical well-being. I can conceive nothing better prepared for subjection, in case of defeat, than a democratic people without free institutions. Formerly it was customary to take the field with a small body of troops, to fight in small engagements, and to make long regular sieges. Modern tactics consist in fighting decisive battles and, as soon as a line of march is open before the army, in rushing upon the capital city in order to terminate the war at a single blow. Napoleon, it is said, was the inventor of this new system; but the invention of such a system did not depend on any individual man, whoever he might be. The mode in which Napoleon carried on war was suggested to him by the state of society in his time; that mode was successful because it was eminently adapted to that state of society and because he was the first to employ it. Napoleon was the first commander who marched at the head of an army from capital to capital; but the road was opened for him by the ruin of feudal society. It may fairly be believed that if that extraordinary man had been born three hundred years ago, he would not have derived the same results from his method of warfare, or rather that he would have had a different method.

I shall add but a few words on civil wars, for fear of exhausting the patience of the reader. Most of the remarks that I have made respecting foreign wars are applicable *a fortiori* to civil wars. Men living in democracies have not naturally the military spirit; they sometimes acquire it when they have been dragged by compulsion to the field, but to rise in a body and voluntarily to expose themselves to the horrors of war, and especially of civil war, is a course that the men of democracies are not apt to adopt. None but the most adventurous members of the community consent to run into such risks; the bulk of the

己也享有某些权益,而这些权益曾使贵族国家的贵族们为了国家的幸福做过努力。

民主国家的君主和其他首领们不应当忘记:只有对自由的热爱和习惯才能最有效地抵制对享受的热爱和习惯。我可以想象,在战败的情况下,再没有比不以自由为基础的民主国家的人民最容易投降的了。以前,总是习惯于在兵力不多的情况下就开始作战,战争的规模也很小,并且进行长期的有规律的进攻。现在,一交战就是有决定性的战役,军队在前进的途中没有阻碍,并一直挺进到敌方的首都,以为了一举结束战争。据说,是拿破仑发明了这套新战术;但这种新发明不是只依靠一个人的力量就可以创造出来的,不管这个人是谁。拿破仑采用的战术,是他所在的社会情况提示给他的;这种战术之所以会成功,是因为它特别适应于当时的社会情况,因为拿破仑首次将这种战术应用于战争。拿破仑是第一个率军由这个国家首都打到另一个国家首都的人;但是,为他敞开的这条大道,实际上是封建社会的瓦解。我们可以设想,如果这位非凡的人物生于 300 年前,他是不会从他的战术得出这样的结果的,或者说他将采用另一种战术。

我想就内战问题再补充几句,因为我害怕读者不耐烦。我在前面所讲的关于外战的一些方面同样也有充分理由适用于内战。生活在民主国家的人,天生就没有军事精神;有时,他们在被迫拖上战场的时候,才会有点这种精神。但是,根据自己的意志大家一起奔赴战场,自愿忍受战争的风险,尤其是内战的风险,决不是民主国家的人想要采取的行动。只有最喜欢冒险的人,才会同意去冒这种危险。民主国家的大部分群众都不会去这样做。

population remain motionless.

But even if the population were inclined to act, considerable obstacles would stand in their way; for they can resort to no old and well-established influence that they are willing to obey, no well known leaders to rally the discontented, as well as to discipline and to lead them, no political powers subordinate to the supreme power of the nation which afford an effectual support to the resistance directed against the government.

In democratic countries the moral power of the majority is immense, and the physical resources that it has at its command are out of all proportion to the physical resources that may be combined against it. Therefore the party which occupies the seat of the majority, which speaks in its name and wields its power, triumphs instantaneously and irresistibly over all private resistance; it does not even give such opposition time to exist, but nips it in the bud.

Those who in such nations seek to effect a revolution by force of arms have no other resource than suddenly to seize upon the whole machinery of government as it stands, which can better be done by a single blow than by a war; for as soon as there is a regular war, the party that represents the state is always certain to conquer.

The only case in which a civil war could arise is if the army should divide itself into two factions, the one raising the standard of rebellion, the other remaining true to its allegiance. An army constitutes a small community, very closely knit together, endowed with great powers of vitality, and able to supply its own wants for some time. Such a war might be bloody, but it could not be long; for either the rebellious army would gain over the government by the sole display of its resources or by its first victory, and then the war would be over; or the struggle would take place, and then that portion of the army which was not supported by the organized powers of the state would speedily either disband itself or be destroyed. It may therefore be admitted as a general truth that in ages of equality civil wars will become much less frequent and less protracted. [1]

---

[1] It should be borne in mind that I speak here of sovereign and independent democratic nations, not of confederate democracies; in confederacies, as the preponderating power always resides, in spite of all political fictions, in the state governments and not in the federal government, civil wars are in fact nothing but foreign wars in disguise.

　　甚至是当人民愿意行动的时候,也会考虑到在他们前进途中的障碍物;因为他们在国内已经找不到长久的和早已确立的他们愿意服从的权威,没有大家都公认的领袖来集合、统帅和领导希望起来行动的人,没有在国家政权领导下的政治力量去有效地支持政府进行抵抗。

　　在民主国家里,多数的道德力量是很巨大的,而多数拥有的物质力量,也是为了抵制它而首先可以联合起来的力量所无法比的。因此,占据多数位置的,以多数的名义和利用多数的权力发言的党派,可以在瞬间取得胜利,并且是所有的个人力量所无法抵抗的;这些党派甚至不让个别抵抗存在,在萌芽期间就把它掐死。

　　因此,在这样的国家里,凡是想以武力进行革命的人,除了在突然间占领政府的全部机关外,已没有其他选择了。能够达到这个目的的办法最好是通过政变,而不是通过战争,因为一旦进行正规战争,胜利者几乎准是代表政府的党派。

　　要想引发内战,只有将军队分成两方,一方举旗进行反叛,另一方仍保留他对政府的忠诚。军队本身就是一个小社会,组织严密,有强大的生命力,在一定的期间内能自给自足。战争可能是血腥的,但不会持续很久;因为叛军通过显示其武力,或经过初战的胜利,就能控制政府,于是战争随之结束;或者最好是因为战争一开始,没有得到政府的有组织的力量支持的那一派军队很快就自行瓦解或被消灭。因此,可以把内战在平等时代将会非常稀少和非常短暂看作是一个普遍真理。①

---

　　① 应当切记,我在这里所讲的民主国家的主权与独立,并不是指联邦民主;在联邦国家中,除过所有政治机构,那里的大多数权力都来自州政府而不是联邦政府,因此,内战实际上就是被掩饰过的外战。

FOURTH BOOK
Influence Of Democratic Ideas
And Feelings On Political Society

I Should imperfectly fulfill the purpose of this book if, after having shown what ideas and feelings are suggested by the principle of equality, I did not point out, before I conclude, the general influence that these same ideas and feelings may exercise upon the government of human societies. To succeed in this object I shall frequently have to retrace my steps, but I trust the reader will not refuse to follow me through paths already known to him, which may lead to some new truth.

CHAPTER I
Equality Naturally Gives
Men A Taste For Free Institutions

The principle of equality, which makes men independent of each other, gives them a habit and a taste for following in their private actions no other guide than their own will. This complete independence, which they constantly enjoy in regard to their equals and in the intercourse of private life, tends to make them look upon all authority with a jealous eye and speedily suggests to them the notion and the love of political freedom. Men living at such times have a natural bias towards free institutions. Take any one of them at a venture and search if you can his most deepseated instincts, and you will find that, of all

第四部 民主思想的影响和
政治社会的观念

  我在讲述了平等原则的主张和观念后,并没有完全实现本书的目的,在进行总结之前,我没有指出平等原则的主张和观念可能对人类政体所产生的一般影响。为了能很好地讲述这一观点,我需要经常折回脚步,但我相信读者不会拒绝再跟随我穿越已经探索过的小路,因为这样可以得到新知。

第一章 平等自然使人爱好自由制度

  使人们之间彼此独立的平等的原则,也使人养成只按自己的意志进行个人活动的习惯和爱好。人在与自己相等的人的交流中和作为个人的生活习惯而永远享有的这样完全独立,使人用偏激的眼光看待一切权威,并很快激起关于政治自由的思想和对于政治自由的爱好。因此,生活在这个时代的人们都自然地对民主制度有一种偏见。请你随便找一个人并试图研究一下他的最主要的本能,你会发现在所有政府中,他首先考虑的和给予最高评

governments, he will soonest conceive and most highly value that government whose head he has himself elected and whose administration he may control.

Of all the political effects produced by the equality of conditions, this love of independence is the first to strike the observing and to alarm the timid; nor can it be said that their alarm is wholly misplaced, for anarchy has a more formidable aspect in democratic countries than elsewhere. As the citizens have no direct influence on each other, as soon as the supreme power of the nation fails, which kept them all in their several stations, it would seem that disorder must instantly reach its utmost pitch and that. every man drawing aside in a different direction, the fabric of society must at once crumble away.

I am convinced, however, that anarchy is not the principal evil that democratic ages have to fear, but the least. For the principle of equality begets two tendencies: the one leads men straight to independence and may suddenly drive them into anarchy; the other conducts them by a longer, more secret, but more certain road to servitude. Nations readily discern the former tendency and are prepared to resist it; they are led away by the latter, without perceiving its drift; hence it is peculiarly important to point it out.

Personally, far from finding fault with equality because it inspires a spirit of independence, I praise it primarily for that very reason. I admire it because it lodges in the very depths of each man's mind and heart that indefinable feeling, the instinctive inclination for political independence, and thus prepares the remedy for the ill which it engenders. It is precisely for this reason that I cling to it.

价的政府,是由他选举首脑并由他监督首脑行动的政府。

在所有因身份平等而产生的政治效果中,首先引起人们注意的和使胆怯的人害怕的,就是对独立的这种热爱;我们不能说这种恐惧是完全错误的,因为无政府状态在民主国家比在其他任何国家都表现得更为可怕。由于公民在彼此之间没有直接的影响,所以一旦能使公民们各得其所的国家政权不复存在时,混乱状态就必然立即达到其顶峰状态。公民们被拉向不同的方向,社会组织就立即化为灰烬。

但是,我深信无政府状态并不是民主时代应当害怕的最主要的弊端,而是最不值得害怕的弊端。因为平等的原则会产生两种倾向:一种倾向是直接使人们走向独立,并且可能会突然使人们陷入无政府状态;另一种倾向是使人们沿着一条漫长的,但确实存在的道路走上被奴役的状态。人民容易分辨出第一种倾向,并准备加以抵制;但对于第二种倾向,则由于发现不了而误入歧途。因此,向人们提出这一点是特别重要的。

至于我,决不会因为平等提倡独立而挑平等的毛病,我恰恰是因为它提倡独立而赞扬它。我之所以赞美平等,是因为它深深地在每个人的思想和心灵深处灌输了关于政治独立的模糊观念和本能的冲动,并为它造成的弊端提供补救措施。正是由于这一点,我才爱慕平等。

CHAPTER II

That The Opinions Of Democratic Nations About Government Are Naturally Favorable To The Concentration Of Power

The notion of secondary powers placed between the sovereign and his subjects occurred naturally to the imagination of aristocratic nations, because those communities contained individuals or families raised above the common level and apparently destined to command by their birth, their education, and their wealth. This same notion is naturally wanting in the minds of men in democratic ages, for converse reasons; it can only be introduced artificially, it can only be kept there with difficulty, whereas they conceive, as it were without thinking about the subject, the notion of a single and central power which governs the whole community by its direct influence. Moreover, in politics as well as in philosophy and in religion the intellect of democratic nations is peculiarly open to simple and general notions. Complicated systems are repugnant to it, and its favorite conception is that of a great nation composed of citizens all formed upon one pattern and all governed by a single power.

The very next notion to that of a single and central power which presents itself to the minds of men in the ages of equality is the notion of uniformity of legislation. As every man sees that he differs but little from those about him, he cannot understand why a rule that is applicable to one man should not be equally applicable to all others. Hence the slightest privileges are repugnant to his reason; the faintest dissimilarities in the political institutions of the same people offend him, and uniformity of legislation appears to him to be the first condition of good government.

第二章 民主国家关于政府的观点自然有利于中央集权

关于在君主和臣民之间存在的次要权力的观念,自然浮现于贵族国家人民的想象中,因为这种权力是某些个人或家庭觉得自己的出身、教育和财产高于他人或家庭而应当拥有的,而且这种个人和家庭似乎认为自己生来就是指挥他人的。民主时代的人的头脑里,由于与此相反的原因而自然会不存在这种观点;而只能人为地引进这种观点,而且要想保留它还会有很大的困难,但是,民主时代的人,可以不加思考地想出关于由政府亲自直接领导全体公民的单一的中央权力的观念。另外,在政治方面,也同在哲学和宗教方面一样,民主国家人民的头脑对一些简单而普遍的观念特别容易接受。他们厌恶复杂的制度,他们所倾向的观念是一个大国由同一模式的公民组成并由一个权力当局领导。

在平等时代,继代表人们思想的单一的中央权力的观念之后,自然又要产生关于统一的立法的观念。由于每个人都知道自己同他人没有太大的差别,所以他很难理解为什么应用于一个人的法规不能同等地应用于其他一切人。即使是最微不足道的特权,也让他们从理性上难以接受;同一国家的政治制度上的最微小差异,也使他们感到不快;在他们看来,立法的统一是一个好政府的首要条件。

I find, on the contrary, that this notion of a uniform rule equally binding on all the members of the community was almost unknown to the human mind in aristocratic ages; either it was never broached, or it was rejected.

These contrary tendencies of opinion ultimately turn on both sides to such blind instincts and ungovernable habits that they still direct the actions of men, in spite of particular exceptions. Notwithstanding the immense variety of conditions in the Middle Ages, a certain number of persons existed at that period in precisely similar circumstances; but this did not prevent the laws then in force from assigning to each of them distinct duties and different rights. On the contrary, at the present time all the powers of government are exerted to impose the same customs and the same laws on populations which have as yet but few points of resemblance.

As the conditions of men become equal among a people, individuals seem of less and society of greater importance; or rather every citizen, being assimilated to all the rest, is lost in the crowd, and nothing stands conspicuous but the great and imposing image of the people at large. This naturally gives the men of democratic periods a lofty opinion of the privileges of society and a very humble notion of the rights of individuals; they are ready to admit that the interests of the former are everything and those of the latter nothing. They are willing to acknowledge that the power which represents the community has far more information and wisdom than any of the members of that community; and that it is the duty, as well as the right, of that power to guide as well as govern each private citizen.

If we closely scrutinize our contemporaries and penetrate to the root of their political opinions, we shall detect some of the notions that I have just pointed out, and we shall perhaps be surprised to find so much accordance between men who are so often at variance. The Americans hold that in every state the supreme power ought to emanate from the people; but when once that power is constituted, they can conceive, as it were, no limits to it, and they are ready to admit that it has the right to do whatever it pleases. They have not the slightest notion of peculiar privileges granted to cities, families, or

相反地，我发现在贵族制时代，这种对全体社会成员同等地实行统一的法制的观点在人们的思想里是根本不存在的；人们不是从来没有提出过它就是抛弃它。

这两种互相对立的思想倾向，最终都变成盲目的本能和无法克服的习惯，以致除了一些特殊的情况外，它们仍在支配人们的行动。尽管中世纪各国的情况有着很大的多样性，有时各国正好也有一些完全相同的个人；但这并没有阻止法律对其中的每个人规定不同的义务和不同的权利。相反，在现今这个时代，一些国家的政府将其全部的能力都用于将同样的习惯和同样的法律加于还没有变得相同的全体居民身上。

随着人们的身份逐渐趋于平等，个人便显得很渺小，而社会却显得日益强大；或者说，每个公民都变得与其他一切公民相同，在人群中失去自我，除了人民本身高大宏伟的形象以外，什么也见不到了。这自然要使民主时代的人产生社会的特权是至高无上的观念，而个人的权利则是非常卑微的观点；他们容易承认社会的利益是一切，而个人的利益则什么也不是。他们也愿意承认，代表社会的权力比任何一个社会成员的权力都更有知识和更高明；指导和统治每个公民既是它的义务，也是它的权利。

要是我们仔细研究一下我们的同时代人，并深入到他们政治观念的根源，便会发现他们中的一些有我刚才所讲的观念中的某几个观念，并为发现见解经常不一致的人们中间竟有如此的一致而感到吃惊。美国人认为，在各个州里，社会的最高权力应当来源于人民；但是，当这项权力一旦被设立，可以说没有什么可以限制它，并可以心甘情愿承认它有权去做任何它想做的事情。他们对赋予城市、家庭或个人的特殊权力，并没有什么概念；他们的思

persons; their minds appear never to have foreseen that it might be possible not to apply with strict uniformity the same laws to every part of the state and to all its inhabitants.

These same opinions are more and more diffused in Europe; they even insinuate themselves among those nations that most vehemently reject the principle of the sovereignty of the people. Such nations assign a different origin to the supreme power, but they ascribe to that power the same characteristics. Among them all the idea of intermediate powers is weakened and obliterated; the idea of rights inherent in certain individuals is rapidly disappearing from the minds of men; the idea of the omnipotence and sole authority of society at large rises to fill its place. These ideas take root and spread in proportion as social conditions become more equal and men more alike. They are produced by equality, and in turn they hasten the progress of equality.

In France, where the revolution of which I am speaking has gone further than in any other European country, these opinions have got complete hold of the public mind. If we listen attentively to the language of the various parties in France, we find that there is not one which has not adopted them. Most of these parties censure the conduct of the government, but they all hold that the government ought perpetually to act and interfere in everything that is done. Even those which are most at variance are nevertheless agreed on this head. The unity, the ubiquity, the omnipotence of the supreme power, and the uniformity of its rules constitute the principal characteristics of all the political systems that have been put forward in our age. They recur even in the wildest visions of political regeneration; the human mind pursues them in its dreams.

If these notions spontaneously arise in the minds of private individuals, they suggest themselves still more forcibly to the minds of princes. While the ancient fabric of European society is altered and dissolved, sovereigns acquire new conceptions of their opportunities and their duties; they learn for the first time that the central power which they represent may and ought to administer, by its own agency and on a uniform plan, all the concerns of the whole community. This opinion, which, I will venture to say, was never conceived before our time by the monarchs of Europe, now sinks

想里并没有闪现过可以不把同一法律的一致性严格地用于国内的各地和全体居民。

这样的见解正越来越广地在欧洲传播着；甚至渗入到最强烈反对人民主权学说的国家。这些国家与美国有着不同的最高权力来源，但对权力的特点的看法却与美国的一样。在所有国家，中间权力的观念已经被削弱和逐渐消失；一些个人所与生俱来的关于权利的思想，正迅速从人们的头脑里消失；而关于社会具有无限权威和唯一权威的思想正在逐步代替这种观念。后一种思想正随着社会身份的日益平等和人们的日益相同而生根和蔓延。平等使这种思想产生，而这种思想又反过来加速平等的发展。

我刚才所讲的革命在法国的发展比欧洲其他任何国家都先进，所以这种思想已经完全深入到人们的头脑。如果我们认真听一听法国各政党的心声，就会发现没有一个政党不采用这种思想。大部分政党指责政府的行为，但所有的政党都认为政府应当一直工作下去并参与一切事务。甚至那些意见不统一的也在这一点上保持一致。社会权力的统一性、普遍性和无限权威性，以及法制的一致性，是在我们这个时代产生的各种政治制度的显著特点。甚至这些特点会重现在各种各样的政治体系的深处；人在做梦的时候都在幻想这些东西。

如果每个人的思想中会自然地浮现出这些观点，那么，它会更容易地出现于君主们的想象之中。当欧洲社会的旧制度正在转变和瓦解时，君主们对于他们的权能和责任也在产生新的认识。他们初次知道，他们所代表的中央权力可以而且应当按照统一的计划亲自管理国家的一切事务和所有的人。我敢说这种见解在我们这个时代以前是欧洲的君主们从来没有过的，而现在却

deeply into the minds of kings and abides there amid all the agitation of more unsettled thoughts.

Our contemporaries are therefore much less divided than is commonly supposed; they are constantly disputing as to the hands in which supremacy is to be vested, but they readily agree upon the duties and the rights of that supremacy. The notion they all form of government is that of a sole, simple, providential, and creative power.

All secondary opinions in politics are unsettled; this one remains fixed, invariable, and consistent. It is adopted by statesmen and political philosophers; it is eagerly laid hold of by the multitude; those who govern and those who are governed agree to pursue it with equal ardor; it is the earliest notion of their minds, it seems innate. It originates, therefore, in no caprice of the human intellect, but it is a necessary condition of the present state of mankind. ①

---

① See Appendix Y.

日益深入到这些君主的思想中,并坚守在很多不坚固的思想中。

因此,我们这个时代的人,并不像人们想象中的那样分散;他们虽然一直都在争论应将最高主权置于谁的手中,但他们都一致同意主权的责任和权利的易得性。所有的人都认为政府是一种唯一的、简明的、及时的和具有创造力的权力。

所有关于政治方面的次要观点都是不定的;只有上述的思想是固定的、不变的和具有一致性的。政治家和政治哲学家都借用这个思想;而且也被群众积极拥护;统治者和被统治者都以同样的热情去追求它;它虽是他们思想中最早期的观念,但却好像是生来就有的。因此,它不是人的精神任意形成的,而是人类的现实情况和自然要求。①

---

① 见附录 Y。

CHAPTER III

That The Sentiments Of Democratic Nations Accord With Their Opinions In Leading Them To Concentrate Political Power

If it is true that in ages of equality men readily adopt the notion of a great central power, it cannot be doubted, on the other hand, that their habits and sentiments predispose them to recognize such a power and to give it their support. This may be demonstrated in a few words, as the greater part of the reasons to which the fact may be attributed have been previously stated.

As the men who inhabit democratic countries have no superiors, no inferiors, and no habitual or necessary partners in their undertakings, they readily fall back upon themselves and consider themselves as beings apart. I had occasion to point this out at considerable length in treating of individualism. Hence such men can never, without an effort, tear themselves from their private affairs to engage in public business; their natural bias leads them to abandon the latter to the sole visible and permanent representative of the interests of the community; that is to say, to the state. Not only are they naturally wanting in a taste for public business, but they have frequently no time to attend to it. Private life in democratic times is so busy, so excited, so full of wishes and of work, that hardly any energy or leisure remains to each individual for public life. I am the last man to contend that these propensities are unconquerable, since my chief object in writing this book has been to combat them. I maintain only that at the present day a secret power is fostering them in the human heart, and that if they are not checked, they will wholly overgrow it.

第三章 民主国家人民的感情和思想 一致引导他们走向中央集权

如果说在平等时代人们确实能轻易接受关于建立强大的中央政权的思想，那么，另一方面也不应当怀疑，他们的习惯和感情已经事先承认了这样的权力并对此表示支持。用几句话就可以说明这一点，因为大部分理由已在前面讲过了。

生活在民主国家的人没有高级与低级的差别，在干事业时，也没有习惯的和必不可少的伙伴，所以他们愿意自我反省，并进行独立思考。我在讨论个人主义时曾有机会谈过这一点。因此，这些人从来不会放弃自己的个人事业而参与到公共事业中；他们的自然倾向，是把公共事业交给唯一明显的和集体利益的永久代表去管理；也就是说，交给国家去管理。他们不但天生缺乏对公共事业管理的喜好，而且往往没有时间去管理。在民主时代，个人生活是极其繁忙的，欲求很大，工作很多，以致每个人几乎没有精力和余暇再去参与政治活动。我绝不认为这种倾向是不可克服的，因为我写此书的主要目的就是与这种倾向进行战斗。我只认为，在我们这个时代，有一种神秘的力量在培养这种倾向在人心中的增长，如果不及时加以阻止，它们将会完全控制人心。

I have also had occasion to show how the increasing love of well-being and the fluctuating character of property cause democratic nations to dread all violent disturbances. The love of public tranquillity is frequently the only passion which these nations retain, and it becomes more active and powerful among them in proportion as all other passions droop and die. This naturally disposes the members of the community constantly to give or to surrender additional rights to the central power, which alone seems to be interested in defending them by the same means that it uses to defend itself.

As in periods of equality no man is compelled to lend his assistance to his fellow men, and none has any right to expect much support from them, everyone is at once independent and powerless. These two conditions, which must never be either separately considered or confounded together, inspire the citizen of a democratic country with very contrary propensities. His independence fills him with self-reliance and pride among his equals; his debility makes him feel from time to time the want of some outward assistance, which he cannot expect from any of them, because they are all impotent and unsympathizing. In this predicament he naturally turns his eyes to that imposing power which alone rises above the level of universal depression. Of that power his wants and especially his desires continually remind him, until he ultimately views it as the sole and necessary support of his own weakness. ①

---

① In democratic communities nothing but the central power has any stability in its position or any permanence in its undertakings. All the citizens are in ceaseless stir and transformation. Now, it is in the nature of all governments to seek constantly to enlarge their sphere of action; hence it is almost impossible that such a government should not ultimately succeed, because it acts with a fixed principle and a constant will upon men whose position, ideas, and desires are constantly changing.

It frequently happens that the members of the community promote the influence of the central power without intending to. Democratic eras are periods of experiment, innovation, and adventure. There is always a multitude of men engaged in difficult or novel undertakings, which they follow by themselves without shackling themselves to their fellows. Such persons will admit, as a general principle, that the public authority ought not to interfere in private

我也曾指出,人们日益增长的对安宁的喜爱和财产的起伏不定性,是怎样使民主国家的人民害怕所有的暴力倾向的。对社会安宁的热爱往往成了民主国家人民所保存的唯一政治激情,并随着其他激情的减弱和消失而变得更加积极和强大。这自然使公民们将一些额外的权利赠予或让给中央政权,认为似乎只有中央政权才有兴趣和办法保卫自己,从而使他们免遭无政府状态的侵害。

在平等时代,没有人会被迫去援助他人,也没有人会有要求他人支援的权利,所以每个人都会很独立,而同时又很软弱。这两种情况既不能被分开考虑,也不能混为一谈,它使民主国家的公民具有了十分矛盾的性格。他们的独立性,使他们在与自己平等的人们中间充满自信心和自豪感;而他们的软弱,使他们时不时会感到需要外界的帮助,但他们却不能指望任何人给予他们援助,因为大家都是同样软弱无力的和没有同情心的。在这种困境中,他们自然将视线转向那个在这种普遍感到无能为力的情况下唯一能够超然屹立的伟大权力。他们的需求,特别是他们的欲望,使他们不断想起这个伟大的权力,直到最后,他们终于把这个权力视为拯救个人的软弱的唯一的和必要的依靠。①

---

① 在民主国家,只有中央集权具有其地位上的稳定性和事业上的持久性。在那里,所有公民都处在无休止的变动和变革中。目前,所有政府都本能地不断试图想要扩大自己的活动范围;因此,如果说这些政府最终不会成功,那几乎是不可能的,因为它的行为总是在已确立原则的指导下和人们的坚定意志上,而这些人的地位、思想和欲望又是不断改变的。

常常会发生人们在无准备的情况下大大促进了中央集权的影响。民主时代是一个富有实验性、创新性、和冒险性的时代。这个时代的大多数人都参与到一些艰巨的和新奇的事业中,在这期间,他们总是跟随自己的想法行动,而从不会被同伙的思想所束缚。作为一个普遍原则,这些人将承认公共权威不应干涉个人活动;但是也有例外,因为每个人都希望公共权威能对自己所参与的事业

This may more completely explain what frequently takes place in democratic countries, where the very men who are so impatient of superiors patiently submit to a master, exhibiting at once their pride and their servility. The hatred that men bear to privilege increases in proportion as privileges become fewer and less considerable, so that democratic passions would seem to burn most fiercely just when they have least fuel. I have already given the reason for this phenomenon. When all conditions are unequal, no inequality is so great as to offend the eye, whereas the slightest dissimilarity is odious in the midst of general uniformity; the more complete this uniformity is, the more insupportable the sight of such a difference becomes. Hence it is natural that the love of equality should constantly increase together with equality itself, and that it should grow by what it feeds on.

This never dying, ever kindling hatred which sets a democratic people against the smallest privileges is peculiarly favorable to the gradual concentration of all political rights in the hands of the representative of the state alone. The sovereign, being necessarily and incontestably above all the citizens, does not excite their envy, and each of them thinks that he strips his equals of the prerogative that he concedes to the crown. The man of a democratic age is extremely reluctant to obey his neighbor, who is his equal; he refuses to acknowledge superior ability in such a person; he mistrusts his justice and is jealous of his power; he fears and he despises him; and he loves continually to remind him of the common dependence in which both of them stand to the same master.

Every central power, which follows its natural tendencies, courts

---

concerns; but, by an exception to that rule, each of them craves its assistance in the particular concern on which he is engaged and seeks to draw upon the influence of the government for his own benefit, although he would restrict it on all other occasions. If a large number of men applies this particular exception to a great variety of different purposes, the sphere of the central power extends itself imperceptibly in all directions, although everyone wishes it to be circumscribed.

Thus a democratic government increases its power simply by the fact of its permanence. Time is on its side; every incident befriends it; the passions of individuals unconsciously promote it; and it may be asserted that the older a democratic community is, the more centralized will its government become.

这就可以完全解释民主国家经常发生的现象:人们一面无法忍受掌权者,一面又不得不耐心服从长官的命令,这立即会显示出他们的傲慢和卑屈。随着特权逐渐减少和缩小,人们对特权的憎恶反而日益增强,所以可以说民主的激情在只有很少燃料时似乎会烧得更猛烈。我在前面已经说明过这种现象的原因。当人人的身份都很不平等时,没有什么大的不平等会刺激到眼睛;而在人人都一致时,轻微的差异也会令人讨厌;这种统一越完善,这种厌恶也会更加使人难以忍受。因此,对平等的热爱将会自然随着平等本身的发展而不断增加,而在这种热情得到满足的时候又促进了平等发展。

使民主国家人民反对一切特权的这种永不消失的憎恶,特别有利于一切政治权利逐步集中于国家的唯一代表手里。必然地和无可争议地高于全体公民的最高权力,不会激起公民们的嫉妒,因为每个公民都认为与他平等的人可以剥夺他们从最高权力那里取得的任何特权。民主时代的人极其不愿意服从与自己平等的邻居的意见;不愿意承认邻居在能力上高于自己;不相信邻居正直,并嫉妒邻居的权力;他既担心又鄙视邻居;喜欢让邻居时时刻刻感到他们双方是属于同一个主人管辖的。

顺应自然倾向的各项中央权力,都喜欢和鼓励平等的原则;

给予特别的援助,并利用政府的影响为自己谋利,尽管在所有其他的场合人们会限制这种影响。如果大多数人将这一特别的例外用于其他各种各样的不同的目的,虽然人人都希望这种权力是要被限制的,但中央集权还会在不知不觉中在所有方面扩大了自己的范围。

所以,民主政府仅是简单地通过自己的永久性增加其权力。时间对它有利;而每个小事件也在帮助它;个人激情在不知不觉中促进着它;因此我们可以推断,民主国家的时代越久远,其政府的中央集权就越强。

and encourages the principle of equality; for equality singularly facilitates, extends, and secures the influence of a central power.

In like manner it may be said that every central government worships uniformity; uniformity relieves it from inquiry into an infinity of details, which must be attended to if rules have to be adapted to different men, instead of indiscriminately subjecting all men to the same rule. Thus the government likes what the citizens like and naturally hates what they hate. These common sentiments, which in democratic nations constantly unite the sovereign and every member of the community in one and the same conviction, establish a secret and lasting sympathy between them. The faults of the government are pardoned for the sake of its inclinations; public confidence is only reluctantly withdrawn in the midst even of its excesses and its errors, and it is restored at the first call. Democratic nations often hate those in whose hands the central power is vested, but they always love that power itself.

Thus by two separate paths I have reached the same conclusion. I have shown that the principle of equality suggests to men the notion of a sole, uniform, and strong government; I have now shown that the principle of equality imparts to them a taste for it. To governments of this kind the nations of our age are therefore tending. They are drawn thither by the natural inclination of mind and heart; and in order to reach that result, it is enough that they do not check themselves in their course.

I am of the opinion that, in the democratic ages which are opening upon us, individual independence and local liberties will ever be the products of art; that centralization will be the natural government. ①

---

① See Appendix Z.

因为平等特别便于推动,扩大和保护中央权力的影响。

　　也可以说每个中央政府都崇拜统一;统一可减轻政府在制定无数细节方面的操劳,如果不对所有的人规定同一制度,而对不同人采用不同的制度,则必须规定这些细则。因此,政府自然会爱公民之所爱,恨公民之所恨。这种共同的感情,在民主国家不断将每个公民和国家主权结合在同一思想下,并在两者之间建立起隐秘的和持久的同情。出于自己的爱好,公民原谅政府的缺点;只有政府做得太过分或犯严重错误时,公民才会不信任政府;但只要政府改正错误,就可以恢复公民对它的信任。民主国家的人民虽然经常憎恨那些掌握中央政权的人,但他们通常对这个权力本身是热爱的。

　　因此,我可以从两条不同的途径得出同样的结论。我在前面指出,平等的原则使人产生了关于单一的、统一的和强大的政府的观念;我现在又要指出,平等的原则使人们爱上了这样的政府,因此,现今这个时代的各个国家都想要建立这样的政府。思想和感情的自然倾向,都在驱使人们朝着这个方面迈进;只要不加阻止,人们就可以达到目的地。

　　我认为,在展现于我们眼前的民主时代,个人独立和地方自由将永远是艺术的杰作,而中央集权化则是政府的自然趋势。①

---

　　①　见附录Z。

CHAPTER IV

Of Certain Peculiar And Accidental Causes Which Either Lead A People To Complete The Centralization Of Government Or Divert Them From It

If all democratic nations are instinctively led to the centralization of government, they tend to this result in an unequal manner. This depends on the particular circumstances which may promote or prevent the natural consequences of that state of society, circumstances which are exceedingly numerous, but of which I shall mention only a few.

Among men who have lived free long before they became equal, the tendencies derived from free institutions combat, to a certain extent, the propensities superinduced by the principle of equality; and although the central power may increase its privileges among such a people, the private members of such a community will never entirely forfeit their independence. But when equality of conditions grows up among a people who have never known or have long ceased to know what freedom is (and such is the case on the continent of Europe), as the former habits of the nation are suddenly combined, by some sort of natural attraction, with the new habits and principles engendered by the state of society, all powers seem spontaneously to rush to the center. These powers accumulate there with astonishing rapidity, and the state instantly attains the utmost limits of its strength, while private persons allow themselves to sink as suddenly to the lowest degree of weakness.

The English who emigrated three hundred years ago to found a democratic commonwealth on the shores of the New World had all learned to take a part in public affairs in their mother country; they were conversant with trial by jury; they were accustomed to liberty of speech and of the press, to personal freedom, to the notion of rights and the practice of asserting them. They carried with them to America

第四章 导致民主国家走上中央集权或避免走上中央集权的一些特殊的和偶然的原因

如果所有的民主国家都本能地走向中央集权制度,那它们也要采取不一样的方式。这取决于该国的特殊环境是可以促进还是阻止社会情况的自然发展。这种特殊环境有很多种,但我只想谈及一二。

在获得平等身份以前长期生活在自由中的人民那里,来自自由制度的倾向与平等原则所造成的倾向之间有一定的冲突。尽管中央政权在这些人们当中增加了自己的特权,但社会的个人是永远都不会放弃自己的独立权力的。但是,当平等在一个从来不知道或长期以来已经停止了解自由是什么的国家里(比如像在欧洲大陆人们所见到的那样)发展起来的时候,民族以前的习惯就要突然通过某种自然的吸引力而与社会情况造成的新习惯和新信念突然结合起来,以致所有的权力都好像本能地冲向中央。这些权力以惊人的速度集聚于中央,国家立刻达到其力量的最大极限,而个人也允许他们自己被陷入其弱小的最后限界。

三百多年前移居到新大陆岸上的英国人,想要建立民主共和国,并且他们都养成了在自己的母国参与公共事务的习惯;他们熟悉陪审制度;他们习惯于言论自由、出版自由和人身自由,他们具有权利观念并有权行使它们。他们把这些自由制度和坚毅的

these free institutions and manly customs, and these institutions preserved them against the encroachments of the state. Thus among the
Americans it is freedom that is old; equality is of comparatively modern date. The reverse is occurring in Europe, where equality, introduced by absolute power and under the rule of kings, was already infused into the habits of nations long before freedom had entered into
their thoughts.

I have said that, among democratic nations the notion of government naturally presents itself to the mind under the form of a sole and
central power, and that the notion of intermediate powers is not familiar to them. This is peculiarly applicable to the democratic nations
which have witnessed the triumph of the principle of equality by
means of a violent revolution. As the classes that managed local affairs have been suddenly swept away by the storm, and as the confused mass that remains has as yet neither the organization nor the habits
which fit it to assume the administration of these affairs, the state a-
lone seems capable of taking upon itself all the details of government,
and centralization becomes, as it were, the unavoidable state of the
country.

Napoleon deserves neither praise nor censure for having centered
in his own hands almost all the administrative power of France; for after the abrupt disappearance of the nobility and the higher rank of the
middle classes, these powers devolved on him of course: it would
have been almost as difficult for him to reject as to assume them. But
a similar necessity has never been felt by the Americans, who, having
passed through no revolution, and having governed themselves from
the first, never had to call upon the state to act for a time as their
guardian. Thus the progress of centralization among a democratic people depends not only on the progress of equality, but on the manner in
which this equality has been established.

At the commencement of a great democratic revolution, when
hostilities have but just broken out between the different classes of
society, the people endeavor to centralize the public administration
in the hands of the government, in order to wrest the management
of local affairs from the aristocracy. Towards the close of such a
revolution, on the contrary, it is usually the conquered aristocracy that endeavors to make over the management of all affairs to
the state, because such an aristocracy dreads the tyranny of a
people that has become its equal and not infrequently its master.

习俗带到美洲,并用这些制度抵制政府对他们的侵犯。因此,在美国,自由已经是很古老的东西了;而平等相对则是比较现代的。欧洲的情形与此相反。在欧洲,平等是被专制权力引进的并且在国王的统治之下,在自由进入人民的思想很久以前,平等早已深入人民的习惯。

我已经讲过,在民主国家,人们认为政府自然地代表着唯一的中央政权,而他们并不熟悉什么是中间权力。这一点也特别适用于通过暴力革命而见证到平等原则胜利的民主国家。那些管理地方事务的阶级被这场暴风雪一扫而光,而剩下来的大众既没有组织,也没有可以管好自己事务的习惯,所以看来似乎只有国家才能够担负起管理一切政府工作细节的重任,结果,中央集权成了国家的一种不可避免的事实。

对于拿破仑独揽法国的几乎所有行政大权的行为,我既不赞扬,也不排斥,因为在贵族和大资产阶级突然消失以后,这些权力便落入他的手中。对他来讲,拒绝这些权力和接受这些权力几乎是同样的困难。美国人就不曾感到有这样的必要,因为他们没有经历过革命,从一开始就是自己治理自己,从不需要请国家作他们的临时保卫者。因此,中央集权在民主国家的发展,不仅依靠于平等的进展,而且要看这种平等是以什么方式建立起来的。

在一场民主大革命的开始阶段,当仇视的斗争在社会各个不同阶级中爆发时,人民都努力想把全国的行政权集中到中央政府手里,以能从贵族手中夺取对地方事务的管理权。而相反地,在这样的革命快接近尾声的时候,常常是被打败的贵族竭力想把一切事务的领导权交给国家,因为他们害怕已经变得与他们平等并常常变成了他们的主人的人民所实行的暴政。因此,并不是社会

Thus it is not always the same class of the community that strives to increase the prerogative of the government; but as long as the democratic revolution lasts, there is always one class in the nation, powerful in numbers or in wealth, which is induced, by peculiar passions or interests, to centralize the public administration, independently of that hatred of being governed by one's neighbor which is a general and permanent feeling among democratic nations.

It may be remarked that at the present day the lower orders in England are striving with all their might to destroy local independence and to transfer the administration from all the points of the circumference to the center; whereas the higher classes are endeavoring to retain this administration within its ancient boundaries. I venture to predict that a time will come when the very reverse will happen. These observations explain why the supreme power is always stronger, and private individuals weaker, among a democratic people that has passed through a long and arduous struggle to reach a state. of equality than among a democratic community in which the citizens have been equal from the first. The example of the Americans completely demonstrates the fact. The inhabitants of the United States were never divided by any privileges; they have never known the mutual relation of master and inferior; and as they neither dread nor hate each other, they have never known the necessity of calling in the supreme power to manage their affairs. The lot of the Americans is singular: they have derived from the aristocracy of England the notion of private rights and the taste for local freedom; and they have been able to retain both because they have had no aristocracy to combat.

If education enables men at all times to defend their independence, this is most especially true in democratic times. When all men are alike, it is easy to found a sole and all-powerful government by the aid of mere instinct. But men require much intelligence, knowledge, and art to organize and to maintain secondary powers under similar circumstances and to create, amid the independence and individual weakness of the citizens, such free associations as may be able to struggle

里的同一阶级努力想要加强政府的特权,但只要民主革命继续进行下去,国内总要出现一个在人数上或在财富上强大的阶级,它被一种特殊的激情和利益所驱使,想把国家的管理大权集于中央,它的这种感情和利益是完全独立于民主国家一般具有的那种经常憎恶被邻国统治的感情。

我们可以看到,目前英国的底层阶级都尽自己所有努力去摧毁地方的独立,而将各地的行政权转移到中央手中;然而,上层阶级则试图把地方的行政权保留在原来的界定范围中。我敢预言,总有一天会出现完全相反的情景。上面所叙述的可以清楚地解释,为什么社会权力在经过民主国家人民的长期而艰苦的奋斗之后所获得平等的国家里总要比民主国家人民一开始就总是平等的国家里强大,而个人的权力在前者总要比在后者软弱。美国人的例子就可以完全证明这一事实。美国的居民从未被任何特权所划分过;他们从来不知道主人与仆人之间的相互关系;由于他们彼此间既没有害怕,也没有憎恨,所以从来不知道有请求最高权力来指导他们自己的事务的需要。美国人的命运是特殊的:他们从英国的贵族那里取得了关于个人权利的思想和地方自由的爱好,并能把两者全都保存下来,因为他们不需同贵族进行斗争。

如果说教育在任何时候都使人们能够保护自己的独立,那么这个说法在民主时代就尤为真实。当所有人都相同的时候,便很容易建立起一个单一的和全能的政府,而且只凭本能就可以做到这一点。但是,这要求人们具备更丰富的智能、知识和技能,以便在这种环境下组织和维持次要的权力,以及在公民都是独立而个人又都是软弱无力的条件下建立既可以反抗暴政又可以维持秩序的自由社团。

against tyranny without destroying public order.

Hence the concentration of power and the subjection of individuals will increase among democratic nations, not only in the same proportion as their equality, but in the same proportion as their ignorance. It is true that in ages of imperfect civilization the government is frequently as wanting in the knowledge required to impose a despotism upon the people as the people are wanting in the knowledge required to shake it off; but the effect is not the same on both sides. However rude a democratic people may be, the central power that rules them is never completely devoid of cultivation, because it readily draws to its own uses what little cultivation is to be found in the country, and, if necessary, may seek assistance elsewhere. Hence among a nation which is ignorant as well as democratic an amazing difference cannot fail speedily to arise between the intellectual capacity of the ruler and that of each of his subjects. This completes the easy concentration of all power in his hands: the administrative function of the state is perpetually extended because the state alone is competent to administer the affairs of the country.

Aristocratic nations, however unenlightened they may be, never afford the same spectacle, because in them instruction is nearly equally diffused between the monarch and the leading members of the community.

The Pasha who now rules in Egypt found the population of that country composed of men exceedingly ignorant and equal, and he has borrowed the science and ability of Europe to govern that people. As the personal attainments of the sovereign are thus combined with the ignorance and democratic weakness of his subjects, the utmost centralization has been established without impediment, and the Pasha has made the country his factory, and the inhabitants his workmen.

I think that extreme centralization of government ultimately enervates society and thus, after a length of time, weakens the government itself; but I do not deny that a centralized social power may be able to execute great undertakings with facility in a given time and on a particular point. This is more especially true of war, in which success depends much more on the means of transferring all the resources of a nation to one single point than on the extent of those resources. Hence it is chiefly in war that nations desire, and frequently need, to increase the powers of the central government. All men of military genius are fond of centralization, which increases their strength; and all

因此,中央集权和个人服从在民主国家里不仅随平等的增加而增强,而且随公民的愚昧无知而增强。不错,在不太文明的时代,政府经常缺乏去完善其专制统治的知识,而人民也同样缺乏去摆脱专制统治的知识;但是,两者的后果并不相同。无论民主国家的人民多么粗俗,统治他们的中央政权从来不会完全没有教养,因为它容易吸取它从全国发现的少量知识,如果有必要,它可以到任何地方去寻求帮助。因此,在一个既愚昧又民主的国家里,国家领导和每个被统治者之间的巨大智力差距,便不能不立即暴露出来。这便容易使一切权力集中到国家领导手里。国家的行政权力将不断扩大,因为只有国家能够胜任行政管理工作。

而贵族国家,不管它会是多么的无知,它也永远不会出现这种情况,因为在贵族国家,知识都是同样被普及到君主和一些主要公民之中。

如今统治埃及的帕夏发现他的人民都是极度的无知和极度的平等,于是便从欧洲学来统治其人民的知识和经验。君主的个人成就与其子民的愚昧和民主弱点是结合在一起的,中央集权便在没有阻碍的情况下无限加强,而帕夏也将自己的国家变成他的工厂,把臣民变成他的工人。

我认为极度的中央集权最终会削弱社会活力,久而久之,还会使政府本身软弱无能;但是,我并不否认集权的社会权力能够在一定时期和特定场所轻易实现巨大的事业。这一点对于战争是尤为真实的,因为战争的胜负主要取决于将全国资源迅速地投于规定的目的的方法,其次才取决于资源的多少。因此,主要是在战争时期人民才希望并常常需要要扩大中央政府的权力。所有的军事天才都喜欢中央集权,因为中央集权可以增强他们的势

men of centralizing genius are fond of war, which compels nations to combine all their powers in the hands of the government. Thus the democratic tendency that leads men unceasingly to multiply the privileges of the state and to circumscribe the rights of private persons is much more rapid and constant among those democratic nations that are exposed by their position to great and frequent wars than among all others.

I have shown how the dread of disturbance and the love of well-being insensibly lead democratic nations to increase the functions of central government as the only power which appears to be intrinsically sufficiently strong, enlightened, and secure to protect them from anarchy. I would now add that all the particular circumstances which tend to make the state of a democratic community agitated and precarious enhance this general propensity and lead private persons more and more to sacrifice their rights to their tranquillity.

A people is therefore never so disposed to increase the functions of central government as at the close of a long and bloody revolution, which, after having wrested property from the hands of its former possessors, has shaken all belief and filled the nation with fierce hatreds, conflicting interests, and contending factions. The love of public tranquillity becomes at such times an indiscriminate passion, and the members of the community are apt to conceive a most inordinate devotion to order.

I have already examined several of the incidents that may concur to promote the centralization of power, but the principal cause still remains to be noticed. The foremost of the incidental causes which may draw the management of all affairs into the hands of the ruler in democratic countries is the origin of that ruler himself and his own propensities. Men who live in the ages of equality are naturally fond of central power and are willing to extend its privileges; but if it happens that this same power faithfully represents their own interests and exactly copies their own inclinations, the confidence they place in it knows no bounds, and they think that whatever they bestow upon it is bestowed upon themselves.

The attraction of administrative powers to the center will always be less easy and less rapid under the reign of kings who are still in some way connected with the old aristocratic order than under new

力;而所有中央集权的天才则都喜欢战争,因为战争将迫使国家将所有权力都集中到政府手里。因此,在经常准备发动大规模战争和生存可能经常遭到危险的民主国家,使人们不断扩大国家的特权而限制个人权利的民主倾向,要比在其他一切国家迅速和持久。

我已经说过,对动乱的害怕和对安宁的喜爱已在不知不觉中使民主国家增加了中央政府的职能,以致中央政府自以为是强大的、开明的和安全的足以防止国家陷入无政府状态的唯一力量。我几乎不必补充大家就会知道,使民主国家动荡不安和不稳定的所有的社会的特殊情况加强了中央集权的这种一般倾向,并使个人为了社会安定而牺牲越来越多的权利。

因此,一个国家在即将结束一场长期的血腥革命的时候决不会去扩大中央政府的职能,并且这样的革命在把财产从前任所有者手里夺下来以后便动摇了人民的信心,并使国家陷入猛烈地仇恨、相互冲突和党派的倾轧中。于是,在那时,对社会安定的热爱变成了一种盲目的激情,而公民则对秩序产生了一种反常的热爱。

我在上面只讲了几个可以促进中央集权发展的偶然原因,而对主要的偶然原因我还没有谈到。在民主国家可能使国家统治者拥有对一切事务领导权的一个首要的偶然原因,就是国家首领本人的出身及其爱好。生活在平等时代的人自然喜欢中央政权,并愿意扩大它的特权;而且,如果这个政权忠实地代表了他们自己的利益,并确切地表现出他们的自然倾向时,他们对它的信任就几乎是无限的,并准备将自己所能付出的一切献给它。

同旧贵族制度仍然保持某些联系的国王实行行政集权,将不如在出身、偏见、本性和习惯等方面似乎与平等的运动有不可分割联系的自创新业的国王容易和迅速。我并不是要说出身于贵

princes, the children of their own achievements, whose birth, prejudices, propensities, and habits appear to bind them indissolubly to
the cause of equality. I do not mean that princes of aristocratic origin
who live in democratic ages do not attempt to centralize; I believe
they apply themselves as diligently as any others to that object. For
them the sole advantages of equality lie in that direction; but their opportunities are less great, because the community, instead of volun-
teering compliance with their desires, frequently obey them with reluctance. In democratic communities the rule is that centralization
must increase in proportion as the sovereign is less aristocratic.

When an ancient race of kings stands at the head of an aristocracy, as the natural prejudices of the sovereign perfectly accord with the
natural prejudices of the nobility, the vices inherent in aristocratic
communities have a free course and meet with no corrective. The reverse is the case when the scion of a feudal stock is placed at the head
of a democratic people. The sovereign is constantly led, by his education, his habits, and his associations, to adopt sentiments suggested
by the inequality of conditions, and the people tend as constantly, by
their social condition, to those manners which are engendered by e-
quality. At such times it often happens that the citizens seek to control the central power far less as a tyrannical than as an aristocratic
power, and that they persist in the firm defense of their independence, not only because they would remain free, but especially because they are determined to remain equal.

A revolution that overthrows an ancient regal family in order to
place new men at the head of a democratic people may temporarily
weaken the central power; but however anarchical such a revolution
may appear at first, we need not hesitate to predict that its final and
certain consequence will be to extend and to secure the prerogatives of
that power.

The foremost or indeed the sole condition required in order to
succeed in centralizing the supreme power in a democratic community
is to love equality, or to get men to believe you love it. Thus the science of despotism, which was once so complex, is simplified, and reduced, as it were, to a single principle.

族而生活在民主时代的君主们不想实行中央集权。我相信他们
会同其他君主一样坚持不懈地致力于中央集权制度。对于他们
来说，平等的唯一好处就在于能够中央集权。但是，他们的机遇
却不是很大，因为公民不会自动地服从他们的意旨，而常常只是
不情愿地接受他们的要求。在民主时代，贵族的权力越少，中央
集权的可能性也就越大，这是一条规律。

　　当一个古代的王朝领导贵族国家时，君主天生的偏见必然与
贵族天生的偏见完全一致，而贵族社会的内在弊端将会自由发
展，并且没有可以纠正的办法。当封建世家的子孙成为民主国家
的领袖时，情况就会相反。君主会不断受自己的教育、习惯和感
情的影响，每天都适用由不平等的身份所造成的情感，而人民则
出于自己的社会情况，时时都在追求平等所产生的民情。这时，
公民们常常试图抑制中央政权，把它视为专制的政权远远胜过把
它视为贵族的政权。他们坚决维护自己的独立，这不仅是因为他
们要维护自由，而特别是因为他们决心维护平等。

　　颠覆古代帝王家族而使新人出任民主国家首领的革命，会暂
时削弱中央政权；但是，在革命开始所出现的某些无政府状态，可
以让我们毫不犹豫地预言，这个革命的最终的而且也是必然的结
果，将是扩大和保护这个政权的特权。

　　使民主社会的政治权力集中的第一个而且可以说是唯一的
必要条件，就是它对平等的喜爱并叫人相信他喜爱平等。因此，
本来十分复杂的专制的艺术，现在已经简单了，可以说它已简化
为一项单一的原则。

CHAPTER V

That Among The European Nations Of Our Time The Sovereign Power Is Increasing, Although The Sovereigns Are Less Stable

On reflecting upon what has already been said, the reader will be startled and alarmed to find that in Europe everything seems to conduce to the indefinite extension of the prerogatives of government and to render every day private independence more weak, more subordinate, and more precarious.

The democratic nations of Europe have all the general and permanent tendencies which urge the Americans to the centralization of government, and they are moreover exposed to a number of secondary and incidental causes with which the Americans are unacquainted. It would seem as if every step they make towards equality brings them nearer to despotism.

And, indeed, if we only look around, we shall be convinced that such is the fact. During the aristocratic ages that preceded the present time, the sovereigns of Europe had been deprived of, or had relinquished, many of the rights inherent in their power. Not a hundred years ago, among the greater part of European nations, numerous private persons and corporations were sufficiently independent to administer justice, to raise and maintain troops, to levy taxes, and frequently even to make or interpret the law. The state has everywhere resumed to itself alone these natural attributes of sovereign power; in all matters of government the state tolerates no intermediate agent between itself and the people, and it directs them by itself in general affairs. I am far from blaming this concentration of power, I simply point it out.

At the same period a great number of secondary powers existed

第五章 在现今的欧洲国家中,尽管统治者的地位不如以前稳定,但最高权力却在日益加强

如果让读者再仔细思考一下我刚才所讲的一切,读者便会吃惊地发现,在欧洲,所有的一切都好像在促进中央政权特权的无限增加,使个人的独立日益软弱,日益处于从属的地位,和日益地不稳定。

欧洲的各个民主国家,都具有能促使美国人走向中央集权的所有一般的和长期的倾向,此外,欧洲的民主国家还有许多为美国人所不知道的次要的和偶然的原因,在促进它们走向中央集权。可以说它们每向平等迈进一步,就越接近专制一步。

实际上,只要环顾一下四周,我们便可以确信这个事实。在以前的贵族时代,欧洲的一些君主被剥夺或自动放弃了他们的权力所固有的一些职权。距今不到100年以前,在欧洲的大多数国家里,许多私人或团体还是相当独立的,他们能够自己审理案件,自己招募和培养军队,自己征税,甚至常常自己制定和解释法律。现在,各国均已收回这些本属于国家主权的权限;在有关国家管理的一切事务方面,国家不能容忍在它与公民之间有任何中间代表,而由自己对公民进行全面领导。我并不是要谴责这种中央集权,而只是要指出这个事实。

在同一时期,欧洲到处存在着大量的代表地方利益和管理地

in Europe, which represented local interests and administered local affairs. Most of these local authorities have already disappeared; all are speedily tending to disappear or to fall into the most complete dependence. From one end of Europe to the other the privileges of the nobility, the liberties of cities, and the powers of provincial bodies are either destroyed or are upon the verge of destruction.

In the course of the last half-century Europe has endured many revolutions and counter-revolutions, which have agitated it in opposite directions; but all these perturbations resemble each other in one respect: they have all shaken or destroyed the secondary powers of government. The local privileges which the French did not abolish in the countries they conquered have finally succumbed to the policy of the princes who conquered the French. Those princes rejected all the innovations of the French Revolution except centralization; that is the only principle they consented to receive from such a source.

My object is to remark that all these various rights which have been successively wrested, in our time, from classes, guilds, and individuals have not served to raise new secondary powers on a more democratic basis, but have uniformly been concentrated in the hands of the sovereign. Everywhere the state acquires more and more direct control over the humblest members of the community and a more exclusive power of governing each of them in his smallest concerns. ①

Almost all the charitable establishments of Europe were formerly in the hands of private persons or of guilds; they are now almost all dependent on the supreme government, and in many countries are actually administered by that power. The state almost exclusively undertakes to

---

① This gradual weakening of the individual in relation to society at large may be traced in a thousand things. I shall select from among these examples one derived from the law of wills.

In aristocracies it is common to profess the greatest reverence for the last wishes of a dying man. This feeling sometimes even became superstitious among the elder nations of Europe: the power of the state, far from interfering with the caprices of a dying man, gave full force to the very least of them and ensured to him a perpetual power.

When all the living men are weak, the will of the dead is less respected; it is circumscribed within a narrow range, beyond which it is annulled or checked by the supreme power of the laws. In the Middle Ages testamentary power had, so to speak, no limits; among the French at the present day a man cannot distribute his fortune among his children without the interference of the state; after having domineered over a man's whole life, the law insists upon regulating even his very last act.

方事务的次要权力。目前,这些地方当局的大部分已经不存在了,而其余的不是正在迅速消失之中,就是要陷入完全的依赖中。从欧洲的一端到另一端,贵族的特权、城市的自由和地方的行政权,不是已经消失,便是在毁灭的边缘。

在近半世纪的时间里,欧洲已经经历了多次革命和刺激它走向反面的反革命;但所有这些运动在一点上是共同的:那就是它们都动摇或破坏了政府的次要权力。法国在被它征服的地区所没有废除的地方特权,最终屈从于征服法国的君主的政策。这些君主拒绝所有来自法国革命的新鲜事物,唯独把中央集权留为己用;这是他们肯从革命里接受的唯一东西。

我的目的是想指出,在我们这个时代,那些相继从某些阶级、团体和个人手里夺过来的各种各样的权利并没有在更为民主的基础上建立新的次要权力,而是被全部集中到君主的手里。在任何地方,各国都要求越来越直接地领导最卑微的公民,并对他们每个人的小事也越来越加强管理。①

在古代欧洲,几乎所有的慈善事业都归私人或团体掌管;而在今天,几乎所有的慈善事业都依赖于国家的最高权力,在某些国家实际上是由这些权力管理的。国家几乎承担了向饥

---

① 我们在很多事情上都能够找到个人权力被逐渐减小的痕迹。我将根据法律的意愿从中选一个例子来说明这个问题。

在贵族社会,对即将死去的人的临终愿望表示极大的尊敬是很常见的。有时,这种感情在古老的欧洲国家甚至变得很神圣,国家的权力远远不能干涉一个临终的人的任何反复无常的行为,它给予其中极少数人全部力量并且保证给予他永久的权力。

当所有活着的人的力量都很软弱时,他们的临终遗愿也不会受到太多的尊敬;它被限制在很狭窄的范围内,如有超越就会受到最高权力的阻止和废除。在中世纪,可以说遗嘱权是不受任何限制的;而在今天的法国,在没有国家的参与下,一个人无法对自己的子女进行财产分配;在支配了一个人的一生后,法律甚至连这个人的最终遗愿也不放过。

supply bread to the hungry, assistance and shelter to the sick, work to the idle, and to act as the sole reliever of all kinds of misery.

Education, as well as charity, has become in most countries at the present day a national concern. The state receives, and often takes, the child from the arms of the mother to hand it over to official agents; the state undertakes to train the heart and to instruct the mind of each generation. Uniformity prevails in the courses of public instruction as in everything else; diversity as well as freedom is disappearing day by day.

Nor do I hesitate to affirm that among almost all the Christian nations of our days, Catholic as well as Protestant, religion is in danger of falling into the hands of the government. Not that rulers are over-jealous of the right of settling points of doctrine, but they get more and more hold upon the will of those by whom doctrines are expounded; they deprive the clergy of their property and pay them salaries; they divert to their own use the influence of the priesthood, they make them their own ministers, often their own servants, and by this alliance with religion they reach the inner depths of the soul of man. ①

But this is as yet only one side of the picture. The authority of government has not only spread, as we have just seen, throughout the sphere of all existing powers, till that sphere can no longer contain it, but it goes further and invades the domain heretofore reserved to private independence. A multitude of actions which were formerly entirely beyond the control of the public administration have been subjected to that control in our time, and the number of them is constantly increasing.

Among aristocratic nations the supreme government usually contented itself with managing and superintending the community in whatever directly and ostensibly concerned the national honor, but in all other respects the people were left to work out their own free will. Among these nations the government often seemed to forget that there is a point at which the faults and the sufferings of private persons involved the general prosperity, and that to prevent the ruin of a private individual must sometimes be a matter of public importance.

---

① In proportion as the functions of the central power are augmented, the number of public officers by whom that power is represented must increase also. They form a nation within each nation; and as they share the stability of the government, they more and more fill up the place of an aristocracy.

In almost every part of Europe the government rules in two ways: it rules one portion of the citizens by the fear which they feel for its agents, and the other by the hope they have of becoming its agents.

饿者施舍面包,救济和收容病残和安排无业者就业等事业,国家成了一切灾难的几乎唯一的救济者。今天,在大多数欧洲国家。

教育事业也同慈善事业一样,成为一项民族性的事业。国家从母亲的怀抱里把孩子接过来,而且常常是要过来,并交到它所设立的官方机构里,由这些机构负责对每一代人进行感情陶冶和思想教育。同其他制度一样,教育制度也是统一的。其差异也和自由一样,在一天天地消失。

我会毫不犹豫的承认,在现今的几乎所有基督教国家,无论是天主教还是新教,都有落入政府手中的危险。这不是指统治者对教会自行决定教义表示非常嫉妒,而是指他们控制了教义宣讲者的意志,并剥夺教士的财产而付给教士薪水;他们还把教士的影响转为己用,任命教士而且往往是任命自己的仆从,通过与宗教的联合,他们深入到每个人的心灵深处。①

但是,这仅仅是整个画面的一个侧面。正如我们所看到的,政府的权威不仅扩大到已存在的权力的每个领域,直到这些领域已不能满足它,它除要充分行使现有的全部职权以外,还要更进一步,把自己的统治扩展到个人的独立这至今尚未被它侵占的领域。曾经完全不受政府控制的许多行动,现在都在政府的控制中,而且被控制的行动在不断增加。

在贵族国家,政府的最高权力通常只限于管理与监督与国家荣誉有着直接的和显著的关系的事务的公民,而在其他方面,公民都按照自己的意愿行动。在这些国家里,政府好像常常忽略了个人的错误和苦难会危害全国的幸福,忽略了防止个人的破产有时也是关系国家的重要任务。

---

① 中央集权的不断扩大,代表中央集权的公共官员的数量也在日益增加。他们在每个国家里都形成了自己的小国家;因为他们享有政府的稳定性,他们越来越多地占据了贵族的职位。

在欧洲,政府的每个部分几乎都用两种方式进行统治:对于一部分公民,利用其对于自己政府的恐惧心理来实施统治,而对另一部分人,则利用了他们梦想成为统治阶层一分子的心理。

The democratic nations of our time lean to the opposite extreme. It is evident that most of our rulers will not content themselves with governing the people collectively; it would seem as if they thought themselves responsible for the actions and private condition of their subjects, as if they had undertaken to guide and to instruct each of them in the various incidents of life and to secure their happiness quite independently of their own consent. On the other hand, private individuals grow more and more apt to look upon the supreme power in the same light; they invoke its assistance in all their necessities, and they fix their eyes upon the administration as their mentor or their guide.

I assert that there is no country in Europe in which the public administration has not become, not only more centralized, but more inquisitive and more minute: it everywhere interferes in private concerns more than it did; it regulates more undertakings, and undertakings of a lesser kind; and it gains a firmer footing every day about, above, and around all private persons, to assist, to advise, and to coerce them.

Formerly a sovereign lived upon the income of his lands or the revenue of his taxes; this is no longer the case now that his wants have increased as well as his power. Under the same circumstances that formerly compelled a prince to put on a new tax, he now has recourse to a loan. Thus the state gradually becomes the debtor of most of the wealthier members of the community and centralizes the largest amounts of capital in its own hands.

Small capital is drawn into its keeping by another method. As men are intermingled and conditions become more equal, the poor have more resources, more education, and more desires; they conceive the notion of bettering their condition, and this teaches them to save. These savings are daily producing an infinite number of small capitals, the slow and gradual produce of labor, which are always increasing. But the greater part of this money would be unproductive if it remained scattered in the hands of its owners. This circumstance has given rise to a philanthropic institution

当今的民主国家偏向另一个极端。很明显,当代的大部分统治者不会满足于仅治理整个国家;他们认为应当对自己所统治的人民的行动和个人状况负责,认为自己已经承担了指导和指点每个人在一生中的各种各样的行动的责任,并且在必要的时候,不管人们愿意不愿意,还教导每个人如何获得幸福。另一方面,人民也越来越多地倾向于以这样的方式看待政府;一有需要就去找政府援助,并时时刻刻把政府视为导师和向导。

我敢说在欧洲,没有一个国家的政府不是不仅越来越中央集权,而且越来越集中于微小事情和管得越来越严。各国的政府越来越比以前更深入到私人活动领域;并越来越多地直接控制个人的行动,而且是微不足道的行动;每天都站在每个公民的身边协助和引导他们,或站在公民的头上强迫他们行动。

以前,君主依靠他的土地的收入和税收生活。而现在的情况就不同了,因为他的需求和权力都增加了。以前,一个君主如果要被迫制定一种新税,那么现在他可以举债。于是,国家就逐渐变成大多数富人的债务人,并把最大部分的资金集中到自己手里。

对于小额资金,它用另一种办法吸收。随着人们彼此间的逐渐混合,身份也日益接近平等,穷人也开始拥有了一些财产、一些教养和一些欲望。他们希望改善自己的境遇,而这就教会了他们去储蓄。于是,储蓄每天都会产生出无数的小额资金,其慢慢地和逐渐地积累起来的劳动果实在不断地增加。但是,如果这么多钱分散在个人手里,便不会产生任何收益。于是,这种情况便会出现一种慈善组织,如果我没有看错的

which will soon become, if I am not mistaken, one of our most important political institutions. Some charitable persons conceived the notion of collecting the savings of the poor and placing them out at interest. In some countries these benevolent associations are still completely distinct from the state; but in almost all they manifestly tend to identify themselves with the government; and in some of them, the government has superseded them, taking upon itself the enormous task of centralizing in one place, and putting out at interest, on its own responsibility, the daily savings of many millions of the working classes.

Thus the state draws to itself the wealth of the rich by loans and has the poor man's mite at its disposal in the savings banks. The wealth of the country is perpetually flowing around the government and passing through its hands; the accumulation increases in the same proportion as the equality of conditions; for in a democratic country the state alone inspires private individuals with confidence, because the state alone appears to be endowed with strength and durability. ①

Thus the sovereign does not confine himself to the management of the public treasury; he interferes in private money matters; he is the superior, and often the master, of all the members of the community; and in addition to this he assumes the part of their steward and paymaster.

The central power not only fulfills of itself the whole of the duties formerly discharged by various authorities, extending those duties, and surpassing those authorities, but it performs them with more alertness, strength, and independence than it displayed before. All the governments of Europe have, in our time, singularly improved the science of administration: they do more things, and they do everything with more order, more celerity, and at less expense; they seem to be constantly enriched by all the experience of which they have

---

① On the one hand, the taste for worldly welfare is perpetually increasing; and, on the other, the government gets more and more complete possession of the sources of that welfare.

Thus men are following two separate roads to servitude; the taste for their own well-being withholds them from taking a part in the government, and their love of that well-being forces them to closer and closer dependence upon those who govern.

话,这个组织不久便会成为我们的一个重要政治机构。一些有慈善之心的人想出一个办法,把穷人的储蓄收集在一起,使其产生效益。在某些国家里,这种慈善组织仍然与国家有着完全的区别;但几乎在所有国家里,这种团体有归顺于政府的倾向;甚至在个别国家里,政府已经取代了它,并亲自承担起把数百万劳动者的日常储蓄集中在一个场所,并独家经营其生息业务的庞大工作。

于是,国家既可以通过举债的办法吸收富人的资金,又可以通过储蓄的办法随意使用穷人的存款。这样一来,国家的财富就会不断地在政府里循环;并随着身份日趋平等而相应地增加;因为在一个民主国家里,只有政府能赋予个人以自信,而每个人之所以相信政府,是因为他们觉得只有政府才拥有力量且才会持久。[①]

因此,统治者并不是只把自己限制在管理公共财产的范围里,而且还在干预私人财产。他是所有公民的首领,而且往往是他们的主人。另外,他还是公民的管家和发薪人员。

现在的中央政权不仅要实行原来政权的全部职责,而且超过了它的工作范围,扩大其责任,但是,它比以前所执行得更灵活、更有力量和更有独立性。在我们这个时代,欧洲所有国家的政府已经大大改进其管理技巧:它们做的事情比以前多了,而且每件事都做得比以前更有条理、更敏捷和更节省经费;他们似乎在不断用从私人那里得来的所有的丰富经验来提升自己。欧洲的君主们日复一日地在他们的管辖地区派有其下属进行严格管理,并

---

① 一方面,人们对幸福和平的喜好在不断增长;另一方面,政府越来越多地完全占有了幸福的来源。

于是,人们逐渐走向两条不同的奴役的道路:一是他们对自己幸福的喜爱阻止他们参与政府事业;二是他们对幸福的喜爱强迫他们越来越依靠于政府的统治。

stripped private persons. From day to day, the princes of Europe hold their subordinate officers under stricter control and invent new methods for guiding them more closely and inspecting them with less trouble. Not content with managing everything by their agents, they undertake to manage the conduct of their agents in everything; so that the public administration not only depends upon one and the same power, but it is more and more confined to one spot and concentrated in the same hands. The government centralizes its agency while it increases its prerogative; hence a twofold increase of strength.

In examining the ancient constitution of the judicial power among most European nations, two things strike the mind: the independence of that power and the extent of its functions. Not only did the courts of justice decide almost all differences between private persons, but in very many cases they acted as arbiters between private persons and the state.

I do not here allude to the political and administrative functions that courts of judicature had usurped in some countries, but to the judicial duties common to them all. In most of the countries of Europe there were, and there still are, many private rights, connected for the most part with the general right of property, which stood under the protection of the courts of justice, and which the state could not violate without their sanction. It was this semipolitical power that mainly distinguished the European courts of judicature from all others; for all nations have had judges, but all have not invested their judges with the same privileges.

Upon examining what is now occurring among the democratic nations of Europe that are called free, as well as among the others, it will be observed that new and more dependent courts are everywhere springing up by the side of the old ones, for the express purpose of deciding, by an extraordinary jurisdiction, such litigated matters as may arise between the government and private persons. The elder judicial power retains its independence, but its jurisdiction is narrowed; and there is a growing tendency to reduce it to be exclusively the arbiter between private interests.

The number of these special courts of justice is continually increasing, and their functions increase likewise. Thus the government ismore and more absolved from the necessity of subjecting its policy and its rights to the sanction of another power. As judges cannot be dispensed with, at least the state is to select them and always to hold

且发明了一些新方法来直接领导这些代表和便于监督他们。他们还不满足于让自己的代表管理一切事务,于是便直接参与其代表所管理的一切事务;结果,公共行政不但依赖于同一个政权,而且越来越集中于同一地方和控制在少数人手里。政府在集中其代理的同时,也加强了它的特权。这是使它力量强大的两个原因。

在考察大多数欧洲国家在古代所实行的司法制度时,有两件事情使我们感到吃惊:它们是司法权的独立和司法权限的扩大。法院不仅在审理私人间的几乎一切纠纷,而且在大多数情况下是充当私人与国家间的仲裁人。

在这里,我并不想谈法院在某些国家所篡夺的政治职能和行政职能,而只谈各国法院所拥有的普遍职能。在欧洲的大部分国家里,仍存在着很多大部分是与一般财产权有关的私人权利,这项权利受到法院的保护,不经法院许可国家不得剥夺。正是这种半政治权力使欧洲的法院与所有其他国家的法院区分开来,因为其他所有国家虽然设有法官,但都没有授予法官以这样的特权。

如果我们考察一下被称作自由的欧洲民主国家以及其他国家所发生的一切,就会发现所有的国家除普通法院外,还另外设立了不如普通法院独立的专门审理国家与公民间可能发生的纠纷的法院。原有的法院还保有其独立性,但它们的审判权越来越小了;而且人们越来越倾向于叫它们只充当私人利益冲突的仲裁者。

这种特殊法院的数目在不断增加,它们的职权也在增加。因此,政府可以越来越免于让另一个权力机关来批准它的计划和权力的需要了。政府虽然不能绕过法官,但它至少可以选任法官,并永远控制住他们;也就是说,在政府和私人之间,与其说它们是主持正义,不如说是在名义上主持正义。因此,国家并不满足于

them under its control; so that between the government and private individuals they place the effigy of justice rather than justice itself. The state is not satisfied with drawing all concerns to itself, but it acquires an ever increasing power of deciding on them all, without restriction and without appeal. ①

There exists among the modern nations of Europe one great cause, independent of all those which have already been pointed out, which perpetually contributes to extend the agency or to strengthen the prerogative of the supreme power, though it has not been sufficiently attended to: I mean the growth of manufactures, which is fostered by the progress of social equality. Manufacturers generally collect a multitude of men on the same spot, among whom new and complex relations spring up. These men are exposed by their calling to great and sudden alternations of plenty and want, during which public tranquillity is endangered. It may also happen that these employments sacrifice the health and even the life of those who gain by them or of those who live by them. Thus the manufacturing classes require more regulation, superintendence, and restraint than the other classes of society, and it is natural that the powers of government should increase in the same proportion as those classes.

This is a truth of general application; what follows more especially concerns the nations of Europe. In the centuries which preceded that in which we live, the aristocracy was in possession of the soil, and was competent to defend it; landed property was therefore surrounded by ample securities, and its possessors enjoyed great independence. This gave rise to laws and customs that have been perpetuated, notwithstanding the subdivision of lands and the ruin of the nobility; and at the present time landowners and agriculturists are still those among the community who most easily escape from the control of the supreme power. In these same aristocratic ages, in which all the sources of our history are to be traced, personal property was of small importance and those who possessed it were despised and weak. The manufacturing class formed an exception in the midst of those aristocratic communities; as it had no certain patronage, it was not outwardly protected and was often unable to protect itself. Hence a habit sprang up of

---

① A strange sophism has been uttered on this subject in France. When a suit arises between the government and a private person, it is not to be tried before an ordinary judge, in order, they say, not to mix the administrative and the judicial powers; as if it were not to confuse those powers and in the most dangerous and oppressive manner to invest the government with the office of judging and administering at the same time.

总揽一切事务,它还越来越多地要求在没有限制和没有被控诉的情况下自行决定一切。①

在现代的欧洲各国,除了我刚才讲过的各项原因以外,还存在着一个重大原因使它们不断扩大最高当局的代理或增加其特权,但这些还没有引起人们足够的注意:这个原因是社会平等的进步所促成的工业发展。工业制造者通常将许多人集聚在同一地方,在这些人之间形成了新型的和复杂的关系。工业使他们辗转于大富和大贫的突然变化中,而这种时穷时富的变化,自然危害着社会的安定。最后还会出现工业劳动损害靠此盈利者和靠此生活者的健康,甚至危害到他们的生命。因此,工业阶级比其他阶级更需要制度,更需要监督和限制,而随着这个阶级的壮大,政府的权限也自然会随之增加。

这是一项适用于普遍应用的真理;但是我要强调的是与欧洲各国有特别关系的部分。在以前的许多世纪里,只有贵族拥有土地,而且他们有能力保护其土地;因此,当时的地产有着充足的保障,所有者享有极大的独立性。于是,尽管土地被分割且贵族也没落了,但仍有生效的法律和习惯;而在今天,土地所有者和农户仍然是最容易逃避中央政权控制的公民。在可以发现我们历史的一切根源的贵族时代,个人财产并不重要,其所有者也被轻视,而且力量薄弱。工业阶级形成了贵族社会里的一个例外;因为他们没有特定的赞助者,所以受不到保护,而且往往不能自保。因此,人们习惯性地认为工业财产是一种具有特殊性质的财产,不

---

① 在法国对这方面有一种奇怪的辩论。当在政府和个人间发生诉讼案件时,一般不会由普通法庭审理,他们认为这样做是为了不把行政权和司法权混合在一起;就好像不是混淆这些权力,并以一种最危险和最压迫的方式让政府同时享有审判和行政的职能。

considering manufacturing property as something of a peculiar nature, not entitled to the same deference and not worthy of the same securities as property in general; and manufacturers were looked upon as a small class in the social hierarchy, whose independence was of small importance and who might with propriety be abandoned to the disciplinary passions of princes. On glancing over the codes of the Middle Ages, one is surprised to see, in those periods of personal independence, with what incessant royal regulations manufactures were hampered, even in their smallest details; on this point centralization was as active and as minute as it can ever be.

Since that time a great revolution has taken place in the world; manufacturing property, which was then only in the germ, has spread till it covers Europe: the manufacturing class has been multiplied and enriched by the remnants of all other ranks; it has grown and is still perpetually growing in number, in importance, in wealth. Almost all those who do not belong to it are connected with it at least on some one point; after having been an exception in society, it threatens to become the chief, if not the only class. Nevertheless, the notions and political habits created by it of old still continue. These notions and habits remain unchanged, because they are old, and also because they happen to be in perfect accordance with the new notions and general habits of our contemporaries.

Manufacturing property, then, does not extend its rights in the same ratio as its importance. The manufacturing classes do not become less dependent while they become more numerous, but, on the contrary, it would seem as if despotism lurked within them and naturally grew with their growth. ①

---

① I shall cite a few facts in support of this. Mines are the natural sources of manufacturing wealth; as manufactures have grown up in Europe, as the produce of mines has become of more general importance, and profitable mining more difficult because of the subdivision of property which is a consequence of the equality of conditions, most governments have asserted a right of owning the soil in which the mines lie, and of inspecting the works, which has never been the case with any other kind of property.

Thus mines, which were private property, subject to the same obligations and sheltered by the same guarantees as all other landed property, have fallen under the control of the state. The state either works them or leases them; their owners become mere tenants, deriving their rights from the state. Moreover, the state almost everywhere claims the power of directing their operations: it lays down rules, enforces the adoption of particular methods,

像一般财产那样受到同样的尊敬和得到同样的保护;工业制造者被看作是社会里的一个小阶层,他们的独立并不太重要,并会随着君主的情绪被任意踢开。如果我们浏览一下中世纪的法典,便会吃惊地看到,在那个时代的个人独立中,国王竟不断限制工业,甚至管到工业的最微小细节;在这方面,中央集权正是像它所能达到的那样积极和细致。

从那以后,世界上发生了一场大的革命;刚刚出现的工业财产已经逐渐发展到整个欧洲:工业阶级在不断扩大并以其他阶级的残余壮大了自己的力量;工业阶级的人数、重要性和财富均大大增加,而且不断增加下去。原先与它没有关系的人,至少在某个方面也都差不多与它结合。这个原先被人视为例外阶级的阶级,现在有了变为主要阶级而且可以说是变为唯一阶级的趋势。然而,它所形成的政治思想和政治习惯仍在持续。这些思想和习惯之所以没有改变,一方面是因为它们很古老,另一方面是因为它们与现代人的新思想和一般习惯完全一致。

因此,工业财产并没有随着其重要性的提高而扩大其权利。工业阶级的人数虽然增加了,而它的依赖性并没有减少,但是相反的,专制似乎已经潜伏在它的内部,并随着它的发展而自然而然地加强。①

---

① 我将引用少数的事实来证明这个现象。矿产是制造业财富的自然源泉;随着制造业在欧洲的壮大,矿产的开发也变得越来越重要,而矿产的利润也变得越来越困难,因为对财产的划分是社会平等的结果,政府已经宣布了对矿产所在地的土地所有权,并且监察其操作,这在其他类型的财产中是没有的。

因此,作为私有财产的矿产,与其他土地财产一样,要服从相同的义务,享有相同的保护,也归入国家的掌控之下。国家要么自己经营,要么出租,业主就变成了租客而已,从国家那里享受权利。几乎所有国家都要求控制矿产业操作的权力:国家放弃规则,强制采用特殊条例,迫使业主受到

As a nation becomes more engaged in manufactures, the lack of roads, canals, harbors, and other works of a semi-public nature, which facilitate the acquisition of wealth, is more strongly felt; and as a nation becomes more democratic, private individuals are less able, and the state more able, to execute works of such magnitude. I do not hesitate to assert that the manifest tendency of all governments at the present time is to take upon themselves alone the execution of these undertakings, by which means they daily hold in closer dependence the population which they govern.

On the other hand, in proportion as the power of a state increases and its necessities are augmented, the state consumption of manufactured produce is always growing larger; and these commodities are generally made in the arsenals or establishments of the government. Thus in every kingdom the ruler becomes the principal manufacturer: he collects and retains in his service a vast number of engineers, architects, mechanics, and handicraftsmen.

Not only is he the principal manufacturer, but he tends more and more to become the chief, or rather the master, of all other manufacturers. As private persons become powerless by becoming more equal, they can effect nothing in manufactures without combination; but the government naturally seeks to place these combinations under its own control.

It must be admitted that these collective beings, which are called companies, are stronger and more formidable than a private individual can ever be, and that they have less of the responsibility for their own actions; whence it seems reasonable that they should not be allowed to retain so great an independence of the supreme government as might be conceded to a private individual.

Rulers are the more apt to follow this line of policy as their own inclinations invite them to it. Among democratic nations it is only by association that the resistance of the people to the government can ever display itself; hence the latter always looks with ill favor on those associations which are not in its own power; and it is well

---

subjects the miners to constant supervision, and, if refractory, they are ousted by a government court of justice, and the government transfers their contract to other hands; so that the government not only possesses the mines, but has all the men who work them in its power. Nevertheless, as industry increases, the working of old mines increases also; new ones are opened; the mining population expands and grows; day by day governments augment their subterranean dominions, and people them with their agents.

随着国家工业化的加强,它就越是强烈地需要便利于致富的道路、运河、港口和其他半公用性工程;而随着国家越来越民主化,个人就越是不可能进行这样的工程,但国家却是越有可能进行。我会毫不犹豫地声称,当前各国政府的明显倾向是单独承担这些工程,它们这样做是为了越来越近地控制它所统治的人民。

另一方面,随着国力的增强和需求的增加,国家所消耗的工业品也在不断增加;这些工业品一般均由国家的兵工厂和工厂制造。因此,在每个王国,统治者便成了最大的工业家。他召集了一大批工程师、建筑师、技师和技工为他服务。

他不仅是最大的工业家,而且越来越想成为其他一切产业的首领,或者说是主人。公民们由于日益平等而变得越来越没有能力,如果他们不联合起来就不会在工业方面有任何作为;但是,政府自然想把他们的联合组织掌握在自己的控制中。

应当承认,被称为合伙组织的这种集体,比个人更加强大和更加可怕,但对自己的行为却承担很小的责任。因此,不让它们像私人那样可以对政府有较大的独立性,似乎是合理的。

统治者们也越来越倾向于这种政策,因为他们的喜好就在于此。在民主国家里,公民只有通过联合,才能有效地抵制中央政权,所以中央政府从来不喜欢不受它控制的结社。但是,特别值得指出的是,在民主国家里,公民们却往往在内心里对他们本来

其持续监控。如果业主难以控制,他们将会被政府法庭剥夺其经营权,并将其矿产交给他人管理。所以,政府不仅拥有矿产,还有对所有工作人员的控制权。不过,随着工业增长,对旧矿开发的增加,以及新矿的不断涌出,使矿业的人数不断扩大和增长。各国政府也日益扩大对地下领土及人民和代理的统治。

worthy of remark that among democratic nations the people themselves often entertain against these very associations a secret feeling of fear and jealousy, which prevents the citizens from defending the institutions of which they stand so much in need. The power and the duration of these small private bodies in the midst of the weakness and instability of the whole community astonish and alarm the people, and the free use which each association makes of its natural powers is almost regarded as a dangerous privilege. All the associations that spring up in our age are, moreover, new corporate powers, whose rights have not been sanctioned by time; they come into existence at a time when the notion of private rights is weak and when the power of government is unbounded. Hence it is not surprising that they lose their freedom at their birth.

Among all European nations there are some kinds of associations or companies which cannot be formed until the state has examined their by-laws and authorized their existence. In several others attempts are made to extend this rule to all associations; the consequences of such a policy, if it were successful, may easily be foreseen.

If once the sovereign had a general right of authorizing associations of all kinds upon certain conditions, he would not be long without claiming the right of superintending and managing them, in order to prevent them from departing from the rules laid down by himself. In this manner the state, after having reduced all who are desirous of forming associations into dependence, would proceed to reduce into the same condition all who belong to associations already formed; that is to say, almost all the men who are now in existence.

Governments thus appropriate to themselves and convert to their own purposes the greater part of this new power which manufacturing interests have in our time brought into the world. Manufactures govern us, they govern manufactures.

I attach so much importance to all that I have just been saying that I am tormented by the fear of having impaired my meaning in seeking to render it more clear. If the reader thinks that the examples I have adduced to support my observations are insufficient or ill-chosen, if he imagines that I have anywhere exaggerated the encroachments of the supreme power, and, on the other hand, that I have underrated the extent of the sphere which still remains open to the exertions of individual independence, I entreat him to lay down the book for a moment and to turn his mind to reflect upon the subjects I have

很需要的结社怀有恐惧感和嫉妒感,从而阻止了他们保卫需要结成的社团。这些私人小团体在整个社会的普遍软弱和不稳定性中的权力和长期存在,使公民们感到吃惊和不安,所以不得不将每个团体自由应用其能力看作是一种危险的特权。另外,所有在我们这个时代出现的社团,都是新式的社团力量,它们的权力还没有得到时间的认可;它们是在个人权力的观念微弱时和国家权力无限大的时代出生的。因此,它们自出世以后就没有自由,是不足为奇的。

在所有的欧洲国家,有几种类型的社团或组织在不经国家审查其章程和批准其成立的情况下是不能创设的。有些国家正努力把这套办法扩大到所有种类的社团上。如果成功的话,这种办法的后果是很容易被预见的。

一旦统治者拥有根据一定的条件批准各种社团成立的权力,他不久就会要求监督和管理这些社团的权力,以阻止社团背离他所定的规则。在这种情况下,国家在限制了所有渴望形成独立的社团后,还将继续限制那些属于已经成立社团的人。也就是说,几乎要把现在所有存在的人都限制起来。

各国政府就这样逐渐把工业在现今世界创造出来的新力量的大部分转化为自己的利益。工业引领我们,他们引领工业。

对于刚才所讲的一切,我赋予很大的重视,一直害怕在我想把自己的想法好好地表达出来时却没能很好地表达清楚。因此,如果读者认为我所引证的例子不足以或是不能恰当说明我的观点,认为我过度地夸张了中央政权的范围,而在另一方面,又对个人独立仍能活动的范围过于轻视,我恳请读者先暂时放下此书,自己试着回顾一下我努力想向读者说明的东西。让读者仔细考察一下在法国和在其他国家所发生的一切,让读者同周围的人交

attempted to explain. Let him attentively examine what is taking place in France and in other countries, let him inquire of those about him, let him search himself, and I am much mistaken if he does not arrive, without my guidance, and by other paths, at the point to which I have sought to lead him.

He will perceive that, for the last half-century, centralization has everywhere increased in a thousand different ways. Wars, revolutions, conquests, have served to promote it; all men have labored to increase it. In the course of the same period, during which men have succeeded one another with singular rapidity at the head of affairs, their notions, interests, and passions have been infinitely diversified; but all have, by some means or other, sought to centralize. This instinctive centralization has been the only settled point amid the extreme mutability of their lives and their thoughts.

If the reader, after having investigated these details of human affairs, will seek to survey the wide prospect as a whole, he will be struck by the result. On the one hand, the most settled dynasties shaken or overthrown; the people everywhere escaping by violence from the sway of their laws, abolishing or limiting the authority of their rulers or their princes; the nations which are not in open revolution restless at least, and excited, all of them animated by the same spirit of revolt; and, on the other hand, at this very period of anarchy, and among these untractable nations, the incessant increase of the prerogative of the supreme government, becoming more centralized, more adventurous, more absolute, more extensive, the people perpetually falling under the control of the public administration, led insensibly to surrender to it some further portion of their individual independence, till the very men who from time to time upset a throne and trample on a race of kings bend more and more obsequiously to the slightest dictate of a clerk. Thus in our days two contrary revolutions appear to be going on, the one continually weakening the supreme power, the other as continually strengthening it; at no other period in our history has it appeared so weak or so strong.

But upon a more attentive examination of the state of the world, it appears that these two revolutions are intimately connected together,

谈交谈,让读者自己最后深思一下,如果读者没有在我的引导下或通过其他途径而达不到我想引导他去的地方,那就是我大错而特错了。

读者会发觉,在过去的半个世纪中,中央集权已在各处以成千上万种不同的形式增加了。战争、革命、征服都促进了中央集权的发展;所有的人都为增加中央集权出了力。在这个期间,人们一个接着一个地以异常快的速度相继主持事务,他们的观点、利益和感情都经历着无穷的变化;但所有人都想以某种方式或其他方式实行中央集权。中央集权的本性就好像是他们的生活和思想的多端变化中的唯一一个。

如果读者在研究完人间诸事的这些细节之后,会再综观一下全景,这时他会为结果吃惊。一方面,最牢固的王朝已经被动摇和被颠覆;各国人民以暴力推翻他们国王的统治,废除或限制他们的领主或君主的权威;没有发生革命的各国至少也得不到安宁,人人都受到同样的造反精神的鼓舞而兴奋。另一方面,在这个无政府状态的特别时期,在人民如此不驯服的国家里,最高政府的特权却在不断扩大,并日益集权化,日益胆大妄为,日益走向专制,日益扩大范围;而公民永远都处于国家行政机关的控制下,每天都在不知不觉之中将自己的独立一点一点地让给国家,那些刚刚推翻王权和践踏国王的人,现在却越来越趋于对新政权的一个小办事员的微小的指令都不敢违背。因此,在我们这个时代,似乎有两种截然相反的革命在进行着:一种革命在持续不断地削弱政权,而另一种革命则在继续巩固政权;在我们的历史上,没有一个时期的政权会如此软弱,或如此强大。

但是,在更仔细地研究过整个世界的状况后,便会发现这两

that they originate in the same source, and that, after having followed a separate course, they lead men at last to the same result.

I may venture once more to repeat what I have already said or implied in several parts of this book: great care must be taken not to confound the principle of equality itself with the revolution which finally establishes that principle in the social condition and the laws of a nation. Here lies the reason for almost all the phenomena that occasion our astonishment.

All the old political powers of Europe, the greatest as well as the least, were founded in ages of aristocracy, and they more or less represented or defended the principles of inequality and of privilege. To make the novel wants and interests which the growing principle of equality introduced preponderate in government, our contemporaries had to overturn or to coerce the established powers. This led men to make revolutions and breathed into many of them that fierce love of disturbance and independence which all revolutions, whatever be their object, always engender. I do not believe that there is a single country in Europe in which the progress of equality has not been preceded or followed by some violent changes in the state of property and persons; and almost all these changes have been attended with much anarchy and license, because they have been made by the least civilized portion of the nation against that which is most civilized.

Hence proceeded the twofold contrary tendencies that I have just pointed out. As long as the democratic revolution was glowing with heat, the men who were bent upon the destruction of old aristocratic powers hostile to that revolution displayed a strong spirit of independence; but as the victory of the principle of equality became more complete, they gradually surrendered themselves to the propensities natural to that condition of equality, and they strengthened and centralized their governments. They had sought to be free in order to make themselves equal; but in proportion as equality was more established by the aid of freedom, freedom itself was thereby rendered more difficult of attainment.

These two states of a nation have sometimes been contemporaneous: the last generation in France showed how a people might organize a stupendous tyranny in the community at the very time when they were baffling the authority of the nobility and braving the power of all kings, at once teaching the world the way to win freedom and the way

种革命是密切地联系在一起的,它们有着同样的来源,虽然路线不同,但最后都把人引向同一结果。

我又一次大胆重复我在本书许多地方已经说过和指出的一点:一定要注意不能把平等的原则与把平等带进社会情况和法制的革命混淆在一起。而人们之所以对所见的几乎一切现象表示惊讶,原因就在于此。

欧洲所有的古老的政治权力,无论是最强大的还是最弱小的,都建立于贵族时代,它们都或多或少地代表或维护不平等和特权的原则。为了使平等原则的日益增长所带来的新需要和新利益在政府中占居优势,我们同时代的人不得不推翻和压迫已建立的政权。这就促使人们要进行革命,使其中的大多数人产生无论以什么为目的的革命都总要具有的那种敢于闹事和热爱独立的激情。我认为,无论是欧洲的哪一个国家,都是经过财产和人的情况的激烈变化之后或紧接着这种变化,才使平等发展起来的,而且几乎所有的这种变化都伴随着严重的无政府状态和放纵行为,因为这些变化是国内的那些反对文明的人的缺乏文明的人创造的。

因此,这就产生了我刚才指出的那两个完全相反的倾向。只要民主革命继续升温,那些倾向于摧毁敌对民主革命的老的贵族政权的人,便会表现出巨大的独立精神,并随着平等的胜利,而逐渐完全地投降于这个平等所产生的自然本性,努力加强和集中其中央政权。他们本来想寻求自由以使自己平等;但随着平等在自由的帮助下得到进一步发展,自由本身就更难达到了。

国家的这两种情况有时可能同时发生:在法国,上一代人就曾经表示过一个民族在打击贵族的权威和藐视国王的权力的同时能够在国内建立巨大的暴政,在教会了世界赢得自由的同时还

to lose it.

In our days men see that constituted powers are crumbling down on every side; they see all ancient authority dying out, all ancient barriers tottering to their fall, and the judgment of the wisest is troubled at the sight: they attend only to the amazing revolution that is taking place before their eyes, and they imagine that mankind is about to fall into perpetual anarchy. If they looked to the final consequences of this revolution, their fears would perhaps assume a different shape. For myself, I confess that I put no trust in the spirit of freedom which appears to animate my contemporaries. I see well enough that the nations of this age are turbulent, but I do not clearly perceive that they are liberal; and I fear lest, at the close of those perturbations which rock the base of thrones, the dominion of sovereigns may prove more powerful than it ever was before.

教会了其失去自由的方法。

在我们这个时代,所有已建立的政权在各个方面都已被粉碎;所有的旧势力正在灭亡,所有的旧障碍正在摇摇欲坠,这种情况使一些见多识广之士感到困惑不解。他们只注意发生在他们眼前的不可思议的革命,认为人类将因此陷入永远的无政府状态。如果他们再观望这场革命的最终结果,他们的恐惧或许会增加。至于我,我承认我并不相信那种似乎在鼓舞当代人的自由精神。我清楚地看到当代国家都处在动乱中,但我并不认为它们是自由的;而是担心在动摇王权的那些动乱接近尾声时,统治者们会得到比以前更为强大的权力。

CHAPTER VI
What Sort Of Despotism
Democratic Nations Have To Fear

I had remarked during my stay in the United States that a democratic state of society, similar to that of the Americans, might offer singular facilities for the establishment of despotism; and I perceived, upon my return to Europe, how much use had already been made, by most of our rulers, of the notions, the sentiments, and the wants created by this same social condition, for the purpose of extending the circle of their power. This led me to think that the nations of Christendom would perhaps eventually undergo some oppression like that which hung over several of the nations of the ancient world.

A more accurate examination of the subject, and five years of further meditation, have not diminished my fears, but have changed their object.

No sovereign ever lived in former ages so absolute or so powerful as to undertake to administer by his own agency, and without the assistance of intermediate powers, all the parts of a great empire; none ever attempted to subject all his subjects indiscriminately to strict uniformity of regulation and personally to tutor and direct every member of the community. The notion of such an undertaking never occurred to the human mind; and if any man had conceived it, the want of information, the imperfection of the administrative system, and, above all, the natural obstacles caused by the inequality of conditions would speedily have checked the execution of so vast a design.

When the Roman emperors were at the height of their power, the different nations of the empire still preserved usages and customs of great diversity; although they were subject to the same monarch, most

第六章　民主国家害怕哪种专制

在我留美期间，就已经注意到，像美国那样的民主社会情况，会为专制的建立提供非常便利的条件；在我回欧洲后，我发现欧洲的大部分君主已在利用这种社会情况所产生的思想、感情和需要去扩大他们的权力范围。这使我感到，基督教国家最终或许也会承受类似古代的一些国家曾经受到过的某种压力。

对这个问题进行的精确的考察，以及五年来更进一步的思考，都没有减轻我的担心，但却改变了我担心的对象。

在以往的时代，没有一个君主会如此专制地和如此强大地能够不用次级君主政权的帮助而亲自管理一个大帝国的所有部分；也没有一位君主曾试图不加选择地让他的子民一律严格遵守统一的制度，或亲自辅导或直接指导国家的每个臣民。人的头脑里从来没有产生过这个念头；即使有人产生过这个想法，知识的不足，管理方法的不完整性，特别是身份不平等带来的自然障碍，也要使他很快停止实行如此庞大的计划。

在罗马帝国处于势力鼎盛的时期时，居住在罗马帝国里的不同民族仍然保持各自不同的习惯和风俗；虽然它们受控于同一君主，但大部分地区实行独自管理，拥有许多有力的和积极的自治城市；虽然对帝国的整个统治都被集中在皇帝一个人手里，必要

of the provinces were separately administered; they abounded in powerful and active municipalities; and although the whole government of the empire was centered in the hands of the Emperor alone and he always remained, in case of need, the supreme arbiter in all matters, yet the details of social life and private occupations lay for the most part beyond his control. The emperors possessed, it is true, an immense and unchecked power, which allowed them to gratify all their whimsical tastes and to employ for that purpose the whole strength of the state. They frequently abused that power arbitrarily to deprive their subjects of property or of life; their tyranny was extremely onerous to the few, but it did not reach the many; it was confined to some few main objects and neglected the rest; it was violent, but its range was limited.

It would seem that if despotism were to be established among the democratic nations of our days, it might assume a different character; it would be more extensive and more mild; it would degrade men without tormenting them. I do not question that, in an age of instruction and equality like our own, sovereigns might more easily succeed in collecting all political power into their own hands and might interfere more habitually and decidedly with the circle of private interests than any sovereign of antiquity could ever do. But this same principle of equality which facilitates despotism tempers its rigor. We have seen how the customs of society become more humane and gentle in proportion as men become more equal and alike. When no member of the community has much power or much wealth, tyranny is, as it were, without opportunities and a field of action. As all fortunes are scanty, the passions of men are naturally circumscribed, their imagination limited, their pleasures simple. This universal moderation moderates the sovereign himself and checks within certain limits the inordinate stretch of his desires.

Independently of these reasons, drawn from the nature of the state of society itself, I might add many others arising from causes beyond my subject; but I shall keep within the limits I have laid down.

Democratic governments may become violent and even cruel at certain periods of extreme effervescence or of great danger, but these crises will be rare and brief. When I consider the petty passions of our contemporaries, the mildness of their manners, the extent of their

时皇帝总是享有对一切事情的专断权,但社会生活的细节和个人的日常生活,一般都不受皇帝的控制。罗马皇帝确实拥有无限巨大的权力,这可以使他们满足自己任何奇特的喜好并因此而动用全国的力量。他们往往滥用这种权力,专横地去剥夺一个公民的财产或生命;他的暴政对某些人来说是极其沉重的压迫,但并未扩及大多数人;暴政只被限制在几个主要的对象中,而不针对于其他人;暴政是残酷的,但它的范围是有限的。

看来,如果在我们今天的民主国家建立专制,那专制将呈现出另一种特性:它的范围将会很大,但它的方法将会很温和;它会在不使人痛苦的情况下使人堕落。我不怀疑,在像我们今天这样的文明和平等的时代,统治者们可能比古代的任何一个统治者更容易把一切政治权力集中在自己手里,会更习惯和更坚决地介入到私人利益中。但是,这个便于专制的平等的原则,又能缓和专制的严厉性。我们知道,随着人们的日益平等和日益相似,社会的民情会更加具有人情味和更加温和。当没有一个公民具有巨大的权力和巨大的财富时,专制几乎没有出现的机会和其行动的舞台。如果所有的财富都很缺乏时,人们的激情就自然有所节制,他们的想象,他们的快乐也很简朴。这种普遍的克制也在节制统治者本人,使他的无休止伸展的欲望也被限定在一定范围内。

除了这些来自社会本身的自然原因以外,我还可以举出许多其他的超越本书主题的例子;但是,我需要保留在我所规定的范围内。

民主政府在极度活跃和出现重大危机的一定时期可能变得暴力,甚至是残忍,但这种危险是少见的和短暂的。当我一想到同时代人的温和的激情,温顺的品行,知识的广泛,对宗教的虔

education, the purity of their religion, the gentleness of their morality, their regular and industrious habits, and the restraint which they almost all observe in their vices no less than in their virtues, I have no fear that they will meet with tyrants in their rulers, but rather with guardians. [1]

I think, then, that the species of oppression by which democratic nations are menaced is unlike anything that ever before existed in the world; our contemporaries will find no prototype of it in their memories. I seek in vain for an expression that will accurately convey the whole of the idea I have formed of it; the old words *despotism* and *tyranny* are inappropriate: the thing itself is new, and since I cannot name, I must attempt to define it.

I seek to trace the novel features under which despotism may appear in the world. The first thing that strikes the observation is an innumerable multitude of men, all equal and alike, incessantly endeavoring to procure the petty and paltry pleasures with which they glut their lives. Each of them, living apart, is as a stranger to the fate of all the rest; his children and his private friends constitute to him the whole of mankind. As for the rest of his fellow citizens, he is close to them, but he does not see them; he touches them, but he does not feel them; he exists only in himself and for himself alone; and if his kindred still remain to him, he may be said at any rate to have lost his country.

Above this race of men stands an immense and tutelary power, which takes upon itself alone to secure their gratifications and to watch over their fate. That power is absolute, minute, regular, provident, and mild. It would be like the authority of a parent if, like that authority, its object was to prepare men for manhood; but it seeks, on the contrary, to keep them in perpetual childhood: it is well content

---

[1] See Appendix AA.

诚,良好的道德,有序而勤奋的习惯,及其他们明辨善恶的能力,我就不担心他们将受到暴君的统治,而主要害怕他们的监护人变成他们的统治者。①

因此我认为,使民主国家受到威胁的那种压迫,不同于至今世界上所出现过的任何压迫;我们同时代的人不会在他们的记忆中找到这种压迫的原型。我曾试图用一个词精确地表达我对这种压迫所形成的完整观念,但是没有成功;那些古老的关于专制或暴政的词汇都不适用。这个事物本身是崭新的,所以在不能定名以前,就得努力说明它的特点。

我想寻找这种专制再现于世界所出现的新特点。我认为,首先引起注意的是到那时候将出现无数的平等的和相同的人,永无止境地努力追逐他们心中所想的小小的庸俗的快乐。他们中的每个人都离开群体,单独居住,对他人的命运漠不关心;他们认为,他们的子女和亲友就构成了整个人类。至于剩下的其他人,即使站在他们的身旁,他们也不屑一顾;他们虽与这些人接触,但并没有感到这些人的存在;每个人都生活在自我中,并且只是为了自己而生存。如果说他们还有一个家庭,那么在某种程度上可以说他们已经失去了祖国。

在这样的一群人之上,站立着一个只负责保证他们的享乐和监护他们一生命运的拥有无限权力的监护性当局。这个当局的权威是绝对的、无微不至的、有条理的、有远见的,而且是十分和善的。如果说这种权威像是父权,那它的目的就是要教导人们如何长大成人。但是相反地,它却想让人们永远停留在孩童时期。

---

① 　见附录 AA。

that the people should rejoice, provided they think of nothing but rejoicing. For their happiness such a government willingly labors, but it chooses to be the sole agent and the only arbiter of that happiness; it provides for their security, foresees and supplies their necessities, facilitates their pleasures, manages their principal concerns, directs their industry, regulates the descent of property, and subdivides their inheritances: what remains, but to spare them all the care of thinking and all the trouble of living?

Thus it every day renders the exercise of the free agency of man less useful and less frequent; it circumscribes the will within a narrower range and gradually robs a man of all the uses of himself. The principle of equality has prepared men for these things; it has predisposed men to endure them and often to look on them as benefits.

After having thus successively taken each member of the community in its powerful grasp and fashioned him at will, the supreme power then extends its arm over the whole community. It covers the surface of society with a network of small complicated rules, minute and uniform, through which the most original minds and the most energetic characters cannot penetrate, to rise above the crowd. The will of man is not shattered, but softened, bent, and guided; men are seldom forced by it to act, but they are constantly restrained from acting. Such a power does not destroy, but it prevents existence; it does not tyrannize, but it compresses, enervates, extinguishes, and stupefies a people, till each nation is reduced to nothing better than a flock of timid and industrious animals, of which the government is the shepherd.

I have always thought that servitude of the regular, quiet, and gentle kind which I have just described might be combined more easily than is commonly believed with some of the outward forms of freedom, and that it might even establish itself under the wing of the sovereignty of the people. Our contemporaries are constantly excited by two conflicting passions: they want to be led, and they wish to remain free. As they cannot destroy either the one or the other of these contrary propensities, they strive to satisfy them both at once. They devise

它喜欢公民们享乐,而且认为没有什么比享乐更重要了。它愿意努力为公民造福,但它要充当公民幸福的唯一代理人和仲裁者。它可以使公民安全,预见并提供公民的需要,为公民的娱乐提供方便,指挥公民的主要活动,领导公民的工商业,规定公民的遗产继承,分配公民的遗产。而剩下来的,不就是完全不让公民开动脑筋和为生活操劳吗?

因此,每天它都使公民很少运用和不太运用自己的自由意志,把他们的意志限制在很小的范围内,并最终剥夺了每个公民的自我活动能力。平等使人养成了接受这一切的习惯,强迫人们忍受这一切,甚至往往把这一切视为利益。

统治者在把每个人一个一个地控制在自己的权力下,并按照自己的想法塑造他们后,统治者便将手扩向了整个社会。他用一张其中织有详尽的、细微的和全面统一的规则的密网覆盖在社会的表面,即使是最具独创思想和最具坚强意志的人也不能冲破这张网,从而成为出类拔萃的人物。人们的意志并没有被粉碎,但却被软化、驯服和支配着。他不强迫人行动,但却不断限制人行动。这样的一种政权并没有破坏,而只是阻止新生事物的存在。他不实行暴政,但限制和削弱人,使人们颓靡和麻木不仁,最后使全体人民变成一群胆小而只会干活的牲畜,而政府则是牧人。

我一直认为,刚才描述的这种规律的、温和的和平稳的奴役状态,可能比某些人的想象更容易具有自由的外貌,它甚至可以建立在人民主权的幌子下。我们同时代的人经常为两种互相冲突的激情所兴奋:一方面他们需要被人指导,另一方面他们又希望保持自由。因为他们不能破坏这两种相反的倾向中的任何一个,所以他们努力使两者同时得到满足。他们想出一种唯一的、

a sole, tutelary, and all-powerful form of government, but elected by the people. They combine the principle of centralization and that of popular sovereignty; this gives them a respite: they console themselves for being in tutelage by the reflection that they have chosen their own guardians. Every man allows himself to be put in leading-strings, because he sees that it is not a person or a class of persons, but the people at large who hold the end of his chain.

By this system the people shake off their state of dependence just long enough to select their master and then relapse into it again. A great many persons at the present day are quite contented with this sort of compromise between administrative despotism and the sovereignty of the people; and they think they have done enough for the protection of individual freedom when they have surrendered it to the power of the nation at large. This does not satisfy me: the nature of him I am to obey signifies less to me than the fact of extorted obedience.

I do not deny, however, that a constitution of this kind appears to me to be infinitely preferable to one which, after having concentrated all the powers of government, should vest them in the hands of an irresponsible person or body of persons. Of all the forms that democratic despotism could assume, the latter would assuredly be the worst.

When the sovereign is elective, or narrowly watched by a legislature which is really elective and independent, the oppression that he exercises over individuals is sometimes greater, but it is always less degrading; because every man, when he is oppressed and disarmed, may still imagine that, while he yields obedience, it is to himself he yields it, and that it is to one of his own inclinations that all the rest give way. In like manner, I can understand that when the sovereign represents the nation and is dependent upon the people, the rights and the power of which every citizen is deprived serve not only the head of the state, but the state itself; and that private persons derive some return from the sacrifice of their independence which they have made to the public. To create a representation of the people in every centralized country is, therefore, to diminish the evil that extreme centralization may produce, but not to get rid of it.

I admit that, by this means, room is left for the intervention of individuals in the more important affairs; but it is not the less suppressed in the smaller and more privates ones. It must not be forgotten that it is especially dangerous to enslave men in the minor details of life. For my own part, I should be inclined to think free

具有监护性的、全能的,但要由公民选举的权力机构。他们把中央集权和人民主权结合起来。这就使他们有了一定的缓解:他们认为是由他们自己选举监护人,所以安于被监护。每个人都能忍受捆在身上的链子,因为他们看到握着链子的末端的不是一个人或一个阶级,而是人民自己。

通过这种制度,公民刚刚摆脱从属的状态后,由于为自己指定了主人而又陷入到原来的地位。现今,有很多人都满足于行政专制与人民主权之间的这种妥协,认为把个人自由完全托付给国家时,就为保护个人自由做了很大的努力。这一点并不能使我满足:在我看来,主人的本性远远不如服从的事实重要。

但是我并不否认,这种政体远比那种把一切权力集中之后交给一个不负责任的人或团体管理的政体好得多。在民主的专制可能采取的所有形式中,后一种政体无疑是最坏的。

当国家的元首是通过真正的选举并在独立的立法机构的监督下选举产生的时候,他对个人的压迫有时会更大,但这种压迫经常很少使人名誉扫地,因为当每个人在受到压迫和侮辱的时候,还会认为自己在表示服从时等于服从自己,并且是他自己的倾向想要放弃一切。我也可以理解,在国家元首代表国家并依赖于人民时,剥夺每个公民的权力和力量不仅为国家元首服务,也为国家本身服务,而个人为公牺牲自己的独立也会得到某些补偿。因此,在每个集权的国家里建立国民代表制度,可以减少极端中央集权可能产生的弊端,但不能彻底根除弊端。

我承认,通过这种办法可以为个人参与国家更为重要的事件留有空间,但很少能对小事和私人事件产生影响。但我们一定不能忘记使人在很细微的小事上受奴役是很危险的。至于我,既然看到两

dom less necessary in great things than in little ones, if it were possible to be secure of the one without possessing the other.

Subjection in minor affairs breaks out every day and is felt by the whole community indiscriminately. It does not drive men to resistance, but it crosses them at every turn, till they are led to surrender the exercise of their own will. Thus their spirit is gradually broken and their character enervated; whereas that obedience which is exacted on a few important but rare occasions only exhibits servitude at certain intervals and throws the burden of it upon a small number of men. It is in vain to summon a people who have been rendered so dependent on the central power to choose from time to time the representatives of that power; this rare and brief exercise of their free choice, however important it may be, will not prevent them from gradually losing the faculties of thinking, feeling, and acting for themselves, and thus gradually falling below the level of humanity.

I add that they will soon become incapable of exercising the great and only privilege which remains to them. The democratic nations that have introduced freedom into their political constitution at the very time when they were augmenting the despotism of their administrative constitution have been led into strange paradoxes. To manage those minor affairs in which good sense is all that is wanted, the people are held to be unequal to the task; but when the government of the country is at stake, the people are invested with immense powers; they are alternately made the playthings of their ruler, and his masters, more than kings and less than men. After having exhausted all the different modes of election without finding one to suit their purpose, they are still amazed and still bent on seeking further; as if the evil they notice did not originate in the constitution of the country far more than in that of the electoral body.

It is indeed difficult to conceive how men who have entirely given up the habit of self-government should succeed in making a proper choice of those by whom they are to be governed; and no one

者不能兼顾而只能顾一方,那就只有认为大事之需要自由不如小事之需要自由。

在小事上出现的服从每天都会发生,而且所有的公民都能同样感受到。这种服从并没有使公民一致抵抗,但它一直限制公民的行动,直到使公民完全放弃用自己的意志。于是,公民的精神在逐渐被控制,特性也日益被抹去;然而,只被要求在少数的情况所必需的服从虽然非常严格,但极为稀少,而且绝不同于奴役,它只是把负担扔给一些特定的人。号召曾经如此依附于中央政权的公民如今又去选举这个政权的代表是无用的;让公民们如此少见的而又如此短暂地行使自己的自由意志,不管它有多么重要,也防止不了他们逐渐失去独立思考、独自感受和独立行动的能力,只能使他们慢慢下降到人类的一般水平之下。

我再补充一点:他们很快就将失去行使他们仅有的重大的和唯一的特权的能力。当民主国家在把自由引进政治领域和加强行政领域的专制以后,必然产生一些非常矛盾的现象。一些只凭常识就可以处理的小事,它却认为公民没有能力办理,而要亲自承揽起来;但当国家政府处于危急时刻时,它又赋予公民以无限特权。于是,它有时会把主权视为自己的玩具,有时又会视主权为自己的主人;而国家元首的权力有时比国王还大,有时又不如普通老百姓。在经过了各种选举制度后,为始终没能找到适合自己的而感到吃惊,但又接着去找,好像它所发现的弊端不是来自本国的政治制度,而是来自选举制度。

我们确实很难想象那些完全放弃了自治习惯的人,能够很好地选举出将要治理他们的人;也没有人会认为处于奴隶

will ever believe that a liberal, wise, and energetic government can spring from the suffrages of a subservient people. ①

A constitution republican in its head and ultra-monarchical in all its other parts has always appeared to me to be a shortlived monster. The vices of rulers and the ineptitude of the people would speedily bring about its ruin; and the nation, weary of its representatives and of itself, would create freer institutions or soon return to stretch itself at the feet of a single master.

---

① See Appendix BB.

状态的人民有一天会选出一个自由的、精干的和精力充沛的政府。①

对我来说,上层为共和制的而其余部分为极端君主制的政体始终是个短命的魔鬼。统治者的缺点和人民的无能,很快会打倒这个魔鬼;而厌烦了自己和自己的代表的人民,不是创造出更自由的制度,便是不久又伏在一个独夫的脚下。

---

① 见附录 BB。

CHAPTER VII
Continuation Of The Preceding Chapters

I Believe that it is easier to establish an absolute and despotic government among a people in which the conditions of society are equal than among any other; and I think that if such a government were once established among such a people, it not only would oppress men, but would eventually strip each of them of several of the highest qualities of humanity. Despotism, therefore, appears to me peculiarly to be dreaded in democratic times. I should have loved freedom, I believe, at all times, but in the time in which we live I am ready to worship it.

On the other hand, I am persuaded that all who attempt, in the ages upon which we are entering, to base freedom upon aristocratic privilege will fail; that all who attempt to draw and to retain authority within a single class will fail. At the present day no ruler is skillful or strong enough to found a despotism by re-establishing permanent distinctions of rank among his subjects; no legislator is wise or powerful enough to preserve free institutions if he does not take equality for his first principle and his watchword. All of our contemporaries who would establish or secure the independence and the dignity of their fellow men must show themselves the friends of equality; and the only worthy means of showing themselves as such is to be so: upon this depends the success of their holy enterprise. Thus the question is not how to reconstruct aristocratic society, but how to make liberty proceed out of that democratic state of society in which God has placed us.

These two truths appear to me simple, clear, and fertile in consequences; and they naturally lead me to consider what kind of free government can be established among a people in which social conditions are equal.

第七章　以上各章的延续

我认为在社会身份平等的国家比在其他国家更容易建立绝对专制的政府；并且我还认为一旦在这样的国家建立起这样的政府，那它不但要压迫人民，而且要永久剥夺人类的一些最高品质。因此，我认为专制在民主时代特别让人恐惧。我相信我在任何时候都是爱自由的，而在我们生活的这个时代，我甚至想崇拜它。

另一方面，我相信在我们即将进入的时代，那些试图以贵族特权作为基础的人，都会失败；那些想在单一的阶级里建立并保持权威的人，也终究会失败。在现今这个时代，没有一个统治者有足够的能力和足够的力量以重新建立臣民之间的永久差别的办法来建立专制；也没有一个立法者有足够的智慧和足够的权力能不以平等作为自己的第一原则和格言而维护自由制度。因此，如果我们同时代的所有人，想要确立和保护自己的同类的独立和尊严时，就必须表明自己是平等的朋友，而能够证明自己是平等的朋友的唯一办法，就是平等待人。也正是这一点决定了他们事业的成败。因此，问题不在于怎样重建贵族社会，而在于从上帝安排给我们的民主社会的内部发掘自由。

在我看来，这两个事实是简单的，清楚的，而且是会有成效的；它们自然使我要去考察的哪种自由政府可以建立于身份平等的国家。

It results from the very constitution of democratic nations and from their necessities that the power of government among them must be more uniform, more centralized, more extensive, more searching, and more efficient than in other countries. Society at large is naturally stronger and more active, the individual more subordinate and weak; the former does more, the latter less; and this is inevitably the case.

It is not, therefore, to be expected that the range of private independence will ever be so extensive in democratic as in aristocratic countries; nor is this to be desired; for among aristocratic nations the mass is often sacrificed to the individual, and the prosperity of the greater number to the greatness of the few. It is both necessary and desirable that the government of a democratic people should be active and powerful; and our object should not be to render it weak or indolent, but solely to prevent it from abusing its aptitude and its strength.

The circumstance which most contributed to secure the independence of private persons in aristocratic ages was that the supreme power did not affect to take upon itself alone the government and administration of the community. Those functions were necessarily partially left to the members of the aristocracy; so that, as the supreme power was always divided, it never weighed with its whole weight and in the same manner on each individual.

Not only did the government not perform everything by its immediate agency, but as most of the agents who discharged its duties derived their power, not from the state, but from the circumstance of their birth, they were not perpetually under its control. The government could not make or unmake them in an instant, at pleasure, or bend them in strict uniformity to its slightest caprice; this was an additional guarantee of private independence.

I readily admit that recourse cannot be had to the same means at the present time, but I discover certain democratic expedients that may be substituted for them. Instead of vesting in the government alone all the administrative powers of which guilds and nobles have been deprived, a portion of them may be entrusted to secondary public bodies temporarily composed of private citizens: thus the liberty of private persons will be more secure, and their equality will not be diminished. The Americans, who care less for words than the French, still designate by the name of County the largest of their administrative districts; but the duties of the count or lord-lieutenant are in part performed by a provincial assembly.

在民主国家,是民主国家的制度本身和国家的需要,使得其政府的权力要比其他国家更一致、更集中、更广泛、更透彻和更有效。它的社会自然比较强壮和活跃,而个人则比较次要和软弱;也就是说,社会做的事情多,个人做的事情少;并且这种情况是不可避免的。

因此,不要期望个人独立的范围在民主国家里会像在贵族制国家里那样广泛;而且这也不是人们所渴望的;因为在贵族国家里社会经常因为个人的利益而作出牺牲,大多数人的荣华往往让步于少数人的富贵。使民主国家的政府积极和强大,既是必需的,又是人们所希望的;我们的目的不是让中央政权变得软弱无力或懒惰,但要阻止它滥用其机智和权力。

在贵族时代,最有利于确保个人独立的因素,是君主不独揽治理公民的任务。这项任务被部分地交给贵族的成员,所以中央政权总是分权的,从不以整个权力和同样的管理方式来对待每个人。

不仅君主不通过他的直接代理控制一切事情,就连他的大部分代理也不总是受他的控制,因为他们的权力并非来自君主,而是来自他们的家庭出身。君主任何时候都不能任意设置或废除这些官职,也不能强迫他们严格服从他的随意的想法。这对个人的独立也起到了额外的保护作用。

我十分清楚,在现今这个时代不能求助于这样的办法,但我想出一些可以取代这种办法的民主措施。把从各种自治团体或贵族收回的所有管理权不完全交给主权者,而部分地分给由普通公民临时组成的次级团体。于是,个人的自由将会有更多保障,而他们的平等也不会被减弱。美国人很少注重对词语的应用,这一点不像法国人,他们仍用县一词来表示州以下的最大行政单位,但它的一部分职权却由州议会来执行。

At a period of equality like our own, it would be unjust and unreasonable to institute hereditary officers; but there is nothing to prevent us from substituting elective public officers to a certain extent. Election is a democratic expedient, which ensures the independence of the public officer in relation to the government as much as hereditary rank can ensure it among aristocratic nations, and even more so.

Aristocratic countries abound in wealthy and influential persons who are competent to provide for themselves and who cannot be easily or secretly oppressed; such persons restrain a government within general habits of moderation and reserve. I am well aware that democratic countries contain no such persons naturally, but something analogous to them may be created by artificial means. I firmly believe that an aristocracy cannot again be founded in the world, but I think that private citizens, by combining together, may constitute bodies of great wealth, influence, and strength, corresponding to the persons of an aristocracy. By this means many of the greatest political advantages of aristocracy would be obtained without its injustice or its dangers. An association for political, commercial, or manufacturing purposes, or even for those of science and literature, is a powerful and enlightened member of the community, which cannot be disposed of at pleasure or oppressed without remonstrance, and which, by defending its own rights against the encroachments of the government, savesthe common liberties of the country.

In periods of aristocracy every man is always bound so closely to many of his fellow citizens that he cannot be assailed without their coming to his assistance. In ages of equality every man naturally stands alone; he has no hereditary friends whose co-operation he may demand, no class upon whose sympathy he may rely; he is easily got rid of, and he is trampled on with impunity. At the present time an oppressed member of the community has therefore only one method of self-defense: he may appeal to the whole nation, and if the whole nation is deaf to his complaint, he may appeal to mankind. The only means he has of making this appeal is by the press. Thus the liberty of the press is infinitely more valuable among democratic nations than among all others; it is the only cure for the evils that equality may

　　像在我们这样的平等时代,设立世袭的官员是不公正的和不合理的,但没有什么能阻碍我们在一定的范围内以选举办法选用官员。选举是一种民主的办法,它可以保证选出的官员会像贵族国家的世袭官员那样,对中央政权具有独立性,甚至超过世袭官员的独立性。

　　贵族国家有许多有钱人和有一定影响力的人,他们能够足够负担起自己的生活,不会轻易忍受压迫或受压迫而不反抗。这些人可使政府具有一般习惯上的温和的态度与谨慎的作风。我完全知道,民主国家自然不会有这样的人,但它可以人为地创造出某种类似的人物。我深信,世界上不会再建立又一个贵族制度,但我认为,如果把公民联合在一起,就有可能建立非常富裕、非常有影响、非常强大的社团,也就是建立具有贵族性质的人。这样,他们就可以不在贵族制度的不公正和危险下,获得很多贵族性质的重大政治好处。以政治、商业和工业为目的的社团,甚至是科学和文艺的社团,都像是既有力量又有知识的公民,它们不能被随意限制或被暗中加以迫害,它们在维护自己的权益而反对政府的无理要求的时候,也保护了全体公民的自由。

　　在贵族时代,每个人都与其他的同胞有着密切的联系,因而他们一受到攻击,这些人就会来帮助他。在平等时代,每个人自然是孤立的;他们既没有可以合作的世代相传的朋友,又没有确实能够给予他们同情的阶级;他们容易被人置之不理,被人随意践踏。因此,在现今这个时代,公民只有一种方法可以保护自己不受压迫:这就是他可以向全国呼吁,如果国人对他的抗议置之不理,他则可以全人类呼吁。他们用来进行呼吁的唯一方法就是报刊。因此,出版自由在民主国家比在其他国家都更加无限珍贵,它是可以救治平等可能产生的大部分弊端的唯一手段。平等

produce. Equality sets men apart and weakens them; but the press places a powerful weapon within every man's reach, which the weakest and loneliest of them all may use. Equality deprives a man of the support of his connections, but the press enables him to summon all his fellow countrymen and all his fellow men to his assistance. Printing has accelerated the progress of equality, and it is also one of its best correctives.

I think that men living in aristocracies may, strictly speaking, do without the liberty of the press; but such is not the case with those who live in democratic countries. To protect their personal independence I do not trust to great political assemblies, to parliamentary privilege, or to the assertion of popular sovereignty. All these things may, to a certain extent, be reconciled with personal servitude. But that servitude cannot be complete if the press is free; the press is the chief democratic instrument of freedom. Something analogous may be said of the judicial power. It is a part of the essence of judicial power to attend to private interests and to fix itself with predilection on minute objects submitted to its observation. Another essential quality of judicial power is never to volunteer its assistance to the oppressed, but always to be at the disposal of the humblest of those who solicit it; their complaint, however feeble they may themselves be, will force itself upon the ear of justice and claim redress, for this is inherent in the very constitution of courts of justice.

A power of this kind is therefore peculiarly adapted to the wants of freedom, at a time when the eye and finger of the government are constantly intruding into the minutest details of human actions, and when private persons are at once too weak to protect themselves and too much isolated for them to reckon upon the assistance of their fellows. The strength of the courts of law has always been the greatest security that can be offered to personal independence; but this is more especially the case in democratic ages. Private rights and interests are in constant danger if the judicial power does not grow more extensive and stronger to keep pace with the growing equality of conditions.

Equality awakens in men several propensities extremely dangerous to freedom, to which the attention of the legislator ought constantly be directed. I shall only remind the reader of the most important among them.

使人孤立并使人软弱,但报刊是在每个人都可以达到的并能被最软弱和最孤立的人利用的最有力的武器。平等使每个人失去其亲友的支援,但报刊可以使他们唤回自己国家公民和全人类的援助。印刷术促进了平等的发展,而同时又是平等的最好缓和剂之一。

严格地讲,我认为,生活在贵族国家的人民可以不要出版自由,而生活在民主国家的人却不能如此。我不相信大规模的政治集会、议会的特权和人民主权的宣言能够保护民主国家人民的独立。所有这一切,在一定程度内可以和解个人的奴役状态。但如果出版是自由的,这种奴役就不可能完整。报刊是保护自由的主要民主手段。我现在要谈一谈有着类似作用的司法权。参与私人的权益纠纷和仔细研究所处理的每一件小事,属于司法权的本质;对受压迫的人不主动进行援助,但对其中的最微贱者不断进行援助,也是司法权的本质。这些人的控诉,也由于这些人本身的软弱无能而变得很无力,但也永远能迫使法官听取他们的控诉并要求做出答复。这是受司法权的固有性质所驱使。

因此,当统治者不断监视和干预个人的最细小的行动,当个人又软弱得无法保护自己和孤立得无法得到自己同伴的援助时,司法权特别适用于自由的需要。法院的力量总是可以作为个人独立的最强大保障,而这在民主时代又尤为真实。在民主时代,如果司法权不随着身份的日益平等而更加广泛和强大,个人的权利和利益就永远处于危险状态。

平等使人产生了一些对自由极其有害的倾向,立法者应当将注意力经常放到这一点上。我现在只想向读者谈一谈其中的几个主要倾向。

Men living in democratic ages do not readily comprehend the u-
tility of forms: they feel an instinctive contempt for them, I have elsewhere shown for what reasons. Forms excite their contempt and often
their hatred; as they commonly aspire to none but easy and present
gratifications, they rush onwards to the object of their desires, and the
slightest delay exasperates them. This same temper, carried with
them into political life, renders them hostile to forms, which perpetually retard or arrest them in some of their projects. Yet this objection
which the men of democracies make to forms is the very thing which
renders forms so useful to freedom; for their chief merit is to serve as
a barrier between the strong and the weak, the ruler and the people,
to retard the one and give the other time to look about him. Forms become more necessary in proportion as the government becomes more
active and more powerful, while private persons are becoming more
indolent and more feeble. Thus democratic nations naturally stand
more in need of forms than other nations, and they naturally respect
them less. This deserves most serious attention.

Nothing is more pitiful than the arrogant disdain of most of our
contemporaries for questions of form, for the smallest questions of
form have acquired in our time an importance which they never had
before; many of the greatest interests of mankind depend upon them.
I think that if the statesmen of aristocratic ages could sometimes despise forms with impunity and frequently rise above them, the statesmen to whom the government of nations is now confided ought to treat
the very least among them with respect and not neglect them without
imperious necessity. In aristocracies the observance of forms was superstitious; among us they ought to be kept up with a deliberate and
enlightened deference. Another tendency which is extremely natural
to democratic nations and extremely dangerous is that which leads
them to despise and undervalue the rights of private persons. The attachment that men feel to a right and the respect that they display for
it are generally proportioned to its importance or to the length of time
during which they have enjoyed it. The rights of private persons a-
mong democratic nations are commonly of small importance, of recent
growth, and extremely precarious; the consequence is that they are
often sacrificed without regret and almost always violated without remorse.

生活在民主时代的人,不容易理解规章制度的有利性,并对规章有一种本能的轻视,我已经在其他地方讲过其原因。规章常常引起他们的蔑视,并常常遭到他们的憎恨。由于他们通常是不顾一切,而只在乎眼前的享乐,所以便匆匆地奔向他们所追求的每一享乐对象,稍有延误就会使他们愤怒。把这种性格带进政治生活以后,便对时常拖延或阻止他们实现某些计划的规章持有敌对情绪。但是,规章对生活在民主时代的人的这种阻碍,恰恰是规章有利于自由的地方,因为规章的主要功用就是要成为强者和弱者之间、统治者和被统治者之间的一道屏障,阻止一方的行动,而使另一方有时间再好好考虑对策。随着统治者更加积极和更加强大,个人日益孤立和软弱,规章变得更为必需。因此,民主国家的人民本来比其他国家的人民更需要规章,但他们却又很自然地不太尊重规章。这是一个值得认真注意的问题。

再没有什么事情比大部分当代人盲目轻视规章的问题更可悲的了,因为即使是最小的规章问题在现在也具有了以往所没有过的重要性。人类的很多重大的利益都取决于规章问题。我认为,如果生活在贵族时代的政治家有时可以随便轻视规章,并且常常不受规章的约束,那么今天各国的政治家则认为对于最细微的规章都应当尊敬,不到迫不得已时决不能忽视其中任何一点。在贵族制度下,人们有过迷信规章的现象;而我们,则应当对规章采取明智的和审慎的尊重。在民主国家里,另一个非常自然而又非常危险的本能,就是使人轻视和低估了个人的权利。一般说来,人们对一种权利的热爱和对这种权利的尊重,与这种权利的重要性或是它长期被人们享用的时间成正比。民主国家的个人权利一般都不太重要,而且是刚刚成长起来的和非常不稳定的。因此,往往容易被人放弃,受到侵犯也几乎永不怀恨在心。

But it happens that, at the same period and among the same nations in which men conceive a natural contempt for the rights of private persons, the rights of society at large are naturally extended and consolidated; in other words, men become less attached to private rights just when it is most necessary to retain and defend what little remains of them. It is therefore most especially in the present democratic times, that the true friends of the liberty and the greatness of man ought constantly to be on the alert to prevent the power of government from lightly sacrificing the private rights of individuals to the general execution of its designs. At such times no citizen is so obscure that it is not very dangerous to allow him to be oppressed; no private rights are so unimportant that they can be surrendered with impunity to the caprices of a government. The reason is plain: if the private right of an individual is violated at a time when the human mind is fully impressed with the importance and the sanctity of such rights, the injury done is confined to the individual whose right is infringed; but to violate such a right at the present day is deeply to corrupt the manners of the nation and to put the whole community in jeopardy, because the very notion of this kind of right constantly tends among us to be impaired and lost.

There are certain habits, certain notions, and certain vices which are peculiar to a state of revolution and which a protracted revolution cannot fail to create and to propagate, whatever, in other respects, are its character, its purpose, and the scene on which it takes place. When any nation has, within a short space of time, repeatedly varied its rulers, its opinions, and its laws, the men of whom it is composed eventually contract a taste for change and grow accustomed to see all changes effected by sudden violence. Thus they naturally conceive a contempt for forms which daily prove ineffectual; and they do not support without impatience the dominion of rules which they have so often seen infringed.

As the ordinary notions of equity and morality no longer suffice to explain and justify all the innovations daily begotten by a revolution, the principle of public utility is called in, the doctrine of political necessity is conjured up, and men accustom themselves to sacrifice private interests without scruple and to trample on the rights of individuals in order more speedily to accomplish any public purpose.

These habits and notions, which I shall call revolutionary because all

但是,在人们轻视个人权利的那个时代和那个国家,社会权利却自然地扩大和加强了。也就是说,在人们最需要保持和维护仅余的特殊权利的时候,却越来越不爱护它了。因此,特别是在现在的民主时代,人类的自由和伟大的真正的朋友,应当持续不断地处在警戒中,设法防止国家权力为全面推行其计划而随意牺牲某些个人的特殊权利。在这样一个时代,没有一个默默无闻的公民不会有被压迫的危险,也没有什么个人权利会如此微不足道地拱手交给专横的当局。理由很简单:当个人的特殊权利在被人们视为重要的和神圣的权利的时代,侵犯这种权利只会伤害被侵犯的人;但在现今这个时代,侵犯这种权利就是严重败坏国家的民情,并将整个社会置于危险中,因为关于这种权利的观念将在我们中间被削弱,直到消失。

不管革命的性质、目的和其发生的场景是什么,革命的一些特殊的习惯、特殊的思想和特殊的弊病,必然在一个长期的革命当中产生出来,并在全国范围内推广。任何一个国家如果在短期内多次更换首领,改变观念和法制,其人民最终要染上喜欢变动的爱好,并逐渐习惯于突然暴力所产生的一切变动。于是,他们自然会对每天都在表明其无用性的规章产生轻视的态度,只是出于无奈才忍受他们常常看到的被人们违反的法规的约束。

由于关于平等和道德的普通观念已不能解释和论证革命每天都在创造的新鲜事物,所以人们便去追求关于公共事业效益的原则,创造关于政治的必要性的学说,习惯于毫不犹豫地牺牲个人的利益和践踏个人的权利,以求用最快的速度达到他们所设想的一般目的。

我之所以把这些习惯和思想称为革命的习惯和思想,是因为

revolutions produce them, occur in aristocracies just as much as a-
mong democratic nations; but among the former they are often less
powerful and always less lasting, because there they meet with habits,
notions, defects, and impediments that counteract them. They consequently disappear as soon as the revolution is terminated, and the nation reverts to its former political courses. This is not always the case
in democratic countries, in which it is ever to be feared that revolutionary tendencies, becoming more gentle and more regular, without
entirely disappearing from society, will be gradually transformed into
habits of subjection to the administrative authority of the government.
I know of no countries in which revolutions are more dangerous than
in democratic countries, because, independently of the accidental and
transient evils that must always attend them, they may always create
some evils that are permanent and unending.

I believe that there are such things as justifiable resistance and
legitimate rebellion; I do not therefore assert as an absolute proposition that the men of democratic ages ought never to make revolutions;
but I think that they have especial reason to hesitate before they embark on them and that it is far better to endure many grievances in
their present condition than to have recourse to so perilous a remedy.

I shall conclude with one general idea, which comprises not only
all the particular ideas that have been expressed in the present chapter, but also most of those of which it is the object of this book to
treat. In the ages of aristocracy which preceded our own, there were
private persons of great power and a social authority of extreme weakness. The outline of society itself was not easily discernible and was
constantly confounded with the different powers by which the community was ruled. The principal efforts of the men of those times were
required to strengthen, aggrandize, and secure the supreme power;
and, on the other hand, to circumscribe individual independence
within narrower limits and to subject private interests to the interests
of the public. Other perils and other cares await the men of our age.
Among the greater part of modern nations the government, whatever
may be its origin, its constitution, or its name, has become almost
omnipotent, and private persons are falling more and more into the
lowest stage of weakness and dependence.

革命创造了这种习惯和思想。它们既发生在贵族国家,也发生在民主国家,但在前者它们往往是软弱无力的,并且总是不能持久,因为有贵族国家原有的习惯、思想、缺陷和障碍在阻止它们。因此,只要革命一结束,它们就会立即消失,而国家也就又恢复了其原来的政治路线。但民主国家的情况就不总是如此,因为人们总是担心革命的趋势虽然会变得更温和与更有规律,但不会完全从社会中消失,而逐渐转变成政府的统治作风和行政习惯。我不知道还有什么国家的革命比民主国家的革命更危险,因为民主国家的革命除了必然造成一些偶然的和短暂的灾难以外,还经常会制造长期的、也可以说是永久的灾难。

我相信一定会发生公正的抵抗和合理的造反。因此,我不能绝对地断言民主时代的人永远不会革命;但我认为他们在革命前有更多的理由进行思考,并会感到与其求助于如此危险的救治手段,不如忍受目前的种种委屈。

最后,我以一个一般观点来作总结。这个一般观点不仅包括本章所述的所有特别的观点,而且包括本书想要表达的大部分观点。在我们这个世纪以前的贵族时代,个人权力是极其强大的,而社会权威则是十分软弱的。连社会本身的轮廓也很难分辨清楚,经常混淆在统治公民的各式各样的权力之间。因此,这个时代的人的主要努力,就是要去加强、扩大和保护社会权力;另一方面,又要把个人的独立限制在极小的范围内,使个别利益服从公共利益。还有另一种危险和另一种顾虑在等待着我们这个时代的人。在大部分现代国家里,不管统治者是什么出身,身体是否健康,或叫什么名称,他们几乎都是总揽一切大权的;而个人则逐渐陷入最底层,变成最软弱和最有依赖性的人。

In olden society everything was different; unity and uniformity were nowhere to be met with. In modern society everything threatens to become so much alike that the peculiar characteristics of each individual will soon be entirely lost in the general aspect of the world. Our forefathers were always prone to make an improper use of the notion that private rights ought to be respected; and we are naturally prone, on the other hand, to exaggerate the idea that the interest of a private individual ought always to bend to the interest of the many.

The political world is metamorphosed; new remedies must henceforth be sought for new disorders. To lay down extensive but distinct and settled limits to the action of the government; to confer certain rights on private persons, and to secure to them the undisputed enjoyment of those rights; to enable individual man to maintain whatever independence, strength, and original power he still possesses; to raise him by the side of society at large, and uphold him in that position; these appear to me the main objects of legislators in the ages upon which we are now entering.

It would seem as if the rulers of our time sought only to use men in order to make things great; I wish that they would try a little more to make great men; that they would set less value on the work and more upon the workman; that they would never forget that a nation cannot long remain strong when every man belonging to it is individually weak; and that no form or combination of social polity has yet been devised to make an energetic people out of a community of pusillanimous and enfeebled citizens. I trace among our contemporaries two contrary notions which are equally injurious. One set of men can perceive nothing in the principle of equality but the anarchical tendencies that it engenders; they dread their own free agency, they fear themselves. Other thinkers, less numerous but more enlightened, take a different view: beside that track which starts from the principle of equality to terminate in anarchy, they have at last discovered the road that seems to lead men to inevitable servitude. They shape their souls beforehand to this necessary condition; and, despairing of remaining free, they already do

在旧社会里，一切都有所不同。在那里，到处都不会有和谐与统一的景象。在现代社会里，所有的一切都在迫使人们变得越来越相似，以致每个人的个性很快就将完全消失在普遍的万人中间。我们的祖先总是倾向于认为个人的权利应当受到尊重的观点很重要，而我们则自然喜欢夸大个人的利益应当经常服从多数人的利益的观点。

政治世界是会改变的，对于新的弊端我们必须寻找新的办法去救治。给社会权力规定广泛的、明确的、固定的界限，为个人授予一定的权利，并保证他们会不受打扰地享受这项权利，让个人维持少量的独立性、影响力和独创精神，使个人与社会能在最大程度上平等，并在社会面前支持个人；在我看来，这些就是我们行将进入的时代的立法者的主要目标。

现代的统治者们似乎只想率领人民去干伟大的事业。我希望他们应当多考虑一下去造就伟大的人物，应该把少部分的精力放在工作上，而把大多数精力放在工作的人身上，永远要切记当一个国家的每个居民都很软弱的时候，这个国家也不会长久强大下去，而且绝不会找到能使由一群胆怯和萎靡不振的公民组成的国家变成精力充沛国家的社会形式和政治组织。我发现在我们这代人中，有两种对立的但又都同样有害的观念。一些人只从平等中看到它所产生的无政府状态的倾向。他们害怕自己的自由意志，也就是他们自己害怕自己。另一些思考者，虽然人数很少但很有知识，他们则持有另一种看法。他们在由平等出发走向无政府状态的大路旁，终于又发现一条似乎会不可阻挡地使人走向受奴役状态的小路。他们事先就让自己的灵魂适应于这种必然的状况，并由于对保持自由已经绝望，便早就开始从内心屈服于不久就将出现的主人。前一种

obeisance in their hearts to the master who is soon to appear. The former abandon freedom because they think it dangerous; the latter, because they hold it to be impossible.

If I had entertained the latter conviction, I should not have written this book, but I should have confined myself to deploring in secret the destiny of mankind. I have sought to point out the dangers to which the principle of equality exposes the independence of man, because I firmly believe that these dangers are the most formidable as well as the least foreseen of all those which futurity holds in store, but I do not think that they are insurmountable.

The men who live in the democratic ages upon which we are entering have naturally a taste for independence; they are naturally impatient of regulation, and they are wearied by the permanence even of the condition they themselves prefer. They are fond of power, but they are prone to despise and hate those who wield it, and they easily elude its grasp by their own mobility and insignificance.

These propensities will always manifest themselves, because they originate in the groundwork of society, which will undergo no change; for a long time they will prevent the establishment of any despotism, and they will furnish fresh weapons to each succeeding generation that struggles in favor of the liberty of mankind. Let us, then, look forward to the future with that salutary fear which makes men keep watch and ward for freedom, not with that faint and idle terror which depresses and enervates the heart.

人放弃自由是因为他们认为自由很危险,而后一种放弃自由是因为断定自由不可能实现。

如果我持有后一种人的观点,就不会写这本书,而只让自己在内心深处为我们人类的命运表示默哀。我之所以要指出平等给人的独立造成的危害,是因为我坚信这种危害是未来的隐患中最可怕的,而且是最难预测的。但我并不认为它是不可克服的。

生活在我们正在进入的民主时代的人,会自然地爱好独立。他们自然也对规章制度忍无可忍了,即对他们自己选定的社会情况的长久不变感到厌烦。他们喜爱权力,但又轻视和憎恨那些倾向于挥霍权力的人,并由于他们的灵活性并且很渺小,他们则很容易逃脱权力的控制。

这些本性总是会将他们的自我表现出来,因为它们来自将来也不会改变的社会的根基。在一个很长的时期内,它们将会阻止任何一种专制的建立,并向愿意为人的自由而奋斗的每一代新人提供新的武器。因此,让我们以一种有益的担心面对未来,而这种担心可以使人们提高警惕和进行战斗,而不要抱有可以使人们丧失信心和毅力的畏缩无能的恐惧。

CHAPTER VIII
General Survey Of The Subject

Before finally closing the subject that I have now discussed, I should like to take a parting survey of all the different characteristics of modern society and appreciate at last the general influence to be exercised by the principle of equality upon the fate of mankind; but I am stopped by the difficulty of the task, and, in presence of so great a theme, my sight is troubled and my reason fails.

The society of the modern world, which I have sought to delineate and which I seek to judge, has but just come into existence. Time has not yet shaped it into perfect form; the great revolution by which it has been created is not yet over; and amid the occurrences of our time it is almost impossible to discern what will pass away with the revolution itself and what will survive its close. The world that is rising into existence is still half encumbered by the remains of the world that is waning into decay; and amid the vast perplexity of human affairs none can say how much of ancient institutions and former customs will remain or how much will completely disappear.

Although the revolution that is taking place in the social condition, the laws, the opinions, and the feelings of men is still very far from being terminated, yet its results already admit of no comparison with anything that the world has ever before witnessed. I go back from age to age up to the remotest antiquity, but I find no parallel to what is occurring before my eyes; as the past has ceased to throw its light

第八章 对主题的总体概括

在最后完成我所讨论的研究之前,我想对新世界的各种不同面貌进行最后一次综述,并最终判断一下平等对人的命运产生的一般影响。但是,这项工作的艰巨性使我止步了;在如此重大的题目面前,我感到自己的知识水平不够宽阔和自己的智力无法胜任。我试图描绘和打算判断的新社会还只是刚刚诞生。

时间还没有赋予它很好的外形,创造新社会的大革命还没有结束,从现今所发生的一切当中,我们几乎还不能分辨出哪些东西将要随着革命本身的结束而消失,哪些东西在革命结束之后还要存在下去。刚刚存在的世界中,还有一半受到正在衰败的世界的腐朽事务的阻碍,在世间万物的巨大混乱中没有人能说得清楚,有哪些古老的制度和习俗还会保留下来,又有哪些制度和习俗会完全消失。

尽管在社会情况、法制、观念和人的感情方面发生的革命至今还没有结束,但它所产生的后果是世界上以前所发生的任何事情所无法对比的。我一个时代一个时代地向前追溯,一直到最原始的古代,也没有发现任何一个与我现在看到的变化相似的变化。过去已经不再能为未来照明道路,人类的灵魂正在徘徊于黑

upon the future, the mind of man wanders in obscurity.

Nevertheless, in the midst of a prospect so wide, so novel, and so confused, some of the more prominent characteristics may already be discerned and pointed out. The good things and the evils of life are more equally distributed in the world: great wealth tends to disappear, the number of small fortunes to increase; desires and gratifications are multiplied, but extraordinary prosperity and irremediable penury are alike unknown. The sentiment of ambition is universal, but the scope of ambition is seldom vast. Each individual stands apart in solitary weakness, but society at large is active, provident, and powerful; the performances of private persons are insignificant, those of the state immense.

There is little energy of character, but customs are mild and laws humane. If there are few instances of exalted heroism or of virtues of the highest, brightest, and purest temper, men's habits are regular, violence is rare, and cruelty almost unknown. Human existence becomes longer and property more secure; life is not adorned with brilliant trophies, but it is extremely easy and tranquil. Few pleasures are either very refined or very coarse, and highly polished manners are as uncommon as great brutality of tastes. Neither men of great learning nor extremely ignorant communities are to be met with; genius becomes more rare, information more diffused. The human mind is impelled by the small efforts of all mankind combined together, not by the strenuous activity of a few men. There is less perfection, but more abundance, in all the productions of the arts. The ties of race, of rank, and of country are relaxed; the great bond of humanity is strengthened.

If I endeavor to find out the most general and most prominent of all these different characteristics, I perceive that what is taking place in men's fortunes manifests itself under a thousand other forms. Almost all extremes are softened or blunted: all that was most prominent is superseded by some middle term, at once less lofty and less low, less brilliant and less obscure, than what before existed in the world.

When I survey this countless multitude of beings, shaped in each other's likeness, amid whom nothing rises and nothing falls, the sight of such universal uniformity saddens and chills me and I

暗中。

然而，在这片如此广阔、如此新奇和如此混杂的景象中，一些主要的特征总是会被显现出来。人世间的善与恶都非常平等的分布在世界上。拥有巨大财产的人已经不见了，小康之家日益增加。欲求和享受在成倍的增加，但还没有出现空前的繁荣和极端的贫穷。人们普遍都有奋进之心，但胸怀大志者不多。每一个人都是孤立而软弱的，但整个社会是积极的、有远见的和强大有力的。个人都做无意义的小事，而国家做大事。

品质具有很少的力量，但民情温和，立法仁慈。尽管没有伟大的英雄事迹的例子或最高尚、最光辉和最纯洁的德行，但人们的习惯是规律的，很少有暴力现象发生，残酷更是闻所未闻。人的寿命越来越长，人的财富也越来越有保障。生活虽然没有闪亮饰品的装饰，但却非常安逸和舒适。没有什么享乐会既高雅又粗鄙。不讲究繁文缛节，没有低级趣味的嗜好。既没有博学的绅士，也没有极其无知的愚夫。天才越来越少，但知识日益普及。人类所作的微小努力的联合促进了人们思想的发展，而不是某几个人的强大推动的结果。文艺作品的杰作虽然不会太多，但作品的数量将会大增。束缚着种族、等级和国家的各种纽带将会被松开，而人类的大团结却要加强。

如果我努力从这些特征中找出最普遍和最主要的特点，我发现它将表现在财产具有的成千上万种不同的形式方面。几乎所有的极端现象将会日趋减少或消失；所有的最突出的东西都将被中等的东西所取代；这些中等的东西比起世界上存在过的类似东西既不华贵也不低俗，既不光彩也不逊色。

当我审视彼此之间都很相似的芸芸众生，看到在他们中间既没有大起也没有大落时，这种普遍一致的情景真让我感到悲伤和

am tempted to regret that state of society which has ceased to be. When the world was full of men of great importance and extreme insignificance, of great wealth and extreme poverty, of great learning and extreme ignorance, I turned aside from the latter to fix my observation on the former alone, who gratified my sympathies. But I admit that this gratification arose from my own weakness; it is because I am unable to see at once all that is around me that I am allowed thus to select and separate the objects of my predilection from among so many others. Such is not the case with that Almighty and Eternal Being whose gaze necessarily includes the whole of created things and who surveys distinctly, though all at once, mankind and man.

We may naturally believe that it is not the singular prosperity of the few, but the greater well-being of all that is most pleasing in the sight of the Creator and Preserver of men. What appears to me to be man's decline is, to His eye, advancement; what afflicts me is acceptable to Him. A state of equality is perhaps less elevated, but it is more just: and its justice constitutes its greatness and its beauty. I would strive, then, to raise myself to this point of the divine contemplation and thence to view and to judge the concerns of men.

No man on the earth can as yet affirm, absolutely and generally, that the new state of the world is better than its former one; but it is already easy to perceive that this state is different. Some vices and some virtues were so inherent in the constitution of an aristocratic nation and are so opposite to the character of a modern people that they can never be infused into it; some good tendencies and some bad propensities which were unknown to the former are natural to the latter; some ideas suggest themselves spontaneously to the imagination of the one which are utterly repugnant to the mind of the other. They are like two distinct orders of human beings, each of which has its own merits and defects, its own advantages and its own evils. Care must therefore be taken not to judge the state of society that is now coming into existence by notions derived from a state of society that no longer exists; for as these states of society are exceedingly different in their structure, they cannot be submitted to a just or fair comparison. It would be scarcely more reasonable to require of our contemporaries the

心寒,并为这里已不复有社会而遗憾。当世界上充满了最伟大重
要的人和最微不足道的人、最富裕的人和最贫穷的人、最博学的
人和最无知的人的时候,我总把视线离开后者而只看使我看起来
喜欢的前者。但是,我知道这种喜欢来自于我的弱点,因为我不
可能立刻了解在我周围的所有一切,而只能从这么多的对象当中
选择和分离出我最喜欢的对象。这种情况不会发生在全能和永
恒的上帝面前,他必然将目光集中到全体事物上,而且把整个人
类和每一个人都同时看得清清楚楚。

　　我们自然相信,使这位造物主和人类保护者最愉悦的,并不
是个别人的非凡的荣华富贵,而是全体人的巨大幸福。因此,使
我认为是会使人类衰退的东西,在上帝看来都是进步的东西;使
我受折磨的东西,却是他喜爱的东西。平等也许并不怎么崇高,
但却非常正义,也正是它的正义构成了它的伟大和美丽。我要努
力使自己达到上帝的这个观点,并试图用这个观点去考察和判断
世间的事物。

　　世界上没有一个人能够既绝对又全面地断言新的社会情况
会比旧的社会情况更好,但已经不难看到它们是不同的。贵族国
家的制度里所固有的一些缺陷和美德,与现代人的性格恰好相
反,因而从来不能灌入他们当中。前者所不知的一些良好的喜好
和恶劣的习性,在后者看来却是很自然的。有些思想是从一方的
想象中自然产生出来的,但却与另一方的思想完全不一致。它们
就像两个完全不同的人,每一方都有自己的优点和缺点,有自己
的优势和弊端。因此,我们必须要注意,不能用已不存在的社会
留下的观点去判断正在产生的社会。因为这两种社会的结构是
截然不同的,它们无法忍受这么不公平的对比。要求现代人具有

peculiar virtues which originated in the social condition of their forefathers, since that social condition is itself fallen and has drawn into one promiscuous ruin the good and evil that belonged to it.

But as yet these things are imperfectly understood. I find that a great number of my contemporaries undertake to make a selection from among the institutions, the opinions, and the ideas that originated in the aristocratic constitution of society as it was; a portion of these elements they would willingly relinquish, but they would keep the remainder and transplant them into their new world. I fear that such men are wasting their time and their strength in virtuous but unprofitable efforts. The object is, not to retain the peculiar advantages which the inequality of conditions bestows upon mankind, but to secure the new benefits which equality may supply. We have not to seek to make ourselves like our progenitors, but to strive to work out that species of greatness and happiness which is our own.

For myself, who now look back from this extreme limit of my task and discover from afar, but at once, the various objects which have attracted my more attentive investigation upon my way, I am full of apprehensions and of hopes. I perceive mighty dangers which it is possible to ward off, mighty evils which may be avoided or alleviated; and I cling with a firmer hold to the belief that for democratic nations to be virtuous and prosperous, they require but to will it.

I am aware that many of my contemporaries maintain that nations are never their own masters here below, and that they necessarily obey some insurmountable and unintelligent power, arising from anterior events, from their race, or from the soil and climate of their country. Such principles are false and cowardly; such principles can never produce aught but feeble men and pusillanimous nations. Providence has not created mankind entirely independent or entirely free. It is true that around every man a fatal circle is traced beyond which he cannot pass; but within the wide verge of that circle he is powerful and free; as it is with man, so with communities. The nations of our time cannot prevent the conditions of men from becoming equal, but it depends upon themselves whether the principle of equality

适合他们祖辈的社会情况的特殊美德，也是很不合理的，因为祖辈的社会情况已经衰落了，而属于它的一切善和一切恶，也随着它的衰落陷入完全的混乱中。

但是，这些情况至今还不能被完全了解。我已看到，大多数我的同代人正从旧社会的贵族制度产生的章程、观念和思想中进行选择。对于其中的一部分，他们会愿意放弃，但还想保留另一部分，并把这一部分带到新世界。我担心这些人是在浪费自己的时间并做着毫无效果的努力。问题是不应当再保持身份的不平等给人们带来的那些特殊利益，而是应当确保平等可能为人们提供的新利益。我们并不是要让自己与祖先相同，而应当努力走向属于我们自己的那种伟大和幸福。

至于我，在达到我的任务的终点后，远远地、但是全面地回顾一下我曾分别深入研究的所有不同对象时，我既充满着忧郁，又满怀希望。我看到一些可能被排除的严重危险；我还看到一些能够被避免或抵制的重大弊端。因此，我越来越深深地坚信，只要民主国家想要并愿意干，还是能够建成高尚而繁荣的社会的。

我知道，很多当代人坚持认为人民从来不能成为自己的主人，他们必然服从一些不可抗拒的和无法理解的力量的支配，有种族、土地和气候所产生的力量。这是一种错误的和消极的观点，它什么用都没有，而只能使人永远软弱和使国家永远优柔寡断。上帝并没有创造出完全独立或完全自由的人类。不错，上帝是在每个人的周围画了一个他不可能越出的命运所注定的圈子，但是在这个广泛的圈子里，人还是强大的和自由的。人类既然如此，国家也会如此。现代的各国已不能阻止人们身份日益平等的趋势了。但是，平等将导致奴役还是导致自由，导致文明还是导致野蛮，导

is to lead them to servitude or freedom, to knowledge or barbarism, to prosperity or wretchedness.

Appendix I

APPENDIX A. -Vol. I, p. 19

For information concerning all the countries of the West which have not yet been visited by Europeans, consult the account of two expeditions undertaken at the expense of Congress by Major Long. This traveler particularly mentions, on the subject of the great American desert, that a line may be drawn nearly parallel to the 20th degree of longitude (meridian of Washington),[①] beginning from the Red River and ending at the River Platte. From this imaginary line to the Rocky Mountains, which bound the valley of the Mississippi on the west, lie immense plains, which are generally covered with sand incapable of cultivation, or scattered over with masses of granite. In summer these plains are destitute of water, and nothing is to be seen on them but herds of buffaloes and wild horses. Some tribes of Indians are also found there, but in no great numbers.

Major Long was told that in traveling northwards from the River Platte you find the same desert lying constantly on the left; but he was unable to ascertain the truth of this report. (Long's *Expedition*, Vol. II, p. 361.)

However worthy of confidence may be the narrative of Major Long, it must be remembered that he passed through only the country of which he speaks, without deviating widely from the line which he had traced out for his journey.

APPENDIX B. -Vol. I, p. 20

South America, in the regions between the tropics, produces an incredible profusion of climbing plants, of which the flora of the Antilles alone furnishes forty different species.

Among the most graceful of these shrubs is the passion-flower, which, according to Descourtiz, climbs trees by means of the tendrils

---

① The 20th degree of longitude, meridian of Washington, corresponds to about 99° of the meridian of Paris.

致繁荣还是导致贫困,这就全靠各国自己了。

附录 I

附录 A。——第一卷,第 19 页

参考朗少校在国会的资助下到欧洲人尚未拜访过的整个西部地区去的两次考察报告。朗少校在讲到美国的大沙漠时特别指出,可以划一条紧靠甚至是平行于东经 20 度的线(以华盛顿为 0 度)①从鲁日河开始到普拉特河结束。从这条假定线到密西西比河谷的西界落基山之间,有一些面积很大的平地,平地上一般覆有一层植物无法生长的沙子,或散布着有花岗岩的石块。夏季,这里有许多成群的野牛和野马。还可以发现一些为数不多的印第安人部落。

朗少校听说,在普拉特河岸上游走,会发现上游左岸也会常遇到这样的沙漠,但他未能以亲自考察来证实这个传闻(参阅朗少校的考察报告第 2 章第 361 页。共 2 卷,费城,1823 年)。

不管朗少校的叙述有哪些是可信的,我们必须切记,他只是横越了他所说的地区,而没有走到他所经过的路线的两侧做反复细致的考察。

附录 B。——第一卷,第 20 页

生活在南北回归线之间的南美洲,到处都盛产这种品类繁多的通称为美洲野藤的攀绕植物。只单单在安德列斯群岛的植物区系中,这种美洲野藤现在就有四十多种。

在这种攀绕植物中,最优美的是西番莲。据德库蒂兹在其记述安德列斯群岛植物界的著作中说,这种植物利用其身上生长的

---

① 　东经 20 度,以华盛顿为 0 度,与巴黎子午线的大约 99 度相一致。

with which it is provided, and forms moving bowers of rich and elegant festoons, decorated with blue and purple flowers, and fragrant with perfume. (Vol. I, p. 265.)

The *Acacia àgrandes gousses* is a creeper of enormous and rapid growth, which climbs from tree to tree and sometimes covers more than half a league. (Vol. III, p. 227.)

APPENDIX C. -Vol. I, p. 22

The languages that are spoken by the Indians of America, from the Pole to Cape Horn, are said to be all formed on the same model and subject to the same grammatical rules; whence it may fairly be concluded that all the Indian nations sprang from the same stock. Each tribe of the American continent speaks a different dialect; but the number of languages, properly so called, is very small, a fact which tends to prove that the nations of the New World had not a very remote origin.

Moreover, the languages of America have a great degree of regularity, from which it seems probable that the tribes which employ them had not undergone any great revolutions or been incorporated, voluntarily or by constraint, into foreign nations; for it is generally the union of several languages into one that produces grammatical irregularities.

It is not long since the American languages, especially those of the North, first attracted the serious attention of philologists. When they were carefully studied, the discovery was made that this idiom of a barbarous people was the product of a very complicated system of ideas and of exceedingly well-conceived systems. These languages were found to be very rich, and great pains had been taken at their formation to render them agreeable to the ear. The grammatical system of the Americans differs from all others in several points, but especially in the following: Some nations of Europe, among others the Germans, have the power of combining at pleasure different expressions, and thus giving a complex sense to certain words. The Indians have given a most surprising extension to this power, so as to connect a great number of ideas with a single term. This will be easily understood with the help of an example quoted by Mr. Duponceau, in the

卷须爬上大树,在林中形成一条条优美的植物的长廊。这些长廊不仅被深红间蓝的美丽花朵点缀着,而且因花朵散发的香味而发出芬芳(见第 1 卷第 265 页)。

大豆荚金合欢,是一种非常粗的藤本植物。它生长得很快,由一棵树爬向另一棵树,有时可以蔓延约半里以上(见第 3 卷第 227 页)。

附录 C。——第一卷,第 22 页

关于土著的美洲印第安人所讲的语言,无论是在北极圈还是到合恩角,都已经定型在同样的模式上,并有着相同的语法规则。因此,基本上可以断定,所有的印第安人都出于同一血统。美洲大陆的各个部落,都有自己不同的方言。但是,确切地讲,符合严格定义的语言却少之又少,所以有人仍在试图证明新大陆的各族并没有特别古老的族源。

然而,美洲土著的语言有着很强的规律性。大概,现存的各个部落还未经历过巨大的革命,没有被迫或自愿与外来的民族混合,因为在通常情况下,当几种语言混合在一起之后,就会出现语法规则的混乱。

不久以后,美洲土著的语言,特别是北美土著的语言,首次吸引了语言学家的注意。当他们认真研究时,立即发现,野蛮人的这种土语是一套非常复杂的观念的产物,组织得极其合理。他们认为,这种语言极其丰富多彩,在创造它的时候特别努力地使听觉赋予一些辨别能力。美洲语言的语法体系,在许多方面都不同于其他语言。但在以下几点尤为突出:在欧洲的一些民族之间,德语就有一个不同于其他语言的特点,它可以随意把几个词联结在一起,并形成了不同的含义。印第安语更令人惊奇地扩大了这个特点,甚至达到可以说只用一个词就能表达很多含义的地步。利用杜邦索先生在《美国哲学学会报告》中引用的下述例子,就可以很容易地说明这一点。

Memoirs of the American Philosophical Society.

"A Delaware woman playing with a cat or a young dog," says this writer, "is heard to pronounce the word *kuligatschis*, which is composed thus: *k* is the sign of the second person, and signifies 'thou' or 'thy'; *uli* (pronounced *ouli*) is a part of the word *wulit*, which signifies 'beautiful,' 'pretty'; *gat* is another fragment of the word *wichgat*, which means 'paw'; and, lastly, *schis* (pronounced *chise*) is a diminutive giving the idea of smallness. Thus, in one word, the Indian woman has expressed 'Thy pretty little paw.'"

Take another example of the felicity with which the savages of A-merica have composed their words. A young man, in the Delaware tongue, is called *piapé*. This word is formed from *pilsit*, chaste, inno-cent; and *lenapé*, man; hence man in his purity and innocence.

This facility of combining words is most remarkable in the strange formation of their verbs. The most complex action is often expressed by a single verb, which serves to convey all the shades of an idea by the modification of its construction. Those who may wish to examine more in detail this subject, which I have only glanced at superficial-ly, should read: 1. "The Correspondence of Mr. Duponceau and the Rev. Mr. Heckewelder [*sic*, Bowen] relative to the Indian langua-ges," found in Volume I of the *Memoirs of the American Philosophical Society*, published at Philadelphia, by Abraham Small, 1819, pp. 356-464. 2. The grammar of the Delaware or Lenape language by Geiberger, and its preface by Mr. Duponceau. All these are in the same collection, Vol. III. 3. An excellent account of these works, which is at the end of Volume VI of the *American Encyclopæ* dia.

APPENDIX D. -Vol. I, p. 24

See, in Charlevoix, Vol. I, p. 235, the history of the first war which the French inhabitants of Canada carried on, in 1610, against the Iroquois. The latter, armed with bows and arrows, offered a des-perate resistance to the French and their allies. Charlevoix is not a great painter, yet he exhibits clearly enough in this narrative the contrast between the European manners and those of savages, as

作者说道:"在一个特拉华族的女人逗弄一只小猫或小狗时,可以听到她反复说 kuligatschis 一词,这就是一个合成词。其中的 k 代表第二人称,意为'你'或'你的';uli 读作 ouli(乌利),是 wulit 一词的一部分,意为'美丽的'和'可爱的';gat 是 wichgat 一词的末段,意为'爪子';最后是 schis 一词,读作西斯,是一个表示小形的爱称。于是,这个印第安妇女只用一词,就表达了'你的可爱的小爪子'这层意思。"

这里,再举一个更充分例子,可以很好地说明美洲的野蛮民族是善于组织他们的单词的。一个特拉华族的男青年,用纯洁一词和 lenape 一词描述自己,而 lenape 的意思是人。也就是说,他自称是"纯洁的人"。

这种对几个词的联合,尤其常见于动词的合成方面。一个非常复杂的动作,经常只由一个简单的动词来表示。几乎所有的意思上的细微差别,都能用动词和动词的变形表示出来。那些希望更详细地了解我只是很浅地提及的这个问题的人,可读: 1. 杜邦索先生与赫克维尔德牧师关于印第安语的通信。这封通信见于阿伯拉罕·斯莫尔主编的 1819 年在费城出版的《美国哲学学会报告》第 1 卷第 356—464 页。2.《特拉华语或勒纳普语语法》。此书共三卷,全面地分析了特拉华族的语言,前面有杜邦索先生的序言。3.《美国百科全书》第 5 卷末尾所收上述语法书的摘要。

附录 D。——第一卷,第 24 页

见夏尔瓦的《新法兰西的历史》的第 1 卷第 235 页,上面记载有 1610 年加拿大法国人反对易洛魁人的第一次战争历史。尽管易洛魁人使用的是弓箭,但他们却对法国人及其同盟者进行了拼死的抵抗。夏尔瓦并不是伟大的画家,但在记述欧洲人和野蛮人

well as the different sense which the two races had of honor.

"When the French," says he, "seized upon the beaver-skins which covered the Indians who had fallen, the Hurons, their allies, were greatly offended at this proceeding; but they set to work in their usual manner, inflicting horrid cruelties upon the prisoners, and devouring one of those who had been killed, which made the Frenchmen shudder. Thus the barbarians prided themselves upon a disinterestedness which they were surprised at not finding in our nation, and could not understand that there was less to reprehend in stripping dead bodies than in devouring their flesh like wild beasts."

Charlevoix, in another place (Vol. I, p. 230), thus describes the first torture of which Champlain was an eyewitness, and the return of the Hurons into their own village.

"Having proceeded eight leagues," says he, "our allies halted; and having singled out one of their captives, they reproached him with all the cruelties that he had practised upon the warriors of their nation who had fallen into his hands, and told him that he might expect to be treated in like manner, adding that if he had any spirit, he would prove it by singing. He thereupon chanted his war-song, and all the songs he knew, but in a very mournful strain," says Champlain, who was not then aware that all savage music has a melancholy character. "The tortures which succeeded, accompanied by all the horrors which we shall mention hereafter, terrified the French, who made every effort to put a stop to them, but in vain. The following night, one of the Hurons having dreamt that they were pursued, the retreat was changed to a real flight, and the savages never stopped until they were out of the reach of danger.

"The moment they perceived the huts of their own village, they cut themselves long sticks, to which they fastened the scalps which had fallen to their share, and carried them in triumph. At this sight, the women swam to the canoes, where they took the bloody scalps from the hands of their husbands and tied them round their necks.

的品德的对比时,却用了很鲜明及其很美妙的手法描写,还进一步叙述了这两个种族对待荣誉的不同态度。

他写道:"当法国人纷纷争抢战死在战场上的印第安人的海狸皮衣时,他们的同盟者休伦人则极力鄙视这种行为。但他们却按照惯例,对俘虏施以严酷的刑罚,并吃掉了一个被他们杀死的人,这可使法国人害怕极了。这些野蛮人为自己的无私行为感到光荣,并为我们没有这种想法表示惊奇,而且不理解扒死人的衣服为什么远远不如吃死人的肉那么坏,因为在他们看来,这同吃野兽的肉没有什么不同。"

夏尔瓦在另一处(第1卷,第230页),还曾描述过尚普兰首次目睹的这种酷刑和休伦人回到自己村舍时的情景。

他写道:"在走了约八里格以后,我们的同盟者们停下了脚步。他们选出一名俘虏,对他施以他们的同族战士落到这个俘虏的所在部族手中时受过的一切酷刑,宣布这个俘虏也会受到同样的刑罚;并补充说:如果他有勇气,可以用歌声来伴奏。这个俘虏立即唱起战歌,他会用悲惨的声音把自己知道的一切歌都唱完。尚普兰说,他从来都不知道野蛮人的所有音乐竟有如此悲伤的调子。这种酷刑还伴有我们随后即将谈到的各种惨事,这一切都把法国人吓呆了。他们尽力想止步于这个场面,但是没有用。当天夜里,一个休伦人梦到他们被追击,他们的退却,简直变成了逃命;而野蛮人紧追不舍,完全把危险置于度外。"

"他们一望见自己的村庄,就砍了一些长竿子,把各自分得的被处死俘虏的头发拴在竿子上,摇动着以表示凯旋。妇女们看到此景便都开始奔跑,并纷纷跳进水里,登上几条独木舟,从自己丈夫的手里接过沾满血污的头发,系在自己的脖子上。"

"The warriors offered one of these horrible tiophies to Champlain; they also presented him with some bows and arrows, the only spoils of the Iroquois which they had ventured to seize, entreating him to show them to the King of France. "

Champlain lived a whole winter quite alone among these barbarians, without being under any alarm for his person or property.

APPENDIX E. -Vol. I, p. 39

Although the puritanical strictness which presided over the establishment of the English colonies in America is now much relaxed, remarkable traces of it are still found in their habits and laws. In 1792, at the very time when the antichristian republic of France began its ephemeral existence, the legislative body of Massachusetts promulgated the following law, to compel the citizens to observe the Sabbath. I give the preamble and a few articles of this law, which is worthy of the reader's attention.

"Whereas," says the legislator, "the observation of the Sabbath is an affair of public interest; inasmuch as it produces a necessary suspension of labor, leads men to reflect upon the duties of life and the errors to which human nature is liable, and provides for the public and private worship of God, the Creator and Governor of the universe, and for the performance of such acts of charity as are the ornament and comfort of Christian societies;

"Whereas irreligious or light-minded persons, forgetting the duties which the Sabbath imposes, and the benefits which these duties confer on society, are known to profane its sanctity, by following their pleasures or their affairs; this way of acting being contrary to their own interest as Christians, and calculated to annov those who do not follow their example; being also of great injury to society at large, by spreading a taste for dissipation and dissolute manners;

Be it enacted and ordained by the Governor, Council, and Representatives convened in General Court of Assembly, that:

1. No one will be permitted on Sunday to keep his store or workshop open. No one will be permitted on that day to look after any business, to go to a concert, dance, or show of any sort, or to engage in any kind of hunting, game, recreation, without penalty of fine. The fine will not be less than 10 nor exceed 20 shillings for

"休伦人的战士把这样一件让人害怕的战利品赠给了尚普兰。此外,还送给他几张弓、几支箭和他们本来打算自己留下的那张仅有的易洛魁人皮,并托他把这张人皮呈给法兰西国王。"

尚普兰独身在这些野蛮人中间生活了整整一个冬天,他的人身和财产始终没有受到侵害。

附录 E。——第一卷,第 39 页

虽然在美洲的英国殖民地建立时就具有统治地位的清教徒的教规的严谨性早已大大松弛,但在他们的习惯和法律上仍会看到明显的痕迹。在 1792 年,当反对基督教的法兰西共和国开始它短暂的统治,马萨诸塞的立法团就公布了一项强制公民遵守礼拜日的法律。下面我将给出该法序言和主要条款,这是值得引起读者注意的。

立法者写道:"鉴于遵守礼拜日是一项公共活动,因为它可给劳动者带来必要的中断,使人们反思生存的职责和人类不可避免的错误的机会,让公共和个人都崇拜创造和管理世界的上帝,并使人们履行这种使基督教社会富丽和安宁的慈善事业;

"鉴于无宗教信仰或轻浮的人忘记礼拜日应尽的义务和社会带给他们的好处时,会亵渎神的圣洁而沉溺于自己的享乐或事务中;这样的行为违背了他们作为基督教徒的义务,具有干扰不仿效他们的人的作用,将给整个社会带来真正危害,并传播给社会放荡的风气和浮夸的习惯;

参议院和众议院兹命令如下:

"第一条,在礼拜日,任何人不得营业自己的店铺或作坊。在这一天,任何人也不得从事任何劳动和公务,不得出席任何音乐会、舞会或观看任何性质的演出,或参与任何种类的狩猎、游戏或娱乐,违者罚款。罚款的金额每次不低于 10 先令,但也不超过 20

each infraction.

"2. No traveller, conductor, or driver shall be allowed to travel on Sunday unless necessary, under the same penalty.

"3. Tavernkeepers, storekeepers, and innkeepers will prevent anyone living in their district from coming to pass the time there for pleasure or business. The innkeeper and his guest will pay a fine in case of disobedience. Furthermore, the innkeeper may lose his license.

"4. Those who, being in good health, without sufficient reason, fail to worship God publicly for three months, shall be fined 10 shillings.

"5. Those who behave improperly within the precincts of a church shall pay from 5 to 10 shillings fine.

"6. The tything men of the township are charged with the execution of the law. ① They have the right to visit on Sunday all the rooms of hotels or public places. The innkeeper who refuses them admission will be fined 40 shillings.

"The tything men may stop travellers and ask their reasons for travelling on Sunday. Those who refuse to answer will be fined 5 pounds stirling.

"If the reason given by the traveller does not seem sufficient to the tything man, he may prosecute said traveller before the district justice of the peace. " Law of March 8, 1792; *General Laws of Massachusetts*, Vol. 1, p. 410.

On the 11th of March 1797 a new law increased the amount of fines, half of which was to be given to the informer (same collection, Vol. I, p. 525).

On the 16th of February 1816 a new law confirmed these same measures (same collection, Vol II, p. 405).

Similar enactments exist in the laws of the state of New York, revised in 1827 and 1828 (see *Revised Statutes*, Part I, Chap. XX,

---

① These are officers, elected annually, who according to their functions resemble both the warden and the officer attached to the police magistrate in France.

先令。

"第二条,任何外出旅行者,列车员或驾驶者,除非必要,不得在礼拜日出行。违者处以与第一条相同的罚款。

"第三条,酒馆经营者、店铺经营者和客栈经营者应阻止本区域的任何定居居民在礼拜日到其店铺消遣娱乐或办事。如有违反,店主和客人同被罚款,而且可以吊销店主的执照。

"第四条,那些身体健康而又无充足理由在三个月内未能向上帝进行一次公开礼拜的人,将被罚款 10 先令。

"第五条,那些在教堂的围墙以内做出不当行为的人,将被处以 5—10 先令的罚款。

"第六条,乡镇的十户长负责执行本法。[①] 他们有权在礼拜日巡视所有的旅店或公共场所。拒绝让十户长进本店铺巡视的店主,将处以 40 先令的罚款。

"十户长有权拘留旅客,问明其在礼拜日旅行的原因。拒不回答的人,将处以金额可达 5 英镑的罚款。

"如果旅行者的答案不能使十户长满意,十户长可将此旅客送到区域治安法官处理。"(1792 年 3 月 8 日法令,载《马萨诸塞普通法》第 1 卷第 410 页)

在 1797 年 3 月 11 日,一项新的法律增加了罚款的金额,其一半归拘留该轻罪犯人的人所有(见上述法令汇编第 1 卷第 525 页)。

而在 1816 年 2 月 16 日,又有一项新法批准这些措施(见上述法令汇编第 2 卷第 405 页)。

在纽约州也存在着类似的法律,修订于 1827 年和 1828 年

---

① 这些官员每年选举一次,依据职责,他们即类似典狱长又类似于法国的违警罪法庭推事官员。

p. 675). In these it is declared that no one is allowed on the Sabbath to hunt, to fish, to play at games, or to frequent houses where liquor is sold. No one can travel, except in case of necessity. And this is not the only trace which the religious strictness and austere manners of the first emigrants have left behind them in the American laws.

In the *Revised Statutes of the State of New York*, Vol. I, p. 662, is the following clause:

"Whoever shall win or lose in the space of twenty-four hours, by gaming or betting, the sum of twenty-five dollars (about 132 francs), shall be found guilty of a misdemeanor, and, upon conviction, shall be condemned to pay a fine equal to at least five times the value of the sum lost or won; which shall be paid to the inspector of the poor of the township. He that loses twenty-five dollars or more may bring an action to recover them; and if he neglects to do so, the inspector of the poor may prosecute the winner, and oblige him to pay into the poor's box both the sum he has gained and three times as much besides."

The laws I quote are of recent date, but they are unintelligible without going back to the very origin of the colonies. I have no doubt that in our days the penal part of these laws is very rarely applied. Laws preserve their inflexibility long after the customs of a nation have yielded to the influence of progress. It is still true, however, that nothing strikes a foreigner on his arrival in America more forcibly than the regard paid to the Sabbath. There is one, in particular, of the large American cities in which all social movement begins to be suspended even on Saturday evening. You traverse its streets at the hour when you expect men in the middle of life to be engaged in business, and young people in pleasure; and you meet with solitude and silence. Not only have all ceased to work, but they appear to have ceased to exist. You can hear neither the movements of industry, nor the accents of joy, nor even the confused murmur that arises from the midst of a great city. Chains are hung across the streets in the neighborhood of the churches; the half-closed shutters of the houses scarcely admit a ray of sun into the dwellings of the citizens. Now and then you perceive a solitary individual, who glides silently along thedeserted streets and lanes.

(见《增订纽约州法令集》第 1 编第 20 章第 675 页)。其中规定,任何人在礼拜日不得出去打猎、钓鱼,不得在酒店逗留和进进出出。除非特殊情况,任何人不得在礼拜日出行。上述这些,还不是初期移民的宗教的严谨性和习俗的严肃性留在美国法律上的唯一痕迹。

在纽约州修订的法律文集第 1 卷第 662 页,可以见到以下的条款:

"因赌博或打赌而在 24 小时内输赢的总量达到 25 美元(约132 法郎)时,应被视为轻罪,并根据确凿的证据处以等同于至少是所赢所输金额五倍的罚款。此项罚款将被交给本乡镇济贫工作视察员管理。输 25 美元或以上的人可以向法院申诉。如不申诉,济贫工作视察员则可以作为赢方,迫使输方交出输款和相当于输款三倍的罚款,供济贫工作使用。"

我引述的这几项法律都是新近实施的,但如果不追溯到这些殖民地的初始时期,我们又怎能理解这些法律呢? 我毫不怀疑,在我们这个时代,这些法律中所制定的刑法部分已经很少被使用了。在民情已经发生很大变化的时代,法律仍然保留其原有特性。当然,最使外来人感到惊奇的还是美国人严守礼拜日的做法。特别是美国有一个大城市,一到星期六晚上整个社会就像停止运动一样。当你认为在本应是成年人忙着赶去应酬和青年人急着赶去娱乐的时刻去逛一逛这座城市,迎接你的将是孤独与寂静。所有的事务不仅是好像停止了工作,而且好像停止了存在。你既听不到工业的"轰隆"声,也听不到高兴的欢呼声,更听不到闹市区的喧嚣声。生活的锁链穿过街区,绷紧在教堂的周围。半闭着的百叶窗,只允许一缕缕的阳光射进居民的室内。好不容易才能看到远方有一个人独自默默地穿过十字路口,长长的一条大街竟无一个人影。

But on Monday at early dawn the rolling of carriages, the noise of hammers, the cries of the population, begin again to make themselves heard. The city is awake once more. An eager crowd hastens towards the resort of commerce and industry; everything around you bespeaks motion, bustle, hurry. A feverish activity succeeds to the lethargic stupor of yesterday; you might almost suppose that they had but one day to acquire wealth and to enjoy it.

APPENDIX F. -Vol. I, p. 44

It is unnecessary to say that in the chapter which has just been read I have not pretended to give a history of America. My only object has been to enable the reader to appreciate the influence that the opinions and manners of the first immigrants have exercised upon the fate of the different colonies and of the Union in general. I have therefore cited only a few detached fragments. I do not know whether I am deceived, but it appears to me that by pursuing the path which I have merely pointed out, it would be easy to present such pictures of the American republics as would not be unworthy the attention of the public and could not fail to suggest to the statesman matter for reflection. Not being able to devote myself to this labor, I am anxious at least to render it easy to others; and for this purpose I append a short catalogue and analysis of the works which seem to me the most important to consult.

At the head of the general documents which it would be advantageous to examine, I place the work entitled: *Historical Collection of State Papers and Other Authentic Documents, intended as materials for an hystory of the United States of America*, by Ebenezer Hazard. The first volume of this compilation, which was printed at Philadelphia in 1792, contains a literal copy of all the charters granted by the Crown of England to the emigrants, as well as the principal acts of the colonial governments, during the first period of their existence. One can find there, among other things, a great number of authentic documents on the affairs of New England and Virginia during this period. The second volume is almost entirely devoted to the acts of the Confederation of 1643.

This federal compact, which was entered into by the colonies of New England with the view of resisting the Indians, was the first instance of union afforded by the Anglo-Americans. There were several other such compacts, up to the one of 1776, which led to the independence of the colonies.

但在星期一的清晨,车辆的开动声、铁锤的敲打声、人们的叫喊声,又一次传入你的耳朵。整个城市又醒来了。急匆匆的人群不断地赶往城市的工商业中心;所有的人都在行动,行色匆忙,仓促赶路。在昨天昏昏欲睡的状态之后,又开始了繁忙的一天,好像人人觉得要想发财和由此享乐,只有今天一天似的。

附录 F。——第一卷,第 44 页

在这一章里,已经没有必要让我再去叙述美国的历史。我的目的只想让读者由此了解初期移民的观点和民情对于各个不同的殖民地和整个美国的后来命运所产生的影响。因此,我只引用了少数有关的片段。我不知道这样做是否正确,但我认为通过我引用的这些片段,可以很容易描绘出美国各共和州的早期画面。这幅画面不仅会引起一般读者的注意,而且无疑会向国务活动家提供供他们深入研究的资料。虽然我本人不能致力于美国的历史研究,但我至少愿意为别人提供方便。因此,我认为应当在这里附加上一篇简短的书目,并对我觉得最宜于引用的几部著作进行扼要的分析。

在对考察有利的一般性文献中,我首先要推荐埃伯尼泽·哈泽德编的收有各州文件和其他可靠文献的《美利坚合众国历史资料汇编》。这部汇编的第一卷在 1792 年出版于费城,包括英国国王颁给移民的所有宪章的书面文本,以及各殖民地政府自成立以来的主要法规。此外,还有关于这一时期的新英格兰和弗吉尼亚事务的大量可信的文件。第二卷几乎全是关于 1643 年联邦的文件。

这个联盟和约,是新英格兰各殖民地之间为抵抗印第安人而结成的,是英籍美国人宣布联合的第一个实例。直到 1776 年,有其他一些相同的联盟使殖民地宣布独立。

The Philadelphia historical collection is in the Library of Congress.

Each colony has, besides, its own historic monuments, some of which are extremely curious, beginning with Virginia, the state that was first peopled. The earliest historian of Virginia was its founder, Captain John Smith. Captain Smith has left us a quarto volume, entitled *The general Historie of Virginia and New-England, by Captain John Smith, some time Governor in those Countries, and Admiral of New England*; printed at London in 1627. (This volume is to be found in the Biblioth èque royale.) Smith's work is illustrated with very curious maps and engravings which date from the period when it was printed. The historian's account extends from 1584 to 1626. Smith's book is well thought of and merits being so. The author is one of the most celebrated adventurers who has appeared in a century full of adventurers; he lived at its end. The book itself breathes that ardor of discovery, that spirit of enterprise, which characterizes such men; there one finds those chivalric manners which are often mingled with trade and made to serve the acquisition of riches.

But what is remarkable about Captain Smith is that he combined the virtues of his contemporaries with qualities which were alien to most of them; his style is simple and clear, his accounts have the mark of truth, his descriptions are not elaborated. This author throws valuable light on the state of the Indians at the time of the discovery of North America.

The second historian to consult is Beverley. Beverley's work, a volume in duodecimo, was translated into French, and published at Amsterdam, in 1707. The author begins his narrative in 1585 and ends it in 1700. The first part of his book contains historical documents, properly so called, relative to the infancy of the colony. The second affords a most curious picture of the state of the Indians at this remote period. The third conveys very clear ideas concerning the manners, social condition, laws, and political customs of the Virginians in the author's lifetime.

Beverley was a Virginian, which leads him to say, in opening. that he begs the reader "not to examine my work in too critical a

在国会图书馆中藏有费城出版的这部历史文献汇编。

此外,各殖民地还有自己的历史文献,其中有些是极其古怪的。我要从最早被人们移民的弗吉尼亚州开始。在弗吉尼亚的所有历史家当中,最早的奠基者是约翰·史密斯船长。史密斯船长给我们留下一部 16 开本的著作,书名为《弗吉尼亚和新英格兰通史》,1627 年于伦敦出版(本书亦藏于王家图书馆)。史密斯的这部著作里插入了多幅地图和一些雕版图,并标有制作的日期。这位历史学家的著作从 1584 年一直到 1626 年。史密斯的著作得到很高的评价,而且受之无愧。这位作者是一位有名的冒险家,他生于冒险家辈出的时代,并最终取得了胜利。这本书处处都散发着冒险的热情,而这种冒险进取精神是那个时代的人们所特有的。我们从这部书中,还可以发现混有经商致富味道的武士气概的精神。

但是,史密斯船长最突出的特点,是他除具有同时代人的美德之外,还具备他们当中的大部分人所没有的一些品质。他的风格既简单又清楚,叙述也很逼真,没有一点矫饰。这位作者使我们知道了印第安人在欧洲人发现北美时期的有价值的情况。

第二位历史学家是贝弗利。他的著作为 48 开本,1707 年出版于阿姆斯特丹,已被译为法文。作者的叙述始于 1585 年,止于 1707 年。这本书的第一部分载有殖民初期的历史文献。第二部分,对印第安人在这个远古时期的生活情景,做了有趣的报道。第三部分,清晰地表达了在作者生活的时期,弗吉尼亚当时的民情、社会情况、法律和政治习惯。

贝弗利出生于弗吉尼亚,所以他一开始就说:“由于我出生在印度,没有专注于语言的纯洁性,故请读者不要以过于严格的

spirit for, since I was born in the Indies, I cannot aspire to purity of language. " Despite this colonist's modesty, the author shows throughout his book that he vigorously supports the supremacy of the mother country. Numerous instances of that spirit of civil liberty that has since then inspired the English colonies in America are also found in Beverley's work. Evidence of the divisions which so long existed among them and delayed their independence is likewise to be found. Beverley detests his Catholic neighbors in Maryland more than the English government. This author's style is simple; his descriptions are often full of interest and inspire confidence. The French translation of Beverley's history may be found in the Bibiloth èque royale.

I saw in America, but was unable to find in France, another work which ought to be consulted entitled *The History of Virginia*, by William Stith. This book affords some curious details, but I thought it long and diffuse.

The oldest as well as the best document to be consulted on the history of Carolina is a work in small quarto, entitled *The History of Carolina*, by John Lawson, printed at London in 1718. This work contains, in the first part, a journey of discovery in the west of Carolina, the account of which, given in the form of a journal, is in general confused and superficial; but it contains a very striking description of the mortality caused among the savages of that time by both smallpox and the immoderate use of brandy; with a curious picture of the corruption of manners prevalent among them, which was increased by the presence of Europeans. The second part of Lawson's book is devoted to a description of the physical condition of Carolina and its products.

In the third part the author gives an interesting description of the customs, habits, and government of the Indians at that time. Wit and originality are often to be found in this part of the book. Lawson's history concludes with the Charter granted Carolina in the reign of Charles II. This work is light in tone, often licentious, and presents a complete contrast to the very serious style of works

批判观点来审查我的著作。"尽管这位移民很谦虚,但他在自己著作的整篇都在证明,他是情不自禁地维护母国的最高主权的。我们从贝弗利的著作中,还可以看到当时曾经鼓舞美洲英国殖民地前进的那种公民自由精神的许多痕迹。书中还可以找到各殖民地之间长期以来存在的并且一直延续到独立时的不睦的痕迹。贝弗利对他的邻居马里兰的天主教徒表示的憎恨,远远大于对英国政府的憎恨。这位作者的风格简朴,他的叙述总是充满着同情心而且令人信服。贝弗利著作的法文译本,可在王家图书馆找到。

还有一本值得考虑的著作,我在美国读过,但还没有在法国找到,它就是威廉斯蒂思写的《弗吉尼亚最初发现与定居开发史》。这本书提供了很多有趣的细节,但我觉得有些冗长和啰嗦。

关于卡罗来纳的历史,一部值得考虑的最早的和最好的著作,是约翰劳森的一部 16 开本的薄书《卡罗来纳史》,此书 1718 年出版于伦敦。这部著作的第一部分首先记述了卡罗来纳西部的发现旅程。这部书是以游记的形式写成的,作者的叙述普遍有些混乱和肤浅。但却极其深刻地描写了在当时野蛮部落中由天花和酗酒所造成的死亡,并用极其有趣的图片描写了风行在这些部落的并因欧洲人的到来而又加剧的道德败坏行为。劳森著作的第二部分,是专门描述卡罗来纳的自然状况和其物产的。

在这本著作的第三部分,作者对当时印第安人的风尚、习俗和管理组织做了生动有趣的描述。在该书的这一部分,到处都可以发现作者的智慧和创新之处。劳森的这部历史,到查理二世时期赐给卡罗林纳宪章时结束。这部著作的基调是轻快的,但往往随意过度,与当时在新英格兰出版的著作的非常严肃的风格完全

published at the same time in New England. Lawson's history is an extremely rare volume in America, and cannot be acquired in Europe. Nevertheless, there is a copy in the Biblioth èque royale.

From the southern I pass at once to the northern extremity of the United States, as the intermediate space was not peopled till a later period.

I would first mention a very curious compilation, entitled *Collections of the Massachusetts Historical Society*, printed for the first time at Boston in 1792, and reprinted in 1806. This work is not in the Biblioth èque royale, nor, I believe, in any other library. This collection, which is continued to the present day, contains a great number of very valuable documents relating to the history of the different states of New England. Among them are letters which have never been published, and authentic pieces which had been buried in provincial archives. The whole work of Gookin, concerning the Indians, is inserted there.

I have mentioned several times, in the chapter to which this note relates, the work of Nathaniel Morton, entitled *New England's Memorial*; sufficiently, perhaps, to prove that it deserves the attention of those who would be conversant with the history of New England. Nathaniel Morton's book is an octavo volume, reprinted at Boston in 1826. It is not in the Biblioth èque royale.

The most valuable and important authority that exists on the history of New England is the work of the Rev. Cotton Mather, entitled *Magnalia Christi Americana, or the Ecclesiastical History of New England*, 1620-1698, 2 vols. , 8 vo, reprinted at Hartford, in 1820. I do not believe it is in the Biblioth èque royale. The author divided his work into seven books. The first presents the history of the events which prepared and brought about the establishment of New England. The second contains the lives of the first governors and chief magistrates who presided over the country. The third is devoted to the lives and labors of the evangelical ministers who during the same period had the care of souls. In the fourth the author relates the institution and progress of the university at Cambridge (Massachusetts). In the fifth he describes the principles and the discipline of the Church of New England, The sixth is taken up in retracing certain facts which, in the opinion of Mather, prove the merciful interposition of Providence in behalf of the inhabitants of New England. Lastly, in the seventh, the author gives an account of the heresies and the troubles to

不同。劳森的这部历史,在美国已是极其罕见的,而在欧洲就更是难于找到了。但在王家图书馆还有一部副本。

我从美国的最南部分一直游历到它的最北部分,其间的广大地区直到很晚以后才有移民涌进。

我首先要提到一部非常值得一读的汇编,它的题名为《马萨诸塞历史学会论丛》,1792 年出版于波士顿,1806 年再版。王家图书馆没有收藏这部著作,而且我相信其他图书馆也不会有。这部至今仍在继续编辑的汇编,收载了关于新英格兰各州历史的大量珍贵文献,其中有从未被出版过的信件和被收藏在地方档案馆的原始文件。古金主编的这部论丛,也收有关于印第安人的材料。

我在与本注的相关章节中,曾多次提到纳撒尼尔莫尔顿的《新英格兰回忆录》。或许,我已经充足的证明了:凡想了解新英格兰历史的人,都应当读一读这部著作。莫尔顿的著作为 32 开本,1826 年出版于波士顿。王家图书馆没有收藏此书。

讲述新英格兰历史的最有价值和最重要的权威著作,是大教士科顿马瑟的《基督教美洲传教史》,或《1620—1698 年新英格兰教会史》。这部书为 32 开本,共两卷,1820 年出版于哈特福德。我认为王家图书馆也不会有此藏书。作者将此书分为七册。第一册讲述新英格兰的筹建和建设的历史。第二册记述新英格兰的几位初期的统治者和主要行政官员的生平。第三册叙述当时指导人们思想的福音会牧师们的生平和事迹。在第四册中,作者讲述了剑桥(在马萨诸塞)大学的成立和发展过程。他在第五册中描述了新英格兰教会的教义和教规。第六册再次追述了根据马瑟的观点,表明仁慈上帝向新英格兰居民施福的某些事件。最后,在第七册,作者向我们讲述了当时的异教和新英格兰教会加

which the Church of New England was exposed. Cotton Mather was an evangelical minister, who was born at Boston and passed his life there. His narratives are distinguished by the same ardor and religious zeal which led to the foundation of the colonies of New England. Traces of bad taste often occur in his manner of writing; but he interests because he is full of enthusiasm. He is often intolerant, still oftener credulous, but he never betrays an intention to deceive.

Sometimes there are even brilliant passages, and even true and profound reflections, such as these: "Before the arrival of the Puritans," he says (Vol. I, chap. iv, p. 61), "there were more than a few attempts of the *English*, to people and improve the parts of *New-England*, which were to the northward of *New-Plymouth*; but the designs of those attempts being aimed no higher than the advancement of some *worldly interests*, a constant series of disasters has confounded them, until there was a plantation erected upon the nobler designs of *christianity* [*sic*]; and that plantation, though it has had more adversaries than perhaps any one upon earth; yet, *having obtained help from God, it continues to this day.*"

Mather sometimes softens the severity of his story with touches of warmth and tenderness: after talking of an English woman who, with her husband, was brought to America by religious zeal, and shortly after died from the fatigue and suffering of exile, he adds: "As to her virtuous spouse, Isaac Johnson, he tried to live without her, and being unable to, he died" (Vol. I, p. 71) [*sic*].

Mather's book admirably portrays the times and country he wishes to describe. Desiring to show us what motives led the Puritans to seek a refuge beyond the seas, he says:

"Briefly, the God of Heaven served as it were, a *summons* upon the *spirits* of his people in the English nation; stirring up the spirits of thousands which never saw the *faces* of each other, with a most unanimous inclination to leave all the pleasant accommodations of their native country, and go over a terrible *ocean*, into a more terrible *desart*, for the *pure enjoyment of all his ordinances.* It is now reasonable that before we pass any further, the *reasons* of this undertaking should be more exactly made known unto *posterity*, especially unto the *posterity* of those that were the *under*

以反对的动乱。马瑟是一个福音会牧师,生于波士顿,并在那里度过其一生。在他的叙述中,以引导人们建设新英格兰殖民地的那种宗教热心和激情为特征。一些不够典雅的习惯还在他的文章中留有痕迹,因为他只想靠满腔的热情去打动读者。他常常过于偏执,而最经常的是过于轻信,但他从来没有过欺骗的企图。

在他的这部著作里,偶尔也有很精彩的片段和真实深刻的思想。比如,他在第一卷第四章第61页说道:"在清教徒到来之前,英国人就曾不止一次地试图向北方的新普利茅斯移居,但他们的努力从来没有超越过现有的物质利益,所以持续不断的困难,会使他们一再的困惑。而在崇高的基督教思想的推动和支持下来到美洲的人,绝不会如此。虽然这些人遇到的敌人远比任何殖民地的创建者遇到的敌人要强大得多,但他们能够坚持自己的信念,以致使他们创建的东西依然存在于今天。"

有时,马瑟也会用温和与亲切的手法来缓和其严肃的叙述。比如,他谈到一位英国妇女,在宗教热情的鼓舞下同她的丈夫一起来到美洲,但不久便死于疲劳和由流亡所带来的苦难中。然后他接着说:"至于她的道德高尚的丈夫,艾萨克约翰逊却试图独自一人生活,但他未能活下来而最终死去。"(第一卷第71页)

马瑟在他的著作中,极其精致地描述了他想要描述的时代和地区。他想要让我们知道清教徒是出于什么动机到大洋彼岸去寻找避难所,他写道:

"上帝召唤着居住于英国的人们的思想;在鼓舞着成千上万的不相识的人们的精神时候,要求他们下定决心放弃在故乡的安适生活,横渡到大洋彼岸,到一片令人望而生畏的荒野去安家立业;而这样做的唯一目的,就是无条件地服从上帝的所有条例。在做长篇大论之前,

takers, lest they come at length to forget and neglect *the true interest of New-England*. Wherefore I shall now transcribe some of *them* from a manuscript, wherein they were then tendred unto consideration.

"*First*, It will be a service unto the *Church* of great consequence, to carry the *Gospel* into *those* parts of the world, and raise a *bulwark* against the kingdom of *antichrist*, which the *Jesuites* labour to rear up in *all* parts of the world.

"*Secondly*, All other Churches of *Europe* have been brought under *desolations*; and it may be feared that the like judgments are coming upon *us*; and who knows but God hath provided this place to be a *refuge* for many, whom he means to save out of the *General Destruction* .

"*Thirdly*, The land grows weary of her *inhabitants*, insomuch that *man*, which is the most precious of all creatures, is here more vile and base than the earth he treads upon: *children*, *neighbours* and *friends*, especially the *poor*, are counted the greatest *burdens*, which if things were right would be the chiefest earthly *blessings*.

"*Fourthly*, We are grown to that intemperance in all *excess of riot*, as no mean estate almost will suffice a man to keep sail with his *equals*, and he that fails in it, must live in scorn and contempt: hence it comes to pass, that all *arts* and *trades* are *carried* in that deceitful manner, and unrighteous course, as it is almost impossible for a good upright man to maintain his constant charge, and live comfortably in them.

"*Fifthly*, The *schools* of learning and religion are so corrupted, as (besides the unsupportable charge of education) most children, even the best, wittiest, and of the fairest hopes, are perverted, corrupted, and utterly overthrown, by the multitude of evil examples and licentious behaviours in these *seminaries*.

"*Sixthly*, *The whole earth is the Lord's garden*, and he hath given it to the sons of *Adam*, to be tilled and improved by them: why then should we stand starving here for places of habitation, and in the mean time suffer whole countries, as profitable for the use of man, to lye waste without any improvement?

应当精确地说明他们进行这种冒险的原因是什么,而特别是让后代清楚地知道他们的动机,以免使他们不要忘记或忽视新英格兰的真正利益。因此,我要在这里转述一部手稿里谈到的某些人的当时动机。

"第一个动机:最大程度地服务于教会,即向世界的这一部分传播福音,建起一所反对基督教敌人的堡垒,以反对企图在世界的其余部分建立统治的非基督徒。

"第二个动机:欧洲的其余所有教会已被破坏,害怕上帝也会将同样的惩罚指向我们,故决心开辟这个地方,为大多数人提供免遭大破坏的避难场所。

"第三个动机:我们所在的国土好像在折磨居民,最珍视财物的人却最轻视他们所踏的土地。人们将子女、邻居和朋友,特别是穷人视为最大的负担。如果事物按照这样的秩序发展,最能创造享乐的人要被排挤出这个世界。

"第四个动机:在所有的暴动中,我们的放纵日益增长,好像有钱才能在同类中保持应有的地位,而无钱就要被人轻视。因此,各种行业和各种交易都在以欺诈的方式,以及不道德的方法进行,从而使一个诚实守信的人几乎不可能在这种情况下继续维持自己的作风,并安逸地生活。

"第五个动机:讲授科学和宗教知识的学校太腐败(除了让人不能忍受教育费用以外),以致使大部分儿童,甚至是最优秀和最有才华的儿童和那些人们认为最有希望成才的儿童,在他们周围的大量邪恶事例和大量腐败行为的影响下学坏了。

"第六个动机:大地是上帝的花园,他把大地赐给他的儿子亚当,让他自己去耕种,而我们为什么要让自己因为没有土地而饿死,并叫这片本来应当供人使用的广阔土地无人居住和如此荒芜呢?

"*Seventhly*, What can be a better or nobler work, and more worthy of a *christian*, than to erect and support a *reformed particular Church* in its infancy, and unite our forces with such a company of faithful people, as by a timely assistance may grow stronger and prosper; but for want of it, may be put to great hazards, if not be wholly ruined.

"*Eighthly*, If any such as are known to be godly, and live in wealth and prosperity here, shall forsake all this to join with this *reformed church*, and with it run the hazard of an hard and mean condition, it will be an example of great use, both for the removing of *scandal*, and to give more *life* unto the *faith* of God's people in their prayers for the plantation, and also to encourage others to join the more willingly in it. "

Later, in stating the principles of the Church of New England with respect to morals, Mather inveighs with violence against the custom of drinking healths at table, which he denounces as a pagan and abominable practice. He proscribes with the same rigor all ornaments for the hair used by the female sex, as well as their custom of having the arms and neck uncovered. In another part of his work he relates several instances of witchcraft which had alarmed New England. It is plain that the visible action of the Devil in the affairs of this world appeared to him an incontestable and evident fact. At many points this book reveals the spirit of civil liberty and political independence that characterized the author's contemporaries. Their principles in matters of government are in evidence throughout. Thus, for example, we find that in the year 1630 [*sic*], ten years after the settlement of Plymouth, the inhabitants of Massachusetts contributed 400 pounds sterling toward the establishment of the university at Cambridge.

In passing from the general documents relative to the history of New England to those which describe the several states comprised within its limits, I ought first to mention *The History of the Colony of Massachusetts*, by Thomas Hutchinson, Lieutenant-Governor of the Massachusetts Province, 2 vols. , 8vo. There is a copy of this

"第七个动机：要成立一个革新的教会，并深深地支持它；要把我们的力量与一个虔诚的民族的力量联合起来，并在适当时候巩固和发展这个教会，使它摆脱那些没有这种支持就可能成为它的大灾大难的危险。对于一个基督徒来说，有什么工作能比这项工作更为高尚和壮丽的呢？有什么事业能比这项事业更值得做的呢？

"第八个动机：一个正直的并在这里享有荣华富贵的人如能放弃因加入这个革新的教会而获得的好处，并愿意在艰苦的环境中承担苦难，他将为人们做出一个伟大而高尚的榜样，这不仅是为了消除流言蜚语，而且使人们学习他在向上帝为殖民地祷告时表示自己的虔诚信仰，并把大多数人联合过来。"

最后，在叙述新英格兰教会在道德方面的原则时，马瑟强烈地抨击了在宴会上为健康而干杯的作法，说这是异教徒的令人厌恶的习俗。他也同样严厉地反对妇女对头发进行任何装饰，无情地谴责妇女穿着袒胸露臂的时装。他在其著作的某一部分里，向我们举出了一些曾震惊了整个新英格兰的妖魔作怪的事例。在他看来，恶魔在这个世界兴妖作怪，是毋庸置疑的明显事实。这本书在很多方面都揭示了他的同时代人所特有的追求公民自由和政治独立的精神，说他们每前进一步都遵循他们的自治原则。比如，我们发现在 1630 年以后，即在建立普利茅斯殖民地后的 10 里，马萨诸塞的居民就用去 400 英镑在剑桥创办一所大学。

如果我们从对新英格兰的历史的研究转向对新英格兰各州历史的研究，则首先应当提到马萨诸塞地方副总督哈钦森的《马萨诸塞殖民地史》。此书为 32 开本，共两卷。王家图书馆藏有此

work at the Biblioth éque royale, a second edition printed at London in 1765. The history by Hutchinson, which I have several times quoted in the chapter to which this note relates, commences in the year 1628 and ends in 1750. Throughout the work there is a striking air of truth and the greatest simplicity of style; it is full of minute details.

The best history to consult concerning Connecticut is that of Benjamin Trumbull, entitled A *Complete History of Connecticut*, *Civil and Ecclesiastical*, 1630-1764, 2 vols. , 8vo, printed in 1818, at New Haven. I do not believe that Trumbull's work is in the Biblioth éque royale. This history contains a clear and calm account of all the events which happened in Connecticut during the period given in the title. The author drew from the best sources, and his narrative bears the stamp of truth. His remarks on the early days of Connecticut are extremely interesting. See, especially, in his work, "The Constitution of 1639 ," Vol. I, chap. vi, p. 100, and also "The Penal Laws of Connecticut," Vol. I, chap. vii, p. 125.

The History of New Hampshire, by Jeremy Belknap, is a work held in merited esteem. It was printed at Boston in 1792, in 2 vols. , 8vo. The third chapter of the first volume is particularly worthy of attention for the valuable details it affords on the political and religious principles of the Puritans, on the causes of their emigration, and on their laws. Here we may find a curious quotation from a sermon delivered in 1663: "New England must always remember that she was founded with a religious and not a commercial aim. Her visage shows that purity in doctrine and discipline is her vocation. Let tradesmen and all those who are engaged in heaping penny upon penny remember that religion and not profit was the aim in founding these colonies. If there is anyone among us who, in his valuation of the world and of religion, regards the former as thirteen and the latter as only twelve, he is not inspired by the feelings of a true son of New England. " The reader of Belknap will find in his work more general ideas and more strength of thought than are to be met with in other American historians even to the present day. I do not know whether this book is in the Biblioth éque royale.

Among the central states which deserve our attention for their

书一部,这本书的第二版在 1765 年出版于伦敦。我在与本注相关的章节曾多次引用过这部著作,其叙述始于 1628 年,而结束于 1750 年。本书写得十分真实,并且风格简练,是一部对细节也叙述得很到位的历史著作。

一部可以参考康涅狄格的历史的最好著作,是本杰明·特朗布尔的《康涅狄格全史:世俗史和宗教史,1630—1764》。此书为 32 开本,共两卷,1818 年出版于纽黑文。我认为这部著作不会被收藏在王家图书馆里。这部书历史清晰而深刻地描述了康涅狄格在书名所指期间内发生的一切重大事件。作者有着最好的出处来源,而且其叙述极为真实。他十分有趣地描写了康涅狄格早期的事件。特别是应当读一读第一卷第五章(《一六三九年的康涅狄格》)第 100 页,以及第一卷第七章(《康涅狄格的刑法》)第 125 页。

杰理米·贝尔纳普的《新罕布什尔史》是一部值得一读的著作。此书为 32 开本,共两卷,1792 年出版于波士顿。特别值得读者注意的是第一卷第三章。因为在这一章里,作者对于清教徒的政治原则和宗教教义,他们的移居原因和法律,做了极其详细的叙述。下边是在 1663 年一位说教者的讲话:"新英格兰必须永久记住它创建宗教的目的不在于商业。人们在前进中要坚持清教徒的教义和纪律。因此,商人和靠一个个铜板攒钱的人也应当切记,创建这些殖民地的目的在于宗教,而不在于金钱。如果我们当中有人在评价世界和宗教时认为世界值 13,而宗教只值 12,那么,这个人就没有被赋予新英格兰的真正男儿的情感。"读者从贝尔纳普的著作里可以看到,他比那些至今在研究美国历史的其他作者更多地提到观念的普遍性和思想的权威性。我不知道这本书是否被藏在皇家图书馆里。

在吸引我们注意的存在很久的几个主要州中,纽约州和宾夕法

early origin, New York and Pennsylvania are the foremost. The best history we have of the former is entitled: *A History of New York*, by William Smith, printed at London in 1757. There is a French translation, also printed at London, in 1767, one vol. , duodecimo. Smith gives us important details of the wars between the French and English in America. His is the best account of the famous confederation of the Iroquois.

With respect to Pennsylvania, I cannot do better than point out the work of Proud, entitled the *History of Pennsylvania, from the original Institution and Settlement of that Province, under the first Proprietor and Governor, William Penn, in* 1681, *till after the Year* 1742, by Robert Proud, 2 vols. , 8 vo, printed at Philadelphia in 1797. This work is deserving of the especial attention of the reader; it contains a mass of curious documents concerning Penn, the doctrine of the Quakers, and the character, manners, and customs of the first inhabitants of Pennsylvania. As far as I know, there is no copy at the Biblioth éque. I need not add that among the most important documents relating to this state are the works of Penn himself and those of Franklin. These works are familiar to a great many readers. I consulted most of the works just cited during my stay in America. Some were made available to me by the Biblioth#éque royale, and others were lent me by M. Warden, author of an excellent book on America, former Consul General of the United States at Paris. I cannot close this note without expressing my gratitude to M. Warden.

APPENDIX G. -Vol. I, p. 50

We read in Jefferson's *Memoirs* as follows:

"At the time of the first settlement of the English in Virginia, when land was to be had for little or nothing, some provident persons having obtained large grants of it, and being desirous of maintaining the splendor of their families, entailed their property upon their descendants. The transmission of these estates from generation to generation, to men who bore the same name, had the effect of raising up a distinct class of families, who, possessing by law the privilege of perpetuating their wealth, formed by these means a sort of patrician order, distinguished by the

尼亚州最为突出。关于纽约州的历史,最好的一部著作是威廉·史密斯的《纽约史》。此书为 48 开本,共一卷,1757 年出版于伦敦;1767 年出了法译本,亦出版于伦敦。史密斯为我们提供了法英两国在美洲进行战争的细节。他最成功的报道,是对著名的易洛魁联盟的报道。

至于宾夕法尼亚的历史,我只想推荐罗伯特·普劳特的《宾夕法尼亚自创建与定居:1861 年威廉·佩恩就任第一任领主与总督直至 1742 年以后的历史》。此书为 32 开本,共两卷,1797 年出版于费城。这部书值得读者去认真读一读,其中收有关于佩恩的大批珍贵文献,以及教友派信徒的教义以及宾夕法尼亚初期移民的性格、风尚和习惯。据我所知,王家图书馆没有此书。我不需要再补充,在与宾夕法尼亚相关的主要著作中,也包括佩恩本人的著作和富兰克林的著作。广大读者都熟悉他们的著作。我在留美期间就已阅读过大量的以上介绍的这些著作。其中的一些是从王家图书馆里借到的,而其余的几部,是美国前驻巴黎总领事沃登先生给我找到的,沃登先生也写有一部关于美国历史的杰出著作。在结束这个注的时候,我要表达对沃登先生的谢意。

附录 G。——第一卷,第 50 页

我们在阅读杰斐逊的自传时会看到:

“在英国人初次在弗吉尼亚建立殖民地的时候,当土地还只有很少的用途或什么也不是的时候,一些有远见的人便获得了大量的租让地,并为了维持其家庭的荣华富贵,而把财产传给了后代。财产从一代同姓人的手中传向下一代同姓人手中,从而产生一些独特的家族集团。家族集团依法享有永久保持财富的特权,进而依靠自己州的强大和富饶而形成显赫的贵族阶层。而国王

grandeur and luxury of their establishments. From this order it was that the King usually chose his councillors of state. "

In the United States the principal provisions of English law respecting inheritance have been universally rejected. "The first rule that we follow," says Chancellor Kent, "touching inheritance, is the following: If a man dies intestate, his property goes to his heirs in a direct line. If he has but one heir or heiress, he or she succeeds to the whole. If there are several heirs of the same degree, they divide the inheritance equally among them, without distinction of sex. "

This rule was prescribed for the first time in the state of New York, by a statute of the 23d of February 1786. (See *Revised Statutes*, Vol. III, Appendix, p. 48.) At the present day this law holds good throughout the whole of the United States, with the exception of the state of Vermont, where the male heir inherits a double portion. (Kent's *Commentaries*, Vol. IV, p. 370.) Chancellor Kent, in the same work (Vol. IV, pp. 1-22), gives a historical account of American legislation on the subject of entail; by this we learn that previous to the Revolution the colonies followed the English law of entail. Estates tail were abolished in Virginia in 1776, on motion of Mr. Jefferson. (See Jefferson's *Memoirs*.) They were suppressed in New York in 1786, and have since been abolished in North Carolina, Kentucky, Tennessee, Georgia, and Missouri. In Vermont, Indiana, Illinois, South Carolina, and Louisiana entail was never introduced. Those states which thought proper to preserve the English law of entail modified it in such a way as to deprive it of its most aristocratic tendencies. "Our general principles on the subject of government," says Kent, "tend to favor the free circulation of property. "

It cannot fail to strike the French reader who studies the law of inheritance that on these questions French legislation is infinitely more democratic than even the American.

American law makes an equal division of the father's property, but only in the case of his will not being known; "for every man," says the law (*Revised Statutes*, Vol. III, Appendix, p. 51) , "in the State of New York, has entire liberty, power, and

也照例经常是从这个阶层中选派州的议员。"

美国人对英国法律中关于遗产继承的一些主要规定全部否定。肯特先生说："我们在遗产继承问题上做的第一个规定是,如果一个人死后而没有立遗嘱时,其财产由直接亲属继承;要是这个人只有一个男性或一个女性继承人,他或她独自获得全部遗产;如有数名同顺序的继承人,则不分性别,由数人平分遗产。"

最初,纽约州以1786年2月23日法令通过这项规定,后来又进行过修订(见《增订纽约州法令集》第三卷;附录,第48页)。直到今天,美国各州都仍在采用这项规定,但佛蒙特州有些例外,那里的男性继承人可得两份遗产(见《美国法释义》第4卷第370页)。肯特先生在该书第四卷第1—22页,对美国的限定继承立法史进行了一系列的叙述。通过他的叙述,使我们知道了美国在独立前,各殖民地都采用英国的限定继承法。后来,弗吉尼亚根据杰斐逊的提议(见《杰斐逊自传》),于1776年在弗吉尼亚废除了遗产限定继承制度。纽约州也于1786年禁止了这种制度。接着,北卡罗来纳、肯塔基、田纳西、佐治亚和密苏里,也相继废除了限定继承法。而在佛蒙特、印第安纳、伊利诺伊、南卡罗来纳和路易斯安那,从来就没有采用过限定继承制度。那些认为应当保留英国的限定继承法的各州,也对限定继承制加以修改,并去掉了其中的贵族立法倾向。肯特先生写道:"我们在国家管理方面的一般原则,是要有利于促进财产的自由流通。"

使研究美国遗产继承立法的法国人大为吃惊的是,法国的继承法比美国的继承法更加民主。

美国的法律规定对父亲的遗产要进行平等的划分,但只是在父亲没有另立遗嘱的情况下,因为纽约州的法律规定(《增订纽

authority to dispose of his property by will, to leave it entire, or divided in favor of any persons he chooses as his heirs, provided he does not leave it to a political body or any corporation. " The French law obliges the testator to divide his property equally, or nearly so, among his heirs. Most of the American republics still admit of entails, under certain restrictions; but the French law prohibits entail in all cases. If the social condition of the Americans is more democratic than that of the French, the laws of the latter are the more democratic of the two. This may be explained more easily than at first appears to be possible. In France democracy is still occupied in the work of destruction; in America it reigns quietly over the ruins it has made.

APPENDIX H. -Vol. I, p. 58

Simmary Of The Qualifications Of Voters In The United States

All the states agree in granting the right of voting at the age of twenty-one. In all of them it is necessary to have resided for a certain time in the district where the vote is cast. This period varies from three months to two years. As to qualifications, in the state of Massachusetts it is necessary to have an income of three pounds sterling, or a capital of sixty pounds. In Rhode Island a man must possess landed property to the amount of 133 dollars (704 francs). In Connecticut he must have property which gives an income of seventeen dollars (about 90 francs). A year of service in the militia also gives the electoral privilege. In New Jersey an elector must have a property of fifty pounds. In South Carolina and Maryland the elector must possess fifty acres of land. In Tennessee he must possess some property. In the states of Mississippi, Ohio, Georgia, Virginia, Pennsylvania, Delaware, and New York the only necessary qualification for voting is that of paying the taxes; and in most of the states, service in the militia is equivalent to the payment of taxes. In Maine and New Hampshire any man can vote who is not on the pauper list. Lastly, in the states of Missouri, Alabama, Illinois, Louisiana, Indiana, Kentucky, and Vermont voting requirements have no reference to the property of the elector.

约州法令集》,第三卷,附录,第51页):"每个纽约州的公民都有完全的自由、权力和资格通过立遗嘱来处理自己的财产,即对某一政治机关或社会团体留下遗言,将其财产全部或部分遗赠给任何一个他想要赠送的人。"法国的法律规定立遗嘱人可将其财产平分或近于平分各继承人和受遗赠人。现在,美国的大部分州还在实行限定继承制度,但在一定的范围内。但法国的法律在任何情况下都禁止限定继承。如果美国的社会情况比法国的民主,那么法国的法律则比美国的民主。这最能说明一个值得人们深思的问题:即在法国,民主安于遭受破坏;而在美国,民主能在废墟之上泰然自立。

附录 H。——第一卷,第58页

对美国选举资格的概要

所有的州都同意赋予年满21岁的人选举权。在各州,选举人应在其参加选举的区域居住过一定时间,这个时间通常为三个月或两年。关于财产资格:在马萨诸塞州,选举人必须有 3 英镑收入或60英镑资产。在罗得岛,选举人必须拥有价值133 美元(约合704法郎)的地产。在康涅狄格,选举人必须拥有收入可达到17 美元(约合90法郎)的财产。在民兵中服役一年,亦可享有选举权。在新泽西,选举人应有50 英镑财产。在南卡罗来纳和马里兰,选举人必须拥有50 英亩土地。在田纳西,选举人必须拥有一定数量的财产,其形式可随意。在密西西比州、俄亥俄州、佐治亚州、弗吉尼亚州、宾夕法尼亚州、特拉华州和纽约州,只要是纳税,就可以成为选举人,但其中的大部分州,民兵服役就等同于纳税。在缅因和新罕布什尔,凡是没有被列入贫困名单的,都可成为选举人。最后,在密苏里州、阿拉巴马州、伊利诺伊州、路易斯安那州、印第安纳州、肯塔基州和佛蒙特州,对于选举人的财产没有规定任何条件。

I believe there is no other state beside that of North Carolina in which different requirements govern voting for the Senate and electing the House of Representatives. The electors of the former, in this case, must possess a property of fifty acres of land; to vote for the latter, nothing more is required than to pay taxes.

APPENDIX I. -Vol. I, p. 94

The United States has a prohibitive tariff. The small number of custom-house officers employed in the United States, and the great extent of the coast, render smuggling very easy; notwithstanding, it is less practiced than elsewhere because everybody endeavors to repress it. In America there is no fire-prevention service, and fires are more frequent than in Europe; but, in general, they are more speedily extinguished, because the surrounding population is prompt to lend assistance.

APPENDIX K. -Vol. I, p. 96

It is incorrect to say that centralization was produced by the French Revolution: the Revolution brought it to perfection, but did not create it. The mania for centralization and government regulation dates from the period when jurists began to take a share in the government, in the time of Philip the Fair; ever since this period they have been on the increase. In the year 1775 M. de Malesherbes, speaking in the name of the *Cour des Aides*, said to Louis XVI: ①

"Every corporation and every community of citizens retained the right of administering its own affairs, a right which not only forms part of the primitive constitution of the kingdom, but has a still higher origin; for it is the right of nature and of reason. Nevertheless, your subjects, Sire, have been deprived of it; and we do not fear to say that, in this respect, your government has fallen into

---

① See *Mémoires pour servir àl' histoire de la France en matiére d' impôts*, *Brussels*, 1779, p. 654.

我相信,除了北卡罗来纳州,再不会有任何一个州对参议员的选举人规定的资格与众议员的不同:前者必须拥有 50 英亩土地,而对后者没有什么特殊的要求,只要是纳税公民就可以了。

附录 I。——第一卷,第 94 页

美国实行保护关税政策,所以只雇佣了少数海关人员,它的大部分海岸地区最容易走私,但并不像其他国家那样无法无天,因为任何人都可以缉私。美国不设消防警察,所以火灾比欧洲的频繁,但一般说来,火灾都可以被及时扑灭,因为周围的居民不会置之不理,而会伸出援助之手。

附录 K。——第一卷,第 96 页[1]

说中央集权产生于法国大革命,是极其不正确的。法国大革命只是使中央集权更加完善,但并没有创造中央集权。在法国,对中央集权的爱好和对典章制度的狂信,是开始于法学家进入政府的时期,也就是美男子腓力四世统治法国的时代。从那个时期以后,这两种倾向一直在持续增加。下面是马尔泽尔布先生 1775 年代表最高税务法院向路易十六国王的进言摘录:[①]

"每个社团和每个公民组织都保留自己管理自己事务的权利;这项权利不仅会成为王国的第一部宪法的一部分,而且会有更高的出处;因为它是一项自然的并且是合情合理的权利。但是,它已夺走您的主要东西。陛下和我们都不要害怕说:在这方

---

① 见 1779 年于布鲁塞尔的"Mémoires pour servirā l'histoire de la France en matière d'impôts",第 654 页。

[1] 托克维尔并没有包含字母 J 的附录。

puerile extremes. From the time when powerful ministers made it a political principle to prevent the convocation of a national assembly, one consequence has succeeded another, until the deliberations of the inhabitants of a village are declared null if they have not been authorized by the Intendant. Of course, if the community has an expensive undertaking to carry through, it must remain under the control of the sub-delegate of the Intendant, and, consequently, follow the plan he proposes, employ his favorite workmen, pay them according to his pleasure; and if an action at law is deemed necessary, the Intendant's permission must be obtained. The cause must be pleaded before this first tribunal previous to its being carried into a public court; and if the opinion of the Intendant is opposed to that of the inhabitants, or if their adversary enjoys his favor, the community is deprived of the power of defending its rights. Such are the means, Sire, which have been exerted to extinguish the municipal spirit in France and to stifle, if possible, the opinions of the citizens. The nation may be said to lie under an interdict, and to be in wardship under guardians. "

What could be said more to the purpose at the present day, when the Revolution has achieved what are called *its victories* in centralization?

In 1789 Jefferson wrote from Paris to one of his friends: "There is no country where the mania for over-governing has taken deeper root than in France, or been the source of greater mischief. " (*Letter to Madison*, August 28, 1789.)

The fact is that for several centuries the central power of France has done everything it could to extend central administration; it has acknowledged no other limits than its own strength. The central power to which the Revolution gave birth made more rapid advances than any of its predecessors, because it was stronger and wiser than they had been. Louis XVI committed the welfare of the municipal communities to the caprice of an Intendant; Napoleon left them to that of the Minister. The same principle governed both, though its consequences were more or less far- reaching.

APPENDIX L. -Vol. I, p. 100

This immutability of the Constitution in France is a necessary consequence of the laws.

To begin with the most important of all the laws, that which de

面,我们的政府已经陷入了极其不成熟的阶段。自从几位有权势的大臣提出禁止召集国民议会的政治原则以来,一些结论便层出不穷,以致村镇的居民不经总督的批准,什么决定也不能做出。因此,如果某个村镇要想实施一项花费巨大的事业,就必须受到总督的下属官员的控制,从而要根据官员同意的计划进行,雇佣他们喜欢的工人,随着他们的意思支付工资;如果审理什么案件,也得经总督批准,即在向法院起诉之前,要把案件先送到那里进行初审。如果总督的意见同居民的相反,或诉讼的对方是总督的亲信,村镇就失去保卫自己权力的能力。总督就是通过这些办法尽力熄灭法国全部地方的自治精神的,如果有可能,则将使公民的心中的这种精神窒息。也可以说,全国人民都会受到阻断,并给他们指定了监护人。"

那么今天怎么能说法国大革命在中央集权方面所做的一切是所谓的胜利呢?

1789 年杰斐逊在巴黎给一位友人写信说道:"没有一个国家会像法国那样,对统治的狂热会那样的根深蒂固和造成了许多灾难。"(见 1789 年 8 月 28 日致麦迪逊的信中。)

实际上,几个世纪以来,法国的中央政权,已经做到了一切能够扩大其行政集权的事务;在这方面,它的权力从来没有受到过限制。法国大革命产生的中央政权,比其他任何一个先行者都具有更快的进步,因为它比它们都更强壮和更有智慧。比如,路易十四只是使村镇生活的一切服从于一位总督的享乐;拿破仑只是使村镇生活的一切服从于一位大臣。原则始终相同,只是后来的发展有大有小。

附录 L。——第一卷,第 100 页

法国宪法的这种不变性,是法律的必然结果。

先从一切法律中最重要的法律开始,也就是规定王位继承的法

cides the order of succession to the throne, what can be more immutable in its principle than a political order founded upon the natural succession of father to son? In 1814 Louis XVIII established the perpetual law of hereditary succession in favor of his own family. Those who controlled the outcome of the Revolution of 1830 followed his example; they merely established the perpetuity of the law in favor of another family. In this respect they imitated Chancellor Maupeou, who, when he erected the new Parliament upon the ruins of the old, took care to declare in the same ordinance that the rights of the new magistrates should be as inalienable as those of their predecessors had been.

The laws of 1830, like those of 1814, point out no way of changing the Constitution, and it is evident that the ordinary means of legislation are insufficient for this purpose. As the King, the Peers, and the Deputies all derive their authority from the Constitution, these three powers united cannot alter a law by virtue of which alone they govern. Without the Constitution they are nothing; where, then, could they take their stand to effect a change in its provisions? The alternative is clear: either their efforts are powerless against the Charter, which continues to exist in spite of them, in which case they only reign in the name of the Charter; or they succeed in changing the Charter, and then, the law by which they existed being annulled, they themselves cease to exist. By destroying the Charter they destroy themselves.

This is much more evident in the laws of 1830 than in those of 1814. In 1814 the royal prerogative took its stand above and beyond the Constitution; but in 1830 it was avowedly created by and dependent on the Constitution.

A part, therefore, of the French Constitution is immutable, because it is united to the destiny of a family; and the body of the Constitution is equally immutable, because there appear to be no legal means of changing it.

These remarks are not applicable to England. That country having no written Constitution, who can tell when its Constitution is changed?

律。有什么法律比这个以父传子的以自然顺序为基础的政治规定在原则上更不可改变的呢？1814 年，路易十八建立了对自己家族有利的永久性的继承权。控制 1830 年 7 月革命爆发结果的那些人，以路易十八为榜样，并效仿他的做法，只不过建立了对另一个家族有利的永久继承权罢了。在这方面，他们也仿效了大法官莫普。莫普在旧的最高法院的废墟上建立起新的最高法院时，没有忘记宣布在国王的诏令中，新的大法官也同他们的前任一样是不可罢免的。

1830 年的法律也同 1814 年的法律一样，根本没有提到有关修改宪法的问题。而且很明显，一般的立法手段已经满足了这个要求。国王，贵族院议员和众议院议员是依靠宪法来取得他们的权力吗？在这种情况下，这三种权力的联合也不可能对他们的权力所唯一依靠的法律进行任何改革。离开了宪法，他们就什么也没有了。那么，在什么状况下他们才会坚持修改宪法呢？下述两种条件必居其一：不是在他们无力反对人民的一些行为，但却是以他们的名义继续实行宪法的某些条款的时候；就是在他们借以掌权的法律不复存在，他们自己不再有什么地位，而要求改变宪法的时候。后来，由于破坏了宪法，他们便自己毁灭了自己。

这一点，在 1830 年的法律中比在 1814 年的法律中表现得更加明显。在 1814 年，王权可以说是超越了宪法的范围；但在 1830年，王权已经受宪法控制，并完全依赖于宪法。

因此，法国宪法的各个部分都是不可变的，因为它与一个家族的命运联系在一起了；法国宪法的外体也同样是不可变的，因为人们还没有找到修改宪法的合法手段。

这些论述都不适用于英国。英国没有成文宪法，谁能说英国的成文宪法被修改过呢？

APPENDIX M. -Vol. I, p. 100

The most esteemed authors who have written upon the English Constitution agree with each other in establishing the omnipotence of Parliament.

Delolme says (Chap. X, p. 77) : "It is a fundamental principle with the English lawyers, that Parliament can do everything except make a woman a man, or a man a woman. "

Blackstone expresses himself more in detail, if not more energetically, than Delolme, in the following terms:

" The power and jurisdiction of Parliament, says Sir Edward Coke (4 Inst. , 36), is so transcendent and absolute, that it cannot be confined, either for causes or persons, within any bounds. And of this high Court, he adds, may truly be said, ' *Si antiquitatem spectes, est vetustissima; si dignitatem, est honoratissima; si jurisdictionem, est capacissima.* ' It hath sovereign and uncontrollable authority in the making, confirming, enlarging, restraining, abrogating, repealing, reviving, and expounding of laws, concerning matters of all possible denominations; ecclesiastical or temporal; civil, military, maritime, or criminal; this being the place where that absolute despotic power which must, in all governments, reside somewhere, is intrusted by the Constitution of these kingdoms. All mischiefs and grievances, operations and remedies, that transcend the ordinary course of the laws, are within the reach of this extraordinary tribunal. It can regulate or new-model the succession to the Crown; as was done in the reign of Henry VIII and William III. It can alter the established religion of the land; as was done in a variety of instances in the reigns of King Henry VIII and his three children. It can *change and create afresh even the Constitution of the kingdom*, and of parliaments themselves; as was done by the Act of Union and the several statutes for triennial and septennial elections. It can, in short, do everything that is not naturally impossible to be done; and, therefore, some have not scrupled to call its power, by a figure rather too bold, the omnipotence of Parliament. "

附录 M。——第一卷,第 100 页

几位研究英国宪法的著名学者,也相互讨论过关于建立议会的这种无限权威。

德洛姆在其著作第 10 章第 77 页中写道:"英国法学家们所坚持的基本原则,就是认为议会除了不能把女人变成男人或把男人变成女人以外,其他任何事情都能做到。"

布莱克斯通虽然说得不像德洛姆这样坚定,但也十分细致地表达了自己的观点。下面,就是他说的:

"爱德华·科克爵士认为议会的权力和司法权(第 4 项第 36 款),无论是对人,还是对事,都是如此的广泛和如此的专制,以致它不能被限制在任何范围里。他补充说,对于这个最高的法院简直可以说是:Si antiquitatem spectes, est vetustissiC ma; si dignitatem, est honoratissima; si jurisdictionem, est capacissima。议会在制定、批准、扩大、限制、废除、恢复使用和解释教会法令方面都享有至高无上和不可控制的权威;或是在世俗法令、民法、军事法、海运法或刑法等名目众多的法律方面,也拥有同样巨大的权力;而授予议会以这种可以左右政府各部门的绝对专制权力的,正是这个王国的宪法。所有的冤情和损害以及要求赔偿损失的案件,都可越过普通法院而送到这个特殊的法院去解决。它能调整或重新编制王位继承法,就像在亨利八世和威廉三世所发生的一样。它可以改变某一国家的宗教信仰,比如在亨利八世及其三个子女统治时期,它就曾以各种方法使国家改变宗教。它可以改变和创造王国的宪法和议会本身,比如它曾通过联盟的法案,以及关于三年和七年举行一次选举的各项法令,而且这样做过。简而言之,它能做到本来不能做到的一切,因此它毫不犹豫地使用了自己的权力,以过于大胆的形式表现了议会万能。"

APPENDIX N. -Vol. I, p. 111

There is no question on which the American Constitutions agree more fully than on that of political jurisdiction. All the Constitutions which take cognizance of this matter give to the House of Representatives the exclusive right of impeachment; excepting only the Constitution of North Carolina, which grants the same privilege to grand juries. (Article 23.)

Almost all the Constitutions give to the Senate, or to the legislative body which occupies its place, the exclusive right of trying the impeachment and pronouncing judgment. The only punishments which the political tribunals can inflict are removal from office, and exclusion from public functions for the future. The Constitution of Virginia alone enables them to inflict any kind of punishment.

The crimes which are subject to political jurisdiction are, in the Federal Constitution (Article I, Section 4), in that of Indiana (Art. 3, paragraphs 23 and 24), of New York (Art. 5), of Delaware (Art. 5): high treason, bribery, and other high crimes or misdemeanors.

In the Constitution of Massachusetts (Chap. I, Section 2), that of North Carolina (Art. 23), of Virginia (p. 252): misconduct and maladministration.

In the Constitution of New Hampshire (p. 105): corruption, intrigue, and maladministration.

In Vermont (Chap. 2, Art. 24): maladministration.

In South Carolina (Art. 5), Kentucky (Art. 5), Tennessee (Art. 4), Ohio (Art. 1, 23, 24), Louisiana (Art. 5), Mississippi (Art. 5), Alabama (Art. 6), Pennsylvania (Art. 4): crimes committed in the performance of official duties. In the states of Illinois, Georgia, Maine, and Connecticut no particular offenses are specified.

APPENDIX O. -Vol. I, p. 172

It is true that the powers of Europe may carry on maritime wars against the Union; but it is always easier and less dangerous to undertake a maritime than a continental war. Maritime warfare requires only one species of effort. A commercial people which consents to fur

附录 N。——第一卷,第 111 页

美国各州的宪法,都在政治审判制度方面的规定表现得非常一致。各州的宪法都定有这种制度,并授予州众议院以弹劾的专权,只有北卡罗来纳州宪法把这项权利授予大陪审团(第 23 条)。

几乎所有州的宪法,都授予州参议院或有州参议员出席的立法机构以政治审判的专权。政治法院可以作出的唯一处罚,就是撤职或以后不准再任公职。只有弗吉尼亚宪法准许政治法院可以做出各种不同处罚。

可以送交政治审判的罪行有:在联邦宪法第一条第 4 项、印第安纳州宪法第三条第 23 项和第 24 项、纽约州宪法第五条和特拉华州宪法第五条规定的叛国罪、贿赂罪和其他重罪或轻罪;

在马萨诸塞州宪法第一章第二条、北卡罗来纳州宪法第二十三条和弗吉尼亚州宪法第 252 页,所列出的渎职罪和玩忽职守罪;

在新罕布什尔州宪法第 105 页规定的贿赂罪、私通罪和玩忽职守罪;

在佛蒙特州宪法第二章第二十四条规定的玩忽职守罪;

在南卡罗来纳州宪法第五条、肯塔基州宪法第五条、田纳西州宪法第四条、俄亥俄州宪法第一条第 23 项和第 24 项、路易斯安那州宪法第五条、密西西比州宪法第五条、亚拉巴马州宪法第六条和宾夕法尼亚州宪法第四条规定的渎职罪。在伊利诺伊州、佐治亚州、缅因州和康涅狄格州的宪法中没有特别列明罪行。

附录 O。——第一卷,第 172 页

不错,欧洲各国可以对美国进行大规模的海战;但对于美国,海战往往比陆战更容易对付,而且危险较小。海战只需要一种武力。在商业国家,只要人民同意向政府提供必要的资金,就肯定

nish its government with the necessary funds is sure to possess a fleet. And it is far easier to induce a nation to part with its money, almost unconsciously, than to reconcile it to sacrifices of men and personal efforts. Moreover, defeat by sea rarely compromises the existence or independence of the people which endures it.

As for continental wars, it is evident that the nations of Europe cannot threaten the American Union in this way. It would be very difficult to transport and maintain in America more than 25,000 soldiers, an army which may be considered to represent a nation of about 2,000,000 men. The most populous nation of Europe, contending in this way against the Union, is in the position of a nation of 2,000,000inhabitants at war with one of 12,000,000. Add to this that America has all its resources within reach, while the European is 4,000 miles distant from his, and that the immensity of the American continent would of itself present an insurmountable obstacle to its conquest.

APPENDIX P. -Vol. I, p. 188

The first American newspaper appeared in April 1704, and was published at Boston. (See *Collections of the Historical Society of Massachusetts*, Vol. VI, p. 66.)

It would be a mistake to suppose that the press has always been entirely free in the American colonies: an attempt was made to establish something like censorship and posting of bonds. (Consult the *Legislative Documents of Massachusetts, January* 14, 1722.)

The Committee appointed by the General Court (the legislative body of the province) for the purpose of examining an affair relative to a paper entitled *The New England Courant* expresses its opinion that "the tendency of the said journal is to turn religion into derision, and bring it into contempt; that it mentions the sacred writers in a profane and irreligious manner; that it puts malicious interpretations upon the conduct of the ministers of the Gospel; and that the government of His Majesty is insulted, and the peace and tranquillity of the Province disturbed, by the said journal. The Committee is consequently of opinion that the printer and publisher, James Franklin, should be forbidden to print and publish the said journal or any other work in future, without having previously submitted it to the Secretary of the Province; and that the justices of the peace for the county of Suffolk should be commissioned to require bail of the said James Franklin for his good conduct during the ensuing year. "

The suggestion of the Committee was adopted, and passed into a law; but the effect was null, for the journal eluded the prohibition by

会拥有强大的舰队。而且让人民几乎是在不知不觉中,牺牲一些金钱远比让他们牺牲生命和人力要容易得多。另外,海战的败绩也很少损害战败国的生存和独立。

至于陆战,欧洲国家显然不能威胁到美国。即使一个拥有将近200万人口的国家,也很难向美国运去并在那里供养 25000 名士兵。如果一个这样的欧洲大国同美国交战,就等于一个拥有 200 万人口的国家同拥有 1200 万人口的国家打仗。并且,美国人拥有各种类型的资源,欧洲人距离他们还有 4000 英里的路程,何况美国广袤无垠的土地是在征服它时将要遇到的不可克服的障碍。

附录 D。——第一卷,第 188 页

美国的第一份报纸,在 1704 年 4 月出版于波士顿(见《马萨诸塞历史学会集刊》第六卷第 66 页)。

如果认为出版业在美国殖民地是完全自由的,那就错了。在那里,也曾试图设立过审查机构和提交保证金之类的制度(马萨诸塞州 1722 年 1 月 14 日法令就有这类规定)。

由一般法庭(县立法机关)委派的检查新闻工作的“新英格兰报刊委员会”的观点如下:“被告的报纸有轻视宗教和使人鄙视宗教的倾向,准许一些著名作者以亵渎宗教和对神不敬的方式在上面发表文章,并恶意咒骂福音会教士的行为,侮辱国王陛下的政府,扰乱本地的和平和安宁。因此结果是,或禁止该报出版人兼发行人詹姆斯·富兰克林继续出版和发行该报,或令其将要发表的一切文章送交本地行政长官审查;命令萨福克县治安法官令富兰克林先生交纳保证金并担保自己今后一年之内保持良好的行为。”

委员会的建议被采纳并通过了法律,但未产生任何效果。报纸为了躲避禁令,在边栏将发行人詹姆斯·富兰克林的姓名改为本

putting the name of Benjamin Franklin instead of James Franklin at the bottom of its columns, and this maneuver was supported by public opinion.

APPENDIX Q. -Vol. I, p. 283

To be a voter in the county (those who represent landed property) before the Reform Bill passed in 1832, it was necessary to have unencumbered, in one's own ownership or on lease for life, land bringing in at least 40 shillings' income. This law was enacted about 1450 under Henry VI. It has been reckoned that 40 shillings in the time of Henry VI might be the equivalent of 30 sterling of our time. The English, however, have allowed this qualification, adopted in the fifteenth century, to persist up to 1832, which proves how democratic the English Constitution became with the passage of time even while it appeared static. (See Delolme, Bk. I, ch. 4; see also Blackstone, Bk. I, ch. 4.)

English juries are chosen by the sheriff of the county (Delolme, Bk. I, ch. 12). The sheriff is generally an important man in the county; he discharges judicial and administrative duties; he represents the king and is named by him every year (Blackstone, Bk. I, ch. 9). His position places him above the suspicion of corruption on the part of any litigants; besides, if his impartiality is questioned, they can dismiss the entire jury which he has chosen, and then another officer is entrusted with the task of choosing new jurymen (see Blackstone, Bk. III, ch. 23).

In order to have the right to be a juryman, you have to be the owner of a piece of land yielding a minimum of 10 shillings' income (Blackstone, Bk. III, ch. 23). It will be noted that the qualification was required under the reign of William and Mary, that is to say about 1700, a period when the value of money was infinitely greater than it is today. It is obvious that the English have based their jury system not on ability but on landed property, as is the case with all their other political institutions.

They have finally admitted farmers to serve on juries, but they have required that their leases be very long and that they have a net income of 20 shillings, independent of rents (Blackstone, idem.).

杰明·富兰克林,并且受到舆论的支持。

附录 Q。——第一卷,第 283 页

在 1832 年通过改革法案以前,县的选举人(土地财产的代表者)必须拥有 40 先令纯收入,是来自维持生计的自有地产或租用地产。这项法案是在亨利四世时期于 1450 年前后制定的。亨利四世时期的 40 先令,相当于现今的 30 英镑。但是,英国人一直采用 15 世纪定下的这个金额,一直持续到 1832 年,这就表明英国的宪法是日趋民主了,经过了这么长的时间,为选举人规定的财产资格还没有变动过(参看:德洛姆著作第一卷第四章;布莱克斯通著作第一卷第四章)。

英国的陪审员由县治安官选举(德洛姆著作第一卷第十二章)。县治安官一般是本县的重要人士,主管司法和行政工作;他在可以代表国王,每年由国王任命(布莱克斯通著作第一卷第九章)。他的地位容易被人怀疑受诉讼当事人的贿赂,而且当他的公正受到质疑时,人民可以解散由他任命的整个陪审团,改由另一名官员负责推选新的陪审员(参看布莱克斯通著作第三卷第二十三章)。

为了得到当选陪审员的权力,一个人必须拥有可以获得不少于 10 先令收入的地产(布莱克斯通著作第三卷第二十三章)。值得注意的是,这个条款必须是在威廉和玛丽统治时期,也就是说在 1700 年先后规定的,这个时期的货币的价值比现在要高很多。很明显,英国的陪审制度,也像该国的其他一切政治制度一样,不是根据人的能力而是根据人的地产建立的。

最后,农民也可以担任陪审员,但是要求他必须是有着长期租约的人,而且除过地租后,他的纯收入要达 20 先令(布莱克斯通著作第三卷第二十三章)。

APPENDIX R. -Vol. I, p. 283

The Federal Constitution has introduced the jury into the tribunals of the Union, just as the states had introduced it into their own several courts; but as it has not established any fixed rules for the choice of jurors, the Federal courts select them from the ordinary jury list which each state makes for itself. The laws of the states must thereforebe examined for the theory of the formation of juries. See Story's *Commentaries on the Constitution*, Book III, Chap. xxxviii, pp. 654-9; Sergeant's *Constitutional Law*, p. 165. See also the Federal laws of 1789, 1800, and 1802 on this subject.

In order thoroughly to understand American principles with respect to the formation of juries, I examined the laws of widely separated states, and the following observations were the result of my inquiries:

In America all the citizens who exercise the elective franchise have the right of serving on a jury. The great state of New York, however, has made a slight difference between the two privileges, but in a spirit quite contrary to that of the laws of France; for in the state of New York there are fewer persons eligible as jurymen than there are electors. It may be said, in general, that the right of forming part of a jury, like the right of electing representatives, is open to all the citizens; the exercise of this right, however, is not put indiscriminately into any hands.

Every year a body of town or county magistrates (called *selectmen in* New England, *supervisors* in New York, *trustees* in Ohio, and *sheriffs of the parish* in Louisiana) chooses for each county a certain number of citizens who have the right of serving as jurymen, and who are supposed to be capable of doing so. These magistrates, being themselves elective, excite no distrust; their powers, like those of most republican magistrates, are very extensive and very arbitrary, and they frequently make use of them, especially in New England, to remove

附录 R。——第一卷,第 283 页

联邦宪法已将陪审制度引进到联邦系统的法院中,就像各州也将陪审制度引入到本州系统的法院一样。但是,联邦宪法没有具体规定如何推选陪审员。联邦法院从每个州按该州规定的办法选定的常任陪审员中抽调陪审员。因此,各州的法律有必要用来说明陪审制度形成的原理。参阅斯托里:《美国宪法释义》第 3 卷第 38 章第 654—659 页;萨金特:《美国宪法》第165 页;以及 1789 年、1800 年和 1802 年联邦有关这个问题颁布的法令。

为了完全详细地了解美国陪审制度的原则,我查阅过几个相距很远的州的法律。下面就是我查阅的结果。

在美国,凡是具有选举权的公民都有担任陪审员的权利。但在纽约那样的大州,推选人的法定资格与陪审员的法定资格只是略有不同,而且这种不同与法国的法律完全相反,因为在纽约州,陪审员的法定资格比推选人的法定资格要低很多。总的说来,在美国,推选陪审员的权利,也同选举议员的权利一样,对所有公民都是公开的。但是,对这项权利的行使,在任何人手中并不是都一样的。

每年,乡镇或县的行政当局会为本地区推选一定数量的有权担任陪审员和预计有此种能力的公民为陪审员的公民(在新英格兰是请乡镇的行政委员,在纽约州是请乡镇行政长官,在俄亥俄州是请遗孤财产保管人,在路易斯安那州是县治安长官)。如这些官员本人当选为陪审员时,也不会引起他人反对。他们的权力同其他共和政体的行政官员的权力一样,具有非常广泛和非常专断的性质,尤其在新英格兰,他们往往

unworthy or incompetent jurymen.

The names of the jurymen thus chosen are transmitted to the county court; and the jury who have to decide any case are drawn by lot from the whole list of names.

The Americans have endeavored in every way to make the common people eligible for the jury and to render the service as little onerous as possible. The jurors being very numerous, each one's turn does not come round oftener than once in three years. The sessions are held in the chief town of every county. The county is roughly equivalent to our arrondissement. Thus the court comes to the jury, instead of bring the jury to it, as in France. Finally, the jury are indemnified for their attendance either by the state or by the parties concerned. They receive in general a dollar per day (5.42 francs), besides their traveling-expenses. In America being placed upon the jury is looked upon as a burden, but it is a burden that is easily borne, and to which everyone readily submits.

See Brevard's *Digest of the Public Statute Law of South Carolina*, Vol. II, p. 338; idem. , Vol. I, pp. 454, 456; idem. , Vol. II, p. 218.

See *The General Laws of Massachusetts Revised and Published by Authority of the Legislature*, Vol. II, pp. 331, 187.

See *The Revised Statutes of the State of New York*, Vol. II, pp. 720, 411, 717, 643.

See *The Statute Law of the State of Tennessee*, Vol. I, p. 209.

See *Acts of the State of Ohio*, pp. 95, 210.

See *Digeste générale des actes de la législature de la Louisiane*, Vol. II, p. 55.

APPENDIX S. -Vol. I, p. 286

If we attentively examine the constitution of the jury in civil proceedings in England, we shall readily perceive that the jurors are under the immediate control of the judge. It is true that the verdict of

有权罢免不称职的或无能力的陪审员。

将被选出的陪审员的名单送交县法院,然后用抽签办法从中选出有权参加各种案件审理的陪审团。

此外,美国人还尽力通过一切办法使普通人民都具有陪审员的资格,并尽可能减轻陪审团的负担。陪审员的人数很多,每人最多只能连任三年。法院在每个县的县城开庭审理案件。美国的县大致相当于法国的区。因此,法院离陪审团很近,而不像法国那样在法院开庭时去召集陪审团。最后,陪审员的报酬或者是由州支付,或者是由诉讼当事人支付,这要取决于案件本身。一般说来,除去旅费外,每人每天可收入一美元(相当于5.42法郎)。在美国,把做陪审员看成是一项负担,但这项负担很容易被承受。参阅布雷瓦德:

《南卡罗来纳州法令汇编》第二卷第 338 页,第一卷第 454 和第 456 页,以及第二卷第 218 页。

参阅立法机构编辑和出版的《马萨诸塞普通法》第二卷第 331 页和第 187 页。

参阅《增订纽约州法令集》第二卷第 720 页、第 411 页、第 717 页和第 643 页。

参阅《田纳西州法令集》第一卷第 209 页。参阅《俄亥俄州法令集》第 95 和 210 页。

参阅《路易斯安那州立法汇编》第二卷第 55 页。

附录 S。——第一卷,第 286 页

如果我们仔细研究英国的民事陪审制度,就会轻易地发现陪审员直接受到法官的控制。当然,陪审团对民事案件和刑事案件所作的判决,也包括对事实和法律的质问。例如:有

known this to happen. (See Blackstone, the jury, in civil as well as in criminal cases, comprises the questions of fact and of law in the same reply. Thus a house is claimed by Peter as having been purchased by him; this is the fact to be decided. The defendant puts in a plea of incompetency on the part of the vendor; this is the legal question to be resolved. The jury simply says that the house shall be delivered to Peter, and thus decides both the questions of fact and of law. But according to the practice of the English courts, the opinion of the jury is not held to be infallible in civil as it is in criminal cases, if the verdict is for acquittal. If the judge thinks that their verdict has made a wrong application of the law, he may refuse to receive it, and send back the jury to deliberate over again. Even if the judge allows the verdict to pass without observation, the case is not yet finally determined; there are still many modes of arresting judgment. The principal one consists in asking the court to set aside the verdict and order a new trial before another jury. It is true that such a request is seldom granted, and never more than twice; yet I have actually Book III, Chap. xxiv; idem. , Book IV, Chap. xxv.)

APPENDIX T. -Vol. II, p. 155

Some aristocracies, however, have devoted themselves eagerly to commerce and have cultivated manufactures with success. The history of the world furnishes several conspicuous examples. But, generally speaking, the aristocratic principle is not favorable to the growth of trade and manufactures. Moneyed aristocracies are the only exception to the rule. Among such aristocracies there are hardly any desires that do not require wealth to satisfy them; the love of riches becomes, so to speak, the high road of human passions, which is crossed by or connected with all lesser tracks. The love of money and the thirst for that distinction which attaches to power are then so closely intermixed in the same souls that it becomes difficult to discover whether men grow covetous from ambition or whether they are ambitious from covetousness. This is the case in England, where men seek to get rich in order to arrive at distinction, and seek distinctions as a manifestation of their wealth. The mind is then seized by both ends, and hurried into trade and manufactures, which are the shortest roads that lead to opulence.

一所住宅,彼得说是他花钱购买的,这就是需要决定的事实问题;但是,他的反对者对他说,出售人没有行为能力,这就是权利问题。陪审团只要说这所住宅将归彼得所有,这就等于认定事实和权利。如果陪审团的判决是宣告被告无罪,英国人就同意陪审团的判决没有错误;但在民事方面应用陪审制度时,英国人就没有保留这种想法。如果法官认为陪审团的判决在法律的应用方面有错误,他可以拒绝接受,驳回给陪审员重新审理。如果法官允许陪审团将案件先搁置起来,不予复审,那么诉讼就不能宣告结束,因为仍旧有很多办法可以抵制陪审团的判决。主要的方法是,要求法院撤销原判和成立新的陪审团。实际上,这样的要求很少能得到满足,而且也不会再出现两次。我就切实地看到过这样的事情(参看布莱克斯通著作第三卷第二十四章和第四卷第二十五章)。

附录 T。——第二卷,第 155 页

但是,有些贵族曾热心致力于商业并在工业方面取得了成就。世界历史为这方面提供了若干显著的范例。然而,一般来说,贵族原则向来不利于工商业的发展。金钱贵族只是这一规律的例外。金钱贵族从来没有不想用财富来满足自己的需要。对财富的热爱,可以说是人类的最大激情,其他一切次要的激情都与此交错或与此交织。如果爱财之心和对权力的渴望之心都混合在同一个人身上,则很难辨别这个人变得如此贪婪是出于他的野心还是他的野心是来自他的贪婪。英国就有这种情况,在那里,人们希望通过财富来获得更多的荣誉,并认为荣誉是财富的标志。因此,人的思想完全被工商业抓住和吸引过去,工商业成了致富的最好捷径。

This, however, strikes me as an exceptional and transitory circumstance. When wealth has become the only symbol of aristocracy, it is very difficult for the wealthy to maintain sole possession of political power, to the exclusion of all other men. The aristocracy of birth and pure democracy are the two extremes of the social and political state of nations; between them moneyed aristocracy finds its place. The latter approximates the aristocracy of birth by conferring great privileges on a small number of persons; it so far belongs to the democratic element that these privileges may be successfully acquired by all. It frequently forms a natural transition between these two conditions of society, and it is difficult to say whether it closes the reign of aristocratic institutions or whether it even now ushers in the new era of democracy.

APPENDIX U. -Vol. II, p. 203

I find in my traveling-journal a passage that may serve to convey a more complete notion of the trials to which the women of America, who consent to follow their husbands into the wilds, are often subjected. This description has nothing to recommend it but its perfect truth.

"From time to time we come to fresh clearings; all these places are alike; I shall describe the one at which we halted tonight, since it will serve me for a picture of all the others.

"The bell which the pioneers hang round the necks of their cattle, in order to find them again in the woods, announced from afar our approach to a clearing; and we soon afterwards heard the stroke of the axe, hewing down the trees of the forest. As we came nearer, traces of destruction marked the presence of civilized man: the road was strewn with cut boughs; trunks of trees, half consumed by fire, or mutilated by the axe, were still standing in our way. We proceeded till we reached a wood in which all the trees seemed to have been sud

但是,在我看来,这是一种例外的和暂时的现象,因为当财富仅仅成为贵族的标志的时候,就很难让富人在维持这唯一的政治权力,并排斥其他一切人的实施。世袭的贵族制度和纯正的民主制度,是国家的社会和政治情况的两个极端,在这两个极端之间存在着金钱贵族。金钱贵族与世袭贵族有些相似,但同意给予少数公民以某些重大特权;到目前为止,它依旧具有民主性质,但要求人人都可以继承特权。这个阶级往往是世袭的贵族制度和纯正的民主制度之间的最自然的过渡,而且人们很难说它是在结束贵族的等级制度还是已经在开辟民主制度的新纪元。

附录 U。——第二卷,第 203 页

在我的旅行日记里,我找到下述几段记载。这些记载可以更完整地让读者了解同意跟随丈夫前往荒凉地区定居的美国妇女都经受了哪些考验。我向读者推荐这几段记载,仅仅是因为它们的真实性。

"我们时常遇到一些新的被开垦的土地。所有这些新居民点都很相似。我要描述我们今天晚上留宿的这个居民点,它给我留下使我想起其他一切居民点的印象。

"开拓者们在自己家牲畜的脖子上拴上了小铃铛,为了能在广袤的森林里找到它们。我们在离居民点还很远的时候,就已听到这种铃声。并且很快地,我们又听到森林里传来砍伐树木的斧头声。随着我们逐渐地靠近,那些伐木的痕迹明显的表示了这里有文明人在劳动。被砍掉的枝干挡住了道路;被火烧毁的残余树干或伐木留下的树墩,还立在我们所走的道路上。我们继续往前走,来到一片森林里,其中所有的树好像突然死去了一样。在正是盛夏的季节里,它们的枝干却

denly struck dead; in the middle of summer their boughs were as leaf-less as in winter; and upon closer examination we found that a deep circle had been cut through the bark, which, by stopping the circula-tion of the sap, soon kills the tree. We were informed that this is commonly the first thing a pioneer does, as he cannot, in the first year, cut down all the trees that cover his new domain; he sows Indi-an corn under their branches, and puts the trees to death in order to prevent them from injuring his crop. Beyond this field, at present im-perfectly traced out, the first work of civilization in the desert, we suddenly came upon the cabin of its owner, situated in the center of a plot of ground more carefully cultivated than the rest, but where man was still waging unequal warfare with the forest; there the trees were cut down, but not uprooted, and the trunks still encumbered the ground which they so recently shaded. Around these dry blocks, wheat, oak seedlings, and plants of every kind grow and intertwine in all the luxuriance of wild, untutored nature. Amid this vigorous and varied vegetation stands the house of the pioneer, or, as they call it, the *log house*. Like the ground about it, this rustic dwelling bore marks of recent and hasty labor: its length seemed not to exceed thirty feet, its height fifteen; the walls as well as the roof were formed of rough trunks of trees, between which a little moss and clay had been inserted to keep out the cold and rain.

"As night was coming on, we determined to ask the master of the log house for a lodging. At the sound of our footsteps the children who were playing among the scattered branches sprang up, and ran towards the house, as if they were frightened at the sight of man; while two large dogs, half wild, with ears erect and outstretched nose, came growling out of their hut to cover the retreat of their young masters. The pioneer himself appeared at the door of his dwelling; he looked at us with a rapid and inquisitive glance, made a sign to the dogs to go into the house, and set them the example, without betra-ying either curiosity or apprehension at our arrival.

光秃秃的像是在严冬。我走进森林仔细观察这些树,这才发现树干上有一圈被深深的刮光树皮的痕迹。由于切断了树内汁液的循环,所以树很快就枯死了。我们因此才知道,这通常是开拓者要做的第一件事。第一年,他们还不能将全部的树木都砍倒,使它们变为自己的新财产,而是要在留下的树木之间播种玉米。如果把树全都砍光,则失去为作物遮阴的保护。走过这片由文明在荒野中建造的初具规模的田地,我们立刻看到田地主人的房舍。它位于一片比人们尚在滥伐的林地管理得好得多的田地中央。在滥伐的林地上,树木已被伐倒,但其根部尚未被破坏,树墩还挡在昔日有绿荫覆盖的土地上。在这片杂乱的树木丛中,小麦、橡树以及各种各样的多年生植物和野草混合在一片仍旧很粗野的原始土地上。开拓者的房屋,或如当地人所称的"圆木小屋",就掩藏在这片由各种植物组成的茂密的树荫中间。这座简陋的房屋也同它周围的田野一样,表明它是在匆忙中刚刚建成不久。它的长度不超过30英尺,高度在15英尺以内。房层的墙壁和顶部,都是用粗糙的大树干筑成的,在缝隙之间填满碎干草,敷以泥土,用以防寒和防雨。

"夜幕降临的时候,我们决定去问问圆木小屋的主人是否可以借宿。一听到我们的脚步声,几个在零星分散的树干间玩耍的小孩,马上爬起来,慌忙地向家里跑去,好像害怕见生人似的。这时,两条尚有一半野性的大狗,竖着耳朵,伸长脖子,一面吠叫着,一面从狗舍里窜出来,想来保护它们的小主人。这家的主人出现在门前,他先迅速并好奇地扫了我们一眼,随后就打手势,叫他的狗回狗舍去,并以自己的行动向狗表示,我们的光临并未引起他的惊恐或不安。

"We entered the log house: the inside is quite unlike that of the cottages of the peasantry of Europe; it contains more that is superfluous, less that is necessary. A single window with a muslin curtain; on a hearth of trodden clay an immense fire, which lights the whole interior; above the hearth, a good rifle, a deerskin, and plumes of eagles' feathers; on the right hand of the chimney, a map of the United States, raised and shaken by the wind through the crannies in the wall; near the map, on a shelf formed of a roughly hewn plank, a few volumes of books: a Bible, the first six books of Milton, and two of Shakespeare's plays; along the wall, trunks instead of closets; in the center of the room, a rude table, with legs of green wood with the bark still on them, looking as if they grew out of the ground on which they stood; but on this table a teapot of British china, silver spoons, cracked teacups, and some newspapers.

"The master of this dwelling has the angular features and lank limbs peculiar to the native of New England. It is evident that this man was not born in the solitude in which we have found him: his physical constitution suffices to show that his earlier years were spent in the midst of civilized society and that he belongs to that restless, calculating, and adventurous race of men who do with the utmost coolness things only to be accounted for by the ardor of passion, and who endure the life of savages for a time in order to conquer and civilize the backwoods.

"When the pioneer perceived that we were crossing his threshold, he came to meet us and shake hands, as is their custom; but his face was quite unmoved. He opened the conversation by inquiring what was going on in the world; and when his curiosity was satisfied, he held his peace, as if he were tired of the noise and importunity of mankind. When we questioned him in our turn, he gave us all the information we asked; he then attended sedulously, but without eager

"我们走进圆木小屋。屋里的景象与欧洲农家的完全不同，摆着许多多余的东西，而没有几件是必要的。只有一个窗户挂着细布窗帘；在土坯砌成的壁炉炉台上放着一盏大灯，灯光照亮了全屋；在这个壁炉炉台的上方，挂着一支漂亮的步枪，一张鹿皮，一串鹰的羽毛；在壁炉的右侧墙上，挂着一张美国地图，而风通过墙缝吹动着地图乱晃；在地图附近，架着一个粗糙的木搁板，上面放着几本书：其中有一部《圣经》，弥尔顿的最初 6 篇长诗和莎士比亚的两个剧本；沿着墙放着几个木柜，而没有皮箱；在房屋中央，有一张简陋的桌子，桌子的四条腿是用刚刚砍伐的小树干做的，上面未剥掉的树皮还在发绿，好像是就地生长出来的；在桌子上面有一个英国制的陶瓷茶壶，几把银制的钥匙，几个已经有裂纹的茶杯，还有几张报纸。

"这所房子的主人，面部很有棱角，四肢修长，这表明他原来是新英格兰的居民。显而易见，这个男子并不是出现在我们发现他的这个荒凉的地区，因为他的行为举止足以证明他的早年是在文明社会中度过的。他属于一个活泼好动、有头脑和敢于冒险的民族，能够冷静处理靠热烈激情而发动起来的事物。他之所以要在这里体验一段时间野蛮生活，是为了更好地征服荒野，并使其开化。

"当这位开拓者看出我们想跨进他房屋的门槛时，他走上前来同我们对话，并按他的习惯同我们握了握手，但他脸上的表情依旧很平静。他首先向我们询问世界上发生的事情。当他的好奇心得到满足后，他便默不作声了。就好像他早已厌倦了人类的喧嚣和一些纠缠不清的事情。当转向我们向他提问的时候，他向我们提供了我们所需的资料。接着，他虽然没有很大的热情，但

ness, to our wants. While he was engaged in providing thus kindly for us, how did it happen that, in spite of ourselves, we felt our gratitude die on our lips? It is that our host, while he performs the duties of hospitality, seems to be obeying a painful obligation of his station; he treats it as a duty imposed upon him by his situation, not as a pleasure.

"By the side of the hearth sits a woman with a baby on her lap; she nods to us without disturbing herself. Like the pioneer, this woman is in the prime of life; her appearance seems superior to her condition, and her apparel even betrays a lingering taste for dress; but her delicate limbs appear shrunken, her features are drawn in, her eye is mild and melancholy; her whole physiognomy bears marks of religious resignation, a deep quiet of all passions, and some sort of natural and tranquil firmness, ready to meet all the ills of life without fearing and without braving them.

"Her children cluster about her, full of health, turbulence, and energy: they are true children of the wilderness. Their mother watches them from time to time with mingled melancholy and joy: to look at their strength and her languor, one might imagine that the life she has given them has exhausted her own, and still she does not regret what they have cost her.

"The house inhabited by these emigrants has no internal partition or loft. In the one chamber of which it consists the whole family is gathered for the night. The dwelling is itself a little world, an ark of civilization amid an ocean of foliage: a hundred steps beyond it the primeval forest spreads its shades, and solitude resumes its sway."

APPENDIX V. -Vol. II, p. 204

It is not the equality of condition that makes men immoral and irreligious; but when men, being equal, are also immoral and irreli

还是很诚恳地满足我们的需要。当我们看到他能如此热心待客时，为什么又感到他的好客有些冷淡呢？他履行一个主人的职责似乎是出于无奈，要痛苦的服从他作为一个主人的义务，他将招待客人看成是自己的职责，而不是一种快乐。

"在壁炉炉台的另一端，坐着一位妇女抱着一个小男孩在她的膝盖上。她向我们点头，但并没有加入我们的谈话。像那位开拓者一样，这位妇女也正值其人生的壮年时期。她的举止表明她原来也很高雅，她的服饰说明她是一个喜爱打扮的女人。但是，她的四肢已经不如昔日纤美，她的面容显得有些疲惫，她的眼光温和中带有忧郁。她的外表给人的整个印象，是她有一颗虔诚的信奉宗教之心，有安和宁静的心态，一种自然而泰然自若的毅力使她敢于面对生活中的一切艰难困苦，从不畏惧，也从不轻视困难。

"她的孩子促膝在她的身旁，身体健康，性格活泼，精力旺盛。这些孩子是真真实实地在这片荒野中生长起来的，他们的母亲时不时地用忧郁而又欣慰的眼光望着他们。孩子们的强壮和母亲的衰弱无力，让我们可以想象到她为抚育他们已经费尽了心血，并对为此付出的代价毫不后悔。

"这座被移民们居住的房屋既无室内隔挡，也无阁楼，全家都住在一个大统屋子里，夜间共同在里面安息。这所房屋本身已经成了一个小世界。它是漂浮在林海中的一叶文明方舟。在它的百步以外，就是无边无际的茂密森林，而且又开始没有人烟了。"

附录 V。——第二卷，第 204 页

并不是由身份的平等使人没有道德和不信宗教。但是，当人们变得没有道德和不信宗教，而同时又都是平等的时候，不道德

gious, the effects of immorality and irreligion more easily manifest themselves, because men have but little influence over each other, and no class exists which can undertake to keep society in order. Equality of condition never creates profligacy of morals, but it sometimes allows that profligacy to show itself.

APPENDIX W. -Vol. II, p. 225

Aside from all those who do not think at all and those who dare not say what they think, the immense majority of Americans will still be found to appear satisfied with their political institutions; and I believe they really are so. I look on this state of public opinion as an indication, but not as a proof, of the absolute excellence of American laws. National pride, the gratification, by legislation, of certain ruling passions, fortuitous circumstances, unperceived defects, and, more than all the rest, the influence of the majority which shuts the mouth of all opponents, may long perpetuate the delusions of a people as well as those of a man.

Look at England throughout the eighteenth century. No nation was ever more prodigal of self-applause, no people were ever better satisfied with themselves; then every part of their constitution was right, everything, even to its most obvious defects, was irreproachable. At the present day a vast number of Englishmen seem to be occupied only in proving that this constitution was faulty in a thousand respects. Which was right, the English people of the last century, or the English people of the present day?

The same thing occurred in France. It is certain that, during the reign of Louis XIV the great bulk of the nation was devotedly attached to the form of government which then governed the community. It is a vast error to suppose that there was anything degraded in the character of the French of that age, There might have been some instances of servitude in France at that time, but assuredly there was no servile spirit among the people. The writers of that age felt a species of genuine enthusiasm in raising the power of their King over all other authority; and there was no peasant so obscure in his hovel as not to take a pride in the glory of his sovereign, or who would not die cheerfully with the cry "*Vive le Roi*!" upon his lips. These same forms of loyalty

和无信仰的行为就容易表现出来,因为人们对彼此之间的相互影响已经减少,已没有一个阶级能够承担起维持社会治安的责任。身份的平等并不能使道德变坏,但有时听任其变坏表面化。

附录 W。——第二卷,第 225 页

即使排除那些根本就什么也不想的人和那些不敢说出自己想法的人,你也会发现美国的绝大多数人似乎满意他们的政治制度;我也确实认为如此。我认为公共舆论的这种倾向是表明美国法制十分良好的标志,而不是它的证明。民族的自豪感,立法对某些激情、偶然事件、未被发觉的弊端的放纵,特别是可以封住反对派之口的多数的利益,可以长期给整个民族和每个公民造成一种错觉。

我们现在来看一看 18 世纪的英国。当时,没有一个国家会像这个国家一样喜欢自我吹捧,也没有任何一个国家的人民会像这里的人民一样对自己都很满意,所以认为他们制度的每个方面都是正确的,并且觉得一切事情甚至是它的一些明显缺欠也是好的。但在今天,绝大多数英国人好像都认为他们的制度在许多方面都是错误的。究竟是上一世纪的英国人是正确的? 还是今天的英国人是正确的呢?

法国的情况也是如此。在路易十四统治时期,议会的多数曾热烈致力于支持统治当时社会的政府,并认为那些说这个政府贬低了当时法国人人格的人是错误的。而在我们这个时代,却有人认为当时的法国受到了奴役,但在人们中间并不一定存在奴役思想。当时的作家极其热忱地赞扬了高于其他一切权力的王权,农民们在他们的茅屋里也以其国家君主的荣誉为自豪,在高喊“国王万岁!”而死时亦未感到光荣。这种形式的忠诚已日益让法国

have now become odious to the French people. Which were wrong, the French of the age of Louis XIV or their descendants of the present day?

Our judgment of the laws of a people, then, must not be founded exclusively uponits inclinations, since those inclinations change from age to age; but upon more elevated principles and a more general experience. The love which a people may show for its laws proves only this: that we should not be in a hurry to change them.

APPENDIX X -Vol. II, p. 276

In the chapter to which this note relates I have pointed out one source of danger; I am now about to point out another, more rare indeed, but more formidable if it were ever to appear.

If the love of physical gratification and the taste for well-being, which are naturally suggested to men by a state of equality, were to possess the mind of a democratic people and to fill it completely, the manners of the nation would become so totally opposed to military pursuits that perhaps even the army would eventually acquire a love of peace, in spite of the peculiar interest which leads it to desire war. Living amid a state of general relaxation, the troops would ultimately think it better to rise without efforts, by the slow but commodious advancement of a period of peace, than to purchase more rapid promotionat the cost of all the toils and privations of the field. With these feelings, they would take up arms without enthusiasm and use them without energy; they would allow themselves to be led to meet the foe, instead of marching to attack him.

It must not be supposed that this pacific state of the army would render it adverse to revolutions; for revolutions, and especially military revolutions, which are generally very rapid, are attended indeed with great dangers, but not with protracted toil; they gratify ambition at less cost than war; life only is at stake, and the men of democracies care less for their lives than for their comfort.

Nothing is more dangerous for the freedom and the tranquillity of a people than an army afraid of war, because as such an army no lon

人厌恶。究竟是路易十四时期的法国人错了,还是我们今天的法国人错了?

于是,我们对一个国家法制的判断不应当只根据舆论的倾向,而且还要根据最主要的动机和最普遍的经验去评定,因为舆论的倾向从一个时代到另一个时代都在发生变化。但在普遍原则和持久的经验中,一个国家的人民对法制的热爱只证明了一件事,那就是他们希望不要很快就改变已定的法律。

附录 X。——第二卷,第 276 页

在与这个注释相关的章节里,我只指出一种危险。现在,我想指出另一种非常罕见,但一旦出现便会非常可怕的危险。

当平等使人们自然产生的对物质热爱和对舒适生活的喜爱,并在控制着一个民主国家人民的精神并最终会完全支配这种精神时,尽管这个国家的自身利益会使它渴望战争,但民族的习俗会让军队逐渐反对在军事上的追求,而最终爱好和平。生活在这种舒适环境下的士兵,将会意识到,与其在战场上通过艰难险阻的方式去获得快速的晋升,还不如在和平的环境中一步一步地、顺顺利利地和毫不费力地晋升。在这种精神状态下,军队虽有武器但缺乏热情,在使用武器时也没有活力。他们宁愿引狼入室,也不愿冲到前线去杀敌。

不要以为军队的这种平静的状态会对革命不利。因为革命,尤其是军事革命,一般都非常迅速,并且伴有很大的危险,但不必付出艰苦的劳动。至少在革命中比在战争中更能让他们满足自己的野心,只要拿生命去冒险就可以了,而民主国家的人对于生命的重视不如对于舒适生活的重视。

没有什么比一个害怕战争的军队更不利于国家的自由和

ger seeks to maintain its importance and its influence on the field of battle, it seeks to assert them elsewhere. Thus it might happen that the men of whom a democratic army consists would lose the interests of citizens without acquiring the virtues of soldiers; and that the army would cease to be fit for war without ceasing to be turbulent. I shall here repeat what I have said in the text: the remedy for these dangers is not to be found in the army, but in the country; a democratic people which has preserved the manliness of its character will never be at a loss for military prowess in its soldiers.

APPENDIX Y. Vol. II, p. 292

Men place the greatness of their idea of unity in the means, God in the ends; hence this idea of greatness, as men conceive it, leads us to infinite littleness. To compel all men to follow the same course towards the same object is a human conception; to introduce infinite variety of action, but so combined that all these acts lead in a thousand different ways to the accomplishment of one great design, is a divine conception.

The human idea of unity is almost always barren; the divine idea is infinitely fruitful. Men think they manifest their greatness by simplifying the means they use; but it is the purpose of God which is simple; his means are infinitely varied.

APPENDIX Z. Vol. II, p. 296

Not only is a democratic people led by its own taste to centralize its government, but the passions of all the men by whom it is governed constantly urge it in the same direction. It may easily be foreseen that almost all the able and ambitious members of a democratic community will labor unceasingly to extend the powers of government, because they all hope at some time or other to wield those powers themselves. It would be a waste of time to attempt to prove to them that extreme centralization may be injurious to the state, since they are centralizing it for their own benefit. Among the public men of democracies, there are hardly any but men of great disinterestedness or extreme mediocrity who seek to oppose the centralization of government; the former are scarce, the latter powerless.

安宁,因为这样的军队不想在战场上表现其伟大和力量时,便要到其他地方去表现伟大和力量了。因此,民主国家军队的官兵有可能不顾公民的利益而失去军人的品质,而军队则不再具有战斗力并不断发生暴乱。我在这里再重复一遍我在前面已经说过的一句话:对于这种危险的补救办法不在军队,而在国家。保留着英勇气概的民主国家,将永远不会为军队士兵没有英勇士气而感到茫然不知所措。

附录 Y。——第二卷,第 292 页

人认为统一这一观点的伟大之处就在于方法,而神则认为在于目的。结果,这种关于伟大的观点使我们只注意无数的小事情。强制人们经过同样的努力朝向同一目标,是人的观点;而引导多种多样的人的行动,并结合他们的所有行动通过数以千计的不同道路去完成伟大的计划,则是神的观点。

人关于一致性的观点几乎总是贫乏无力的,而神关于单一性的观点则是丰富而有活力的。人以为简化手段可以显示出自己的伟大;而神的目标很简单,那就是使手段无限多样化。

附录 Z。——第二卷,第 296 页

民主国家不仅是由于自己的喜好而走向中央集权,而且领导它的人的激情也在不断把它推向同一方向。我们很容易预见,在民主国家里,几乎所有有才能和有野心的人,将会不断地扩大社会的权力,因为他们都希望有朝一日能自己领导社会权力。要想试图向他们证明过分中央集权可能会对国家有害,那简直是浪费时间,因为他们是在为自己的利益集权。在民主国家的官员中,除了一些大公无私的或极其平庸的人以外,几乎没有人想要反对中央集权。反对中央集权的,不是少数就是无力。

APPENDIX AA. -Vol. II, p. 318

I have often asked myself what would happen if, amid the laxity of democratic customs, and as a consequence of the restless spirit of the army, a military government were ever to be established among any of the nations of our times. I think that such a government would not differ much from the outline I have drawn in the chapter to which this note refers, and that it would retain none of the fierce characteristics of a military oligarchy. I am persuaded that in such a case a sort of fusion would take place between the practices of civil officials and those of the military service. The administration would assume something of a military character, and the army some of the practices of the civil administration. The result would be a regular, clear, exact, and absolute system of government; the people would become the reflection of the army, and the community be regimented like a garrison.

APPENDIX BB. -Vol. II, p. 321

It cannot be absolutely or generally affirmed that the greatest danger of the present age is license or tyranny, anarchy or despotism. Both are equally to be feared; and the one may proceed as easily as the other from one and the same cause: namely, that *general apathy* which is the consequence of individualism. It is because this apathy exists that the executive government, having mustered a few troops, is able to commit acts of oppression one day; and the next day a party which has mustered some thirty men in its ranks can also commit acts of oppression. Neither the one nor the other can establish anything which will last; and the causes which enable them to succeed easily prevent them from succeeding for long; they rise because nothing opposes them, and they sink because nothing supports them. The proper object, therefore, of our most strenuous resistance is far less either anarchy or despotism than that apathy which may almost indifferently beget either the one or the other.

附录 AA。——第二卷,第 318 页

我常常自己问自己,如果在民主民情的松懈中,再加上军队里出现的不安情绪,一个军事政府将建立在我们今天的某些国家里,那么会发生什么。我认为,这样的政府本身不会出现在本注所在的章节里所描绘的现象,也不会保留在军事垄断上的野蛮作风。但我深信,在这种情况下,会在文职官员的办事习惯与军人的办事习惯之间产生某种融合。在行政方面采纳某些军人精神,在军队方面也要吸收某些文官的办事习惯。这样融合的结果,将会实现有条不紊、纪律严明、条理分明和绝对服从的指挥,人民的身上有军人的风范,而社会也将类似于一个大部队。

附录 BB。——第二卷,第 321 页

我不能绝对地或普遍地断言当代的最大危险是胡作非为或暴政,是无政府状态或专制。这些东西都是同样让人感到恐惧的,而且很容易都来自同一个原因。这就是个人主义造成的普遍的漠不关心的结果。正是因为有这种漠不关心的存在,才使行政权可以总揽某些权力而实行压迫;也正是这种漠不关心,能使一个政党在以后的某一天召集 30 个人投入战斗而且也实行压迫。但是,不论是前者还是后者,都不能长期存在下去,使它们容易获得成功的那些原因也在妨碍它们长期保持成功。它们之所以会成功,是因为没有什么力量反对它们,而他们之所以会垮台,是因为没有什么力量支持他们。因此,最应当反对的是漠不关心,而不是无政府状态或专制,因为漠不关心可以几乎分毫不差地创造无政府状态和专制。

译者后记

托克维尔是法国政治思想家和历史学家。本书的基本思想在于承认贵族制度衰落的必然性和平等与民主势不可当的发展趋势。它既是第一部对美国社会、政治制度和民情进行综合研究的著作,也是第一部记述美国民主制度的专著。作者把民主作为一个对象来观察,没有掺杂自己的观点加以论证,使读者得以看到那个时代美国社会的真实面貌。《论美国民主》是托克维尔的代表作,这部作品出版后,立即受到了社会各界的好评,使他名扬海外。《论美国民主》分为上卷和下卷,这两卷写于不同时期,其间相隔了 5 年,因而在笔调、结构、叙述上有所不同。但是作者的文字十分优美。笔者为了更好地完成这部伟大著作的翻译工作,在翻译期间查阅了大量的资料,拜访了多位学者,得到了专家的支持,在这里一并表示感谢。如今笔者终于完成了《论美国民主》的翻译。由于笔者水平所限,错误之处在所难免,在此请教于方家,也请广大读者不吝赐教,批评指正。

朱尾声

2006 年 9 月